The Columbia Checklist

The Columbia Checklist

*The Feature Films, Serials,
Cartoons and Short Subjects
of Columbia Pictures Corporation,
1922–1988*

by Len D. Martin

McFarland & Company, Inc., Publishers
Jefferson, North Carolina, and London

Acknowledgments. I would like to thank the following institutions and individuals for their invaluable assistance in providing books, films, and other research materials in the compilation of this book: Rice University, University of Houston, Mr. Dane Wilsonne at Kit Parker Films, Budget Films, Film Favorites, Roy Bonario of Roy's Collectors Showcase, Fred Castro, Al Davis, G. B. Love, Bill Mooney, Pat Mooney, Bob Selig, Marc Schooley, Chuck Bixler, DeWayne Dickey, Herman Taylor, and especially Pat Ray, who helped fill in missing gaps and clarify contradictory data regarding Columbia releases.

A very special thanks to my wife, Ann, for her patience and understanding; she aided immensely in the editing of this book.

British Library Cataloguing-in-Publication data are available

Library of Congress Cataloguing-in-Publication Data

Martin, Len D., 1939–
    The Columbia checklist : the feature films, serials, cartoons and short subjects of Columbia Pictures Corporation, 1922–1988 / by Len D. Martin.
    p.   cm.
    Includes bibliographical references and index.
    ISBN 0-89950-556-2 (lib. bdg. : 50# alk. paper) ∞
    1. Columbia Pictures Corporation—Catalogs.   2. Motion pictures—United States—Catalogs.   I. Title.
    PN1999.C57M37   1991
    016.79143'75—dc20   90-53507
                                                                            CIP

Manufactured in the United States of America

McFarland & Company, Inc., Publishers
Box 611, Jefferson, North Carolina 28640

Table of Contents

Preface

This book is not intended to be an in-depth examination of Columbia Pictures Corporation or its product; rather it is intended as a reference checklist to the entire output of the studio.

Beginning with the decade of the sixties and continuing today, Columbia began to acquire and distribute films which were produced by independent producers and foreign-language studios, the "art films," which bore the Columbia logo and brought in added revenue for the studio. From the sixties until the mid-seventies, Columbia was sole distributor for Royal Films; from the mid-seventies to the eighties, Triumph Films. For the sake of completeness, all of these films are included here.

In doing research for this book (using mostly *The New York Times, The Los Angeles Times,* and *Variety*), it was not uncommon to find different running times and release dates for certain titles. I have tried to furnish the reader with information that is as accurate as possible.

It has become difficult to determine which films were released to theaters and which directly to home video or cable television. While many films in 1989 went directly to the home video or cable market, some were given a one- or two-day run on the East or West coast beforehand. I have chosen not to continue this listing past 1988 until more accurate information on film releases becomes available. Two films listed in the book, *Dream One,* as yet unreleased, and *White Water Summer,* which may or may not have had a theatrical release, are included for completeness.

These abbreviations are used in this book: *DIR* (director), *PRO* (producer), *SP* (screenplay), *B&W* (black & white), and *Scope* — any of the wide screen processes (CinemaScope, TechniScope, HammerScope, MegaScope, HorrorScope, etc.).

A work of this size will probably contain minor errors, despite my best efforts. Readers are encouraged to send their queries, suggestions, corrections, complaints, and so forth, to me in care of the publisher.

Len D. Martin
Houston, Texas
December 1990

Historical Overview

Columbia Pictures had its beginnings back in 1920 when Jack Cohn, Joe Brandt, and Harry Cohn set up C.B.C. Film Sales in New York to handle their production of a series of shorts called *Screen Snapshots*, which showed the offscreen activities of the movie stars and helped publicize their movies. Harry Cohn, who was more a producer than a businessman, decided to move to California and set up shop there as an independent producer, and let his brother Jack and Joe Brandt handle the money end of the business from New York.

Harry Cohn found a place at Gower Street and Sunset Boulevard in the middle of Poverty Row. He called his company C.B.C. Pictures, for Cohn, Brandt, and Cohn, but the competition in the business called it "Corned Beef and Cabbage." Harry Cohn, however, was to prove he was there to stay and would not disappear from Poverty Row as some of the studios would in later years.

In 1924, C.B.C. Pictures incorporated and became Columbia Pictures Corporation, with Joe Brandt as president, Jack Cohn as executive vice-president, and Harry Cohn as vice-president in charge of production. It was Joe Brandt who decreed that Columbia build no theaters, but confine itself to the production of motion pictures. This meant that Columbia had to make better movies than the other studios and make movies that the theaters wanted to show.

Columbia grew steadily during the 1920s, turning out a stream of small-budget dramas, comedies, action pictures (usually starring Jack Holt) and shorts. When a young director named Frank Capra arrived at the studio in 1927, Columbia would no longer be another Poverty Row studio. Capra began by turning out comedies such as *That Certain Thing* and *So This Is Love?* and then settled into directing dramas, like *Ladies of Leisure,* and action pictures (*Flight* and *Dirigible* e.g.), along with the comedies.

When Joe Brandt left the company in 1932, Harry Cohn became president of Columbia, and for the next 26 years under his leadership Columbia would grow into a major studio.

By the mid–30s Columbia was producing over 40 features a year along with a larger number of "A" pictures. Its successes were with the "screwball" comedies including *The Awful Truth* and its first big Oscar winner, *It Happened One Night,* directed by Capra. The list of Columbia's most memorable comedies between 1933 and 1943 is an impressive one. Along the way the studio had acquired its own special group of directors and stars, either contractually or for a one or two picture deal.

But there was another side to Columbia, the B pictures and the shorts. Harry Cohn believed in making lots of movies and shorts and his B unit was there to do it. There were the first B westerns with Buck Jones and Tim McCoy in the '30s, Bill Elliott in the late '30s and early '40s, and Charles Starrett, who was to reign as the Columbia B western king from 1935 to 1952, with his "Durango Kid" westerns. Even Gene Autry did a stint at Columbia from 1947 to 1953.

There were also the series films based on radio programs such as *The Whistler, I Love a Mystery, Crime Doctor;* detective characters such as *Boston Blackie,* the *Lone Wolf, Ellery Queen;* and the comic strip series such as *Blondie* and *Jungle Jim.*

The comedy shorts unit was headed by Jules White, who produced them from 1934 until the late '50s. Among the best known were those by Andy Clyde (1934–1956), the Three Stooges (1934–1959), Vera Vague (1943–1952), and countless others with such stars as Buster Keaton, Charlie Chase, and El Brendel.

Columbia also produced many other short subjects throughout its history including *Screen Snapshots,* which started in 1920 under the C.B.C. banner, as well as travelogues, musicals, historical and sports shorts.

For a short time Columbia even distributed the Disney cartoons until it lost out to United Artists over a contractual dispute with Walt Disney. Charles Mintz and his successors then provided Columbia with the Krazy Kat, Scrappy, and Color Rhapsodies cartoons in the 1930s and early '40s along with other cartoons including the Fox and the Crow in the late '40s and early '50s. When Columbia closed its cartoon studio in 1948, it was Stephen Bosustow and his UPA Productions that supplied Columbia with its cartoon output until 1959. From 1959 to 1965 it was Hanna and Barbera that produced the final Columbia cartoon output.

Columbia's venture into serial production in 1937 lasted until 1956. Like the series, the main sources for these were the radio programs — "The Shadow," "Jack Armstrong," "Captain Midnight"; the comic strips — *Batman, Superman, Blackhawk;* and various westerns and thrillers.

By the 1940s Columbia's A unit began to move in the direction of Technicolor filming. Their first Technicolor film in 1943 was a beautiful outdoor western, *The Desperadoes,* directed by Charles Vidor, and starring Randolph Scott and Glenn Ford.

Columbia's least interest was in musicals, but with stars like Rita

Hayworth and Ann Miller, it began to produce them. Many were low-budget programmers in black and white, but the most notable were the Technicolor musicals such as *Cover Girl* with Rita Hayworth and Gene Kelly, *A Song to Remember* with Cornel Wilde, and *The Jolson Story* and *Jolson Sings Again*, both starring Larry Parks.

By the early 1950s Columbia acquired a number of leading stars and its A picture quality began to resemble the output of the other major studios. The studio offered the moviegoing public the Rita Hayworth musicals, the Randolph Scott westerns, the Judy Holliday and Jack Lemmon comedies, the *film noir* thrillers of Glenn Ford, and the dramas, whose stars included Humphrey Bogart, William Holden, Broderick Crawford, and Marlon Brando.

Columbia also ventured into the newest innovation, 3-D, with an output of nine pictures during 1953 and 1954, but was quick to drop it when audiences lost interest in the fad. In 1955 Columbia entered the CinemaScope field with the release of *The Violent Men*.

In 1956 Jack Cohn died and Harry was ill with cancer. No longer was he able to control the studio as he had done in the past. The profit margins on the shorts and B pictures had fallen and were no longer viable productions. The new medium of television was also becoming a competitor for this type of program. Harry Cohn died in February 1958 and for the first time in its history Columbia Studios fell into the red.

In later years Columbia would undergo many different changes—presidents, mergers, acquisitions, losses, scandals; their releases would range from foreign to independent productions to studio. But Columbia would never be the same without Harry Cohn—the Hollywood mogul who so firmly put his personal stamp on his studio's output. In his own colorful words was his philosophy: "Every Friday the front door opens and I spit a movie out into Gower Street . . . I want one good picture a year. That's my policy . . . and I won't let an exhibitor have it unless he takes the bread-and-butter product, the Boston Blackies, the Blondies, the low budget westerns and the rest of the junk we make. I like good pictures too, but to get one I have to shoot five or six, and to shoot five or six I have to keep the plant going with the programmer pictures."

Feature Films
(1922–1988)

Following is a complete list of feature films produced and or distributed by Columbia Pictures. Producer and Screenwriter are given, where known. Not included in this listing are those films Columbia jointly produced, but were released by other studios.

1. A Nos Amours (To Our Loves) (10/84) Eastman Color — 102 mins. (Drama). *DIR/PRO:* Maurice Pialat. *SP:* Maurice Pialat, Arlette Langmann. A Les Films du Livardois–Gaumont–FR3–Triumph Films Production. *CAST:* Sandrine Bonnaire, Dominique Besnehard, Maurice Pialat, Evelyne Ker, Anne-Sophie Maille, Christophe Odent, Cyr Boitard, Maite Maille, Pierre-Loup Rajot, Cyril Collard, Tom Stevens.

A young teenage girl (Bonnaire) causes dissension with her family and friends because of her amoral attitude toward sex. *NOTES:* Limited theatrical release; in French with English subtitles. [British title: *To Our Loves*].

2. Aaron Loves Angela (12/75) Metrocolor — 99 mins. (Romance). *DIR:* Gordon Parks, Jr. *PRO:* Robert J. Anderson. *SP:* Gerald Sanford. *CAST:* Kevin Hooks, Irene Cara, Moses Gunn, Robert Hooks, Ernestine Jackson, Leon Pinkney, Wanda Velez, Charles McGregor, Norman Evans, Alex Stevens, Jose Feliciano, Walt Frazier, Frank Aldrich.

A black youth (Kevin Hooks) and a Puerto Rican girl (Cara) struggle to make their feelings known to each other but are hampered by their ghetto peers.

3. Abandon Ship (3/57) B&W — 95 mins. (Adventure). *DIR/SP:* Richard Sale. *PRO:* John R. Sloan. *CAST:* Tyrone Power, Mai Zetterling, Lloyd Nolan, Stephen Boyd, Moira Lister, James Hayter, Victor Maddern, Gordon Jackson, Clive Morton, Laurence Naismith, John Stratton, Eddie Byrne, Jill Melford, Claire Austin, Finlay Currie.

A British seaman (Power) commands a lifeboat of survivors following a disaster at sea and must exercise the survival-of-the-fittest rule as he tries to save as many lives as possible. [British title: *Seven Waves Away*].

4. Abdul the Damned (5/11/36) B&W — 111 mins. (Drama). *DIR:* Karl Grune. *SP:* Ashley Dukes, Warren Chetham-Strode, Roger Burford. Story by Robert Neumann. A British International–Capitol Film Production. *CAST:* Fritz Kortner, Nils Asther, Adrienne Ames, John Stuart, Walter Rilla, Charles Carson, Patric

Knowles, Eric Portman, Clifford Heatherley, Annie Esmond, Arthur Hardy, Robert Naylor, Warren Jenkins, George Zucco.

In the early 1900's, a Turkish ruler (Kortner) ruthlessly sets out to destroy all those who he believes are conspiring against him.

5. Above the Clouds (12/19/33) B&W—68 mins. (Adventure). *DIR:* Roy William Neill. *SP:* Albert DeMond. Story by George B. Seitz. *CAST:* Robert Armstrong, Richard Cromwell, Dorothy Wilson, Edmund Breese, Morgan Wallace, Dorothy Revier, Bessie Barriscale, Geneva Mitchell, Luis Alberni, Sherry Hall.

A cameraman's assistant (Cromwell) saves the day for his boss (Armstrong) and gets the girl (Wilson) when he records the destruction of a dirigible. [British title: *Winged Devils*].

6. Absence of Malice (11/81) Eastman Color—116 mins. (Drama). *DIR/PRO:* Sydney Pollack. *SP:* Kurt Luedtke. A Mirage Enterprises Production. *Cast:* Paul Newman, Sally Field, Bob Balaban, Melinda Dillon, Luther Adler, Barry Primus, Wilford Brimley, Arnie Ross, Josef Sommer, Don Hood, John Harkins, Anna Marie Napoles, Shelley Spurlock.

An investigative reporter (Field) is set up by an unscrupulous federal investigator (Balaban) to discredit the son (Newman) of a dead mobster.

7. Abused Confidence (12/7/38) B&W—88 mins. (Drama). *DIR:* Henry Decoin. *SP:* Henry Decoin, Jean Boyer. Story by Pierre Wolff. A UDIF Production. *CAST:* Danielle Darrieux, Charles Vanel, Valentine Tessier, Therese Dorny, Jean Worms, Pierre Mingand, Gilbert Gil, Yvette Lebon, Svetlana Pitoeff, Nicole de Rouves.

A young woman (Darrieux) pretends to be the daughter of a writer's (Vanel) dead mistress so that he will finance her education through law school. *NOTES:* In French with English subtitles. [Original French title: *Abus de Confiance*].

8. Acqua e Sapone (Acqua and Sapone) (10/85) Eastman Color—105 mins. (Comedy). *DIR:* Carlo Verdone. *PRO:* Mario Cecchi Gori, Vittorio Cecchi Gori. *SP:* Carlo Verdone, Enrico Oldoini, Franco Ferrini. A Triumph Films Production. *CAST:* Carlo Verdone, Natasha Hovey, Florinda Bolkan, Elena Fabrizi, Fabrizio Bracconeri.

A janitor (Verdone) poses as a priest at a girls' school in order to be near the girl (Hovey) he loves. *NOTES:* Limited theatrical release; in Italian with English subtitles.

9. Acquitted (10/26/29) B&W—62 mins. (Crime). *DIR:* Frank R. Strayer. *PRO:* Harry Cohn. *SP:* Keene Thompson, James Seymour. *CAST:* Lloyd Hughes, Margaret Livingston, Sam Hardy, Charles West, George Regas, Otto Hoffman, Charles Wilson.

A gangster's moll (Livingston), framed for murder by her gangster boyfriend (Hardy), falls for a doctor (Hughes) while in prison, and vows revenge when she gets out.

10. Across the Badlands (9/14/50) B&W—55 mins. (Western). *DIR:* Fred F. Sears. *PRO:* Colbert Clark. *SP:* Barry Shipman. *CAST:* Charles Starrett, Helen Mowery, Smiley Burnette, Stanley Andrews, Bob Wilke, Dick Elliott, Dick Alexander, Hugh Prosser, Robert W. Cavendish, Charles Evans, Paul Campbell, Harmonica Bill.

The Durango Kid (Starrett) tracks down a gang of outlaws who have been harassing railroad surveyors to prevent them from finding a lost stagecoach trail. [British title: *The Challenge*].

11. Across the Sierras (2/13/41) B&W—58 mins. (Western). *DIR:* D. Ross Lederman. *PRO:* Leon Barsha.

SP: Paul Franklin. *CAST*: Bill Elliott, Luana Walters, Dub Taylor, Dick Curtis, Richard Fiske, LeRoy Mason, Tom London, Edmund Cobb, Art Mix, John Dilson, Jim Pierce, Ralph Peters, Eddie Laughton, Milton Kibbee, Ruth Robinson, Tex Cooper, Carl Knowles.

When a gunfighter (Curtis) is released from prison, he sets out to get revenge on Wild Bill Hickok (Elliott). [British title: *Welcome Stranger*].

12. Adam Had Four Sons (2/24/41) B&W—108 mins. (Drama). *DIR*: Gregory Ratoff. *PRO*: Robert Sherwood. *SP*: William Hurlbut, Michael Blankfort. Based on *Legacy* by Charles Bonner. *CAST*: Ingrid Bergman, Warner Baxter, Susan Hayward, Fay Wray, Richard Denning, Johnny Downs, Robert Shaw, Charles Lind, Billy Ray, Steven Muller, Wallace Chadweel, Bobby Walberg, Helen Westley, June Lockhart, Pietro Sosso, Gilbert Emery, Renie Riano, Clarence Muse.

A widower (Baxter) hires a housekeeper (Bergman) to help raise his four sons. *NOTES*: Ingrid Bergman's second U.S. film.

13. Address Unknown (4/24/44) B&W—80 mins. (War). *DIR*: William Cameron Menzies. *SP*: Herbert Dalmas. Story by Kressmann Taylor. *CAST*: Paul Lukas, Carl Esmond, Peter Van Eyck, Mady Christians, Morris Camovsky, K.T. Stevens, Emory Parnell, Mary Young, Frank Faylen, Charles Halton, Erwin Kalser, Frank Reicher, Dale Cornell, Peter Newmeyer.

A German-American (Lukas) returns to Germany and becomes swept up in the new Nazi order.

14. Adventure in Manhattan (10/23/36) B&W—73 mins. (Crime-Comedy). *DIR*: Edward Ludwig. *SP*: Sidney Buchman, Harry Sauber, Jack Kirkland. Story by Joseph Krumgold. Based on *Purple and Fine Linen* by

May Edington. *CAST*: Jean Arthur, Joel McCrea, Reginald Owen, Thomas Mitchell, Herman Bing, Victor Kilian, John Gallaudet, Emmett Vogan, George Cooper, Robert Warwick.

A newspaper editor (Mitchell) hires an art connoisseur and criminologist (McCrea) to track down a gang of art thieves. [British title: *Manhattan Madness*].

15. Adventure in Sahara (12/23/38) B&W—60 mins. (Adventure). *DIR*: D. Ross Lederman. *PRO*: Louis B. Appleton. *SP*: Maxwell Shane. Story by Samuel Fuller. *CAST*: Paul Kelly, Lorna Gray, Robert Fiske, Dwight Frye, Marc Lawrence, C. Henry Gordon, Dick Curtis, Stanley Brown, Al Bridge, Raphael Bennett, Charles Moore, Stanley Andrews.

A brutal Legionnaire commandant (Gordon) is sent into the desert with a few loyal soldiers to die. He manages to survive, and when he returns for revenge, he finds the fort under attack by Arabs.

16. Adventure in Washington (5/29/41) B&W—82 mins. (Drama). *DIR*: Alfred E. Green. *PRO*: Charles R. "Buddy" Rogers. *SP*: Lewis R. Foster, Arthur Caesar. Story by Albert Benham, Jeanne Spencer. *CAST*: Herbert Marshall, Virginia Bruce, Gene Reynolds, Samuel S. Hinds, Ralph Morgan, Vaughn Glaser, Charles Smith, Dickie Jones, Pierre Watkin, J. M. Kerrigan, Tommy Bond, Billy Dawson, Charles Lind, Mary Currier.

A Senator (Marshall) and his girlfriend (Bruce), a radio personality, expose a Senate page (Reynolds) who is selling government secrets to manipulative stockholders. [British title: *Female Correspondent*].

17. Adventures in Silverado (2/25/48) B&W—75 mins. (Western). *DIR*: Phil Karlson. *PRO*: Ted Richmond, Robert Cohn. *SP:* Kenneth Gamet, Tom Kilpatrick, Joe Pagano. Based on *Silverado Squatters* by Robert Louis Stevenson. *CAST:* William Bishop, Gloria Henry, Forrest Tucker, Edgar Buchanan, Edgar Barrier, Paul E. Burns, Eddy Waller, Trevor Bardette, Fred F. Sears, Irving Bacon.

A stagecoach passenger (Bishop) sets out to capture a notorious bandit known as "The Monk." [British title: *Above All Laws*].

18. Adventures of Martin Eden (2/26/42) B&W — 87 mins. (Adventure). *DIR:* Sidney Salkow. *PRO:* B. P. Schulberg. *SP:* W. L. River. Based on the book by Jack London. *CAST:* Glenn Ford, Claire Trevor, Evelyn Keyes, Stuart Erwin, Dickie Moore, Ian MacDonald, Frank Conroy, Rafaela Ottiano, Pierre Watkin, Regina Wallace, Robert J. MacDonald.

After enduring hardship and brutal treatment, a sailor (Ford) campaigns for the publication of his memoirs exposing brutal conditions aboard ship.

19. Adventures of Rusty (9/6/45) B&W — 69 mins. (Children). *DIR:* Paul Bumford. *PRO:* Rudolph C. Flothow. *SP:* Aubrey Wisberg. Story by Al Martin. *CAST:* Ted Donaldson, Margaret Lindsay, Conrad Nagel, Gloria Holden, Robert Williams, Addison Richards, Arno Frey, Eddie Parker, Bobby Larson, Douglas Madore, Gary Gray, Ruth Warren, "Ace" the dog.

A young boy (Donaldson) must adjust to a new stepmother (Lindsay) while trying to prove that his new pet German shepherd is not vicious.

20. Advise and Consent (6/62) B&W/Panavision — 140 mins. (Drama). *DIR/PRO:* Otto Preminger. *SP:* Wendell Mayes. Based on the book by Allen Drury. *CAST:* Henry Fonda, Charles Laughton, Don Murray, Walter Pidgeon, Peter Lawford, Gene Tierney, Franchot Tone, Lew Ayres,

Burgess Meredith, Eddie Hodges, Paul Ford, George Grizzard, Inga Swenson, Paul McGrath, Will Geer, Betty White, Malcolm Atterbury, Edward Andrews, Tom Helmore.

A group of Senators wheel and deal as they try to push for the confirmation of the newly appointed Secretary of State.

21. Affair in Trinidad (6/30/52) B&W — 98 mins. (Spy-Drama). *DIR/PRO:* Vincent Sherman. *SP:* Oscar Saul, James Gunn. Story by Virginia Van Upp, Berne Giler. A Beckworth Production. *CAST:* Rita Hayworth, Glenn Ford, Alexander Scourby, Valerie Bettis, Torin Thatcher, Howard Wendell, Karel Stepanek, George Voskovec, Steven Geray, Walter Kohler, Juanita Moore, Gregg Martell, Mort Mills, Robert Boon, Ralph Moody, Ross Elliott, Don Kohler.

When her husband is killed, a nightclub singer (Hayworth) and her brother-in-law (Ford) become entangled in a serious game of espionage.

22. The Affairs of a Rogue (2/17/49) B&W — 111 mins. (Drama). *DIR:* Alberto Cavalcanti. *PRO:* Joseph Friedman. *SP:* Nicholas Phipps, Reginald Long. Based on a play by Norman Ginsbury. A Two Cities Production. *CAST:* Jean Pierre Aumont, Joan Hopkins, Cecil Parker, Ronald Squire, Athene Seyler, Anthony Hawtrey, Gerard Heinz, Margaretta Scott, Jack Livesey, Hugh Griffith, Joan Young, Betty Huntley-Wright.

The story of British royalty in the early 19th century as the Prince Regent (Parker) tries unsuccessfully to marry off his unruly daughter (Hopkins) to a number of nobles until a German prince (Aumont) wins her hand. [British title: *The First Gentleman*].

23. The Affairs of Messalina (11/54) B&W — 116 mins. (Historical-Drama). *DIR/PRO/SP:* Carmine Gallone. Adapted by Albert Valentin, Nino Novarese. *CAST:* Memo Benassi, Maria Felix, Georges Marchal, Jean Chevrier, Jean Tissier, Michel Vitold.

The story of Messalina (Felix), wife of Roman Emperor Claudius, and her many love affairs.

24. Africa Speaks (9/21/30) B&W — 77 mins. (Documentary). *DIR:* Walter Futter. *PRO:* Lowell Thomas. *SP:* Lowell Thomas, Walter Futter. *CAST:* Narrated by Lowell Thomas.

A documentary about African wildlife and the Ubangi tribe.

25. After Business Hours (12/15/24) B&W — 56 mins. (Drama). *DIR:* Mal St. Clair. *PRO:* Harry Cohn. *SP:* Douglas Z. Doty. Based on *Everything Money Can Buy* by Ethel Watts Mumford. *CAST:* Elaine Hammerstein, Lou Tellegen, Phyllis Haver, John Patrick, Lillian Langdon, William Scott, Lee Moran.

A husband (Tellegen) who believes his wife (Hammerstein) shouldn't be trusted with money causes her to turn to shoplifting. *NOTES:* Columbia's first feature to play a major first run theater.

26. After Midnight with Boston Blackie (3/18/43) B&W — 64 mins. (Crime). *DIR:* Lew Landers. *PRO:* Sam White. *SP:* Howard J. Green. Story by Aubrey Wisberg. Based on the book and characters created by Jack Boyle. *CAST:* Chester Morris, Ann Savage, George E. Stone, Richard Lane, Al Hill, Walter Sande, Lloyd Corrigan, George McKay, Cy Kendall, Jan Buckingham, Dick Elliott, Walter Baldwin, Don Barclay, John Harmon.

Blackie (Morris) is asked by an old girlfriend (Savage) to return a sack of diamonds stolen by her convict father (Baldwin), and when he turns up dead, Blackie is accused of the murder and sets out to find the real killer. [British title: *After Midnight*].

27. After the Dance (8/14/35) B&W — 60 mins. (Drama-Musical). *DIR:* Leo Bulgakov. *PRO:* Irving Briskin. *SP:* Harold Shumate, Bruce Manning. Story by Harrison Jacobs. *CAST:* Nancy Carroll, George Murphy, Thelma Todd, Jack LaRue, Arthur Hohl, Wyrley Birch, Victor Kilian, George McKay, Thurston Hall, Robert Middlemass, Harry Barris, Virginia Sale.

After escaping from prison for a crime he didn't commit, a man (Murphy) is taken in by a dancer (Carroll). They form a dance team and at the height of their success, her jealous boyfriend (LaRue) turns him over to the cops.

28. After the Rehearsal (6/84) Eastman Color — 72 mins. (Drama). *DIR/SP:* Ingmar Bergman. *PRO:* Jorn Donner. A Cinematograph-Personafilm-Triumph Films Production. *CAST:* Erland Josephson, Ingrid Thulin, Lena Olin, Bertil Guve, Nadja Palmstjerna-Weiss.

An aging theater director (Josephson), looking back on his past, discusses esoteric life and theater with a young actress (Olin). *NOTES:* Originally filmed for Swedish television. Limited theatrical release; in Swedish with English subtitles. [British title: *The Rehearsal*]. [Original Swedish title: *Efter Repetitionen*].

29. After the Storm (4/19/28) B&W — 55 mins. (Drama). *DIR:* George B. Seitz. *PRO:* Harry Cohn. *SP:* Will M. Ritchie. Story by Harold Shumate. *CAST:* Hobart Bosworth, Eugenia Gilbert, Charles Delaney, Maude George, George Kuwa, Linda Loredo.

A sea captain (Bosworth) deserts his wife (George) and takes his young son

(Delaney) to sea. Twenty years later the wife stows away aboard ship to be near her son.

30. Against All Odds (3/84) Metrocolor—128 mins. (Crime-Drama). *DIR:* Taylor Hackford. *PRO:* Taylor Hackford, William S. Gilmore. *SP:* Eric Hughes. Based on the screenplay *Out of the Past* by Daniel Mainwaring and *Build My Gallows High* by William Morrow. A New Visions Production. *CAST:* Rachel Ward, Jeff Bridges, James Woods, Alex Karras, Jane Greer, Richard Widmark, Dorian Harewood, Swoosie Kurtz, Saul Rubinek, Pat Corley, Bill McKinney, Allen Williams.

A fading professional football player (Bridges) falls in love with the girlfriend (Ward) of a small-time hood (Woods) and becomes involved with shady, high-stakes real estate dealings. *NOTES:* A remake of the 1947 RKO film *Out of the Past.*

31. Against the Law (11/21/34) B&W—61 mins. (Crime). *DIR:* Lambert Hillyer. *PRO:* Irving Briskin. *SP:* Harold Shumate. *CAST:* Johnny Mack Brown, Sally Blane, Arthur Hohl, George Meeker, James Bush, Bradley Page, Ward Bond, Al Hill, Hooper Atchley, Joseph Crehan.

An ambulance driver (Brown) seeks revenge against the underworld when his best friend (Meeker) is killed by the mob. [British title: *Urgent Call*].

32. Age of Consent (12/69) Pathe Color—98 mins. (Drama). *DIR:* Michael Powell. *PRO:* Michael Powell, James Mason. *SP:* Peter Yeldham. Based on the book by Norman Lindsay. A Nautilus Production. *CAST:* James Mason, Helen Mirren, Jack MacGowran, Neva Carr-Glyn, Frank Thring, Andonia Katsaros, Michael Boddy, Harold Hopkins, Max Meldrum, Judy McGrath, Slim Da Gray, Clarissa Kaye.

A disillusioned artist (Mason) returns to an island off the Great Barrier Reef and while there asks a young girl (Mirren) to become his model.

33. Agnes of God (10/85) Metrocolor—98 mins. (Crime-Drama). *DIR:* Norman Jewison. *PRO:* Patrick Palmer, Norman Jewison. *SP:* John Pielmier. Based on the play by John Pielmier. *CAST:* Jane Fonda, Meg Tilly, Anne Bancroft, Anne Pitoniak, Winston Rekert, Gratien Gelinas, Guy Hoffman, Gabriel Arcand, Francoise Faucher, Jacques Tourangeau.

A psychiatrist (Fonda) probes the mind of a nun (Tilly) to find the reason a newborn infant was found murdered in her room.

Agua en el Suelo, El *see* **El Agua en el Suelo**

34. Air Hawks (6/1/35) B&W—68 mins. (Adventure). *DIR:* Albert S. Rogell. *PRO:* Ben Pivar. *SP:* Griffin Jay, Grace Neville. *CAST:* Ralph Bellamy, Wiley Post, Douglas Dumbrille, Tala Birell, Robert Allen, Billie Seward, Victor Kilian, Robert Middlemass, Geneva Mitchell, Wyrley Birch, Edward Van Sloan, Bill Irving, C. Franklin Parker, Peggy Terry, Al Hill.

A pilot (Bellamy) must stop a rival airline company, using a motor-immobilizing ray, from downing his company's planes.

35. Air Hostess (1/21/33) B&W—67 mins. (Drama). *DIR:* Albert S. Rogell. *SP:* Keene Thompson, Milton Raison. Story by Grace Perkins. *CAST:* Evalyn Knapp, James Murray, Arthur Pierson, Jane Darwell, Thelma Todd, J. M. Kerrigan, Mike Donlin, Dutch Hendrian.

An air hostess (Knapp) discovers her husband (Murray) with another woman (Todd), leaves him, but he ends up saving her life when the train she is on is headed for destruction.

36. Air Hostess (8/25/49) B&W—60 mins. (Drama). *DIR:* Lew Landers. *PRO:* Wallace MacDonald. *SP:* Robert Libott, Frank Burt. Story by Louise Rousseau. *CAST:* Gloria Henry, Audrey Ford, Marjorie Lord, Ann Doran, Ross Ford, William Wright, Olive Dearing, Laetrice Joy, Barbara Billingsley, Harry Tyler, Jessie Arnold, Irene Tedrow, Grady Sutton.

Three girls (Henry, Ford, Lord) become air hostesses for various reasons.

37. Al Jennings of Oklahoma (1/17/51) Technicolor—79 mins. (Western). *DIR:* Ray Nazarro. *PRO:* Rudolph C. Flothow. *SP:* George Bricker. Original story by Al Jennings and Will Irwin. *CAST:* Dan Duryea, Gale Storm, Dick Foran, Guinn "Big Boy" Williams, Gloria Henry, Stanley Andrews, John Dehner, Harry Shannon, James Millican, Raymond Greenleaf, Helen Brown, Robert Phillips, Charles Meredith, John Ridgely, Robert Bice, George J. Lewis, Jimmie Dodd, Edwin Parker, James Griffith, William "Bill" Phillips, William Norton Bailey, Louis Jean Heydt, Harry Cording, Theresa Harris.

Al Jennings (Duryea) rises from train robber to successful lawyer.

Alamein, El *see* **El Alamein**

38. Alias Boston Blackie (4/2/42) B&W—67 mins. (Crime). *DIR:* Lew Landers. *PRO:* Wallace MacDonald. *SP:* Paul Yawitz. Based on characters created by Jack Boyle. *CAST:* Chester Morris, Adele Mara, George E. Stone, Larry Parks, Richard Lane, Walter Sande, Lloyd Corrigan, Paul Fix, Cy Kendall, Ben Taggart, Lloyd Bridges, George McKay, Ernie Adams, Edmund Cobb, Sidney Miller, Bud Geary, Duke York.

Blackie (Morris) helps an escaped prisoner (Parks) to clear himself of a murder charge.

39. Alias Mr. Twilight (12/24/46) B&W—71 mins. (Drama). *DIR:* John Sturges. *PRO:* John Haggott. *SP:* Brenda Weisberg, Malcolm Stuart Boylan. Story by Arthur E. Orloff. *CAST:* Michael Duane, Trudy Marshall, Lloyd Corrigan, Gigi Perreau, Rosalind Ivan, Jeff York, Peter Brocco, Torben Meyer.

An old rogue (Corrigan) loses custody of his orphaned granddaughter (Perreau) when he is sent to jail.

40. Alias the Lone Wolf (8/22/27) B&W—65 mins. (Crime). *DIR:* Edward H. Griffith. *PRO:* Harry Cohn. *SP:* Edward H. Griffith, Dorothy Howell. Based on the book by Louis Joseph Vance. *CAST:* Bert Lytell, Lois Wilson, Paulette Duvall, William V. Mong, Ned Sparks, Ann Brody, Alphonz Ethier, James Mason.

The Lone Wolf (Lytell) helps a woman (Wilson) smuggle her jewels through customs to prevent jewel thieves from getting them.

Alibi, L' *see* **L'Alibi**

41. Alibi for Murder (10/2/36) B&W—61 mins. (Crime-Mystery). *DIR:* D. Ross Lederman. *PRO:* Ralph Cohn. *SP:* Tom Van Dycke. *CAST:* William Gargan, Marguerite Churchill, Gene Morgan, Dwight Frye, Egon Brecher, John Gallaudet, Romaine Callender, Drue Leyton, Wade Boteler, Raymond Lawrence.

A radio newsman (Gargan) sets out to find the murderer of a scientist (Brecher) he has been sent to interview.

42. All American Sweetheart (12/20/37) B&W—62 mins. (Crime). *DIR:* Lambert Hillyer. *PRO:* Wallace MacDonald. *SP:* Grace Neville, Fred Niblo, Jr., Michael L. Simmons. Story by Robert E. Kent. *CAST:* Patricia Farr, Scott Colton, Gene Morgan, Jimmy Eagles, Arthur Loft, Joe Twerp, Ruth Hilliard, Donald Briggs, Louis

Da Pron, Allen Brook, Frank C. Wilson, Deane Janis, The Four Esquires.

Racketeers try to take over the local college rowing team by kidnapping the crew's coxswain (Eagles). He is rescued by his best friend (Colton) and they go on to win the big race.

43. All Ashore (3/20/53) Technicolor—80 mins. (Musical-Comedy). *DIR*: Richard Quine. *PRO*: Jonie Taps. *SP*: Blake Edwards, Richard Quine. Story by Blake Edwards, Robert Wells. *CAST*: Mickey Rooney, Dick Haymes, Peggy Ryan, Ray McDonald, Barbara Bates, Jody Lawrence, Fay Roope, Jean Willes, Rica Owen, Patricia Walker, Edwin Parker, Dick Crockett, Frank Kreig, Ben Welden, Gloria Pall, Joan Shawlee.

Three sailors (Rooney, Haymes, McDonald) pose as entertainers to earn money while on shore leave.

44. All the King's Men (10/7/49) B&W—109 mins. (Drama). *DIR/ PRO/SP*: Robert Rossen. Based on the book by Robert Penn Warren. *CAST*: Broderick Crawford, Joanne Dru, John Ireland, John Derek, Ralph Dumke, Mercedes McCambridge, Shepperd Strudwick, Anne Seymour, Katharine Warren, Raymond Greenleaf, Walter Burke, Will Wright, Grandon Rhodes, Paul Ford, Richard Hale, Ted French, Houseley Stevenson, Judd Holdren.

An honest man (Crawford) is elected mayor and then governor, but becomes corrupted by power and ruins his life and those of his friends before being assassinated.

45. All the Young Men (8/60) B&W—86 mins. (War). *DIR/PRO/ SP*: Hall Bartlett. A Jaguar Production. *CAST*: Alan Ladd, Sidney Poitier, James Darren, Glenn Corbett, Mort Sahl, Ana St. Clair, Paul Richards, Dick Davalos, Lee Kingsolving, Joe Gallison, Paul Baxley, Charles Quin-

livan, Michael Davis, Ingemar Johansson.

During the Korean War, a black man (Poitier) must fight the prejudice and resentment of a platoon when he is given command over a professional sergeant (Ladd).

46. Aloha, Bobby and Rose (4/ 75) Metrocolor—88 mins. (Drama). *DIR/SP*: Floyd Mutrux. *PRO*: Fouad Said. A Cine Artists International Production. *CAST*: Paul LeMat, Dianne Hull, Tim McIntire, Leigh French, Robert Carradine, Noble Willingham, Martine Bartlett, Mario Gallo, Erick Hines, Tony Gardenas, Edward James Olmos, William Dooley, Cliff Emmich, David Bond.

An auto mechanic (LeMat) and a car wash worker (Hull) get mixed up in a robbery and find themselves on the run.

47. Alvarez Kelly (10/66) Eastman Color/Panavision—110 mins. (Western). *DIR*: Edward Dmytryk. *PRO*: Sol C. Siegel. *SP*: Franklin Coen, Elliott Arnold. Story by Franklin Coen. *CAST*: William Holden, Janice Rule, Richard Widmark, Victoria Shaw, Richard Rust, Arthur Franz, Donald "Red" Barry, Harry Carey, Jr., Mauritz Hugo, Duke Hobbie, Roger C. Carmel, Howard Caine, G. B. Atwater, Robert Morgan, Clint Ritchie, Stephanie Hill, Paul Lukather, Indus Arthur.

A cattleman (Holden) sells his cattle to the Union Army, but en route to deliver them he is waylaid by a Confederate officer (Widmark) and his men.

48. The Amazing Mr. Williams (11/22/39) B&W—80 mins. (Crime-Comedy). *DIR*: Alexander Hall. *PRO*: Everett Riskin. *SP*: Dwight Taylor, Sy Bartlett, Richard Maibaum. Story by Sy Bartlett. *CAST*: Melvyn Douglas, Joan Blondell, Clarence Kolb, Maude Eburne, Edward Brophy, Ruth Donnelly, Donald MacBride, Don Beddoe, Jonathan Hale, John Wray.

A detective (Douglas) postpones his marriage as he investigates a murder.

49. Ambush at Tomahawk Gap (5/1/53) Technicolor — 73 mins. (Western). *DIR:* Fred F. Sears. *PRO:* Wallace MacDonald. *SP:* David Lang. *CAST:* John Hodiak, Maria Elena Marques, John Derek, David Brian, Ray Teal, John Qualen, Percy Helton, Trevor Bardette, John Doucette, Otto Hulett.

Four ex-convicts (Hodiak, Derek, Brian, Teal), searching for their hidden loot in a ghost town, get caught in an Indian attack.

50. Ambush in Leopard Street (5/62) B&W — 60 mins. (Crime). *DIR:* J. Henry Piperno. *PRO:* Bill Luckwell, Jock McGregor. *SP:* Bernard Spicer, Ahmed Faroughy. Story by Bernard Spicer. A Luckwell Production. *CAST:* James Kenney, Michael Brennan, Bruce Seton, Norman Rodway, Jean Harvey, Pauline Delany, Marie Conmee.

An aging thief (Brennan) comes out of retirement to plan his last big job, enlisting the aid of his old friends and novices. *NOTES:* Limited theatrical release.

51. The Ambushers (12/67) Technicolor — 101 mins. (Spy-Drama). *DIR:* Henry Levin. *PRO:* Irving Allen. *SP:* Herbert Baker. Based on the book by Donald Hamilton. A Meadway-Claude Production. *CAST:* Dean Martin, Senta Berger, Janice Rule, James Gregory, Albert Salmi, Kurt Kazner, Beverly Adams, David Mauro, Roy Jenson, John Brascia, Linda Foster.

Matt Helm (Martin) is sent to Mexico to retrieve an experimental flying saucer from the enemy.

52. American Anthem (7/86) MGM Color/Panavision — 100 mins. (Sports-Drama). *DIR:* Albert Magnoli.

PRO: Robert Schaffel, Doug Chapin. *SP:* Evan Archerd, Jeff Benjamin. Story by Evan Archerd, Jeff Benjamin, Susan Williams. A Fields-Doug Chapin-Lorimar Production. *CAST:* Mitch Gaylord, Janet Jones, Michelle Phillips, R. J. Williams, Michael Pataki, Patrice Donnelly, Stacey Maloney, Maria Anz, Andrew White.

Two young people (Gaylord, Jones) overcome overwhelming odds to win a place on the national gymnastic team.

53. American Madness (8/15/32) B&W — 75 mins. (Drama). *DIR:* Frank Capra. *PRO:* Harry Cohn. *SP:* Robert Riskin. A Frank Capra Production. *CAST:* Walter Huston, Pat O'Brien, Kay Johnson, Constance Cummings, Gavin Gordon, Arthur Hoyt, Robert Emmett O'Conner, Robert Ellis, Edwin Maxwell, Edward Martindale, Berton Churchill, Ralph Lewis, Pat O' Malley, Jeanne Sorel, Walter Walker, Anderson Lawlor, Sterling Holloway.

An idealistic bank president (Huston), ignoring his board of directors, makes loans on faith to businessmen.

54. American Pop (2/81) Eastman Color — 97 mins. (Animated-Musical). *DIR:* Ralph Bakshi. *PRO:* Martin Ransohoff, Ralph Bakshi. *SP:* Ronni Kern. *CAST:* Voices of Ron Thompson, Marya Small, Jerry Holland, Lisa Jane Persky, Jeffrey Lippa, Roz Kelly, Frank DeKova.

The history of American pop music, from vaudeville to rock 'n' roll, traced through several generations of a family of musicians.

American Success *see* **The American Success Company**

55. The American Success Company (3/80) Eastman Color — 94 mins. (Comedy-Drama). *DIR:* William Richert. *PRO:* Daniel H. Blatt, Edgar J. Scherick. *SP:* Larry Cohen, William Richert. Story by Larry Cohen. *CAST:*

Jeff Bridges, Belinda Bauer, Ned Beatty, Steven Keats, Bianca Jagger, John Glover, Mascha Gonska, Michael Durrell, David Brooks, Judy Brown, Michael Burger, Pater Capell, Lloyd Catlett.

A loser (Bridges) becomes a tough guy to impress his father (Beatty) and succeed in life. NOTES: Re-edited and re-released in 1981 as *American Success* and 1983 as *Success.*

56. Among the Missing (9/25/34) B&W — 62 mins. (Crime). DIR: Albert S. Rogell. PRO: Harry Cohn. SP: Fred Niblo, Jr., Herbert Asbury. Story by Florence Wagner. CAST: Henrietta Crosman, Richard Cromwell, Billie Seward, Arthur Hohl, Ivan Simpson, Ben Taggart, Wade Boteler, Harry C. Bradley, Claire DuBrey, Douglas Cosgrove, Paul Hurst.

An old lady (Crosman) leaves her family, takes a job as a cook for an antique dealer who is also a jewel thief, and helps one of the gang members (Cromwell) to reform.

Among Vultures see **Frontier Hellcat**

57. The Amsterdam Kill (3/78) Technicolor/Panavision — 89 mins. (Crime). DIR: Robert Clouse. PRO: Andre Morgan. SP: Robert Clouse, Gregory Teifer. Story by Gregory Teifer. A Golden Harvest Production. CAST: Robert Mitchum, Bradford Dillman, Richard Egan, Leslie Nielsen, Keye Luke, George Cheung, Chan Sing.

An ex-narcotics investigator (Mitchum) is brought out of retirement to track down a traitor within the Drug Enforcement Agency in Hong Kong.

An Evening with Batman and Robin see **Batman**

58. Anatomy of a Murder (7/59) B&W — 160 mins. (Crime-Drama). DIR/PRO: Otto Preminger. SP: Wendell Mayes. Based on the book by Robert Traver. CAST: James Stewart, Lee Remick, Ben Gazzara, Arthur O'Connell, Eve Arden, Kathryn Grant, George C. Scott, Joseph N. Welch, Brooks West, Murray Hamilton, Orson Bean, Alexander Campbell, Joseph Kearns, Howard McNear, Ken Lynch, John Qualen, Duke Ellington.

A small town lawyer (Stewart) defends an Army lieutenant (Gazzara) accused of murdering a bartender who had assaulted his wife (Remick).

59. And Baby Makes Three (12/20/49) B&W — 84 mins. (Comedy). DIR: Henry Levin. PRO: Robert Lord. SP: Lou Breslow, Joseph Hoffman. CAST: Robert Young, Barbara Hale, Robert Hutton, Janis Carter, Billie Burke, Nicholas Joy, Lloyd Corrigan, Howland Chamberlin, Melville Cooper, Louise Currie, Grandon Rhodes, Katherine Warren, Wilton Graff, Joe Sawyer.

When a recently divorced couple (Young, Hale) discover they are to have a baby, the wife tries to get out of her second marriage and get her husband back.

60. . . . And Justice for All (9/79) Metrocolor — 120 mins. (Drama). DIR: Norman Jewison. PRO: Norman Jewison, Patrick Palmer. SP: Valerie Curtain, Barry Levinson. CAST: Al Pacino, Jack Warden, John Forsythe, Lee Strasberg, Jeffrey Tambor, Christine Lahti, Sam Levene, Robert Christian, Thomas Waites, Larry Bryggman, Craig T. Nelson, Beverly Sanders, Connie Sawyer, Keith Andes, Robert Symonds, Charles Siebert, Alan North.

An idealistic lawyer (Pacino) defends a self-righteous judge (Forsythe) against an assault charge.

61. And Now for Something Completely Different (8/72) Eastman Color — 88 mins. (Comedy). DIR:

Ian MacNaughton. *PRO*: Patricia Casey. *SP*: Graham Chapman, John Cleese, Terry Gilliam, Eric Idle, Terry Jones, Michael Palin. A Kettledrum-Python Productions Film. *CAST*: Graham Chapman, John Cleese, Eric Idle, Terry Jones, Michael Palin, Carol Cleveland, Connie Booth.

First feature for the Monty Python troupe of TV fame. Includes some of their best skits, "The World's Deadliest Joke," "Upper-Class Twit of the Year," "Dead Parrot," and the "Lumberjack Song."

62. And So They Were Married (5/14/36) B&W — 72 mins. (Comedy). *DIR*: Elliott Nugent. *PRO*: B. P. Schulberg. *SP*: Doris Anderson, Joseph Anthony, A. Laurie Brazee. Story by Sarah Addington. *CAST*: Melvyn Douglas, Mary Astor, Edith Fellows, Jackie Moran, Donald Meek, Dorothy Stickney, Romaine Callender, Douglas Scott, Margaret Armstrong, George McKay, Wade Boteler, Charles Irwin, Dennis O'Keefe, Charles Arnt, Al Bridge, Hooper Atchley.

When two single parents (Douglas, Astor) meet at a winter resort and fall in love, their children try to keep them from marrying.

63. . . . And Suddenly It's Murder (1/64) B&W — 90 mins. (Comedy). *DIR*: Mario Camerini. *PRO*: Dino De Laurentiis. *SP*: Rodolfo Sonego, Giorgio Artorio, Stefano Strucchi, Luciano Vincenzoni. A Royal Films International Production. *CAST*: Alberto Sordi, Vittorio Gassman, Silvana Mangano, Dorian Gray, Nino Manfredi, Franca Valeri, Bernard Blier, Georges Rivere.

Three couples (Sordi, Gray, Gassman, Mangano, Manfredi, Valeri), on holiday in Monte Carlo, become suspects in a murder case when a corpse is found in one of their trunks. *NOTES*: In Italian with English sub-

titles. [Original Italian title: *Crimen*]. [Original French title: *Chacun Son Alibi*].

64. And the Ship Sails On (1/84) Eastman Color — 130 mins. (Comedy). *DIR*: Federico Fellini. *PRO*: Franco Cristaldi. *SP*: Federico Fellini, Tonino Guerra. An RAI-VIDES-Triumph Films Production. *CAST*: Freddie Jones, Barbara Jefford, Victor Poletti, Peter Cellier, Elsa Marinardi, Norma West, Paolo Paolini, Sarah Jane Varley, Phillip Locke, Pina Bausch, Fiorenzo Serra, Linda Polan, Maurice Barrier, Fred Williams, Janet Suzman.

In 1914, a shipload of passengers set sail to a small island to scatter the ashes of a great soprano who recently died. Trouble arises when it is learned that there are Serbian freedom fighters on board, and the ship is halted. *NOTES*: Limited theatrical release; in Italian with English subtitles. [Original Italian title: *E la Nave Va*].

65. The Anderson Tapes (6/71) Eastman Color — 98 mins. (Crime). *DIR*: Sidney Lumet. *PRO*: Robert M. Weitman. *SP*: Frank R. Pierson. Based on the book by Lawrence Sanders. *CAST*: Sean Connery, Dyan Cannon, Martin Balsam, Ralph Meeker, Alan King, Christopher Walken, Val Avery, Dick Anthony Williams, Garrett Morris, Stan Gottlieb, Richard B. Shull, Margaret Hamilton, Conrad Bain, Janet Ward, Judith Lowry, Anthony Holland.

An ex-convict (Connery) plans to rob a posh apartment building, unaware that the police are recording his every move.

Angel *see* **Danny Boy**

66. Angels Over Broadway (9/27/40) B&W — 78 mins. (Drama). *DIR*: Ben Hecht, Lee Garmes. *PRO/SP*: Ben Hecht. *CAST*: Douglas Fairbanks, Jr., Rita Hayworth, Thomas

Mitchell, John Qualen, George Watts, Ralph Theodore, Eddie Foster, Jack Roper, Constance Worth, Frank Conlan, Walter Baldwin, Jack Carr, Al Seymour, Richard Bon.

An alcoholic playwright (Mitchell) and an embezzler (Qualen) plan to take a card shark (Fairbanks) for all he has.

67. Ann Carver's Profession (6/9/33) B&W — 71 mins. (Drama). DIR: Edward Buzzell. PRO: Harry Cohn. SP: Robert Riskin. CAST: Fay Wray, Gene Raymond, Claire Dodd, Arthur Pierson, Frank Conroy, Claude Gillingwater, Frank Albertson, Jessie Ralph, Robert Barrat, Edward Keane, Diana Bori.

A female lawyer (Wray) defends her husband (Raymond) when he is accused of murdering his lover (Dodd).

68. Anna Lucasta (7/11/49) B&W — 86 mins. (Drama). DIR: Irving Rapper. PRO: Philip Yordan. SP: Philip Yordan, Arthur Laurents. Based on the play by Philip Yordan. CAST: William Bishop, Paulette Goddard, Oscar Homolka, John Ireland, Broderick Crawford, Will Geer, Gale Page, Mary Wickes, Whit Bissell, Lisa Golm, James Brown, Dennie Moore, Anthony Caruso.

A young streetwalker (Goddard) is married off by her father (Holmolka) when he sees a chance to make big money. NOTES: Remade in 1958 by United Artists with an all-black cast.

69. Annie (5/82) Metrocolor/Panavision — 130 mins. (Musical). DIR: John Huston. PRO: Ray Stark. SP: Carol Sobieski. Based on the stage production that was based on the comic strip *Little Orphan Annie* by Harold Gray. CAST: Albert Finney, Carol Burnett, Bernadette Peters, Ann Reinking, Tim Curry, Aileen Quinn, Geoffrey Holder, Roger Minami, Edward Herrmann, Peter Marshall, Ken Swof-

ford, Lois DeBanzie, I.M. Hobson, Lu Leonard, Mavis Ray.

An orphan waif (Quinn) is adopted by a billionaire (Finney).

70. Anzio (7/68) Eastman Color/Panavision — 117 mins. (War). DIR: Edward Dmytryk. PRO: Dino De Laurentiis. SP: Harry A. L. Craig. Based on the book by Wynford Vaughn-Thomas. CAST: Robert Mitchum, Peter Falk, Robert Ryan, Earl Holliman, Mark Damon, Arthur Kennedy, Reni Santoni, Joseph Walsh, Thomas Hunter, Anthony Steel, Giancarlo Giannini, Patrick Magee, Arthur Franz, Wolfgang Preiss, Tonio Selwart, Elsa Albani, Wade Preston.

A war correspondent (Mitchum) covers the Allied invasion of Italy. [British title: *The Battle for Anzio*]. [Original Italian title: *Lo Sbarco di Anzio*].

71. The Apache (11/19/28) B&W — 57 mins. (Mystery). DIR: Philip E. Rosen. PRO: Jack Cohn. SP: Harriet Hinsdale. Story by Ramon Romero. CAST: Margaret Livingston, Warner Richmond, Philo McCullough, Don Alvarado.

Set in the Apache dens of Paris and Marseilles, a professional knife-thrower (Livingston) threatens her partner with death during their act unless he confesses to a crime he committed and saves the man she loves.

72. Apache Ambush (9/55) B&W — 68 mins. (Western). DIR: Fred F. Sears. PRO: Wallace MacDonald. SP: David Lang. CAST: Bill Williams, Movita, Richard Jaeckel, Alex Montoya, Tex Ritter, Ray "Crash" Corrigan, Ray Teal, Don C. Harvey, James Griffith, George Chandler, Harry Lauter, Adelle August, Bill Hale, Robert C. Foulk, James Flavin, George Keymas, Victor Millan, Kermit Maynard.

A mixed group of Confederate and Union soldiers, driving cattle from Texas to the northern states, locate a shipment of repeating rifles to be used by renegades and/or Indians in capturing Texas.

73. Apache Country (5/30/52) Sepiatone—62 mins. (Western). *DIR:* George Archainbaud. *PRO:* Armand Schaefer. *SP:* Norman S. Hall. A Gene Autry Production. *CAST:* Gene Autry, Mary Scott, Pat Buttram, Francis X. Bushman, Gregg Barton, Tom London, Byron Foulger, Mickey Simpson, Iron Eyes Cody, Sidney Mason, Harry Lauter, Frank Matts, The Cass County Boys, Carolina Cotton, Tony Whitecloud's Jemez Indians.

Autry is sent by the government to break up a gang of outlaws using the Indians to cover up its activities.

74. Apache Gold (5/65) Eastman Color/Scope—91 mins. (Western). *DIR:* Harald Reinl. *PRO:* Horst Wendlandt. *SP:* Harald G. Petersson. Based on *Winnetou* by Karl Friedrich May. A Rialto-Jadran-Preben Philipsen Production. *CAST:* Lex Barker, Mario Adorf, Pierre Brice, Marie Versini, Ralf Wolter, Walter Barnes, Chris Howland.

Old Shatterhand (Barker) and Winnetou (Brice) set out to stop a railroad magnate (Adorf) from extending his railroad through Apache country. [British title: *Winnetou the Warrior*]. [Original French title: *La Revolte des Indiens Apaches*]. [Original Italian title: *La Valle dei Lunghi Coltelli*]. [Original German title: *Winnetou—I. Teil*]. [Original Yugoslavian title: *Vinetu*].

75. Apache Territory (9/58) B&W—75 mins. (Western). *DIR:* Ray Nazarro. *PRO:* Rory Calhoun, Victor M. Orsatti. *SP:* Charles R. Marion, George W. George. Based on a story by Louis L'Amour. A Rorvic Production. *CAST:* Rory Calhoun, Barbara Bates, John Dehner, Carolyn Craig, Leo Gordon, Myron Healey, Francis De Sales, Frank DeKova, Tom Pitt-

man, Reg Parton, Bob Woodward, Fred Krone.

A drifter (Calhoun) helps a group of settlers fight off an Indian attack.

76. Appointment in Berlin (7/26/43) B&W—77 mins. (War). *DIR:* Alfred E. Green. *PRO:* Samuel Bischoff. *SP:* Horace McCoy, Michael Hogan. Story by B. P. Fineman. *CAST:* George Sanders, Marguerite Chapman, Onslow Stevens, Alan Napier, Gale Sondergaard, H. P. Sanders, Don Douglas, Jack Lee, Alec Craig, Leonard Mudie, Frederic Worlock, Steven Geray.

An ex–RAF officer (Sanders), pretending to be a traitor, flees to Berlin to become a radio propagandist, where he sends secret messages to England via word/phrase codes.

Arizona *see* **Men Are Like That**

77. Arizona (12/25/40) B&W—125 mins. (Western). *DIR/PRO:* Wesley Ruggles. *SP:* Claude Binyon. Story by Clarence Budington Kelland. *CAST:* William Holden, Jean Arthur, Warren William, Paul Harvey, George Chandler, Byron Foulger, Syd Saylor, Addison Richards, Edgar Buchanan, Regis Toomey, Carleton Young, Frank Darien, Porter Hall, Paul Lopez, Griff Barnett, Earl Crawford.

A drifter (Holden) helps a struggling freight line owner (Arthur) battle Indians and villains as they settle the town of Tucson. *NOTES:* William Holden's role was originally intended for Gary Cooper.

78. Arizona Raiders (7/65) Technicolor/Scope—88 mins. (Western). *DIR:* William Whitney. *PRO:* Grant Whytock. *SP:* Alex Gottlieb, Mary and Willard Willingham. Story by Frank Gruber, Richard Schayer. An Admiral Pictures Production. *CAST:* Audie Murphy, Gloria Talbot, Michael Dante, Ben Cooper, Buster Crabbe,

Ray Stricklyn, Fred Graham, Boyd "Red" Morgan, George Keymas, Fred Krone, Willard Willingham.

Two ex-Confederates (Murphy, Cooper) are offered a pardon if they will join the Arizona Raiders and help round up Quantrill (Graham) and his men.

79. The Arkansas Swing (7/29/ 48) B&W — 63 mins. (Comedy-Musical). *DIR:* Ray Nazarro. *PRO:* Colbert Clark. *SP:* Barry Shipman. *CAST:* Gloria Henry, Stuart Hart, June Vincent, Eleanor Donahue, The Hoosier Hotshots.

The Hoosier Hotshots help a girl (Henry) make her horse a trotting champion. [British title: *Wrong Number*].

80. Armed and Dangerous (8/86) DeLuxe Color — 88 mins. (Comedy). *DIR:* Mark L. Lester. *PRO:* Brian Grazer, James Keach. *SP:* Harold Ramis, Peter Torokvei. Story by Harold Ramis, Peter Torokvei, James Keach. A Frostbacks Production. *CAST:* John Candy, Eugene Levy, Robert Loggia, Kenneth McMillan, Meg Ryan, Brion James, Jonathan Banks, Don Stroud, Larry Hankin, Steve Railsback, Judy Landers, Bruce Kirby, Stacy Keach, Sr., Tom "Tiny" Lester.

An out-of-work cop (Candy) and a disbarred attorney (Levy) wind up working as security guards, getting mixed up with crooks and a mob union boss (Loggia).

81. Around the Corner (5/4/30) B&W — 71 mins. (Comedy). *DIR:* Bert Glennon. *SP:* Jo Swerling. *CAST:* George Sidney, Charlie Murray, Joan Peers, Charles Delaney, Larry Kent, Fred Sullivan, Harry Strang, Jess Devorska.

A Jewish pawnbroker (Sidney) and an Irish cop (Murray) adopt a foundling. Eighteen years later, when she (Peers) is ready to marry, she has to choose between a prize fighter (Delaney) and a rich boy (Kent).

82. As the Devil Commands (9/ 1/33) B&W — 70 mins. (Mystery). *DIR:* Roy William Neill. *SP:* Dan Nelson. Story by Jo Swerling. *CAST:* Alan Dinehart, Mae Clarke, Neil Hamilton, Charles Sellon, Charles Coleman, John Sheehan.

A crooked lawyer (Hamilton) murders a rich invalid (Sellon) and then frames the invalid's aide (Dinehart) in order to get his fortune.

83. As the Sea Rages (9/60) B&W — 76 mins. (Drama). *DIR:* Horst Haechler. *PRO:* Carl Szokoll. *SP:* Jeffery Dell, Jo Eisinger. Based on the screenplay by Walter Ulbrich and the book *Raubfischer in Hellas* by Werner Helwig. *CAST:* Cliff Robertson, Maria Schell, Cameron Mitchell.

A fisherman (Robertson) sacrifices his life to save a fishing village. [Original German title: *Raubfischer in Hellas*].

84. Assignment K (6/68) Technicolor — 97 mins. (Spy-Drama). *DIR:* Val Guest. *PRO:* Ben Arbeid, Maurice Foster. *SP:* Val Guest, Bill Strutton, Maurice Foster. Based on *Department K* by Hartley Howard. *CAST:* Stephen Boyd, Camilla Sparv, Michael Redgrave, Leo McKern, Jeremy Kemp, Robert Hoffman, Jane Merrow, Carl Mohner, Werner Peters, David Healy, Basil Dignam, Geoffrey Bayldon, Peter Capell, John Alderton.

A British agent (Boyd), posing as a European toy manufacturer, learns that his girl (Sparv) and his friends are double agents.

85. Assignment — Paris (9/4/52) B&W — 84 mins. (Spy-Drama). *DIR:* Robert Parrish. *PRO:* Sam Marx, Jerry Bresler. *SP:* William Bowers, Walter Goetz, Jack Palmer White. Based on *Trial by Terror* by Paul Gallico, Pauline

Gallico. *CAST:* Dana Andrews, Marta Toren, George Sanders, Audrey Totter, Sandro Giglio, Donald Randolph, Herbert Berghof, Ben Astar, Willis Bouchey, Earl Lee, Maurice Doner, Leon Askin, Paul Hoffman, Jay Adler, Mari Blanchard.

An American newsman (Andrews), assigned to Budapest, is arrested as a spy when he uncovers a Communist conspiracy.

86. Atlantic Adventure (9/10/35) B&W—68 mins. (Crime). *DIR:* Albert S. Rogell. *SP:* John Thomas Neville, Nat Dorfman. Story by Diana Bourbon. *CAST:* Lloyd Nolan, Nancy Carroll, Harry Langdon, Arthur Hohl, Robert Middlemass, Dwight Frye, John Wray, E. E. Clive, Nana Bryant.

An ex-reporter (Nolan), with his fiancee (Carroll) and his assistant (Langdon), sneak aboard an ocean liner to capture a murderer.

87. Atlantic Convoy (7/10/42) B&W—66 mins. (War). *DIR:* Lew Landers. *PRO:* Colbert Clark. *SP:* Robert Lee Johnson. *CAST:* Bruce Bennett, Virginia Field, John Beal, Clifford Severn, Larry Parks, Stanley Brown, Lloyd Bridges, Victor Kilian, Hans Schumm, Erik Rolf, Eddie Laughton.

A weather operator (Beal) with the U.S. air patrol off the coast of Iceland, is suspected of being a Nazi spy.

88. Attorney for the Defense (5/8/32) B&W—70 mins. (Drama). *DIR:* Irving Cummings. *SP:* Jo Swerling. Story by J. K. McGuinness. *CAST:* Edmund Lowe, Evelyn Brent, Constance Cummings, Donald Dillaway, Dorothy Peterson, Bradley Page, Nat Pendleton, Dwight Frye, Douglas Haig, Wallis Clark, Clarence Muse.

When a lawyer (Lowe) learns he had sent an innocent man (Frye) to his death, he tries to make up for it by educating the man's son (Dillaway).

89. Autumn Leaves (8/56) B&W—107 mins. (Drama). *DIR:* Robert Aldrich. *PRO:* William Goetz. *SP:* Jack Jevne, Lewis Meltzer, Robert Blees. *CAST:* Joan Crawford, Cliff Robertson, Vera Miles, Lorne Greene, Ruth Donnelly, Shepperd Strudwick, Selmer Jackson, Maxine Cooper, Marjorie Bennett, Frank Gerstle, Leonard Mudie, Maurice Manson.

A middle-aged spinster (Crawford) marries a younger man (Robertson) only to discover he is mentally unstable and already married.

90. The Avenger (4/19/31) B&W—65 mins. (Western). *DIR:* Roy William Neill. *PRO:* Sol Lesser. *SP:* George Morgan, Jack Townley. Story by Jack Townley. A Beverly Production. *CAST:* Buck Jones, Otto Hoffman, Dorothy Revier, Sidney Bracey, Paul Fix, Edward Hearn, Frank Ellis, Walter Percival, Edward Piel, Sr., Slim Whitaker, Al Taylor.

Joaquin Murrieta (Jones) seeks to avenge the death of his brother and bring justice to those responsible.

91. Avenging Waters (7/8/36) B&W—57 mins. (Western). *DIR:* Spencer G. Bennet. *PRO:* Larry Darmour. *SP:* Nate Gatzert. *CAST:* Ken Maynard, Beth Marion, Ward Bond, John Elliott, Tom London, Edmund Cobb, Hal Taliaferro (Wally Wales), Glenn Strange, Sterling Holloway, Buffalo Bill, Jr. (Jay Wilsey), Jack King, Zella Russell, Bud McClure, Edward Hearn, Buck Moulton, Cactus Mack, Buck Bucko.

A cowboy (Maynard) gets involved in a range war over fencing rights, manages to straighten everything out, and gets the girl (Marion).

92. The Awakening of Jim Burke (5/18/35) B&W—70 mins. (Drama). *DIR:* Lambert Hillyer. *SP:* Michael L. Simmons. Story by G. Gardner Sullivan. *CAST:* Jack Holt,

Florence Rice, Kathleen Burke, Jimmie Butler, Robert Middlemass, Wyrley Birch, George McKay, Ralph M. Remley, Frank Yaconelli.

A construction foreman (Holt) tries to make a man of his violin-playing son (Butler). [British title: *Iron Fist*].

93. The Awful Truth (10/15/37) B&W — 90 mins. (Comedy). *DIR/PRO:* Leo McCarey. *SP:* Vina Delmar. Based on the play by Arthur Richman. *CAST:* Irene Dunne, Cary Grant, Ralph Bellamy, Alexander D'Arcy, Cecil Cunningham, Molly Lamont, Esther Dale, Joyce Compton, Robert Allen, Robert Warwick, Mary Forbes, Al Bridge, Edgar Dearing, Vernon Dent, Byron Foulger, Edward Piel, Sr., Bess Flowers, John Tyrrell.

When a couple divorce (Grant, Dunne), they realize they still love each other and try to spoil each other's plans for re-marriage. *NOTES:* This was a stage play in 1922 and was filmed as a silent in 1925 with Agnes Ayres and Warner Baxter, then in 1929 with Henry Daniell and Ina Claire. Remade by Columbia in 1953 as *Let's Do It Again*.

94. Babette Goes to War (3/60) Eastman Color/Scope — 106 mins. (Satire-Comedy). *DIR:* Christian Jaque. *PRO:* Raoul J. Levy. *SP:* Jean Ferry. Story by Gerard Oury, Raoul J. Levy. *CAST:* Brigitte Bardot, Jacques Charrier, Hans Messemer, Yves Vincent, Ronald Howard, Francis Blanche, Rene Havard, Pierre Bertin.

In 1940, a French refugee girl (Bardot) is sent by the British to France to kidnap a Nazi general and delay the invasion of England. [Original French title: *Babette S'en Va-t-en Guerre*].

95. Babies for Sale (6/14/40) B&W — 65 mins. (Drama). *DIR:* Charles Barton. *PRO:* Ralph Cohn. *SP:* Robert D. Andrews. Story by Robert Chapin, Joseph Carole. *CAST:* Rochelle Hudson, Glenn Ford, Miles Mander, Joseph DeStefani, Georgia Caine, Isabel Jewell, Eva Hyde, Selmer Jackson, Mary Currier, Edwin Stanley, Douglas Wood, John Qualen, Helen Brown.

A crusading reporter (Ford) sets out to expose a doctor (Mander) operating an illegal adoption business.

96. Baby Blue Marine (5/76) Eastman Color/Panavision — 90 mins. (Drama). *DIR:* John Hancock. *PRO:* Aaron Spelling, Leonard Goldberg. *SP:* Stanford Whitmore. *CAST:* Jan-Michael Vincent, Glynnis O'Conner, Katherine Helmond, Dana Elcar, Bert Remsen, Bruno Kirby, Jr., Richard Gere, Art Lund, Michael Conrad, Kenneth Tobey, Adam Arkin, Allan Miller, Will Seltzer, Michael LeClair.

In 1943, a Marine dropout (Vincent) is mistaken for a hero when he returns home.

97. Baby, the Rain Must Fall (1/65) B&W — 100 mins. (Drama). *DIR:* Robert Mulligan. *PRO:* Alan J. Pakula. *SP:* Horton Foote. Based on the play *The Traveling Lady* by Horton Foote. *CAST:* Steve McQueen, Lee Remick, Don Murray, Paul Fix, Ruth White, Carol Veazie, Charles White, Josephine Hutchinson, Estelle Hemsley, George Dunn, Kimberly Block, Zamah Cunningham.

A parolee (McQueen) returns home to his wife (Remick) and daughter (Block), but is unable to change his ways.

98. The Bachelor Girl (5/20/29) B&W — 65 mins. (Drama). *DIR:* Richard Thorpe. *PRO:* Harry Cohn. *SP:* Jack Townley. Story by Frederic Hatton, Fanny Hatton, Weldon Melick. *CAST:* William Collier, Jr., Jacqueline Logan, Thelma Todd, Edward Hearn.

When a salesman (Collier) is fired for being incompetent, his girl (Logan) gets him a job with a rival company.

NOTES: Only three talking sequences in the movie.

99. The Bachelor's Baby (2/20/27) B&W — 56 mins. (Comedy). *DIR:* Frank R. Strayer. *PRO:* Harry Cohn. *SP:* Julian Sands. Story by Garrett Elsden Fort. *CAST:* Helene Chadwick, Harry Myers, Midget Gustav, Edith Yorke, Blanche Payson, Pat Harmon, James Marcus.

A couple (Myers, Chadwick) hire a midget (Gustav) to impersonate their supposedly sick child. All goes well until the girl's parents and the midget's wife arrive.

100. Backfire (4/65) B&W — 97 mins. (Crime-Thriller). *DIR:* Jean Becker. *PRO:* Paul-Edmond Decharme. *SP:* Didier Goulard, Maurice Fabre, Jean Becker. Based on the book by Clet Coroner. A Royal Films International Production. *CAST:* Jean-Paul Belmondo, Jean Seberg, Gert Frobe, Enrico Maria Salerno, Renate Emert, Jean-Pierre Marielle, Wolfgang Preiss, Fernando Rey, Diana Lorys, Michel Beaune, Roberto Camardiel.

A man (Belmondo) and his mistress (Seberg) are hired to smuggle a shipment of gold from one country to another. NOTES: In French with English subtitles. [Original French title: *Echappement Libre*]. [Original Italian title: *Scappamento Aperto*]. [Original Spanish title: *Escape Libre*].

101. Bad for Each Other (1/54) B&W — 83 mins. (Drama). *DIR:* Irving Rapper. *PRO:* William Fadiman. *SP:* Irving Wallace, Horace McCoy. Based on *Scapel* by Horace McCoy. *CAST:* Charlton Heston, Lizabeth Scott, Dianne Foster, Mildred Dunnock, Arthur Franz, Ray Collins, Marjorie Rambeau, Lester Matthews, Rhys Williams, Lydia Clarke, Chris Alcaide, Robert Keys, Frank Tully, Ann Robinson.

An idealistic man (Heston) chooses a career as a society doctor, until a mine disaster reverses his decision.

102. Bad Men of the Hills (8/13/42) B&W — 58 mins. (Western). *DIR:* William Berke. *PRO:* Jack Fier. *SP:* Luci Ward. *CAST:* Charles Starrett, Luana Walters, Cliff Edwards, Jack Ingram, Russell Hayden, Guy Usher, Al Bridge, Ben Corbett, Dick Botiller, Frank Ellis, Art Mix, John Cason, Joel Friedkin, Norma Jean Wooters, John Shay, Carl Sepulveda.

A U.S. marshal (Starrett) is assigned to stop a murderous sheriff (Bridge) from taking over the local ranches. [British title: *Wrongly Accused*].

103. Bait (3/54) B&W — 79 mins. (Drama). *DIR/PRO:* Hugo Haas. *SP:* Samuel W. Taylor. *CAST:* Cleo Moore, John Agar, Hugo Haas, Emmett Lynn, Bruno VeSota, Jan Englund, George Keymas. Prolog by Sir Cedric Hardwicke.

A prospector (Haas) uses his wife (Moore) as bait to try and kill his partner (Agar) when they discover a lost gold mine.

Bamba, La *see* **La Bamba**

104. Bambole! (The Dolls) (6/65) B&W — 111 mins. (Drama). *DIR:* Dino Risi. *SP:* Gianni Polidori — "The Telephone Call." *DIR:* Luigi Comencini. *SP:* Gianni Polidori — "Treatise on Eugenics." *DIR:* Franco Rossi. *SP:* Rodolfo Sonego — "The Soup." *DIR:* Mauro Bolognini. *SP:* Leo Benvenuti, Piero De Bernardi — "Monsignor Cupid." *PRO:* Gianni Hecht Lucari. Based on *Tales of the Decameron* by Giovanni Boccaccio. A Royal Films International Production. *CAST:* "The Telephone Call" — Virna Lisi, Nino Manfredi, Alicia Bradet. "Treatise on Eugenics" — Elke Sommer, Maurizio Arena, Piero Focaccia. "The Soup" — Monica Vitti, John Karlsen, Orazio Orlando, Roberto De Simone. "Monsignor Cupid"—Gina Lollobrigida, Jean Sorel, Akim Tamiroff.

A quartet of stories focusing on everyday Italian life. [British title: *Four Kinds of Love*].

105. The Bamboo Prison (12/54) B&W—79 mins. (War). *DIR*: Lewis Seiler. *PRO*: Bryan Foy. *SP*: Edwin Blum, Jack DeWitt. Story by Jack De-Witt. *CAST*: Robert Francis, Dianne Foster, Brian Keith, Jerome Courtland, Jack Kelly, E. G. Marshall, Earle Hyman, Murray Matheson, King Donovan, Leo Gordon, Dick Jones, Richard Loo, Keye Luke, George Keymas, Pepe Hern.

In a North Korean P.O.W. camp, a prisoner (Francis) poses as a traitor to obtain secret information from the enemy.

106. Band of Outsiders (3/66) B&W—95 mins. (Crime-Drama). *DIR/SP*: Jean-Luc Godard. *PRO*: Philippe Dussart. Based on *Fool's Gold/Pigeon Vole* by Dolores Hitchens. An Anouchka-Orsay-Royal Films International Production. *CAST*: Anna Karina, Claude Brasseur, Sami Frey, Louisa Colpeyn, Daniele Girard, Ernest Menzer, Chantal Darget, Michele Seghers, Georges Staquet.

A group of youths (Karina, Brasseur, Frey) sever relations with their parents and turn to a life of crime. [Original French title: *Bande a Parte*].

107. The Bandit of Sherwood Forest (2/21/46) Technicolor—86 mins. (Adventure). *DIR*: George Sherman, Henry Levin. *PRO*: Leonard S. Picker, Clifford Sanforth. *SP*: Wilfrid H. Pettitt, Melvin Levy. Story by Paul A. Castleton, Wilfrid H. Pettitt. Based on *The Son of Robin Hood* by Paul A. Castleton. *CAST*: Cornel Wilde, Anita Louise, Jill Esmond, Edgar Buchanan, Henry Daniell, George Macready, Russell Hicks, John Abbott, Lloyd Corrigan, Eva Moore, Ray Teal, Ian Wolfe, Mauritz Hugo, Philip Van Zandt, Ralph Dunn, Dick Curtis, George Eldredge, Lane Chandler, Gene Roth, Holmes Herbert, Leslie Denison, Maurice R. Tauzin, Harry Cording, Nelson Leigh, Robert Scott, Ross Hunter, Jimmy Lloyd, Ted Allan, Ferdinand Munier.

The son (Wilde) of Robin Hood (Hicks) returns to Sherwood Forest, and with his father and his band, vows to save England's young king (Tauzin).

108. The Bandit of Zhobe (4/59) Eastman Color/Scope—81 mins. (Adventure). *DIR/SP*: John Gilling. *PRO*: Irving Allen, Albert R. Broccoli. Story by Richard Maibaum. A Warick Film Production. *CAST*: Victor Mature, Anne Aubrey, Anthony Newley, Norman Woodland, Dermot Walsh, Walter Gotell, Sean Kelly, Paul Stassino, Laurence Taylor, Denis Shaw.

In 19th century India, an Indian leader (Mature) turns outlaw when he believes his family has been wiped out by the British.

109. Bandits of El Dorado (10/20/49) B&W—56 mins. (Western). *DIR*: Ray Nazarro. *PRO*: Colbert Clark. *SP*: Barry Shipman. *CAST*: Charles Starrett, George J. Lewis, Smiley Burnette, John Dehner, Clayton Moore, Fred F. Sears, Jock Mahoney, John Doucette, Max Wagner, Henry Kulky, Mustard and Gravy.

The Durango Kid (Starrett) goes undercover to find out why outlaws have been disappearing into Mexico. [British title: *Tricked*].

110. Barabbas (12/62) Technicolor/Technirama—144 mins. (Historical-Drama). *DIR*: Richard Fleischer. *PRO*: Dino De Laurentiis. *SP*: Christopher Fry. Based on the novel by Par Lagerkvist. *CAST*: Anthony Quinn, Silvana Mangano, Arthur Kennedy, Katy Jurado, Harry Andrews, Vittorio Gassman, Jack Palance, Ernest Borgnine, Norman Wooland, Valentina Cortese, Michael Gwynn, Douglas Fowley, Robert Hall, Lawrence Payne, Ivan Triesault.

Pardoned instead of Christ, Barabbas (Quinn) is sentenced to the silver mines, becomes a gladiator, and turns Christian.

111. Barbary Pirate (11/10/49) B&W—65 mins. (Adventure). *DIR:* Lew Landers. *PRO:* Sam Katzman. *SP:* Robert Libott, Frank Burt. *CAST:* Donald Woods, Trudy Marshall, Lenore Aubert, Stefan Schnabel, Ross Ford, John Dehner, Matthew Boulton, Nelson Leigh, Joe Mantell, Frank Reicher, Holmes Herbert, Frank Jacquet, William Fawcett, Russell Hicks.

An Army officer (Woods) is sent to Tripoli to uncover a traitor who has been supplying the pirates with shipping information.

112. Barbed Wire (7/25/52) Sepiatone—61 mins. (Western). *DIR:* George Archainbaud. *PRO:* Armand Schaefer. *SP:* Gerald Geraghty. A Gene Autry Production. *CAST:* Gene Autry, Anne James, Pat Buttram, Clayton Moore, William Fawcett, Leonard Penn, Edwin Parker, Pat O'Malley, Stuart Whitman, Al Bridge, Bud Osborne, Harry Harvey, Zon Murray, Terry Frost, Victor Cox, Sandy Sanders, Frankie Marvin, Michael Vallon, Bobby Clark, Bob Woodward, Duke York, Wesley Hudman.

Gene, with the help of his pal (Buttram) and a newspaper editor (James), foils a plot by cattlemen to fence off large sections of land. [British title: *False News*].

113. The Barefoot Boy (8/15/23) B&W—58 mins. (Drama). *DIR/SP:* David Kirkland. *PRO:* Harry Cohn. Story by Wallace Clifton. Suggested by the poem by John Greenleaf Whittier. A C.B.C. Release. *CAST:* Frankie Lee, George Periolat, Harry Todd,

Tully Marshall, Raymond Hatton, Virginia True Boardman, George McDaniel, Brinsley Shaw, John Bowers, Marjorie Daw, Otis Harlan, Rex Lease, Gertrude Messinger.

A young boy (Lee) runs away after being accused of setting the schoolhouse afire. Years later, he (Bowers) returns seeking vengeance but is persuaded by his sweetheart (Daw) to change his mind.

114. The Barefoot Mailman (11/5/51) Super CineColor—83 mins. (Adventure). *DIR:* Earl McEvoy. *PRO:* Robert Cohn. *SP:* James Gunn, Francis Swann. Based on the novel by Theodore Pratt. *CAST:* Robert Cummings, Terry Moore, Jerome Courtland, Mary Field, Will Geer, John Russell, Arthur Shields, Ellen Corby, Trevor Bardette, Arthur Space, Frank Ferguson, Percy Helton, Robert Lynn.

In 19th century Florida, a mailman (Courtland), a conman (Cummings), and a girl (Moore) team up for several adventures on their walk from Palm Beach to Miami.

115. Battle in Outer Space (6/60) Eastman Color/Scope—90 mins. (Science Fiction). *DIR:* Inoshiro Honda. *PRO:* Tomoyuki Tanaka. *SP:* Shinichi Sekizawa. Story by Jotaro Okami. A Toho Company Production. *CAST:* Ryo Ikebe, Kyoko Anzai, Koreya Senda, Yoshio Tsuchiya, Kisaya Ito, Kozo Nomura, Minoru Takada, Fuyuki Murakami, Leonard Stanford, Harold Conway, George Wyman, Elise Richter, Leonard Walsh, Malcolm Pearce.

Earth retaliates when threatened by an alien invasion. [Original Japanese title: *Uchu Dai Senso*].

116. Battle of Rogue River (3/54) Technicolor—71 mins. (Western). *DIR:* William Castle. *PRO:* Sam Katzman. *SP:* Douglas Heyes. *CAST:* George Montgomery, Martha Hyer,

Richard Denning, John Crawford, Emory Parnell, Frank Sully, Willis Bouchey, Michael Granger, Freeman Morse, Bill Bryant, Charles Evans, Lee Roberts, Steve Ritch, Bill Hale, Wesley Hudman, Jimmy Lloyd.

An Army major (Montgomery) learns that his friend (Denning) is stirring up the Indians for personal reasons.

117. Battle of the Coral Sea (11/59) B&W—80 mins. (War). *DIR*: Paul Wendkos. *PRO*: Charles H. Schneer. *SP*: Daniel B. Ullman, Stephen Kandel. Story by Stephen Kandel. *CAST*: Cliff Robertson, Gia Scala, Teru Shimada, Patricia Cutts, Rian Garrick, Gene Blakely, L. Q. Jones, Robin Hughes, Tom Laughlin, Eiji Yamashiro, James T. Goto, K. L. Smith, Carlyle Mitchell.

A submarine commander (Robertson) and his crew are captured by the Japanese when they return from a recon patrol.

118. Battle Stations (2/56) B&W—81 mins. (War). *DIR*: Lewis Seiler. *PRO*: Bryan Foy. *SP*: Crane Wilbur. Story by Ben Finney. *CAST*: John Lund, William Bendix, Richard Boone, Keefe Brasselle, William Leslie, James Lydon, George O'Hanlon, Claude Akins, John Craven, Jack Diamond, Eddie Foy, III, Dick Cathcart, Chris G. Randall, Robert Forrest.

A chaplain (Lund) witnesses life aboard an aircraft carrier during World War II.

119. The Battling Fool (7/1/24) B&W—51 mins. (Drama). *DIR/SP*: W. S. Van Dyke. *PRO*: Harry Cohn. *CAST*: William Fairbanks, Eva Novak, Fred J. Butler, Laura Winston, Pat Harmon.

A minister's son (Fairbanks) becomes a champion prizefighter with the help of an ex-fighter (Harmon).

120. Be My Guest (3/65) B&W—82 mins. (Musical-Drama). *DIR/PRO*: Lance Comfort. *SP*: Lyn Fairhurst. A Three Kings Production. *CAST*: David Hemmings, Stephen Marriot, John Pike, Andrea Monet, Ivor Salter, Anna King, Avril Angers, Joyce Blair, David Healy, Tony Wagner, David L. Lander, Robin Stewart, Monica Evans, Douglas Ives, Jerry Lee Lewis.

A London family purchases a hotel and, to attract guests, they decide to sponsor a talent contest with several British pop groups and, as guest star, Jerry Lee Lewis. *NOTES*: Filmed when Jerry Lee Lewis went to London to do his concert. Limited theatrical release.

121. Bear Island (8/80) Eastman Color—108 mins. (Drama). *DIR*: Don Sharp. *PRO*: Peter Snell. *SP*: Don Sharp, David Butler, Murray Smith. Based on the book by Alistair MacLean. A Selkirk-Bear Island-Taft International Production. *CAST*: Donald Sutherland, Vanessa Redgrave, Richard Widmark, Christopher Lee, Barbara Parkins, Lloyd Bridges, Lawrence Dane, Patricia Collins, Michael Reynolds, Nicholas Cortland.

A United Nations expedition to an obscure North Atlantic island has to deal with sabotage and murder as a sunken German submarine is located with gold bullion on board. *NOTES*: Limited theatrical release. Home video and cable distribution rights reverted to Taft International. Originally released at a running time of 118 mins.

122. The Beast (10/88) Rank Color—109 mins. (War). *DIR*: Kevin Reynolds. *PRO*: John Fiedler. *SP*: William Mastrosimone. Based on the play *Nanawatai* by William Mastrosimone. An A&M Production. *CAST*: George Dzundza, Jason Patric, Steven Bauer, Stephen Baldwin, Don Harvey, Kabir Bedi, Erick Avari, Shosh Marciano.

During the Soviet-Afghan war, a tank, nicknamed "The Beast," gets separated from its unit, thereby causing friction between the tank commander (Dzundza) and his crew (Patric, Bedi, Harvey, Baldwin). *NOTES*: Limited theatrical release.

123. Beautiful But Broke (1/28/44) B&W — 74 mins. (Musical-Comedy). *DIR*: Charles Barton. *PRO*: Irving Briskin. *SP*: Monte Brice, Manny Seff. Story by Arthur Housman. *CAST*: Joan Davis, John Hubbard, Jane Frazee, Judy Clark, Bob Haymes, Danny Mummert, Byron Foulger, George McKay, Forrest Taylor, Isabel Withers, John Eldredge, Grace Hayle, John Dilson, Joe King, Emmett Vogan.

A lady booking agent (Davis) has trouble booking an all-girl band.

124. Beautiful Sinner (10/1/24) B&W — 53 mins. (Crime-Drama). *DIR*: W. S. Van Dyke. *PRO*: Harry Cohn. *SP*: Wilfred Lucas. *CAST*: William Fairbanks, Eva Novak, George Nichols, Kate Lester, Carl Stockdale.

A criminologist (Fairbanks) and Secret Service agent (Stockdale) set out to trap a gang of waterfront thieves.

125. Beauty on Parade (5/4/50) B&W — 66 mins. (Drama). *DIR*: Lew Landers. *PRO*: Wallace MacDonald. *SP*: Arthur E. Orloff, George Bricker. Story by Arthur E. Orloff. *CAST*: Robert Hutton, Ruth Warrick, Lola Albright, John Ridgely, Hillary Brooke, Wally Vernon, Jimmy Lloyd, Donna Gibson, Frank Sully.

An ex-beauty queen (Warrick) almost ruins her marriage and her daughter's life (Albright) as she pushes her to win the Miss USA contest.

126. Because They're Young (4/60) B&W — 102 mins. (Drama). *DIR*: Paul Wendkos. *PRO*: Jerry Bresler. *SP*: James Gunn. Based on *Harrison High* by John Farris. *CAST*: Dick Clark, Michael Callan, Tuesday Weld, Victoria Shaw, Roberta Shore, Warren Berlinger, Doug McClure, Linda Watkins, Chris Robinson, Rudy Bond, Wendell Holmes, Philip Coolidge, James Darren, Duane Eddy and the Rebels.

A teacher (Clark) takes an interest in the lives of his pupils and prevents them from going astray.

127. Bed and Board (1/71) Eastman Color — 95 mins. (Drama). *DIR/PRO*: Francois Truffaut. *SP*: Francois Truffaut, Claude De Givray, Bernard Revon. A Co-Production of Les Films du Carrosse-Valoria Films and Fida Cinematofrafic. *CAST*: Jean-Pierre Leaud, Claude Jade, Hiroko Berghauer, Barbara Laage, Daniel Ceccaldi, Claire Duhamel, Claude Vega, Bill Kerns, Pierre Fabre.

A fun-loving Frenchman (Leaud) experiments with life as he marries and has an affair. [Original French title: *Domicile Conjugal*].

128. The Bedford Incident (10/65) B&W — 102 mins. (Drama-Adventure). *DIR/PRO*: James B. Harris. *SP*: James Poe. Based on the book by Mark Rascovich. *CAST*: Richard Widmark, Sidney Poitier, James MacArthur, Martin Balsam, Wally Cox, Eric Portman, Michael Kane, Phil Brown, Gary Cockrell, Brian Davies, Warren Stanhope, Donald Sutherland, Colin Maitland, Edward Bishop, George Roubicek.

A destroyer captain (Widmark) plays cat-and-mouse with a Russian sub in the North Atlantic with disastrous results.

129. Bedtime Story (3/19/42) B&W — 83 mins. (Comedy). *DIR*: Alexander Hall. *PRO*: B. P. Schulberg. *SP*: Richard Flournoy. Story by Horace Jackson, Grant Garrett. *CAST*: Frederic March, Loretta Young, Robert Benchley, Allyn Joslyn, Eve Arden, Helen Westley, Joyce Compton, Tim Ryan, Olaf Hytten, Dorothy Adams, Clarence Kolb, Andrew Tombes.

A playwright's (March) insistence

that his wife (Young) star in his new play puts a strain on their marriage.

130. Before I Hang (10/4/40) B&W—62 mins. (Horror). *DIR:* Nick Grinde. *PRO:* Wallace MacDonald. *SP:* Robert D. Andrews. Story by Robert D. Andrews, Karl Brown. *CAST:* Boris Karloff, Evelyn Keyes, Bruce Bennett, Edward Van Sloan, Ben Taggart, Pedro de Cordoba, Wright Kramer, Barton Yarborough, Don Beddoe, Robert Fiske, Kenneth MacDonald, Frank Richards.

A scientist (Karloff) injects himself with a serum that turns him into a killer.

131. Before Midnight (3/19/34) B&W—63 mins. (Mystery). *DIR:* Lambert Hillyer. *PRO:* Irving Briskin. *SP:* Robert Quigley. *CAST:* Ralph Bellamy, June Collyer, Claude Gillingwater, Betty Blythe.

Inspector Trent (Bellamy) is called in to solve the slayings at an old house where the men met their fate at exactly one minute before midnight.

132. Before Winter Comes (3/69) Eastman Color—107 mins. (Drama). *DIR:* J. Lee Thompson. *PRO:* Robert Emmett Ginna. *SP:* Andrew Sinclair. Based on *The Interpreter* by Frederick L. Keefe. A Windward Film Production. *CAST:* David Niven, Topol, Anna Karina, John Hurt, Anthony Quayle, John Collin, George Innes, Ori Levy, Tony Selby, Hugh Futcher, Guy Deghy, Larry Dann, Colin Spaull, Christopher Sandford.

In 1945, a British major (Niven) at a displaced persons camp is helped, then hindered by an interpreter (Topol) who turns out to be Russian.

133. Behind Closed Doors (2/24/29) B&W—56 mins. (Mystery). *DIR:* Roy William Neill. *PRO:* Harry Cohn. *SP:* Howard J. Green. Story by Lillian Ducey, H. Milner Kitchin.

CAST: Virginia Valli, Gaston Glass, Otto Matiesen, Andres De Segurola, Fanny Midgley.

A mysterious figure, known as the "Eagle" (Midgley), sets out to thwart a plot in a foreign embassy in Washington to return a deposed ruler to the throne. *NOTES:* Released as a silent film only.

134. Behind Prison Gates (9/8/39) B&W—63 mins. (Crime-Drama). *DIR:* Charles Barton. *PRO:* Wallace MacDonald. *SP:* Arthur T. Horman. Story by Leslie T. White. *CAST:* Brian Donlevy, Jacqueline Wells (Julie Bishop), Joseph Crehan, Paul Fix, George Lloyd, Dick Curtis, Richard Fiske.

A federal agent (Donlevy) goes to prison to locate where a pair of robbers have hidden their loot.

135. Behind the Evidence (1/8/35) B&W—70 mins. (Drama). *DIR:* Lambert Hillyer. *SP:* Harold Shumate. *CAST:* Norman Foster, Donald Cook, Sheila Mannors, Geneva Mitchell, Samuel S. Hinds, Frank Darien, Pat O'Malley, Gordon DeMain, Edward Keane.

A playboy (Foster) becomes a newspaper reporter and solves a series of holdups.

Behind the Iron Mask *see* **The Fifth Musketeer**

136. Behind the Mask (5/1/32) B&W—68 mins. (Crime-Drama). *DIR:* John Francis Dillon. *PRO:* Harry Cohn. *SP:* Jo Swerling. Based on *In the Secret Service* by Jo Swerling. *CAST:* Jack Holt, Boris Karloff, Constance Cummings, Claude King, Bertha Mann, Edward Van Sloan, Willard Robertson.

A Secret Service agent (Holt) goes after a drug syndicate head (Van Sloan).

137. Behold a Pale Horse (8/64) B&W—113 mins. (War-Drama). *DIR/*

PRO: Fred Zinnemann. *SP:* J. P. Miller. Based on *Killing a Mouse on Sunday* by Emeric Pressburger. A Brentwood-Highland Production. *CAST:* Gregory Peck, Omar Sharif, Anthony Quinn, Mildred Dunnock, Raymond Pellegrin, Paolo Stoppa, Daniela Rocca, Christian Marquand, Michael Lonsdale.

A Spanish guerrilla (Peck) returns home after twenty years to see his dying mother (Dunnock), not realizing a trap has been set by the local police chief (Quinn) to capture him.

138. Bell, Book and Candle (10/58) Technicolor — 103 mins. (Comedy). *DIR:* Richard Quine. *PRO:* Julian Blaustein. *SP:* Daniel Taradash. Based on the play by Jan Van Druten. *CAST:* James Stewart, Kim Novak, Jack Lemmon, Ernie Kovacs, Hermione Gingold, Elsa Lanchester, Janice Rule, Howard McNear.

A publisher (Stewart) falls under the spell of a witch (Novak).

139. Bell-Bottom George (12/43) B&W — 97 mins. (Comedy). *DIR:* Marcel Varnel. *PRO:* Ben Henry. *SP:* Peter Fraser, Edward Dryhurst. Story by Richard Fisher, Peter Cresswell. A Columbia-British Production. *CAST:* George Formby, Anne Firth, Reginald Purdell, Peter Murray Hill, Charles Farrell, Eliot Makeham, Manning Whiley, Hugh Dempster, Dennis Wyndham, Jane Welsh, Peter Gawthorne.

George (Formby) becomes a hero and gets the girl (Firth) when he impersonates a sailor and captures some spies.

140. The Belle of Broadway (9/5/26) B&W — 55 mins. (Drama). *DIR:* Harry O. Hoyt. *PRO:* Harry Cohn. *SP:* Jean Peary. Story by J. Grubb Alexander. *CAST:* Betty Compson, Herbert Rawlinson, Edith Yorke, Armand Kaliz.

An American actress (Compson) takes the place of a fading star (Yorke) and becomes the rage of Paris.

141. Belle Sommers (5/62) B&W — 62 mins. (Drama). *DIR:* Elliott Silverstein. *PRO:* William B. Sackheim. *SP:* Richard Alan Simmons. An Astron Productions Ltd. Production. *CAST:* David Janssen, Polly Bergen, Warren Stevens, Carroll O'Conner, Jay Adler, Joan Staley.

A press agent (Janssen) tries to help a singer (Bergen) whom the mob is after.

142. The Beloved Vagabond (9/36) B&W — 78 mins. (Musical-Drama). *DIR:* Kurt Bernhardt. *PRO:* Ludovico Toeplitz. *SP:* Hugh Mills, Walter Creighton, Arthur Wimperis. Based on the book by William J. Locke. A Toeplitz Production. *CAST:* Maurice Chevalier, Betty Stockfield, Margaret Lockwood, Desmond Tester, Austin Trevor, Peter Haddon, Charles Carson, Kathleen Nesbitt.

A jilted architect (Chevalier) returns to Paris and falls in love with a gypsy (Lockwood).

143. Below the Sea (6/3/33) B&W — 78 mins. (Adventure). *DIR:* Albert S. Rogell. *SP:* Jo Swerling. *CAST:* Ralph Bellamy, Fay Wray, Frederick Vogeding, Esther Howard, Trevor Bland, William J. Kelly, Paul Page.

A soldier of fortune (Vogeding) hires a diver (Bellamy) to locate a sunken German U-boat containing three million in gold. *NOTES:* Two underwater sequences filmed in Technicolor.

144. Bermuda Affair (7/56) B&W — 77 mins. (Drama). *DIR:* Edward Sutherland. *PRO:* Coolidge Adams. *SP:* Robert J. Shaw. Story by A. C. Ward, Donald Hyde. A Bermuda Studios Production. *CAST:* Gary Merrill, Ron Randell, Zena Marshall, Kim Hunter, Don Gibson, Robert Arden.

A pilot (Merrill) sacrifices his life to save his partner (Randell).

145. Berserk (12/67) Technicolor — 96 mins. (Crime-Horror-Mystery). *DIR:* Jim O'Connolly. *PRO:* Herman Cohen. *SP:* Aben Kandel, Herman Cohen. *CAST:* Joan Crawford, Ty Hardin, Diana Dors, Michael Gough, Judy Geeson, Robert Hardy, Geoffrey Keen, Peter Burton, George Claydon, Sidney Tafler, Philip Madoc, Ambrosine Phillpotts, Thomas Cimarro.

Suspicion falls on a circus owner (Crawford) when a series of bizarre murders begin happening. *NOTES:* A loose remake of the 1937 Columbia film *The Shadow.*

146. Best Man Wins (1/2/35) B&W — 75 mins. (Adventure). *DIR:* Erle C. Kenton. *SP:* Ethel Hill, Bruce Manning. Story by Ben G. Kohn. *CAST:* Jack Holt, Florence Rice, Edmund Lowe, Bela Lugosi, J. Farrell MacDonald, Forrester Harvey, Bradley Page, Mitchell Lewis, Frank Sheridan, Selmer Jackson, Esther Howard, Oscar Apfel.

A harbor patrolman (Holt) goes after his friend (Lowe) when he gets mixed up with a jewel smuggler (Lugosi).

147. The Best Man Wins (5/6/48) B&W — 73 mins. (Drama). *DIR:* John Sturges. *PRO:* Ted Richmond. *SP:* Edward Huebsch. Based on *The Celebrated Jumping Frog of Calaveras County* by Mark Twain. *CAST:* Edgar Buchanan, Anna Lee, Robert Shayne, Gary Gray, George Lynn, Hobart Cavanaugh, Stanley Andrews, Bill Sheffield, Paul E. Burns.

With the help of his son (Gray), a wandering father (Buchanan) tries to win back his wife (Lee).

148. The Best of Enemies (9/62) Technicolor/Technirama — 104 mins. (War-Comedy). *DIR:* Guy Hamilton. *PRO:* Dino De Laurentiis. *SP:* Jack Pulman. Story by Luciano Vincenzoni. *CAST:* David Niven, Michael Wilding, Harry Andrews, Noel Harrison, Ronald Fraser, Bernard Cribbins, Duncan MacRae, Robert Desmond, Kenneth Fortescue, Michael Trubshawe, Alberto Sordi, David Opatoshu.

In 1941 Ethiopia, a British officer (Niven) and an Italian soldier (Sordi) learn mutual respect for each other. [Original Italian title: *I Due Nemici*].

149. The Better Way (12/5/26) B&W — 58 mins. (Comedy). *DIR:* Ralph Ince. *PRO:* Harry Cohn. *SP:* Dorothy Howell. Story by William H. Osborne. *CAST:* Dorothy Revier, Ralph Ince, Eugene Strong, Armand Kaliz.

A young secretary (Revier) makes a killing in the stock market and is pursued by the office bookkeeper (Ince).

150. Betty Co-Ed (11/28/46) B&W — 71 mins. (Drama). *DIR:* Arthur Dreifuss. *PRO:* Sam Katzman. *SP:* George H. Plympton, Arthur Dreifuss. *CAST:* Jean Porter, Shirley Mills, William Mason, Rosemary La Planche, Karen Morley, Jackie Moran, Edward Van Sloan, George Meader, Daisy Moran, Ray Bennett.

A carnival singer (Porter) gets accepted into a college sorority and reforms the snobbish attitudes of the other girls. [British title: *The Melting Pot*].

151. Between Midnight and Dawn (9/28/50) B&W — 89 mins. (Crime). *DIR:* Gordon Douglas. *PRO:* Hunt Stromberg. *SP:* Eugene Ling. Story by Gerald Drayson Adams, Leo Katcher. *CAST:* Mark Stevens, Gale Storm, Edmond O'Brien, Donald Buka, Gale Robbins, Anthony Ross, Roland Winters, Tito Vuolo, Madge Blake, Philip Van Zandt, Lora Lee Michel.

A radio patrolman (O'Brien) goes after a killer (Buka) when his partner (Stevens) is killed.

152. Beware of Blondes (7/1/28) B&W — 59 mins. (Drama). *DIR:* George

B. Seitz. *PRO*: Harry Cohn. *SP*: Peter Milne. Story by George Hull, Harvey Thew. *CAST*: Dorothy Revier, Matt Moore, Roy D'Arcy, Robert Edeson, Hazel Howell.

A jewelry store clerk (Moore) transports a valuable gem to the Islands and mistakes a young blonde girl (Revier) for a notorious gem thief.

153. Beware of Blondie (4/13/50) B&W — 66 mins. (Comedy). *DIR*: Edward Bernds. *PRO*: Milton Feldman. *SP*: Jack Henley. Based on the comic strip created by Chic Young. *CAST*: Penny Singleton, Arthur Lake, Larry Simms, Marjorie Kent, Danny Mummert, Adele Jergens, Dick Wessel, Jack Rice, Alyn Lockwood, Emory Parnell, Isabel Withers, Douglas Fowley, William E. Green.

Blondie (Singleton) saves the day when Dagwood (Lake) almost gets swindled by a beautiful woman (Jergens). *NOTES*: The last film of the *Blondie* series.

154. Beware Spooks! (11/9/39) B&W — 65 mins. (Comedy). *DIR*: Edward Sedgwick. *PRO*: Robert Sparks. *SP*: Richard Flournoy, Albert Duffy, Brian Marlow. *CAST*: Joe E. Brown, Mary Carlisle, Clarence Kolb, Marc Lawrence, Don Beddoe, George J. Lewis.

A nervous policeman (Brown) captures a gang of crooks in the spookhouse at Coney Island.

155. Beyond Mombasa (6/57) B&W — 90 mins. (Adventure). *DIR*: George Marshall. *PRO*: Tony Owen. *SP*: Richard English, Gene Levitt. Based on *The Mark of the Leopard* by James Eastwood. A Hemisphere Production. *CAST*: Cornel Wilde, Donna Reed, Leo Genn, Ron Randell, Christopher Lee, Dan Jackson, Eddie Calvert, Roy Purcell.

While searching for a uranium mine in East Africa, a man (Wilde) seeks to avenge his brother's death by the Leopard Men.

156. Beyond the Law (7/31/34) B&W — 60 mins. (Western). *DIR*: D. Ross Lederman. *SP*: Harold Shumate. *CAST*: Tim McCoy, Shirley Grey, Lane Chandler, Addison Richards, Dick Rush, Harry C. Bradley, John Merton.

A railroad detective (McCoy) sets out to prove an ex-con (Richards) innocent of robbery and murder.

157. Beyond the Purple Hills (7/18/50) Sepiatone — 69 mins. (Western). *DIR*: John English. *PRO*: Armand Schaefer. *SP*: Norman S. Hall. A Gene Autry Production. *CAST*: Gene Autry, Jo Carroll Dennison, Pat Buttram, Don Beddoe, Hugh O'Brian, Bob Wilke, Harry Harvey, Gregg Barton, Pat O'Malley, Merrill McCormack, Frank Ellis, Maudie Prickett, Victor Cox, Jerry Ambler, Lynton Brent, James Millican, Don Kay Reynolds, Roy Gordon, Sandy Sanders, Tex Terry, Ralph Peters, Fenton Jones, Herman Hack, Cliff Barnett, Frank O'Conner, Frankie Marvin, Bobby Clark, Boyd Stockman.

Gene sets out to prove that a son (O'Brian) is innocent of the murder of his father (Gordon).

158. Beyond the Sacramento (11/14/40) B&W — 58 mins. (Western). *DIR*: Lambert Hillyer. *PRO*: Leon Barsha. *SP*: Luci Ward. *CAST*: Bill Elliott, Evelyn Keyes, Dub Taylor, John Dilson, Bradley Page, Frank LaRue, Norman Willis, Steve Clark, Jack Clifford, Don Beddoe, Harry Bailey, Art Mix, George McKay, Bud Osborne, Ned Glass, Clem Horton, Tex Cooper, Blackjack Ward, Jack Low, Olin Francis.

Wild Bill Hickok (Elliott), his pal (Taylor), and a banker's daughter (Keyes) save a town from a couple of confidence men (LaRue, Page). [British title: *Power of Justice*].

159. The Big Blue (8/88) B&W-Eastman Color/Panavision—119 mins. (Drama). *DIR:* Luc Besson. *PRO:* Patrice Ledoux. *SP:* Luc Besson, Robert Garland, Marilyn Goldin, Jacques Mayol, Marc Perrier. Story by Luc Besson. A Gaumont-Weintraub Production. *CAST:* Rosanna Arquette, Jean-Marc Barr, Jean Reno, Paul Shenar, Sergio Castellitto, Jean Bouise, Griffin Dunne.

A World Champion Free Diver (Reno), and his best friend (Barr), compete against each other in the World Championship Free Diving competition in Sicily.

160. The Big Boss (5/20/41) B&W—70 mins. (Drama). *DIR:* Charles Barton. *PRO:* Wallace MacDonald. *SP:* Howard J. Green. *CAST:* Otto Kruger, Gloria Dickson, John Litel, Don Beddoe, Robert Fiske, George Lessey, Joe Conti.

Two brothers (Kruger, Litel) become pitted against each other on opposite sides of the political fence.

161. The Big Chill (9/83) Metrocolor—104 mins. (Drama). *DIR:* Lawrence Kasdan. *PRO:* Michael Shamberg. *SP:* Lawrence Kasdan, Barbara Benedek. A Carson Productions Group Ltd. Production. *CAST:* Tom Berenger, Glenn Close, Jeff Goldblum, William Hurt, Meg Tilly, Kevin Kline, Mary Kay Place, JoBeth Williams, Don Galloway, James Gillis.

Eight friends get together and reminisce about old times when they attend the funeral of a friend.

162. The Big Easy (8/87) DeLuxe Color—108 mins. (Crime-Thriller). *DIR:* Jim McBride. *PRO:* Stephen J. Friedman. *SP:* Daniel Petrie, Jr., Jack Baran. A Kings Road Entertainment Production. *CAST:* Dennis Quaid, Ellen Barkin, Ned Beatty, Ebbe Roe Smith, John Goodman, Lisa Jane Persky, Charles Ludlam, Marc Lawrence, Thomas O'Brien, Carole Sutton, Nick Hagler, Jim Chimento.

A New Orleans homicide detective (Quaid), investigating a series of mob murders, falls for an investigator (Barkin) assigned to uncover suspected departmental corruption.

163. The Big Gundown (8/68) Technicolor/Scope—84 mins. (Western). *DIR:* Sergio Sollima. *PRO:* Alberto Grimaldi. *SP:* Sergio Donati, Sergio Sollima. Story by Franco Solinas, Fernando Morandi. A PEA-Tulio Demicheli Production. *CAST:* Lee Van Cleef, Tomas Milian, Luisa Rivelli, Fernando Sancho, Walter Barnes, Maria Granada, Nieves Navarro.

A Texas lawman (Van Cleef) is hired to catch a Mexican outlaw (Milian) and to supervise the building of a railroad across Texas into Mexico. [Original Italian title: *La Resa dei Conti*]. [Original Spanish title: *El Halcon y la Presa*].

164. The Big Gusher (7/9/51) B&W—68 mins. (Adventure). *DIR:* Lew Landers. *PRO:* Wallace MacDonald. *SP:* Daniel B. Ullman. Story by Harold R. Greene. *CAST:* Wayne Morris, Preston Foster, Dorothy Patrick, Paul E. Burns, Eddie Parker, Emmett Vogan, Fred F. Sears.

Two oilfield roughnecks (Morris, Foster) must bring in a well or lose their savings.

165. The Big Heat (7/6/53) B&W—89 mins. (Crime-Drama). *DIR:* Fritz Lang. *PRO:* Robert Arthur. *SP:* Sydney Boehm. Based on the serial in the *Saturday Evening Post* by William P. McGivern. *CAST:* Glenn Ford, Gloria Grahame, Jocelyn Brando, Alexander Scourby, Lee Marvin, Jeanette Nolan, Peter Whitney, Willis Bouchey, Robert Burton, Adam Williams, Chris Alcaide, Carolyn Jones,

John Crawford, John Doucette, Harry Lauter, Dorothy Green, Dan Seymour, Ric Roman, Howard Wendell.

A police detective (Ford) sets out to get the mob when his wife (Brando) dies in a bomb blast meant for him.

166. The Big Mouth (7/67) Pathe Color — 107 mins. (Comedy). *DIR/PRO*: Jerry Lewis. *SP*: Jerry Lewis, Bill Richmond. Story by Bill Richmond. *CAST*: Jerry Lewis, Harold J. Stone, Susan Day, Buddy Lester, Del Moore, Paul Lambert, Jeannine Riley, Charlie Callas, Frank DeVol, John Nolan.

Crooks chase a fisherman (Lewis) who has found a map to some stolen diamonds.

167. The Big Sombrero (3/49) CineColor — 82 mins. (Western). *DIR*: Frank McDonald. *PRO*: Armand Schaefer. *SP*: Olive Cooper. A Gene Autry Production. *CAST*: Gene Autry, Elena Verdugo, Stephen Dunne, George J. Lewis, Gene Roth, John Cason, Pierce Lyden, William Edmunds, Vera Marshe, Joe Kirk, Alex Montoya, Martin Garralaga, Jose Alvarado.

Gene goes to Mexico and helps a ranch owner (Verdugo) to save her ranch.

168. The Big Timer (7/11/32) B&W — 60 mins. (Sports-Drama). *DIR*: Edward Buzzell. *SP*: Robert Riskin, Dorothy Howell. Story by Robert Riskin. *CAST*: Ben Lyon, Thelma Todd, Constance Cummings, Charles Delaney, Tom Dugan, Charley Grapewin, Russell Hopton, Robert Emmett O'Conner, Jack Miller.

A female fight promoter (Cummings) turns a hamburger stand operator (Lyon) into a champion, but he forsakes the ring for a society girl (Todd).

169. The Big Town (9/87) Medallion Film Labs Color — 109 mins. (Drama). *DIR*: Ben Bolt. *PRO*: Martin Ransohoff, Don Carmody. *SP*: Robert Roy Pool. Based on *The Arm* by Clark Howard. *CAST*: Matt Dillon, Diane Lane, Tommy Lee Jones, Bruce Dern, Lee Grant, Tom Skerritt, Suzy Amis, David Marshall, Don Francks, Del Close, Meg Hogarth, Cherry Jones, Mark Danton.

A small-town crapshooter (Dillon) moves into the world of highstakes gambling in 1957 Chicago.

170. Big Trouble (5/86) Metrocolor/Panavision — 93 mins. (Comedy). *DIR*: John Cassavetes. *PRO*: Michael Lobell. *SP*: Warren Bogle. A Columbia-Delphi III Production. *CAST*: Peter Falk, Alan Arkin, Beverly D'Angelo, Charles Durning, Paul Dooley, Robert Stack, Valerie Curtain, Richard Libertini, Steve Alterman, Jerry Pavlon, Paul LaGreca, John Finnegan, Karl Lukas, Rosemarie Stack, Al White, Barbara Tarbuck, Edith Fields.

A harried insurance salesman (Arkin), needing money to send his children to Yale, becomes involved with a dizzy blonde (D'Angelo) in a plot to murder her looney husband (Falk) for a share of the insurance money. *NOTES*: Completed in 1985, but had limited theatrical release.

171. Birds Do It (8/66) Pathe Color — 88 mins. (Comedy). *DIR*: Andrew Marton. *PRO*: Ivan Tors. *SP*: Arnie Kogen, Art Arthur. Story by Leonard Kaufman. *CAST*: Soupy Sales, Tab Hunter, Arthur O'Connell, Edward Andrews, Beverly Adams, Doris Dowling, Louis Quinn, Frank Nastasi, Burt Taylor, Courtney Brown, Russell Saunders, Julian Voloshin, Bob Bersell, Warren Day, Burt Leigh, Jay Laskay.

A janitor (Sales) at an atomic plant is accidentally ionized and finds he can fly.

172. Birds Do It, Bees Do It (6/74) Eastman Color — 89 mins. (Documentary). *DIR/PRO/SP*: Nicholas

Noxon. CAST: Narrated by Lee Bergere.

A documentary that examines the various ways in which members of the animal kingdom reproduce.

173. Birds of Prey (3/20/27) B&W—56 mins. (Crime-Drama). DIR: William James Craft. PRO: Harry Cohn. SP: Dorothy Howell. Story by George B. Howard. CAST: Priscilla Dean, Hugh Allan, Gustav von Seyffertitz, Ben Hendricks, William H. Tooker.

An ex-con banker (Tooker) plots a bank robbery with a gang of thieves and ends up trapped in an earthquake.

174. Bite the Bullet (7/75) Metrocolor/Panavision—131 mins. (Western). DIR/PRO/SP: Richard Brooks. CAST: Gene Hackman, Candace Bergen, James Coburn, Ben Johnson, Ian Bannen, Jan-Michael Vincent, Dabney Coleman, Jean Willes, Paul Stewart.

A varied group of Westerners compete in a grueling 600 mile horse race at the turn of the century.

175. The Bitter Tea of General Yen (1/6/33) B&W—88 mins. (Drama). DIR: Frank Capra. PRO: Walter Wanger. SP: Edward Paramore. Based on the book by Grace Zaring Stone. A Frank Capra Production. CAST: Barbara Stanwyck, Nils Asther, Toshia Mori, Walter Connolly, Gavin Gordon, Lucien Littlefield, Richard Loo, Helen Jerome Eddy, Emmett Corrigan, Clara Blandick, Moy Ming, Robert Wayne, Knute Erickson, Ella Hall, Arthur Millette, Martha Mattox, Jessie Arnold, Ray Young.

An American missionary (Stanwyck) is captured by a Chinese warlord (Asther) and finds herself falling in love with him. NOTES: This film was chosen as the premiere film to open Radio City Music Hall in New York.

176. Bitter Victory (3/58) B&W/Scope—90 mins. (War-Adventure). DIR: Nicholas Ray. PRO: Paul Graetz, Robert Laffont. SP: Nicholas Ray, Rene Hardy, Gavin Lambert. Based on the book by Rene Hardy. CAST: Curt Jurgens, Richard Burton, Ruth Roman, Raymond Pellegrin, Nigel Green, Anthony Bushell, Alfred Burke, Christopher Lee, Sean Kelly, Harry Landis, Ramon De Larrocha, Sumner Williams.

During World War II, an unfit soldier (Jurgens) returns home a hero, but his wife (Roman) knows he had murdered his best friend (Burton). NOTES: Originally released at a running time of 103 mins. [Original French title: *Amere Victorie*].

Bizet's Carmen *see* **Carmen**

177. The Black Arrow (6/30/48) B&W—76 mins. (Adventure). DIR: Gordon Douglas. PRO: Edward Small. SP: Richard Schayer, Thomas Seller, David P. Sheppard. Based on the book by Robert Louis Stevenson. CAST: Louis Hayward, Janet Blair, George Macready, Edgar Buchanan, Lowell Gilmore, Russell Hicks, Paul Cavanagh, Rhys Williams, Walter Kingsford.

An English knight (Hayward) returns home from the Thirty Years War and seeks the murderer of his father. [British title: *The Black Arrow Strikes*].

178. The Black Bird (12/75) Metrocolor—98 mins. (Comedy). DIR/SP: David Giler. PRO: Michael Levee, Lou Lombardo. Based on a story by Don M. Mankiewicz and Gordon Cotler. CAST: George Segal, Stephane Audran, Lionel Stander, Elisha Cook, Jr., Lee Patrick, Felix Silla, Signe Hasso, John Abbott, Connie Kreski, Howard Jeffrey, Richard B. Shull, Ken Swofford.

Sam Spade, Jr. (Segal) and several crooks are on the trail of the elusive Maltese Falcon statuette.

179. The Black Dakotas (9/54) Technicolor—65 mins. (Western). DIR: Ray Nazarro. PRO: Wallace MacDonald. *SP*: Ray Buffam, DeVallon Scott. Story by Ray Buffam. *CAST*: Gary Merrill, Wanda Hendrix, John Bromfield, Noah Beery, Jr., Richard Webb, James Griffith, Clayton Moore, Jay Silverheels, Chris Alcaide, Peter Whitney, Howard Wendell, Frank Wilcox, Fay Roope, Robert F. Simon, John War Eagle, George Keymas, Robert Griffin.

A Confederate spy (Merrill) poses as a Yankee to steal gold from the Indians and start a war.

180. Black Eagle (9/16/48) B&W — 76 mins. (Western-Drama). *DIR*: Robert Gordon. *PRO*: Robin Cohn. *SP*: Edward Huebsch, Hal Smith. Based on *The Passing of Black Eagle* by O. Henry. *CAST*: William Bishop, Virginia Patton, Gordon Jones, James Bell, Trevor Bardette, Edmund MacDonald, Ted Mapes, Richard Talmadge, Paul E. Burns, Will Wright, Al Eben, Harry Cheshire.

A drifter (Bishop) becomes involved in a range war.

181. Black Gunn (12/72) Eastman Color — 94 mins. (Crime). *DIR*: Robert Hartford-Davis. *PRO*: John Heyman, Norman Priggen. *SP*: Franklin Coen. Based on the screenplay by Robert Sherere from an idea by Robert Hartford-Davis. A Champion Production Company Film. *CAST*: Jim Brown, Martin Landau, Brenda Sykes, Luciana Paluzzi, Herbert Jefferson, Jr., Jim Watkins, Vida Blue, Stephen McNally, Keefe Brasselle, Timothy Brown, William Campbell, Bernie Casey, Gary Conway, Bruce Glover.

A black nightclub owner (Brown) goes after the mobs top man (Landau) when his brother is killed.

182. The Black Knight (10/54) Technicolor — 85 mins. (Historical-Drama). *DIR*: Tay Garnett. *PRO*: Irving Allen, Albert R. Broccoli. *SP*: Alec Coppel. A Warwick Film Production. *CAST*: Alan Ladd, Patricia Medina,

Andre Morell, Harry Andrews, Peter Cushing, Anthony Bushell, Laurence Naismith, Patrick Troughton, Bill Brandor, Ronald Adam, Basil Appleby, Jean Lodge.

A blacksmith (Ladd) becomes the mysterious Black Knight, and reveals a traitor to King Arthur (Bushell).

183. Black Moon (6/28/34) B&W — 68 mins. (Drama). *DIR*: Roy William Neill. *PRO*: Everett Riskin. *SP*: Wells Root. Story by Clements Ripley. *CAST*: Jack Holt, Fay Wray, Dorothy Burgess, Clarence Muse, Cora Sue Collins, Arnold Korff, Lawrence Criner, Lumsden Hare.

A man (Holt) stands by helplessly as his wife (Burgess) becomes obsessed with voodoo rituals.

184. The Black Parachute (5/4/44) B&W — 67 mins. (Spy-War). *DIR*: Lew Landers. *PRO*: Jack Fier. *SP*: Clarence Upson Young. Story by Paul Gangelin. *CAST*: Larry Parks, Jeanne Bates, Jonathan Hale, Osa Massen, Art Smith, John Carradine, Trevor Bardette, Ivan Triesault, Robert Lowell, Charles Wagenheim, Charles Waldron, Ernie Adams.

During World War II, an American soldier (Parks) parachutes into an unnamed European country to free its king (Hale) from the Nazis.

185. The Black Room (8/13/35) B&W — 73 mins. (Horror). *DIR*: Roy William Neill. *PRO*: Robert North. *SP*: Arthur Strawn, Henry Meyers. Story by Arthur Strawn. *CAST*: Boris Karloff, Marian Marsh, Robert Allen, Thurston Hall, John Buckler, Katherine DeMille, Henry Kolker, Colin Tapley, Egon Brecher, John Bleifer, Edward Van Sloan, Frederick Vogeding.

An evil twin (Karloff) kills his brother and assumes his identity in order to continue ruling his subjects. [British title: *The Black Room Mystery*].

186. Blackjack Ketchum, Desperado (4/1/56) B&W — 76 mins. (Western). *DIR:* Earl Bellamy. *PRO:* Sam Katzman. *SP:* Luci Ward, Jack Natteford. Story by Louis L'Amour. A Clover Production. *CAST:* Howard Duff, Maggie Mahoney, Victor Jory, Angela Stevens, Pat O'Malley, Don C. Harvey, Charles Wagenheim, Kermit Maynard, David Orrick, William Tannen, Ken Christy, Robert Roark, Martin Garralaga, Ralph Sanford, Jack V. Littlefield, Wesley Hudman, George Edward Mather.

A former gunfighter (Duff) must strap on his guns once more to defeat the local cattle baron (Jory) before he can settle down to a peaceful life.

187. The Blackmailer (7/23/36) B&W — 66 mins. (Comedy-Mystery). *DIR:* Gordon Wiles. *PRO:* Irving Briskin. *SP:* Joseph Krumgold, Lee Loeb, Harold Buchman. *CAST:* William Gargan, Florence Rice, H. B. Warner, Nana Bryant, George McKay, Wyrley Birch, Drue Leyton, Paul Hurst, Kenneth Thompson, Alexander Cross, Boyd Irwin.

A police inspector (Hurst) and an amateur detective (Gargan) work together to locate the blackmailer of a prominent family.

Blake Edwards' That's Life! *see* **That's Life!**

188. Blazing Across the Pecos (7/1/48) B&W — 55 mins. (Western). *DIR:* Ray Nazarro. *PRO:* Colbert Clark. *SP:* Norman S. Hall. *CAST:* Charles Starrett, Patricia White (Patricia Barry), Smiley Burnette, Paul Campbell, Charles Wilson, Chief Thunder Cloud, Jock Mahoney, Pat O'Malley, Jack Ingram, Pierce Lyden, Thomas Jackson, Frank McCarroll, Paul Conrad, Red Arnell and His Western Aces.

The Durango Kid (Starrett) sets out to track down the men who have been raiding the trading posts and selling guns to the Indians in order to get their land.

189. Blazing Six Shooters (4/4/40) B&W — 61 mins. (Western). *DIR:* Joseph H. Lewis. *PRO:* Irving Briskin. *SP:* Paul Franklin. *CAST:* Charles Starrett, Iris Meredith, Bob Nolan, Al Bridge, George Cleveland, Dick Curtis, Henry Hall, Stanley Brown, John Tyrrell, Eddie Laughton, Francis Walker, Edmund Cobb, Bruce Bennett, Sons of the Pioneers.

Starrett is out to stop an outlaw (Curtis) from gaining control of ranch land when a silver mine is discovered on one of the ranches. [British title: *Stolen Wealth*].

190. The Blazing Sun (11/20/50) Sepiatone — 70 mins. (Western). *DIR:* John English. *PRO:* Armand Schaefer. *SP:* Jack Townley. A Gene Autry Production. *CAST:* Gene Autry, Lynne Roberts,.Pat Buttram, Edward Norris, Gregg Barton, Alan Hale, Jr., Kenne Duncan, Tom London, Pat O'Malley, Nolan Leary, Sam Flint, Anne Gwynne, Steve Darrell, Sandy Sanders, Frankie Marvin, Bob Woodward, Boyd Stockman, Virginia Carroll, Chris Allen, Lewis Martin, Almira Sessions, Charles Coleman.

Set in the modern West, Gene goes after two bank robbers who use modern devices to try and stop him.

191. Blazing the Western Trail (9/18/45) B&W — 60 mins. (Western). *DIR:* Vernon Keays. *PRO:* Colbert Clark. *SP:* J. Benton Cheney. *CAST:* Charles Starrett, Carole Mathews, Tex Harding, Nolan Leary, Dub Taylor, Al Bridge, Virginia Sale, Steve Clark, Ted Mapes, Ethan Laidlaw, Budd Buster, Frank LaRue, Edmund Cobb, Mauritz Hugo, John Tyrrell, James T. Nelson, Bob Wills and His Texas Playboys.

The Durango Kid (Starrett), in order to stop an unscrupulous stage line owner (Bridge) from gaining a monopoly on the the transportation system, helps the rival stage line win the stage coach race and postal contract. [British title: *Who Killed Waring?*].

192. The Blazing Trail (7/5/49) B&W — 56 mins. (Western). *DIR:* Ray Nazarro. *PRO:* Colbert Clark. *SP:* Barry Shipman. *CAST:* Charles Starrett, Marjorie Stapp, Smiley Burnette, Jock Mahoney, Trevor Bardette, Fred F. Sears, Steve Darrell, John Cason, Hank Penny, Slim Duncan, Robert Malcolm, Steve Pendleton.

The Durango Kid (Starrett) tracks down the murderer of a wealthy ranch owner, with the help of the ranch owner's brother (Darrell). [British title: *The Forged Will*].

193. Bless the Beasts and Children (7/71) Eastman Color — 109 mins. (Children-Drama). *DIR/PRO:* Stanley Kramer. *SP:* Mac Benoff. Based on the book by Glendon F. Swarthout. *CAST:* Bill Mumy, Barry Robins, Miles Chapin, Darel Glaser, Bob Kramer, Jesse White, Ken Swofford, Dave Ketchum, Marc Vahanian, Bruce Glover, Elaine Devry, Vanessa Brown.

Six boys (Mumy, Robins, Chapin, Glaser, Kramer, Vahanian) set out to free a herd of buffalo who are to be slaughtered.

194. Blind Alley (5/29/39) B&W — 68 mins. (Crime-Drama). *DIR:* Charles Vidor. *PRO:* Fred Kohlmar. *SP:* Philip MacDonald, Michael Blankfort, Albert Duffy. Based on the play by James Warwick. *CAST:* Chester Morris,. Ralph Bellamy, Ann Dvorak, Melville Cooper, Joan Perry, Rose Stradner, Marc Lawrence, John Eldredge, Ann Doran, Stanley Brown, Scotty Beckett, Milburn Stone, Marie Blake.

A psychiatrist (Bellamy) explores the subconscious mind of an escaped killer (Morris) when he takes refuge in his home. *NOTES:* Remade in 1948 by Columbia as *The Dark Past.*

195. Blind Date (8/31/34) B&W — 71 mins. (Drama). *DIR:* Roy William Neill. *SP:* Ethel Hill. Story by Vida Hurst. *CAST:* Ann Sothern, Neil Hamilton, Paul Kelly, Mickey Rooney, Spencer Charters, Jane Darwell, Joan Gale, Theodore Newton, Geneva Mitchell.

When her marriage to a department store owner (Hamilton) fails, a working girl (Sothern) goes back to the garageman (Kelly) she jilted. [British title: *Her Sacrifice*].

196. Blind Spot (2/6/47) B&W — 73 mins. (Thriller). *DIR:* Robert Gordon. *PRO:* Ted Richmond. *SP:* Martin M. Goldsmith. Story by Harry Perowne. *CAST:* Chester Morris, Constance Dowling, Steven Geray, Sid Tomack, James Bell, Paul E. Burns.

A mystery writer (Morris), framed for the murder of his publisher, sets out to find the real murderer.

197. Blonde Captive (2/29/32) B&W — 75 mins. (Documentary). *DIR:* Dr. Paul C. Withington, Clinton Childs. *PRO:* William M. Pizor. *SP:* Lowell Thomas. *CAST:* Narrated by Lowell Thomas.

A journey into the Aborigine land of Australia in search of natives supposed to be descendants of Neanderthal man and the discovery of a white woman living among the natives.

198. Blonde from Brooklyn (6/21/45) B&W — 65 mins. (Musical-Comedy). *DIR:* Del Lord. *PRO:* Ted Richmond. *SP:* Erna Lazarus. *CAST:* Robert Stanton (Bob Haymes), Lynn Merrick, Thurston Hall, Mary Treen, Walter Soderling, Arthur Loft, Regina Wallace, Byron Foulger, Myrtle Ferguson, John Kelly, Matt Willis, Eddie Bartell.

An ex-GI (Stanton) teams up with a singer (Merrick) pretending to be a

Southern belle, to form a singing duo, but winds up in hot water with a Southern colonel (Hall).

199. The Blonde from Singapore (8/29/41) B&W—67 mins. (Adventure). *DIR:* Edward Dmytryk. *PRO:* Jack Fier. *SP:* George Bricker. Story by Houston Branch. *CAST:* Leif Erickson, Florence Rice, Gordon Jones, Dwight Frye, Don Beddoe, Alexander D'Arcy, Adele Rowland, Lumsden Hare, Emory Parnell.

Two pilots (Erikson, Jones) use an adventuress (Rice) to smuggle their pearls. [British title: *Hot Pearls*].

200. Blondie (11/7/38) B&W—68 mins. (Comedy). *DIR:* Frank R. Strayer. *PRO:* Robert Sparks. *SP:* Richard Flournoy. Story by Kay Van Riper. Based on the comic strip created by Chic Young. *CAST:* Penny Singleton, Arthur Lake, Larry Simms, Jonathan Hale, Danny Mummert, Irving Bacon, Gene Lockhart, Stanley Andrews, Gordon Oliver, Ian Wolfe, Ann Doran, Kathleen Lockhart, Dorothy Moore, Fay Helm, Richard Fiske.

Dagwood (Lake) loses his job on the eve of his and Blondie's (Singleton) fifth wedding anniversary, but Blondie saves the day. *NOTES:* The first film of the *Blondie* series.

201. Blondie Brings Up Baby (11/8/39) B&W—67 mins. (Comedy). *DIR:* Frank R. Strayer. *PRO:* Robert Sparks. *SP:* Richard Flournoy, Gladys Lehman. Story by Robert Chapin, Karen DeWolf, Richard Flournoy. Based on the comic strip created by Chic Young. *CAST:* Penny Singleton, Arthur Lake, Larry Simms, Jonathan Hale, Danny Mummert, Irving Bacon, Robert Middlemass, Olin Howlin, Fay Helm, Roy Gordon, Peggy Ann Garner, Grace Stafford, Helen Jerome Eddy, Robert Sterling, Bruce Bennett, Ian Wolfe.

Blondie (Singleton) enrolls Baby Dumpling (Simms) in a special school when she thinks he is a genius.

202. Blondie for Victory (8/6/42) B&W—72 mins. (Comedy). *DIR:* Frank R. Strayer. *PRO:* Robert Sparks. *SP:* Karen DeWolf, Connie Lee. Story by Fay Kanin. Based on the comic strip created by Chic Young. *CAST:* Penny Singleton, Arthur Lake, Larry Simms, Irving Bacon, Danny Mummert, Jonathan Hale, Majelle White, Stuart Erwin, Edward Gargan, Renie Riano, Harrison Greene, Charles Wagenheim, Sylvia Field, Georgia Backus.

Blondie (Singleton) organizes the Housewives of America to guard the local dam, but gives it up when Dagwood (Lake) pretends to join the Army. [British title: *Troubles Through Billets*].

203. Blondie Goes Latin (2/27/41) B&W—70 mins. (Comedy). *DIR:* Frank R. Strayer. *PRO:* Robert Sparks. *SP:* Karen DeWolf, Richard Flournoy. Story by Quinn Martin. Based on the comic strip created by Chic Young. *CAST:* Penny Singleton, Arthur Lake, Larry Simms, Irving Bacon, Danny Mummert, Jonathan Hale, Ruth Terry, Tito Guizar, Janet Burston, Kirby Grant, Joseph King, Eddie Acuff.

Blondie (Singleton) and Dagwood (Lake) slip off on a cruise to South America. [British title: *Conga Swing*].

204. Blondie Goes to College (1/15/42) B&W—74 mins. (Comedy). *DIR:* Frank R. Strayer. *PRO:* Robert Sparks. *SP:* Lou Breslow. Story by Warren Wilson, Clyde Bruckman. Based on the comic strip created by Chic Young. *CAST:* Penny Singleton, Arthur Lake, Larry Simms, Irving Bacon, Danny Mummert, Jonathan Hale, Larry Parks, Adele Mara, Lloyd Bridges, Sidney Melton, Andrew Tombes, Esther Dale, Janet Blair, Bill Goodwin.

Blondie (Singleton) tags along when Dagwood (Lake) enrolls in college. [British title: *The Boss Said "No"*].

205. Blondie Has Servant Trouble (10/9/40) B&W — 69 mins. (Comedy). *DIR*: Frank R. Strayer. *PRO*: Robert Sparks. *SP*: Richard Flournoy. Story by Albert Duffy. Based on the comic strip created by Chic Young. *CAST*: Penny Singleton, Arthur Lake, Larry Simms, Irving Bacon, Danny Mummert, Jonathan Hale, Arthur Hohl, Esther Dale, Ray Turner, Fay Helm, Walter Soderling, Murray Alper, Eddie Laughton.

Mr. Dithers (Hale) asks Dagwood (Lake) and Blondie (Singleton) to move into a house to prove it isn't haunted.

206. Blondie Hits the Jackpot (10/6/49) B&W — 66 mins. (Comedy). *DIR*: Edward Bernds. *PRO*: Ted Richmond. *SP*: Jack Henley. Based on the comic strip created by Chic Young. *CAST*: Penny Singleton, Arthur Lake, Larry Simms, Marjorie Kent, Jerome Cowan, Danny Mummert, Lloyd Corrigan, James Flavin, Dick Wessel, Ray Teal, Alyn Lockwood.

Dagwood (Lake) makes a mistake in a construction deal, is fired by Mr. Dithers (Cowan), and winds up on a labor gang. Blondie (Singleton) eventually saves the day. [British title: *Hitting the Jackpot*].

207. Blondie in Society (6/14/41) B&W — 77 mins. (Comedy). *DIR*: Frank R. Strayer. *PRO*: Robert Sparks. *SP*: Karen DeWolf. Story by Eleanor Griffin. Based on the comic strip created by Chic Young. *CAST*: Penny Singleton, Arthur Lake, Larry Simms, Irving Bacon, Danny Mummert, Jonathan Hale, William Frawley, Edgar Kennedy, Chick Chandler, Bill Goodwin, Gary Owen, Tommy Dixon.

When Dagwood (Lake) brings home a pedigreed Great Dane, Blondie (Singleton) decides to enter it in the local dog show. [British title: *Henpecked*].

208. Blondie in the Dough (10/16/47) B&W — 69 mins. (Comedy). *DIR*: Abby Berlin. *PRO*: Burt Kelly. *SP*: Arthur Marx, Jack Henley. Based on the comic strip created by Chic Young. *CAST*: Penny Singleton, Arthur Lake, Larry Simms, Marjorie Kent, Jerome Cowan, Danny Mummert, Hugh Herbert, Clarence Kolb, William Forrest, Eddie Acuff, Norman Phillips, Kernan Cripps, Fred F. Sears, Boyd Davis, Mary Emery.

A sudden windfall of money creates problems for Dagwood (Lake) and Blondie (Singleton).

209. Blondie Knows Best (10/17/46) B&W — 69 mins. (Comedy). *DIR*: Abby Berlin. *PRO*: Burt Kelly. *SP*: Edward Bernds, Al Martin. Story by Edward Bernds. Based on the comic strip created by Chic Young. *CAST*: Penny Singleton, Arthur Lake, Larry Simms, Alyn Lockwood, Danny Mummert, Jonathan Hale, Steven Geray, Marjorie Kent, Shemp Howard, Jerome Cowan, Ludwig Donath, Arthur Loft, Edwin Cooper, Jack Rice, Carol Hughes, Kay Mallory.

Dagwood (Lake) tries to avoid a half-blind process server (Howard), while he impersonates his boss (Hale) in order to close a business deal.

210. Blondie Meets the Boss (5/1/39) B&W — 58 mins. (Comedy). *DIR*: Frank R. Strayer. *PRO*: Robert Sparks. *SP*: Richard Flournoy. Story by Kay Van Riper, Richard Flournoy. Based on the comic strip created by Chic Young. *CAST*: Penny Singleton, Arthur Lake, Larry Simms, Jonathan Hale, Danny Mummert, Irving Bacon, Dorothy Moore, Don Beddoe, Linda Winters (Dorothy Comingore), Stanley Brown, Joel Dean, Richard Fiske, Inez Courtney, Eddie Acuff, James Craig, George Chandler, Robert Sterling.

Blondie (Singleton) takes over Dagwood's (Lake) job when he gets into trouble on a fishing trip.

211. Blondie on a Budget (4/10/40) B&W—72 mins. (Comedy). *DIR:* Frank R. Strayer. *PRO:* Robert Sparks. *SP:* Richard Flournoy. Story by Charles M. Brown. Based on the comic strip created by Chic Young. *CAST:* Penny Singleton, Arthur Lake, Larry Simms, Irving Bacon, Danny Mummert, Don Beddoe, John Qualen, Rita Hayworth, Fay Helm, Thurston Hall, William Brisbane, Emory Parnell, Willie Best, Dick Curtis.

Blondie (Singleton) becomes jealous when an old flame (Hayworth) of Dagwood's (Lake) comes into town.

212. Blondie Plays Cupid (12/5/40) B&W—67 mins. (Comedy). *DIR:* Frank R. Strayer. *PRO:* Robert Sparks. *SP:* Richard Flournoy, Karen DeWolf. Story by Karen DeWolf, Charles M. Brown. Based on the comic strip created by Chic Young. *CAST:* Penny Singleton, Arthur Lake, Larry Simms, Irving Bacon, Danny Mummert, Jonathan Hale, Glenn Ford, Luana Walters, Will Wright, Spencer Charters, Leona Roberts, Tommy Dixon.

While on a trip to visit their relatives in the country, Dagwood (Lake) and Blondie (Singleton) help an eloping couple (Ford, Walters).

213. Blondie Takes a Vacation (9/14/39) B&W—58 mins. (Comedy). *DIR:* Frank R. Strayer. *PRO:* Robert Sparks. *SP:* Richard Flournoy. Story by Karen DeWolf, Richard Flournoy, Robert Chapin. Based on the comic strip created by Chic Young. *CAST:* Penny Singleton, Arthur Lake, Larry Simms, Donald Meek, Danny Mummert, Irving Bacon, Donald MacBride, Thomas W. Ross, Elizabeth Dunn, Milton Kibbee, Robert Wilcox, Harlan Briggs.

Blondie (Singleton) and Dagwood (Lake) help an aging couple run a mountain hotel so they won't lose their life savings.

214. Blondie's Anniversary (12/18/47) B&W—75 mins. (Comedy). *DIR:* Abby Berlin. *PRO:* Burt Kelly. *SP:* Jack Henley. Based on the comic strip created by Chic Young. *CAST:* Penny Singleton, Arthur Lake, Larry Simms, Marjorie Kent, Jerome Cowan, Adele Jergens, Grant Mitchell, William Frawley, Eddie Acuff, Edmund MacDonald, Jack Rice, Alyn Lockwood, Frank Wilcox, Fred F. Sears.

Blondie (Singleton) mistakenly thinks the watch that Dagwood (Lake) brought home is her anniversary present.

215. Blondie's Big Deal (3/10/49) B&W—66 mins. (Comedy). *DIR:* Edward Bernds. *PRO:* Ted Richmond. *SP:* Lucile Watson Henley. Based on the comic strip created by Chic Young. *CAST:* Penny Singleton, Arthur Lake, Larry Simms, Marjorie Kent, Jerome Cowan, Danny Mummert, Collette Lyons, Wilton Graff, Alyn Lockwood, Ray Walker, Stanley Andrews, Alan Dinehart, III, Eddie Acuff, Jack Rice, Chester Clute, George Lloyd.

Blondie (Singleton) saves the day when Dagwood (Lake) loses his nonflammable paint invention to a couple of rival contractors (Graff, Walker). [British title: *The Big Deal*].

216. Blondie's Big Moment (1/9/47) B&W—69 mins. (Comedy). *DIR:* Abby Berlin. *PRO:* Burt Kelly. *SP:* Connie Lee. Based on the comic strip created by Chic Young. *CAST:* Penny Singleton, Arthur Lake, Larry Simms, Marjorie Kent, Jerome Cowan, Danny Mummert, Anita Louise, Jack Rice, Jack Davis, Dick Wessel, Johnny Granath, Hal K. Dawson, Eddie Acuff, Alyn Lockwood, Robert Stevens, Douglas Wood, Robert De Haven.

Blondie (Singleton) creates havoc in the Bumstead household when she has a chance to become a big star. NOTES: In a contract dispute with the studio, Jonathan Hale (J. C. Dithers) was replaced by Jerome Cowan (George Radcliffe) as Dagwood's new boss for the remainder of the series.

217. Blondie's Blessed Event (4/9/42) B&W—69 mins. (Comedy). *DIR*: Frank R. Strayer. *PRO*: Robert Sparks. *SP*: Connie Lee, Karen DeWolf, Richard Flournoy. Based on the comic strip created by Chic Young. *CAST*: Penny Singleton, Arthur Lake, Larry Simms, Irving Bacon, Danny Mummert, Jonathan Hale, Hans Conreid, Olin Howlin, Stanley Brown, Eileen O'Hearn, Norma Jean Wayne, Mary Wickes, Arthur O'Connell, Paul Harvey.

When Cookie (Norma Jean Wayne) is born, a cynical author (Conreid) comes to the Bumstead household to write a baby book. [British title: *A Bundle of Trouble*].

218. Blondie's Hero (3/9/50) B&W—67 mins. (Comedy). *DIR*: Edward Bernds. *PRO*: Ted Richmond. *SP*: Jack Henley. Based on the comic strip created by Chic Young. *CAST*: Penny Singleton, Arthur Lake, Larry Simms, Danny Mummert, William Frawley, Iris Adrian, Edward Earle, Joe Sawyer, Alyn Lockwood, Teddy Infuhr, Frank Jenks, Dick Wessel, Frank Sully, Jimmy Lloyd, Robert Emmett Keane, Mary Newton, Pat Flaherty, Ted Mapes, Frank Wilcox.

Dagwood (Lake) almost causes a civil war when he signs up for the Army Reserve.

219. Blondie's Holiday (4/10/47) B&W—61 mins. (Comedy). *DIR*: Abby Berlin. *PRO*: Burt Kelly. *SP*: Connie Lee. Based on the comic strip created by Chic Young. *CAST*: Penny Singleton, Arthur Lake, Larry Simms, Marjorie Kent, Jerome Cowan, Grant

Mitchell, Sid Tomack, Mary Young, Jeff York, Bobby Larson, Jody Gilbert, Jack Rice, Alyn Lockwood, Eddie Acuff, Tim Ryan, Anne Nagel.

Dagwood (Lake) gets mixed up with bookies and winds up rescuing the local banker's wife (Young).

220. Blondie's Lucky Day (4/4/46) B&W—69 mins. (Comedy). *DIR*: Abby Berlin. *PRO*: Burt Kelly. *SP*: Connie Lee. Based on the comic strip created by Chic Young. *CAST*: Penny Singleton, Arthur Lake, Larry Simms, Marjorie Kent, Robert Stanton, Jonathan Hale, Angelyn Orr, Paul Harvey, Jack Rice, Bobby Larson, Charles Arnt, Marjorie Liszt, Frank Orth, Frank Jenks.

Dagwood (Lake) takes over the office during his boss's absence and hires a former WAC (Orr) with predictable complications.

221. Blondie's Reward (6/3/48) B&W—65 mins. (Comedy). *DIR*: Abby Berlin. *PRO*: Burt Kelly. *SP*: Edward Bernds. Based on the comic strip created by Chic Young. *CAST*: Penny Singleton, Arthur Lake, Larry Simms, Marjorie Kent, Jerome Cowan, Danny Mummert, Gay Nelson, Ross Ford, Paul Harvey, Frank Jenks, Chick Chandler, Jack Rice, Eddie Acuff, Alyn Lockwood, Frank Sully, Myron Healey, Chester Clute.

Dagwood (Lake) gets into trouble when he buys the wrong property and gets into a fight with a client's son.

222. Blondie's Secret (12/23/48) B&W—68 mins. (Comedy). *DIR*: Edward Bernds. *PRO*: Ted Richmond. *SP*: Jack Henley. Based on the comic strip created by Chic Young. *CAST*: Penny Singleton, Arthur Lake, Larry Simms, Marjorie Kent, Jerome Cowan, Danny Mummert, Thurston Hall, Jack Rice, Alyn Lockwood, Frank Orth, Murray Alper, William "Bill" Phillips,

Eddie Acuff, Greta Granstedt, Grandon Rhodes, Joseph Crehan.

Problems arise when Blondie (Singleton) and Dagwood (Lake) decide to take a vacation.

Blood Money see **The Stranger and the Gunfighter**

223. The Blood Ship (8/10/27) B&W—65 mins. (Adventure). DIR: George B. Seitz. PRO: Harry Cohn. SP: Fred Myton. Story by Norman Springer. CAST: Hobart Bosworth, Jacqueline Logan, Richard Arlen, Walter James, Fred Kohler, Arthur Rankin, Sydney Crossley.

A cruel sea captain (James) kidnaps a man's wife and daughter (Logan), and years later, is finally confronted by the man (Bosworth).

224. Blue Canadian Rockies (11/20/52) Sepiatone—58 mins. (Western). DIR: George Archainbaud. PRO: Armand Schaefer. SP: Gerald Geraghty. A Gene Autry Production. CAST: Gene Autry, Gail Davis, Pat Buttram, Ross Ford, Tom London, Mauritz Hugo, Don Beddoe, Gene Roth, John Merton, David Garcia, Bob Woodward, Bill Wilkerson, Carolina Cotton, The Cass County Boys.

Gene heads to Canada to save his employer's daughter (Davis) from marrying a fortune hunter (Hugo).

225. The Blue Lagoon (6/80) Metrocolor—104 mins. (Drama-Romance). DIR/PRO: Randal Kleiser. SP: Douglas Day Stewart. Based on the book by Henry Devere Stacpoole. CAST: Christopher Atkins, Brooke Shields, Leo McKern, William Daniels, Elva Josephson, Glenn Kohan, Alan Hopgood, Gus Mercurio, Jeffrey Means, Bradley Pryce, Chad Timmerman.

Two young people (Shields, Atkins) are shipwrecked on an island, grow to be adults, have a child, and are rescued.

226. Blue Thunder (5/83) DeLuxe Color/Panavision—110 mins. (Adventure). DIR: John Badham. PRO: Gordon Carroll. SP: Dan O'Bannon, Don Jakoby. A Rastar Production. CAST: Roy Scheider, Warren Oates, Candy Clark, Daniel Stern, Joe Santos, Paul Roebling, David S. Sheiner, Malcolm McDowell, Ed Bernard, Anthony James, James Murtaugh, Patrick McNamara, Jack Murdock.

A policeman (Scheider) and his partner (Stern) try to stop a fanatic (McDowell) from destroying their helicopter, the Blue Thunder, and from overthrowing the U.S.

227. Bob and Carol and Ted and Alice (11/69) Technicolor—104 mins. (Comedy). DIR: Paul Mazursky. PRO: Larry Tucker. SP: Paul Mazursky, Larry Tucker. A Frankovich Production. CAST: Natalie Wood, Robert Culp, Elliott Gould, Dyan Cannon, Lee Bergere, Horst Ebersberg, K. T. Stevens, Gregg Mullavey, Celeste Yarnell, Lynn Borden, Diana Berghoff, John Halloran, Jeffery Walker.

Two California couples (Culp & Wood, Gould & Cannon), influenced by a group therapy session advocating sexual freedom, almost get caught up in a wife-swapping party. NOTES: The directorial debut of Paul Mazursky.

228. Bob, Le Flambeur (**Bob, the Gambler**) (6/82) B&W—100 mins. (Crime). DIR/PRO/SP: Jean-Pierre Melville. A Triumph Films Production. CAST: Roger Duchesne, Isabel Corey, Daniel Cauchy, Guy Decombie, Andre Garet, Claude Cerval, Colette Fleury, Gerard Buhr, Simone Paris.

Everything goes wrong when a hard-luck gambler (Duchesne) enlists the aid of his pals to rob a French casino. NOTES: Originally released in France in 1956. Limited theatrical release; in French with English subtitles.

229. Bobby Deerfield (9/77) Metrocolor/Panavision — 124 mins. (Romance). *DIR/PRO:* Sydney Pollack. *SP:* Alvin Sargent. Based on *Heaven Has No Favorites* by Erich Maria Remarque. *CAST:* Al Pacino, Marthe Keller, Anny Duperey, Walter McGinn, Romolo Valli, Stephan Meldegg, Jaime Sanchez, Norm Nielson, Monique Lejeune, Steve Gadler.

A top-flight racing driver (Pacino) falls for a jet-setter (Keller) with an incurable disease.

230. Body Double (10/84) Metrocolor — 109 mins. (Mystery-Crime). *DIR/PRO:* Brian De Palma. *SP:* Brian De Palma, Robert J. Avrech. Story by Brian De Palma. A Columbia-Delphi II Production. *CAST:* Craig Wasson, Melanie Griffith, Gregg Henry, Deborah Shelton, Guy Boyd, Dennis Franz, David Haskell, Rebecca Stanley, Barbara Crampton, Russ Marin, Linda Shaw.

An out of work actor (Wasson) uncovers an elaborate murder plot when he spies on his neighbor (Shelton).

231. Bodyhold (3/21/50) B&W — 63 mins. (Crime). *DIR:* Seymour Friedman. *PRO:* Rudolph C. Flothow. *SP:* George Bricker. *CAST:* Willard Parker, Lola Albright, Hillary Brooke, Allen Jenkins, Roy Roberts, Gordon Jones, Sammy Menacker, Frank Sully, John Dehner, Henry Kulky, Ruth Warren, John Hamilton, George Lloyd.

A plumber (Parker) gets mixed up with a crooked promoter (Roberts), becomes a professional wrestler, and sets out to get the promoter.

232. Bonanza Town (7/18/51) B&W — 56 mins. (Western). *DIR:* Fred F. Sears. *PRO:* Colbert Clark. *SP:* Barry Shipman, Bert Hoswell. *CAST:* Charles Starrett, Fred F. Sears, Smiley Burnette, Myron Healey, Luther Crockett, Paul McGuire, Charles Horvath, Vernon Dent, Ted Jordan, Al Wyatt, Slim Duncan.

The Durango Kid (Starrett), through some marked money taken in a robbery, discovers that an outlaw (Sears), believed to be dead, is alive and hiding at the home of his brother (Crockett), a judge, in Bonanza Town. [British title: *Two-Fisted Agent*].

233. Bonjour Tristesse (4/58) Technicolor/Scope — 93 mins. (Drama). *DIR:* Otto Preminger, John Palmer. *PRO:* Otto Preminger. *SP:* Arthur Laurents. Based on the book by Francoise Sagan. *CAST:* Deborah Kerr, David Niven, Jean Seberg, Mylene Demongeot, Geoffrey Horne, Juliette Greco, Walter Chiari, Marita Hunt, Roland Culver, Jean Kent, David Oxley, Tutte Lemkow, Elga Anderson, Jeremy Burnham.

A teenage girl (Seberg) becomes involved with her father's (Niven) love affairs, and causes the death of his mistress (Kerr).

234. The Boogie Man Will Get You (10/22/42) B&W — 66 mins. (Comedy). *DIR:* Lew Landers. *PRO:* Colbert Clark. *SP:* Edwin Blum. Story by Hal Fimberg, Robert E. Hunt. Adapted by Paul Gangelin. *CAST:* Boris Karloff, Peter Lorre, Maxie Rosenbloom, Larry Parks, Jeff Donnell, Maude Eburne, Don Beddoe, George McKay, Frank Puglia, Eddie Laughton, Frank Sully, James Morton.

A couple (Parks, Donnell) buy a New England hotel from a wacky scientist (Karloff) who is trying to turn traveling salesmen into a race of supermen.

235. Boomerang (3/34) B&W — 82 mins. (Drama). *DIR:* Arthur Maude. *SP:* John Paddy Carstairs. Based on the play by David Evans. A Maude Production. *CAST:* Nora Swinburne, Lester Matthews, Millicent Wolf, Henry Braban, Wallace Geoffrey, Charles Mortimer.

A blind author (Matthews) sets out to find the blackmailer of his wife (Swinburne).

Boot, Das see **Das Boot**

236. Boots Malone (1/11/52) B&W — 102 mins. (Sports-Drama). DIR: William Dieterle. PRO/SP: Milton Holmes. CAST: William Holden, Johnny Stewart, Stanley Clements, Basil Ruysdael, Carl Benton Reid, Ralph Dumke, Ed Begley, Hugh Sanders, Henry (Harry) Morgan, Anna Lee, Anthony Caruso, Billy Pearson, Milton Kibbee, Frank Ferguson, Earle Hodgins, Carleton Young, Emory Parnell, Hank Worden.

A jockey's agent (Holden), down on his luck, trains a young jockey (Stewart) to win the big race.

237. Border Law (9/15/31) B&W — 63 mins. (Western). DIR: Louis King. PRO: Irving Briskin. SP: Stuart Anthony. CAST: Buck Jones, F. R. Smith, Lupita Tovar, John Wallace, James Mason, Robert Burns, Frank Rice, Glenn Strange, Don Chapman, Fred Burns, Louis Hickus, Art Mix.

A Texas Ranger (Jones) is granted a leave of absence to go after the head of an outlaw gang (Mason) when his brother is killed. NOTES: Remade by Columbia in 1934 as The Fighting Ranger.

238. Born Free (9/66) Technicolor/Panavision — 95 mins. (Outdoors-Drama). DIR: James Hill. PRO: Sam Jaffe, Paul Radin. SP: Gerald L. C. Copley. Based on the book by Joy Adamson. An Open Road-High Road-Atlas Production. CAST: Virginia McKenna, William Travers, Geoffrey Keen, Peter Lukoye, Bill Godden, Bryan Epsom, Robert Cheetham, Robert Young, Geoffrey Best.

A Kenya game warden (Travers) and his wife (McKenna) adopt the cubs of a slain lioness.

239. Born Yesterday (11/20/50) B&W — 103 mins. (Comedy). DIR: George Cukor. PRO: S. Sylvan Simon. SP: Albert Mannheimer. Based on the play by Garson Kanin. CAST: Judy Holliday, Broderick Crawford, William Holden, Howard St. John, Frank Otto, Larry Oliver, Barbara Brown, Grandon Rhodes, Claire Carleton.

A scrap iron tycoon (Crawford) hires a tutor (Holden) to teach his girlfriend (Holliday) culture.

240. Borrowed Clothes (2/34) B&W — 70 mins. (Comedy). DIR: Arthur Maude. SP: Aimee and Philip Stuart. Based on the play Her Shop by Aimee and Philip Stuart. A Maude Production. CAST: Anne Grey, Lester Matthews, Sunday Wilshin, Joe Hayman, Renee Macready, P. G. Clark, Philip Strange, Anthony Holles.

An extravagant English lady (Grey) accidentally buys a failing fashion shop and turns it into a success.

241. Boston Blackie and the Law (12/12/46) B&W — 65 mins. (Crime). DIR: D. Ross Lederman. PRO: Ted Richmond. SP: Harry J. Essex. Based on the characters created by Jack Boyle. CAST: Chester Morris, Trudy Marshall, George E. Stone, Constance Dowling, Richard Lane, Frank Sully, Warren Ashe, Selmer Jackson, Fred Graff, Edward F. Dunn, Ted Hecht, Eddie Fetherstone, Frank O'Conner, Brian O'Hara.

During a magic show at the women's prison, Blackie (Morris) inadvertently allows a woman prisoner to escape, who is later found murdered. [British title: Blackie and the Law].

242. Boston Blackie Booked on Suspicion (5/10/45) B&W — 66 mins. (Crime). DIR: Arthur Dreifuss. PRO: Michael Kraike. SP: Paul Yawitz. Story by Malcolm Stuart Boylan. Based on the characters created by Jack Boyle. CAST: Chester Morris, Lynn

Merrick, George E. Stone, Frank Sully, Richard Lane, Lloyd Corrigan, Steve Cochran, George Carleton, George Meader, Douglas Wood, George Lloyd, Robert Williams, Jessie Arnold.

Murder ensues when Blackie (Morris) poses as an auctioneer to help a friend and mistakenly sells a fake Charles Dickens first edition. [British title: *Booked on Suspicion*].

243. Boston Blackie Goes Hollywood (11/5/42) B&W—68 mins. (Crime). DIR: Michael Gordon. PRO: Wallace MacDonald. SP: Paul Yawitz. Based on the characters created by Jack Boyle. CAST: Chester Morris, Constance Worth, George E. Stone, William Wright, Richard Lane, Walter Sande, Lloyd Corrigan, Forrest Tucker, Cy Kendall, John Tyrrell, Shirley Patterson, Ralph Dunn, Jessie Arnold.

Blackie (Morris) goes to Hollywood to help a friend (Corrigan) and locate the lost Monterey Diamond. [British title: *Blackie Goes Hollywood*].

244. Boston Blackie's Chinese Venture (3/3/49) B&W—59 mins. (Crime). DIR: Seymour Friedman. PRO: Rudolph C. Flothow. SP: Maurice Tombragel. Based on the characters created by Jack Boyle. CAST: Chester Morris, Joan Woodbury, Richard Lane, Sid Tomack, Maylia, Don McGuire, Frank Sully, Luis Van Rooten, Benson Fong, Philip Ahn, Charles Arnt, Peter Brocco, Edgar Dearing, Fred F. Sears, Pat O'Malley, George Lloyd.

Blackie (Morris) goes to Chinatown to solve a murder and uncovers a diamond smuggling operation. [British title: *Chinese Adventure*].

245. Boston Blackie's Rendezvous (7/5/45) B&W—64 mins. (Crime). DIR: Arthur Dreifuss. PRO: Alexis Thurn-Taxis. SP: Edward Dein. Story by Fred Schiller. Based on char-

acters created by Jack Boyle. CAST: Chester Morris, Nina Foch, George E. Stone, Steve Cochran, Richard Lane, Frank Sully, Iris Adrian, Philip Van Zandt, Richard Alexander, Harry Hayden, Adelle Roberts, Joe Devlin, John Tyrrell.

Blackie must protect a young girl (Foch) when a crazed killer (Cochran) escapes from an asylum. [British title: *Blackie's Rendezvous*].

246. Both Barrels Blazing (5/17/45) B&W—57 mins. (Western). DIR: Derwin Abrahams. PRO: Colbert Clark. SP: William Lively. CAST: Charles Starrett, Pat Parrish, Tex Harding, Emmett Lynn, Dub Taylor, Al Bridge, Dan White, Edward Howard, Jack Rockwell, Charles King, Robert Barron, James T. Nelson, Hansel Warner, John Cason, The Jesters.

The Durango Kid (Starrett), with the help of an old prospector (Lynn), uncovers a plot to transport a fortune in stolen gold. [British title: *The Yellow Streak*].

Boum, La *see* La Boum

247. The Boy and the Bridge (7/59) B&W—91 mins. (Drama). DIR: Kevin McClory. PRO: Kevin McClory, David Eady. SP: Kevin McClory, Desmond O'Donovan, Geoffrey Orme. Story by Leon Ware. A Xanadu Production. CAST: Ian MacLaine, Liam Redmond, James Hayter, Norman MacOwan, Geoffrey Keen, Jack Mac-Gowran, Royal Dano, Rita Webb, Jack Stewart.

A boy (MacLaine) runs away from home and hides in the ramparts of Tower Bridge when he thinks his father (Redmond) has been arrested for murder.

248. The Boy from Stalingrad (5/20/43) B&W—69 mins. (War). DIR: Sidney Salkow. PRO: Colbert Clark. SP: Ferdinand Reyher. Story by Robert Arden, Robert Lee Johnson. CAST: Bobby Samarzich, Conrad Binyon, Mary Lou Harrington, Scotty Beckett, Steven Muller, Donald Mayo, John Wengraf, Erik Rolf.

An English boy (Beckett), together with a group of Russian boys, helps to hold a Russian village against a German attack.

The Boy Next Door *see* **To Find a Man**

249. The Boys in Company C (2/78) Technicolor/Panavision—125 mins. (War-Drama). *DIR*: Sidney J. Furie. *PRO*: Andrew Morgan. *SP*: Sidney J. Furie, Richard Natkin. A Golden Harvest Production. *CAST*: Stan Shaw, Andrew Stevens, James Canning, Michael Lembeck, Craig Wasson, Scott Hylands, James Whitmore, Jr., Noble Willingham, Lee Ermey, Santos Morales, Drew Michaels, Karen Hilger, Peggy O'Neal, Claude Wilson, Chuck Doherty, Stan Johns, Don Bell.

Five young men (Shaw, Stevens, Canning, Lembeck, Wasson) find their lives altered drastically by the Vietnam War.

250. Boys' School (6/29/39) B&W—103 mins. (Mystery). *DIR*: Christian Jaque. *SP*: J. H. Blanchon. Based on the book by Pierre Very. A Francinex-Vog Production. *CAST*: Erich von Stroheim, Michel Simon, Armand Bernard, Serge Grave, Marcel Mouloudji, Jean Claudio, Aime Clariond, Pierre Labry, Robert LaVigan, R. Genin, Jean Bouquet, Claude Roy.

At the boarding school of St. Agil in France, a member (Grave) of the secret "Skull and Crossbones Society" suspects that one of his teachers, Simon (von Stroheim), is a forger and murderer and is responsible for the disappearance of his fellow members (Claudio, Mouloudji). *NOTES*: In French with English subtitles. [Original French title: *Les Disparus de St Agil*].

251. Branded (9/1/31) B&W—59 mins. (Western). *DIR*: D. Ross Lederman. *SP*: Randall Faye. *CAST*: Buck Jones, Philo McCullough, Ethel Kenyon, John Oscar, Al Smith, Wallace MacDonald, Bob Kortman, Fred Burns, Clark Burroughs, Sam MacDonald.

A cowboy (Jones) is branded a rustler when he refuses to sell out to his neighbor (Kenyon).

252. The Brave Bulls (4/18/51) B&W—106 mins. (Drama). *DIR/PRO*: Robert Rossen. *SP*: John Bright. Based on the book by Tom Lea. *CAST*: Mel Ferrer, Miroslava, Anthony Quinn, Eugene Iglesias, Jose Torvay, Charlita, Jose-Luis Lopez Vasquez, Alfonso Alvirez, Alfredo Aguilar.

A matador (Ferrer) loses faith in himself when his manager (Quinn) and girl (Miroslava) are killed in an auto crash, but makes a comeback when his brother (Iglesias) is gored in the ring.

253. Brave Warrior (6/1/52) Technicolor—73 mins. (Western). *DIR*: Spencer G. Bennet. *PRO*: Sam Katzman. *SP*: Robert E. Kent. *CAST*: Jon Hall, Christine Larson, Michael Ansara, Jay Silverheels, Harry Cording, George Eldredge, James Seay, Leslie Denison, Rory Mallison, Rusty Wescoatt, Bert Davidson, William P. Wilkerson, Gilbert V. Perkins.

A government agent (Hall) is sent west to find those responsible for stirring up the Indians.

254. Breakout (5/75) Eastman Color—96 mins. (Adventure). *DIR*: Tom Gries. *PRO*: Robert Chartoff, Irwin Winkler. *SP*: Marc Norman, Elliott Baker, Howard B. Kreitsek. Based on the book by Warren Hinckle, Eliot Asinof, and William Turner. *CAST*: Charles Bronson, Jill Ireland, Robert Duvall, John Huston, Randy Quaid, Sheree North, Alejandro Rey,

Paul Mantee, Roy Jenson, Alan Vint, Jorge Moreno.

A pilot (Bronson) is hired to spring an innocent man (Duvall) from a Mexican prison.

255. Brian's Song (1972) Eastman Color—73 mins. (Drama). *DIR:* Buzz Kulik. *PRO:* Paul Junger Witt. *SP:* William E. Blinn. Based on *I Am Third* by Gale Sayers. A Screen Gems-Columbia Pictures Production. *CAST:* James Caan, Billy Dee Williams, Jack Warden, Shelley Fabares, Judy Pace, Bernie Casey, David Huddleston, Ron Feinberg, Jack Concannon, Abe Gibron, Ed O'Bradovich, Dick Butkas, The Chicago Bears.

The story of Brian Piccolo (Caan), running back of the Chicago Bears, his lasting rivalry and friendship with teammate Gale Sayers (Williams), and his losing battle with cancer. *NOTES:* Originally released Nov. 30, 1971, as a made for TV movie. This film is included in this list because the following year, 1972, Columbia released this film theatrically, with a major premiere in Chicago. It was withdrawn because of poor attendance, since almost everyone had seen it free on television.

256. The Bride (8/85) Rank Film Lab Color—119 mins. (Horror-Drama). *DIR:* Franc Roddam. *PRO:* Victor Drai. *SP:* Lloyd Fonvielle. Based on *Frankenstein* by Mary Shelley. *CAST:* Sting, Jennifer Beals, Anthony Higgins, Clancy Brown, Veruschka, David Rappaport, Geraldine Page, Alexei Sayle, Phil Daniels, Quentin Crisp, Gary Elwes, Tom Spaull, Ken Campbell, Guy Rolfe.

Frankenstein (Sting) seeks to create the perfect, independent woman (Beals) with disastrous results. *NOTES:* A loose remake of the 1935 Universal film *The Bride of Frankenstein.*

257. The Bridge on the River Kwai (12/57) Technicolor/Scope—161 mins. (War-Drama). *DIR:* David Lean. *PRO:* Sam Spiegel. *SP:* Pierre Boule. Based on *The Bridge on the River Kwai* by Pierre Boule. *CAST:* William Holden, Alec Guinness, Jack Hawkins, Sessue Hayakawa, James Donald, Geoffrey Horne, Andre Morell, Peter Williams, Percy Herbert, Ann Sears, John Boxer, Harold Goodwin.

In 1943 Burma, a British colonel (Guinness) convinces a Japanese commander (Hayakawa) to let his men build the bridge across the Kwai River; meanwhile British agents are sent to destroy it.

258. Brief Moment (8/31/33) B&W—69 mins. (Drama). *DIR:* David Burton. *SP:* Brian Marlow, Edith Fitzgerald. Based on the play by Samuel Nathaniel Behrman. *CAST:* Carole Lombard, Gene Raymond, Monroe Owsley, Donald Cook, Arthur Hohl, Reginald Mason, Jameson Thomas, Theresa Maxwell Conover, Florence Britton, Irene Ware, Herbert Evans.

A nightclub singer (Lombard) seeks to reform her playboy husband (Raymond).

259. The Brigand (6/25/52) Technicolor—93 mins. (Adventure-Drama). *DIR:* Phil Karlson. *PRO:* Edward Small. *SP:* Jesse L. Lasky, Jr. Story by George Bruce. Adapted from *Brigand, a Romance of the Reign of Don Carlos* by Alexandre Dumas. *CAST:* Anthony Dexter, Jody Lawrence, Anthony Quinn, Gale Robbins, Ron Randell, Carl Benton Reid, Fay Roope, Carleton Young, Ian MacDonald, Holmes Herbert, Lester Matthews, Barbara Brown, Walter Kingsford, Donald Randolph, Mari Blanchard.

A wanted adventurer (Dexter) takes the place of a wounded king (Dexter) in order to expose his enemies. *NOTES:* A loose remake of *The*

Prisoner of Zenda and *The Mask of the Avenger.*

260. The Brigand of Kandahar (5/65) Technicolor/Scope—81 mins. (Adventure). *DIR/SP:* John Gilling. *PRO:* Anthony Nelson-Keys. A Hammer Production. *CAST:* Ronald Lewis, Oliver Reed, Duncan Lamont, Yvonne Romain, Catherine Woodville, Glyn Houston, Sean Lynch, Walter Brown, Jeremy Burnham.

A Bengal Lancer (Lewis) joins up with a bandit chief (Reed) when he is sacked by the Army.

261. Bring Your Smile Along (8/55) Technicolor—83 mins. (Musical-Comedy). *DIR/SP:* Blake Edwards. *PRO:* Jonie Taps. Story by Blake Edwards, Richard Quine. *CAST:* Frankie Laine, Keefe Brasselle, Constance Towers, Lucy Marlow, William Leslie, Mario Siletti, Ruth Warren, Jack Albertson, Bobby Clark, Murray Leonard, Ida Smeraldo.

A schoolteacher (Towers) travels to New York and teams up with a tunesmith (Brasselle) to turn out hit songs recorded by Frankie Laine. NOTES: Blake Edwards' debut as film director.

262. Broadway Bill (11/21/34) B&W—90 mins. (Comedy). *DIR:* Frank Capra. *PRO:* Harry Cohn. *SP:* Robert Riskin. Story by Mark Hellinger. A Frank Capra Production. *CAST:* Warner Baxter, Myrna Loy, Walter Connolly, Helen Vinson, Douglas Dumbrille, Raymond Walburn, Lynne Overman, Clarence Muse, Margaret Hamilton, Frankie Darro, George Cooper, George Meeker, Jason Robards, Sr., Edmund Breese, Lucille Ball, Ward Bond, Charles Lane, Alan Hale, Charles Middleton, Irving Bacon.

A businessman (Baxter) quits his job and marriage to start a new life as the owner of a racehorse, Broadway Bill. [British title: *Strictly Confidential*].

263. Broadway Daddies (3/26/28) B&W—55 mins. (Drama). *DIR:* Fred Windemere. *PRO:* Harry Cohn. *SP:* Anthony Coldeway. Story by Victoria Moore. *CAST:* Jacqueline Logan, Alec B. Francis, Rex Lease, Phillips Smalley, Betty Francisco, Clarissa Selwynne, De Sacia Mooers.

A nightclub dancer (Logan) falls in love with a poor boy (Lease) who turns out to be rich.

264. The Broadway Hoofer (12/15/29) B&W—63 mins. (Musical-Drama). *DIR:* George Archainbaud. *PRO:* Harry Cohn. *SP:* Gladys Lehman. *CAST:* Marie Saxon, Jack Egan, Louise Fazenda, Howard Hickman, Ernest Hilliard, Gertrude Short, Eileen Percy, Charlotte Merriam, Fred MacKaye.

A Broadway dancing star (Saxon), while on vacation, lands a role in a small town play and falls in love with the show's manager (Egan). [British title: *Dancing Feet*].

265. Broadway Scandals (11/10/29) B&W—73 mins. (Musical). *DIR:* George Archainbaud. *PRO:* Harry Cohn. *SP:* Norman Houston, Gladys Lehman. Story by Howard J. Green. *CAST:* Sally O'Neil, Jack Egan, Carmel Myers, J. Barney Sherry, John Hyams, Charles Wilson, Doris Dawson, Gordon (Bill) Elliott, Charles Lane.

Two girls (O'Neil, Myers) fall in love with the same guy (Egan) and compete for his affections.

266. Brother John (3/71) Eastman Color—94 mins. (Drama). *DIR:* James Goldstone. *PRO:* Joel Glickman. *SP:* Ernest Kinoy. An E&R Production. *CAST:* Sidney Poitier, Will Geer, Bradford Dillman, Beverly Todd, Ramon Bieri, Lincoln Kilpatrick, Paul Winfield, Warren J. Kemmerling, Richard Ward, Bill Crane, Michael Bell, P. Jay Sidney.

A mysterious man's (Poitier) return

to his home town touches off a series of violent reactions among the townsfolk.

267. The Brotherhood of Satan (8/71) Technicolor/Scope—92 mins. (Horror). *DIR:* Bernard McEveety. *PRO:* L. Q. Jones, Alvy Moore. *SP:* William Welch. Story by Sean McGregor. An LQJAF Production. *CAST:* Strother Martin, L. Q. Jones, Charles Bateman, Alvy Moore, Charles Robinson, Ahna Capri, Geri Reischi, Helen Winston, Jeff Williams, Joyce Easton, Debi Storm, Judy McConnell, Robert Ward.

A small town is cut off from all communications when witchcraft and demonic forces are unleashed.

268. Brothers (10/19/30) B&W—63 mins. (Drama). *DIR:* Walter Lang. *PRO:* Harry Cohn. *SP:* Sidney Lazarus, John Thomas Neville, Charles R. Condon. Based on the play by Herbert Ashton, Jr. *CAST:* Bert Lytell, Dorothy Sebastian, William Morris, Richard Tucker, Maurice Black, Frank McCormack, Claire McDowell, Howard Hickman, Francis McDonald, Rita Carlyle, Jessie Arnold.

Two identical twin brothers (Lytell), separated as children, are brought together when one brother frames the other for murder. [British title: *Blood Brothers*].

269. The Brothers Rico (9/57) B&W—92 mins. (Crime-Drama). *DIR:* Phil Karlson. *PRO:* Lewis J. Rachmil. *SP:* Lewis Meltzer, Ben Perry. Based on *Les Freres Rico* by Georges Simenon. *CAST:* Richard Conte, Dianne Foster, Kathryn Grant, Larry Gates, James Darren, Argentina Brunetti, Lamont Johnson, Harry Bellaver, Paul Picerni, Paul Dubov, Rudy Bond, William Phipps, Richard Bakalyan.

An accountant (Conte) goes to New York to stop the mob from killing his two brothers (Darren, Picerni).

Brownie *see* **The Daring Young Man**

270. Buchanan Rides Alone (8/1/58) Technicolor—78 mins. (Western). *DIR:* Oscar (Budd) Boetticher. *PRO:* Harry Joe Brown, Randolph Scott. *SP:* Charles Lang, Jr. Based on *The Name's Buchanan* by Jonas Wood. A Scott-Brown Production. *CAST:* Randolph Scott, Jennifer Holden, Craig Stevens, Barry Kelley, Peter Whitney, L. Q. Jones, Robert Anderson, Joe de Santis, Terry Frost, Roy Jenson, Tol Avery, Manual Rojas, William Leslie, Don C. Harvey, Barbara James, Leo Ogletree, Jim B. Leon, Nacho Galindo, Frank Scannell, Al Wyatt, Riley Hill.

A drifter (Scott) winds up helping a Mexican (Rojas) accused of murder and gets mixed up in a town feud.

271. Buck and the Preacher (4/72) Eastman Color—102 mins. (Western). *DIR:* Sidney Poitier. *PRO:* Joel Glickman. *SP:* Ernest Kinroy. Story by Ernest Kinroy and Drake Walker. An E&R Productions Corp.-Belafonte Enterprises Co-Production. *CAST:* Sidney Poitier, Ruby Dee, Harry Belafonte, Nita Talbot, Cameron Mitchell, Denny Miller, James McEachin, John Kelly, Tony Brubaker, Bobby Johnson, Clarence Muse, Lynn Hamilton, Ken Menard, Pamela Jones, Dennis Hines, Enrique Lucerno, Julie Robinson.

A con-man preacher (Belafonte) teams up with a wagonmaster (Poitier) to help escaped slaves.

272. Buckaroo from Powder River (10/14/47) B&W—55 mins. (Western). *DIR:* Ray Nazarro. *PRO:* Colbert Clark. *SP:* Norman S. Hall. *CAST:* Charles Starrett, Eve Miller, Smiley Burnette, Paul Campbell, Kermit Maynard, Doug Coppin, Ted Adams, Forrest Taylor, Frank McCarroll, Ethan Laidlaw, Philip

Morris, Casey MacGregor, Roy Butler, Phil Arnold, Buster Brodie, The Cass County Boys.

The Durango Kid (Starrett), in pursuit of a gang of bank robbers, ends up saving a son (Coppin) who has been marked for death by his outlaw father (Taylor).

273. The Buddy Holly Story (7/78) Eastman Color—113 mins. (Biography-Musical). *DIR:* Steve Rash. *PRO:* Fred Bauer. *SP:* Robert Gittler. Based on the book by John Coldrosen. *CAST:* Gary Busey, Don Stroud, Charles Martin Smith, Bill Jordan, Maria Richwine, Conrad Janis, Albert Popwell, Amy Johnston, Jim Beach, John F. Goff, Fred Travalena, Stymie Beard, Arch Johnson, Freeman King.

The story of rock 'n' roll legend Buddy Holly (Busey), from his youth in Lubbock, to his death in an airplane crash with the Big Bopper and Ritchie Valens.

274. Bulldog Drummond at Bay (5/15/47) B&W—70 mins. (Crime). *DIR:* Sidney Salkow. *PRO:* Louis B. Appleton, Jr., Bernard Small. *SP:* Frank Gruber. Based on the character created by Herman Cyril McNeile ("Sapper"). *CAST:* Ron Randell, Anita Louise, Pat O'Moore, Terence Kilburn, Holmes Herbert, Lester Matthews, Leonard Mudie, Dave Thursby, Oliver Thorndike, Aminta Dyne.

Bulldog Drummond (Randell) goes after a murderer who has stolen a valuable set of diamonds.

275. Bulldog Drummond Strikes Back (9/4/47) B&W—65 mins. (Crime). *DIR:* Frank McDonald. *PRO:* Louis B. Appleton, Jr., Bernard Small. *SP:* Lawrence Edmund Taylor. Story by Edna Anhalt, Edward Anhalt, Based on the character created by Herman Cyril McNeile ("Sapper"). *CAST:* Ron Randell, Gloria Henry, Pat O'Moore, Terence Kilburn, Anabel Shaw, Holmes Herbert, Wilton Graff, Matthew Boulton, Barry Bernard, Carl Harbord, Leslie Denison, Elspeth Dudgeon.

Bulldog Drummond (Randell) finds himself involved in murder when he goes after a woman impersonating an heiress (Henry).

276. A Bullet Is Waiting (9/54) Technicolor—82 mins. (Drama). *DIR:* John Farrow. *PRO:* Howard Welsch. *SP:* Thames Williamson, Casey Robinson. Story by Thames Williamson. *CAST:* Rory Calhoun, Jean Simmons, Stephen McNally, Brian Aherne.

A plane crash forces a sheriff (McNally) and his prisoner (Calhoun) to hole up in a cabin with a girl (Simmons) and her father (Aherne).

277. Bullets for Bandits (2/12/42) B&W—55 mins. (Western). *DIR:* Wallace W. Fox. *PRO:* Leon Barsha. *SP:* Robert Lee Johnson. *CAST:* Bill Elliott, Dorothy Short, Tex Ritter, Ralph Theodore, Frank Mitchell, Edythe Elliott, Forrest Taylor, Hal Taliaferro (Wally Wales), Eddie Laughton, Bud Osborne, Art Mix, John Tyrrell, Harry Harvey, Joe McQuinn, Tom Moray.

Wild Bill Hickok (Elliott) and his pal Cannonball (Taylor) help to save a ranch from an outlaw gang.

278. Bullets for Rustlers (3/5/40) B&W—58 mins. (Western). *DIR:* Sam Nelson. *PRO:* Jack Fier. *SP:* John Rathmell. *CAST:* Charles Starrett, Lorna Gray, Bob Nolan, Kenneth MacDonald, Dick Curtis, Edward J. LeSaint, Hal Taliaferro (Wally Wales), Jack Rockwell, Eddie Laughton, Lee Prather, Francis Walker, Sons of the Pioneers.

A detective for the Cattlemen's Association (Starrett) must crack a ring of cattle rustlers. [British title: *On Special Duty*].

279. Bunny Lake Is Missing (10/65) B&W/Panavision—107 mins. (Mystery). *DIR/PRO:* Otto Preminger. *SP:* John and Penelope Mortimer. Based on the book by Evelyn Piper. *CAST:* Carol Lynley, Keir Dullea, Laurence Olivier, Noel Coward, Marita Hunt, Anna Massey, Finlay Currie, Richard Wattis, Lucie Mannheim, Clive Revill, Megs Jenkins.

A Scotland Yard inspector (Olivier) tries to find the missing daughter of an American woman (Lynley), but wonders if she ever existed.

280. The Burglar (6/57) B&W—90 mins. (Crime). *DIR:* Paul Wendkos. *PRO:* Louis W. Kellman. *SP:* David Goodis. Based on the book by David Goodis. *CAST:* Dan Duryea, Jayne Mansfield, Martha Vickers, Peter Capell, Mickey Shaughnessy, Wendell Phillips, Phoebe Mackay, Stewart Bradley.

When a trio of crooks (Duryea, Capell, Shaughnessy) steals a valuable necklace, a crooked cop (Bradley) kills them to get the necklace. *NOTES:* Remade in 1972 as *The Burglars*.

281. The Burglars (6/72) Eastman Color/Panavision—117 mins. (Crime). *DIR/PRO:* Henri Verneuil. *SP:* Henri Verneuil, Vahe Katcha. Based on the book by David Goodis. *CAST:* Jean-Paul Belmondo, Omar Sharif, Dyan Cannon, Robert Hossein, Nicole Calfan, Renato Salvatori, Myriam Colombi, Steve Eckardt, Roberto Duranton, Daniel Verite.

A corrupt police official (Sharif) meets a violent end when he tries to get stolen emeralds from a thief (Belmondo). *NOTES:* Loose remake of the 1957 Columbia film *The Burglar*. [Original French title: *Le Casse*].

282. Buster and Billie (6/74) CFI Color—100 mins. (Drama). *DIR:* Daniel Petrie. *PRO:* Ron Silverman. *SP:* Ron Turbeville. Based on a story by Ron Turbeville and Ron Baron. *CAST:* Jan-Michael Vincent, Joan Goodfellow, Pamela Sue Martin, Robert Englund, Clifton James, Jessie Lee Fulton, J. B. Joiner, Dell C. Payne.

In 1948 rural Georgia, tragedy strikes when a sensitive high school senior (Vincent) marries a girl (Goodfellow) from the wrong side of the tracks.

283. The Buttercup Chain (3/71) Eastman Color/Panavision—95 mins. (Drama). *DIR:* Robert Ellis Miller. *PRO:* John Whitney, Philip Waddilove. *SP:* Peter Draper. Based on the book by Janice Elliott. *CAST:* Hywel Bennett, Leigh Taylor-Young, Jane Asher, Sven-Bertil Taube, Clive Revill, Michael Elphick.

While touring Europe, four friends decide to exchange partners.

284. Butterflies Are Free (7/72) Eastman Color—109 mins. (Drama). *DIR:* Milton Katselas. *PRO:* M. J. Frankovich. *SP:* Leonard Gershe. Based on the play by Leonard Gershe. *CAST:* Goldie Hawn, Edward Albert, Eileen Heckart, Michael Glaser, Mike Warren.

A neighbor (Hawn) helps a young blind man (Albert) break free from his over-protective mother (Heckart).

285. By Whose Hand? (9/15/27) B&W—57 mins. (Crime). *DIR:* Walter Lang. *PRO:* Harry Cohn. *SP:* Marion Orth. *CAST:* Ricardo Cortez, Eugenia Gilbert, J. Thornton Baston, Tom Dugan, Edgar Washington Blue, Lillian Leighton, William Scott, John Steppling, De Sacia Mooers.

Agent X-9 (Cortez), suspecting the girl (Gilbert) he loves is a jewel thief, sets out to expose the real jewel thief (Scott).

286. By Whose Hand? (5/1/32) B&W—65 mins. (Crime-Drama). *DIR:* Ben Stoloff. *SP:* Isadore Bernstein, Stephen Roe. Story by Harry Adler. *CAST:* Ben Lyon, Barbara Weeks,

William V. Mong, Ethel Kenyon, Kenneth Thompson, Tom Dugan, William Halligan, Helene Millard, Dwight Frye, Dolores Rey, Nat Pendleton.

An innocent bystander (Lyon) becomes involved in murder while on a train ride from Los Angeles to San Francisco.

287. Bye Bye Birdie (4/63) Technicolor/Panavision—112 mins. (Musical). *DIR*: George Sidney. *PRO*: Fred Kohlmar. *SP*: Irving Brecher. Based on the musical comedy by Michael Stewart. *CAST*: Janet Leigh, Dick Van Dyke, Ann-Margret, Maureen Stapleton, Paul Lynde, Bobby Rydell, Jesse Pearson, Ed Sullivan, Mary La Roche, Michael Evans, Robert Paige, Gregory Morton, Bryan Russell, Milton Frome, Ben Astar, Frank Albertson, Frank Sully, Trudi Ames.

When a small Iowa town wins the opportunity to host the nationally televised final performance of a teen idol (Pearson) about to enter the military service, a songwriter (Van Dyke) tries to get him to record one of his tunes.

288. Cactus Flower (12/69) Technicolor—103 mins. (Comedy). *DIR*: Gene Saks. *PRO*: M.J. Frankovich. *SP*: I. A. L. Diamond. Based on the play by Abe Burrows. A Frankovich Production. *CAST*: Walter Matthau, Ingrid Bergman, Goldie Hawn, Jack Weston, Rick Lenz, Vito Scotti, Irene Hervey, Eve Bruce, Irwin Charone, Matthew Saks.

A dentist (Matthau) falls for his nurse (Bergman) when he asks her to pose as his wife so he can get out of marriage to his mistress (Hawn).

Cactus Jack *see* **The Villain**

289. Cadets on Parade (1/22/42) B&W—64 mins. (Drama). *DIR*: Lew Landers. *PRO*: Wallace MacDonald.

SP: Howard J. Green. Story by Frank Fenton, Martha Barnett. *CAST*: Freddie Bartholomew, Jimmy Lydon, Joseph Crehan, Raymond Hatton, Minna Gombell, Robert Warwick, Kenneth MacDonald, Lloyd Bridges.

A young boy (Bartholomew), ashamed to face his father (Warwick) because he is a coward, is expelled from military school, runs away, and becomes friends with a newsboy (Lydon).

290. Cafe Hostess (1/11/40) B&W—65 mins. (Crime). *DIR*: Sidney Salkow. *SP*: Harold Shumate. Story by Tay Garnett, Howard Higgin. *CAST*: Preston Foster, Ann Dvorak, Douglas Fowley, Wynne Gibson, Arthur Loft, Bruce Bennett, Eddie Acuff, Bradley Page, Linda Winters (Dorothy Comingore), Beatrice Blinn, Dick Wessel, Peggy Shannon.

A sailor (Foster) risks his life to save the girl he loves (Dvorak) from a gang-run nightspot.

291. The Caine Mutiny (6/54) Technicolor—123 mins. (Drama). *DIR*: Edward Dmytryk. *PRO*: Stanley Kramer. *SP*: Stanley Roberts. Based on the play and book by Herman Wouk. *CAST*: Humphrey Bogart, Jose Ferrer, Van Johnson, Fred MacMurray, Robert Francis, May Wynn, Tom Tully, E. G. Marshall, Arthur Franz, Lee Marvin, Warner Anderson, Claude Akins, Katharine Warren, Jerry Paris, Steve Brodie, Whit Bissell, James Best, Guy Anderson, James Edwards, Don Dubbins.

A paranoid captain (Bogart) of a destroyer drives his men to mutiny when he panics during a typhoon.

292. California Conquest (7/1/52) Technicolor—79 mins. (Western). *DIR*: Lew Landers. *PRO*: Sam Katzman. *SP*: Robert E. Kent. *CAST*: Cornel Wilde, Teresa Wright, Alfonso Bedoya, Eugene Iglesias, John Dehner, George Eldredge, Lisa Ferraday, Alex

Montoya, Hank Patterson, William P. Wilkerson, Ivan Lebedeff, Baynes Barron.

In the early 1800's, a Spanish-Californian (Wilde) joins forces with a gun shop owner (Wright) to save California from a Russian takeover.

293. California Frontier (12/15/38) B&W — 54 mins. (Western). *DIR:* Elmer Clifton. *PRO:* Monroe Shaff. *SP:* Monroe Shaff, Arthur Hoerl. A Coronet Production. *CAST:* Buck Jones, Carmen Bailey, Milburn Stone, Stanley Blystone, Glenn Strange, Ernie Adams, Forrest Taylor, Paul Ellis, Jose Perez, Carlos Villanos.

A U.S. Army captain (Jones) is sent to California to stop a band of outlaws from stealing land from the Mexican ranchers.

294. California Split (6/74) Metrocolor/Panavision — 108 mins. (Comedy). *DIR:* Robert Altman. *PRO:* Robert Altman, Joseph Walsh. *SP:* Joseph Walsh. *CAST:* George Segal, Elliott Gould, Ann Prentiss, Gwen Welles, Edward Walsh, Joseph Walsh, Bert Remsen, Barbara London, Barbara Ruick, Jay Fletcher, Jeff Goldblum.

Two gamblers (Segal, Gould) go for broke in the gambling palaces of Reno. *NOTES:* Barbara Ruick's last film.

295. California Suite (12/78) Eastman Color/Panavision — 103 mins. (Comedy). *DIR:* Herbert Ross. *PRO:* Ray Stark. *SP:* Neil Simon. Based on the play by Neil Simon. A Rastar Production. *CAST:* Alan Alda, Michael Caine, Bill Cosby, Jane Fonda, Walter Matthau, Elaine May, Richard Pryor, Maggie Smith, Gloria Gifford, Sheila Frazier, Herb Edelman.

A quartet of stories in which a couple (Fonda, Alda) are divorced and argue over child custody; a couple (Caine, Smith) wait for the Academy Awards ceremony to begin; the vacations of two couples (Cosby, Frazier, Pryor, Gifford) turn into a hilarious situation; a husband (Matthau) is found in his room with another woman by his wife (May).

296. The California Trail (3/24/33) B&W — 67 mins. (Western). *DIR/SP:* Lambert Hillyer. Story by Jack Natteford. *CAST:* Buck Jones, Helen Mack, George Humbart, Luis Alberni, Charles Stevens, Emile Chautard, Evelyn Sherman, Chris-Pin Martin, William Steele, Allan Garcia, Carmen LaRoux, Carlo Villar, John Paul Jones.

A drifter (Jones) saves a town from a corrupt mayor (Humbart) and his brother (Alberni).

297. Call of the Rockies (4/30/38) B&W — 54 mins. (Western). *DIR:* Allan James. *PRO:* Harry L. Decker. *SP:* Ed Earl Repp. *CAST:* Charles Starrett, Iris Meredith, Donald Grayson, Bob Nolan, Edward J. LeSaint, George Chesebro, Dick Curtis, Glenn Strange, John Tyrrell, Art Mix, Edmund Cobb, Sons of the Pioneers.

A cowboy (Starrett) helps a ranch owner (Meredith) to save her ranch.

298. Call of the West (5/10/30) B&W — 73 mins. (Western). *DIR:* Albert Ray. *SP:* Florence Ryerson, Colin Clements. *CAST:* Dorothy Revier, Blanche Rose, Matt Moore, Katherine Claire Ward, Tom O'Brien, Gertrude Bennett, Vic Potel, Allan Roscoe, Buff Jones, Joe de la Cruz, Nick DeCruz, Bud Osborne, Connie LaMont.

A Broadway singer (Revier) returns to New York when a Texas rancher (Moore) leaves her at the altar to go after cattle rustlers, but follows her to the city to bring her back.

Calling All G-Men *see* **You May Be Next**

299. The Calling of Dan Matthews (1/25/36) B&W — 65 mins.

(Drama). *DIR:* Philip E. Rosen. *PRO:* Sol Lesser. *SP:* Dan Jarrett, Don Swift, Karl Brown. Based on the book by Harold Bell Wright. *CAST:* Richard Arlen, Mary Kornman, Douglass Dumbrille, Charlotte Wynters, Donald Cook, Frederick Burton, Lee Moran, Tom Dugan, Edward McWade, Carlyle Blackwell, Jr.

A crusading minister (Arlen) sets out to clean up a lurid red-light district known as "Old Town."

300. Calypso Heat Wave (6/57) B&W — 86 mins. (Musical). *DIR:* Fred F. Sears. *PRO:* Sam Katzman. *SP:* David Chandler. Story by Orville H. Hampton. *CAST:* Johnny Desmond, Merry Anders, Meg Myles, Paul Langton, Joel Grey, Michael Granger, George E. Stone, Pierce Lyden, Darla Hood, The Tarriers, The Hi-Lo's, Maya Angelou, Dick Wittinghill, The Treniers, Mac Niles and the Calypsonians.

A jukebox baron (Granger) tries to take over a recording company and its top star (Desmond) to cash in on the calypso fad. *NOTES:* The film debut of Johnny Desmond.

301. The Camp on Blood Island (7/58) B&W/Scope — 82 mins. (War). *DIR:* Val Guest. *PRO:* Anthony Hinds. *SP:* Jon Manchip White, Val Guest. Story by Jon Manchip White. A Hammer Production. *CAST:* Andre Morell, Carl Mohner, Edward Underdown, Walter Fitzgerald, Phil Brown, Barbara Shelley, Michael Goodliffe, Michael Gwynn, Ronald Radd, Richard Wordsworth.

When a sadistic Japanese commandant (Radd) vows to kill all prisoners of war in his camp should Japan lose the war, the prisoners decide to keep the end of the war a secret. *NOTES:* Originally released in Britain at a running time of 91 mins.

302. Canal Zone (3/19/42) B&W — 79 mins. (Drama). *DIR:* Lew

Landers. *PRO:* Colbert Clark. *SP:* Robert Lee Johnson. Story by Blaine Miller, Jean DuPont Miller. *CAST:* Chester Morris, Harriet Hilliard, John Hubbard, Larry Parks, Forrest Tucker, Eddie Laughton, Lloyd Bridges, George McKay, Stanley Andrews, John Tyrrell, Stanley Brown, John Shay.

A pilot (Morris), who believes in high gains and low losses, pushes his men as they ferry bombers across the Atlantic.

The Candy Web *see* **13 Frightened Girls**

303. Cangaceiro — The Story of an Outlaw (The Bandit) (9/3/54) B&W — 91 mins. (Western). *DIR/SP:* Lima Barreto. A Vera Cruz Production. *CAST:* Alberto Ruschel, Marisa Prado, Milton Ribeiro, Vanja Orico.

A bandit leader (Ribeiro) attacks a village, kidnaps a schoolteacher (Prado), and then must pursue one of his men (Ruschel) when he falls in love with her and tries to help her escape. [Original Brazilian title: *O Cangacieros*].

304. Cannibal Attack (11/54) B&W — 69 mins. (Adventure). *DIR:* Lee Sholem. *PRO:* Sam Katzman. *SP:* Carroll Young. *CAST:* Johnny Weissmuller, Judy Walsh, David Bruce, Bruce Cowling, Charles Evans, Steve Darrell, Joseph Allen, Jr.

Weissmuller sets out to stop a gang of crooks from selling cobalt to a foreign government. *NOTES:* Beginning with this film, Columbia lost the rights to the "Jungle Jim" character, and starred Weissmuller as himself for the last three features of the series.

305. The Captain Hates the Sea (11/30/34) B&W — 80 mins. (Comedy). *DIR:* Lewis Milestone. *SP:* Wallace Smith. *CAST:* Victor McLaglen, Helen Vinson, John Gilbert, Alison

Skipworth, Wynne Gibson, Walter Connolly, Fred Keating, Tala Birell, Leon Errol, Walter Catlett, Donald Meek, Arthur Treacher, Akim Tamiroff, Claude Gillingwater, Luis Alberni, the Three Stooges (Moe Howard, Larry Fine, Curly Howard).

An ocean liner captain (Connolly) has to deal with a variety of people as he ferries them across the ocean. *NOTES:* 1) John Gilbert's last film. 2) When Harry Cohn received word that the cost of this film was over budget, he wired director Milestone, "the cost is staggering" and, as several of the cast members, including Milestone, were known to be heavy drinkers, he wired back to Cohn "So is the cast."

306. Captain Pirate (8/27/52) Technicolor – 85 mins. (Historical-Drama-Adventure). *DIR:* Ralph Murphy. *PRO:* Harry Joe Brown. *SP:* Robert Libott, Frank Burt, John Meredyth Lucas. Based on *Captain Blood Returns* by Rafael Sabatini. *CAST:* Louis Hayward, Patricia Medina, John Sutton, Charles Irwin, George Givot, Rex Evans, Ted de Corsia, Lester Matthews, Ian Wolfe, Jay Novello, Robert Bice, Genevieve Aumont.

Reformed pirate Captain Blood (Hayward) steals a ship, and with his old crew, seeks the imposter who framed him for piracy. [British title: *Captain Blood, Fugitive*].

307. Captive Girl (4/27/50) B&W – 73 mins. (Adventure). *DIR:* William Berke. *PRO:* Sam Katzman. *SP:* Carroll Young. Based on the *Jungle Jim* newspaper comic strip created by Alex Raymond. *CAST:* Johnny Weissmuller, Anita Lhoest, Buster Crabbe, John Dehner, Rick Vallin, Rusty Wescoatt, Nelson Leigh.

Jungle Jim (Weissmuller) sets out to rescue a blonde goddess (Lhoest) who has grown up in the jungle, while an explorer (Crabbe) seeks hidden loot.

308. The Cardinal (12/63) Technicolor/Super Panavision 70 – 173 mins. (Drama). *DIR/PRO:* Otto Preminger. *SP:* Robert Dozier. Based on the book by Henry Morton Robinson. *CAST:* Tom Tryon, Carol Lynley, Dorothy Gish, Maggie McNamara, Bill Hayes, Cameron Prud'Homme, Cecil Kellaway, Loring Smith, John Saxon, John Huston, Robert Morse, James Hickman, Burgess Meredith, Jill Haworth, Raf Vallone, Ossie Davis, Chill Wills, Arthur Hunnicutt, Patrick O'Neal, Murray Hamilton, Romy Schneider, Wolfgang Preiss.

The rise of an Irish-American (Tryon), from the priesthood to the college of Cardinals.

309. Care Bears Movie II: A New Generation (3/86) Eastman Color – 77 mins. (Children-Animated). *DIR:* Dale Schott. *PRO:* Michael Hirsh, Patrick Loubert, Clive A. Smith. *SP:* Peter Sauder. A Nelvana Production. *CAST:* Voices of Hadley Kay, Chris Wiggins, Jim Henshaw, Michael Fantini, Dan Hennessey, Maxine Miller.

The adventures of True Heart Bear and his friend Noble Heart Horse as they try to stop their nemesis, Dark Heart, from working his sinister tricks on a group of summer campers.

310. Careless (1/82) B&W – 110 mins. (Drama). *DIR/PRO:* Mauro Bolognini. *SP:* Mauro Bolognini, Tullio Pinelli, Goffredo Parise. Based on the book by Italo Svevo. A Zebra-Aera Production. *CAST:* Anthony Franciosa, Claudia Cardinale, Betsy Blair, Philippe Leroy, Raimondo Magni.

In 1920 Trieste, a middle-aged clerk (Franciosa) who lives with his spinster sister (Blair), becomes infatuated with a younger amoral woman (Cardinale) who humiliates and destroys him. *NOTES:* Limited theatrical release. Originally released in Italy in 1961. [Original Italian title: *Senilita*].

311. Cargo to Capetown (4/50) B&W—80 mins. (Drama). *DIR*: Earl McEvoy. *PRO/SP*: Lionel Houser. *CAST*: Broderick Crawford, John Ireland, Ellen Drew, Edgar Buchanan, King Donovan, Ted de Corsia, Frank Reicher, Gregory Gay, Leonard Strong.

A ship's captain (Ireland) and his engineer (Crawford) are at odds over the love of a woman (Drew).

312. Carmen (9/84) Eastman Color/Panavision—152 mins. (Opera). *DIR*: Francesco Rosi. *PRO*: Patrice Ledoux. *SP*: Francesco Rosi, Tonino Guerra. Based on the story by Prosper Merimee and the opera by Georges Bizet. A Gaumont-Dassault-Opera Film Produzione-Triumph Films Production. *CAST*: Julia Migenes-Johnson, Placido Domingo, Ruggero Raimondi, Faith Esham, Jean-Philippe Lafont, Gerard Garino, Susan Daniel, Lilian Watson, John Paul Bogart, Francois Le Roux, Julien Guiomar.

A filmed version of the famous opera by Georges Bizet. *NOTES*: Limited theatrical release; in French with English subtitles.

313. Carnival (2/15/35) B&W—77 mins. (Drama-Comedy). *DIR*: Walter Lang. *SP*: Robert Riskin. Story by Compton Mackenzie. *CAST*: Lee Tracy, Sally Eilers, Jimmy Durante, Dickie Walters, Thomas Jackson, Florence Rice, Fred Kelsey, Lucille Ball.

A widowed carnival puppeteer (Tracy) tries to keep his son from the hands of his paternal grandfather (Jackson). [British title: *Carnival Nights*].

314. Carolina Blues (9/26/44) B&W—81 mins. (Musical). *DIR*: Leigh Jason. *PRO*: Samuel Bischoff. *SP*: Joseph Hoffman, Al Martin. Story by M. M. Musselman, Kenneth Earl. *CAST*: Kay Kyser, Ann Miller, Victor Moore, Jeff Donnell, Howard Freeman, Georgia Carroll, Harry Babbitt, Sully Mason, Doodles Weaver, Diane Pendleton, M. A. Bogue, Robert Williams, Dorothea Kent, Frank Orth, Eddie Acuff, Harold Nicholas, The Cristianis, The Layson Brothers, The Four Step Brothers.

A band leader (Kyser) is persuaded to hire a girl singer (Miller) while giving a show at a war plant.

315. Carthage in Flames (3/61) Technicolor—111 mins. (Historical-Drama). *DIR*: Carmine Gallone. *PRO*: Guido Luzzato, Carmine Gallone. *SP*: Ennio De Concini, Duccio Tessari, Carmine Gallone, William De Lane Lea. *CAST*: Anne Heywood, Jose Saurez, Pierre Brasseur, Ilaria Occhini, Daniel Gelin, Paolo Stoppa, Mario Girotti, Aldo Silvani.

Love and intrigue amid the Rome-Carthage wars of 200 B.C. [Original Italian title: *Cartagine in Fiamme*]. [Original French title: *Carthage en Flammes*].

316. The Case Against Brooklyn (6/58) B&W—82 mins. (Crime). *DIR*: Paul Wendkos. *PRO*: Charles H. Schneer. *SP*: Raymond T. Marcus. Story by Daniel B. Ullman. Based on a magazine article by Ed Reid. *CAST*: Darren McGavin, Margaret Hayes, Warren Stevens, Peggy McCay, Tol Avery, Emile Meyer, Nestor Paiva, Robert Osterloh, Brian G. Hutton, Joseph Turkel, Bobby Helms, Herb Vigran.

A rookie policeman (McGavin) goes undercover to expose payoffs to the police department by the gambling syndicate.

317. The Case of the Missing Man (11/22/35) B&W—58 mins. (Mystery). *DIR*: D. Ross Lederman. *PRO*: Irving Briskin. *SP*: Lee Loeb, Harold Buchman. *CAST*: Roger Pryor, Joan Perry, Thuston Hall, Arthur

Hohl, George McKay, Tom Dugan, James Burke, Arthur Rankin.

A photographer (Pryor) has the mob after him when he accidentally snaps a picture of a jewel thief leaving the scene of the crime.

318. Casey's Shadow (3/78) Eastman Color/Panavision—116 mins. (Drama). *DIR:* Martin Ritt. *PRO:* Ray Stark. *SP:* Carol Sobieski. Based on *Ruidoso* by John Mcphee. A Rastar Production. *CAST:* Walter Matthau, Alexis Smith, Robert Webber, Murray Hamilton, Whit Bissell, Stephen Burns, Susan Myers, Michael Hershewe, Harry Caesar, Joel Fluellen, Jimmy Halty, William Pitt, Dean Turpitt, Richard Thompson.

A Cajun horse trainer (Matthau) in New Mexico tries to raise his three sons when his wife leaves him.

319. Cash on Demand (2/62) B&W—66 mins. (Crime). *DIR:* Quentin Lawrence. *PRO:* Michael Carreras. *SP:* David T. Chantler, Lewis Greifer. Based on the TV play *The Gold Inside* by Jacques Gillies. A Woodpecker-Hammer Production. *CAST:* Peter Cushing, Andre Morell, Richard Vernon, Barry Lowe, Norman Bird, Kevin Stoney, Edith Sharpe, Lois Daine, Alan Haywood, Charles Morgan, Vera Cook, Gareth Tandy, Fred Stone.

A bank president (Cushing) is forced into aiding a bank robber when his wife and son are kidnapped.

320. Casino Royale (1/67) Technicolor/Panavision—131 mins. (Comedy-Adventure). *DIR:* John Huston, Val Guest, Ken Hughes, Robert Parrish, Joseph McGrath. *PRO:* Charles K. Feldman, Jerry Bresler. *SP:* Wolf Mankowitz, John Law, Michael Sayers. Suggested by the book by Ian Fleming. A Famous Artists Production. *CAST:* Peter Sellers, Ursula Andress, David Niven, Orson Welles, Joanna Pettet, Daliah Lavi, Woody Allen, Deborah Kerr, William Holden, Charles Boyer, John Huston, Kurt Kasznar, George Raft, Jean-Paul Belmondo, Terence Cooper, Barbara Bouchet, Hermione Baddeley, Bernard Cribbins, Percy Herbert, Graham Stark, Richard Wattis, Geoffrey Bayldon, Jacqueline Bisset.

Agent 007 (Niven) is brought out of retirement to fight SMERSH in this spoof of James Bond pictures.

Castle in the Air see **Rainbow 'Round My Shoulder**

321. Castle Keep (7/69) Eastman Color/Panavision—108 mins. (War-Drama). *DIR:* Sydney Pollack. *PRO:* Martin Ransohoff, John Calley. *SP:* Daniel Taradash, David Rayfiel. Based on the book by William Eastlake. *CAST:* Burt Lancaster, Peter Falk, Patrick O'Neal, Jean Pierre Aumont, Astrid Heeren, Scott Wilson, Tony Bill, Michael Conrad, Bruce Dern, James Patterson, Al Freeman, Jr., Ernest Clark, Harry Baird, Dave Jones.

In 1944, a group of Allied soldiers take refuge in a 10th century castle.

322. Cat Ballou (6/65) Eastman Color—96 mins. (Western-Comedy). *DIR:* Elliott Silverstein. *PRO:* Harold Hecht. *SP:* Frank R. Pierson, Walter Newman. Based on a story by Roy Chanslor. *CAST:* Jane Fonda, Lee Marvin, Michael Callan, Dwayne Hickman, Tom Nardini, John Marley, Stubby Kaye, Nat "King" Cole, Reginald Denny, Jay C. Flippen, Arthur Hunnicutt, Bruce Cabot, Paul Gilbert, Burt Mustin, Charles Wagenheim, Harry Harvey, Charles Horvath, Chuck Roberson, Nick Cravat.

Cat Ballou (Fonda), schoolteacher turned outlaw, hires a drunken gunfighter (Marvin) to avenge her father's death. *NOTES:* 1) Nat "King" Cole's last film. 2) The only Columbia film in which their logo becomes an animated cowgirl.

323. Cattle Raiders (2/12/38) B&W—61 mins. (Western). *DIR:* Sam Nelson. *PRO:* Harry L. Decker. *SP:* Joseph F. Poland, Ed Earl Repp. Story by Folmer Blangsted. *CAST:* Charles Starrett, Iris Meredith, Donald Grayson, Dick Curtis, Edward J. LeSaint, George Chesebro, Alan Sears, Jack Kirk, Art Mix, Edmund Cobb, Frank Ellis, Jim Thorpe, James Mason, Wally West, Blackie Whiteford, Forrest Taylor, Bob Nolan, Steve Clark, Hank Bell, Allen Brook, Edward Piel, Sr., Merrill McCormack, Robert Burns, George Morrell, Jack Clifford, Horace B. Carpenter, Sons of the Pioneers.

A cowboy (Starrett) sets out to prove himself innocent of the murder of a sheriff (Piel).

324. The Cattle Thief (2/26/36) B&W—58 mins. (Western). *DIR:* Spencer G. Bennet. *PRO:* Larry Darmour. *SP:* Nate Gatzert. Story by Jesse A. Duffy. *CAST:* Ken Maynard, Geneva Mitchell, Ward Bond, Roger Williams, Jim Marcus, Sheldon Lewis, Edward Cecil, Jack Kirk, Glenn Strange, Edward Hearn, Jack King, Al Taylor, Dick Rush, Bud McClure.

A cattle detective (Maynard) masquerades as a peddler during the day and a masked rider at night.

325. Cell 2455, Death Row (5/55) B&W—77 mins. (Biography-Drama). *DIR:* Fred F. Sears. *PRO:* Wallace MacDonald. *SP:* Jack De Witt. Based on the autobiography of Caryl Chessman. *CAST:* William Campbell, Robert Campbell, Marian Carr, Kathryn Grant, Paul Dubov, Harvey Stephens, Vince Edwards, Allen Nourse, Diane De Laire, Tyler MacDuff, Eleanor Audley, Howard Wright.

The story of convicted murderer and rapist Caryl Chessman (William Campbell), from his teen years to his adult years on death row.

326. Cha-Cha-Cha Boom! (10/56) B&W—78 mins. (Musical). *DIR:* Fred F. Sears. *PRO:* Sam Katzman. *SP:* James B. Gordon. *CAST:* Prez Prado, Mary Kay Trio, Helen Grayco, Luis Arcaraz, Manny Lopez, Stephen Dunne, Alix Talton, Jose Gonzales Gonzales, Sylvia Lewis, Charles Evans, Howard Wright.

A talent scout (Dunne) travels to Cuba to find new talent for his recording studio.

327. Chain Gang (9/28/50) B&W—70 mins. (Crime-Drama). *DIR:* Lew Landers. *PRO:* Sam Katzman. *SP:* Howard J. Green. *CAST:* Douglas Kennedy, Marjorie Lord, Emory Parnell, William "Bill" Phillips, Thurston Hall, Harry Cheshire, Don C. Harvey, George Eldredge, William Tannen, Frank Wilcox, Rusty Wescoatt, Dorothy Vaughn, William Fawcett, George Robotham.

A reporter (Kennedy) almost gets killed when he goes undercover to expose chain gang brutality.

328. Chain of Circumstance (8/23/51) B&W—68 mins. (Drama). *DIR:* Will Jason. *PRO:* Wallace MacDonald. *SP:* David Lang. Based on an article in *True Story* magazine. *CAST:* Richard Grayson, Margaret Field, Marta Mitrovich, Harold J. Kennedy, Helen Wallace, Connie Gilchrist, Lawrence Dobkin, Sumner Getchell, James Griffith, Oliver Blake, Percy Helton, Douglas Fowley, Carleton Young.

A young married couple (Grayson, Field) almost get convicted for theft.

329. Challenge of the Range (2/3/49) B&W—54 mins. (Western). *DIR:* Ray Nazarro. *PRO:* Colbert Clark. *SP:* Ed Earl Repp. *CAST:* Charles Starrett, Paula Raymond, Smiley Burnette, Billy Halop, George Chesebro, Steve Darrell, Henry Hall, John Cason, John R. McKee, Frank

McCarroll, Robert W. Filmer, Pat O'Malley, The Sunshine Boys. The Durango Kid (Starrett), working with the Farmer's Association, sets out to find the outlaws responsible for terrorizing the ranchers. [British title: *Moonlight Raid*].

330. Champagne for Breakfast (7/6/35) B&W—69 mins. (Drama). *DIR*: Melville Brown. *SP*: George Waggner. Story by E. Morton Hough. *CAST*: Mary Carlisle, Hardie Albright, Joan Marsh, Lila Lee, Sidney Toler, Bradley Page, Emerson Tracy, Adrian Rosley, Wallis Clark, Clarence Wilson, Lucien Prival, Vince Barnett, Edward Martindel.

A lawyer (Albright) helps a young girl (Carlisle) to keep her fortune from a con-man (Toler).

331. The Chance of a Lifetime (10/26/43) B&W—65 mins. (Mystery-Crime). *DIR*: William Castle. *PRO*: Wallace MacDonald. *SP*: Paul Yawitz. Based on characters created by Jack Boyle. *CAST*: Chester Morris, Jeanne Bates, George E. Stone, William Wright, Richard Lane, Erik Rolf, Lloyd Corrigan, Walter Sande, Douglas Fowley, Cy Kendall, Larry Joe Olsen, Sally Cairns, Trevor Bardette, Harry Semels, Arthur Hunnicutt, Maude Eburne, Pierre Watkin, George Magrill, Ray Teal, Jessie Arnold.

Blackie (Morris) sponsors a group of parolees so they can work in a war plant, and when a parolee (Rolf) is accused of murder, Blackie uncovers the real murderer.

332. Chapter Two (12/79) Metrocolor—124 mins. (Comedy). *DIR*: Robert Moore. *PRO*: Ray Stark. *SP*: Neil Simon. A Rastar Production. *CAST*: James Caan, Marsha Mason, Joseph Bologna, Valerie Harper, Alan Fudge, Judy Farrell, Debra Mooney, Isabel Cooley, Imogene Bliss, Ray Young, George Rondo.

A widowed author (Caan), still mourning his first wife, tries not to fall in love with a divorcee (Mason).

333. Charge of the Lancers (2/54) Technicolor—73 mins. (Spy-Drama). *DIR*: William Castle. *PRO*: Sam Katzman. *SP*: Robert E. Kent. *CAST*: Paulette Goddard, Jean Pierre Aumont, Richard Stapley, Karin Booth, Charles Irwin, Ben Astar, Lester Matthews, Gregory Gay, Ivan Triesault, Lou Merrill, Charles Horvath.

During the Crimean War, a British major (Aumont) and a gypsy (Goddard) help the British capture the Russian naval base at Sebastopol.

334. Charley's Aunt (12/28/30) B&W—88 mins. (Comedy). *DIR/PRO*: Al Christie. *SP*: F. McGrew Willis. Based on the play and story by Brandon Thomas. *CAST*: Charlie Ruggles, June Collyer, Hugh Williams, Doris Lloyd, Halliwell Hobbes, Flora Le Breton, Rodney McLennon, Flora Sheffield, Phillips Smalley, Wilson Benge.

An Oxford student (Ruggles) acts as his classmate's matronly aunt and chaperone. *NOTES*: Filmed in 1925 with Sydney Chaplin, in 1941 with Jack Benny, and in 1952 as a musical with Ray Bolger.

Charrette Fantôme, La *see* **La Charrette Fantôme**

335. The Chase (2/66) Technicolor/Panavision—135 mins. (Drama). *DIR*: Arthur Penn. *PRO*: Sam Spiegel. *SP*: Lillian Hellman. Based on the book and play by Horton Foote. A Horizon Production. *CAST*: Marlon Brando, Jane Fonda, Robert Redford, E. G. Marshall, Angie Dickinson, Janice Rule, Miriam Hopkins, Martha Hyer, Robert Duvall, James Fox, Diana Hyland, Henry Hull, Jocelyn Brando, Steve Ihnat, Bruce Cabot, Richard Bradford, Katherine Walsh, Clifton James.

A sheriff (Brando) tries to prevent the meeting of an escaped convict (Redford) and his adulterous wife (Fonda) with tragic results.

336. The Cheap Detective (6/78) Metrocolor/Panavision — 92 mins. (Comedy). *DIR:* Robert Moore. *PRO:* Ray Stark. *SP:* Neil Simon. A Rastar Production. *CAST:* Peter Falk, Ann-Margret, Eileen Brennan, Sid Caesar, Stockard Channing, James Coco, Dom DeLuise, Louise Fletcher, John Houseman, Madeline Kahn, Fernando Lamas, Marsha Mason, Phil Silvers, Abe Vigoda, Paul Williams, Nicol Williamson, Scatman Crothers, David Ogden Stiers, Vic Tayback, Carole Wells, Lew Gallo, James Cromwell.

A forties private eye, Lou Peckinpaugh (Falk), is involved in a complex murder case spoofing "Casablanca," "The Maltese Falcon," "The Big Sleep," and "Murder, My Sweet."

The Checker Player *see* **The Devil Is an Empress**

337. Cheech and Chong's Nice Dreams (6/81) Metrocolor — 110 mins. (Comedy). *DIR:* Thomas Chong. *PRO:* Howard Brown. *SP:* Thomas Chong, Richard "Cheech" Marin. *CAST:* Thomas Chong, Richard "Cheech" Marin, Dr. Timothy Leary, Evelyn Gunero, Stacy Keach, Robert Maffei, Rikki Marin, Louis Guss, Danny Kwan, Michael Lansing, Paul Zegler, Roderick E. Daniels, Paul Reubens (Pee Wee Herman).

Two zanies (Cheech, Chong) use an ice-cream truck as a front to sell their drugs.

The Chess Player *see* **The Devil Is an Empress**

338. Chicago Syndicate (7/55) B&W — 84 mins. (Crime). *DIR:* Fred F. Sears. *PRO:* Sam Katzman. *SP:* Joseph Hoffman. Story by William B. Sackheim. A Clover Production. *CAST:*

Dennis O'Keefe, Abbe Lane, Paul Stewart, Xavier Cugat, Allison Hayes, Dick Cutting, Chris Alcaide, William Challee, John Zaremba, George Brand, Mark Hanna, Carroll McComas, Hugh Sanders.

An accountant (O'Keefe) is sent to uncover the mob's secret bookkeeping operation to stop their racketeering.

339. Child of Manhattan (2/11/33) B&W — 70 mins. (Drama). *DIR:* Edward Buzzell. *SP:* Gertrude Purcell. Based on a play by Preston Sturges. *CAST:* Nancy Carroll, John Boles, Warburton Gamble, Clara Burdick, Jane Darwell, Gary Owen, Betty Grable, Luis Alberni, Jessie Ralph, Charles (Buck) Jones, Tyler Brooke, Betty Kendall.

A dance hall hostess (Carroll) asserts her independence from her millionaire husband (Boles).

340. China Corsair (6/12/51) B&W — 76 mins. (Adventure). *DIR:* Ray Nazarro. *PRO:* Rudolph C. Flothow. *SP:* Harold R. Greene. *CAST:* Jon Hall, Lisa Ferraday, Ron Randell, Douglas Kennedy, Ernest Borgnine, John Dehner, Marya Marco, Philip Ahn, Peter Mamakos, Weaver Levy.

A ship's engineer (Hall) falls for a Eurasian girl (Ferraday) and helps her get the killer of her uncle. *NOTES:* The film debut of Ernest Borgnine.

341. China Is Near (12/67) B&W — 108 mins. (Comedy). *DIR:* Marco Bellocchio. *PRO:* Franco Cristaldi. *SP:* Marco Bellocchio, Elda Tattoli. Story by Marco Bellocchio. A Vides-Royal Films International Production. *CAST:* Glauco Mauri, Elda Tattoli, Paolo Graziosi, Daniela Surina, Pierluigi Apra, Alessandro Haber, Claudio Trionfo, Laura De Marchi, Claudio Cassinelli, Renato Jalenti.

A political science professor (Mauri) campaigns for public office on the Socialist Party ticket. [Original Italian title: *La Cina e Vicina*].

342. The China Syndrome (3/79) Metrocolor—122 mins. (Drama). *DIR:* James Bridges. *PRO:* Michael Douglas. *SP:* T. S. Cook, Mike Gray, James Bridges. An IPC Production. *CAST:* Michael Douglas, Jane Fonda, Jack Lemmon, Scott Brady, Wilford Brimley, James Hampton, Peter Donat, Richard Herd, Daniel Valdez, Stan Bohrman, James Karen, Michael Alaimo, Donald Hotton, Paul Larson.

A TV reporter (Fonda) and cameraman (Douglas) learn about the cover-up of a near disaster at a nuclear plant from the plant engineer (Lemmon).

343. China Venture (9/53) B&W—83 mins. (War). *DIR:* Don Siegel. *PRO:* Anson Bond. *SP:* George Worthing Yates, Richard Collins. Story by Anson Bond. *CAST:* Edmond O'Brien, Barry Sullivan, Jocelyn Brando, Leo Gordon, Richard Loo, Dayton Lummis, Leon Askin, Dabbs Greer, Alvy Moore, Philip Ahn, Frank Wilcox, James Anderson, Rex Reason, Todd Karns.

In 1945, a Marine (O'Brien) and a Naval officer (Sullivan) are sent to the China coast to kidnap a Japanese general (Ahn).

344. Chinatown at Midnight (1/19/50) B&W—67 mins. (Crime). *DIR:* Seymour Friedman. *PRO:* Sam Katzman. *SP:* Robert Libott, Frank Burt. *CAST:* Hurd Hatfield, Jean Willes, Tom Powers, Ray Walker, Charles Russell, Jacqueline DeWit, Maylia, Ross Elliott, Benson Fong, Barbara Jean Wong, Victor San Yen, Josephine Whitell.

Police search San Francisco Chinatown for a killer (Hatfield).

345. Chinatown Nights (3/38) B&W—70 mins. (Crime). *DIR:* Tony Frenguelli. *PRO:* Neil Emerald. *SP:*

Nigel Byass. A Victory Production. *CAST:* H. Agar Lyons, Anne Grey, Robert Hobbs, Neil Emerald.

A Chinese master criminal (Lyons) kidnaps the sister (Grey) of an inventor to obtain his invention.

346. Chloe in the Afternoon (9/72) B&W—97 mins. (Drama). *DIR/SP:* Eric Rohmer. *PRO:* Pierre Cottrell. A Les Films du Losange-Barbet Schroeder Production. *CAST:* Bernard Verly, Zouzou, Francoise Verly, Daniel Ceccaldi, Malvina Penne, Babette Ferrier, Tina Michelino, Jean-Louis Livi, Pierre Nunzi.

A married man (Verly) spends his afternoons in conversation with a kooky girl (Zouzou). *NOTES:* The sixth installment of Rohmer's *Six Moral Tales*. [British title: *Love in the Afternoon*]. [Original French title: *L'Apres-Midi*].

347. A Chorus Line (12/85) Technicolor/Panavision—113 mins. (Musical). *DIR:* Richard Attenborough. *PRO:* Cy Feuer, Ernest Martin. *SP:* Arnold Schulman. Based on the play by Michael Bennett. An EM-Polygram Production. *CAST:* Michael Douglas, Alyson Reed, Vicki Frederick, Cameron English, Yamil Borges, Gregg Burge, Audrey Landers, Pam Klinger, Blane Savage, Janet Jones, Michelle Johnston, Jan Gan Boyd, Michael Blevins, Sharon Brown, Tony Fields, Terrence Mann, Nicole Fosse.

A Broadway producer (Douglas) auditions several young singers and dancers for a new show.

348. Chosen Survivors (5/74) Eastman Color—99 mins. (Science-Fiction). *DIR:* Sutton Roley. *PRO:* Charles Fries, Leon Benson. *SP:* H. B. Cross, Joe Reb Moffly. Story by H. B. Cross. An Alpine Production in association with Churubusco Studios. *CAST:* Jackie Cooper, Alex Cord, Richard Jaeckel, Bradford Dillman, Diana Muldaur, Pedro Armendariz,

Jr., Lincoln Kilpatrick, Gwen Mitchell, Barbara Babcock, Christina Moreno, Nancy Rodman, Kelly Lange.

A group of people are sent underground to test human reaction to a thermo-nuclear disaster, but find themselves at the mercy of vampire bats.

349. Christine (12/83) Metrocolor/Panavision — 116 mins. (Horror). *DIR:* John Carpenter. *PRO:* Richard Kobritz. *SP:* Bill Phillips. Based on the book by Stephen King. *CAST:* Keith Gordon, John Stockwell, Alexandra Paul, Robert Prosky, Harry Dean Stanton, Christine Belford, Roberts Blossom, David Spielberg, William Ostrander, Malcolm Danare, Kelly Preston, Steven Tash.

A killer Plymouth Fury car has a will of its own and dispatches the enemies of its owner (Gordon).

350. Cigarette Girl (2/13/47) B&W — 74 mins. (Musical). *DIR:* Guenther V. Fritsch. *PRO:* William Bloom. *SP:* Henry K. Moritz. Story by Edward Huebsch. *CAST:* Leslie Brooks, Jimmy Lloyd, Ludwig Donath, Doris Colleen, Howard Freeman, Joan Barton, Mary Forbes, Francis Pierlot, Eugene Borden, Arthur Loft, Emmett Vogan, David Bond, Russ Morgan and His Orchestra.

A would-be oil baron (Lloyd) and a would-be nightclub singer (Brooks) fall in love after lying to each other about their occupations.

351. The Circus Queen Murder (5/6/33) B&W — 65 mins. (Mystery). *DIR:* Roy William Neill. *SP:* Jo Swerling. Based on the book by Anthony Abbot. *CAST:* Adolphe Menjou, Greta Nissen, Donald Cook, Ruthelma Stevens, Harry Holman, Dwight Frye, George Rosener.

While on vacation, New York police commissioner Thatcher Colt (Menjou) investigates the murder of a trapeze artist at a traveling circus.

352. Cisco Pike (1/72) Eastman Color — 94 mins. (Crime). *DIR/SP:* Bill L. Norton. *PRO:* Gerald Ayres. An Acrobat Film Production. *CAST:* Kris Kristofferson, Karen Black, Gene Hackman, Harry Dean Stanton, Viva, Joy Bang, Roscoe Lee Browne, Severn Darden, Antonio Fargas, Douglas Sahm, Alan Arbus, Herb Weil, Lorna Thayer.

A former rock star (Kristofferson), vowing to go straight after his release from prison, is blackmailed by a crooked cop (Hackman) into selling drugs. *NOTES:* Kris Kristofferson's film debut.

353. City of Fear (2/59) B&W — 75 mins. (Crime-Drama). *DIR:* Irving Lerner. *PRO:* Leon Chooluck. *SP:* Steven Ritch, Robert Dillon. *CAST:* Vince Edwards, Lyle Talbot, John Archer, Steven Ritch, Patricia Blair, Joseph Mell, Sherwood Price, Cathy Browne, Kelly Thordsen.

An escaped convict (Edwards) places a city in danger when he steals a container of radioactive material, which he believes to be heroin.

354. City Streets (7/29/38) B&W — 88 mins. (Drama). *DIR:* Albert S. Rogell. *PRO:* Wallace MacDonald. *SP:* Fred Niblo, Jr., Lou Breslow. Story by Isadore Bernstein. *CAST:* Edith Fellows, Leo Carrillo, Tommy Bond, Mary Gordon, Helen Jerome Eddy, Joseph King, Frank Sheridan, Arthur Loft, George Humbert, Frank Reicher, Grace Goodall.

A kindly man (Carrillo) cares for a crippled orphan girl (Fellows), but loses her to the state when he becomes impoverished.

355. City Without Men (1/14/43) B&W — 75 mins. (Drama). *DIR:* Sidney Salkow. *PRO:* B. P. Schulberg. *SP:* W. L. River, George Sklar, Donald Davis. Story by Budd Schulberg, Martin Berkeley. A Samuel Bronston Production. *CAST:* Linda Darnell, Michael Duane, Sara Allgood, Edgar Buchanan, Leslie Brooks, Glenda Farrell, Margaret Hamilton, Sheldon Leonard.

A boarding house, near a prison, is filled with women awaiting the release of their imprisoned menfolk.

356. Claire's Knee (2/71) Eastman Color — 103 mins. (Comedy-Drama). *DIR/SP:* Eric Rohmer. *PRO:* Pierre Cottrell. A Les Films du Losange Production. *CAST:* Jean-Claude Brialy, Aurora Cornu, Beatrice Romand, Michele Montel, Laurence De Monaghan, Gerard Falconetti, Fabrice Luchini.

A young man (Brialy), engaged to be married, meets a girl (De Monaghan) and becomes fascinated with her knee. *NOTES:* The fifth installment of Rohmer's *Six Moral Tales*. [Original French title: *Le Genou de Claire*].

357. A Close Call for Boston Blackie (1/24/46) B&W — 60 mins. (Mystery). *DIR:* Lew Landers. *PRO:* John Stone. *SP:* Ben Markson, Paul Yawitz. Story by Paul Yawitz. Based on characters created by Jack Boyle. *CAST:* Chester Morris, Lynn Merrick, George E. Stone, Frank Sully, Richard Lane, Russell Hicks, Claire Carleton, Erik Rolf, Charles Lane, Robert Scott, Emmett Vogan, Doris Houck, Ruth Warren, Jack Gordon.

Blackie (Morris) is accused of murder when a corpse is found in his room. [British title: *Lady of Mystery*].

358. A Close Call for Ellery Queen (1/29/42) B&W — 65 mins. (Mystery). *DIR:* James Hogan. *PRO:* Larry Darmour. *SP:* Eric Taylor. Based on *The Dragon's Teeth, A Problem in Deduction* by Ellery Queen (Frederic Dannay, Manfred Lee). *CAST:* William Gargan, Margaret Lindsay, Charley Grapewin, Ralph Morgan, Kay Linaker, Edward Norris, James Burke, Addison Richards,

Charles Judels, Andrew Tombes, Claire DuBrey, Micheline Cheirel, Ben Welden, Milton Parsons.

Ellery (Gargan) and his secretary (Lindsay) help the owner (Morgan) of an estate prove his innocence of murder and expose a plot to replace a missing heir. [British title: *A Close Call*].

359. Close Encounters of the 3rd Kind (11/77) Metrocolor — 135 mins. (Science Fiction). *DIR/SP:* Steven Spielberg. *PRO:* Michael Phillips, Julia Phillips. *CAST:* Richard Dreyfuss, Francois Truffaut, Teri Garr, Melinda Dillon, Cary Guffey, Bob Balaban, J. Patrick McNamara, Warren J. Kemmerling, Philip Dodds, Lance Hendricksen, George Di Cenzo, Merrill Connally.

An Indiana lineman (Dreyfuss) is led by intuition and detection to the landing site of UFO's at Devil's Tower, Wyoming. *NOTES:* Re-released in 1980 with additional footage.

360. The Clouded Yellow (8/52) B&W — 96 mins. (Drama). *DIR:* Ralph Thomas. *PRO:* Betty E. Box. *SP:* Eric Ambler. Story by Janet Green. A Carillon Production. *CAST:* Jean Simmons, Trevor Howard, Sonia Dresdel, Barry Jones, Maxwell Reed, Kenneth More, Andre Morell, Gerard Heinz, Lily Kann, Geoffrey Keen, Eric Pohlmann, Richard Wattis, Michael Brennan.

A fired British Secret Service agent (Howard) helps a girl (Simmons) clear herself of a murder charge.

361. Clouds Over Europe (6/19/39) B&W — 82 mins. (Spy-Comedy). *DIR:* Tim Whelan. *PRO:* Irving Asher, Alexander Korda. *SP:* Ian Dalrymple. Story by Jack Wittingham, Brock Williams, Arthur Wimperis. A Harefield-London Production. *CAST:* Laurence Olivier, Valerie Hobson, Ralph Richardson, George Curzon, George Merritt, Gus McNaughton, David Tree, Sandra Storme, Frank Fox.

A Scotland Yard inspector (Richardson) and a pilot (Olivier) learn that Germans are using a radio beam aboard ship to down test aircraft. [British title: Q-Planes].

362. The Clown (6/20/27) B&W—57 mins. (Drama). DIR: William James Craft. PRO: Harry Cohn. SP: Harry O. Hoyt, Dorothy Howell. CAST: Johnnie Walker, Dorothy Revier, William V. Mong, John Miljan, Barbara Tennant, Charlotte Walker.

A circus clown (Walker), sent to prison for accidentally killing his wife (Tennant) instead of her lover (Miljan), escapes to kill his wife's former lover.

363. Coast Guard (8/4/39) B&W—72 mins. (Drama). DIR: Edward Ludwig. PRO: Fred Kohlmar. SP: Richard Maibaum, Albert Duffy, Harry Segall. CAST: Randolph Scott, Frances Dee, Ralph Bellamy, Lorna Gray, Walter Connolly, Stanley Andrews, Ned Glass, Edmund MacDonald, Robert Middlemass, Ray Mala, John Tyrrell, Don Beddoe, Ann Doran, J. Farrell MacDonald.

Two Coast Guardsmen (Scott, Bellamy) clash over the love of a woman (Dee), but when one of them crashes in the Arctic the other must decide whether or not to rescue him.

364. The Cockleshell Heroes (5/56) Technicolor/Scope—98 mins. (War-Drama). DIR: Jose Ferrer. PRO: Irving Allen, Albert R. Broccoli. SP: Bryan Forbes, Richard Maibaum. Story by George Kent. A Warwick Films Production. CAST: Jose Ferrer, Trevor Howard, Victor Maddern, Anthony Newley, David Lodge, Peter Arne, Percy Herbert, Karel Stepanek, Christopher Lee, Graham Stewart, John Fabian.

During World War II, ten Royal Marines travel by canoe to the Bordeaux docks to plant mines on German ships.

365. Cocktail Hour (5/29/33) B&W—74 mins. (Drama). DIR: Victor Schertzinger. SP: Gertrude Purcell, Richard Schayer. Story by J. K. McGuinness. CAST: Randolph Scott, Bebe Daniels, Jessie Ralph, Muriel Kirkland, Sidney Blackmer, Barry Norton, Marjorie Gateson, George Nardelli.

A young painter (Daniels) gets away from it all to experience life, and almost loses the man she loves (Scott).

366. Code of the Range (10/9/36) B&W—55 mins. (Western). DIR: C. C. Coleman, Jr. PRO: Harry L. Decker. SP: Ford Beebe. Story by Peter B. Kyne. CAST: Charles Starrett, Mary Blake, Ed Coxen, Allen Caven, Edmund Cobb, Edward Piel, Sr., Edward J. LeSaint, Ralph McCullough, George Chesebro, Art Mix, Albert J. Smith.

A rancher (Starrett), framed for murder by a crooked cattle baron (Smith), sets out to prove his innocence and open the range to sheepmen.

367. Code 7 . . . Victim 5 (12/64) Technicolor/Scope—88 mins. (Crime). DIR: Robert Lynn. PRO: Harry Alan Towers. SP: Peter Yeldham. Story by Peter Welbeck (Harry Alan Towers). A Towers of London Film Production. CAST: Lex Barker, Ronald Fraser, Walter Rilla, Veronique Vendell, Ann Smyrner, Dietmar Schonherr, Howard Davies, Sophia Spentzos.

A private detective (Barker) journeys to South Africa to find a murderer, and uncovers a group of Nazi war criminals linked to the murder. [British title: Victim Five].

368. The Collector (6/65) Technicolor—117 mins. (Drama). DIR: William Wyler. PRO: Jud Kinberg. SP: Stanley Mann, John Kohn. Story by John Fowles. A William Wyler Production. CAST: Terence Stamp, Samantha Eggar, Mona Washbourne, Maurice Dallimore, William Beckley, Gordon Barclay, David Holland.

A demented butterfly collector (Stamp) kidnaps an art student (Eggar) to add to his collection.

369. The College Coquette (8/5/29) B&W — 68 mins. (Drama). *DIR:* George Archainbaud. *PRO:* Harry Cohn. *SP:* Ralph Graves. Story by Norman Houston. *CAST:* Ruth Taylor, William Collier, Jr., Jobyna Ralston, John Holland, Adda Gleason, Gretchen Hartman, Frances Lyons, Edward Piel, Sr., Eddie Clayton, Morris Murphy.

A young girl (Ralston), wanting to be accepted by the college crowd, gives herself to the local college boy (Collier) with tragic results. NOTES: Released as both silent and sound.

370. The College Hero (10/9/27) B&W — 54 mins. (Comedy). *DIR:* Walter Lang. *PRO:* Harry Cohn. *SP:* Dorothy Howell. Story by Henry R. Symonds. *CAST:* Bobby Agnew, Pauline Garon, Ben Turpin, Rex Lease, Churchill Ross, Joan Standing, Charles Paddock.

A college freshman (Agnew) proves himself a hero by winning the big game despite being injured.

371. The Colorado Trail (9/8/38) B&W — 55 mins. (Western). *DIR:* Sam Nelson. *PRO:* Harry L. Decker. *SP:* Charles F. Royal. *CAST:* Charles Starrett, Iris Meredith, Bob Nolan, Dick Curtis, Al Bridge, Edward J. LeSaint, Robert Fiske, Hank Bell, Edward Piel, Sr., Stanley Brown, Edmund Cobb, Dick Botiller, Jack Clifford, Sons of the Pioneers.

A wandering gunfighter (Starrett) gets mixed up in range war when it is revealed that he is the son of one of the rival ranchers.

372. Comanche Station (3/60) Eastman Color/Scope — 74 mins.

(Western). *DIR:* Budd Boetticher. *PRO:* Harry Joe Brown, Budd Boetticher. *SP:* Burt Kennedy. A Renown Production. *CAST:* Randolph Scott, Nancy Gates, Claude Akins, Skip Homeier, Richard Rust, Rand Brooks, Duke Johnson, Foster Hood, Joe Molina, Vince St. Cyr, Paul Holland.

A rancher, while searching for his wife, rescues a woman (Gates) kidnapped by the Comanches, and guides her and three outlaws (Akins, Rust, Homeier) through Comanche territory.

373. Combat Squad (10/19/53) B&W — 72 mins. (War-Drama). *DIR:* Cy Roth. *PRO:* Jerry Thomas. *SP:* Wyatt Ordung. *CAST:* John Ireland, Lon McCallister, Hal March, George E. Stone, Norman Leavitt, Myron Healey, Don Haggerty, Tristram Coffin, David Holt, Robert Easton, Dick Fortune, Jill Hollingsworth, Linda Danson, Neva Gilbert, Eileen Howe, Paul Keast.

A young soldier (McCallister) learns the meaning of bravery during the Korean War.

374. Come Closer, Folks (11/24/36) B&W — 61 mins. (Comedy). *DIR:* D. Ross Lederman. *PRO:* Ben Pivar. *SP:* Lee Loeb, Harold Buchman. Story by Aben Kandel. *CAST:* James Dunn, Marian Marsh, Wynne Gibson, Herman Bing, George McKay, Gene Lockhart, John Gallaudet, Gene Morgan, Wallis Clark.

A street hawker (Dunn) rises from department store salesman to assistant manager.

375. Come Dance with Me (5/50) B&W — 58 mins. (Musical). *DIR/PRO:* Mario Zampi. *SP:* Cyril Roberts. An Anglofilm Production. *CAST:* Max Wall, Gordon Humphris, Yvonne Marsh, Barbara Hamilton, Vincent Ball, Anne Shelton, Derek Roy, Anton Karas, The Marquis Trio.

A nightclub valet (Humphris), pretending to be a Baronet, falls in love with a maid (Marsh), pretending to be a Lady.

376. The Comic (11/69) Pathe Color—95 mins. (Comedy-Drama). *DIR/PRO:* Carl Reiner. *SP:* Carl Reiner, Aaron Ruben. An Acre Enterprises Production. *CAST:* Dick Van Dyke, Michele Lee, Mickey Rooney, Cornel Wilde, Nina Wayne, Pert Kelton, Steve Allen, Barbara Heller, Ed Peck, Jeannine Riley, Gavin McLeod, Jay Novello, Fritz Feld, Jerome Cowan, Isabel Sanford, Jeff Donnell, Carl Reiner.

The rise and fall of a silent film comedian (Van Dyke), as told in flashbacks during his funeral.

377. Coming of Age (3/38) B&W—68 mins. (Comedy). *DIR:* Manning Haynes. *PRO:* George Smith. *SP:* Paul White, Rowan Kennedy. A GS Enterprises Production. *CAST:* Eliot Makeham, Joyce Bland, Jack Melford, Ruby Miller, Jimmy Hanley, Evelyn Ankers, Annie Esmond, Aubrey Mallalieu.

Two couples (Makeham, Bland; Melford, Ankers) try to have an affair with each other's spouse.

378. The Commandos Strike at Dawn (1/7/43) B&W—98 mins. (War-Drama). *DIR:* John Farrow. *PRO:* Lester Cowan. *SP:* Irwin Shaw. Story by C. S. Forester. *CAST:* Paul Muni, Lillian Gish, Robert Coote, Anna Lee, Ray Collins, Sir Cedric Hardwicke, Rosemary DeCamp, Alexander Knox, Elizabeth Fraser, Richard Derr, Rod Cameron, George Macready, Erville Alderson, Louis Jean Heydt, Lloyd Bridges, Walter Sande, Philip Van Zandt, Ann Carter.

A Norwegian fisherman (Muni) leads British commandos on a raid to destroy a German airfield in Norway, and to free the village where his daughter (Carter) is held hostage.

379. The Competition (12/80) Metrocolor—129 mins. (Musical-Drama). *DIR/SP:* Joel Oliansky. *PRO:* William B. Sackheim. Story by Joel Oliansky, William B. Sackheim. *CAST:* Richard Dreyfuss, Amy Irving, Lee Remick, Sam Wanamaker, Joseph Cali, Ty Henderson, Vickie Kriegler, Adam Stern, James B. Sikking, Priscilla Pointer, Bea Silvern, Philip Sterling.

An aging piano competitor (Dreyfuss) tries for a comeback in a San Francisco piano competition.

380. Confessions from a Holiday Camp (8/77) Eastman Color—88 mins. (Comedy). *DIR:* Norman Cohen. *PRO:* Greg Smith. *SP:* Christopher Wood. Based on the book by Timothy Lea. *CAST:* Robin Askwith, Anthony Booth, Doris Hare, Bill Maynard, Sheila White, Colin Crompton, Liz Fraser, Linda Hayden, John Junkens, Lance Percival, Nicholas Owen, Janet Ede, Mike Savage.

At a British Holiday Camp, an entertainment officer (Askwith) turns the place topsy-turvy with his antics. *NOTES:* Limited theatrical release.

381. Confessions of a Driving Instructor (7/76) Eastman Color—90 mins. (Comedy). *DIR:* Norman Cohen. *PRO:* Greg Smith. *SP:* Christopher Wood. Based on the book by Timothy Lea. *CAST:* Robin Askwith, Anthony Booth, Bill Maynard, Doris Hare, Sheila White, Windsor Davies, Liz Fraser, Irene Handl, George Layton, Linda Bellingham, Avril Angers, Maxine Casson, Chrissy Iddon, Peter Godfrey, John Junkin, Suzy Mandel, Ballard Berkeley.

A driving instructor (Askwith) has to fight off the ladies while trying to teach them how to drive a car. *NOTES:* Limited theatrical release.

382. Confessions of a Pop Performer (8/75) Eastman Color—91 mins. (Comedy). *DIR:* Norman Cohen. *PRO:* Greg Smith. *SP:* Christopher Wood. Based on the book by Timothy Lea. *CAST:* Robin Askwith, Anthony Booth, Bill Maynard, Doris Hare, Sheila White, Bob Todd, Jill Gascoine, Peter Cleall, Peter Jones, Carol Hawkins.

Disaster plagues a man (Askwith) and his brother-in-law (Booth) when they try to promote an unknown pop group. *NOTES:* Limited theatrical release.

383. Confessions of a Window Cleaner (11/74) Eastman Color—90 mins. (Comedy). *DIR:* Val Guest. *PRO:* Greg Smith. *SP:* Christopher Wood, Val Guest. Based on the book by Timothy Lea. *CAST:* Robin Askwith, Anthony Booth, Sheila White, Dandy Nichols, Bill Maynard, Linda Hayden, John Le Mesurier, Joan Hickson, Richard Wattis, Anita Graham, Christine Donna, Sue Longhurst.

An apprentice window washer (Askwith) has several misadventures while applying his trade. *NOTES:* Limited theatrical release.

384. Confessions of Boston Blackie (12/28/41) B&W—65 mins. (Mystery). *DIR:* Edward Dmytryk. *PRO:* William Berke. *SP:* Paul Yawitz, Jay Dratler. Based on characters created by Jack Boyle. *CAST:* Chester Morris, Harriet Hilliard, George E. Stone, Joan Woodbury, Richard Lane, Walter Sande, Lloyd Corrigan, Kenneth MacDonald, Billy Benedict, Walter Soderling, Ralph Theodore, Eddie Laughton, Ralph Dunn, Eddie Fetherstone, Stanley Brown, Jessie Arnold.

Blackie (Morris), framed for the murder of an art dealer, tries to clear himself and locate a valuable statue stolen from a woman (Hilliard). [British title: *Confessions*].

385. Conquest of Cochise (9/53) Technicolor—70 mins. (Western). *DIR:* William Castle. *PRO:* Sam Katzman. *SP:* Arthur Lewis, DeVallon Scott. Story by DeVallon Scott. *CAST:* John Hodiak, Joy Page, Robert Stack, Fortunio Bonanova, Rico Alaniz, Edward Colemans, Alex Montoya, Joseph Waring, Steven Ritch, Carol Thurston, Rodd Redwing, Robert Griffin, John Crawford.

An Army major (Stack) is sent to make peace with Cochise (Hodiak).

386. Convicted (8/24/38) B&W—58 mins. (Crime). *DIR:* Leon Barsha. *PRO:* Kenneth J. Bishop. *SP:* Edgar Edwards. Based on *Face Work* by Cornell Woolrich. A Central Film Production. *CAST:* Charles Quigley, Rita Hayworth, Marc Lawrence, George McKay, Doreen McGregor, Bill Irving, Eddie Laughton, Edgar Edwards, Phyllis Clare, Bob Rideout, Michael Heppell, Noel Cusack, Grant MacDonald, Don Douglas.

A private detective (Quigley) and a nightclub singer (Hayworth) set out to clear her brother (Edwards) of a murder charge.

387. Convicted (8/50) B&W—91 mins. (Prison Drama). *DIR:* Henry Levin. *PRO:* Jerry Bresler. *SP:* William Bowers, Fred Niblo, Jr., Seton I. Miller. Based on the play *The Criminal Code* by Martin Flavin. *CAST:* Glenn Ford, Broderick Crawford, Millard Mitchell, Dorothy Malone, Carl Benton Reid, Frank Faylen, Will Geer, Martha Stewart, Henry O'Neill, Douglas Kennedy, Ed Begley, John Doucette, Ilka Gruning, Whit Bissell, Fred F. Sears, Fred Graham, Eddie Parker, James Millican, Ray Teal, Clancy Cooper, Harry Cording, Griff Barnett.

A district attorney (Crawford) works to free an innocent man (Ford) from prison. *NOTES:* A remake of the 1931 Columbia film *The Criminal Code*.

388. Convicted Woman (3/8/40) B&W—66 mins. (Drama). *DIR:* Nick Grinde. *PRO:* Ralph Cohn. *SP:* Joseph

Carole. Story by Martin Mooney, Alex Gottlieb. *CAST:* Rochelle Hudson, Frieda Inescort, June Lang, Lola Lane, Mary Field, Lorna Gray, Iris Meredith, Glenn Ford, Esther Dale, William Farnum, Beatrice Blinn, June Gittleson, Dorothy Appleby.

Women try to establish a form of self-government while confined in prison.

389. Corky of Gasoline Alley (9/17/51) B&W—80 mins. (Comedy). *DIR/SP:* Edward Bernds. *PRO:* Wallace MacDonald. Based on the comic strip *Gasoline Alley* by Frank O. King. *CAST:* Scotty Beckett, Jimmy Lydon, Don Beddoe, Gordon Jones, Patti Brady, Susan Morrow, Kay Christopher, Madelon Mitchel, Dick Wessel, Harry Tyler, Ralph Votrian, John Doucette, Charles Williams, Lester Matthews, Jack Rice, Ludwig Stossel, John Dehner, Lewis Russell.

The Wallet household is thrown into turmoil when a cousin (Jones) of Nina's (Christopher) comes for a visit. [British title: *Corky*].

390. Cornered (8/5/32) B&W—58 mins. (Western). *DIR:* B. Reeves Eason. *SP:* Wallace MacDonald. Story by Ruth Todd. *CAST:* Tim McCoy, Shirley Grey, Niles Welch, Raymond Hatton, Charles King, Lloyd Ingraham, Claire McDowell, John Eberts, John Elliott, Walter Long, Bob Kortman, Art Mix, Merrill McCormack, Noah Beery, Sr., Artie Ortego, Jim Corey, Edward Piel, Sr., Ray Jones, Jack Evans, Blackie Whiteford.

A ranch foreman (McCoy), framed for murder, escapes from jail and seeks those who framed him.

391. Coroner Creek (7/1/48) CineColor—90 mins. (Western). *DIR:* Ray Enright. *PRO:* Harry Joe Brown. *SP:* Kenneth Gamet. Based on the book by Luke Short. A Producers-Actors Production. *CAST:* Randolph Scott, Marguerite Chapman, George

Macready, Edgar Buchanan, Wallace Ford, Forrest Tucker, William Bishop, Joe Sawyer, Russell Simpson, Douglas Fowley, Forrest Taylor, Lee Bennett, Sally Eilers, Barbara Reed, Phil Shumaker, Warren Jackson.

When his fiancee commits suicide in a stage holdup, a rancher (Scott) trails the outlaws to Coroner Creek to exact justice.

392. The Corpse Came C.O.D. (6/10/47) B&W—87 mins. (Mystery-Comedy). *DIR:* Henry Levin. *PRO:* Samuel Bischoff. *SP:* George Bricker, Dwight V. Babcock. Based on the book by Jimmy Starr. *CAST:* George Brent, Joan Blondell, Jim Bannon, Adele Jergens, Leslie Brooks, Mary Field, John Berkes, Grant Mitchell, Una O'Conner, Fred F. Sears, William Trenk, Marvin Miller, William Forrest, Wilton Graff, Lane Chandler, Robert Kellard, Myron Healy.

Two rival reporters (Brent, Blondell) try to solve the mystery of why a dead body was sent to an actress (Jergens).

393. Corruption (12/68) Eastman Color—91 mins. (Horror). *DIR:* Robert Hartford-Davis. *PRO:* Peter Newbrook. *SP:* Donald Ford, Derek Ford. A Titan Production. *CAST:* Peter Cushing, Sue Lloyd, Noel Trevarthen, Kate O'Mara, Anthony Booth, David Lodge, Wendy Varnals, Vanessa Howard, Jan Waters, Diana Ashley, Phillip Manikum, Alexandra Dane.

A surgeon (Cushing) must obtain the pituitary glands of young women to keep his wife (Lloyd) beautiful.

394. Counsel for Crime (10/18/37) B&W—61 mins. (Drama). *DIR:* John Brahm. *PRO:* Irving Briskin. *SP:* Fred Niblo, Jr., Grace Neville, Lee Loeb, Harold Buchman. Story by Harold Shumate. *CAST:* Otto Kruger, Douglass Montgomery, Jacqueline Wells (Julie Bishop), Thurston Hall, Nana Bryant, Gene Morgan, Marc

Lawrence, Robert Warwick, Stanley Fields.

A crooked lawyer (Kruger), who provides alibis for gangsters, is tried for murder by his son (Montgomery).

395. Count Three and Pray (10/55) Technicolor/Scope—102 mins. (Western-Drama). *DIR*: George Sherman. *PRO*: Ted Richmond. *SP*: Herb Meadow. Based on *Calico Pony* by Herb Meadow. A Copa Productions Incorporated Production. *CAST*: Van Heflin, Joanne Woodward, Phil Carey, Raymond Burr, Allison Hayes, Myron Healey, Nancy Kulp, James Griffith, Richard Webb, John Cason, Jean Willes, Robert Burton, Steve Raines.

After the Civil War, a Southerner (Heflin) returns home and becomes the town's parson. *NOTES*: Joanne Woodward's film debut.

396. Countdown at Kusini (4/76) Metrocolor—99 mins. (Drama). *DIR*: Ossie Davis. *PRO*: Ladi Ladebo. *SP*: Ossie Davis, Ladi Ladebo, Al Freeman, Jr. Based on a story by John Storm Roberts. A Tan International Ltd. of Nigeria-Glipp Production. *CAST*: Ruby Dee, Ossie Davis, Greg Morris, Tom Aldredge, Michael Ebert, Thomas Baptiste, Jab Adu, Elsie Olusola, Funso Adeolu.

An African revolutionary (Davis) is sought by a mercenary (Aldredge) because of his political activities.

397. Counter-Attack (4/26/45) B&W—90 mins. (War). *DIR/PRO*: Zoltan Korda. *SP*: John Howard Lawson. Based on the play by Janet Stevenson and Philip Stevenson. Story by Ilya Vershinin, Mikhail Ruderman. *CAST*: Paul Muni, Marguerite Chapman, Larry Parks, Virginia Christine, Philip Van Zandt, George Macready, Roman Bohnen, Harro Meller, Erik Rolf, Rudolph Anders, Ian Wolfe, Ivan Triesault, Ludwig Donath, Trevor Bardette.

A Russian paratrooper (Muni) and a Russian woman (Chapman) hold Germans at bay in a bombed out basement. [British title: *One Against Seven*].

398. Counter-Espionage (9/3/42) B&W—72 mins. (Spy-Drama). *DIR*: Edward Dmytryk. *PRO*: Wallace MacDonald. *SP*: Aubrey Wisberg. Based on characters created by Louis Joseph Vance. *CAST*: Warren William, Hillary Brooke, Eric Blore, Thurston Hall, Fred Kelsey, Forrest Tucker, Matthew Boulton, Kurt Katch, Morton Lowry, Leslie Denison, Billy Bevan, Stanley Logan, Tom Stevenson, Eddie Laughton, Keith Hitchcock, Wyndham Standing, Guy Kingsford, Heather Wilde.

The Lone Wolf (William), a member of British Intelligence in London, sets out to stop a gang of Nazis from stealing a secret beam detector.

399. Counterfeit (6/5/36) B&W—73 mins. (Crime). *DIR*: Erle C. Kenton. *PRO*: B. P. Schulberg. *SP*: William Rankin, Bruce Manning. Story by William Rankin. *CAST*: Chester Morris, Margot Grahame, Lloyd Nolan, Marian Marsh, Claude Gillingwater, George McKay, John Gallaudet, Gene Morgan, Pierre Watkin, Marc Lawrence.

A T-Man (Morris) goes undercover to rescue a kidnapped Treasury engraver from a gang of crooks.

400. Counterfeit Lady (1/12/37) B&W—56 mins. (Crime). *DIR*: D. Ross Lederman. *PRO*: Ralph Cohn. *SP*: Tom Van Dycke. Story by Harold Shumate. *CAST*: Ralph Bellamy, Joan Perry, Douglas Dumbrille, George McKay, Gene Morgan, Henry Mollison, John Tyrrell, Max Hoffman, Jr., Edward J. LeSaint, John Harrington.

A lady jewel thief (Perry) is pursued by the cops, a private detective (Bellamy), and gangster friends of the jewelry store owner.

401. Counterspy Meets Scotland Yard (11/21/50) B&W — 67 mins. (Spy-Drama). *DIR*: Seymour Friedman. *PRO*: Wallace MacDonald. *SP*: Harold R. Greene. Based on the *Counterspy* radio program created by Phillips H. Lord. *CAST*: Howard St. John, Amanda Blake, Ron Randell, June Vincent, Fred F. Sears, John Dehner, Lewis Martin, Rick Vallin, Jimmy Lloyd, Ted Jordan, Paul Marton, Gregory Gay, Robert Bice, John Doucette, Douglas Evans.

David Harding (St. John), with the help of Scotland Yard, tracks down the killer of one of his agents at a guided missile base.

402. Court-Martial (8/12/28) B&W — 65 mins. (Western-Historical-Drama). *DIR*: George B. Seitz. *PRO*: Harry Cohn. *SP*: Anthony Coldeway. Story by Elmer Harris. *CAST*: Jack Holt, Betty Compson, Pat Harmon, Doris Hill, Frank Lackteen, Frank Austin, George Cowl, Zack Williams.

A Union officer (Holt) is ordered by President Lincoln (Austin) to break up a Confederate band of outlaws led by Belle Starr (Compson).

403. Cover Girl (4/6/44) Technicolor — 105 mins. (Musical-Comedy). *DIR*: Charles Vidor. *PRO*: Arthur Schwartz. *SP*: Virginia Van Upp, Marion Parsonnet, Paul Gangelin. Story by Erwin Gelsey. *CAST*: Rita Hayworth, Gene Kelly, Lee Bowman, Phil Silvers, Leslie Brooks, Jinx Falkenburg, Eve Arden, Otto Kruger, Jess Barker, Anita Colby, Edward Brophy, Thurston Hall, Jack Norton, Sam Flint, Shelley Winters, John Tyrrell, Barbara Pepper, Grace Lenard, Billy Benedict.

A magazine publisher (Kruger) spots a nightclub dancer (Hayworth) and uses her as a cover girl on his magazine.

404. Cow Town (5/19/50) Sepiatone — 70 mins. (Western). *DIR*: John English. *PRO*: Armand Schaefer. *SP*: Gerald Geraghty. A Gene Autry Production. *CAST*: Gene Autry, Gail Davis, Harry Shannon, Jock Mahoney, Harry Harvey, Steve Darrell, Bud Osborne, Blackie Whiteford, Pat O'Malley, Sandy Sanders, Chuck Roberson, House Peters, Jr., Ted Mapes, Clark Burroughs, Ralph Sanford, Robert Hilton, Herman Hack, Victor Cox, Frank McCarroll, Felice Raymond, Holly Bane, Frankie Marvin.

A range war erupts when Gene puts barbed wire around his ranch to stop cattle rustling.

405. Cowboy (3/58) Technicolor — 92 mins. (Western). *DIR*: Delmer Daves. *PRO*: Julian Blaustein. *SP*: Edmund H. North. Based on *My Reminiscences As a Cowboy* by Frank Harris. *CAST*: Glenn Ford, Anna Kashfi, Jack Lemmon, Dick York, Brian Donlevy, Richard Jaeckel, King Donovan, Vaughn Taylor, Eugene Iglesias, Victor Manuel Mendoza, James Westerfield, Robert "Buzz" Henry, Frank DeKova, Donald Randolph.

A tenderfoot (Lemmon) matures from a weak city boy to a hardened trail boss when he joins a cattle drive.

406. The Cowboy and the Indians (9/15/49) B&W — 70 mins. (Western). *DIR*: John English. *PRO*: Armand Schaefer. *SP*: Dwight Cummins, Dorothy Yost. A Gene Autry Production. *CAST*: Gene Autry, Sheila Ryan, Frank Richards, Hank Patterson, Jay Silverheels, Frank Lackteen, Iron Eyes Cody, Chief Yowlachie, Shooting Star, Nolan Leary, Claudia Drake, Maudie Prickett, Charles Quigley, Lee Roberts, George Nokes, Charles Stevens, Alex Frazer, Harry Mackin, Roy Gordon.

Gene and a lady doctor (Ryan) thwart a crooked Indian agent's (Richards) attempt to drive the Indians from their land.

407. Cowboy Blues (7/18/46) B&W—62 mins. (Western-Musical). *DIR*: Ray Nazarro. *PRO*: Colbert Clark. *SP*: J. Benton Cheney. *CAST*: Ken Curtis, Jeff Donnell, Guy Kibbee, Guinn "Big Boy" Williams, Jack Rockwell, Forbes Murray, Vernon Dent, Robert Scott, Peg LaCentra, Coulter Irwin, Al Bridge, Carolina Cotton, The Plainsmen, The Town Criers, The Hoosier Hotshots, Deuce Spriggins and His Band.

A father (Kibbee) pretends to be a big ranch owner to impress the daughter (Donnell) he has not seen for years. *NOTES*: Peg LaCentra played the role of Mrs. Uppington on radio's Fibber McGee and Molly. [British title: *Beneath the Starry Skies*].

408. Cowboy Canteen (2/8/44) B&W—72 mins. (Western-Musical). *DIR*: Lew Landers. *PRO*: Jack Fier. *SP*: Paul Gangelin, Felix Adler. *CAST*: Charles Starrett, Jane Frazee, Tex Ritter, Barbara Jo Allen (Vera Vague), Dub Taylor, Guinn "Big Boy" Williams, Max Terhune, Dick Curtis, Jeff Donnell, Edythe Elliott, The Mills Brothers, The Tailor Maids, Emmett Lynn, Chickie and Buck, Jimmy Wakely and His Saddle Pals, Roy Acuff and His Smokey Mountain Boys and Girls.

A ranch owner (Starrett) transforms his ranch into a canteen for soldiers when he is called to active duty. [British title: *Close Harmony*].

409. Cowboy from Lonesome River (9/21/44) B&W—55 mins. (Western). *DIR*: Benjamin Kline. *PRO*: Jack Fier. *SP*: Luci Ward. *CAST*: Charles Starrett, Vi Athens, Dub Taylor, Jimmy Wakely, Ozie Waters, Kenneth MacDonald, Arthur Wentzel, Jack Rockwell, Shelby Atkinson, Al Sloey, Steve Clark, Foy Willing, Bud Geary, John Tyrrell, Ian Keith, Craig Woods.

A cowboy (Starrett) leads the local ranch owners against an unscrupulous land baron (MacDonald). [British title: *Signed Judgement*].

410. Cowboy in the Clouds (12/23/43) B&W—58 mins. (Western). *DIR*: Benjamin Kline. *PRO*: Jack Fier. *SP*: Elizabeth Beecher. *CAST*: Charles Starrett, Julie Duncan, Dub Taylor, Jimmy Wakely, Hal Taliaferro (Wally Wales), Charles King, Lane Chandler, Dick Curtis, Ted Mapes, John Tyrrell, Ed Cassidy, Davidson Clark, Paul Zaremba, The Jesters.

A cowboy (Starrett) extols the merits of the Civil Air Patrol when he uses a CAP plane to rescue a rancher's daughter (Duncan) from a forest fire and to catch a murderer.

411. The Cowboy Star (11/20/36) B&W—56 mins. (Western). *DIR*: David Selman. *PRO*: Harry L. Decker. *SP*: Francis Guihan. Story by Frank Melford, Cornelius Reece. *CAST*: Charles Starrett, Iris Meredith, Si Jenks, Marc Lawrence, Edward Piel, Sr., Wally Albright, Dick Terry, Ralph McCullough, Lew Meehan, Nick Copeland, Landers Stevens, Winifred Hari.

A cowboy movie star (Starrett) and his sidekick (Jenks), fed up with Hollywood, settle in Arizona; he uses his Hollywood training when he has to rescue a young boy (Albright) kidnapped by bandits.

412. Craig's Wife (10/2/36) B&W—73 mins. (Drama). *DIR*: Dorothy Arzner. *PRO*: Edward Chodorov. *SP*: Mary C. McCall, Jr. Based on the play by George Edward Kelly. *CAST*: Rosalind Russell, John Boles, Billie Burke, Jane Darwell, Dorothy Wilson, Alma Kruger, Thomas Mitchell, Raymond Walburn, Robert Allen, Elisabeth Risdon, Nydia Westman, Kathleen Burke.

A domineering wife (Russell) loses her husband (Boles) and her friends when she begins to think more of material objects than their welfare. *NOTES:* First made as a silent in 1928 with Irene Rich and Warner Baxter, and then remade by Columbia in 1950 as *Harriet Craig*.

413. Crash Landing (7/58) B&W — 76 mins. (Drama). *DIR:* Fred F. Sears. *PRO:* Sam Katzman. *SP:* Fred Frieberger. A Clover Production. *CAST:* Gary Merrill, Nancy Davis, Irene Hervey, Roger Smith, Bek Nelson, Jewell Lain, Sheridan Comerate, Richard Keith, Celia Lovsky, Lewis Martin, Hal Torey, John McNamara, Dayle Rodney, Rodolfo Hoyos, Kim Charney, Robin Warga, Robert Whiteside, Ronald Green, Richard Newton.

Passengers of an airliner reveal their innermost feelings when they learn their plane is doomed to crash.

414. Crazy Joe (2/74) Eastman Color — 100 mins. (Crime-Drama). *DIR:* Carlo Lizzani. *PRO:* Nino E. Krisman. *SP:* Lewis John Carlino. Based on the book by Nicholas Gage. A Dino De Laurentiis Presentation of a B-P Associates Production. *CAST:* Peter Boyle, Paula Prentiss, Fred Williamson, Charles Cioffi, Rip Torn, Luther Adler, Fausto Tozzi, Franco Lanteri, Eli Wallach, Louis Guss, Henry Winkler, Adam Wade, Peter Savage, Herve Villechaize.

The rise and fall of a New York Mafia hood, "Crazy" Joey Gallo (Boyle).

415. Creature with the Atom Brain (7/55) B&W — 69 mins. (Horror). *DIR:* Edward L. Cahn. *PRO:* Sam Katzman. *SP:* Curt Siodmak. A Clover Production. *CAST:* Richard Denning, Angela Stevens, S. John Launer, Michael Granger, Gregory Gay, Linda Bennett, Tristram Coffin, Harry Lauter, Larry Blake, Charles Evans, Pierre Watkin, Lane Chandler, Nelson Leigh, Don C. Harvey.

A scientist (Gay) creates an army of zombies using atomic radiation, then teams with a gangster (Granger) who uses them for revenge.

416. Creatures the World Forgot (7/71) Technicolor — 95 mins. (Horror). *DIR:* Don Chaffey. *PRO/SP:* Michael Carreras. A Hammer Production. *CAST:* Julie Ege, Brian O'Shaughnessy, Tony Bonner, Robert John, Sue Wilson, Rosalie Crutchley, Marcia Fox, Beverly Blake, Don Leonard, Frank Hayden, Fred Swart, Ken Hare.

In prehistoric times, two brothers (Bonner, John) fight for the right to be leader of their tribe.

417. The Creeping Flesh (2/73) Eastman Color — 91 mins. (Horror). *DIR:* Freddie Francis. *PRO:* Michael Redbourn. *SP:* Peter Spenceley, Jonathan Rumbold. A Tigon British World Film Services Production. *CAST:* Peter Cushing, Christopher Lee, Lorna Heilbron, George Benson, Kenneth J. Warren.

A Victorian scientist (Cushing) discovers that water causes flesh to grow on a Neanderthal skeleton.

418. Crime and Punishment (11/21/35) B&W — 88 mins. (Crime-Drama). *DIR:* Josef von Sternberg. *PRO:* B. P. Schulberg. *SP:* S. K. Lauren, Joseph Anthony. Based on the book by Feodor Dostoyevsky. *CAST:* Edward Arnold, Peter Lorre, Marian Marsh, Tala Birell, Elisabeth Risdon, Robert Allen, Douglas Dumbrille, Gene Lockhart, Charles Waldron, Thurston Hall, Johnny Arthur.

A Russian student (Lorre) murders a pawnbroker and, because of self-remorse, turns himself in to the policeman (Arnold) who has been trailing him. *NOTES:* The French version of this film opened one week before Columbia released their version. There were four silent versions filmed; three by Russia in 1913, 1922, and 1926, and one by Pathe in 1917. Three sound remakes were also filmed; by Sweden in 1948, by Allied Artists in 1959, and by Russia, once again, in 1975.

419. Crime Doctor (6/22/43) B&W—66 mins. (Crime-Mystery). DIR: Michael Gordon. PRO: Ralph Cohn. SP: Graham Baker, Louise Lantz, Jerome Odlum. Based on the CBS radio program *Crime Doctor* by Max Marcin. CAST: Warner Baxter, Margaret Lindsay, John Litel, Ray Collins, Harold Huber, Don Costello, Leon Ames, Constance Worth, Dorothy Tree, Vi Athens.

The head of a burglary ring (Baxter) suffers amnesia and becomes a successful psychiatrist, Dr. Robert Ordway, the Crime Doctor; when he regains his memory he turns himself in and receives a suspended sentence. NOTES: In 1940, Ray Collins was the first to portray Dr. Robert Ordway, the Crime Doctor, on radio.

420. The Crime Doctor's Courage (2/27/45) B&W—70 mins. (Crime-Mystery). DIR: George Sherman. PRO: Rudolph C. Flothow. SP: Eric Taylor. Based on the CBS radio program *Crime Doctor* by Max Marcin. CAST: Warner Baxter, Hillary Brooke, Jerome Cowan, Robert Scott, Lloyd Corrigan, Emory Parnell, Stephen Crane, Charles Arnt, Anthony Caruso, Dennis Moore, Lupita Tovar, Jack Carrington, "King Kong" Kashay.

While on vacation in California, Dr. Ordway (Baxter) is called upon to solve the murder of a girl's (Brooke) husband and suspects that a dance team (Caruso, Tovar) may have been responsible, since they are suspected of being vampires. [British title: *The Doctor's Courage*].

421. The Crime Doctor's Diary (5/18/49) B&W—61 mins. (Crime-Mystery). DIR: Seymour Friedman. PRO: Rudolph C. Flothow. SP: Ed-

ward Anhalt. Story by David Dressler. Based on the CBS radio program *Crime Doctor* by Max Marcin. CAST: Warner Baxter, Lois Maxwell, Stephen Dunne, Adele Jergens, Robert Armstrong, Don Beddoe, Whit Bissell, Cliff Clark, Lois Fields, George Meeker, Crane Whitley, Claire Carleton, Selmer Jackson, Sid Tomack, Robert Emmett Keane.

Dr. Ordway (Baxter) comes to the aid of a framed arsonist (Dunne), when he is suspected of murdering the man who framed him.

422. Crime Doctor's Gamble (11/27/47) B&W—66 mins. (Crime-Mystery). DIR: William Castle. PRO: Rudolph C. Flothow. SP: Edward Bock. Story by Raymond L. Schrock. Based on the CBS radio program *Crime Doctor* by Max Marcin. CAST: Warner Baxter, Micheline Cheirel, Roger Dann, Steven Geray, Marcel Journet, Eduardo Ciannelli, Maurice Marsac, Henri Letondal, Jean Del Val, Leon Lenoir, Wheaton Chambers, Emory Parnell, George Davis.

While vacationing in Paris, Dr. Ordway (Baxter) becomes involved in a murder and stolen paintings. [British title: *The Doctor's Gamble*].

423. Crime Doctor's Man Hunt (10/24/46) B&W—64 mins. (Crime-Mystery). DIR: William Castle. PRO: Rudolph C. Flothow. SP: Leigh Brackett. Story by Eric Taylor. Based on the CBS radio program *Crime Doctor* by Max Marcin. CAST: Warner Baxter, Ellen Drew, William Frawley, Claire Carleton, Frank Sully, Bernard Nedell, Jack Lee, Francis Pierlot, Myron Healey, Olin Howlin, Ivan Triesault, Paul E. Burns, Mary Newton, Leon Lenoir.

When a World War II vet is murdered by two hoods, and the hoods are murdered by a mysterious woman (Drew), Dr. Ordway (Baxter) sets out to solve the mystery.

424. Crime Doctor's Strangest Case (12/9/43) B&W—68 mins. (Crime-Mystery). *DIR:* Eugene J. Forde. *PRO:* Rudolph C. Flothow. *SP:* Eric Taylor. Based on the CBS radio program *Crime Doctor* by Max Marcin. *CAST:* Warner Baxter, Lynn Merrick, Lloyd Bridges, Rose Hobart, Barton MacLane, Virginia Brissac, Gloria Dickson, Reginald Denny, Sam Flint, Jerome Cowan, Constance Worth, Thomas Jackson, George Lynn.

Dr. Ordway (Baxter) is called upon to solve the murder of a realty operator and prove the innocence of his business partner (Bridges). [British title: *The Strangest Case*].

The Crime Doctor's Vacation *see* **The Millerson Case**

425. Crime Doctor's Warning (9/27/45) B&W—69 mins. (Crime-Mystery). *DIR:* William Castle. *PRO:* Rudolph C. Flothow. *SP:* Eric Taylor. Based on the CBS radio program *Crime Doctor* by Max Marcin. *CAST:* Warner Baxter, Dusty Anderson, John Litel, Coulter Irwin, Miles Mander, John Abbott, Eduardo Ciannelli, Alma Kruger, J. M. Kerrigan, Franco Corsaro.

When several artist models are found murdered, Dr. Ordway (Baxter) sets out to help a young artist (Irwin) clear himself of the murders. [British title: *The Doctor's Warning*].

426. Crime of Helen Stanley (7/3/34) B&W—58 mins. (Mystery). *DIR:* D. Ross Lederman. *PRO:* Irving Briskin. *SP:* Harold Shumate. Story by Charles R. Condon. *CAST:* Ralph Bellamy, Shirley Grey, Gail Patrick, Kane Richmond, Bradley Page, Vincent Sherman, Clifford Jones, Arthur Rankin, Lucien Prival, Ward Bond, Helen Eby-Rock.

Inspector Trent (Bellamy) is called in to solve the murder of an actress at a film studio.

427. Crime Takes a Holiday (5/9/38) B&W—59 mins. (Crime). *DIR:* Lewis D. Collins. *PRO:* Larry Darmour. *SP:* Jefferson Parker, Henry Altimus, Charles Logue. Story by Henry Altimus. *CAST:* Jack Holt, Marcia Ralston, Paul Fix, Arthur Hohl, Thomas Jackson, John Wray, Douglass Dumbrille, Russell Hopton, William Pawley, Harry Woods, Joseph Crehan.

A district attorney (Holt) sets out to break up the mob when he is urged into politics.

Criminal Cargo *see* **Outside the Three-Mile Limit**

428. The Criminal Code (1/4/31) B&W—96 mins. (Prison-Drama). *DIR:* Howard Hawks. *PRO:* Harry Cohn. *SP:* Fred Niblo, Jr., Seton I. Miller. Based on the play by Martin Flavin. *CAST:* Walter Huston, Phillips Holmes, Constance Cummings, Mary Doran, Boris Karloff, DeWitt Jennings, John Sheehan, Otto Hoffman, Clark Marshall, Arthur Hoyt, Ethel Wales, Lee Phelps, Paul Porcasi, Hugh Walker.

A district attorney (Huston) is made warden of a prison and, once there, tries to befriend the man he had convicted (Holmes). When an inmate is murdered the man remains true to the criminal code by refusing to tell who did it. *NOTES:* Remade by Columbia in 1938 as *Penitentiary* and in 1950 as *Convicted*.

429. Criminal Lawyer (8/24/51) B&W—73 mins. (Drama). *DIR:* Seymour Friedman. *PRO:* Rudolph C. Flothow. *SP:* Harold R. Greene. *CAST:* Pat O'Brien, Jane Wyatt, Carl Benton Reid, Mary Castle, Robert Shayne, Mike Mazurki, Jerome Cowan, Marvin Kaplan, Douglas Fowley, Mickey Knox, Louis Jean Heydt, Wallis Clark, Grandon Rhodes, Darryl Hickman.

An attorney (O'Brien), who has been buying judges and juries, takes to the bottle when he is refused endorsement by the bar association; he sobers up long enough to defend a friend accused of murder.

430. Criminals of the Air (11/1/37) B&W—61 mins. (Crime). *DIR:* C. C. Coleman, Jr. *PRO:* Wallace MacDonald. *SP:* Owen Francis. Story by Jack Cooper. *CAST:* Rosalind Keith, Charles Quigley, Rita Hayworth, John Gallaudet, Marc Lawrence, Patricia Farr, John Hamilton, Ralph Byrd, Walter Soderling, Russell Hicks, John Tyrrell, Lester Dorr, Frank Sully, Robert Fiske, Sam Flint, Eddie Fetherstone, Martha Tibbetts, Howard Hickman, Lucille Lund, Crawford Weaver, Jay Eaton, Sammy Blum, Dick Botiller, Matty Kemp, Herbert Heywood, Ruth Hilliard.

A detective (Quigley) and newspaper woman (Keith) go south of the border to expose a smuggling operation.

431. The Crimson Blade (3/64) Technicolor/Scope—82 mins. (Historical-Drama). *DIR/SP:* John Gilling. *PRO:* Anthony Nelson-Keys. A Hammer Production. *CAST:* Lionel Jeffries, Oliver Reed, Jack Hedley, June Thorburn, Duncan Lamont, Susan Farmer, Michael Ripper, Harold Goldblatt, Michael Byrne, John Stewart, John Harvey, Charles Houston.

During Cromwell's struggle for power in the 17th century, two young people (Reed, Thorburn), on opposite sides of the struggle, fall in love. [British title: *The Scarlet Blade*].

432. The Crimson Kimono (10/59) B&W—81 mins. (Crime). *DIR/PRO/SP:* Samuel Fuller. A Glove Enterprises Production. *CAST:* Victoria Shaw, Glenn Corbett, James Shigeta, Anna Lee, Paul Dubov, Neyle Morrow, Jaclynne Greene, Gloria Pall, Barbara Hayden, Walter Burke.

Two detectives (Corbett, Shigeta) set out to solve the murder of a stripper in the Little Tokyo section of Los Angeles.

433. Cripple Creek (7/1/52) Technicolor—78 mins. (Western). *DIR:* Ray Nazarro. *PRO:* Edward Small. *SP:* Richard Schayer. A Resolute Production. *CAST:* George Montgomery, Karin Booth, Jerome Courtland, William Bishop, Richard Egan, Don Porter, John Dehner, Roy Roberts, George Cleveland, Byron Foulger, Zon Murray, Harry Cording, Chris Alcaide, Robert Armstrong, Robert Bice, Grandon Rhodes, Peter Brocco, Cliff Clark.

Two government agents (Montgomery, Courtland) go undercover to stop a gold smuggling operation.

434. Cromwell (10/70) Technicolor/Panavision—140 mins. (Historical-Drama). *DIR:* Ken Hughes. *PRO:* Irving Allen. *SP:* Ken Hughes, Ronald Harwood. *CAST:* Richard Harris, Alec Guinness, Robert Morley, Dorothy Tutin, Frank Finlay, Timothy Dalton, Patrick Wymark, Patrick Magee, Nigel Stock, Charles Gray, Michael Goodliffe, Anna Cropper, Geoffrey Keen, Richard Cornish, Jack Gwillim, Patrick Holt, Anthony May, Ian McCulloch, Robin Stewart, Zena Walker, Douglas Wilmer, Anthony Kemp, George Merritt.

Cromwell (Harris) decides to rid England of the tyrannical rule of Charles I (Guinness), and thereby causes a Civil War.

435. The Crooked Web (12/55) B&W—77 mins. (Drama). *DIR:*Nathan Hertz. *PRO:* Sam Katzman. *SP:* Lou Breslow. A Clover Production. *CAST:* Frank Lovejoy, Mari Blanchard, Richard Denning, John Mylong, Harry Lauter, Steven Ritch, Louis Merrill, Roy Gordon, John Hart, Richard Emory, Van Des Autels, George Cezar.

Two government agents (Blanchard, Denning) are hired to bring an ex-GI (Lovejoy) back to Germany to face a murder charge.

436. Crossroads (3/86) Technicolor/Panavision—98 mins. (Drama). DIR: Walter Hill. PRO: Mark Carliner. SP: John Fusco. A Columbia-Delphi IV Production. CAST: Ralph Macchio, Joe Seneca, Jami Gertz, Joe Morton, Robert Judd, Steve Vai, Dennis Lipscomb, Tim Russ, Harry Carey, Jr.

A young musician (Macchio) tracks down a legendary blues singer (Seneca) and agrees to help him back to his Mississippi home in exchange for a legendary lost song.

437. Cruisin' Down the River (7/23/53) Technicolor—79 mins. (Musical). DIR: Richard Quine. PRO: Jonie Taps. SP: Blake Edwards, Richard Quine. CAST: Dick Haymes, Audrey Totter, Billy Daniels, Cecil Kellaway, Connie Russell, Douglas Fowley, Larry Blake, Johnny Downs, Benny Payne, Byron Foulger, Dick Crockett, The Bell Sisters.

A New York crooner (Haymes) inherits a riverboat and turns it into a floating nightclub.

438. Cruz Diablo (The Devil's Cross) (4/6/35) B&W—??? mins. (Romance-Adventure). DIR: Fernando de Fuentes. PRO: Paul H. Bush. CAST: Lupita Gallardo, Ramon Pereda, Matilde Brillas, Juan Jose Martinez-Casado, Rosita Arriaga, Julian Soler, Vicente Orona, Paco Martinez, Manuel Tames, Emilio Fernandez.

In seventeenth century Mexico, a mysterious figure, believed in league with the devil, puts a cross on the foreheads of his enemies with his sword. NOTES: Released to Spanish language theaters.

439. Cry for Happy (3/61) Eastman Color/Scope—110 mins. (Romance-Comedy). DIR: George Marshall. PRO: William Goetz. SP: Irving Brecher. Based on the book by George Campbell. CAST: Glenn Ford, Donald O'Conner, Miiko Taka, James Shigeta, Miyoshi Umeki, Howard St. John, Joe Flynn, Chet Douglas, Nancy Kovack, Ted Knight, Bob Quinn, Harriet E. MacGibbon, Harlan Warde.

Four Navy men (Ford, O'Conner, Flynn, Douglas) hole up in a geisha house and turn it into an orphanage. NOTES: A loose remake of the 1956 M-G-M feature *The Teahouse of the August Moon.*

440. Cry of the Werewolf (8/17/44) B&W—63 mins. (Horror). DIR: Henry Levin. PRO: Wallace MacDonald. SP: Griffin Jay, Charles O'Neal. CAST: Nina Foch, Stephen Crane, Osa Massen, Blanche Yurka, Fred Graff, Ivan Triesault, Barton MacLane, John Abbott, John Tyrrell, Robert Williams, Fritz Leiber, Milton Parsons.

A young girl (Foch) inherits the crown as Queen of the Gypsies, and also inherits the werewolf curse when she learns her mother was one.

441. Curse of the Demon (7/58) B&W—95 mins. (Horror). DIR: Jacques Tourneur. PRO: Hal E. Chester. SP: Hal E. Chester, Charles Bennett. Based on *Casting the Runes* by Montague R. James. A Sabre Film Productions Limited Production. CAST: Dana Andrews, Peggy Cummins, Niall MacGinnis, Maurice Denham, Athene Seyler, Liam Redmond, Reginald Beckwith, Ewan Roberts, Percy Herbert, Peter Elliott, Richard Leech, Janet Barrow.

A psychologist (Andrews) sets out to expose an occultist (MacGinnis) as the leader of a devil cult. NOTES: Originally released in the U.S. at a running time of 82 mins. [British title: *Night of the Demon*].

442. The Curse of the Mummy's Tomb (2/65) Technicolor/Scope—80 mins. (Horror). DIR/PRO: Michael Carreras. SP: Henry Younger. A Hammer-Swallow Production. *CAST:* Terence Morgan, Ronald Howard, Fred Clark, Jeanne Roland, George Pastell, Jack Gwillim, John Paul, Michael Ripper, Dickie Owen, Harold Goodwin.

An Egyptian mummy is brought back to England and comes to life, killing members of the expedition that unearthed it.

The Custer Massacre *see* **The Great Sioux Massacre**

443. Customs Agent (5/18/50) B&W—71 mins. (Crime). *DIR:* Seymour Friedman. *PRO:* Rudolph C. Flothow. *SP:* Russell S. Hughes, Malcolm Stuart Boylan. Story by Hal Smith. *CAST:* William Eythe, Marjorie Reynolds, Griff Barnett, Howard St. John, Jim Backus, Robert Shayne, Denver Pyle, John Doucette, Harlan Warde, James Fairfax, Clark Howat, Marya Marco, Guy Kingsford, William "Bill" Phillips.

A customs agent (Eythe) goes undercover to stop the flow of drugs into the U.S. from China.

444. Cyclone Fury (8/19/51) B&W—54 mins. (Western). *DIR:* Ray Nazarro. *PRO:* Colbert Clark. *SP:* Barry Shipman, Ed Earl Repp. *CAST:* Charles Starrett, Fred F. Sears, Smiley Burnette, Clayton Moore, Bob Wilke, George Chesebro, Frank O'Conner, Louis Lettieri, Merle Travis and His Bronco Busters.

The Durango Kid (Starrett) saves a young Indian boy (Lettieri) from being murdered and having his ranch and wild horse herd stolen from him.

445. Cyclone Prairie Rangers (11/9/44) B&W—56 mins. (Western). *DIR:* Benjamin Kline. *PRO:* Jack Fier. *SP:* Elizabeth Beecher. *CAST:* Charles Starrett, Constance Worth, Dub Taylor, Jimmy Davis, Foy Willing, I. Stanford Jolley, Robert Fiske, Clancy Cooper, Edmund Cobb, Ray Bennett,

Forrest Taylor, John Tyrrell, Ted Mapes, Eddie Phillips, Paul Zaremba, Jimmy Wakely and His Saddle Pals.

A drifter (Starrett) and his sidekick (Taylor) come to the aid of a woman rancher (Worth) whose herd is being rustled by outlaws.

446. Dad's Army (9/71) Technicolor—95 mins. (Comedy). *DIR:* Norman Cohen. *PRO:* John R. Sloan. *SP:* Jimmy Perry, David Croft. Based on the BBC television series of the same name. *CAST:* Arthur Lowe, John Le Mesurier, Clive Dunn, John Laurie, Arnold Ridley, Ian Lavender, Liz Fraser, Bernard Archard, Derek Newark, Bill Pertwee, Frank Williams, Edward Sinclair.

The elderly Home Guard protect the shores of England during World War II, and wind up capturing three German aviators.

447. Damn the Defiant! (9/62) Eastman Color/Scope—101 mins. (War). *DIR:* Lewis Gilbert. *PRO:* John Brabourne. *SP:* Edmund H. North, Nigel Kneale. Based on *Mutiny* by Frank Tilsley. A GW Films Limited Production. *CAST:* Alec Guinness, Dirk Bogarde, Maurice Denham, Nigel Stock, Richard Carpenter, Peter Gill, David Robinson, Robin Stewart, Ray Brooks, Peter Greenspan, Anthony Quayle, Tom Bell, Murray Melvin, Victor Maddern.

During the Napoleonic war, mutiny erupts on a warship when a captain (Guinness) is unaware of the brutal treatment of his men by his lieutenant (Bogarde). [British title: *H.M.S. Defiant*].

Dan Matthews *see* **The Calling of Dan Matthews**

448. Dancing in Manhattan (2/1/45) B&W—60 mins. (Comedy). *DIR:* Henry Levin. *PRO:* Wallace MacDonald. *SP:* Erna Lazarus. *CAST:*

Fred Brady, Jeff Donnell, William Wright, Ann Savage, Cy Kendall, Howard Freeman, Eddie Kane, Sally Bliss, Adelle Roberts, Jean Stevens, George McKay, Dorothy Vaughn.

A truck driver (Brady) finds a blackmailer's payoff, and rather than return it, decides to spend it with his girl (Donnell).

449. A Dandy in Aspic (4/68) Technicolor/Panavision—107 mins. (Drama). *DIR/PRO:* Anthony Mann. *SP:* Derek Marlowe. Based on the book by Derek Marlowe. *CAST:* Laurence Harvey, Tom Courtenay, Mia Farrow, Lionel Stander, Harry Andrews, Peter Cook, Per Oscarsson, Barbara Murray, Norman Bird, Michael Trubshawe, Richard O'Sullivan, Calvin Lockhart, Geoffrey Bayldon, Michael Pratt, Arthur Hewlett, Paulene Stone, James Cossins, Geoffrey Denton.

A Russian agent (Harvey), posing as a British agent, is given the assignment to kill his counterpart. *NOTES:* Director Anthony Mann died during filming, and the directorial duties were taken over by Harvey.

450. The Danger Signal (7/1/25) B&W—56 mins. (Drama). *DIR:* Erle C. Kenton. *PRO:* Harry Cohn. *SP:* Douglas Z. Doty. *CAST:* Jane Novak, Dorothy Revier, Robert Edeson, Gaston Glass, Robert Gordon.

Two brothers (Glass, Gordon), separated as youngsters, grow up to love the same girl (Revier).

451. A Dangerous Adventure (7/22/37) B&W—58 mins. (Drama). *DIR:* D. Ross Lederman. *PRO:* Wallace MacDonald. *SP:* John Rathmell, Owen Francis. Story by Owen Francis. *CAST:* Don Terry, Rosalind Keith, Nana Bryant, John Gallaudet, Frank C. Wilson, Marc Lawrence, Russell Hicks, Joe Sawyer.

An heiress (Keith) inherits a steel mill and tries to make a go of it with the help of one of the steel workers (Terry).

452. A Dangerous Affair (9/30/31) B&W—75 mins. (Mystery-Comedy). *DIR:* Edward Sedgwick. *PRO:* Harry Cohn. *SP:* Howard J. Green. *CAST:* Jack Holt, Ralph Graves, Sally Blane, Susan Fleming, Edward Brophy, William V. Mong, Charles Middleton, Blanche Frederici, DeWitt Jennings, Tyler Brooks, Fred Santley, Sidney Bracey, Esther Muir.

A policeman (Holt) and reporter (Graves), usually at odds with each other, work together to solve the murder of a prominent lawyer.

453. Dangerous Blondes (9/23/43) B&W—81 mins. (Comedy). *DIR:* Leigh Jason. *PRO:* Samuel Bischoff. *SP:* Richard Flournoy, Jack Henley. Story by Kelley Roos. *CAST:* Allyn Joslyn, Evelyn Keyes, Edmund Lowe, Anita Louise, John Hubbard, Ann Savage, William Demarest, Dwight Frye, Frank Craven, Michael Duane, Hobart Cavanaugh, Frank Sully, Lynn Merrick, Stanley Brown, Bess Flowers, Mary Forbes, John Abbott.

A mystery writer (Joslyn) and his wife (Keyes) set out to solve a murder at a fashion studio.

454. Dangerous Business (6/20/46) B&W—59 mins. (Crime). *DIR:* D. Ross Lederman. *PRO:* Ted Richmond. *SP:* Hal Smith. Based on *Corpus Delecti* by Harry J. Essex. *CAST:* Forrest Tucker, Lynn Merrick, Gerald Mohr, Gus Schilling, Shemp Howard, Frank Sully, Cora Witherspoon, Thurston Hall, William Forrest, Matt Willis, Ben Welden.

Two attorneys (Tucker, Mohr) try to prove a utility president innocent of embezzlement charges.

455. Dangerous Crossroads (6/22/33) B&W—62 mins. (Crime). *DIR:*

Lambert Hillyer. *SP:* Lew Levenson. Story by Horace McCoy. *CAST:* Jackie Searle, Diane Sinclair, Chic Sale, Frank Albertson, Preston Foster, Niles Welch, Eddie Kane.

A detective's son (Searle) helps to round up a gang of freight train robbers.

456. Dangerous Intrigue (1/18/36) B&W—59 mins. (Drama). *DIR:* David Selman. *PRO:* Robert North. *SP:* Grace Neville. Story by Harold Shumate. *CAST:* Ralph Bellamy, Gloria Shea, Joan Perry, Fred Kohler, Frederik Vogeding, Edward J. LeSaint, George Billings, Boyd Irwin, Gene Morgan, Stanley Andrews.

A famous surgeon (Bellamy) suffers a case of amnesia, and winds up working as a doctor at a steel mill.

457. Danny Boy (5/84) Technicolor—92 mins. (Drama). *DIR/SP:* Neil Jordan. *PRO:* Barry Blackmore. A Triumph Films Production. *CAST:* Stephen Rea, Veronica Quilligan, Alan Devlin, Peter Caffrey, Honor Heffernan, Ray McAnally, Donal McCann, Marie Kean, Dan Foley, Tony Rohr, Anita Reeves, Michael Lally, Macrea Clarke, Derek Lord, Lise-Ann McLaughlin, Ian McElhinney.

A saxophone player (Rea) witnesses the murder of two innocent people and becomes obsessed with finding the killers and seeking revenge. *NOTES:* Limited theatrical release. Originally released in Ireland in 1982.

458. Danton (9/83) Eastman Color—136 mins. (Biography-Drama). *DIR:* Andrzej Wajda. *PRO:* Margaret Menegoz. *SP:* Jean-Claude Carriere, Andrzej Wajda, Agnieszka Holland, Boleslaw Michalek, Jacek Gasiorowski. Based on *The Danton Affair* by Stanislawa Przybyszewska. A Gaumont-Triumph Films Production. *CAST:* Gerard Depardieu, Wojciech Pszoniak, Anne Alvaro, Roland Blanche,

Patrice Chereau, Emmanuelle Debever, Boguslaw Linda, Stephane Jobert, Ronald Guttmann, Gerard Hardy, Angela Winkler, Alain Mace, Bernard Maitre, Serge Merlin.

In 1793, Danton (Depardieu) returns to France to battle Robespierre (Pszoniak) over his decision to execute the citizens en masse. *NOTES:* Limited theatrical release; in French with English subtitles.

459. Daring Danger (7/27/32) B&W—57 mins. (Western). *DIR:* D. Ross Lederman. *PRO:* Irving Briskin. *SP:* Michael Trevelyan. Based on a story by William Colt MacDonald. *CAST:* Tim McCoy, Alberta Vaughn, Wallace MacDonald, Robert Ellis, Bobby Nelson, Edward J. LeSaint, Max Davidson, Richard Alexander, Vernon Dent, Edmund Cobb, Murdock McQuarrie.

A cowboy (McCoy) goes after an outlaw (Alexander) who beat him up, and learns that he is with a group of rustlers, so he goes after the rustlers also.

460. The Daring Young Man (10/8/42) B&W—73 mins. (Comedy). *DIR:* Frank R. Strayer. *PRO:* Robert Sparks. *SP:* Karen DeWolf, Connie Lee. *CAST:* Joe E. Brown, Marguerite Chapman, William Wright, Claire Dodd, Lloyd Bridges, Don Douglas, Robert Middlemass, Arthur Lake, Minerva Urecal, Irving Bacon, Philip Van Zandt, Danny Mummert, Carl Stockdale, Robert Emmett Keane.

Rejected by the draft, a man (Brown) becomes a hero when he rounds up a Nazi spy ring in New York.

461. The Dark Past (1/11/49) B&W—75 mins. (Crime). *DIR:* Rudolph Mate. *PRO:* Buddy Adler. *SP:* Philip MacDonald, Michael Blankfort, Albert Duffy. Adapted by Malvin Wald, Oscar Saul. Based on the play *Blind Alley* by James Warwick. *CAST:* William Holden, Lee J. Cobb, Nina Foch, Adele Jergens, Stephen Dunne, Lois Maxwell, Barry Kroeger, Steven Geray, Wilton Graff, Robert Osterloh, Kathryn Card, Bobby Hyatt, Ellen Corby, Harry Harvey.

A psychiatrist (Cobb) probes the sub-conscious mind of an escaped killer (Holden) hiding out in his home. *NOTES:* A remake of the 1939 Columbia film *Blind Alley*.

462. Das Boot (The Boat) (2/82) Eastman Color—150 mins. (War-Drama). *DIR/SP:* Wolfgang Petersen. *PRO:* Gunter Rohrbach, Michael Bittins. Based on the book by Lothar-Gunther Buchheim. A Bavaria Atelier Production. *CAST:* Jurgen Prochnow, Herbert Gronemeyer, Klaus Wennemann, Hubertus Bengsch, Martin Semmelrogge, Bernd Tauber, Erwin Leder, Martin May, Heinz Honig, Jan Fedder, Ralph Richter.

A German commander (Prochnow) commands a U-boat during the Second World War.

463. David Harding, Counterspy (5/22/50) B&W—70 mins. (Spy-Drama). *DIR:* Ray Nazarro. *PRO:* Milton Feldman. *SP:* Clint Johnson, Tom Reed. Based on the *Counterspy* radio program created by Phillips H. Lord. *CAST:* Willard Parker, Audrey Long, Howard St. John, Raymond Greenleaf, Harlan Warde, Alex Gerry, Fred F. Sears, John Dehner, Anthony Jochim, Jock Mahoney, John Pickard, Steve Darrell, Jimmy Lloyd, Charles Quigley, Allen Mathews.

David Harding (St. John) and a naval officer (Parker) investigate the murder of a torpedo plant manager.

464. Dawn (6/3/28) B&W—75 mins. (Historical-Drama). *DIR/PRO:* Herbert Wilcox. *SP:* Herbert Wilcox, Robert J. Cullen. Based on the play by Reginald Berkeley. A British Domin-

ions Production. *CAST:* Sybil Thorndike, Marie Ault, Mary Brough, Ada Bodart, Dacia Deane, Haddon Mason, Mickey Brantford, Cecil Barry, Frank Perfitt, Edward O'Neill, Maurice Braddell, Griffith Humphreys.

In 1914 Brussels, nurse Edith Cavell (Thorndike) helps British military prisoners escape to England before she is caught by the Germans and executed.

465. The Dawn Trail (11/23/30) B&W—60 mins. (Western). *DIR:* Christy Cabanne. *PRO:* Harry Cohn. *SP:* John Thomas Neville. Story by Forrest Sheldon. A Beverly Production. *CAST:* Buck Jones, Vester Pegg, Miriam Seegar, Charles Brinley, Charles Morton, Slim Whitaker, Charles King, Inez Gomez, Hank Mann, Robert Fleming, Robert Burns, Buck Conners, Erville Alderson, Edward J. LeSaint, Jack Curtis, Violet Axzelle.

A sheriff (Jones) tries to bring peace between the cattlemen and sheepherders.

466. A Day in the Death of Joe Egg (6/72) Eastman Color—106 mins. (Comedy-Drama). *DIR:* Peter Medak. *PRO:* David Deutsch. *SP:* Peter Nichols. Based on the play by Peter Nichols. A Domino Production. *CAST:* Alan Bates, Janet Suzman, Peter Bowles, Sheila Gish, Joan Hickson, Elizabeth Robillard, Murray Melvin, Fanny Carby, Constance Chapman, Elizabeth Tyrell.

A teacher (Bates) and his wife (Suzman) become frustrated with their inability to cope with their spastic daughter (Robillard).

Day of the Landgrabbers *see* **Land Raiders**

467. Dead Heat on a Merry-Go-Round (11/66) Eastman Color—107 mins. (Crime-Comedy). *DIR/SP:* Bernard Girard. *PRO:* Carter De Haven III. *CAST:* James Coburn, Camilla Sparv, Aldo Ray, Nina Wayne, Robert Webber, Rose-Marie, Todd Armstrong, James Westerfield, Ben Astar, Marian Moses, Michael Strong, Severn Darden, Philip Pine, Simon Scott, Lawrence Mann, Roy Glenn, Tyler McVey, Alex Rodine.

After his release from prison, a con artist (Coburn) gets back to work planning an airport robbery that will occur simultaneously with the arrival of a Russian dignitary.

468. Dead Reckoning (1/2/47) B&W—100 mins. (Crime-Mystery). *DIR:* John Cromwell. *PRO:* Sidney Biddell. *SP:* Oliver H. P. Garrett, Steve Fisher, Allen Rivkin. Story by Gerald Drayson Adams, Sidney Biddell. *CAST:* Humphrey Bogart, Lizabeth Scott, Morris Carnovsky, Charles Cane, William Prince, Marvin Miller, Wallace Ford, James Bell, George Chandler, William Forrest, Ruby Dandridge, Syd Saylor, George Eldredge, Joseph Crehan, Gary Owen, Stymie Beard, Ray Teal, Charles Hamilton, Robert Ryan, Grady Sutton, Byron Foulger, Wilton Graff.

A war veteran (Bogart) gets mixed up in conspiracy and murder when he tries to find his missing friend (Prince).

469. The Deadline (10/14/31) B&W—64 mins. (Western). *DIR/SP:* Lambert Hillyer. *PRO:* Irving Briskin. *CAST:* Buck Jones, Knute Erickson, Loretta Sayers, George Ernest, Robert Ellis, Harry Todd, Ed Brady, Jack Curtis, Raymond Nye, James Farley, Edward J. LeSaint.

Paroled from prison for a killing he didn't commit, a man (Jones) returns home and is ostracized by the townspeople; he eventually finds the killer and foils a bank robbery.

470. The Deadly Affair (2/67) Technicolor—107 mins. (Spy-Drama).

DIR/PRO: Sidney Lumet. *SP:* Paul Dehn. Based on *Call for the Dead* by John Le Carre. *CAST:* James Mason, Simone Signoret, Maximilian Schell, Harriet Andersson, Harry Andrews, Kenneth Haigh, Lynn Redgrave, Roy Kinnear, Max Adrian, Robert Flemying, Corin Redgrave, Kenneth Ives, Denis Shaw, Sheraton Blount, David Warner, Michael Bryant.

A British agent (Mason) uncovers a spy ring when he tries to learn the reason why a foreign office official (Flemying) committed suicide.

471. Death Flies East (2/27/35) B&W—65 mins. (Mystery). *DIR:* Philip E. Rosen. *PRO:* Sid Rogell. *SP:* Albert DeMond, Fred Niblo, Jr. Story by Philip Wylie. *CAST:* Conrad Nagel, Florence Rice, Raymond Walburn, Geneva Mitchell, Robert Allen, Oscar Apfel, Mike Morita, Purnell Pratt, Irene Franklin, George Irving, Adrian Rosley, George "Gabby" Hayes.

On a transcontinental flight from California to New York, a nurse (Rice) tries to clear herself of murder and robbery with the help of a professor (Nagel).

472. Death Goes North (3/1/39) B&W—56 mins. (Mystery). *DIR:* Frank McDonald. *PRO:* Kenneth J. Bishop. *SP:* Edward R. Austin. A Warwick Production. *CAST:* Edgar Edwards, Sheila Bromley, Dorothy Bradshaw, Jameson Thomas, Walter Byron, Arthur Kerr, James McGrath, Vivian Combe, Reginald Hincks, "Rin-Tin-Tin, Jr.," the dog.

A Mountie (Edwards) comes to the rescue of a lumber heiress (Bromley) when it is learned that her uncle was murdered and an imposter (Thomas) has taken his place.

473. Death of a Salesman (12/10/51) B&W—115 mins. (Drama). *DIR:* Laslo Benedek. *PRO:* Stanley Kramer. *SP:* Stanley Roberts. Based on the play by Arthur Miller. A Stanley Kramer Production. CAST: Frederic March, Mildred Dunnock, Kevin McCarthy, Cameron Mitchell, Howard Smith, Royal Beal, Don Keefer, Jesse White, Claire Carleton, David Alpert, Elizabeth Fraser, Patricia Walker.

An aging traveling salesman (March) ponders the reasons for his failure as a businessman and as a family man.

474. The Deceiver (11/29/31) B&W—66 mins. (Mystery). DIR: Louis King. PRO: Harry Cohn. SP: Charles Logue, Jack Cunningham, Jo Swerling. Based on Unwanted by Bella Muni and Abem Finkel. CAST: Lloyd Hughes, Dorothy Sebastian, Ian Keith, Natalie Moorhead, Richard Tucker, George Byron, Greta Granstedt, Murray Kinnell, DeWitt Jennings, Allan Garcia, Harvey Clark, Sidney Bracey, Frank Halliday, Colin Campbell, Nick Copeland.

Police are called in when a noted Shakespearian actor (Keith) is found dead. NOTES: John Wayne played an un-billed bit part as the corpse.

475. Deception (1/10/33) B&W—65 mins. (Crime-Sports). DIR: Lewis Seiler. PRO: Bryan Foy. SP: Harold Tarshis. Story by Nat Pendleton. CAST: Leo Carrillo, Dickie Moore, Nat Pendleton, Thelma Todd, Barbara Weeks, Frank Sheridan, Henry Armetta, Hans Steinke.

When a professional wrestler (Pendleton) realizes he has been used by his manager (Carrillo), he decides to turn the tables. NOTES: Nat Pendleton won an Olympic medal in the 1922 Olympics for wrestling.

476. Decision at Sundown (11/10/57) Technicolor—77 mins. (Western). DIR: Budd Boetticher. PRO: Harry Joe Brown, Randolph Scott. SP: Charles Lang, Jr. Story by Vernon L. Flaharty. A Scott-Brown Production. CAST: Randolph Scott, Karen Steele,

John Carroll, Valerie French, John Archer, Noah Beery, Jr., Andrew Duggan, John Litel, Ray Teal, Vaughn Taylor, Richard Deacon, H. M. Wynant, Guy Wilkerson, James Westerfield.

A gunman (Scott) tracks down the man responsible (Carroll) for his wife's suicide.

477. The Deep (6/77) Eastman Color—123 mins. (Crime-Adventure). DIR: Peter Yates. PRO: Peter Guber. SP: Peter Benchley, Tracy Keenan Wynn. Based on the book by Peter Benchley. A Casablanca Filmworks Production. CAST: Robert Shaw, Jacqueline Bisset, Nick Nolte, Louis Gossett, Jr., Eli Wallach, Robert Tessier, Dick Anthony Williams, Earl Maynard, Bob Minor, Peter Benchley, Peter Wallach, Colin Shaw.

A young couple (Bisset, Nolte), vacationing in Bermuda, become involved in intrigue and terror when they locate a cache of drugs on a sunken ship.

478. The Defense Rests (8/15/34) B&W—70 mins. (Drama). DIR: Lambert Hillyer. PRO: Robert North. SP: Jo Swerling. CAST: Jack Holt, Jean Arthur, Harold Huber, Shirley Grey, Arthur Hohl, Nat Pendleton, Raymond Hatton, John Wray, Raymond Walburn, Robert Glecker, Sarah Padden, Donald Meek, Vivian Oakland, Selmer Jackson, J. Carrol Naish, Samuel S. Hinds.

A lawyer (Arthur) wants to expose her boss (Holt), a legal wizard, because of his questionable courtroom tactics.

479. Demonstrator (7/71) Eastman Color—112 mins. (Drama). DIR: Warwick Freeman. PRO: James Fishburn, David Brice. SP: Kit Denton. Story by Elizabeth Campbell, Don Campbell. A Freeburn-Fishburn International Production. CAST: Joe James, Irene Inescort, Gerard Maguire, Wendy Lingham, Kenneth Tsang, Michael Long, Harold Hopkins, Elizabeth Hall, Kerry Dwyer, John Warwick, Slim Da Gray, Stewart Ginn.

A Minister of Defense (James) tries to rally the Asian nations to ratify a military alliance for mutual protection. NOTES: Limited theatrical release.

480. The Deputy Drummer (9/35) B&W — 71 mins. (Musical). DIR: Henry W. George. PRO: Ian Sutherland. SP: Reginald Long, Arthur Rigby. A St. Georges Pictures Production. CAST: Lupino Lane, Jean Denis, Kathleen Kelly, Wallace Lupino, Margaret Yarde, Arthur Rigby, Syd Crossley, Reginald Long, Fred Leslie.

A composer (Lane) impersonates an aristocrat in order to crash a party and encounters a gang of jewel thieves at work.

Dernier Combat, Le *see* **Le Dernier Combat**

481. Desert Bloom (4/86) Metrocolor/Panavision — 104 mins. (Drama). DIR/SP: Eugene Corr. PRO: Michael Hausman. Story by Eugene Corr, Linda Remy. A Carson-Sundance Institute-Columbia-Delphi IV Production. CAST: Annabeth Gish, Jon Voight, JoBeth Williams, Ellen Barkin, Desiree Joseph, Jay D. Underwood, Allen Garfield, Dusty Balcerzak, Tressi Loria, Laura Ramussen, William Lang.

Living near the atomic test sites in Nevada, a young girl (Gish) tries to cope with her turbulent home life.

482. The Desert Bride (3/26/28) B&W — 56 mins. (Drama). DIR: Walter Lang. PRO: Harry Cohn. SP: Ewart Adamson. Story by Elmer Harris. CAST: Betty Compson, Allan Forrest, Edward Martindel, Otto Matiesen.

A French spy (Forrest) and his girl (Compson) are captured and tortured by an Arab nationalist (Matiesen), but are finally rescued when French troops storm his fortress and he is killed.

483. The Desert Horseman (7/11/46) B&W — 57 mins. (Western). DIR: Ray Nazarro. PRO: Colbert Clark. SP: Sherman L. Lowe. CAST: Charles Starrett, Adelle Roberts, Smiley Burnette, Richard Bailey, John Merton, George Morgan, Bud Osborne, Tommy Coates, Jack Kirk, Riley Hill, Walt Shrum and His Colorado Hillbillies.

An Army officer (Starrett) is framed for robbery; disguised as the Durango Kid he goes after the outlaws who framed him and clears his name. [British title: *Checkmate*].

484. Desert Vengeance (1/25/31) B&W — 62 mins. (Western). DIR: Louis King. PRO: Sol Lesser. SP: Stuart Anthony. CAST: Buck Jones, Al Smith, Barbara Bedford, Ed Brady, Buck Conners, Robert Ellis, Pee Wee Holmes, Bob Fleming, Slim Whitaker, Joe Girard, Douglas Gilmore, Barney Bearsley.

The leader of an outlaw gang (Jones) kidnaps a swindler's sister (Bedford), takes her to his hideout, and puts her to work to earn her keep.

485. Desert Vigilante (11/8/49) B&W — 56 mins. (Western). DIR: Fred F. Sears. PRO: Colbert Clark. SP: Earle Snell. CAST: Charles Starrett, Peggy Stewart, Smiley Burnette, Tristram Coffin, Paul Campbell, George Chesebro, Ted Mapes, Jack Ingram, I. Stanford Jolley, Mary Newton, Tex Harding, The Georgia Crackers.

The Durango Kid (Starrett) sets out to break up a band of smugglers who are illegally shipping silver bars into the United States from Mexico. NOTES: Fred F. Sears' debut as a film director.

486. Design for Loving (6/62) B&W — 68 mins. (Comedy). DIR: Godfrey Grayson. PRO: John Ingram. SP: Mark Grantham. A Danziger Production. CAST: June Thorburn, Pete

Murray, Soraya Rafat, James Maxwell, June Cunningham, Prudence Hyman, Michael Balfour, Edward Palmer, Humphrey Lestocq, Mary Malcolm.

A fashion executive (Thorburn) hires an artistic beatnik (Rafat) to be her chief designer.

487. The Desperado Trail (10/65) Eastman Color—93 mins. (Western). *DIR:* Harald Reinl. *PRO:* Horst Wendlandt. *SP:* Harald G. Petersson, Joachim Bartsch. Based on *Winnetou, the Red Gentleman* by Karl Friedrich May. A Rialto-Film Philipsen-Jadran Production. *CAST:* Lex Barker, Pierre Brice, Rik Battaglia, Ralf Wolter, Carl Lange, Sophie Hardy.

Winnetou (Brice), framed for the murder of an Apache by a land baron (Battaglia), sacrifices his life to save his friend Shatterhand (Barker) and avert an Indian war. *NOTES:* Although Brice's character was killed off in this film, he was resurrected for future installments of the series.

488. The Desperadoes (3/25/43) Technicolor—85 mins. (Western). *DIR:* Charles Vidor. *PRO:* Harry Joe Brown. *SP:* Robert Carson. Story by Max Brand. *CAST:* Randolph Scott, Claire Trevor, Glenn Ford, Evelyn Keyes, Edgar Buchanan, Guinn "Big Boy" Williams, Joan Woodbury, Slim Whitaker, Glenn Strange, Jack Kinney, Ethan Laidlaw, Raymond Walburn, Francis Ford, Bill Wolfe, Porter Hall, Bernard Nedell, Irving Bacon, Edward Pawley, Chester Clute, Tom Smith, Charles King.

A sheriff (Scott) helps an old friend (Ford), convicted of bank robbery, escape from jail, and together, they set out to bring those responsible to justice. *NOTES:* Columbia's first full-length Technicolor feature.

489. The Desperados (5/69) Technicolor—90 mins. (Western). *DIR:* Henry Levin. *PRO:* Irving Allen.

SP: Walter Brough. Based on a story by Clarke Reynolds. *CAST:* Vince Edwards, Jack Palance, George Maharis, Neville Brand, Sylvia Syms, Christian Roberts, Kate O'Mara, Kenneth Cope, John Paul, Patrick Holt, Christopher Malcolm, John Clarke, Benjamin Edney.

A son (Edwards) breaks with his fanatic father (Palance) and family when they continue to loot and kill after the Civil War is over. He moves to Texas to start a new life and six years later his marauding family arrive in town and a showdown is imminent.

490. A Desperate Chance for Ellery Queen (5/7/42) B&W—70 mins. (Mystery). *DIR:* James Hogan. *PRO:* Larry Darmour. *SP:* Eric Taylor. Based on the radio play *A Good Samaritan* by Ellery Queen (Frederic Dannay, Manfred Lee). *CAST:* William Gargan, Margaret Lindsay, Charley Grapewin, John Litel, James Burke, Lillian Bond, Jack LaRue, Morgan Conway, Noel Madison, Frank M. Thomas, Charlotte Wynters.

Ellery (Gargan) is hired by a banker's wife (Wynters) to locate her missing husband (Litel) and becomes involved in murder. [British title: *A Desperate Chance*].

491. Destroyer (9/2/43) B&W—99 mins. (War-Drama). *DIR:* William A. Seiter. *PRO:* Louis F. Edelman. *SP:* Frank W. Wead, Lewis Meltzer, Borden Chase. Story by Frank W. Wead. *CAST:* Edward G. Robinson, Glenn Ford, Marguerite Chapman, Edgar Buchanan, Leo Gorcey, Regis Toomey, Edward Brophy, Warren Ashe, Craig Woods, Bobby Jordan, Pierre Watkin, Roger Clark, John Merton, Virginia Sale, Lloyd Bridges, Dale Van Sickel, Addison Richards, Dennis Moore, Edmund Cobb, Tristram Coffin, Lester Dorr, Bud Geary, Eddy Waller, Charles McGraw.

A welder (Robinson) re-enlists in the Navy to serve on the ship he helped build, but runs afoul of his men when he drives them too hard; once in battle he shows his true colors and earns the respect of his men.

492. The Detective (10/54) B&W—91 mins. (Comedy-Crime). *DIR:* Robert Hamer. *PRO:* Paul F. Moss, Vivian A. Cox. *SP:* Thelma Schnee, Robert Hamer. Based on the *Father Brown* stories by G. K. Chesterton. A Facet Production. *CAST:* Alec Guinness, Joan Greenwood, Peter Finch, Cecil Parker, Bernard Lee, Sidney James, Gerard Oury, Eugene Deckers, Austin Trevor.

A Catholic priest (Guinness) turns detective to recover a priceless cross when it is stolen in transit from London to Rome. [British title: *Father Brown*].

493. The Devil at 4 O'clock (10/61) Eastman Color—125 mins. (Drama). *DIR:* Mervyn LeRoy. *PRO:* Fred Kohlmar. *SP:* Liam O'Brien. Based on the book by Max Catto. *CAST:* Frank Sinatra, Spencer Tracy, Kerwin Mathews, Jean Pierre Aumont, Gregoire Aslan, Alexander Scourby, Barbara Luna, Cathy Lewis, Bernie Hamilton, Martin Brandt, Lou Merrill, Marcel Dalio, Tom Middleton, Ann Dugan.

A drunken priest (Tracy) and three convicts (Sinatra, Aslan, Hamilton), on a South Seas volcanic island, lead a colony of leper children to safety at the cost of their own lives.

494. The Devil Commands (2/14/41) B&W—65 mins. (Horror). *DIR:* Edward Dmytryk. *PRO:* Wallace MacDonald. *SP:* Robert D. Andrews, Milton Gunzberg. Based on *The Edge of Running Water* by William Sloane. *CAST:* Boris Karloff, Richard Fiske, Amanda Duff, Anne Revere, Ralph Penny, Dorothy Adams, Walter Bald-

win, Kenneth MacDonald, Shirley Warde.

A demented scientist (Karloff) tries to communicate with his dead wife through the use of electricity and stolen corpses.

495. Devil Goddess (10/55) B&W—70 mins. (Jungle-Adventure). *DIR:* Spencer G. Bennet. *PRO:* Sam Katzman. *SP:* George H. Plympton. Story by Dwight V. Babcock. *CAST:* Johnny Weissmuller, Angela Stevens, Selmer Jackson, William Tannen, Ed Hilton, William M. Griffith, Frank Lackteen, Abel Fernandez, Vera M. Francis, George Berkeley.

Weissmuller leads a professor (Jackson) and his daughter (Stevens) through the jungle in search of the professor's associate who has set himself up as a native god.

496. The Devil Is an Empress (12/4/39) B&W—70 mins. (Drama). *DIR/SP:* Jean Dreville. Based on *The Chess Player of Vilna* by H. Dupuy-Mazuel. *CAST:* Conrad Veidt, Francoise Rosay, Micheline Francey, Edmonde Guy, Bernard Lancret, Paul Cambo, Gaston Modot, Jacques Gretillat.

Young lovers (Guy, Francey) escape from the clutches of Catherine II of Russia (Rosay) and her henchman (Veidt). [Original French title: *Le Jouer d'Echecs*].

497. The Devil Is Driving (7/20/37) B&W—69 mins. (Drama). *DIR:* Harry Lachman. *PRO:* William Perlberg. *SP:* Jo Milward, Richard Blake. Story by Lee Loeb, Harold Buchman. *CAST:* Richard Dix, Joan Perry, Nana Bryant, Frank C. Wilson, Ian Wolfe, Elisha Cook, Jr., Henry Kolker, Walter Kingsford, Ann Rutherford, Paul Harvey, John Wray, Charles C. Wilson.

A district attorney (Dix) commits perjury when he defends a friend's son (Cook) on a drunk driving charge.

498. Devil Ship (12/11/47) B&W—61 mins. (Drama). *DIR:* Lew Landers. *PRO:* Martin Mooney. *SP:* Lawrence Edmund Taylor. *CAST:* Richard Lane, Louise Campbell, William Bishop, Damian O'Flynn, Myrna Liles, Anthony Caruso, Anthony Warde, Denver Pyle, William Forrest, Marjorie Wordworth, Joseph Kim, Sam Bernard.

A tuna fisherman (Lane) supplements his income by hauling prisoners to Alcatraz.

499. The Devil-Ship Pirates (5/64) Technicolor/Scope—86 mins. (Drama). *DIR:* Don Sharp. *PRO:* Anthony Nelson-Keys. *SP:* Jimmy Sangster. A Hammer Production. *CAST:* Christopher Lee, John Cairney, Barry Warren, Ernest Clark, Andrew Keir, Duncan Lamont, Michael Ripper, Susan Farmer, Natasha Pyne, Annette Whiteley, Charles Houston, Philip Latham, Harry Locke, Leonard Fenton.

When an English village is attacked by pirates, a sailor (Warren) jumps ship and organizes the villagers in revolt against the pirates' evil rule.

500. The Devil's Henchman (9/15/49) B&W—68 mins. (Crime). *DIR:* Seymour Friedman. *PRO:* Rudolph C. Flothow. *SP:* Eric Taylor. *CAST:* Warner Baxter, Mary Beth Hughes, Mike Mazurki, Peggy Converse, Regis Toomey, Harry Shannon, James Flavin, Julian Rivero, Ken Christy, Al Bridge, William Forrest, Paul Marion, George Lloyd.

A detective (Baxter) disguises himself as a seaman to infiltrate a gang of fur smugglers.

The Devil's Imposter *see* **Pope Joan**

501. The Devil's Mask (5/23/46) B&W—68 mins. (Mystery-Crime). *DIR:* Henry Levin. *PRO:* Wallace

MacDonald. *SP:* Charles O'Neal, Dwight V. Babcock. Based on the radio program *I Love a Mystery* by Carleton E. Morse. *CAST:* Jim Bannon, Anita Louise, Barton Yarborough, Mona Barrie, Michael Duane, Ludwig Donath, Edward Earle, Thomas Jackson, Paul E. Burns, Richard Hale, John Elliott, Frank Mayo.

An explorer's daughter (Louise) hires two detectives (Bannon, Yarborough) to investigate the possibility that a shrunken head with red hair found in a plane crash was that of her father.

502. Devil's Playground (2/16/37) B&W—74 mins. (Adventure-Drama). *DIR:* Erle C. Kenton. *PRO:* Robert North. *SP:* Liam O'Flaherty, Jerome Chodorov, Dalton Trumbo. Story by Norman Springer. *CAST:* Richard Dix, Dolores Del Rio, Chester Morris, George McKay, John Gallaudet, Pierre Watkin, Ward Bond, Don Rowan, Francis McDonald, Stanley Andrews, Gene Morgan, Gary Owen, Edward Hern, Ann Doran, Wesley Hopper.

Two Navy buddies (Dix, Morris) have a falling out over a woman (Del Rio), but when one becomes trapped in a sunken submarine, the other puts his feelings aside and comes to his rescue. *NOTES:* A remake of the 1928 Columbia film *Submarine*.

503. Devil's Rock (3/38) B&W—54 mins. (Drama-Musical). *DIR/PRO:* Germain Gerard Burger. *SP:* Richard Hayward. *CAST:* Richard Hayward, Geraldine Mitchell, Gloria Grainger, Terence Grainger, Nancy Cullen, Charles Fagan, Tom Casement.

A concert play in Ireland finds itself without payment when the box office is held up and the money stolen.

504. Devil's Squadron (5/12/36) B&W—80 mins. (Drama). *DIR:* Erle C. Kenton. *PRO:* Robert North. *SP:* Howard J. Green, Bruce Manning,

Lionel Houser. Story by Richard V. Grace. *CAST:* Richard Dix, Karen Morley, Lloyd Nolan, Shirley Ross, Gene Morgan, Henry Mollison, Gordon Jones, William Stelling, Thurston Hall, Gertrude Green, Boyd Irwin, Cora Sue Collins.

When a girl (Morley) inherits an airplane plant, she decides to close the plant because too many test pilots have died; a test pilot (Dix) makes a successful flight, convincing her to keep the plant open.

505. The Devil's Trail (5/14/42) B&W—61 mins. (Western). *DIR:* Lambert Hillyer. *PRO:* Leon Barsha. *SP:* Philip Ketchum. Based on *The Town in Hell's Backyard* by Robert Lee Johnson. *CAST:* Bill Elliott, Eileen O'Hearn, Tex Ritter, Ruth Ford, Art Mix, Noah Beery, Sr., Frank Mitchell, Joe McGuinn, Edmund Cobb, Bud Osborne, Tristram Coffin, Stanley Brown, Steve Clark, Buck Moulton, Joel Friedkin, Paul Newlan, Sarah Padden.

When Wild Bill Hickok (Elliott) is framed for murder by an outlaw leader (Beery), he joins forces with a Federal Marshal (Ritter) to clear his name and bring the outlaws to justice. [British title: *Rogue's Gallery*].

506. Diamond Head (1/63) Eastman Color/Panavision—107 mins. (Drama). *DIR:* Guy Green. *PRO:* Jerry Bresler. *SP:* Marguerite Roberts. Based on the book by Peter Gilman. *CAST:* Charlton Heston, Yvette Mimieux, George Chakiris, France Nuyen, James Darren, Aline MacMahon, Elizabeth Allen, Vaughn Taylor, Philip Ahn, Harold Fong, Clarence Kim.

A domineering plantation owner in Hawaii (Heston), wishing to keep his blood-lines pure, sets out to ruin his sister's (Mimieux) plans to marry a Hawaiian (Darren), even though he has an Hawaiian mistress (Nuyen).

Diary of a Voyage in the South Pacific *see* **Nude Odyssey**

507. Die! Die! My Darling (5/65) Eastman Color—96 mins. (Horror). *DIR:* Silvio Narizzano. *PRO:* Anthony Hinds. *SP:* Richard Matheson. Based on *Nightmare* by Anne Blaisdell. A Hammer-Seven Arts Production. *CAST:* Tallulah Bankhead, Stefanie Powers, Peter Vaughn, Maurice Kaufmann, Yootha Joyce, Donald Sutherland, Gwendolyn Watts, Robert Dorning, Philip Gilbert, Winifred Dennis, Diana King.

An American girl (Powers) visits the mother (Bankhead) of her dead fiance, and finds herself a prisoner of the mother who is a religious fanatic. *NOTES:* Tallulah Bankhead's last film. [British title: *Fanatic*].

The Dion Brothers *see* **The Gravy Train**

508. Dirigible (4/18/31) B&W—100 mins. (Drama-Adventure). *DIR:* Frank Capra. *PRO:* Harry Cohn. *SP:* Dorothy Howell, Jo Swerling. Story by Frank W. Wead. A Frank Capra Production. *CAST:* Jack Holt, Ralph Graves, Fay Wray, Hobart Bosworth, Roscoe Karns, Clarence Muse, Harold Goodwin, Emmett Corrigan, Alan Roscoe, Selmer Jackson.

A dirigible commander (Holt), in love with his best friend's wife (Wray), volunteers to go to the South Pole to rescue him (Graves) when he crashes and is presumed lost.

509. Dirty Little Billy (11/72) Eastman Color—100 mins. (Western). *DIR:* Stan Dragoti. *PRO:* Jack L. Warner. *SP:* Stan Dragoti, Charles Moss. A WRG-Dragoti Production. *CAST:* Michael J. Pollard, Lee Purcell, Richard Evans, Charles Aidman, Gary Busey, Ronnie Graham, Dick Van Patten, Dran Hamilton, Willard Sage, Josip Elic, Mills Watson, Alex Wilson, Dick Stahl, Cherie Franklin.

An offbeat, violent western, based on the early life of Billy the Kid (Pollard), portraying him as a mentally deficient psychopath; the film ends as Billy is beginning his legendary career.

510. Discontented Husbands (1/1/24) B&W—58 mins. (Drama). DIR: Edward J. LeSaint. PRO: Harry Cohn. SP: Jack Sturmwasser. Story by Evelyn Campbell. A C.B.C. Release. CAST: James Kirkwood, Cleo Madison, Grace Darmond, Arthur Rankin.

An inventor (Kirkwood) encounters domestic problems when his new invention turns him into a wealthy man.

511. Divorce American Style (7/67) Technicolor—109 mins. (Comedy-Satire). DIR: Bud Yorkin. PRO/SP: Norman Lear. Story by Robert Kaufman. A Tandem-National General Production. CAST: Dick Van Dyke, Debbie Reynolds, Jason Robards, Jr., Jean Simmons, Van Johnson, Joe Flynn, Shelley Berman, Martin Gabel, Lee Grant, Pat Collins, Tom Bosley, Emmaline Henry, Dick Gautier, Eileen Brennan, Tim Matthieson, Gary Goetzman, Shelley Morrison.

Concerned friends create problems for a divorced couple (Van Dyke, Reynolds) when they try to get them back together.

512. Do You Know This Voice? (6/64) B&W—80 mins. (Crime-Mystery). DIR: Frank Nesbitt. PRO: Jack Parsons. SP: Neil McCallum. Based on the book by Evelyn Berckman. A Lippert-Parroch-McCallum Production. A British Lion Film. CAST: Dan Duryea, Isa Miranda, Gwen Watford, Alan Edwards, Peter Madden, Shirley Cameron, Barry Warren, Jean Aubrey.

A kidnapper and murderer (Duryea) sets out to kill his neighbor, an Italian widow (Miranda), who, he thinks, knows that he is a killer. NOTES: Although this film was released theatrically to American audiences, it was re-

leased in Britain for television viewing only.

513. Doctor Faustus (2/68) Technicolor—93 mins. (Fantasy). DIR: Richard Burton, Nevill Coghill. PRO: Richard Burton, Richard McWhorter. SP: Nevill Coghill. Adapted from the play by Christopher Marlowe. An Oxford University Screen Production in association with Nassau Films and Venfilms Rome. CAST: Richard Burton, Elizabeth Taylor, Andreas Teuber, Ian Marter, David McIntosh, Richard Carwardine, Jeremy Eccles, Adrian Benjamin.

A medical student (Burton) conjures up Mephistopheles (Teuber) and agrees to sell his soul for a life of decadence.

514. Dr. Strangelove: or How I Learned to Stop Worrying and Love the Bomb (1/64) B&W—102 mins. (Comedy). DIR/PRO: Stanley Kubrick. SP: Stanley Kubrick, Terry Southern, Peter George. Based on Red Alert by Peter George. CAST: Peter Sellers, George C. Scott, Sterling Hayden, Keenan Wynn, Slim Pickens, Peter Bull, Tracy Reed, James Earl Jones, Jack Creley, Frank Berry, Glenn Beck, Shane Rimmer, Paul Tamarin, Gordon Tanner, Robert O'Neil, voice of Vera Lynn.

A mad Air Force general (Hayden) launches an attack on Russia; the President (Sellers) tries to deal with the Russians and his own military; a British colonel (Sellers) tries to deal with the mad general; and a German scientist, Dr. Strangelove (Sellers) suggests the ultimate solution.

515. The Doctor Takes a Wife (6/17/40) B&W—89 mins. (Comedy). DIR: Alexander Hall. PRO: William Perlberg. SP: George Seaton, Ken Englund. Story by Aleen Leslie. CAST: Loretta Young, Ray Milland, Reginald Gardiner, Gail Patrick, Edmund Gwenn, Frank Sully, Gordon Jones, Georges Metaxa, Charles Halton, Chester Clute, Edward Van Sloan, John Wray, Edgar Dearing, Irving Bacon, Don Beddoe, Charles Lane, Edward Gargan, Virginia Sale, Edgar Buchanan, Vernon Dent.

A lady author (Young), who hates marriage and dominating males, and a medical college professor (Milland) pretend to be married as a publicity stunt; they eventually fall in love and do get married.

516. Doctors' Wives (2/71) Eastman Color — 102 mins. (Drama). *DIR*: George Schaefer. *PRO*: M. J. Frankovich. *SP*: Daniel Taradash. Based on the book by Frank G. Slaughter. *CAST*: Dyan Cannon, Richard Crenna, Gene Hackman, Carroll O'Conner, Diana Sands, Rachel Roberts, Janice Rule, Cara Williams, Richard Anderson, Ralph Bellamy, John Colicos, George Gaynes, Marion McCargo.

When the cheating wife (Cannon) of a doctor is murdered, suspicion falls on the medical staff of the hospital.

517. Dodge City Trail (12/1/36) B&W — 62 mins. (Western). *DIR*: C. C. Coleman, Jr. *PRO*: Harry L. Decker. *SP*: Harold Shumate. *CAST*: Charles Starrett, Marion Weldon, Donald Grayson, Russell Hicks, Si Jenks, Al Bridge, Art Mix, Ernie Adams, Lew Meehan, Hank Bell, Jack Rockwell, George Chesebro, Blackie Whiteford.

A cowboy (Starrett) sets out to rescue his future bride (Weldon) from a fake kidnapping arranged by her father (Hicks), the leader of an outlaw gang.

518. $ (Dollars) (12/71) Technicolor — 119 mins. (Crime-Comedy). *DIR/SP*: Richard Brooks. *PRO*: M. J. Frankovich. *CAST*: Warren Beatty, Goldie Hawn, Gert Frobe, Robert Webber, Scott Brady, Arthur Brauss, Robert Stiles, Robert Herron, Wolf-

gang Kieling, Christiane Maybach, Hans Hutter, Monica Stender, Horst Hesslein.

A security expert (Beatty) and his assistant (Hawn) plan to rob the safety deposit boxes of known criminals, in a bank where he has installed the alarm system. [British title: *The Heist*].

519. The Domino Kid (10/57) B&W — 74 mins. (Western). *DIR*: Ray Nazarro. *PRO*: Rory Calhoun, Victor M. Orsatti. *SP*: Kenneth Gamet, Hal Biller. Based on a story by Rory Calhoun. A Rorvic Production. *CAST*: Rory Calhoun, Kristine Miller, Andrew Duggan, Yvette Dugay, Peter Whitney, Eugene Iglesias, James Griffith, Roy Barcroft, Denver Pyle, Ray "Crash" Corrigan, William Christensen, Don Orlando, Robert Burton, Bart Bradley.

An ex-Confederate soldier (Calhoun) seeks revenge against the outlaws who killed his father and stole his cattle.

520. The Donovan Affair (4/11/29) B&W — 83 mins. (Mystery-Comedy). *DIR*: Frank Capra. *PRO*: Harry Cohn. *SP*: Howard J. Green, Dorothy Howell. Based on the play *The Donovan Affair* by Owen Davis. *CAST*: Jack Holt, Dorothy Revier, William Collier, Jr., Agnes Ayres, John Roche, Fred Kelsey, Hank Mann, Wheeler Oakman, Virginia Brown Faire, Ethel Wales, Alphonse Ethier, Edward Hearn, John Wallace.

Inspector Killian (Holt) and his partner (Kelsey) try to find the killer of Jack Donovan (Roche), gambler and ladies' man. *NOTES*: Columbia's first all-talking picture. A silent version was also made for theaters not yet equipped for sound.

521. Don't Gamble with Love (2/28/36) B&W — 65 mins. (Drama). *DIR*: Dudley Murphy. *PRO*: Irving Briskin. *SP*: Lee Loeb, Harold Buchman. *CAST*: Ann Sothern, Bruce

Cabot, Irving Pichel, Ian Keith, Thurston Hall, George McKay, Elisabeth Risdon, Clifford Jones, Franklin Pangborn.

When a gambling house owner (Cabot) is persuaded by his wife (Sothern) to get out of the business, he gets swindled when he invests his money in a legitimate venture.

522. Don't Knock the Rock (1/57) B&W—85 mins. (Musical). *DIR:* Fred F. Sears. *PRO:* Sam Katzman. *SP:* Robert E. Kent, James B. Gordon. A Clover Production. *CAST:* Alan Dale, Patricia Hardy, Fay Baker, Jana Lund, Gail Ganley, Pierre Watkin, George Cisar, Dick Elliott, Alan Freed, Bill Haley, Little Richard, The Treniers, Dave Appell and His Applejacks.

A rock 'n' roller (Dale) comes back to his home town to put on a show, but meets opposition from the local townsfolk. *NOTES:* A sequel to the 1956 Columbia film *Rock Around the Clock*.

523. Don't Knock the Twist (4/62) B&W—86 mins. (Musical). *DIR:* Oscar Rudolph. *PRO:* Sam Katzman. *SP:* James B. Gordon. A Four Leaf Production. *CAST:* Lang Jeffries, Mari Blanchard, Georgine Darcy, Stephen Preston, Barbara Morrison, Nydia Westman, James Chandler, Frank Albertson, Hortense Petra, Elizabeth Harrower, Chubby Checker, Gene Chandler, Vic Dana, Linda Scott, The Carroll Brothers, The Dovells.

A TV producer (Jeffries) decides to put on a special promoting the dance craze, the "Twist."

524. Don't Panic Chaps! (10/59) B&W—85 mins. (War-Comedy). *DIR:* George Pollack. *PRO:* Terry Baird. *SP:* Jack Davies. Based on a story by Michael Corston and Ronald Holroyd. A Hammer-A.C.T. Production. *CAST:* Dennis Price, George Cole, Thorley

Walters, Harry Fowler, Nadja Regin, Nicholas Phipps, Percy Herbert, George Murcell, Gertan Klauber, Terence Alexander, Thomas Foulkes.

British and German observation units, on an Adriatic island, agree to a truce and live comfortably on the island; all goes well until a castaway (Regin) arrives, then fighting begins anew.

525. Don't Raise the Bridge, Lower the River (6/68) Technicolor—99 mins. (Comedy). *DIR:* Jerry Paris. *PRO:* Walter Shenson. *SP:* Max Wilk. Based on the book by Max Wilk. *CAST:* Jerry Lewis, Terry-Thomas, Jacqueline Pearce, Bernard Cribbins, Patricia Routledge, Nicholas Parsons, Michael Bates, Colin Gordon, John Bluthal, Sandra Caron, Margaret Nolan, Pippa Benedict, Harold Goodwin, Al Mancini, John Moore, Jerry Paris, John Barrard.

An American (Lewis), living in England, gets mixed up with a confidence man (Terry-Thomas), and almost loses his wife (Pearce) because of his get-rich-quick schemes.

526. The Doolins of Oklahoma (7/49) B&W—90 mins. (Western). *DIR:* Gordon Douglas. *PRO:* Harry Joe Brown. *SP:* Kenneth Gamet. A Producers Actors Corporation Production. *CAST:* Randolph Scott, Louise Allbritton, George Macready, Virginia Huston, John Ireland, Noah Beery, Jr., Lee Patrick, Jock Mahoney, Dona Drake, Charles Kemper, Robert H. Barrat, Griff Barnett, Frank Fenton, James Kirkwood, Robert Osterloh, Virginia Brissac, John Sheehan.

Bill Doolin (Scott) organizes a new gang and takes to the outlaw trail, once again, when his close friends, the Daltons, are massacred. [British title: *The Great Manhunt*].

Dorado Pass, El *see* **El Dorado Pass**

Feature Films 85

527. **Doughboys in Ireland** (10/
7/43) B&W — 61 mins. (Musical). *DIR:*
Lew Landers. *PRO:* Jack Fier. *SP:*
Howard J. Green, Monte Brice. *CAST:*
Kenny Baker, Jeff Donnell, Lynn Mer-
rick, Guy Bonham, Red Latham,
Wamp Carlson, Robert Mitchum,
Buddy Yarus, Harry Shannon, Dor-
othy Vaughn, Larry Thompson, Syd
Saylor, Herbert Rawlinson, Neil
Regan, Constance Purdy, The Jesters.
A bandleader and vocalist (Baker) is
inducted into the Army and winds up
stationed in Ireland, where he ro-
mances an Irish girl (Donnell).

528. **Down Rio Grande Way** (4/
23/42) B&W — 57 mins. (Western).
DIR: William Berke. *PRO:* Jack Fier.
SP: Paul Franklin. *CAST:* Charles
Starrett, Rose Ann Stevens, Russell
Hayden, Britt Wood, Norman Willis,
Forrest Taylor, Edmund Cobb, Ker-
mit Maynard, Budd Buster, Edward
Piel, Sr., William Desmond, Steve
Clark, Art Mix, John Cason, Davidson
Clark, Joseph Eggenton, Paul Newlan,
Betty Roadman, Jim Corey, Tom
Smith, Frank McCarroll.
Sam Houston (Newlan), wanting to
make sure Texas is admitted to the
Union, sends a couple of Texas Ran-
gers (Starrett, Hayden) to deal with the
anti-statehood faction. [British title:
The Double Punch].

529. **Down to Earth** (3/30/47)
Technicolor — 101 mins. (Musical-
Comedy-Fantasy). *DIR:* Alexander
Hall. *PRO:* Don Hartman. *SP:* Edwin
Blum, Don Hartman. Based on charac-
ters created by Harry Segall in his play
Heaven Can Wait. CAST: Rita Hay-
worth, Larry Parks, Marc Platt, Roland
Culver, James Gleason, Edward Ever-
ett Horton, Adele Jergens, George
Macready, William Frawley, Jean Don-
ahue, Kathleen O'Malley, William
Haade, James Burke, Fred F. Sears,
Lynn Merrick, Lucien Littlefield,

Myron Healey, Cora Witherspoon,
Forbes Murray, Billy Bletcher, Al
Bridge, Eddie Acuff, Jack Norton.
The Greek goddess of dance, Terp-
sichore (Hayworth), comes to earth to
help a Broadway producer (Parks) with
his show. *NOTES:* Remade by Universal Studios in 1980 as *Xanadu.*

530. **Dream One** (1984) Eastman
Color — 97 mins. (Fantasy). *DIR:* Ar-
naud Selignac. *PRO:* John Boorman,
Claude Nedjar. *SP:* Arnaud Selignac,
Jean-Pierre Esquenazi, Telshe Boorman. Based on *Vingt Mille Lieues sous
les Mers* by Jules Verne. An NEF Dif-
fusion-Christel-Films A2-Channel 4
Production. *CAST:* Jason Connery,
Seth Kibel, Mathilda May, Nipsey
Russell, Harvey Keitel, Carole Bouquet, Michel Blanc, Katrine Boorman,
Charley Boorman, Dominique Pinon,
Gaetan Bloom.
A teenage boy (Connery) lets his imagination take him to another planet
where he meets an assortment of
storybook characters. *NOTES:* As of
this writing Columbia, the American
distributor of this film, has chosen
NOT to release it, for whatever reason,
to theaters, cable, or home video.

531. **The Dresser** (11/83) East-
man Color — 118 mins. (Drama). *DIR/
PRO:* Peter Yates. *SP:* Ronald Har-
wood. Based on the play by Ronald
Harwood. A Goldcrest-World Film
Services Production. *CAST:* Albert
Finney, Tom Courtenay, Edward Fox,
Zena Walker, Eileen Atkins, Michael
Gough, Cathryn Harrison, Betty Mars-
den, Guy Manning, Sheila Reid, Lock-
wood West, Donald Eccles, John Sharp.
During World War II, an aging
Shakespearian actor-manager (Finney)
depends on his dresser (Courtenay) for
constant pampering and prodding.
NOTES: Based on the touring life of
actor Donald Wolfit, whose dresser
was Ronald Harwood.

532. The Dreyfus Case (8/30/31) B&W—90 mins. (Historical-Drama). *DIR*: F. W. Kraemer, Milton Rosmer. *PRO*: F. W. Kraemer. *SP*: Reginald Berkeley, Walter Mycroft. Based on the play by Herzog and Rehfisch. A British International Production. *CAST*: Cedric Hardwicke, Beatrix Thomson, Charles Carson, Garry Marsh, Sam Livesey, George Merritt, Henry Caine, George Zucco, Randle Ayrton, George Skillan, Abraham Sofaer, Nigel Barrie, Violet Howard, Reginald Dance, Arthur Hardy, Alexander Sarner, Frederick Leister.

A Jewish French officer, Alfred Dreyfus (Hardwicke), is framed for spying and is defended by Emile Zola (Merritt). [British title: *Dreyfus*].

533. Driftwood (10/15/28) B&W—65 mins. (Drama). *DIR*: Christy Cabanne. *PRO*: Harry Cohn. *SP*: Lillie Hayward. Story by Richard Harding Davis. *CAST*: Don Alvarado, Marceline Day, Alan Roscoe, J. W. Johnston.

An alcoholic beachcomber (Alvarado) meets a woman (Day) on an island, falls in love, and tries to start life anew.

534. Drive a Crooked Road (4/54) B&W—83 mins. (Crime). *DIR*: Richard Quine. *PRO*: Jonie Taps. *SP*: Blake Edwards. Story by James Benson Nablo. Adapted by Richard Quine. *CAST*: Mickey Rooney, Dianne Foster, Kevin McCarthy, Jack Kelly, Harry Landers, Jerry Paris, Paul Picerni, Dick Crockett, Mort Mills, Peggy Maley.

A garage mechanic and race car driver (Rooney) is forced by two gangsters (McCarthy, Kelly) to be their getaway driver because of his ability to handle cars.

535. Drive, He Said (6/71) Metrocolor—90 mins. (Drama). *DIR*: Jack Nicholson. *PRO*: Jack Nicholson, Steve Blauner. *SP*: Jeremy Larner, Jack Nicholson. Based on the book by Jeremy Larner. A BBS Production. *CAST*: Bruce Dern, Karen Black, William Tepper, Michael Margotta, Robert Towne, Mike Warren, June Fairchild, David Ogden Stiers, Henry Jaglom, Cindy Williams, Bill Kenney.

A college basketball star (Tepper) cannot decide whether to turn pro or join the campus radicals, while his best friend (Margotta) pretends to be crazy to get out of the draft. *NOTES*: William Tepper's only film.

536. Drive-In (5/76) Metrocolor/Panavision—96 mins. (Comedy). *DIR*: Rod Amateau. *PRO*: Alex Rose, Tamara Asseyev. *SP*: Bob Peete. *CAST*: Lisa Lemole, Glenn Morshower, Gary Cavagnaro, Billy Milliken, Lee Newsom, Regan Kee, Andy Parks, Trey Wilson, Gordon Hurst, Kent Perkins, Ashley Cox, Louis Zito, Linda Larimer.

The activities of teenagers at a Texas drive-in where a campy disaster movie, "Disaster '76," is showing on screen.

537. Drums of Tahiti (1/54) Technicolor/3-D—73 mins. (Adventure). *DIR*: William Castle. *PRO*: Sam Katzman. *SP*: Robert E. Kent, Douglas Heyes. *CAST*: Dennis O'Keefe, Patricia Medina, Francis L. Sullivan, George Keymas, Sylvia Lewis, Cicely Browne, Raymond Lawrence, Frances Brandt.

An American gunrunner (O'Keefe) supplies arms to the natives of Tahiti in their fight against the French.

538. Drylanders (4/63) B&W/Scope—70 mins. (Drama). *DIR*: Donald Haldane. *PRO*: Peter Jones. *SP*: M. Charles Cohen. A National Film Board of Canada Production. *CAST*: Frances Hyland, James Douglas, Lester Nixon, Mary Savage, William Fruete, Don Francks, Irena Mayeska, William Weintraub.

An ex-soldier (Douglas), back from

the Boer War, decides to move his family from the city to the country and become a wheat farmer. *NOTES:* The first feature film from Canada's Film Board was originally written for TV, but was released to theaters and had a limited theatrical release in the U.S.

Duchess of Broadway *see* **Talk About a Lady**

539. Duel on the Mississippi (10/55) Technicolor—72 mins. (Adventure). *DIR:* William Castle. *PRO:* Sam Katzman. *SP:* Gerald Drayson Adams. A Clover Production. *CAST:* Lex Barker, Patricia Medina, Warren Stevens, Craig Stevens, John Dehner, Ian Keith, Chris Alcaide, John Mansfield, Celia Lovsky, Lou Merrill, Mel Welles.

In 1820, a gambling ship owner (Medina) and her crew seek revenge on the Southern plantation owners who have shunned her.

540. Duffy (9/68) Technicolor—101 mins. (Crime-Comedy). *DIR:* Robert Parrish. *PRO:* Martin Manulis. *SP:* Donald Cammell, Harry Joe Brown, Jr. Story by Donald Cammell, Harry Joe Brown, Jr., Pierre de la Salle. *CAST:* James Coburn, James Mason, James Fox, Susannah York, John Alderton, Barry Shawzin, Marne Maitland, Guy Deghy, Andre Maranne, Tutte Lemkow, Carl Duering, Julie Mendez.

Two half-brothers (Fox, Alderton) contract with an aging hippie (Coburn) to rob their father (Mason) of his bank notes while in transit from Tangiers to Marseilles.

541. The Durango Kid (8/23/40) B&W—61 mins. (Western). *DIR:* Lambert Hillyer. *PRO:* Jack Fier. *SP:* Paul Franklin. *CAST:* Charles Starrett, Luana Walters, Bob Nolan, Kenneth MacDonald, Forrest Taylor, Melvin Lang, Frank LaRue, Pat Brady, Jack Rockwell, John Tyrrell, Francis

Walker, Steve Clark, Ben Taggart, Tim Spencer, Roger Gray, Marin Sais, Ralph Peters, Sons of the Pioneers.

The Durango Kid (Starrett), with the help of a homesteader's daughter (Walters), sets out to find the rancher (MacDonald) who killed his father and has been terrorizing the local homesteaders. *NOTES:* Charles Starrett's first western as "The Durango Kid." [British title: *The Masked Stranger*].

542. Eadie Was a Lady (2/23/45) B&W—67 mins. (Musical). *DIR:* Arthur Dreifuss. *PRO:* Michael Kraike. *SP:* Monte Brice. *CAST:* Ann Miller, Joe Besser, William Wright, Jeff Donnell, Jimmy Little, Marion Martin, Kathleen Howard, Tom Dugan, Douglas Wood, George Meeker, Ida Moore, Jack Cole, George Lessey, Hal McIntyre and His Orchestra.

By day, a girl (Miller) is a straight-laced student, but by night is a top attraction at a burlesque show.

543. The Eagle Has Landed (3/77) Eastman Color/Panavision—134 mins. (War). *DIR:* John Sturges. *PRO:* Jack Winer, David Niven, Jr. *SP:* Tom Mankiewicz. Based on the book by Jack Higgins. An ITC Entertainment-Associated General Film-Filmways Australasian Production. *CAST:* Michael Caine, Donald Sutherland, Robert Duvall, Jenny Agutter, Donald Pleasence, Anthony Quayle, Jean Marsh, Sven-Bertil Taube, Judy Geeson, John Standing, Treat Williams, Larry Hagman, Sigfried Rauch, Jeff Conaway.

A Nazi colonel (Duvall), under direct orders from Himmler (Pleasence), invades England with his men to kidnap Churchill.

544. Earth Vs. the Flying Saucers (7/56) B&W—82 mins. (Science-Fiction). *DIR:* Fred F. Sears. *PRO:* Charles H. Schneer. *SP:* George Worthing Yates, Raymond T. Marcus. Story by Curt Siodmak. Suggested by

Flying Saucers from Outer Space by Maj. Donald E. Keyhoe. CAST: Hugh Marlowe, Joan Taylor, Donald Curtis, Morris Ankrum, John Zaremba, Thomas B. Henry, Grandon Rhodes, Larry Blake, Harry Lauter, Charles Evans, Clark Howat, Frank Wilcox, Alan Reynolds.

A scientist (Marlowe) saves the earth from alien invasion when he invents an anti-saucer sound ray to defeat the aliens. NOTES: Special effects by Ray Harryhausen.

545. East of Fifth Avenue (11/ 28/33) B&W — 73 mins. (Drama). DIR: Albert S. Rogell. SP: Jo Swerling. Story by Lew Levenson. CAST: Wallace Ford, Dorothy Tree, Walter Connolly, Maude Eburne, Walter Byron, Mary Carlisle, Lucien Littlefield, Willard Robertson, Louise Carter, Harry Holman, Fern Emmett.

In a New York boardinghouse, the lives of several people are drawn together through an old couple's suicide (Connolly, Carter). [British title: *Two in a Million*].

546. East of Sudan (7/65) Technicolor/Scope — 85 mins. (Adventure). DIR: Nathan Juran. PRO: Charles H. Schneer, Nathan Juran. SP: Jud Kinberg. A British Lion Production. CAST: Anthony Quayle, Sylvia Syms, Derek Fowlds, Jenny Agutter, Johnny Sekka, Harold Coyne, Joseph Layode, Desmond Davies, Derek Bloomfield, Edward Ellis.

In 1880 India, when a British outpost is overrun by Arabs, a British trooper (Quayle) and his rookie lieutenant (Fowlds) lead a governess (Syms) and her charge (Agutter) to safety.

547. Easy Rider (7/69) Eastman Color — 94 mins. (Drama). DIR: Dennis Hopper. PRO: Peter Fonda. SP: Peter Fonda, Dennis Hopper, Terry Southern. A Pando-Raybert Production. CAST: Peter Fonda, Dennis Hopper, Antonio Mendoza, Phil Spector, Luke Askew, Luana Anders, Jack Nicholson, Sabrina Scharf, Sandy Wyeth, Robert Walker, Jr., Keith Green, George Fowler, Jr.

Two drop-outs (Fonda, Hopper) ride their motorcycles across America searching for a way of life they can never attain.

548. The Eavesdropper (9/66) B&W — 102 mins. (Drama). DIR: Leopoldo Torre Nilsson. PRO: Paul M. Heller. SP: Beatriz Guido, Edmundo Eichelbaum, Joe Goldberg, Leopoldo Torre Nilsson, Mabel Itzcovich. Story by Beatriz Guido, Leopoldo Torre Nilsson. A Royal Films International Production. CAST: Stathis Giallelis, Janet Margolin, Lautaro Murua, Leonardo Favio, Nelly Meden, Elena Cortesina, Ignacio de Soroa.

In Buenos Aires, a fascist (Giallelis) goes into hiding in a hotel and overhears a plot to assassinate a visiting dignitary, not realizing it is a rehearsal for a play. [Original Argentine title: *El Ojo de la Cerradura*].

549. The Eddy Duchin Story (2/ 56) Technicolor/Scope — 123 mins. (Musical-Biography). DIR: George Sidney. PRO: Jerry Wald. SP: Samuel Taylor. Story by Leo Katcher. CAST: Tyrone Power, Kim Novak, Victoria Shaw, James Whitmore, Shepperd Strudwick, Rex Thompson, Frieda Inescort, Gloria Holden, Larry Keating, John Mylong, Gregory Gay, Richard Crane, Kirk Alyn, Jack Albertson, Xavier Cugat.

Biography of pianist-bandleader Eddy Duchin (Power), beginning with his arrival in New York, thru the 30's and 40's, and ending with his death.

550. Edge of Eternity (11/59) Technicolor/Scope — 80 mins. (Action). DIR: Don Siegel. PRO: Kendrick Sweet. SP: Knut Swenson, Richard Collins. Story by Knut Swenson, Ben Markson. A Thunderbird Production. *CAST:* Cornel Wilde, Victoria Shaw, Mickey Shaughnessy, Edgar Buchanan, Rian Garrick, Jack Elam, Dabbs Greer, Alexander Lockwood, Tom Fadden, John Roy, Wendell Holmes.

A sheriff (Wilde), out to solve the murder of a mining executive, corners the murderer (Shaughnessy) in a tram car above the Grand Canyon.

551. Educating Rita (9/83) Technicolor—110 mins. (Drama-Comedy). *DIR/PRO:* Lewis Gilbert. *SP:* Willy Russell. Based on the play by Willy Russell. An Acorn Pictures Production. *CAST:* Michael Caine, Julie Walters, Michael Williams, Maureen Lipman, Jeananne Crowley, Malcolm Douglas, Godfrey Quigley, Pat Daly, Kim Fortune, Philip Hurdwood, Hilary Reynolds, Jack Walsh.

A young hairdresser (Walters), wanting to better herself, enrolls in college and selects an alcoholic professor (Caine) as her tutor.

552. Eight Bells (5/11/35) B&W—69 mins. (Drama). *DIR:* Roy William Neill. *PRO:* J. G. Bachman. *SP:* Ethel Hill, Bruce Manning. Based on the play by Percy G. Mandley. *CAST:* Ann Sothern, Ralph Bellamy, John Buckler, Catherine Doucet, Arthur Hohl, Charley Grapewin, Franklin Pangborn, John Darrow.

A girl (Sothern) sneaks aboard ship to be near her fiance (Buckler), but complications arise when she falls in love with the first mate (Bellamy).

553. Eight Iron Men (12/52) B&W—80 mins. (War). *DIR:* Edward Dmytryk. *PRO:* Stanley Kramer. *SP:* Harry Brown. Based on the play *A Sound of Hunting* by Harry Brown. A Stanley Kramer Company Production. *CAST:* Bonar Colleano, Arthur Franz, Lee Marvin, Richard Kiley, Nick Dennis, James Griffith, Dick

Moore, George Cooper, Barney Phillips, Robert Nichols, Richard Grayson, Douglas Henderson, Mary Castle, David McMahon.

A squad of eight infantrymen are trapped in a bombed-out house behind enemy lines and await relief.

554. 84 Charing Cross Road (2/87) Rank-TVC Color—97 mins. (Drama). *DIR:* David Jones. *PRO:* Geoffrey Helman. *SP:* Hugh Whitemore. Based on the book by Helene Hanff. A Brooksfilm Production. *CAST:* Anne Bancroft, Anthony Hopkins, Judi Dench, Jean De Baer, Maurice Denham, Eleanor David, Mercedes Ruehl, Daniel Gerroll, Wendy Morgan, Ian McNeice, J. Smith-Cameron, Tom Isbell, Anne Dyson.

A New York writer (Bancroft) and a British bookseller (Hopkins) share a mutual friendship and correspondence over a twenty year period.

555. El Agua en el Suelo (Water in the Ground) (2/4/35) B&W—??? mins. (Drama). *DIR:* Eusebio F. Ardavin. *CAST:* Maruchi Fresno, Luis Pena, Nicolas Navarro.

In Madrid, a woman (Fresno) must leave her village when malicious gossip spreads about her and her spiritual advisor. *NOTES:* Released to Spanish language theaters. The title comes from an old Spanish proverb that "to stop scandalous gossip, once started, is as difficult as trying to recover water spilled on the ground."

556. El Alamein (1/54) B&W—66 mins. (War). *DIR:* Fred F. Sears. *PRO:* Wallace MacDonald. *SP:* Herbert Purdum, George Worthing Yates. Story by Herbert Purdum. *CAST:* Scott Brady, Edward Ashley, Robin Hughes, Rita Moreno, Michael Pate, Peter Brocco, Peter Mamakos, Ray Page, Benny Rubin, Henry Rowland.

A civilian (Brady), delivering tanks to the British, becomes trapped with a small group of men at a desert oasis the Germans are using as a fuel dump. [British title: *Desert Patrol*].

557. El Dorado Pass (10/14/48) B&W — 56 mins. (Western). *DIR*: Ray Nazarro. *PRO*: Colbert Clark. *SP*: Earle Snell. *CAST*: Charles Starrett, Elena Verdugo, Smiley Burnette, Steve Darrell, Ted Mapes, Blackie Whiteford, Rory Mallison, Stanley Blystone, Harry Vejar, Russell Meeker, Gertrude Chorre, Shorty Thompson and His Saddle Rockin' Rhythm.

A drifter (Starrett) accused of robbing a stagecoach becomes the Durango Kid and brings the gang to justice and recovers the money. [British title: *Desperate Men*.].

558. El Pasado Acusa (The Accusing Past) (10/15/38) B&W — ??? mins. (Crime). *DIR*: David Selman. Story by Winifred Van Duzer. *CAST*: Carlos Villarias, Barry Norton, Luana Alcaniz, Julio Villarreal, Alfredo de Diestro.

A woman (Alcaniz) is forced to give up her husband (Norton) and baby when it is learned her ex-boyfriend (Villarias) was a gangster. *NOTES*: Released to Spanish language theaters. A Spanish remake of the 1931 Columbia film *The Good Bad Girl*.

559. El Valor de Vivar (The Price of Living) (4/54) DuoColor/ 3-D — 105 mins. (Drama). *DIR*: Tito Davidson. *PRO*: Sergio Kogan. *SP*: Julio Alejandro, Tito Davidson. Based on the screen play *'Til We Meet Again* by Warren Duff and the screen story *S.S. Atlantic* by Robert Lord. An Internacional Cinematografica Production. *CAST*: Arturo de Cordova, Rosita Quintana, Maria Douglas, Miguel Angel Ferriz, Julio Villarreal, Jose Baviera, Jose Maria Linares Rivas, Delia Magana, Jose Pardave, Fernando Wagner.

A convicted murderer (de Cordova) and a woman (Quintana) with a fatal heart condition fall in love knowing that each has not long to live. *NOTES*: Released to Spanish language theaters. A Spanish remake of the 1940 Warner Bros. film *'Til We Meet Again*.

560. The Electronic Monster (5/ 60) B&W — 76 mins. (Science Fiction). *DIR*: Montgomery Tully. *PRO*: Alec C. Snowden. *SP*: Charles Eric Maine, J. MacLaren-Ross. Based on *Escapement* by Charles Eric Maine. An Ango-Amalgamated-Merton Park Production. *CAST*: Rod Cameron, Mary Murphy, Peter Illing, Meredith Edwards, Carl Jaffe, Kay Callard, Carl Duering, Roberta Huby, Felix Felton, Larry Cross.

Investigating the death of an actress at a clinic, an insurance investigator (Cameron) uncovers a plot by a doctor (Illing) to control the minds of his patients. [British title: *Escapement*].

561. Ellery Queen and the Murder Ring (11/18/41) B&W — 70 mins. (Mystery). *DIR*: James Hogan. *PRO*: Larry Darmour. *SP*: Eric Taylor, Gertrude Purcell. Based on *The Dutch Shoe Mystery* by Ellery Queen (Frederic Dannay, Manfred Lee). *CAST*: Ralph Bellamy, Margaret Lindsay, Charley Grapewin, Mona Barrie, George Zucco, Paul Hurst, James Burke, Blanche Yurka, Leon Ames, Tom Dugan, Jean Fenwick, Olin Howlin, Dennis Moore, Charlotte Wynters, Pierre Watkin.

Ellery (Bellamy) is asked by his father (Grapewin) to help solve the murder of the owner (Yurka) of a private hospital and gets more than he bargained for when other murders turn up. [British title: *The Murder Ring*].

562. Ellery Queen and the Perfect Crime (8/14/41) B&W — 67 mins. (Mystery). *DIR*: James Hogan. *PRO*: Larry Darmour. *SP*: Eric Taylor. Based on *The Perfect Crime* by

Ellery Queen (Frederic Dannay, Manfred Lee). CAST: Ralph Bellamy, Margaret Lindsay, Charley Grapewin, Spring Byington, H. B. Warner, James Burke, Douglass Dumbrille, John Beal, Linda Hayes, Sidney Blackmer, Walter Kingsford, Charles Lane, Honorable Wu.

Ellery (Bellamy) sets out to solve the murder of a shady utilities promoter (Dumbrille). [British title: *The Perfect Crime*].

563. Ellery Queen, Master Detective (11/28/40) B&W—58 mins. (Mystery). DIR: Kurt Neumann. PRO: Larry Darmour. SP: Eric Taylor. Based on *Ellery Queen, Master Detective* by Ellery Queen (Frederic Dannay, Manfred Lee). CAST: Ralph Bellamy, Margaret Lindsay, Charley Grapewin, James Burke, Michael Whalen, Marsha Hunt, Fred Niblo, Charles Lane, Ann Shoemaker, Marion Martin, Douglas Fowley, Morgan Wallace, Byron Foulger, Katherine DeMille, Lee Phelps, Jack Rice.

Ellery (Bellamy) has to put up with a rival writer (Lindsay) when he is called in to solve the murder of a millionaire (Niblo) at a health resort. NOTES: Margaret Lindsay, who played the part of Nikki Porter—a rival writer, agrees to give up her job and become Ellery's secretary in this film.

564. Ellery Queen's Penthouse Mystery (3/24/41) B&W—69 mins. (Mystery). DIR: James Hogan. PRO: Larry Darmour. SP: Eric Taylor. Based on *The Penthouse Mystery* by Ellery Queen (Frederic Dannay, Manfred Lee). CAST: Ralph Bellamy, Margaret Lindsay, Charley Grapewin, Anna May Wong, James Burke, Eduardo Ciannelli, Russell Hicks, Charles Lane, Ann Doran, Frank Albertson, Noel Madison, Tom Dugan, Mantan Moreland, Theodore Von Eltz.

Ellery (Bellamy) and his father (Grapewin) are called in to solve the murder of a Chinese vaudeville performer (Madison) who was, in reality, a jewel smuggler.

565. Emergency Wedding (11/15/50) B&W—78 mins. (Romantic-Comedy). DIR: Edward Buzzell. PRO: Nat Perrin. SP: Nat Perrin, Claude Binyon. Story by Dalton Trumbo. CAST: Larry Parks, Barbara Hale, Willard Parker, Una Merkel, Alan Reed, Eduard Franz, Irving Bacon, Don Beddoe, Jim Backus, Ian Wolfe, Helen Spring, Greg McClure, Boyd Davis, Pierre Watkin, Myron Healey, Jean Willes, Harry Harvey, William Forrest, Queenie Smith.

A millionaire playboy (Parks) thinks his wife (Hale), a lady doctor, spends too much time with her male patients, so he buys a hospital so he can keep an eye on her. NOTES: A remake of the 1941 Columbia film *You Belong to Me*. [British title: *Jealousy*].

566. Emmanuelle (12/74) Eastman Color—92 mins. (Drama). DIR: Just Jaeckin. PRO: Yves Rousset-Rouard. SP: Jean-Louis Richard. Based on the book by Emmanuelle Arsan. A Trinacra Films-Orphee Production. CAST: Sylvia Kristel, Alain Cuny, Daniel Sarky, Marika Green, Jeanne Colletin, Christine Boisson.

In Thailand, the bored wife (Kristel) of a French official is initiated into the joys of sex. NOTES: Columbia's first and only distribution of a soft X-rated film.

567. The End of the Affair (5/55) B&W—105 mins. (Drama). DIR: Edward Dmytryk. PRO: David Lewis. SP: Lenore Coffee. Based on the book by Graham Greene. A Coronado Production. CAST: Deborah Kerr, Van Johnson, John Mills, Peter Cushing, Michael Goodliffe, Stephen Murray, Charles Goldner, Nora Swinburne, Frederick Leister, Mary Williams.

In wartime London, the wife (Kerr) of a British official has an illicit love affair with an American writer (Johnson).

568. End of the Trail (12/9/32) B&W—61 mins. (Western). DIR: D. Ross Lederman. PRO: Irving Briskin. SP: Stuart Anthony. CAST: Tim McCoy, Luana Walters, Wheeler Oakman, Wally Albright, Lafe McKee, Wade Boteler, Chief White Eagle.

An Army officer (McCoy), sympathetic to the Indian cause, is framed for selling guns to the Indians. He is court-martialed, thrown out of the Army, and loses all his friends. His son (Albright) and best friend (Boteler) are killed. In the end he is wounded trying to bring peace between the Indians and whites. NOTES: In the original ending of the film, McCoy was supposed to be killed. Columbia felt this ending was too depressing and shot another ending in which McCoy recovers.

569. End of the Trail (10/31/36) B&W—72 mins. (Western). DIR: Erle C. Kenton. PRO: Irving Briskin. SP: Harold Shumate. Based on *Outlaws of Palouse* by Zane Grey. CAST: Jack Holt, Louise Henry, Douglass Dumbrille, George McKay, Gene Morgan, Guinn "Big Boy" Williams, John McGuire, Edward J. LeSaint, Frank Shannon, Erle C. Kenton, Hank Bell, Art Mix, Edgar Dearing, Blackjack Ward, Blackie Whiteford.

A veteran of the Spanish-American War (Holt) returns home, and not being able to find work, turns to rustling. When the younger brother (McGuire) of his sweetheart (Henry) is murdered, he shoots the killer and ends up going to the gallows. [British title: *Revenge*].

570. The Endless Summer (7/66) Technicolor—95 mins. (Documentary). DIR/PRO/SP: Bruce Brown. A Cinema 5 Production. CAST: Mike Hynson, Robert August. Narrated by Bruce Brown.

Two surfers (Hynson, August) search the world for the perfect wave. NOTES: Distribution rights reverted to Cinema 5 when Columbia failed to properly distribute this film.

571. Enemy Agents Meet Ellery Queen (7/30/42) B&W—64 mins. (Mystery). DIR: James Hogan. PRO: Larry Darmour. SP: Eric Taylor. Based on *The Greek Coffin Mystery* by Ellery Queen (Frederic Dannay, Manfred Lee). CAST: William Gargan, Margaret Lindsay, Charley Grapewin, Gilbert Roland, Gale Sondergaard, Sig Rumann, James Burke, Ernest Dorian, Felix Basch, Minor Watson, John Hamilton, James Seay, Ludwig Donath, Dick Wessel.

Ellery (Gargan) must solve the murder of an Allied agent (Roland) and deal with Nazi spies when he helps transport a valuable Egyptian collection to the U.S. [British title: *The Lido Mystery*].

572. The Enemy General (9/60) B&W—75 mins. (War). DIR: George Sherman. PRO: Sam Katzman. SP: Dan Pepper, Burt Picard. Story by Dan Pepper. A Clover Production. CAST: Van Johnson, Jean Pierre Aumont, Dany Carrel, John Van Dreelan, Francoise Prevost, Hubert Noel, Jacques Marin, Gerard Landry, Edward Fleming, Paul Bonifas, Paul Muller.

An O.S.S. agent (Johnson) and a French resistance leader (Aumont) join forces to transport a defecting German general (Van Dreelan) from France to England.

573. An Enemy of Men (7/1/25) B&W—56 mins. (Drama). DIR: Frank R. Strayer. PRO: Harry Cohn. SP: Douglas Bronston. CAST: Cullen Landis, Dorothy Revier, Charles Clary, Barbara Luddy.

A woman (Revier) becomes a hater of all men because of her sister's

(Luddy) death and refuses to marry until she learns that the man (Clary) who killed her sister is dead.

574. Enter Inspector Duval (12/61) B&W — 64 mins. (Crime). *DIR:* Max Varnel. *PRO:* Bill Luckwell, Jock McGregor. *SP:* J. Henry Piperno. Story by Jacques Monteux. A Bill & Michael Luckwell Production. *CAST:* Anton Diffring, Diane Hart, Mark Singleton, Charles Mitchell, Aiden Grennell, Susan Hallinan, Charles Roberts.

A French police detective (Diffring) assists Scotland Yard in solving the murder of a socialite during a jewel robbery.

575. Enter Laughing (7/67) Eastman Color — 112 mins. (Comedy). *DIR:* Carl Reiner. *PRO/SP:* Carl Reiner, Joseph Stein. Based on the play by Joseph Stein. An Acre-Sajo Production. *CAST:* Jose Ferrer, Shelley Winters, Elaine May, Jack Gilford, Janet Margolin, Reni Santoni, David Opatoshu, Michael J. Pollard, Don Rickles, Rob Reiner, Nancy Kovack, Richard Deacon, Herbie Faye, Milton Frome, Danny Stein, Lillian Adams, Mantan Moreland, Peter Brocco, Patrick Campbell.

A young man (Santoni) gives up a career in pharmacy and decides to become an actor. *NOTES:* Based on the early life of Carl Reiner.

576. Escape from Devil's Island (11/26/35) B&W — 64 mins. (Crime-Drama). *DIR:* Albert S. Rogell. *SP:* Earle Snell, Fred Niblo, Jr. Story by Fred De Gresac. *CAST:* Victor Jory, Florence Rice, Norman Foster, Stanley Andrews, Daniel Haynes, Herbert Heywood, Frank Lackteen, Arthur Aylesworth, Noble Johnson.

Two prisoners (Jory, Foster) escape from Devil's Island, but because they fight over a woman (Rice), miss their ship to freedom.

577. Escape from San Quentin (9/57) B&W — 81 mins. (Crime-Drama). *DIR:* Fred F. Sears. *PRO:* Sam Katzman. *SP:* Raymond T. Marcus. *CAST:* Johnny Desmond, Merry Anders, Richard Devon, Roy Engel, William Bryant, Ken Christy, Larry Blake, Don Devlin, Victor Millan, John Merrick, Norman Frederic, Barry Brooks, Lennie Smith.

Three convicts (Desmond, Devon, Engel) escape from San Quentin, try to locate hidden loot, but are eventually captured.

578. Escape in the Fog (4/5/45) B&W — 65 mins. (Crime-Drama). *DIR:* Oscar (Budd) Boetticher, Jr. *PRO:* Wallace MacDonald. *SP:* Aubrey Wisberg. *CAST:* Nina Foch, William Wright, Otto Kruger, Konstantin Shayne, Ivan Triesault, Ernie Adams, Mary Newton, Ralph Dunn, John Tyrrell, Charles Jordan, Noel Cravat, John Elliott.

A nurse (Foch) sees a man being murdered in a dream, and sets out to locate and warn him before the murder happens.

579. Escape to Glory (5/20/40) B&W — 74 mins. (War-Drama). *DIR:* John Brahm. *PRO:* Samuel Bischoff. *SP:* P. J. Wolfson. Story by Sidney Biddell, Fredric Frank. *CAST:* Pat O'Brien, Constance Bennett, John Halliday, Melville Cooper, Alan Baxter, Edgar Buchanan, Marjorie Gateson, Francis Pierlot, Frank Sully, Don Beddoe, Bruce Bennett, Arno Frey, Olaf Hytten.

At the outbreak of World War II, a merchant ship, with a variety of passengers, is stalked by a Nazi submarine.

580. The Eternal Woman (4/18/29) B&W — 57 mins. (Drama). *DIR:* John P. McCarthy. *PRO:* Harry Cohn. *SP:* Wellyn Totman. *CAST:* Olive Borden, Ralph Graves, Ruth Clifford,

John Miljan, Nena Quartero, Josef Swickard, Julia Swayne Gordon.

A young woman (Borden) saves a man (Graves) from a shipwreck and believing him to be the man who murdered her father, sets out to kill him. Upon discovering that he is innocent, they set out to find the real killer.

581. Eve Knew Her Apples (4/12/45) B&W — 64 mins. (Musical). DIR: Will Jason. PRO: Wallace MacDonald. SP: E. Edwin Moran. Story by Rian James. CAST: Ann Miller, William Wright, Robert Williams, Ray Walker, Charles D. Brown, John Eldredge, Eddie Bruce, Frank Jacquet, Jessie Arnold, Boyd Davis, Syd Saylor, Si Jenks, Harry Semels, Jack Rice, Hank Bell, John Tyrrell.

A radio singing star (Miller) runs away from money and fame by hiding out in the trunk of a reporter's (Wright) car.

582. Ever Since Venus (9/14/44) B&W — 74 mins. (Musical). DIR: Arthur Dreifuss. SP: McElbert Moore, Arthur Dreifuss. CAST: Ina Ray Hutton, Hugh Herbert, Ann Savage, Billy Gilbert, Glenda Farrell, Ross Hunter, Alan Mowbray, Marjorie Gateson, Thurston Hall, Fritz Feld, Dudley Dickerson, Ralph Dunn, Kernan Cripps, Isabel Withers, Mary Gordon, Byron Foulger, Chester Clute, Jack Rice, Anne Loos.

An inventor (Hunter) sets out to market a new type of lipstick at a cosmetics show, but runs into trouble with a cosmetics king (Mowbray).

583. Every Day Is a Holiday (7/66) Eastman Color — 76 mins. (Comedy-Drama). DIR/PRO: Mel Ferrer. SP: Mel Ferrer, Jose Maria Palacio. A Guion Films Production. CAST: Marisol, Angel Peralta, Rafel De Cordova, Jose Marco Davo, Vala Clifton, Pedro Mari Sanchez.

A girl (Marisol) masquerades as a boy and becomes a bullfighter to impress her idol (Peralta). [Original Spanish title: *Cabriola*].

Every Man's Woman see **A Rose for Everyone**

584. Everybody Go Home! (11/62) B&W — 105 mins. (War-Comedy). DIR: Luigi Comencini. PRO: Dino De Laurentiis. SP: Marcello Fondato, Luigi Comencini. A De Laurentiis Cinematografica-Orsay-Davis-Royal Films International Production. CAST: Alberto Sordi, Martin Balsam, Serge Reggiani, Nino Castelnuovo, Mario Feliciani, Carla Gravina, Jole Mauro, Alex Nicol, Eduardo De Filippo, Mino Doro, Claudio Gora.

Two Italian soldiers (Sordi, Reggiani) become involved with Germans and partisans as they try to return to their lines. [Original Italian title: *Tutti a Casa*]. [Original French title: *La Grande Pagaille*].

Everyman's Woman see **A Rose for Everyone**

585. Everything in Life (11/36) B&W — 70 mins. (Musical-Comedy). DIR: J. Elder Wills. PRO: Marquis of Ely. SP: James E. Lewis. A Tudor Films Production. CAST: Gitta Alpar, Neil Hamilton, Lawrence Grossmith, H. F. Maltby, Gerald Barry, Dorothy Boyd, Wyn Weaver, Clarissa Selwynne, Bruce Winston, Vera Bogetti, John Deverell.

An opera singer (Alpar) gives up her career, falls in love with a musical conductor (Hamilton), and backs his new show.

586. Everything's Ducky (11/61) B&W — 80 mins. (Comedy). DIR: Don Taylor. PRO: Red Doff. SP: John Fenton Murray, Benedict Freedman. A Barboo Enterprises Production. CAST: Mickey Rooney, Buddy Hackett, Jackie Cooper, Joanie Sommers, Roland Winters, Elizabeth McRae,

Gene Blakely, Gordon Jones, Richard Deacon, Alvy Moore, James Milhollin. Two sailors (Rooney, Hackett) are entrusted with a talking duck, and the trio wind up on a space capsule orbiting the earth.

587. The Executioner (6/70) Technicolor/Panavision—111 mins. (Spy-Drama). *DIR:* Sam Wanamaker. *PRO:* Charles H. Schneer. *SP:* Jack Pulman. Story by Gordon McDonell. *CAST:* George Peppard, Joan Collins, Judy Geeson, Oscar Homolka, Charles Gray, Nigel Patrick, Keith Mitchell, Alexander Scourby, Peter Bull, Ernest Clark, George Baker.

A British spy (Peppard) sets out to prove that his partner (Mitchell) is a double agent.

588. Experiment in Terror (4/62) B&W—123 mins. (Crime-Drama). *DIR/PRO:* Blake Edwards. *SP:* Gordon Gordon, Mildred Gordon. Based on *Operation Terror* by Gordon Gordon, Mildred Gordon. *CAST:* Glenn Ford, Lee Remick, Stefanie Powers, Roy Poole, Ned Glass, Ross Martin, Gilbert Green, Clifton James, William Bryant, Dick Crockett, Sidney Miller, Ray Kellogg.

A bank teller (Remick) assists an FBI agent (Ford) to trap an asthmatic killer (Martin) when her sister (Powers) is kidnapped. [British title: *The Grip of Fear*].

589. Extortion (5/9/38) B&W—57 mins. (Mystery). *DIR:* Lambert Hillyer. *PRO:* Ralph Cohn. *SP:* Earl Felton. *CAST:* Scott Colton, Mary Russell, Thurston Hall, Arthur Loft, Gene Morgan, Frank C. Wilson, Ann Doran, J. Farrell MacDonald, George Offerman, Jr., Nick Lucats, Roland Got, Albert Van Dekker, Ruth Hilliard.

When a proctor (Van Dekker) of the local college is murdered, the school paper editor (Colton) sets out to find the murderer.

590. The Eyes, the Mouth (12/83) Eastman Color—100 mins. (Drama). *DIR:* Marco Bellocchio. *PRO:* Enzo Porcelli, Enea Ferrario. *SP:* Marco Bellocchio, Vincenzo Cerami. An RAI TV-Gaumont-Triumph Films Production. *CAST:* Lou Castel, Angela Molina, Emanuelle Riva, Michel Piccoli, Antonio Piovanelli, Giampaolo Saccorola, Viviana Toni, Antonio Petrocelli.

A man (Castel) attends his brother's funeral and ends up falling in love with the girl (Molina) his brother killed himself over. *NOTES:* Limited theatrical release; in Italian with English subtitles. [Original Italian title: *Gli Occhi, la Bocca*].

591. Eyes of Laura Mars (8/78) Eastman Color/Panavision—104 mins. (Crime-Mystery). *DIR:* Irvin Kershner. *PRO:* Jon Peters. *SP:* John Carpenter, David Zelag Goodman. Based on a story by John Carpenter. *CAST:* Faye Dunaway, Tommy Lee Jones, Brad Dourif, Rene Auberjonois, Raul Julia, Frank Adonis, Lisa Taylor, Darlanne Fluegel, Rose Gregorio, Michael Tucker, Marilyn Meyers, Meg Mundy.

A fashion photographer (Dunaway) has visions of violent death as experienced through the eyes of the killer.

592. The Face Behind the Mask (2/10/41) B&W—69 mins. (Drama-Horror). *DIR:* Robert Florey. *PRO:* Wallace MacDonald. *SP:* Allen Vincent, Paul Jarrico. Story by Arthur Levinson. Based on the radio play *Interem* by Thomas Edward O'Connell. *CAST:* Peter Lorre, Evelyn Keyes, Don Beddoe, George E. Stone, John Tyrrell, Stanley Brown, Al Seymour, James Seay, Warren Ashe, Charles Wilson, George McKay, Ben Taggart, Frank Reicher, Walter Soderling, Lee Prather, Al Bridge, John Dilson, Joel Friedkin, Harry Strang, Lee Shumway, Ernie Adams.

A Hungarian immigrant (Lorre) turns to a life of crime when his face is disfigured in a fire; he seeks revenge against his gang when his blind girlfriend (Keyes) dies in a car bombing meant for him.

593. Face of a Fugitive (5/59) Eastman Color—81 mins. (Western). *DIR:* Paul Wendkos. *PRO:* David Heilwell. *SP:* Daniel B. Ullman, David T. Chantler. Based on *Long Gone* by Peter Dawson. A Morningside Production. *CAST:* Fred MacMurray, Dorothy Green, Lin McCarthy, Myrna Fahey, Alan Baxter, James Coburn, Francis De Sales, Paul E. Burns, Gina Gillespie, Ron Hayes, Robert "Buzz" Henry, John Milford, James Gavin, Hal K. Dawson, Rankin Mansfield, Stanley Farrar, Harrison Lewis.

A bank robber (MacMurray), falsely accused of murder, tries to make a new start in another town, until his past catches up with him.

594. The Facts of Love (2/49) B&W—83 mins. (Comedy). *DIR:* Henry Cass. *PRO:* Sydney Box. *SP:* Muriel Box, Sydney Box. Based on the play 29 *Acacia Avenue* by Denis and Mabel Constanduros. A Boca-Oxford Production. *CAST:* Gordon Harker, Betty Balfour, Jimmy Hanley, Carla Lehmann, Hubert Gregg, Jill Evans, Henry Kendall, Dinah Sheridan, Megs Jenkins, Noele Gordon, Guy Middleton, Aubrey Mallalieu.

A middle-aged couple (Harker, Balfour) try to cope with the courting plans of their son (Hanley) and daughter (Lehmann). *NOTES:* Originally released in England in 1945. [British title: 29 *Acacia Avenue*].

595. Fail-Safe (10/64) B&W—111 mins. (Drama). *DIR:* Sidney Lumet. *PRO:* Max E. Youngstein. *SP:* Walter Bernstein. Based on the book by Eugene Burdick and Harvey Wheeler. *CAST:* Dan O'Herlihy, Walter Matthau, Frank Overton, Edward Binns, Fritz Weaver, Henry Fonda, Larry Hagman, William Hansen, Russell Hardie, Russell Collins, Sorrell Booke, Hildy Parks, Dom DeLuise, Dana Elcar.

A mechanical malfunction sends SAC bombers to bomb Moscow; a political nightmare develops as the president (Fonda) and his military advisors, unable to stop the impending disaster, try to avert an all out retaliatory escalation of nuclear war.

596. The Faker (1/2/29) B&W—55 mins. (Drama). *DIR:* Philip E. Rosen. *PRO:* Harry Cohn. *SP:* Howard J. Green. *CAST:* Jacqueline Logan, Charles Delaney, Warner Oland, Charles Hill Mailes, Gaston Glass.

A disinherited son (Glass) contacts a phony spiritualist (Oland) to conduct a fake seance in the hopes that an invented message from his dead mother will make his father (Mailes) take him back.

597. The Fall of Eve (6/25/29) B&W—67 mins. (Comedy). *DIR:* Frank R. Strayer. *PRO:* Harry Cohn. *SP:* Gladys Lehman, Frederic Hatton, Fanny Hatton. Story by John Emerson, Anita Loos. *CAST:* Patsy Ruth Miller, Ford Sterling, Gertrude Astor, Arthur Rankin, Jed Prouty, Betty Harrington, Fred Kelsey, Hank Mann.

A secretary (Miller) creates chaos at a nightclub when she pretends to be the wife of a businessman (Prouty). *NOTES:* Released as both a silent and sound film.

598. The False Alarm (9/25/26) B&W—57 mins. (Drama). *DIR:* Frank O'Conner. *PRO:* Harry Cohn. *SP:* J. Grubb Alexander. *CAST:* Ralph Lewis, Dorothy Revier, John Harron, Mary Carr, George O'Hara, Patricia Bonner.

A fireman (Harron) is branded a coward when he fails to rescue his father (Lewis) from a burning building, but redeems himself when he saves a fellow fireman from another blaze.

Familia Dressel, La *see* **La Familia Dressel**

599. The Family Secret (10/24/51) B&W — 85 mins. (Drama-Crime). *DIR*: Henry Levin. *PRO*: Robert Lord. *SP*: Francis Cockrell, Andrew Solt. Story by Marie Baumer, James Cavanaugh. A Santana Production. *CAST*: John Derek, Lee J. Cobb, Jody Lawrence, Erin O'Brien-Moore, Santos Ortega, Henry O'Neill, Carl Benton Reid, Peggy Converse, Jean Alexander, Dorothy Tree, Onslow Stevens, Whit Bissell.

When a boy (Derek) kills his best friend by mistake, his father (Cobb) defends the man charged with the crime, knowing his son is guilty.

600. The Farmer (3/77) Eastman Color/Panavision — 98 mins. (Crime-Action). *DIR*: David Berlatsky. *PRO*: Gary Conway. *SP*: Janice Colson-Dodge, John Carmody, Patrick Regan, George Fargo. Story by George Fargo. An FIA-Cinema-Milway Production. *CAST*: Gary Conway, Angel Tompkins, Michael Dante, George Memmoli, Timothy Scott, Jack Waltzer, Ken Renard, John Popwell, Stratton Leopold, Don Payne, Sonny Shroyer, Eric Weston.

A World War II vet (Conway) tries to start a farm, but becomes a hit man for the mob when he is unable to make the payments on his farm.

601. Fashion Madness (2/26/28) B&W — 57 mins. (Drama). *DIR*: Louis J. Gasnier. *PRO*: Harry Cohn. *SP*: Victoria Moore. Story by Olga Printzlau. *CAST*: Claire Windsor, Reed Howes, Laska Winters, Donald McNamee.

A woman (Windsor) drags her dying lover (Howes) through the Canadian wilds and saves his life.

602. Fast and Sexy (9/60) Technicolor/Technirama — 99 mins. (Comedy). *DIR*: Reginald Denham. *PRO*: Milko Skofic. *SP*: E. M. Margadonna, Lucianna Corda, Joseph Stefano. A Circeo Cinematografic Production. *CAST*: Gina Lollobrigida, Dale Robertson, Vittorio de Sica, Amadeo Nazzari, Renzo Cesana.

A Brooklyn widow (Lollobrigida), desiring a new husband, returns to her village in Italy and tries to romance the local blacksmith (Robertson). [British title: *Anna of Brooklyn*]. [Original Italian title: *Anna di Brooklyn*].

603. Fast Break (3/79) Metrocolor — 97 mins. (Comedy). *DIR*: Jack Smight. *PRO*: Stephen J. Friedman. *SP*: Sandor Stern. Story by Marc Kaplan. *CAST*: Gabe Kaplan, Harold Sylvester, Michael Warren, Bernard King, Reb Brown, Mavis Washington, Bert Remsen, John Chappell, Rhonda Bates, Marty Zagon, Connie Sawyer, James Jeter, Randee Heller.

A New York college coach (Kaplan) accepts a coaching job at a Nevada college and brings his street basketball players with him.

604. Fast Forward (2/85) Metrocolor — 110 mins. (Musical). *DIR*: Sidney Poitier. *PRO*: John Patrick Veitch. *SP*: Richard Wesley. Story by Timothy March. A Verdon-Cedric Production. *CAST*: John Scott Clough, Don Franklin, Tamara Mark, Tracy Silver, Cindy McGee, Gretchen F. Palmer, Monique Cintron, Debra Varnado, Noel Conlon, Irene Worth, Constance Towers, David White, Karen Kopins, Sam McMurry.

A high school pop group from Ohio travel to New York in the hopes of auditioning for a big show.

605. Fat City (7/72) Eastman Color — 100 mins. (Drama). *DIR*: John Huston. *PRO*: Ray Stark. *SP*: Leonard Gardner. Based on the book by Leonard Gardner. A John Huston-Ray Stark Production. *CAST*: Stacy Keach, Jeff Bridges, Susan Tyrell, Candy Clark, Nicholas Colasanto, Art Aragon, Curtis Cokes, Sixto Rodriguez, Billy Walker, Wayne Mahan, Ruben Navarro.

An alcoholic ex-fighter (Keach) tries for a comeback with his protege (Bridges), but fails and goes back to his old way of life.

606. The Fatal Mistake (9/1/24) B&W – 50 mins. (Crime-Drama). *DIR*: Scott R. Dunlap. *PRO*: Harry Cohn. *SP*: Walter Anthony. *CAST*: William Fairbanks, Eva Novak, Wilfred Lucas, Dot Farley.

A cub reporter (Fairbanks) joins forces with a police woman (Novak) to recover a valuable jewel.

607. The Fatal Night (4/48) B&W – 50 mins. (Drama-Mystery). *DIR/PRO*: Mario Zampi. *SP*: Gerald Butler, Kathleen Conners. Based on *The Gentleman from America* by Michael Arlen. An Anglofilm Production. *CAST*: Lester Ferguson, Jean Short, Leslie Armstrong, Brenda Hogan, Patrick Macnee, Aubrey Mallalieu.

While visiting England, a man (Ferguson) accepts a bet to spend the night in a haunted house.

608. The Fate of a Flirt (4/1/26) B&W – 57 mins. (Comedy). *DIR/SP*: Frank R. Strayer. *PRO*: Harry Cohn. *CAST*: Dorothy Revier, Forrest Stanley, Tom Ricketts, Phillips Smalley, Clarissa Selwynne.

An English lord (Stanley) takes a job as a chauffeur to be near the girl (Revier) he loves.

609. Father and Son (5/13/29) B&W – 68 mins. (Drama). *DIR*: Erle C. Kenton. *PRO*: Harry Cohn. *SP*: Jack Townley. Story by Elmer Harris. *CAST*: Jack Holt, Dorothy Revier, Helene Chadwick, Mickey McBan, Wheeler Oakman.

When a man (Holt) is put on trial for the murder of his wife (Revier), his son (McBan) proves his innocence through a phonograph recording. *NOTES*: Columbia's first picture with talking sequences, music score, and sound effects.

610. Father Is a Bachelor (2/14/50) B&W – 83 mins. (Drama). *DIR*: Norman Foster, Abby Berlin. *PRO*: S. Sylvan Simon. *SP*: Aleen Leslie, James Edward Grant. Story by James Edward Grant. *CAST*: William Holden, Coleen Gray, Mary Jane Saunders, Charles Winninger, Stuart Erwin, Clinton Sundberg, Gary Gray, Sig Rumann, Billy Gray, Tommy Ivo, Lloyd Corrigan, Peggy Converse, Arthur Space, Hank Worden, Dooley Wilson, William Tannen, Ruby Dandridge, Eddy Waller.

A tramp (Holden), who enjoys fishing more than work, adopts five orphans who change him and, in the process, prompt him to seek a wife.

611. Faust and the Devil (4/26/50) B&W – 87 mins. (Opera). *DIR*: Carmine Gallone. *PRO*: Gregor Rabinovitch. *SP*: Leopold Marchand. Based on the opera *Faust* by Charles Gounod and the dramatic poem *Faust, eine Tragödie* by Wolfgang von Goethe. A Cineopera Production. *CAST*: Italo Tajo, Nelly Corradi, Gino Mattera, Giles Queant, Therese Dorny, Cesare Barbetti.

A filmed version of the opera by Gounod. [Original Italian title: *La Leggenda di Faust*].

612. The Fearless Lover (12/1/24) B&W – 53 mins. (Drama). *DIR*: Henry MacRae. *PRO*: Harry Cohn. *SP*: Scott R. Dunlap. *CAST*: William Fairbanks, Eva Novak, Tom Kennedy, Frankie Darro.

When a cop (Fairbanks) learns that his future brother-in-law (Darro) was forced into a life of crime against his will, he sets out to get the head crook (Kennedy).

613. A Feather in Her Hat (10/25/33) B&W — 72 mins. (Drama). *DIR:* Alfred Santell. *PRO:* Everett Riskin. *SP:* Lawrence Hazard. Based on the book by Ida Alexa Ross Wylie. *CAST:* Pauline Lord, Basil Rathbone, Louis Hayward, Billie Burke, Wendy Barrie, Victor Varconi, Nydia Westman, Thurston Hall, Nana Bryant, J. M. Kerrigan, David Niven, Lawrence Grant, Doris Lloyd, Olaf Hytten.

A shopkeeper (Lord), wanting her son (Hayward) to climb out of his poor surroundings, convinces him that his real mother is an actress.

614. The Feathered Serpent (12/34) B&W — 72 mins. (Crime). *DIR:* Maclean Rogers. *PRO:* A. George Smith. *SP:* Maclean Rogers, Kathleen Butler. Based on *The Feathered Serpent* by Edgar Wallace. A GS Enterprises Production. *CAST:* Enid Stamp-Taylor, Tom Helmore, D. A. Clarke-Smith, Moore Marriott, Molly Fisher, Vincent Holman, Evelyn Roberts, Iris Baker, O. B. Clarence.

When an actress (Stamp-Taylor) is wanted for the murder of a fence, a reporter (Helmore) comes to her aid and helps her prove her innocence.

615. Feudin' Rhythm (12/10/49) B&W — 66 mins. (Musical-Western). *DIR:* Edward Bernds. *PRO:* Colbert Clark. *SP:* Barry Shipman. *CAST:* Eddy Arnold, Gloria Henry, Kirby Grant, Isabel Randolph, Tommy Ivo, Fuzzy Knight, Edward Gargan, Dick Elliott, Emil Sitka, George Lloyd, Carolina Cotton, Mustard and Gravy, The Oklahoma Wranglers.

A radio deejay (Grant) decides to move his show to television, but when the station burns down he puts on his show at the ranch of a wealthy backer (Randolph) who wants to be in his show; meanwhile a country singer (Ar-nold) is reunited with his son (Ivo). [British title: *Ace Lucky*].

Fever Heat *see* **Bob, Le Flambeur**

Fielder's Field *see* **Girls Can Play**

616. The Fifth Musketeer (9/79) Eastman Color — 103 mins. (Adventure). *DIR:* Ken Annakin. *PRO:* Ted Richmond. *SP:* David Ambrose. Based on *The Man in the Iron Mask* by Alexandre Dumas and a screenplay by George Brace. *CAST:* Sylvia Kristel, Beau Bridges, Ursula Andress, Cornel Wilde, Ian McShane, Lloyd Bridges, Alan Hale, Jr., Helmut Dantine, Olivia De Havilland, Jose Ferrer, Rex Harrison, Bernard Bresslaw, Stephan Bastian.

The three musketeers (Lloyd Bridges, Ferrer, Hale) and D'Artagnan (Wilde) help a twin (Beau Bridges) regain his rightful place on the throne. *NOTES:* A loose remake of the 1939 United Artists film *The Man in the Iron Mask.*

617. Fifty Fathoms Deep (8/16/31) B&W — 68 mins. (Adventure). *DIR:* Roy William Neill. *SP:* Dorothy Howell, Roy Chanslor. Story by Dorothy Howell. *CAST:* Jack Holt, Mary Doran, Richard Cromwell, Loretta Sayers, Wallace MacDonald, Christine Montt, Henry Mowbray.

Two divers (Holt, Cromwell) have a falling out when one of them marries a fortune hunter (Sayers), but, when danger threatens, all feelings are put aside.

618. A Fight for Honor (8/1/24) B&W — 50 mins. (Drama). *DIR:* Henry MacRae. *PRO:* Harry Cohn. *SP:* Henry W. George. *CAST:* William Fairbanks, Eva Novak, Claire McDowell, Jack Byron, Wilfred Lucas.

A station master (Lucas) discovers a plot to blow up a railway bridge.

619. The Fight for Life (3/11/40) B&W — 72 mins. (Documentary).

DIR/SP: Pare Lorentz. PRO: United States Film Service. Based on the book by Dr. Paul de Kruif. CAST: Myron McCormick, Will Geer, Storrs Haynes, Dorothy Adams, Dudley Digges, Dorothy Urban. Narration by Morris Carnovsky.

A documentary that focuses on pregnancy, motherhood, and health care in the Chicago ghettos. NOTES: This documentary was commissioned by the U.S. Department of Health under the Roosevelt Administration. It was withdrawn from circulation in 1944, since government funds for producing such documentaries were at an end. It was made available again for circulation in 1947, as an edited 16mm film, after certain cuts were made. It was policy during the war years that a major studio (Paramount, RKO, etc.) release at least one documentary by the U.S. Film Service and the government was to share in the profits for a stipulated number of years.

620. A Fight to the Finish (11/1/25) B&W—50 mins. (Drama). DIR: B. Reeves Eason. PRO: Harry Cohn. SP: Douglas Z. Doty. CAST: William Fairbanks, Phyllis Haver, Tom Ricketts, Pat Harmon.

A millionaire (Ricketts) pretends to be poor so that his playboy son (Fairbanks) will straighten up.

621. A Fight to the Finish (6/30/37) B&W—58 mins. (Drama). DIR: C. C. Coleman, Jr. PRO: Ralph Cohn. SP: Harold Shumate. CAST: Don Terry, Rosalind Keith, George McKay, Ward Bond, Wade Boteler, Lucille Lund, Ivan Miller, Tom Chatterton, Frank Sheridan, Harold Goodwin.

A taxi superintendent (Terry), released from prison for a crime he didn't commit, starts a rival taxi company and declares an all-out taxi war against the man (Bond) who framed him.

622. The Fighting Buckaroo (2/1/43) B&W—58 mins. (Western). DIR: William Berke. PRO: Jack Fier. SP: Luci Ward. CAST: Charles Starrett, Kay Harris, Arthur Hunnicutt, Stanley Brown, Wheeler Oakman, Forrest Taylor, Lane Bradford, Robert Stevens (Kellard), Norma Jean Wooters, Roy Butler, Ernest Tubb, Johnny Luther and His Ranch Boys.

A stranger (Starrett) sets out to clear his friend (Brown) of cattle rustling with the help of a rancher's daughter (Harris).

623. The Fighting Code (12/30/33) B&W—65 mins. (Western). DIR/SP: Lambert Hillyer. PRO: Irving Briskin. CAST: Buck Jones, Diane Sinclair, Dick Alexander, Louis Natheaux, Ward Bond, Niles Welch, Alf James, Erville Alderson, Gertrude Howard, Bob Kortman, Charles Brinley, Buck Moulton.

A cowboy (Jones) helps a rancher's daughter (Sinclair) find the murderer of her father.

624. The Fighting Fool (1/20/32) B&W—57 mins. (Western). DIR: Lambert Hillyer. SP: Frank Howard Clark. CAST: Tim McCoy, Marceline Day, William V. Mong, Robert Ellis, Arthur Rankin, Dorothy Granger, Harry Todd, Bob Kortman, Ethel Wales, Mary Carr.

A sheriff (McCoy) sets out to avenge the death of his brother by going after the outlaw responsible, a mysterious figure known as "The Shadow."

625. Fighting for Justice (10/29/32) B&W—61 mins. (Western). DIR: Otto Brower. SP: Robert Quigley. Story by Gladwell Richardson. CAST: Tim McCoy, Joyce Compton, Hooper Atchley, William Norton Bailey, Walter Brennan, Lafe McKee, Harry Todd, Harry Cording, Robert Frazer, Charles King, William V. Mong, Murdock McQuarrie.

A cowboy (McCoy) sets out to get back his father's ranch which was illegally sold.

626. The Fighting Frontiersman (12/19/46) B&W—61 mins. (Western). *DIR:* Ray Nazarro. *PRO:* Colbert Clark. *SP:* Ed Earl Repp. *CAST:* Charles Starrett, Helen Mowery, Smiley Burnette, Emmett Lynn, Robert W. Filmer, George Chesebro, Jock Mahoney, Frank LaRue, Frank Ellis, Ernie Adams, Maudie Prickett, Russell Meeker, Zon Murray, Jim Diehl, Hank Newman and the Georgia Crackers.

The Durango Kid (Starrett) helps an old prospector friend (Lynn) keep his gold mine, and bring to justice the outlaws who tried to steal it. [British title: *Golden Lady*].

627. The Fighting Guardsman (1/4/46) B&W—84 mins. (Historical-Drama). *DIR:* Henry Levin. *PRO:* Michael Kraike. *SP:* Edward Dein, Franz Spencer. Based on *The Companions of Jehu* by Alexandre Dumas. *CAST:* Willard Parker, Anita Louise, Janis Carter, John Loder, Edgar Buchanan, George Macready, Lloyd Corrigan, Elisabeth Risdon, Ian Wolfe, Ray Teal, Victor Kilian, Charles Halton, Maurice R. Tauzin, Charles Waldron.

During the reign of Louis XVI (Corrigan), a nobleman (Parker) gathers together a group of revolutionaries to fight the king's tyrannical rule.

628. The Fighting Marshal (11/25/31) B&W—58 mins. (Western). *DIR:* D. Ross Lederman. *SP:* Frank Howard Clark. *CAST:* Tim McCoy, Blackie Whiteford, Dorothy Gulliver, Harry Todd, Bob Perry, Mathew Betz, Mary Carr, Edward J. LeSaint, Pat O'Malley, Lafe McKee, W. A. Howell, Dick Dickenson, Ethan Laidlaw, Lee Shumway, Blackjack Ward.

An escaped convict (McCoy) assumes the identity of a dead marshal to find the men who framed him.

629. The Fighting Ranger (3/17/34) B&W—60 mins. (Western). *DIR:* George B. Seitz. *PRO:* Irving Briskin. *SP:* Harry O. Hoyt. Story by Stuart Anthony. *CAST:* Buck Jones, Dorothy Revier, Frank Rice, Bradley Page, Ward Bond, Paddy O'Flynn, Art Smith, Denver Dixon, Frank LaRue, Bud Osborne, Jim Corey, Jack Wallace, Mozelle Britton, Lew Meehan, Steve Clemente, Frank Ellis.

A Texas Ranger (Jones) and his partner (Rice) travel to Mexico to search for the killer of his brother. *NOTES:* A remake of Buck Jones's 1931 Columbia film *Border Law.*

630. Fighting Shadows (4/18/35) B&W—58 mins. (Western). *DIR:* David Selman. *SP:* Ford Beebe. *CAST:* Tim McCoy, Geneva Mitchell, Ward Bond, Bob Allen, Si Jenks, Otto Hoffman, Edward J. LeSaint, Bud Osborne, Alan Sears, Ethan Laidlaw.

A lawman (McCoy) sets out to rid his town of an unscrupulous bandit gang.

631. The Fighting Sheriff (5/15/31) B&W—67 mins. (Western). *DIR:* Louis King. *PRO:* Sol Lesser. *SP:* Stuart Anthony. A Beverly Production. *CAST:* Buck Jones, Lillian Worth, Loretta Sayers, Nena Quartero, Robert Ellis, Clarence Muse, Harlan E. Knight, Lilliane Leighton, Paul Fix, Tom Bay.

A society debutante (Sayers) gets mixed up in a series of adventures with a rough and tumble sheriff (Jones).

632. Fighting the Flames (8/23/24) B&W—55 mins. (Action-Drama). *DIR:* B. Reeves Eason. *PRO:* Harry Cohn. *SP:* Douglas Z. Doty. *CAST:* William Haines, Dorothy Devore, Frankie Darro, David Torrence.

The son (Haines) of a judge (Torrence), disowned by his father because of his obstructing firemen during a blaze, redeems himself by rescuing a youngster (Darro) from a burning building.

633. Fighting Youth (7/1/25) B&W—50 mins. (Action-Drama). DIR: B. Reeves Eason. PRO: Harry Cohn. SP: Dorothy Howell. Story by Paul Archer. CAST: William Fairbanks, Pauline Garon, George Periolat, William Norton Bailey, Frank Hagney.

A young man (Fairbanks) gets into numerous fights and loses his fiancee (Garon), but gets her back when, in a charity fight, he defeats the man (Hagney) who brutally beat up her brother.

634. Final Edition (2/28/32) B&W—66 mins. (Crime). DIR: Howard Higgin. SP: Dorothy Howell. Story by Roy Chanslor. CAST: Pat O'Brien, Mae Clarke, Mary Doran, Bradley Page, Morgan Wallace, James Donlan, Phil Tead, Wallis Clark, Bertha Mann.

A girl reporter (Clarke), out to get a story, almost gets herself killed when she decides to go after the head of the town's crime syndicate (Wallace). [British title: *Determination*].

635. The Final Hour (8/1/36) B&W—57 mins. (Drama). DIR: D. Ross Lederman. PRO: Irving Briskin. SP: Harold Shumate. CAST: Ralph Bellamy, Marguerite Churchill, John Gallaudet, George McKay, Elisabeth Risdon, Marc Lawrence, Lina Basquette.

An alcoholic lawyer (Bellamy) sobers up long enough to defend a woman (Churchill) accused of murder.

636. Find the Witness (1/8/37) B&W—55 mins. (Crime-Mystery). DIR: David Selman. PRO: Ralph Cohn. SP: Grace Neville, Fred Niblo, Jr. Story by Richard Sale. CAST: Charles Quigley, Rosalind Keith, Henry Mollison, Rita La Roy, Jimmy Conlin, Charles Wilson, Wade Boteler, Harry Depp, Edward Earle, Alyce Ardell.

A reporter (Quigley) turns detective to catch a murderer at a seaside resort.

637. A Fine Mess (8/86) DeLuxe Color/Panavision—88 mins. (Comedy). DIR/SP: Blake Edwards. PRO: Tony Adams. A Columbia-Delphi V-Blake Edwards Entertainment Production. CAST: Ted Danson, Howie Mandel, Richard Mulligan, Stuart Margolin, Maria Conchita Alonso, Jennifer Edwards, Paul Sorvino, Keye Luke, Ed Herlihy, Larry Storch, Walter Charles, Rick Ducommun.

A movie extra (Danson), overhearing a plot at the racetrack to dope a horse, persuades his friend (Mandel) to place a bet on the horse. When they win, the big boss (Sorvino) has his gang go after them, and the chase begins.

638. The Finest Hours (10/64) Technicolor—116 mins. (Documentary). DIR: Peter Baylis. PRO: Jack Le Vien. SP: Victor Wolfsen. Based on the writings of Winston Churchill. CAST: Narrated by Orson Welles.

The life of Sir Winston Churchill as told through newsreels and feature film clips.

639. Fire Down Below (5/57) Technicolor/Scope—115 mins. (Adventure-Drama). DIR: Robert Parrish. PRO: Irving Allen, Albert R. Broccoli. SP: Irwin Shaw. Based on the book by Max Catto. A Warwick Production. CAST: Rita Hayworth, Jack Lemmon, Robert Mitchum, Herbert Lom, Bonar Colleano, Bernard Lee, Edric Conner, Peter Illing, Joan Miller, Anthony Newley, Eric Pohlmann.

Two partners (Lemmon, Mitchum) who are in the smuggling business have a falling out over a woman (Hayworth). NOTES: Jack Lemmon provided the film's harmonica theme.

640. Fire Over Africa (11/54) Technicolor—84 mins. (Adventure-Action). DIR: Richard Sale. PRO: Colin Lesslie, M. J. Frankovich. SP: Robert Westerby. A Film Locations Production. CAST: Macdonald Carey,

Maureen O'Hara, Guy Middleton, Hugh McDermott, James Lilburn, Harry Lane, Binnie Barnes, Leonard Sachs, Ferdy Mayne, Eric Corrie, Bruce Beeby, Gerard Tichy, Derek Sydney, Jacques Cey, Mike Brendall.

A female secret agent (O'Hara) is sent to Africa to break up a dope smuggling ring, which she does with the help of another agent (Carey). [British title: *Malaga*].

641. First Comes Courage (9/10/43) B&W–88 mins. (War). *DIR:* Dorothy Arzner. *PRO:* Harry Joe Brown. *SP:* Lewis Meltzer, Melvin Levy, George Sklar. Based on *The Commandos* by Elliott Arnold. *CAST:* Merle Oberon, Brian Aherne, Carl Esmond, Fritz Leiber, Erville Alderson, Erik Rolf, Richard Ryen, Lewis Wilson, John H. Elliott, Greta Granstedt, William "Bill" Phillips, Arno Frey, Lloyd Ingraham, Louis Jean Heydt, Miles Mander, Larry Parks, Byron Foulger, Paul Langton, Charles Irwin, Sven-Hugo Borg, Marten Lamont.

A member of the Norwegian underground (Oberon) romances a Nazi agent (Esmond) to gather vital information and aids in the rescue of a captured British commando (Aherne).

642. First Men in the Moon (10/64) Technicolor–103 mins. (Science Fiction). *DIR:* Nathan Juran. *PRO:* Charles H. Schneer. *SP:* Nigel Kneale, Jan Read. Based on the book by Jules Verne. An Ameran Production. *CAST:* Edward Judd, Martha Hyer, Lionel Jeffries, Eric Chitty, Betty McDowall, Miles Malleson, Lawrence Herder, Marne Maitland, Hugh McDermott, Gordon Robinson, Sean Kelly.

In 1899, a British trio (Judd, Hyer, Jeffries) are the first to land on the moon and encounter a race of moonmen. *NOTES:* Special effects by Ray Harryhausen.

643. First Offenders (3/15/39) B&W–63 mins. (Drama). *DIR:* Frank McDonald. *PRO:* Louis B. Appleton. *SP:* Walter Wise. Story by J. Edward Slavin. *CAST:* Walter Abel, Beverly Roberts, Iris Meredith, Johnny Downs, Diana Lewis, John Hamilton, Forbes Murray, Pierre Watkin, John Tyrrell, George Offerman, Jr., Robert Sterling, Warren Douglas, Michael Conroy, Donald "Red" Barry.

A district attorney (Abel) quits his job to start a farm where young city boys have a chance to learn a trade instead of criminal ways.

644. The First Time (1/31/52) B&W–89 mins. (Comedy). *DIR:* Frank Tashlin. *PRO:* Harold Hecht. *SP:* Frank Tashlin, Jean Rouverol, Hugo Butler, Dane Lussier. Story by Jean Rouverol, Hugo Butler. A Norma Production. *CAST:* Robert Cummings, Barbara Hale, Bill Goodwin, Jeff Donnell, Carl Benton Reid, Mona Barrie, Cora Witherspoon, Virginia Christine, Paul Harvey, Bea Benaderet, Kathleen Comegys.

A young couple (Cummings, Hale) experience the standard problems in raising a baby.

645. Five (10/51) B&W–93 mins. (Drama-Science Fiction). *DIR/PRO/SP:* Arch Obler. A Lobo Production. *CAST:* William Phipps, Susan Douglas, James Anderson, Charles Lampkin, Earl Lee.

Five people survive a nuclear holocaust; an idealist (Phipps), a mountain climber (Anderson), a black (Lampkin), a banker (Lee), and a pregnant woman (Douglas). The woman loses her baby when she goes into town to look for her husband and three of the men die of radiation poisoning. She returns to start a new life with the idealist.

646. Five Against the House (3/55) B&W–84 mins. (Crime-Drama). *DIR:* Phil Karlson. *PRO:* Stirling Silliphant. SP: Stirling Silliphant, William Bowers, John Barnwell. Story by Jack Finney. A Doyle Production. CAST: Guy Madison, Kim Novak, Brian Keith, Alvy Moore, William Conrad, Kerwin Mathews, Jack Diamond, Jean Willes, John Zaremba, George Brand, Mark Hanna, Hugh Sanders, Carroll McComas.

Five college students (Madison, Keith, Moore, Mathews, Novak) devise a plan to rob a Reno, Nevada, casino.

647. Five Angles on Murder (10/50) B&W—88 mins. (Crime). DIR: Anthony Asquith. PRO: Edward Baird. SP: John Cresswell. A J. Arthur Rank-Javelin Film Production. CAST: Jean Kent, Dirk Bogarde, John McCallum, Susan Shaw, Hermione Baddeley, Charles Victor, Duncan MacRae, Lana Morris, Vida Hope, Duncan Lamont, Anthony Dawson, Josephine Middleton, Albert Chevalier.

When a fairground fortune teller (Kent) is murdered, the police get five different views of the woman's life through interviews with the peole who knew her. [British title: The Woman in Question].

648. Five Easy Pieces (9/70) Eastman Color—96 mins. (Drama). DIR: Bob Rafelson. PRO: Bob Rafelson, Richard Wechsler. SP: Adrien Joyce (Carol Eastman). Based on a story by Bob Rafelson and Adrien Joyce. A BBS Production. CAST: Jack Nicholson, Karen Black, Billy Green Bush, Fannie Flagg, Sally Ann Struthers, Marlena MacGuire, Lorna Thayer, Susan Anspach, Ralph Waite, William Challee, Irene Dailey, Toni Basil, Helena Kallianiotes.

A middle-class man (Nicholson), who gave up being a classical pianist for a different life, and his pregnant girlfriend (Black) head home to visit his family and his dying father.

649. Five Finger Exercise (6/62) B&W—108 mins. (Drama). DIR: Daniel Mann. PRO: Fredrick Brisson. SP: Francis Goodrich, Albert Hackett. Based on the play by Peter Shaffer. CAST: Rosalind Russell, Jack Hawkins, Maximilian Schell, Richard Beymer, Annette Gorman, Lana Wood, Todd Armstrong, Terry Huntington, William Quinn, Mary Benoit, Bart Conrad, Jeannine Riley, Kathy West.

A neurotic California family (Russell, Hawkins, Beymer, Gorman) take in a German refugee (Schell) as a tutor, which adds to increased tensions within the family.

650. Five Golden Hours (2/61) B&W—90 mins. (Comedy). DIR/PRO: Mario Zampi. SP: Hans Wilheim. An Anglofilm Production. CAST: Ernie Kovacs, Cyd Charisse, George Sanders, Kay Hammond, Dennis Price, John Le Mesurier, Finlay Currie, Reginald Beckwith, Ron Moody, Leonard Sachs, Martin Benson, Clelia Matania, Bruno Barnabe.

A professional mourner and con man (Kovacs) teams with a baroness (Charisse) in a swindling scheme, but when it backfires he tries to murder the three widows he swindled. [Original Italian title: Cinque Ore in Contanti].

651. Five Little Peppers and How They Grew (11/28/39) B&W—58 mins. (Comedy-Drama). DIR: Charles Barton. PRO: Jack Fier. SP: Nathalie Bucknall, Jefferson Parker. Based on Five Little Peppers and How They Grew by Margaret Sidney. CAST: Edith Fellows, Dorothy Ann Seese, Dorothy Peterson, Charles Peck, Tommy Bond, Jimmy Leake, Ronald Sinclair, Harry Bernard, Clarence Kolb, Bruce Bennett, Paul Everton, George Lloyd, Edward J. LeSaint, Harry Hayden, Linda Winters (Dorothy Comingore), Betty Roadman, Bessie Wade, Maurice Costello, Flo Campbell, Leonard Carey.

The five Pepper kids (Fellows, Seese, Peck, Bond, Leake) and their mother (Peterson) move in with their friend (Sinclair) and his grandfather (Kolb) when the mother becomes ill and cannot work.

652. Five Little Peppers at Home (4/10/40) B&W – 67 mins. (Comedy-Drama). DIR: Charles Barton. PRO: Jack Fier. SP: Harry Sauber. Based on *Five Little Peppers and How They Grew* by Margaret Sidney. CAST: Edith Fellows, Dorothy Ann Seese, Dorothy Peterson, Charles Peck, Tommy Bond, Bobby Larson, Ronald Sinclair, Rex Evans, Clarence Kolb, Herbert Rawlinson, Laura Treadwell, Bruce Bennett, Spencer Charters, Jack Rice, Ann Doran, Edward J. Le-Saint, Paul Everton, John Dilson, Joseph DeStefani, Richard Fiske, Tom London, Sam Ash, Marin Sais.

The Pepper kids and Jasper (Sinclair) try to help their mother (Peterson) and Mr. King (Kolb) keep their jobs.

653. Five Little Peppers in Trouble (11/15/40) B&W – 63 mins. (Comedy-Drama). DIR: Charles Barton. PRO: Jack Fier. SP: Harry Rebuas. Based on *Five Little Peppers and How They Grew* by Margaret Sidney. CAST: Edith Fellows, Dorothy Ann Seese, Dorothy Peterson, Charles Peck, Tommy Bond, Bobby Larson, Ronald Sinclair, Pierre Watkin, Rex Evans, Eddie Laughton, Kathleen Howard, Mary Currier, Helen Brown, Betty Jane Graham, Shirley Mills, Shirley Jean Rickert, Antonia Oland, Rita Quigley, Beverly Michaelson, Judy Lynn, Bess Flowers, Reginald Simpson, Carlton Griffin, Sue Ann Barnett, Fred Mercer, Billy Lechner, Ruth Robinson, Robert Carson, Ann Barlow.

Mrs. Pepper (Peterson) and Mr. King (Watkin) send the Pepper kids

and Jasper (Sinclair) off to boarding school where they get into trouble.

654. The 5000 Fingers of Dr. T (7/1/53) Technicolor – 89 mins. (Fantasy-Musical). DIR: Roy Rowland. PRO: Stanley Kramer. SP: Theodore Geisel (Dr. Seuss), Allan Scott. A Stanley Kramer Production. CAST: Peter Lind Hayes, Mary Healy, Hans Conreid, Tommy Rettig, John Heasley, Robert Heasley, Noel Cravat, Henry Kulky.

A young boy (Rettig), who hates taking piano lessons, dreams he is captive of an evil doctor (Conreid) who keeps five hundred boys prisoner in his castle of musical instruments.

655. Flame of Calcutta (7/20/53) Technicolor – 70 mins. (Adventure-Drama). DIR: Seymour Friedman. PRO: Sam Katzman. SP: Robert E. Kent. Story by Sol Shor. An Esskay Pictures Production. CAST: Denise Darcel, Patric Knowles, Paul Cavanagh, George Keymas, Joseph Mell, Ted Thorpe, Leonard Penn, Gregory Gay, Edward Clark, Robin Hughes.

In 18th century India, a mysterious girl (Darcel), known as the "Flame," joins forces with a British officer (Knowles) to wipe out a villainous prince (Keymas).

656. Flame of Stamboul (3/5/51) B&W – 68 mins. (Spy-Drama). DIR: Ray Nazarro. PRO: Wallace MacDonald. SP: Daniel B. Ullman. CAST: Richard Denning, Lisa Ferraday, Norman Lloyd, Nestor Paiva, George Zucco, Donald Randolph, Peter Brocco, Peter Mamakos, Paul Marion.

A U.S. intelligence agent (Denning) is sent to the city of Stamboul to stop a mysterious spy, known as the "Voice" (Zucco), from stealing defense plans of the Suez Canal.

657. Flight (11/1/29) B&W – 110 mins. (Aviation-Drama). DIR: Frank

Capra. *PRO:* Harry Cohn. *SP:* Howard J. Green. Story by Ralph Graves. A Frank Capra Production. *CAST:* Jack Holt, Lila Lee, Ralph Graves, Alan Roscoe, Harold Goodwin, Jimmy De La Cruze.

A football player (Graves) joins the Marine Corps to forget about his career, and he and his best friend (Holt) are sent to Nicaragua to stop a revolutionary uprising. NOTE: Columbia's first outdoor sound picture.

658. Flight (6/60) B&W—72 mins. (Drama). *DIR:* Louis Bispo. *SP:* Barnaby Conrad. Based on *Flight* by John Steinbeck. A San Francisco Films Incorporated Production. *CAST:* Efrain Ramirez, Ester Cortez, Maria Gonzales, Endrew Cortez, Ed Smith, Susan Jane Darby, Richard Crommie, Edward O'Brien, Barnaby Conrad.

A Mexican youth (Ramirez) kills a drunk in a bar and flees to the mountains where he is hunted by the police and the drunk's friend.

659. Flight Into Nowhere (4/19/38) B&W—63 mins. (Aviation-Drama). *DIR:* Lewis D. Collins. *PRO:* Larry Darmour. *SP:* Jefferson Parker, Gordon Rigby. Story by William Bloom, Clarence Jay Schneider. *CAST:* Jack Holt, Jacqueline Wells (Julie Bishop), Dick Purcell, James Burke, Karen Sorrell, Fritz Leiber, Howard Hickman, Robert Fiske, Hector V. Sarno.

A hot-shot pilot (Purcell), after being grounded for his reckless stunts, steals a plane and ends up crashing in an uncharted jungle.

660. Flight Lieutenant (6/29/42) B&W—80 mins. (Aviation-Drama). *DIR:* Sidney Salkow. *PRO:* B. P. Schulberg. *SP:* Michael Blankfort. Story by Richard Carroll, Betty Hopkins. *CAST:* Glenn Ford, Pat O'Brien, Evelyn Keyes, Jonathan Hale, Minor Watson, Frank Puglia, Edward Pawley, Gregory Gay, Clancy Cooper, Trevor Bardette,

Marcel Dalio, John Gallaudet, Larry Parks, Lloyd Bridges, Hugh Beaumont, Douglas Croft, William Forrest.

While his son (Ford) makes his way up in the ranks of the Air Force, the father (O'Brien), a disgraced pilot, attempts to rebuild his self-image and esteem.

661. Flight of the Doves (4/71) Eastman Color—101 mins. (Children-Drama). *DIR/PRO:* Ralph Nelson. *SP:* Frank Gabrielson, Ralph Nelson. Based on the book by Walter Macken. A Rainbow Production. *CAST:* Ron Moody, Jack Wild, Dorothy McGuire, Stanley Holloway, Helen Raye, William Rushton, James Barclay, Brendan O'Reilly, Brendan Cauldwell.

Two youngsters (Wild, Raye), who run away from their cruel stepfather to join their Irish grandmother (McGuire), are pursued by their wicked uncle (Moody) who wants their inheritance.

662. Flight to Fame (12/21/38) B&W—67 mins. (Science Fiction). *DIR:* C. C. Coleman, Jr. *PRO:* Ralph Cohn. *SP:* Michael L. Simmons. *CAST:* Charles Farrell, Jacqueline Wells (Julie Bishop), Hugh Sothern, Alexander D'Arcy, Jason Robards, Sr., Charles D. Brown, Addison Richards, Frederick Burton, Selmer Jackson, Reed Howes.

A crazed pilot (Robards) steals a death ray and uses it to down the planes of other pilots until he is stopped by a pilot (Farrell) and the inventor's daughter (Wells).

663. The Flood (5/3/31) B&W—65 mins. (Drama). *DIR:* James Tinling. *SP:* John Thomas Neville. *CAST:* Eleanor Boardman, Monte Blue, Frank Sheridan, William V. Mong, Violet Barlowe, Eddie Tamblyn, Arthur Hoyt, Ethel Wales, Buddy Ray, Ethan Allen, David Newell.

Set against the backdrop of a faltering dam in the Mississippi Valley, a young girl (Boardman) is torn between two loves.

664. The Flying Fontaines (12/ 59) Eastman Color — 73 mins. (Drama). *DIR:* George Sherman. *PRO:* Sam Katzman. *SP:* Lee Erwin, Don Mullally. A Clover Production. *CAST:* Michael Callan, Evy Norlund, Joan Evans, Rian Garrick, Roger Perry, Joe de Santis, John Van Dreelan, Jeanne Manet, Barbara Kelly, Dorothy Johnson, Pierre Watkin, Murray Parker, William Quinn.

A high-wire artist (Callan) returns home from the war, finds his girl married, and resumes his career with the circus, only to become seriously injured while performing his act.

665. The Flying Marine (6/5/29) B&W — 60 mins. (Drama). *DIR:* Albert S. Rogell. *PRO:* Harry Cohn. *SP:* Jack Natteford. Story by Norman Houston. *CAST:* Ben Lyon, Shirley Mason, Jason Robards, Sr.

When a man (Robards) learns that his girl (Mason) is in love with his brother (Lyon), he sacrifices his life to save his brother. *NOTES:* Released as both a silent and sound film.

666. The Flying Missile (12/27/ 50) B&W — 91 mins. (War-Drama). *DIR:* Henry Levin. *PRO:* Jerry Bresler. *SP:* Richard English, James Gunn. Story by N. Richard Nash, Harvey S. Haislip. *CAST:* Glenn Ford, Viveca Lindfors, Henry O'Neill, Carl Benton Reid, Joe Sawyer, John Qualen, Anthony Ross, Harry Shannon, Ross Ford, Jerry Paris, Kenneth Tobey, Paul Harvey, Grandon Rhodes, James Seay, Richard Quine, Charles Evans, Zachary A. Charles.

A submarine commander (Ford) defies Navy authority to prove that guided missiles can be launched from submarines.

Fog *see* **A Study in Terror**

667. Fog (1/6/34) B&W — 70 mins. (Mystery). *DIR:* Albert S. Rogell. *SP:* Ethel Hill, Dore Schary. Based on *Fog* by Valentine Williams, Dorothy Rice Sims. *CAST:* Donald Cook, Mary Brian, Reginald Denny, Maude Eburne, Robert McQuade, Helen Freeman, Samuel S. Hinds, G. Pat Collins, Edwin Maxwell, Marjorie Gateson.

On an ocean liner enveloped in fog, a couple of passengers (Cook, Brian) try to solve three murders with the help of a soothsayer (Freeman).

668. A Fool and His Money (3/ 1/24) B&W — 56 mins. (Drama). *DIR:* Erle C. Kenton. *PRO:* Harry Cohn. *SP:* Douglas Z. Doty. Story by George B. McCutcheon. *CAST:* Madge Bellamy, William Haines, Stuart Holmes, Alma Bennett.

A writer (Haines) buys a castle and encounters what he thinks is a woman's ghost, but in reality she (Bellamy) is the wife of the castle's previous owner (Holmes).

669. Foolin' Around (3/80) DeLuxe Color — 111 mins. (Romance-Comedy). *DIR:* Richard T. Heffron. *PRO:* Arnold Kopelson. *SP:* Michael Kane. Story by David Swift. *CAST:* Gary Busey, Annette O'Toole, John Calvin, Eddie Albert, Shirley Kane, Tony Randall, Cloris Leachman, Michael Talbott, W. H. Macy, Beth Rosacker, Roy Jenson, Gene Lebell.

A ranch hand (Busey) goes to college in Minnesota, falls for a rich heiress (O'Toole) and tries to win her even though she is engaged to someone else.

670. The Foolish Virgin (2/1/24) B&W — 58 mins. (Drama). *DIR:* George W. Hill. *PRO:* Harry Cohn. *SP:* Lois Zellner. A C.B.C. Release. *CAST:* Elaine Hammerstein, Robert Frazer, Gladys Brockwell, Phyllis Haver.

When a reformed thief (Frazer) is

spurned by his sweetheart (Hammerstein), he redeems himself by rescuing
her from a forest fire.

671. Fools' Parade (7/71) East-
man Color—98 mins. (Drama). *DIR/
PRO:* Andrew V. McLaglen. *SP:*
James Lee Barrett. Based on the book
by Davis Grubb. A Stanmore-Penbar
Production. *CAST:* James Stewart,
George Kennedy, Anne Baxter, Stro-
ther Martin, Kurt Russell, William
Windom, Mike Kellin, Kathy Cannon,
Morgan Paull, Robert Donner, David
Huddleston, James Lee Barrett.

Three ex-cons (Stewart, Martin,
Russell) try to open a business with the
money one of them has saved, but are
stalked by their ex-guard (Kennedy)
and his men who want the money.
NOTES: James Stewart's last film for
Columbia. [British title: *Dynamite
Man from Glory Jail*].

672. Footlight Glamour (9/30/
43) B&W—68 mins. (Comedy). *DIR/
PRO:* Frank R. Strayer. *SP:* Karen De-
Wolf, Connie Lee. Based on the comic
strip created by Chic Young. *CAST:*
Penny Singleton, Arthur Lake, Larry
Simms, Irving Bacon, Danny Mum-
mert, Jonathan Hale, Ann Savage,
Thurston Hall, Grace Hayle, Marjorie
Ann Mutchie, Rafael Storm, Arthur
Loft, James Flavin.

When Dagwood (Lake) is hired by a
tool manufacturer (Hall) for another
job, Blondie (Singleton) tries to stop it
by casting the boss's daughter (Savage)
in a play.

673. Footsteps in the Fog (9/55)
Technicolor—90 mins. (Drama). *DIR:*
Arthur Lubin. *PRO:* M. J. Frankovich,
Maxwell Sutton. *SP:* Dorothy Reid,
Lenore Coffee, Arthur Pierson. Based
on *The Interruption* by William Wy-
mark Jacobs. A Films Location Lim-
ited Production. *CAST:* Stewart Gran-
ger, Jean Simmons, Bill Travers,
Finlay Currie, Ronald Squire, Belinda

Lee, William Hartnell, Frederick Leister, Peter Bull, Victor Maddern, Cameron Hall, Sheila Manahan.

In London at the turn of the century, a maid (Simmons) blackmails her
employer (Granger) when she learns
he has killed his wife.

674. For Ladies Only (7/20/27)
B&W—57 mins. (Comedy). *DIR:*
Scott Pembroke. *PRO:* Harry Cohn.
SP: Robert Lord. Story by George F.
Worts. *CAST:* John Bowers, Jac-
queline Logan, Edna Marion, Ben
Hall.

A secretary (Logan) outsmarts her
boss (Bowers) when he fires all his
female employees.

675. For Pete's Sake (6/74) East-
man Color—90 mins. (Comedy). *DIR:*
Peter Yates. *PRO:* Martin Erlichman,
Stanley Shapiro. *SP:* Stanley Shapiro,
Maurice Richlin. A Rastar Production.
CAST: Barbra Streisand, Michael Sar-
razin, Estelle Parsons, William Red-
field, Molly Picon, Louis Zorich, Vivian
Bonnell, Haywood Hale Broun, Richard
Ward, Joseph Maher, Anne Ramsey.

A devoted wife (Streisand) involves
herself in several wacky schemes to
raise some extra money so that her cab
driver husband (Sarrazin) can finish his
education.

676. For Singles Only (5/68)
Pathe Color—91 mins. (Musical-Com-
edy-Drama). *DIR:* Arthur Dreifuss.
PRO: Sam Katzman. *SP:* Arthur
Dreifuss, Hal Collins. Story by Arthur
Hoerl and Albert Derr. A Four Leaf
Production. *CAST:* John Saxon, Mary
Ann Mobley, Milton Berle, Lana
Wood, Ann Elder, Mark Richman,
Chris Noel, Marty Ingels, Hortense
Petra, Charles Robinson, Dick Castle,
Norman Wells, Duke Hobbie, Walter
Wanderley Trio, Cal Tjader Band,
Nitty Gritty Dirt Band, Lewis & Clark
Expedition, The Sunshine Company.

Two girls (Mobley, Wood) move into

a "singles" apartment complex and have several misadventures while fighting off the men.

677. For the Love O' Lil (11/30/ 30) B&W—67 mins. (Drama). *DIR:* James Tinling. *PRO:* Harry Cohn. *SP:* Dorothy Howell, Bella Cohen, Robert Bruckner. Story by J. Leslie Thrasher. *CAST:* Jack Mulhall, Elliott Nugent, Sally Starr, Margaret Livingston, Joan Standing, Charles Sellon, Julia Swayne Gordon, Billy Bevan, Claire Du Brey.

A lawyer (Mulhall) tries to settle down but is used as a scapegoat in a divorce trial.

678. For the Love of Rusty (5/1/ 47) B&W—68 mins. (Children). *DIR:* John Sturges. *PRO:* John Haggott. *SP:* Malcolm Stuart Boylan. Based on characters created by Al Martin. *CAST:* Ted Donaldson, Tom Powers, Ann Doran, Aubrey Mather, Sid Tomack, George Meader, Mickey McGuire, Harry Hayden, Dick Elliott, Olin Howlin, Teddy Infuhr, Fred F. Sears, Dwayne Hickman, George Nokes, Almira Sessions, "Flame," the Dog.

When a boy (Donaldson) has a falling out with his father (Powers), they are brought back together through the boy's dog and a kind hearted veterinarian (Mather).

679. Forbidden (1/15/32) B&W— 87 mins. (Drama). *DIR:* Frank Capra. *PRO:* Harry Cohn. *SP:* Jo Swerling. Story by Frank Capra. A Frank Capra Production. *CAST:* Barbara Stanwyck, Adolphe Menjou, Ralph Bellamy, Dorothy Peterson, Thomas Jefferson, Myrna Fresholt, Charlotte Henry, Oliver Eckhardt, Halliwell Hobbes, Flo Wix, Claude King, Robert Graves, Harry Holman.

A librarian (Stanwyck) has an affair with a married man (Menjou) and bears his child. When, years later, he is to become governor, her husband (Bel-

lamy) threatens to expose her affair and she shoots him. Later, she is pardoned by the dying governor.

680. Forbidden Island (3/59) Columbia Color—66 mins. (Adventure). *DIR/PRO/SP:* Charles B. Griffith. *CAST:* Jon Hall, Nan Adams, John Farrow, Jonathan Haze, Greigh Phillips, Dave "Howdy" Peters, Tookie Evans, Martin Denny, Bob LaVarre, Bill Anderson, Abraham Kaluna.

A psychotic treasure hunter (Farrow) hires a frogman (Hall) to locate a hidden treasure in a shipwreck.

681. Forbidden Trail (11/18/32) B&W—71 mins. (Western). *DIR:* Lambert Hillyer. *SP:* Milton Krims. *CAST:* Buck Jones, Barbara Weeks, Mary Carr, George Cooper, Ed Brady, Al Smith, Frank Rice, Frank LaRue, Wong Chung, Wallis Clark, Tom Forman, Dick Rush, Charles Berner, Gertrude Howard.

A cowboy (Jones) pretends to be a fool in order to catch the outlaw gang terrorizing the territory.

682. Forgive and Forget (9/16/ 23) B&W—57 mins. (Crime-Drama). *DIR:* Howard M. Mitchell. *PRO:* Harry Cohn. *SP:* Jack Sturmwasser. Story by Charles Furthman. A C.B.C. Release. *CAST:* Estelle Taylor, Pauline Garon, Philo McCullough, Josef Swickard, Wyndham Standing, Vernon Steele.

A woman (Taylor) is being blackmailed by her lover's roommate (McCullough). When her lover is found murdered, her husband (Standing) is accused of the crime.

683. Fort Savage Raiders (3/15/ 51) B&W—54 mins. (Western). *DIR:* Ray Nazarro. *PRO:* Colbert Clark. *SP:* Barry Shipman. *CAST:* Charles Starrett, John Dehner, Smiley Burnette, Trevor Bardette, Fred F. Sears, Sam

Flint, John Cason, Dusty Walker, Peter Thompson, Frank Griffin.

The Durango Kid (Starrett) tracks down an Army deserter (Dehner) and his gang who have been terrorizing the plains.

684. Fort Ti (5/1/53) Technicolor/3-D—73 mins. (Western). *DIR:* William Castle. *PRO:* Sam Katzman. *SP:* Robert E. Kent. An Esskay Picture Production. *CAST:* George Montgomery, Joan Vohs, Irving Bacon, James Seay, Howard Petrie, Lester Matthews, Louis D. Merrill, Cicely Browne, Ben Astar, Phyllis Fowler, George Lee.

During the French and Indian wars, an Indian scout (Montgomery) leads Rogers' Rangers to oust the French from Fort Ticonderoga.

685. The Fortune (6/75) Technicolor—88 mins. (Comedy). *DIR:* Mike Nichols. *PRO:* Mike Nichols, Don Devlin. *SP:* Adrien Joyce (Carol Eastman). *CAST:* Jack Nicholson, Warren Beatty, Stockard Channing, Florence Stanley, Richard B. Shull, Tom Newman, John Fiedler, Scatman Crothers, Dub Taylor, Ian Wolfe, Brian Avery, Christopher Guest.

Two con men (Nicholson, Beatty) plan to kidnap an heiress (Channing), romance her, then bilk her out of her fortune, but when things go wrong, they try to murder her with comic results.

686. Fortunes of Captain Blood (5/19/50) B&W—90 mins. (Adventure). *DIR:* Gordon Douglas. *PRO:* Harry Joe Brown. *SP:* Michael Hogan, Robert Libott, Frank Burt. Based on *The Fortunes of Captain Blood* by Rafael Sabatini. *CAST:* Louis Hayward, Patricia Medina, George Macready, Alfonso Bedoya, Dona Drake, Lowell Gilmore, Wilton Graff, Curt Bois, Lumsden Hare, Billy Bevan,

Harry Cording, Duke York, Sven-Hugo Borg, Charles Irwin, Terry Kilburn.

Peter Blood (Hayward), physician, turns pirate when he is convicted of helping a rebel and sails the seven seas to revenge wrongdoings.

687. 40 Carats (6/73) Eastman Color—108 mins. (Comedy). *DIR:* Milton Katselas. *PRO:* M. J. Frankovich. *SP:* Leonard Gershe. Based on the play adapted by Jay Allen from the French play by Pierre Barillet and Jean-Pierre Gredy. *CAST:* Liv Ullmann, Edward Albert, Gene Kelly, Binnie Barnes, Deborah Raffin, Billy Green Bush, Nancy Walker, Don Porter, Rosemary Murphy, Natalie Schafer, Claudia Jennings, Brooke Palance, Sam Chew, Jr.

While vacationing in Greece, a woman of 40 (Ullmann) finds romance with a much younger man (Albert).

688. Forty Guns to Apache Pass (5/67) Pathe Color—95 mins. (Western). *DIR:* William Whitney. *PRO:* Grant Whytock. *SP:* Mary Willingham, Willard Willingham. An Admiral Production. *CAST:* Audie Murphy, Laraine Stevens, Michael Burns, Kenneth Tobey, Ted Gehring, Kenneth MacDonald, Robert Brubaker, Michael Blodgett, Michael Keep, Kay Stewart, Byron Morrow, Willard Willingham, James Beck.

A cavalry captain (Murphy) must stop one of his men (Tobey) from selling guns to the Indians, while trying to stop Cochise (Keep) from attacking the homesteaders.

689. The 49th Man (5/12/53) B&W—73 mins. (Spy-Drama). *DIR:* Fred F. Sears. *PRO:* Sam Katzman. *SP:* Harry J. Essex. Story by Ivan Tors. *CAST:* John Ireland, Richard Denning, Suzanne Dalbert, Robert C. Foulk, Michael (Touch) Conners, Richard Avonde, William R. Klein, Cicely Browne, Tommy Farrell, Peter

Marshall, Genevieve Aumont, Chris Alcaide, George Milan.

A U.S. security investigator (Ireland) tracks down foreign spies smuggling A-bomb parts into the U.S.

690. The Four-Poster (10/8/52) B&W — 103 mins. (Comedy-Drama). *DIR*: Irving Reis. *PRO*: Stanley Kramer. *SP*: Allan Scott. Based on the play by Jan de Hartog. A Stanley Kramer Production. *CAST*: Rex Harrison, Lili Palmer.

A married couple (Harrison, Palmer) go through their lives, from marriage to death, played out in scenes around their four-poster bed. *NOTES*: Animated sequences by UPA Studios.

691. Fragment of Fear (9/70) Eastman Color — 95 mins. (Crime-Mystery). *DIR*: Richard C. Sarafian. *PRO*: John R. Sloan. *SP*: Paul Dehn. Based on the book by John Bingham. *CAST*: David Hemmings, Gayle Hunnicutt, Flora Robson, Wilfrid Hyde-White, Daniel Massey, Roland Culver, Adolfo Celi, Mona Washbourne, Glyn Edwards, Mary Wimbush, Derek Newkirk, Arthur Lowe, John Rae.

A reformed junkie (Hemmings), now a writer, begins to question his own sanity when he goes to Pompeii to investigate the murder of his aunt.

692. The Frame-Up (8/12/37) B&W — 59 mins. (Crime). *DIR*: D. Ross Lederman. *PRO*: Ralph Cohn. *SP*: Harold Shumate. Based on *Right Guy* by Richard E. Wormser. *CAST*: Paul Kelly, Jacqueline Wells (Julie Bishop), George McKay, Robert Emmett O'Conner, Raphael Bennett, Wade Boteler, Edward Earle, John Tyrrell, Ted Oliver, C. Montague Shaw, Horace Murphy.

When his girl (Wells) is kidnapped by the mob, a race track detective (Kelly) must submit to their criminal plans until he can find the chance to outwit them.

693. Framed (3/7/47) B&W — 82 mins. (Crime-Drama). *DIR*: Richard Wallace. *PRO*: Jules Schermer. *SP*: Ben Maddow. Story by Jack Patrick. *CAST*: Glenn Ford, Janis Carter, Barry Sullivan, Edgar Buchanan, Karen Morley, Jim Bannon, Sid Tomack, Barbara Woodell, Paul E. Burns, Charles Cane, Robert Stevens, Fred Graff, Kenneth MacDonald, Al Bridge, Gene Roth, Snub Pollard, Stanley Andrews, Harry Strang, Nacho Galindo, Eugene Borden.

A truck driver (Ford) is set up as a fall guy by two thieves (Carter, Sullivan) when they plan to rob a bank. [British title: *Paula*].

694. Fresh Horses (10/88) CFI Color — 105 mins. (Romance-Drama). *DIR*: David Anspaugh. *PRO*: Dick Berg. *SP*: Larry Ketron. Based on the play by Larry Ketron. A Weintraub Entertainment Production. *CAST*: Molly Ringwald, Andrew McCarthy, Patti D'Arbanville, Ben Stiller, Leon Russom, Molly Hagen, Doug Hutchinson, Larry Ketron.

A rich college kid (McCarthy) decides to give up college and his friends when he falls in love with a girl (Ringwald) from the wrong side of the tracks.

695. Fright Night (7/85) Metrocolor — 106 mins. (Horror). *DIR/SP*: Tom Holland. *PRO*: Herb Jaffe. *CAST*: Chris Sarandon, William Ragsdale, Amanda Bearse, Roddy McDowall, Stephen Geoffreys, Jonathan Stark, Dorothy Fielding, Art Evans, Stewart Stern, Robert Corff, Pamela Brown.

A teenager (Ragsdale) enlists the help of an aging horror-film star (McDowall) to help prove that his neighbor (Sarandon) is a vampire and must be destroyed.

696. From Here to Eternity (9/29/53) B&W — 118 mins. (Drama). *DIR*: Fred Zinnemann. *PRO*: Buddy

Adler. SP: Daniel Taradash. Based on the book by James Jones. CAST: Burt Lancaster, Deborah Kerr, Frank Sinatra, Donna Reed, Montgomery Clift, Ernest Borgnine, Philip Ober, Jack Warden, Mickey Shaughnessy, Harry Bellaver, George Reeves, John Dennis, Tim Ryan, Barbara Morrison, Kristine Miller, Jean Willes, Merle Travis, Claude Akins, Robert Wilke, Don Dubbins, John Cason, Joan Shawlee, Angela Stevens.

The lives of five people (Lancaster, Kerr, Sinatra, Reed, Clift) are drastically changed during the days before Pearl Harbor is attacked. NOTES: The original cast slated for this film was to be (in cast order as shown above): Edmond O'Brien, Joan Crawford, Eli Wallach, Julie Harris and either John Derek or Aldo Ray. Due to other commitments or the objections of Harry Cohn and/or director Zinnemann over the originally selected cast, the above cast was finally selected for this film.

697. The Front (9/76) Eastman Color/Panavision—94 mins. (Drama-Comedy). DIR/PRO: Martin Ritt. SP: Walter Bernstein. CAST: Woody Allen, Zero Mostel, Herschel Bernardi, Andrea Marcovicci, Michael Murphy, Lloyd Gough, Joshua Shelley, Norman Rose, Danny Aiello, Remak Ramsay, Marvin Lichterman, David Margulies, Scott McKay, Julie Garfield.

During the 1950's McCarthy witch-hunt era, a New York bookkeeper (Allen) is hired by blacklisted television writers to put his name to their scripts.

698. Frontier Fury (6/24/43) B&W—55 mins. (Western). DIR: William Berke. PRO: Jack Fier. SP: Betty Burbridge. CAST: Charles Starrett, Roma Aldrich, Arthur Hunnicutt, Stanley Brown, Clancy Cooper, Bruce Bennett, I. Stanford Jolley, Ted Mapes, Edmund Cobb, Bill Wilkerson, Frank LaRue, Lew Meehan, Stanley

Brown, Joel Friedkin, Johnny Bond, Chief Yowlachie, Jimmy Davis and His Singing Buckaroos.

When an Indian agent (Starrett) is robbed of the money allocated to the Indian tribe, he sets out to find those responsible and bring them to justice.

699. Frontier Gunlaw (1/31/46) B&W—60 mins. (Western). DIR: Derwin Abrahams. PRO: Colbert Clark. SP: Bennett R. Cohen. Story by Victor McLeod. CAST: Charles Starrett, Jean Stevens, Tex Harding, Frank LaRue, Dub Taylor, John Elliott, Jack Rockwell, Bob Kortman, Stanley Price, Weldon Heyburn, Hank Worden, John Tyrrell, Bill Nestell, Al Trace and His Silly Symphonists.

The Durango Kid (Starrett) brings to justice the outlaw gang known as the "Phantoms" who have been plaguing the ranchers. [British title: Menacing Shadows].

700. Frontier Hellcat (11/66) Eastman Color/Scope—98 mins. (Western). DIR: Alfred Vohrer. PRO: Preben Philipsen. SP: Eberhard Keindorff, Johanna Sibelius. Based on the book by Karl Friedrich May. A Rialto-Atlantis-S.N.J.-Jadran Production. CAST: Stewart Granger, Pierre Brice, Elke Sommer, Gotz George, Walter Barnes, Sieghardt Rupp, Renato Baldini, Mario Girotti, Louis Velle, Paddy Fox, Miha Baloh.

Old Surehand (Granger) and Winnetou (Brice) rescue a kidnapped woman (Sommer) from a band of outlaws known as the "Vultures." NOTES: Released in Germany in 1964 at a running time of 102 mins. [Original German title: Unter Geiern]. [Original French title: Parmi les Vautours]. [Original Yugoslavian title: Medju Jastrebovima].

701. Frontier Outpost (12/29/49) B&W—55 mins. (Western). DIR: Ray Nazarro. PRO: Colbert Clark. SP: Barry Shipman. CAST: Charles Starrett, Lois Hall, Smiley Burnette, Steve Darrell, Fred F. Sears, Bob Wilke, Jock Mahoney, Bud Osborne, Dick Wessel, Paul Campbell, Pierre Watkin, Chuck Roberson, Hank Penny, Slim Duncan, Everett Glass.

A U.S. Marshal (Starrett), accused of intercepting gold shipments, disguises himself as The Durango Kid and tracks down the real outlaws responsible.

702. Frontiers of '49 (1/19/39) B&W — 54 mins. (Western). *DIR:* Joseph Levering. *PRO:* Larry Darmour. *SP:* Nate Gatzert. *CAST:* Bill Elliott, Luana DeAlcaniz, Hal Taliaferro (Wally Wales), Charles King, Slim Whitaker, Al Ferguson, Jack Walters, Bud Osborne, Jack Ingram, Kit Guard, Frank Ellis, Lee Shumway, Joe de la Cruz, Tex Palmer, Carlos Villarias, Ed Cassidy, Octavio Giraud.

An Army major (Elliott) is sent to Spanish territory to stop a land agent (King) from stealing the settlers' land.

703. Fugitive at Large (8/22/39) B&W — 66 mins. (Drama). *DIR:* Lewis D. Collins. *PRO:* Larry Darmour. *SP:* Eric Taylor, Harvey Gates. Story by Eric Taylor. *CAST:* Jack Holt, Patricia Ellis, Stanley Fields, Arthur Hohl, Leon Ames, Cy Kendall, Weldon Heyburn, Guinn "Big Boy" Williams, Jonathan Hale, Don Douglas, Ben Welden, Leon Beaumon.

A robber (Holt) sees a civil engineer (Holt) who looks like him, and sets him up to take the rap for his crimes.

704. Fugitive from a Prison Camp (8/6/40) B&W — 58 mins. (Prison-Drama). *DIR:* Lewis D. Collins. *PRO:* Larry Darmour. *SP:* Albert DeMond. Story by Stanley Roberts. *CAST:* Jack Holt, Marian Marsh, Jack LaRue, Robert Barrat, Phillip Terry, Dennis Moore, George Offerman, Jr., Frank Burke, Donald Haines, Alan Baldwin, Frank LaRue, Ernest Morrison.

A sheriff (Holt), out to prove that prisoners can be rehabilitated, gets them jobs on a road construction project.

705. Fugitive Lady (12/10/34) B&W — 66 mins. (Drama). *DIR:* Albert S. Rogell. *PRO:* Sid Rogell. *SP:* Fred Niblo, Jr., Herbert Asbury. *CAST:* Neil Hamilton, Florence Rice, Donald Cook, Clara Blandick, Nella Walker, William Demarest, Wade Boteler, Rita La Roy, Howard Hickman, Billie Seward, Edward J. LeSaint, Phillips Smalley, Sam Flint, Pat O'Malley, Bess Flowers, Lucille Ball, Harry Holman.

A girl (Rice) unknowingly marries a jewel thief (Hamilton) and gets blamed for his crimes. While being sent to prison she is involved in a train wreck and assumes a new identity.

706. The Fugitive Sheriff (10/20/36) B&W — 58 mins. (Western). *DIR:* Spencer G. Bennet. *PRO:* Larry Darmour. *SP:* Nate Gatzert. *CAST:* Ken Maynard, Beth Marion, Walter Miller, Hal Price, Edmund Cobb, Lafe McKee, Art Mix, Vernon Dent, Bud Osborne, Glenn Strange, John Elliott, Slim Whitaker, Frank Ellis, Arthur Millette, Virginia True Boardman, Frank Ball, William Gould, Bob Burns, Horace Murphy, Tex Palmer, Al Taylor, Horace B. Carpenter, Oscar Gahan, Fred Burns, Lew Meehan, Blackjack Ward, Tex Cooper, Roy Bucko, Buck Bucko, Art Dillard, Jack King, Bud Jamison, Bud McClure.

A newly elected sheriff (Maynard) is framed for a crime by the opposition, but wins out when he catches the real crooks responsible for the crime. [British title: *Law and Order*].

707. Full of Life (4/57) B&W — 91 mins. (Comedy-Drama). *DIR:* Richard Quine. *PRO:* Fred Kohlmar. *SP:* John Fante. Based on the book by John Fante. *CAST:* Judy Holliday, Richard Conte, Salvatore Baccaloni, Esther Minciotti, Joe de Santis, Silvio Minciotti, Penny Santon, Arthur Lovejoy, Eleanor Audley, Trudy Marshall, Walter Conrad, Sam Gilman.

A wife (Holliday), about to have a baby, must put up with the antics of her husband's (Conte) father (Baccaloni) when he moves in with them.

708. The Fuller Brush Girl (9/15/50) B&W—85 mins. (Comedy). *DIR:* Lloyd Bacon. *SP:* Frank Tashlin. *CAST:* Eddie Albert, Lucille Ball, Carl Benton Reid, Gale Robbins, Jeff Donnell, Lee Patrick, Jerome Cowan, John Litel, Fred Graham, Jack Perrin, Arthur Space, Sid Tomack, Billy Vincent, Lorin Raker, Lelah Taylor, Sarah Edwards, Lois Austin, Isabel Randolph, Isabel Withers, Donna Boswell, Gregory Marshall, Sumner Getchell, Red Skelton, John Doucette, Charles Hamilton, Myron Healey, Barbara Pepper, Bud Osborne, Paul E. Burns, Jean Willes, George Lloyd, Joseph Crehan.

A Fuller Brush saleswoman (Ball) and her boyfriend (Albert) get mixed up with thieves and murder. [British title: *The Affairs of Sally*].

709. The Fuller Brush Man (6/3/48) B&W—93 mins. (Comedy-Crime). *DIR/PRO:* S. Sylvan Simon. *SP:* Frank Tashlin, Devery Freeman. Based on *Now You See It* by Roy Huggins. An Edward Small Production. *CAST:* Red Skelton, Janet Blair, Don McGuire, Hillary Brooke, Ross Ford, Adele Jergens, Trudy Marshall, Mary Field, Nicholas Joy, Donald Curtis, Arthur Space, Selmer Jackson, Roger Moore, Stanley Andrews, David Sharpe, Bud Wolfe, Jimmy Hunt, Dick Wessel, Jimmy Logan.

A Fuller Brush salesman (Skelton) stumbles into a murder and, with the help of his girl (Blair), tries to clear himself and find the murderer. [British title: *That Mad Mr. Jones*].

710. Fun with Dick and Jane (5/77) Metrocolor—95 mins. (Comedy).

DIR: Ted Kotcheff. *PRO:* Peter Bart, Max Palevsky. *SP:* David Gilber, Jerry Belson, Mordecai Richler. Based on a story by Gerald Gaiser. *CAST:* George Segal, Jane Fonda, Ed McMahon, Dick Gautier, Allan Miller, Hank Garcia, John Dehner, Mary Jackson, Walter Brooke, Fred Willard, Sean Frye, James Jeter, Maxine Stuart.

When an aerospace worker (Segal) loses his job, he and his wife (Fonda) turn to a life of crime to make ends meet.

711. Funny Girl (9/68) Technicolor/Panavision—150 mins. (Musical-Comedy). *DIR:* William Wyler. *PRO:* Ray Stark. *SP:* Isobel Lennart. Based on the play by Jule Styne, Bob Merrill, Isobel Lennart. A Rastar Production. *CAST:* Barbra Streisand, Omar Sharif, Kay Medford, Anne Francis, Walter Pidgeon, Lee Allen, Mae Questel, Gerald Mohr, Frank Faylen, Penny Santon, Mittie Lawrence, Gertrude Flynn, John Harmon.

Fanny Brice (Streisand) rises from her Jewish ghetto to become a Broadway star, but loses her husband (Sharif) because of her career.

712. Funny Lady (3/75) Technicolor/Panavision—140 mins. (Musical-Comedy). *DIR:* Herbert Ross. *PRO:* Ray Stark. *SP:* Jay Presson Allen, Arnold Schulman. Story by Arnold Schulman. A Rastar Production. *CAST:* Barbra Streisand, James Caan, Omar Sharif, Roddy McDowall, Ben Vereen, Carole Wells, Larry Gates, Hedi O'Rourke, Samantha Huffaker, Matt Emery, Joshua Shelley, Corey Fischer.

Fanny Brice (Streisand) continues her rise to stardom and marries Billy Rose (Caan), but their separate careers keep them apart and eventually lead to their breakup. *NOTES:* A sequel to the 1968 Columbia film *Funny Girl*.

713. Further Up the Creek! (10/58) B&W/Scope—91 mins. (Comedy). *DIR*: Val Guest. *PRO*: Henry Halsted. *SP*: Val Guest, John Warren, Len Heath. A Byron-Hammer Production. *CAST*: David Tomlinson, Frankie Howerd, Shirley Eaton, Thora Hird, Eric Pohlmann, Lionel Jeffries, John Warren, David Lodge, Lionel Murton, Sam Kydd, Ian Whittaker, Tom Gill, Michael Goodliffe, Michael Ripper, Basil Dingham, Desmond Llewellyn, Jack Le White, Max Day.

When a naval officer (Tomlinson) is assigned to deliver a war ship to another country, he learns that his bo's'n (Howerd) has sold tickets to passengers for a luxury cruise. *NOTES*: A sequel to the 1958 British film *Up the Creek*.

714. Fury at Gunsight Pass (2/15/56) B&W—68 mins. (Western). *DIR*: Fred F. Sears. *PRO*: Wallace MacDonald. *SP*: David Lang. *CAST*: David Brian, Lisa Davis, Neville Brand, Katharine Warren, Percy Helton, Morris Ankrum, Addison Richards, Wally Vernon, Paul E. Burns, James Anderson, Richard Long, Joe Forte, Frank Fenton, George Keymas, Robert Anderson, Frank Coby, John Lehmann, Guy Teague.

When two outlaws (Brian, Brand) try to double-cross each other after a bank robbery, they lose the money to an outsider and decide to hold the whole town for ransom until the missing money is turned over.

715. Fury of the Congo (2/26/51) B&W—69 mins. (Adventure). *DIR*: William Berke. *PRO*: Sam Katzman. *SP*: Carroll Young. Based on the *Jungle Jim* newspaper comic strip by Alex Raymond. *CAST*: Johnny Weissmuller, Sherry Moreland, Lyle Talbot, Bill Henry, Joel Friedkin, Paul Marion, George Eldredge, Rusty Wescoatt, Pierce Lyden, Blanca Vischer, John Hart.

Jungle Jim (Weissmuller) searches for a missing professor (Friedkin) while trying to stop a narcotics gang from exploiting a native tribe in their search for a giant spider that produces a potent narcotic.

716. Fury of the Jungle (2/8/34) B&W—55 mins. (Drama). *DIR*: Roy William Neill. *PRO*: Robert North. *SP*: Ethel Hill, Dore Schary. Story by Horace McCoy. *CAST*: Donald Cook, Peggy Shannon, Alan Dinehart, Harold Huber, Dudley Digges, Clarence Muse, Frederik Vogeding, Charles Stevens, Toshia Mori.

A white woman (Shannon) arrives in a native village and creates tensions and jealousies as the males vie for her attention. [British title: *Jury of the Jungle*].

717. Fury of the Pagans (7/62) Eastman Color/Scope—86 mins. (Action-Drama). *DIR*: Guido Malatesta. *SP*: Gino Mangini, Umberto Scarpelli. Story by Gino Mangini. An Arion Production. *CAST*: Edmund Purdom, Rossana Podesta, Livio Lorenzon, Carla Calo, Daniele Vargas, Andrea Fantasia, Vittorio Feri.

During the sixth century in northern Italy, two warring tribes and their leaders (Purdom, Lorenzon) fight for control of each other's village. [Original Italian title: *La Furia del Barbari*].

718. The Gallant Blade (10/15/48) CineColor—81 mins. (Action-Adventure). *DIR*: Henry Levin. *PRO*: Irving Starr. *SP*: Walter Ferris, Morton Grant, Wilfrid H. Pettitt. Story by Ted Thomas, Edward Dein. *CAST*: Larry Parks, Marguerite Chapman, Victor Jory, George Macready, Edith King, Michael Duane, Onslow Stevens, Peter Brocco, Tim Huntley, Ross Ford, Paul Campbell, Fred F. Sears, Wilton Graff.

In 17th century France, a young

116   The Columbia Checklist

lieutenant (Parks) rescues his general (Macready) from a revolutionary (Jory).

719. Gallant Defender (10/30/35) B&W—60 mins. (Western). DIR: David Selman. PRO: Harry L. Decker. SP: Ford Beebe. Story by Peter B. Kyne. CAST: Charles Starrett, Joan Perry, Harry Woods, Edward J. Le-Saint, Jack Clifford, Al Bridge, George Chesebro, Edmund Cobb, Frank Ellis, Jack Rockwell, George Billings, Tom London, Glenn Strange, Slim Whitaker, Al Ferguson, Bud Osborne, Stanley Blystone, Lew Meehan, Merrill McCormack, Sons of the Pioneers (Roy Rogers, Bob Nolan, Tim Spencer, Hugh Farr, Carl Farr).

A cowboy (Starrett) sets out to prove his innocence of a crime while helping to bring peace between the cattlemen and homesteaders. NOTES: The first of Starrett's westerns for Columbia. He would stay with the studio for 131 westerns ending with *The Kid from Broken Gun* (1952).

720. Gallant Journey (9/24/46) B&W—86 mins. (Aviation-Biography). DIR/PRO: William A. Wellman. SP: William A. Wellman, Byron Morgan. CAST: Glenn Ford, Janet Blair, Charlie Ruggles, Henry Travers, Jimmy Lloyd, Charles Kemper, Arthur Shields, Willard Robertson, Selena Royale, Byron Morgan, Paul Marion, Paul E. Burns, Chris-Pin Martin, Tommy Cook.

The story of 19th century aviation pioneer John Montgomery (Ford), who pioneered the development of glider flight.

721. Galloping Thunder (4/25/46) B&W—54 mins. (Western). DIR: Ray Nazarro. PRO: Colbert Clark. SP: Ed Earl Repp. CAST: Charles Starrett, Adelle Roberts, Smiley Burnette, Kermit Maynard, Richard Bailey, John Merton, Ray Bennett, Budd Buster, Edmund Cobb, Forrest Taylor, Curt

Barrett, Nolan Leary, Gordon Harrison, Merle Travis and His Bronco Busters.

An undercover agent (Starrett) goes to work for the Arizona Stockman's Syndicate to find out why they are having trouble getting horses from a certain region. As The Durango Kid he uncovers a plot by a gang of outlaws to break the ranchers and claim the horses for themselves. [British title: *On Boot Hill*].

722. The Game Is Over (1/67) Technicolor/Panavision—98 mins. (Drama). DIR/PRO: Roger Vadim. SP: Roger Vadim, Jean Cau, Bernard Frechtman. Based on *La Curee* by Emile Zola. A Marceau-Cocinor-Royal Films International Production. CAST: Jane Fonda, Peter McEnery, Michel Piccoli, Tina Marquand, Jacque Monod, Simone Valerie, Howard Vernon, Ham Chao Luong, Douglas Read.

A wealthy woman (Fonda) falls in love with her step-son (McEnery); when she returns from obtaining a divorce from her husband (Piccoli), she learns that the step-son is engaged to someone else and, after a near suicide attempt, must accept her fate to live life alone. [Original French title: *La Curee*].

723. Game of Death (6/79) Eastman Color/Panavision—102 mins. (Martial Arts). DIR: Robert Clouse. PRO: Raymond Chow. SP: Jan Spears. CAST: Bruce Lee, Gig Young, Dean Jagger, Hugh O'Brian, Colleen Camp, Mel Novack, Robert Wall, Kareem Abdul-Jabbar, Chuck Norris, Billy McGill, Roy Chaio, Danny Inosanto, Hung Kim Po.

A martial arts expert (Lee) takes on a crime syndicate in Hong Kong. NOTES: Bruce Lee died during production of this film. It was later reassembled using outtakes from other

Bruce Lee films and a Bruce Lee double.

724. The Game That Kills (9/30/37) B&W — 55 mins. (Drama). *DIR:* D. Ross Lederman. *PRO:* Harry L. Decker. *SP:* Fred Niblo, Jr., Grace Neville. Story by J. Benton Cheney. *CAST:* Charles Quigley, Rita Hayworth, John Gallaudet, Arthur Loft, Paul Fix, J. Farrell MacDonald, John Tyrrell, Dick Wessel, Harry Strang, Dick Curtis, Lee Prather, Edmund Cobb, Ralph Dunn, Ethan Laidlaw, Clyde Dilson, George Chesebro, Eddie Fetherstone, Sammy McKim.

A man (Quigley) joins a professional hockey team to learn who killed his brother in a faked ring accident.

725. The Gamma People (1/56) B&W — 79 mins. (Science Fiction). *DIR:* John Gilling. *PRO:* John W. Gossage. *SP:* John Gilling, John W. Gossage. Story by Louis Pollock. A Warwick Production. *CAST:* Paul Douglas, Eva Bartok, Leslie Phillips, Walter Rilla, Philip Leaver, Marvin Miller, Leonard Sachs, Cyril Chamberlain, Olaf Pooley, Michael Caridia, Pauline Drewett, Jackie Lane.

A newsman (Douglas) and his photographer (Bartok), while traveling through a communist country, learn that scientists are turning the children into geniuses or idiots through the use of gamma rays.

726. Gandhi (12/82) Eastman Color/Panavision — 188 mins. (Biography). *DIR/PRO:* Richard Attenborough. *SP:* John Briley. Presented by Goldcrest Films International-International Film Investors-Indo-British Films-National Film Development Corp. *CAST:* Ben Kingsley, Candice Bergen, Edward Fox, John Gielgud, Trevor Howard, John Mills, Martin Sheen, Rohini Hattangady, Ian Charleston, Athol Fugard, Ian Bannen, Michael Bryant, Michael Hordern.

The biography of Mohandas K. Gandhi (Kingsley), who rose from lawyer to leader of his nation and a symbol of international peace.

727. The Garment Jungle (6/57) B&W — 88 mins. (Crime). *DIR:* Vincent Sherman. *PRO/SP:* Harry Kleiner. Based on the article *Gangsters in the Dress Business* by Lester Velie. *CAST:* Lee J. Cobb, Kerwin Mathews, Gia Scala, Richard Boone, Valerie French, Robert Loggia, Joseph Wiseman, Harold J. Stone, Adam Williams, Wesley Addy, Willis Bouchey, Dick Crockett, Robert Ellenstein, Celia Lovsky, Jon Shepodd, Betsy Jones Moreland, Dale Van Sickel, George Robotham.

A son (Mathews) goes after the mob boss (Boone) who killed his father (Cobb) and a union leader (Loggia).

728. Gasoline Alley (1/16/51) B&W — 76 mins. (Comedy). *DIR/SP:* Edward Bernds. *PRO:* Milton Feldman. Based on the newspaper comic strip *Gasoline Alley* created by Frank O. King. *CAST:* Scotty Beckett, Jimmy Lydon, Susan Morrow, Don Beddoe, Patti Brady, Madelon Mitchel, Dick Wessel, Gus Schilling, Kay Christopher, Byron Foulger, Virginia Toland, Jimmy Lloyd, William Forrest, Ralph Peters, Charles Halton, Charles Williams, Christine McIntyre.

Corky (Beckett) and Hope (Morrow) get married, open a diner, and, with the help of the Wallett clan and friends, make it successful.

729. The Gay Senorita (8/21/45) B&W — 69 mins. (Musical-Drama). *DIR:* Arthur Dreifuss. *PRO:* Jay Gorney. *SP:* Edward Eliscu. Story by J. Robert Bren. *CAST:* Jinx Falkenburg, Jim Bannon, Steve Cochran, Corinna Mura, Thurston Hall, Isabelita (Lita Baron), Isabel Withers, Marguerita Sylva, Lusite Triana, Lola Mentes, Tommy Cook, Nina Bara, Leander de Cordova, Antonio Triama.

A businessman (Bannon) sets out to convert a Mexican section of a California town into a factory site, but changes his plans when he falls in love with a local senorita (Falkenburg).

730. Gene Autry and the Mounties (1/30/51) Sepiatone—70 mins. (Western). DIR: John English. PRO: Armand Schaefer. SP: Norman S. Hall. A Gene Autry Production. CAST: Gene Autry, Elena Verdugo, Pat Buttram, Carleton Young, Gregg Barton, House Peters, Jr., Trevor Bardette, Francis McDonald, Boyd Stockman, Nolan Leary, Richard Emory, Herbert Rawlinson, Jim Frasher, Jody Gilbert, Bruce Carruthers, Robert Hilton, Teddy Infuhr, Billy Gray, John R. McKee, Roy Butler, Stephen Elliott, Chris Allen.

Gene and his sidekick (Buttram) go north of the border and enlist the help of the Mounties to round up a gang of bank robbers.

731. The Gene Krupa Story (12/59) B&W—102 mins. (Musical-Biography). DIR: Don Weis. PRO: Philip A. Waxman. SP: Orin Jannings. CAST: Sal Mineo, Susan Kohner, James Darren, Susan Oliver, Yvonne Craig, Lawrence Dobkin, Celia Lovsky, Gavin McLeod, John Bleifer, Shelley Manne, Buddy Lester, Red Nichols, Bobby Troup, Anita O'Day.

The story of Gene Krupa's (Mineo) rise to jazz drummer and his subsequent fall due to drug charges. [British title: Drum Crazy].

732. Genghis Khan (7/65) Eastman Color/Panavision—124 mins. (Adventure). DIR: Henry Levin. PRO: Irving Allen. SP: Clarke Reynolds, Beverley Cross. Based on a story by Berkely Mather. An Irving Allen-CCC-Avala Production. CAST: Stephen Boyd, Omar Sharif, James Mason, Eli Wallach, Telly Savalas, Francoise Dorleac, Robert Morley, Michael Hor-

dern, Yvonne Mitchell, Woody Strode, Kenneth Cope, Roger Croucher, George Savalas, Suzanne Hsaio.

Genghis Khan (Sharif) revenges himself on his enemy Jamuga (Boyd) and leaves his mountain tribe for China, where he gains the respect of the Chinese leader (Mason).

733. The Gentleman from Nowhere (9/9/48) B&W—65 mins. (Crime). DIR: William Castle. PRO: Rudolph C. Flothow. SP: Edward Anhalt. CAST: Warner Baxter, Fay Baker, Luis Van Rooten, Charles Lane, Wilton Graff, Grandon Rhodes, Noel Madison, Victoria Horne, Don Haggerty, William Forrest, Pierre Watkin, Robert Emmett Keane.

A boxer (Baxter), presumed dead, resurfaces during a chemical company robbery after a lengthy disappearance and tries to clear his name so he can start life anew.

734. The Gentleman Misbehaves (2/28/46) B&W—70 mins. (Comedy). DIR: George Sherman. PRO: Alexis Thurn-Taxis. SP: Robert Wyler, Richard Weil. Story by Robert Wyler, John B. Clymer. CAST: Robert Stanton, Osa Massen, Hillary Brooke, Frank Sully, Dusty Anderson, Shemp Howard, Sheldon Leonard, Jimmy Lloyd, Chester Clute.

A Broadway producer (Stanton) seeks help from gamblers to finance his show.

735. George in Civvy Street (2/46) B&W—79 mins. (Comedy). DIR: Marcel Varnel. PRO: Marcel Varnel, Ben Henry. SP: Peter Fraser, Ted Kavanagh, Max Kester, Gale Pedrick. Story by Howard Irving Young. A Columbia-British Production. CAST: George Formby, Rosalyn Boulter, Ronald Shiner, Ian Fleming, Wally Patch, Philippa Hiatt, Enid Cruickshank, Mike Johnson, Frank Drew.

A tavern owner (Formby), in love

with a waitress (Boulter) from a rival tavern, starts a war with the rival owner to win the girl. NOTES: Last screen appearance of George Formby.

736. Georgy Girl (5/66) B&W— 99 mins. (Comedy-Drama). DIR: Silvio Narizzano. PRO: Robert A. Goldston, Otto Plaschkes. SP: Peter Nichols, Margaret Forster. Based on the book by Margaret Forster. An Everglades Production. CAST: James Mason, Alan Bates, Lynn Redgrave, Charlotte Rampling, Bill Owen, Claire Kelly, Rachel Kempson, Denise Coffey.

An unattractive girl (Redgrave) grows from a self-conscious waif to a woman of responsibilities. NOTES: Lynn Redgrave's first starring film.

737. Get Cracking (3/43) B&W— 96 mins. (Comedy). DIR: Marcel Varnel. PRO: Ben Henry. SP: L. DuGarde Peach. A Columbia-British Production. CAST: George Formby, Edward Rigby, Frank Pettingell, Ronald Shiner, Dinah Sheridan, Wally Patch, Mike Johnson, Irene Handl, Vera Frances.

A crazy mechanic (Formby) enters the Home Guard and defeats the neighboring village rival in a Home Guard exercise.

738. Getting Straight (6/70) Eastman Color— 126 mins. (Comedy-Drama). DIR/PRO: Richard Rush. SP: Robert Kaufman. Based on the book by Ken Kolb. A Film by The Organization. CAST: Elliott Gould, Candice Bergen, Jeff Corey, Max Julien, Leonard Stone, Robert F. Lyons, Cecil Kellaway, William Bramley, Brenda Sykes, Jon Lormer, Gregory Sierra, Hilarie Thompson, Harrison Ford, Irene Tedrow.

A Vietnam veteran (Gould) returns to college to finish his education and he and his girlfriend (Bergen) get caught up in a clash between students and faculty.

Ghengis Khan *see* **Genghis Khan**

739. Ghost of the China Sea (9/58) B&W—73 mins. (War-Drama). DIR: Fred F. Sears. PRO/SP: Charles B. Griffith. A Polynesian Production. CAST: David Brian, Lynn Bernay, Jonathan Haze, Harry Chang, Gene Bergman, Kam Fong Chun, Mel Prestige, Jamie Del Rosario, Dan Taba, Bud Pente.

The captain of a freighter (Brian) and his crew try to escape the Japanese invasion of the Philippines.

740. The Ghost That Walks Alone (2/10/44) B&W—63 mins. (Mystery-Comedy). DIR: Lew Landers. PRO: Jack Fier. SP: Clarence Upson Young. Based on *The Wedding Guest Sat on a Stone* by Richard Shattuck. CAST: Arthur Lake, Janis Carter, Lynne Roberts, Frank Sully, Warren Ashe, Arthur Space, Barbara Brown, Matt Willis, Ida Moore, Jack Lee, Paul Hurst, Robert Williams, John Tyrrell.

While on their honeymoon, a married couple (Lake, Carter) find a dead body in their hotel room.

741. Ghostbusters (6/84) Metro-color/Panavision—107 mins. (Comedy-Drama). DIR/PRO: Ivan Reitman. SP: Dan Aykroyd, Harold Ramis. CAST: Bill Murray, Dan Aykroyd, Harold Ramis, Sigourney Weaver, Rick Moranis, Annie Potts, William Atherton, Ernie Hudson, David Margulies, Roger Grimsby, Larry King, Joe Franklin, Casey Kasem, Michael Ensign.

A trio of "paranormal investigators" (Murray, Aykroyd, Ramis) go into business to rid New York City of ghosts and spirits.

742. The Giant Claw (6/57) B&W—76 mins. (Science Fiction). DIR: Fred F. Sears. PRO: Sam Katzman. SP: Samuel Newman, Paul Gangelin. A Clover Production. CAST: Jeff Morrow, Mara Corday,

Morris Ankrum, Louis D. Merrill, Edgar Barrier, Robert Shayne, Morgan Jones, Clark Howat, Ruell Shayne. Scientists (Morrow, Ankrum, Corday) save the world when it is threatened by a giant bird from outer space. NOTES: Many people regard this film (and the monster bird) as one of the worst science fiction films ever made.

743. Gideon of Scotland Yard (2/59) B&W—57 mins. (Crime-Comedy). DIR: John Ford. PRO: John Ford, Michael Killanin. SP: T. E. B. Clarke. Based on *Gideon's Day* by J. J. Marric (John Creasley). CAST: Jack Hawkins, Dianne Foster, Anna Lee, Anna Massey, Andrew Ray, Cyril Cusack, James Hayter, Ronald Howard, Howard Marion-Crawford, Laurence Naismith, Derek Bond, John Loder, Marjorie Rhodes, Hermione Bell, Michael Trubshawe, John Le Mesurier, Jack Watling, John Warwick.

A day in the life of Inspector Gideon (Hawkins), which includes a cop on the take, a maniacal killer, and incurring the wrath of his family. NOTES: European distribution was Technicolor and a running time of 91 mins; U.S. distribution was Black & White and a running time of 57 mins. It has since been restored to its original form thru American television prints. [British title: *Gideon's Day*].

744. Gidget (4/59) Eastman Color/Scope—95 mins. (Comedy). DIR: Paul Wendkos. PRO: Lewis J. Rachmil. SP: Gabrielle Upton. Based on the book by Frederick Kohner. CAST: Sandra Dee, James Darren, Cliff Robertson, Arthur O'Connell, Mary La Roche, Joby Baker, Tom Laughlin, Sue George, Robert Ellis, Jo Morrow, Doug McClure, Yvonne Craig, Burt Metcalfe, Patti Kane, The Four Preps.

A teenage girl (Dee) hits the beach one summer and falls in love with a surfer (Darren), while being pursued by another (Robertson).

745. Gidget Goes Hawaiian (6/61) Eastman Color—101 mins. (Comedy). DIR: Paul Wendkos. PRO: Jerry Bresler. SP: Ruth Brooks Flippen. Based on characters created by Frederick Kohner. CAST: Deborah Walley, James Darren, Michael Callan, Peggy Cass, Carl Reiner, Eddie Foy, Jr., Jeff Donnell, Vicki Trickett, Joby Baker, Don Edmonds, Bart Patton, Jan Conaway, Robin Lory, Arnold Merritt, Vivian Marshall, Johnny Gilbert.

Gidget (Walley) goes to Hawaii for a vacation with her parents and is pursued by her boyfriend (Darren).

746. Gidget Goes to Rome (8/63) Eastman Color—103 mins. (Comedy). DIR: Paul Wendkos. PRO: Jerry Bresler. SP: Ruth Brooks Flippen, Katherine Eunson, Dale Eunson. Based on characters created by Frederick Kohner. CAST: Cindy Carol, James Darren, Jessie Royce Landis, Cesare Danova, Joby Baker, Danielle De Metz, Trudi Ames, Noreen Corcoran, Peter Brooks, Jeff Donnell, Don Porter, Claudio Gora, Lisa Gastoni.

Gidget (Carol) and her boyfriend (Darren) go to Rome on a vacation and allow their love to wander, but in the end are reunited. NOTES: Columbia's television branch, Screen Gems, made two Gidget films exclusively for television, *Gidget Grows Up* (1969) with Karen Valentine, and *Gidget Gets Married* (1972) with Monie Ellis.

747. Gilda (2/14/46) B&W—110 mins. (Drama). DIR: Charles Vidor. PRO: Virginia Van Upp. SP: Marion Parsonnet. Story by E. A. Ellington. Adapted by Jo Eisinger. CAST: Glenn Ford, Rita Hayworth, George Macready, Joseph Calleia, Steven Geray, Joe Sawyer, Gerald Mohr, Robert Scott, Ludwig Donath, Don Douglas, Lionel Royce, George J. Lewis, Ruth

Roman, Forbes Murray, Sam Flint, Eduardo Ciannelli, Rodolfo Hoyos, Robert Kellard, Philip Van Zandt, John Tyrrell.

A gambler (Ford) becomes the right-hand man to a casino owner (Macready) and resumes an affair with the casino owner's wife (Hayworth). NOTES: It was this film that made Rita Hayworth a superstar and Hollywood sex goddess.

748. The Girl Friend (9/28/35) B&W—67 mins. (Musical). DIR: Edward Buzzell. PRO: Samuel J. Briskin. SP: Gertrude Purcell, Benny Rubin. Story by Gene Towne, Graham Baker. CAST: Ann Sothern, Jack Haley, Roger Pryor, Thurston Hall, Ray Walker, Victor Kilian, Margaret Seddon, Inez Courtney, Geneva Mitchell, Vic Potel, Lee D. Kohlmar, John T. Murray.

A writer (Haley) has his play about Napoleon turned into a musical by three composers (Pryor, Hall, Kilian) posing as producers.

749. Girl in Danger (9/11/34) B&W—57 mins. (Crime). DIR: D. Ross Lederman. PRO: Irving Briskin. SP: Harold Shumate. CAST: Ralph Bellamy, Shirley Grey, J. Carrol Naish, Charles Sabin, Ward Bond, Arthur Hohl, Edward J. LeSaint, Vincent Sherman, Francis McDonald, Edward Keane, Eddy Chandler, Pat O'Malley.

Inspector Trent (Bellamy) goes after a gang of jewel thieves, and must prevent the murder of one of the thieves (Grey) who absconded with one of the jewels.

750. Girl in the Case (4/20/44) B&W—65 mins. (Mystery-Comedy). DIR: William Berke. PRO: Sam White. SP: Joseph Hoffman, Dorcas Cochran. Story by Charles F. Royal. CAST: Edmund Lowe, Janis Carter, Robert Williams, Richard Hale, Stanley Clements, Carole Mathews, Robert Scott, Dick Elliott, Gene Roth.

A lawyer (Lowe), who is an expert lock picker, and his wife (Carter), get involved in espionage when he is hired to pick the lock on an old chest. [British title: *The Silver Key*].

751. The Girl of the Limberlost (10/11/45) B&W—60 mins. (Drama). DIR: Melchor G. Ferrer. PRO: Alexis Thurn-Taxis. SP: Erna Lazarus. Based on *A Girl of the Limberlost* by Gene Stratton Porter. CAST: Ruth Nelson, Dorinda Clifton, Loren Tindall, Gloria Holden, Ernest Cossart, Vanessa Brown, James Bell, Joyce Arling, Charles Arnt, Warren Mills, Gloria Patrice, Lillian Bronson, Peggy Converse, Jimmy Clark, Carol Morris.

A vengeful mother (Nelson) physically and mentally tortures her daughter (Clifton), because she blames her for the death of her husband.

752. Girls Can Play (6/23/37) B&W—59 mins. (Crime). DIR/SP: Lambert Hillyer. PRO: Ralph Cohn. Story by Albert DeMond. CAST: Jacqueline Wells (Julie Bishop), Charles Quigley, Rita Hayworth, John Gallaudet, George McKay, Gene Morgan, Patricia Farr, Guinn "Big Boy" Williams, Joseph Crehan, John Tyrrell, Richard Terry, James Flavin, Beatrice Curtis, Ruth Hilliard, Lee Prather, George Lloyd, Michael Breen, Lee Shumway, Ann Doran.

When one of the members of a girls' baseball team is murdered, a policeman (Williams) and reporter (Quigley) set out to solve the crime.

753. Girls of the Road (7/24/40) B&W—61 mins. (Drama). DIR: Nick Grinde. PRO: Wallace MacDonald. SP: Robert D. Andrews. CAST: Ann Dvorak, Helen Mack, Lola Lane, Ann Doran, Mary Field, Marjorie Cooley, Mary Booth, Madelon Grayson, Grace Lenard, Evelyn Young, Bruce Bennett, Eddie Laughton, Don Beddoe, Howard Hickman.

During the Depression, a governor's daughter (Dvorak) takes to the road to learn first hand of the plight of female hoboes.

754. Girls' School (9/27/38) B&W—71 mins. (Comedy). *DIR:* John Brahm. *PRO:* Sam Marx. *SP:* Tess Slesinger, Richard Sherman. Based on *The Answer on the Magnolia Tree* by Tess Slesinger. *CAST:* Anne Shirley, Nan Grey, Ralph Bellamy, Dorothy Moore, Gloria Holden, Marjorie Main, Margaret Tallichet, Peggy Moran, Kenneth Howell, Doris Kenyon, Cecil Cunningham, Pierre Watkin, Virginia Howell.

Turmoil erupts at a boarding school for wealthy girls when a scandal is uncovered.

755. Girls' School (2/9/50) B&W—61 mins. (Drama). *DIR:* Lew Landers. *PRO:* Wallace MacDonald. *SP:* Brenda Weisberg. Story by Jack Henley. *CAST:* Joyce Reynolds, Ross Ford, Laura Elliott, Julia Dean, Thurston Hall, Leslie Banning, Joyce Otis, Louise Beavers, Sam McDaniel, Wilton Graff, Grant Calhoun, Mary Ellen Kay, Boyd Davis, Harry Cheshire, Joan Vohs, Diantha Patterson, Toni Newman.

A gambler's daughter (Reynolds) seeks safety in a girls' finishing school when she learns that the money her father left her has been stolen. [British title: *Dangerous Inheritance*].

756. Girls Under 21 (11/15/40) B&W—64 mins. (Crime). *DIR:* Max Nosseck. *PRO:* Ralph Cohn. *SP:* Jay Dratler, Fanya Foss. *CAST:* Bruce Cabot, Rochelle Hudson, Paul Kelly, Tina Thayer, Roberta Smith, Lois Verner, Beryl Vaughan, Joanne Tree, Debbie Ellis, William Edmunds, John Dilson, John Tyrrell.

A gangster's ex-wife (Hudson) tries to start a new life by returning to her neighborhood where she tries to reform a gang of female shoplifters.

757. The Gladiator (8/8/38) B&W—70 mins. (Comedy). *DIR:* Edward Sedgwick. *PRO:* David L. Loew. *SP:* Charles Melson, Arthur Sheckman. Based on the book by Philip Wylie. *CAST:* Joe E. Brown, Man Mountain Dean, June Travis, Dickie Moore, Lucien Littlefield, Robert Kent, Ethel Wales, Don Douglas, Lee Phelps, Eddie Kane, Wright Kramer.

A timid college man (Brown) drinks a serum that gives him superpowers, enabling him to become a campus hero.

758. Glamour for Sale (11/5/40) B&W—60 mins. (Drama). *DIR:* D. Ross Lederman. *PRO:* Wallace MacDonald. *SP:* John Bright. *CAST:* Anita Louise, Roger Pryor, Frances Robinson, June MacCloy, Paul Fix, Don Beddoe, Arthur Loft, Veda Ann Borg, Myra Marsh, Evelyn Young, Madelon Grayson, Ann Doran, Dorothy Fay, Jeanne Hart.

A nice girl (Louise) gets caught up in the escort service racket and, with the help of a policeman (Pryor), manages to clear her name and bring the leader (MacCloy) to justice.

759. Glamour Girl (1/16/48) B&W—68 mins. (Musical-Drama). *DIR:* Arthur Dreifuss. *PRO:* Sam Katzman. *SP:* M. Coates Webster, Lee Gold. Story by Lee Gold. A Kay Picture Production. *CAST:* Virginia Grey, Michael Duane, Susan Reed, Jimmy Lloyd, Jack E. Leonard, Pierre Watkin, Eugene Borden, Netta Packer, Noel Neill, Jeanne Bell, Carolyn Grey, Gene Krupa.

A talent agent (Grey) and her boyfriend (Duane) form their own company and make a musician (Reed) an overnight sensation. [British title: *Nightclub Girl*].

760. Glass Houses (1/72) Eastman Color—90 mins. (Drama). *DIR:* Alexander Singer. *PRO:* George Folsey, Jr. *SP:* Alexander Singer, Judith

Singer. A Magellan Production. *CAST:* Bernard Barrow, Jennifer O'Neill, Deirdre Lenihan, Ann Summers, Philip Pine, Lloyd Kino, Logan Ramsey, Eve McVeagh, Clarke Gordon, Lorna Thayer, Holly Irving, Gar Campbell, Maury Hill, Tom Toner, Joan Kaye.

Several couples explore different relationships with each other's spouses at a California retreat. *NOTES:* Jennifer O'Neill's first film. It was filmed in 1970, but not released until 1972, possibly to capitalize on Miss O'Neill's stardom.

761. The Glass Wall (4/53) B&W — 78 mins. (Drama). *DIR:* Maxwell Shane. *PRO:* Ivan Tors. *SP:* Ivan Tors, Maxwell Shane. *CAST:* Vittorio Gassman, Gloria Grahame, Ann Robinson, Douglas Spencer, Robin Raymond, Jerry Paris, Elizabeth Slifer, Richard Reeves, Joseph Turkel, Else Neft, Michael Fox, Ned Booth, Kathleen Freeman, Juney Ellis, Jack Teagarden, Shorty Rogers and His Band.

A European refugee (Gassman), facing deportation, goes into hiding in New York City and is helped by a social outcast (Grahame) and a musician (Paris).

762. Gloria (9/80) Eastman Color — 123 mins. (Crime-Drama). *DIR/PRO/SP:* John Cassavetes. *CAST:* Gena Rowlands, Juan Adames, Buck Henry, Julie Carmen, Jessica Castillo, Lupe Guarnica, Tony Knesich, Tom Noonan.

A former gun moll (Rowlands) protects an eight-year-old Puerto Rican boy (Adames) from the Mafia after his family is killed by hit men.

763. The Go-Between (7/71) Technicolor — 116 mins. (Drama). *DIR:* Joseph Losey. *PRO:* John Heyman, Norman Priggen. *SP:* Harold Pinter. Based on the book by L. P. Hartley. An MGM-EMI World Film Services Production. *CAST:* Julie Christie, Alan Bates, Dominic Guard, Margaret

Leighton, Michael Redgrave, Michael Gough, Edward Fox, Simon Hume-Kendall, Richard Gibson.

A man (Redgrave) reminisces about his past when, as a young boy (Guard), he carried love letters between two lovers (Christie, Bates), leading to tragic results.

764. Go West, Young Lady (11/27/41) B&W — 70 mins. (Comedy-Musical-Western). *DIR:* Frank R. Strayer. *PRO:* Robert Sparks. *SP:* Richard Flournoy, Karen DeWolf. Story by Karen DeWolf. *CAST:* Glenn Ford, Penny Singleton, Ann Miller, Charlie Ruggles, Allen Jenkins, Onslow Stevens, Edith Meiser, Bill Hazlett, Jed Prouty, The Foursome, Bob Wills and His Texas Playboys.

Two singers (Singleton, Miller) vie for a marshal's attention (Ford) when he is sent to clean up a western town.

765. Goal! (2/67) Technicolor/Scope — 93 mins. (Documentary). *DIR:* Abidine Dino, Ross Devenish. *PRO:* Octavio Senoret. *SP:* Brian Glanville. *CAST:* Narrated by Nigel Patrick.

Documentary on the World Cup soccer series in England in July of 1966, covering all 16 nations that participated. [British title: *Goal! World Cup 1966*].

766. The Goddess (5/58) B&W — 104 mins. (Drama). *DIR:* John Cromwell. *PRO:* Milton Perlman. *SP:* Paddy Chayefsky. *CAST:* Kim Stanley, Betty Lou Holland, Joan Copeland, Gerald Hiken, Steven Hill, Joyce Van Patten, Lloyd Bridges, Bert Freed, Donald McKee, Louise Beavers, Elizabeth Wilson, Werner Klemperer, Joan Linville, Patty Duke.

Loosely based on the Marilyn Monroe legend, a Southern girl (Stanley) rises to become one of Hollywood's hottest stars, but falls from the spotlight because of her dependency on drugs and alcohol. NOTES: Kim Stanley and Patty Duke's first starring role.

767. Godspell (3/73) Eastman Color—103 mins. (Musical). DIR: David Greene. PRO: Edgar Lansbury. SP: David Greene, John-Michael Tebelak. Based on the stage play by John-Michael Tebelak. CAST: Victor Garber, David Haskell, Jerry Sroka, Lynne Thigpen, Katie Hanley, Robin Lamont, Gilmer McCormick, Joanne Jonas, Merrell Jackson, Jeffrey Mylett.

The Gospel according to Saint Matthew is played against the contemporary backdrop of New York City.

768. Going Steady (2/58) B&W—82 mins. (Comedy). DIR: Fred F. Sears. PRO: Sam Katzman. SP: Budd Grossman. Story by Budd Grossman, Sumner A. Long. A Clover Production. CAST: Molly Bee, Alan Reed, Jr., Irene Hervey, Bill Goodwin, Ken Miller, Susan Easter, Linda Watkins, Byron Foulger, Hugh Sanders, Florence Ravenel, Ralph Moody, Carlyle Mitchell.

High school sweethearts (Bee, Reed) run off to get married and then move in with her parents (Hervey, Goodwin).

769. Golden Boy (8/31/39) B&W—99 mins. (Drama). DIR: Rouben Mamoulian. PRO: William Perlberg. SP: Lewis Meltzer, Daniel Taradash, Sarah Y. Mason, Victor Heerman. Based on the play by Clifford Odets. CAST: Barbara Stanwyck, Adolphe Menjou, William Holden, Lee J. Cobb, Sam Levene, Joseph Calleia, Edward Brophy, Beatrice Blinn, Don Beddoe, William H. Strauss, Frank Jenks, Charles Halton, John Wray, Charles Lane, Harry Tyler, Stanley Andrews, Robert Sterling, Minerva Urecal, Eddie Fetherstone, Lee Phelps, George Lloyd.

A violinist (Holden) becomes a prizefighter and is manipulated by his manager (Menjou) and girl (Stanwyck).

NOTES: William Holden's first starring role.

770. The Golden Hawk (10/52) Technicolor—83 mins. (Adventure). DIR: Sidney Salkow. PRO: Sam Katzman. SP: Robert E. Kent. Based on the book by Frank Yerby. CAST: Rhonda Fleming, Sterling Hayden, Helena Carter, John Sutton, Paul Cavanagh, Michael Ansara, Raymond Hatton, Alex Montoya, Albert Pollet, David Bond, Donna Martell, Mary Munday.

A pirate (Hayden) sails to Cartagena to rescue a female pirate (Fleming) and avenge himself on the governor (Sutton) for the murder of his mother.

The Golden Virgin see The Story of Esther Costello

771. The Golden Voyage of Sinbad (4/74) Eastman Color/Dynarama—105 mins. (Fantasy-Adventure). DIR: Gordon Hessler. PRO: Charles H. Schneer, Ray Harryhausen. SP: Brian Clemens. A Morningside Production. CAST: John Phillip Law, Caroline Munro, Tom Baker, Douglas Wilmer, Martin Shaw, Gregoire Aslan, Kurt Christian, Takis Emmanuel, John D. Garfield, Aldo Sambrell.

Sinbad (Law) battles demons, devils, sorcerers, and swordsmen while searching for a golden amulet. NOTES: Special effects by Ray Harryhausen.

772. Goldtown Ghost Raiders (5/30/53) Sepiatone—57 mins. (Western). DIR: George Archainbaud. PRO: Armand Schaefer. SP: Gerald Geraghty. A Gene Autry Production. CAST: Gene Autry, Gail Davis, Smiley Burnette, Kirk Riley, Carleton Young, John Doucette, Denver Pyle, Steve Conte, Neyle Morrow.

Gene is a circuit court judge presiding over a murder trial where the accused admits he has already served time for the killing.

773. Golf Widows (5/1/28) B&W — 56 mins. (Comedy). *DIR:* Erle C. Kenton. *PRO:* Harry Cohn. *SP:* W. Scott Darling. *CAST:* Kathleen Key, Vera Reynolds, John Patrick, Sally Rand, Harrison Ford, Will Stanton, Vernon Dent.

Complications arise when two golf widows (Key, Rand) decide to get even with their husbands (Dent, Stanton) by going to the racetrack with two men (Patrick, Ford).

774. The Good Bad Girl (5/17/31) B&W — 67 mins. (Crime-Drama). *DIR:* Roy William Neill. *SP:* Jo Swerling. Story by Winifred Van Duzer. *CAST:* Mae Clarke, James Hall, Marie Prevost, Robert Ellis, Nance O'Neil, Edmund Breese, James Donlan, Paul Porcasi, Paul Fix, Wheeler Oakman, George Berlinger.

A woman (Clarke) is forced to give up her husband (Hall) and baby when it is learned her ex-boyfriend (Ellis) was a gangster.

775. Good Day for a Hanging (1/59) Columbia Color — 85 mins. (Western). *DIR:* Nathan Juran. *PRO:* Charles H. Schneer. *SP:* Daniel B. Ullman, Maurice Zimm. Story by John Reese. A Morningside Production. *CAST:* Fred MacMurray, Margaret Hayes, Robert Vaughn, Joan Blackman, James Drury, Wendell Holmes, Stacy Harris, Emile Meyer, Denver Pyle, Bing Russell, Gregg Barton, Harry Lauter, Edmon Ryan, Kathryn Card, Tom London, William Fawcett, Howard McNear, Russell Thorsen, William Baskin, Robert Bice, Phil Chambers, Rusty Swope, Michael Garth.

A sheriff (MacMurray) tries to convince his daughter (Blackman) and the townspeople that a charming youngster (Vaughn) is really a murderer.

776. Good Girls Go to Paris (6/20/39) B&W — 75 mins. (Comedy). *DIR:* Alexander Hall. *PRO:* William Perlberg. *SP:* Gladys Lehman, Ken Englund. Based on *Miss Aesop Butters Her Bread* by Lenore Coffee, William Joyce Cowen. *CAST:* Melvyn Douglas, Joan Blondell, Walter Connolly, Alan Curtis, Joan Perry, Isabel Jeans, Stanley Brown, Alexander D'Arcy, Clarence Kolb, Henry Hunter, Howard Hickman, Helen Jerome Eddy, Forbes Murray, John Tyrrell, James Craig, Robert Fiske, Robert Sterling, Linda Winters (Dorothy Comingore), Ann Doran, Lorna Gray, Don Beddoe, George Lloyd, Dave Willock.

A campus waitress (Blondell), who yearns to see Paris, sees her chance when she meets a British professor (Douglas) on an exchange program.

777. The Good Humor Man (6/1/50) B&W — 79 mins. (Comedy). *DIR:* Lloyd Bacon. *PRO:* S. Sylvan Simon. *SP:* Frank Tashlin. Based on *Appointment with Fear* by Roy Huggins. *CAST:* Jack Carson, Lola Albright, George Reeves, Jean Wallace, Peter Miles, Frank Ferguson, David Sharpe, Chick Collins, Eddie Parker, Pat Flaherty, Arthur Space, Richard Egan, Jack Overman, Victoria Horne.

A Good Humor man (Carson) innocently gets involved in a payroll robbery, but with the help of his girl (Albright) and his regular customers, manages to round up the crooks and turn them over to the police.

778. Good Luck, Mr. Yates (6/29/43) B&W — 89 mins. (Drama). *DIR:* Ray Enright. *PRO:* David J. Chatkin. *SP:* Adele Commandini, Lou Breslow. Story by Hal Smith, Sam Rudd. *CAST:* Claire Trevor, Edgar Buchanan, Jess Barker, Tom Neal, Tommy Cook, Albert Basserman, Scotty Beckett, Frank Sully, Henry Armetta, Bobby Larson, Conrad Binyon, Rosina Galli, The Bob Mitchell Boys Choir, The Sheriff's Boys Band.

A military school teacher (Barker),

who is 4-F, pretends to be in the army but is actually a welder in a shipyard. NOTES: A deleted comedy sequence, filmed with the Three Stooges, was later used in their comedy short *Gents Without Cents* (1944).

779. Good Neighbor Sam (6/64) Eastman Color—130 mins. (Comedy). DIR/PRO: David Swift. SP: James Fritzell, Everett Greenbaum, David Swift. Based on the book by Jack Finney. CAST: Jack Lemmon, Romy Schneider, Edward G. Robinson, Dorothy Provine, Michael Conners, Anne Seymour, Charles Lane, Louis Nye, Edward Andrews, Joyce Jameson, Robert Q. Lewis, Peter Hobbs, Tristram Coffin, Neil Hamilton, William Forrest, Bernie Kopell, Bess Flowers, Barbara Bouchet, The Hi-Lo's.

An advertising man (Lemmon) pretends to be married to his wife's (Provine) college chum (Schneider) so she can inherit her grandfather's estate and he can land a top account.

780. Good Times (5/67) DeLuxe Color—92 mins. (Musical). DIR: William Friedkin. PRO: Lindsley Parsons. SP: Tony Barrett. Story by Nicholas Hyams. A Motion Pictures International Production. CAST: Sonny Bono, Cher Bono, George Sanders, Norman Alden, Larry Duran, Edy Williams, Hank Worden, Kelly Thordsen, Peter Robbins, James Flavin, Joe Devlin, Hank Reardon, Bruce Tegner, China Lee, Diane Haggerty.

When a singing duo (Sonny, Cher) are approached by a producer (Sanders) to become movie stars, they fantasize about the type of movies to star in.

Goodbye Bruce Lee: His Last Game of Death *see* **Game of Death**

781. Gorath (6/64) Eastman Color/Scope—83 mins. (Science Fiction). DIR: Inoshiro Honda. SP: Takeshi Kimura. A Toho Company Produc-

tion. CAST: Ryo Ikebe, Akihiko Hirata, Jun Tazaki, Yumi Shirakawa, Takashi Shimura, Kumi Mizuno. A Toho Company Production.

Scientists use rockets to move the Earth to a new orbit when a planetary body, known as "Gorath," hurtles on a collision course with Earth. NOTES: American prints ended with the Earth in a new orbit. Japanese prints showed the destruction caused by the change in Earth's orbit. [Original Japanese title: *Yosei Gorasu*].

782. The Gorgon (2/65) Technicolor—83 mins. (Horror). DIR: Terence Fisher. PRO: Anthony Nelson-Keys. SP: John Gilling. Based on a story by J. Llewellyn Devine. A Hammer Production. CAST: Peter Cushing, Christopher Lee, Richard Pasco, Michael Goodliffe, Barbara Shelley, Patrick Troughton, Jack Watson, Jenny Longhurst, Toni Gilpin, Redmond Phillips, Joseph O'Connor, Alister Williamson, Michael Peake.

In 1910 Germany, a professor (Lee) arrives in a village to investigate a series of mysterious murders.

783. Grand Exit (11/5/35) B&W—68 mins. (Crime). DIR: Erle C. Kenton. PRO: Robert North. SP: Bruce Manning, Lionel Houser. Story by Gene Towne, Graham Baker. CAST: Edmund Lowe, Ann Sothern, Onslow Stevens, Robert Middlemass, Guy Usher, Wyrley Birch, Selmer Jackson, Miki Morita, Arthur Rankin, Russell Hicks, Edward Van Sloan.

An insurance investigator (Lowe) sets out to stop an arsonist.

784. Grand Prix (3/34) B&W—70 mins. (Drama). DIR/SP: St. John L. Clowes. PRO: L. S. Stock. A Clowes-Stock Production. CAST: John Stuart, Gillian Sande, Milton Rosmer, Peter Gawthorne, Wilson Coleman, Lawrence Andrews.

A race car driver (Stuart) redeems

himself in the eyes of his girl (Sande) by winning the big race in a car which killed his girl's father (Gawthorne).

785. The Gravy Train (6/74) Eastman Color—95 mins. (Crime). *DIR*: Jack Starrett. *PRO*: Jonathan Taplin. *SP*: David Whitney, Bill Kerby. A Tomorrow Entertainment Production. *CAST*: Stacy Keach, Frederic Forrest, Margot Kidder, Barry Primus, Denny Miller, Richard Romanus, Clay Tanner, Robert Phillips, Jack Starrett, Lorna Thayer, Francesca Bellini.

Two brothers (Keach, Forrest) leave their coal-mining community to strike it rich and get involved in an armored-car robbery; a gun battle ensues when the leader (Primus) double-crosses the gang and skips with the money.

786. The Great Battle (10/74) Eastman Color—118 mins. (War). *DIR/PRO*: Yuri Ozerov. *SP*: Yuri Bondarev, Oscar Kurganov, Yuri Ozerov. A Mosfilm Production. *CAST*: Nikolai Olyalin, Larissa Golubkina, Boris Zaidenbergh, Nikolai Ribnikov, Mihall Ulyanov, Vladion Strzholchik, Sergei Harchenko, Alfred Shtravo, Fritz Ditz.

A reconstruction of the lengthy and bloody Kursk tank and infantry battle that ended Hitler's last hope of victory on the Russian front. *NOTES*: This film was reduced from two Russian 70mm features. Director Yuri Ozerov actually fought in this battle.

787. The Great Manhunt (4/50) B&W—104 mins. (Adventure-Spy-Drama). *DIR/SP*: Sidney Gilliat. *PRO*: Frank Launder, Sidney Gilliat. A London Films Production. *CAST*: Douglas Fairbanks, Jr., Glynis Johns, Jack Hawkins, Herbert Lom, Walter Rilla, Carl Jaffe, Karel Stepanek, Gerard Heinz, Hans Moser, Anton Diffring, Peter Illing.

A doctor (Fairbanks) is invited to a mythical country to perform an opera-tion on the head of the government. When he becomes aware of the true political climate of the country he attempts an escape along with a girl (Johns) and a gangster (Lom). They are eventually captured and freedom comes only when the government changes hands. [British title: *State Secret*].

788. The Great Plane Robbery (12/9/40) B&W—55 mins. (Crime). *DIR*: Lewis D. Collins. *PRO*: Larry Darmour. *SP*: Albert DeMond. Story by Harold R. Greene. *CAST*: Jack Holt, Stanley Fields, Vicki Lester, Noel Madison, Granville Owens, Theodore Von Eltz, Hobart Cavanaugh, Milburn Stone, Paul Fix, Harry Cording, John Hamilton, Doris Lloyd, Lane Chandler.

On board a plane, an insurance investigator (Holt) must protect a racketeer (Madison) when his gang hijacks the plane to kill him.

789. The Great Sensation (10/1/25) B&W—50 mins. (Drama). *DIR*: Jay Marchant. *PRO*: Harry Cohn. *SP*: Douglas Z. Doty. *CAST*: William Fairbanks, Pauline Garon, Lloyd Whitlock, William Franey, Adelaide Hallock.

A rich young man (Fairbanks) pretends to be a chauffeur to be near his sweetheart (Garon) and ends up saving her from drowning and recovering her mother's (Hallock) jewels from a crook (Whitlock).

790. The Great Sioux Massacre (9/1/65) Pathe Color/Scope—91 mins. (Western). *DIR*: Sidney Salkow. *PRO*: Leon Fromkess. *SP*: Fred C. Dobbs (Marvin Gluck). Story by Sidney Salkow and Marvin Gluck. *CAST*: Joseph Cotten, Julie Sommars, Darren McGavin, Nancy Kovack, Phil Carey, Michael Pate, Don Haggerty, Frank Ferguson, Iron Eyes Cody, Stacy Harris, John Matthews, House Peters, Jr.,

John Napier, William Tannen, Blair Davis, Louise Serpa.

At a military inquiry, two of Custer's (Carey) officers, Maj. Reno (Cotten) and Capt. Benton (McGavin), relate the events of the battle of Little Big Horn.

791. The Great Swindle (4/10/41) B&W—58 mins. (Mystery). *DIR:* Lewis D. Collins. *PRO:* Larry Darmour. *SP:* Albert DeMond. Story by Eric Taylor. *CAST:* Jack Holt, Jonathan Hale, Marjorie Reynolds, Sidney Blackmer, Douglas Fowley, Tom Kennedy, Henry Kolker, Don Douglas, Boyd Irwin.

An insurance investigator (Holt) sets out to track down the culprit who stole crucial evidence regarding a warehouse arson. *NOTES:* Jack Holt's last starring feature film for Columbia. His only serial, *Holt of the Secret Service,* would be released later in the year. He would come back to Columbia in 1948 to co-star with Gene Autry.

792. The Greatest (5/77) Metrocolor—101 mins. (Biography-Sports-Drama). *DIR:* Tom Gries. *PRO:* John Marshall. *SP:* Ring Lardner, Jr. Based on *The Greatest—My Own Story* by Muhammad Ali, Herbert Muhammad, Richard Durham. *CAST:* Muhammad Ali, Ernest Borgnine, Lloyd Haynes, John Marley, Robert Duvall, David Huddleston, Ben Johnson, James Earl Jones, Dina Merrill, Paul Winfield, Roger E. Mosley, Annazette Chase, Mira Waters, Skip Homeier, Phillip MacAllister, Arthur Adams.

Muhammad Ali tells his own story of his rise to the top and his battles in and out of the ring. *NOTES:* Director Tom Gries' last film.

793. Guard That Girl (11/2/35) B&W—67 mins. (Mystery). *DIR/SP:* Lambert Hillyer. *PRO:* Harry L. Decker. *CAST:* Robert Allen, Florence Rice, Ward Bond, Wyrley Birch, Barbara Kent, Arthur Hohl, Elisabeth

Risdon, Nana Bryant, Thurston Hall, Bert Roach.

A detective (Allen) is hired to protect an heiress (Kent) marked for murder.

794. Guess Who's Coming to Dinner (12/67) Technicolor—108 mins. (Drama). *DIR/PRO:* Stanley Kramer. *SP:* William Rose. *CAST:* Spencer Tracy, Sidney Poitier, Katharine Hepburn, Cecil Kellaway, Katharine Houghton, Beah Richards, Roy Glenn, Virginia Christine, Isabel Sanford, Alexandra Hay, Barbara Randolph, D'Urville Martin, Tom Heaton, Grace Gaynor, John Hudkins.

When a white San Francisco girl (Houghton) brings home her black fiance (Poitier) to meet her parents (Tracy, Hepburn), they must confront their liberal attitudes. *NOTES:* Spencer Tracy's last film.

795. The Guilt of Janet Ames (3/6/47) B&W—83 mins. (Drama). *DIR:* Henry Levin. *SP:* Louella MacFarlane, Allen Rivkin, Devery Freeman. Story by Lenore Coffee. *CAST:* Rosalind Russell, Melvyn Douglas, Sid Caesar, Betsy Blair, Nina Foch, Charles Cane, Harry Von Zell, Bruce Harper, Arthur Space, Richard Benedict, Frank Orth, Hugh Beaumont, Emory Parnell, Victoria Horne, William Forrest, Isabel Withers, Denver Pyle.

An embittered woman (Russell), with the help of a journalist (Douglas), seeks to learn whether her husband's sacrifice during the war was worthwhile.

796. Guilty? (4/13/30) B&W—67 mins. (Drama). *DIR:* George B. Seitz. *SP:* Dorothy Howell. Based on *Black Sheep* by Dorothy Howell. *CAST:* Virginia Valli, John Holland, John St. Polis, Lydia Knott, Erville Alderson, Richard Carlyle, Robert Haynes, Clarence Muse, Eddie Clayton, Edward Cecil, Gertrude Howard.

A group of people gather together

and each relates their version of a man's suicide.

797. The Guilty Generation (11/19/31) B&W—82 mins. (Crime). *DIR:* Rowland V. Lee. *PRO:* Harry Cohn. *SP:* Jack Cunningham. Based on the play by Jo Milward and J. Kirby Hawkes. *CAST:* Leo Carrillo, Constance Cummings, Robert Young, Boris Karloff, Emma Dunn, Leslie Fenton, Ruth Warren, Murray Kinnell, Elliott Roth, Jimmy Wilcox, Phil Tead, Frederick Howard, Eddie Roland.

A gangster (Carrillo), at war with his rival (Karloff), seeks revenge against his rival's son (Young) when he learns that his daughter (Cummings) is married to him.

798. Gumshoe (3/72) Eastman Color—84 mins. (Satire-Crime). *DIR:* Stephen Frears. *PRO:* Michael Medwin. *SP:* Neville Smith. A Memorial Enterprises Film Production. *CAST:* Albert Finney, Billie Whitelaw, Frank Finlay, Janice Rule, Carolyn Seymour, George Innes, Billy Dean, Fulton Mackay, George Silver, Maureen Lipman, Wendy Richard, Oscar James, Joey Kenyon, Bert King, Chris Cunningham.

A Liverpool bingo caller (Finney) who envisions himself as a tough 40's detective, places an ad in the newspaper, and becomes involved in a murder case.

799. Gun Fury (10/30/53) Technicolor/3-D—83 mins. (Western). *DIR:* Raoul Walsh. *PRO:* Lewis J. Rachmil. *SP:* Irving Wallace, Roy Huggins. Based on *Ten Against Caesar* by Kathleen B. George, Robert A. Granger. *CAST:* Rock Hudson, Donna Reed, Phil Carey, Roberta Haynes, Leo Gordon, Lee Marvin, Neville Brand, John Cason, Ray Thomas, Robert Herron, Phil Rawlins, Forrest Lewis, Don Carlos, Pat Hogan, Mel Welles, Post Park.

A psychotic outlaw (Carey) robs a stagecoach and kidnaps a young bride (Reed), forcing her husband (Hudson) to pursue them.

800. The Gun That Won the West (9/55) Technicolor—71 mins. (Western). *DIR:* William Castle. *PRO:* Sam Katzman. *SP:* James B. Gordon. A Clover Production. *CAST:* Dennis Morgan, Paula Raymond, Richard Denning, Chris O'Brien, Kenneth MacDonald, Robert Bice, Michael Morgan, Roy Gordon, Howard Wright, Richard H. Cutting, Howard Negley.

Two cavalry scouts (Morgan, Denning), armed with the new Springfield rifles, are sent to protect railroad crewmen from Indian attacks.

801. The Gunfighters (7/1/47) CineColor—87 mins. (Western). *DIR:* George Waggner. *PRO:* Harry Joe Brown. *SP:* Alan LeMay. Based on *Twin Sombreros* by Zane Grey. A Producers Actors Corporation Production. *CAST:* Randolph Scott, Barbara Britton, Dorothy Hart, Bruce Cabot, Charley Grapewin, Steven Geray, Forrest Tucker, Charles Kemper, Grant Withers, John Miles, Griff Barnett.

When his best friend is killed, a retired gunfighter (Scott) puts on his guns once again and goes after a corrupt cattle baron (Barnett), his gunmen, and a corrupt sheriff (Kemper). [British title: *The Assassin*].

802. Gunman's Walk (7/58) Technicolor/Scope—97 mins. (Western). *DIR:* Phil Karlson. *PRO:* Fred Kohlmar. *SP:* Frank Nugent. Story by Rick Hardman. *CAST:* Van Heflin, Kathryn Grant, Tab Hunter, James Darren, Mickey Shaughnessy, Edward Platt, Ray Teal, Paul Birch, Bert Convy, Paul E. Burns, Robert F. Simon, Michael Granger, Will Wright, Chief Blue Eagle, Paul Bryar, Everett Glass, Dorothy Adams, Willis Bouchey, Ewing Mitchell, Sam Flint.

A rancher (Heflin), who brought law

and order to the West with his guns, tries to raise his two sons (Darren, Hunter) to be respectable, but one son wants to follow his father's way.

803. Gunmen from Laredo (3/59) Columbia Color—67 mins. (Western). DIR/PRO: Wallace MacDonald. SP: Clarke Reynolds. CAST: Robert Knapp, Jana Davi, Walter Coy, Paul Birch, X. Brands, Ron Hayes, Don C. Harvey, Clarence Straight, Jerry Barclay, Charles Horvath, Jean Moorehead, Harry Antrim.

A rancher (Knapp), sent to jail by a bar owner (Coy) who killed his wife, escapes with the help of an Indian girl (Davi) and seeks revenge.

804. Gunning for Vengeance (3/21/46) B&W—53 mins. (Western). DIR: Ray Nazarro. PRO: Colbert Clark. SP: Ed Earl Repp, Louise Rousseau. Story by Louise Rousseau. CAST: Charles Starrett, Marjean Neville, Smiley Burnette, Bob Kortman, George Chesebro, Lane Chandler, Frank LaRue, John Tyrrell, Robert Williams, Jack Kirk, Phyllis Adair, Nolan Leary, Frank Fanning, The Trailsmen.

The Durango Kid (Starrett) stops an outlaw gang from extorting protection money from the ranchers and townspeople. [British title: *Jail Break*].

805. The Guns of Fort Petticoat (4/57) Technicolor—82 mins. (Western). DIR: George Marshall. PRO: Harry Joe Brown. SP: Walter Doniger. Story by C. William Harrison. A Brown-Murphy Pictures Incorporated Production. CAST: Audie Murphy, Kathryn Grant, Sean McClory, Hope Emerson, James Griffith, Jeanette Nolan, Jeff Donnell, Dorothy Crider, Madge Meredith, Ernestine Wade, Ray Teal, Nestor Paiva, Ainslie Pryor, Charles Horvath, Peggy Maley, Isobel Elsom, Patricia Livingston, Kim Charney.

A cavalry officer (Murphy) heads to

Texas and trains a group of townswomen to fight off an Indian attack.

806. The Guns of Navarone (7/61) Eastman Color/Scope—157 mins. (War-Drama-Adventure). DIR: J. Lee Thompson. PRO: Carl Foreman. SP: Carl Foreman. Based on the book by Alistair MacLean. An Open Road Films Production. CAST: Gregory Peck, David Niven, Anthony Quinn, Stanley Baker, Anthony Quayle, James Darren, Irene Papas, Gia Scala. James Robertson Justice, Richard Harris, Bryan Forbes, Allan Cuthbertson, Michael Trubshawe, Percy Herbert, George Mikell, Walter Gotell, Tutte Lemkow, Christopher Rhodes.

During World War II, six men are sent on a hazardous mission to destroy two long-range German guns that have been installed on an Aegean island. NOTES: With a different cast, American International Pictures, in 1978, released a sequel, *Force 10 from Navarone*.

807. A Guy, a Gal, and a Pal (3/8/45) B&W—62 mins. (Comedy-Romance). DIR: Oscar (Budd) Boetticher, Jr. PRO: Wallace MacDonald. SP: Monte Brice. Story by Gerald Drayson Adams. CAST: Ross Hunter, Lynn Merrick, Ted Donaldson, George Meeker, Jack Norton, Will Stanton, Sam McDaniel, Al Bridge, Mary McLeod, Mary Forbes, Russell Hicks, Nella Walker.

During the war years, a girl (Merrick) falls in love and must choose between a Marine (Hunter) and a civilian (Meeker).

808. A Guy Called Caesar (10/62) B&W—62 mins. (Crime). DIR: Frank Marshall. PRO: Bill Luckwell, Umesh Mallik. SP: Umesh Mallik, Tom Burdon. Story by Umesh Mallick. A Luckwell Production. CAST: Conrad Phillips, George Moon, Philip

O'Flynn, Maureen Toal, Desmond Perry, Peter Maycock.

A policeman (Phillips) goes undercover to trap a gang of jewel thieves.

809. The H-Man (6/59) Eastman Color/Scope—79 mins. (Science Fiction). *DIR:* Inoshiro Honda. *PRO:* Tomoyuki Tanaka. *SP:* Takeshi Kimura. Story by Hideo Kaijo. A Toho Company Production. *CAST:* Yumi Shirakawa, Kenji Sahara, Akihiko Hirata, Eitaro Ozawa, Koreya Senda, Mitsuru Sato.

Radioactive liquid turns humans into blobs that live in the sewers of Tokyo. [Original Japanese titles: *Uomini H; Biyo to Ekitainingen*].

810. Hail to the Rangers (9/16/43) B&W—58 mins. (Western). *DIR:* William Berke. *PRO:* Jack Fier. *SP:* Gerald Geraghty. *CAST:* Charles Starrett, Leota Atcher, Arthur Hunnicutt, Robert Atcher, Lloyd Bridges, Norman Willis, Budd Buster, Tom London, Edmund Cobb, Ted Adams, Art Mix, Dick Botiller, Eddie Laughton, Ernie Adams, Davidson Clark, Jack Kirk.

A Texas Ranger (Starrett) and his men help save the local ranchers from an outlaw gang. [British title: *Illegal Rights*].

811. Hamlet (12/69) Technicolor—117 mins. (Drama). *DIR:* Tony Richardson. *PRO:* Neil Hartley. From the play by William Shakespeare. A Woodfall-Filmways Production. *CAST:* Nicol Williamson, Gordon Jackson, Anthony Hopkins, Judy Parfitt, Mark Dignam, Michael Pennington, Marianne Faithfull, Ben Aris, Clive Graham, Roger Livesey, Anjelica Huston, Mark Griffith, Peter Gale, Robin Chadwick.

Hamlet (Williamson) is depicted as a symbol of modern despair in this interpretation of Shakespeare's play.

812. Hammerhead (7/68) Technicolor—99 mins. (Spy-Drama). *DIR:* David Miller. *PRO:* Irving Allen. *SP:* William Bast, Herbert Baker. Based on the book by James Mayo. *CAST:* Vince Edwards, Judy Geeson, Peter Vaughn, Diana Dors, Michael Bates, Beverly Adams, Douglas Wilmer, Tracy Reed, Patrick Cargill, Patrick Holt, David Prowse, Veronica Carlson, Joseph Furst, William Mervyn.

A secret agent (Edwards) goes undercover to stop an arch-criminal (Vaughn) intent on world domination.

813. Hand in Hand (12/60) B&W—80 mins. (Drama-Children). *DIR:* Philip Leacock. *PRO:* Helen Winston. *SP:* Diana Morgan. Story by Sidney Harmon. A Winston Production. *CAST:* Loretta Parry, Philip Needs, John Gregson, Sybil Thorndike, Finlay Currie, Derek Sydney, Miriam Karlin, Arnold Diamond, Kathleen Byron, Barry Keegan, Martin Lawrence, Barbara Hicks, Dennis Gilmore, Peter Pike, Susan Reid, Donald Tandy.

A Jewish girl (Parry) and a Catholic boy (Needs) become friends and must endure the racial prejudice of their parents and friends.

814. Hands Across the Rockies (6/19/41) B&W—57 mins. (Western). *DIR:* Lambert Hillyer. *PRO:* Leon Barsha. *SP:* Paul Franklin. Based on *A Gunsmoke Case for Major Cain* by Norbert Davis. *CAST:* Bill Elliott, Mary Daily, Dub Taylor, Kenneth MacDonald, Ethan Laidlaw, Frank LaRue, George Chesebro, Donald Curtis, Art Mix, Stanley Brown, Edmund Cobb, Slim Whitaker, Eddie Laughton, Eddy Waller, Steve Clark, Tex Cooper, Tom Moray, Harrison Greene, Hugh Prosser, George Morrell, Curley Dresden, Kathryn Bates, Buck Moulton.

Wild Bill Hickok (Elliott) and Cannonball (Taylor) help two young people in love (Daily, Brown) and bring the murderer (MacDonald) of Cannonball's father to justice.

815. The Handsome Brute (12/1/25) B&W—50 mins. (Action). *DIR:* Robert Eddy. *PRO:* Harry Cohn. *SP:* Lillian Taft Maize. *CAST:* William Fairbanks, Virginia Lee Corbin, Lee Shumway, Robert Bolder, J. J. Bryson, Daniel Belmont.

A cop (Fairbanks) is removed from the police force but redeems himself by rounding up a gang of jewel thieves.

816. Hangman's Knot (11/15/52) Technicolor—84 mins. (Western). *DIR/SP:* Roy Huggins. *PRO:* Harry Joe Brown. A Scott-Brown Production. *CAST:* Randolph Scott, Donna Reed, Claude Jarman, Jr., Frank Faylen, Glenn Langan, Richard Denning, Lee Marvin, Jeanette Nolan, Ray Teal, Monte Blue, Guinn "Big Boy" Williams, Frank Yaconelli, Clem Bevans, Reed Howes, John Call, Edward Earle, Post Park, Frank Hagney.

A Confederate officer (Scott) and his men, after robbing a Union gold shipment, learn that the war was over. On their way back home they take refuge at a stagecoach stop and are waylaid by bandits. NOTES: The only film directed by future television producer Roy Huggins.

817. Hanky Panky (6/82) Metrocolor—105 mins. (Comedy). *DIR:* Sidney Poitier. *PRO:* Martin Ransohoff. *SP:* Henry Rosenbaum, David Taylor. *CAST:* Gene Wilder, Gilda Radner, Kathleen Quinlan, Richard Widmark, Sam Gray, Robert Prosky, Josef Sommer, Johnny Sekka, Jay O. Sanders, Pat Corley, Larry Bryggman, Bill Moor.

An innocent architect (Wilder) is chased by spies, assassins, and the cops when a girl (Radner) on a spy mission asks for his help.

818. Hanover Street (5/79) Technicolor/Panavision—108 mins. (Romance-War-Drama). *DIR/SP:* Peter Hyams. *PRO:* Paul N. Lazarus III. *CAST:* Harrison Ford, Lesley-Anne Down, Christopher Plummer, Alec McCowen, Richard Masur, Michael Sacks, Patsy Kensit, Max Wall, Shane Rimmer, Keith Buckley, Sherrie Hewson, Keith Alexander, John Ratzenberger, Hugh Fraser.

In 1943 London, an American bomber pilot (Ford) falls in love with a married Englishwoman (Down). When he flies her husband (Plummer) on a mission behind enemy lines and is shot down, he painfully decides to save the husband's life and return him to the woman they both love.

819. The Happening (3/67) Technicolor—101 mins. (Comedy). *DIR:* Elliott Silverstein. *PRO:* Jud Kinberg. *SP:* Frank R. Pierson, Ronald Austin, James D. Buchanan. A Horizon Picture. *CAST:* Anthony Quinn, George Maharis, Michael Parks, Robert Walker, Jr., Martha Hyer, Faye Dunaway, Milton Berle, Oscar Homolka, Jack Kruschen, Luke Askew, Eugene Roche, Clifton James, James Randolph Kuhl.

Four hippies (Maharis, Parks, Walker, Dunaway) kidnap a Mafia don (Quinn) and hold him for ransom. When no one wants to pay to get him back, the don decides to turn the tables and handle the kidnapping his way.

820. Happy Birthday to Me (5/81) Metrocolor—108 mins. (Horror). *DIR:* J. Lee Thompson. *PRO:* John Dunning, Andre Link. *SP:* John Saxton, Peter Jobin, Timothy Bond. Story by John Saxton. *CAST:* Melissa Sue Anderson, Glenn Ford, Lawrence Dane, Sharon Acker, Frances Hyland, Tracy Bergman, Jack Blum, Matt Craven, Lenore Zann, David Eisner, Lisa Langlois, Richard Rabiere.

A psychiatrist (Ford) tries to help a

young girl (Anderson) who thinks she might be the killer of her friends.

821. Happy Birthday, Wanda June (12/71) Eastman Color – 105 mins. (Comedy). *DIR*: Mark Robson. *PRO*: Lester M. Goldsmith. *SP*: Kurt Vonnegut, Jr. Based on the play by Kurt Vonnegut, Jr. A Filmmakers Group-Sourdough Ltd.-Red Lion Production. *CAST*: Rod Steiger, Susannah York, George Grizzard, Don Murray, William Hickey, Steven Paul, Pamelyn Ferdin, Pamela Saunders, Louis Turenne, Lester M. Goldsmith, C. C. Whitney.

Returning home after being lost in the jungle for eight years, a big game hunter (Steiger) finds his carhop wife (York) educated, liberated and about to remarry.

822. Happy New Year (8/87) De-Luxe Color – 86 mins. (Comedy). *DIR*: John G. Avildsen. *PRO*: Jerry Weintraub. *SP*: Warren Lane. Based on Claude LeLouch's film *La Bonne Anne*. A Columbia-Delphi IV Production. *CAST*: Peter Falk, Charles Durning, Claude Lelouch, Wendy Hughes, Gary Maas, Tom Courtenay, Bruce Kirby, Bruce Malmuth, Tracy Brooks Swope.

Two jewel thieves (Falk, Durning) plan to rob a Palm Beach jewelry store but romance complicates matters. *NOTES*: Originally filmed in 1985, but not released by Columbia until 1987 due to changes in upper management. It also had limited theatrical release.

823. The Happy Time (8/26/52) B&W – 94 mins. (Comedy). *DIR*: Richard Fleischer. *PRO*: Stanley Kramer. *SP*: Earl Felton. Based on the play *Happy Time* by Samuel Taylor and on the book by Robert L. Fontaine. *CAST*: Charles Boyer, Louis Jourdan, Marsha Hunt, Kurt Kasznar, Linda Christian, Bobby Driscoll, Marcel Dalio, Jeanette Nolan, Jack

Raine, Richard Erdman, Will Wright, Eugene Borden, Marlene Cameron, Gene Collins, Ann Faber, Kathryn Sheldon, Maurice Marsac.

Set in 1920 Canada, a French-Canadian family, the father (Boyer), the grandfather (Dalio), two uncles (Kasznar, Jourdan) and the son (Driscoll), chase the opposite sex.

824. The Hard Man (12/57) Technicolor – 80 mins. (Western). *DIR*: George Sherman. *PRO*: Helen Ainsworth. *SP*: Leo Katcher. Based on the book by Leo Katcher. A Romsom Production. *CAST*: Guy Madison, Valerie French, Lorne Greene, Barry Atwater, Trevor Bardette, Myron Healey, Robert Burton, Rudy Bond, Renata Vanni, Rickie Sorenson, Frank Richards, Robert B. Williams.

An ex-Ranger (Madison) takes a job as a deputy sheriff, winds up in the middle of a range war with a local rancher (Greene), and has an affair with the rancher's wife (French).

825. Hard Times (10/75) Metrocolor/Panavision – 92 mins. (Sports-Drama). *DIR*: Walter Hill. *PRO*: Lawrence Gordon. *SP*: Walter Hill, Bryan Gindorff, Bruce Henstell. Story by Bruce Henstell, Bryan Gindorff. *CAST*: Charles Bronson, James Coburn, Jill Ireland, Strother Martin, Nick Dimitri, Maggie Blye, Michael McGuire, Robert Tessier, Bruce Glover, Felice Orlandi, Edward Walsh.

In the 1930's, a New Orleans promoter (Coburn) arranges bare-knuckle bouts for his streetfighter (Bronson). [British title: *The Streetfighter*].

Hard to Handle *see* **Paid to Dance**

826. Hardbodies (5/84) DeLuxe Color – 88 mins. (Comedy). *DIR*: Mark Griffiths. *PRO*: Jeff Begun, Ken Dalton. *SP*: Steve Greene, Eric Alter, Mark Griffiths. A Chroma III Production. *CAST*: Grant Cramer, Teal Roberts,

Gary Wood, Michael Rapport, Sorrels Pickard, Roberta Collins, Cindy Silver, Courtney Gaines, Crystal Shaw.

Three middle-aged men (Wood, Rapport, Pickard) rent a beach house and try to score with the girls; when they fail they hire a pro (Cramer) to give them pointers.

827. Hardcore (2/79)Metrocolor— 105 mins. (Drama). *DIR/SP:* Paul Schrader. *PRO:* Buzz Feitshans. An A-Team Production. *CAST:* George C. Scott, Peter Boyle, Season Hubley, Dick Sargent, Leonard Gaines, David Nichols, Gary Rand Graham, Larry Block, Marc Alaimo, Leslie Ackerman, Charlotte McGinnis, Paul Marin, Bibi Besch, Reb Brown, Roy London, Ed Begley, Jr., Ilah Davis.

A father (Scott) searches for his missing teenage daughter (Davis) in the pornography underworld. [British title: *The Hardcore Life*].

828. The Harder They Fall (4/ 56) B&W—109 mins. (Sports-Drama). *DIR:* Mark Robson. *PRO/SP:* Philip Yordan. Based on the book by Budd Schulberg. *CAST:* Humphrey Bogart, Rod Steiger, Jan Sterling, Mike Lane, Max Baer, Jersey Joe Walcott, Edward Andrews, Harold J. Stone, Carlos Montalban, Felice Orlandi, Nehemiah Persoff, Herbie Faye, Rusty Lane, Jack Albertson, Abel Fernandez, Marion Carr, Sandy Sanders, Paul Frees, Frank Hagney, Pat Comiskey.

A cynical sportswriter (Bogart) turns press agent for a mob-connected fight promoter (Steiger) by publicizing an Argentinian boxer (Lane). When he sees how the fighter is manipulated by the mob, he decides to quit and write a series of articles exposing the mobsters and the fight racket. *NOTES:* Humphrey Bogart's last film.

829. Harem Girl(1/21/52)B&W— 70 mins. (Comedy). *DIR:* Edward Bernds. *PRO:* Wallace MacDonald.

SP: Edward Bernds, Elwood Ullman. Story by Edward Bernds. *CAST:* Joan Davis, Peggie Castle, Arthur Blake, Paul Marion, Henry Brandon, Donald Randolph, Minerva Urecal, Peter Mamoks, John Dehner, Peter Brocco, Russ Conklin, Guy Teague, Alan Foster, Ric Roman, Nick Thompson.

A sheik (Randolph) tries to take over the oil supply of a mythical kingdom by killing its princess (Castle), but his plans are thwarted by the princess' secretary (Davis).

830. Harlem Globetrotters (10/ 24/51) B&W—75 mins.(Sports-Drama). *DIR:* Phil Brown, Will Jason. *PRO:* Buddy Adler. *SP:* Alfred Palca. A Sidney Buchman Enterprises Production. *CAST:* Thomas Gomez, Dorothy Dandridge, Bill Walker, Angela Clarke, Peter Thompson, Steve Roberts, Peter Virgo, Ray Walker, Al Eben, William Forrest, Ann E. Allen, Tom Greenway, The Harlem Globetrotters: Billy Brown, Roscoe Cumberland, William "Pop" Gates, Marques Haynes, Louis "Babe" Pressley, Ermer Robinson, Ted Strong, Reese "Goose" Tatum, Frank Washington, Clarence Wilson, Inman Jackson.

A college student (Brown) drops out to become a member of the Harlem Globetrotters basketball team.

831. Harmon of Michigan (10/2/ 41) B&W—65 mins. (Sports-Drama-Biography). *DIR:* Charles Barton. *PRO:* Wallace MacDonald. *SP:* Howard J. Green. Story by Richard Goldstone, Stanley Rauh, Fredric Frank. *CAST:* Tom Harmon, Anita Louise, Forest Evashevski, Oscar O'Shea, Warren Ashe, Stanley Brown, Ken Christy, Tim Ryan, William Hall, Lloyd Bridges, Chester Conklin, Larry Parks, Bill Henry, Sam Balter, Wendell Niles, Tom Hanlon, Ken Niles.

The story follows Tom Harmon's early career as he drifts in and out of the pros, marries his college sweetheart (Louise), takes a series of coaching jobs, and finally ends up as assistant to his old coach (O'Shea) at Michigan.

832. Harriet Craig (10/31/50) B&W—94 mins. (Drama). *DIR*: Vincent Sherman. *PRO*: William Dozier. *SP*: Anne Froelick, James Gunn. Based on the play *Craig's Wife* by George Edward Kelly. *CAST*: Joan Crawford, Wendell Corey, Lucile Watson, Allyn Joslyn, William Bishop, K. T. Stevens, Raymond Greenleaf, Ellen Corby, Virginia Brissac, Douglas Wood, Mira McKinney.

A domineering wife (Crawford) loses her husband (Corey) and her friends when she begins to think more of her house and possessions than their welfare. *NOTES*: A remake of the 1936 Columbia film *Craig's Wife*.

833. Harry and Walter Go to New York (6/76) Metrocolor/Panavision—123 mins. (Comedy). *DIR*: Mark Rydell. *PRO*: Don Devlin, Harry Gittes. *SP*: Robert Kaufman, John Byrum. Story by Don Devlin and John Byrum. *CAST*: James Caan, Elliott Gould, Michael Caine, Diane Keaton, Charles Durning, Lesley Ann Warren, Val Avery, Jack Gilford, Carol Kane, Burt Young, Bert Remsen, Ted Cassidy, Dennis Dugan, Kathryn Grody, Michael Conrad, David Shire, Michael Greene, Nicky Blair, George Gaynes, Warren Berlinger.

In 1890 New York, a couple of vaudeville performers (Caan, Gould) get put in jail, meet a petty thief (Caine), and get involved in his plans to rob a bank.

834. Harvard, Here I Come (3/31/42) B&W—64 mins. (Comedy). *DIR*: Lew Landers. *PRO*: Wallace MacDonald. *SP*: Albert Duffy. Story by Karl Brown. *CAST*: Maxie Rosenbloom, Arline Judge, Stanley Brown, Don Beddoe, Marie Wilson, Virginia

Sale, Byron Foulger, Boyd Davis, Julius Tannen, Walter Baldwin, Tom Herbert, Larry Parks, George McKay, John Tyrrell, Mary Ainslee, Lloyd Bridges, Al Hill, Yvonne De Carlo, Jack Mulhall, Marion Murray.

A nightclub owner (Rosenbloom) returns to college and is given the run of the college when professors decide he is the missing link in their project. [British title: *Here I Come*].

835. Harvey Middleman, Fireman (7/65) Eastman Color—76 mins. (Drama). *DIR/SP*: Ernest Pintoff. *PRO*: Robert L. Lawrence. *CAST*: Gene Troobnick, Hermione Gingold, Patricia Harty, Arlene Golonka, Will MacKenzie, Ruth Jaroslow, Charles Durning, Peter Carew, Stanley Myron Handelman, Trudy Bordoff, Neil Rouda, Gigi Chevalier, Stacy Graham, Maurice Shrog.

A married fireman (Troobnick) seeks help from a psychiatrist when his life becomes complicated after rescuing a girl (Harty) from a burning building and falling in love with her.

836. Have Rocket, Will Travel (8/59) B&W—76 mins. (Comedy). *DIR*: David L. Rich. *PRO*: Harry Romm. *SP*: Raphael Hayes. *CAST*: The Three Stooges (Moe Howard, Larry Fine, Joe DeRita), Jerome Cowan, Anna-Lisa, Robert Colbert, Don Lamond.

Three janitors (The Stooges) at a research space complex get launched into orbit, land on Venus, discover a talking unicorn, and return to Earth heroes. *NOTES*: At the time of this release, Columbia had decided not to renew the Stooges' contract; but with the success of this, their first feature, they were to star in 5 more, 4 for Columbia and 1 for 20th Century–Fox, before their retirement.

837. The Hawk of Wild River (2/28/52) B&W—54 mins. (Western).

DIR: Fred F. Sears. *PRO:* Colbert Clark. *SP:* Howard J. Green. *CAST:* Charles Starrett, Donna Hall, Smiley Burnette, Jock Mahoney, Jim Diehl, Clayton Moore, Lane Chandler, Syd Saylor, John Cason, Sam Flint, LeRoy Johnson, Edwin Parker, Jack Carry.

The Durango Kid (Starrett) pits his six-gun against the bow and arrow of the outlaw known as the "Hawk" (Moore) and brings him to justice.

838. He Laughed Last (8/56) Technicolor — 76 mins. (Comedy). *DIR/SP:* Blake Edwards. *PRO:* Jonie Taps. Story by Richard Quine, Blake Edwards. *CAST:* Frankie Laine, Lucy Marlow, Anthony Dexter, Richard Long, Alan Reed, Jesse White, Florenz Ames, Henry Slate, Paul Dubov, Peter Brocco, Joe Forte, Robin Morse, Dale Van Sickel, Mara McAfee, John Cason, Richard Benedict, David Tomack, John Truex.

In the twenties, New York gangsters battle for control of a nightclub, inherited by a flapper (Marlow).

He Lived to Kill *see* **Night of Terror**

839. He Snoops to Conquer (12/44) B&W — 103 mins. (Comedy). *DIR:* Marcel Varnel. *PRO:* Marcel Varnel, Ben Henry. *SP:* Stephen Black, Howard Irving Young, Norman Lee, Michael Vaughn, Langford Reed. A Columbia-British Production. *CAST:* George Formby, Robertson Hare, Elizabeth Allen, Claude Bailey, James Harcourt, Aubrey Mallalieu, George McLeod, Vincent Holman, Ian Fleming, Katie Johnson, William Rodwell, James Page, Robert Clive.

With the help of a crackpot inventor (Hare), the town's handyman (Formby) exposes corruption in the town council.

840. He Stayed for Breakfast (8/22/40) B&W — 86 mins. (Comedy).

DIR: Alexander Hall. *PRO:* B. P. Schulberg. *SP:* P. J. Wolfson, Michael Fessier, Ernest Vajda. Based on the play *Liberte Provisoire* by Michel Duran. Adapted by Sidney Howard. *CAST:* Loretta Young, Melvyn Douglas, Alan Marshall, Eugene Pallette, Curt Bois, Una O'Conner, Leonid Kinsiey, Trevor Bardette, Grady Sutton, Frank Sully, Evelyn Young, William Castle, Ernie Adams, Jack Rice, Harry Semels, Nestor Paiva, Charles Wagenheim, Vernon Dent, Leonard Mudie, Art Miles.

A Parisian communist (Douglas) takes a shot at a banker, is pursued by the police, and ends up in the apartment of the banker's ex-wife (Young), who converts him to capitalism.

841. Head (11/68) Technicolor — 85 mins. (Musical-Comedy). *DIR:* Bob Rafelson. *PRO/SP:* Bob Rafelson, Jack Nicholson. A Raybert Production. *CAST:* The Monkees (Peter Tork, David Jones, Mickey Dolenz, Michael Nesmith), Victor Mature, Annette Funicello, Timothy Carey, Logan Ramsey, Abraham Sofaer, Vito Scotti, Charles Macaulay, T. C. Jones, Charles Irving, Percy Helton, Sonny Liston, Ray Nitschke, Carol Doda, Frank Zappa, Teri Garr, June Fairchild.

The Monkees cavort through a series of endless skits using old film clips and lots of guest stars.

842. Headin' East (12/13/37) B&W — 63 mins. (Western-Crime). *DIR:* Ewing Scott. *PRO:* L. G. Leonard. *SP:* Ethel La Branche, Paul Franklin. Story by Joseph Hoffman and Monroe Shaff. *CAST:* Buck Jones, Ruth Coleman, Don Douglas, Shemp Howard, Elaine Arden, Earle Hodgins, John Elliott, Stanley Blystone, Frank Faylen, Al Herman, Dick Rich, Harry Lash.

A cowboy (Jones) heads to the big city to smash a produce racket that has been ruining his father's lettuce shipments.

843. Heading West (8/15/46) B&W—54 mins. (Western). *DIR:* Ray Nazarro. *PRO:* Colbert Clark. *SP:* Ed Earl Repp. *CAST:* Charles Starrett, Doris Houck, Smiley Burnette, Norman Willis, Frank McCarroll, John Merton, Tom Chatterton, Hal Taliaferro (Wally Wales), Nolan Leary, Bud Geary, Stanley Price, Tommy Coates, Hank Penny and His Plantation Boys. The Durango Kid (Starrett) goes to Bonanza City to find out who has been impersonating him and robbing the local mine owners. [British title: *The Cheat's Last Throw*].

844. Heat of Desire (5/84) B&W—90 mins. (Drama). *DIR:* Luc Beraud. *PRO:* Lise Fayolle, Giorgio Silvagni. *SP:* Luc Beraud, Claude Miller. A Triumph Films Production. *CAST:* Patrick Dewaere, Clio Goldsmith, Jeanne Moreau, Guy Marchand, Pierre Dux, Jose-Luis Lopez Vasquez. When a lecturer (Dewaere) travels to Barcelona for a speaking engagement, he becomes involved in a steamy affair with a woman (Goldsmith), which leads him to devote all his time and money to her knowing that the affair cannot last. *NOTES:* Released in France in 1980. Limited theatrical release; in French with English subtitles. Patrick Dewaere committed suicide shortly after the completion of this film.

845. The Heat's On (10/29/43) B&W—80 mins. (Musical-Comedy). *DIR:* Gregory Ratoff. *PRO:* Milton Carter. *SP:* Fitzroy Davis, George S. George, Fred Schiller. Story by Lou Breslow, Boris Ingster. *CAST:* Mae West, Victor Moore, William Gaxton, Lester Allen, Mary Roche, Almira Sessions, Hazel Scott, Alan Dinehart, Lloyd Bridges, Sam Ash, Lina Romay, Harry Shannon, Harry Harvey, Edward Earle, Harry Tyler, Xavier Cugat and His Orchestra. A Broadway producer (Gaxton) concocts a plan to have his show closed by a morals group because it is bad, but his star (West) has other plans and convinces the leader of the morals group (Sessions) to back the show or she will expose her brother's (Moore) unwholesome activities. *NOTES:* Mae West would not appear on screen again until 1970. [British title: *Tropicana*].

846. Heavy Metal (8/81) Eastman Color—91 mins. (Animated-Fantasy). *DIR:* Gerald Potterton. *PRO:* Ivan Reitman. *SP:* Dan Goldberg, Len Blum. Based on original art and stories by Richard Corben, Angus McKie, Thomas Warkentin, Dan O'Bannon, Berni Wrightson. *CAST:* Voices of John Candy, Don Francks, Roger Bumpass, Jackie Burroughs, Joe Flaherty, Eugene Levy, Harold Ramis, Richard Romanus, John Vernon. A series of animated stories centered around a green glowing stone called the Loc-Nar; "Soft Landing," "Harry Canyon," "Gremlins," "Captain Sternn," "So Beautiful and So Dangerous," "Den," and "Taarna."

847. Heir to Trouble (12/17/35) B&W—59 mins. (Western). *DIR:* Spencer G. Bennet. *PRO:* Larry Darmour. *SP:* Nate Gatzert. Story by Ken Maynard. *CAST:* Ken Maynard, Joan Perry, Harry Woods, Hal Taliaferro (Wally Wales), Pat O'Malley, Art Mix, Jack Rockwell, Bud McClure, Frank Yaconelli, Lafe McKee, Frank LaRue, Slim Whitaker, Hal Price, Dorothy Wolbert, Jim Corey, Jack Ward, Martin Faust, Harold Brown, Fern Emmett, Roy Bucko, Buck Bucko, Artie Ortego. A cowboy (Maynard) inherits his friend's gold mine and baby when he is killed, and sets out to find the outlaw gang responsible.

848. Hell Below Zero (7/54) Technicolor—90 mins. (Adventure). DIR: Mark Robson. PRO: Albert R. Broccoli, Irving Allen. SP: Alec Coppel, Max Trell. Adapted by Richard Maibaum. Based on *The White South* by Hammond Innes. A Warwick Film Production. CAST: Alan Ladd, Joan Tetzel, Basil Sydney, Stanley Baker, Joseph Tomelty, Niall MacGinnis, Jill Bennett, Peter Dyneley, Susan Rayne, Philo Hauser, Ivan Craig, Paddy Ryan.

An American adventurer (Ladd) sails to the Antarctic with the daughter (Tetzel) of a whaling captain to help her find the murderer of her father.

849. Hell Bent for Love (5/10/34) B&W—55 mins. (Crime). DIR: D. Ross Lederman. PRO: Irving Briskin. SP: Harold Shumate. CAST: Tim McCoy, Lillian Bond, Bradley Page, Vincent Sherman, Lafe McKee, Guy Usher, Harry C. Bradley, Edward J. LeSaint, Ernie Adams, Hal Price, Wedgewood Newell, Gloria Warner, Max Wagner.

A state trooper (McCoy) uses ex-cons to gather evidence against a nightclub owner (Page) suspected of being in the rackets.

850. The Hell Cat (7/7/34) B&W—70 mins. (Drama). DIR: Albert S. Rogell. PRO: Sid Rogell. SP: Fred Niblo, Jr. Story by Adele Buffington. CAST: Robert Armstrong, Ann Sothern, Benny Baker, Minna Gombell, Purnell Pratt, Charles Wilson, J. Carrol Naish, Irving Bacon, Henry Kolker, Guy Usher, Joseph Crehan, Huey White, Nick Copeland.

A newspaper reporter (Armstrong) and his girl (Sothern) help break up a Chinese smuggling racket.

851. Hell Is a City (11/60) B&W/Scope—98 mins. (Crime). DIR/SP: Val Guest. PRO: Michael Carreras. Based on *Hell Is a City* by Maurice Procter. An Associated British-Ham-

mer Production. CAST: Stanley Baker, John Crawford, Donald Pleasence, Maxine Audley, Billie Whitelaw, Joseph Tomelty, George A. Cooper, Geoffrey Frederick, Vanda Godsell, Charles Houston, Joby Blanshard, Charles Morgan, Peter Madden, Dickie Owen, Lois Dane.

A British detective (Baker) tracks an escaped convict (Crawford) who he thinks will return to the city to get his stolen jewels.

852. Hell-Ship Morgan (3/10/36) B&W—64 mins. (Adventure-Romance). DIR: D. Ross Lederman. PRO: Irving Briskin. SP: Harold Shumate. CAST: George Bancroft, Ann Sothern, Victor Jory, George Regas, Howard Hickman, Ralph Byrd, Rollo Lloyd, Fred "Snowflake" Toones.

A fishing boat captain (Bancroft) sacrifices his life when he learns that his wife (Sothern) does not love him, but his first mate (Jory).

853. Hellcats of the Navy (5/57) B&W—81 mins. (War). DIR: Nathan Juran. PRO: Charles H. Schneer. SP: David Lang, Raymond T. Marcus. Based on *Hellcats of the Sea* by Charles A. Lockwood, Hans Christian Adamson. A Morningside Production. CAST: Ronald Reagan, Nancy Davis, Arthur Franz, Robert Arthur, William Leslie, William "Bill" Phillips, Harry Lauter, Joseph Turkel, Michael Garth, Don Keefer, Selmer Jackson, Maurice Manson. Introduction by Fleet Admiral Chester W. Nimitz.

During World War II, a submarine commander (Reagan) is accused of cowardice when he leaves one of his men (Lauter) behind to save the rest of his crew. NOTES: Ronald Reagan's last theatrical feature and the only film to star him and his wife Nancy Davis.

854. The Hellions (5/62) Technicolor/Technirama—80 mins. (Adventure). DIR: Ken Annakin. PRO: Harold Huth. *SP:* Patrick Kirwan, Harold Huth, Harold Swanton. Based on the television play *Nobody's Town* by Harold Swanton. An Irving Allen-Jamie Ulys Production. *CAST:* Richard Todd, Anne Aubrey, Jamie Ulys, Marty Wilde, Lionel Jeffries, James Booth, Al Mulock, Colin Blakely, Ronald Fraser, Zena Walker, George Moore, Bill Brewer, Jan Bryuns, Lorna Cowell, Ricky Arden.

In 1900 South Africa, a police sergeant (Todd) appeals to the townspeople for help when a father (Jeffries) and his four sons (Wilde, Booth, Mulock, Blakely) threaten to kill him and take over the town. *NOTES:* A South African version of the 1952 United Artists film *High Noon*.

855. Hello Annapolis (8/5/42) B&W — 62 mins. (Comedy). *DIR:* Charles Barton. *PRO:* Wallace MacDonald. *SP:* Donald Davis, Tom Reed. Story by Tom Reed. *CAST:* Tom Brown, Jean Parker, Larry Parks, Phil Brown, Joseph Crehan, Thurston Hall, Ferris Taylor, Herbert Rawlinson, Mae Busch, Robert Stevens, Stanley Brown, William Blees, Georgia Caine, Lloyd Bridges.

Two high school pals (Tom Brown, Parks) enter the Naval Academy and carry their rivalry for the same girl (Parker) with them. [British title: *Personal Honour*].

856. Hello Trouble (7/15/32) B&W — 61 mins. (Western). *DIR/SP:* Lambert Hillyer. *PRO:* Irving Briskin. *CAST:* Buck Jones, Lina Basquette, Russell Simpson, Otto Hoffman, Allan Roscoe, Wallace MacDonald, Morgan Galloway, Ruth Warren, Frank Rice, Lafe McKee, Ward Bond, Al Smith, Spec O'Donnell, King Baggott.

An ex-Ranger (Jones) hangs up his guns when he accidentally kills a boy he once knew. He goes to work at a ranch and when the owner is killed he straps on his guns and goes after the murderer.

857. Hell's Horizon (12/55) B&W — 78 mins. (War). *DIR/SP:* Tom Gries. *PRO:* Wray Davis. A Gravis Production. *CAST:* John Ireland, Marla English, Bill Williams, Hugh Beaumont, Larry Pennell, Chet Baker, William Schallert, Jerry Paris, Paul Levitt, John Murphy, Wray Davis, Mark Scott, Kenne Duncan, Don Burnett, Stanley Adams.

During the Korean War, a bomber pilot (Ireland) and his crew set out on a mission to bomb a bridge over the Yalu River.

858. Hell's Island (7/20/30) B&W — 77 mins. (Adventure). *DIR:* Edward Sloman. *PRO:* Harry Cohn. *SP:* Jo Swerling. Story by Thomas Buckingham. *CAST:* Jack Holt, Ralph Graves, Dorothy Sebastian, Richard Cramer, Harry Allen, Lionel Belmore, Otto Lang, Carl Stockdale.

A legionnaire (Graves) is sent to Devil's Island when he attacks his sergeant (Cramer) for wounding his best friend (Holt).

859. Her Accidental Husband (3/1/23) B&W — 63 mins. (Drama). *DIR:* Dallas M. Fitzgerald. *PRO:* Harry Cohn. *SP:* Lois Zellner. A C.B.C. Release. *CAST:* Forrest Stanley, Miriam Cooper, Maude Wayne, Mitchell Lewis, Kate Lester, Richard Tucker.

A girl (Cooper) saves a man (Stanley) from drowning and convinces him to marry her after her father dies, but when she decides to leave him he wins her back.

860. Her First Beau (6/11/41) B&W — 76 mins. (Drama). *DIR:* Theodore Reed. *PRO:* B. B. Kahane. *SP:* Gladys Lehman, Karen DeWolf. Based on the play *June Mad* by Florence Ryerson, Colin Clements. *CAST:* Jackie

Cooper, Jane Withers, Edith Fellows, Josephine Hutchinson, William Tracy, Martha O'Driscoll, Edgar Buchanan, Una O'Conner, Jonathan Hale, Kenneth Howell, Addison Richards.

A teenage girl (Withers) tries to get her childhood sweetheart (Cooper) to pay more attention to her and forget his hobbies.

861. Her First Romance (5/4/51) B&W—72 mins. (Romance-Drama). *DIR*: Seymour Friedman. *SP*: Albert Mannheimer. Based on *City Boy* by Herman Wouk. *CAST*: Margaret O'Brien, Allen Martin, Jr., Jimmy Hunt, Sharyn Moffett, Ann Doran, Lloyd Corrigan, Eleanor Donahue, Susan Stevens, Marissa O'Brien, Arthur Space, Otto Hulett, Lois Pace, Harlan Warde, Maudie Prickett.

A schoolgirl (Margaret O'Brien) pursues an older boy (Martin) to summer camp and gets in trouble when she steals money from her father's (Space) safe to help him with his camp project. *NOTES*: This film marked Margaret O'Brien's first grown up role and her first screen kiss. [British title: *Girls Never Tell*].

862. Her Husband's Affairs (7/22/47) B&W—84 mins. (Comedy). *DIR*: S. Sylvan Simon. *PRO*: Raphael Hakim. *SP*: Ben Hecht, Charles Lederer. A Cornell Production. *CAST*: Lucille Ball, Franchot Tone, Edward Everett Horton, Nana Bryant, Mikhail Rasumny, Gene Lockhart, Jonathan Hale, Paul Stanton, Mabel Paige, Frank Mayo, Pierre Watkin, Jack Rice, Clancy Cooper, Charles C. Wilson, Charles Trowbridge, Selmer Jackson, Arthur Space, Stanley Blystone, Larry Parks, Fred F. Sears, Robert Emmett Keane, Harry Cheshire, John Cason, Teddy Infuhr, Dwayne Hickman, Charles Hamilton.

A wife (Ball) tries to help her advertising executive husband (Tone)

market a depilatory for women but instead it turns out to grow hair.

863. Her Wonderful Lie (7/17/50) B&W—90 mins. (Drama). *DIR*: Carmine Gallone. *PRO*: Gregor Rabinovitch. *SP*: Ernst Marischka, Hamilton Benz, Rowland Leigh. Story by Ernst Marischka, Gustav Holm. Based on *Latin Quarter* by Henri Murger and the opera *La Boheme* by Giacomo Puccini. A Cineopera Production. *CAST*: Marta Eggerth, Jan Kiepura, Janis Carter, John Abbott, Sterling Holloway, Marc Platt, Isobel Elsom, Gil Lamb, Franklin Pangborn, Douglass Dumbrille, Constance Dowling, John Hamilton, Lester Matthews, Milada Miadova.

Based on the opera by Puccini, tragedy befalls two lovers (Eggerth, Kiepura) on the left bank of Paris.

864. Here Comes Mr. Jordan (7/23/41) B&W—93 mins. (Fantasy-Comedy). *DIR*: Alexander Hall. *PRO*: Everett Riskin. *SP*: Seton I. Miller, Sidney Buchman. Based on the play *Heaven Can Wait* by Harry Segall. *CAST*: Robert Montgomery, Evelyn Keyes, Claude Rains, Rita Johnson, Edward Everett Horton, James Gleason, John Emery, Donald MacBride, Don Costello, Halliwell Hobbes, Benny Rubin, Joseph Crehan, Warren Ashe, Joe Hickey, Bobby Larson, Mary Currier, William Forrest, Selmer Jackson, Chester Conklin, Lloyd Bridges, John Ince, Ken Christy.

A saxophone-playing boxer (Montgomery) is sent to Heaven ahead of schedule by an overeager angel (Horton), and must be found a new body by Mr. Jordan (Rains) after his old body has been cremated. *NOTES*: Remade by Paramount Pictures in 1978 as *Heaven Can Wait*.

865. The Heroes of Telemark (7/65) Columbia Color/Panavision—131 mins. (War). *DIR*: Anthony Mann.

PRO: S. Benjamin Fisz. SP: Ivan Moffat, Ben Barzman. Based on *Skis Against the Atom* by Knut Hauklid and *But for These Men* by John Drummond. A Rank-Benton Film Production. CAST: Kirk Douglas, Richard Harris, Michael Redgrave, Ulla Jackson, Roy Dotrice, Eric Porter, Anton Diffring, Mervyn Johns, Barry Jones, Geoffrey Keen, Jennifer Hilary, David Weston, Maurice Denham, Ralph Michael, William Marlowe, Alan Howard, John Golightly, Patrick Jordan.

In 1942 Norway, the leader of the Norwegian underground (Harris) and a scientist (Douglas) try to stop the Nazis from producing "heavy water," an essential element for A-bomb development. NOTES: Director Anthony Mann's last completed film.

866. Heroes of the Alamo (4/2/38) B&W—74 mins. (Western). DIR: Harry Fraser. PRO: Anthony J. Xydias. SP: Roby Wentz. A Sunset Film Corporation Production. CAST: Lane Chandler, Earle Hodgins, Ruth Findlay, Roger Williams, Rex Lease, Edward Piel, Sr., Bruce Warren, Julian Rivero, Steve Clark, Denver Dixon, George Morrell, Tex Cooper, Oscar Gahan, Ben Corbett.

Crockett (Chandler), Bowie (Williams), and Travis (Lease) valiantly defend the Alamo against Santa Anna (Rivero) and his men. NOTES: This film was originally a Sunset Film Corporation release and was released on 8/16/37. Columbia purchased this film and released it in their 1938 film schedule.

867. Heroes of the Range (8/18/36) B&W—58 mins. (Western). DIR: Spencer G. Bennet. PRO: Larry Darmour. SP: Nate Gatzert. CAST: Ken Maynard, June Gale, Harry Woods, Bob Kortman, Tom London, Hal Taliaferro (Wally Wales), Buffalo Bill, Jr. (Jay Wilsey), Lafe McKee, Jack Rockwell, Bud Jamison, Bud McClure, Bud

Osborne, Harry Ernest, Jack King, Frank Hagney, Jerome Ward, Bob Reeves.

An FBI agent (Maynard) goes undercover to stop an outlaw gang from robbing a gold shipment.

868. Heroina (Heroin) (11/65) B&W—105 mins. (Drama). DIR/PRO: Jeronimo Mitchell Melendez. SP: Enrique de la Torre. Story by Jeronimo Mitchell Melendez. A Royal Films International Production. CAST: Kitty de Hoyas, Jaime Sanchez, Otto Sirgo, Jeddu Mascorieto, Marta Casanas, Jose de San Anton, Nidia Caro, Felix Monclova, Freddie Baez, Raul Davila, Olga Guillot.

When a young man (Sanchez) becomes an addict, his father (de San Anton) accepts responsibility for his son's situation and tries to help him. NOTES: Released to Spanish language theaters. In Spanish with English subtitles.

869. He's a Cockeyed Wonder (10/31/50) B&W—76 mins. (Comedy). DIR: Peter Godfrey. PRO: Rudolph C. Flothow. SP: John Henley. CAST: Mickey Rooney, Terry Moore, William Demarest, Charles Arnt, Ross Ford, Ned Glass, Mike Mazurki, Douglas Fowley, William "Bill" Phillips, Ruth Warren, Eddy Waller, Frank Ferguson.

A would-be magician (Rooney) and his girl (Moore) foil a gang of robbers at an orange plant and win the approval of her father (Demarest).

870. Hey Boy! Hey Girl! (5/59) B&W—83 mins. (Musical). DIR: David L. Rich. PRO: Harry Romm. SP: Raphael Hayes, James West. CAST: Louis Prima, Keely Smith, James Gregory, Henry Slate, Kim Charney, Barbara Heller, Asa Maynor, Sam Butera and the Witnesses.

A parishioner (Smith) helps her parish priest (Gregory) by asking a musician (Prima) to perform at their church benefit to boost attendance.

871. Hey Rookie (3/9/44) B&W – 71 mins. (Musical). *DIR*: Charles Barton. *PRO*: Irving Briskin. *SP*: Henry Meyers, Edward Eliscu, Jay Gorney. Based on the play by K. E. B. Culvan, Doris Culvan. *CAST*: Joe Besser, Ann Miller, Larry Parks, Joe Sawyer, Jimmy Little, Selmer Jackson, Larry Thompson, Barbara Brown, Charles Trowbridge, Charles Wilson, Syd Saylor, Doodles Weaver, Hi, Lo, Jack and a Dame, Condos Brothers, The Vagabonds, Jack Gilford, Johnson Brothers, Judy Clark and the Solid Senders, Bob Evans.

A musical comedy producer (Parks) gets drafted and is assigned to put on a stage show at an Army base.

872. Hey There, It's Yogi Bear (6/64) Eastman Color – 89 mins. (Animated). *DIR/PRO*: William Hanna, Joseph Barbera. *SP*: William Hanna, Joseph Barbera, Warren Foster. *CAST*: Voices of Daws Butler, Don Messick, Julie Bennett, Mel Blanc, Hal Smith, J. Pat O'Malley, James Darren, Jean Vander Pyl.

Yogi Bear and Boo-Boo set out to rescue Cindi Bear from a circus and have several adventures on their way back to Jellystone Park.

873. Hidden Power (9/7/39) B&W – 61 mins. (Drama). *DIR*: Lewis D. Collins. *PRO*: Larry Darmour. *SP*: Gordon Rigby. *CAST*: Jack Holt, Gertrude Michael, Dickie Moore, Henry Kolker, Regis Toomey, William B. Davidson, Helen Browne, Marilyn Knowlden, Harry Hayden, Holmes Herbert, Christian Rub.

A scientist (Holt) loses his wife (Michael) and son (Moore) when he spends all his time trying to develop an anti-toxin burn serum, but gets them back when he saves his son's life by using the serum.

874. High Flight (4/58) Technicolor/Scope – 102 mins. (Action-Drama). *DIR*: John Gilling. *PRO*: Irving Allen, Albert R. Broccoli. *SP*: Joseph Landon, Ken Hughes. Story by Jack Davies. A Warwick Film Production. *CAST*: Ray Milland, Bernard Lee, Kenneth Haigh, Anthony Newley, Kenneth Fortescue, Sean Kelly, Helen Cherry, Leslie Phillips, Duncan Lamont, Jan Brooks, John Le Mesurier, Frank Atkinson, Ian Fleming, Anne Aubrey, Andrew Keir, Richard Wattis.

An R.A.F. flight instructor (Milland) tries to straighten out a rebellious cadet (Haigh) and only does so after the cadet is injured in maneuvers.

875. High Speed (4/10/32) B&W – 60 mins. (Crime-Sports). *DIR*: D. Ross Lederman. *SP*: Adele Buffington. Story by Harold Shumate. *CAST*: Buck Jones, Loretta Sayers, Mickey McGuire (Mickey Rooney), William Walling, Edward J. LeSaint, Ward Bond, Dick Dickenson, Martin Faust, Joe Bordeaux, Pat O'Malley, Eddie Chandler, Wallace MacDonald.

In his off hours, a policeman (Jones) races cars. When a driver is killed, he takes in his crippled son (McGuire), and while in the line of duty he rounds up a mob of crooks, goes back to racing, and wins the big race.

876. Highway Patrol (8/5/38) B&W – 56 mins. (Crime). *DIR*: C. C. Coleman, Jr. *PRO*: Wallace MacDonald. *SP*: Robert E. Kent, Stuart Anthony. Story by Lambert Hillyer. *CAST*: Robert Paige, Jacqueline Wells (Julie Bishop), Robert Middlemass, Arthur Loft, Al Bridge, Eddie Foster, George McKay, Eddie Laughton, Ann Doran.

A cop (Paige) helps a refinery owner (Middlemass) find out who is behind the bombing of his refinery and hijacking of his trucks.

877. Hills of Utah (9/30/51) Sepiatone—70 mins. (Western). *DIR:* John English. *PRO:* Armand Schaefer. *SP:* Gerald Geraghty. Story by Les Savage, Jr. A Gene Autry Production. *CAST:* Gene Autry, Elaine Riley, Pat Buttram, Onslow Stevens, Denver Pyle, Harry Lauter, William Fawcett, Tom London, Tommy Ivo, Stanley Price, Boyd Stockman, Kenne Duncan, Donna Martell, Sandy Sanders, Teddy Infuhr, Lee Morgan, Billy Griffith, Bob Woodward.

Gene, a newly arrived doctor in a small Utah community, becomes tired of the bloodshed between the cattle ranchers and copper miners, and goes after the outlaws who are stirring them up.

878. The Hireling (6/73) Eastman Color—108 mins. (Drama). *DIR:* Alan Bridges. *PRO:* Ben Arbeid. *SP:* Wolf Mankowitz. Based on the book by L. P. Hartley. A World Film Services/Champion Production. *CAST:* Robert Shaw, Sarah Miles, Peter Egan, Elizabeth Sellars, Caroline Mortimer, Patricia Lawrence, Petra Markham, Ian Hogg, Christine Hargreaves.

In 1920 England, a wealthy young widow (Miles) falls in love with her chauffeur (Shaw) but, because of class barriers, their relationship is doomed.

879. His Girl Friday (1/5/40) B&W—92 mins. (Comedy). *DIR/ PRO:* Howard Hawks. *SP:* Charles Lederer. Based on the play *The Front Page* by Ben Hecht, Charles MacArthur. *CAST:* Cary Grant, Rosalind Russell, Ralph Bellamy, Gene Lockhart, Helen Mack, Porter Hall, Ernest Truex, Cliff Edwards, Clarence Kolb, Roscoe Karns, Frank Jenks, Regis Toomey, Abner Biberman, Frank Orth, John Qualen, Alma Kruger, Billy Gilbert, Irving Bacon, Edmund Cobb, Wade Boteler.

Ace reporter Hildy Johnson (Russell) decides to quit the newspaper and get married, but her editor and ex-husband (Grant) has other plans and sends her to cover an execution as her final story. *NOTES:* A remake of the 1931 United Artists film *The Front Page.*

880. Hit the Hay (11/29/45) B&W—75 mins. (Musical-Comedy). *DIR:* Del Lord. *PRO:* Ted Richmond. *SP:* Richard Weil, Charles R. Marion. *CAST:* Judy Canova, Ross Hunter, Fortunio Bonanova, Doris Merrick, Gloria Holden, Francis Pierlot, Grady Sutton, Louis Mason, Paul Stanton, Clyde Pillmore, Maurice Cass, Luis Alberni.

An operatic agent (Hunter) discovers a hillbilly girl (Canova) singing arias while milking cows and takes her back to the city. Since she can't act, he hires an actress (Canova) who looks like her to be on stage while she sings in the background. Tired of this, the hillbilly wows the crowd with her rendition of "William Tell," dubbed "Tillie Tell."

881. Hoedown (6/6/50) B&W—64 mins. (Musical-Western). *DIR:* Ray Nazarro. *PRO:* Colbert Clark. *SP:* Barry Shipman. *CAST:* Eddy Arnold, Jeff Donnell, Jock Mahoney, Guinn "Big Boy" Williams, Carolina Cotton, Fred F. Sears, Don C. Harvey, Charles Sullivan, Ray Walker, Douglas Fowley, Harry Harvey, The Pied Pipers, The Oklahoma Wranglers.

An ex-movie cowboy (Mahoney) and a girl reporter (Donnell) round up a gang of bank robbers at Eddy Arnold's "Singing Dude Ranch."

882. Hold the Press (11/5/33) B&W—65 mins. (Crime). *DIR:* Philip E. Rosen. *SP:* Horace McCoy. *CAST:* Tim McCoy, Shirley Grey, Henry Wadsworth, Wheeler Oakman, Joseph Crehan, Edward J. LeSaint, Bradley Page, Julian Rivero, Samuel S. Hinds, Oscar Apfel.

A reporter (McCoy) sets out to trap a murderer.

883. Holiday (5/24/38) B&W — 93 mins. (Comedy). *DIR:* George Cukor. *PRO:* Everett Riskin. *SP:* Donald Ogden Stewart, Sidney Buchman. Based on the play by Philip Barry. *CAST:* Cary Grant, Katharine Hepburn, Doris Nolan, Lew Ayres, Edward Everett Horton, Henry Kolker, Binnie Barnes, Jean Dixon, Henry Daniell, Charles Trowbridge, Howard Hickman, Frank Shannon, Bess Flowers.

An engaged man (Grant) breaks off with his fiancee (Nolan) when she wants him in her father's banking business. He then falls for her free-spirited sister (Hepburn). [British titles: *Free to Live; Unconventional Linda*].

884. Holiday in Havana (10/13/49) B&W — 70 mins. (Musical). *DIR:* Jean Yarbrough. *PRO:* Ted Richmond. *SP:* Robert Lees, Karen DeWolf, Frederic I. Rinaldo. Story by Morton Grant. *CAST:* Desi Arnaz, Mary Hatcher, Ann Doran, Steven Geray, Minerva Urecal, Sig Arno, Ray Walker, Nacho Galindo, Tito Renaldo, Martin Garralaga.

A Cuban bandleader (Arnaz) is in love with a dancer (Hatcher) at the club where he performs. Through a misunderstanding they break up, but are reunited at a Havana musical festival.

885. The Hollywood Knights (5/80) Metrocolor — 85 mins. (Comedy). *DIR/SP:* Floyd Mutrux. *PRO:* Richard Lederer. Story by Floyd Mutrux, Richard Lederer, William Tennant. A Poly-Gram Production. *CAST:* Fran Drescher, Leigh French, Randy Gornel, Gary Graham, Sandy Helberg, James Jeter, Stuart Pankin, Michelle Pfeiffer, Richard Schaal, Robert Wuhl, Tony Danza.

In 1965, a group of teenagers decide to get back at the adults for closing down their local drive-in hangout.

886. Hollywood Roundup (11/6/37) B&W — 62 mins. (Western). *DIR:*
Ewing Scott. *PRO:* L. G. Leonard. *SP:* Joseph Hoffman, Monroe Shaff. *CAST:* Buck Jones, Helen Twelvetrees, Grant Withers, Shemp Howard, George Berlinger, Dickie Jones, Eddie Kane, Monty Collins, Warren Jackson, Lester Dorr, Lee Shumway, Edward Keane, Bob Woodward.

A temperamental cowboy star (Withers) tries to get back at his stunt double (Buck Jones) when the double falls for the leading lady (Twelvetrees).

887. Hollywood Speaks (7/1/32) B&W — 71 mins. (Drama). *DIR:* Edward Buzzell. *SP:* Norman Krasna, Jo Swerling. Story by Norman Krasna. *CAST:* Pat O'Brien, Genevieve Tobin, Lucien Prival, Rita La Roy, Leni Stengel, Ralf Harolde, Anderson Lawlor.

A Hollywood columnist (O'Brien) stops a despondent actress (Tobin) from committing suicide, gets her a test with a notorious director (Prival), and ends up marrying her when scandal threatens.

888. Home in San Antone (4/15/49) B&W — 62 mins. (Western-Musical). *DIR:* Ray Nazarro. *PRO:* Colbert Clark. *SP:* Barry Shipman. *CAST:* Roy Acuff, Jacqueline Thomas, Bill Edwards, George Cleveland, William Frawley, Dorothy Vaughn, Matt Willis, Sam Flint, Fred F. Sears, Ivan Triesault, Lloyd Corrigan, Doye O'Dell, The Modernaires, The Smoky Mountain Boys.

The owner (Acuff) of a country inn has to keep bailing his kleptomaniac uncle (Cleveland) out of trouble. [British title: *Harmony Inn*].

889. Homicidal (6/61) B&W — 87 mins. (Horror). *DIR/PRO:* William Castle. *SP:* Robb White. *CAST:* Glenn Corbett, Patricia Breslin, Jean Arless, Eugenie Leontovich, Alan Bunce, Richard Rust, James Westerfield, Gilbert Green, Wolfe Barzell, Hope Summers, Teri Brooks, Ralph Moody, Joe Forte.

To secure an inheritance, a psychotic blonde (Arless) moves in with an old lady (Leontovich) and her strange young son (Arless). NOTES: This film was based on a true story, a 10-year-old Scandinavian case. William Castle's gimmick: A "Fright Break" five minutes before the film ends; the audience is given 45 seconds to go to the "coward's corner."

890. Homicide Bureau (2/2/39) B&W – 56 mins. (Crime). DIR: C. C. Coleman, Jr. PRO: Jack Fier. SP: Earle Snell. CAST: Bruce Cabot, Rita Hayworth, Robert Paige, Marc Lawrence, Richard Fiske, Moroni Olsen, Norman Willis, Gene Morgan, Lee Prather, Stanley Andrews, Eddie Fetherstone, John Tyrrell, Charles Trowbridge, George Lloyd, Ann Doran, Dick Curtis, Stanley Brown, George DeNormand, Beatrice Curtis, Joseph DeStefani, Beatrice Blinn, Harry Bernard, Nell Craig, Kit Guard, George Cooper, Ky Robinson, Dick Rush, Lee Shumway, Lester Dorr, Wedgewood Nowell, Gene Stone.

A detective (Cabot), who believes in using force to get results, tracks down gangsters who are preying on junk dealers and shipping their scrap iron to a foreign power.

891. Honolulu Lu (12/11/41) B&W – 72 mins. (Musical-Comedy). DIR: Charles Barton. PRO: Wallace MacDonald. SP: Eliot Gibbons, Paul Yawitz, Ned Dandy. Story by Eliot Gibbons. CAST: Lupe Velez, Bruce Bennett, Leo Carrillo, Marjorie Gateson, Don Beddoe, Forrest Tucker, George McKay, Helen Dickson, Romaine Callender, Nina Campana, John Tyrrell, Lloyd Bridges, Kit Guard, Chester Conklin, Ray Mala, Ernie Adams, Mickey Simpson, Al Bridge, Roger Clark.

A girl (Velez) becomes involved with a group of sailors who transform her from risque nightclub singer to beauty queen.

892. Hook, Line and Sinker (5/69) Technicolor – 91 mins. (Comedy). DIR: George Marshall. PRO: Jerry Lewis. SP: Rod Amateau. Based on a story by Rod Amateau and David Davis. CAST: Jerry Lewis, Peter Lawford, Anne Francis, Pedro Gonzalez-Gonzalez, Jimmy Miller, Jennifer Edwards, Eleanor Audley, Henry Corden, Sylvia Lewis, Philip Pine, Kathleen Freeman.

A dying man (Lewis) runs up $100,000 in credit card charges and then is told by his doctor (Lawford) that in order to get out of debt he must fake his own "death" since he is not dying.

893. Hope and Glory (10/87) Eastman Color – 113 mins. (Drama-Comedy). DIR/SP: John Boorman. PRO: John Boorman, Michael Dryhurst. A Nelson Entertainment Production. CAST: Sarah Miles, Sebastian Rice-Edwards, Geraldine Muir, David Hayman, Sammi Davis, Derek O'Conner, Susan Woolridge, Ian Bannen, Jean-Marc Barr.

John Boorman's fictionalized autobiographical account of growing up in suburban London during World War II as seen through the eyes of a young boy (Rice-Edwards).

894. The Horsemen (7/71) Eastman Color/Super Panavision – 105 mins. (Drama). DIR: John Frankenheimer. PRO: Edward Lewis. SP: Dalton Trumbo. Based on the book by Joseph Kessel. A Frankenheimer-Lewis Production. CAST: Omar Sharif, Leigh Taylor-Young, Jack Palance, Peter Jeffrey, David De, George Murcell, Eric Pohlmann, John Ruddock, Mark Colleano, Milton Reid.

An Afghan tribesman (Sharif), to prove his manhood to his father (Palance) and rival his father's horsemanship, plays the deadly game of buzkashi, a brutal version of soccer, played on horses and using the headless carcass of a calf.

895. Horsemen of the Sierras (11/22/49) B&W—59 mins. (Western). DIR: Fred F. Sears. PRO: Colbert Clark. SP: Barry Shipman. CAST: Charles Starrett, Lois Hall, Smiley Burnette, T. Texas Tyler, Tommy Ivo, John Dehner, Jason Robards, Sr., Jock Mahoney, George Chesebro, Dan Sheridan, Al Wyatt.

The Durango Kid (Starrett), investigating the murder of a government surveyor, runs into a ranch feud started by two local ranchers (Dehner, Robards), so they can claim the oil rich ranch land. [British title: *Remember Me*].

896. Hot Blood (3/56) Technicolor/Scope—85 mins. (Drama-Musical). DIR: Nicholas Ray. PRO: Howard Welsch, Harry Tatelman. SP: Jesse L. Lasky, Jr. Story by Jean Evans. CAST: Jane Russell, Cornel Wilde, Luther Adler, Joseph Calleia, Mikhail Rasumny, Nina Koshetz, Helen Wescott, Wally Russell, Nick Dennis, Richard Deacon, Robert C. Foulk, John Raven, Joe Merritt, Ethan Laidlaw, Peter Brocco, Ross Bagdasarian.

A dying gypsy king (Adler) arranges a marriage between his brother (Wilde) and a hot blooded gypsy girl (Russell) so that he can succeed him.

897. Hot News (3/36) B&W—77 mins. (Comedy). DIR: W. P. Kellino. PRO: Ian Sutherland. SP: Reginald Long, Arthur Rigby. A St. George's Production. CAST: Lupino Lane, Phyllis Clare, Wallace Lupino, Barbara Kilner, Ben Welden, Glen Raynham, Reginald Long, Fred Leslie, George Pughe, Edward Pierce, Scott Harold, Geoffrey Clarke, Henry Longhurst.

A British newspaper reporter (Lane), heading to America as a guest journalist, gets mixed up with criminals and rescues an heiress (Kilner).

898. Hot Stuff (5/79) Metrocolor/Panavision—91 mins. (Comedy). DIR: Dom DeLuise. PRO: Mort Engelberg. SP: Donald E. Westlake, Michael Kane. A Rastar-Mort Engleberg Production. CAST: Dom DeLuise, Suzanne Pleshette, Jerry Reed, Ossie Davis, Luis Avalos, Marc Lawrence, Dick Davalos, Alfie Wise, Bill McCutcheon, Sydney Lassick, Barney Martin, Pat McCormick, Sid Gould, Mike Falco.

Four undercover cops (DeLuise, Reed, Pleshette, Avalos) set up a fencing operation to trap thieves, but to their surprise it turns into a success money-wise, and the mob wants in.

House of Mystery *see* **Making the Headlines**

899. The Householder (3/63) B&W—100 mins. (Comedy). DIR: James Ivory. PRO: Ismail Merchant. SP: Ruth Prawer Jhabvala. Based on the book by Ruth Prawer Jhabvala. A Royal Films International Production. CAST: Shashi Kapoor, Leela Naidu, Hariendernath Chattopadaya, Durga Khote, Romesh Thappar, Patsy Dance, Walter King, Ernest Castaldo.

An Indian school teacher (Kapoor) has an affair with an American girl (Dance) and comes to realize that it is his wife (Naidu) that he loves. [Original Indian title: *Gharbar*].

900. Housekeeping (11/87) Rank Color—116 mins. (Drama). DIR/SP: Bill Forsyth. PRO: Robert L. Colesberry. Based on the book by Marilynne Robinson. CAST: Christine Lahti, Sara Walker, Andrea Burchill, Anne Pitoniak, Barbara Reese, Bill Smillie, Wayne Robson, Margot Pinvidic.

The lives of two orphaned girls (Walker, Burchill) are drastically changed when their eccentric aunt (Lahti) comes to take care of them.

901. The Houston Story (2/56) B&W — 79 mins. (Crime). *DIR:* William Castle. *PRO:* Sam Katzman. *SP:* James B. Gordon. A Clover Production. *CAST:* Gene Barry, Barbara Hale, Edward Arnold, Paul Richards, Jeanne Cooper, Frank Jenks, John Zaremba, Chris Alcaide, Jack V. Littlefield, Paul Levitt, Fred Krone, Pete Kellett, Leslie Hunt, Claudia Bryar, Larry W. Fultz, Charles Gray.

An oilfield employee (Barry) devises a way to siphon oil and gasoline from the big companies and sell it himself, but he and his discovery are sought after by the mob.

902. How to Murder a Rich Uncle (12/57) B&W/Scope — 79 mins. (Comedy). *DIR:* Nigel Patrick. *PRO/ SP:* John Paxton. Based on *Il Faut Tuer Julie* by Didier Daix. A Warwick Film Production. *CAST:* Charles Coburn, Nigel Patrick, Wendy Hiller, Katie Johnson, Anthony Newley, Athene Seyler, Noel Hood, Kenneth Fortescue, Patricia Webster, Michael Caine, Trevor Reid, Cyril Luckham.

A destitute English nobleman (Patrick) plans to kill his rich uncle (Coburn), but his plan backfires, and he winds up killing off family members with traps he has set for the uncle.

903. How to Save a Marriage — And Ruin Your Life (1/68) Pathe Color/Panavision — 102 mins. (Comedy). *DIR:* Fielder Cook. *PRO:* Stanley Shapiro. *SP:* Stanley Shapiro, Nate Monaster. A Nob Hill Production. *CAST:* Dean Martin, Stella Stevens, Eli Wallach, Anne Jackson, Betty Field, Jack Albertson, George Furth, Monroe Arnold, Katharine Bard, Alan Oppenheimer, Shelley Morrison, Woodrow Parfrey.

An unmarried lawyer (Martin) tries to help his friend (Wallach) save his marriage by romancing his mistress (Jackson) away from him, but mistak-enly romances his secretary (Stevens) with unexpected results. [British title: *Band of Gold*].

904. The Howards of Virginia (9/3/40) B&W — 116 mins. (Historical-Drama). *DIR/PRO:* Frank Lloyd. *SP:* Sidney Buchman. Based on *The Tree of Liberty* by Elizabeth Page. *CAST:* Cary Grant, Martha Scott, Sir Cedric Hardwicke, Alan Marshall, Paul Kelly, Richard Carlson, Irving Bacon, Elisabeth Risdon, Anne Revere, Tom Drake, Phil Taylor, Rita Quigley, George Houston, Richard Gaines, Libby Taylor, Sam McDaniel, Virginia Sale, Ralph Byrd, Dickie Jones, Wade Boteler, Mary Field, Olaf Hytten, Emmett Vogan, Lane Chandler, James Westerfield.

During the Colonial period, a surveyor (Grant) marries a Virginia aristocrat (Scott) and when the Revolutionary War comes, their relationship is strained by their divided loyalties. [British title: *The Tree of Liberty*].

905. Human Desire (9/54) B&W — 90 mins. (Crime-Drama). *DIR:* Fritz Lang. *PRO:* Lewis J. Rachmil. *SP:* Alfred Hayes. Based on *La Bete Humaine* by Emile Zola. *CAST:* Glenn Ford, Gloria Grahame, Broderick Crawford, Edgar Buchanan, Kathleen Case, Peggy Maley, Diane DeLaire, Grandon Rhodes, Dan Seymour, John Pickard, Paul Brinegar, Dan Riss, Victor Hugo Greene, John Zaremba, Olan Soule.

A railroad employee (Ford) is drawn into a murder plot by the wife (Grahame) of a fellow employee (Crawford). *NOTES:* A remake of the 1938 French film *La Bete Humaine*, and released in the U.S. as *The Human Beast*.

906. The Humanoid (7/79) Eastman Color — 100 mins. (Science Fiction). *DIR:* George B. Lewis. *PRO:* Giorgio Venturini. *SP:* Aldo Lado, Adriano Bolzoni. A Merope Production. CAST: Richard Kiel, Corinne Clery, Leonard Mann, Barbara Bach, Arthur Kennedy, Marco Yeh, Ivan Rassimov.

A group of people (Kiel, Clery, Kennedy, Yeh) try to stop an evil scientist (Mann) from carrying out his plans for world domination. NOTES: limited theatrical release.

907. The Hunchback of Rome (8/63) B&W — 84 mins. (War-Drama). DIR: Carlo Lizzani. PRO: Dino De Laurentiis. SP: Luciano Vincenzoni, Ugo Pirro, Elio Petri, Tommaso Chiaretti, Vittoriano Petrilli, Mario Socrate, Carlo Lizzani. An Orsay-Royal Films International Production. CAST: Gerard Blain, Anna Maria Ferrero, Ivo Garrani, Bernard Blier, Pier Paolo Pasolini, Teresa Pellati, Luba Bodine, Enzo Cerusico.

In 1944 Rome, a top resistance leader (Blain) tries to rally the people against the Fascists, but because he is hunchback, is laughed at and is eventually killed when he tries to escape. NOTES: Director Pier Paolo Pasolini in one of his two film roles; limited theatrical release.

908. Hurricane (9/30/29) B&W — 60 mins. (Action). DIR: Ralph Ince. PRO: Harry Cohn. SP: Norman Houston. Story by Norman Springer. CAST: Johnny Mack Brown, Leila Hyams, Hobart Bosworth, Tom O'Brien, Allan Roscoe, Leila McIntyre, Eddy Chandler, Jack Bourdeaux.

Captain Black (Roscoe) and his men, stranded on a South Sea island, plan to steal aboard the vessel of Captain Hurricane Martin (Bosworth), incite a mutiny, and steal the cargo. NOTES: Sound effects and dialog only, no musical background. Also released as a silent film.

909. Hurricane Island (7/16/51) Super CineColor — 71 mins. (Adventure). DIR: Lew Landers. PRO: Sam

Katzman. SP: David Mathews. CAST: Jon Hall, Marie Windsor, Marc Lawrence, Romo Vincent, Karen Randle, Edgar Barrier, Jo Gilbert, Nelson Leigh, Marshall Reed, Don C. Harvey, Rick Vallin, Russ Conklin, Lyle Talbot, Alex Montoya, Rusty Wescoatt, Zon Murray.

Ponce de Leon (Barrier), his captain (Hall), a female pirate (Windsor), and his men search for the Fountain of Youth and encounter an Indian (Gilbert) seer who uses her powers to guide them to the Fountain.

910. Husbands (12/70) DeLuxe Color — 138 mins. (Drama). DIR/SP: John Cassavetes. PRO: Al Ruban. A Faces Music Inc. Production. CAST: Ben Gazzara, Peter Falk, John Cassavetes, Jenny Runacre, Jenny Lee Wright, David Rowlands, Noelle Kao, Leola Harlow, Meta Shaw, John Kullers.

Shocked at the death of their best friend, three married men (Falk, Gazzara, Cassavetes) go on a drinking binge, fly to Europe, and bare their souls to strangers. NOTES: Originally released at a running time of 154 mins.

911. I Aim at the Stars (10/60) B&W — 106 mins. (Biography-Drama). DIR: J. Lee Thompson. PRO: Charles H. Schneer. SP: Jay Dratler. Story by H. W. John, U. Wolter, George Froeschel. A Morningside-Worldwide Production. CAST: Curt Jurgens, Victoria Shaw, Herbert Lom, Gia Scala, James Daly, Adrian Hoven, Gunther Mruwka, Hans Schumm, Lea Seidl, Gerard Heinz, Karel Stepanek, Peter Capell, Eric Zuckmann, Austin Willis.

A fictional account of the life of German scientist Wernher von Braun (Jurgens), his creation of the V-2 rocket, his adjustment to life in the U.S., and his later work in the space program.

912. I Am the Law (8/24/38) B&W — 83 mins. (Crime-Drama). DIR:

Alexander Hall. *PRO:* Everett Riskin. *SP:* Jo Swerling. Based on *Trailing New York's Crime Boss* by Fred Allhoff. *CAST:* Edward G. Robinson, Barbara O'Neil, John Beal, Wendy Barrie, Otto Kruger, Arthur Loft, Marc Lawrence, Douglas Wood, Robert Middlemass, Charles Halton, Louis Jean Heydt, Ivan Miller, Emory Parnell, Theodore Von Eltz, Horace MacMahon, Lucien Littlefield, Frederick Burton, Edward Keane, Kane Richmond, Edward J. LeSaint, Eddie Fetherstone, James Millican, Bud Jamison, Walter Soderling, Iris Meredith, Joseph DeStefani, Lane Chandler, Lee Shumway, Lester Dorr, Lloyd Whitlock, Bess Flowers, Fay Helm.

A law professor (Robinson) is hired as a special prosecutor to clean up the rackets, unaware that the civic leader (Kruger) who hired him is involved in the rackets.

913. I Didn't Do It (6/45) B&W— 97 mins. (Comedy-Crime). *DIR:* Marcel Varnel. *PRO:* Marcel Varnel, Ben Henry. *SP:* Norman Lee, Howard Irving Young, Stephen Black, Peter Fraser, Michael Vaughn. A Columbia-British Production. *CAST:* George Formby, Billy Caryll, Hilda Mundy, Gaston Palmer, Jack Daly, Carl Jaffe, Marjorie Browne, Wally Patch, Ian Fleming, Vincent Holman, Dennis Wyndham, Jack Raine.

A would-be stage actor (Formby) takes a room in an actor's boarding house and finds himself accused of murder.

914. I Love a Bandleader (9/13/45) B&W—70 mins. (Musical-Comedy). *DIR:* Del Lord. *PRO:* Michael Kraike. *SP:* Paul Yawitz. Story by John Grey. *CAST:* Phil Harris, Eddie "Rochester" Anderson, Leslie Brooks, Walter Catlett, Frank Sully, James Burke, Pierre Watkin, Philip Van

Zandt, Nick Stewart, Robin Short, The Four V's.

A nightclub painter (Harris) suffers a case of amnesia and becomes a bandleader. [British title: *Memory for Two*].

915. I Love a Mystery (1/25/45) B&W—69 mins. (Mystery). *DIR:* Henry Levin. *PRO:* Wallace MacDonald. *SP:* Charles O'Neal. Based on the *I Love a Mystery* radio program and book by Carleton E. Morse. *CAST:* Jim Bannon, Nina Foch, Barton Yarborough, Carole Mathews, George Macready, Lester Matthews, Gregory Gay, Frank O'Conner, Joseph Crehan, Isabel Withers, Leo Mostovoy, Kay Dowd, Ernie Adams.

Two detectives (Bannon, Yarborough) must protect a businessman (Macready) marked for death by an Oriental cult who want his head because it resembles their dead leader.

916. I Love Trouble (1/10/48) B&W—93 mins. (Mystery). *DIR/PRO:* S. Sylvan Simon. *SP:* Roy Huggins. Based on *Double Take* by Roy Huggins. A Cornell Production. *CAST:* Franchot Tone, Janet Blair, Janis Carter, Adele Jergens, Glenda Farrell, Steven Geray, Tom Powers, Lynn Merrick, John Ireland, Donald Curtis, Eduardo Ciannelli, Robert H. Barrat, Raymond Burr, Arthur Space, Sid Tomack, Eddie Marr.

A private detective (Tone) is hired by a politician (Powers) to investigate his wife's (Merrick) background.

917. I Love, You Love (11/62) Eastman Color—90 mins. (Documentary-Revue). *DIR/SP:* Alessandro Blasetti. *PRO:* Dino De Laurentiis. A Davis-Royal Films Production. *CAST:* The Moissiev Ballet, Don Yada's Japanese Dance Troupe, The Benitez Sisters, The Norman Davis Dancers, Obrazov and His Puppet Theatre, The Soviet Army Choir, George Lafaye, Fattini and Cairoli, Chaz Chase, the voice of Edith Piaf, The Marney Trio. Narrated by Peter Marshall.

A documentary surveying love in various capitals of the world, spliced with newsreel, feature, and short subject footage. [Original Italian title: *Io Amo, Tu Ami*]. [Original French title: *J'Aime, Tu Aimes*].

918. I Married Adventure (7/24/40) B&W — 78 mins. (Documentary). *EDITOR:* Ralph Dixon. *PRO:* Osa Johnson. *SP:* Albert Duffy, Don Clark. Based on the book by Martin and Osa Johnson. *CAST:* Narrated by Jim Bannon.

A pictorial account of the adventures of famed 30's explorers Martin and Osa Johnson.

919. I Never Sang for My Father (10/70) Technicolor — 92 mins. (Drama). *DIR/PRO:* Gilbert Cates. *SP:* Robert Anderson. Based on the play by Robert Anderson. *CAST:* Melvyn Douglas, Dorothy Stickney, Gene Hackman, Estelle Parsons, Elizabeth Hubbard, Daniel Keyes, Jon Richards, Conrad Bain.

When his mother (Stickney) dies, a middle-aged man (Hackman) is saddled with his tyrannical father (Douglas).

920. I Only Arsked! (6/58) B&W — 82 mins. (Comedy). *DIR:* Montgomery Tully. *PRO:* Anthony Hinds. *SP:* Sid Colin, Jack Davies. From the Granada TV series *The Army Game*. A Hammer-Granada Production. *CAST:* Bernard Bresslaw, Michael Medwin, Alfie Bass, Geoffrey Summer, Charles Hawtrey, Norman Rossington, David Lodge, Arthur Howard, Michael Bentine, Francis Matthews, Marne Maitland, Ewen McDuff, Michael Ripper.

A bumbling British Army squad, sent to a Middle East country to prevent a revolution, wind up finding oil.

921. I Promise to Pay (2/18/37) B&W — 68 mins. (Crime-Drama). *DIR:* D. Ross Lederman. *PRO:* Myles Connolly. *SP:* Mary C. McCall, Jr., Lionel Houser. *CAST:* Chester Morris, Leo Carrillo, Helen Mack, Thomas Mitchell, Thurston Hall, John Gallaudet, Patsy O'Conner, Wallis Clark, James Flavin, Edward Keane, Harry Woods, Henry Brandon, Marc Lawrence.

A family man (Morris) gets involved with loan sharks when he borrows money to take his family on a vacation.

922. I Surrender Dear (10/7/48) B&W — 67 mins. (Musical). *DIR:* Arthur Dreifuss. *PRO:* Sam Katzman. *SP:* M. Coates Webster. A Kay Picture Production. *CAST:* Gloria Jean, David Street, Don McGuire, Alice Tyrrell, Robert Emmett Keane, Douglas Wood, Regina Wallace, Byron Foulger, Jack Eigen, Peter Potter, Dave Garroway, The Novelties.

Complications develop when an orchestra leader (Street) replaces his girlfriend's (Jean) father (Keane) as a disc jockey.

923. I Walk the Line (10/70) Eastman Color/Panavision — 95 mins. (Drama). *DIR:* John Frankenheimer. *PRO:* Harold D. Cohen. *SP:* Alvin Sargent. Based on *An Exile* by Madison Jones. A Frankenheimer-Lewis Production. *CAST:* Gregory Peck, Tuesday Weld, Estelle Parsons, Ralph Meeker, Lonny Chapman, Charles Durning, Freddie McCloud, Jane Rose, J. C. Evans, Jeff Dalton, Bill Littleton.

A Tennessee sheriff (Peck) destroys his professional and personal life when he falls in love with a moonshiner's daughter (Weld).

924. I Was a Prisoner on Devil's Island (8/4/41) B&W — 71 mins. (Drama). *DIR:* Lew Landers. *PRO:* Wallace MacDonald. *SP:* Karl Brown. Story by Otto Van Eyss, Edgar Van Eyss. *CAST:* Donald Woods, Eduardo Ciannelli, Victor Kilian, Sally Eilers,

Dick Curtis, Charles Halton, John Tyrrell, Eddie Laughton, Edmund Cobb, Robert Warwick, Lloyd Bridges.

An American seaman (Woods) kills his captain, is sentenced to Devil's Island, and later escapes with the wife (Eilers) of the prison doctor (Ciannelli).

925. I'll Fix It (11/10/34) B&W— 68 mins. (Drama). *DIR:* Roy William Neill. *SP:* Ethel Hill, Dorothy Howell. Story by Leonard Spiegelgass. *CAST:* Jack Holt, Mona Barrie, Edward Brophy, Winnie Lightner, John Wray, Jimmy Butler, Charles Moore, Edward Van Sloan, Clarence Wilson, Selmer Jackson, Harry Holman, Robert Gunn, Dorian Johnston, Wallis Clark, Nedda Harrigan, Helena Phillips Evans, Charles Levison.

A town politician (Holt) causes a teacher revolt when he has the school principal (Barrie) fired for not letting his younger brother (Butler) play on the football team.

926. I'll Love You Always (3/30/ 35) B&W—75 mins. (Drama). *DIR:* Leo Bulgakov. *PRO:* Everett Riskin. *SP:* Vera Caspary, Sidney Buchman. Story by Lawrence Hazard. *CAST:* Nancy Carroll, George Murphy, Raymond Walburn, Jean Dixon, Arthur Hohl, Paul Harvey, Harry Bresford, Robert Allen.

An engineer (Murphy) turns to theft when his marriage starts falling apart. He is captured and sentenced to prison, keeping the secret from his wife (Carroll) until he is paroled.

927. I'll Take Romance (11/17/37) B&W—85 mins. (Musical). *DIR:* Edward H. Griffith. *PRO:* Everett Riskin. *SP:* George Oppenheimer, Jane Murfin. Story by Stephen Morehouse Avery. *CAST:* Grace Moore, Melvyn Douglas, Helen Westley, Stuart Erwin, Margaret Hamilton, Walter Kingsford, Richard Carle, Ferdinand Gottschalk, Esther Muir, Frank Forest, Walter Stahl, Barry Orton, Franklin Pangborn, Greta Meyer, Albert Conti, John Gallaudet, Gennaro Curci, Mavek Windheim, Allan Garcia.

An American promoter (Douglas) tries to persuade an opera singer (Moore) to open the Buenos Aires opera season.

928. I'm All Right Jack (10/60) B&W—104 mins. (Comedy). *DIR:* John Boulting. *PRO:* Roy Boulting. *SP:* Frank Harvey, Alan Hackney, John Boulting. Based on *Private Life* by Alan Hackney. A Boulting Brothers Production. *CAST:* Peter Sellers, Ian Carmichael, Terry-Thomas, Richard Attenborough, Dennis Price, Margaret Rutherford, Irene Handl, Liz Fraser, Miles Malleson, Marne Maitland, John Le Mesurier, Raymond Huntley, Victor Maddern, Kenneth Griffith, Malcolm Muggeridge, Basil Dignam, Stringer Davis, Wally Patch.

A young man (Carmichael) goes to work for his uncle (Price), streamlines factory operations, and causes national strife between labor and management.

929. I'm Going to Get You . . . Elliot Boy (5/71) Eastman Color—97 mins. (Drama). *DIR:* Edward J. Forsyth. *PRO:* J. M. Slutker. *SP:* Joseph E. Duhamel. A Cinepro Production. *CAST:* Ross Stephenson, Maureen McGill, Richard Gishler, Jeremy Hart.

Released from prison, a man (Stephenson) kills his girl (McGill) when she tries to steal the money he had stolen earlier. *NOTES:* Limited theatrical release.

930. Ice Castles (12/78) Metrocolor—113 mins. (Drama). *DIR:* Donald Wrye. *PRO:* John Kemeny, Rodger Olenicoff. *SP:* Donald Wrye, Gary L. Baim. Story by Gary L. Baim. *CAST:* Lynn-Holly Johnson, Robby Benson, Colleen Dewhurst, Tom Skerritt, Jennifer Warren, David Huffman, Diane Reilly, Brian Foley, Leonard Lillyholm,

Craig T. McMullen, Kelsey Ufford, Jean-Claude Bleuze, Teresa Willmus. An Olympic hopeful (Johnson), blinded by an accident, continues her ice skating training with the help of her boyfriend (Benson).

931. Idol on Parade (4/59) B&W/ Scope—92 mins. (Comedy). *DIR:* John Gilling. *PRO:* Harold Huth. *SP:* John Antrobus. Based on the book by William Camp. A Warwick Films Production. *CAST:* William Bendix, Anthony Newley, Anne Aubrey, Lionel Jeffries, David Lodge, Sidney James, Dilys Laye, William Kendall, Bernie Winters, Harry Fowler, Percy Herbert, John Wood, Rupert Davies.

A pop singer (Newley) creates chaos with his fans and with the British Army when he is drafted.

932. If Ever I See You Again (5/ 78) Technicolor—105 mins. (Romance). *DIR/PRO:* Joseph Brooks. *SP:* Joseph Brooks, Martin Davidson. *CAST:* Joseph Brooks, Shelley Hack, Jimmy Breslin, Jerry Keller, George Plimpton, Michael Decker, Julie Ann Gordon, Shannon Bolin, Bob Kaliban, Gordon Ramsey, Vinnie Bell, Peter Billingsley, Dan Resin.

A music composer (Brooks) tries to rekindle a romance with his old girlfriend (Hack).

933. If I Were Boss (3/38) B&W—72 mins. (Drama). *DIR:* Maclean Rogers. *PRO:* George Smith. *SP:* Basil Mason. A GS Enterprises Production. *CAST:* Bruce Seton, Googie Withers, Ian Fleming, Zillah Bateman, Julie Suedo, Charles Oliver, Paul Sheridan, Michael Ripper.

A clerk (Seton) at an egg company almost causes financial ruin for his boss (Fleming) when he listens to the advice of a shady rival (Oliver).

934. If You Could Only Cook (12/17/35) B&W—70 mins. (Comedy-

Romance). *DIR:* William A. Seiter. *PRO:* Everett Riskin. *SP:* Howard J. Green, Gertrude Purcell. Story by F. Hugh Herbert. *CAST:* Herbert Marshall, Jean Arthur, Leo Carrillo, Lionel Stander, Alan Edwards, Frieda Inescort, Gene Morgan, Ralf Harolde, Matt McHugh, Richard Powell.

An auto tycoon (Marshall), pretending to be unemployed, meets an unemployed girl (Arthur) and both take jobs as butler and maid in the house of a gourmet gangster (Carrillo). *NOTES:* When this film opened in London, it was advertised as being a Frank Capra Production, which it was not. Capra was furious when he found out about it and sued for libel. The incident was resolved when Harry Cohn called on Capra and promised to purchase the rights to *You Can't Take It With You,* which Capra was anxious to direct.

935. Images (12/72) Technicolor/ Panavision—101 mins. (Psychological-Drama). *DIR/SP:* Robert Altman. *PRO:* Tommy Thompson. Based on *In Search of Unicorns* by Susannah York. A Lion's Gate-Hemdale Film Production. *CAST:* Susannah York, Rene Auberjonois, Marcel Bozzuffi, Hugh Millias, Cathryn Harrison.

A troubled young woman (York), haunted by images of her husband (Auberjonois) and former lovers (Bozzuffi, Millias), tries to distinguish reality from fantasy.

936. The Impatient Years (9/7/ 44) B&W—91 mins. (Romance). *DIR/ PRO:* Irving Cummings. *SP:* Virginia Van Upp. *CAST:* Jean Arthur, Lee Bowman, Charles Coburn, Edgar Buchanan, Charley Grapewin, Phil Brown, Harry Davenport, Jane Darwell, Grant Mitchell, Frank Jenks, Frank Orth, Charles Arnt, Robert Emmett Keane.

A young housewife (Arthur), unsure of her love for her husband (Bowman), who has just returned from the war, files for divorce, but through the efforts of her father (Coburn) and a judge (Buchanan), the couple are reconciled.

937. In a Lonely Place (8/50) B&W—94 mins. (Drama). *DIR:* Nicholas Ray. *PRO:* Robert Lord, Henry S. Kesler. *SP:* Andrew Solt. Story by Edmund H. North. Based on the book by Dorothy B. Hughes. A Santana Pictures Production. *CAST:* Humphrey Bogart, Gloria Grahame, Frank Lovejoy, Carl Benton Reid, Art Smith, Jeff Donnell, Martha Stewart, Robert Warwick, Morris Ankrum, William Ching, Steven Geray, Hadda Brooks, Alice Talton, Ruth Warren, Jack Reynolds, Ruth Gillette, Prince Michael Romanoff, Arno Frey, Billy Gray, Myron Healey.

When a screenwriter (Bogart) finds himself accused of murder and is hounded by the police, his friends and girl (Grahame) begin to question his innocence when they learn about his violent past.

938. In Cold Blood (12/67) B&W/ Panavision—134 mins. (Crime-Drama). *DIR/PRO/SP:* Richard Brooks. Based on the book by Truman Capote. A Pax Enterprises Production. *CAST:* Robert Blake, Scott Wilson, John Forsythe, Paul Stewart, Jeff Corey, Gerald S. O'Loughlin, James Flavin, Charles McGraw, John Gallaudet, Will Geer, Ruth Storey, Vaughn Taylor, Duke Hobbie, Raymond Hatton.

Semi-documentary account which traces the lives of two killers, Perry Smith (Blake) and Dick Hickock (Wilson); their motives, eventual arrest, and execution for slaughtering the Clutter family in Holcomb, Kansas, on November 15, 1959.

939. In Early Arizona (11/2/38) B&W—53 mins. (Western). *DIR:* Joseph Levering. *PRO:* Larry Darmour. *SP:* Nate Gatzert. *CAST:* Bill Elliott,

Dorothy Gulliver, Harry Woods, Jack Ingram, Franklyn Farnum, Frank Ellis, Charles King, Slim Whitaker, Art Davis, Bud Osborne, Al Ferguson, Tom London, Buzz Barton, Ed Cassidy, Lester Dorr, Kit Guard, Jack O'Shea, Frank Ball, Tex Palmer, Sherry Tansey, Dick Dorrell, Oscar Gahan, Jess Caven, Symona Boniface.

Whit Gordon (Elliott) is appointed marshal of Tombstone when the former marshal (Ingram) is killed. He sets out to rid the town of an outlaw gang and crooked politicians controlling the town.

940. In Spite of Danger (4/9/35) B&W—53 mins. (Action). *DIR:* Lambert Hillyer. *PRO:* Irving Briskin. *SP:* Anthony Coldeway. *CAST:* Wallace Ford, Marian Marsh, Arthur Hohl, Charles Middleton, Dick Wessel, Edward J. LeSaint, Jay Walter Ward.

An ex-race car driver (Ford) meets a waitress (Marsh) and is persuaded to join her father (Ward) in the trucking business, where they compete against a rival trucking firm.

941. In the French Style (9/63) B&W—104 mins. (Romance). *DIR:* Robert Parrish. *PRO:* Irwin Shaw, Robert Parrish. *SP:* Irwin Shaw. Based on the short stories *In the French Style* and *A Year to Learn the Language* by Irwin Shaw. A Casanna-Orsay Production. *CAST:* Jean Seberg, Stanley Baker, Philippe Forquet, Addison Powell, Jack Hedley, Maurice Teynac, James Leo Herlihy, Ann Lewis, Jacques Charon, Claudine Auger, Barbara Somers, Moustache.

An American girl (Seberg), studying painting in Paris, has affairs with a student (Forquet) and correspondent (Baker), but eventually marries a doctor (Herlihy) and returns to the U.S. [Original French title: *A la Francaise*].

942. In the Nick (8/60) B&W/ Scope—105 mins. (Comedy). *DIR/SP:*

Ken Hughes. *PRO:* Harold Huth. Story by Frank Norman. A Warwick Films Production. *CAST:* Anthony Newley, Anne Aubrey, Bernie Winters, James Booth, Harry Andrews, Al Mulock, Derren Nesbitt, Victor Brooks, Ian Hendry, Barry Keegan, Niall MacGinnis, Kynaston Reeves.

A prison psychologist (Newley) sets out to reform a tough prison inmate (Booth) and attempts to reach him through his girl (Aubrey).

943. The Incredible Invasion (4/71) Eastman Color—90 mins. (Horror). *DIR:* Jack Hill, Juan Ibanez. *PRO:* Luis Enrique Vergara. *SP:* Karl Schanzer, Luis Enrique Vergara. *CAST:* Boris Karloff, Enrique Guzman, Christa Linder, Maura Monti, Yerye Beirute, Tere Valez, Sergio Kleiner, Mariela Flores, Griselda Mejia, Tito Novarro, Rosangela Balbo.

Two aliens from outer space come to earth to destroy a powerful machine and secretly enter the bodies of a scientist (Karloff) and an escaped convict (Beirute). Before they can destroy the machine the scientist regains his will and destroys the aliens and the machine so that no other aliens can come to earth. *NOTES:* Originally filmed in 1968, this was the last feature film Boris Karloff made to be released theatrically. Owing to the death of producer Vergara, the remaining Karloff films, *The Fear Chamber* and *House of Evil* have never been released theatrically. This film played to Spanish language theaters only, before being dubbed and released to television. All of Karloff's scenes were filmed in Los Angeles and later edited into the film. [Original Spanish titles: *Invasion Siniestra; La Invasion Siniestro*].

944. Indian Territory (9/30/50) Sepiatone—70 mins. (Western). *DIR:* John English. *PRO:* Armand Schaefer. *SP:* Norman S. Hall. *CAST:* Gene

Autry, Gail Davis, Pat Buttram, Kirby Grant, James Griffith, Philip Van Zandt, Chief Thunder Cloud, Chief Yowlachie, Frank Lackteen, Pat Collins, Kenne Duncan, Frank Ellis, Charles Stevens, Roy Gordon, Robert Carson, Boyd Stockman, Sandy Sanders, Frankie Marvin, John R. McKee, Bert Dodson, Nick Rodman, Wesley Hudman, Robert Hilton, Roy Butler, Chief Thundersky.

Gene, working undercover with the Union Army, is sent to make peace between the Indians and whites. Learning that an ex-Austrian officer (Van Zandt) is working with the outlaws to stir up the Indians, he sets out to bring them to justice.

945. Indian Uprising (1/2/52) Super CineColor—75 mins. (Western). *DIR:* Ray Nazarro. *PRO:* Edward Small. *SP:* Kenneth Gamet, Richard Schayer. *CAST:* George Montgomery, Audrey Long, Carl Benton Reid, Eugene Iglesias, John Baer, Joe Sawyer, Eddy Waller, Douglas Kennedy, Robert Shayne, Robert Dover, Miguel Inclan, Hugh Sanders, John Call, Robert Griffin, Fay Roope, Hank Patterson, Peter Thompson.

Geronimo (Inclan) goes on the warpath when white men (Kennedy, Sanders) try to take gold from the reservation. An Army captain (Montgomery) manages to bring peace between Geronimo and the settlers.

946. Indiscretion of an American Wife (7/54) B&W—63 mins. (Drama). *DIR/PRO:* Vittorio de Sica. *SP:* Caesare Zavattini, Luigi Chiarini, Giorgio Prosperi, Truman Capote. Based on *Terminal Station* by Caesare Zavattini. *CAST:* Jennifer Jones, Montgomery Clift, Gino Cervi, Richard Beymer, Paolo Stoppa, Mando Bruno.

An adulterous wife (Jones) meets her lover (Clift) at a railway station for one final affair before she leaves

Rome. NOTES: Released to the European market at a running time of 120 mins. [British title: Indiscretion]. [Original Italian title: Stazione Termini].

947. Innocence (12/1/23) B&W— 58 mins. (Drama). DIR: Edward J. Le-Saint. PRO: Harry Cohn. SP: Jack Sturmwasser. Based on Circumstances Alter Divorce Cases by Lewis Allen Browne. A C.B.C. Release. CAST: Anna Q. Nilsson, Freeman Wood, Earle Foxe, Wilfred Lucas, William Scott, Marion Harlan.

A millionaire (Wood) marries a show girl (Nilsson) against his parents' will and complications develop when her old boyfriend (Foxe) shows up.

948. Inside Detroit (1/56) B&W— 80 mins. (Drama). DIR: Fred F. Sears. PRO: Sam Katzman. SP: Robert E. Kent, James B. Gordon. A Clover Production. CAST: Dennis O'Keefe, Pat O'Brien, Tina Carver, Margaret Field, Mark Damon, Larry Blake, Ken Christy, Joseph Turkel, Paul Bryar, Guy Kingsford, Robert Griffin, Dick Rich, Norman Leavitt, Katherine Warren.

A racketeer (O'Brien) is released from prison and tries to regain control of the United Auto Workers union from an honest labor leader (O'Keefe).

949. Interlude (7/68) Technicolor—113 mins. (Drama). DIR: Kevin Billington. PRO: David Deutsch. SP: Lee Langley, Hugh Leonard. A Domino Production. CAST: Oskar Werner, Barbara Ferris, Virginia Maskell, Donald Sutherland, Nora Swinburne, Alan Webb, Geraldine Sherman, Derek Jacobi, Richard Pescud, Janet Davies, Robert Lang, Bernard Kay, John Cleese.

Told in flashback, an orchestra leader (Werner) falls in love with a lady journalist (Ferris), but eventually returns to his wife (Maskell). NOTES: A remake of the 1939 Universal film When Tomorrow Comes and the 1957 Universal film Interlude.

International Police see **Pickup Alley**

950. The Interns (8/62) B&W— 130 mins. (Drama-Romance). DIR: David Swift. PRO: Robert Cohn. SP: Walter Newman, David Swift. Based on the book by Richard Frede. CAST: Michael Callan, Cliff Robertson, James MacArthur, Nick Adams, Suzy Parker, Haya Harareet, Anne Helm, Stefanie Powers, Buddy Ebsen, Telly Savalas, Katharine Bard, Kay Stevens, Gregory Morton, Angela Clarke, Connie Gilchrist, Ellen Davalos, Charles Robinson, John Banner, Mari Lynn, Brian G. Hutton, Peter Brocco, Michael Fox, William O. Douglas.

The careers and loves of four interns (Callan, Robertson, MacArthur, Adams) during their first year of practice at a large hospital.

951. The Invaders (12/18/41) B&W—105 mins. (War-Drama). DIR: Michael Powell. PRO: Michael Powell, John Sutro. SP: Rodney Ackland, Emeric Pressburger. Story by Emeric Pressburger. A GFD-Ortus Production. CAST: Leslie Howard, Raymond Massey, Laurence Olivier, Anton Walbrook, Eric Portman, Glynis Johns, Niall MacGinnis, Finlay Currie, Raymond Lovell, John Chandos, Basil Appleby, Eric Clavering, Charles Victor, Richard George, Peter Moore, Frederick Piper, Charles Rolfe.

During the early days of World War II, a German submarine is sunk in the Gulf of St. Lawrence, leaving the captain (Portman) and six of his crew, who try to escape across Canada to the U.S. NOTES: Original British running time was 123 mins. [British title: The Forty-Ninth Parallel].

Invasion of the Flying Saucers see **Earth vs. the Flying Saucers**

952. Invasion U.S.A. (12/10/52) B&W—73 mins. (Drama). *DIR:* Alfred E. Green. *PRO:* Albert Zugsmith, Robert Smith. *SP:* Robert Smith. Story by Robert Smith, Franz Spencer. An American Production. *CAST:* Gerald Mohr, Peggie Castle, Dan O'Herlihy, Robert Bice, Tom Kennedy, Wade Crosby, Erik Blythe, Phyllis Coates, Aram Katcher, Noel Neill, Edward G. Robinson, Jr.

A stranger (O'Herlihy) convinces people in a bar that the U.S. is engaged in nuclear war and each reacts accordingly, until they realize they have been hypnotized.

953. Investigation of a Citizen Above Suspicion (12/70) Technicolor—112 mins. (Crime-Drama). *DIR:* Elio Petri. *PRO:* Daniele Senatore. *SP:* Ugo Pirro, Elio Petri. A Vera Film Production. *CAST:* Gian Maria Volonte, Florinda Bolkan, Salvo Randone, Gianni Santuccio, Arturo Dominici, Orazio Orlando, Sergio Tramonti, Massimo Foschi, Aldo Rendine.

A mentally disturbed police inspector (Volonte) kills his mistress, and thinking himself above suspicion, plants clues that point to him as the killer. He even confesses the crime, thinking he will get an acquittal. *NOTES:* In Italian with English subtitles. [Original Italian title: *Indagine Su un Cittadino al di Sopra di Ogni Sospetto*].

954. Invitation au Voyage (Invitation to the Voyage) (4/83) Eastman Color—93 mins. (Drama). *DIR:* Peter Del Monte. *PRO:* Claude Nedjar. *SP:* Peter Del Monte, Franco Ferrini. Based on *Moi, Ma Soeur* by Jean Bany. A Triumph Films Production. *CAST:* Laurent Malet, Aurore Clement, Mario Adorf, Nina Scott, Raymond Bussieres.

A young man (Malet) refuses to accept the death of his sister (Scott) and drives across France with her body encountering a dream-like world. *NOTES:* Limited theatrical release; in French with English subtitles.

955. The Iron Glove (4/54) Technicolor—77 mins. (Action-Romance). *DIR:* William Castle. *PRO:* Sam Katzman. *SP:* Jesse L. Lasky, Jr., DeVallon Scott, Douglas Heyes. Story by Robert E. Kent, Samuel J. Jacoby. *CAST:* Robert Stack, Ursula Thiess, Richard Stapley, Charles Irwin, Leslie Bradley, Alan Hale, Jr., Paul Cavanagh, Otto Waldis, Rica Owen, Eric Feldary, David Bruce, Shirley Whitney, Ingard Dawson, Louis D. Merrill.

An Irish swordsman (Stack) and a Scottish prince (Stapley) try to seize the throne of George I (Waldis).

956. Is Everybody Happy? (10/28/43) B&W—73 mins. (Musical). *DIR:* Charles Barton. *PRO:* Irving Briskin. *SP:* Monte Brice. *CAST:* Ted Lewis, Michael Duane, Nan Wynn, Larry Parks, Lynn Merrick, Bob Haymes, Dick Winslow, Harry Barris, Frank Stanford, Fern Emmett, Eddie Kane, Ray Walker, Anthony Marlowe, George Reed, Perc Launders, Paul Bryant, Billy Bletcher, Charles D. Wilson, George McKay, Tom Kennedy, Vi Athens, John Tyrrell, Eddie Laughton, Kirk Alyn.

A young soldier (Parks) refuses to marry his girl (Wynn) because he fears he will return home from the war an invalid. At an Army camp he meets an old friend of his father, Ted Lewis, who helps him make the decision to marry his girl.

957. Ishtar (5/87) Technicolor—107 mins. (Comedy). *DIR/SP:* Elaine May. *PRO:* Warren Beatty. A Columbia-Delphi V Production. *CAST:* Warren Beatty, Dustin Hoffman, Isabelle Adjani, Charles Grodin, Jack Weston, Tess Harper, Carol Kane, David Margulies, Rose Arrick, Julie Garfield,

Christine Rose, Herb Gardner, Bill Moor, Edgar Smith.

Two untalented singer-songwriters (Hoffman, Beatty) get involved with international intrigue in North Africa.

958. Island of Doomed Men (5/20/40) B&W — 68 mins. (Drama). *DIR:* Charles Barton. *PRO:* Wallace MacDonald. *SP:* Robert D. Andrews. *CAST:* Peter Lorre, Rochelle Hudson, Robert Wilcox, Don Beddoe, Kenneth MacDonald, George E. Stone, Charles Middleton, Stanley Brown, Earl Gunn, Don Douglas, Bruce Bennett, Sam Ash, Eddie Laughton, John Tyrrell, Al Hill, Richard Fiske, Trevor Bardette, Howard Hickman, Addison Richards, Lee Prather, Raymond Bailey, Forbes Murray, George McKay, Harry Strang, Charles Hamilton.

An undercover agent (Wilcox) gets sent to Dead Man's Isle, to stop the owner (Lorre) from using paroled convicts to mine for diamonds.

959. Isle of Forgotten Women (9/27/27) B&W — 58 mins. (Drama). *DIR:* George B. Seitz. *PRO:* Harry Cohn. *SP:* Norman Springer. Story by Louella Parsons. *CAST:* Conway Tearle, Dorothy Sebastian, Gibson Gowland, Alice Calhoun, Harry Semels, William Welch, Eddie Harris.

A man (Tearle) flees to a desert island after confessing to a crime he believed his father committed. There he encounters the wrath of the local bully (Gowland) and the love of the bully's native mistress (Sebastian).

Isle of the Dead; Isle of the Snake People *see* **The Snake People**

960. It Came from Beneath the Sea (7/55) B&W — 79 mins. (Science Fiction). *DIR:* Robert Gordon. *PRO:* Charles H. Schneer. *SP:* George Worthing Yates, Hal Smith. Story by George Worthing Yates. A Clover Production. *CAST:* Kenneth Tobey,

Faith Domergue, Donald Curtis, Ian Keith, Harry Lauter, Del Courtney, Dean Maddox, Jr., Tol Avery, Ray Storey, Ed Fisher, Jack V. Littlefield, Jules Irving, Rudy Puteska.

Awakened from the ocean depths by an H-bomb blast, a giant octopus wreaks havoc on the shipping lanes and San Francisco until a submarine commander (Tobey) destroys him. *NOTES:* Special effects by Ray Harryhausen.

961. It Can't Last Forever (7/30/37) B&W — 68 mins. (Comedy-Crime). *DIR:* Hamilton MacFadden. *PRO:* Harry L. Decker. *SP:* Lee Loeb, Harold Buchman. *CAST:* Ralph Bellamy, Betty Furness, Robert Armstrong, Raymond Walburn, Thurston Hall, Edward Pawley, Wade Boteler, Charles Judels, Barbara Burbank.

A theatrical agent (Bellamy) and news girl (Furness) get mixed up with racketeers, double as a radio act, and locate a missing jewel for the police.

962. It Had to Be You (10/22/47) B&W — 98 mins. (Comedy). *DIR:* Don Hartman, Rudolph Mate. *PRO:* Don Hartman. *SP:* Norman Panama, Melvin Frank. Story by Allen Boretz, Don Hartman. *CAST:* Cornel Wilde, Ginger Rogers, Percy Waram, Spring Byington, Thurston Hall, Ron Randell, Charles Evans, Douglas Wood, Mary Forbes, Doug Coppin, Virginia Hunter, Fred F. Sears, Harlan Warde, Myron Healey, Jack Rice, George Chandler, Vernon Dent.

A socialite (Rogers), about to be married for the fourth time, runs out on her prospective groom (Randell) and falls for the man of her dreams, a fireman (Wilde).

963. It Happened in Hollywood (10/6/37) B&W — 67 mins. (Drama). *DIR:* Harry Lachman. *PRO:* Myles Connolly. *SP:* Samuel Fuller, Ethel Hill, Harvey Fergusson. Based on *Once a Hero* by Myles Connolly.

CAST: Richard Dix, Fay Wray, Victor Kilian, Franklin Pangborn, Charles Arnt, Granville Bates, William B. Davidson, Arthur Loft, Edgar Dearing, James Donlan, Billy Burrud, Harold Goodwin, Charles Brinley, Zeffie Tilbury.

A silent western star (Dix) tries to make the transition to talkies, but feels ill at ease in evening clothes and refuses to play gangster roles. Years later, when he foils a bank robbery and becomes a hero, he is in demand again and producers find suitable roles for him and his former leading lady (Wray). [British title: Once a Hero].

It Happened in Paris see **The Lady in Question**

964. It Happened One Night (2/23/34) B&W—105 mins. (Comedy). DIR: Frank Capra. PRO: Harry Cohn. SP: Robert Riskin. Based on Night Bus by Samuel Hopkins Adams. A Frank Capra Production. CAST: Clark Gable, Claudette Colbert, Walter Connolly, Roscoe Karns, Jameson Thomas, Ward Bond, Eddy Chandler, Alan Hale, Arthur Hoyt, Blanche Frederici, Charles C. Wilson, Wallis Clark, Irving Bacon, Hal Price, Frank Yaconelli, Harry C. Bradley, Joseph Crehan, Milton Kibbee, Mickey Daniels, Bess Flowers, Eddie Kane, Harry Todd, Ernie Adams, Kit Guard.

An heiress (Colbert) runs away from her father (Connolly) when he tries to stop her marriage to a scoundrel (Thomas) and gets involved with a reporter (Gable) on her journey across the country. NOTES: Remade by Columbia in 1956 as You Can't Run Away from It.

965. It Happened to Jane (5/59) Eastman Color/Scope—98 mins. (Comedy). DIR/PRO: Richard Quine. SP: Norman Katkov. Story by Norman Katkov, Max Wilk. An Arwin Production. CAST: Jack Lemmon, Doris Day, Ernie Kovacs, Steve Forrest, Teddy Rooney, Russ Brown, Parker Fennelly, Mary Wickes, Walter Greaza, Philip Coolidge, Casey Adams, John Cecil Holm, Gina Gillespie, Dick Crockett, Robert Paige, Dave Garroway, Garry Moore, Bill Cullen, Jayne Meadows, Henry Morgan, Betsy Palmer, Gene Rayburn, Bess Myerson, Steve McCormick.

A lady lobster company owner (Day) and a lawyer (Lemmon) take on a railroad tycoon (Kovacs) when he sabotages her shipment of lobsters. NOTES: Re-released by Columbia in 1960 as Twinkle and Shine and with a running time of 90 mins.

966. It Should Happen to You (3/54) B&W—86 mins. (Comedy). DIR: George Cukor. PRO: Fred Kohlmar. SP: Garson Kanin. CAST: Judy Holliday, Jack Lemmon, Peter Lawford, Michael O'Shea, Connie Gilchrist, Vaughn Taylor, Heywood Hale Broun, Rex Evans, Art Gilmore, Whit Bissell, Melville Cooper, Constance Bennett, Ilka Chase, Wendy Barrie, Ralph Dumke, Chick Chandler, Cora Witherspoon, Jack Kruschen, John Saxon.

A New York model (Holliday), with an urge to become famous, rents a billboard and puts her name on it. NOTES: Jack Lemmon's film debut.

967. It's a Great Life (5/27/43) B&W—68 mins. (Comedy). DIR/PRO: Frank R. Strayer. SP: Connie Lee, Karen DeWolf. Based on the comic strip created by Chic Young. CAST: Penny Singleton, Arthur Lake, Larry Simms, Irving Bacon, Danny Mummert, Jonathan Hale, Hugh Herbert, Alan Dinehart, Douglas Leavitt, Marjorie Ann Mutchie, Frank Sully, Hal Taliaferro (Wally Wales).

Blondie (Singleton) saves the day for Dagwood (Lake) when he mistakenly buys a horse for a client instead of a house.

968. It's All Yours (7/26/37) B&W—80 mins. (Comedy). *DIR:* Elliott Nugent. *PRO:* William Perlberg. *SP:* Mary C. McCall, Jr. Story by Adelaide Heilbron. *CAST:* Madeleine Carroll, Francis Lederer, Mischa Auer, Grace Bradley, Victor Kilian, George McKay, J. C. Nugent, Richard Carle, Arthur Hoyt, Charles Waldron, Connie Boswell.

When a secretary (Carroll) comes into a large inheritance, her male secretary (Lederer) decides to protect her from a baron (Auer) out to steal her money.

969. It's Great to Be Young (9/12/46) B&W—69 mins. (Musical). *DIR:* Del Lord. *PRO:* Ted Richmond. *SP:* Jack Henley. Story by Karen DeWolf. *CAST:* Leslie Brooks, Jimmy Lloyd, Jeff Donnell, Robert Stanton, Jack Williams, Jack Fina, Frank Orth, Ann Codee, Pat Yankee, Frank Sully, Grady Sutton, Vernon Dent, Milton DeLugg and His Swing Wing Band.

A group of ex-GI's, with show business in their veins, stage a show at a summer resort and finish up on Broadway.

970. It's My Turn (10/80) Metrocolor—91 mins. (Romance-Comedy). *DIR:* Claudia Weill. *PRO:* Martin Elfand. *SP:* Eleanor Bergstein. A Rastar-Martin Elfand Production. *CAST:* Michael Douglas, Jill Clayburgh, Charles Grodin, Beverly Garland, Steven Hill, Teresa Baxter, Joan Copeland, John Gabriel, Jennifer Salt, Daniel Stern, Roger Robinson, Charles Kimbrough, Dianne Wiest, Ralph Mauro, Noah Hathaway, Robert Ackerman.

A mathematics professor (Clayburgh) finds herself falling in love with the son (Douglas) of her father's new bride. *NOTES:* The film debut of Dianne Wiest.

971. J. W. Coop (1/72) Eastman Color—112 mins. (Drama). *DIR/PRO:*

Cliff Robertson. *SP:* Cliff Robertson, Gary Cartwright, Edwin "Bud" Shrake. A Robertson & Associates Production. *CAST:* Cliff Robertson, Geraldine Page, R. C. Armstrong, John Crawford, Christina Ferrare, Wade Crosby, Marjorie Durant Dye, Paul Harper, Son Hooker, Richard Kennedy, Bruce Kirby, Larry Mahan, Mary Robin Redd, Larry Clayman, R.L. Armstrong.

A rodeo rider (Robertson), after spending 10 years in prison, tries to adjust to a new way of life in society and on the rodeo circuit.

972. Jack and the Beanstalk (2/76) Eastman Color—92 mins. (Animated-Musical). *DIR:* Gisaburo Sugii. *PRO:* Katsumi Furukawa. *SP:* Shuji Hirami. A Nippon Herald Films Inc.-Group TAC Production. (Japanese version). *DIR/SP:* Peter J. Solmo. *PRO:* Film Rite, Inc. (English version). *CAST:* Not available.

A musical version of the familiar story of Jack and the Beanstalk; how he rescues the golden goose and a princess, and kills the giant. *NOTES:* Originally released in Japan in 1974; no Japanese title available.

973. Jack McCall, Desperado (4/1/53) Technicolor—76 mins. (Western). *DIR:* Sidney Salkow. *PRO:* Sam Katzman. *SP:* John O'Dea. Story by David Chandler. *CAST:* George Montgomery, Angela Stevens, Douglas Kennedy, James Seay, Eugene Iglesias, Jay Silverheels, Gene Roth, John Hamilton, Joe McGuinn, Stanley Blystone, William Tannen, Selmer Jackson, Alva Lacy.

Jack McCall (Montgomery) goes after the men (Kennedy, Seay) who framed him as a spy and killed his parents.

974. Jagged Edge (10/85) Metrocolor—108 mins. (Mystery-Thriller). *DIR:* Richard Marquand. *PRO:* Martin Ransohoff. *SP:* Joe Eszterhas. *CAST:* Peter Coyote, Glenn Close,

Jeff Bridges, Robert Loggia, Maria Mayenzet, Lance Henriksen, William Allen Young, Ben Hammer, James Karen, Sanford Jensen, James Winkler, Leigh Taylor-Young, John Dehner, Guy Boyd.

A woman attorney (Close) falls in love with her client (Bridges), a San Francisco newspaper editor, who may be guilty of murder.

975. Jam Session (6/9/44) B&W — 78 mins. (Musical). *DIR*: Charles Barton. *PRO*: Irving Briskin. *SP*: Manny Seff. Story by Harlan Ware, Patterson McNutt. *CAST*: Ann Miller, Jess Barker, Charles D. Brown, Eddie Kane, George Eldredge, Renie Riano, Clarence Muse, Pauline Drake, Charles La Torre, Ray Walker, George McKay, Vernon Dent, John Dilson, Ethan Laidlaw, Ted Mapes, Hank Bell, John Tyrrell, Terry Frost, Paul Zaremba, Eddie Laughton, Nan Wynn, Constance Worth, Louis Armstrong, Charlie Barnet, Jan Garber, Teddy Powell, Alvino Ray, Glen Gray and His Casa Loma Orchestra, The Pied Pipers.

A girl (Miller) wins a dance contest and a round-trip ticket to Hollywood. While there she meets a screen writer (Barker) and almost causes him his job through a series of unintentional mishaps.

976. Jason and the Argonauts (6/63) Eastman Color/Dynamation — 104 mins. (Fantasy-Adventure). *DIR*: Don Chaffey. *PRO*: Charles H. Schneer. *SP*: Jan Read, Beverley Cross. A Morningside Production. *CAST*: Todd Armstrong, Nancy Kovack, Gary Raymond, Laurence Naismith, Niall MacGinnis, Michael Gwynn, Douglas Wilmer, Jack Gwillim, Honor Blackman, John Cairney, Patrick Troughton, Andrew Faulds, Nigel Green, John Crawford.

Jason (Armstrong) and his crew encounter winged harpies, Triton the

Merman, a bronze giant, and a seven-headed Hydra as they sail the Argo to find the Golden Fleece. *NOTES*: Special effects by Ray Harryhausen.

Jason and the Golden Fleece *see* **Jason and the Argonauts**

977. Jazz Boat (11/60) B&W/ Scope — 96 mins. (Crime-Musical). *DIR*: Ken Hughes. *PRO*: Harold Huth. *SP*: Ken Hughes, John Antrobus. Story by Rex Rienits. A Warwick Production. *CAST*: Anthony Newley, Anne Aubrey, Lionel Jeffries, David Lodge, Bernie Winters, James Booth, Al Mulock, Joyce Blair, Leo McKern, Jean Phillippe, Liam Gaffney, Henry Webb, Ted Heath and His Orchestra.

A handyman and jazz musician (Newley) pretends to be a crook, gets involved with a gang of rookie "Teddy Boy" crooks, and then leads the police to the gang. [Great Britain title: *Jazzboat*].

978. Jealousy (11/23/34) B&W — 66 mins. (Drama). *DIR*: Roy William Neill. *SP*: Joseph Moncure, Kubec Glasmon. Based on the play *Spring 3100* by Argyle Campbell, Willard Mack. *CAST*: Nancy Carroll, George Murphy, Donald Cook, Raymond Walburn, Arthur Hohl, Inez Courtney, Josephine Whittell, Arthur Vinton, Edward Keane, Tom London, Charles King, Edward J. LeSaint, Emmett Vogan, C. Montague Shaw, Ethan Laidlaw, Lucille Ball, Arthur Hoyt.

A professional boxer (Murphy) lets his temper get the best of him when he kills his fiancee's (Carroll) boss (Cook) and is sentenced to death.

979. Jeanne Eagels (8/57) B&W — 109 mins. (Biography-Drama). *DIR/PRO*: George Sidney. *SP*: Daniel Fuchs, Sonya Levien, John Fante. Story by Daniel Fuchs. *CAST*: Kim Novak, Jeff Chandler, Agnes Moorehead, Charles Drake, Larry Gates,

Virginia Grey, Gene Lockhart, Joe de Santis, Murray Hamilton, Will Wright, Snub Pollard, Michael Dante, Joseph Turkel, Judd Holdren, Alyn Lockwood, George J. Lewis, Myrna Fahey, Nanette Fabares, Larry Blake.

In the 1920's, Jeanne Eagels (Novak) rises from sideshow performer to celebrated actress and then begins her decline into alcohol, drugs, and eventually death.

980. Jesse James Vs. the Daltons (4/54) Technicolor/3-D—65 mins. (Western). DIR: William Castle. PRO: Sam Katzman. SP: Robert E. Kent, Samuel Newman. Story by Edwin Westrate. CAST: Brett King, Barbara Lawrence, James Griffith, William Phipps, John Cliff, Rory Mallison, William Tannen, Richard Garland, Nelson Leigh, Raymond Largay.

A man (King), supposedly the son of Jesse James, joins the Dalton gang to learn whether his father is really Jesse James and is still alive. NOTES: Columbia's last 3-D western.

981. Jo Jo Dancer, Your Life Is Calling (5/86) DeLuxe Color—97 mins. (Comedy-Drama). DIR/PRO: Richard Pryor. SP: Richard Pryor, Rocco Urbisci, Paul Mooney. A Columbia-Delphi V Production. CAST: Richard Pryor, Debbie Allen, Art Evans, Fay Hauser, Barbara Williams, Carmen McRae, Paula Kelly, Diahnne Abbott, Scoey Mitchell, Billy Eckstine, Tanya Boyd, Wings Hauser, Michael Ironside, Dennis Farina, E'Lon Cox, J. J. Barry, Michael Genovese, Marlene Warfield, Virginia Capers.

Largely autobiographical account of a comedian's life (Pryor), as seen in flashbacks through his alter ego (Pryor), from his show business success to his drug related accident.

982. Joe Macbeth (2/56) B&W—90 mins. (Crime). DIR: Ken Hughes. PRO: M. J. Frankovich. SP: Philip Yor-

dan. Based on the play *Macbeth* by William Shakespeare. A Film Locations Limited Production. CAST: Paul Douglas, Ruth Roman, Bonar Colleano, Gregoire Aslan, Sidney James, Nick Stuart, Robert Arden, Minerva Pious, Harry Green, Bill Nagy, Kay Callard, Walter Crisham, Mark Baker.

The wife (Roman) of a gangster (Douglas) pushes her husband into becoming a top crime figure, but he eventually meets his downfall at the hands of a rival gangster (Colleano).

983. Johnny Allegro (5/26/49) B&W—80 mins. (Crime-Drama). DIR: Ted Tetzlaff. PRO: Irving Starr. SP: Karen DeWolf, Guy Endore. Story by James Edward Grant. CAST: George Raft, Nina Foch, George Macready, Will Geer, Gloria Henry, Ivan Triesault, Harry Antrim, William "Bill" Phillips, Walter Rode, Thomas B. Henry, Paul E. Burns, Charles Hamilton, George Offerman, Jr., Fred F. Sears, Eddie Acuff, Harlan Warde.

An ex-gangster (Raft) is hired by the Treasury Department as an undercover agent to stop a counterfeiter (Macready) from flooding the U.S. with counterfeit currency. [Great Britain title: *Hounded*].

984. Johnny Nobody (10/61) B&W/Scope—88 mins. (Crime). DIR: Nigel Patrick. PRO: John R. Sloan. SP: Patrick Kirwan. Based on *The Trial of Johnny Nobody* by Albert Z. Carr. CAST: Nigel Patrick, Yvonne Mitchell, Aldo Ray, William Bendix, Cyril Cusack, Bernie Winters, Niall MacGinnis, Noel Purcell, Eddie Byrne, John Welsh, Michael Brennan.

A priest (Patrick) sets out to prove that an explorer (Ray) is guilty of murder.

985. Johnny O'Clock (1/10/47) B&W—95 mins. (Crime-Drama). DIR/SP: Robert Rossen. PRO: Edward G. Nealis. Story by Milton

Holmes. A J.E.M. Production. *CAST:* Dick Powell, Evelyn Keyes, Lee J. Cobb, Ellen Drew, Nina Foch, Thomas Gomez, John Kellogg, Jim Bannon, Mabel Paige, Jeff Chandler, Kit Guard, Robert Ryan, Al Hill, George Lloyd, Kenneth MacDonald.

A gambler (Powell), accused of the murder of a crooked policeman (Bannon) and his girl (Foch), sets out to prove his innocence with the help of the murdered girl's sister (Keyes). *NOTES:* Robert Rossen's first directorial assignment.

986. Jolson Sings Again (8/12/49) Technicolor—96 mins. (Biography-Musical). *DIR:* Henry Levin. *PRO/SP:* Sidney Buchman. *CAST:* Larry Parks, Barbara Hale, William Demarest, Ludwig Donath, Bill Goodwin, Myron McCormick, Tamara Shayne, Eric Wilton, Robert Emmett Keane, Jock Mahoney, Marjorie Stapp, Peter Brocco, Morris Stoloff and His Orchestra, voice of Al Jolson.

This film traces the later life of Al Jolson (Parks), from the break-up of his first marriage, entertaining the troops in Africa, his second marriage to a nurse (Hale), and finally, meeting the actor, Larry Parks, who will portray his life in the making of the first movie *The Jolson Story. NOTES:* A sequel to the 1946 Columbia film *The Jolson Story;* Larry Parks plays a dual role in this film.

987. The Jolson Story (7/16/46) Technicolor—128 mins. (Biography-Musical). *DIR:* Alfred E. Green. *PRO:* Sidney Skolsky. *SP:* Stephen Longstreet, Harry Chandlee, Andrew Solt. *CAST:* Larry Parks, Evelyn Keyes, William Demarest, Bill Goodwin, Ludwig Donath, Tamara Shayne, John Alexander, Jo Carroll Dennison, Ernest Cossart, Scotty Beckett, William Forrest, Edwin Maxwell, Emmett Vogan, Adelle Roberts, Harry Shannon, Pierre Watkin, Will Wright, Arthur Loft, Ed-

ward Keane, Eddie Fetherstone, Jessie Arnold, Fred F. Sears, voice of Al Jolson.

The life of entertainer Al Jolson (Parks), from his boyhood to his success on the stage and in the movies.

Joseph Desa *see* **The Reluctant Saint**

988. Josepha (9/82) Eastman Color—146 mins. (Drama). *DIR/SP:* Christopher Frank. *PRO:* Albina du Boisrouvray, Robert Amon. Based on the book by Christopher Frank. A Triumph Films Production. *CAST:* Miou-Miou, Claude Brasseur, Bruno Cremer.

A woman (Miou-Miou) cannot decide which of her two husbands (Brasseur, Cremer) she really loves. *NOTES:* Limited theatrical release. In French with English subtitles.

989. Juarez y Maximiliano (Juarez and Maximilian) (2/15/35) B&W—??? mins. (Historical). *DIR:* Miguel Contreras Torres. *CAST:* Enrique Herrera, Medea de Novara, Froilan Tenes, Matilde Palou, Antonio R. Frauato, Alfredo de Diestro, Maria Luisa Zea, F. Nava Ferriz, J. Enriquez, Roberto Guzman.

The story of the rise and fall of Emperor Maximilian (Herrera) of Austria. *NOTES:* Released to Spanish language theaters.

990. Jubal (1/56) Technicolor/Scope—101 mins. (Western). *DIR:* Delmer Daves. *PRO:* William Fadiman. *SP:* Russell S. Hughes, Delmar Daves. Based on *Jubal Troop* by Paul I. Wellman. *CAST:* Glenn Ford, Felicia Farr, Ernest Borgnine, Valerie French, Rod Steiger, Basil Ruysdael, Noah Beery, Jr., Charles Bronson, Jack Elam, John Dierkes, Robert "Buzz" Henry, Robert Burton, Robert Knapp, Juney Ellis, Don C. Harvey, Guy Wilkerson, Larry Hudson, Mike Lawrence.

A rancher's wife (French) causes the

death of her husband (Borgnine) when she falls for a drifter (Ford) and is herself, in turn, killed when she spurns the advances of a sadistic ranch hand (Steiger).

991. The Juggler (5/12/53) B&W—84 mins. (Drama). *DIR:* Edward Dmytryk. *PRO:* Stanley Kramer. *SP:* Michael Blankfort. Based on the book by Michael Blankfort. A Stanley Kramer Production. *CAST:* Kirk Douglas, Millie Vitale, Paul Stewart, Joey Walsh, Alf Kjellin, Beverly Washburn, Charles Lane, John Banner, Richard Benedict, Jay Adler, Oscar Karlweis, John Bleifer, Greta Granstedt.

A once famous juggler (Douglas), now a displaced Jew in Israel, believes he has killed a policeman (Benedict) and, while being pursued across Israel by a policeman (Stewart), befriends a small boy (Walsh).

992. Juke Box Rhythm (7/59) B&W—82 mins. (Musical). *DIR:* Arthur Dreifuss. *PRO:* Sam Katzman. *SP:* Mary C. McCall, Jr., Earl Baldwin. Story by Lou Morheim. A Clover Production. *CAST:* Jo Morrow, Jack Jones, Brian Donlevy, Hans Conreid, Karin Booth, Marjorie Reynolds, Frieda Inescort, Edgar Barrier, Fritz Feld, Hortense Petra, George Jessel, Earl Grant Trio, The Nitwits, Johnny Otis, The Treniers.

A European princess (Morrow) arrives in New York to purchase her coronation wardrobe, but a young man (Jones) tries to get her to buy it from his friend (Conreid), while his father (Donlevy) tries to use the princess as a publicity stunt for his Broadway show.

July Pork Bellies *see* **For Pete's Sake**

993. Junction City (7/12/52) B&W—54 mins. (Western). *DIR:* Ray Nazarro. *PRO:* Colbert Clark. *SP:* Barry Shipman. *CAST:* Charles Starrett, Kathleen Case, Smiley Burnette, Jock Mahoney, John Dehner, Hal Taliaferro (Wally Wales), Steve Darrell, George Chesebro, Chris Alcaide, Frank Ellis, Anita Castle, Mary Newton, Robert Bice, Hal Price, Bob Woodward, Joel Friedkin, Harry Tyler.

The Durango Kid (Starrett) prevents the murder of a young girl (Case) who has inherited a gold mine, by her two guardians (Dehner, Newton) and their hired killer (Bice).

994. Jungle Jim (12/26/48) B&W—71 mins. (Adventure). *DIR:* William Berke. *PRO:* Sam Katzman. *SP:* Carroll Young. Based on the *Jungle Jim* newspaper comic strip created by Alex Raymond. *CAST:* Johnny Weissmuller, Virginia Grey, George Reeves, Lita Baron, Rick Vallin, Holmes Herbert, Tex Mooney.

Jungle Jim (Weissmuller) leads a lady scientist (Grey) to a remote jungle village to locate a drug that will combat polio and thwarts the attempt of an explorer (Reeves) to steal the natives' diamonds.

995. Jungle Jim in the Forbidden Land (3/17/52) B&W—64 mins. (Adventure). *DIR:* Lew Landers. *PRO:* Sam Katzman. *SP:* Samuel Newman. Based on the *Jungle Jim* newspaper comic strip created by Alex Raymond. *CAST:* Johnny Weissmuller, Angela Greene, Lester Matthews, Jean Willes, William Tannen, George Eldredge, Frederic Berest, Clem Erickson, William Fawcett, Frank Jacquet.

Jungle Jim (Weissmuller) leads an anthropologist (Greene) and a territory commissioner (Matthews) to the land of the giant people to find the "missing link."

996. Jungle Man-Eaters (6/54) B&W—67 mins. (Adventure). *DIR:* Lee Sholem. *PRO:* Sam Katzman. *SP:* Samuel Newman. Based on the *Jungle Jim* newspaper comic strip created by

Alex Raymond. *CAST:* Johnny Weissmuller, Karin Booth, Richard Stapley, Bernie Hamilton, Lester Matthews, Paul Thompson, Louise Franklin, Gregory Gay, Vince M. Townsend, Jr.

Jungle Jim (Weissmuller) goes on a mission to round up a gang of diamond smugglers and has to fight a tribe of cannibals.

997. Jungle Manhunt (10/4/51) B&W—66 mins. (Adventure). *DIR:* Lew Landers. *PRO:* Sam Katzman. *SP:* Samuel Newman. Based on the *Jungle Jim* newspaper comic strip created by Alex Raymond. *CAST:* Johnny Weissmuller, Sheila Ryan, Bob Waterfield, Rick Vallin, Lyle Talbot, William P. Wilkerson.

Jungle Jim (Weissmuller) leads a photographer (Ryan) into the jungle to find a missing football star (Waterfield), and comes across a gang of smugglers forcing the natives to make synthetic diamonds.

998. Jungle Moon Men (4/55) B&W—70 mins. (Adventure). *DIR:* Charles S. Gould. *PRO:* Sam Katzman. *SP:* Dwight V. Babcock, Joe Pagano. Story by Joe Pagano. *CAST:* Johnny Weissmuller, Jean Byron, Bill Henry, Helene Stanton, Myron Healey, Billy Curtis, Frank Sully, Michael Granger, Benjamin F. Chapman, Jr., Kenneth L. Smith, Ed Hinton.

Weissmuller saves a female writer (Byron) from the clutches of a blonde priestess (Stanton) who has the secret of eternal life.

999. Junior Army (11/26/42) B&W—70 mins. (Drama). *DIR:* Lew Landers. *PRO:* Colbert Clark. *SP:* Paul Gangelin. Story by Albert Bein. *CAST:* Freddie Bartholomew, Billy Halop, Bobby Jordan, Huntz Hall, Boyd Davis, William Blees, Richard Noyes, Joseph Crehan, Don Beddoe, Charles Lind, Billy Lechner, Peter Lawford, Robert O. Davis, Bernard Punsly.

An English boy (Bartholomew), staying with his uncle (Crehan) in America while in a military academy, saves the life of his friend (Halop) and, through the efforts of his uncle, gets his friend enrolled in the military academy.

1000. Just Before Dawn (3/7/46) B&W—65 mins. (Crime-Mystery). *DIR:* William Castle. *PRO:* Rudolph C. Flothow. *SP:* Eric Taylor, Aubrey Wisberg. Based on the CBS radio program *Crime Doctor* by Max Marcin. *CAST:* Warner Baxter, Adelle Roberts, Martin Kosleck, Mona Barrie, Marvin Miller, Charles D. Brown, Craig Reynolds, Robert Barrat, Wilton Graff, Charles Lane, Charles Arnt, Ted Hecht, Peggy Converse, Irene Tedrow, Thomas Jackson.

Dr. Ordway (Baxter), Crime Doctor, solves a kidnapping and a murder, and saves a young woman's (Roberts) life from a psychopath (Kosleck).

1001. Just for Fun (6/63) B&W—85 mins. (Musical). *DIR:* Gordon Flemying. *PRO/SP:* Milton Subotsky. An Amicus Production. *CAST:* Mark Wynter, Cherry Roland, Richard Vernon, Reginald Beckwith, John Wood, Jeremy Lloyd, Harry Fowler, Edwin Richfield, Irene Handl, Hugh Lloyd, Dick Emery, Bobby Vee, The Crickets, Freddy Cannon, Johnny Tillotson, Kitty Lester, Joe Brown and the Breakaways, Karl Denve, Kenny Lynch, Jed Harris, Tony Meehan, Cloda Rogers, Louise Cordet, Lyn Cornell, The Tornados, The Springfields, The Spotniks, Jimmy Powell, Brian Poole and the Tremeloes, Sounds Incorporated, The Vernon Girls.

When teens are given the vote in England, two of them (Wynter, Roland) form their own party and throw the election with the help of popular recording artists.

1002. Just One of the Guys (4/85) Metrocolor—101 mins. (Comedy).

DIR: Lisa Gottlieb. *PRO:* Andrew Fogelson, Dennis Feldman. *SP:* Dennis Feldman, Jeff Franklin. Story by Dennis Feldman. A Summa-Triton Production. *CAST:* Joyce Hyser, Clayton Rohner, Billy Jacoby, Toni Hudson, William Zabka, Leigh McCloskey, Sherilyn Fenn, Deborah Goodrich, Arye Gross, Robert Fieldsteel, Stuart Charno, Steve Basil, John Blanton. Determined to prove herself as an investigative reporter, a young girl (Hyser) enrolls at a nearby school disguised as a boy to see how the other half lives.

1003. Just You and Me, Kid (7/79) Eastman Color—93 mins. (Comedy). *DIR:* Leonard Stern. *PRO:* Irving Fein, Jerome M. Zeitman. *SP:* Oliver Hailey, Leonard Stern. Story by Tom Lazarus. *CAST:* George Burns, Brooke Shields, Burl Ives, Lorraine Gary, Nicolas Coster, Keye Luke, Carl Ballentine, Leon Ames, Ray Bolger, John Schuck, Andrea Howard, Christopher Knight, William Russ, Robert Doran. An elderly comedian (Burns) finds a runaway girl (Shields) in the trunk of his car and winds up protecting her from a dope pusher and the police.

1004. Justice of the Far North (3/15/25) B&W—57 mins. (Adventure). *DIR/SP:* Norman Dawn. *PRO:* Harry Cohn. *CAST:* Arthur Jasmine, Marcia Manon, Laska Winters, Chuck Reisner, Max Davidson, George Fisher, Katherine Dawn, Steve Murphy. An eskimo chief (Jasmine) trails his enemies across the frozen wasteland to rescue his sister (Winters), whom they have kidnapped.

1005. Justice of the Range (5/25/35) B&W—58 mins. (Western). *DIR:* Davie Selman. *PRO:* Irving Briskin. *SP:* Ford Beebe. *CAST:* Tim McCoy, Billie Seward, Ward Bond, Guy Usher, Jack Rockwell, George "Gabby" Hayes, Edward J. LeSaint, Bud Osborne, Alan Sears, Tom London, Jack Rutherford, Stanley Blystone, Dick Botiller, Bill Patton, Earl Dwire, Dick Rush, J. Frank Glendon, Frank Ellis. A cattle detective (McCoy), hired by the local ranchers to end a range feud, must prove himself innocent of murder while putting an end to the range war.

1006. Juvenile Court (9/7/38) B&W—60 mins. (Drama). *DIR:* D. Ross Lederman. *PRO:* Ralph Cohn. *SP:* Michael L. Simmons, Henry Taylor, Robert E. Kent. *CAST:* Paul Kelly, Rita Hayworth, Frankie Darro, Hally Chester, Don Latorre, David Gorcey, Dick Selzer, Allan Ramsey, Charles Hart, Howard Hickman, John Tyrrell, Joseph DeStefani, Dick Curtis, Kane Richmond, Lee Shumway, Edmund Cobb, Tom London, Harry Strang, George Chesebro, Edward Hearn, Lee Prather, Edward J. LeSaint, Gloria Blondell, Stanley Andrews, Steve Clark, Kernan Cripps, Ethan Laidlaw, Bud Osborne, Vernon Dent. A public defender (Kelly) organizes a Police Athletic League to give the juveniles an honest way to spend their time.

1007. Kansas City Kitty (9/1/44) B&W—72 mins. (Musical). *DIR:* Del Lord. *PRO:* Ted Richmond. *SP:* Manny Seff. *CAST:* Joan Davis, Bob Crosby, Jane Frazee, Erik Rolf, Tim Ryan, Robert Emmett Keane, Matt Willis, Johnny Bond, Charles Wilson, Lee Gotch, Charles Williams, William Newell, Edward Earle, Vivian Mason, Doodles Weaver, Vic Potel, The Williams Brothers. A song plugger (Davis) is tricked into buying a music publishing house, and finds herself in a lawsuit with a composer (Willis) over the song "Kansas City Kitty."

1008. The Karate Kid (5/84) Metrocolor—126 mins. (Sports-Drama). *DIR:* John G. Avildsen. *PRO:* Jerry Weintraub. *SP:* Robert Mark

Kamen. *CAST:* Ralph Macchio, Noriyuki "Pat" Morita, Elisabeth Shue, Martin Kove, Randee Heller, William Zabka, Ron Thomas, Rob Garrison, Chad McQueen, Tony O'Dell, William Bassett, Israel Juarbe, Larry B. Scott.

A teenager (Macchio) seeks help from his apartment building's maintenance man (Morita), a karate master, who teaches him self-confidence and karate that he needs in order to win the Valley Karate Championship.

1009. The Karate Kid Part II (6/86) DeLuxe Color—113 mins. (Sports-Drama). *DIR:* John G. Avildsen. *PRO:* Jerry Weintraub. *SP:* Robert Mark Kamen. *CAST:* Ralph Macchio, Noriyuki "Pat" Morita, Martin Kove, William Zabka, Chad McQueen, Tony O'Dell, Ron Thomas, Rob Garrison, Yuji Okumoto, Joey Miyashima, Danny Kamekona, Tamlyn Tomita, Nobu McCarthy.

After winning the Valley Karate Championship, a teenager (Macchio) and his karate master (Morita) journey to Japan where the karate master must settle a score with an old friend (Kamekona).

1010. Kazan (7/14/49) B&W—65 mins. (Adventure). *DIR:* Will Jason. *PRO:* Robert Cohn. *SP:* Arthur A. Ross. Based on *Kazan, the Wolf Dog* by James Oliver Curwood. *CAST:* Stephen Dunne, Lois Maxwell, Joe Sawyer, Roman Bohnen, Ray Teal, George Cleveland, John Dehner, Loren Gage, "Zoro," the dog.

In the Canadian northwoods, a wild white dog, trained as a killer by his master (Sawyer), is rescued by a wildlife expert (Dunne) and turned into a pet.

Keep Him Alive *see* **The Great Plane Robbery**

1011. Keeper of the Bees (7/18/47) B&W—68 mins. (Drama). *DIR:* John Sturges. *PRO:* John Haggott. *SP:*
Lawrence E. Watkin, Malcolm Stuart Boylan. Adapted by Ralph Rose, Jr. Based on the book by Gene Stratton Porter. *CAST:* Michael Duane, Jo Ann Marlowe, J. Farrell MacDonald, Will Wright, Frances Robinson, George Meader, Gloria Henry, Harry Davenport, Jane Darwell.

An artist (Duane), who has lost the will to live, has his faith restored in humanity through the influence of an ailing beekeeper (Davenport) and an orphan (Marlowe). *NOTES:* Originally made by Monogram Pictures in 1935.

1012. The Key (7/58) B&W/Scope—125 mins. (Drama). *DIR:* Sir Carol Reed. *PRO:* Aubrey Baring. *SP:* Carl Foreman. Based on *Stella* by Jan de Hartog. An Open Road Films Production. *CAST:* William Holden, Sophia Loren, Trevor Howard, Oscar Homolka, Kieron Moore, Bernard Lee, Beatrix Lehmann, Noel Purcell, Bryan Forbes, Russell Waters, Irene Handl, John Crawford, Jameson Clark, Sidney Vivian, Rupert Davies, James Hayter.

During World War II, a tugboat captain (Howard), who feels that his next mission may be his last, passes the key to his flat and the woman (Loren) that goes with it to the next captain (Holden).

1013. Key Witness (10/9/47) B&W—67 mins. (Crime-Drama). *DIR:* D. Ross Lederman. *PRO:* Rudolph C. Flothow. *SP:* Raymond L. Schrock, Edward Bock. Story by J. Donald Wilson. *CAST:* John Beal, Trudy Marshall, Jimmy Lloyd, Helen Mowery, Wilton Graff, Barbara Reed, Charles Trowbridge, Harry Hayden, William Newell, Selmer Jackson, Robert Williams, Victoria Horne.

An inventor (Beal), accused of the murder of a young girl, runs away, becomes a hobo and almost gets lynched when he accidentally kills a man.

1014. The Kid from Amarillo (10/30/51) B&W — 56 mins. (Western). DIR: Ray Nazarro. PRO: Colbert Clark. SP: Barry Shipman. CAST: Charles Starrett, Fred F. Sears, Smiley Burnette, Harry Lauter, Don Megowan, George Chesebro, George J. Lewis, Henry Kulky, Scott Lee, Guy Teague, Charles Evans, Jerry Scroggins, The Cass County Boys.

The Durango Kid (Starrett), with the help of the Mexican authorities, breaks up a gang of silver smugglers operating across the Mexican border. [British title: *Silver Chains*].

1015. The Kid from Broken Gun (8/15/52) B&W — 56 mins. (Western). DIR: Fred F. Sears. PRO: Colbert Clark. SP: Ed Earl Repp, Barry Shipman. CAST: Charles Starrett, Angela Stevens, Smiley Burnette, Jock Mahoney, Tristram Coffin, Myron Healey, Pat O'Malley, Edgar Dearing, Chris Alcaide, Mauritz Hugo, Helen Mowery, John Cason, Eddie Parker, Edward Hearn, Charles Horvath.

The Durango Kid (Starrett) goes all out to prove his friend (Mahoney) innocent of murder and robbery. NOTES: The last of Starrett's westerns for Columbia in which he played "The Durango Kid" for seven years.

1016. The Kid Sister (7/5/27) B&W — 58 mins. (Drama). DIR: Ralph Graves. PRO: Harry Cohn. SP: Harry O. Hoyt. Based on *The Lost House* by Dorothy Howell. CAST: Marguerite De La Motte, Ann Christy, Malcolm McGregor, Brooks Benedict, Tom Dugan, Sally Long, Barrett Greenwood.

A young girl (Christy) leaves her small town to be with her sister (De La Motte) in the big city. Once there she gets into trouble and has to have her sister's boyfriend (McGregor) bail her out. Wiser, she returns home.

1017. Kill Her Gently (10/58) B&W — 75 mins. (Suspense). DIR:

Charles Saunders. PRO: Guido Coen. SP: Paul Erickson. A Fortress Production. CAST: Marc Lawrence, George Mikell, Griffith Jones, John Gaylord, Roger Avon, Maureen Connell, Shay Gorman, Marianne Brauns, Frank Hawkins, Patrick Conner, David Lawton, Elaine Wells.

A mental patient (Jones), who believes his wife (Connell) is responsible for his internment, enlists the aid of two convicts (Lawrence, Mikell) in a plot to kill his wife.

1018. Kill the Umpire (4/27/50) B&W — 77 mins. (Sports-Comedy). DIR: Lloyd Bacon. PRO: John Beck. SP: Frank Tashlin. CAST: William Bendix, Una Merkel, Ray Collins, Gloria Henry, Richard Taylor (Jeff Richards), Connie Marshall, William Frawley, Tom D'Andrea, Luther Crockett, Jeff York, Glenn Thompson, Bob Wilke, Jim Bannon, Alan Hale, Jr.

A baseball lover (Bendix), who can't hold a job during baseball season, goes to umpire training school, joins the Texas league, and becomes the world's most hated man because of his calls.

1019. Killer Ape (12/4/53) B&W — 68 mins. (Adventure). DIR: Spencer G. Bennet. PRO: Sam Katzman. SP: Carroll Young, Arthur Hoerl. Story by Carroll Young. Based on the *Jungle Jim* newspaper comic strip created by Alex Raymond. CAST: Johnny Weissmuller, Carol Thurston, Nestor Paiva, Ray "Crash" Corrigan, Paul Marion, Burt Wenland, Nick Stuart, Eddie Foster, Rory Mallison, Max Palmer.

Jungle Jim (Weissmuller) sets out to rescue a couple of natives (Thurston, Marion) from a giant caveman (Palmer) and stop a scientist (Paiva) from killing animals to produce a mind control drug.

1020. Killer at Large (10/27/36) B&W — 54 mins. (Crime-Suspense).

DIR: David Selman. *SP:* Harold Shumate. Based on *Poker Face* by Carl Clausen. *CAST:* Mary Brian, Russell Hardie, Betty Compson, George McKay, Thurston Hall, Henry Brandon, Harry Hayden, Boyd Irwin.

A store detective (Brian) sets out to trap a killer known as "Mr. Zero."

1021. The Killer That Stalked New York (12/1/50) B&W — 79 mins. (Drama). *DIR:* Earl McEvoy. *PRO:* Robert Cohn. *SP:* Harry J. Essex. Based on a magazine article by Milton Lehman. *CAST:* Evelyn Keyes, Charles Korvin, William Bishop, Dorothy Malone, Lola Albright, Barry Kelley, Carl Benton Reid, Ludwig Donath, Art Smith, Roy Roberts, Whit Bissell, Connie Gilchrist, Dan Riss, Harry Shannon, Beverly Washburn, Celia Lovsky, Richard Egan, Walter Burke, Arthur Space, Jim Backus, Peter Brocco, Tommy Ivo, Angela Clarke, Peter Virgo, Don Kohler.

A doctor (Bishop) works with Treasury agents to track down a couple (Keyes, Korvin) who have not only smuggled diamonds into the country, but are smallpox carriers. [British title: *Frightened City*].

1022. Killers of Kilimanjaro (4/60) Eastman Color/Scope — 91 mins. (Adventure). *DIR:* Richard Thorpe. *PRO:* John R. Sloan. *SP:* John Gilling, Earl Felton, Richard Maibaum, Cyril Hume. Based on *African Bush Adventures* by John A. Hunter, Dan P. Mannix. A Warwick Films Production. *CAST:* Robert Taylor, Anthony Newley, Anne Aubrey, Gregoire Aslan, Allan Cuthbertson, Martin Benson, Orlando Martins, Donald Pleasence, John Dimech, Martin Boddey, Earl Cameron, Harry Baird, Anthony Jacobs, Joyce Blair, Barbara Joyce, Christine Pockett.

A civil engineer (Taylor), surveying the Kenya bush for the first African railway, takes a young English girl (Aubrey) along as they search for her missing father and fiance.

1023. King of Dodge City (8/14/41) B&W — 59 mins. (Western). *DIR:* Lambert Hillyer. *PRO:* Leon Barsha. *SP:* Gerald Geraghty. *CAST:* Bill Elliott, Judith Linden, Tex Ritter, Dub Taylor, Pierce Lyden, Francis Walker, Jack Rockwell, Edmund Cobb, George Chesebro, Tristram Coffin, Steve Clark, Jack Ingram, Tex Cooper, Ned Glass, Ed Coxen, Lee Prather, Russ Powell, Rich Anderson, Kenneth Harlan, Guy Usher, Harrison Greene, Frosty Royce, Jay Lawrence.

Wild Bill Hickok (Elliott), with the help of a blacksmith (Taylor) and the sheriff (Ritter), breaks up an outlaw gang terrorizing the town of Abilene.

1024. The King of Marvin Gardens (10/72) Eastman Color — 103 mins. (Drama). *DIR/PRO:* Bob Rafelson. *SP:* Jacob Brackman. Story by Bob Rafelson, Jacob Brackman. A BBS Production. *CAST:* Jack Nicholson, Bruce Dern, Ellen Burstyn, Julia Anne Robinson, Scatman Crothers, Charles Lavine, Arnold Williams, John Ryan, Josh Mostel, Sally Boyar, William Pabst, Imogene Bliss.

A radio talk jockey (Nicholson) heads for Atlantic City to see his brother (Dern) and becomes embroiled in his financial schemes.

1025. King of the Wild Horses (11/10/33) B&W — 62 mins. (Western). *DIR:* Earl Haley. *SP:* Fred Myton. Story by Earl Haley. *CAST:* "Rex," "Lady," "Marquis," William Janney, Dorothy Appleby, Wallace MacDonald, Harry Semels, Art Mix, Ford West.

A rare story in which the hero (Rex), the heroine (Lady), and the villain (Marquis) are horses. [British title: *King of the Wild*].

1026. King of the Wild Horses (3/29/47) B&W — 79 mins. (Adventure). *DIR:* George Archainbaud. *PRO:* Ted Richmond. *SP:* Brenda Weisberg. Story by Ted Thomas. *CAST:* Preston Foster, Gail Patrick, Bill Sheffield, Guinn "Big Boy" Williams, Robert "Buzz" Henry, Charles Kemper, Patti Brady, John Kellogg, Ruth Warren, Louis Faust.

After being rescued by a wild horse, a young boy (Sheffield) sets out to capture and tame him.

1027. King Rat (11/65) B&W— 134 mins. (War-Drama). *DIR/SP:* Bryan Forbes. *PRO:* James Woolf. Based on the book by James Clavell. A Coleytown Production. *CAST:* George Segal, Tom Courtenay, James Fox, Patrick O'Neal, Denholm Elliott, James Donald, Todd Armstrong, John Mills, Alan Webb, Gerald Sim, Leonard Rossiter, John Standing, John Ronane, Joseph Turkel, Hamilton Dyce, Geoffrey Bayldon, Richard Dawson, William Fawcett, Roy Deane, John Barclay, John Warburton, David Frankham.

During World War II, an American corporal (Segal) wheels and deals his way to a more comfortable life in a Japanese prison camp.

1028. The King Steps Out (5/12/36) B&W—85 mins. (Musical). *DIR:* Josef von Sternberg. *PRO:* William Perlberg. Based on the operetta *Cissy* by Hubert and Ernst Marischka, and the play by Gustav Holm, Ernest Decsey. *CAST:* Grace Moore, Franchot Tone, Walter Connolly, Raymond Walburn, Victor Jory, Nana Bryant, Elisabeth Risdon, Frieda Inescort, Thurston Hall, Herman Bing, George Hassell, Johnny Arthur.

Emperor Franz Josef (Tone) falls in love with the sister (Moore) of the princess (Inescort) to whom he is betrothed.

1029. Kiss and Tell (7/12/45) B&W—90 mins. (Comedy-Romance). *DIR:* Richard Wallace. *PRO:* Sol C.

Siegel. *SP:* F. Hugh Herbert. Based on the play by F. Hugh Herbert. An Abbott Production. *CAST:* Shirley Temple, Jerome Courtland, Walter Abel, Katharine Alexander, Robert Benchley, Porter Hall, Edna Holland, Virginia Welles, Tom Tully, Darryl Hickman, Scott McKay, Scott Elliott, Kathryn Card, Mary Phillips, Darren McGavin, Jessie Arnold, Frank Darien, Isabel Withers.

Corliss Archer (Temple) tries to protect her brother's (Elliott) secret marriage when it is learned her sister-in-law (Welles) is pregnant. NOTES: A sequel was released in 1949 by United Artists, *A Kiss for Corliss*, which was Shirley Temple's last screen appearance.

1030. Kiss the Girls and Make Them Die (12/66) Technicolor—105 mins. (Spy-Drama). *DIR:* Henry Levin, Dino Mauri. *PRO:* Dino De Laurentiis. *SP:* Jack Pulman, Dino Mauri. Story by Dino Mauri. *CAST:* Michael Conners, Dorothy Provine, Terry-Thomas, Raf Vallone, Oliver McGreevy, Sandro Dori, Beverly Adams, Margaret Lee, Marilu Tolo, Seyna Seyn, Nicoletta Machiavelli.

Two undercover agents (Conners, Provine) set out to stop a power mad industrialist (Vallone) from taking over the world by sterilizing mankind through ultrasonic waves. [Original Italian titles: *Se Tutte le Donne del Mondo*; *Operazione Paradiso*].

1031. Klondike Kate (12/16/43) B&W—64 mins. (Western). *DIR:* William Castle. *PRO:* Irving Briskin. *SP:* M. Coates Webster. Story by M. Coates Webster, Houston Branch. *CAST:* Tom Neal, Ann Savage, Glenda Farrell, Constance Worth, Sheldon Leonard, Lester Allen, George Cleveland, Dan Seymour, George McKay.

Kate Rockwell Mason (Savage), queen of the Alaskan gold rush of the

1890's, helps a prospector (Neal), accused of murder, prove his innocence.

1032. Knock on Any Door (2/21/49) B&W — 100 mins. (Crime-Drama). *DIR:* Nicholas Ray. *PRO:* Robert Lord. *SP:* Daniel Taradash, John Monks, Jr. Based on the book by Willard Motley. A Santana Pictures Production. *CAST:* Humphrey Bogart, John Derek, George Macready, Allene Roberts, Susan Perry, Mickey Knox, Barry Kelley, Dooley Wilson, Cara Williams, Jimmy Conlin, Sumner Williams, Dewey Martin, Houseley Stevenson, Vince Barnett, Pierre Watkin, Charles Hamilton, Myron Healey, Blackie Whiteford, Franklyn Farnum, Jeff York, Chester Conklin, George Chandler, Sid Tomack, Frank Hagney, Peter Virgo, Helen Mowery, Jody Gilbert.

A defense attorney (Bogart) tries to save a slum youth (Derek), who has been charged with killing a policeman, from the electric chair.

1033. Konga, the Wild Stallion (4/10/40) B&W — 62 mins. (Western). *DIR:* Sam Nelson. *PRO:* Wallace MacDonald. *SP:* Harold Shumate. *CAST:* Fred Stone, Rochelle Hudson, Richard Fiske, Eddy Waller, Robert Warwick, Don Beddoe, Carl Stockdale, George Cleveland, Burr Caruth.

A feud develops between a rancher (Stone) and farmer (Warwick) when horses trample the farmer's wheat fields and the rancher's favorite stallion is shot. [British title: *Konga*].

1034. Kramer Vs. Kramer (12/79) Technicolor — 105 mins. (Drama). *DIR/SP:* Robert Benton. *PRO:* Stanley R. Jaffe. Based on the book by Avery Corman. *CAST:* Dustin Hoffman, Meryl Streep, Jane Alexander, Justin Henry, Howard Duff, George Coe, Jo-Beth Williams, Bill Moor, Howard Chamberlain, Jess Osuna, Jack Ramage, Ellen Parker.

When his wife (Streep) walks out on him, a father (Hoffman) must provide for himself and his young son (Henry).

1035. Krull (7/83) Metrocolor/Panavision — 117 mins. (Fantasy). *DIR:* Peter Yates. *PRO:* Ron Silverman. *SP:* Stanford Sherman. *CAST:* Ken Marshall, Lysette Anthony, Freddie Jones, Francesca Annis, Alan Armstrong, David Battley, Bernard Bresslaw, Liam Neeson, John Welsh, Graham McGrath, Tony Church, Bernard Archard, Belinda Mayne.

A prince (Marshall) and his followers encounter mythical creatures when they set out to rescue his fiancee (Anthony) from the "Black Beast."

1036. The L-Shaped Room (6/63) B&W — 124 mins. (Drama). *DIR/SP:* Bryan Forbes. *PRO:* James Woolf, Richard Attenborough. Based on the book by Lynne Reid Banks. A Romulus-Davis-Royal Film Ltd. Production. *CAST:* Leslie Caron, Anthony Booth, Avis Bunnage, Patricia Phoenix, Verity Edmett, Tom Bell, Cicely Courtneidge, Harry Locke, Emlyn Williams, Jenny White, Brock Peters, Gerry Duggan, Bernard Lee, Nanette Newman, Arthur White.

A pregnant girl (Caron) journeys to London from Paris, takes a room in a boarding house full of odd characters, and falls in love with a writer (Bell). *NOTES:* Released to the European market at a running time of 142 mins.

1037. La Bamba (7/87) Deluxe Color — 108 mins. (Musical-Biography). *DIR/SP:* Luis Valdez. *PRO:* Taylor Hackford, Bill Borden. A New Visions Production. *CAST:* Lou Diamond Phillips, Esai Morales, Rosanna De Soto, Elizabeth Pena, Danielle von Zerneck, Joe Pantoliano, Rick Dees, Marshall Crenshaw, Howard Huntsberry, Brian Setzer, Daniel Valdez.

The musical biography of Ritchie Valens (Phillips), whose life was cut short by his death in the plane crash that also took the lives of Buddy Holly and the Big Bopper. The story follows Richie's career as a writer-performer, the rivalry that existed between him and his half-brother Bob (Morales), and his short rise to stardom.

1038. La Boum (The Party) (5/83) Eastman Color — 108 mins. (Drama). DIR: Claude Pinoteau. PRO: Alain Poire. SP: Daniele Thompson, Claude Pinoteau. A Triumph Films Production. CAST: Claude Brasseur, Brigitte Fossey, Sophie Marceau, Denise Grey, Dominique Lavanant, Bernard Giraudeau.

A young French girl (Marceau) tries to make it through adolescence despite the shaky relationship of her parents (Brasseur, Fossey). NOTES: Limited theatrical release; in French with English subtitles. A sequel La Boum 2 was relesed the following year in France.

1039. La Charrette Fantôme (The Phantom Wagon) (5/27/40) B&W — 90 mins. (Drama). DIR/SP: Julien Duvivier. Based on La Charretier de la Mort by Selma Lagerlof. A Transcontinental Films of Paris Production. CAST: Pierre Fresnay, Marie Bell, Louis Jouvet, Micheline Francey, Jean Mercanton, Ariane Borg.

A drunkard (Fresnay) has an accident on New Year's Eve, relives his life before it was ruined by drink, and is reformed when he sees the wagon of death. NOTES: In French with English subtitles.

1040. La Familia Dressel (The Family Dressel) (5/3/36) B&W — ??? mins. (Drama). DIR: Fernando de Fuentes. CAST: Rosita Arriaga, Jorge Velez, Julian Soler, Consuelo Frank, Ramon Armengod.

A mother (Arriaga) opposes her son's (Velez) choice of a wife (Frank) and tries to break up his marriage.

NOTES: Released to Spanish language theatres.

1041. La Noche del Pecado (The Night of Sin) (12/24/33) B&W — ??? mins. (Drama). DIR: Miguel Contreras Torres. CAST: Medea de Novara, Ramon Pereda, Virginia Zuri, Ernesto Vilches, Julio Villarreal, Enrique Herrera.

A wife (de Novara) gets into a desperate situation when she decides to get even with her husband (Perada), whom she thinks is deceiving her, and has to be rescued from her predicament by a family friend (Vilches). NOTES: Released to Spanish language theatres.

1042. La Nuit de Varennes (The Night at Varennes) (2/83) Eastman Color — 135 mins. (Comedy-Historical Drama). DIR: Ettore Scola. PRO: Renzo Rossellini. SP: Sergio Amidei, Ettore Scola. A Gaumont-Columbia-Triumph Films Production. CAST: Marcello Mastroianni, Jean-Louis Barrault, Hanna Schygulla, Harvey Keitel, Jean-Claude Brialy, Daniel Gelin, Jean-Louis Trintignanat, Michel Piccoli, Eleanore Hirt, Andrea Ferreol, Michel Vitold, Laura Betti, Pierre Malet.

King Louis XVI (Piccoli) and the Queen, Marie Antoinette (Hirt), flee Paris before the Revolution to the safety of Varennes followed by Casanova (Mastroianni) and Thomas Paine (Keitel) who bicker about life and politics as they travel. NOTES: Limited theatrical release.

1043. La Petite Bande (The Little Bunch) (11/84) Eastman Color — 91 mins. (Comedy). DIR: Michel Deville. PRO: Bob Kellett. SP: Gilles Perrault, Michel Deville. Story by Gilles Perrault. A Triumph Films Production. CAST: Yveline Ailhaud, Michel Amphoux, Roland Amstutz, Pierre Ascaride, Nathalie Becue, Jean-Pierre Bagot, Didier Benureau, Liliane Berrand, Jean Bois, Jacques Blot, Jacques Cancelier, Georges Carmier, Marie-Pierre Casey, Pierre Chevalier, Francois Clavier, Josine Comellas, Dominique Constantin, Roger Cornillac, Monique Couturier, Roger Desmare.

A group of trouble-making school children drive their parents and everyone crazy with their antics. NOTES: Limited theatrical release; in French with English subtitles.

1044. La Sombra de Pancho Villa (The Shadow of Pancho Villa) (1/7/34) B&W—??? mins. (Drama-Historical). DIR: Miguel Contreras Torres. CAST: Luis G. Barreiro, Carmen Guerrero, Manuel Telez.

Two brothers (Barreiro, Telez), one a revolutionist, the other a soldier, meet on the battlefield in the fight to free Mexico from the despotic rule of Porfirio Diaz. NOTES: Released to Spanish language theaters.

1045. La Traviata (2/68) Eastman Color—110 mins. (Opera). DIR/SP: Mario Lafranchi. PRO: Afro Taccari. Based on the libretto by Francisco Maria Piave. Based on The Lady of the Camellias by Alexandre Dumas. A Royal Films International Production. CAST: Anna Moffo, Gino Bechi, Franco Bonisolli, Mafalda Micheluzzi, Afro Poli, Glauco Scarlini, Arturo La Porta, Athos Cesarini, Maurizio Piacenti, Gianna Lollini, Chorus and Orchestra of the Rome Opera.

A filmed version of Verdi's opera, filmed at the Rome Opera house.

1046. La Ultima Cita (The Last Date) (1/21/36) B&W—??? mins. (Drama-Comedy). DIR: Bernard B. Ray. CAST: Jose Crespo, Luana Alcaniz, Andrea de Palma, Rafael Storm, Paul Ellis.

A violinist (Crespo) loses his true love (Alcaniz) when he becomes infatuated with a rich socialite (de Palma). NOTES: Released to Spanish language theaters.

1047. La Verbena Tragica (The Tragic Festival) (3/12/39) B&W—??? mins. (Drama). DIR: Charles Lamont. CAST: Fernando Soler, Luana Alcaniz, Juan Torena, Pilar Arcos.

A prize-fighter (Soler) returns from prison and learns that his wife (Alcaniz) is having an affair with his best friend (Torena). NOTES: Released to Spanish language theaters.

1048. La Vie Continue (Life Goes On) (5/82) Eastman Color—93 mins. (Drama). DIR: Moshe Mizrahi. PRO: Lise Fayolle, Giorgio Silvagni. SP: Moshe Mizrahi, Rachael Fabien. A Triumph Films Production. CAST: Annie Girardot, Jean-Pierre Cassel, Pierre Dux, Michel Aumont, Giulia Salvatori, Paulette Dubost, Emmanuel Gayet, Rivera Andres.

A woman (Girardot) must learn to face life alone when her husband dies of a heart attack. NOTES: Limited theatrical release.

1049. La Vie de Château (Life at Home) (3/67) B&W—92 mins. (Comedy). DIR: Jean-Paul Rappeneau. PRO: Nicole Stephane. SP: Alain Cavalier, Claude Sautet, Jean-Paul Rappeneau, Daniel Boulanger. An Anicex-Cobela-Productions de la Gueville-Royal Films International Production. CAST: Catherine Deneuve, Philippe Noiret, Pierre Brasseur, Mary Marquet, Henri Garcin, Carlos Thompson, Marc Dudicort, Alexis Micha, Robert Moor, Donald O'Brien, Paul Le Person, Pierre Rousseau.

During the German occupation of France in World War II, a bored housewife (Deneuve) hides the local resistance leader (Garcin) in her chateau, while playing cat and mouse with the German commander (Dudicort) who occupies it as his headquarters.

Labyrinth see **A Reflection of Fear**

1050. Ladies in Retirement (9/9/41) B&W—92 mins. (Crime-Drama). DIR: Charles Vidor. PRO: Lester Cowan, Gilbert Miller. SP: Garrett Elsden Fort, Reginald Denham. Based on the play by Reginald Denham, Edward Percy and based on *French Crime and Criminals* by H. B. Irving. CAST: Louis Hayward, Ida Lupino, Evelyn Keyes, Elsa Lanchester, Edith Barrett, Isobel Elsom, Emma Dunn, Queenie Leonard, Clyde Cook.

In an attempt to prevent her two sisters (Lanchester, Barrett) from being placed in a mental institution, a housekeeper (Lupino) murders her employer (Elsom). NOTES: Remade by Columbia in 1969 as *The Mad Room*.

1051. Ladies Must Play (8/24/30) B&W—70 mins. (Comedy-Drama). DIR/PRO: Raymond Cannon. SP: Jo Swerling, Dorothy Howell, Lucille Gleason. Story by Paul Hervey Fox. CAST: Dorothy Sebastian, Neil Hamilton, Natalie Moorhead, John Holland, Harry Stubbs, Shirley Palmer, Pauline Neff.

A businessman (Hamilton) plans to marry off his secretary (Sebastian) to a wealthy bachelor (Holland) for a commission, but instead, ends up marrying her himself.

1052. Ladies of Leisure (3/1/26) B&W—57 mins. (Drama). DIR: Thomas Buckingham. PRO: Harry Cohn. SP: Dorothy Howell. CAST: Elaine Hammerstein, T. Roy Barnes, Robert Ellis, Gertrude Short.

A confirmed bachelor (Barnes) marries a woman (Hammerstein) in order to protect her reputation.

1053. Ladies of Leisure (4/5/30) B&W—98 mins. (Comedy-Drama).

DIR: Frank Capra. PRO: Harry Cohn. SP: Jo Swerling. Based on the play *Ladies of the Evening* by Milton Herbert Grooper. A Frank Capra Production. CAST: Barbara Stanwyck, Lowell Sherman, Ralph Graves, Marie Prevost, Nance O'Neil, George Fawcett, Juliette Compton, Johnnie Walker, Charles Butterworth.

An artist (Graves) finds true love with a gold-digging model (Stanwyck), but loses her when his parents (O'Neil, Fawcett) force her to give him up. NOTES: Remade by Columbia in 1937 as *Women of Glamour*.

1054. Ladies of the Chorus (2/10/48) B&W—59 mins. (Musical-Romance). DIR: Phil Karlson. PRO: Harry Romm. SP: Harry Sauber, Joseph Carole. Story by Harry Sauber. CAST: Adele Jergens, Marilyn Monroe, Rand Brooks, Nana Bryant, Eddie Carr, Steven Geray, Bill Edwards, Marjorie Hoshelle, Frank Scannell, Dave Barry, Alan Barry, Myron Healey, Gladys Blake, Almira Sessions, Claire Whitney, Robert Clarke, Emmett Vogan.

A burlesque queen (Jergens) tries to dissuade her showgirl daughter (Monroe) from falling in love with a wealthy socialite (Brooks). NOTES: Marilyn Monroe's second film appearance.

1055. The Lady and the Bandit (8/14/51) B&W—79 mins. (Adventure-Drama). DIR: Ralph Murphy. PRO: Harry Joe Brown. SP: Robert Libott, Frank Burt. Story by Jack DeWitt, Duncan Renaldo. Based on the poem *The Highwayman* by Alfred Noyes. CAST: Louis Hayward, Patricia Medina, Suzanne Dalbert, Tom Tully, John Williams, Malu Gatcia, Alan Mowbray, Lumsden Hare, Barbara Brown, Malcolm Keen, Stapleton Kent, Sheldon Jett, George Baxter, Ivan Triesault, Norman Leavitt, Frank Reicher.

A highwayman (Hayward) sacrifices his own life to protect his wife (Medina) and avenge his father. [British title: *Dick Turpin's Ride*].

1056. The Lady and the Mob (4/13/39) B&W—65 mins. (Crime-Comedy). DIR: Ben Stoloff. PRO: Fred Kohlmar. SP: Richard Maibaum, Gertrude Purcell. Story by George Bradshaw, Price Day. CAST: Lee Bowman, Ida Lupino, Henry Armetta, Fay Bainter, Warren Hymer, Harold Huber, Forbes Murray, Joe Sawyer, Tom Dugan, Jim Toney, Joe Caits, Tommy Mack, Brandon Tynen, George Meeker.

An old lady (Bainter), menaced by the mob, forms her own mob to get rid of the town's protection racket.

1057. Lady by Choice (10/2/34) B&W—74 mins. (Comedy). DIR: David Burton. PRO: Robert North. SP: Jo Swerling. Based on *Orchids and Onions* by Dwight Taylor. CAST: Carole Lombard, May Robson, Roger Pryor, Walter Connolly, Arthur Hohl, Raymond Walburn, James Burke, Mariska Aldrich, William Faversham, John Boyle, Henry Kolker, Lillian Harmer, Fred "Snowflake" Toones, Charles Coleman, Abe Dinovitch, Gino Corrado, Kit Guard, Charles King, Lee Shumway, Edward Hearn, Dennis O'Keefe.

A fan-dancer (Lombard) adopts an alcoholic old lady (Robson) as her "mother" for a Mother's Day publicity stunt. NOTES: A sequel to the 1933 Columbia film *Lady for a Day*.

1058. Lady for a Day (9/13/33) B&W—95 mins. (Comedy-Drama). DIR: Frank Capra. PRO: Harry Cohn. SP: Robert Riskin. Based on *Madame La Gimp* by Damon Runyon. CAST: Warren William, May Robson, Guy Kibbee, Glenda Farrell, Jean Parker, Ned Sparks, Walter Connolly, Barry Norton, Nat Pendleton, Hobart Bos-

worth, Wallis Clark, Robert Emmett O'Conner, Halliwell Hobbes, Samuel S. Hinds, Irving Bacon.

A gangster (William) and his friends help an old apple seller (Robson) pose as a wealthy New York lady for the arrival of her daughter (Parker) and fiancee (Norton) from Spain. NOTES: Remade by Frank Capra for United Artists in 1961 as *Pocketful of Miracles*.

1059. Lady from Nowhere (12/23/36) B&W—60 mins. (Crime-Drama). DIR: Gordon Wiles. PRO: Irving Briskin. SP: Fred Niblo, Jr., Arthur Strawn, Joseph Krumgold. Story by Ben G. Kohn. CAST: Charles Quigley, Mary Astor, Thurston Hall, Victor Kilian, Spencer Charters, Norman Willis, Gene Morgan, Rita La Roy, Claudia Coleman, Matty Fain, John Tyrrell.

A newspaperman (Quigley) protects a woman (Astor) from the mob and cops after she witnessed a murder.

1060. The Lady from Shanghai (10/9/48) B&W—87 mins. (Crime-Drama). DIR/PRO/SP: Orson Welles. Based on *The Lady from Shanghai* by Sherwood King. CAST: Rita Hayworth, Orson Welles, Everett Sloane, Ted de Corsia, Glenn Anders, Erskine Sanford, Gus Schilling, Carl Frank, Louis D. Merrill, Evelyn Ellis, Harry Shannon, Edythe Elliott, Harry Strang, Milton Kibbee, Philip Van Zandt, Edward Piel, Sr., Jessie Arnold.

A sailor (Welles) becomes involved in murder with a mysterious woman (Hayworth) and her crippled husband (Sloane).

1061. The Lady in Question (7/31/40) B&W—78 mins. (Drama). DIR: Charles Vidor. PRO: B. B. Kahane. SP: Lewis Meltzer. Based on the screenplay for *Hearts of Paris* by H. G. Lustig, Marcel Archard. CAST: Rita Hayworth, Glenn Ford, Brian Aherne, Irene Rich, George Coulouris, Lloyd

Corrigan, Evelyn Keyes, Edward Norris, Curt Bois, Frank Reicher, Sumner Getchell, Theodore Lorch, Eddie Laughton, Vernon Dent, Jack Rice, Harrison Greene, William Castle, Earl Gunn.

A Parisian shopkeeper (Aherne) on a jury helps to acquit a woman (Hayworth) of a murder charge, gets her a job in his store, and then begins to worry when his son (Ford) starts showing an interest in her. NOTES: This was the first film to pair Rita Hayworth and Glenn Ford.

1062. The Lady in the Car with Glasses and a Gun (12/70) Eastman Color/Panavision—105 mins. (Drama). DIR: Anatole Litvak. PRO: Anatole Litvak, Raymond Danon. SP: Richard Harris, Eleanor Perry. Based on the book by Sebastien Japrisot. A Lira-Columbia Production. CAST: Samantha Eggar, Oliver Reed, John McEnery, Stephane Audran, Billie Dixon, Bernard Fresson, Philippe Nicaud, Marcel Bozzuffi, Jacques Fabbri, Yves Pignot, Maria Meriko.

An English secretary (Eggar) leaves Paris for the Riviera, and along the way encounters bizarre occurrences that make her believe she is either mad or suffering from amnesia. [Original French title: *La Dame dans l'Auto avec des Lunettes et un Fusil*].

The Lady Is Waiting *see* **Full of Life**

1063. The Lady Is Willing (8/11/34) B&W—66 mins. (Comedy). DIR: Gilbert Miller. PRO: Joseph Friedman. SP: Guy Bolton. Based on the play by Louis Verneuil. CAST: Leslie Howard, Cedric Hardwicke, Binnie Barnes, Sir Nigel Playfair, Nigel Bruce, Claude Allister, W. Graham Browne, Kendall Lee, Arthur Howard, Virginia Field, John Trumball.

A private detective (Howard), hired to get the goods on a businessman (Hardwicke), kidnaps his wife (Barnes) and finds himself falling in love with her. NOTES: Columbia's first film produced at Columbia-British studios.

1064. The Lady Is Willing (2/17/42) B&W—92 mins. (Comedy). DIR/PRO: Mitchell Leisen. SP: James Edward Grant, Albert McCleery. Story by James Edward Grant. CAST: Marlene Dietrich, Fred MacMurray, Aline MacMahon, Stanley Ridges, Arline Judge, Roger Clark, Marietta Canty, David James, Ruth Ford, Sterling Holloway, Harvey Stephens, Harry Shannon, Elisabeth Risdon, Charles Lane, Murray Alper, Kitty Kelly, Chester Clute, Robert Emmett Keane, Eddie Acuff, Eugene Borden, Neil Hamilton, Charles Halton, Romaine Callender, Ernie Adams.

A Broadway musical star (Dietrich) adopts an abandoned baby and falls in love with the pediatrician (MacMurray) who cares for him.

1065. The Lady Objects (10/12/38) B&W—62 mins. (Musical-Drama). DIR: Erle C. Kenton. PRO: William Perlberg. SP: Gladys Lehman, Charles Kenyon. CAST: Lanny Ross, Gloria Stuart, Joan Marsh, Roy Benson, Pierre Watkin, Robert Paige, Arthur Loft, Stanley Andrews, Jan Buckingham, Bess Flowers, Ann Doran, Vessy O'Davoren.

A college football star (Ross) marries his college sweetheart (Stuart), but they drift apart as she becomes a successful criminal lawyer and he a nightclub singer. Later, she is called upon to defend him when he is accused of murder.

1066. Lady of Secrets (2/21/36) B&W—73 mins. (Drama). DIR: Marion Gering. PRO: B. P. Schulberg. SP: Joseph Anthony, Zoe Akins. Based on *Maid of Honor* by Katherine Brush. CAST: Ruth Chatterton, Otto Kruger, Lionel Atwell, Marian Marsh, Lloyd

Nolan, Robert Allen, Elisabeth Risdon, Nana Bryant, Esther Dale. A mother (Chatterton) exposes a dark family secret to her daughter (Marsh) to keep her from marrying the man she does not love.

1067. The Lady on the Tracks (12/68) Eastman Color/Scope—83 mins. (Musical-Comedy). *DIR:* Ladislav Rychman. *PRO:* Barrandov Films. *SP:* Vratislav Blazek. A Barrandov-Royal Films International Production. *CAST:* Jirina Bohdalova, Radoslav Brzobohaty, Frantisek Peterka, Libuse Geprtova, Stanislav Fiser.

When a woman (Bohdalova) sees her husband (Brzobohaty) with another woman, she takes all their money and becomes more fashionable to try and win her husband back. *NOTES:* Limited theatrical release. [Original Czech title: *Dama No Kolejich*].

1068. Lady Raffles (1/25/28) B&W—57 mins. (Comedy). *DIR:* Roy William Neill. *PRO:* Harry Cohn. *SP:* Dorothy Howell. Story by Jack Jungmeyer, Fred Stanley. *CAST:* Estelle Taylor, Roland Drew, Lilyan Tashman, Ernest Hilliard.

A Scotland Yard investigator (Taylor) pretends to be a notorious jewel thief, "Lady Raffles," in order to capture a couple of real jewel thieves (Tashman, Hilliard).

1069. L'Alibi (The Alibi) (4/14/39) B&W—82 mins. (Crime-Mystery). *DIR:* Pierre Chenal. *SP:* Marcel Achard, J. Companeez, R. Juttke. A British National Films Production. *CAST:* Erich von Stroheim, Louis Jouvet, Albert Prejean, Jany Holt, Margo Lico, Phillippe Richard.

A nightclub mind-reader (von Stroheim) believes he has set up the perfect alibi when he kills an old enemy. *NOTES:* In French with English subtitles.

1070. Lamp in the Desert (1/15/23) B&W—58 mins. (Drama). *DIR:* F. Martin Thornton. *SP:* Leslie Howard Gordon. Based on the book by Ethel M. Dell. A British-Stoll Production. *CAST:* Gladys Jennings, Lewis Willoughby, George K. Arthur, J. R. Tozer, Teddy Arundell, Lewis Gilbert, Gladys Mason, Tony Fraser.

In India, a Captain (Willoughby) forces a bigamist (Arthur) to pretend he is dead so that he can marry his wife (Jennings).

1071. Land Raiders (12/69) Technicolor—101 mins. (Western). *DIR:* Nathan Juran. *PRO:* Charles H. Schneer. *SP:* Ken Pettus. Story by Ken Pettus, Jesse L. Lasky, Jr., Pat Silver. *CAST:* Telly Savalas, George Maharis, Arlene Dahl, Janet Landgard, Guy Rolfe, Jocelyn Lane, George Coulouris, Phil Brown, Marcella St. Amant, Paul Picerni, Robert Carricart, Fernando Rey, Gustavo Rojo, John Clark, Susan Harvey, Charles Stalnaker.

A rancher (Savalas), intent on driving the Indians off their land so he can claim it, renews an old feud with his brothers (Maharis) when he exposes his plans.

1072. Landrush (10/18/46) B&W—53 mins. (Western). *DIR:* Vernon Keays. *PRO:* Colbert Clark. *SP:* Michael L. Simmons. *CAST:* Charles Starrett, Doris Houck, Smiley Burnette, Emmett Lynn, Bud Osborne, Bud Geary, Bob Kortman, George Chesebro, Stephen Barclay, Victor French, George Russell, George Hoey, Ethan Laidlaw, John Tyrrell, Russell Meeker, Roy Butler, Curt Barrett, John Hawks, Sam Garrett, Ozie Waters and His Colorado Rangers.

The Durango Kid (Starrett) stops the outlaw domination of a section of the western frontier which is made open to homesteaders in a planned landrush. [British title: *The Claw Strikes*].

1073. Laramie (5/19/49) B&W—55 mins. (Western). *DIR:* Ray Nazarro. *PRO:* Colbert Clark. *SP:* Barry Shipman. *CAST:* Charles Starrett, Smiley Burnette, Fred F. Sears, Tommy Ivo, Nolan Leary, Bob Wilke, Jay Silverheels, John (Bob) Cason, Myron Healey, George Lloyd, Ethan Laidlaw, Elton Britt, Rodd Redwing, Jim Diehl, Shooting Star.

The Durango Kid (Starrett) prevents an Indian war by bringing to justice an army scout (Wilke) who kills one of the Indian chiefs while selling guns to the Indians.

1074. Laramie Mountains (4/20/52) B&W—54 mins. (Western). *DIR:* Ray Nazarro. *PRO:* Colbert Clark. *SP:* Barry Shipman. *CAST:* Charles Starrett, Fred F. Sears, Smiley Burnette, Jock Mahoney, Marshall Reed, Zon Murray, Bob Wilke, John War Eagle, Rory Mallison, Boyd Morgan, Chris Alcaide.

The Durango Kid (Starrett) sets out to prove that a series of wagon train raids are the work of white men and not Indians. [British title: *Mountain Desperadoes*].

1075. The Last Angry Man (11/59) B&W—100 mins. (Drama). *DIR:* Daniel Mann. *PRO:* Fred Kohlmar. *SP:* Gerald Green, Richard Murphy. Based on the book by Gerald Green. *CAST:* Paul Muni, David Wayne, Betsy Palmer, Luther Adler, Joby Baker, Joanna Moore, Nancy R. Pollock, Billy Dee Williams, Claudia McNeil, Dan Tobin, Robert F. Simon, Godfrey Cambridge, Helen Champan, Cicely Tyson, David Winters.

An old doctor (Muni), working in a Brooklyn slum for the past 45 years, becomes the subject of a TV documentary. *NOTES:* The film debut of Billy Dee Williams; the last film of Paul Muni.

1076. The Last Blitzkreig (1/59) B&W—85 mins. (War). *DIR:* Arthur Dreifuss. *PRO:* Sam Katzman. *SP:* Lou Morheim. *CAST:* Van Johnson, Kerwin Mathews, Dick York, Larry Storch, Lise Bourdin, Hans Bentz van der Berg, Leon Askin, Robert Boon, Howard B. Jaffe, Ton Van Duinhoven, Charles Rosenblum, Gijsbert Tersteeg, Steve Van Brandenberg, Herb Grika, Montgomery Ford, Chris Baay, Fred Oster, Karl Kent, Jan Verkoren.

During the Battle of the Bulge, a German (Johnson) and his men infiltrate American troops in the hopes of sabotaging the war effort.

1077. Last Days of Boot Hill (11/11/47) B&W—55 mins. (Western). *DIR:* Ray Nazarro. *PRO:* Colbert Clark. *SP:* Norman S. Hall. *CAST:* Charles Starrett, Virginia Hunter, Smiley Burnette, Paul Campbell, Mary Newton, Bill Free, Bob Wilke, Al Bridge, J. Courtland Lytton, Syd Saylor, The Cass County Boys.

The Durango Kid (Starrett) sets out to find a stolen gold shipment and in the process must keep the daughter (Hunter) of the outlaw who stole the gold from being killed since she might know the location of the stolen gold.

1078. The Last Detail (12/73) Metrocolor—103 mins. (Drama). *DIR:* Hal Ashby. *PRO:* Gerald Ayres. *SP:* Robert Towne. Based on the book by Darryl Ponicsan. An Acrobat Film Production. *CAST:* Jack Nicholson, Otis Young, Randy Quaid, Clifton James, Carol Kane, Michael Moriarty, Luana Anders, Nancy Allen, Gilda Radner, Kathleen Miller, Gerry Salsberg, Don McGovern, Michael Chapman.

Two sailors (Nicholson, Young), given the duty of escorting a young seaman (Quaid), convicted of thievery, from their Virginia base to a federal prison decide to take him on a last fling before imprisonment.

1079. **The Last Emperor** (11/87)
Technicolor/Technovision – 160
mins. (Biography). *DIR:* Bernardo Bertolucci. *PRO:* Jeremy Thomas. *SP:*
Mark Peploe, Bernardo Bertolucci,
Enzo Ungari. Based on *From Emperor
to Citizen* by Henry Pu Yi. A Hemdale
Film Corporation Production. *CAST:*
John Lone, Joan Chen, Peter O'Toole,
Dennis Dun, Maggie Han, Ric Young.
   In 1908, Pu Yi (Lone), at the age of
three, is named emperor of China,
only three years before a republic is
declared. He grows up without power
within the confines of the Forbidden
City, only to be ousted in 1924. The invading Japanese make him a puppet
emperor and when the Chinese regain
control he is sent to prison for ten
years. Finally, in 1960, he returns to
Beijing as a gardener, free at last, to
work until his death in 1967.

1080. **The Last Frontier** (12/55)
Technicolor/Scope – 97 mins. (West-
ern). *DIR:* Anthony Mann. *PRO:* Wil-
liam Fadiman. *SP:* Russell S. Hughes,
Philip Yordan. Based on *The Gilded
Rooster* by Richard Emery Roberts.
CAST: Victor Mature, Anne Bancroft,
Robert Preston, Guy Madison, James
Whitmore, Peter Whitney, Russell
Collins, Mickey Kuhn, Pat Hogan,
Manuel Donde, Guy Williams, Wil-
liam Calles.
   Three fur trappers (Mature, Whit-
more, Hogan) arrive at a cavalry out-
post, become scouts, and save the fort
from an Indian attack caused by the
fort commander (Preston).

1081. **The Last Horseman** (6/
22/44) B&W – 54 mins. (Western).
DIR: William Berke. *PRO:* Leon Barsha. *SP:* Ed Earl Repp. *CAST:* Russell
Hayden, Ann Savage, Dub Taylor,
John Maxwell, Frank LaRue, Ted
Mapes, Curley Dresden, Forrest Taylor, Nick Thompson, Blackie Whiteford, Bob Wills and His Texas Playboys.

A ranch foreman (Hayden) and his
pals (Taylor, Wills) disguise themselves
as women to nab the crooks who stole
their money.

1082. **The Last Hurrah** (11/58)
B&W – 121 mins. (Drama). *DIR/PRO:*
John Ford. *SP:* Frank Nugent. Based
on the book by Edwin O'Conner.
CAST: Spencer Tracy, Jeffrey Hunter,
Dianne Foster, Pat O'Brien, Basil
Rathbone, Donald Crisp, James Glea-
son, Edward Brophy, John Carradine,
Willis Bouchey, Basil Ruysdael, Ri-
cardo Cortez, Wallace Ford, Frank
McHugh, Anna Lee, Jane Darwell,
Frank Albertson, Charles FitzSimons,
Carleton Young, Bob Sweeney, Ed-
mund Lowe, William Leslie, Ken Cur-
tis, O. Z. Whitehead, Ruth Warren,
James Flavin, Dan Borzage, Frank
Sully, William Forrest, Richard Dea-
con, Bill Henry, Harry Lauter, Rand
Brooks, Edmund Cobb, Charles Trow-
bridge, Harry Tyler, Arthur Walsh.
   A political boss (Tracy) fights his last
campaign for mayor amidst his loyal
supporters, ruthless opponents, and
domestic turmoil with his son (Walsh).
NOTES: Loosely based on the life of
Boston mayor James Curley.

1083. **The Last Man** (9/17/32)
B&W-Color – 65 mins. (Mystery).
DIR: Howard Higgin. *SP:* Keene
Thompson. Story by Francis Edwards
Faragoh, Sam Nelson. *CAST:* Charles
Bickford, Constance Cummings, Alec
B. Francis, Alan Roscoe, Robert Ellis,
Jimmy Wang, John Eberts, Bill Wil-
liams, Al Smith, Hal Price, Kit Guard,
Jack Carlisle, Edward J. LeSaint,
George Magrill, Jack Richardson,
William Sundholm, Robert St. Angelo.
   A detective (Bickford) investigates
the mystery of a derelict ship, floating
off the coast of Port Said, with only
two people left alive.

1084. **The Last Man to Hang**
(12/56) B&W – 75 mins. (Drama).

DIR: Terence Fisher. PRO: John W. Gossage. SP: Gerald Bullett, Ivor Montagu, Max Trell, Maurice Elvey. Based on *The Jury* by Gerald Bullett. An ACT Films Production. CAST: Tom Conway, Elizabeth Sellars, Eunice Gayson, Freda Jackson, Hugh Latimer, Ronald Simpson, Victor Maddern, Anthony Newley, Margaretta Scott, Leslie Weston, Harold Goodwin, Anna Turner, Joan Hickson, Joan Newell.

A man (Conway) is placed on trial for the death of his wife (Sellars), and the jury must decide whether it was premeditated or accidental.

1085. Last of the Buccaneers (10/18/50) Technicolor — 78 mins. (Adventure). DIR: Lew Landers. PRO: Sam Katzman. SP: Robert E. Kent. CAST: Paul Henreid, Jack Oakie, Karin Booth, Mary Anderson, John Dehner, Edgar Barrier, Harry Cording, Eugene Borden, Pierre Watkin, Sumner Getchell, Paul Marion, Rusty Wescoatt, Jean Del Val.

After the Battle of New Orleans, Jean LaFitte (Henreid) sets up shop on a small island off the coast of Louisiana and continues his plunder of foreign ships. Later, he and his bride (Booth) escape to safety when one of his captains attacks an American ship.

1086. Last of the Comanches (2/1/53) Technicolor — 85 mins. (Western). DIR: Andre De Toth. PRO: Buddy Adler. SP: Kenneth Gamet. CAST: Broderick Crawford, Barbara Hale, Lloyd Bridges, George Mathews, Mickey Shaughnessy, Chubby Johnson, Martin Milner, Carleton Young, Johnny Stewart, Hugh Sanders, Ric Roman, Milton Parsons, Jack Woody, John War Eagle, William Andrews, Bud Osborne, George Chesebro, Rodd Redwing, Jay Silverheels.

An Army sergeant (Crawford) leads a group of survivors across the desert, and when an Indian attack occurs, they hole up in an abandoned mission and wait until help comes. NOTES: A western remake of the 1943 Columbia film *Sahara*. [British title: *The Sabre and the Arrow*].

1087. Last of the Lone Wolf (10/19/30) B&W — 70 mins. (Adventure). DIR: Richard Boleslawski. PRO: Harry Cohn. SP: John Thomas Neville, James Whitaker. Based on the book and characters created by Louis Joseph Vance. CAST: Bert Lytell, Patsy Ruth Miller, Lucien Prival, Otto Matiesen, Alfred Hickman, Maryland Morne, Haley Sullivan, Pietro Sosso, Henry Daniell, James Liddy.

The Lone Wolf (Lytell), while visiting a foreign country, helps a queen (Morne) recover a ring given to her by the king (Hickman). NOTES: The first all-talking Lone Wolf film; Bert Lytell's final appearance as the "Lone Wolf."

1088. Last of the Pony Riders (11/30/53) Sepiatone — 59 mins. (Western). DIR: George Archainbaud. PRO: Armand Schaefer. SP: Ruth Woodman. A Gene Autry Production. CAST: Gene Autry, Kathleen Case, Smiley Burnette, Dick Jones, Howard Wright, Arthur Space, Gregg Barton, Robert "Buzz" Henry, Harry Mackin, Harry Hines, John Downey.

Gene fights a local banker (Wright) who is trying to stop him from setting up a stage line to continue his mail franchise. NOTES: Gene Autry's last Columbia feature.

1089. Last of the Redmen (8/1/47) VitaColor — 77 mins. (Western). DIR: George Sherman. PRO: Sam Katzman. SP: Herbert Dalmas, George H. Plympton. Based on *The Last of the Mohicans* by James Fenimore Cooper. CAST: Jon Hall, Evelyn Ankers, Michael O'Shea, Jacqueline Wells (Julie Bishop), Buster Crabbe, Rick Vallin, Robert "Buzz"

Henry, Guy Hedlund, Frederick Worlock, Emmett Vogan, Chief Many Treaties.

A British major (Hall), with the help of his Indian guide (O'Shea), leads three children (Wells, Ankers, Henry) through dangerous Indian territory at the request of their general father (Hedlund). [British title: *Last of the Redskins*].

1090. Last of the Renegades (9/66) Eastman Color/Scope—93 mins. (Western). *DIR*: Harald Reinl. *PRO*: Horst Wendlandt, Wolfgang Kuhnlenz. *SP*: Harald G. Petersson. Based on the book by Karl Friedrich May. A Rialto-SNC-Jadran-Atlantis Production. *CAST*: Lex Barker, Pierre Brice, Anthony Steel, Karin Dor, Klaus Kinski, Mario Girotti, Renato Baldini, Eddi Arent, Marie Noelle.

Old Shatterhand (Barker) and Winnetou (Brice) foil the attempts of a couple of outlaws (Kinski, Steel) to drive the Indians off their land to get the oil underneath it. *NOTES*: Filmed in 1964, but not released in the U.S. until 1966. [Original French title: *Le Tresor des Montagnes*]. [Original Italian title: *Giorni di Fuoco*]. [Original German title: *Winnetou II-Teil*]. [Original Yugoslavian title: *Vinetu II*].

1091. The Last Parade (3/1/31) B&W—82 mins. (Crime). *DIR*: Erle C. Kenton. *PRO*: Jack Cohn. *SP*: Dorothy Howell. Story by Casey Robinson. *CAST*: Jack Holt, Tom Moore, Constance Cummings, Edmund Breese, Clarence Muse, Gino Corrado, Gaylord Pendleton, Robert Ellis, Edward J. LeSaint, Earle D. Bunn, Robert Graham.

Two pals return home from World War I, and one becomes a policeman (Moore) while the other (Holt) turns to crime and becomes a bootlegger.

1092. The Last Picture Show (10/71) B&W—118 mins. (Drama).

DIR: Peter Bogdanovich. *PRO*: Stephen J. Friedman. *SP*: Peter Bogdanovich. Larry McMurtry. Based on the book by Larry McMurtry. A BBS Production. *CAST*: Timothy Bottoms, Jeff Bridges, Cybill Shepherd, Ben Johnson, Cloris Leachman, Ellen Burstyn, Eileen Brennan, Clu Gulager, Sam Bottoms, Randy Quaid, Joe Heathcock, Bill Thurman, John Hillerman, Robert Glenn, Sharon Taggart.

In 1951, two teenagers (Timothy Bottoms, Jeff Bridges) experience life, love, separation and sorrow as they grow up in Archer City, Texas. *NOTES*: The film debuts of Randy Quaid, Cybill Shepherd, and Sam Bottoms.

1093. The Last Posse (7/53) B&W—73 mins. (Western). *DIR*: Alfred L. Werker. *PRO*: Harry Joe Brown. *SP*: Seymour Bennett, Connie Lee Bennett, Kenneth Gamet. Story by Seymour and Connie Lee Bennett. *CAST*: Broderick Crawford, Wanda Hendrix, John Derek, Charles Bickford, Warner Anderson, Henry Hull, Tom Powers, Skip Homeier, Monte Blue, Eddy Waller, Will Wright, Raymond Greenleaf, James Kirkwood, James Bell, Guy Wilkerson, Mira McKinney, Helen Wallace, Harry Hayden.

A posse of upstanding citizens steal a cattle baron's (Bickford) money from the outlaws who stole it, and the sheriff's (Crawford) son (Derek) tries to right the wrong.

1094. The Last Rebel (8/71) Technicolor—90 mins. (Western). *DIR*: Denys McCoy. *PRO*: Larry G. Spangler. *SP*: Warren Kiefer. A Glendinning U.S. Capital Film Production. *CAST*: Joe Namath, Jack Elam, Woody Strode, Ty Hardin, Victoria George, Renato Romano, Marina Coffa, Annamaria Chio, Mike Forrest, Jessica Dublin, Herb Andress, Larry Laurence.

At the end of the Civil War, a Confederate soldier (Namath) and his partner (Elam) raise havoc in a Missouri town, and rescue a man (Strode) from being lynched.

1095. The Last Round-Up (11/5/47) B&W—77 mins. (Western). DIR: John English. PRO: Armand Schaefer. SP: Jack Townley, Earle Snell. Story by Jack Townley. A Gene Autry Production. CAST: Gene Autry, Jean Heather, Ralph Morgan, Carol Thurston, Bobby Blake, John (Bob) Cason, Trevor Bardette, Dale Van Sickel, Edward Piel, Sr., Nolan Leary, Ted Adams, Steve Clark, Bud Osborne, Iron Eyes Cody, Mark Daniels, Blackie Whiteford, Charles Hamilton, Russ Vincent, Shug Fisher, Lee Bennett, John Halloran, Sandy Sanders, Roy Gordon, Silverheels Smith, Francis Rey, Billy Wilkinson, George Carleton, Don Kay Reynolds, Jack Baxley, Frankie Marvin, Kernan Cripps, Jose Alvarado, J. W. Cody, Robert Walker, Virginia Carroll, Arline Archuletta, Louis Crosby, Brian O'Hara, Alex Montoya, Rodd Redwing, The Texas Rangers.

Gene sets out to relocate a tribe of Indians so that an aqueduct can be built on their barren land. NOTES: Gene Autry's first western for Columbia.

1096. The Last Ten Days (4/56) B&W—113 mins. (Drama). DIR: G. W. Pabst. PRO: Carl Szokoll. SP: Erich Maria Remarque. Based on *Ten Days to Die* by Michael Angelo Musmanno. A Cosmopolfilm Production. CAST: Albin Skoda, Oskar Werner, Lotte Tobisch, Willy Krause, Erich Stuckmann, Edmund Erlandsen, Kurt Eilers, Leopold Hainisch, Otto Schmoele, Herbert Herbe, Hannes Schiel, Erik Frey, Otto Woegerer.

Adolf Hitler (Skoda), Eva Braun (Tobish), and Hitler's closest friends spend their last ten years in a bunker as Germany falls. [Original German title: *Der Letzte Akt*].

The Last Ten Days of Adolf Hitler *see* **The Last Ten Days**

1097. Last Train from Bombay (8/52) B&W—73 mins. (Adventure). DIR: Fred F. Sears. PRO: Sam Katzman. SP: Robert Libott. An Esskay Production. CAST: Jon Hall, Christine Larson, Lisa Ferraday, Douglas Kennedy, Michael Fox, Donna Martell, Matthew Boulton, James Fairfax, Gregory Gay.

An American diplomat (Hall), in India, becomes a target for the police and assassins as he tries to clear himself of the murder of his friend (Kennedy) and save a prince's life.

1098. The Last Woman (6/76) Eastman Color—112 mins. (Drama). DIR: Marco Ferreri. PRO: Jacques Roitfeld. SP: Marco Ferreri, Rafael Azacona, Dante Matelli. CAST: Gerard Depardieu, Ornella Muti, Michel Piccoli, Zouzou, Renato Salvatori, Giuliana Calandra, Carole Lepers, Nathalie Baye.

A young French engineer (Depardieu) feels threatened when his wife (Zouzou) leaves him and their son, joins the feminist movement with her friend (Lepers), and then plots to take her son away from him. NOTES: Limited theatrical release. [Original French title: *La Derniere Femme*]. [Original Italian title: *L'Ultima Donna*].

1099. Laugh Your Blues Away (11/12/42) B&W—65 mins. (Comedy). DIR: Charles Barton. PRO: Jack Fier. SP: Harry Sauber, Ned Dandy. CAST: Jinx Falkenburg, Bert Gordon, Douglas Drake, Joel Friedkin, Isobel Elsom, Roger Clark, George Lessey, Vivian Oakland, Dick Elliott, Phyllis Kennedy, Robert Greig, Frank Sully, Barbara Brown, Edward Earle, Eddie Kane, Clyde Fillmore, Shirley Patterson, Bess Flowers, Ken Christy, John Tyrrell, Eddie Laughton.

A woman (Elsom) hires a couple of unemployed actors (Falkenburg, Gordon) to pose as Russian royalty to impress her future daughter-in-law's (Kennedy) parents (Elliott, Oakland).

1100. Law and Disorder (10/74) Eastman Color/Panavision—103 mins. (Comedy-Drama). *DIR:* Ivan Passer. *PRO:* William Richert. *SP:* Ivan Passer, William Richert, Kenneth Harris Fishman. A Memorial-Leroy Street-Ugo-Fadsin Production. A Palomar Presentation. *CAST:* Carroll O'Conner, Ernest Borgnine, Ann Wedgeworth, Anita Dangler, Leslie Ackerman, Karen Black, Jack Kehoe, David Spielberg, Joe Ragno, Ed Grover, J. Frank Lucas, Rita Gam.

Two middle-aged New Yorkers (O'Conner, Borgnine) form a police auxiliary group to combat crime in their community.

1101. Law Beyond the Range (2/15/35) B&W—60 mins. (Western). *DIR/SP:* Ford Beebe. *PRO:* Harry L. Decker. Story by Lambert Hillyer. *CAST:* Tim McCoy, Billie Seward, Walter Brennan, Robert Allen, Guy Usher, Harry Todd, Si Jenks, J. B. Kenton, Tom London, Jack Rockwell, Alan Sears, Jules Cowles, Ben Hendricks, Jr.

A cowboy (McCoy) regains territory taken over by outlaws for the law-abiding citizens.

1102. The Law Comes to Texas (4/16/39) B&W—61 mins. (Western). *DIR:* Joseph Levering. *PRO:* Larry Darmour. *SP:* Nate Gatzert. *CAST:* Bill Elliott, Veda Ann Borg, Bud Osborne, Leon Beaumon, Edmund Cobb, Paul Everton, Charles King, Slim Whitaker, David Sharpe, Frank Ellis, Budd Buster, Jack Rockwell, Lee Shumway, Jack Ingram, Frank LaRue,

Forrest Taylor, Lane Chandler, Ben Corbett, Dan White.

An attorney (Elliott) becomes a Texas state trooper, and with his sidekick (King), captures a gang of outlaws.

1103. Law of the Barbary Coast (7/21/49) B&W—65 mins. (Crime). *DIR:* Lew Landers. *PRO:* Wallace MacDonald. *SP:* Robert Libott, Frank Burt. *CAST:* Stephen Dunne, Gloria Henry, Adele Jergens, Robert Shayne, Edwin Max, J. Farrell MacDonald, Ross Ford, Stefan Schnabel.

A crusading district attorney (Dunne) sets out to stop a mobster's (Schnabel) operation on the San Francisco Barbary Coast.

1104. Law of the Canyon (4/24/47) B&W—55 mins. (Western). *DIR:* Ray Nazarro. *PRO:* Colbert Clark. *SP:* Eileen Gary. *CAST:* Charles Starrett, Nancy Saunders, Smiley Burnette, Fred F. Sears, Robert "Buzz" Henry, Jack Kirk, George Chesebro, Bob Wilke, Edmund Cobb, Frank Marlo, Zon Murray, Stanley Price, Frank LaRue, Joseph Palma, Doug Coppin, Texas Jim Lewis and His Lone Star Cowboys.

The Durango Kid (Starrett) stops an outlaw gang from demanding protection money from the local ranchers. [British title: *The Price of Crime*].

1105. Law of the Northwest (5/27/43) B&W—57 mins. (Western). *DIR:* William Berke. *PRO:* Jack Fier. *SP:* Luci Ward. *CAST:* Charles Starrett, Shirley Patterson, Arthur Hunnicutt, Stanley Brown, Davidson Clarke, Donald Curtis, Douglas Levitt, Reginald Barlow, Douglas Drake.

A Mountie (Starrett) and his sidekick (Hunnicutt) set out to stop a group of Nazis from sabotaging the transportation of valuable minerals for the Allied forces.

1106. Law of the Plains (5/12/38) B&W—56 mins. (Western). *DIR:* Sam

Nelson. *PRO:* Harry L. Decker. *SP:* Maurice Geraghty. *CAST:* Charles Starrett, Iris Meredith, Bob Nolan, Dick Curtis, Art Mix, Edward J. Le-Saint, George Chesebro, Robert Warwick, Jack Rockwell, Edmund Cobb, Jack Long, John Tyrrell, Sons of the Pioneers.

A cowboy (Starrett) stops a crooked banker (Warwick) and his gang from stealing the farmers' land.

1107. Law of the Ranger (5/11/37) B&W — 58 mins. (Western). *DIR:* Spencer G. Bennet. *PRO:* Larry Darmour. *SP:* Nate Gatzert. Story by Jesse A. Duffy and Joseph Levering. *CAST:* Bob Allen, Elaine Shepard, Hal Taliaferro (Wally Wales), Lafe McKee, John Merton, Tom London, Lane Chandler, Slim Whitaker, Ernie Adams, Bud Osborne, Jimmy Aubrey.

When a newspaper editor (McKee) is murdered for exposing a crook (Merton) trying to steal the town's water rights, a ranger (Allen) and his men ride into town and bring the crook to justice.

1108. Law of the Texan (10/24/38) B&W — 54 mins. (Western). *DIR:* Elmer Clifton. *PRO:* Monroe Shaff. *SP:* Monroe Shaff, Arthur Hoerl. A Coronet Production. *CAST:* Buck Jones, Dorothy Fay, Kenneth Harlan, Don Douglas, Matty Kemp, Joe Whitehead, Forrest Taylor, Bob Kortman, Dave O'Brien, Tommy Mack, Jose Tortosa, Melissa Sierra.

A sheriff (Jones) goes undercover to stop a gang of outlaws from stealing the town's silver bullion.

1109. The Law Vs. Billy the Kid (8/54) Technicolor — 72 mins. (Western). *DIR:* William Castle. *PRO:* Sam Katzman. *SP:* John Williams. *CAST:* Scott Brady, Betta St. John, James Griffith, Alan Hale, Jr., William "Bill" Phillips, Benny Rubin, Steve Darrell, Frank Sully, William Fawcett, Robert Griffin, Paul Cavanagh, George Berke-

ley, William Tannen, Martin Garralaga, Richard H. Cutting, John Cliff, Otis Garth.

Sheriff Pat Garrett (Griffith) goes after Billy the Kid (Brady) when he commits a string of murders.

1110. Lawless Empire (11/15/45) B&W — 58 mins. (Western). *DIR:* Vernon Keays. *PRO:* Colbert Clark. *SP:* Bennett R. Cohen. Story by Elizabeth Beecher. *CAST:* Charles Starrett, Mildred Law, Tex Harding, Johnny Walsh, Dub Taylor, John Calvert, Jack Rockwell, George Chesebro, Forrest Taylor, Ethan Laidlaw, Lloyd Ingraham, Tom Chatterton, Jessie Arnold, Boyd Stockman, Frank LaRue, Ray Jones, John Tyrrell, James T. Nelson, Edward Howard, Jack Kirk, Joe Galbreath, Bob Wills and His Texas Playboys.

The Durango Kid (Starrett), with the help of a minister (Harding), prevents a gang of outlaws from chasing homesteaders from their land. [British title: *Power of Possession*].

1111. Lawless Plainsmen (3/17/42) B&W — 59 mins. (Western). *DIR:* William Berke. *PRO:* Jack Fier. *SP:* Luci Ward. *CAST:* Charles Starrett, Luana Walters, Cliff Edwards, Ray Bennett, Russell Hayden, Gwen Kenyon, Stanley Brown, Frank LaRue, Carl Mathews, Eddie Laughton, Nick Thompson.

A ranch foreman (Starrett) and his sidekick (Hayden) protect a wagon train from Indian attacks until the cavalry arrives. [British title: *Roll On*].

1112. Lawless Riders (12/6/35) B&W — 58 mins. (Western). *DIR:* Spencer G. Bennet. *PRO:* Larry Darmour. *SP:* Nate Gatzert. *CAST:* Ken Maynard, Geneva Mitchell, Harry Woods, Frank Ellis, Frank Yaconelli, Jack Rockwell, Hal Taliaferro (Wally Wales), Hank Bell, Slim Whitaker, Bud Jamison, Bob McKenzie, Bud Mc-

Clure, Jack King, Horace B. Carpenter, Oscar Gahan, Pascale Perry.

A cowboy (Maynard) tries to prove his innocence when he is accused of murder.

1113. A Lawless Street (12/15/ 55) Technicolor—78 mins. (Western). *DIR:* Joseph H. Lewis. *PRO:* Harry Joe Brown, Randolph Scott. *SP:* Kenneth Gamet. Based on *Marshal of Medicine Bend* by Brad Ward. A Scott-Brown Production. *CAST:* Randolph Scott, Angela Lansbury, Warner Anderson, Jean Parker, Wallace Ford, John Emery, James Bell, Michael Pate, Don Megowan, Jeanette Nolan, Stanley Blystone, Edwin Chandler, Kermit Maynard, Jack Perrin, Ruth Donnelly, Frank Hagney, Frank Ferguson, Reed Howes, Jay Lawrence, Harry Tyler, Guy Teague, Peter Ortiz, Don Carlos, Charles Williams, Harry Antrim, Hal K. Dawson, Pat Collins, Frank Scannell, Barry Brooks.

A marshal (Scott) refuses to hang up his guns, even when his wife (Lansbury) leaves him, until he cleans up the town of Medicine Bend.

1114. Lawrence of Arabia (12/ 62) Technicolor/Super Panavision 70—220 mins. (Biography-Adventure). *DIR:* David Lean. *PRO:* Sam Spiegel, David Lean. *SP:* Robert Bolt, Michael Wilson. Based on *Seven Pillars of Wisdom* by T. E. Lawrence. A Horizon Production. *CAST:* Peter O'Toole, Alec Guinness, Anthony Quinn, Jack Hawkins, Jose Ferrer, Anthony Quayle, Claude Rains, Arthur Kennedy, Donald Wolfit, Omar Sharif, I. S. Johar, Howard Marion Crawford, Kenneth Fortescue, Norman Rossington, Michel Ray, John Dimech.

Told in flashback, T. E. Lawrence (O'Toole) unites the Arabs in their fight with the Turks during World War I.

1115. Le Dernier Combat (The Last Battle) (6/84) B&W/Panavision—90 mins. (Science Fiction). *DIR:* Luc Besson. *PRO/SP:* Luc Besson, Pierre Jolivet. A Les Films du Loup-Triumph Films Production. *CAST:* Pierre Jolivet, Jean Bouise, Fritz Wepper, Jean Reno, Maurice Lamy, Petra Muller, Christiane Kruger, Pierre Carrive, Bernard Havet, Jean-Michel Castanie, Michel Doset, Garry Jode, Marcel Berthomier.

In the post-apocalyptic future, a man (Jolivet) lives in a half-buried skyscraper and must fight his adversary (Wepper) to become ruler of this new domain. *NOTES:* Limited theatrical release; in French with English subtitles.

1116. The League of Frightened Men (5/25/37) B&W—71 mins. (Mystery). *DIR:* Alfred E. Green. *SP:* Eugene Solow, Guy Endore. Based on *The League of Frightened Men* by Rex Stout. *CAST:* Walter Connolly, Irene Hervey, Lionel Stander, Nana Bryant, Eduardo Ciannelli, Victor Kilian, Walter Kingsford, Allen Brook, Leonard Mudie, Kenneth Hunter, Rafaela Ottiano, Edward McNamara, Jameson Thomas, Ian Wolfe, Jonathan Hale, Herbert Ashley, James Flavin, Charles Irwin.

Nero Wolfe (Connolly) sets out to solve the murder of three Harvard alumni with the help of his assistant Archie (Stander).

1117. Leather Gloves (11/11/48) B&W—75 mins. (Drama). *DIR:* William Asher. *PRO:* Richard Quine, William Asher. *SP:* Brown Holmes. Based on *No Place to Go* by Richard English. *CAST:* Cameron Mitchell, Virginia Grey, Jane Nigh, Sam Levene, Henry O'Neill, Blake Edwards, Bob Castro, Sally Corner, Stanley Andrews, Eddie Acuff, Ralph Volkie, Walter Soderling.

An on-the-skids boxer (Mitchell) signs up to throw a fight and then has second thoughts. [British title: *Loser Take All*].

1118. Leave It to Blondie (2/22/45) B&W — 75 mins. (Comedy). *DIR:* Abby Berlin. *PRO:* Burt Kelly. *SP:* Connie Lee. Based on the comic strip created by Chic Young. *CAST:* Penny Singleton, Arthur Lake, Larry Simms, Maude Eburne, Danny Mummert, Jonathan Hale, Chick Chandler, Marjorie Weaver, Arthur Space, Marjorie Ann Mutchie, Eddie Acuff, Eula Morgan, Fred Graff, Jack Rice, Anne Loos, Marilyn Johnson.

Dagwood (Lake) and Blondie (Singleton) enter a song writing contest hoping to win the prize money to cover bad checks.

1119. The Legend of Tom Dooley (7/59) B&W — 79 mins. (Western). *DIR:* Ted Post. *PRO/SP:* Stan Shpetner. Based on the folk song *The Legend of Tom Dooley* as sung by The Kingston Trio. *CAST:* Michael Landon, Jo Morrow, Jack Hogan, Richard Rust, Dee Pollack, Ken Lynch, Howard Wright, Ralph Moody, John Cliff, Cheerio Meredith, Gary Hunley, Anthony Jochim, Jeff Morris, Jason Johnson, Joe Yrigoyen, Sandy Sanders, Juney Ellis, Maudie Prickett.

A Confederate soldier (Landon) robs a Union stagecoach and kills two soldiers, only to find out the war is over. He becomes a hunted man and, when his girl (Morrow) is killed, he is captured and hanged.

1120. Legion of Terror (11/3/36) B&W — 62 mins. (Crime-Drama). *DIR:* C. C. Coleman, Jr. *PRO:* Ralph Cohn. *SP:* Bert Granet. *CAST:* Bruce Cabot, Marguerite Churchill, Crawford Weaver, Ward Bond, Charles Wilson, John Hamilton, Arthur Loft, Nick Copeland, John Tyrrell, Edward J. Le-Saint.

When the brother (Bond) of his girlfriend (Churchill) is murdered by the Klan, a post office investigator (Cabot) sets out to put an end to them.

1121. Leonard Part 6 (12/87) DeLuxe Color — 85 mins. (Comedy). *DIR:* Paul Weiland. *PRO:* Bill Cosby. *SP:* Jonathan Reynolds. Story by Bill Cosby. A SAH Enterprises Production. *CAST:* Bill Cosby, Tom Courtenay, Joe Don Baker, Moses Gunn, Pat Colbert, Gloria Foster, Victoria Rowell, Anna Levine, David Maier, George Kirby.

A secret agent (Cosby) is brought out of retirement to battle a madwoman (Foster) bent on world domination.

1122. Let No Man Write My Epitaph (10/60) B&W — 105 mins. (Drama). *DIR:* Philip Leacock. *PRO:* Boris D. Kaplan. *SP:* Robert Presnell, Jr. Based on the book by Willard Motley. *CAST:* Burl Ives, Shelley Winters, James Darren, Jean Seberg, Ricardo Montalban, Ella Fitzgerald, Rudolfo Acosta, Philip Ober, Jeanne Cooper, Bernie Hamilton, Walter Burke, Francis De Sales.

In order to help a Chicago slum kid (Darren) and his mother (Winters), a judge (Ives) kills the drug dealer (Montalban) who has been supplying her with drugs. *NOTES:* A sequel to the 1949 Columbia film *Knock on Any Door.*

1123. Let the Good Times Roll (5/73) Eastman Color — 99 mins. (Documentary). *DIR:* Sid Levin, Robert Abel. *PRO:* Gerald I. Isenberg. A Metromedia Producers Corp. and Richard Nader Production. A Cinema Associates Film. *CAST:* Richard Nader — MC, Chuck Berry, Little Richard, Fats Domino, Chubby Checker, Bo Diddley, The Shirelles, The Five Satins, The Coasters, Danny and the Juniors, Bill Haley and the Comets, Bobby Comstock Rock and Roll Band.

A compilation rock 'n' roll concert culled from several 1972 stage shows, newsreel, feature film, and television footage from the '50's.

1124. Let Us Live (2/20/39) B&W—66 mins. (Crime). *DIR:* John Brahm. *PRO:* William Perlberg. *SP:* Anthony Veiller, Allen Rivkin. Story by Joseph F. Dineen. *CAST:* Maureen O'Sullivan, Henry Fonda, Ralph Bellamy, Alan Baxter, Henry Kolker, Stanley Ridges, Peter Lynn, George Douglas, Philip Trent, Martin Spellman, Charles Trowbridge, Dick Elliott, Byron Foulger, Emmett Vogan, Arthur Loft, John Qualen, William V. Mong, Eddie Laughton, Ann Doran, Dick Curtis, William Royle, Edmund Cobb, Tom London, George Chesebro, Lee Shumway, Clarence Wilson.
A woman (O'Sullivan) seeks help from a detective (Bellamy) to prove her fiance (Fonda) innocent of robbery and murder.

1125. Let's Do It Again (6/18/53) Technicolor—95 mins. (Musical-Comedy). *DIR:* Alexander Hall. *PRO:* Oscar Saul. *SP:* Mary Loos, Richard Sale. Based on the play *The Awful Truth* by Arthur Richman. *CAST:* Ray Milland, Jane Wyman, Aldo Ray, Valerie Bettis, Leon Ames, Tom Helmore, Karin Booth, Mary Treen, Dick Wessel, Kathryn Givney, Herbert Hayes, Herb Vigran.
A divorced couple (Milland, Wyman) try to win each other back by making one another jealous. *NOTES:* A musical remake of the 1937 Columbia film *The Awful Truth*.

1126. Let's Fall in Love (1/20/34) B&W—64 mins. (Musical-Comedy). *DIR:* David Burton. *PRO:* Felix Young. *SP:* Herbert Fields. *CAST:* Edmund Lowe, Ann Sothern, Miriam Jordan, Gregory Ratoff, Tala Birell, Arthur Jarrett, Marjorie Gateson, Betty Furness, Ruth Warren, Greta Meyer, Kane Richmond, John Qualen, Selmer Jackson, Sven-Hugo Borg.
A producer (Ratoff) and director (Lowe) try to promote a sideshow performer (Sothern) as their newest Swedish discovery. *NOTES:* Remade by Columbia in 1949 as *Slightly French*.

1127. Let's Get Married (4/14/37) B&W—68 mins. (Comedy). *DIR:* Alfred E. Green. *PRO:* Everett Riskin. *SP:* Ethel Hill. Story by A. H. Z. Carr. *CAST:* Walter Connolly, Ida Lupino, Ralph Bellamy, Nana Bryant, Raymond Walburn, Robert Allen, Reginald Denny, Edward McWade, Granville Bates, Arthur Hoyt, Emmett Vogan, Will Morgan, Charles Irwin, George Ernest, James Flavin.
A politician's daughter (Lupino) falls for a weatherman (Bellamy) instead of the socialite her father (Connolly) has picked for her.

1128. Let's Go Steady (1/4/45) B&W—60 mins. (Musical-Comedy). *DIR:* Del Lord. *PRO:* Ted Richmond. *SP:* Erna Lazarus. Story by William B. Sackheim. *CAST:* Pat Parrish, Jackie Moran, June Preisser, Jimmy Lloyd, Arnold Stang, Skinnay Ennis, Mel Torme, William Moss, Byron Foulger, Gladys Blake, Eddie Bruce, William Frambes, The Skinnay Ennis Band.
A group of kids from a small town are swindled out of fifty dollars by a New York publisher, so they promote themselves by getting a bandleader and radio station to air their songs.

1129. Let's Have Fun (3/4/43) B&W—65 mins. (Comedy). *DIR:* Charles Barton. *PRO:* Jack Fier. *SP:* Harry Sauber. *CAST:* Margaret Lindsay, John Beal, Bert Gordon, Dorothy Ann Seese, Constance Worth, Leonid Kinskey, Sig Arno, Edward Keane, Ernest Hilliard, John Tyrrell.
An out of work actor (Gordon) tries to find work in his profession.

1130. Let's Live Tonight (3/16/35) B&W—75 mins. (Romance-Comedy). *DIR:* Victor Schertzinger. *PRO:* Robert North. *SP:* Gene Markey.

Based on *Once a Gentleman* by Bradley King. CAST: Lillian Harvey, Tullio Carminati, Janet Beecher, Hugh Williams, Tala Birell, Luis Alberni, Claudia Coleman, Arthur Treacher, Gilbert Emery.

Two millionaire brothers (Carminati, Williams) pursue the same woman (Harvey) while in Monte Carlo.

1131. Let's Rock (6/58) B&W – 78 mins. (Musical-Drama). DIR/PRO: Harry Foster. SP: Hal Hackady. CAST: Julius La Rosa, Phyllis Newman, Conrad Janis, Joy Harmon, Fred Kareman, Pete Paull, Charles Shelander, Harold Grey, Jerry Hackady, Wink Martindale, Paul Anka, Della Reese, Roy Hamilton, Danny and the Juniors, The Royal Teens, The Tyrones.

A ballad singer (La Rosa) is convinced by his agent (Janis) and sweetheart (Newman) that the only way to sell records is change his style and perform rock'n'roll. [British title: *Keep It Cool*].

1132. The Liberation of L. B. Jones (3/70) Eastman Color – 102 mins. (Drama). DIR: William Wyler. PRO: Ronald Lubin. SP: Stirling Silliphant, Jesse Hill Ford. Based on *The Liberation of Lord Byron Jones* by Jesse Hill Ford. A Liberation Production. CAST: Lee J. Cobb, Anthony Zerbe, Roscoe Lee Browne, Lola Falana, Lee Majors, Barbara Hershey, Yaphet Kotto, Arch Johnson, Chill Wills, Dub Taylor, Lauren Jones, Ray Teal, Eve McVeagh, Brenda Sykes, Larry D. Mann.

Racial tensions flare when a black undertaker (Browne) decides to divorce his wife (Falana) because she has a white lover (Zerbe) and he asks a white lawyer (Cobb) to handle his case. NOTES: The American film debut of Lola Falana; director William Wyler's final film.

1133. Lies My Father Told Me (11/75) Eastman Color – 103 mins. (Drama). DIR: Jan Kadar. PRO: Anthony Bedrich, Harry Gulkin. SP: Ted Allan. A Pentimento-Pentacle VIII Production. CAST: Yossi Yadin, Len Birman, Marilyn Lightstone, Jeffrey Lynas, Ted Allan, Barbara Chilcott, Mignon Elkins, Henry Gamer, Carole Lazare, Cleo Paskal.

In 1920 Montreal, a young boy (Lynas), who cannot relate to his parents, seeks solace with his grandfather (Yadin) as he accompanies him on his rides about the city on his horse drawn wagon.

1134. Life at the Top (8/65) B&W – 117 mins. (Drama). DIR: Ted Kotcheff. PRO: James Woolf. SP: Mordecai Richler. Based on the book by John Braine. A Romulus Production. CAST: Laurence Harvey, Honor Blackman, Jean Simmons, Michael Craig, Donald Wolfit, Robert Morley, Margaret Johnson, Ambrosine Phillpotts, Allan Cuthbertson, George A. Cooper, Nigel Davenport, Geoffrey Bayldon, Charles Lamb, David Oxley, Paul A. Martin, Ian Shand, Francis Cosslet.

It is ten years later and Joe Lampton (Harvey) now has everything he has schemed and cheated to get: a wealthy wife (Simmons), a home in the suburbs, and a top position in the company run by his father-in-law (Wolfit). NOTES: A sequel to the 1958 Continental (Walter Reade) film *Room at the Top*.

1135. Life Begins at 17 (7/58) B&W – 75 mins. (Teenage-Drama-Romance). DIR: Arthur Dreifuss. PRO: Sam Katzman. SP: Richard Baer. A Clover Production. CAST: Mark Damon, Dorothy Johnson, Edward (Edd) Byrnes, Ann Doran, Hugh Sanders, Luana Anders, Cathy O'Neill, George Eldredge, Tommy Ivo, Bob Dennis, Robert Moechel, Maurice Manson.

To get back at a boy (Damon) for throwing her over for her sister (Johnson), a girl (Anders) announces that the boy is the father of her non-existent child-to-be.

1136. Life Begins with Love (4/1/37) B&W—72 mins. (Romance). DIR: Raymond B. McCarey. PRO: Myles Connolly. SP: Thomas Mitchell, Brown Holmes. Story by Dorothy Bennett. CAST: Jean Parker, Douglass Montgomery, Edith Fellows, Leona Maricle, Lumsden Hare, Aubrey Mather, James Burke, Minerva Urecal, Scotty Beckett, Joel Davis, Joyce Kay, Si Wills.

A millionaire (Montgomery) hides out in a nursery school to avoid a pledge he made to give away his millions, and falls for the teacher (Parker).

1137. Life with Blondie (3/27/46) B&W—69 mins. (Comedy). DIR: Abby Berlin. PRO: Burt Kelly. SP: Connie Lee. Based on the comic strip created by Chic Young. CAST: Penny Singleton, Arthur Lake, Larry Simms, Ray Walker, Ernest Truex, Jonathan Hale, Marc Lawrence, Marjorie Kent, Veda Ann Borg, Bobby Larson, Douglas Fowley, George Tyne, Edward Gargan, Jack Rice, Francis Pierlot, Eddie Acuff, Robert Ryan, Steve Benton.

Dagwood (Lake) becomes upset and jealous when their dog, Daisy, wins a contest to become a canine photographic pinup, and threatens his position as breadwinner.

1138. Light Fingers (7/29/29) B&W—60 mins. (Crime-Romance). DIR: Joseph Henabery. PRO: Harry Cohn. SP: Jack Natteford. Story by Alfred Henry Lewis. CAST: Ian Keith, Dorothy Revier, Carroll Nye, Ralph Theodore, Tom Ricketts, Charles Gerrard, Pietro Sosso.

A jewel thief (Keith) meets a girl (Revier) who gets him to reform his ways. NOTES: Released as both a silent and sound film.

1139. The Lightning Flyer (4/5/31) B&W—65 mins. (Drama). DIR:

William Nigh. PRO: Harry Cohn. SP: Barry Barringer. CAST: James Hall, Dorothy Sebastian, Walter Merrill, Robert E. Homans, Albert J. Smith, Ethan Allen, Eddie Boland, George Meadows.

A son (Hall) assumes a false identity as he works for the railroad to impress his owner father.

1140. Lightning Guns (12/11/50) B&W—55 mins. (Western). DIR: Fred F. Sears. PRO: Colbert Clark. SP: Victor Arthur. CAST: Charles Starrett, Gloria Henry, Smiley Burnette, Edgar Dearing, Jock Mahoney, George Chesebro, William Norton Bailey, Chuck Roberson, Joel Friedkin, Raymond Bond, Frank Griffin, Ken Houchins.

The Durango Kid (Starrett) exposes the real culprit (Bailey) behind the raids on a dam under construction and thereby prevents a feud from erupting into bloodshed. [British title: *Taking Sides*].

1141. Lightning Swords of Death (3/74) Eastman Color/ Scope—83 mins. (Martial Arts). DIR: Kenji Misumi. PRO: Shintaro Katsu. SP: Kazuo Koike. A Katsu Production in association with Toho Company Productions. CAST: Tomisaburo Wakayama, Goh Kato, Yuko Hama, Akihiro Tanikawa.

A discredited samurai (Wakayama) roams medieval Japan righting wrongs while pushing his young son ahead of him in a baby carriage. NOTES: This film, and its 1980 New Line Cinema sequel *Shogun Assassin*, was edited from the Japanese Lone Wolf and Cub series, *Sword of Vengeance*. [Original Japanese title: *Kozure Ohkami-Ko Wo Kashi Ude Kashi Tsukamatsuru*].

1142. Lilith (10/64) B&W—110 mins. (Drama). DIR/PRO/SP: Robert Rossen. Based on the book by J. R. Salamanca. CAST: Warren Beatty,

Jean Seberg, Peter Fonda, Kim Hunter, Anne Meacham, Robert Reilly, James Patterson, Jessica Walters, Gene Hackman, Lucy Smith, Rene Auberjonois, Maurice Brenner, Jeanne Barr, Richard Higgs, Olympia Dukakis.

A trainee therapist (Beatty) falls in love with a mental patient (Seberg) with tragic consequences. *NOTES:* Robert Rossen's last film.

1143. The Line-Up (4/17/34) B&W—75 mins. (Crime). *DIR:* Howard Higgin. *PRO:* Sid Rogell. *SP:* George Waggner. *CAST:* William Gargan, Marian Nixon, Paul Hurst, John Miljan, Greta Meyer, Harold Huber, Joseph Crehan, Noel Francis, Francis McDonald, Charles Browne.

A detective (Gargan) helps a checkroom girl (Nixon) at a nightclub prove her innocence when she is accused of stealing furs for a gang of crooks. [British title: *Identity Parade*].

1144. The Lineup (6/58) B&W—85 mins. (Crime-Drama). *DIR:* Don Siegel. *PRO:* Jaime De Valle. *SP:* Stirling Silliphant. Based on characters created by Lawrence L. Klee in the TV series *The Lineup*. A Pajemer Production. *CAST:* Eli Wallach, Robert Keith, Warner Anderson, Richard Jaeckel, William Leslie, Mary La Roche, Emile Meyer, Marshall Reed, Raymond Bailey, Vaughn Taylor, Cheryl Callaway, George Eldredge, Robert Bailey, Francis De Sales.

San Francisco detectives (Anderson, Meyer) try to stop a ruthless killer (Wallach) on the trail of a shipment of smuggled heroin.

1145. The Lion and the Lamb (4/5/31) B&W—74 mins. (Crime). *DIR:* George B. Seitz. *SP:* Matt Taylor. Story by E. Phillips Oppenheim. *CAST:* Walter Byron, Carmel Myers, Raymond Hatton, Montague Love, Miriam Seegar, Charles Gerrard, Will Stanton, Charles Wildish, Harry

Semels, Robert Milasch, Yorke Sherwood, Sidney Bracey.

An earl (Byron) accidentally gets mixed up with a gang of kidnappers, and tries to stop them when they kidnap a wealthy heiress (Myers).

1146. The Little Adventuress (12/9/38) B&W—60 mins. (Drama). *DIR:* D. Ross Lederman. *PRO:* Ralph Cohn. *SP:* Michael L. Simmons. Story by Michael L. Simmons, Paul Jarrico. *CAST:* Edith Fellows, Richard Fiske, Jacqueline Wells (Julie Bishop), Cliff Edwards, Virginia Howell, Harry C. Bradley, Charles Waldron, Kenneth Harlan.

When her parents are killed, a young girl (Fellows) takes her horse, goes to live with her cousin (Fiske), and trains the horse for a big race.

1147. Little Miss Broadway (6/19/47) B&W—70 mins. (Musical-Comedy). *DIR:* Arthur Dreifuss. *PRO:* Sam Katzman. *SP:* Arthur Dreifuss, Betty Wright, Victor McLeod. *CAST:* Jean Porter, John Shelton, Ruth Donnelly, Doris Colleen, Edward Gargan, Vince Barnett, Douglas Wood, Milton Kibbee, Dick Nichols, Charles Jordan, Kirk Alyn, Ben Welden, Jack Norman, Stan Ross, Jack George, Jerry Wald and His Orchestra.

An orphaned girl (Porter) thinks her relatives are socialites, but they are really Broadway actors who rent a mansion to impress her and her fiance (Nichols).

1148. Little Miss Roughneck (7/1/38) B&W—64 mins. (Comedy). *DIR:* Aubrey Scotto. *PRO:* Wallace MacDonald. *SP:* Fred Niblo, Jr., Grace Neville, Michael L. Simmons. *CAST:* Edith Fellows, Leo Carrillo, Jacqueline Wells (Julie Bishop), Scott Colton, Margaret Irving, Inez Palange, George McKay, Frank C. Wilson, John Gallaudet, Walter Stahl, Ivan Miller, Al Bridge, Wade Boteler, Guy Usher.

A child star (Fellows) devises a publicity stunt to get back into the movies after her mother's (Irving) behavior has her booted out of every studio.

1149. Little Nikita (1/88) DeLuxe Color—98 mins. (Spy-Thriller). *DIR:* Richard Benjamin. *PRO:* Harry Gittes. *SP:* John Hill, Bo Goldman. Story by Tom Musca, Terry Schwartz. *CAST:* Sidney Poitier, River Phoenix, Richard Lynch, Richard Jenkins, Caroline Kava, Richard Bradford, Loretta Devine, Lucy Deakins, Jerry Hardin, Albert Fortell, Ronald Guttmann, Jacob Vargas.

An FBI agent's (Poitier) investigation into the activities of a renegade Soviet agent (Lynch) leads to a teenager's (Phoenix) discovery that his parents (Kava, Jenkins) are Russian spies.

1150. The Little Ones (4/65) B&W—66 mins. (Children's-Drama). *DIR/SP:* Jim O'Connolly. *PRO:* Freddie Robertson. A Goldhawk Production. *CAST:* Carl Gonzales, Kim Smith, Dudley Foster, Derek Newark, Jean Marlow, Peter Thomas, Derek Francis, Cyril Shaps, John Chandos, Diane Aubrey, George Betton, Tom Crossman, Norman Mitchell, Michael McKenzie, Anne Padwick.

Two London boys (Gonzales, Smith) attempt to leave their unhappy homes by stowing away on a ship bound for Jamaica.

1151. The Little Prince and the Eight-Headed Dragon (2/64) Eastman Color/Scope—86 mins. (Animated). *DIR:* Yugo Serikawa. *PRO:* Toei Animation Studios. *SP:* Ichiro Ikeda, Shin Yoshida, Isamu Takaheshi, Takashi Iijima. A Toei Production. *CAST:* Not available.

A young prince journeys to the heavens, beneath the sea, and a distant land ruled by an eight-headed serpent as he searches for his mother. *NOTES:* Originally released in Japan in 1963. [Original Japanese title: *Wanpaku Ogi No Orochitaiji*].

The Living Death *see* **The Snake People**

1152. Living Free (4/72) Eastman Color—92 mins. (Drama). *DIR:* Jack Couffer. *PRO:* Paul Radmin. *SP:* Millard Kaufman. Based on the book by Joy Adamson. An Open Road-High Road Production. *CAST:* Susan Hampshire, Nigel Davenport, Geoffrey Keen, Peter Lukoye, Shane De Louvres, Robert Beaumont, Charles Hayes, Jean Hayes.

When Elsa the lioness dies, Joy (Hampshire) and George (Davenport) Adamson attempt to keep her lion cubs free. *NOTES:* A sequel to the 1966 Columbia film *Born Free*.

1153. Loaded Pistols (1/15/49) B&W—79 mins. (Western). *DIR:* John English. *PRO:* Armand Schaefer. *SP:* Dwight Cummins, Dorothy Yost. A Gene Autry Production. *CAST:* Gene Autry, Barbara Britton, Chill Wills, Jack Holt, Russell Arms, Robert Shayne, Budd Buster, Dick Alexander, Snub Pollard, Reed Howes, Vince Barnett, Clem Bevans, Hank Bell, Stanley Blystone, Fred Kohler, Jr., Leon Weaver, Sandy Sanders, John R. McKee, Felice Raymond, Frank O'Conner, William Sundholm, Heinie Conklin.

When a friend of his is killed, Gene sets out to prove a youngster (Arms) innocent of the crime and find the real murderer. *NOTES:* Jack Holt's last film for Columbia.

1154. Lock Up Your Daughters! (10/69) Technicolor—103 mins. (Comedy). *DIR:* Peter Coe. *PRO:* David Deutsch. *SP:* Keith Waterhouse, Willis Hall. Based on the Lionel Bart, Laurie Johnson, and Bernard Miles musical. Based on the plays *Rape Upon Rape* by Henry Fielding and *The Relapse* by John Vanbrugh. A Domino

Production. CAST: Christopher Plummer, Susannah York, Glynis Johns, Ian Bannen, Tom Bell, Elaine Taylor, Jim Dale, Roy Kinnear, Georgia Brown, Roy Dotrice, Peter Bull, Paul Dawkins, Vanessa Howard, Peter Bayliss, Fenella Fielding.

In 18th century London, an aristocrat (Plummer) and several of his friends seek female companionship.

1155. The Lone Hand Texan (3/6/47) B&W – 54 mins. (Western). DIR: Ray Nazarro. PRO: Colbert Clark. SP: Ed Earl Repp. CAST: Charles Starrett, Mary Newton, Smiley Burnette, Fred F. Sears, Jim Diehl, George Chesebro, Robert Stevens, John Cason, George Russell, Jasper Weldon, Maudie Prickett, Post Park, Mustard and Gravy (Frank Rice and Ernest Stokes).

The Durango Kid (Starrett) helps an old friend (Sears) to keep his oil rich land when an outlaw gang tries to get control of it. NOTES: The first appearance of Frank Rice and Ernest Stokes as the comedy team of "Mustard and Gravy." [British title: *The Cheat*].

1156. The Lone Prairie (10/15/42) B&W – 58 mins. (Western). DIR: William Berke. PRO: Leon Barsha. SP: Fred Myton. Story by Ed Earl Repp and J. Benton Cheney. CAST: Russell Hayden, Lucille Lambert, Dub Taylor, Kermit Maynard, John Merton, Edmund Cobb, Jack Kirk, Ernie Adams, John Maxwell, Bob Wills and His Texas Playboys.

A sheriff (Hayden) and his sidekick (Taylor) make the prairie safe by rounding up an outlaw gang preying on homesteaders. [British title: *Inside Information*].

1157. The Lone Rider (6/13/30) B&W – 57 mins. (Western). DIR: Louis King. PRO: Sol Lesser. SP: Forrest Sheldon. Story by Frank Howard Clark. A Beverly Production. CAST: Buck Jones, Vera Reynolds, Harry Woods, George Pearce.

The leader of the Vigilante Committee (Jones) is an ex-outlaw whose past is revealed by another outlaw (Woods). He is chased by both the outlaw and the Committee, but redeems himself by bringing the outlaw to justice. NOTES: Jones' first all-talking western; remade by Columbia in 1934 as *The Man Trailer*, and in 1939 as *The Thundering West*.

1158. Lone Star Moonlight (12/12/46) B&W – 66 mins. (Western). DIR: Ray Nazarro. PRO: Colbert Clark. SP: Louise Rousseau. Story by Ande Lamb. CAST: Ken Curtis, Joan Barton, Guy Kibbee, Robert Stevens, Claudia Drake, Arthur Loft, Vernon Dent, Sam Flint, The Smart Set, Merle Travis Trio, The Hoosier Hotshots, Judy Clark and Her Rhythm Cowgirls.

A GI (Curtis) returns home to find his radio station in neglect and learns that a rival station has been opened and is broadcasting. [British title: *Amongst the Thieves*].

1159. Lone Star Pioneers (3/16/39) B&W – 54 mins. (Western). DIR: Joseph Levering. PRO: Larry Darmour. SP: Nate Gatzert. CAST: Bill Elliott, Dorothy Gulliver, Lee Shumway, Jack Ingram, Harry Harvey, Frank LaRue, Charles King, Slim Whitaker, David Sharpe, Frank Ellis, Budd Buster, Jack Rockwell, Tex Palmer, Merrill McCormack, Buzz Barton, Kit Guard.

A U.S. Marshal (Elliott) goes undercover to track down a gang of outlaws raiding supply shipments. [British title: *Unwelcome Visitors*].

1160. The Lone Star Vigilantes (1/1/42) B&W – 58 mins. (Western). DIR: Wallace W. Fox. PRO: Leon Barsha. SP: Luci Ward. CAST: Bill Elliott, Virginia Carpenter, Tex Ritter, Luana Walters, Ethan Laidlaw, Gavin Gordon, Budd Buster, Rich Anderson, Forrest Taylor, George Chesebro, Edmund Cobb, Steve Clark, Frank Mitchell, Lowell Drew, Paul Mulvey, Al Haskell.

Wild Bill Hickok (Elliott) and his friends (Ritter, Mitchell) arrive home after the Civil War and set out to smash a bandit gang led by a phony major (Gordon) who is holding their town under martial law. [British title: *The Devil's Price*].

1161. The Lone Wolf and His Lady (8/1/49) B&W — 60 mins. (Mystery). *DIR*: John Hoffman. *PRO*: Rudolph C. Flothow. *SP*: Malcolm Stuart Boylan. Story by Edward Dein. Based on characters created by Louis Joseph Vance. *CAST*: Ron Randell, June Vincent, Alan Mowbray, William Frawley, Collette Lyons, Douglas Dumbrille, James Todd, Steven Geray, Robert H. Barrat, Arthur Space, Philip Van Zandt, Jack Overman, Lee Phelps, Fred F. Sears, William Newell, Lane Chandler, Harry Hayden, George Tyne.

The Lone Wolf (Randell), covering a diamond exhibition, sets out to find a jewel thief when he is accused of stealing the diamond. *NOTES*: The final film in the Lone Wolf series.

1162. The Lone Wolf in London (11/13/47) B&W — 64 mins. (Mystery). *DIR*: Leslie Goodwins. *PRO*: Ted Richmond. *SP*: Arthur E. Orloff. Story by Brenda Weisberg, Arthur E. Orloff. Based on characters created by Louis Joseph Vance. *CAST*: Gerald Mohr, Nancy Saunders, Eric Blore, Evelyn Ankers, Richard Fraser, Queenie Leonard, Alan Napier, Denis Green, Frederic Worlock, Tom Stevenson, Vernon Steele, Paul Fung, Guy Kingsford.

The Lone Wolf (Mohr), accused by Scotland Yard of stealing a fabulous gem collection, sets out to find the real crooks.

1163. The Lone Wolf in Mexico (1/16/47) B&W — 69 mins. (Mystery). *DIR*: D. Ross Lederman. *PRO*: Sanford Cummings. *SP*: Maurice Tombragel, Martin M. Goldsmith. Based on a story by Louis Joseph Vance. *CAST*: Gerald Mohr, Sheila Ryan, Jacqueline DeWit, Eric Blore, Nestor Paiva, John Gallaudet, Bernard Nedell, Winifred Harris, Peter Brocco, Alan Edwards, Fred Godoy, Theodore Gottlieb.

The Lone Wolf (Mohr) finds himself accused of murder as he tracks down a gang of diamond smugglers.

1164. The Lone Wolf in Paris (5/25/38) B&W — 67 mins. (Mystery). *DIR*: Albert S. Rogell. *SP*: Arthur T. Horman. Based on a story by Louis Joseph Vance. *CAST*: Francis Lederer, Frances Drake, Olaf Hytten, Walter Kingsford, Leona Maricle, Albert (Van) Dekker, Maurice Cass, Bess Flowers, Ruth Robinson, Pio Peretti, Eddie Fetherstone, Dick Curtis, Al Herman.

The Lone Wolf (Lederer) falls for a princess (Drake) when he is hired to steal back her crown jewels from a grand duke (Kingsford).

1165. The Lone Wolf Keeps a Date (1/10/41) B&W — 65 mins. (Mystery). *DIR*: Sidney Salkow. *PRO*: Ralph Cohn. *SP*: Earl Felton. Based on characters created by Louis Joseph Vance. *CAST*: Warren William, Frances Robinson, Bruce Bennett, Eric Blore, Thurston Hall, Jed Prouty, Fred Kelsey, Don Beddoe, Lester Matthews, Edward Gargan, Eddie Laughton, Mary Servoss, Francis McDonald.

The Lone Wolf (William), in Havana, battles a gang of crooks as he tries to recover money stolen from a lady (Robinson) that was to be used to free her boyfriend (Bennett) from prison.

1166. The Lone Wolf Meets a Lady (5/3/40) B&W — 71 mins. (Mystery). *DIR*: Sidney Salkow. *PRO*:

Ralph Cohn. *SP*: John Larkin. Story by John Larkin, Wolfe Kaufman. Based on characters created by Louis Joseph Vance. *CAST*: Warren William, Jean Muir, Eric Blore, Victor Jory, Roger Pryor, Warren Hull, Thurston Hall, Fred Kelsey, Robert Emmett Keane, Georgia Caine, William Forrest, Marla Shelton, Bruce Bennett, Luis Alberni.

The Lone Wolf (William) comes to the aid of a young society girl (Muir) charged with murder, when her ex-husband (Hull) and his pal (Jory) steal her valuable necklace.

1167. The Lone Wolf Returns (8/25/26) B&W — 70 mins. (Mystery). *DIR*: Ralph Ince. *PRO*: Harry Cohn. *SP*: J. Grubb Alexander. Based on characters created by Louis Joseph Vance. *CAST*: Bert Lytell, Billie Dove, Freeman Wood, Gustav von Seyffertitz, Gwendolyn Lee, Alphonse Ethier.

The Lone Wolf (Lytell) sets out to help a lady (Dove) recover her stolen necklace.

1168. The Lone Wolf Returns (2/4/36) B&W — 68 mins. (Mystery). *DIR*: Roy William Neill. *SP*: Joseph Krumgold, Bruce Manning, Lionel Houser, Robert O'Connell. Based on a story by Louis Joseph Vance. *CAST*: Melvyn Douglas, Gail Patrick, Tala Birell, Henry Mollison, Thurston Hall, Raymond Walburn, Douglass Dumbrille, Nana Bryant, Robert Middlemass, Robert Emmett O'Conner, Wyrley Birch, Eddy Chandler, George McKay, Frank Reicher, Olaf Hytten, Roger Gray, Hal Price, Kernan Cripps, Lee Shumway, John Piccori, Arthur Loft, Eddie Fetherstone, Harry Harvey, Lloyd Whitlock.

The Lone Wolf (Douglas) goes after a master jewel thief (Dumbrille) and his mob.

1169. The Lone Wolf Spy Hunt (1/24/39) B&W — 67 mins. (Mystery). *DIR*: Peter Godfrey. *PRO*: Joseph Sis-

trom. *SP*: Jonathan Latimer. Based on *The Lone Wolf's Daughter* by Louis Joseph Vance. *CAST*: Warren William, Ida Lupino, Ralph Morgan, Rita Hayworth, Tom Dugan, Leonard Carey, Virginia Weidler, Don Beddoe, Ben Welden, Irving Bacon, Jack Norton, Marc Lawrence, James Craig, Lorna Gray, Edmund Cobb, I. Stanford Jolley, Edward Hearn, Eddie Fetherstone, Vernon Dent, Lee Phelps, Eddie Laughton, Bud Jamison, Brandon Tynen, Helen Lynd, John Tyrrell, Dick Curtis, Stanley Brown, Forbes Murray.

The Lone Wolf (William), forced to steal secret anti-aircraft plans, only steals half of the plans in order to track down the crooks with the help of his girlfriend (Lupino) and daughter (Weidler). *NOTES*: Warren William's debut as the Lone Wolf. A loose remake of the 1928 Columbia film *The Lone Wolf's Daughter*. [British title: *The Lone Wolf's Daughter*].

1170. The Lone Wolf Strikes (1/26/40) B&W — 57 mins. (Mystery). *DIR*: Sidney Salkow. *PRO*: Fred Kohlmar. *SP*: Harry Segall, Albert Duffy. Story by Dalton Trumbo. Based on characters created by Louis Joseph Vance. *CAST*: Warren William, Joan Perry, Eric Blore, Alan Baxter, Astrid Allwyn, Montague Love, Robert Wilcox, Don Beddoe, Fred Kelsey, Addison Richards, Roy Gordon, Harlan Tucker, Peter Lynn, Murray Alper, Edmund Cobb.

The Lone Wolf (William) helps an heiress (Perry) recover her diamond necklace and proves that her fiance (Wilcox) was part of the mob.

1171. The Lone Wolf Takes a Chance (3/6/41) B&W — 76 mins. (Mystery). *DIR*: Sidney Salkow. *PRO*: Ralph Cohn. *SP*: Sidney Salkow, Earl Felton. Based on characters created by Louis Joseph Vance. *CAST*: Warren

William, June Storey, Henry Wilcoxon, Eric Blore, Thurston Hall, Don Beddoe, Evalyn Knapp, Fred Kelsey, William Forrest, Lloyd Bridges, Walter Kingsford, Richard Fiske, Regis Toomey, Irving Bacon, Tom London, Ben Taggart.

The Lone Wolf (William) tries to stay out of trouble but gets involved in murder, the kidnapping of an inventor (Bridges), and the theft of stolen engraving plates.

1172. The Lone Wolf's Daughter (11/20/28) B&W — 72 mins. (Mystery). *DIR:* Albert S. Rogell. *PRO:* Harry Cohn. *SP:* Sig Herzig, Harry Revier. Based on characters created by Louis Joseph Vance. *CAST:* Bert Lytell, Gertrude Olmstead, Charles Gerrard, Lilyan Tashman, Donald Keith, Florence Allen, Robert Elliott, Ruth Cherrington.

The Lone Wolf (Lytell) travels to England to see his adopted daughter (Allen) and ends up stopping a jewel robbery and capturing two crooks (Gerrard, Tashman) wanted by Scotland Yard. *NOTES:* Released in silent (11/20/28) and sound versions (2/18/29).

1173. The Long Grey Line (2/9/55) Technicolor/Scope — 138 mins. (Biography). *DIR:* John Ford. *PRO:* Robert Arthur. *SP:* Edward Hope. Based on *Bringing Up the Brass* by Marty Maher, Nardi Reeder Champion. A Rotha Production. *CAST:* Tyrone Power, Maureen O'Hara, Robert Francis, Donald Crisp, Ward Bond, Betsy Palmer, Phil Carey, William Leslie, Harry Carey, Jr., Patrick Wayne, Sean McClory, Peter Graves, Milburn Stone, Erin O'Brien-Moore, Willis Bouchey, Walter D. Ehlers, Don Barclay, Martin Milner, Ken Curtis, Mickey Simpson, Pat O'Malley.

Told in flashback, Martin Maher (Power) becomes athletic director at West Point and lives out his life there.

1174. The Long Haul (12/57) B&W — 88 mins. (Drama). *DIR/SP:* Ken Hughes. *PRO:* Maxwell Setton. Based on the book by Mervyn Mills. A Marksman Production. *CAST:* Victor Mature, Gene Anderson, Patrick Allen, Diana Dors, Liam Redmond, Peter Reynolds, Michael Wade, Dervis Ward, Murray Kash, Jameson Clark, John Harvey, Roland Brand, Susan Campbell.

An ex-GI truck driver (Mature) gets involved with a racketeer (Allen) and his girl (Dors) when he stops a phony robbery. *NOTES:* Released to the European market at a running time of 100 mins.

1175. The Long Ships (6/64) Technicolor/Technirama — 124 mins. (Adventure). *DIR:* Jack Cardiff. *PRO:* Irving Allen. *SP:* Berkely Mather, Beverley Cross. Based on the book by Frans T. Bengtsson. A Warwick-Avala Production. *CAST:* Sidney Poitier, Richard Widmark, Rosanna Schiaffino, Russ Tamblyn, Oscar Homolka, Lionel Jeffries, Edward Judd, Beba Loncar, Clifford Evans, Colin Blakely, Gordon Jackson, David Lodge, Paul Stassino, Jeanne Moody.

A Viking (Widmark) adventurer and a Moorish chieftain (Poitier) clash as they search for the Golden Bell of St. James. [Original Yugoslavian title: *Dugi Brodovi*].

1176. The Looking Glass War (2/70) Technicolor/Panavision — 107 mins. (Spy-Drama). *DIR/SP:* Frank R. Pierson. *PRO:* John Box. Based on the book by John Le Carre. A Frankovich Production. *CAST:* Christopher Jones, Pia Degermark, Ralph Richardson, Paul Rogers, Anthony Hopkins, Susan George, Robert Urquhart, Maxine Audley, Anna Massey, Frederick Jaeger, Paul Maxwell, Guy Deghy.

A Polish refugee (Jones) is recruited by the head of British intelligence

(Richardson) to verify the existence of missile sites in East Germany.

1177. Lord Jim (6/65) Technicolor/Super Panavision 70—154 mins. (Drama). *DIR/PRO/SP:* Richard Brooks. Based on the book by Joseph Conrad. A Columbia-Keep Films Co-Production. *CAST:* Peter O'Toole, James Mason, Curt Jurgens, Eli Wallach, Paul Lukas, Jack Hawkins, Daliah Lavi, Akim Tamiroff, Andrew Keir, Jack MacGowran, Eric Young, Noel Purcell, Walter Gotell, A. J. Brown, Christian Marquand, Marne Maitland.

A sailor (O'Toole) is branded a coward when he jumps ship because he thinks it will sink during a storm. He redeems himself when he saves an island of natives from pirates and loses his life in an act of charity.

1178. The Lords of Flatbush (5/74) Eastman Color—86 mins. (Drama). *DIR:* Stephen F. Verona, Martin Davidson. *PRO:* Stephen F. Verona. *SP:* Gayle Glecker, Stephen F. Verona, Martin Davidson, Sylvester Stallone. *CAST:* Perry King, Sylvester Stallone, Henry Winkler, Paul Mace, Susan Blakely, Maria Smith, Renee Paris, Paul Jabara, Bruce Reed, Frank Stiefel, Martin Davidson, Joe Stern, Ruth Klinger, Joan Neumann, Dolph Sweet, Ray Sharkey, Armand Assanti, Margaret Bauer.

In 1950's Brooklyn, three members (King, Stallone, Winkler) of a social club, the Lords of Flatbush, try to avoid the breakup of their club when one of the members decides to marry.

1179. Lorna Doone (5/31/51) Technicolor—88 mins. (Drama). *DIR:* Phil Karlson. *PRO:* Edward Small. *SP:* Jesse L. Lasky, Jr., Richard Schayer. Adapted by George Bruce. Based on the book by Richard D. Blackmore. *CAST:* Barbara Hale, Richard Greene, Carl Benton Reid, William Bishop, Ron Randell, Sean McClory, Onslow Stevens, Lester Matthews, John Dehner, Dick Curtis, Anne Howard, Queenie Leonard, Trevor Bardette, Myron Healey, Harry Lauter, Leonard Mudie, Ray Teal, Fred Graham, Sherry Jackson, House Peters, Jr., Gloria Petroff, Orley Lindgren.

An English farmer (Greene) falls in love with Lorna Doone (Hale) while trying to overthrow her ruthless family.

1180. Loss of Innocence (10/61) Eastman Color—99 mins. (Romance-Drama). *DIR:* Lewis Gilbert. *PRO:* Victor Saville, Edward Small. *SP:* Howard Koch. Based on *The Greengage Summer* by Rumer Godden. A PKL Pictures Ltd. Production. *CAST:* Kenneth More, Danielle Darrieux, Susannah York, Claude Nollier, Jane Asher, Elizabeth Dear, Richard Williams, David Saire, Raymond Gerome, Maurice Denham, Andre Maranne, Harold Kasket, Jacques Brunius, Joy Shelton, Will Stamp.

A young British girl (York), staying at a French hotel, falls in love with a jewel thief (More) and inadvertently is responsible for his capture. [British title: *The Greengage Summer*].

1181. Lost and Found (7/79) Technicolor/Panavision—105 mins. (Comedy). *DIR/PRO:* Melvin Frank. *SP:* Melvin Frank, Jack Rose. *CAST:* George Segal, Glenda Jackson, Maureen Stapleton, Hollis McLaren, John Cunningham, Paul Sorvino, Kenneth Pogue, Janie Sell, John Candy, James Morris, Lois Maxwell, Leslie Carlson, Martin Short, Douglas Campbell.

A widowed professor (Segal) meets a divorced Englishwoman (Jackson) at a French ski resort and they decide to get married, only to find out they are incompatible.

1182. The Lost Command (5/66) Pathe Color/Panavision—129 mins. (Action-Adventure). *DIR/PRO:* Mark Robson. *SP:* Nelson Gidding. Based on *The Centurions* by Jean Larteguy. A Red Lion Production. *CAST:* Anthony Quinn, Alain Delon, George Segal, Michele Morgan, Maurice Ronet, Claudia Cardinale, Gregoire Aslan, Burt Kwouk, Jean Servais, Gordon Heath, Maurice Sarfati, Jean-Claude Bercq.

A French officer (Quinn) leads his old paratroop regiment in Algeria as they fight the Arabs and learn that a former member of their regiment (Segal) is the Arab's leader.

1183. Lost Horizon (2/17/37) B&W—118 mins. (Adventure-Drama). *DIR/PRO:* Frank Capra. *SP:* Robert Riskin. Based on the book by James Hilton. A Frank Capra Production. *CAST:* Ronald Colman, Jane Wyatt, John Howard, Margo, Thomas Mitchell, Edward Everett Horton, Isabel Jewell, H. B. Warner, Sam Jaffe, Hugh Buckler, David Torrence, Willie Fung, Wyrley Birch, Leonard Mudie, Noble Johnson, Carl Stockdale, Richard Loo.

A group of travelers are kidnapped and taken to the mountains of Tibet where they encounter the lost city of Shangri-La and its inhabitants. *NOTES:* Released in 1937 at a running time of 133 mins.

1184. Lost Horizon (3/73) Metrocolor/Panavision—150 mins. (Musical). *DIR:* Charles Jarrott. *PRO:* Ross Hunter. *SP:* Larry Kramer. Based on the book by James Hilton. *CAST:* Peter Finch, Liv Ullmann, Sally Kellerman, George Kennedy, Michael York, Olivia Hussey, Bobby Van, James Shigeta, Charles Boyer, John Gielgud, Larry Duran, Kent Smith, John Van Dreelan.

A group of travelers are kidnapped and taken to the mountains of Tibet where they encounter the lost city of Shangri-La and its inhabitants. *NOTES:* A musical remake of the 1937 Columbia film.

1185. The Lost One (La Traviata) (3/30/48) B&W—90 mins. (Opera). *DIR:* Carmine Gallone. *PRO:* Gregor Rabinovitch. *SP:* Hamilton Benz. Based on the libretto by Francisco Maria Piave and the opera *La Traviata* by Giuseppe Verdi. Based on *The Lady of the Camellias* by Alexandre Dumas. A Cineopera Production. *CAST:* Nelly Corradi, Gino Mattera, Manfredi Polverosi, Flora Marino, Carlo Lombardi, Massimo Serato, Nerio Bernardi.

A filmed version of the opera by Verdi. [Original Italian title: *La Signora dalle Camelie*].

1186. The Lost Tribe (4/19/49) B&W—72 mins. (Adventure). *DIR:* William Berke. *PRO:* Sam Katzman. *SP:* Arthur Hoerl, Don Martin. Based on the *Jungle Jim* newspaper comic strip created by Alex Raymond. *CAST:* Johnny Weissmuller, Myrna Dell, Joseph Vitale, Elena Verdugo, Nelson Leigh, Ralph Dunn, Paul Marion, George J. Lewis, Wally West, George DeNormand, Rube Schaffer.

Jungle Jim (Weissmuller) comes to the rescue of an African city when a couple of crooks (Verdugo, Dunn) seek to steal its treasure.

Lou Costello and His 30-Foot Bride *see* **The 30-Foot Bride of Candy Rock**

1187. Louisiana Hayride (9/1/44) B&W—67 mins. (Comedy). *DIR/PRO:* Charles Barton. *SP:* Paul Yawitz. Story by Paul Yawitz, Manny Seff. *CAST:* Judy Canova, Ross Hunter, Richard Lane, Lloyd Bridges, Matt Willis, George McKay, Minerva Urecal, Hobart Cavanaugh, Eddie Kane, Nelson Leigh, Arthur Loft, Russell Hicks, Si Jenks, Syd Saylor, Ernie Adams, Jack Rice, Bud Jamison, Lane Chandler, Eddy Chandler, Frank Hagney, Christine McIntyre, Jessie Arnold, Gene Roth, Art Miles.

A hillbilly girl (Canova) comes to Hollywood to pursue a film career and gets tangled up with a couple of con men (Lane, McKay).

1188. Love Affair (4/17/32) B&W—68 mins. (Drama). *DIR:* Thornton Freeland. *SP:* Jo Swerling, Dorothy Howell. Story by Ursula Parrott. *CAST:* Dorothy Mackaill, Humphrey Bogart, Jack Kennedy, Barbara Leonard, Astrid Allwyn, Bradley Page, Halliwell Hobbes, Hale Hamilton, Harold Minjir.

An aviator (Bogart) falls for a wealthy heiress (Mackaill) and tries to get her to back his new engine design. *NOTES:* Humphrey Bogart's first Columbia film.

1189. Love and Pain and the Whole Darn Thing (4/73) Eastman Color—110 mins. (Drama). *DIR/PRO:* Alan J. Pakula. *SP:* Alvin Sargent. *CAST:* Maggie Smith, Timothy Bottoms, Jaime de Mora y Aragon, Charles Baxter, Margaret Modlin, May Heatherly, Lloyd Brimhall, Elmer Modlin.

An American (Bottoms), on vacation in Spain, has a doomed affair with an aging spinster (Smith).

1190. Love Has Many Faces (3/65) Eastman Color—104 mins. (Drama). *DIR:* Alexander Singer. *PRO:* Jerry Bresler. *SP:* Marguerite Roberts. *CAST:* Lana Turner, Cliff Robertson, Hugh O'Brian, Ruth Roman, Stefanie Powers, Virginia Grey, Ron Husmann, Enrique Lucero, Carlos Montalban, Jamie Bravo, Fannie Schiller, Rene Dupreyon.

In Acapulco, a wealthy woman (Turner) tries to win back her beachboy husband (Robertson) when he begins to show interest in a younger woman (Powers).

1191. A Love in Germany (11/84) Eastman Color—110 mins. (War-Drama). *DIR:* Andrzej Wajda. *PRO:* Arthur Brauner. *SP:* Andrzej Wajda, Boleslaw Michalek, Agnieszka Holland. Based on the book by Rolf Hochhuth. A Triumph Films Production. *CAST:* Hanna Schygulla, Marie-Christine Barrault, Armin Mueller-Stahl, Elisabeth Trissenaar, Daniel Olbrychski, Piotr Lysak, Gerard Desarthe, Bernhard Wicki, Ralf Wolter, Otto Sander, Ben Becker, Serge Merlin.

A German woman (Schygulla) tries to hide her love for a Polish laborer (Lysak) in Germany during World War II. *NOTES:* Limited theatrical release. In German and French with English subtitles. [Original French title: *Un Amour en Allemagne*]. [Original German title: *Eine Liebe in Deutschland*].

1192. The Love-Ins (8/67) Pathe Color—85 mins. (Drama). *DIR:* Arthur Dreifuss. *PRO:* Sam Katzman. *SP:* Hal Collins, Arthur Dreifuss. A Four Leaf Production. *CAST:* Richard Todd, James MacArthur, Susan Oliver, Mark Goddard, Carol Booth, Marc Cavell, Janee Michelle, Ronnie Eckstine, Michael Evans, Hortense Petra, James Lloyd, Mario Roccuzzo, Joe Pyne, The Chocolate Watch Band, The U.F.O.'s, The New Age, Donnie Brooks.

In the 1960's, a college professor (Todd) resigns his position and moves in with a couple of his students (MacArthur, Oliver) when they are expelled.

1193. The Love Machine (8/71) Eastman Color—108 mins. (Drama). *DIR:* Jack Haley, Jr. *PRO:* M. J. Frankovich. *SP:* Samuel Taylor. Based on the book by Jacqueline Susann. *CAST:* John Phillip Law, Dyan Cannon, Robert Ryan, Jackie Cooper, David Hemmings, Shecky Greene, Alexandra Hay, Jodi Wexler, William Roerick, Sharon Farrell, Clinton Grey, Gregg Mullavey, Claudia Jennings, Ann Ford, Madeleine Collinson, Mary Collinson, Gayle Hunnicutt.

The wife (Cannon) of a top TV executive (Ryan) uses her influence to push a TV newsman (Law) to the top, and once there he doesn't care whom he uses for his self-gain.

1194. Love Me Forever (6/26/35) B&W—91 mins. (Crime-Musical). DIR: Victor Schertzinger. SP: Jo Swerling, Sidney Buchman. Story by Victor Schertzinger. CAST: Grace Moore, Leo Carrillo, Michael Bartlett, Robert Allen, Spring Byington, Thurston Hall, Douglas Dumbrille, Luis Alberni, Gavin Gordon, Harry Barris, Arthur Kaye.

A mobster (Carrillo) falls for an opera singer (Moore), promotes her career, and builds a nightclub for her, but loses her to another man (Bartlett). [British title: On Wings of Song].

1195. Love on a Pillow (12/63) Eastman Color/Scope—102 mins. (Drama). DIR: Roger Vadim. PRO: Francis Cosne. SP: Roger Vadim, Claude Choublier. Based on Les Repos de Guerrier by Christine Rochefort. A Francos-Incei-Royal Films International Production. CAST: Brigitte Bardot, Robert Hossein, James Robertson Justice, Macha Meril, Yves Barsacq, Jacqueline Porel, Jean-Marc Bory, Michel Serrault.

A young woman (Bardot) goes to Dijon, France, to collect an inheritance and, while there, falls in love with an alcoholic (Hossein), whom she saves from a suicide attempt. [Original French title: Le Repos du Guerrier]. [Original Italian title: Il Riposo del Guerriero].

Love—Tahiti Style see **Nude Odyssey**

1196. Lover Come Back (6/7/31) B&W—73 mins. (Drama). DIR: Erle C. Kenton. SP: Robert Shannon, Dorothy Howell. Story by Helen Topping Miller. CAST: Constance Cummings, Jack Mulhall, Betty Bronson,

Jameson Thomas, Fred Santley, Jack Mack, Kathryn Givney, Loretta Sayers, Susan Fleming.

When a man (Mulhall) learns that his wife (Bronson) is having an affair with another man (Thomas), he divorces her and returns to his true love (Cummings).

1197. The Loves of Carmen (8/23/48) Technicolor—99 mins. (Drama). DIR/PRO: Charles Vidor. SP: Helen Deutsch. Based on Carmen by Prosper Merimee. A Beckwith Production. CAST: Rita Hayworth, Glenn Ford, Ron Randell, Victor Jory, Luther Adler, Arnold Moss, Joseph Buloff, Margaret Wycherly, Bernard Nedell, John Baragrey, Philip Van Zandt, Anthony Dante, Leona Roberts, Francis Pierlot, Trevor Bardette, Paul Marion.

In 1820's Seville, Spain, a corporal (Ford) falls for a gypsy girl (Hayworth), becomes a criminal when he kills a fellow officer (Moss) in a fight, and eventually kills the gypsy and her husband (Jory).

1198. Lovin' Molly (3/74) Eastman Color—98 mins. (Drama). DIR: Sidney Lumet. PRO/SP: Stephen J. Friedman. Based on Leaving Cheyenne by Larry McMurtry. CAST: Anthony Perkins, Blythe Danner, Beau Bridges, Susan Sarandon, Edward Binns, John Henry Faulk, Conrad Fowkes, Claude Traverse.

In Texas, between 1925 and 1945, two men (Perkins, Bridges) share a lifelong long love and relationship with the same woman (Danner).

1199. Loving (3/70) Eastman Color—89 mins. (Comedy-Drama). DIR: Irving Kershner. PRO/SP: Don Devlin. Based on Brooks Wilson, Ltd. by J. M. Ryan. CAST: George Segal, Eva Marie Saint, Sterling Hayden, Keenan Wynn, Janis Young, Nancie Phillips, David Doyle, Andrew Duncan, Sherry Lansing, Roland Winters, Edgar Stehli, Roy Scheider, William Duffy, John Fink, Diana Douglas.

A commercial artist (Segal) reaches a crisis point as he vacillates between his wife (Saint), mistress (Young), and landing a large account.

1200. Lucky Legs (10/1/1942) B&W−64 mins. (Comedy). *DIR:* Charles Barton. *PRO:* Wallace Mac-Donald. *SP:* Stanley Rubin, Jack Hart-field. *CAST:* Jinx Falkenburg, Leslie Brooks, Kay Harris, Elizabeth Patterson, Russell Hayden, William Wright, Don Beddoe, Adele Rowland, Edward Marr, George McKay, Eddie Kane, Shirley Patterson, Richard Talmadge, Adele Mara, John Tyrrell, Romaine Callender, Ethan Laidlaw, Jack Rice, Frank Sully.

A woman (Falkenburg) finds she gets more than she bargained for when she inherits a million dollars.

1201. Lulu Belle (6/11/48) B&W−86 mins. (Musical-Drama). *DIR:* Leslie Fenton. *PRO:* Benedict Bogeaus. *SP:* Everett Freeman, Karl Kamb. Based on the play by Charles MacArthur, Edward Shelton. *CAST:* Dorothy Lamour, George Montgomery, Albert Dekker, Otto Kruger, Greg McClure, Glenda Farrell, Charlotte Wynters, Addison Richards, William Haade, Ben Erway, Clancy Cooper.

In 1900, a Broadway star (Lamour) is shot and her rise from saloon singer to Broadway star is told in flashback.

1202. The Lure of the Wild (12/12/25) B&W−58 mins. (Adventure-Drama). *DIR:* Frank R. Strayer. *PRO:* Harry Cohn. *SP:* Thomas J. Hopkins. *CAST:* Jane Novak, Alan Roscoe, Billie Jean, Richard Tucker, Mario Carillo, Pat Harmon, "Lightning," the dog.

In the Canadian wilds, the young daughter (Jean) of a murdered man (Roscoe) is protected by a dog until she is found.

1203. Lust for Gold (5/31/49) B&W−90 mins. (Western). *DIR/PRO:* S. Sylvan Simon. *SP:* Ted Sherdeman, Richard English. Based on *Thunder God's Gold* by Barry Storm. *CAST:* Glenn Ford, Ida Lupino, Gig Young, William Prince, Edgar Buchanan, Will Geer, Paul Ford, Jay Silverheels, Eddy Waller, Tom Tyler, Hayden Rorke, Paul E. Burns, Will Wright, Virginia Mullen, Antonio Moreno, Myrna Dell, Elspeth Dudgeon, George Chesebro, Arthur Space, Edmund Cobb, Richard Alexander, Arthur Hunnicutt, Fred F. Sears, Kermit Maynard, Percy Helton.

A young man (Prince) searches for the Lost Dutchman mine discovered by his grandfather (Ford), while the story of the mine's discovery is told in flashback. *NOTES:* The name of the main character (Prince) was Barry Storm, the same name as the author of the story the film was based on.

1204. Luv (8/67) Eastman Color/Panavision−93 mins. (Comedy). *DIR:* Clive Donner. *PRO:* Martin Manulis. *SP:* Elliott Baker. Based on the play by Murray Schisgal. *CAST:* Jack Lemmon, Peter Falk, Elaine May, Nina Wayne, Eddie Mayhoff, Paul Hartman, Severn Darden, Alan DeWitt.

In the hopes of relieving himself of his neurotic wife (May) and marrying his mistress (Wayne), a man (Falk) brings home a suicidal derelict (Lemmon) and introduces the derelict to his wife.

1205. M (3/5/51) B&W−88 mins. (Crime). *DIR:* Joseph Losey. *PRO:*

Seymour Nebenzal. *SP:* Norman Reilly Raine, Leo Katcher, Waldo Salt. Based on the screenplay by Thea von Harbou, Fritz Lang, Paul Falkenberg, Adolf Jansen, Karl Vash, and based on an article by Egon Jackson. A Seymour Picture Production. *CAST:* David Wayne, Howard Da Silva, Luther Adler, Martin Gabel, Steve Brodie, Raymond Burr, Glenn Anders, Karen Morley, Norman Lloyd, John Miljan, Walter Burke, Roy Engel, Jim Backus, Benny Burt.

In Los Angeles, a psychotic child murderer (Wayne) eludes the police but is caught by the city's criminals who find that his activities are giving them a bad name. *NOTES:* A remake of Fritz Lang's 1931 German masterpiece, *M.*

1206. Macbeth (12/71) Technicolor/Todd-AO 35 — 140 mins. (Drama). *DIR:* Roman Polanski. *PRO:* Andrew Braunsberg. *SP:* Roman Polanski, Kenneth Tynan. Based on the play by William Shakespeare. A Playboy Production. *CAST:* Jon Finch, Francesca Annis, Martin Shaw, Nicholas Selby, John Stride, Stephan Chase, Paul Shelley, Andrew Laurence, Terence Bayler, Frank Wylie, Vic Abbott, Bill Drysdale, Bernard Archard.

An extremely violent and atmospheric re-telling of Shakespeare's tragedy of a young Scot (Finch) lusting for power who is driven on by his crazed wife (Annis) and prophecies.

1207. Machine Gun McCain (9/70) Technicolor/Scope — 94 mins. (Crime). *DIR:* Giuliano Montaldo. *PRO:* Marco Vicario, Bino Cicogna. *SP:* Mino Roli, Giuliano Montaldo. Based on *Candyleg* by Ovid Demaris. A Euroatlantica Production. *CAST:* John Cassavetes, Britt Ekland, Peter Falk, Gabriele Ferzetti, Salvo Randone, Gena Rowlands, Pierluigi Apra,

Jim Morrison, Tony Kendall, Val Avery, Jack Ackerman, Claudio Biava, Luigi Pistilli, Florinda Bolkan, Stephen Zacharias.

A gangster (Cassavetes) is chased by the Mafia when he robs a Las Vegas casino. *NOTES:* Originally filmed in Italy in 1968. [Original Italian title: *Gli Intoccabili*].

1208. MacKenna's Gold (5/69) Technicolor/Super Panavision 70 — 128 mins. (Western). *DIR:* J. Lee Thompson. *PRO/SP:* Carl Foreman. Based on the book by Will Henry. A Highroad Production. *CAST:* Gregory Peck, Camilla Sparv, Omar Sharif, Julie Newmar, Keenan Wynn, Telly Savalas, Dick Peabody, Ted Cassidy, Eduardo Ciannelli, Lee J. Cobb, Burgess Meredith, Edward G. Robinson, Anthony Quayle, Eli Wallach, Raymond Massey, Trevor Bardette, Rudy Diaz, Robert Phillips, Shelley Morrison, J. Robert Porter, John Garfield, Jr., Pepe Callahan, Madeline Taylor-Holmes, Duke Hobbie. Narrated by Victor Jory.

A dying Indian (Ciannelli) entrusts a sheriff (Peck) with a map of the legendary Valley of Gold and every treasure hunter in the territory wants to be part of the hunt for the Valley.

1209. McKenna of the Mounted (8/26/32) B&W — 66 mins. (Western). *DIR:* D. Ross Lederman. *SP:* Stuart Anthony. Story by Randall Faye. *CAST:* Buck Jones, Greta Granstedt, James Glavin, Walter McGrail, Niles Welch, Mitchell Lewis, Claude King, Glenn Strange, Bud Osborne, Edmund Cobb.

A Mountie (Jones), framed and kicked out of the Mounties, joins an outlaw band in order to prove his innocence and bring the outlaws to justice.

1210. Mad Dog Coll (5/61) B&W — 88 mins. (Biography-Crime).

DIR: Burt Balaban. *PRO/SP:* Edward Schreiber. Based on material by Leo Lieberman. *CAST:* John Davis Chandler, Neil Nephew, Brooke Hayward, Joy Harmon, Jerry Orbach, Telly Savalas, Glenn Cannon, Tom Castronova, Kay Doubleday, Vincent Gardenia, Ron Weyland, Peggy Furey, Gene Hackman, Stephanie King, Gilbert Leigh.

Vincent "Mad Dog" Coll (Chandler) starts a gang war to take over the mob and bootlegging business of Dutch Schultz (Gardenia). *NOTES:* John Davis Chandler's film debut; Gene Hackman's first bit part.

1211. The Mad Magician (5/54) B&W/3-D—72 mins. (Horror). *DIR:* John Brahm. *PRO:* Bryan Foy. *SP:* Crane Wilbur. *CAST:* Vincent Price, Mary Murphy, Eva Gabor, John Emery, Donald Randolph, Lenita Lane, Patrick O'Neal, Jay Novello.

A magician (Price) goes berserk and becomes homicidal when his best kept secrets and wife (Gabor) are stolen by a rival magician (Emery). *NOTES:* Columbia's last 3-D feature until the 80's.

1212. Mad Men of Europe (6/26/40) B&W—79 mins. (Spy-Drama). *DIR:* Albert de Courville. *PRO:* Neville E. Neville. *SP:* Ian Hay, Edward Knoblock, Rodney Ackland, Bob Edmunds, Dennis Wheatley, Dora Nirva, Clifford Grey, Richard Llewellyn. Based on a play by Guy du Maurier. An Aldwych Production. *CAST:* Edmund Gwenn, Mary Maguire, Paul Henreid, Geoffrey Toone, Richard Ainley, Desmond Tester, Carl Jaffe, Meinhart Maur, Mavis Villiers, Mark Lester, Norah Howard, John Wood.

A Nazi spy (Henreid) sneaks into England to pinpoint British targets and is unwittingly harbored by a British family. [British title: *An Englishman's Home*].

1213. The Mad Room (4/69) Pathe Color—93 mins. (Drama). *DIR:* Bernard Girard. *PRO:* Norman Maurer. *SP:* A. Z. Martin, Bernard Girard. Based on the screenplay by Garrett Elsden Fort, Reginald Denham, and based on the play *Ladies in Retirement* by Reginald Denham. *CAST:* Stella Stevens, Shelley Winters, Skip Ward, Carol Cole, Severn Darden, Beverly Garland, Michael Burns, Barbara Sammeth, Jennifer Bishop, Gloria Manon, Lloyd Haynes, Lou Kane.

A companion (Stevens) murders her employer (Winters) so that her demented brother (Burns) and sister (Sammeth) will have a home. *NOTES:* A remake of the 1941 Columbia film *Ladies in Retirement*.

1214. Made in Italy (5/67) Technicolor/Scope—101 mins. (Comedy). *DIR:* Nanni Loy. *PRO:* Gianni Hecht Lucari. *SP:* Ettore Scola, Ruggero Maccari, Nanni Loy. Story by Ettore Scola, Ruggero Maccari. A Documento-Orsay-Royal Films International Production. *CAST:* Marina Breti, Claudio Gora, Lando Buzzanca, Iolanda Modio, Walter Chiari, Virna Lisi, Catherine Spaak, Sylva Koscina, Jean Sorel, Nino Manfredi, Rosella Falk, Alberto Sordi, Anna Magnani, Lea Massari, Fabrizio Moroni.

A series of vignettes illustrating the ups and downs of life in modern-day Italy. [Original Italian title: *A l'Italienne*].

1215. Madonna of the Streets (11/30/30) B&W—79 mins. (Drama). *DIR:* John S. Robertson. *PRO:* Harry Cohn. *SP:* Jo Swerling. Based on *The Ragged Messenger* by William B. Maxwell. *CAST:* Evelyn Brent, Robert Ames, Ivan Linlow, Josephine Dunn, Zack Williams, J. Edwards Davis, Ed Brady, Richard Tucker.

The mistress (Brent) of a tycoon finds herself penniless after he is killed and searches for his heir (Ames) as her meal ticket.

1216. The Magic Carpet (10/51) Super CineColor—84 mins. (Adventure). DIR: Lew Landers. PRO: Sam Katzman. SP: David Mathews. An Eskay Production. CAST: Lucille Ball, John Agar, Patricia Medina, George Tobias, Raymond Burr, Gregory Gay, Rick Vallin, Jo Gilbert, William Fawcett, Doretta Johnson, Linda Williams, Perry Sheehan, Eileen Howe.

A deposed prince (Agar) enlists the aid of a harem girl (Ball) as he fights to regain his throne from an evil vizier (Burr).

1217. The Magic Face (9/1/51) B&W—88 mins. (War-Drama). DIR: Frank Tuttle. PRO/SP: Mort Briskin, Robert Smith. CAST: Luther Adler, Patricia Knight, William L. Shirer, Ilka Windish, Heinz Moog, Jasper Von Oertzen, Charles Koenig, Toni Mitterwurzer, Annie Maiers, Herman Ehrhardt.

A master German impersonator (Adler) is captured by the Nazis, escapes his captors, kills Hitler, and takes his place to deliberately lead Germany to defeat.

1218. The Magic World of Topo Gigio (1/66) Eastman Color—75 mins. (Children-Puppets). DIR: Luca De Rico. PRO: Richard Davis. SP: Maria Perego, Guido Stagnaro, Mario Faustinelli. A Richard Davis-Jolly Film Production. CAST: Voices of Peppino Mazzulo, Ermanno Roveri, Ignazio Colnaghi, Federica Milani, Armando Benetti, Ignazio Dolce, Milena Zini, Carlo Delfini.

Topo Gigio, the Italian mouse, and his two friends end up at an amusement park and become the stars of a puppet show. [Original Italian title: *Le Avventure di Topo Gigio*].

The Magnificent Seven *see* **Seven Samurai**

1219. A Maiden for a Prince (9/67) Technicolor/Scope—92 mins. (Comedy). DIR: Pasquale Festa Campanile. PRO: Mario Cecchi Gori. SP: Giorgio Prosperi, Stefano Strucchi, Ugo Liberatore, Pasquale Festa Campanile. A Fair-Orsay-Royal Films International Production. CAST: Vittorio Gassman, Virna Lisi, Philippe Leroy, Tino Buazzelli, Maria Grazia Buccella, Vittorio Caprioli, Paola Barboni, Anna Maria Guarnieri, Luciano Mandolfo.

In 16th century Italy, a prince (Gassman) must prove his manhood with the women or lose his fortune. [Original French title: *Une Vierge pour le Prince*]. [Original Italian title: *Una Vergine per il Principe*].

1220. The Main Event (6/22/38) B&W—55 mins. (Action-Drama). DIR: Danny Dare. PRO: Ralph Cohn. SP: Lee Loeb. Story by Harold Shumate. CAST: Robert Paige, Jacqueline Wells (Julie Bishop), Arthur Loft, John Gallaudet, Thurston Hall, Gene Morgan, Dick Curtis, Oscar O'Shea, Pat Flaherty, John Tyrrell, Nick Copeland, Lester Dorr.

A detective (Paige) tracks down a fighter (Morgan) that has faked his own kidnapping on the eve of the big fight.

1221. Major Dundee (4/65) Eastman Color/Panavision—134 mins. (Western). DIR: Sam Peckinpah. PRO: Jerry Bresler. SP: Harry Julian Fink, Oscar Saul, Sam Peckinpah. Story by Harry Julian Fink. CAST: Charlton Heston, Senta Berger, Richard Harris, Warren Oates, Jim Hutton, Brock Peters, James Coburn, Ben Johnson, Michael Anderson, Jr., L. Q. Jones, R. G. Armstrong, Slim Pickens, Karl Swenson, Michael Pate, Dub Taylor,

Mario Adorf, John Davis Chandler, Albert Carter, Jose Carlos Ruiz, Aurora Clavell, Regonia Palacious, Enrique Lucero, Francisco Reyguera.

A Union officer (Heston) leads a renegade bunch of Confederate prisoners into Mexico after marauding Apaches.

1222. Make Believe Ballroom (4/1/49) B&W—79 mins. (Musical). *DIR:* Joseph Santley. *PRO:* Ted Richmond. *SP:* Albert Duffy, Karen De-Wolf. Story by Albert Duffy. Based on the radio program by Al Jarvis, Martin Block. *CAST:* Jerome Courtland, Ruth Warrick, Ron Randell, Virginia Welles, Al Jarvis, Adele Jergens, Paul Harvey, Louis Jean Heydt, Frank Orth, Vernon Dent, Sid Tomack, Frankie Laine, Charlie Barnet, The Nat "King" Cole Trio, Jimmy Dorsey, Toni Harper, Jan Garber, Jack Smith, Pee Wee Hunt, Kay Starr, Gene Krupa, The Sportsmen, Ray McKinley.

Two collegiate carhops (Courtland, Welles) enter a musical quiz show and win the top prize.

1223. Maker of Men (12/24/31) B&W—71 mins. (Drama). *DIR:* Edward Sedgwick. *PRO:* Harry Cohn. *SP:* Howard J. Green. Story by Edward Sedgwick, Howard J. Green. *CAST:* Jack Holt, Joan Marsh, Richard Cromwell, Robert Alden, John Wayne, Walter Catlett, Natalie Moorhead, Ethel Wales, Richard Tucker, Mike McKay.

A football coach (Holt) forces his son (Cromwell) to play for the team in the crucial game of the season and his bad playing brings defeat to the team. The son then goes to a rival college and wins the game from his father's team.

1224. Making the Headlines (3/10/38) B&W—60 mins. (Mystery). *DIR:* Lewis D. Collins. *PRO:* Larry

Darmour. *SP:* Howard J. Green, Jefferson Parker. Story by Howard J. Green. *CAST:* Jack Holt, Beverly Roberts, Craig Reynolds, Marjorie Gateson, Tom Kennedy, Dorothy Appleby, Gilbert Emery, Corbet Morris, Sheila Bromley, John Wray, Maurice Cass, Tully Marshall.

A cop (Holt) is sent to another district when he receives too much press from a reporter (Roberts) and becomes involved in a double murder.

1225. Man Against Woman (12/17/32) B&W—70 mins. (Crime-Drama). *DIR:* Irving Cummings. *SP:* Jo Swerling. Story by Keene Thompson. *CAST:* Jack Holt, Lillian Miles, Walter Connolly, Gavin Gordon, Arthur Vinton, Jack LaRue, Clarence Muse, Emmett Corrigan, Harry Seymour, Katherine Claire Ward.

A detective (Holt), in love with a mobster's girl (Miles), frames the mobster (Gordon) to get the girl. When she helps her mobster boyfriend escape from the detective while en route to prison, he vows justice and pursues them both.

1226. The Man Called Flintstone (8/66) Eastman Color—90 mins. (Animated). *DIR/PRO:* Joseph Barbera, William Hanna. *SP:* Harvey Bullock, Ray S. Allen. Story and material by Harvey Bullock, Ray S. Allen, William Hanna, Joseph Barbera, Warren Foster, Alex Lovy. *CAST:* Voices of Alan Reed, Mel Blanc, Jean Vander Pyl, Gerry Johnson, Don Messick, Janet Waldo, Paul Frees, Harvey Korman, John Stephenson, June Foray.

Fred Flintstone, who resembles secret agent Rock Slag, is recruited by the Stone Age Secret Service to go to Paris and locate the Green Goose, the head of SMIRK.

1227. A Man Called Sledge (3/71) Technicolor—93 mins. (Western).

DIR: Vic Morrow. *PRO:* Dino De Laurentiis. *SP:* Vic Morrow, Frank Kowalski. *CAST:* James Garner, Dennis Weaver, Claude Akins, John Marley, Wade Preston, Laura Antonelli, Ken Clark, Tony Young.

A bandit (Garner) and his henchman (Weaver) seek revenge against the outlaws who stole their gold.

1228. A Man for All Seasons (12/66) Technicolor—120 mins. (Drama). *DIR/PRO:* Fred Zinnemann. *SP:* Robert Bolt, Constance Willis. Based on the play by Robert Bolt. A Highland Production. *CAST:* Paul Scofield, Wendy Hiller, Leo McKern, Robert Shaw, Orson Welles, Susannah York, Nigel Davenport, John Hurt, Vanessa Redgrave, Colin Blakely, Corin Redgrave, John Nettleton, Paul Hardwick.

Sir Thomas More's (Scofield) opposition to Henry VIII's (Shaw) divorce and formation of the Church of England eventually leads to his execution.

1229. The Man from Chicago (11/31) B&W—74 mins. (Crime-Drama). *DIR:* Walter Summers. *PRO:* John Maxwell. *SP:* Walter Summers, Walter Mycroft. Based on *Speed* by Reginald Berkeley. A British International Pictures Production. *CAST:* Bernard Nedell, Dodo Watts, Joyce Kennedy, Morris Harvey, Albert Whelan, Austin Trevor, Billy Milton, O. B. Clarence, Dennis Hoey, Ben Welden, Leonard Dainton, Syd Crossley, Frederick Lloyd, Matthew Boulton.

An American criminal (Nedell) is trailed by Scotland Yard when he robs a bank and kills a policeman.

1230. The Man from Colorado (11/18/48) Technicolor—99 mins. (Western). *DIR:* Henry Levin. *PRO:* Jules Schermer. *SP:* Robert D. Andrews, Ben Maddow. Story by Borden Chase. *CAST:* Glenn Ford, Ellen Drew, William Holden, Edgar Bu-

chanan, Jim Bannon, Ray Collins, Jerome Courtland, William "Bill" Phillips, Myron Healey, Ian MacDonald, Denver Pyle, James Millican, Craig Reynolds, Mikel Conrad, James Bush, David Clarke, Clarence Chase, Stanley Andrews, David York, Eddie Fetherstone, Symona Boniface, Pat O'Malley.

A sadistic Civil War colonel (Ford) is appointed federal judge of the Colorado territory with his former aide as marshal (Holden), who tries to keep him in line, but rebels when the judge teeters on the brink of insanity.

1231. The Man from Laramie (8/55) Technicolor/Scope—104 mins. (Western). *DIR:* Anthony Mann. *PRO:* William Goetz. *SP:* Philip Yordan, Frank Burt. Story by Thomas T. Flynn. *CAST:* James Stewart, Cathy O'Donnell, Arthur Kennedy, Donald Crisp, Alex Nicol, Aline MacMahon, Wallace Ford, Jack Elam, Boyd Stockman, Gregg Barton, Frank DeKova, James Millican, John War Eagle, Eddy Waller.

A wandering cowboy (Stewart) searches for his brother's killer and ends up in the middle of a range war between two ranchers (Crisp, MacMahon).

1232. The Man from Sundown (7/15/39) B&W—58 mins. (Western). *DIR:* Sam Nelson. *PRO:* Harry L. Decker. *SP:* Paul Franklin. *CAST:* Charles Starrett, Iris Meredith, Bob Nolan, Dick Curtis, Richard Fiske, Jack Rockwell, Edward J. LeSaint, Clem Horton, Ernie Adams, Dick Botiller, George Chesebro, Frank Ellis, Al Bridge, Tex Cooper, Al Haskell, Edward Piel, Sr., Robert Fiske, Forrest Dillon, Kit Guard, Oscar Gahan, Sons of the Pioneers.

A cowboy (Starrett), with the help of a rancher's daughter (Meredith), goes after a ruthless outlaw and his gang. [British title: *A Woman's Vengeance*].

1233. The Man from the Diner's Club (4/63/) B&W—93 mins. (Comedy). *DIR*: Frank Tashlin. *PRO*: Bill Bloom. *SP*: William Peter Blatty. Story by William Peter Blatty, John Fenton Murray. A Dena Pictures-Ampersand Production. *CAST*: Danny Kaye, Cara Williams, Martha Hyer, Telly Savalas, Everett Sloane, Kay Stevens, Howard Caine, George Kennedy, Jay Novello, Ann Morgan Guilbert, Ronald Long, Mark Tobin, Edmund Williams, Harry Dean Stanton, Cliff Carnell.

A clerk (Kaye) at the Diner's Club inadvertently issues a credit card to a notorious gangster (Savalas), and makes a desperate effort to get it back.

1234. The Man from Tumbleweeds (6/14/40) B&W—59 mins. (Western). *DIR*: Joseph H. Lewis. *PRO*: Leon Barsha. *SP*: Charles F. Royal. *CAST*: Bill Elliott, Iris Meredith, Raphael Bennett, Dub Taylor, Stanley Brown, Edward J. LeSaint, Richard Fiske, Ernie Adams, Al Hill, Don Beddoe, Eddie Laughton, Edward Cecil, Jack Low, John Tyrrell, Buel Bryant, Olin Francis, Jay Lawrence, Francis Walker.

Wild Bill Saunders (Elliott) recruits prisoners from the local penitentiary to clean up a town when the local citizens refuse to help.

1235. Man in the Dark (4/8/53) B&W/3-D—70 mins. (Crime). *DIR*: Lew Landers. *PRO*: Wallace MacDonald. *SP*: George Bricker, Jack Leonard, William B. Sackheim. Story by Tom Van Dycke, Henry Altimus. *CAST*: Edmond O'Brien, Audrey Totter, Ted de Corsia, Horace MacMahon, Nick Dennis, Dayton Lummis, Dan Riss, Shepard Menken, John Harmon, Ruth Warren.

A mobster (O'Brien) has plastic surgery and his memory altered to forget his past, but his former gang kidnaps him and tries to force him to remember where he has hidden his stolen loot. *NOTES*: A remake of the 1936 Columbia film *The Man Who Lived Twice*. This picture was Columbia's first 3-D feature, the first 3-D feature to be released by a major studio, and the second 3-D feature to be released in the 1950's.

1236. Man in the Saddle (12/2/51) Technicolor—87 mins. (Western). *DIR*: Andre De Toth. *PRO*: Harry Joe Brown. *SP*: Kenneth Gamet. Story by Ernest Haycox. A Scott-Brown Production. *CAST*: Randolph Scott, Joan Leslie, Ellen Drew, Alexander Knox, John Russell, Guinn "Big Boy" Williams, Alfonso Bedoya, Don Beddoe, Cameron Mitchell, Clem Bevans, Richard Crane, Tennessee Ernie Ford, Richard Rober, Frank Sully, George Lloyd, James Kirkwood, Frank Hagney.

A rancher (Scott), forced off the range by his neighbor (Knox), takes to the hills with the local schoolteacher (Drew), but must eventually settle the score with his neighbor. [British title: *The Outcast*].

1237. The Man Inside (12/58) B&W/Scope—97 mins. (Crime). *DIR*: John Gilling. *PRO*: Irving Allen, Albert R. Broccoli, Harold Huth. *SP*: Richard Maibaum, David Shaw, John Gilling. Based on the book by M. E. Chaber. A Warwick Films Production. *CAST*: Jack Palance, Anita Ekberg, Nigel Patrick, Anthony Newley, Bonar Colleano, Sean Kelly, Sidney James, Donald Pleasence, Eric Pohlmann, Gerard Heinz, Josephine Brown, Anne Aubrey, Bill Shine, Walter Gotell.

A private investigator (Palance), a girl (Ekberg), and two hoodlums (Kelly, Colleano) chase a diamond thief (Patrick) across Europe. *NOTES*: The last film of Bonar Colleano.

1238. Man of Action (1/20/33) B&W—57 mins. (Western). DIR: George Melford. SP: Robert Quigley. Story by William Colt MacDonald. CAST: Tim McCoy, Caryl Lincoln, Wheeler Oakman, Stanley Blystone, Walter Brennan, Charles K. French, Julian Rivero.

A ranger (McCoy) sets out on the trail of bank robbers.

1239. Man on a String (5/60) B&W—92 mins. (Spy-Drama). DIR: Andre De Toth. PRO: Louis deRochemont. SP: John Kafka, Virginia Shaler. Based on *Ten Years a Counterspy* by Boris Morris and Charles Samuels. CAST: Ernest Borgnine, Kerwin Mathews, Colleen Dewhurst, Glenn Corbett, Alexander Scourby, Vladimir Sokoloff, Friedrich Joloff, Richard Kendrick, Ed Prentiss, Carl Jaffe.

A Russian born American citizen (Borgnine), spying for the Soviets, is pressured by the U.S. to become a double agent. [British title: *Confessions of a Counterspy*].

1240. The Man They Could Not Hang (9/28/39) B&W—64 mins. (Horror). DIR: Nick Grinde. PRO: Wallace MacDonald. SP: Karl Brown. Story by Leslie T. White, George W. Sayre. CAST: Boris Karloff, Lorna Gray, Robert Wilcox, Roger Pryor, Don Beddoe, Ann Doran, Joseph DeStephani, Dick Curtis, Byron Foulger, James Craig, John Tyrrell, Charles Trowbridge.

A scientist (Karloff) tries to bring a student back to life using an artificial heart, but is arrested and executed. He is brought back to life with the heart by his assistant (Foulger), and he seeks revenge against the judge, jury, and witnesses who convicted him.

1241. The Man Trailer (3/24/34) B&W—59 mins. (Western). DIR/SP: Lambert Hillyer. PRO: Irving Briskin.

CAST: Buck Jones, Cecilia Parker, Arthur Vinton, Clarence Geldert, Lew Meehan, Steve Clark, Charles West, Dick Botiller, Artie Ortego, Tom Forman.

An ex-outlaw (Jones) saves a girl (Parker) in a stagecoach robbery, becomes marshal of the town, and foils a plot to expose his past. NOTES: A remake of the 1930 Columbia film *The Lone Rider.*

1242. The Man Who Dared (5/30/46) B&W—66 mins. (Crime-Drama). DIR: John Sturges. PRO: Leonard S. Picker. SP: Edward Bock, Malcolm Stuart Boylan. Story by Maxwell Shane, Alex Gottlieb. CAST: Forrest Tucker, Leslie Brooks, George Macready, Richard Hale, Trevor Bardette, Jack Perrin, Ralph Dunn, William Newell, Charles D. Brown, Warren Mills, Charles Evans, Arthur Space, George Lloyd, Harry Tyler, Phil Arnold.

A crusading reporter (Macready), out to prove errors in the judicial system, sets himself up as a prime suspect in a murder case. NOTES: The feature film debut of director John Sturges.

1243. The Man Who Lived Twice (10/13/36) B&W—73 mins. (Crime-Drama). DIR: Harry Lachman. PRO: Ben Pivar. SP: Fred Niblo, Jr., Arthur Strawn, Tom Van Dycke. Story by Tom Van Dycke, Henry Altimus. CAST: Ralph Bellamy, Marian Marsh, Thurston Hall, Isabel Jewell, Nana Bryant, Ward Bond, Henry Kolker, Willard Robertson, Edward Keane.

A murderer (Bellamy) seeks refuge in a hospital, has plastic surgery to alter his brain and face, and rises to the top of the medical profession, only to have his past catch up with him. NOTES: Remade by Columbia in 1953 as *Man in the Dark.*

1244. The Man Who Loved Women (12/83) Metrocolor—118 mins. (Comedy). *DIR:* Blake Edwards. *PRO:* Blake Edwards, Tony Adams. *SP:* Blake Edwards, Milton Wexler, Geoffrey Edwards. Based on Francois Truffaut's 1977 French comedy. *CAST:* Burt Reynolds, Julie Andrews, Kim Basinger, Marilu Henner, Cynthia Sikes, Jennifer Edwards, Sela Ward, Ellen Baur, Denise Crosby, Barry Corbin, Ben Powers, Regis Philbin.

A womanizer (Reynolds) turns to a psychiatrist (Andrews) for help only to find that he is falling for her and she for him.

1245. The Man Who Returned to Life (2/5/42) B&W—61 mins. (Drama). *DIR:* Lew Landers. *PRO:* Wallace MacDonald. *SP:* Gordon Rigby. Based on *The Man Who Came to Life* by Samuel W. Taylor. *CAST:* John Howard, Lucille Fairbanks, Ruth Ford, Marcelle Martin, Roger Clark, Elisabeth Risdon, Paul Guilfoyle, Clancy Cooper, Helen MacKellar, Kenneth MacDonald, Carol Coombs.

A man (Howard) returns to his home town to free another man (Guilfoyle) who is to be executed for his murder.

1246. The Man Who Turned to Stone (3/57) B&W—80 mins. (Horror). *DIR:* Leslie Kardos. *PRO:* Sam Katzman. *SP:* Raymond T. Marcus. A Clover Production. *CAST:* Victor Jory, Ann Doran, Charlotte Austin, William Hudson, Paul Cavanagh, Tina Carver, Jean Willes, Victor Varconi, Frederick Ledebur, George Lynn, Barbara Wilson.

An ageless scientist (Jory) and his assistants take over a girls' reformatory as they use the life force of girls' bodies to keep from aging.

1247. The Man with Connections (12/70) Eastman Color—91 mins. (Comedy). *DIR/PRO/SP:* Claude Berri. A Columbia-Renn-Royal Films International Production. *CAST:* Guy Bedos, Yves Robert, Rosy Varte, Georges Geret, Jean-Pierre Marielle, Zorica Lozic, Claude Pieplu, Claude Melki, Nina Demestre.

A French actor (Bedos), drafted into the French army, uses every means possible to make his life comfortable while in the army. [Original French title: *Le Pistonne*].

1248. The Man with Nine Lives (5/3/40) B&W—73 mins. (Science Fiction). *DIR:* Nick Grinde. *PRO:* Wallace MacDonald. *SP:* Karl Brown. Story by Harold Shumate. *CAST:* Boris Karloff, Roger Pryor, Jo Ann Sayers, Stanley Brown, Byron Foulger, Hal Taliaferro (Wally Wales), Charles Trowbridge, Ernie Adams, Lee Willard, Ivan Miller, Bruce Bennett, John Dilson.

A crazed scientist (Karloff), trying to find a cure for cancer, freezes his patients then experiments on them while they are in a state of suspended animation. [British title: *Behind the Door*].

1249. A Man's Castle (11/20/33) B&W—70 mins. (Drama). *DIR:* Frank Borzage. *SP:* Jo Swerling. Based on the play by Lawrence Hazard. *CAST:* Spencer Tracy, Loretta Young, Glenda Farrell, Walter Connolly, Arthur Hohl, Marjorie Rambeau, Dickie Moore, Harvey Clark, Henry Roquemore, Hector V. Sarno, Helen Jerome Eddy, Robert Grey, Tony Merlo, Harry Watson.

A shantytown roughneck (Tracy) takes in a homeless girl (Young), does odd jobs to support her, and when he learns she is pregnant, tries to commit a robbery but is wounded. Returning home, he realizes how much he needs her and they go off to start a new life together. *NOTES:* This picture was released a year before the Hays Code went into effect and the picture was considered very risque for its time.

1250. A Man's Game (6/18/34) B&W—59 mins. (Action). DIR: D. Ross Lederman. PRO: Irving Briskin. SP: Harold Shumate. CAST: Tim McCoy, Evalyn Knapp, Ward Bond, DeWitt Jennings, Wade Boteler, Bob Kortman, Alden Chase, Nick Copeland.

Two firemen (McCoy, Bond) join forces to help a secretary (Knapp) prove her innocence of embezzlement.

1251. A Man's World (9/17/42) B&W—60 mins. (Drama). DIR: Charles Barton. PRO: Wallace MacDonald. SP: Edward T. Lowe, Jack Roberts. Story by Jack Roberts, George Bricker. CAST: William Wright, Marguerite Chapman, Larry Parks, Wynne Gibson, Roger Pryor, Frank Sully, Ferris Taylor, Edward Van Sloan, Clancy Cooper, James Millican, Lloyd Bridges, Al Hill, Ralph Peters, Al Bridge, Eddie Kane, Grace Lenard, Shirley Patterson.

A nurse (Chapman) is kidnapped after witnessing a murder in a hospital and is sent to an unnamed country where she falls for the owner (Wright) of a mine.

1252. Manhattan Angel (3/17/49) B&W—68 mins. (Musical). DIR: Arthur Dreifuss. PRO: Sam Katzman. SP: Albert Derr. Story by Albert Derr, George H. Plympton. CAST: Gloria Jean, Ross Ford, Patricia White (Patricia Barry), Thurston Hall, Benny Baker, Alice Tyrrell, Russell Hicks, Fay Baker, Toni Harper, Jimmy Lloyd, Leonard Sues, Ralph Hodges, Dorothy Vaughn, Isabel Withers, Peggy Wynne, Barbara Brier, Ida Moore, Robert Cherry.

A young girl (Jean) sets out to stop a businessman (Hall) from tearing down a youth center to build a factory.

1253. Manhattan Shakedown (10/27/39) B&W—56 mins. (Drama). DIR: Leon Barsha. PRO: Kenneth J. Bishop. SP: Edgar Edwards. Based on *Manhattan Whirligig* by Theodore Tinsley. A Warwick Picture Production. CAST: John Gallaudet, Rosalind Keith, George McKay, Reginald Hincks, Bob Rideout, Phyllis Clare, Don Douglas, Michael Heppell.

A crusading reporter (Gallaudet) sets out to stop a blackmailing doctor (Hincks).

1254. Maniac (10/63) B&W/Scope—87 mins. (Thriller). DIR: Michael Carreras. PRO/SP: Jimmy Sangster. Based on *A Time of the Fire* by Marc Brandel. A Hammer Production. CAST: Kerwin Mathews, Nadia Gray, Donald Houston, Liliane Brousse, George Pastell, Arnold Diamond, Norman Bird, Justine Lord, Jerold Wells, Leon Peers.

An artist (Mathews) becomes involved in murder when he helps a woman (Brousse) break her husband (Houston) out of an insane asylum.

1255. March or Die (8/77) Technicolor—107 mins. (Adventure). DIR: Dick Richards. PRO: Dick Richards, Jerry Bruckheimer. SP: David Zelag Goodman. Story by David Zelag Goodman and Dick Richards. An ITC Entertainment-Associated General Film Production. CAST: Gene Hackman, Terence Hill, Max von Sydow, Catherine Deneuve, Ian Holm, Jack O'Halloran, Marcel Bozzuffi, Paul Sherman, Andre Penvern, Vernon Dobtcheff, Walter Gotell, Albert Woods, Wolf Kahler, Guy Deghy, Arnold Diamond, Marne Maitland.

A Legionnaire commander (Hackman) and his men lead a group of archeologists to a dig and, while there, must fight off an Arab attack.

1256. Maria Elena (2/18/36) B&W—??? mins. (Drama). DIR:

Raphael J. Sevilla. *PRO:* Paul H. Bush. *CAST:* Carmen Guerrero, J. J. Martinez Casado, Adolfo Giron, Beatriz Ramos, Lucy Delgado, Guillermo Calles.

A young girl (Guerrero) experiences tragedy in a remote fishing village on the Gulf of Mexico. *NOTES:* Released to Spanish language theaters.

1257. Mark of the Gorilla (2/10/50) B&W—68 mins. (Adventure). *DIR:* William Berke. *PRO:* Sam Katzman. *SP:* Carroll Young. Based on the *Jungle Jim* newspaper comic strip created by Alex Raymond. *CAST:* Johnny Weissmuller, Trudy Marshall, Onslow Stevens, Suzanne Dalbert, Robert Purcell, Selmer Jackson, Pierce Lyden, Neyle Morrow.

Jungle Jim (Weissmuller) sets out to stop a gang of Nazis, who disguise themselves as gorillas to scare the natives, from retrieving buried Nazi loot on a game preserve.

1258. The Mark of the Whistler (10/9/44) B&W—60 mins. (Drama). *DIR:* William Castle. *PRO:* Rudolph C. Flothow. *SP:* George Bricker. Story by Cornell Woolrich. Based on *The Whistler* radio program. *CAST:* Richard Dix, Janis Carter, Porter Hall, Paul Guilfoyle, John Calvert, Matt Willis, Matt McHugh, Howard Freeman.

A drifter (Dix) finds himself the target for revenge when he tries to lay claim to a dormant bank account. [British title: *The Marked Man*].

1259. Marooned (12/69) Technicolor/Panavision—134 mins. (Science Fiction). *DIR:* John Sturges. *PRO:* M. J. Frankovich, John Sturges. *SP:* Mayo Simon. Based on the book by Martin Caidin. *CAST:* Gregory Peck, Richard Crenna, David Janssen, James Franciscus, Gene Hackman, Lee Grant, Nancy Kovack, Mariette Hartley, Scott Brady, George Gaynes, Duke Hobbie, Walter Brooke, Tom Stewart, Mauritz Hugo.

Three astronauts (Hackman, Crenna, Franciscus), on an extended space mission, become marooned in orbit when their spacecraft fails to fire.

1260. The Marriage Came Tumbling Down (11/68) Eastman Color—88 mins. (Comedy-Drama). *DIR:* Jacques Poitrenaud. *PRO:* Jules Borkon. *SP:* Jacques Poitrenaud, Albert Cossery. Based on *I Am Called Jericho* by Catherine Paysan. A Champs Elysees-Isabelle-Royal Films International Production. *CAST:* Michel Simon, Marie Dubois, Yves Lefebvre, Thalie Fruges, Serge Gainsbourg, Mary Marquet, Jeanne Helia.

A couple (Dubois, Lefevbre), whose marriage is failing, go to visit the husband's grandfather (Simon) and, while there, rekindle their relationship. [Original French title: *Ce Sacre Grand-Pere*].

1261. The Marriage Market (10/25/23) B&W—58 mins. (Comedy). *DIR:* Edward J. LeSaint. *PRO:* Harry Cohn. *SP:* Jack Sturmwasser. Story by Evelyn Campbell. A C.B.C. Release. *CAST:* Kate Lester, Mayme Kelso, Pauline Garon, Marc Robbins, Jack Mulhall.

A wealthy young girl (Garon) is expelled from boarding school and heads for the big city.

1262. The Married Woman (8/65) B&W—94 mins. (Drama). *DIR/PRO/SP:* Jean-Luc Godard. An Anouchka-Orsay-Royal Films International Production. *CAST:* Macha Meril, Bernard Noel, Philippe Leroy, Rita Maiden, Chris Tophe, Georges Liron, Roger Leenhardt. Narrated by Jean-Luc Godard.

A married woman (Meril) must choose which is the father of her unborn child, her husband (Leroy) or her lover (Noel). NOTES: The film ends leaving the choice up to the viewer. In French with English subtitles. [British title: A Married Woman]. [Original French title: La Femme Mariee].

1263. The Marrying Kind (2/52) B&W — 92 mins. (Comedy-Drama). DIR: George Cukor. PRO: Bert Granet. SP: Garson Kanin, Ruth Gordon. CAST: Judy Holliday, Aldo Ray, Madge Kennedy, Sheila Bond, John Alexander, Rex Williams, Phyllis Povah, Peggy Cass, Mickey Shaughnessy, Griff Barnett, Joan Shawlee, Frank Ferguson, Larry Blake, Gordon Jones, Joe McGuinn, Charles Bronson (Buchinski), Nancy Kulp.

A couple (Ray, Holliday) seek a divorce but, as each tells their side of the story, through flashback, they realize they still love each other and reconcile.

Martin Eden see **Adventures of Martin Eden**

1264. Mary Lou (1/29/48) B&W — 65 mins. (Musical). DIR: Arthur Dreifuss. PRO: Sam Katzman. SP: M. Coates Webster. A Kay Picture Production. CAST: Robert Lowery, Joan Barton, Glenda Farrell, Abigail Adams, Frank Jenks, Emmett Vogan, Thelma White, Pierre Watkin, Charles Jordan, Leslie Turner, Frankie Carle and His Orchestra.

Two singers (Barton, Adams) bicker with each other over who has the right to use the name "Mary Lou."

1265. Mary of the Movies (5/27/23) B&W — 57 mins. (Drama). DIR: John McDermott. PRO: Jack Cohn. SP: Louis Lewyn. A C.B.C. Release. CAST: Harry Cornelli, Marion Mack, John Geough, Raymond Cannon, Zasu Pitts, Anna May Wong, Rex Ingram, Francis McDonald, Jack Perrin, Florence Lee, Mary Kane, Rosemary Cooper, Creighton Hale, Ray Harford, John McDermott, Henry Burrows.

Mary (Mack) comes to Hollywood to get into the movies. While in Hollywood she meets all the famous stars, and eventually, she gets the break she needs and makes good. She returns home a star. NOTES: This movie combined a sort of travelog, "behind the scenes," and fiction to make it appealing to the film fans.

1266. Mary Ryan, Detective (12/26/49) B&W — 68 mins. (Crime). DIR: Abby Berlin. PRO: Rudolph C. Flothow. SP: George Bricker. Story by Harry Fried. CAST: Marsha Hunt, John Litel, June Vincent, Harry Shannon, William "Bill" Phillips, Katharine Warren, Victoria Horne, Arthur Space, John Dehner, Kernan Cripps, Chester Clute, Clancy Cooper, Ben Welden, Paul Bryar, Charles Russell, Isabel Randolph, Robert Emmett Keane, Ralph Dunn.

A female detective (Hunt) goes undercover as she tries to get the goods on a notorious fence.

1267. Masculine Feminine (9/66) B&W — 103 mins. (Drama). DIR/SP: Jean-Luc Godard. Based on The Signal and Paul's Mistress by Guy de Maupassant. An Anouchka-Argos-Svensk-Sandrews-Royal Films International Production. CAST: Jean-Pierre Leaud, Chantal Goya, Marlene Jobert, Michel Deborb, Chantal Darget, Catherine-Isabelle Duport, Eva-Britt Strandberg, Francoise Hardy, Birger Malmsten, Elsa Leroy, Brigitte Bardot, Antoine Bourseiller.

During the 60's, a confused young man (Leaud) searches for the perfect love by taking up with a singer (Goya) and her two roommates (Jobert, Deborb). [Original French title: Masculin Feminin]. [Original Swedish title: Maskulinum-Feminimum].

1268. Mask of the Avenger (6/27/51) Technicolor — 83 mins. (Adven-

Feature Films 211

ture). *DIR:* Phil Karlson. *PRO:* Hunt Stromberg. *SP:* Jesse L. Lasky, Jr., Ralph Bettinson, Philip MacDonald. Story by George Bruce. Based on *The Count of Monte Cristo* by Alexandre Dumas. *CAST:* Anthony Quinn, John Derek, Jody Lawrence, Arnold Moss, Eugene Iglesias, Dick LeRoy, Harry Cording, Ian Wolfe, Wilton Graff, Tristram Coffin, Ric Roman, Philip Van Zandt, Mickey Simpson, Minerva Urecal, Trevor Bardette, Gregory Gay, Lester Sharpe, David Bond, Carlo Tricoli.

In 1848 Italy, a young aristocrat (Derek) dons a disguise as he searches for the murderer of his father.

Mask of the Himalayas *see* **Storm Over Tibet**

The Massacre at the Rosebud *see* **The Great Sioux Massacre**

1269. Massacre Canyon (5/54) Sepiatone—66 mins. (Western). *DIR:* Fred F. Sears. *PRO:* Wallace MacDonald. *SP:* David Lang. *CAST:* Phil Carey, Audrey Totter, Douglas Kennedy, Jeff Donnell, Ross Elliott, Guinn "Big Boy" Williams, Chris Alcaide, John Pickard, Charlita, Ralph Dumke, Mel Welles, Steve Ritch, James Flavin, Bill Hale.

An Army scout (Carey) tries to keep a load of rifles from falling into the hands of the Indians.

1270. Master of Men (5/25/33) B&W—65 mins. (Drama). *DIR:* Lambert Hillyer. *SP:* Edward Paramore, Seton I. Miller. Story by Chester Erskine, Eugene Solow. *CAST:* Jack Holt, Fay Wray, Walter Connolly, Berton Churchill, Theodore Von Eltz.

A financial wizard (Holt), involved in the stock market, loses everything when his wife (Wray) lets his enemies know about his activities.

1271. Masterson of Kansas (12/54) Technicolor—72 mins. (Western).

DIR: William Castle. *PRO:* Sam Katzman. *SP:* Douglas Heyes. A Clover Production. *CAST:* George Montgomery, Nancy Gates, James Griffith, Jean Willes, Benny Rubin, Bill Henry, Gregg Barton, Jay Silverheels, Leonard Geer, David Bruce, Bruce Cowling, Donald Murphy, Sandy Sanders, Gregg Martell, John Maxwell, Wesley Hudman.

Three lawmen (Montgomery, Griffith, Cowling) set out to stop an outlaw (Henry) from inciting an Indian war.

1272. The Matinee Idol (3/14/28) B&W—66 mins. (Comedy). *DIR:* Frank Capra. *PRO:* Harry Cohn. *SP:* Elmer Harris, Peter Milne. Based on *Come Back to Aaron* by Robert Lord and Ernest S. Pagano. *CAST:* Bessie Love, Johnnie Walker, Lionel Belmore, Ernest Hilliard, David Mir, Sidney D'Albrook.

A famous Broadway star (Walker) becomes a member of a traveling tent show and decides to use the play in his Broadway show as a comedy. *NOTES:* Remade as a musical by Columbia in 1936 as *The Music Goes 'Round.*

1273. The Mating of Millie (3/8/48) B&W—87 mins. (Comedy). *DIR:* Henry Levin. *PRO:* Casey Robinson. *SP:* Louella MacFarlane, St. Clair McKelway. Story by Adele Commandini. *CAST:* Glenn Ford, Evelyn Keyes, Ron Randell, Willard Parker, Virginia Hunter, Jimmy Hunt, Mabel Paige, Virginia Brissac, Patsy Creighton, Tom Stevenson.

A career woman (Keyes), wanting to adopt an orphan (Hunt), must first try to get a husband (Ford).

1274. A Matter of Days (6/69) Eastman Color—98 mins. (Drama). *DIR/PRO:* Yves Ciampi. *SP:* Yves Ciampi, Rodolphe M. Arlaud, Vladimir Kalina, Alena Vostra. Story by

Yves Ciampi. A Telcia Films-Czecheslovak Films-Royal Films International Production. CAST: Thalie Fruges, Vit Olmer, Philippe Baronnet, Jana Sulcova, Milan Mach, Michel Ducrocq, Josef Cap, Valerie Vienne, Ota Ornest, Petr Svojtka, Daniele Garnier, Jean-Pierre Marichal, Alexandre Kilimenko, Ladislav Jansky.

Set against the political student turmoil in Prague in 1967–68, a married French student (Fruges) becomes involved with her professor (Olmer) but, when he begins to show interest in the government that she opposes, she leaves him to go back to her husband (Baronnet) who no longer wants her. [Original French title: A Quelques Jours Pres...].

A Matter of Resistance see **La Vie de Chateau**

1275. Me and the Colonel (10/ 58) B&W—109 mins. (Comedy). DIR: Peter Glenville. PRO: William Goetz. SP: Samuel Nathaniel Behrman, George Froeschel. Based on the play *Jacobowsky and the Colonel* by Franz Werfel. A William Goetz-Count Enterprises Production. CAST: Danny Kaye, Curt Jurgens, Nicole Maurey, Francoise Rosay, Akim Tamiroff, Marita Hunt, Alexander Scourby, Liliane Montevecchi, Ludwig Stossel, Gerard Buhr, Celia Rovsky, Eugene Borden.

In 1940, a Jewish refugee (Kaye), a Polish colonel (Jurgens), and a girl (Maurey) flee Paris before the Germans arrive.

1276. The Medico of Painted Springs (6/26/41) B&W—58 mins. (Western). DIR: Lambert Hillyer. PRO: Jack Fier. SP: Winston Miller, Wyndham Gittens. Based on the book by James L. Rubel. CAST: Charles Starrett, Terry Walker, Richard Fiske, Ray Bennett, Ben Taggart, Bud Osborne, Edmund Cobb, Steve Clark,

Lloyd Bridges, George Chesebro, Charles Hamilton, Edythe Elliott, Jim Corey, The Simp-Phonies.

Dr. Steven Monroe (Starrett) makes a stop in a town to examine Rough Rider recruits and ends up settling a range war between cattlemen and sheepmen. [British title: *Doctor's Alibi*].

1277. Meet Boston Blackie (2/ 27/41) B&W—61 mins. (Crime-Mystery). DIR: Robert Florey. PRO: Ralph Cohn. SP: Jay Dratler. Based on characters created by Jack Boyle. CAST: Chester Morris, Rochelle Hudson, Charles Wagenheim, Constance Worth, Richard Lane, Walter Sande, Jack O'Malley, George Magrill, Michael Hand, Eddie Laughton, John Tyrrell, Harry Anderson, Byron Foulger.

Blackie (Morris) sets out to stop an undercover spy ring operating at an ocean front carnival.

1278. Meet Me on Broadway (3/ 27/46) B&W—78 mins. (Musical). DIR: Leigh Jason. PRO: Burt Kelly. SP: George Bricker, Jack Henley. Story by George Bricker. CAST: Marjorie Reynolds, Fred Brady, Jinx Falkenburg, Spring Byington, Loren Tindall, Gene Lockhart, Allen Jenkins, William Forrest, Jack Rice.

An arrogant director (Brady), who wants to make it big on Broadway, stages an amateur show at a country club and falls for the daughter (Reynolds) of the owner.

1279. Meet Miss Bobby Socks (12/22/44) B&W—68 mins. (Musical). DIR: Glenn Tryon. PRO: Ted Richmond. SP: Muriel Roy Bolton. CAST: Bob Crosby, Lynn Merrick, Louise Erickson, Robert White, Howard Freeman, Mary Currier, Pat Parrish, Sally Bliss, John Hamilton, Douglas Wood, Pierre Watkin, Louis Jordan and the Tympany Five, The Kim Loo Sisters.

A soldier (Crosby) returns home and, with the help of his girl (Merrick) and his fans, makes it big as a nightclub singer.

1280. Meet Nero Wolf (7/17/36) B&W—73 mins. (Mystery). *DIR:* Herbert Biberman. *PRO:* B. P. Schulberg. *SP:* Howard J. Green, Bruce Manning, Joseph Anthony. Based on *Fer de Lance: A Nero Wolfe Mystery* by Rex Stout. *CAST:* Edward Arnold, Joan Perry, Lionel Stander, Victor Jory, Walter Kingsford, Nana Bryant, Dennie Moore, Rita Cansino (Rita Hayworth), John Qualen, Gene Morgan, Frank Conroy, Boyd Irwin, Russell Hardie, George Offerman, Jr., Eddy Waller, Billy Benedict, Raymond Borgaze, William Anderson.

Nero Wolfe (Arnold) and Archie (Stander) set out to solve the murder of a college president and an inventor. *NOTES:* Rita Hayworth's first Columbia film.

1281. Meet the Stewarts (5/21/42) B&W—72 mins. (Comedy). *DIR:* Alfred E. Green. *PRO:* Robert Sparks. *SP:* Karen DeWolf. Based on *Something Borrowed* from the *Candy and Mike Stewart* stories by Elizabeth Dunn. *CAST:* William Holden, Frances Dee, Grant Mitchell, Marjorie Gateson, Anne Revere, Roger Clark, Danny Mummert, Ann Gillis, Margaret Hamilton, Don Beddoe, Mary Gordon, Edward Gargan, Tom Dugan, Marguerite Chapman, William Wright, Arthur Loft, Ed Thomas, Barbara Brown, Ralph Sanford, Boyd Davis, Willie Fung, Chester Clute, Lloyd Bridges.

When a rich wife (Dee) fails to live within the budget set up by her husband (Holden), they split but eventually they get back together.

1282. Meet the Wife (6/21/31) B&W—76 mins. (Comedy). *DIR:* A.

Leslie Pearce. *SP:* F. McGrew Willis, Walter DeLeon. Based on the play by Lynn Starling. A Christie Comedy Production. *CAST:* Laura La Plante, Lew Cody, Joan Marsh, Harry Myers, Claude Allister, William Janney, Edgar Norton.

A wife (La Plante) finds herself in trouble when her supposedly dead husband (Cody) returns home and finds her married to another man (Myers).

1283. Mein Kampf (5/61) B&W—117 mins. (Documentary). *DIR/SP:* Erwin Leiser. *PRO:* Tore Sjoberg. Based on the book by Adolf Hitler. A Minerva Films International Production. *CAST:* Narrated by Claude Stephenson.

Old newsreel footage and film clips illustrate Hitler's rise to power. [Original German title: *Den Blodiga Tiden*].

1284. Melody Man (2/16/30) B&W-Technicolor—75 mins. (Musical-Drama). *DIR:* Roy William Neill. *PRO:* Harry Cohn. *SP:* Howard J. Green. Based on the play by Richard Rodgers, Lorenz Hart. *CAST:* William Collier, Jr., Alice Day, John St. Polis, Johnnie Walker, Mildred Harris, Albert Conti, Tenen Holtz, Lee D. Kohlmar, Bertram Marburgh, Anton Averka.

A Viennese composer (St. Polis) kills his wife and her lover, flees to the United States with his daughter (Day), but is eventually brought to justice when one of his musical compositions is recognized. *NOTES:* The film briefly used the 2-Strip Technicolor process for a 12-minute opening sequence.

1285. The Member of the Wedding (3/53) B&W—91 mins. (Drama). *DIR:* Fred Zinnemann. *PRO:* Stanley Kramer. *SP:* Edna Anhalt, Edward Anhalt. Based on the book and play by

Carson McCullers. *CAST*: Ethel Waters, Julie Harris, Brandon de Wilde, Arthur Franz, Nancy Gates, William Hansen, James Edwards, Harry Bolden, Dick Moore, Danny Mummert, June Hedin, Ann Carter.

In 1945 Georgia, a 12-year-old girl (Harris) finds comfort in her relationship with the family cook (Waters) as she copes with adolescence.

1286. Men Are Like That (10/16/31) B&W—70 mins. (Drama). *DIR*: George B. Seitz. *PRO*: Harry Cohn. *SP*: Robert Riskin, Dorothy Howell. Based on the play *Arizona* by Augustus Thomas. *CAST*: John Wayne, Laura La Plante, Forrest Stanley, June Clyde, Nena Quartero, Susan Fleming, Loretta Sayers, Hugh Cummings.

A West Point graduate (Wayne) breaks off with his girl (La Plante), is transferred to Arizona, and again meets her as the wife of his commanding officer (Stanley). [British title: *The Virtuous Wife*].

1287. Men in Her Life (12/6/31) B&W—70 mins. (Drama). *DIR*: William Beaudine. *SP*: Robert Riskin, Dorothy Howell. Based on the book by Warner Fabian. *CAST*: Lois Moran, Charles Bickford, Victor Varconi, Donald Dillaway, Luis Alberni, Adrienne D'Ambricourt, Barbara Weeks, Wilson Benge, Oscar Apfel, Hooper Atchley.

A woman (Moran) with a shady past is being blackmailed on the eve of her wedding by an unscrupulous count (Varconi). She seeks the help of a bootlegger (Bickford) friend and, when he is put on trial for murder, she comes to his defense.

1288. The Men in Her Life (10/23/41) B&W—89 mins. (Drama). *DIR/PRO*: Gregory Ratoff. *SP*: Frederick Kohner, Michael Wilson, Paul Trivers. Based on *Ballerina* by

Lady Eleanor Smith. *CAST*: Loretta Young, Conrad Veidt, Dean Jagger, Eugenie Leontovich, Shepperd Strudwick, Otto Kruger, Paul Baratoff, Ann Todd, Billy Rayes, Ludmila Toretzka.

A woman (Young) is transformed from a circus performer to a great ballerina through her instructor husband (Veidt). When he dies, she marries a shipping magnate (Jagger) but, when she resumes her career, he takes their daughter and leaves her. Eventually she follows him for a reconciliation.

1289. Men of the Hour (5/9/35) B&W—61 mins. (Action-Drama). *DIR*: Lambert Hillyer. *PRO*: Irving Briskin. *SP*: Anthony Coldeway. *CAST*: Richard Cromwell, Billie Seward, Wallace Ford, Jack LaRue, Wesley Barry, Charles Wilson, Pat O'Malley, Ernie Adams, Eddie Hart, Marc Lawrence, Gene Morgan, Stanley Taylor.

Two newsreel cameramen (Cromwell, Ford) photograph a murder and go after the killers.

1290. Men of the Night (11/28/34) B&W—58 mins. (Crime-Drama). *DIR/SP*: Lambert Hillyer. *CAST*: Bruce Cabot, Judith Allen, Ward Bond, Charles Sabin, John Kelly, Mathew Betz, Walter McGrail, Maidel Turner, Arthur Rankin, Charles C. Wilson, Frank Darien, Harry Holman, Tom London, Lucille Ball, Lee Shumway, Ernie Adams, Mitchell Ingraham, Robert Graves, Pearl Eaton.

A Hollywood detective (Cabot) sets out to capture a gang of thieves, but runs into trouble when he believes his girl (Allen) has tipped off the thieves to his plans.

1291. Men Without Law (10/15/30) B&W—65 mins. (Western). *DIR*: Louis King. *PRO*: Sol Lesser. *SP*: Dorothy Howell. Story by Lewis

Seiler. A Beverly Production. *CAST:* Buck Jones, Fred Kelsey, Carmelita Geraghty, Harry Woods, Thomas Carr, Victor Sarno, Fred Burns, Ben Corbett, Syd Saylor, Lydia Knott, Lafe McKee, Art Mix.

A soldier (Jones), returning home to find the sister (Geraghty) of his friend killed in the war, learns that his brother (Carr) has joined an outlaw gang and that they have kidnapped the sister. After many chases he finally rescues her and brings the gang to justice.

1292. Men Without Souls (5/20/40) B&W—62 mins. (Crime-Drama). *DIR:* Nick Grinde. *PRO:* Wallace MacDonald. *SP:* Robert D. Andrews, Joseph Carole. Story by Harvey Gates. *CAST:* John Litel, Barton MacLane, Rochelle Hudson, Glenn Ford, Don Beddoe, Cy Kendall, Eddie Laughton, Dick Curtis, Richard Fiske, Walter Soderling.

A young man (Ford) has himself sent to prison so that he can kill the prison guard (Kendall) who murdered his father, but the prison chaplain (Litel) helps to save his life and steer him straight.

1293. The Menace (1/31/32) B&W—71 mins. (Crime-Drama). *DIR:* Roy William Neill. *PRO:* Sam Nelson. *SP:* Dorothy Howell, Charles Logue, Roy Chanslor. Based on *The Feathered Serpent* by Edgar Wallace. *CAST:* H. B. Warner, Bette Davis, Walter Byron, Natalie Moorhead, Crawford Kent, William B. Davidson, Halliwell Hobbes, Charles Gerrard, Murray Kinnell.

A young man (Byron), framed for the murder of his father, escapes from jail and has to have plastic surgery when his face is burned. Now looking like someone else, he decides to return home and find the murderer of his father.

Messalina *see* **Affairs of Messalina**

1294. Mexicali Rose (12/26/29) B&W—60 mins. (Drama). *DIR:* Erle C. Kenton. *PRO:* Harry Cohn. *SP:* Gladys Lehman, Norman Houston. *CAST:* Barbara Stanwyck, Sam Hardy, William Janney, Louis Natheaux, Arthur Rankin, Harry Vejar, Louis King, Julia Beharano, Jerry Miley.

A woman (Stanwyck) seeks revenge against the saloon owner (Hardy) who kicked her out of town by marrying his brother (Janney). She meets her fate when she starts playing around with the town idiot (Rankin). *NOTES:* Barbara Stanwyck's first film for Columbia. This film was also released as a silent. [British title: *The Girl from Mexico*].

1295. Miami Expose (9/56) B&W—73 mins. (Crime). *DIR:* Fred F. Sears. *PRO:* Sam Katzman. *SP:* James B. Gordon. A Clover Production. *CAST:* Lee J. Cobb, Patricia Medina, Edward Arnold, Michael Granger, Eleanore Tanin, Alan Napier, Harry Lauter, Chris Alcaide, Hugh Sanders, Barry L. Conners.

A police detective (Cobb) sets out to stop two gamblers (Napier, Granger) who are out to control the gambling action in Florida. *NOTES:* Edward Arnold died at the age of 66 during the production of this film.

1296. The Miami Story (5/54) B&W—75 mins. (Crime). *DIR:* Fred F. Sears. *PRO:* Sam Katzman. *SP:* Robert E. Kent. *CAST:* Barry Sullivan, Luther Adler, John Baer, Adele Jergens, Beverly Garland, Dan Riss, Damian O'Flynn, Chris Alcaide, Gene D'Arcy, David Kasday, George E. Stone, Tom Greenway.

An ex-gangster (Sullivan), hired by a citizen's committee, poses as a Cuban racketeer to get evidence against a

216   The Columbia Checklist

Miami crime boss (Adler). *NOTES:* Introduction by then Florida Senator George A. Smathers.

1297. Michael Kohlhaas (5/69) Eastman Color—97 mins. (Drama). *DIR:* Volker Schlondorff. *PRO:* Jerry Bick. *SP:* Edward Bond, Clement Biddle Wood, Volker Schlondorff. Based on the novella by Heinrich von Kleist. An Oceanic Production. *CAST:* David Warner, Anna Karina, Reila Basic, Anita Pallenberg, Inigo Jackson, Michael Gothard, Anton Diffring, Anthony May, Tim Ray, Ivan Palluch, Kurt Meisel, Emanuel Schmeid, Thomas Holtzman, Vaclav Lohninsky.

A 16th-century horse trader (Warner) becomes a symbol of revolt against injustice when he stands up to a landowner (Jackson) who defrauds him and causes the death of his wife (Karina). *NOTES:* Originally released in both German and English versions. Re-released in 1980. [Original German title: *Michael Kohlhaas—Der Rebell*].

1298. Mickey One (10/65) B&W—93 mins. (Crime-Drama). *DIR/PRO:* Arthur Penn. *SP:* Alan M. Surgal. A Florin-Tatira Production. *CAST:* Warren Beatty, Hurd Hatfield, Alexandra Stewart, Teddy Hart, Jeff Corey, Franchot Tone.

A nightclub comic (Beatty) tries to escape from the mob after he runs up gambling debts but becomes bound for life to a mobster (Hatfield) when his debts are paid by him.

1299. Micki and Maude (12/84) Metrocolor/Panavision—118 mins. (Comedy). *DIR:* Blake Edwards. *PRO:* Tony Adams. *SP:* Jonathan Reynolds. A Columbia-Delphi III-Blake Edwards Entertainment Production. *CAST:* Dudley Moore, Amy Irving, Ann Reinking, Richard Mulligan, George Gaynes, Wallace Shawn, John Pleshette, H. B. Haggerty, Lu Leonard, George Coe, Priscilla Pointer.

A man (Moore) tries to keep his pregnant wife (Reinking) and pregnant girlfriend (Irving) from finding out about each other when they go to the same doctor and are admitted to the same hospital.

1300. Middle of the Night (7/59) B&W—118 mins. (Drama). *DIR:* Delbert Mann. *PRO:* George Justin. *SP:* Paddy Chayefsky. Based on the play by Paddy Chayefsky. A Sundan Company Inc. Production. *CAST:* Kim Novak, Glenda Farrell, Frederic March, Jan Norris, Lee Grant, Lee Philips, Martin Balsam, Joan Copeland, Edith Meiser, David Ford, Audrey Peters, Betty Walker, Albert Dekker, Rudy Bond, Lou Gilbert, Dora Weissman, Lee Richardson, Anna Berger.

A widowed businessman (March) falls in love with a younger woman (Novak) and his family tries to break up the romance. *NOTES:* This was first a TV play in 1954 with E. G. Marshall and Eva Marie Saint, then a Broadway play in 1956 with Edward G. Robinson and Gena Rowlands.

1301. Midnight Episode (3/51) B&W—78 mins. (Mystery). *DIR:* Gordon Parry. *PRO:* Theo Lageard. *SP:* Rita Barisse, Reeve Taylor, Paul Vincent Carroll, David Evans, William P. Templeton. Based on *Monsieur la Souris* by Georges Simenon. A Triangle Production. *CAST:* Stanley Holloway, Leslie Dwyer, Reginald Tate, Meredith Edwards, Wilfrid Hyde-White, Joy Shelton, Ray Young, Leslie Perrins, Sebastian Cabot, Campbell Copelin, Natasha Parry.

A doorman (Holloway) is pursued by murderers when he finds a dead body in a car and keeps the dead man's wallet. *NOTES:* This film was re-released in 1955 with 11 minutes cut.

1302. The Midnight Express (6/1/24) B&W—56 mins. (Drama). *DIR/*

SP: George W. Hill. *PRO:* Harry Cohn. A C.B.C. Release. *CAST:* Elaine Hammerstein, William Haines, George Nichols, Lloyd Whitlock, Edwin Booth Tilton, Pat Harmon, Bertram Grassby, Phyllis Haver, Roscoe Karns, Jack Richardson, Noble Johnson, Dan Crimmins, George Meadows.

A railroad president's son (Haines) gives up the playboy life to become a train engineer. He proves himself by capturing a criminal and by saving the "Midnight Express" from disaster.

1303. Midnight Express (10/78) Eastman Color—120 mins. (Drama). *DIR:* Alan Parker. *PRO:* Alan Marshall, David Puttnam. *SP:* Oliver Stone. Based on the book by Billy Hayes and William Hoffer. A Casablanca Production. *CAST:* Brad Davis, Randy Quaid, Bo Hopkins, John Hurt, Paul Smith, Mike Kellin, Norbert Weisser, Irene Miracle, Palo Bonacelli, Michael Ensign, Tony Boyd, Peter Jeffrey.

Based on the true story of Billy Hayes (Davis), who was sent to a Turkish prison for trying to smuggle two kilos of hashish out of Turkey.

1304. A Midsummer Night's Dream (4/67) Pathe Color—93 mins. (Ballet). *DIR:* Dan Eriksen. *PRO:* Richard Davis. Based on the play by William Shakespeare. An Oberon Productions, Ltd. Production presented in association with the New York City Center of Music and Drama, Inc. *CAST:* Suzanne Farrell, Edward Villella, Arthur Mitchell, Mimi Paul, Nicholas Magallanes, Patricia McBrice, Roland Vazquez, Francisco Monclan, Gloria Govrin, Jacques d'Ambrose, Allegra Kent, The New York City Ballet, the Children of the School of American Ballet.

The famed George Balanchine ballet with music by Felix Mendelssohn.

Military Academy *see* **Military Academy with That 10th Ave. Gang**

1305. Military Academy (8/6/40) B&W—66 mins. (Drama). *DIR:* D. Ross Lederman. *PRO:* Wallace MacDonald. *SP:* Karl Brown, David Silverstein. Story by Richard English. *CAST:* Tommy Kelly, Bobby Jordan, David Holt, Jackie Searl, Don Beddoe, Jimmy Butler, Walter Tetley, Earle Fox, Edward Dew, Warren Ashe, Joan Leslie.

A gangster's son (Kelly) and a showoff (Jordan) learn how to become men at a military academy.

1306. Military Academy with That 10th Ave. Gang (4/27/50) B&W—64 mins. (Drama). *DIR:* D. Ross Lederman. *PRO:* Wallace MacDonald. *SP:* Howard J. Green. *CAST:* Stanley Clements, Myron Welton, Gene Collins, Leon Tyler, James Millican, William Johnstone, James Seay, John Hamilton, Dick Jones, Buddy Swan, Conrad Binyon, John Michaels, Buddy Burroughs, John McGuire, Jack Reynolds, Russ Conway, Tim Ryan.

A judge (Hamilton) sends four delinquents (Clements, Welton, Tyler, Collins) to a military academy, instead of reform school, where they can be shaped into good citizens. [British title: *Sentence Suspended*].

1307. The Millerson Case (5/29/47) B&W—72 mins. (Crime-Drama). *DIR:* George Archainbaud. *PRO:* Rudolph C. Flothow. *SP:* Raymond L. Schrock. Story by Gordon Rigby, Carleton Sand. Based on the CBS radio program *Crime Doctor* by Max Marcin. *CAST:* Warner Baxter, Nancy Saunders, Clem Bevans, Griff Barnett, Paul Guilfoyle, James Bell, Addison Richards, Mark Dennis, Robert Stevens, Eddie Parker, Vic

Potel, Russell Simpson, Sarah Padden, Barbara Pepper, Eddy Waller, Frances Morris.

Dr. Ordway (Baxter), Crime Doctor, on vacation in the Blue Ridge Mountains, discovers that a typhoid epidemic is being used to cover up the murder of a doctor (Barnett) and sets out to solve the murder.

1308. Millie's Daughter (3/20/47) B&W—70 mins. (Drama). *DIR:* Sidney Salkow. *PRO:* William Bloom. *SP:* Edward Huebsch. Story by Donald Henderson Clarke. *CAST:* Gladys George, Gay Nelson, Paul Campbell, Arthur Space, Norma Varden, Nana Bryant, Ethel Griffies, Harry Hayden, Paul Maxey, Robert Emmett Keane.

A mother (George) goes to extremes to protect her daughter (Nelson) from a life of crime.

1309. Mills of the Gods (1/9/35) B&W—67 mins. (Drama). *DIR:* Roy William Neill. *PRO:* Robert North. *SP:* Garrett Elsden Fort. Based on *A Hundred Million Dollars* by Melville Baker, John S. Kirkland. *CAST:* May Robson, Fay Wray, Victor Jory, Raymond Wilburn, James Blakely, Josephine Whittell, Mayo Methot, Albert Conti, Samuel S. Hinds, Willard Robertson, Edward Van Sloan, Frank Reicher, Frederik Vogeding, Edward Keane.

A woman (Robson) tries to save the family business after the stock market crash.

1310. The Mind of Mr. Soames (10/70) Technicolor—98 mins. (Science Fiction). *DIR:* Alan Cooke. *PRO:* Max J. Rosenberg, Milton Subotsky. *SP:* John Hale, Edward Simpson. Based on the book by Charles Eric Maine. An Amicus Production. *CAST:* Terence Stamp, Robert Vaughn, Nigel Davenport, Christian Roberts, Donal Donnelly, Norman Jones, Dan Jackson, Vickery

Turner, Judy Parfitt, Scott Forbes, Joe McPartland.

A 30-year-old man (Stamp), who has been in a coma since birth, awakes with the brain of an infant, is unable to cope with the hostilities of the outside world, and kills his doctor (Vaughn) while being filmed for TV.

1311. The Mine with the Iron Door (5/6/36) B&W—66 mins. (Drama). *DIR:* David Howard. *PRO:* Sol Lesser. *SP:* Don Swift, Dan Jarrett. Based on the book by Harold Bell Wright. A Principal Production. *CAST:* Richard Arlen, Cecilia Parker, Henry B. Walthall, Horace Murphy, Stanley Fields, Spencer Charters, Charles Wilson, Barbara Bedford.

A prospector (Arlen) buys some land in Arizona and it is revealed that the legendary "Mine with the Iron Door," a cache of mission gold, lies somewhere on the property.

1312. A Miracle on Main Street (12/19/39) B&W—78 mins. (Drama). *DIR:* Steven Sekeley. *PRO:* Jack Shirball. *SP:* Frederick Jackson. Story by Samuel Ornitz, Boris Ingster. *CAST:* Margo, Walter Abel, Lyle Talbot, Wynne Gibson, Veda Ann Borg, William Collier, Sr., Jane Darwell, Pat Flaherty, George Humbert, Jeanne Kelly, Susan Miller.

During Christmas time, a dance hall girl (Margo) finds an abandoned baby on the streets of Los Angeles and takes it home.

1313. The Miracle Woman (7/21/31) B&W—90 mins. (Drama). *DIR:* Frank Capra. *PRO:* Harry Cohn. *SP:* Dorothy Howell, Jo Swerling. Based on the play *Bless You, Sister* by John Meehan, Robert Riskin. A Frank Capra Production. *CAST:* Barbara Stanwyck, David Manners, Sam Hardy, Beryl Mercer, Russell Hopton, Charles Middleton, Eddie Boland,

Thelma Hill, Aileen Carlyle, Al Stewart, Harry Todd, Edward J. Le-Saint, John Kelly, Dennis O'Keefe, Fred Warren, Mary Doran.

A con-man and promoter (Hardy) sets up a pastor's daughter (Stanwyck) as an evangelist, and hires phony cripples for her to cure, but his plans are thwarted when she falls in love with a blind ex-pilot (Manners) and decides to confess all to her congregation.

1314. Miss Grant Takes Richmond (9/22/49) B&W — 87 mins. (Crime-Comedy). DIR: Lloyd Bacon. PRO: S. Sylvan Simon. SP: Nat Perrin, Devery Freeman, Frank Tashlin. Story by Everett Freeman. CAST: Lucille Ball, William Holden, Janis Carter, James Gleason, Gloria Henry, Frank McHugh, George Cleveland, Stephen Dunne, Arthur Space, Will Wright, Jimmy Lloyd, Loren Tindall, Roy Roberts, Charles Lane, Harry Harvey, Harry Cheshire, Peter Brocco, Syd Saylor, Eddie Acuff, Charles Hamilton.

A secretary (Ball), unaware of her boss's (Holden) bookmaking activities, is hired as a "front" for their phony real estate office, and when she begins to sell houses to the homeless, they find themselves promoting a low-cost housing scheme. [British title: *Innocence Is Bliss*].

1315. Miss Sadie Thompson (10/53) Technicolor/3-D — 91 mins. (Drama). DIR: Curtis Bernhardt. PRO: Jerry Wald. SP: Harry Kleiner. Based on *Rain* by W. Somerset Maugham. A Beckworth Production. CAST: Rita Hayworth, Jose Ferrer, Aldo Ray, Russell Collins, Diosa Costello, Harry Bellaver, Wilton Graff, Peggy Converse, Rudy Bond, Charles Bronson (Buchinski), Frances Morris, Charles Horvath, John Duncan, Al Kikume.

Sadie Thompson (Hayworth) is run out of Honolulu and lands on a Pacific island inhabited by Marines where she falls prey to a local missionary (Ferrer) and falls in love with a Marine (Ray).

1316. Missing Daughters (6/20/39) B&W — 63 mins. (Crime). DIR: C. C. Coleman, Jr. SP: Michael L. Simmons, George Bricker. CAST: Richard Arlen, Rochelle Hudson, Marian Marsh, Isabel Jewell, Dick Wessel, Edward Raquello, Eddie Kane, Wade Boteler, Don Beddoe, Claire Rochelle.

A reporter (Arlen) joins forces with a woman (Hudson) to expose a gang operating a dance hall and using hostesses recruited through phoney talent agents.

1317. The Missing Juror (11/16/44) B&W — 66 mins. (Mystery). DIR: Oscar (Budd) Boetticher, Jr. PRO: Wallace MacDonald. SP: Charles O'Neal. Story by Leon Abrams, Richard Hill Wilkinson. CAST: Jim Bannon, Janis Carter, George Macready, Jean Stevens, Joseph Crehan, Carole Mathews, Cliff Clark, Edmund Cobb, Mike Mazurki, George Lloyd.

When a murderer is sent to the chair, six members of the jury that convicted him are found dead. A reporter (Bannon) then sets out to find who killed them by trailing the remaining members of the jury.

1318. Missing Ten Days (4/24/41) B&W — 82 mins. (Spy-Drama). DIR: Tim Whelan. PRO: Irving Asher. SP: John Meehan, Jr., James Curtis. Based on *The Disappearance of Roger Tremayne* by Bruce Graeme. CAST: Rex Harrison, Karen Verne, C. V. France, Leo Genn, Joan Marion, Anthony Holles, John Abbott, Robert Rendel, Mavis Clair, Andre Morell, Hay Petrie, Frank Atkinson.

After a plane crash, a man (Harrison) wakes up in Paris, is told about the crash, and cannot remember what he did for the last ten days from the plane crash to when he awoke. [British title: *Ten Days in Paris*].

1319. Mission Over Korea (8/53) B&W—85 mins. (War). *DIR*: Fred F. Sears. *PRO*: Robert Cohn. *SP*: Jesse L. Lasky, Jr., Eugene Ling, Martin M. Goldsmith. Story by Richard Tregaskis. *CAST*: John Hodiak, John Derek, Audrey Totter, Maureen O'Sullivan, Harvey Lembeck, Richard Erdman, William Chun, Rex Reason, Richard Bowers, Todd Karns.

During the Korean War, personal hostilities erupt between two military officers (Hodiak, Derek). [British title: *Eyes of the Skies*].

1320. The Missionary (11/82) Eastman Color/Panavision—90 mins. (Comedy). *DIR*: Richard Loncraine. *PRO*: Neville C. Thompson, Michael Palin. *SP*: Michael Palin. A Hand Made Films Production. *CAST*: Michael Palin, Maggie Smith, Trevor Howard, Denholm Elliott, Graham Crowden, Michael Hordern, Phoebe Nicholls, Tricia George, John Barrett, Peter Vaughn, Valerie Whittington.

After spending 10 years in an African village, a missionary (Palin) is called back to Victorian London to run a slum mission for "fallen women" and finds himself the recipient of fringe benefits.

1321. Mr. Deeds Goes to Town (3/27/36) B&W—115 mins. (Comedy). *DIR/PRO*: Frank Capra. *SP*: Robert Riskin. Based on *Opera Hat* by Clarence Budington Kelland. A Frank Capra Production. *CAST*: Gary Cooper, Jean Arthur, George Bancroft, Lionel Stander, Douglass Dumbrille, H. B. Warner, Raymond Walburn, Margaret Matzenauer, Warren Hymer, Muriel Evans, Ruth Donnelly, Spencer Charters, Arthur Hoyt, Jameson Thomas, Walter Catlett, Stanley

Andrews, Pierre Watkin, Russell Hicks, Charles Lane, Edward J. LeSaint, Irving Bacon, Margaret Seddon, Margaret McWade, Wyrley Birch, John Wray, Gustav von Seyffertitz, Gene Morgan, Dennis O'Keefe, Paul Hurst, Franklin Pangborn, Paul Porcasi, George "Gabby" Hayes, Dale Van Sickel, Billy Bevan, Ann Doran, Bess Flowers, Mayo Methot.

Longfellow Deeds (Cooper) inherits $20 million, goes to New York to take up residence with his benefactor, is pursued and ridiculed by a reporter (Arthur), and finally is taken to court to be declared insane when he wants to use his fortune to help the farmers.

1322. Mr. District Attorney (2/20/47) B&W—81 mins. (Crime). *DIR*: Robert B. Sinclair. *PRO*: Samuel Bischoff. *SP*: Ian McClellan Hunter, Ben Markson. Story by Sidney Marshall. Based on the radio program by Phillips H. Lord. *CAST*: Dennis O'Keefe, Adolphe Menjou, Marguerite Chapman, Michael O'Shea, George Coulouris, Jeff Donnell, Steven Geray, Ralph Morgan, John Kellogg, Charles Trowbridge, Frank Reicher.

An assistant DA (O'Keefe) falls for a woman (Chapman), unaware that she is a murderess.

1323. Mr. Sardonicus (10/61) B&W—89 mins. (Horror). *DIR/PRO*: William Castle. *SP*: Ray Russell. Based on *Sardonicus* by Ray Russell. *CAST*: Ronald Lewis, Audrey Dalton, Guy Rolfe, Oscar Homolka, Vladimir Sokoloff, Erika Peters, Tina Woodward, Constance Cavendish, Mavis Neal.

A wealthy baron (Rolfe) has his face frozen in horror when he opens his father's coffin while searching for a winning lottery ticket. He enlists the aid of a neurosurgeon (Lewis), a former lover of his wife (Dalton), to cure him. His surgery is successful but it leaves the baron without the ability to eat or speak. NOTES: Castle's gimmick for this film was a "punishment poll" in which the audience was furnished a luminous card with a thumb printed on it. Just before the picture ends the audience would vote whether the villain would be spared (thumbs up) or punished (thumbs down). Castle would pretend he was counting the votes but, no matter how one voted, there was only one ending filmed.

1324. Mr. Smith Goes to Washington (10/20/39) B&W—125 mins. (Drama). *DIR/PRO:* Frank Capra. *SP:* Sidney Buchman. Based on *The Gentleman from Montana* by Lewis R. Foster. *CAST:* James Stewart, Jean Arthur, Claude Rains, Edward Arnold, Guy Kibbee, Thomas Mitchell, Eugene Pallette, Beulah Bondi, H. B. Warner, Harry Carey, Ruth Donnelly, Grant Mitchell, Porter Hall, Pierre Watkin, Charles Lane, William Demarest, Al Bridge, Edmund Cobb, Jack Carson, Stanley Andrews, Russell Simpson, Harry Bailey, Dick Elliott, Astrid Allwyn, H. V. Kaltenborn, Maurice Costello, Ann Doran, Walter Soderling, Carl Stockdale, Larry Simms, Vernon Dent, Eddie Kane, George McKay, Gene Morgan, Eddie Fetherstone, Milton Kibbee, James Millican, Fred "Snowflake" Toones, Lorna Gray, Mary Gordon.

Jefferson Smith (Stewart), a naive, idealistic Boy Scout leader, is made Senator by a corrupt political machine. He proves to be far from controllable as he exposes the political machine and filibusters for 23 hours to prevent passage of a bill that would benefit the political machine. NOTES: Frank Capra's last film for Columbia after an 11 year association. This film was updated and remade in 1977 by Taylor-Laughlin Films as *Billy*

Jack Goes to Washington and the producer was Frank Capra, Jr.

1325. Mr. Soft Touch (8/1/49) B&W—92 mins. (Drama). *DIR:* Henry Levin, Gordon Douglas. *PRO:* Milton Holmes. *SP:* Orin Jannings. Story by Milton Holmes. *CAST:* Glenn Ford, Evelyn Keyes, John Ireland, Beulah Bondi, Percy Kilbride, Clara Blandick, Ted de Corsia, Stanley Clements, Roman Bohnen, Harry Shannon, Gordon Jones, Angela Clarke, Charles Trowbridge, Jack Gordon, Ray Mayer, Mikel Conrad, William Rinehart, Leon Tyler, William Edmunds.

A hunted gambler (Ford) takes refuge in a settlement house, falls for the social worker (Keyes), and devotes himself to helping the needy. [British title: *House of Settlement*].

1326. Mr. Winkle Goes to War (8/3/44) B&W—80 mins. (War). *DIR:* Alfred E. Green. *PRO:* Jack Moss. *SP:* Waldo Salt, George Corey, Louis Solomon. Based on the book by Theodore Pratt. *CAST:* Edward G. Robinson, Ruth Warrick, Ted Donaldson, Bob Haymes, Richard Lane, Robert Armstrong, Richard Gaines, Walter Baldwin, Art Smith, Ann Shoemaker, Paul Stanton, William Forrest, Jeff Donnell, Howard Freeman, Warren Ashe, Robert Mitchum, Ben Taggart, Sam Flint, Nelson Leigh, Forbes Murray, Terry Frost, Hugh Beaumont, Dennis Moore, Emmett Vogan, Tommy Cook.

A meek bank clerk (Robinson) is inducted into the Army and becomes a hero when he drives a bulldozer into a foxhole of Japanese. [British title: *Arms and the Woman*].

1327. The Mob (9/7/51) B&W—87 mins. (Crime). *DIR:* Robert Parrish. *PRO:* Jerry Bresler. *SP:* William Bowers. Based on *Waterfront* by Ferguson Findley. *CAST:* Broderick

Crawford, Betty Buehler, Richard Kiley, Otto Hulett, Matt Crowley, Neville Brand, Ernest Borgnine, Walter Klavun, Lynne Baggett, Jean Alexander, Ralph Dumke, John Marley, Frank DeKova, Jay Adler, Emile Meyer, Carleton Young, Fred Coby, Ric Roman, Paul Bryar, Don Megowan, Charles Bronson (Buchinski), Harry Lauter, Paul Dubov, Lawrence Dobkin, Jess Kirkpatrick.

A cop (Crawford) goes undercover as a corrupt dock worker to get the goods on mobsters and their leader (Crowley), who run the docks. [British title: Remember That Face].

1328. Model Shop (2/69) Perfect Color — 90 mins. (Drama). DIR/PRO: Jacques Demy. SP: Jacques Demy, Adrien Joyce (Carol Eastman). CAST: Anouk Aimee, Gary Lockwood, Alexandra Hay, Carol Cole, Severn Darden, Tom Fielding, Neil Elliott, Jacqueline Miller, Anne Randall, Duke Hobbie, Craig Littler, Hilarie Thompson, Jon Lawson, Fred Willard.

A young man (Lockwood), knowing he is about to be drafted, spends his last 24 hours of freedom borrowing money to keep his car from being repossessed, meeting and bedding a French model (Aimee) and giving her his car money so she can get home to Paris. He returns home and finds his girl (Hay) and his car gone, receives his draft notice and resigns himself to face the future. NOTES: The first American film for French director Jacques Demy.

1329. Moderato Cantabile (1/64) B&W/Scope — 95 mins. (Drama). DIR: Peter Brook. PRO: Raoul J. Levy. SP: Marguerite Duras, Gerard Jarlot, Peter Brook. Based on the book by Marguerite Duras. A Lena-Companeez-Documento-Royal Films International Production. CAST: Jean-Paul Belmondo, Jeanne Moreau,

Didier Haudepin, Valerie Dobuzinsky, Pascale de Boysson, Collette Regis.

A woman (Moreau) witnesses a murder at a cafe and then, for several days, meets with a man (Belmondo) at the cafe to discuss the murder. NOTES: Originally released in France in 1960. [British title: Seven Days...Seven Nights].

1330. Modern Mothers (5/13/28) B&W — 59 mins. (Drama). DIR: Philip E. Rosen. PRO: Harry Cohn. SP: Peter Milne. CAST: Helene Chadwick, Douglas Fairbanks, Jr., Ethel Grey Terry, Barbara Kent.

A mother (Chadwick) visits her daughter (Kent), falls in love with her playwright boyfriend (Fairbanks), but gives him up when she sees the hurt it has caused her daughter.

1331. Modern Romance (3/81) Metrocolor — 93 mins. (Comedy). DIR: Albert Brooks. PRO: Andrew Scheinman, Martin Shafer. SP: Albert Brooks, Monica Johnson. CAST: Albert Brooks, Kathryn Harrold, Tyann Means, Bruno Kirby, Jr., Jane Hallaren, Karen Chandler, Dennis Kort, George Kennedy, Meadowlark Lemon, Bob Einstein, Virginia Feingold, Thelma Leeds.

A film editor (Brooks) cannot commit himself to marriage and breaks up with his girl (Harrold). He tries to forget her, but cannot, and tries to win her back, which he does. They marry and divorce and marry and...

The Molester see **Never Take Candy from a Stranger**

1332. Montana Territory (6/1/52) Technicolor — 64 mins. (Western). DIR: Ray Nazarro. PRO: Colbert Clark. SP: Barry Shipman. CAST: Lon McCallister, Wanda Hendrix, Preston Foster, Hugh Sanders, Jack Elam, Clayton Moore, Myron Healey, Eddy Waller, Ethan Laidlaw, Ruth Warren,

Trevor Bardette, George Chesebro, Robert Griffin, George Russell, Frank Matts.

When a sheriff (Foster) turns crooked and uses his badge to commit crimes, it is up to his deputy sheriff (McCallister) to stop him and bring him to justice.

1333. Monty Python Live at the Hollywood Bowl (6/82) Eastman Color—77 mins. (Comedy). *DIR/PRO:* Terry Hughes. Staged and presented by the Monty Python troupe. A Handmade Films Production. *CAST:* Graham Chapman, John Cleese, Terry Gilliam, Eric Idle, Terry Jones, Michael Palin, Neil Innes, Carol Cleveland.

The Monty Python troupe in concert doing some of their best TV skits.

1334. The Moon in the Gutter (9/83) Eastman Color—137 mins. (Drama). *DIR/SP:* Jean-Jacques Beineix. *PRO:* Lise Fayolle. A Gaumont-TFI-Opera-SFPC-Triumph Films Production. *CAST:* Gerard Depardieu, Nastassia Kinski, Victoria Abril, Vittorio Mezzogiorno, Dominique Pinon, Bertice Reading, Gabriel Monnet, Milena Vukotic, Bernard Farcy, Anne-Marie Coffinet.

A dock worker (Depardieu) sets out to find who raped his sister and caused her to commit suicide. *NOTES:* Limited theatrical release. [Original French title: *La Lune dans le Caniveau*].

1335. More Than a Secretary (12/11/26) B&W—77 mins. (Comedy). *DIR:* Alfred E. Green. *PRO:* Everett Riskin. *SP:* Dale Van Every, Ethel Hill, Aben Kandel, Lynn Starling. Based on *From Safari in Manhattan* by Matt Taylor. *CAST:* Jean Arthur, George Brent, Lionel Stander, Ruth Donnelly, Reginald Denny, Dorothea Kent, Charles Halton, Geraldine Hall, Charles Irwin, Francis Sayles, Nick

Copeland, Frances Morris, Tom Ricketts, Josephine McKim.

The owner of a secretarial establishment (Arthur) takes a job as secretary to a publisher (Brent) of a health magazine and, in due time, wins him over and revolutionizes the magazine.

1336. The More the Merrier (3/26/43) B&W—104 mins. (Comedy). *DIR/PRO:* George Stevens. *SP:* Robert Russell, Frank Ross, Richard Flournoy, Lewis R. Foster. Story by Robert Russell, Frank Ross, Garson Kanin. *CAST:* Jean Arthur, Joel McCrea, Charles Coburn, Richard Gaines, Bruce Bennett, Frank Sully, Clyde Fillmore, Stanley Clements, Don Douglas, Ann Savage, Grady Sutton, Shirley Patterson, Ann Doran, Vic Potel, Frank LaRue, Douglas Wood, Chester Clute.

During the World War II housing shortage in Washington, a retired millionaire (Coburn) plays matchmaker for two young people (McCrea, Arthur). *NOTES:* Remade by Columbia in 1966 as *Walk, Don't Run.*

1337. More to Be Pitied Than Scorned (9/24/22) B&W—58 mins. (Drama). *DIR:* Edward J. LeSaint. *PRO:* Harry Cohn. *SP:* Charles E. Blaney. A C.B.C. Production. *CAST:* J. Frank Glendon, Rosemary Theby, Philo McCullough, Alice Lake, Gordon S. Griffith, Josephine Adaire.

An actor (Glendon) mistakenly believes his wife (Lake) has been unfaithful, but in reality she is acting out the plot of a stage play as though it is real life. *NOTES:* Columbia's first feature film release.

1338. Moscow on the Hudson (3/84) Metrocolor—115 mins. (Comedy-Drama). *DIR/PRO:* Paul Mazursky. *SP:* Paul Mazursky, Leon Capetanos. *CAST:* Robin Williams, Maria Conchita Alonso, Cleavant Derricks,

Alejandro Rey, Savely Kramarov, Elya Baskin, Oleg Rudnik, Paul Mazursky, Alexander Beniaminov, Yakov Smirnoff, Michael Greene.

A saxophonist (Williams) with a touring Russian circus eludes the watchful eyes of the KGB and defects to the U.S.

1339. The Most Dangerous Man Alive (6/61) B&W — 82 mins. (Science Fiction). *DIR:* Allan Dwan. *PRO:* Benedict Bogeaus. *SP:* James Leicester, Phillip Rock. Based on *The Steel Monster* by Phillip Rock, Michael Pate. A Trans-Global Production. *CAST:* Ron Randell, Debra Paget, Elaine Stewart, Anthony Caruso, Gregg Palmer, Morris Ankrum, Tudor Owen, Steve Mitchell, Joel Donte.

Escaping from prison, a convict (Randell) wanders into a desert test site and becomes exposed to cobalt rays which turn him to steel. He then seeks the men who framed him knowing that nothing can harm him. *NOTES:* This film was shot in Mexico in 1958 but was not released in the U.S. until 1961. This was the last film to be directed by veteran director Allan Dwan.

1340. Most Precious Thing in Life (11/13/34) B&W — 64 mins. (Drama). *DIR:* Lambert Hillyer. *PRO:* Robert North. *SP:* Ethel Hill, Dore Schary. Based on *Biddy* by Travis Ingham. *CAST:* Jean Arthur, Donald Cook, Richard Cromwell, Anita Louise, Mary Forbes, Jane Darwell, Ben Alexander, John Wray, Dutch Hendrian, Ward Bond, Paul Stanton.

A woman (Arthur), rejected by her husband's (Cook) parents, takes a job at his old college where, twenty years later, she meets her son (Cromwell) and saves his romance.

1341. Mothra (5/62) Eastman Color/Scope — 101 mins. (Science Fic-

tion). *DIR:* Inoshiro Honda. *PRO:* Tomoyuki Tanaka. *SP:* Shinichi Sekizawa. Story by Shincichiro Nakamura, Takehiko Fukunaga, Yoshie Hotta. A Toho Company Production. *CAST:* Frankie Sakai, Hiroshi Koizumim, Kyoko Kagawa, Emi Ito, Yumi Ito, Jerry Ito, Ken Uehara, Takashi Shimura, Kenji Sahara.

When two tiny 6-inch princesses (Emi Ito, Yumi Ito) are kidnapped from their island and taken to Japan, their god, Mothra, a monster size moth, comes to their rescue. [Original Japanese title: *Mosura*].

1342. Motor Madness (5/4/37) B&W — 61 mins. (Crime-Drama). *DIR:* D. Ross Lederman. *PRO:* Harry L. Decker. *SP:* Fred Niblo, Jr., Grace Neville. *CAST:* Rosalind Keith, Allen Brook, Marc Lawrence, Richard Terry, Arthur Loft, J. M. Kerrigan, Joe Sawyer, George Ernest, Al Hill, John Tyrrell, Ralph Byrd.

A boat manufacturer (Brook) falls in with crooks and, with the help of his girl (Keith), manages to escape from their clutches and win the big international boat race.

1343. The Mountain Men (7/80) Metrocolor/Panavision — 102 mins. (Western). *DIR:* Richard Lang. *PRO:* Martin Shafer, Andrew Scheinman. *SP:* Fraser Clarke Heston. *CAST:* Charlton Heston, Brian Keith, Victoria Racimo, Stephen Macht, John Glover, Seymour Cassel, David Ackroyd, Cal Bellini, William Lucking, Ken Ruta, Victor Jory, Danny Zapien, Michael Greene, Terry Leonard.

Two fur trappers (Heston, Keith) enjoy the freedom of the wilderness in the last few years before the encroachment of civilization.

1344. The Mountain Road (6/60) B&W — 102 mins. (War). *DIR:* Daniel Mann. *PRO:* William Goetz.

SP: Alfred Hayes. Based on the book by Theodore White. CAST: James Stewart, Lisa Lu, Glenn Corbett, Henry (Harry) Morgan, Frank Silvera, James Best, Rudy Bond, Mike Kellin, Frank Maxwell, Eddie Firestone, Alan Baxter, William Quinn, Peter Chong.

During World War II in China, an Army major (Stewart) must destroy bridges and roads which are vital to the Japanese.

1345. The Mouse That Roared (11/59) Eastman Color—83 mins. (Comedy). DIR: Jack Arnold. PRO: Walter Senson, Jon Pennington. SP: Stanley Mann, Roger MacDougall. Based on The Wrath of the Grapes by Leonard Wibberly. An Open Roads Film Ltd. Production. CAST: Peter Sellers, Jean Seberg, David Kossoff, William Hartnell, Timothy Bateson, MacDonald Parke, Monty Landis, Leo McKern, Harold Krasket, Colin Gordon, Bill Nagy, Charles Clay, Austin Willis, Guy Deghy.

When the wine industry of the Grand Duchy of Fenwick is threatened by the California vineyards, the Prime Minister (Sellers) persuades the Queen (Sellers) to declare war on the U.S. so they can be defeated and receive foreign aid. NOTES: The only Columbia film in which their logo was a live actress, who left the screen when frightened by a mouse. A sequel, The Mouse on the Moon, was released by United Artists in 1963.

1346. Much Too Shy (7/42) B&W—92 mins. (Comedy). DIR: Marcel Varnel. PRO: Ben Henry. SP: Ronald Krankau. A Gainsborough Production. CAST: George Formby, Kathleen Harrison, Hilda Bayley, Eileen Bennett, Joss Ambler, Jimmy Clitheroe, Frederick Burtwell, Brefni O'Rorke, Eric Clavering, Gibb McLaughlin, Gus McNaughton, Peter Gawthorne.

A painter (Formby), who only paints heads, gets into trouble with his models when bodies are added to the heads and one of his paintings is used as a soap advertisement.

1347. Mule Train (2/22/50) Sepiatone—70 mins. (Western). DIR: John English. PRO: Armand Schaefer. SP: Gerald Geraghty. Based on a story by Alan James. A Gene Autry Production. CAST: Gene Autry, Sheila Ryan, Pat Buttram, Robert Livingston, Vince Barnett, Syd Saylor, Gregg Barton, Stanley Andrews, Pat O'Malley, Kenne Duncan, Bob Wilke, John Miljan, Frank Jacquet, Sandy Sanders, Roy Gordon, Robert Hilton, Robert Carson, Eddie Parker, George Morrell, John R. McKee, George Slocum, Frank O'Conner, Norman Leavitt.

Gene helps an old friend save his cement claim from a villainous contractor and freight shipper (Livingston). NOTES: This film was loosely based on the best selling song by Frankie Laine.

1348. Murder by Contract (12/58) B&W—81 mins. (Crime-Suspense). DIR: Irving Lerner. PRO: Leon Chooluck. SP: Ben Simcoe. CAST: Vince Edwards, Philip Pine, Herschel Bernardi, Michael Granger, Caprice Toriel, Frances Osborne, Cathy Browne, Steven Ritch, Joseph Mell, Janet Brandt, Davis Roberts, Don Garrett, Gloria Victor.

A hit man (Edwards) is sent to California to kill a woman (Toriel) who is to testify against the mob.

1349. Murder by Death (6/76) Eastman Color/Panavision—94 mins. (Comedy). DIR: Robert Moore. PRO: Ray Stark. SP: Neil Simon. A Rastar Production. CAST: Eileen Brennan, Truman Capote, James Coco, Peter Falk, David Niven, Alec Guinness, Elsa Lanchester, Peter Sellers, Maggie

Smith, Nancy Walker, Estelle Winwood, James Cromwell, Richard Narita.

Millionaire Lionel Twain (Capote) invites the world's greatest detectives (Coco, Falk, Niven, Smith, Lanchester, Sellers) to his house for the weekend in order to eliminate them. NOTES: The film debut of director Robert Moore and author Truman Capote.

1350. Murder Czech Style (8/68) B&W-Eastman Color—90 mins. (Comedy-Drama). DIR: Jiri Weiss. PRO: Barrandov Film Studios. SP: Jiri Weiss, Jan Otcenasek. A Barrandov-Ceskoslovensky-Royal Films International Production. CAST: Rudolf Hrusinsky, Kveta Fialova, Vaclav Voska, Vladimir Mensik, Vera Uzlacova, Libuse Svormova, Vjacheslav Irmanov.

When a man (Hrusinsky) learns that his boss (Voska) is having an affair with his wife (Fialova), he entertains thoughts of a double murder and suicide, but instead, decides to blackmail his boss for a better paying position. NOTES: Limited theatrical release. [Original Czech title: *Vrazda Po Cesku, Vrazda Po Nasem*].

1351. Murder in Greenwich Village (11/3/37) B&W—68 mins. (Mystery). DIR: Albert S. Rogell. PRO: Wallace MacDonald. SP: Michael L. Simmons. Story by Robert Shannon. CAST: Richard Arlen, Fay Wray, Raymond Walburn, Wyn Cahoon, Scott Colton, Thurston Hall, Marc Lawrence, Gene Morgan, Mary Russell, George McKay, Leon Ames, Marjorie Reynolds, Barry Macollum.

A photographer (Arlen) sets out to prove the innocence of of a woman (Wray) accused of murder.

1352. Murder in Times Square (6/4/43) B&W—65 mins. (Mystery).

DIR: Lew Landers. PRO: Colbert Clark. SP: Paul Gangelin. Story by Stuart Palmer. CAST: Edmund Lowe, Marguerite Chapman, John Litel, William Wright, Bruce Bennett, Esther Dale, Veda Ann Borg, Gerald Mohr, Sidney Blackmer, Leslie Denison, Douglas Leavitt, George McKay.

A Broadway actor (Lowe), accused of killing four people, sets out to find the real culprit with the help of a press agent (Chapman).

1353. Murder Is News (3/1/39) B&W—55 mins. (Mystery). DIR: Leon Barsha. PRO: Kenneth J. Bishop. SP: Edgar Edwards. Story by Theodore Tinsley. A Warwick Picture, Inc. Production. CAST: John Gallaudet, Iris Meredith, George McKay, John Hamilton, Doris Lloyd, Frank C. Wilson, William McIntyre, John Spacey, Colin Kenny, Fred Baes.

A radio newsman (Gallaudet) sets out to uncover a series of murders when he breaks a story about a society scandal.

1354. Murder on the Roof (2/9/30) B&W—60 mins. (Mystery). DIR: George B. Seitz. SP: F. Hugh Herbert. Story by Edward Doherty. CAST: Dorothy Revier, Raymond Hatton, Margaret Livingston, David Newell, Paul Porcasi, Virginia Brown, William V. Mong, Louis Natheaux, Fred Kelsey, Richard Cramer, Pietro Sosso, Hazel Howell, William Desmond.

When a lawyer (Mong) is jailed for killing a man on a nightclub roof, his daughter (Revier) takes a job there in order to find the real killer. NOTES: Only two sets were used for this film, the nightclub and the penthouse.

1355. Murder Reported (11/58) B&W—58 mins. (Mystery). DIR: Charles Saunders. PRO: Guido Coen. SP: Doreen Montgomery. Based on *Murder for the Millions* by Robert

Chapman. A Fortress Production. CAST: Paul Carpenter, Melissa Stribling, John Laurie, Peter Swanwick, Patrick Holt, Maurice Durant, Georgia Brown, Yvonne Romain, Trevor Reid, Anne Blake, Edna Kove, Hal Osmonde, Joe Robinson.

An ace reporter (Carpenter) and his editor's daughter (Stribling) set out to find the killer of a politician.

1356. Murderer's Row (12/66) Technicolor−108 mins. (Thriller). DIR: Henry Levin. PRO: Irving Allen. SP: Herbert Baker. Based on the book by Donald Hamilton. CAST: Dean Martin, Ann-Margaret, Karl Malden, Camilla Sparv, James Gregory, Beverly Adams, Richard Eastham, Tom Reese, Duke Howard, Ted Hartley, Marcel Hillaire, Corinne Cole, Robert Terry.

Matt Helm (Martin) sets out to rescue an inventor (Eastham) from a madman (Malden) who plans to use the inventor's ray to destroy Washington, D.C.

1357. Murphy's Romance (12/ 85) Metrocolor/Panavision−103 mins. (Romance). DIR: Martin Ritt. PRO: Laura Ziskin. SP: Harriet Frank, Jr., Irving Ravetch. Based on the novella by Max Schott. A Martin Ritt/Fogwood Films Ltd. Production. CAST: James Garner, Sally Field, Brian Kerwin, Corey Haim, Dennis Burkley, Georgann Johnson, Dortha Duckworth, Michael Prokopuk, Billy Ray Sharkey, Michael Crabtree, Anna Levine, Charles Lane, Carole King, Ted Gehring, Peggy McCay.

When a young divorcee (Field) arrives in town with her 13-year-old son (Haim) to rebuild her life, the widowed town pharmacist (Garner) begins a courtship with her.

1358. The Music Goes 'Round (2/24/36) B&W−80 mins. (Musical-Drama). DIR: Victor Schertzinger. PRO: Max Winslow. SP: Jo Swerling. Story by Sidney Buchman. CAST: Harry Richman, Rochelle Hudson, Walter Connolly, Douglass Dumbrille, Lionel Stander, Henry Mollison, Etienne Girardot, Walter Kingsford, Wyrley Birch, Victor Kilian, Dora Early, Gene Morgan, Herman Bing, Michael Bartlett, Eddie Farley, Mike Riley, The Onyx Club Band.

A Broadway star (Richman), on vacation from his show, encounters a troupe of untalented showboat performers and takes them back to New York to be part of his show. NOTES: A musical remake of the 1928 Columbia film *The Matinee Idol*.

1359. Music in My Heart (1/5/ 40) B&W−69 mins. (Musical). DIR: Joseph Stanley. PRO: Irving Starr. SP: James Edward Grant. Based on *Passport to Happiness* by James Edward Grant. CAST: Tony Martin, Rita Hayworth, Edith Fellows, Alan Mowbray, Eric Blore, George Tobias, Joseph Crehan, George Humbert, Joey Ray, Don Brodie, Julieta Novis, Eddie Kane, Phil Tead, Marten Lamont, Andre Kostelanetz and His Orchestra.

A foreign crooner (Martin) seeks to avoid deportation by appearing in a Broadway show with a singer (Hayworth).

1360. Mussolini Speaks (3/11/ 33) B&W−74 mins. (Documentary). DIR/PRO: Jack Cohn. SP: Lowell Thomas. Based on the writings of Benito Mussolini. CAST: Narrated by Lowell Thomas.

Old newsreel clips and still photographs show Mussolini's rise to power.

1361. The Mutations (9/74) Technicolor−91 mins. (Horror). DIR: Jack Cardiff. PRO: Robert D. Weinbach. SP: Robert D. Weinbach, Edward Mann. A Getty Production. CAST: Donald Pleasence, Tom Baker, Brad Harris, Julie Ege, Michael Dunn, Scott Anthony, Jill Haworth, Olga Anthony, Lisa Collins, Joan Scott, Toby Lennon, Richard Davies, John Werford, Eithne Dunne.

A scientist (Pleasence), trying to create a new species, half-plant, half-animal, sends his assistant (Baker) to kidnap humans for each experiment. When the experiments fail, the mutations wind up as freaks in a side show.

1362. The Mutineers (4/22/49) B&W — 60 mins. (Adventure). DIR: Jean Yarbrough. PRO: Sam Katzman. SP: Ben Bengal, Joseph Carole. Story by Dan Gordon. CAST: Jon Hall, Adele Jergens, George Reeves, Noel Cravat, Don C. Harvey, Matt Willis, Tom Kennedy, Pat Gleason, Frank Jacquet, Lyle Talbot, Smith Ballew, Ted Adams, Allen Mathews, Rusty Wescoatt, James Somers, Lee Roberts.

A sailor (Hall) manages to save his ship after it is taken over by a gang of gun runners and counterfeiters.

1363. My Dog, Buddy (8/60) B&W — 76 mins. (Children). DIR/SP: Ray Kellogg. PRO: Ken Curtis. A B.R.-Gordon McLendon Production. CAST: Travis Lemmond, Ken Curtis, Ken Knox, James H. Foster, Jane Murchison, Bob Thompson, Jo Palmie, Judge Dupree, Chuck Eisenmann, Gerry Johnson, Don Keyes, Bart McLendon, Desmond Dhooge, C. B. Lemmond, Lila Lemmond, "London," the dog.

A German shepherd goes in search of his master (Travis Lemmond) after they become separated.

1364. My Dog Rusty (4/8/48) B&W — 67 mins. (Children). DIR: Lew Landers. PRO: Wallace MacDonald. SP: Brenda Weisberg. Story by William B. Sackheim, Brenda Weisberg.

Based on characters created by Al Martin. CAST: Ted Donaldson, John Litel, Ann Doran, Mona Barrie, Whitford Kane, Jimmy Lloyd, Lewis Russell, Harry Harvey, Olin Howlin, Ferris Taylor, Mickey McGuire, Dwayne Hickman, David Ackles, Teddy Infurh, "Flame," the dog.

A young boy (Donaldson) gets his father (Litel), the local mayor, in trouble with his lying and causes him to lose the local election.

1365. My Kingdom for a Cook (10/27/43) B&W — 81 mins. (Comedy). DIR: Richard Wallace. PRO: P. J. Wolfson. SP: Harold Goldman, Andrew Solt, Joseph Hoffman, Jack Henley. Story by Andrew Solt, Lili Hatvany. CAST: Charles Coburn, Isobel Elsom, Bill Carter, Marguerite Chapman, Lucille Scott, Mary Wickes, Edward Gargan, Norma Varden, Almira Sessions, Eddy Waller, Ralph Peters, Ivan Simpson, Betty Brewer, Melville Cooper, Kathleen Howard, Charles Halton, Andrew Tombes.

Complications develop when an author and gourmet (Coburn), on tour in the U.S. without his favorite cook, steals the cook (Sessions) of a New England socialite (Elsom).

1366. My Name Is Julia Ross (11/9/45) B&W — 64 mins. (Mystery). DIR: Joseph H. Lewis. PRO: Wallace MacDonald. SP: Muriel Roy Bolton. Based on *The Woman in Red* by Anthony Gilbert. CAST: Nina Foch, Dame May Whitty, George Macready, Roland Varno, Anita Bolster, Doris Lloyd, Leonard Mudie, Joy Harrington, Queenie Leonard, Harry Hayes Morgan, Ottola Nesmith, Olaf Hytten, Evan Thomas, Reginald Sheffield.

A woman (Foch) accepts a job as a private secretary to a woman (Whitty) and her son (Macready), unaware that she is a dead ringer for the son's murdered wife. She later learns that her employers plan to drive her crazy, make her commit suicide, and replace her as the wife's corpse. NOTES: This film was reworked and remade in 1987 by MGM as *Dead of Winter*.

1367. My Other "Husband" (8/85) Eastman Color—110 mins. (Drama-Comedy). DIR: Georges Lautner. PRO: Alain Poire. SP: Jean-Loup Dabadie. A Triumph Films Production. CAST: Miou-Miou, Roger Hanlin, Eddy Mitchell, Dominique Lavanant, Charlotte de Turckheim, Rachid Ferrache, Ingrid Lurienne, Vincent Barazzoni, Venantino Venantini, Francois Perrot, Renee Saint-Cyr, Florence Giorgetti, Philippe Khorsand, Jean Rougerie.

A woman (Miou-Miou) leads a dual life as she holds down two jobs, two husbands (Hanlin, Mitchell), and two families in two different cities. NOTES: Originally released in France in 1983. Limited theatrical release. In French with English subtitles. [Original French title: *Attention! Une Femme Peut en Cacher une Autre*].

1368. My Sister Eileen (8/27/42) B&W—96 mins. (Comedy). DIR: Alexander Hall. PRO: Max Gordon. SP: Joseph Fields, Jerome Chodorov. Based on the play by Jerome Fields, Jerome Chodorov and stories by Ruth McKenney. CAST: Rosalind Russell, Brian Aherne, Janet Blair, George Tobias, Allyn Joslyn, Elizabeth Patterson, Grant Mitchell, Richard Quine, June Havoc, Donald MacBride, Gordon Jones, Jeff Donnell, Clyde Fillmore, Minna Phillips, Frank Sully, Danny Mummert, Almira Sessions, Kirk Alyn, Ann Doran, Robert Kellard, Forrest Tucker, Walter Sande, Ralph Dunn, Arnold Stang, The Three Stooges (Moe Howard, Larry Fine, Curly Howard).

Two sisters (Russell, Blair) arrive in New York from Ohio and rent a base-ment apartment in Greenwich Village where they encounter their kooky neighbors. NOTES: Remade by Columbia in 1955 as a musical comedy and it became a Broadway musical in 1953, *Wonderful Town* also starring Rosalind Russell.

1369. My Sister Eileen (10/55) Technicolor/Scope—108 mins. (Musical-Comedy). DIR: Richard Quine. PRO: Fred Kohlmar. SP: Blake Edwards, Richard Quine. Based on the play by Joseph Fields, Jerome Chodorov and stories by Ruth McKenney. CAST: Janet Leigh, Betty Garrett, Jack Lemmon, Bob Fosse, Kurt Kasznar, Dick York, Lucy Marlow, Tommy Rall, Barbara Brown, Horace MacMahon, Henry Slate, Hal March, Albert Morin, Queenie Smith, Richard Deacon, Ken Christy.

Two sisters (Garrett, Leigh) arrive in New York from Ohio and rent a base-ment apartment in Greenwich Village where they encounter their kooky neighbors. NOTES: A musical remake of the 1942 Columbia film.

1370. My Six Convicts (3/12/52) B&W—104 mins. (Prison-Drama). DIR: Hugo Fregonese. PRO: Stanley Kramer. SP: Michael Blankfort. Based on the book by Donald Powell Wilson. CAST: Millard Mitchell, Gilbert Roland, John Beal, Marshall Thompson, Alf Kjellin, Henry (Harry) Morgan, Jay Adler, Regis Toomey, Fay Roope, Carleton Young, John Marley, Russ Conway, Byron Foulger, Charles Bronson (Buchinski), George Eldredge, Peter Virgo, Carol Savage, Fred Kelsey, Barney Phillips, Dick Curtis.

A prison psychologist (Beal) probes the psyches of six convicts (Mitchell, Roland, Thompson, Kjellin, Morgan, Adler) to find out what makes them the way they are.

1371. My Son Is a Criminal (3/21/39) B&W—59 mins. (Crime). DIR:

C. C. Coleman, Jr. *PRO:* Wallace MacDonald. *SP:* Arthur T. Horman. *CAST:* Alan Baxter, Jacqueline Wells (Julie Bishop), Gordon Oliver, Willard Robertson, Joseph King, Eddie Laughton, John Tyrrell.

The son (Baxter) of a retired policeman (Robertson) takes to a life of crime, leading to a confrontation between father and son.

1372. My Son Is Guilty (1/24/40) B&W — 63 mins. (Crime). *DIR:* Charles Barton. *PRO:* Jack Fier. *SP:* Harold Shumate, Joseph Carole. Story by Karl Brown. *CAST:* Bruce Cabot, Jacqueline Wells (Julie Bishop), Harry Carey, Glenn Ford, Dick Curtis, Wynne Gibson, Don Beddoe, John Tyrrell, Bruce Bennett, Edgar Buchanan, Al Bridge, Robert Sterling, Edmund Cobb, Howard Hickman, Mary Gordon, Stanley Brown, Richard Fiske, Eddie Fetherstone, Hal Price, Forrest Taylor, Edward Piel, Sr.

A policeman (Carey) tries to get his son (Cabot) to go straight when he is released from prison, but the son returns to a life of crime and kills a police officer, sending the father after his son. [British title: *Crime's End*].

1373. My Stepmother Is an Alien (11/88) DeLuxe Color — 108 mins. (Comedy-Science Fiction). *DIR:* Richard Benjamin. *PRO:* Ronald Parker, Franklin R. Levy. *SP:* Jerico Weingrod, Herschel Weingrod, Timothy Harris, Jonathan Reynolds. A Weintraub Entertainment-Levy-Parker-Catalina Production. *CAST:* Dan Aykroyd, Kim Basinger, Jon Lovitz, Alyson Hannigan, Joseph Maher, Seth Green, Wesley Mann, Adrian Sparks, Juliette Lewis.

A widowed astronomer (Aykroyd) falls in love and marries an alien (Basinger) who has come to earth to find information that will save her planet.

1374. My True Story (3/8/51) B&W — 67 mins. (Crime). *DIR:* Mickey Rooney. *PRO:* Milton Feldman. *SP:* Howard J. Green, Brown Holmes. Story by Margit Mantica. Produced in association with *True Story* magazine. *CAST:* Helen Walker, Willard Parker, Elisabeth Risdon, Emory Parnell, Aldo Ray, Wilton Graff, Ivan Triesault, Ben Welden, Fred F. Sears, Mary Newton, Ann Tyrrell.

A convicted jewel thief (Walker), paroled from jail with the help of a mob boss (Graff), is recruited to rob a rich recluse (Risdon). She decides she wants to go straight and, with the help of a policeman (Parker), foils the mob's plans.

1375. My Woman (10/17/33) B&W — 73 mins. (Drama). *DIR:* Victor Schertzinger. *SP:* Brian Marlowe. *CAST:* Helen Twelvetrees, Victor Jory, Wallace Ford, Claire Dodd, Warren Hymer, Raymond Brown, Hobart Cavanaugh, Charles Levison, Ralph Freud, William Jeffrey, Lester Crawford, Boothe Howard, Edwin Stanley, Lorin Raker, Harry Holman.

A song-and-dance man (Ford) allows success to go to his head and opts for a rich lifestyle but, when his ego gets the best of him and leads to his downfall, he returns humbly to his wife (Twelvetrees).

1376. The Mysterious Avenger (1/17/36) B&W — 54 mins. (Western). *DIR:* David Selman. *PRO:* Harry L. Decker. *SP:* Ford Beebe. Story by Peter B. Kyne. *CAST:* Charles Starrett, Joan Perry, Wheeler Oakman, Hal Price, Charles Locher (Jon Hall), Edward J. LeSaint, George Chesebro, Lafe McKee, Jack Rockwell, Dick Botiller, Edmund Cobb, Sons of the Pioneers (Roy Rogers, Bob Nolan, Hugh Farr, Karl Farr, Tim Spencer).

A Texas Ranger (Starrett) returns

home to settle a cattle rustling feud between his father (McKee) and a neighboring rancher (LeSaint). He eventually locates the real rustler (Oakman) and brings him to justice.

1377. The Mysterious Intruder (4/11/46) B&W—61 mins. (Mystery). *DIR:* William Castle. *PRO:* Rudolph C. Flothow. *SP:* Eric Taylor. Based on *The Whistler* radio program. *CAST:* Richard Dix, Barton MacLane, Nina Vale, Regis Toomey, Helen Mowery, Mike Mazurki, Pamela Blake, Charles Lane, Paul E. Burns, Kathleen Howard, Harlan Briggs.

A private detective (Dix), out to recover some rare recordings, finds himself involved in murder.

1378. Mysterious Island (8/61) Eastman Color—100 mins. (Science Fiction). *DIR:* Cy Endfield. *PRO:* Charles H. Schneer. *SP:* John Prebble, Daniel B. Ullman, Crane Wilbur. Based on *L'Ile Mysterieuse* by Jules Verne. *CAST:* Michael Craig, Michael Callan, Gary Merrill, Herbert Lom, Joan Greenwood, Beth Rogan, Percy Herbert, Dan Jackson, Nigel Green.

A group of Union soldiers, including Cyrus Harding (Craig) and a newsman (Merrill), escape from a Confederate prison in a balloon, are blown off course, and land on an uncharted island inhabited by giant creatures which are the experimental results of Captain Nemo (Lom). *NOTES:* Special effects by Ray Harryhausen.

1379. Mystery of Thug Island (5/66) Eastman Color—96 mins. (Adventure). *DIR:* Luigi Capuano. *PRO:* Nino Battiferri. *SP:* Arpad De Riso, Ottavio Poggi. Based on *I Misteri Della Jungla Nera* by Emilio Salgari. A Leiber-Echberg Production. *CAST:* Guy Madison, Peter Van Eyck, Ingeborg Schoner, Giacomo Rossi Stuart, Ivan Desny, Giulia Rubini, Nando Poggi.

The leader of an island cult (Madison) kidnaps the daughter (Schoner) of a British officer (Van Eyck) who sets out to rescue her 15 years later. *NOTES:* Originally released in Italy in 1964. [Original Italian title: *I Misteri Della Giungla Nera*]. [Original German title: *Das Geheimnis Der Lederschlinge*].

1380. Mystery Ship (8/18/41) B&W—65 mins. (Action-Drama). *DIR:* Lew Landers. *PRO:* Jack Fier. *SP:* David Silverstein, Houston Branch. Story by Alex Gottlieb. *CAST:* Paul Kelly, Lola Lane, Larry Parks, Dwight Frye, Trevor Bardette, Cy Kendall, Roger Imhof, Eddie Laughton, Byron Foulger, John Tyrrell, Dick Curtis, Kenneth MacDonald.

Transporting a group of prisoners to an unnamed country, a G-man (Kelly) and his girl reporter (Lane) have their hands full when the prisoners break out of the hold and take over the ship. *NOTES:* The film debut of Larry Parks.

1381. Nacht-Bummler (Night Birds) (3/8/31) B&W—81 mins. (Crime). *DIR:* Richard Eichberg. *SP:* Rudolph Katscher, Egon Eis, Curt I. Braun, Max Erlich. Story by Victor Kendall. *CAST:* Eugen Burg, Harry Hardt, Hans Albers, Margot Walter, Charlotte Susa, Karl Ludwig Diehl, Herman Blass, Erich Schoenfelder, Jack Mylong-Muenz, Hugo Fischer-Keopee, Milo de Sabo, Senta Soeneland, Martha van Walter, Wera Engels, Leo Monosson, Peggy Whit, Charles Roellinghoff.

A detective (Hardt) sets out to trap a notorious crook. *NOTES:* Director Eichberg shot a 76 min. English version of this film with an English cast and Victor Kendall co-writing the screenplay. It was released in England by British International Pictures and was titled *Night Birds*.

1382. Name the Woman (5/25/28) B&W—56 mins. (Drama). DIR: Erle C. Kenton. PRO: Harry Cohn. SP: Erle C. Kenton, Peter Milne, Elmer Harris. CAST: Anita Stewart, Huntley Gordon, Gaston Glass, Chappell Dossett, Jed Prouty, Julanne Johnston.

A man (Glass) is acquitted of murder when a mysterious masked woman (Stewart) comes to his defense. NOTES: Remade by Columbia in 1934 as a talkie.

1383. Name the Woman (10/16/34) B&W—62 mins. (Crime-Mystery). DIR: Albert S. Rogell. PRO: Sid Rogell. SP: Fred Niblo, Jr., Herbert Asbury. CAST: Richard Cromwell, Arline Judge, Rita La Roy, Charles Wilson, Thomas Jackson, Bradley Page, Henry Kolker, Purnell Pratt, Crane Wilbur, Eddie Chandler, Wallis Clark, George Humbert, Al Hill, Stanley Fields.

A reporter (Cromwell) mistakenly involves a woman (Judge) in a murder plot and sets out to clear her name and find the real murderer. NOTES: A loose remake of the silent 1928 Columbia film.

1384. The National Health, or Nurse Norton's Affairs (5/73) Eastman Color—97 mins. (Comedy). DIR: Jack Gold. PRO: Ned Sherrin, Terry Glinwood. SP: Peter Nichols. Based on the play by Peter Nichols. CAST: Lynn Redgrave, Eleanor Brun, Sheila Scott-Wilkinson, Donald Sinden, Jim Dale, Neville Aurelius, Colin Blakely, Clive Swift, Mervyn Johns, David Hutcheson, Bert Palmer, Bob Hoskins, John Hamill, Robert Gillespie, Patience Collier, Maureen Pryor, George Browne, Graham Weston, Don Hawkins.

The British National Health System is spoofed as the staff and patients of a hospital create chaos. NOTES: Many of the cast members play dual roles as this film is two films in one, a spoof of the British Health System and a soap opera, "Nurse Norton's Affairs."

1385. Naval Academy (6/5/41) B&W—67 mins. (Drama). DIR: Erle C. Kenton. PRO: Wallace MacDonald. SP: David Silverstein, Gordon Rigby. Story by Robert James Cosgriff. CAST: Freddie Bartholomew, James Lydon, Billy Cook, Pierre Watkin, Warren Ashe, Douglas Scott, Warren Lloyd, Jimmie Butler, Joe Brown, Jr., David Durand, Tommy Bupp, John Dilson, William Blees.

Three boys (Bartholomew, Lydon, Cook) share a room and adventures while learning to become men at the naval academy.

1386. The Nebraskan (12/1/53) Technicolor/3-D—68 mins. (Western). DIR: Fred F. Sears. PRO: Wallace MacDonald. SP: David Lang, Martin Berkeley. Based on a story by David Lang. CAST: Phil Carey, Roberta Haynes, Wallace Ford, Lee Van Cleef, Pat Hogan, Richard Webb, Boyd "Red" Morgan, Regis Toomey, Jay Silverheels, Dennis Weaver, Maurice Jara.

An Army scout (Carey) tries to prevent an Indian war when his Indian scout (Jara) is accused of murder.

1387. Neighbors (12/81) Technicolor—95 mins. (Comedy). DIR: John G. Avildsen. PRO: Richard D. Zanuck, David Brown. SP: Larry Gelbart. Based on the book by Thomas Berger. CAST: John Belushi, Kathryn Walker, Cathy Moriarty, Dan Aykroyd, Igors Gavan, Dru-Ann Chukron, Tim Kazurinsky, Tino Insana, P. L. Brown, Henry Judd Baker, Lauren-Marie Taylor.

A suburban couple (Belushi, Walker) have their lives thrown into chaos when new neighbors (Aykroyd,

Moriarty) move next door. *NOTES:* John Belushi's last film.

Nemo *see* **Dream One**

1388. The Nevadan (2/50) Cine-Color—81 mins. (Western). *DIR:* Gordon Douglas. *PRO:* Harry Joe Brown. *SP:* George W. George, George F. Slavin, Rowland Brown. *CAST:* Randolph Scott, Dorothy Malone, Forrest Tucker, Frank Faylen, George Macready, Jeff Corey, Tom Powers, Jock Mahoney, Stanley Andrews, James Kirkwood, Charles Kemper, Kate Drain Lawson, Olin Howlin, Louis Mason.

An undercover marshal (Scott) tracks down an outlaw (Tucker) and tries to keep a quarter of a million in gold from falling into the hands of a greedy rancher (Macready). [British title: *The Man from Nevada*].

1389. Never Take Candy from a Stranger (8/60) B&W/Scope—81 mins. (Drama). *DIR:* Cyril Frankel. *PRO:* Anthony Hinds. *SP:* John Hunter. Based on the play *The Pony Cart* by Roger Garis. A Hammer Production. *CAST:* Gwen Watford, Patrick Allen, Felix Aylmer, Niall MacGinnis, Alison Leggatt, Bill Negy, MacDonald Parke, Michael Gwynn, Janina Faye, Frances Green, Estelle Brody, Robert Arden, James Dyrenforth, Vera Cook, Bud Knapp, Hazel Jennings, Cal McCord, Gaylord Cavallaro, Sheila Robins, Larry O'Conner, Helen Horton, Shirley Butler, Michael Hammond.

A British teacher's (Allen) failure in his attempt to have the town elder (Aylmer) convicted for molesting his daughter (Faye) leads to disastrous consequences. [British title: *Never Take Sweets from a Stranger*].

1390. Never Trust a Gambler (7/13/51) B&W—79 mins. (Crime-Drama). *DIR:* Ralph Murphy. *PRO:* Louis B. Appleton, Jr., Monty Shaff. *SP:* Jesse L. Lasky, Jr., Jerome Odlum. Story by Jerome Odlum. *CAST:* Dane Clark, Cathy O'Donnell, Tom Drake, Jeff Corey, Myrna Dell, Rhys Williams, Kathryn Card, Sid Tomack, Ruth Warren, Tom Greenway.

A gambler (Clark) on the run, who is actually a murderer, seeks refuge with his ex-wife (O'Donnell) and ends up killing another man which leads the police to him.

1391. The New Adventures of Pippi Longstocking (7/88) DeLuxe Color—100 mins. (Children). *DIR:* Ken Annakin. *PRO:* Ken Annakin, Walter Moshay, Gary Mehlman. *SP:* Ken Annakin. Based on characters created by Astrid Lindgren. *CAST:* Tami Erin, David Seaman, Jr., Cory Crow, Eileen Brennan, Dennis Dugan, Dianne Hull, George Di Cenzo, Dick Van Patten, John Schuck, J. D. Dickson.

Pippi (Erin) becomes separated from her father, and with her new friends (Seaman, Crow), encourages them to live life in the most irresponsible way possible.

1392. The New Centurions (8/72) Eastman Color/Panavision—103 mins. (Police-Drama). *DIR:* Richard Fleischer. *PRO:* Irwin Winkler, Robert Chartoff. *SP:* Stirling Silliphant. Based on the book by Joseph Wambaugh. *CAST:* George C. Scott, Jane Alexander, Stacy Keach, Scott Wilson, Erik Estrada, Rosalind Cash, Clifton James, Richard Kalk, James B. Sikking, Isabel Sanford, William Atherton, Ed Lauter, Dolph Sweet, Mittie Lawrence, Beverly Hope Atkinson, Roger E. Mosley, Mike Lane.

A law student (Keach) becomes a rookie policeman, teams up with a veteran cop (Scott), neglects his law studies and loses his wife (Alexander) because of his intense devotion to his

234   The Columbia Checklist

police work. [British title: *Precinct 45 — Los Angeles Police*].

1393. The New Champion (9/1/25) B&W — 50 mins. (Action-Drama). *DIR:* B. Reeves Eason. *PRO:* Harry Cohn. *SP:* Dorothy Howell. *CAST:* William Fairbanks, Edith Roberts, Lotus Thompson, Lloyd Whitlock, Frank Hagney, Al Kaufman, Marion Court, Bert Apling.

While visiting a friend (Fairbanks), a prizefighter (Hagney) hurts his hand while training and cannot fight. His blacksmith friend takes his place in the ring and wins the fight.

1394. The New Interns (6/64) B&W — 122 mins. (Drama). *DIR:* John Rich. *PRO:* Robert Cohn. *SP:* Wilton Schiller. Based on characters from the book *The Interns* by Richard Frede. *CAST:* Michael Callan, Dean Jones, Barbara Eden, Stefanie Powers, Inger Stevens, George Segal, Kay Stevens, Telly Savalas, George Furth, Ellie Wood, Greg Morris, Gordon Kee, Jimmy Mathers, Lee Patrick, Adam Williams, Sue Anne Langdon, Dawn Wells, Michael Fox, Gregory Morton, Rusty Lane, Alan Reed, Jr., Peter Hobbs, Charles Lane.

A group of interns (Callan, Jones, Segal) and nurses (Eden, Powers, Inger Stevens) struggle through their first year at a large hospital. *NOTES:* A sequel to the 1962 Columbia film *The Interns*; George Segal's first featured role.

1395. The New Kids (3/85) Metrocolor — 90 mins. (Thriller). *DIR:* Sean S. Cunningham. *PRO:* Sean S. Cunningham, Andrew Fogelson. *SP:* Stephen Gyllenhaal. Story by Brian Taggert and Stephen Gyllenhaal. A Fogbound Production. *CAST:* Shannon Presby, Lori Loughlin, James Spader, John Philbin, Vincent Grant, David H. MacDonald, Theron Mont-

gomery, Eddie Jones, Eric Stolz, Court Miller, Page Lyn Price, Lucy Martin, Tom Atkins, Jean DeBaer, Brad Sullivan.

A brother (Presby) and sister (Loughlin), newly arrived in town, are considered outsiders and are harassed by the local bully (Spader) and his gang until they can take no more and exact their own form of revenge.

1396. New Orleans Uncensored (3/55) B&W — 76 mins. (Crime-Drama). *DIR:* William Castle. *PRO:* Sam Katzman. *SP:* Orville H. Hampton, Lewis Meltzer. Based on *Riot on Pier 6* by Orville H. Hampton. *CAST:* Arthur Franz, Beverly Garland, Helene Stanton, Michael Ansara, Stacy Harris, Bill Henry, Michael Granger, Frankie Ray, Edwin Stafford Nelson, Mike Mazurki, Ralph Dupas, Pete Herman, Al Chittenden, Judge Walter B. Hamlin.

Told in semi-documentary style, a Navy veteran (Franz), working with the police, obtains a job as a dock worker to infiltrate the mob and clean up the docks. [British title: *Riot on Pier 6*].

Nice Dreams *see* **Cheech and Chong's Nice Dreams**

1397. Nicholas and Alexandra (12/71) Eastman Color/Panavision — 183 mins. (Historical-Biography). *DIR:* Franklin J. Schaffner. *PRO:* Sam Spiegel. *SP:* James Goldman, Edward Bond. Based on the book by Robert K. Massie. A Horizon Film Production. *CAST:* Michael Jayson, Janet Suzman, Roderic Noble, Ania Marson, Lynne Frederick, Candace Glendenning, Fiona Fullerton, Harry Andrews, Irene Worth, Tom Baker, Jack Hawkins, Timothy West, Guy Rolfe, John Wood, Eric Porter, Laurence Olivier, Michael Redgrave, Maurice Denham, Ralph Truman, John McEnery, Michael Bryant, Ian Holm, Alan Webb, Richard Warwick, Alexander Knox, Curt Jurgens, Julian Glover, Vernon Dobtcheff, Roy Dotrice.

A biographical account of the tumultuous reign of Russia's last czar, Nicholas II (Jayson), his wife Alexandra (Suzman), and their children (Noble, Marson, Frederick, Glendenning, Fullerton), which ended in the bloody revolution of 1917.

1398. Nickelodeon (12/76) Metrocolor/Panavision—121 mins. (Comedy). DIR: Peter Bogdanovich. PRO: Irwin Winkler, Robert Chartoff. SP: Peter Bogdanovich, W. D. Richter. CAST: Ryan O'Neal, Burt Reynolds, Tatum O'Neal, Brian Keith, Stella Stevens, John Ritter, Jane Hitchcock, Harry Carey, Jr., James Best, George Gaynes, M. Emmet Walsh, Ted Gehring, Hal Needham.

A lawyer turned director (Ryan O'Neal), and a rodeo-rider turned leading man (Reynolds), struggle in the early days of Hollywood to make moving pictures.

1399. Night Caller (11/75) Eastman Color—91 mins. (Crime-Drama). DIR/PRO: Henri Verneuil. SP: Henri Verneuil, Jean Laborde, Francois Verber. English language version by Paulette Rubinstein. A Franco-Italian Production. CAST: Jean-Paul Belmondo, Charles Denner, Lea Massari, Rosy Varte, Adalberto-Maria Merli, Roland Dubillard, Jean Martin, Catherine Morin.

A detective (Belmondo) has his hands full as he pursues a bank robber and an obscene phone caller who murders his victims. NOTES: Limited theatrical release. [Original French title: *Peur Sur la Ville*].

1400. Night Club Lady (8/27/32) B&W—66 mins. (Mystery-Crime). DIR: Irving Cummings. SP: Robert

Riskin. Based on the book by Anthony Abbot. CAST: Adolphe Menjou, Mayo Methot, Skeets Gallagher, Ruthelma Stevens, Blanche Frederici, Gerald Fielding, Nat Pendleton, Albert Conti, Greta Granstedt, Ed Brady, Lee Phelps, George Humbert, Niles Welch, Teru Shimada, William von Brincken.

New York police commissioner Thatcher Colt (Menjou) sets out to solve the murder of a nightclub hostess (Methot) who was under police protection.

1401. Night Editor (4/18/46) B&W—65 mins. (Crime). DIR: Henry Levin. PRO: Ted Richmond. SP: Hal Smith. Based on *Inside Story* by Scott Littleton. Based on the radio program *Night Editor* by Hal Burdick. CAST: William Gargan, Janis Carter, Jeff Donnell, Coulter Irwin, Harry Shannon, Paul E. Burns, Charles D. Brown, Frank Wilcox, Robert Stevens, Roy Gordon, Michael Chapin, Robert Emmett Keane, Anthony Caruso, Edward Keane, Jack Davis, John Tyrrell, Charles Marsh, Jimmy Lloyd, Emmett Vogan, Charles Wagenheim, Harry Tyler, Vernon Dent.

A police detective (Gargan) jeopardizes his career and marriage by becoming involved with a wealthy socialite (Carter) and, when they witness a murder, they keep quiet to avoid scandal. When an innocent man is convicted of the crime, the detective then sets out to redeem himself and find the real killer. [British title: *The Trespasser*].

1402. The Night Holds Terror (9/55) B&W—86 mins. (Crime). DIR/PRO/SP: Andrew Stone. CAST: Jack Kelly, Hildy Parks, Vince Edwards, John Cassavetes, David Cross, Edward Marr, Jack Kruschen, Joyce McCluskey, Jonathan Hale, Barney Phillips, Charles Herbert, Nancy Dee Zane, Joel Marston.

A trio of hoodlums (Edwards, Cassavetes, Cross) hold a family (Kelly, Parks, Herbert, Zane) captive and then kidnap the husband when they learn that his father is rich. NOTES: Based loosely on the 1939 Columbia film *Blind Alley* and the Broadway play *The Desperate Hours* by Joseph Hayes.

1403. The Night Mayor (11/26/32) B&W—68 mins. (Drama). DIR: Ben Stoloff. SP: Gertrude Purcell. Story by Sam Marx. CAST: Lee Tracy, Evalyn Knapp, Eugene Pallette, Warren Hymer, Donald Dillaway, Vince Barnett, Astrid Allwyn, Barbara Weeks, Gloria Shea, Emmett Corrigan, Tom O'Brien, Wade Boteler, Harold Minjir, Wallis Clark.

A mayor (Tracy) forsakes his mayoral duties for the night life, sports, the theater, and his girlfriend actress (Knapp). When a scandal threatens his administration, he has his girlfriend marry a newsman (Dillaway) so the press will leave him alone. NOTES: Based loosely on the life of New York mayor Jimmy Walker.

1404. Night of Terror (6/7/33) B&W—61 mins. (Mystery). DIR: Ben Stoloff. SP: Beatrice Van, William Jacobs. Based on *The Public Be Damned* by Willard Mack. CAST: Bela Lugosi, Sally Blane, Wallace Ford, George Meeker, Tully Marshall, Edwin Maxwell, Bryant Washburn, Gertrude Michael, Mary Frey, Matt McHugh, Pat Harmon, Oscar Smith.

A reporter (Ford) sets out to find a maniacal killer when his girlfriend's (Blane) family are being murdered one by one. NOTES: At the end of this film, the murderer (???) rises from the grave and warns the audience not to reveal his identity or the plot.

1405. The Night of the Generals (2/67) Technicolor/Panavision—148 mins. (War-Crime). DIR: Anatole Lit-

vak. PRO: Sam Spiegel. SP: Joseph Kessel, Paul Dehn. Based on *Die Nacht der Generale* by Hans Hellmut Kirst and *The Wary Transgressor* by James Hadley Chase. A Horizon-Filmsonor Production. CAST: Peter O'Toole, Omar Sharif, Tom Courtenay, Donald Pleasence, Joanna Pettet, Philippe Noiret, Charles Gray, Coral Browne, John Gregson, Nigel Stock, Christopher Plummer, Juliette Greco, Veronique Vendell, Eleonore Hirt, Gordon Jackson, Patrick Allen, Michael Goodliffe, Charles Millot, Harry Andrews, Pierre Mondy.

In 1942 Warsaw, a psychotic German general (O'Toole) murders a prostitute. Two years later another prostitute is murdered in Paris and the German intelligence officer (Sharif), who has been trailing him is also murdered. Twenty years later, at a banquet given in his honor, the general is confronted by a French police inspector (Noiret), who has also been trailing him. [Original French title: *La Nuit des Généraux*].

1406. Night of the Juggler (6/80) Technicolor—101 mins. (Crime). DIR: Robert Butler. PRO: Jay Weston. SP: Bill Norton, Sr., Rick Natkin. Based on the book by William P. McGivern. CAST: James Brolin, Cliff Gorman, Richard Castellano, Linda G. Miller, Barton Heyman, Sully Boyer, Julie Carmen, Abby Bluestone, Dan Hedaya, Mandy Patinkin, Marco St. John, Frank Adu, Nancy Andrews, Rick Anthony, Tony Azito.

An ex-cop (Brolin) tears apart New York City to locate the psychopath (Gorman) who has mistakenly kidnapped his daughter (Bluestone).

Night of the Tiger *see* **Ride Beyond Vengeance**

1407. Night Stage to Galveston (3/8/52) Sepiatone—61 mins. (Western). *DIR:* George Archainbaud. *PRO:* Armand Schaefer. *SP:* Norman S. Hall. A Gene Autry Production. *CAST:* Gene Autry, Virginia Huston, Pat Buttram, Thurston Hall, Robert Livingston, Harry Cording, Clayton Moore, Steve Clark, Harry Lauter, Dick Alexander, Boyd Stockman, Robert Peyton, Frank Sully, Ben Welden, Judy Nugent, Robert Bice, Frank Rawls, Lois Austin, Kathleen O'Malley, Riley Hill, Bob Woodward, Sandy Sanders, Gary Goodwin.

Gene returns to the Texas Rangers to stop the corruption of the State Police.

1408. The Night the World Exploded (6/57) B&W—64 mins. (Science Fiction). *DIR:* Fred F. Sears. *PRO:* Sam Katzman. *SP:* Luci Ward, Jack Natteford. A Clover Production. *CAST:* Kathryn Grant, William Leslie, Tristram Coffin, Raymond Greenleaf, Charles Evans, Frank Scannell, Marshall Reed, Fred Coby, Paul Savage, Terry Frost.

Three scientists (Grant, Leslie, Coffin) try to control a new element, E-112, from the center of the Earth, that explodes rocks when exposed to air.

1409. A Night to Remember (12/10/42) B&W—91 mins. (Crime). *DIR:* Richard Wallace. *PRO:* Samuel Bischoff. *SP:* Richard Flournoy, Jack Henley. Based on *The Frightened Stiff* by Kelley Roos. *CAST:* Brian Aherne, Loretta Young, William Wright, Jeff Donnell, Lee Patrick, Sidney Toler, Gale Sondergaard, Donald MacBride, Blanche Yurka, Don Costello, Richard Gaines, James Burke, Billy Benedict, George Chandler, Cy Kendall, John Dilson.

A Greenwich Village mystery writer (Aherne) and his wife (Young) turn sleuths to discover how a corpse found its way into their apartment.

1410. Nightfall (12/56) B&W—78 mins. (Crime). *DIR:* Jacques Tourneur. *PRO:* Ted Richmond. *SP:* Stirling Silliphant. Based on the book by David Goodis. A Copa Production. *CAST:* Aldo Ray, Brian Keith, Anne Bancroft, Jocelyn Brando, James Gregory, Frank Albertson, Rudy Bond, Eddie McLean, Gene Roth, George Cisar.

An innocent man (Ray), accused of murder and robbery, is pursued by two hoods (Keith, Bond) who believe he might know where the stolen money is located.

1411. The Nights of Lucrezia Borgeia (8/60) Eastman Color/Scope—108 mins. (Historical-Drama). *DIR:* Sergio Grieco. *PRO:* Carlo Caiano. *SP:* Mario Caiano, Aldo Segri. *CAST:* Belinda Lee, Jacques Sernas, Michele Mercier, Arnoldo Foa, Franco Fabrizi, Marco Tulli, Lily Scaringi, Germando Longo.

Lucrezia Borgeia (Lee) begins her downfall when she learns that her lover (Sernas) is in love with another (Mercier). [British title: *Nights of Temptation*]. [Original Italian title: *Le Notti di Lucrezia Borgia*].

1412. Nightwing (6/79) Metrocolor—103 mins. (Horror-Drama). *DIR:* Arthur Hiller. *PRO:* Martin Ransohoff. *SP:* Steve Shagan, Edwin "Bud" Shrake, Martin Cruz Smith. Based on the book by Martin Cruz Smith. *CAST:* Nick Mancuso, David Warner, Kathryn Harrold, Stephen Macht, George Clutesi, Strother Martin, Ben Piazza, Donald Hutton, Charles Hallahan, Alice Hirson, Judith Novgrod, Pat Corley.

When a Southwestern desert region is terrorized by thousands of rabid bats, an English scientist (Warner) sets out to destroy them.

1413. Nine Girls (2/17/44) B&W—78 mins. (Comedy-Suspense).

DIR: Leigh Jason. *PRO:* Burt Kelly. *SP:* Karen DeWolf, Connie Lee. Based on the play by Wilfrid H. Pettitt. *CAST:* Ann Harding, Evelyn Keyes, Jinx Falkenburg, Anita Louise, Leslie Brooks, Lynn Merrick, Jeff Donnell, Nina Foch, Shirley Mills, Marcia Mae Jones, Willard Robertson, William Demarest, Lester Matthews, Grady Sutton.

At a small California sorority college, suspicion falls on the matron (Harding) and several of her girls when one of them (Louise) is found murdered.

1414. 1984 (9/56) B&W—94 mins. (Drama). *DIR:* Michael Anderson. *PRO:* N. Peter Rathvon. *SP:* William P. Templeton, Ralph Bettinson. Based on the book by George Orwell. A Holiday Production. *CAST:* Michael Redgrave, Edmond O'Brien, Jan Sterling, David Kossoff, Mervyn Johns, Donald Pleasence, Carol Wolveridge, Ernest Clark, Patrick Allen, Ronan O'Casey, Michael Ripper, Kenneth Griffith, Ewen Solon.

In 1984, after the first Atomic War, in the community of Oceania, the people are watched and governed by "Big Brother." When a man (O'Brien) and woman (Sterling) fall in love, they plot to overthrow Big Brother but are betrayed. *NOTES:* There were two endings to this film. In the British version, O'Brien and Sterling are killed. In the American version, O'Brien betrays Sterling and declares his love for Big Brother before being killed.

1415. The Ninth Guest (3/3/34) B&W—67 mins. (Mystery). *DIR:* Roy William Neill. *SP:* Garnett Weston. Based on the play by Owen Davis and *The Invisible Host* by Gwen Bristow, Bruce Manning. *CAST:* Donald Cook, Genevieve Tobin, Hardie Albright, Edward Ellis, Edwin Maxwell, Vince Barnett, Helen Flint, Samuel S. Hinds, Nella Walker, Sidney Bracey.

Eight people are invited to a dinner party and when they arrive a mysterious voice announces that the "ninth guest" is dead and that they are to die one by one.

1416. No Greater Glory (3/13/34) B&W—117 mins. (Drama). *DIR:* Frank Borgaze. *SP:* Jo Swerling. Based on *The Paul Street Boys* by Ferenc Molnar. *CAST:* George Breakston, Jimmy Butler, Jackie Searl, Frankie Darro, Donald Haines, Rolf Ernest, Julius Molnar, Wesley Giraud, Beaudine Anderson, Bruce Line, Samuel S. Hinds, Christian Rub, Ralph Morgan, Lois Wilson, Egon Brecher, Frank Reicher, Tom Ricketts.

A frail youngster (Breakston) is given his happiest moment when he is allowed to join a gang and, despite his weaknesses, gains the respect of his fellow gang members and the rival gang leader (Darro). *NOTES:* Jimmy Butler, who played the gang leader, died 11 years later in World War II.

1417. No Greater Love (5/15/32) B&W—70 mins. (Drama). *DIR:* Lewis Seiler. *PRO:* Ben Stoloff. *SP:* Isadore Bernstein, Lou Breslow. *CAST:* Dickie Moore, Alexander Carr, Richard Bennett, Beryl Mercer, Hobart Bosworth, Betty Jane Graham, Alec B. Francis, Mischa Auer, Helen Jerome Eddy, Martha Mattox, Tom McGuire.

A Jewish delicatessen owner (Carr) adopts a crippled Irish girl (Graham) and, through much opposition, proves that he can care for her. [British title: *Divine Love*].

1418. No More Orchids (1/10/33) B&W—71 mins. (Drama). *DIR:* Walter Lang. *SP:* Gertrude Purcell, Keene Thompson. Based on the book by Grace Perkins. *CAST:* Carole Lombard, Lyle Talbot, Walter Connolly, Louise Closser Hale, Allen Vincent, Ruthelma Stevens, C. Aubrey Smith,

Arthur Housman, Jameson Thomas, William V. Mong, Edward J. LeSaint, William Worthington, Charles Hill Mailes, Harold Minjir, Sidney Bracey, Belle Johnstone, Broderick O'Farrell.

A poor-little-rich-girl (Lombard) is forced to marry into royalty to save her father (Connolly) from ruin, but the father sacrifices his life so that she can marry the man she loves (Talbot).

1419. No Place for a Lady (2/11/43) B&W—66 mins. (Mystery). *DIR:* James Hogan. *PRO:* Ralph Cohn. *SP:* Eric Taylor. *CAST:* William Gargan, Margaret Lindsay, Phyllis Brooks, Dick Purcell, Jerome Cowan, Edward Norris, James Burke, Frank M. Thomas, Thomas Jackson, Tom Dugan, Doris Lloyd, Ralph Sanford, William Hunter, Chester Clute.

When a private detective (Gargan) sets out to find the murderer of a wealthy widow (Lloyd), he learns that she was murdered for her collection of tires.

1420. No Sad Songs for Me (4/12/50) B&W—89 mins. (Drama). *DIR:* Rudolph Mate. *PRO:* Buddy Adler. *SP:* Howard Koch. Story by Ruth Southard. *CAST:* Margaret Sullivan, Wendell Corey, Viveca Lindfors, Natalie Wood, John McIntire, Ann Doran, Richard Quine, Jeanette Nolan, Dorothy Tree, Harlan Warde, Raymond Greenleaf, Urylee Leonardos, Margo Wood, Harry Cheshire, Douglas Evans, Sumner Getchell, Lucile Browne.

A woman (Sullivan) hides the fact from her husband (Corey) and daughter (Wood) that she is dying of cancer. *NOTES:* Margaret Sullivan's last film.

1421. No Sex Please—We're British (8/79) Technicolor—91 mins. (Comedy). *DIR:* Cliff Owen. *PRO:* John R. Sloan. *SP:* Anthony Marriott, John Mortimer, Brian Cooke. Based

on the play by Anthony Marriott, Alistair Foot. *CAST:* Ronnie Corbett, Beryl Reid, Arthur Lowe, Ian Igilvy, Michael Bates, Susan Penhaligon, Cheryl Hall, David Swift, Deryck Guyler, Valerie Leon, Margaret Nolan, Gerald Sim, Michael Robbins.

When a packet of pornographic postcards is delivered by mistake to a bank, the uptight employees undergo a drastic change in their sexual outlook.

1422. No Small Affair (11/84) MGM Color—103 mins. (Comedy-Romance). *DIR:* Jerry Schatzberg. *PRO:* William B. Sackheim. *SP:* Charles Bolt, Terence Mulcahy. Story by Charles Bolt. A Columbia-Delphi II Production. *CAST:* Jon Cryer, Demi Moore, George Wendt, Peter Frenchette, Elizabeth Daily, Ann Wedgeworth, Jeffrey Tambor, Tim Robbins, Hamilton Camp, Scott Getlin, Judith Baldwin, Jennifer Tilly, Kene Holliday.

A teen photographer (Cryer) snaps a picture of a nightclub singer (Moore), falls in love with her, and pursues her until she falls in love with him.

1423. No Time to Be Young (8/57) B&W—82 mins. (Drama). *DIR:* David L. Rich. *PRO:* Wallace MacDonald. *SP:* John McPartland, Raphael Hayes. Story by John McPartland. A Screen Gems Inc. Production. *CAST:* Robert Vaughn, Roger Smith, Tom Pittman, Dorothy Green, Merry Anders, Kathy Nolan, Sarah Selby, Fred Sherman, Ralph Clanton, Don C. Harvey, Bonnie Bolding.

A college dropout (Vaughn), in order to avoid the draft, recruits two friends (Smith, Pittman) to hold up a supermarket, with disastrous consequences. [British title: *Teenage Delinquents*].

1424. No Time to Marry (2/5/38) B&W—63 mins. (Comedy). *DIR:*

Harry Lachman. PRO: Nat Perrin. SP: Paul Jarrico. Based on Night Before Christmas by Paul Gallico. CAST: Richard Arlen, Mary Astor, Lionel Stander, Virginia Dale, Marjorie Gateson, Thurston Hall, Arthur Loft, Jay Adler, Matt McHugh, Paul Hurst, George Humbert.

When a pair of reporters (Arlen, Astor) cannot find the time to get married because their assignments keep them apart, one of them locates a missing person (Dale) the other has been searching for and must decide to tell the other or go for a scoop.

1425. Nobody's Children (12/12/40) B&W — 65 mins. (Drama). DIR: Charles Barton. PRO: Jack Fier. SP: Doris Malloy. Based on the radio program by Walter White, Jr. CAST: Edith Fellows, Billy Lee, Georgia Caine, Lois Wilson, Ben Taggart, Walter White, Jr., Mary Currier, Mary Gordon, Lillian West, William Gould, Russell Hicks, Janet Chapman, Mira McKinney, William Forrest, Edythe Elliott, Lloyd Whitlock, Joel Friedkin, Stanley Brown, Ivan Miller, Dorothy Adams.

Set in an orphanage, a boy (Lee), who could easily be adopted, refuses to be separated from his crippled sister (Fellows).

1426. Nobody's Perfekt (8/81) Metrocolor — 96 mins. (Comedy). DIR: Peter Bonerz. PRO: Mort Engelberg. SP: Tony Kenrick. Based on Two for the Price of One by Tony Kenrick. CAST: Gabe Kaplan, Alex Karras, Robert Klein, Susan Clark, Paul Stewart, Alex Rocco, Arthur Rosenberg, Bobby Ramsen, John DiSanti, Peter Bonerz, Luke Halpin, Roz Simmons, Harold Bergman.

Three social misfits (Kaplan, Karras, Klein) drive their car into a pothole and then concoct various schemes to get reimbursed for the damages.

Noche del Pecado, La see **La Noche del Pecado**

1427. None Shall Escape (2/3/44) B&W — 85 mins. (Drama). DIR: Andre De Toth. PRO: Samuel Bischoff. SP: Lester Cole. Story by Alfred Neumann, Joseph Than. CAST: Marsha Hunt, Alexander Knox, Henry Travers, Erik Rolf, Richard Crane, Dorothy Morris, Richard Hale, Ruth Nelson, Kurt Kreuger, Shirley Mills, Elvin Eric Field, Trevor Bardette, Frank Jacquet, Ray Teal, Art Smith, George Lessey.

A German soldier (Knox), crippled in World War I, returns to his village to his teaching duties, but because of his ideologies and his rape of a student, he loses his fiancee (Hunt) and is forced to leave. He then joins the Nazi party and returns to his village as a Nazi commandant and creates a wave of terror in the village.

1428. Norman Rockwell's World ... An American Dream (6/72) Technicolor — 30 mins. (Documentary). DIR: Robert Deubel. PRO: Richard Barclay. SP: Gaby Monet. A Concepts Unlimited Production. CAST: Norman Rockwell.

A documentary look at Norman Rockwell and how he captures his subjects on canvas. NOTES: Re-released by Columbia in October 1987.

1429. North from the Lone Star (3/31/41) B&W — 58 mins. (Western). DIR: Lambert Hillyer. PRO: Leon Barsha. SP: Charles F. Royal. CAST: Bill Elliott, Dorothy Fay, Dub Taylor, Arthur Loft, Richard Fiske, Jack Roper, Steve Clark, Edmund Cobb, Art Mix, Hank Bell, Claire Rochelle, Dick Botiller, Tex Cooper, Chuck Morrison, Al Rhein.

Wild Bill Hickok (Elliott), duped into becoming Marshal of Deadwood by an outlaw (Loft), turns the tables and proceeds to clean up the town.

1430. North of Nome (11/14/36) B&W—63 mins. (Western). *DIR:* William Nigh. *PRO:* Larry Darmour. *SP:* Albert DeMond. Story by Houston Branch. *CAST:* Jack Holt, Evelyn Venable, John Miljan, Guinn "Big Boy" Williams, Roger Imhof, Dorothy Appleby, Paul Hurst, Frank McGlynn, Robert Glecker, Ben Hendricks, Mike Morita, George Cleveland.

A seal hunter (Holt) fights seal-skin hijackers and a company that wants his hunting ground.

1431. North of Shanghai (6/13/ 39) B&W—59 mins. (War-Drama). *DIR:* D. Ross Lederman. *PRO:* Wallace MacDonald. *SP:* Maurice Rapf, Harold Buchman. *CAST:* James Craig, Betty Furness, Keye Luke, Morgan Conway, Russell Hicks, Joseph Danning, Dorothy Gulliver.

A newspaper reporter (Furness) and a cameraman (Craig), covering the Sino-Japanese war, join forces with a Chinese cameraman (Luke) to smash a spy ring north of Shanghai.

1432. North of the Rockies (4/2/ 42) B&W—60 mins. (Western). *DIR:* Lambert Hillyer. *PRO:* Leon Barsha. *SP:* Herbert Dalmas. *CAST:* Bill Elliott, Shirley Patterson, Tex Ritter, Larry Parks, Frank Mitchell, Francis Sayles, Ian MacDonald, Gertrude Hoffman, Lloyd Bridges, Earl Gunn, John Miljan, Boyd Irwin, Art Dillard, Dave Harper.

A Canadian Mountie (Elliott) and a U.S. Marshal (Ritter) go after fur smugglers. [British title: *False Clues*].

1433. North of the Yukon (3/30/ 39) B&W—62 mins. (Western). *DIR:* Sam Nelson. *PRO:* Harry L. Decker. *SP:* Bennett R. Cohen. *CAST:* Charles Starrett, Linda Winters (Dorothy Comingore), Bob Nolan, Lane Chandler, Paul Sutton, Robert Fiske, Vernon Steele, Tom London, Dick Botiller, Edmund Cobb, Kenne Duncan, Hal

Taliaferro (Wally Wales), Harry Cording, Ed Brady, Sons of the Pioneers.

On the trail of fur thieves, a Mountie (Starrett) pretends to be drummed out of the service so that he can infiltrate their gang and bring them to justice.

1434. Not a Ladies Man (5/14/ 42) B&W—60 mins. (Drama). *DIR:* Lew Landers. *PRO:* Leon Barsha. *SP:* Rian James. Based on *Just Another Dame* by Robert Hyde. *CAST:* Paul Kelly, Fay Wray, Douglas Croft, Ruth Lee, Lawrence Dixon, Don Beddoe, Louise Allbritton, Eileen O'Hearn, Jane Inness, Tristram Coffin, Hal Price, William Wright, Marietta Canty, Jimmy Dakan, Dorothy Babb.

A young boy (Croft) almost wrecks his father's (Kelly) marriage to a school teacher (Wray) when he tells her that his father loves someone else.

1435. Nothing But the Best (7/ 64) Eastman Color—99 mins. (Comedy). *DIR:* Clive Donner. *PRO:* David Deutsch. *SP:* Frederic Raphael. Based on *The Best of Everything* by Stanley Ellin. A Domino-Royal Films International Production. *CAST:* Alan Bates, Denholm Elliott, Harry Andrews, Millicent Martin, Pauline Delany, Godfrey Quigley, Alison Leggatt, Lucinda Curtis, Nigel Stock, James Villiers, Drewe Henley, Avice Landon, Ernest Clark, William Rushton, Peter Madden, Robert Bruce, Angus MacKay, Bernard Levin.

A real estate agent (Bates) hires a degenerate character (Elliott) to teach him manners and the proper way to behave in society in order to marry his boss' daughter (Martin). He then kills his tutor and, with the help of his landlady (Delany), hides his body in a trunk in the basement of her home. He then marries the daughter, goes on a honeymoon, and when he returns finds that his landlady is gone and her house is being torn down. He wonders if the trunk will be found.

1436. Nothing to Wear (11/5/28) B&W—56 mins. (Comedy). *DIR:* Erle C. Kenton. *PRO:* Jack Cohn. *SP:* Peter Milne. *CAST:* Jacqueline Logan, Theodore Von Eltz, Bryant Washburn, Jane Winton, William Irving, Edythe Flynn.

A woman (Logan) assumes a new fur coat is from her former boyfriend (Washburn) after her husband (Von Eltz) refused to buy her one. So, she sends it back to the boyfriend but his new girl (Winton) intercepts it. In reality it was the husband who sent his wife the fur coat and now he wonders where it is. A wild chase ensues with everyone trying to get the coat.

1437. The Notorious Landlady (7/62) B&W—123 mins. (Comedy-Mystery). *DIR:* Richard Quine. *PRO:* Fred Kohlmar. *SP:* Blake Edwards, Larry Gelbart. Based on *The Notorious Tenant* by Margery Sharp. *CAST:* Kim Novak, Jack Lemmon, Fred Astaire, Lionel Jeffries, Estelle Winwood, Maxwell Reed, Philippa Bevans, Henry Daniell, Ronald Long, Doris Lloyd, Richard Peel, Queenie Leonard, Florence Wyatt, Frederic Worlock.

A State Department employee (Lemmon), transferred to London, takes a flat where his landlady (Novak) is suspected of killing her husband. They begin a romance and when her husband (Reed) does turn up, she shoots him in self-defense when he can't find the jewels he had stolen. A mad chase then ensues for the missing jewels.

1438. The Notorious Lone Wolf (2/14/46) B&W—64 mins. (Mystery-Crime). *DIR:* D. Ross Lederman. *PRO:* Ted Richmond. *SP:* Martin Berkeley, Edward Dein. Story by William Bowers. Based on characters created by Louis Joseph Vance.

CAST: Gerald Mohr, Janis Carter, Eric Blore, John Abbott, Don Beddoe, William B. Davidson, Adelle Roberts, Robert Scott, Peter Whitney, Olaf Hytten, Ian Wolfe, Edith Evanson, Maurice Cass, Eddie Acuff, Virginia Hunter.

The Lone Wolf (Mohr) becomes the prime suspect when a museum jewel is stolen.

1439. Nude Odyssey (12/62) Eastman Color/Scope—97 mins. (Drama). *DIR:* Franco Rossi. *PRO:* Golfiero Colonna, Luciano Ercoli, Alberto Pugliese. *SP:* Ennio De Concini, Franco Rossi, Golfiero Colonna, Ottavio Alessi. Story by Franco Rossi, Ennio De Concini, Golfiero Colonna. A PCM-Cineriz-Francinex-Royal Films International Production. *CAST:* Enrico Maria Salerno, Venantino Venantini, Patricia Delores Donlan, Elizabeth Logue, Nathalie Gasse, Pauline Rey, Vaea Bennett, Jack Russel.

A film director (Salerno) goes from one adventure to another while filming a movie in Polynesia. [Original French title: *L'Odyssée Nue*]. [Original Italian title: *Odissea Nuda*].

Nuit de Varennes, La *see* **La Nuit de Varennes**

1440. Obey the Law (11/5/26) B&W—57 mins. (Drama). *DIR:* Alfred Raboch. *PRO:* Harry Cohn. *SP:* Max Marcin. *CAST:* Bert Lytell, Edna Murphy, Hedda Hopper, Larry Kent, Eugenia Gilbert.

A man (Kent) confesses to robbery when it is learned that the necklace he gave his friend (Lytell) for his daughter's wedding was stolen.

1441. Obey the Law (3/11/33) B&W—64 mins. (Drama). *DIR:* Ben Stoloff. *SP:* Arthur Caesar. Story by Harry Sauber. *CAST:* Leo Carrillo, Dickie Moore, Lois Wilson, Henry

Clive, Eddie Garr, Gino Corrado, Ward Bond.

An immigrant barber (Carrillo) becomes a citizen, fights for his personal rights, and helps to stop a crooked tenement boss (Clive) from controlling the local vote. [British title: *East of Fifth Avenue*].

1442. Object-Alimony (3/3/29) B&W—68 mins. (Drama). *DIR:* Scott R. Dunlap. *PRO:* Jack Cohn. *SP:* Peter Milne, Sig Herzig. Story by Elmer Harris. *CAST:* Lois Wilson, Hugh Allan, Ethel Grey Terry, Douglas Gilmore, Roscoe Karns, Carmelita Geraghty, Dickie Moore, Jane Keckley, Thomas Curran.

A young girl (Wilson) marries her boss (Allan) against his mother's (Terry) will, is accused of being unfaithful, and is driven from her husband's home. Moving into a boardinghouse she meets an aspiring writer (Gilmore) who turns her tale of woe into a hit novel and play and the husband, after reading and seeing both, goes to beg forgiveness.

1443. Obsession (7/76) Technicolor—98 mins. (Suspense-Romance). *DIR:* Brian De Palma. *PRO:* George Litto, Harry N. Blum. *SP:* Paul Schrader. Story by Brian De Palma, Paul Schrader. *CAST:* Cliff Robertson, Genevieve Bujold, John Lithgow, Wanda Blackman, Sylvia Kuumba Williams, Patrick McNamara, Stanley J. Reyes, Nick Kreiger, Stocker Fontelieu, Don Hood, Andrea Esterhazy.

In 1959, a businessman's (Robertson) wife and daughter are kidnapped and when he refuses to pay the ransom it is believed they are killed. Sixteen years later on a trip to Europe, he meets a young woman (Bujold) who resembles his dead wife. He becomes obsessed by her and we are left to wonder if she is his wife or his

daughter? *NOTES:* The film debut of John Lithgow.

1444. The Odd Job (5/78) Eastman Color—87 mins. (Comedy). *DIR:* Peter Medak. *PRO:* Mark Forstater, Graham Chapman. *SP:* Bernard MacKenna, Graham Chapman. A Tavlorda Production. *CAST:* Graham Chapman, David Jason, Diana Quick, Simon Williams, Edward Hardwicke, Bill Paterson, Michael Elphick, Stewart Harwood, Carolyn Seymour, George Innes.

An insurance man (Chapman), jilted by his wife (Quick), hires a hit man (Jason) to kill him. Realizing he still wants to live, he tries to stop the hit man, but remembers that he has instructed him not to listen to anything he says.

1445. The Odessa File (10/74) Eastman Color/Panavision—128 mins. (Adventure). *DIR:* Ronald Neame. *PRO:* John Woolf. *SP:* Kenneth Ross, George Markstein. Based on the book by Frederick Forsyth. A Domino-Oceanic Production. *CAST:* Jon Voight, Maximilian Schell, Maria Schell, Mary Tamm, Derek Jacobi, Peter Jeffrey, Klaus Lowitsch, Kurt Meisel, Hans Messemer, Garfield Morgan, Ernst Schroder, Gunter Strack, Noel Willman.

In 1963, a reporter (Voight) sets out to track down a former Nazi (Maximilian Schell) who disappeared after the war, and learns of an elite group, the "Odessa" (a real group) that helps ex-Nazis with new identities.

1446. Odongo (11/56) Technicolor/Scope—85 mins. (Drama). *DIR/ SP:* John Gilling. *PRO:* Islin Auster. Story by Islin Auster. A Warwick Production. *CAST:* Rhonda Fleming, Macdonald Carey, Juma, Eleanor Summerfield, Francis DeWolf, Earl Cameron, Dan Jackson, Michael Carridia, Errol John, Leonard Sachs, Paul Hardmuth, Bartholomew Sketch.

A young boy (Juma) is accused of setting free the animals that a big game hunter (Carey) captures for circuses and zoos.

1447. The Officer and the Lady (10/12/41) B&W—59 mins. (Crime). *DIR:* Sam White. *PRO:* Leon Barsha. *SP:* Lambert Hillyer, Joseph Hoffman. Story by Lambert Hillyer. *CAST:* Rochelle Hudson, Bruce Bennett, Roger Pryor, Richard Fiske, Sidney Blackmer, Tom Kennedy, Oscar O'Shea, Joe McGuinn, Charles Wilson, William Hall.

A policeman (Bennett) rescues his girl (Hudson) and her father (O'Shea) from an escaped convict (Blackmer). *NOTES:* The directorial debut of Sam White.

1448. Okinawa (2/28/52) B&W— 67 mins. (War). *DIR:* Leigh Jason. *PRO:* Wallace MacDonald. *SP:* Jameson Brewer, Leonard Stern, Arthur A. Ross. Story by Arthur A. Ross. *CAST:* Pat O'Brien, Cameron Mitchell, Richard Denning, Rhys Williams, James Dobson, Richard Benedict, Rudy Robles, Don Gibson, George Cooper, Alan Dreeban, Norman Budd, Alvy Moore.

In 1945, during the invasion of Okinawa, the commander of a destroyer (O'Brien) and his gun crew fight off repeated kamikaze attacks.

1449. Oklahoma Crude (7/73) Technicolor/Panavision—108 mins. (Comedy-Drama). *DIR/PRO:* Stanley Kramer. *SP:* Marc Norman. *CAST:* George C. Scott, Faye Dunaway, John Mills, Jack Palance, William Lucking, Harvey Jason, Ted Gehring, Cliff Osmond, Rafael Campos, Woodrow Parfrey, Harvey Parry, Larry D. Mann, John Dierkes, Robert Herron.

A drifter (Scott) helps a woman (Dunaway) and her father (Mills) pro-

tect their oil well from the head (Palance) of an oil-trust company that wants their land.

1450. The Old Dark House (10/ 63) Eastman Color—86 mins. (Horror-Comedy). *DIR:* William Castle. *PRO:* William Castle, Anthony Hinds. *SP:* Robert Dillon. Based on *Benighted* by J. B. Priestley. A Hammer-William Castle Production. *CAST:* Tom Poston, Robert Morley, Janette Scott, Joyce Grenfell, Mervyn Johns, Fenella Fielding, Peter Bull, Danny Green, John Harvey.

An American car salesman in London (Poston) gets involved in murder and mayhem when he delivers a car to an eerie mansion and has to spend the night. *NOTES:* 1) An inferior remake of the 1932 Universal film *The Old Dark House*. 2) Originally filmed in Eastman Color, the film was released to theaters in Black & White.

1451. The Old West (1/15/52) B&W—61 mins. (Western). *DIR:* George Archainbaud. *PRO:* Armand Schaefer. *SP:* Gerald Geraghty. A Gene Autry Production. *CAST:* Gene Autry, Gail Davis, Pat Buttram, Lyle Talbot, Dick Jones, House Peters, Sr., House Peters, Jr., Louis Jean Heydt, Don C. Harvey, Tom London, Syd Saylor, Pat O'Malley, John Merton, Frank Ellis, Kathy Johnson, Dee Pollack, Raymond L. Morgan, James Craven, Frankie Marvin, Bob Woodward, Buddy Roosevelt, Tex Terry, Bobby Clark, Robert Hilton.

Gene teams up with a preacher (Peters, Sr.) to stop his competitor (Talbot) from stealing his contract to supply horses to a stagecoach line. *NOTES:* The first Gene Autry film directed by George Archainbaud.

1452. The Old Wyoming Trail (11/8/37) B&W—56 mins. (Western). *DIR:* Folmer Blangsted. *PRO:* Harry L. Decker. *SP:* Ed Earl Repp. Story by

J. Benton Cheney. *CAST:* Charles Starrett, Barbara Weeks, Donald Grayson, Dick Curtis, Art Mix, Edward J. LeSaint, George Chesebro, Edward Piel, Sr., Edward Hearn, Slim Whitaker, Ernie Adams, Tom London, Dick Botiller, Frank Ellis, Si Jenks, Fred Burns, Blackie Whiteford, Ray Whitley, Guy Usher, Alma Chester, Joe Yrigoyen, Charles Brinley, Curley Dresden, Art Dillard, Ray Jones, Jerome Ward, Tex Cooper, Ed Javregi, Sons of the Pioneers (Roy Rogers, Bob Nolan, Tim Spencer, Hugh Farr, Karl Farr).

A cowboy (Starrett) sets out to stop a gang of land-grabbers when it is learned that a railroad is to be built in the territory.

1453. Oliver! (12/68) Technicolor/Panavision — 153 mins. (Musical). *DIR:* Sir Carol Reed. *PRO:* John Woolf. *SP:* Vernon Harris. Based on the musical play with book, music, and lyrics by Lionel Bart and based on *Oliver Twist* by Charles Dickens. A Romulus-Warwick Production. *CAST:* Ron Moody, Oliver Reed, Shani Wallis, Mark Lester, Jack Wild, Hugh Griffith, Harry Secombe, Sheila White, Joseph O'Connor, Peggy Mount, Leonard Rossiter, Megs Jenkins, James Hayter, Hylda Baker.

A musical version of the story by Charles Dickens, in which Fagin (Moody) recruits Oliver Twist (Lester) into his gang of youthful thieves and Oliver becomes friends with the Artful Dodger (Wild).

1454. The Olympics in Mexico (8/70) Technicolor/Scope — 120 mins. (Documentary). *DIR/SP:* Alberto Isaac. *PRO:* Federico Amerigo. *CAST:* Narrated by Allan Jeffreys.

A documentary of the XIXth Olympiad held in Mexico City. [Original Spanish title: *Olimpiada en Mexico*].

1455. On the Isle of Samoa (8/9/50) B&W — 65 mins. (Adventure). *DIR:* William Berke. *PRO:* Wallace MacDonald. *SP:* Brenda Weisberg, Harold R. Greene. Story by Joseph Santley. *CAST:* Jon Hall, Susan Cabot, Raymond Greenleaf, Henry Marco, Al Kikume, Rosa Turich, Leon Lontac, Neyle Morrow, Jacqueline DeWit, Ben Welden.

A thief (Hall), escaping with his partner's loot, crash-lands on a tropical island, and when he falls in love with a native girl (Cabot), he decides to leave to pay his debt to society and return to her.

1456. On the Waterfront (10/54) B&W — 108 mins. (Crime-Drama). *DIR:* Elia Kazan. *PRO:* Sam Spiegel. *SP:* Budd Schulberg. Based on the articles *Crime on the Waterfront* by Malcolm Johnson. A Horizon-American Picture Production. *CAST:* Marlon Brando, Lee J. Cobb, Rod Steiger, Eva Marie Saint, Karl Malden, Pat Henning, Leif Erickson, James Westerfield, Tony Galento, Tami Mauriello, John Hamilton, Rudy Bond, Martin Balsam, Fred Gwynne, Pat Hingle, Nehemiah Persoff, John Heldabrand, Don Blackman, Arthur Keegan, Abe Simon.

When his brother (Steiger) is killed, an ex-boxer and dock worker (Brando), with the help of his girl (Saint) and a priest (Malden), decides to turn the tables on the head mobster (Cobb) and his men who control the New York docks.

1457. On Top of Old Smoky (3/25/53) Sepiatone — 59 mins. (Western). *DIR:* George Archainbaud. *PRO:* Armand Schaefer. *SP:* Gerald Geraghty. A Gene Autry Production. *CAST:* Gene Autry, Gail Davis, Smiley Burnette, Grandon Rhodes, Kenne Duncan, Sheila Ryan, Zon Murray, Pat O'Malley, Fred S. Martin,

Bert Dodson, Robert Bice, Jerry Scroggins, The Cass County Boys.

Gene and the Cass County Boys, mistaken for Texas Rangers, help the owner of a toll road (Davis) save her ranch, rich in mineral deposits, from outlaws.

1458. On Velvet (3/38) B&W—70 mins. (Musical). *DIR/PRO:* Widgey R. Newman. *SP:* John Quin. An Associated Industries Production. *CAST:* Wally Patch, Joe Hayman, Vi Kaley, Mildred Franklin, Jennifer Skinner, Leslie Bradley, Ambrose Day, Nina Mae McKinney, Garland Wilson, Julie Suedo, Sidney Monckton, Olive Delmer, Bob Field, George Sims, Cleo Fauvel, Andre Sacre, Queenie Lucy, Eric Barker, Gordon Little, Mark Stone, Collinson and Dean, Helga and Jo, Rex Burrows and His Orchestra.

A pair of gamblers (Patch, Hayman) try to make a fortune when they buy a television station.

Once a Hero *see* **It Happened in Hollywood**

1459. Once More, With Feeling (2/60) Technicolor—92 mins. (Comedy). *DIR/PRO:* Stanley Donen. *SP:* Harry Kurnitz. Based on the play by Harry Kurnitz. *CAST:* Yul Brynner, Kay Kendall, Gregory Ratoff, Geoffrey Toone, Maxwell Shaw, Mervyn Johns, Martin Benson, Harry Lockhart, Shirley Anne Field, Grace Newcombe, C. S. Stuart, Colin Drake, Andrew Paulds, Barbara Hall, C. E. Joy.

An orchestra conductor (Brynner) and his wife (Kendall), not legally wed, must first get married in order to obtain a divorce. *NOTES:* Kay Kendall's last film.

1460. Once to Every Woman (3/24/34) B&W—70 mins. (Drama). *DIR:* Lambert Hillyer. *SP:* Jo Swerling. Based on *Kaleidoscope in K* by A. J. Cronin. *CAST:* Ralph Bellamy, Fay

Wray, Walter Connolly, Marie Carlisle, Walter Byron, J. Farrell MacDonald, Billie Seward, Katherine Claire Ward, Mary Foy, Ben Alexander, Rebecca Wassam, Jane Darwell, Edward J. LeSaint, Leila Bennett.

A young surgeon (Bellamy) takes over an operation when his older mentor (Connolly) cannot complete it.

1461. Once Upon a Time (4/27/44) B&W—89 mins. (Comedy). *DIR:* Alexander Hall. *PRO:* Louis F. Edelman. *SP:* Lewis Meltzer, Oscar Saul, Irving Fineman. Based on the radio play *My Client Curly* by Norman Corwin. Story by Lucille Fletcher Herrmann. *CAST:* Cary Grant, Janet Blair, James Gleason, Ted Donaldson, Howard Freeman, Mickey McGuire, William Demarest, Art Baker, Paul Stanton, Edward Gargan, Billy Bevan, Harry Strang, Isabel Withers, Lane Chandler, Nolan Leary, John Abbott, Ian Wolfe, Charles Arnt, William Gould, George Eldredge, Lewis Wilson, Mary Currier, Pedro de Cordoba, John Dilson, James Flavin, Vernon Dent, Emmett Vogan, Vi Athens, Murray Alper, Iris Adrian, Pierre Watkin, Tom Kennedy, John Tyrrell, Syd Saylor, Eddie Acuff, Tom Dugan, Mary Field, Barbara Pepper, Ruth Warren, Ray Teal, Frank Hagney, Kirk Alyn, Lloyd Bridges, Henry Armetta, Walter Fenner.

A failed Broadway producer (Grant) discovers a youngster (Donaldson) who owns a dancing caterpillar and sets out to exploit its commercial worth. *NOTES:* The film debut of Ted Donaldson. The caterpillar was never seen in the film.

1462. One Dangerous Night (1/21/43) B&W—77 mins. (Crime). *DIR:* Michael Gordon. *PRO:* David J. Chatkin. *SP:* Donald Davis. Story by Arnold Phillips, Max Nosseck. Based on characters created by Louis Joseph Vance. *CAST:* Warren William, Marguerite Chapman, Eric Blore, Mona Barrie, Tala Birell, Margaret Hayes, Ann Savage, Thurston Hall, Warren Ashe, Fred Kelsey, Frank Sully, Eddie Marr, Gerald Mohr, Louis Jean Heydt, Roger Clark, Gregory Gay, Eddie Laughton, Symona Boniface, John Tyrrell, Joe McGuinn, Charles Hamilton, Hal Price.

The Lone Wolf (William) has to clear himself of a murder charge when he is accused of killing a playboy who was engaged in blackmail.

1463. One from the Heart (2/82) Metrocolor — 101 mins. (Musical-Romance). *DIR:* Francis Ford Coppola. *PRO:* Gary Frederickson, Fred Roos, Barry Armyan Bernstein. *SP:* Barry Armyan Bernstein, Francis Ford Coppola. Story by Barry Armyan Bernstein. A Zoetrope Film Production. *CAST:* Frederic Forrest, Teri Garr, Raul Julia, Nastassia Kinski, Lainie Kazan, Harry Dean Stanton, Allen Garfield, Jeff Hamlin.

A couple (Forrest, Garr) decide to put their love on hold and see what it is like to have another lover. *NOTES:* It was this film that was a bomb for Coppola and caused the downfall of his Zoetrope Studios.

1464. One Girl's Confession (4/6/53) B&W — 74 mins. (Drama). *DIR/PRO/SP:* Hugo Haas. *CAST:* Cleo Moore, Hugo Haas, Glenn Langan, Ellen Stansbury, Burt Mustin, Anthony Jochim, Russ Conway, Leonid Snegoff, Jim Nusser, Mara Lea, Gayne Whitman, Leo Mastovoy, Martha Wentworth.

When a waitress (Moore) steals money from her guardian (Snegoff) and hides it, she confesses to the crime and is sent to jail. When she is paroled, she goes to work for a cafe owner (Haas) as a waitress and waits for the opportunity to recover her money.

1465. One Glorious Night (7/15/24) B&W — 56 mins. (Drama). *DIR:* Scott R. Dunlap. *PRO:* Harry Cohn. *SP:* J. Grubb Alexander. Story by Harvey Gates. *CAST:* Elaine Hammerstein, Alan Roscoe, Phyllis Haver, Freeman Wood, Lillian Elliott, Clarissa Selwynne.

A woman (Hammerstein) marries a lawyer (Wood), divorces him after her baby is born and given up for adoption, and is reunited with her daughter, years later, by her former lover (Roscoe).

1466. One Is Guilty (5/3/34) B&W — 64 mins. (Crime). *DIR:* Lambert Hillyer. *PRO:* Irving Briskin. *SP:* Harold Shumate. *CAST:* Ralph Bellamy, Shirley Grey, Warren Hymer, Rita La Roy, Wheeler Oakman, J. Carroll Naish, Ruth Abbott, Willard Robertson.

Inspector Trent (Bellamy) sets out to find the murderer of a prizefighter and his manager.

1467. One Man Justice (7/1/37) B&W — 59 mins. (Western). *DIR:* Leon Barsha. *PRO:* Harry L. Decker. *SP:* Paul Perez. Story by William Colt MacDonald. *CAST:* Charles Starrett, Barbara Weeks, Hal Taliaferro (Wally Wales), Jack Clifford, Mary Gordon, Al Bridge, Art Mix, Jack Lipson, Frank Ellis, Dick Curtis, Walter Downing, Lew Meehan, Ted Mapes, Hank Bell, Harry Fleischman, Maston Williams, Edmund Cobb, Steve Clark, Merrill McCormack, Eddie Laughton, Ethan Laidlaw.

A rancher (Starrett), having suffered amnesia, returns to the town of Mesa and is mistaken for another rancher believed dead. He slowly recovers his memory and cleans up the lawlessness in the town.

1468. One Man Law (1/11/32) B&W—61 mins. (Western). *DIR/SP:* Lambert Hillyer. *CAST:* Buck Jones, Shirley Grey, Robert Ellis, Murdock McQuarrie, Harry Todd, Henry Sedley, Ernie Adams, Dick Alexander, Edward J. LeSaint, Wesley Giraud.

A sheriff (Jones) sets out to prevent a land speculator (Ellis) from cheating the local ranchers.

1469. One Million Dollars (10/65) Technicolor/Scope—110 mins. (Comedy). *DIR:* Ettore Scola. *PRO:* Mario Cecchi Gori. *SP:* Ettore Scola, Ruggero Maccari. A Ceiad Production. *CAST:* Vittorio Gassman, Joan Collins, Jacques Bergerac, Hilde Barry, Adolfo Eibenstein.

An Italian nobleman (Gassman) goes after a gang of crooks as they smuggle money across the Italian border to be deposited in Swiss banks. [Original Italian title: *La Congiuntura*].

1470. One More Saturday Night (9/86) DeLuxe Color/Panavision—95 mins. (Comedy). *DIR:* Dennis Klein. *PRO:* Tova Laiter, Robert Kosberg, Jonathan Bernstein. *SP:* Al Franken, Tom Davis. An AAR-Tova Laiter/Columbia-Delphi IV Production. *CAST:* Tom Davis, Al Franken, Moira Harris, Frank Howard, Bess Meyer, Dave Reynolds, Chelcie Ross, Eric Saiet, Jessica Schwartz, Sally Tiven, Jonathan Singer, Nan Woods, Dianne B. Shaw.

A series of teenage misadventures on a Saturday night in Minnesota.

1471. One Mysterious Night (10/21/44) B&W—61 mins. (Crime). *DIR:* Oscar (Budd) Boetticher. *PRO:* Ted Richmond. *SP:* Paul Yawitz. Based on the characters created by Jack Boyle. *CAST:* Chester Morris, Janis Carter, George E. Stone, Dorothy Malone, Richard Lane, William Wright, Joseph Crehan, Robert Williams, Robert Scott, Lyle Latell, George McKay, Early Cantrell, John Tyrrell, Henry Jordan, Ben Taggart, Anne Loos.

Blackie (Morris) works with the police and becomes involved with a girl reporter (Carter) while trying to recover a valuable diamond stolen from a war relief exhibit. [British title: *Behind Closed Doors*].

1472. One Night of Love (9/6/34) B&W—84 mins. (Musical). *DIR:* Victor Schertzinger. *PRO:* Everett Riskin. *SP:* S. K. Lauren, James Gow, Edmund H. North. Based on *Don't Fall in Love* by Dorothy Speare, Charles Beahan. *CAST:* Grace Moore, Tullio Carminati, Lyle Talbot, Mona Barrie, Jessie Ralph, Luis Alberni, Andres De Segurola, Rosemary Glosz, Nydia Westman, Jane Darwell, William Burress, Frederick Burton, Henry Armetta, Olaf Hytten, Frederick Vogeding, Herman Bing, Edward Keane, Paul Ellis, Reginald LeBorg.

After losing a radio talent contest, an opera star (Moore) goes to Europe and, with the help of a singing teacher (Carminati), becomes a famous opera star.

1473. 1001 Arabian Nights (12/59) Technicolor—76 mins. (Animated). *DIR:* Jack Kinney. *PRO:* Stephen Bosustow. *SP:* Czeni Ormande. Story by Dick Shaw, Dick Kenney, Leo Salkin, Pete Burness, Lew Keller, Ed Nofziger, Ted Allen, Margaret Schneider, Paul Schneider. A UPA Production. *CAST:* Voices of Jim Backus, Kathryn Grant, Dwayne Hickman, Hans Conreid, Herschel Bernardi, Alan Reed, Daws Butler, The Clark Sisters.

Mr. Magoo plays matchmaker to his nephew and a princess in this loose adaptation of the classic tale "Aladdin and His Lamp."

One Way Out *see* **Convicted** (387)

1474. One-Way Ticket (12/31/35) B&W—72 mins. (Crime-Drama). *DIR*: Herbert Biberman. *PRO*: B. P. Schulberg. *SP*: Vincent Lawrence, Joseph Anthony, Oliver H. P. Garrett, Grover Jones. Based on the book by Ethel Turner. *CAST*: Lloyd Nolan, Peggy Conklin, Walter Connolly, Edith Fellows, Gloria Shea, Nana Bryant, Thurston Hall, George McKay, Robert Middlemass, Willie Fung, Jack Clifford, James Flavin.

A bank clerk (Nolan) decides to rob the bank he works in after being swindled out of his life savings. He is sent to prison where he escapes, marries the warden's daughter (Conklin), and is eventually caught and sent back to prison.

1475. One Way to Love (1/9/46) B&W—83 mins. (Comedy). *DIR*: Ray Enright. *PRO*: Burt Kelly. *SP*: Joseph Hoffman, Jack Henley. Story by Lester Lee, Larry Marks. *CAST*: Willard Parker, Marguerite Chapman, Chester Morris, Janis Carter, Hugh Herbert, Dusty Anderson, Jerome Cowan, Irving Bacon, Roscoe Karns, Frank Sully, Frank Jenks, Lewis Russell.

Two radio writers (Morris, Parker) and their girlfriends (Chapman, Carter) travel from Chicago to Hollywood and get involved with a millionaire (Herbert) and the president of a radio company (Cowan).

1476. The One Way Trail (10/15/31) B&W—60 mins. (Western). *DIR*: Ray Taylor. *PRO*: Irving Briskin. *SP*: George H. Plympton. Story by Claude Rister. *CAST*: Tim McCoy, Bud Osborne, Polly Ann Young, Slim Whitaker, Doris Hill, Jack Ward, Al Ferguson, Herman Hack, Carroll Nye.

A cowboy (McCoy) goes after the man (Ferguson) who killed his brother.

1477. Only a Shop Girl (12/15/22) B&W—68 mins. (Drama). *DIR/SP*: Edward J. LeSaint. *PRO*: Harry Cohn. Story by Charles E. Blaney. A C.B.C. Release. *CAST*: William Scott, Josephine Adaire, Mae Busch, Estelle Taylor, James Morrison, Willard Louis, Claire Du Brey, Wallace Beery, Tully Marshall.

After the owner of a department store (Louis) tries to make advances to one of his employees (Busch) he is found murdered. The girl's sweetheart (Scott), believing her to be guilty, takes the blame for the owner's murder. Later, after being burned in a fire, the real murderer (Taylor) confesses to the crime.

1478. Only Angels Have Wings (5/25/39) B&W—121 mins. (Aviation-Drama). *DIR/PRO*: Howard Hawks. *SP*: Jules Furthman. Story by Howard Hawks. *CAST*: Cary Grant, Jean Arthur, Richard Barthelmess, Rita Hayworth, Thomas Mitchell, Victor Kilian, John Carroll, Allyn Joslyn, Sig Rumann, Donald "Red" Barry, Noah Beery, Jr., Melissa Sierra, Lucio Villegas, Forbes Murray, Cecilia Callejo, Pat Flaherty, Pedro Regas, Candy Candido, James Millican, Curley Dresden, Stanley Brown, Vernon Dent, Dick Botiller.

The owner of an airline company (Grant) in South America sends his courageous fliers over the Andes in decrepit planes. *NOTES*: Screen writers William Rankin and Eleanor Griffin went uncredited. The plot and theme bore a striking resemblance to the 1937 RKO film *Flight from Glory*.

1479. Only Two Can Play (5/62) B&W—106 mins. (Comedy). *DIR*: Sidney Gilliat. *PRO*: Leslie Grant. *SP*: Bryan Forbes. Based on *That Uncertain Feeling* by Kingsley Amis. A Vale-British Lion-Kingsley Production. *CAST*: Peter Sellers, Mai Zetterling, Richard Attenborough, Virginia Maskell, Kenneth Griffith, Maudie Edwards, Frederick Piper, Graham Stark,

John Arnatt, Sheila Manahan, John Le Mesurier, Raymond Huntley, David Davies, Meredith Edwards, Marjorie Lawrence.

In Wales, a librarian (Sellers) tries unsuccessfully to have an affair with the wife (Zetterling) of a local town official.

1480. Only When I Laugh (9/81) Metrocolor—120 mins. (Comedy-Drama). *DIR:* Glenn Jordan. *PRO:* Roger M. Rothstein, Neil Simon. *SP:* Neil Simon. Based on the play *The Gingerbread Lady* by Neil Simon. *CAST:* Marsha Mason, Kristy Mc-Nichol, James Coco, Joan Hackett, David Dukes, John Bennett Perry, Guy Boyd, Ed Moore, Byron Webster, Peter Coffield, Mark Schubb, Dan Monahan, Michael Ross, Kevin Bacon, Ron Levine.

An alcoholic actress (Mason) struggles to stay off the bottle and reestablish her relationship with her teenaged daughter (McNichol). [British title: *It Hurts Only When I Laugh*].

1481. Open Season (8/74) Eastman Color—103 mins. (Action). *DIR:* Peter Collinson. *PRO:* Jose S. Vicuna. *SP:* Liz Charles-Williams, David Osborn. An Impala-Arpa Production. *CAST:* Peter Fonda, William Holden, Cornelia Sharpe, John Phillip Law, Richard Lynch, Albert Mendoza, Helga Line, Didi Sherman, Norma Castel, William Layton, Scott Miller, Loretta Tovar, May Heatherly.

Three hunters (Fonda, Lynch, Law) find more enjoyment in stalking humans than animals. [Original Spanish title: *Los Cazadores*].

1482. The Opening Night (11/14/27) B&W—55 mins. (Drama). *DIR/SP:* Edward H. Griffith. *PRO:* Harry Cohn. Story by Albert Payson Terhune. *CAST:* Claire Windsor, John Bowers, E. Alyn Warren, Grace Goodall.

A producer (Warren), believed drowned, turns up to see his wife (Windsor) marry her leading man (Bowers), and decides to leave them to their new happiness.

1483. Opening Night (2/35) B&W—68 mins. (Musical). *DIR:* Alex Brown. *PRO:* Charles Alexander. An Olympic Production. *CAST:* Douglas Byng, Walter Crisham, Reginald Gardiner, Dolores Dalgarno, Edward Cooper, Doris Hare, Andre Charlot Girls.

A musical revue centered around the opening of a nightclub cabaret.

1484. Operation Mad Ball (11/57) B&W—105 mins. (Comedy). *DIR:* Richard Quine. *PRO:* Jed Harris. *SP:* Jed Harris, Blake Edwards, Arthur Carter. Based on the play by Arthur Carter. *CAST:* Jack Lemmon, Kathryn Grant, Ernie Kovacs, Arthur O'Connell, Mickey Rooney, Dick York, James Darren, Roger Smith, William Leslie, L. Q. Jones, Sheridan Comerate, Jeanne Manet, Mary La Roche, Dick Crockett, Paul Picerni.

Set in France during World War II, a private (Lemmon) in an Army medical unit decides to throw a wild party and keep it a secret from his superior (Kovacs). *NOTES:* The film debut of Ernie Kovacs.

1485. Operation X (2/51) B&W—81 mins. (Drama). *DIR/PRO:* Gregory Ratoff. *SP:* Robert Thoeren, William Rose. Based on *David Golder* by Irene Nemirowsky. A British Lion-London Films Production. *CAST:* Edward G. Robinson, Nora Swinburne, Peggy Cummins, Richard Greene, Finlay Currie, Gregory Ratoff, Ronald Adam, Walter Rilla, James Robertson Justice, David Hutcheson, Peter Illing, Ronald Ward, Robert Villa, Harry Lane.

A megalomaniac businessman (Robinson) tries to marry his daughter (Cummins) off to the son (Villa) of an

Arab sheik (Illing) in order to get control of a rare mineral in his country. [British title: *My Daughter Joy*].

1486. Otley (3/69) Pathe Color— 91 mins. (Spy-Comedy). *DIR:* Dick Clement. *PRO:* Bruce Cohn Curtis. *SP:* Ian Le Frenais, Dick Clement. Based on the book by Martin Waddell. An Open Road Production. *CAST:* Tom Courtenay, Romy Schneider, Alan Badel, James Villiers, Leonard Rossiter, James Bolam, Fiona Lewis, Freddie Jones, James Cossins, James Maxwell, Edward Hardwicke, Ronald Lacey, Geoffrey Bayldon, Maureen Toal.

When his friend is killed, a petty thief (Courtenay) is suspected of being a spy and is pursued by spies (Schneider, Villiers) who believe he is in possession of valuable state secrets.

1487. Our Man in Havana (5/60) B&W—111 mins. (Comedy). *DIR/ PRO:* Sir Carol Reed. *SP:* Graham Greene. Based on the book by Graham Greene. A Kingsmead Production. *CAST:* Alec Guinness, Burl Ives, Maureen O'Hara, Ernie Kovacs, Noel Coward, Ralph Richardson, Jo Morrow, Paul Rogers, Gregoire Aslan, Duncan MacRae, Maurice Denham, Raymond Huntley, Hugh Manning, Maxine Audley, Ferdy Mayne, Karel Stepanek, Rachel Roberts, Elizabeth Welsh, Jose Prieto.

A vacuum cleaner salesman (Guinness) in Havana is recruited as a British spy and, in order to keep his job as a spy so he can send his daughter (Morrow) to finishing school, sends back fictitious information that is taken seriously.

1488. Our Wife (8/4/41) B&W— 95 mins. (Comedy). *DIR/PRO:* John M. Stahl. *SP:* P. J. Wolfson. Based on the play by Lillian Day, Lyon Mearson. *CAST:* Melvyn Douglas, Ruth Hussey, Ellen Drew, Charles Coburn,

John Hubbard, Harvey Stephens, Theresa Harris, Lloyd Bridges.

A musical composer (Douglas), depressed over the failure of his marriage, meets a girl (Hussey) and is inspired by her to write a new composition. When he finds success, his ex-wife (Drew) tries to win him back.

1489. Out of Bounds (7/86) DeLuxe Color—93 mins. (Crime-Thriller). *DIR:* Richard Tuggle. *PRO:* Charles Fries, Mike Rosenfield. *SP:* Tony Kayden. A Columbia-Delphia V-Fries Entertainment Production. *CAST:* Anthony Michael Hall, Jenny Wright, Jeff Kober, Raymond J. Barry, Pepe Serna, Michelle Little, Jerry Levine, Kevin McCorkle, Linda Shayne, Maggie Gwinn, Ted Gehring, Meatloaf, Jennifer Balgobin.

An Iowa farmboy (Hall) goes to visit his older brother in Los Angeles, picks up the wrong bag at the airport, becomes involved in murder, and is hunted by the police and a drug dealer (Kober).

1490. Out of the Depths (12/27/ 45) B&W—61 mins. (War-Drama). *DIR:* D. Ross Lederman. *PRO:* Wallace MacDonald. *SP:* Martin Berkeley, Ted Thomas. Story by Aubrey Wisberg. *CAST:* Jim Bannon, Ross Hunter, Ken Curtis, Loren Tindall, Robert Scott, Frank Sully, George Khan, Coulter Irwin, George Offerman, Jr., Rodd Redwing, Robert Williams, William Newell, Warren Mills, John Tyrrell.

An American submarine captain (Bannon) and his crew set out to stop a Japanese carrier from launching a kamikaze attack on the U.S. fleet.

1491. Out West with the Peppers (6/30/40) B&W—63 mins. (Comedy-Drama). *DIR:* Charles Barton. *SP:* Harry Rebuas. Based on *Five Little Peppers and How They Grew* by Margaret Sidney. *CAST:* Edith Fellows, Dorothy Ann Seese, Dorothy Peterson, Charles Peck, Tommy Bond, Bobby Larson, Victor Kilian, Helen Brown, Emory Parnell, Pierre Watkin, Ronald Sinclair, Walter Soderling, Roger Gray, Hal Price, Rex Evans, Millard Vincent, Wyndham Standing, Andre Cheron, John Rogers, Ernie Adams, Kathryn Sheldon, Eddie Laughton, Harry Bernard.

The Pepper family head for the Pacific Northwest on vacation and get involved in a series of adventures.

1492. Outcast of Black Mesa (4/ 13/50) B&W—54 mins. (Western). *DIR:* Ray Nazarro. *PRO:* Colbert Clark. *SP:* Barry Shipman. Story by Elmer Clifton. *CAST:* Charles Starrett, Martha Hyer, Smiley Burnette, Richard Bailey, Stanley Andrews, Lane Chandler, Chuck Roberson, William Haade, Bob Wilke, William Gould, Ozie Waters and His Colorado Rangers.

The Durango Kid (Starrett) uncovers a plot by a phony doctor (Bailey) to take over a gold mine. [British title: *The Clue*].

1493. The Outlaw Stallion (7/ 54) Technicolor—64 mins. (Western). *DIR:* Fred F. Sears. *PRO:* Wallace MacDonald. *SP:* David Lang. *CAST:* Phil Carey, Dorothy Patrick, Billy Gray, Roy Roberts, Gordon Jones, Trevor Bardette, Chris Alcaide, Harry Harvey, Robert Anderson, Guy Teague.

An outlaw (Roberts) plans to kidnap a mother (Patrick), her son (Gray), and the boy's stallion, when he learns that the boy's stallion killed his stallion.

1494. The Outlaws Is Coming (1/65) B&W—89 mins. (Western-Comedy). *DIR/PRO:* Norman Maurer. *SP:* Elwood Ullman. Story by Norman Maurer. A Normandy Production. *CAST:* The Three Stooges (Moe Howard, Larry Fine, Joe DeRita), Nancy Kovack, Adam West, Emil Sitka, Henry Gibson, Don Lamond, Mort Mills, Rex Holman, Murray Alper, Tiny Brauer, Joe Bolton, Bill Camfield, Hal Fryar, Johnny Ginger, Wayne Mack, Edward T. McDonnell, Bruce Sedley, Paul Shannon, Sally Starr.

The Three Stooges, after being fired from their job with the Preservation of Wildlife Society, travel out West where they meet Annie Oakley (Kovack) and get mixed up in a battle between gunfighters and Indians. *NOTES:* The last feature film of the Three Stooges for Columbia. [British title: *Three Stooges Meet the Gunslinger*].

1495. Outlaws of the Orient (8/ 20/37) B&W—61 mins. (Western). *DIR:* Ernest B. Schoedsack. *PRO:* Larry Darmour. *SP:* Charles F. Royal. Paul Franklin. Story by Ralph Graves. *CAST:* Jack Holt, Mae Clarke, Harold Huber, Ray Walker, James Bush, Harry Worth, Joseph Crehan, Bernice Roberts.

An oil driller (Holt), sent to the Gobi oil fields, sets out to stop a racketeer (Huber) from extorting protection money from the drillers and a rival oil company from taking over the fields.

1496. Outlaws of the Panhandle (2/27/41) B&W—59 mins. (Western). *DIR:* Sam Nelson. *PRO:* Jack Fier. *SP:* Paul Franklin. *CAST:* Charles Starrett, Frances Robinson, Bob Nolan, Richard Fiske, Lee Prather, Ray Teal, Blackie Whiteford, Pat Brady, Norman Willis, Bud Osborne, Jack Low, Steve Clark, Eddie Laughton, Stanley Brown, Sons of the Pioneers.

A cowboy (Starrett) comes to the aid of ranchers when a crooked gambling hall owner (Willis) tries to stop the railroad from coming thru. [British title: *Faro Jack*].

1497. Outlaws of the Prairie (12/1/37) B&W — 59 mins. (Western). *DIR:* Sam Nelson. *PRO:* Harry L. Decker. *SP:* Ed Earl Repp. Story by Harry Olmstead. *CAST:* Charles Starrett, Iris Meredith, Donald Grayson, Dick Curtis, Edward J. LeSaint, George Chesebro, Earle Hodgins, Jack Kirk, Art Mix, Jack Rockwell, Edmund Cobb, Frank Ellis, Lee Shumway, Dick Alexander, Fred Burns, Charles LeMoyne, Frank McCarroll, Curley Dresden, Hank Bell, George Morrell, Buel Bryant, Ray Jones, Jim Corey, Bob Burns, Steve Clark, Blackie Whiteford, Frank Shannon, Vernon Dent, Norman Willis, Sons of the Pioneers (Bob Nolan, Tim Spencer, Pat Brady, Hugh Farr, Karl Farr).

A Texas Ranger (Starrett) comes to the aid of gold shippers who are losing their shipments to stagecoach robbers.

1498. Outlaws of the Rockies (9/18/45) B&W — 54 mins. (Western). *DIR:* Ray Nazarro. *PRO:* Colbert Clark. *SP:* J. Benton Cheney. *CAST:* Charles Starrett, Carole Mathews, Tex Harding, Philip Van Zandt, Dub Taylor, I. Stanford Jolley, George Chesebro, Steve Clark, Jack Rockwell, Frank LaRue, James T. Nelson, Ted Mapes, Frank O'Conner, Carolina Cotton, Spade Cooley.

The Durango Kid (Starrett) has to prove his friend (Harding) innocent of bank robbery and bring the real outlaws to justice. [British title: *A Roving Rogue*].

1499. Outpost of the Mounties (9/14/39) B&W — 63 mins. (Western). *DIR:* C. C. Coleman, Jr. *PRO:* Harry L. Decker. *SP:* Paul Franklin. *CAST:* Charles Starrett, Iris Meredith, Bob Nolan, Dick Curtis, Kenneth MacDonald, Lane Chandler, Albert Morin, Hal Taliaferro (Wally Wales), Edmund Cobb, Pat O'Hara, Stanley Brown, Sons of the Pioneers.

A Mountie (Starrett) sets out to prove that his girlfriend's (Meredith) brother (Brown) is innocent of murder and robbery. [British title: *On Guard*].

Outside the Law *see* **The Strange Case of Dr. Meade**

1500. Outside the Three-Mile Limit (3/7/40) B&W — 63 mins. (Crime-Drama). *DIR:* Lewis D. Collins. *PRO:* Larry Darmour. *SP:* Albert DeMond. Story by Eric Taylor, Albert DeMond. *CAST:* Jack Holt, Irene Ware, Harry Carey, Eduardo Ciannelli, Paul Fix, Dick Purcell, Sig Rumann, Donald Briggs, Ben Welden, George J. Lewis.

Two G-men (Holt, Purcell) go after a gambling ship owner (Ciannelli) who uses his gambling operation to peddle counterfeit money. *NOTES:* Briefly released in 1939 as *Criminal Cargo*. [British title: *Mutiny on the Seas*].

1501. Outside These Walls (7/1/39) B&W — 60 mins. (Drama). *DIR:* Raymond B. McCarey. *PRO:* Ralph Cohn. *SP:* Harold Buchman. Story by Ferdinand Reyher. *CAST:* Michael Whalen, Dolores Costello, Virginia Weidler, Don Beddoe, Selmer Jackson, Mary Forbes, Robert Emmett Keane, Pierre Watkin, Kathleen Lockhart, Dick Curtis.

An ex-convict (Whalen), unable to find work when he is released from prison, buys a printing press and sets up his own newspaper to fight local corruption and, when the prison warden (Jackson) loses his job, he uses his newspaper to help him get elected governor.

The Outsiders *see* **Band of Outsiders**

1502. Over-Exposed (4/56) B&W — 80 mins. (Drama). *DIR:* Lewis Seiler. *PRO:* Lewis J. Rachmil. *SP:* James Gunn, Gil Orlovitz. Story by Richard Sale, Mary Loos. *CAST:* Cleo

Moore, Richard Crenna, Isobel Elsom, Raymond Greenleaf, James O'Rear, Shirley Thomas, Donald Randolph, Dayton Lummis, Jeanne Cooper, Jack Albertson, William McLean, Edna Holland, Edwin Parker, John Cason, Dick Crockett, Geraldine Hall, Voltaire Perkins, Joan Miller, Norma Brooks, Robert B. Williams, Frank Mitchell.

A top commercial photographer (Moore) learns her trade with the help of an alcoholic cameraman (Greenleaf) and a reporter (Crenna).

1503. Over the Santa Fe Trail (2/13/47) B&W — 63 mins. (Musical-Western). *DIR:* Ray Nazarro. *PRO:* Colbert Clark. *SP:* Louise Rousseau. Story by Eileen Gary. *CAST:* Ken Curtis, Jennifer Holt, Guy Kibbee, Guinn "Big Boy" Williams, Holmes Herbert, Jim Diehl, Noel Neill, Frank LaRue, George Chesebro, Steve Clark, Nolan Leary, Julian Rivero, Bud Osborne, The Hoosier Hotshots, The DeCastro Sisters, Art West and His Sunset Riders.

A cowboy (Curtis) falls for a medicine show entertainer (Holt). [British title: *No Escape*].

1504. Over 21 (7/25/45) B&W — 104 mins. (Comedy). *DIR:* Charles Vidor. *PRO/SP:* Sidney Buchman. Based on the play by Ruth Gordon. *CAST:* Alexander Knox, Irene Dunne, Charles Coburn, Jeff Donnell, Loren Tindall, Lee Patrick, Cora Witherspoon, Phil Brown, Charles Evans, Pierre Watkin, Anne Loos, Nanette Parks, Adelle Roberts, Jean Stevens, Carole Mathews, Robert Emmett Keane, Forbes Murray, James Flavin, Charles Hamilton.

A writer (Knox) joins the Army to find out about military life while his wife (Dunne) deals with domestic problems, and his publisher (Coburn) tries to get him back.

1505. The Overland Express (4/11/38) B&W — 55 mins. (Western). *DIR:* Drew Eberson. *PRO:* L. G. Leonard. *SP:* Monroe Shaff. *CAST:* Buck Jones, Marjorie Reynolds, Carlyle Moore, Maston Williams, Ben Corbett, William Arnold, Lew Kelly, Bud Osborne, Ben Taggart, Bob Woodward, Blackie Whiteford, Gene Alsace (Rocky Camron).

A pony express rider (Jones) battles Indians and a rival stage line as he carries the mail from Missouri to California.

1506. Overland to Deadwood (9/25/42) B&W — 59 mins. (Western). *DIR:* William Berke. *PRO:* Jack Fier. *SP:* Paul Franklin. *CAST:* Charles Starrett, Leslie Brooks, Cliff Edwards, Art Mix, Russell Hayden, Bud Osborne, Norman Willis, Bud Geary, Francis Walker, Lynton Brent, Matt Willis, June Pickrell, Gordon DeMain, Herman Hack.

Two cowboys (Starrett, Hayden) help a woman (Brooks) save her freight-hauling franchise from a rival competitor who wants a railroad franchise. [British title: *Falling Stones*].

1507. The Owl and the Pussycat (11/70) Eastman Color/Panavision — 98 mins. (Comedy). *DIR:* Herbert Ross. *PRO:* Ray Stark. *SP:* Buck Henry. Based on the play by Bill Manhoff. A Rastar Production. *CAST:* Barbra Streisand, George Segal, Robert Klein, Allen Garfield, Roz Kelly, Jacques Sandulescu, Jack Manning, Grace Carney, Barbara Anson, Buck Henry, Evelyn Lang (Marilyn Chambers).

A casual hooker (Streisand) forms an off-again on-again relationship with her neighbor (Segal), a would-be author and bookstore clerk.

1508. Pacific Adventure (11/26/47) B&W — 95 mins. (Biography). *DIR:* Kenneth G. Hall. *PRO:* Nick Perry.

SP: John Chandler, Alec Coppel. Based on *Smithy* by Kenneth G. Hall, Max Afford. CAST: Ron Randell, Muriel Steinbeck, John Tate, Joy Nichols, Nan Taylor, Alec Kellaway, John Dease, Joe Volti, Marshall Crosby, John Dunne, Edward Smith, Alan Herbert, John Stannage, Capt. P. G. Taylor, Rt. Hon. W. M. Hughes.

A biography of Australia's pioneer aviator, Sir Charles Kingsford Smith (Randell). NOTES: Released in Australia in 1946 at a running time of 118 mins. [British title: *Smithy*].

1509. Pack Train (7/30/53) Sepiatone — 57 mins. (Western). DIR: George Archainbaud. PRO: Armand Schaefer. SP: Norman S. Hall. A Gene Autry Production. CAST: Gene Autry, Gail Davis, Smiley Burnette, Kenne Duncan, Sheila Ryan, Tom London, Kermit Maynard, Harry Lauter, Frank Ellis, Dick Alexander, Herman Hack, Jill Zeller, Frank O'Conner, Wesley Hudman, Tex Terry, Frankie Marvin, Melinda Plowman, B. G. Norman, Louise Lorimer, Norman E. Westcott.

Gene sets out to stop a couple of crooked storekeepers (Ryan, Duncan) who are selling supplies to miners instead of the settlers in Settlement Valley.

1510. Pagan Lady (9/27/31) B&W — 70 mins. (Drama). DIR: John Francis Dillon. SP: Benjamin Glazer. Based on the play by William DuBois. CAST: Evelyn Brent, Conrad Nagel, Charles Bickford, Roland Young, William Farnum, Lucille Gleason, Leslie Fenton, Gwen Lee, Wallace MacDonald.

A lady of questionable virtue (Brent) leads the nephew (Nagel) of an evangelist (Farnum) astray.

1511. Paid in Error (2/38) B&W — 68 mins. (Comedy). DIR: Maclean Rogers. PRO: George Smith. SP: Basil Mason, H. F. Maltby. Story by John Chancellor. CAST: George Carney, Lillian Christine, Tom Helmore, Marjorie Taylor, Googie Withers, Molly Hamley-Clifford, Jonathan Field, Aubrey Mallalieu.

A bank cashier (Helmore) sets out to recover money credited to a customer (Carney) in error.

1512. Paid to Dance (12/11/37) B&W — 55 mins. (Crime-Drama). DIR: C. C. Coleman, Jr. PRO: Ralph Cohn. SP: Robert E. Kent. Story by Leslie T. White. CAST: Don Terry, Jacqueline Wells (Julie Bishop), Rita Hayworth, Arthur Loft, Paul Stanton, Paul Fix, Louise Stanley, Ralph Byrd, Bess Flowers, Dick Curtis, Beatrice Blinn, Beatrice Curtis, Al Herman, Thurston Hall, John Gallaudet, Horace MacMahon, George Lloyd, Ann Doran, Ruth Hilliard, Bud Jamison, Edward J. LeSaint, Ethan Laidlaw, Edward Piel, Sr., Harry Strang.

An investigator (Terry) and undercover agent (Wells) set out to stop a gang of racketeers who are infiltrating the dance-hall-hostess game. NOTES: This film was released to cash in on the popularity of the 1937 Warner Bros. film *Marked Woman*.

1513. Pal Joey (10/57) Technicolor — 111 mins. (Musical-Comedy). DIR: George Sidney. PRO: Fred Kohlmar. SP: Dorothy Kingsley. Based on the *New Yorker* stories by John O'Hara, and the musical play by John O'Hara, Richard Rodgers, Lorenz Hart. An Essex-Sidney Production. CAST: Rita Hayworth, Frank Sinatra, Kim Novak, Barbara Nichols, Bobby Sherwood, Hank Henry, Elizabeth Patterson, Robin Morse, Frank Wilcox, Pierre Watkin, John Hubbard, James Seay, Hermes Pan, Frank Sully, Bess Flowers, Franklyn Farnum, Barry Bernard, Ellie Kent, Mara McAfee, Henry McCann, Bek Nelson, Betty Urey.

A down-and-outer (Sinatra) comes to San Francisco, tries to con a widow (Hayworth) into backing him to open a nightclub, and falls in love with a chorus girl (Novak). NOTES: The rights to the film version of the 1940 Broadway musical were purchased in 1940 by Harry Cohn and, because he could not get Gene Kelly for the lead, the project was shelved for 17 years.

1514. Pal O'Mine (3/1/24) B&W—56 mins. (Drama). DIR: Edward J. LeSaint. PRO: Harry Cohn. SP: Jack Sturmwasser. Story by Edith Kennedy. A C.B.C. Release. CAST: Irene Rich, Josef Swickard, Willard Louis, Albert Roscoe, Pauline Garon.

An opera star (Rich) returns to the stage after her husband (Swickard) loses his job. He gets a job with her at the opera house and she secretly pays for his work.

1515. The Palomino (3/18/50) Technicolor—73 mins. (Western-Adventure). DIR: Ray Nazarro. PRO: Robert Cohn. SP: Tom Kilpatrick. CAST: Jerome Courtland, Beverly Tyler, Joseph Calleia, Roy Roberts, Tom Trout, Gordon Jones, Trevor Bardette, Robert Osterloh, Harry Garcia, Juan Duval.

When an outlaw (Roberts) steals a girl's (Tyler) prize palomino, a cattleman (Courtland) comes to her aid. [British title: Hills of the Brave].

1516. Panic on the Air (4/23/36) B&W—56 mins. (Crime). DIR: D. Ross Lederman. PRO: Ralph Cohn. SP: Harold Shumate. Based on Five Spot by Theodore Tinsley. CAST: Lew Ayres, Florence Rice, Benny Baker, Edwin Maxwell, Charles Wilson, Wyrley Birch, Robert Emmett Keane, Gene Morgan, Murray Alper, Eddie Lee.

A sports announcer (Ayres), trying to find out why a star pitcher (Morgan) failed to take the mound in the last game of the World Series, becomes embroiled in a murder plot and has to come to the aid of a young girl (Rice) when she is accused of murder.

1517. Papa, Mama, the Maid and I (8/28/56) B&W—94 mins. (Comedy). DIR: Jean-Paul Le Chanois. SP: Marcel Ayme, Pierre Very, Jean-Paul Le Chanois. A Champs-Elysees Production. CAST: Fernand Ledoux, Gaby Morlay, Nicole Courcel, Robert Lamoureux, Louis De Funes, Jean Tissier.

A young man (Lamoureux), in love with a poor girl (Courcel), persuades his parents (Ledoux, Morlay) to hire her as their maid and let her charm win them over. NOTES: In French with English subtitles. [Original French title: Papa, Maman, La Bonne et Moi].

1518. Paper Orchid (4/49) B&W—86 mins. (Crime-Mystery). DIR: Roy Ward Baker. PRO: William Collier, John R. Sloan. SP: Val Guest. Based on the book by Arthur LaBern. A Ganesh Production. CAST: Hugh Williams, Hy Hazell, Sidney James, Garry Marsh, Ivor Barnard, Andrew Cruickshank, Walter Hudd, Ella Retford, Hughie Green, Vida Hope, Frederick Leister, Patricia Owens, Roger Moore, Kenneth Morgan.

When a man is found murdered in the apartment of a gossip columnist (Hazell) known as the "Orchid," two newspapers try to top each other in locating the murderer.

1519. Parachute Nurse (8/6/42) B&W—65 mins. (Drama). DIR: Charles Barton. PRO: Wallace MacDonald. SP: Rian James. Story by Elizabeth Meehan. CAST: Marguerite Chapman, William Wright, Kay Harris, Louise Albritton, Lauretta M. Schimmoler, Frank Sully, Diedra Vale, Evelyn Wahl, Shirley Patterson, Eileen O'Hearn, Roma Aldrich, Marjorie

Reardon, Catherine Craig, Douglas Wood, Forrest Tucker, John Tyrrell, Eddie Laughton, Barbara Brown, Alma Carroll, Elizabeth Dow, Kit Guard.

A group of nurses (Chapman, Albritton, Harris, Vale, Wahl, O'Hearn, Patterson, Aldrich) are trained to parachute into battle to aid injured men.

1520. Paradise Lagoon (4/57) Technicolor—93 mins. (Drama). *DIR:* Lewis Gilbert. *PRO:* Ian Dalrymple. *SP:* Vernon Harris. Based on the play by James M. Barrie. A Modern Screenplays Production. *CAST:* Kenneth More, Diane Cilento, Cecil Parker, Sally Ann Howes, Marita Hunt, Jack Watling, Peter Graves, Gerald Harper, Mercy Haystead, Miranda Connell, Miles Malleson, Eddie Byrne, Joan Young, Brenda Hogan.

A butler (More) proves to be most resourceful when he and his employers are shipwrecked on an island. [British title: *The Admirable Crichton*].

1521. Paratrooper (1/54) Technicolor—88 mins. (War). *DIR:* Terence Young. *PRO:* Irving Allen, Albert R. Broccoli. *SP:* Richard Maibaum, Frank Nugent, Sy Bartlett. Based on *The Red Beret* by Hilary St. George Sanders. A Warwick Film Production. *CAST:* Alan Ladd, Leo Genn, Susan Stephen, Harry Andrews, Donald Houston, Anthony Bushell, Patric Doonan, Stanley Baker, Lana Morris, Tim Turner, Anton Diffring, John Boxer, Victor Maddern, Michael Balfour, Walter Gotell.

A U.S. Army officer (Ladd), who accidentally caused the death of his friend, pretends to be a Canadian and enlists in the British paratroopers so as not to face life or death decisions. [British title: *The Red Beret*].

1522. Pardon My Gun (12/1/42) B&W—56 mins. (Western). *DIR:* William Berke. *PRO:* Jack Fier. *SP:* Wynd-

ham Gittens. *CAST:* Charles Starrett, Alma Carroll, Arthur Hunnicutt, Noah Beery, Sr., Lloyd Bridges, Ted Mapes, Dick Curtis, Roger Gray, Art Mix, Jack Kirk, Dave Harper, George Morrell, Guy Usher, Joel Friedkin, Denver Dixon, Texas Jim Lewis and His Lone Star Cowboys.

A survey engineer (Starrett) helps a rancher's daughter (Carroll) clear herself of murder and robbery charges.

1523. Pardon My Past (12/25/45) B&W—88 mins. (Comedy). *DIR/ PRO:* Leslie Fenton. *SP:* Earl Felton, Karl Lamb. Story by Patterson McNutt, Harlan Ware. *CAST:* Fred MacMurray, Marguerite Chapman, Akim Tamiroff, William Demarest, Rita Johnson, Harry Davenport, Douglass Dumbrille, Karolyn Grimes, Hugh Prosser, Frank Moran, George Chandler, Charles Arnt, Herbert Evans.

An ex-soldier (MacMurray) and his pal (Demarest), on their way to Wisconsin to buy a mink farm, wind up in a complicated mess when he is mistaken by a gambler (Tamiroff) for a playboy (MacMurray). *NOTES:* Fred MacMurray played a dual role in this film.

1524. Parents on Trial (9/21/39) B&W—58 mins. (Drama). *DIR:* Sam Nelson. *PRO:* Ralph Cohn. *SP:* J. Robert Bren, Gladys Atwater, Lambert Hillyer. Story by J. Robert Bren, Gladys Atwater. *CAST:* Jean Parker, Johnny Downs, Linda Terry, Noah Beery, Jr., Henry Kolker, Virginia Brissac, Nana Bryant, Richard Fiske, Mary Gordon.

Parents (Kolker, Brissac, Bryant) assume responsibility when their children (Parker, Downs, Terry, Beery, Jr.) go wrong.

1525. Paris Model (11/10/53) B&W—81 mins. (Drama). *DIR:* Alfred E. Green. *PRO:* Albert Zugsmith. *SP:*

Robert Smith. An American Pictures Production. *CAST:* Eva Gabor, Tom Conway, Laurette Luez, Aram Katcher, Bibs Borman, Marilyn Maxwell, Cecil Kellaway, Florence Bates, Robert Bice, Byron Foulger, Paulette Goddard, Leif Erickson, Gloria Christian, Barbara Lawrence, Robert Hutton, El Brendel, Prince Michael Romanoff.

Four short stories involving a Paris designer gown; (1) a woman (Gabor) purchases the gown to make an impression on a prince (Conway); (2) a woman (Goddard) illegally copies the gown to impress her boss (Erickson); (3) a woman (Maxwell) uses the gown to try and seduce her retiring boss (Kellaway) so that he will appoint her husband (Bice) as new president of the company; (4) a woman (Lawrence) uses the gown to get her boyfriend (Hutton) to propose marriage.

1526. Parole Girl (4/10/33) B&W — 64 mins. (Crime-Drama). *DIR:* Edward Cline. *SP:* Norman Krasna. Based on *Dance of the Millions* by Norman Krasna. *CAST:* Mae Clarke, Ralph Bellamy, Marie Prevost, Hale Hamilton, Ferdinand Gottschalk, Ernest Wood, Sam Godfrey, John Paul Jones, Lee Phelps.

A woman (Clarke), sent to prison for trying to rob a store, is paroled from prison and returns to the store seeking revenge, but instead, falls in love with the store manager (Bellamy).

1527. Parole Racket (3/11/37) B&W — 62 mins. (Crime). *DIR:* C. C. Coleman, Jr. *PRO:* Ralph Cohn. *SP:* Harold Shumate. *CAST:* Paul Kelly, Rosalind Keith, Leona Maricle, Thurston Hall, Gene Morgan, John Spacey, Francis McDonald, Raymond Brown, Jack Daly, Al Hill, C. Montague Shaw.

When it is learned that mobsters control the parole board, a police lieutenant (Kelly) goes undercover to gain their confidence and put an end to their parole racket. *NOTES:* Two other films were released with similar plot, the 1938 Syndicate film, *Paroled from the Big House,* and the 1949 Eagle-Lion film, *Parole, Inc.*

1528. Parsifal (1/83) Eastman Color — 255 mins. (Cine-Opera). *DIR:* Hans-Jurgen Syberberg. *PRO:* Henry Nap, Annie Nap-Oleon. Based on the opera by Richard Wagner. A Gaumont-TMS-Triumph Films Production. *CAST:* Armin Jordan, Martin Sperr, Robert Lloyd, Michael Kutter, Karen Krick, Aage Haugland, Edith Clever.

A filmed version of the Wagnerian opera. *NOTES:* Limited theatrical release.

1529. The Parson and the Outlaw (9/57) Technicolor — 71 mins. (Western). *DIR:* Oliver Drake. *PRO:* Robert Gilbert, Charles R. "Buddy" Rogers. *SP:* Oliver Drake, John Mantley. *CAST:* Sonny Tufts, Marie Windsor, Anthony Dexter, Jean Parker, Robert Lowery, Charles "Buddy" Rogers, Bob Steele, Madalyn Trahey.

Billy the Kid (Dexter) straps on his guns once more and goes after the men that killed his friend, the local preacher (Rogers).

1530. Party Wire (5/17/35) B&W — 66 mins. (Comedy). *DIR:* Erle C. Kenton. *PRO:* Robert North. *SP:* Ethel Hill, John Howard Lawson. Story by Bruce Manning, Vera Caspary. *CAST:* Victor Jory, Jean Arthur, Charley Grapewin, Helen Lowell, Robert Allen, Clara Blandick, Geneva Mitchell, Maude Eburne, Edward J. LeSaint, Robert Middlemass, Oscar Apfel, Matt McHugh.

Town gossips begin to talk when the town's eligible bachelor and dairy owner (Jory) begins a romance with the daughter (Arthur) of the town's leading citizen (Grapewin).

1531. The Party's Over (8/30/34) B&W—64 mins. (Comedy). DIR: Walter Lang. SP: S. K. Lauren. Based on the play by Daniel Kusell. CAST: Stuart Erwin, Ann Sothern, Arline Judge, Chick Chandler, Patsy Kelly, Catherine Doucet, Marjorie Lytell, Henry Travers, William Bakewell, Esther Muir, Rollo Lloyd.

An accountant (Erwin), fed up with his mooching family, does an about-face, dumps them, and makes the decision to marry his girl (Sothern).

Pasado Acusa, El see **El Pasado Acusa**

1532. A Passage to India (12/84) Metrocolor—163 mins. (Drama). DIR/SP: David Lean. PRO: John Brabourne, Richard Goodwin. Based on the book by E. M. Forster and the play by Santha Rama Rau. A John Heyman-Edward Sands-Home Box Office Production. CAST: Judy Davis, Victor Banerjee, Peggy Ashcroft, James Fox, Alec Guinness, Nigel Havers, Richard Wilson, Antonia Pemberton, Michael Culver, Saeed Jaffrey, Art Malik, Clive Swift.

In 1920's India, a sight-seeing excursion for two Englishwomen (Davis, Ashcroft) and their Indian companion (Banerjee) ends in tragedy that serves to aggravate the conditions of British rule.

1533. The Passionate Friends (1/15/23) B&W—70 mins. (Drama). DIR: Jaurice Elvey. SP: Leslie Howard Gordon. Based on the book by H. G. Wells. A British-Stoll Production. CAST: Milton Rosmer, Valia, Fred Raynham, Madge Stuart, Lawford Davidson, Ralph Forster, Teddy Arundell, Annie Esmond.

A woman (Valia) commits suicide in order to save her lover from a divorce scandal.

1534. Passport to Alcatraz (6/6/40) B&W—60 mins. (Action-Adven-

ture). DIR: Lewis D. Collins. PRO: Larry Darmour. SP: Albert DeMond. Story by Eric Taylor, Albert DeMond. CAST: Jack Holt, Noah Beery, Jr., Ivan Lebedeff, Cecilla Callejo, Maxie Rosenbloom, C. Henry Gordon, Guy Usher, Clay Clement, Ben Welden, Robert Fiske, Harry Cording.

A private detective (Holt) poses as a saboteur in order to stop a group of foreign saboteurs from blowing up U.S. munition factories. NOTES: Released in New York only as *Passport to Hell*. [British title: *Alien Sabotage*].

1535. Passport to China (3/61) Technicolor—75 mins. (Adventure). DIR/PRO: Michael Carreras. SP: Gordon Wellesley. A Hammer-Swallow Production. CAST: Richard Basehart, Lisa Gastoni, Athene Seyler, Eric Pohlmann, Alan Gifford, Bernard Cribbins, Burt Kwouk, Marne Maitland.

An American adventurer (Basehart), living in Hong Kong, gets mixed up with a Chinese woman (Seyler) trying to locate her missing son, and an American secret agent (Gastoni). [British title: *Visa to Canton*].

Passport to Hell see **Passport to Alcatraz**

1536. Passport to Suez (8/19/43) B&W—72 mins. (Action-Adventure). DIR: Andre De Toth. PRO: Wallace MacDonald. SP: John Stone. Story by Alden Nash. Based on characters created by Louis Joseph Vance. CAST: Warren William, Ann Savage, Eric Blore, Robert Stanford, Sheldon Leonard, Lloyd Bridges, Gavin Muir, Lou Merrill, Frederick Worlock, Jay Novello, Sig Arno, John Tyrrell, Frank O'Conner, Eddie Kane, Stanley Price, Jack Rice, Frank Lackteen, Nick Thompson.

While in Egypt, the Lone Wolf (William) goes undercover to stop a group of Nazis from stealing the British minefield plans of the Suez Canal. NOTES: Warren William's last film as the "Lone Wolf." In late 1943, his final performances as the Lone Wolf would be in an episode on the CBS radio program *Suspense* entitled "Murder Goes for a Swim"; Eric Blore would also repeat his performance of the faithful butler, Jamison.

1537. The Pathfinder (12/18/52) Technicolor—78 mins. (Western). DIR: Sidney Salkow. PRO: Sam Katzman. SP: Robert E. Kent. Based on *The Pathfinder* by James Fenimore Cooper. CAST: George Montgomery, Helena Carter, Jay Silverheels, Elena Verdugo, Walter Kingsford, Chief Yowlachie, Ed Coch, Jr., Russ Conklin, Rodd Redwing, Stephen Bekassy, Bruce Lester, Vi Ingraham, Adele St. Maur.

A scout (Montgomery) and his companions (Carter, Silverheels) are sent by the British to infiltrate a French stronghold and learn of their plans to take control of the Great Lakes territory.

1538. Paula (6/52) B&W—80 mins. (Drama). DIR: Rudolph Mate. PRO: Buddy Adler. SP: James Poe, William B. Sackheim. Story by Larry Marcus. CAST: Loretta Young, Kent Smith, Alexander Knox, Tommy Rettig, Otto Hulett, Will Wright, Raymond Greenleaf, Eula Gay, William Vedder, Ann Doran, Kathryn Card, Sidney Mason, Keith Larsen, Ann Tyrrell, Clark Howat, Roy Engel, Jeanne Bates, Sam Harris, Edwin Parker, Gertrude Astor, Lawrence Williams, Helen Dickson, Richard Gordon.

A hit-and-run driver (Young) redeems herself when she teaches her victim, a young boy (Rettig), to speak again. [British title: *The Silent Voice*].

1539. Paying the Price (4/5/27) B&W—58 mins. (Crime-Drama). DIR:

David Selman. PRO: Harry Cohn. SP: Dorothy Howell. CAST: Marjorie Bonner, Priscilla Bonner, John Miljan, George Hackathorne, Mary Carr, George Fawcett.

A gambler (Miljan) is accused of the murder of a gambling club owner after he loses a lot of money.

1540. Payment in Blood (12/68) Technicolor/Scope—89 mins. (Western). DIR: E. G. Rowland (Enio Girolami). PRO: F. Orefici. SP: Tito Carpi, E. G. Rowland (Enio Girolami). A Cirsuc-Fono Roma-St. Regis Production. CAST: Edd Byrnes, Guy Madison, Enio Girolami, Louise Barrett, Rick Boyd, Alfred Aysanoa, Mario Donen.

A bounty hunter (Byrnes) goes after a gang of ex-Confederate soldiers and their leader (Madison). [Original Italian title: *7 Winchester Per un Massacro*].

1541. Pearls Bring Tears (3/37) B&W—63 mins. (Comedy). DIR: Manning Haynes. PRO: A. George Smith. SP: Roy Lockwood. Story by Clifford Grey. A GS Enterprises Production. CAST: John Stuart, Dorothy Boyd, Eve Gray, Mark Stone, Googie Withers, Aubrey Mallalieu, Annie Esmond, H. F. Maltby, Hal Walters, Syd Crossley, Michael Ripper, Elizabeth James, Isobel Scaife.

When a woman (Boyd) breaks a strand of pearls that were on loan to her husband (Stone), she takes them to be repaired but they are stolen, and she tries to locate them before her husband learns of their disappearance.

1542. Pecos River (12/15/51) B&W—55 mins. (Western). DIR: Fred F. Sears. PRO: Colbert Clark. SP: Barry Shipman. CAST: Charles Starrett, Dolores Sidener, Smiley Burnette, Jock Mahoney, Paul Campbell, Steve Darrell, Zon Murray, Edgar Dearing, Maudie Prickett, Eddie Fetherstone, Frank Jenks, Harmonica Bill.

The Durango Kid (Starrett) goes to the town of Pecos River to investigate a series of mail robberies. [British title: *Without Risk*].

1543. Pendulum (1/69) Technicolor—106 mins. (Crime). *DIR:* George Schaefer. *PRO/SP:* Stanley Niss. *CAST:* George Peppard, Jean Seberg, Richard Kiley, Charles McGraw, Paul McGrath, Madeline Sherwood, Robert F. Lyons, Stewart Moss, Dana Elcar, Harry Lewis, Isabel Sanford, Frank Marth, Marj Dusay, Logan Ramsey, Robin Raymond, Gene Boland, Jack Grimes, Richard Guizon, Mildred Trares.

A police captain (Peppard), suspected of the murder of his wife (Seberg) and her lover (Lewis), sets out to find the real killer.

1544. Penitentiary (2/5/38) B&W—74 mins. (Prison-Drama). *DIR:* John Brahm. *PRO:* Robert North. *SP:* Seton I. Miller, Fred Niblo, Jr. Based on the play *The Criminal Code* by Martin Flavin. *CAST:* Walter Connolly, John Howard, Jean Parker, Robert Barrat, Marc Lawrence, Arthur Hohl, Dick Curtis, Paul Fix, Marjorie Main, John Gallaudet, Edward Van Sloan, Ann Doran, Dick Elliott, Charles Halton, Ward Bond, James Flavin, Stanley Andrews, Robert Allen, Ethan Laidlaw, Lee Shumway, Bess Flowers, Louise Stanley, Thurston Hall, Lester Dorr, Lee Prather.

A district attorney (Connolly) becomes a prison warden and his daughter (Parker) falls in love with the convict (Howard) he had sent to prison. *NOTES:* A remake of the 1931 Columbia film *The Criminal Code*.

1545. Pennies from Heaven (11/16/36) B&W—80 mins. (Drama-Musical). *DIR:* Norman Z. McLeod. *PRO:* Emmanuel Cohen. *SP:* Jo Swerling. Story by William Rankin. Based on

The Peacock's Feather by Katherine Leslie Moore. *CAST:* Bing Crosby, Madge Evans, Edith Fellows, Donald Meek, John Gallaudet, Tom Dugan, Nana Bryant, Charles Wilson, Harry Tyler, William Stack, Tom Ricketts, Nydia Westman, Louis Armstrong, Lionel Hampton.

When a murderer is about to die in prison, he asks a fellow convict (Crosby) to locate his relatives (Fellows, Meek) and move them to his family estate. He locates them and they move to the family estate, which they turn into a restaurant called the "Haunted House Cafe."

1546. Penny Serenade (4/16/41) B&W—125 mins. (Drama). *DIR/PRO:* George Stevens. *SP:* Morris Ryskind. Story by Martha Cheavens. *CAST:* Irene Dunne, Cary Grant, Beulah Bondi, Edgar Buchanan, Ann Doran, Leonard Willey, Eva Lee Kuney, Wallis Clark, Walter Soderling, Billy Bevan, Grady Sutton, Stanley Brown, John Tyrrell, Ben Taggart, Frank Moran, Dick Wessel, Fred "Snowflake" Toones, Edward Piel, Sr., Eddie Laughton, Bess Flowers.

The trials and tribulations of a married couple (Grant, Dunne) as they lose their unborn baby, then their adopted daughter (Kuney) dies, and, as they are about to split up, they finally get another chance to adopt another child.

1547. Pepe (1/60) Eastman Color/ Panavision—195 mins. (Musical-Comedy). *DIR/PRO:* George Sidney. *SP:* Dorothy Kingsley, Claude Binyon. Story by Leonard Spiegelgass, Sonya Levien. Based on *Broadway Magic* by Ladislas Bus Fekete. *CAST:* Cantinflas, Dan Dailey, Shirley Jones, Carlos Montalban, Vicki Trickett, Matt Mattox, Hank Henry, Suzanne Lloyd, Stephen Bekassy, Ernie Kovacs, William Demarest, Carol Douglas, Francisco Reguerra, Joe Hyams, Carlos Rivas, Bunny Waters, Jack Entratter, Col. E. E. Fogelson, Jane Robinson, Joey Bishop, Michael Callan, Maurice Chevalier, Charles Coburn, Richard Conte, Bing Crosby, Tony Curtis, Bobby Darin, Sammy Davis, Jr., Jimmy Durante, Zsa Zsa Gabor, voice of Judy Garland, Greer Garson, Hedda Hopper, Peter Lawford, Janet Leigh, Jack Lemmon, Dean Martin, Jay North, Kim Novak, Andre Previn, Donna Reed, Debbie Reynolds, Edward G. Robinson, Cesar Romero, Frank Sinatra, Billie Burke, Ann B. Davis.

When a Mexican peasant (Cantinflas) discovers his white stallion has been sold to a Hollywood director (Dailey), he travels to Hollywood to persuade the director to let him tend the horse. NOTES: The running time of 195 mins. is the original release running time. It was later released to theaters at a running time of 157 mins. In addition, it was a bust and put an end to the U.S. career of Cantinflas.

1548. Perfect (6/85) Technicolor/ Panavision—115 mins. (Drama). DIR/ PRO: James Bridges. SP: Aaron Latham. Based on articles in *Rolling Stone* magazine by Aaron Latham. CAST: John Travolta, Stefan Gierasch, Jamie Lee Curtis, Jann Wenner, Anne De Salvo, Murphy Dunne, Kenneth Welsh, Laurie Burton, Ann Travolta, Laraine Newman, Marilu Henner, Mathew Reed.

A reporter for *Rolling Stone* magazine (Travolta) falls in love with an aerobics instructor (Curtis) while doing an expose on the exercise fad.

1549. Peril (8/85) Eastman Color— 110 mins. (Drama). DIR/SP: Michel Deville. PRO: Emmanuel Schlumberger. Based on *Sur La Terre Comme Au Ciel* by Rene Belletto. A Triumph Films Production. CAST: Christophe

Malavoy, Nicole Garcia, Michel Piccoli, Anemone, Richard Bohringer, Anais Jeanneret, Jean-Claude Jay, Helene Roussel.

A man (Malavoy) becomes involved in blackmail, murder, and deceit when he is hired as a musical teacher to a man's (Piccoli) wife (Garcia) and daughter (Jeanneret). NOTES: Limited theatrical release; in French with English subtitles. [British title: *Death in a French Garden*]. [Original French title: *Peril en la Demeure*].

1550. Perilous Holiday (6/19/46) B&W—89 mins. (Crime). DIR: Edward H. Griffith. PRO: Phil L. Ryan. SP: Roy Chanslor. Story by Robert Carson. CAST: Pat O'Brien, Ruth Warrick, Alan Hale, Edgar Buchanan, Audrey Long, Willard Robertson, Eduardo Ciannelli, Minna Gombell, Martin Garralaga, Jay Novello, Al Hill, Pedro Regas, Nacho Galindo, Chris-Pin Martin.

A Treasury agent (O'Brien) and a newspaper reporter (Warrick) join forces to stop counterfeiters who are operating in Mexico.

1551. Personality (2/23/30) B&W—66 mins. (Drama). DIR/SP: Victor Heerman. Story by Gladys Lehman. CAST: Sally Starr, Johnny Arthur, Lee D. Kohlmar, Vivian Oakland, John T. Murray, Blanche Frederici, Frank Hammond, Buck Black, George Pierce.

A couple (Starr, Arthur) experience money and employment problems when they try to live beyond their means.

1552. Personality Kid (8/8/46) B&W—62 mins. (Drama). DIR: George Sherman. PRO: Wallace MacDonald. SP: Lewis H. Herman, William B. Sackheim. Story by Cromwell MacKechnie. CAST: Anita Louise, Michael Duane, Ted Donaldson, Barbara Brown, Bobby Larson, Edythe

Elliott, Paul Maxey, Martin Garralaga, Oscar O'Shea, Harlan Briggs, Regina Wallace.

A commercial photographer (Duane) wins a contest with pictures he has taken of his kid brother (Donaldson) and his pet burro.

Petite Bande, La see **La Petite Bande**

1553. The Petty Girl (8/23/50) Technicolor – 87 mins. (Comedy). *DIR:* Henry Levin. *PRO/SP:* Nat Perrin. Story by Mary E. McCarthy. *CAST:* Robert Cummings, Joan Caulfield, Elsa Lanchester, Tippi Hedren, Melville Cooper, Audrey Long, Frank Orth, Mary Wickes, John Ridgely, Ian Wolfe, Frank Jenks, Mabel Paige, Kathleen Howard, Douglas Wood, Philip Van Zandt, Movita Castaneda, Ray Teal, Pat Flaherty, Russell Hicks, Lois Hall, Mona Knox, Everett Glass, Sarah Edwards, Tim Ryan, Raymond Largay.

A calendar artist (Cummings) falls for a prudish college professor (Caulfield) and follows her back to college to get her to pose for him. When his persistence gets her fired, she agrees to pose for him and they eventually marry. *NOTES:* The film debut of Tippi Hedren. [British title: *Girl of the Year*].

1554. Phantom Gold (8/31/38) B&W – 56 mins. (Western). *DIR:* Joseph Levering. *PRO:* Larry Darmour. *SP:* Nate Gatzert. *CAST:* Jack Luden, Beth Marion, Slim Whitaker, Barry Downing, Art Davis, Hal Taliaferro (Wally Wales), Jimmy Robinson, Jack Ingram, Buzz Barton, Marin Sais, "Tuffy," the dog.

A cowboy (Luden) thwarts an outlaw's (Whitaker) plan to salt a gold mine.

1555. The Phantom Stagecoach (4/1/57) B&W – 79 mins. (Western).

DIR: Ray Nazarro. *PRO:* Wallace MacDonald. *SP:* David Lang. *CAST:* William Bishop, Kathleen Crowley, Richard Webb, Maudie Prickett, Hugh Sanders, John Doucette, Ray Teal, Frank Ferguson, Percy Helton, Lane Bradford, Eddy Waller, John Lehmann, Robert Anderson.

A Wells Fargo investigator (Bishop) sets out to stop a stagecoach war between two rival owners (Ferguson, Sanders).

1556. The Phantom Submarine (2/13/41) B&W – 70 mins. (Adventure). *DIR:* Charles Barton. *PRO:* Ralph Cohn. *SP:* Joseph Krumgold. Based on *Ocean Gold* by Augustus Muir. *CAST:* Anita Louise, Bruce Bennett, Oscar O'Shea, John Tyrrell, Victor Wong, Pedro de Cordoba, Charles McMurphy, Harry Strang, Don Beddoe, Richard Fiske, Eddie Laughton, William Forrest, William Ruhl, Henry Zynda, Budd Fine.

A newspaper reporter (Louise) and a salvage diver (Bennett) investigate the presence of a submarine operating near the Panama Canal.

1557. The Phantom Thief (5/2/46) B&W – 65 mins. (Crime-Mystery). *DIR:* D. Ross Lederman. *PRO:* John Stone. *SP:* Richard Wormer, Richard Weil. Story by G. A. Snow. Based on characters created by Jack Boyle. *CAST:* Chester Morris, Jeff Donnell, George E. Stone, Dusty Anderson, Richard Lane, Marvin Miller, Murray Alper, Frank Sully, Wilton Graff, Forbes Murray, Joseph Crehan, Edward F. Dunn, Eddie Fetherstone, Edmund Cobb, George Magrill.

Blackie (Morris) is suspected of murder when he sets out to recover stolen gems and gets involved with spiritualists.

1558. Phantom Valley (2/19/48) B&W – 53 mins. (Western). *DIR:* Ray Nazarro. *PRO:* Colbert Clark. *SP:* J.

Benton Cheney. *CAST*: Charles Starrett, Virginia Hunter, Smiley Burnette, Sam Flint, Fred F. Sears, Robert W. Filmer, Zon Murray, Jerry Jerome, Joel Friedkin, Teddy Infuhr, Mikel Conrad, Ozie Waters and His Colorado Rangers.

The Durango Kid (Starrett) goes to the town of Phantom Valley to prevent a range war and locate the outlaw gang responsible for attacks on the ranchers and homesteaders.

1559. Phffft (12/54) B&W—91 mins. (Comedy). *DIR*: Mark Robson. *PRO*: Fred Kohlmar. *SP*: George Axelrod. *CAST*: Judy Holliday, Jack Lemmon, Kim Novak, Jack Carson, Luella Gear, Donald Randolph, Donald Curtis, Arny Freeman, Merry Anders, Olan Soule, Geraldine Hall, Harry Cheshire, William Newell, Eugene Borden, Fay Baker, Joyce Jameson, Jimmie Dodd.

A successful couple (Lemmon, Holliday), bored with each other, get a divorce but realize they still love each other, and get back together.

1560. Pickup (8/1/51) B&W—76 mins. (Drama). *DIR*: Hugo Haas. *PRO*: Hugo Haas, Edgar E. Walden *SP*: Hugo Haas, Arnold Phillips. Based on *Watchman 47* by Joseph Kopta. A Forum Production. *CAST*: Hugo Haas, Beverly Michaels, Allan Nixon, Howland Chamberlin, Mark Lowell, Jo Carroll Dennison, Art Lewis, Jack Daly, Bernard Gorcey.

A gold-digger (Michaels) marries a middle-aged railway dispatcher (Haas) for his money and, when he suffers a bout of deafness, she and her lover (Nixon) plot to kill him.

1561. Pickup Alley (8/57) B&W/ Scope—92 mins. (Crime). *DIR*: John Gilling. *PRO*: Irving Allen, Albert R. Broccoli. *SP*: John Paxton. Based on *Interpol* by A. J. Forrest. A Warwick Film Production. *CAST*: Victor Ma-

ture, Anita Ekberg, Trevor Howard, Bonar Colleano, Dorothy Alison, Andre Morell, Martin Benson, Eric Pohlmann, Peter Illing, Sidney Tafler, Sidney James, Lionel Murton, Danny Green, Marne Maitland, Gaylord Cavallaro, Peter Elliott, Yvonne Romain, Alfred Burke, Russell Waters.

An Interpol agent (Mature) travels through Europe on the trail of an international dope smuggler (Howard) who killed his sister. [British title: *Interpol*].

1562. Picnic (11/55) Technicolor/ Scope—115 mins. (Drama). *DIR*: Joshua Logan. *PRO*: Fred Kohlmar. *SP*: Daniel Taradash. Based on the play by William Inge. *CAST*: William Holden, Kim Novak, Rosalind Russell, Arthur O'Connell, Cliff Robertson, Susan Strasberg, Betty Field, Verna Felton, Reta Shaw, Nick Adams, Raymond Bailey, Phyllis Newman, Elizabeth Wilson, Don C. Harvey.

A drifter (Holden) enters a Kansas town on Labor Day, seeks out his college friend (Robertson), and proceeds to steal his fiancee (Novak) from him. *NOTES*: The film debut of director Joshua Logan.

1563. The Pinto Kid (2/5/41) B&W—61 mins. (Western). *DIR*: Lambert Hillyer. *PRO*: Jack Fier. *SP*: Fred Myton. *CAST*: Charles Starrett, Louise Currie, Bob Nolan, Hank Bell, Francis Walker, Ernie Adams, Jack Rockwell, Pat Brady, Roger Gray, Dick Botiller, Steve Clark, Frank Ellis, Paul Sutton, Sons of the Pioneers.

A cowboy (Starrett) must prove his innocence when he is framed by a cattle rustler and bank robber (Sutton). [British title: *All Square*].

1564. Pioneer Trail (7/15/38) B&W—59 mins. (Western). *DIR*: Joseph Levering. *PRO*: Larry Darmour. *SP*: Nate Gatzert. *CAST*: Jack Luden, Joan Barclay, Slim Whitaker, Leon

Beaumon, Marin Sais, Hal Taliaferro (Wally Wales), Eve McKenzie, Hal Price, Dick Botiller, Tom London, Tex Palmer, Art Davis, Fred Burns, Bob McKenzie, "Tuffy," the dog. The foreman (Luden) of a cattle drive is captured by outlaws who hope to use him to lure larger cattle drives through their valley so they can rustle the cattle.

1565. Pioneers of the Frontier (2/14/40) B&W—58 mins. (Western). *DIR*: Sam Nelson. *PRO*: Leon Barsha. *SP*: Fred Myton. *CAST*: Bill Elliott, Linda Winters (Dorothy Comingore), Carl Stockdale, Dick Curtis, Dub Taylor, Stanley Brown, Richard Fiske, Ralph McCullough, Lafe McKee, Al Bridge, Edmund Cobb, George Chesebro, Jack Kirk, Lynton Brent, Ralph Peters.

Wild Bill Saunders (Elliott) goes after a ranch foreman (Curtis) and his band of renegades who murdered his uncle (McKee) and are terrorizing the settlers. [British title: *The Anchor*].

Pirate Ship *see* **The Mutineers**

1566. The Pirates of Blood River (8/62) Eastman Color/Scope—87 mins. (Adventure). *DIR*: John Gilling. *PRO*: Anthony Nelson-Keys. *SP*: John Hunter, John Gilling. Story by Jimmy Sangster. A Hammer Production. *CAST*: Kerwin Mathews, Glenn Corbett, Christopher Lee, Marla Landi, Oliver Reed, Andrew Keir, Peter Arne, Michael Ripper, Jack Stewart, David Lodge, Marie Devereux, Diane Aubrey, Desmond Llewellyn.

A pirate captain (Lee) forces a fugitive from the law (Mathews) to lead him to his Huguenot island.

1567. Pirates of Tripoli (2/55) Technicolor—72 mins. (Adventure). *DIR*: Felix Feist. *PRO*: Sam Katzman. *SP*: Allen March. A Clover Produc-

tion. *CAST*: Paul Henreid, Patricia Medina, Paul Newlan, John Miljan, Lillian Bond, Jean Del Val, Mel Wells, Louis Mercier, Karl Davis, Peter Mamakos, William Fawcett, Eugene Borden, Frank Richards.

In the 16th century, a princess (Medina) enlists the aid of a pirate captain (Henreid) to defeat the invaders of her homeland. *NOTES*: Contains footage from the 1952 Columbia film *The Golden Hawk*.

1568. Platinum Blonde (10/30/31) B&W—88 mins. (Comedy). *DIR*: Frank Capra. *PRO*: Harry Cohn. *SP*: Jo Swerling, Dorothy Howell, Robert Riskin. Story by Harry E. Chandler and Douglas W. Churchill. A Frank Capra Production. *CAST*: Loretta Young, Robert Williams, Jean Harlow, Halliwell Hobbes, Reginald Owen, Edmund Breese, Donald Dillaway, Walter Catlett, Claude Allister, Louise Closser Hale, Bill Elliott, Harry Semels, Olaf Hytten, Tom London, Hal Price, Eddy Chandler, Charles Jordan, Dick Cramer, Wilson Benge.

A wise cracking reporter (Williams) marries a wealthy socialite (Harlow) but grows tired of society life and, when he decides to write a play and bring his reporter friends to stay with him, she throws them out and he goes back to his old girlfriend (Young).

1569. Please Turn Over (12/60) B&W—87 mins. (Comedy). *DIR*: Gerald Thomas. *PRO*: Peter Rogers. *SP*: Norman Hudis. Based on the play *Book of the Month* by Basil Thomas. An Anglo-Amalgamated Production. *CAST*: Ted Ray, Jean Kent, Leslie Phillips, Joan Sims, Julia Lockwood, Tim Seely, Charles Hawtrey, Dilys Laye, Lionel Jeffries, June Jago, Colin Gordon, Joan Hickson, Victor Maddern, Ronald Adam, Cyril Chamberlain, Marianne Stone, Myrtle Reed, Noel Dyson.

A teenage girl (Lockwood) creates havoc in her neighborhood when she writes a steamy novel and her family and neighbors believe that they are the characters portrayed in her novel.

1570. Pleasure Before Business (4/20/27) B&W—55 mins. (Comedy). *DIR:* Frank R. Strayer. *PRO:* Harry Cohn. *SP:* Ernest S. Pagano. Story by William Branch. *CAST:* Pat O'Malley, Virginia Brown Faire, Max Davidson, Rosa Rosanova.

A daughter (Faire) uses her inheritance to keep her father (Davidson) in the style to which he is accustomed after he falls into bad health and cannot manage his business.

1571. The Poisoned Diamond (12/34) B&W—73 mins. (Drama). *DIR/SP:* W. P. Kellino. *PRO:* Fred Browett. A Grafton Production. *CAST:* Anne Grey, Lester Matthews, Patric Knowles, Raymond Raikes, Bryan Powley, Lucius Blake, D. J. Williams.

A bankrupt businessman (Matthews) discovers a diamond mine and uses his newfound wealth to destroy those who ruined him.

1572. Police Car 17 (9/27/33) B&W—57 mins. (Crime). *DIR/SP:* Lambert Hillyer. *CAST:* Tim McCoy, Evalyn Knapp, Wallis Clark, Ward Bond, Harold Huber, Edwin Maxwell, Charles West, Jack Long, DeWitt Jennings.

A policeman (McCoy) goes after his girl (Knapp), held captive by a mobster (Huber) and his men.

1573. Poor Girls (5/5/27) B&W— 58 mins. (Drama). *DIR:* William James Craft. *PRO:* Harry Cohn. *SP:* William Branch. Story by Sophie Bogen. *CAST:* Dorothy Revier, Edmund Burns, Ruth Stonehouse, Lloyd Whitlock.

A young girl (Revier) runs away from home when she learns that her mother (Stonehouse) is the owner of a notorious nightclub.

1574. Pope Joan (8/72) Eastman Color/Panavision—132 mins. (Drama). *DIR:* Michael Anderson. *PRO:* Kurt Unger. *SP:* John Briley. A Big City-Command-Triple Eight Production. *CAST:* Liv Ullmann, Keir Dullea, Robert Beatty, Jeremy Kemp, Peter Arne, Trevor Howard, Duncan Lamont, Philip Ross, Maximilian Schell, Franco Nero, Olivia De Havilland, Andre Morell, George Innes, Lesley-Anne Down, Patrick Magee, Susan Macready, Natasa Nicolescu, Kurt Christian, Mary Healey.

A modern day evangelist (Ullmann) seeks the help of a psychiatrist (Dullea) when she imagines herself to be the reincarnation of "Pope Joan" who, supposedly, held the Papal throne between Leo IV and Benedict III.

1575. Porgy and Bess (6/59) Technicolor/Todd-AO—138 mins. (Musical). *DIR:* Otto Preminger. *PRO:* Samuel Goldwyn. *SP:* N. Richard Nash. Based on the play *Porgy* by DuBose and Dorothy Heyward and the operetta by George Gershwin, Ira Gershwin, DuBose Heyward. A Samuel Goldwyn Production. *CAST:* Sidney Poitier, Dorothy Dandridge, Sammy Davis, Jr., Pearl Bailey, Brock Peters, Leslie Scott, Diahann Carroll, Ruth Attaway, Clarence Muse, Everdinne Wilson, Joel Fluellen, Earl Jackson, Moses LaMarr, Ivan Dixon, Margaret Hairston, Antoine Durousseau, Helen Thigpen, Roy Glenn, Claude Akins.

The loves, dreams, and jealousies of the poor folk, Porgy (Poitier), Bess (Dandridge), and Crown (Peters), in Charleston's "Catfish Row." *NOTES:* The last film to be produced by Samuel Goldwyn. Rouben Mamoulian, who had directed the 1927 drama and

1935 musical operetta, was to direct this picture but, because of creative differences with Goldwyn, was replaced by Otto Preminger after eight months of pre-production work.

1576. Port Afrique (10/56) Technicolor—92 mins. (Mystery). *DIR:* Rudolph Mate. *PRO:* John R. Sloan, David E. Rose. *SP:* Frank Partos, John Cresswell. Based on the book by Bernard Victor Dryer. A Coronado-Production Limited. *CAST:* Pier Angeli, Phil Carey, Dennis Price, Eugene Deckers, James Hayter, Rachel Gurney, Anthony Newley, Guido Lorraine, Denis Shaw, Jacques Cey, Christopher Lee, Richard Molinas, Dorothy White.

Returning to his African plantation after World War II, an American pilot (Carey) learns his wife has been murdered and sets out to find her killer.

1577. Port Said (4/15/48) B&W—69 mins. (Drama). *DIR:* Reginald Leborg. *PRO:* Wallace MacDonald. *SP:* Brenda Weisberg. Story by Louis Pollock. *CAST:* Gloria Henry, William Bishop, Steven Geray, Edgar Barrier, Richard Hale, Ian MacDonald, Blanche Zohar, Robin Hughes, Jay Novello, Ted Hecht, Lester Sharpe, Martin Garralaga.

With his daughter (Henry), a father (Barrier) searches through the Egyptian port for the Fascist murderer (Henry) of his wife. *NOTES:* Gloria Henry played a dual role in this film.

1578. The Power of the Press (10/31/28) B&W—62 mins. (Crime-Drama). *DIR:* Frank Capra. *PRO:* Jack Cohn. *SP:* Frederick A. Thompson, Sonya Levien. A Frank Capra Production. *CAST:* Douglas Fairbanks, Jr., Jobyna Ralston, Mildred Harris, Philo McCullough, Wheeler Oakman, Robert Edeson, Edwards Davis, Del Henderson, Charles Clary.

A cub reporter (Fairbanks) sets out to prove that the daughter (Ralston) of a man (Davis) running for mayor is innocent of murder.

1579. Power of the Press (1/28/43) B&W—64 mins. (Crime-Drama). *DIR:* Lew Landers. *PRO:* Leon Barsha. *SP:* Robert D. Andrews. Story by Samuel Fuller. *CAST:* Guy Kibbee, Gloria Dickson, Lee Tracy, Otto Kruger, Victor Jory, Larry Parks, Rex Williams, Frank Sully, Don Beddoe, Douglas Leavitt, Minor Watson.

The publisher (Kruger) of a big city newspaper, who resorts to murder in his rise to power, is exposed by his managing editor (Tracy) and secretary (Dickson).

1580. The Power of the Whistler (4/19/45) B&W—66 mins. (Mystery). *DIR:* Lew Landers. *PRO:* Leonard S. Picker. *SP:* Aubrey Wisberg. Based on *The Whistler* radio program. *CAST:* Richard Dix, Janis Carter, Jeff Donnell, Loren Tindall, Tala Birell, John Abbott, Murray Alper, Cy Kendall, Kenneth MacDonald.

A woman (Carter) almost falls victim to an amnesiac (Dix) who is, in reality, a homicidal maniac.

1581. Prairie Gunsmoke (7/16/42) B&W—56 mins. (Western). *DIR:* Lambert Hillyer. *PRO:* Leon Barsha. *SP:* Fred Myton. Story by Jack Ganzhorn. *CAST:* Bill Elliott, Virginia Carroll, Tex Ritter, Rich Anderson, Frank Mitchell, Art Mix, Tristram Coffin, Francis Walker, Joe McGuinn, Steve Clark, Glenn Strange, Ray Jones, Hal Price, Frosty Royce, Ted Mapes.

Wild Bill Hickok (Elliott) thwarts the plans of a land baron (Coffin) to gain control of the ranches he holds mortgages on.

1582. Prairie Raiders (5/29/47) B&W—54 mins. (Western). *DIR:* Derwin Abrahams. *PRO:* Colbert Clark. *SP:* Ed Earl Repp. *CAST:* Charles

268		The Columbia Checklist

Starrett, Nancy Saunders, Smiley Burnette, Robert Scott, Steve Clark, Hugh Prosser, Tommy Coates, Lane Bradford, Frank LaRue, Ray Bennett, John Cason, Doug Coppin, Sam Flint, Ozie Waters and His Colorado Rangers.

The Durango Kid (Starrett) stops a crooked land owner (Prosser) from using counterfeit leases to buy up Federal land. [British title: *The Forger*].

1583. Prairie Roundup (1/15/51) B&W—55 mins. (Western). DIR: Fred F. Sears. PRO: Colbert Clark. SP: Joseph O'Donnell. CAST: Charles Starrett, Mary Castle, Smiley Burnette, Frank Fenton, Lane Chandler, Don C. Harvey, Frank Sully, John Cason, Paul Campbell, Al Wyatt, George Baxter, Ace Richmond, Forrest Taylor, Glenn Thompson, The Sunshine Boys.

A former Texas Ranger (Starrett) is arrested for killing the Durango Kid. His arrest and subsequent jail break allow him, as the real Durango Kid, to uncover a plot to steal cattle on the Santa Fe trail.

1584. Prairie Schooners (9/30/40) B&W—58 mins. (Western). DIR: Sam Nelson. PRO: Leon Barsha. SP: Robert Lee Johnson, Fred Myton. Based on *Into the Crimson West* by George Cory Franklin. CAST: Bill Elliott, Evelyn Young, Dub Taylor, Kenneth Harlan, Ray Teal, Bob Burns, Richard Fiske, Edmund Cobb, Jim Thorpe, George Morrell, Ned Glass, Merrill McCormack, Sammy Stein, Lucien Maxwell, Netta Packer.

Wild Bill Hickok (Elliott) and his pal Cannonball (Taylor) lead a wagon train of settlers through Indian territory to the gold fields of Colorado. [British title: *Through the Storm*].

1585. Prairie Stranger (9/18/41) B&W—58 mins. (Western). DIR: Lambert Hillyer. PRO: William Berke. SP: Winston Miller. Based on *Prairie*

Dust by James L. Rubel. CAST: Charles Starrett, Patti McCarty, Cliff Edwards, Forbes Murray, Frank LaRue, Francis Walker, Edmund Cobb, George Morrell, Archie Twitchell, Jim Corey, Russ Powell, Lew Preston and His Ranch Hands.

Dr. Steven Monroe (Starrett) loses his patients to an Eastern doctor (Cobb) and takes a job as a cowboy. When a disease threatens to wipe out a cattle herd, he cures them and rounds up the outlaws responsible for causing the disease. NOTES: Due to legal problems over Columbia's rights to the James L. Rubel stories, this was the last of the "Doctor Monroe" series. [British title: *The Marked Bullet*].

1586. The Prescott Kid (11/8/34) B&W—58 mins. (Western). DIR/PRO: David Selman. SP: Ford Beebe, Claude Rister. Story by Claude Rister. CAST: Tim McCoy, Sheila Mannors, Joe Sawyer, Ward Bond, Walter Brennan, Slim Whitaker, Charles King, Bud Osborne, Tom London, Steve Clark, Edmund Cobb, Ernie Adams, Lew Meehan, Art Mix, Alden Chase, Hooper Atchley, Jack Rockwell, Albert J. Smith, Carlos De Veldez.

A cowboy (McCoy) arrives in town, is mistaken for a sheriff, and goes after a gang of cattle rustlers and their leader (Chase).

1587. The Price of Honor (3/5/27) B&W—57 mins. (Drama). DIR: Edward H. Griffith. PRO: Harry Cohn. SP: Dorothy Howell. CAST: Dorothy Revier, Malcolm McGregor, William V. Mong, Gustav von Seyffertitz.

An innocent man (Mong), convicted on circumstantial evidence, is paroled from prison because he is not expected to live.

1588. The Price of Success (8/15/25) B&W—50 mins. (Drama). DIR: Tony Gaudio. PRO: Harry Cohn.

CAST: Alice Lake, Lee Shumway, Gaston Glass, Florence Turner, Alma Bennett.

A woman (Lake) begins a flirtation with a wealthy man (Glass) to get her husband (Shumway) to come back to her.

1589. The Price She Paid (4/1/24) B&W—55 mins. (Drama). *DIR:* Henry MacRae. *PRO:* Harry Cohn. *SP:* Lois Zellner. *CAST:* Alma Rubens, Frank Mayo, Eugenie Besserer, William Welsh.

A young girl (Rubens) accepts a marriage proposal from a rich man (Welsh) she hates in order to save her mother from bankruptcy.

1590. Pride of the Marines (4/28/36) B&W—66 mins. (Drama). *DIR:* D. Ross Lederman. *PRO:* Irving Briskin. *SP:* Harold Shumate. Based on *United States Smith* by Gerald Beaumont. *CAST:* Charles Bickford, Florence Rice, Billy Burrud, Robert Allen, George McKay, Thurston Hall, Ward Bond, Joe Sawyer.

A Marine sergeant (Bickford) looks after an orphan (Burrud) who shows up on the Marine base until he can be legally adopted by newlyweds (Rice, Allen).

1591. Prince of Diamonds (5/4/30) B&W—67 mins. (Romance). *DIR:* Karl Brown, A. H. Van Buren. *SP:* Paul Hervey Fox. Story by Gene Markey. *CAST:* Aileen Pringle, Ian Keith, Fritzi Ridgeway, Tyrrell Davis, Claude King, Tom Ricketts, E. Alyn Warren, Gilbert Emery, Frederick Sullivan, Sybil Grove, G. L. McDonell.

A diamond merchant (King) and a matinee idol (Keith) from the 20's vie for the affections of a woman (Pringle) with rich tastes.

1592. Prince of Pirates (3/53) Technicolor—78 mins. (Adventure). *DIR:* Sidney Salkow. *PRO:* Sam Katz-man. *SP:* John O'Dea, Samuel Newman. Story by William Copeland, Herman Kline. An Esskay Picture Production. *CAST:* John Derek, Barbara Rush, Carla Balenda, Whitfield Conner, Edgar Barrier, Robert Shayne, Harry Lauter, Don C. Harvey, Henry Rowland, Gene Roth, Sandy Sanders, Joe McGuinn, Glase Lohman.

A prince (Derek) leads a band of volunteers to overthrow the tyranny of his evil brother (Conner).

1593. The Prince of Thieves (1/3/48) CineColor—72 mins. (Adventure). *DIR:* Howard Bretherton. *PRO:* Sam Katzman. *SP:* Charles H. Schneer, Maurice Tombragel. Based on *Credits* by Alexandre Dumas. A Kay Picture Production. *CAST:* Jon Hall, Patricia Morison, Adele Jergens, Alan Mowbray, Michael Duane, H. B. Warner, Lowell Gilmore, Gavin Muir, Robin Raymond, Lewis Russell, Walter Sande, Syd Saylor, I. Stanford Jolley, Fred Santley, Belle Mitchell.

Robin Hood (Hall) sets out to ensure that Lady Christabel (Jergens) marries the man of her choice (Duane).

1594. Prison Breaker (2/36) B&W—69 mins. (Prison-Drama). *DIR:* Adrian Brunel. *PRO:* A. George Smith. *SP:* Frank Witty. Based on the book by Edgar Wallace. A GS Enterprises Production. *CAST:* James Mason, Andrews Englemann, Marguerite Allan, Ian Fleming, George Merritt, Wally Patch, Vincent Holman, Andrea Malandrinos, Tarva Penna, Neville Brook, Aubrey Mallalieu, Michael Ripper, John Counsell, Clifford Buckton.

A Secret Service agent (Mason), sent to prison for killing one of the men employed by an international crook (Englemann), escapes from prison and, with the help of the crook's daughter (Allan), brings him to justice.

Prison Camp *see* **Fugitive from a Prison Camp**

1595. Prison Ship (11/15/45) B&W — 60 mins. (War-Drama). *DIR:* Arthur Dreifuss. *PRO:* Alexis Thurn-Taxis. *SP:* Josef Mischel, Ben Markson. *CAST:* Robert Lowery, Nina Foch, Richard Loo, Ludwig Donath, Robert Scott, Barry Bernard, Erik Rolf, Moy Ming, Louis Mercier, David Hughes, Barbara Pepper, Coulter Irwin.

When POW's learn that the Japanese ship they are being transported to Tokyo on is a decoy for an American submarine, they stage a mutiny and, after many lives are lost, take over the ship and warn the sub of the impending danger.

1596. Prison Warden (12/8/49) B&W — 62 mins. (Prison-Drama). *DIR:* Seymour Friedman. *PRO:* Rudolph C. Flothow. *SP:* Eric Taylor. *CAST:* Warner Baxter, Anna Lee, James Flavin, Harlan Warde, Charles Cane, Reginald Sheffield, Harry Antrim, William "Bill" Phillips, Frank Richards, Jack Overman, Charles Evans, Harry Hayden, John Hamilton, Clancy Cooper, Edgar Dearing.

A public health official (Baxter) takes over as warden of a prison where reforms are needed, while his wife (Lee) plots the escape of her ex-lover (Warde).

1597. The Prisoner (3/56) B&W — 95 mins. (Drama). *DIR:* Peter Glenville. *PRO:* Vivian A. Cox. *SP:* Bridget Boland. Based on the play by Bridget Boland. A London Independent-Facet Production. *CAST:* Alec Guinness, Jack Hawkins, Raymond Huntley, Jeannette Sterke, Ronald Lewis, Kenneth Griffith, Gerard Heinz, Mark Dignam, Wilfred Lawson.

In an unnamed European country, a cardinal (Guinness) is interrogated by his old friend, a psychologist (Hawkins), until he "confesses" to the crimes against him.

1598. Prisoners of the Casbah (11/53) Technicolor — 78 mins. (Adventure). *DIR:* Richard Bare. *PRO:* Sam Katzman. *SP:* DeVallon Scott. Story by William Raynor. *CAST:* Gloria Grahame, Cesar Romero, Turhan Bey, Nestor Paiva, Paul Newlan, Frank Richards, John Parrish, Lucille Barkley, Philip Van Zandt, Wade Crosby, Gloria Saunders, Nelson Leigh, John Marshall, John Mansfield, Ray Singer.

A sheik (Bey) saves a princess (Grahame) from the clutches of an evil villain (Romero).

1599. A Prize of Gold (6/55) Technicolor — 100 mins. (Crime-Adventure). *DIR:* Mark Robson. *PRO:* Irving Allen, Albert R. Broccoli, Phil C. Samuel. *SP:* Robert Buckner, John Paxton. Based on the book by Max Catto. A Warwick Film Production. *CAST:* Richard Widmark, Mai Zetterling, Nigel Patrick, George Cole, Donald Wolfit, Joseph Tomelty, Andrew Ray, Karel Stepanek, Robert Ayres, Eric Pohlmann, Olive Sloane, Leslie Linder, Alan Gifford, Harry Towb, Ivan Craig.

In Berlin, a U.S. Army sergeant (Widmark) plans to hijack a shipment of gold to help a war refugee (Zetterling) transport a group of children from Europe to Brazil.

1600. Problem Girls (4/1/53) B&W — 70 mins. (Drama). *DIR:* E. A. Dupont. *PRO/SP:* Aubrey Wisberg, Jack Pollexfen. *CAST:* Helen Walker, Ross Elliott, Susan Morrow, Anthony Jochim, James Seay, Marjorie Stapp, Ray Regnier, Eileen Stevens, Tom Charlesworth, Beverly Garland, Joyce Jameson, Nan Leslie, Joyce Jarvis, Mara Corday, Tandra Quinn, Norma

Eberhardt, Walter Bonn, John Oger, Gladys Kingston, Juney Ellis.

At a school for problem girls, a psychology instructor (Elliott) learns of a plot by the headmistress (Walker) and athletic director (Seay) to drug one of the girls (Morrow) and pass her off as an oil heiress, whom they have already murdered.

1601. The Professionals (11/66) Technicolor/Panavision—117 mins. (Western). *DIR/PRO/SP:* Richard Brooks. Based on A *Mule for the Marquesa* by Frank O'Rourke. A Pax Enterprises Production. *CAST:* Burt Lancaster, Claudia Cardinale, Lee Marvin, Robert Ryan, Woody Strode, Jack Palance, Ralph Bellamy, Joe de Santis, Vaughn Taylor, Rafael Bertrand, Jorge Martinez de Hoyas, Marie Gomez, Jose Chavez, Carlos Romero.

Four professional ex-soldiers and gunfighters (Lancaster, Ryan, Marvin, Strode) are hired by a rancher (Bellamy) to go into Mexico and rescue his wife (Cardinale) from a bandit chief (Palance).

1602. The Proud and the Damned (12/72) Eastman Color—94 mins. (Adventure). *DIR/PRO/SP:* Ferde Grofe, Jr. A Media Trend-Prestige Production. *CAST:* Chuck Conners, Aron Kincaid, Cesar Romero, Jose Greco, Henry Capps, Peter Ford, Smoky Roberts, Maria Grimm, Anita Quinn, Conrad Parkham.

Five Civil War veterans (Conners, Kincaid, Capps, Ford, Roberts) travel to South America, get involved in a revolution, and hire themselves out as mercenaries to save their lives.

Proud, Damned and Dead *see* **The Proud and the Damned**

1603. Psyche 59 (4/64) B&W—94 mins. (Drama). *DIR:* Alexander Singer. *PRO:* Phillip Hazelton. *SP:* Julian Halevy. Based on the book by Francoise des Ligneris. A Troy-Schenck-Royal Films International Production. *CAST:* Patricia Neal, Curt Jurgens, Samantha Eggar, Ian Bannen, Beatrix Lehmann, Elspeth March, Sandra Lee, Shelley Crowhurst.

A woman (Neal) feigns blindness when she learns that her husband (Jurgens) and sister (Eggar) are having an affair.

1604. The Public Menace (9/24/35) B&W—73 mins. (Crime). *DIR:* Erle C. Kenton. *SP:* Ethel Hill, Lionel Houser. *CAST:* Jean Arthur, George Murphy, Douglass Dumbrille, George McKay, Robert Middlemass, Victor Kilian, Charles C. Wilson, Gene Morgan, Murray Alper, Shirley Grey, Bradley Page, Arthur Rankin, Thurston Hall, Fred Kelsey.

A manicurist (Arthur) helps her reporter husband (Murphy) get his job back when she locates a missing mobster (Dumbrille) believed dead.

1605. Pulse (3/88) DeLuxe Color—91 mins. (Thriller). *DIR/SP:* Paul Golding. *PRO:* Patricia A. Stallone. An Aspen Film Society Production. *CAST:* Cliff De Young, Roxanne Hart, Joey Lawrence, Matthew Lawrence, Charles Tyner, Dennis Redfield, Robert Romanus.

A family (De Young, Hart, Joey Lawrence) experience the horror of their household appliances running amok as alien forces seem to control the "Pulse" of electricity into their home. *NOTES:* Limited theatrical release.

1606. The Pumpkin Eater (11/64) B&W—118 mins. (Drama). *DIR:* Jack Clayton. *PRO:* James Woolf. *SP:* Harold Pinter. Based on the book by Penelope Mortimer. A Romulus-Royal Films International Production. *CAST:* Anne Bancroft, Peter Finch, James Mason, Janine Grey, Rosalind Atkinson, Cedric Hardwicke, Alan

Webb, Richard Johnson, Maggie Smith, Eric Porter, Cyril Luckham, Anthony Nicholls.

A woman (Bancroft) divorces her second husband (Johnson), marries a screen writer (Finch), and has a nervous breakdown after the birth of her seventh child when she learns of her husband's infidelities.

1607. Punchline (2/88) DeLuxe Color—128 mins. (Comedy-Drama). *DIR/SP:* David Seltzer. *PRO:* Daniel Melnick, Nichael Rachmil. *CAST:* Sally Field, Tom Hanks, John Goodman, Mark Rydell, Kim Greist, Paul Mazursky, Pam Matteson, George Michael McGrath.

A New Jersey housewife (Field) and an ex-medical student (Hanks) compete against each other as stand-up comics at the local comedy club.

1608. Purple Haze (11/83) Eastman Color—97 mins. (Drama). *DIR:* David Burton Morris. *PRO:* Thomas Anthony Fucci. *SP:* Victoria Wozniak. Story by Tom Kelsey, Victoria Wozniak, David Burton Morris. A Triumph Films Production. *CAST:* Peter Nelson, Chuck McQuary, Bernard Beldan, Susanna Lack, Bob Breuler, Joanne Bauman, Katy Horsch, Heidi Helman, Tomy O'Brien, Dan Jones, Jean Ashley, Sara Hennessy, Michael Bailey, Peter Thoemke.

In the late 60's, a youth (Nelson) gets expelled from college, experiences drugs, and tries to fight off the draft and "the Establishment."

1609. The Purple Heart Diary (11/12/51) B&W—73 mins. (Drama-Musical). *DIR:* Richard Quine. *PRO:* Sam Katzman. *SP:* William B. Sackheim. Based on the wartime columns of Frances Langford. *CAST:* Judd Holdren, Frances Langford, Ben Lessy, Tony Romano, Aline Towne, Brett King, Warren Mills, Larry Stewart, Joel Marston, Richard Grant,

Rory Mallison, Selmer Jackson, Lyle Talbot, Douglas F. Bank, William R. Klein, Harry Guardino, Marshall Reed, Steve Pendleton, George Offerman, Jr.

Frances Langford plays cupid to an amputee (King) and a nurse (Towne), as she and the rest of her troupe (Romano, Lessy), representing the United Service Organization (USO), entertain the troops in the Pacific. [British title: *No Time for Tears*].

1610. The Pursuers (12/61) B&W—63 mins. (Crime). *DIR:* Godfrey Grayson. *PRO:* Philip Elton, Ralph Goddard. *SP:* Brian Clemens, David Nicholl. A Danziger Production. *CAST:* Cyril Chaps, Francis Matthews, Susan Denny, Sheldon Lawrence, George Murcell, John Gabriel, Tony Doonan, Steve Plytas.

A private investigator (Matthews) tracks down the head (Chaps) of a Nazi concentration camp.

1611. The Pursuit of Happiness (2/71) Eastman Color—93 mins. (Drama). *DIR:* Robert Mulligan. *PRO:* David Susskind. *SP:* George L. Sherman, Jon Boothe. Based on the book by Thomas Rogers. *CAST:* Michael Sarrazin, Barbara Hershey, Robert Klein, Sada Thompson, Ralph Waite, Arthur Hill, E. G. Marshall, Rue McClanahan, Ruth White, David Doyle, Bernard Hughes, Charles Durning, William Devane, Gilbert Lewis.

A radical student (Sarrazin), sentenced to a year in prison after accidentally killing a woman with his car, breaks out of prison and, with his girlfriend (Hershey), escapes to Canada.

1612. Pushover (8/54) B&W—88 mins. (Crime-Drama). *DIR:* Richard Quine. *PRO:* Jules Shermer. *SP:* Roy Huggins. Based on *The Night Watch* by Thomas Walsh and *Rafferty* by William S. Ballinger. *CAST:* Fred MacMurray, Kim Novak, Phil Carey, Dorothy Malone, Allen Nourse, E. G. Marshall, Phil Chambers, Alan Dexter, Robert Forrest, Don C. Harvey, Paul Richards, Ann Morriss, Dick Crockett, Marion Ross, Hal Taggart, Anne Loos, Paul Picerni, Mort Mills.

A gun-moll (Novak) entices a cop (MacMurray) to kill her gangster boyfriend (Richards) for his stolen loot, which leads to disastrous consequences. NOTES: Kim Novak's first Columbia feature and first starring role.

1613. Pygmy Island (11/22/50) B&W—69 mins. (Adventure). *DIR:* William Berke. *PRO:* Sam Katzman. *SP:* Carroll Young. Based on the *Jungle Jim* newspaper comic strip created by Alex Raymond. *CAST:* Johnny Weissmuller, Ann Savage, David Bruce, Steven Geray, William Tannen, Tristram Coffin, Billy Curtis, Rusty Wescoatt, Billy Barty, Pierce Lyden, Tommy Farrell.

Jungle Jim (Weissmuller), with the help of a pygmy chief (Barty) and his tribe, sets out to rescue a lost WAC captain (Savage) and stop a group of enemy agents.

1614. Queen Bee (11/55) B&W—95 mins. (Drama). *DIR/SP:* Randall MacDougall. *PRO:* Jerry Wald. Based on the book by Edna Lee. *CAST:* Joan Crawford, Barry Sullivan, Betsy Palmer, John Ireland, Lucy Marlow, William Leslie, Fay Wray, Katherine Anderson, Tim Hovey, Willa Pearl Curtis, Bill Walker, Olan Soule, Juanita Moore.

A domineering woman (Crawford) manipulates the lives of those around her.

1615. Queen of the Pirates (8/61) Eastman Color/Scope—80 mins. (Action-Adventure). *DIR:* Mario Costa. *PRO:* Ottavio Poggi. *SP:* Nino Stresa. Story by Kurt Nachmann, Rolf Olsen. A Max-Rapid Film Production. *CAST:*

Gianna Maria Canale, Massimo Serato, Scilla Gabel, Paul Muller, Jose Jaspe, Livio Lorenzon, Giustino Durano.

A woman (Canale) and her father (Jaspe), together with her lover (Serato), become pirates to stop a tyrannical ruler (Muller). NOTES: Originally filmed in Eastman Color, it was initially released in the U.S. in black and white. A sequel was released by Embassy Pictures in 1964, *Tiger of the Seven Seas*. [Original Italian title: *La Venere dei Pirati*]. [Original German title: *Venus der Piraten*].

1616. The Queens (3/68) Eastman Color—111 mins. (Drama). *Queen Sabina*—*DIR:* Luciano Salce. *SP:* Ruggero Maccari, Luigi Magni, Luciano Salce. *Queen Armenia*—*DIR:* Mario Monicelli. *SP:* Suso Cecchi D'Amico, Tonino Guerra, Giorgio Salvioni. *Queen Elena*—*DIR:* Mauro Bolognini. *SP:* Rodolfo Sonego. *Queen Marta*—*DIR:* Antonio Pietrangeli. *SP:* Rodolfo Sonego. *PRO:* Gianni Hecht Lucari. A Documento-Orsay-Royal Films International Production. *CAST: Queen Sabina*— Monica Vitti, Enrico Maria Salerno, Franco Balducci, Renzo Giovanpietro. *Queen Armenia*—Claudia Cardinale, Gastone Moschin. *Queen Elena*—Raquel Welch, Jean Sorel, Pia Lindstrom, Massimo Fornari. *Queen Marta*—Capucine, Alberto Sordi, Anthony Steel, Olga Villi, Gigi Ballista, Nino Marchetti.

A quartet of stories focusing on women as "Queens" of their world. NOTES: In Italian with English subtitles. [British title: *Sex Quartet*]. [Original Italian title: *Le Fate*]. [Original French title: *Les Ogresses*].

1617. Querelle (4/83) Eastman Color/Scope—106 mins. (Drama). *DIR/SP:* Rainer Werner Fassbinder. *PRO:* Dieter Schidor. Based on *Querelle De Brest* by Jean Genet. A

Planet-Albatros-Triumph Films Production. CAST: Brad Davis, Franco Nero, Jeanne Moreau, Laurent Malet, Nadja Brunkhorst, Hanno Poschl, Gunther Kaufmann, Burkhard Driest, Dieter Schidor, Roger Fritz, Michael McLeron, Neil Bell, Harry Baer.

A French sailor (Davis) discovers his homosexuality. NOTES: Limited theatrical release. Director Rainer Werner Fassbinder's last film.

1618. A Question of Suspense (4/61) B&W—62 mins. (Crime). DIR: Max Varnel. PRO: Bill Luckwell, Jock McGregor. SP: Lawrence Huntington. Based on the book by Roy Vickers. A Bill and Michael Luckwell Production. CAST: Peter Reynolds, Noelle Middleton, Yvonne Buckingham, Norman Rodway, James Neylin, Pauline Delany, Anne Mulvey.

A woman (Buckingham) seeks revenge on the man (Reynolds) that killed her lover.

1619. The Quick Gun (4/64) Technicolor/Scope—87 mins. (Western). DIR: Sidney Salkow. PRO: Grant Whytock. SP: Robert E. Kent. Based on The Fastest Gun by Steve Fisher. An Admiral Production. CAST: Audie Murphy, Merry Anders, James Best, Ted de Corsia, Walter Sande, Frank Ferguson, Raymond Hatton, William Fawcett, Rex Holman, Charles Meredith, Mort Mills, Gregg Palmer, Frank Gerstle, Stephen Roberts, Paul Bryar.

A gunfighter (Murphy) returns home and aids a sheriff (Best) when a gang of outlaws plan to rob the local bank.

1620. Quick on the Trigger (12/2/48) B&W—55 mins. (Western). DIR: Ray Nazarro. PRO: Colbert Clark. SP: Elmer Clifton. CAST: Charles Starrett, Helen Parrish, Smiley Burnette, Lyle Talbot, George Eldredge, Ted Adams, Russell Arms, Budd Buster, Blackie Whiteford, Al Bridge, Tex Cooper, Bud Osborne, Russell Meeker, The Sunshine Boys.

A sheriff (Starrett), framed for murder by a crooked lawyer (Talbot), escapes from jail and, as the Durango Kid, sets out to prove the lawyer is the real killer and the leader of the outlaws who have been robbing the stagecoaches. [British title: Condemned in Error].

1621. Quicksilver (2/86) Metrocolor—101 mins. (Drama). DIR/SP: Tom Donnelly. PRO: Michael Rachmil, Daniel Melnick. A Columbia-Delphi IV Production. CAST: Kevin Bacon, Jami Gertz, Paul Rodriguez, Rudy Ramos, Andrew Smith, Gerald S. O'Loughlin, Larry Fishburne, Louis Anderson, Charles McCaughan, David Harris, Whitney Kershaw, Joshua Shelley, Georgann Johnson.

After losing his company's money and his parents' savings in a stock market deal, a young stockbroker (Bacon) decides to drop out of the rat race and becomes a bicycle messenger with the Quicksilver Messenger Service.

1622. The Quitter (4/1/29) B&W—58 mins. (Drama). DIR: Joseph Henabery. SP: Dorothy Howell. Based on The Spice of Life by Dorothy Howell. CAST: Ben Lyon, Dorothy Revier, Fred Kohler, Charles McHugh.

A disgraced surgeon (Lyon) redeems himself when he saves the life of a cafe owner (Kohler).

1623. R.P.M. (Revolutions Per Minute) (9/70) Eastman Color—92 mins. (Drama). DIR/PRO: Stanley Kramer. SP: Erich Segal. CAST: Anthony Quinn, Ann-Margret, Gary Lockwood, Paul Winfield, Graham Jarvis, Alan Hewitt, John McLiam, Donald Moffat, David Ladd, John Zaremba, Norman Burton, Don Keefer, Ramon Bieri.

A college president (Quinn) loses the respect of the student body when he fails to meet the demands of a group of radical students.

1624. Racing for Life (5/1/24) B&W — 50 mins. (Action). *DIR:* Henry MacRae. *PRO:* Harry Cohn. *SP:* Wilfred Lucas. A C.B.C. Release. *CAST:* Eva Novak, William Fairbanks, Philo McCullough, Wilfred Lucas, Ralph De Palma, Lydia Knott, Frankie Darro, Edwin Booth Tilton, Frank Whitson, Harley Moore, Larry La Verne, George Atkinson, Paul J. Derkum, Edgar Kennedy.

A young man (Fairbanks) agrees to drive his sweetheart's (Novak) father's car in the big race but is kidnapped the day before the race. He manages to escape and win the race and the girl.

1625. Racing Luck (11/18/48) B&W — 66 mins. (Drama). *DIR:* William Berke. *PRO:* Sam Katzman. *SP:* Joseph Carole, Al Martin, Harvey Gates. *CAST:* Gloria Henry, Stanley Clements, David Bruce, Paula Raymond, Harry Cheshire, Dooley Wilson, Jack Ingram, Nelson Leigh, Bill Cartledge, Syd Saylor.

A brother (Clements) and sister (Henry) enter the horse race game when they inherit a pair of race horses.

1626. The Racket Man (1/18/44) B&W — 65 mins. (Crime). *DIR:* D. Ross Lederman. *PRO:* Wallace MacDonald. *SP:* Howard J. Green, Paul Yawitz. Story by Casey Robinson. *CAST:* Tom Neal, Hugh Beaumont, Jeanne Bates, Larry Parks, Douglas Fowley, Lewis Wilson, Clarence Muse, Mary Gordon, Anthony Caruso, Warren Ashe, Pauline Drake.

A racketeer (Neal), inducted into the Army, goes undercover to stop a gang of black marketeers.

1627. Racketeers in Exile (4/15/37) B&W — 60 mins. (Crime). *DIR:*
Erle C. Kenton. *PRO:* Irving Briskin. *SP:* Harry Sauber, Robert Shannon. Story by Harry Sauber. *CAST:* George Bancroft, Evelyn Venable, Wynne Gibson, Marc Lawrence, John Gallaudet, George McKay, Gary Owen, Jack Clifford, William Burress, Helen Lowell, Richard Carle, Jonathan Hale.

A mobster (Bancroft), hiding out from the police in his home town, encounters a religious revival and decides to become an evangelist.

1628. Rage (12/66) Eastman Color — 103 mins. (Drama). *DIR/PRO:* Gilberto Gazcon. *SP:* Teddi Sherman, Gilberto Gazcon, Fernando Mendez. A Cinematografica Jalisco-Joseph M. Schenck Enterprises Production. *CAST:* Glenn Ford, Stella Stevens, David Reynoso, Armando Silvestre, Ariadne Welter, Jose Elias Moreno, Dacia Gonzalez, Pancho Cordova, Susana Cabrera, David Silva, Quentin Bulnes, Valentin Trujillo.

A doctor (Ford), infected by rabies, races across the Mexican desert to get to a treatment center. [Original Spanish title: *El Mal*].

1629. The Raider Emden (4/30/28) B&W — 65 mins. (War). *DIR:* Louis Ralph. *SP:* Joseph Weil. An Emelka Production produced with the cooperation of the German Admiralty. *CAST:* Not available.

Based on the exploits of the German cruiser *Emden* during World War I, the film depicts the *Emden* sinking Allied vessels and its subsequent capture by the British warship *Sydney*. *NOTES:* A sound version, released in 1931 and entitled *Cruiser Emden,* was also directed by and starred Louis Ralph.

1630. Raiders of Tomahawk Creek (10/25/50) B&W — 55 mins. (Western). *DIR:* Fred F. Sears. *PRO:* Colbert Clark. *SP:* Barry Shipman.

276 The Columbia Checklist

Story by Robert Schafer, Eric Frei-
wald. CAST: Charles Starrett, Kay
Buckley, Smiley Burnette, Edgar
Dearing, Bill Kimbley, Paul Marion,
Paul McGuire, Bill Hale, Lee Morgan,
Ted Mapes.

The Durango Kid (Starrett) sets out
to stop a series of murders near the
area of Tomahawk Creek by a crooked
Indian agent (Dearing) who has
located a lost silver mine on Indian lands. [British title: Circle of
Fear].

1631. Rain or Shine (8/15/30)
B&W — 87 mins. (Drama). DIR: Frank
Capra. PRO: Harry Cohn. SP: Doro-
thy Howell, Jo Swerling. Based on the
book by James Gleason and Maurice
Marks and the play by James Gleason.
A Frank Capra Production. CAST: Joe
Cook, Louise Fazenda, Joan Peers,
William Collier, Jr., Tom Howard,
Dave Chasen, Alan Roscoe, Adolph
Milar, Clarence Muse, Nora Lane, Ed-
ward Martindale, Tyrrell Davis.

A woman (Peers), with the help of
her manager (Cook), tries to salvage
the circus she inherited from her
father.

1632. Rainbow 'Round My
Shoulder (9/52) Technicolor — 78
mins. (Musical). DIR: Richard Quine.
PRO: Jonie Taps. SP: Blake Edwards,
Richard Quine. CAST: Frankie Laine,
Billy Daniels, Charlotte Austin, Arthur Franz, Ida Moore, Lloyd Corrigan, Barbara Whiting, Ross Ford, Arthur Space, Frank Wilcox, Diane Garrett, Chester Marshall, Helen Wallace,
Eleanore Davis, Eugene Baxter, Ken
Garcia, Mira McKinney, Edythe Elliott, Jean Andren.

A young girl (Austin) goes to Hollywood in the hopes of becoming a star
and lands a role in a film with Frankie
Laine. NOTES: This film provided the
viewer with a tour of Columbia's back
lot.

1633. A Raisin in the Sun (4/61)
B&W — 127 mins. (Drama). DIR: Dan-
iel Petrie. PRO: David Susskind,
Philip Rose. SP: Lorraine Hansberry.
Based on the play by Lorraine Hans-
berry. A Paman-Doris Production.
CAST: Sidney Poitier, Claudia Mc-
Neil, Ruby Dee, Diana Sands, Ivan
Dixon, John Fiedler, Louis Gossett,
Jr., Stephen Perry, Joel Fluellen, Roy
Glenn, Ray Stubbs, George DeNor-
mand, Louis Terkel.

A black family (Poitier, McNeil,
Dee, Sands) decide to move out of
their South Chicago slum apartment
into a more affluent neighborhood.

1634. Rampage at Apache Wells
(1/66) Eastman Color/Scope — 91
mins. (Western). DIR: Harald Philipp.
PRO: Horst Wendlandt. SP: Fred
Dinger, Harald Philipp. Based on Der
Olprinz by Karl Friedrich May. A
Rialto-Jadran Production. CAST:
Stewart Granger, Pierre Brice, Harald
Leipnitz, Macha Meril, Mario Girotti,
Walter Barnes, Gerd Frickhoffer,
Paddy Fox, Heinz Erhardt, Vladimir
Leib, Antje Weisgerber.

Winnetou (Brice) leads a wagon
train of settlers through Navaho Indian country while Surehand (Granger) brings to justice the landgrabber
(Leipnitz) responsible for killing the
Navaho chief's son. [Original German
title: Der Olprinz]. [Original Yugoslavian title: Kralj Petroleja].

1635. The Range Feud (11/22/
31) B&W — 64 mins. (Western). DIR:
D. Ross Lederman. PRO: Irving Bris-
kin. SP: Milton Krims. CAST: Buck
Jones, Harry Woods, John Wayne,
Glenn Strange, Susan Fleming, Jim
Corey, Edward J. LeSaint, Lew Mee-
han, William Walling, Frank Austin,
Wallace MacDonald.

A sheriff (Jones) arrests a ranch
owner's son (Wayne) for killing a rival
rancher over a feud involving cattle

rustling. Believing his innocence, he sets out to find the real killer and uncovers him at the scene of a lynching.

1636. Ranger Courage (1/10/37) B&W—58 mins. (Western). *DIR:* Spencer G. Bennet. *PRO:* Larry Darmour. *SP:* Nate Gatzert. *CAST:* Bob Allen, Martha Tibbetts, Walter Miller, Robert "Buzz" Henry, Bud Osborne, Bob Kortman, Harry Strang, Horace Murphy, William Gould, Franklyn Farnum, Buffalo Bill, Jr. (Jay Wilsey), Gene Alsace (Rocky Camron).

A Ranger (Allen) saves a wagon train from outlaws masquerading as Indians.

1637. The Rangers Step In (8/8/37) B&W—58 mins. (Western). *DIR:* Spencer G. Bennet. *PRO:* Larry Darmour. *SP:* Nate Gatzert. Story by Jesse A. Duffy and Joseph Levering. *CAST:* Bob Allen, Eleanor Stewart, Buffalo Bill, Jr. (Jay Wilsey), John Merton, Hal Taliaferro (Wally Wales), Jack Ingram, Jack Rockwell, Lafe McKee, Bob Kortman, Billy Townsend, Ray Jones, Lew Meehan, Harry Harvey, Jr., Herman Hack, Dick Cramer, Joseph Girard, George Plues, Tex Palmer, Francis Walker, Ed Juregi.

A Ranger (Allen) sets out to find the cause of the feud between his family and his girl's (Stewart) family.

1638. Ransom (6/7/28) B&W—58 mins. (Adventure). *DIR:* George B. Seitz. *PRO:* Harry Cohn. *SP:* Dorothy Howell, Elmer Harris. Story by George B. Seitz. *CAST:* Edmund Burns, Lois Wilson, William V. Mong, Blue Washington, Jackie Coombs, James B. Leong.

A chemist (Burns) discovers a deadly nerve gas and the leader of the Chinatown underworld (Mong) resorts to kidnapping and murder in trying to secure the formula.

1639. The Ravagers (5/79) Metrocolor/Panavision—91 mins. (Adventure). *DIR:* Richard Compton. *PRO:* John W. Hyde. *SP:* Donald S. Sanford. Based on *Path to Savagery* by Robert Edmond Alter. *CAST:* Richard Harris, Ann Turkel, Art Carney, Ernest Borgnine, Anthony James, Woody Strode, Alana Hamilton, Seymour Cassel.

In the post-nuclear holocaust world of 1991, a man (Harris) seeks to avenge his wife's death with the help of a band of survivors who are attempting to rebuild civilization.

1640. The Razor's Edge (10/84) Eastman Color/Panavision—130 mins. (Drama). *DIR:* John Byrum. *PRO:* Robert P. Marcucci, Henry Benn. *SP:* John Byrum, Bill Murray. Based on the book by W. Somerset Maugham. A Colgems Production. *CAST:* Bill Murray, Theresa Russell, Catherine Hicks, Denholm Elliott, James Keach, Peter Vaughn, Brian Doyle Murray, Stephen Davies, Saeed Jaffrey, Faith Brook, Andre Maranne.

After surviving World War I, a young American (Bill Murray) tries to find the meaning of life through his journeys to the Himalayas and Paris. *NOTES:* A remake of the 1946 20th Century-Fox film.

1641. Reach for Glory (9/63) B&W—86 mins. (Drama). *DIR:* Philip Leacock. *PRO:* John Kohn, Jud Kinberg. *SP:* John Kohn, John Rae, Jud Kinberg. Based on *The Custard Boys* by John Rae. A Blazer-Royal Films International Production. *CAST:* Harry Andrews, Kay Walsh, Michael Anderson, Jr., Oliver Grimm, Martin Tomlinson, John Coker, Freddy Eldrett, James Luck, Michael Trubshawe, Arthur Hewlett, Allan Jeayes, Richard Vernon, Russell Waters, Pat Hayes, John Rae, Alexis Kanner, George Pravda, Peter Furnell, John Pike.

A group of London boys, evacuated to a coastal town during World War II, form a gang and play war games, but it becomes all too real when one of the boys (Grimm) is accused of cowardice and, during a mock court-martial and execution, he is killed.

1642. The Reckless Moment (10/17/49) B&W—82 mins. (Crime). DIR: Max Ophul. PRO: Walter Wanger. SP: Henry Garson, Robert W. Soderberg, Mel Dinelli, Robert E. Kent. Based on *The Blank Wall* by Elizabeth S. Holding. CAST: James Mason, Joan Bennett, Geraldine Brooks, Henry O'Neill, David Blair, Shepperd Strudwick, Roy Roberts, Frances Williams, Paul E. Burns, Danny Jackson, Claire Carleton, Peter Brocco, Virginia Hunter, Harry Harvey, Boyd Davis, Kathryn Card, Pat O'Malley, Jessie Arnold, William Schallert.

When a woman (Bennett) hides the body of a man she believes her daughter (Brooks) killed, a blackmailer (Mason) enters the picture and demands money for his silence. NOTES: The last American film of Max Ophul and the third American film for James Mason.

1643. The Reckless Ranger (5/30/37) B&W—56 mins. (Western). DIR: Spencer G. Bennet. PRO: Larry Darmour. SP: Nate Gatzert. Story by Joseph Levering, Jesse A. Duffy. CAST: Bob Allen, Louise Small, Jack Perrin, Harry Woods, Bud Osborne, Tom London, Slim Whitaker, Roger Williams, Lafe McKee, Mary MacLaren, Lane Chandler, Buffalo Bill, Jr. (Jay Wilsey), Al Taylor, Bob McKenzie, Buddy Cox, Jack Rockwell, Jim Corey, Hal Price, Tex Cooper, Frank Ball, George Plues, Tex Palmer, Victor Cox, Chick Hannon.

A Ranger (Allen) investigates the murder of his twin brother by a land grabber (Woods).

1644. The Reckoning (1/71) Technicolor—111 mins. (Drama). DIR:

Jack Gold. PRO: Ronald Shedlo. SP: John McGrath. Based on *The Harp That Once* by Patrick Hall. CAST: Nicol Williamson, Ann Bell, Rachel Roberts, Lilita De Barros, Thomas Kempinski, Kenneth Hendel, Douglas Wilmer, Barbara Ewing, Zena Walker, Paul Rogers, Christine Hargreaves, Ernest Jennings, Edward Hardwicke, Desmond Perry, Don Douglas.

An Irishman (Williamson), consumed by ambition, uses and manipulates people in his rise into the world of big business.

1645. Red Lips (3/64) B&W—90 mins. (Drama). DIR: Giuseppe Bennati. PRO: Carmine Bologna. SP: Paolo Levi, Federico Zardi, Giuseppe Bennati. Story by Paolo Levi, Giuseppe Bennati. A Rotot-Gray-Orsay-Royal Films International Production. CAST: Gabriele Ferzetti, Giorgio Albertazzi, Jeanne Valerie, Christine Kaufmann, Marina Bonfigli, Laura Betti, Elvy Lissiak, Gabriella Serafini.

A father (Ferzetti) searches for his lost teenage daughter and, when he finds her and returns her home, he soon realizes that his youngest daughter is following in her sister's footsteps. NOTES: Limited theatrical release. [Original French title: *Fausses Ingenues*; original Italian title: *Labbra Rosse*.]

1646. Red Snow (7/7/52) B&W—75 mins. (Adventure-Spy). DIR: Boris L. Petroff, Harry S. Franklin, Ewing Scott (Alaskan unit director). PRO: Boris L. Petroff. SP: Tom Hubbard, Orville H. Hampton. Story by Robert Peters. An All American Film Corp. Picture Production. CAST: Guy Madison, Ray Mala, Carole Mathews, Gloria Saunders, Robert Peyton, John Bryant, Richard Vath, Philip Ahn, Tony Benroy, Gordon Barnes, John Bleifer, Gene Roth, Muriel Maddox, Robert Bice, Richard Emory, Renny

McEvoy, Bert Arnold, Richard Pinner, George Pembroke, Robert Carson, William Fletcher. Narration by William Shaw.

An American Air Force outpost in Alaska is alerted to the fact that the Russians are testing a new weapon close by. NOTES: The major portion of this film contained stock footage of Eskimo life.

1647. Redhead from Manhattan (5/6/43) B&W — 63 mins. (Musical-Drama). DIR: Lew Landers. PRO: Wallace MacDonald. SP: Joseph Hoffman. Story by Rex Taylor. CAST: Lupe Velez, Michael Duane, Tim Ryan, Gerald Mohr, Lillian Yarbo, Arthur Loft, Lewis Wilson, Douglas Leavitt, Clancy Cooper, Douglas Drake, Ben Carter, Alma Carroll, Shirley Patterson, Stanley Brown, Edythe Elliott, Larry Parks, Adele Mara, Pat O'Malley, Frank Sully, Richard Talmadge, Roger Gray, Frank Richards, Donald Kerr.

When a Broadway star (Velez) becomes pregnant, she has her sister (Velez) impersonate her. NOTES: Lupe Velez played a dual role in this film.

1648. A Reflection of Fear (2/73) Eastman Color — 89 mins. (Horror). DIR: William A. Fraker. PRO: Howard B. Jaffe. SP: Edward Hume, Lewis John Carlino. Based on *Go to Thy Deathbed* by Stanton Forbes. CAST: Robert Shaw, Sally Kellerman, Mary Ure, Signe Hasso, Sondra Locke, Mitchell Ryan, Gordon DeVol, Gordon Anderson, Victoria Risk, Leonard John Crofoot, Michael St. Clair, Liam Dunn, Michelle Marvin, Michele Montau.

A young psychotic girl (Locke), secluded from the world by her grandmother (Hasso), goes over the edge when her father (Shaw) and his mistress (Kellerman) return home for a visit.

1649. Reformatory (7/21/38) B&W — 59 mins. (Crime-Drama). DIR: Lewis D. Collins. PRO: Larry Darmour. SP: Gordon Rigby. CAST: Jack Holt, Bobby Jordan, Ward Bond, Frankie Darro, Grant Mitchell, Charlotte Wynters, Tommy Bupp, Sheila Bromley, Paul Everton, Lloyd Ingraham, Joe Caits, Robert Emmett Keane, Vernon Dent, Greta Granstedt, Guy Usher, Al Bridge, Kent Rogers, John Wray.

A prison warden (Holt), sent to supervise a boys' reformatory, gains their confidence and respect through kindness.

1650. Relentless (2/20/48) Technicolor — 93 mins. (Western). DIR: George Sherman. PRO: Eugene B. Rodney. SP: Winston Miller. Based on *Three Were Thoroughbreds* by Kenneth Perkins. CAST: Robert Young, Marguerite Chapman, Willard Parker, Akim Tamiroff, Barton MacLane, Mike Mazurki, Robert Barrat, Paul E. Burns, Emmett Lynn, Hank Patterson, Will Wright, Frank Fenton, Clem Bevans, John Cason, Byron Foulger, Nacho Galindo, Ethan Laidlaw.

A cowboy (Young), falsely accused of murder, tracks down the man (MacLane) who can clear him of the charges.

1651. The Reluctant Saint (4/62) B&W — 105 mins. (Comedy-Drama). DIR/PRO: Edward Dmytryk. SP: John Fante, Joseph Petracca. A Dmytryk-Weiler-Davis-Royal Films International Production. CAST: Maximilian Schell, Ricardo Montalban, Lea Padovani, Akim Tamiroff, Harold Goldblatt, Arnoldo Foa, Mark Damon, Luciana Paluzzi, Carlo Croccolo, Giulio Bosetti, Elisa Cegani.

A village idiot (Schell), sent through training as a priest, is declared a saint when he is seen floating in a river and praying. NOTES: Limited theatrical release. [Original Italian title: *Cronache di un Convento*].

1652. Remember (12/20/26) B&W — 57 mins. (Romance-Drama). *DIR*: David Selman. *PRO*: Harry Cohn. *SP*: J. Grubb Alexander. Story by Dorothy Perkins. *CAST*: Dorothy Phillips, Earl Metcalfe, Lola Todd, Lincoln Stedman.

A young man (Metcalfe) returns from the war and realizes that the woman he loves is his ex-sweetheart's sister (Phillips).

1653. Remember My Name (2/78) DeLuxe Color — 95 mins. (Drama). *DIR/SP*: Alan Rudolph. *PRO*: Robert Altman. A Lion's Gate Film Production. *CAST*: Geraldine Chaplin, Anthony Perkins, Berry Berenson, Moses Gunn, Jeff Goldblum, Tim Thomerson, Alfre Woodard, Marilyn Coleman, Jeffrey S. Perry, Carlos Brown, Dennis Franz.

Released from prison, a psychotic woman (Chaplin) terrorizes her husband (Perkins) and his new wife (Berenson) in an effort to win him back. *NOTES*: The film debut of Berry Berenson, Anthony Perkins' real-life wife.

Remember the Alamo *see* **Heroes of the Alamo**

1654. Renegades (6/13/46) Technicolor — 87 mins. (Western). *DIR*: George Marshall. *PRO*: Michael Kraike. *SP*: Melvin Levy, Francis Edwards Faragoh. Story by Harold Shumate. *CAST*: Willard Parker, Evelyn Keyes, Larry Parks, Edgar Buchanan, Forrest Tucker, Jim Bannon, Eddy Waller, Francis Ford, Addison Richards, Ludwig Donath, Vernon Dent, Frank Sully, Paul E. Burns, Willard Robertson, Virginia Brissac, Hermine Sterler.

A doctor (Parker) goes after his girl (Keyes) when she runs off with the outlaw son (Parks) of a renegade band (Buchanan, Tucker, Bannon, Brissac).

1655. Renegades of the Sage (11/24/49) B&W — 56 mins. (Western). *DIR*: Ray Nazarro. *PRO*: Colbert Clark. *SP*: Earle Snell. *CAST*: Charles Starrett, Leslie Banning, Smiley Burnette, Trevor Bardette, Douglas Fowley, Fred F. Sears, Jock Mahoney, George Chesebro, Jerry Hunter, Frank McCarroll, Selmer Jackson.

The Durango Kid (Starrett) sets out to stop a gang of outlaws from destroying telegraph lines. [British title: *The Fort*].

1656. Reprisal! (11/56) Technicolor — 74 mins. (Western). *DIR*: George Sherman. *PRO*: Lewis J. Rachmil. *SP*: David P. Harmon, Raphael Hayes, David Dortort. Based on the book by Arthur Gordon. *CAST*: Guy Madison, Felicia Farr, Michael Pate, Kathryn Grant, Edward Platt, Frank DeKova, Addison Richards, Otto Mulett, Wayne Mallory, Robert Burton, Ralph Moody, Paul McGuire, Don Rhodes, Philip Breedlove, Malcolm Atterbury, Eve McVeagh, Victor Zamudia, Pete Kellett, Jack Lomas, John Zaremba.

A half-breed (Madison) buys land to raise cattle but finds he must fight three Indian hating brothers (Pate, Platt, Mallory) who want to drive him off his land.

1657. Repulsion (4/65) B&W — 105 mins. (Thriller). *DIR*: Roman Polanski. *PRO*: Eugene Gutowski. *SP*: Roman Polanski, Gerard Brach. A Compton-Tekli-Royal Films International Production. *CAST*: Catherine Deneuve, Ian Hendry, John Fraser, Patrick Wymark, Yvonne Furneaux, Renee Houston, Helen Fraser, Valerie Taylor, James Villiers, Hugh Futcher, Monica Merlin, Roman Polanski.

A sexually repressed woman (Deneuve), left alone in her sister's (Furneaux) apartment, begins her descent into madness when she starts to imagine men in the apartment and a hallway of arms. She eventually murders her landlord (Wymark) and the man (John Fraser) who loves her before going insane. NOTES: The first English-language film of Roman Polanski.

1658. Requiem for a Heavyweight (10/62) B&W—85 mins. (Drama). DIR: Ralph Nelson. PRO: David Susskind. SP: Rod Serling. Based on the play by Rod Serling. CAST: Anthony Quinn, Jackie Gleason, Mickey Rooney, Julie Harris, Stanley Adams, Herbie Faye, Jack Dempsey, Cassius Clay (Muhammad Ali), Steve Belloise, Lou Gilbert, Madame Spivy, Arthur Mercante, Val Avery, Rory Calhoun, Barney Ross, Michael Conrad, Alex Miteff.

A punch-drunk boxer (Quinn), retired from the ring, loses his self-respect when he resorts to wrestling, dressed as an Indian, to help his manager (Gleason) pay off a bet. NOTES: The film debut of director Ralph Nelson. Fifteen minutes of extra footage were added when this film were released for television showing. [British title: *Blood Money*].

1659. Restless Youth (12/11/28) B&W—65 mins. (Drama). DIR: Christy Cabanne. PRO: Jack Cohn. SP: Howard J. Green. Story by Cosmo Hamilton. CAST: Marceline Day, Ralph Forbes, Norman Trevor, Robert Ellis, Gordon (Bill) Elliott.

A woman (Day), accused of murder, is successfully defended by her sweetheart (Forbes).

1660. The Return of Daniel Boone (5/7/41) B&W—61 mins. (Western). DIR: Lambert Hillyer. PRO: Leon Barsha. SP: Paul Franklin, Joseph Hoffman. Story by Paul Franklin. CAST: Bill Elliott, Betty Miles, Dub Taylor, Ray Bennett, Lee Powell, Bud Osborne, Carl Stockdale, Edmund Cobb, Art Miles, Francis Walker, Tex Cooper, Steve Clark, Tom Carter, Hank Bell, Walter Soderling, Murdock McQuarrie, Melinda Rodik, Matilda Rodik (The Rodik Twins), Roy Butler, Edwin Bryant.

William Boone (Elliott), grandson of Daniel Boone, succeeds in proving that the mayor (Soderling) of Pecos, Arizona, and a hotel owner (Bennett) are behind the crooked tax collection and foreclosure of the ranches in the area. [British title: *The Mayor's Nest*].

1661. The Return of Monte Cristo (12/19/46) B&W—91 mins. (Adventure). DIR: Henry Levin. PRO: Grant Whytock. SP: George Bruce, Alfred Neumann. Story by Curt Siodmak, Arnold Phillips. Based on characters created by Alexandre Dumas. An Edward Small Production. CAST: Louis Hayward, Barbara Britton, George Macready, Una O'Conner, Henry Stephenson, Steven Geray, Ray Collins, Ludwig Donath, Ivan Triesault, Eugene Borden, Crane Whitley, Jean Del Val.

The grandson (Hayward) of the Count of Monte Cristo escapes from Devil's Island and, in a variety of disguises, tracks down those who framed and robbed him of his fortune. [British title: *Monte Cristo's Revenge*].

1662. The Return of October (11/26/48) Technicolor—98 mins. (Comedy). DIR: Joseph H. Lewis. PRO: Rudolph Mate. SP: Melvin Frank, Norman Panama. Story by Connie Lee, Karen DeWolf. CAST: Glenn Ford, Terry Moore, James Gleason, Albert Sharpe, Henry O'Neill, Dame May Whitty, Frederic Tozere, Samuel S. Hinds, Nana Bryant, Lloyd Corrigan, Roland Winters, Stephen Dunne, Gus Schilling, Murray Alper, Horace MacMahon, Victoria Horne, Byron Foulger, Russell Hicks, Billy Pearson, Ray Walker.

A girl's (Moore) inheritance is contested on the grounds that she thinks a horse is the reincarnation of her dead uncle (Gleason). [British title: A Date with Destiny].

1663. The Return of Rusty (6/27/46) B&W — 64 mins. (Drama). DIR: William Castle. PRO: Leonard S. Picker. SP: Lewis H. Herman. Based on characters created by Al Martin. CAST: Ted Donaldson, John Litel, Mark Dennis, Barbara Woodell, Robert Stevens, Mickey Kuhn, Teddy Infuhr, Dwayne Hickman, Mickey McGuire, Gene Collins, David Ackles, Donald Davis, "Flame," the dog.

A war orphan comes to America and is befriended by a boy (Donaldson) and his dog.

1664. The Return of the Durango Kid (4/19/45) B&W — 58 mins. (Western). DIR: Derwin Abrahams. PRO: Colbert Clark. SP: J. Benton Cheney. CAST: Charles Starrett, Jean Stevens, Tex Harding, Betty Roadman, John Calvert, Ray Bennett, Hal Price, Steve Clark, Dick Botiller, Elmo Lincoln, Britt Wood, Ted Mapes, Paul Conrad, Carl Sepulveda, Herman Hack, Dan White, James T. Nelson, The Jesters.

The Durango Kid (Starrett) sets out on a dual mission: to clear his father's name and find the outlaws responsible for the rash of stagecoach robberies in the area of Silver City, Texas. [British title: Stolen Time].

1665. Return of the Vampire (2/25/44) B&W — 69 mins. (Horror). DIR: Lew Landers. PRO: Sam White. SP: Griffin Jay, Randall Faye, Based on an idea by Kurt Neumann. CAST: Bela Lugosi, Frieda Inescort, Nina Foch, Roland Varno, Miles Mander, Matt Willis, Ottola Nesmith, Gilbert Emery, Leslie Denison, Jeanne Bates, Billy Bevan, George McKay, William C. P. Austin, Donald Dewar.

In World War II London, a vampire (Lugosi) is released from his coffin by the bombings and, with the help of a werewolf (Willis), goes in search of fresh young blood. NOTES: Since Universal owned the copyright to the "Dracula" character, the vampire's name used in this film was Armand Tesla. The vampire's demise was considered too graphic for British audiences and was edited out of the British release print. Makeup man Clay Campbell was to reproduce his werewolf makeup 12 years later for the 1956 Columbia film The Werewolf.

1666. Return of the Whistler (3/18/48) B&W — 63 mins. (Mystery). DIR: D. Ross Lederman. PRO: Rudolph C. Flothow. SP: Edward Bock, Maurice Tombragel. Story by Cornell Woolrich. Based on The Whistler radio program. CAST: Michael Duane, Lenore Aubert, Richard Lane, James Cardwell, Ann Shoemaker, Wilton Graff, Olin Howlin, Eddy Waller, Trevor Bardette, Ann Doran, Robert Emmett Keane, Edgar Dearing, Sarah Padden.

A man (Duane) enlists the aid of a private detective (Lane) when his fiancee (Aubert) turns up missing.

1667. The Return of Wild Bill (6/27/40) B&W — 60 mins. (Western). DIR: Joseph H. Lewis. PRO: Leon Barsha. SP: Robert Lee Johnson, Fred Myton. Based on Black K Rides Tonight by Walt Coburn. CAST: Bill Elliott, Iris Meredith, Edward J. Le-Saint, Dub Taylor, Luana Walters, George Lloyd, Frank LaRue, Francis Walker, Chuck Morrison, Buel Bryant, William Kellogg, Jack Rockwell, Jim Corey, John Ince, John Merton, Donald Haines.

Wild Bill Saunders (Elliott) returns home to find his father (LeSaint) shot by brothers (Lloyd, Walker) posing as vigilantes and sets out to bring them and their gang to justice. [British title: *False Evidence*].

1668. Return to Warbow (1/58) Technicolor—67 mins. (Western). *DIR*: Ray Nazarro. *PRO*: Wallace MacDonald. *SP*: Les Savage, Jr. Based on the book by Les Savage, Jr. *CAST*: Phil Carey, Catherine McLeod, Andrew Duggan, William Leslie, Robert J. Wilke, James Griffith, Jay Silverheels, Harry Lauter, Paul Picerni, Francis De Sales, Joe Forte, Chris Olsen.

A man (Carey) escapes from prison to retrieve his stolen loot only to find that his brother (Griffith) has gambled it away.

1669. Reveille with Beverly (2/4/43) B&W—78 mins. (Musical). *DIR*: Charles Barton. *PRO*: Sam White. *SP*: Howard J. Green, Jack Henley, Albert Duffy. *CAST*: Ann Miller, William Wright, Dick Purcell, Franklin Pangborn, Tim Ryan, Larry Parks, Adele Mara, Walter Sande, Wally Vernon, Barbara Brown, Andrew Tombes, Eddie Kane, Boyd Davis, Eddy Chandler, Doodles Weaver, Eugene Jackson, Harry Anderson, Si Jenks, Jack Rice, Irene Ryan, John T. Murray, Virginia Sale, Herbert Rawlinson, Shirley Mills, Maude Eburne, Lee Wilde, Lyn Wilde, Bob Crosby and His Orchestra, Freddie Slack and His Orchestra, Ella Mae Morse, Duke Ellington and His Orchestra, Count Basie and His Orchestra, Frank Sinatra, The Mills Brothers, The Radio Rogues.

A lady disc jockey (Miller) spins records for soldiers at a nearby Army base, while visualized depictions of the artists are shown when she spins the records. NOTES: This film, budgeted at $40,000, returned a huge profit for Columbia. One possible explanation was the one-song appearance of America's teen idol, Frank Sinatra.

1670. The Revenge of Frankenstein (7/58) Technicolor—89 mins. (Horror). *DIR*: Terence Fisher. *PRO*: Anthony Hinds. *SP*: Jimmy Sangster, H. Hurford Janes. Based on characters created by Mary Shelley. A Hammer Production. *CAST*: Peter Cushing, Francis Matthews, Eunice Gayson, Michael Gwynn, John Welsh, Lionel Jeffries, Michael Ripper, Oscar Quitak, John Stuart, Margery Cresley, Arnold Diamond, Anna Walmsley.

Dr. Frankenstein (Cushing) enlists the aid of a German doctor (Matthews) to create a monster with a dwarf's brain.

1671. The Revenge Rider (3/18/35) B&W—60 mins. (Western). *DIR*: David Selman. *PRO*: Harry L. Decker. *SP*: Ford Beebe. *CAST*: Tim McCoy, Billie Seward, Robert Allen, Edward Earle, Frank Sheridan, Jack Clifford, George Pierce, Alan Sears, Harry Semels, Joe Sawyer, Lafe McKee, Jack Mower.

A sheriff (McCoy) goes after the men who killed his parents.

1672. Revenue Agent (12/12/50) B&W—72 mins. (Crime). *DIR*: Lew Landers. *PRO*: Sam Katzman. *SP*: William B. Sackheim, Arthur A. Ross. *CAST*: Douglas Kennedy, Jean Willes, Onslow Stevens, Ray Walker, William "Bill" Phillips, David Bruce, Archie Twitchell, Lyle Talbot, Rick Vallin.

An agent (Kennedy) for the Internal Revenue Service goes undercover to stop a crook (Stevens) from sneaking $1 million in gold dust out of the country.

1673. The Reverse Be My Lot (1/38) B&W—68 mins. (Drama). *DIR*: Raymond Stross. *PRO*: Nat Ross. *SP*: Syd Courtenay. Based on the book by Margaret Morrison. A Rock Production. *CAST*: Ian Fleming, Marjorie Corbett, Mickey Brantford, Georgie

Harris, Jackie Heller, Helen Goss, Audrene Brier, Aubrey Mallalieu.
An actress (Corbett), in love with a doctor's son (Brantford), is used by the doctor (Fleming) as a test subject for his influenza vaccine.

1674. Rhythm Round-Up (6/7/45) B&W—66 mins. (Western). *DIR:* Vernon Keays. *PRO:* Colbert Clark. *SP:* Charles R. Marion. Story by Louise Rousseau. *CAST:* Ken Curtis, Cheryl Walker, Raymond Hatton, Guinn "Big Boy" Williams, Vic Potel, Eddie Bruce, Arthur Loft, Vera Lewis, Walter Baldwin, The Hoosier Hotshots, The Pied Pipers, Bob Wills and His Texas Playboys.
The owner of a hotel (Curtis) tries to stop a group of rowdies (Hoosier Hotshots) from laying claim to his hotel. [British title: *Honest John*].

1675. Rhythm Serenade (7/15/43) B&W—87 mins. (Musical-Romance). *DIR:* Gordon Wellesley. *PRO:* Ben Henry, George Formby. *SP:* Marjorie Deans, Basil Woon, Margaret Kennedy, Edward Dryhurst. Story by Marjorie Deans. A Columbia-British Production. *CAST:* Vera Lynn, Peter Murray Hill, Julien Mitchell, Charles Victor, Jimmy Jewel, Ben Warriss, Joss Ambler, Rosalyn Boulter, Betty Jardine, Irene Handl, Lloyd Pearson, Jimmy Clitheroe, Aubrey Mallalieu, Peter Madden.
A teacher (Lynn) sets up a day school for children of employees working at a munitions factory.

1676. Rich Men's Sons (5/20/27) B&W—57 mins. (Drama). *DIR:* Ralph Graves. *PRO:* Harry Cohn. *SP:* Dorothy Howell. *CAST:* Ralph Graves, Shirley Mason, Robert Cain, Frances Raymond.
The idle son (Graves) of a railroad magnate goes to work in an ironworks and, with the help of the owner's

daughter (Mason), redeems himself with his father.

1677. Richard Pryor Here and Now (10/83) Metrocolor—94 mins. (Comedy). *DIR/SP:* Richard Pryor. *PRO:* Bob Parkinson, Andy Friendly. *CAST:* Richard Pryor.
Richard Pryor in concert in New Orleans.

1678. Richard Pryor Live on Sunset Strip (3/82) Metrocolor—88 mins. (Comedy). *DIR:* Joe Layton. *PRO/SP:* Richard Pryor. A Rastar Production. *CAST:* Richard Pryor.
Richard Pryor in concert at the Hollywood Palladium.

1679. The Richest Man in Town (8/2/41) B&W—70 mins. (Comedy). *DIR:* Charles Barton. *PRO:* Jack Fier. *SP:* Fanya Foss, Jerry Sackheim. Story by Jerry Sackheim. *CAST:* Frank Craven, Edgar Buchanan, Eileen O'Hearn, Roger Pryor, Tom Dugan, George McKay, Jimmie Dodd, Jan Duggan, John Tyrrell, Harry Tyler, Will Wright, Joel Friedkin, Erville Alderson, Edward Earle, Thomas W. Ross, Ferris Taylor, George Guhl, Netta Packer, William Gould, Kathryn Sheldon, Lee Prather, Edythe Elliott, Billy Benedict, Ned Glass, Jessie Arnold, Ernie Adams, Murdock McQuarrie, Richard Fiske.
Complications ensue when a newspaper publisher (Buchanan) publishes an obituary he has written for his pal (Craven), the local banker.

1680. Ride Beyond Vengeance (4/66) Pathe Color—100 mins. (Western). *DIR:* Bernard McEveety. *PRO:* Andrew J. Fenady, Mark Goodson, Bill Todman. *SP:* Andrew J. Fenady. Based on *The Night of the Tiger* by Al Dewlen. A Tiger-Sentinel-Fenady Associates Production. *CAST:* Chuck Conners, Michael Rennie, Kathryn Hays, Joan Blondell, Gloria Grahame,

Gary Merrill, Bill Bixby, Claude Akins, Paul Fix, Buddy Baer, Harry Harvey, Frank Gorshin, Robert Q. Lewis, James MacArthur, Jamie Farr, Ruth Warrick, Arthur O'Connell.

Told in double-flashback, a bartender (O'Connell) relates to a census taker (MacArthur) the story of how a buffalo hunter (Conners) sought vengeance on those who branded him and stole his money. *NOTES:* The film debut of Kathryn Hays.

1681. Ride Lonesome (2/59) Eastman Color/Scope — 75 mins. (Western). *DIR/PRO:* Budd Boetticher. *SP:* Burt Kennedy. A Ranown Production. *CAST:* Randolph Scott, Donna Reed, Pernell Roberts, Karen Steele, James Best, Lee Marvin, Lee Van Cleef, James Coburn, Boyd Stockman, Roy Jenson, Duke Johnson, Boyd "Red" Morgan, Bennie Dobbins.

A bounty hunter (Scott) and two outlaws (Coburn, Roberts) trail a giggling killer (Best) hoping that he will lead them to his killer brother (Van Cleef). *NOTES:* The film debut of James Coburn.

1682. Ride the High Iron (12/56) B&W — 74 mins. (Drama). *DIR:* Don Weis. *PRO:* William Self. *SP:* Milton Gelman. *CAST:* Don Taylor, Sally Forrest, Raymond Burr, Lisa Golm, Otto Waldis, Nestor Paiva, Mae Clarke, Maurice Marsac, Robert Johnson.

A Korean War veteran (Taylor) hides his past as the son of an immigrant railroad worker as he tries to make it in the world of public relations. *NOTES:* Originally scheduled as a television movie, it was withheld from broadcast and released theatrically.

1683. Ride the Wild Surf (7/64) Eastman Color — 101 mins. (Comedy-Drama). *DIR:* Don Taylor. *PRO/SP:* Art Napoleon, Jo Napoleon. *CAST:*

Fabian, Shelley Fabares, Tab Hunter, Barbara Eden, Peter Brown, Susan Hart, James Mitchum, Anthony Hayes, Roger Davis, Catherine McLeod, Murray Rose, Robert Kenneally, David Cadiente, Alan LeBuse, Paul Tremaine, John Kennell.

A trio of surfers (Fabian, Hunter, Brown) head for Hawaii to compete in the surfing finals.

1684. Riders in the Sky (11/1/49) B&W — 70 mins. (Western). *DIR:* John English. *PRO:* Armand Schaefer. *SP:* Gerald Geraghty. Story by Herbert A. Woodbury. A Gene Autry Production. *CAST:* Gene Autry, Gloria Henry, Pat Buttram, Mary Beth Hughes, Robert Livingston, Steve Darrell, Alan Hale, Jr., Tom London, Dennis Moore, Kenne Duncan, Kermit Maynard, Boyd Stockman, Pat O'Malley, Bud Osborne, Hank Patterson, Ben Welden, Joe Forte, Frank Jacquet, Roy Gordon, Lois Bridge, Vernon Johns, John Parrish, Lynton Brent, Isabel Withers, Sandy Sanders, Denver Dixon, Robert Walker.

Gene comes to the aid of his friend (Darrell) who has been framed for murder and exposes a gambler and town boss (Livingston) as the real killer.

1685. Riders of Black River (8/23/39) B&W — 59 mins. (Western). *DIR:* Norman Deming. *PRO:* Harry L. Decker. *SP:* Bennett R. Cohen. Based on the screenplay *The Revenge Rider* by Ford Beebe. *CAST:* Charles Starrett, Iris Meredith, Bob Nolan, Dick Curtis, Stanley Brown, Francis Sayles, Forrest Taylor, George Chesebro, Clem Horton, Edmund Cobb, Ethan Allen, Maston Williams, Carl Sepulveda, Olin Francis, Sons of the Pioneers.

An ex–Ranger (Starrett) helps a girl (Meredith) whose brother (Brown) is mixed up with cattle rustlers. *NOTES:*

A loose remake of the 1935 Columbia film *The Revenge Rider.*

1686. Riders of the Badlands
(12/18/41) B&W — 57 mins. (Western).
DIR: Howard Bretherton. PRO: William Berke. SP: Betty Burbridge. CAST: Charles Starrett, Ilene Brewer, Russell Hayden, Cliff Edwards, Kay Hughes, Roy Barcroft, Ethan Laidlaw, Harry Cording, George J. Lewis, Edmund Cobb, Francis Walker, Ted Mapes, Rich Anderson, Hal Price, Edith Leach, John Cason.

A Texas Ranger (Starrett) almost gets himself lynched when he is mistaken for an outlaw (Starrett). NOTES: Charles Starrett played a dual role in this film.

1687. Riders of the Lone Star
(8/14/47) B&W — 55 mins. (Western). DIR: Derwin Abrahams. PRO: Colbert Clark. SP: Barry Shipman. CAST: Charles Starrett, Virginia Hunter, Smiley Burnette, Steve Darrell, Edmund Cobb, Mark Dennis, Ted Mapes, Lane Bradford, George Chesebro, Eddie Parker, Peter Perkins, Bud Osborne, Nolan Leary, Curly Williams and His Georgia Peach Pickers.

The Durango Kid (Starrett) stops an outlaw gang bent on preventing the opening of a silver mine because it contains stolen money.

1688. Riders of the Northland
(6/18/42) B&W — 58 mins. (Western). DIR: William Berke. PRO: Jack Fier. SP: Paul Franklin. CAST: Charles Starrett, Shirley Patterson, Cliff Edwards, Lloyd Bridges, Russell Hayden, Kenneth MacDonald, Bobby Larson, Joe McGuinn, Paul Sutton, Francis Walker, Robert O. Davis, George Fitz, Blackjack Ward, Dick Jensen.

Three Texas Rangers (Starrett, Hayden, Edwards), anxious to join the Army, are sent to Alaska to stop a group of Nazis from operating a secret base to refuel German subs. NOTES:

One of the first B-Westerns to acknowledge the fact that America was at war. [British title: *Next in Line*].

1689. Riders of the Northwest Mounted (2/15/43) B&W — 57 mins. (Western). DIR: William Berke. PRO: Leon Barsha. SP: Fred Myton. CAST: Russell Hayden, Adele Mara, Dub Taylor, Vernon Steele, Dick Curtis, Richard Bailey, Jack Ingram, Leon McAulfie, Bob Wills and His Texas Playboys.

Two Mounties (Hayden, Taylor) set out to stop a gang of fur thieves.

1690. Riders of the Whistling Pines (5/1/49) B&W — 70 mins. (Western). DIR: John English. PRO: Armand Schaefer. SP: Jack Townley. A Gene Autry Production. CAST: Gene Autry, Patricia White (Patricia Barry), Jimmy Lloyd, Douglas Dumbrille, Clayton Moore, Harry Cheshire, Jason Robards, Sr., Lane Chandler, Emmett Vogan, Nolan Leary, Damian O'Flynn, Britt Wood, Leon Weaver, Lois Bridge, Jerry Scroggins, Fred Martin, Bert Dodson, Roy Gordon, Len Torrey, Lynn Farr, Al Thompson, Virginia Carroll, Steve Benton, The Pinagores, The Cass County Boys.

Gene goes after a trio of outlaws (Dumbrille, O'Flynn, Moore) who are destroying the forestlands for their own gain.

1691. Ridin' for Justice (1/4/32) B&W — 64 mins. (Western). DIR: D. Ross Lederman. PRO: Irving Briskin. SP: Harold Shumate. CAST: Buck Jones, Mary Doran, Russell Simpson, Walter Miller, William Walling, Bob McKenzie, Billy Engle, Hank Mann, Lafe McKee.

A cowboy (Jones), framed for murder, discovers that the marshal's wife (Doran) is the killer.

1692. Ridin' the Outlaw Trail (2/23/51) B&W — 56 mins. (Western).

DIR: Fred F. Sears. *PRO:* Colbert Clark. *SP:* Victor Arthur. *CAST:* Charles Starrett, Sunny Vickers, Smiley Burnette, Edgar Dearing, Jim Bannon, Ethan Laidlaw, Lee Morgan, Chuck Roberson, Peter Thompson, Frank McCarroll, Pee Wee King and His Golden West Cowboys.

The Durango Kid (Starrett) prevents an outlaw (Bannon) from melting down stolen gold pieces into gold bars.

1693. Riding Through Nevada (10/2/42) B&W—59 mins. (Western). *DIR:* William Berke. *PRO:* Jack Fier. *SP:* Gerald Geraghty. *CAST:* Charles Starrett, Shirley Patterson, Arthur Hunnicutt, Edmund Cobb, Minerva Urecal, Kermit Maynard, Ethan Laidlaw, Clancy Cooper, Davidson Clark, Stanley Brown, Art Mix, Jimmy Davis and His Rainbow Ramblers.

A postal inspector (Starrett) goes undercover to stop a rash of stagecoach robberies.

1694. The Riding Tornado (5/4/32) B&W—64 mins. (Western). *DIR:* D. Ross Lederman. *PRO:* Irving Briskin. *SP:* Kurt Kempler. Story by William Colt MacDonald. *CAST:* Tim McCoy, Shirley Grey, Wallace MacDonald, Russell Simpson, Art Mix, Montague Love, Wheeler Oakman, Vernon Dent, Lafe McKee, Bud Osborne, Hank Bell, Silver Tip Baker, Tex Palmer, Artie Ortego.

A cowboy (McCoy) goes after a ranch foreman (Oakman) and his gang of cattle rustlers when they kidnap his girl (Grey).

1695. Riding West (5/18/44) B&W—58 mins. (Western). *DIR:* William Berke. *PRO:* Jack Fier. *SP:* Luci Ward. *CAST:* Charles Starrett, Shirley Patterson, Arthur Hunnicutt, Steve Clark, Clancy Cooper, Wheeler Oakman, Blackie Whiteford, Johnny Bond, Bill Wilkerson, Ernest Tubb.

A cowboy (Starrett) runs into opposition when he tries to start a Pony Express run. *NOTES:* Originally filmed in 1943. [British title: *Fugitive from Time*].

1696. Riding Wild (6/28/35) B&W—57 mins. (Western). *DIR:* David Selman. *SP:* Ford Beebe. *CAST:* Tim McCoy, Billie Seward, Niles Welch, Dick Alexander, Jack Rockwell, Si Jenks, Edward J. LeSaint, Bud Osborne, Al Haskell, Wally West, Edmund Cobb, Dick Botiller.

A ranch foreman (McCoy) stops a crooked ranch owner from running the ranchers off their land.

1697. Rim of the Canyon (7/1/49) B&W—70 mins. (Western). *DIR:* John English. *PRO:* Armand Schaefer. *SP:* John K. Butler. Based on *Phantom .45's Talk Loud* by Joseph Chadwick. A Gene Autry Production. *CAST:* Gene Autry, Nan Leslie, Thurston Hall, Clem Bevans, Walter Sande, Jock Mahoney, Alan Hale, Jr., Denver Pyle, Francis McDonald, John R. McKee, Lynn Farr, Boyd Stockman, Amelita Ward, Bobby Clark, Sandy Sanders, Rory Mallison, Frankie Marvin.

Gene stops three outlaws (Mahoney, McDonald, Sande) when they break jail and return to a ghost town to get the money they stole twenty years earlier. *NOTES:* Gene Autry plays a dual role in this film.

1698. Ring-a-Ding Rhythm! (9/62) B&W—73 mins. (Musical-Comedy). *DIR/PRO:* Richard Lester. *SP:* Milton Subotsky. An Amicus Production. *CAST:* Helen Shapiro, Craig Douglas, Felix Felton, Arthur Mullard, Timothy Bateson, Hugh Lloyd, Mario Fabrizi, Deryck Guyler, The Brooks Brothers, Chubby Checker, Del Shannon, Gary "U.S." Bonds, Gene Vincent, Gene McDaniels, The Paris Sisters, The Dukes of Dixieland, Chris Baker and His Jazz Band, Ottilie

Patterson, Acker Bilk and His Paramount Jazz Band, Kenny Ball and His Jazzmen, Bob Wallis and His Storyville Jazzmen, Terry Lightfoot and His New Orleans Jazz Band, The Temperance Seven, Sounds Incorporated, David Jacobs, Pete Murray, Alan Freeman.

Two teenagers (Shapiro, Douglas) stage a music festival to win over the mayor (Felton) and the town when they oppose their music. NOTES: The film debut of director Richard Lester. [British title: It's Trad, Dad!].

1699. Rings Around the World (9/66) Eastman Color — 90 mins. (Documentary). DIR/PRO: Gilbert Gates. SP: Victor Wolfsen. CAST: Narrated by Don Ameche.

A documentary focusing on circuses around the world.

1700. Rio Grande (12/8/38) B&W — 58 mins. (Western). DIR: Sam Nelson. PRO: Harry L. Decker. SP: Charles F. Royal. CAST: Charles Starrett, Ann Doran, Bob Nolan, Dick Curtis, Pat Brady, Dick Botiller, Edward J. LeSaint, George Chesebro, Art Mix, Hank Bell, Hal Taliaferro (Wally Wales), Edward Piel, Sr., Ted Mapes, Forrest Taylor, Lee Prather, Harry Strang, Fred Burns, Stanley Brown, George Morrell, John Tyrrell, Fred Evans, Sons of the Pioneers.

A cowboy (Starrett) comes to the aid of a lady ranch owner (Doran) when she is forced off her land by land grabbers.

1701. Rio Grande Ranger (12/11/36) B&W — 54 mins. (Western). DIR: Spencer G. Bennet. PRO: Larry Darmour. SP: Nate Gatzert. Story by Jacques and Ceilia Jaccard. CAST: Bob Allen, Iris Meredith, Hal Taliaferro (Wally Wales), Paul Sutton, Robert "Buzz" Henry, John Elliott, Tom London, Slim Whitaker, Jack Rockwell, Dick Botiller, Art Mix, Frank Ellis, Jack Ingram, Al Taylor, Jim Corey, Henry Hall, Jack C. Smith, Ed Cassidy, Ray Jones.

When outlaws cross the state line in their getaway, a Texas Ranger (Allen) goes undercover to lure them back.

The River of Missing Men see **Trapped by G-Men**

1702. Riverrun (4/70) Eastman Color — 95 mins. (Drama). DIR/SP: John Korty. PRO: Stephen Schmidt. A Korty Production. CAST: John McLiam, Louise Ober, Mark Jenkins, Josephine Nichols.

Two students (Ober, Jenkins) leave college for life on a sheep farm and all is peaceful until the girl's father (McLiam) arrives.

1703. Roaming Lady (5/2/36) B&W — 68 mins. (Adventure). DIR: Albert S. Rogell. PRO: Sid Rogell. SP: Fred Niblo, Jr., Earle Snell. Story by Diana Bourbon, Bruce Manning. CAST: Fay Wray, Ralph Bellamy, Thurston Hall, Edward Gargan, Roger Imhof, Paul Guilfoyle, Arthur Rankin, Tetsu Komai.

An aviator (Bellamy) must fly a mission for Chinese rebels when they capture him and his girl (Wray).

1704. Roaring Frontiers (10/16/41) B&W — 60 mins. (Western). DIR: Lambert Hillyer. PRO: Leon Barsha. SP: Robert Lee Johnson. CAST: Bill Elliott, Ruth Ford, Tex Ritter, Frank Mitchell, Bradley Page, Hal Taliaferro (Wally Wales), Francis Walker, Joe McGuinn, George Chesebro, Tristram Coffin, Charles King, Charles Stevens, Hank Bell, Fred Burns, Lew Meehan, Ernie Adams, George Eldredge.

When a man (Ritter) is accused of murdering the sheriff, Wild Bill Hickok (Elliott) saves him from a lynching and exposes the real killer (Page).

1705. Roaring Rangers (2/14/46) B&W—55 mins. (Western). *DIR:* Ray Nazarro. *PRO:* Colbert Clark. *SP:* Barry Shipman. *CAST:* Charles Starrett, Adelle Roberts, Smiley Burnette, Mickey Kuhn, Jack Rockwell, Ted Mapes, Ed Cassidy, Bob Wilke, Edmund Cobb, Gerald Mackey, Herman Hack, Teddy Infuhr, John Tyrrell, Nolan Leary, Ethan Laidlaw, Jack Kirk, Tommy Coates, Merle Travis and His Bronco Busters.

The Durango Kid (Starrett) comes to the aid of a youngster (Kuhn) and his sheriff father (Rockwell) when the sheriff's brother (Cassidy) tries to take over the town. [British title: *False Hero*].

1706. Roaring Timber (7/4/37) B&W—65 mins. (Action-Drama). *DIR:* Philip E. Rosen. *PRO:* Larry Darmour. *SP:* Paul Franklin, Robert James Cosgriff. Story by Robert James Cosgriff. *CAST:* Jack Holt, Grace Bradley, Ruth Donnelly, Raymond Hatton, Willard Robertson, J. Farrell MacDonald, Charles Wilson, Fred Kohler, Jr., Tom London, Philip Ahn, Ben Hendricks, Ernest Wood.

A lumberman (Holt) helps a woman (Bradley) save her lumber business from a pair of swindlers (Wilson, Robertson).

1707. Robin and Marian (3/76) Technicolor—107 mins. (Adventure). *DIR:* Richard Lester. *PRO:* Denis O'Dell. *SP:* James Goldman. *CAST:* Sean Connery, Audrey Hepburn, Robert Shaw, Richard Harris, Nicol Williamson, Denholm Elliott, Kenneth Haigh, Ronnie Barker, Ian Holm, Bill Maynard, Veronica Quilligan, Peter Butterworth, John Barrett.

Robin (Connery) returns to Sherwood Forest after a twenty year Crusade with King Richard (Harris), searches for Marian (Hepburn), and must again battle the Sheriff of Nottingham (Shaw).

1708. Robin Hood of the Range (7/29/43) B&W—57 mins. (Western). *DIR:* William Berke. *PRO:* Jack Fier. *SP:* Betty Burbridge. *CAST:* Charles Starrett, Kay Harris, Arthur Hunnicutt, Stanley Brown, Bud Osborne, Kenneth MacDonald, Edward Piel, Sr., Merrill McCormack, Frank LaRue, Douglas Drake, Johnny Bond, Ray Jones, Frank McCarroll, Jimmy Wakely Trio.

The foster son (Starrett) of a railroad manager (MacDonald) assumes the guise of the "Vulcan" as he helps homesteaders save their land from the railroad.

1709. Rock Around the Clock (4/56) B&W—77 mins. (Musical). *DIR:* Fred F. Sears. *PRO:* Sam Katzman. *SP:* Robert E. Kent, James B. Gordon. *CAST:* Alan Freed, Johnny Johnston, Alix Talton, Lisa Gaye, John Archer, Henry Slate, Earl Barton, Bill Haley and His Comets, The Platters, Tony Martinez and His Band, Freddie Bell and the Bellboys.

A deejay (Freed) discovers a rock band (Bill Haley and His Comets) in a mountain village and brings them back to New York where he promotes them. *NOTES:* The first rock 'n' roll film. Remade by Columbia in 1961 as *Twist Around the Clock*.

1710. Rock City (7/81) B&W-Technicolor—104 mins. (Documentary). *DIR/PRO:* Peter Clifton. A World Films Services Ltd. Production. *CAST:* The Rolling Stones, Otis Redding, Peter Townshend, Cat Stevens, Jimi Hendrix, Joe Cocker, Tina Turner, Pink Floyd, Rod Stewart, The Faces.

A musical concert filmed at the London Palladium.

1711. Rocket Gibraltar (9/88) DuArt Color—100 mins. (Drama). *DIR:* Daniel Petrie. *PRO:* Jeff Weiss, Marcus Viscidi. *SP:* Amos Poe. A

Ulick-Mayo-Weiss Production. *CAST*: Burt Lancaster, Suzy Amis, Patricia Clarkson, Frances Conroy, Sinead Cusack, John Glover, Bill Pullman, John Bell, Dan Corkill, Kevin Spacey, Sara Goethals, Emily Poe.

When his children (Amis, Glover, Clarkson, Conroy) and grandchildren come for a visit, a dying father (Lancaster) asks for a Viking funeral. *NOTES*: Limited theatrical release.

1712. Rockin' in the Rockies (4/17/45) B&W—63 mins. (Comedy-Western). *DIR*: Vernon Keays. *PRO*: Colbert Clark. *SP*: J. Benton Cheney, John Gray. Story by Louise Rousseau, Gail Davenport. *CAST*: Jay Kirby, Mary Beth Hughes, Gladys Blake, The Three Stooges (Moe Howard, Larry Fine, Curly Howard), Jack Clifford, Forrest Taylor, Tim Ryan, Vernon Dent, The Hoosier Hotshots, Spade Cooley, The Cappy Barra Boys.

The Three Stooges head West as termite exterminators and get involved in prospecting and cattle rustling. [British title: *Partners in Fortune*].

1713. Rogues of Sherwood Forest (6/21/50) Technicolor—80 mins. (Adventure). *DIR*: Gordon Douglas. *PRO*: Fred M. Packard. *SP*: George Bruce. Story by Ralph Bettinson. *CAST*: John Derek, Diana Lynn, George Macready, Alan Hale, Paul Cavanagh, Lowell Gilmore, Billy House, Lester Matthews, Billy Bevan, Wilton Graff, John Dehner, Donald Randolph, Gavin Muir, Tim Huntley, Paul Collins, Olaf Hytten, Symona Boniface, Nelson Leigh.

The son (Derek) of Robin Hood returns to Sherwood Forest, rounds up the Merry Men to steal from the rich and give to the poor, and forces King John (Macready) to sign the Magna Carta.

1714. Rolling Caravans (3/7/38) B&W—55 mins. (Western). *DIR*: Joseph Levering. *PRO*: Larry Darmour. *SP*: Nate Gatzert. *CAST*: Jack Luden, Eleanor Stewart, Harry Woods, Buzz Barton, Lafe McKee, Slim Whitaker, Bud Osborne, Jack Rockwell, Francis Walker, Cactus Mack, Tex Palmer, Sherry Tansey, Oscar Gahan, Franklyn Farnum, Curley Dresden, Richard Cramer, Horace Murphy.

A cowboy (Luden) helps settlers save their land from a gang of outlaws.

1715. Romance of the Redwoods (5/17/39) B&W—61 mins. (Drama). *DIR*: Charles Vidor. *PRO*: Wallace MacDonald. *SP*: Michael L. Simmons. Based on *The White Silence* by Jack London. *CAST*: Charles Bickford, Jean Parker, Al Bridge, Gordon Oliver, Lloyd Hughes, Ann Shoemaker, Pat O'Malley, Marc Lawrence, Earl Gunn, Don Beddoe, Erville Alderson, Lee Prather.

A lumberjack (Bickford) is suspected of murder when another lumberjack (Oliver) is killed and it is revealed that both were in love with the same girl (Parker).

1716. The Romantic Age (6/5/27) B&W—56 mins. (Drama). *DIR*: Robert Florey. *PRO*: Harry Cohn. *SP*: Dorothy Howell. *CAST*: Eugene O'Brien, Alberta Vaughn, Stanley Taylor, Bert Woodruff.

A woman (Vaughn) must choose between two brothers (O'Brien, Woodruff) and she chooses the right brother (O'Brien) when he saves her securities from an office fire.

The Roof Garden *see* **The Terrace**

1717. Rookie Fireman (10/19/50) B&W—63 mins. (Drama). *DIR*: Seymour Friedman. *PRO*: Milton Feldman. *SP*: Jerry Sackheim. Story by Harry Field. *CAST*: Bill Williams, Barton MacLane, Marjorie Reynolds, Gloria Henry, Richard Quine, John

Ridgely, Richard Benedict, Cliff Clark, Barry Brooks, George Eldredge, Gaylord Pendleton, Frank Sully, Ted Jordan.

During a dock strike, an ex-dock worker (Williams) takes a job as a fireman and decides he likes this job better.

1718. A Rose for Everyone (7/ 67) Technicolor — 107 mins. (Comedy). *DIR:* Franco Rossi. *PRO:* Franco Cristaldi. *SP:* Eduardo Borras, Ennio De Concini, Nino Manfredi, Franco Rossi. Based on the play *Procura-se Uma Rosa* by Glaucio Gill. A Vides-Royal Films International Production. *CAST:* Claudia Cardinale, Nino Manfredi, Mario Adorf, Akim Tamiroff, Lando Buzzanca, Luis Pellegrini, Milton Rodriguez, Oswaldo Loureiro, Jose Lewgoy, Grande Othelo, Celia Bilar, Laura Soares.

A promiscuous woman (Cardinale) returns to her many lovers when she realizes she cannot settle down with one man (Buzzanca). *NOTES:* Limited theatrical release. [Original Italian title: *Una Rosa per Tutti*].

1719. Rose of Santa Rosa (1/5/ 48) B&W — 65 mins. (Musical-Comedy). *DIR:* Ray Nazarro. *PRO:* Colbert Clark. *SP:* Barry Shipman. *CAST:* Dolores de Garfias (Patricia White), Eduardo Ciannelli, Fortunio Bonanova, Eduardo Noriega, Ann Cordes, Douglas Fowley, The Hoosier Hotshots, The Philharmonica Trio, Aaron Gonzales and His Orchestra.

A man (Bonanova) tries to get out of an arranged marriage with a girl (de Garfias) he has never seen.

1720. Rough Ridin' Justice (3/ 14/45) B&W — 58 mins. (Western). *DIR:* Derwin Abrahams. *PRO:* Jack Fier. *SP:* Elizabeth Beecher. *CAST:* Charles Starrett, Betty Jane Graham, Dub Taylor, Dan White, Wheeler Oakman, Bob Kortman, Jack Ingram,

George Chesebro, Forrest Taylor, Robert Ross, Jack Rockwell, Edmund Cobb, Carl Sepulveda, Jimmy Wakely and His Oklahoma Cowboys, Butch and Buddy.

A cowboy (Starrett) is hired by ranchers to stop a gang of outlaws. [British title: *Decoy*].

1721. Rough, Tough and Ready (4/2/45) B&W — 66 mins. (War-Comedy). *DIR:* Del Lord. *PRO:* Alexis Thurn-Taxis. *SP:* Edward T. Lowe. *CAST:* Chester Morris, Victor McLaglen, Jean Rogers, Veda Ann Borg, John Tyrrell, Amelita Ward, Robert Williams, Fred Graff, Addison Richards, Tex Harding, William Forrest, Loren Tindall, Bob Meredith, Ida Moore, Blackie Whiteford.

A soldier (Morris) is at odds with his best friend (McLaglen) when he steals his girl (Rogers) but their friendship is renewed when he saves his life on a Pacific island. [British title: *Men of the Deep*].

1722. The Rough, Tough West (6/15/52) B&W — 54 mins. (Western). *DIR:* Ray Nazarro. *PRO:* Colbert Clark. *SP:* Barry Shipman. *CAST:* Charles Starrett, Valeria Fisher, Smiley Burnette, Jock Mahoney, Marshall Reed, Fred Sears, Tommy Ivo, Bert Arnold, Boyd Morgan, Thomas Kingston, Carolina Cotton, Pee Wee King and His Band.

The Durango Kid (Starrett) helps an old friend (Mahoney), who has gone crooked, to mend his ways.

1723. Roxanne (6/87) DeLuxe Color — 107 mins. (Comedy). *DIR:* Fred Schepisi. *PRO:* Michael Rachmil, Daniel Melnick. *SP:* Steve Martin. Based on *Cyrano de Bergerac* by Edmond Rostand. A Daniel Melnick-Indieprod-LA Films Production. *CAST:* Steve Martin, Daryl Hannah, Rick Rossovich, Shelley Duvall, John Kapelos, Fred Willard, Max Alexander,

Michael J. Pollard, Shandra Beri, Brian George, Steve Mittleman, Damon Wayans.

A fireman (Rossovich) asks the help of the fire chief (Martin) in wooing the local astronomer (Hannah).

1724. Royal Eagle (6/36) B&W— 69 mins. (Crime). *DIR:* George A. Cooper, Arnold Ridley. *PRO:* Clive Loehnis. *SP:* Arnold Ridley. A Quality Films Production. *CAST:* John Garrick, Nancy Burne, Edmund Willard, Lawrence Anderson, Muriel Aked, Hugh E. Wright, Fred Groves, Felix Aylmer, Betty Shale, Ian Fleming.

A warehouse clerk (Garrick), framed for robbery and murder, locates the real crooks while traveling on a pleasure boat.

1725. The Royal Mounted Patrol (11/13/41) B&W—59 mins. (Western). *DIR:* Lambert Hillyer. *PRO:* William Berke. *SP:* Winston Miller. *CAST:* Charles Starrett, Wanda McKay, Russell Hayden, Donald Curtis, Lloyd Bridges, Kermit Maynard, Evan Thomas, Harrison Greene, Ted Adams, Ted Mapes, George Morrell.

When a crooked lumber camp boss (Curtis) starts a forest fire and kills a Mountie (Bridges), his fellow Mounties (Starrett, Hayden) bring him to justice. [British title: *Giants A'Fire*].

1726. A Royal Romance (4/27/ 30) B&W—66 mins. (Romance). *DIR:* Erle C. Kenton. *SP:* George B. McCutcheon, Norman Houston. Based on *Private Property* by Norman Houston. *CAST:* William Collier, Jr., Pauline Starke, Clarence Muse, Ullrich Haupt, Ann Brody, Eugenie Besserer, Walter P. Lewis.

When a writer (Collier) inherits a fortune, he buys a castle and rescues the woman (Starke) hiding there from her divorced husband (Haupt).

1727. Rumble on the Docks (12/ 56) B&W—82 mins. (Crime-Drama). *DIR:* Fred F. Sears. *PRO:* Sam Katzman. *SP:* Lou Morheim, Jack DeWitt. Based on the book by Frank Paley. A Clover Production. *CAST:* James Darren, Laurie Carroll, Michael Granger, Jerry Janger, Robert Blake, Edgar Barrier, Celia Lovsky, David Bond, Timothy Carey, Barry Froner, Dan Terranova, Don Devlin, Joseph Vitale, David Orrick, Larry Blake, Steve Warren, Don Garrett, Joel Ashley, Freddie Bell and the Bellboys.

The leader of a street gang (Darren) gets involved in murder and graft when he teams up with a crooked union boss (Granger). *NOTES:* The film debut of James Darren. This film ran as a second bill with *Don't Knock the Rock*.

1728. Run Wild, Run Free (6/69) Technicolor—100 mins. (Drama). *DIR:* Richard C. Sarafian. *PRO:* John Danischewsky. *SP:* David Rook. Based on *The White Colt* by David Rook. An Irving Allen Production. *CAST:* John Mills, Mark Lester, Sylvia Syms, Gordon Jackson, Bernard Miles, Fiona Fullerton.

A mute 10-year-old boy (Lester) learns to speak and communicate again through his love of a white colt and the understanding of a retired colonel (Mills). [British title: *Philip*].

1729. The Runaway (11/64) B&W—62 mins. (Drama). *DIR:* Tony Young. *PRO:* Bill Luckwell, David Vigo. *SP:* John Perceval, John Gerrard Sharp. Story by John Perceval. A Luckwell Production. *CAST:* Greta Gynt, Alex Gallier, Paul Williamson, Michael Trubshawe, Tony Quinn, Wendy Varnals, Denis Shaw, Howard Lang, Ross Hutchinson, Stuart Sanders, John Watson, John Dearth, Leonard Dixon.

A British agent (Williamson) saves a

chemist (Gallier), his wife (Gynt), and his secret formula from the Soviets.

1730. Runaway Girls (8/23/28) B&W—58 mins. (Drama). *DIR:* Mark Sandrich. *PRO:* Harry Cohn. *SP:* Dorothy Howell. Story by Lillie Hayward. *CAST:* Shirley Mason, Arthur Rankin, Hedda Hopper, Alice Lake, George Irving, Edward Earle.

When a young girl (Mason) leaves home after her parents separate, she becomes a model and almost gets dragged into a life of white slavery but is rescued in time by her sweetheart (Rankin).

Runaways of St. Agil *see* **Boys' School**

1731. The Running Man (10/63) Eastman Color/Panavision—113 mins. (Drama). *DIR/PRO:* Sir Carol Reed. *SP:* John Mortimer. Based on *The Ballad of the Running Man* by Shelley Smith. A Peet Production. *CAST:* Laurence Harvey, Lee Remick, Alan Bates, Felix Aylmer, Eleanor Summerfield, Allan Cuthbertson, Harold Goldblatt, Noel Purcell, Ramsay Ames, Fernando Rey, Eddie Byrne, Colin Gordon, John Meillon, Shirley Gale, Fortunio Bonanova, Juan Jose Menendez.

A man (Harvey) fakes his own death to collect the insurance, goes to Spain under a new identity to await his wife (Remick), but is placed in danger when an insurance investigator (Bates) arrives.

1732. Rustlers of the Badlands (8/16/45) B&W—55 mins. (Western). *DIR:* Derwin Abrahams. *PRO:* Colbert Clark. *SP:* J. Benton Cheney. Story by Richard Hill Wilkinson. *CAST:* Charles Starrett, Sally Bliss, Tex Harding, George Eldredge, Dub Taylor, Ray Bennett, Dan White, Edward Howard, Karl Hackett, Ted Mapes, Frank McCarroll, Steve Clark, James T. Nelson, Carl Sepulveda, Frank LaRue, Bud Osborne, Edmund Cobb, Ted French, Nolan Leary, Jack Ingram, Frank Ellis, Al Trace and His Silly Symphonists.

The Durango Kid (Starrett), investigating a murder, comes across cattle rustling and kidnapping before he brings the outlaws to justice. [British title: *By Whose Hand?*].

1733. Rusty Leads the Way (10/21/48) B&W—59 mins. (Drama). *DIR:* Will Jason. *PRO:* Robert Cohn. *SP:* Arthur A. Ross. Story by Nedrick Young. Based on characters created by Al Martin. *CAST:* Ted Donaldson, Sharyn Moffett, John Litel, Ann Doran, Paula Raymond, Peggy Converse, Harry Hayden, Ida Moore, Mary Currier, Fred F. Sears, Mickey McGuire, Teddy Infuhr, Dwayne Hickman, David Ackles, "Flame," the dog.

A boy (Donaldson) trains his dog as a seeing-eye dog for a blind girl (Moffett).

1734. Rusty Rides Alone (5/26/33) B&W—58 mins. (Western). *DIR:* D. Ross Lederman. *SP:* Robert Quigley. Story by Walt Coburn. *CAST:* Tim McCoy, Barbara Weeks, Dorothy Burgess, Wheeler Oakman, Edmund Cobb, Edmund Burns, Rockcliffe Fellows, Clarence Geldert.

A cowboy (McCoy) stops a sheepman (Oakman) from driving the cattle ranchers from their land.

1735. Rusty Saves a Life (4/8/49) B&W—68 mins. (Drama). *DIR:* Seymour Friedman. *PRO:* Wallace MacDonald. *SP:* Brenda Weisberg. Based on characters created by Al Martin. *CAST:* Ted Donaldson, Gloria Henry, Stephen Dunne, Ellen Corby, John Litel, Ann Doran, Thurston Hall, Rudy Robles, Harlan Briggs, Dwayne Hickman, David Ackles, Ronnie Ralph, Robert Scott, Harry Harvey, Emmett Vogan, "Flame," the dog.

When a boy (Donaldson) and his friends are to inherit an old house, the owner suddenly dies without a will and his nephew (Dunne) takes the house. The nephew is eventually saved from drowning by the boy's dog and the kids win out.

1736. Rusty's Birthday (11/3/49) B&W—60 mins. (Drama). *DIR:* Seymour Friedman. *PRO:* Wallace MacDonald. *SP:* Brenda Weisberg. Based on characters created by Al Martin. *CAST:* Ted Donaldson, John Litel, Ann Doran, Jimmy Hunt, Mark Dennis, Ray Teal, Lillian Bronson, Ronnie Ralph, Teddy Infuhr, Dwayne Hickman, David Ackles, Robert B. Williams, Myron Healey, Raymond Largay, Lelah Tyler, "Flame," the dog.

A boy (Donaldson) goes in search of his dog when his father (Litel) mistakenly sells him to a couple of tourists.

1737. S.O.S. Perils of the Sea (11/1/25) B&W—58 mins. (Action-Drama). *DIR:* James Hogan. *PRO:* Harry Cohn. *SP:* Thomas J. Hopkins. *CAST:* Elaine Hammerstein, Jean O'Rourke, Robert Ellis, William Franey, Pat Harmon.

A mother (Hammerstein) and daughter (O'Rourke) sail for America unaware that they have inherited a fortune and will lose it if not claimed within ten years.

1738. Sabotage Squad (8/11/42) B&W—64 mins. (Action-Adventure). *DIR:* Lew Landers. *PRO:* Jack Fier. *SP:* Bernice Petkere, Wallace Sullivan, David Silverstein. Story by Bernice Petkere, Wallace Sullivan. *CAST:* Bruce Bennett, Kay Harris, Edward Norris, Sidney Blackmer, Don Beddoe, John Tyrrell, George McKay, Robert Emmett Keane, Eddie Laughton, Byron Foulger, Edward Hearn, Pat Lane, John Dilson, Ethan Laidlaw, Hugh Prosser, Lester Dorr, Richard

Bartell, Stanley Brown, Edmund Cobb, Ernie Adams, Kenneth MacDonald.

An undercover agent (Bennett) battles Nazis and sacrifices his life to save an aviation plant.

1739. Saddle Leather Law (12/21/44) B&W—59 mins. (Western). *DIR:* Benjamin Kline. *PRO:* Jack Fier. *SP:* Elizabeth Beecher. *CAST:* Charles Starrett, Vi Athens, Dub Taylor, Lloyd Bridges, Reed Howes, Jimmy Wakely, Bob Kortman, Steve Clark, Ted French, Ed Cassidy, Frank LaRue, Ted Adams, Budd Buster, Franklyn Farnum, Salty Holmes, Frank O'Conner, Nolan Leary, Joseph Eggenton.

Two cowboys (Starrett, Taylor) are framed for the murder of a rancher by a crooked syndicate boss (Athens). [British title: *The Poisoner*].

1740. Saddles and Sagebrush (4/27/43) B&W—58 mins. (Western). *DIR:* William Berke. *PRO:* Leon Barsha. *SP:* Ed Earl Repp. *CAST:* Russell Hayden, Ann Savage, Dub Taylor, Wheeler Oakman, Edmund Cobb, Frank LaRue, Jack Ingram, Blackie Whiteford, Art Mix, Joe McGuinn, Bob Burns, Ben Corbett, William Wright, Ray Jones, Bob Wills and His Texas Playboys.

A cowboy (Hayden) and his sidekick (Taylor) help a rancher (McGuinn) and his daughter (Savage) save their ranch from a land grabber (Wright). [British title: *The Pay-Off*].

1741. Safari (6/56) Technicolor/Scope—92 mins. (Adventure). *DIR:* Terence Young. *PRO:* Adrian D. Worker. *SP:* Anthony Veiller. Story by Robert Buckner. A Warwick Films Production. *CAST:* Victor Mature, Janet Leigh, John Justin, Roland Culver, Liam Redmond, Earl Cameron, Orlando Martins, Slim Harris, Harry Quashie, Cy Grant, John Wynn, Arthur Lovegrove, May Estelle, Christopher Warbey, John Cook, Bob Isaacs. A white hunter (Mature) takes a client (Culver) and his wife (Leigh) on safari into Mau Mau country to avenge the death of his son at the hands of the Mau Mau.

1742. Safe at Home! (4/62) B&W—84 mins. (Drama). *DIR:* Walter Doniger. *PRO:* Tom Naud. *SP:* Robert Dillon. Story by Tom Naud, Steve Ritch. *CAST:* Mickey Mantle, Roger Maris, Ralph Houk, Whitey Ford, William Frawley, Patricia Barry, Don Collier, Bryan Russell, Eugene Iglesias, Flip Mark, Scott Lane, Charles G. Martin, Desiree Sumarra, Joe Hickman, Chris Hughes, James A. Argyras, Fred A. Schwarb.

A young boy (Russell) brags to his friends that he and his father (Collier) are best friends with Mickey Mantle and Roger Maris and has to make good his boast.

1743. A Safe Place (10/71) Technicolor—94 mins. (Drama). *DIR/SP:* Henry Jaglom. *PRO:* Harold Schneider. A BBS Production. *CAST:* Tuesday Weld, Orson Welles, Jack Nicholson, Philip Proctor, Gwen Welles, Dov Lawrence, Barbara Flood, Roger Garrett, Jordan Hahn, Julie Robinson, Jennifer Walker.

A woman (Weld) lives in a dream world, decides she can never grow up, and seeks out a place where she can be safe. *NOTES:* The film debut of director Henry Jaglom.

1744. Sagebrush Heroes (2/1/45) B&W—56 mins. (Western). *DIR:* Benjamin Kline. *PRO:* Jack Fier. *SP:* Luci Ward. *CAST:* Charles Starrett, Dub Taylor, Constance Worth, Elvin Eric Field, Ozie Waters, Bobby Larson, Forrest Taylor, Joel Friedkin, Lane Chandler, Paul Zaremba, Eddie Laughton, John Tyrrell, Jimmy Wakely and His Saddle Pals.

A cowboy (Starrett) comes to the aid of a boy (Larson) at a correctional institution.

1745. Saginaw Trail (9/20/53) Sepiatone—56 mins. (Western). *DIR:* George Archainbaud. *PRO:* Armand Schaefer. *SP:* Dorothy Yost, Dwight Cummins. A Gene Autry Production. *CAST:* Gene Autry, Connie Marshall, Smiley Burnette, Ralph Reed, Myron Healey, Mickey Simpson, Gregg Barton, John Merton, Eugene Borden, Henry Blair, John War Eagle, Rodd Redwing, Bill Wilkerson, John Parrish, Charlie Hayes.

In 1827 northern Michigan, a captain (Autry) in Hamilton's Rangers goes after a fur trapper (Borden) who is using the Indians to drive out the settlers for his own gain. *NOTES:* The earliest period setting (1827) of any Gene Autry film.

1746. Sahara (10/14/43) B&W—97 mins. (War-Drama). *DIR:* Zoltan Korda. *PRO:* Harry Joe Brown. *SP:* John Howard Lawson, Zoltan Korda, James O'Hanlon. Story by Philip MacDonald. Based on an incident in the Soviet screenplay *The Thirteen*—USSR. *CAST:* Humphrey Bogart, Bruce Bennett, Lloyd Bridges, Rex Ingram, Dan Duryea, J. Carrol Naish, Richard Nugent, Patrick O'Moore, Louis Mercier, Carl Harbord, Guy Kingsford, Kurt Kreuger, John Wengraf, Hans Schumm, Frank Lackteen.

After the fall of Tobruk, an American tank commander (Bogart) leads his men, a group of British soldiers, a Sudanese (Ingram), an Italian prisoner (Naish) and a German prisoner (Kreuger) across the desert where they make a stand at a desert well against a motorized German unit. *NOTES:* Remade by Columbia in 1952 as *Last of the Comanches.*

1747. Sail a Crooked Ship (12/61) B&W—88 mins. (Comedy). *DIR:*

Irving Brecher. *PRO:* Philip Barry, Jr. *SP:* Ruth Brooks Flippen, Bruce Geller. Based on the book by Nathaniel Benchley. *CAST:* Robert Wagner, Dolores Hart, Carolyn Jones, Ernie Kovacs, Frankie Avalon, Frank Gorshin, Jesse White, Harvey Lembeck, Sid Tomack, Guy Raymond, Buck Kartalian, Wilton Graff, Marjorie Bennett.

A crook (Kovacs) and his men kidnap an ex-Navy officer (Wagner) and his girl (Hart) and force him to try and sail their ship from New York to Boston after a bank heist. *NOTES:* The last film of Ernie Kovacs.

1748. Sailor's Holiday (2/24/44) B&W — 60 mins. (Comedy). *DIR:* William Berke. *PRO:* Wallace MacDonald. *SP:* Manny Seff. *CAST:* Arthur Lake, Jane Lawrence, Bob Haymes, Shelley Winters, Lewis Wilson, Edmund MacDonald, Pat O'Malley, Herbert Rawlinson, Vi Athens, George Ford, Buddy Yarus.

A trio of merchant marines (Lake, Haymes, Wilson) go on a tour of the Columbia backlot.

1749. St. Elmo's Fire (6/85) Metrocolor — 110 mins. (Drama). *DIR:* Joel Schumacher. *PRO:* Lauren Shuler. *SP:* Joel Schumacher, Carl Kurlander. *CAST:* Emilio Estevez, Rob Lowe, Andrew McCarthy, Demi Moore, Judd Nelson, Ally Sheedy, Martin Balsam, Mare Winningham, Joyce Van Patten, Jenny Wright, Andie MacDowell, Matthew Lawrence, Blake Clark.

The adventures of a group of friends (Estevez, Lowe, McCarthy, Moore, Nelson, Sheedy, Winningham) trying to cope with life after graduation from college.

1750. Sally in Our Alley (9/3/27) B&W — 56 mins. (Comedy-Drama). *DIR:* Walter Lang. *PRO:* Harry Cohn. *SP:* Dorothy Howell. Story by Edward Clark. *CAST:* Shirley Mason, Richard Arlen, Alec B. Francis, Paul Panzer, Kathlyn Williams, William H. Strauss, Florence Turner, Harry Crocker.

A young girl (Mason) shuns the life of riches and returns to her friends (Francis, Strauss, Panzer) and true love (Arlen).

1751. Salome (2/13/53) Technicolor — 103 mins. (Biblical). *DIR:* William Dieterle. *PRO:* Buddy Adler. *SP:* Harry Kleiner. Story by Harry Kleiner, Jesse L. Lasky, Jr. A Beckworth Production. *CAST:* Rita Hayworth, Stewart Granger, Charles Laughton, Judith Anderson, Sir Cedric Hardwicke, Alan Badel, Basil Sydney, Maurice Schwartz, Rex Reason, Arnold Moss, Robert Warwick, Michael Granger, Karl Davis, Mickey Simpson, Charles Wagenheim, Tristram Coffin, John Crawford, Ralph Moody, George Keymas, Rick Vallin, Carleton Young, Guy Kingsford.

Salome (Hayworth) dances her "Dance of the Seven Veils" for King Herod (Laughton) in order to save John the Baptist (Badel). *NOTES:* The role of Salome was first portrayed by Theda Bara in 1918 and then by the Russian actress Nazimova in 1923.

1752. Salvatore Giuliano (9/64) B&W — 125 mins. (Crime-Historical-Drama). *DIR:* Francesco Rosi. *PRO:* Franco Cristaldi. *SP:* Cecchi D'Amico, Enzo Provenzale, Franco Solinas, Francesco Rosi. A Lux-Vides-Galatea-Royal Films International Production. *CAST:* Pietro Cammarata, Frank Wolff, Salvo Randone, Federico Zardi, Fernando Cicero, Sennuccio Benelli, Bruno Ekmar, Max Cartier, Giuseppe Calandra, Cosimo Torino, Giuseppe Teti, Ugo Torrente.

Based on the true story of Salvatore Giuliano (Cammarata), a Sicilian Mafia chieftain, who took on church, state, and Mafia in his attempt to help Sicily secede from Italy after World

War II. *NOTES:* Limited theatrical release. In 1987, a much inferior version of this story was released by 20th Century–Fox entitled *The Sicilian,* and starred Christopher Lambert as Salvatore Giuliano.

1753. Sandra (1/66) B&W – 100 mins. (Drama). *DIR:* Luchino Visconti. *PRO:* Franco Cristaldi. *SP:* Suso Cecchi D'Amico, Enrico Medioli, Luchino Visconti. A Vides-Royal Films International Production. *CAST:* Claudia Cardinale, Jean Sorel, Michael Craig, Marie Bell, Renzo Ricci, Fred Williams, Amalia Troiani, Vittorio Manfrino, Renato Moretti, Giovanni Rovini, Paolo Pescini.

A woman (Cardinale) returns to her home in Europe with her husband (Craig) and learns that her mother (Bell) was responsible for her father's death. [British title: *Of a Thousand Delights*]. [Original Italian title: *Vaghe Stelle dell'Orsa*].

1754. Sanford Meisner: The Theatre's Best Kept Secret (4/85) B&W-Eastman Color – 60 mins. (Documentary). *DIR:* Nick Doob. *PRO:* Kent Paul. *CAST:* See below.

A documentary profile of veteran drama coach Sanford Meisner, featuring interviews with Robert Duvall, Peter Falk, Lee Grant, Bob Fosse, Anne Jackson, David Mamet, Tony Randall, Mark Rydell, Mary Steenburgen, Frances Sternhagen, Eli Wallach, Gwen Verdon, Jon Voight, Joanne Woodward, Gregory Peck, Elia Kazan, Suzanne Pleshette, Vivian Matlon. *NOTES:* Limited theatrical release.

1755. Santa Fe (4/2/51) Technicolor – 89 mins. (Western). *DIR:* Irving Pichel. *PRO:* Harry Joe Brown. *SP:* Kenneth Gamet. Story by Louis Stevens. Based on the book by James Marshall. *CAST:* Randolph Scott, Janis Carter, Jerome Courtland, John Ar-

cher, Warner Anderson, Jock Mahoney, Harry Cording, Irving Pichel, Paul E. Burns, Chief Thunder Cloud, Blackie Whiteford, Lane Chandler, Charles Hamilton, Roy Roberts, Edgar Dearing, Peter Thompson, Billy House, Olin Howlin, Arlene Roberts, Sven-Hugo Borg, Frank Ferguson, Harry Tyler, Reed Howes, Charles Meredith, Paul Stanton, Richard Cramer, William Haade, Francis McDonald, Frank O'Conner, Harry Tenbrook, James Mason, Guy Wilkerson, Frank Hagney, William Tannen, James Kirkwood, Stanley Blystone, Al Kunde, Art Loeb, Budd Fine, Richard Fortune, Charles Evans, George Sherwood, Louis Mason, Roy Butler, Ralph Sanford, William McCormack.

An ex-Confederate soldier (Scott) heads west after the Civil War, takes a job with the Santa Fe Railroad, and has to fight his three brothers (Courtland, Thompson, Archer) when they plan a train robbery with outlaws.

1756. The Saracen Blade (6/54) Technicolor – 77 mins. (Adventure). *DIR:* William Castle. *PRO:* Sam Katzman. *SP:* DeVallon Scott, George Worthing Yates. Based on the book by Frank Yerby. *CAST:* Ricardo Montalban, Betta St. John, Rick Jason, Carolyn Jones, Whitfield Conner, Michael Ansara, Edgar Barrier, Nelson Leigh, Pamela Duncan, Frank Pulaski, Leonard Penn, Ed Coch, Nyra Monsour, Gene D'Arcy.

In the 13th century, a commoner (Montalban) seeks revenge against a count (Ansara) and his son (Jason) for his father's death. *NOTES:* This film contains black and white footage of the storming of a castle.

1757. Saturday Morning (4/71) Eastman Color – 88 mins. (Documentary). *DIR/PRO:* Kent MacKenzie. A Dimension Film Production. *CAST:* Not available.

On a Saturday morning, four teenagers talk about adolescence. NOTES: Limited theatrical release.

1758. Saturday's Hero (8/23/51) B&W—109 mins. (Drama). DIR: David Miller. PRO: Buddy Adler. SP: Millard Lampell, Sidney Buchman. Based on *The Hero* by Millard Lampell. CAST: John Derek, Donna Reed, Sidney Blackmer, Alexander Knox, Elliott Lewis, Otto Hulett, Howard St. John, Aldo Ray, Alvin Baldock, Wilbur Robertson, Charles Mercer Barnes, Bill Martin, Mickey Knox, Don Gibson, Peter Virgo, Don Gardner, Robert C. Foulk, John W. Bauer, Mervyn Williams, Peter Thompson, Noel Reyburn, Steve Clark, Sandro Giglio, Tito Vuolo.

A college student (Derek) learns the importance of school when he is injured on the football field and cannot play. He comes to realize that those who supported him, his coaches (Hulett, Gibson) and a wealthy alumnus (Blackmer), now turn their backs on him since he is no longer a star. [British title: *Idols in the Dust*].

1759. Savage Mutiny (2/3/53) B&W—73 mins. (Adventure). DIR: Spencer G. Bennet. PRO: Sam Katzman. SP: Sol Shor. Story by Carroll Young. Based on the *Jungle Jim* newspaper comic strip created by Alex Raymond. An Esskay Picture Production. CAST: Johnny Weissmuller, Angela Stevens, Paul Marion, Lester Matthews, Nelson Leigh, Charles Stevens, Gregory Gay, Leonard Penn, Ted Thorpe, George Robotham.

Jungle Jim (Weissmuller) battles enemy agents as he tries to relocate natives from a small island that is to be used for an atom bomb test to the mainland.

Savage Wilderness *see* **The Last Frontier**

1760. Saving Grace (7/86) Technicolor/Technovision—112 mins. (Drama-Comedy). DIR; Robert M. Young. PRO: Herbert F. Solow. SP: David S. Ward, Richard Kramer. Based on the book by Celia Gittelson. An EM Production. CAST: Tom Conti, Fernando Rey, Erland Josephson, Giancarlo Giannini, Donald Hewlett, Edward James Olmos, Patricia Mauceri, Angelo Evans.

A newly elected Pope (Conti) manages to sneak out of the Vatican in everyday clothing and journeys to help a village become self-sufficient.

1761. Say It with Sables (7/13/28) B&W—70 mins. (Drama). DIR: Frank Capra. PRO: Harry Cohn. SP: Frank Capra, Peter Milne, Dorothy Howell. A Frank Capra Production. CAST: Helene Chadwick, Francis X. Bushman, Margaret Livingston, Arthur Rankin, June Nash, Alphonz Ethier, Edna Mae Cooper.

When a gold digger (Livingston) is murdered, a father (Bushman) tries to make it look like suicide to protect his son (Rankin).

1762. Scandal Sheet (1/11/40) B&W—67 mins. (Crime-Drama). DIR: Nick Grinde. PRO: Ralph Cohn. SP: Joseph Carole. CAST: Otto Kruger, Ona Munson, Edward Norris, John Dilson, Don Beddoe, Eddie Laughton, Linda Winters (Dorothy Comingore), Nedda Harrigan, Selmer Jackson, Frank M. Thomas, Edward Marr.

A newspaper editor (Kruger) commits murder in order to protect his illegitimate son (Norris).

1763. Scandal Sheet (3/52) B&W—82 mins. (Crime). DIR: Phil Karlson. PRO: Edward Small. SP: Ted Sherdeman, Eugene Ling, James Poe. Based on *The Dark Page* by Samuel Fuller. CAST: John Derek, Donna Reed, Broderick Crawford, Rosemary DeCamp, Henry O'Neill, Henry Morgan, James Millican, Griff Barnett, Jonathan Hale, Pierre Watkin, Ida Moore, Ralph Reed, Luther Crockett, Charles Cane, Jay Adler, Don Beddoe, Kathryn Card, Victoria Horne, Matt Willis, Peter Virgo, Ric Roman, Eugene Baxter, Katherine Warren.

A reporter (Derek) for a tabloid newspaper uncovers the truth that his editor (Crawford) murdered his wife (DeCamp) and a fellow reporter (O'Neill). [British title: *The Dark Page*].

1764. Scarlet Lady (8/1/28) B&W–59 mins. (Drama). *DIR:* Alan Crosland. *PRO:* Harry Cohn. *SP:* John Goodrich. Story by Bess Meredyth. *CAST:* Lya De Putti, Don Alvarado, Warner Oland, Otto Matiesen, John Peters, Valentina Zimina.

A Russian revolutionist (De Putti) falls in love with a prince (Alvarado) who is marked for death by her former love (Oland), an assassin. In the end she kills her former lover and escapes with the prince to safety.

1765. School Daze (2/88) DuArt Color–120 mins. (Musical-Comedy). *DIR/SP:* Spike Lee. *PRO:* Spike Lee, Monty Ross, Loretha C. Jones. A Forty Acres and a Mule Production. *CAST:* Larry Fishburne, Giancarlo Esposito, Tisha Campbell, Joe Seneca, Ossie Davis, Spike Lee, Art Evans, Bill Nunn, Ellen Holly, Branford Marsalis, Anthony Thompkins, Guy Killum, Dominic Hoffman.

A self-serious activist student (Lee) at an all-black college fights a lonely battle between the administration and his fellow students.

1766. Scream of Fear (9/61) B&W–82 mins. (Mystery-Drama). *DIR:* Seth Holt. *PRO/SP:* Jimmy Sangster. A Hammer Production. *CAST:* Susan Strasberg, Ronald Lewis, Christopher Lee, Ann Todd, Anne Blake, Leonard Sachs, John Ser-

ret, Fred Johnson, Bernard Brown, Richard Klee.

A girl (Strasberg) goes to visit her father and is almost driven mad by her step-mother (Todd) and chauffeur (Lewis). [British title: *Taste of Fear*].

1767. Screaming Mimi (4/58) B&W–79 mins. (Suspense-Drama). *DIR:* Gerd Oswald. *PRO:* Harry Joe Brown, Robert Fellows. *SP:* Robert Blees. Based on the book by Frederic Brown. A Sage Production. *CAST:* Anita Ekberg, Phil Carey, Gypsy Rose Lee, Harry Townes, Linda Cherney, Romney Brent, Alan Gifford, Oliver McGowan, Red Norvo, Stephen Ellsworth, Vaughn Taylor, Frank Scannell.

When a stripper (Ekberg) is attacked by a knife-wielding maniac in the shower, she seeks the help of a psychiatrist (Townes) while a newspaper man (Carey) tries to link the attack to a series of murders. *NOTES:* The shower scene pre-dated the *Psycho* shower scene by two years.

1768. Sealed Lips (9/15/25) B&W–56 mins. (Drama). *DIR:* Tony Gaudio. *PRO:* Harry Cohn. *SP:* Thomas J. Hopkins. *CAST:* Dorothy Revier, Cullen Landis, Lincoln Stedman, Scott Turner.

A suitor (Landis) misunderstands the affections of his sweetheart (Revier) toward a man who happens to be her father (Turner).

1769. Secret Command (7/30/44) B&W–82 mins. (Spy-War-Drama). *DIR:* Edward Sutherland. *PRO:* Phil L. Ryan. *SP:* Roy Chanslor. Based on *The Saboteurs* by John Hawkins, Ward Hawkins. A Torneen Production. *CAST:* Pat O'Brien, Carole Landis, Chester Morris, Ruth Warrick, Barton MacLane, Tom Tully, Wallace Ford, Howard Freeman, Erik Rolf, Matt McHugh, Frank Sully, Frank Fenton,

Charles D. Brown, Carol Nugent, Richard Lane.

A Naval Intelligence officer (O'Brien) goes undercover at a shipyard to stop a group of Nazis from sabotaging the yard and an aircraft carrier.

1770. The Secret of St. Ives (6/30/49) B&W—75 mins. (Adventure). DIR: Philip E. Rosen. PRO: Rudolph C. Flothow. SP: Eric Taylor. Based on *St. Ives* by Robert Louis Stevenson. CAST: Richard Ney, Vanessa Brown, Henry Daniell, Edgar Barrier, Aubrey Mather, Luis Van Rooten, John Dehner, Paul Marion, Douglas Walton, Phyllis Morris, Jean Del Val, Maurice Marsac, Harry Cording, Alex Fraser, Tom Stevenson, Billy Bevan, Charles Andre, Guy de Vestal.

A Frenchman (Ney) escapes from a British prison camp, and with his English fiancee (Brown), makes his way back to Napoleon's lines.

1771. Secret of the Whistler (11/7/46) B&W—65 mins. (Crime). DIR: George Sherman. PRO: Rudolph C. Flothow. SP: Raymond L. Schrock. Story by Richard H. Landau. Based on *The Whistler* radio program. CAST: Richard Dix, Leslie Brooks, Mary Currier, Michael Duane, Mona Barrie, Ray Walker, Claire DuBrey, Charles Trowbridge, Arthur Space, Jack Davis, Barbara Woodell.

A crazed artist (Dix), having killed his first wife, plans to kill his second (Brooks).

1772. Secret of Treasure Mountain (6/56) B&W—68 mins. (Western). DIR: Seymour Friedman. PRO: Wallace MacDonald. SP: David Lang. CAST: Raymond Burr, Valerie French, William Prince, Lance Fuller, Susan Cummings, Rodolfo Hoyos, Pat Hogan, Reginald Sheffield, Paul McGuire, Tom Hubbard, Boyd Stockman.

Two hundred years after Apaches buried gold on their land and put a curse on the land and gold, a gold hunter (Burr) and his men fall victim to the curse.

1773. Secret Patrol (6/3/36) B&W—60 mins. (Western). DIR: David Selman. PRO: Kenneth J. Bishop. SP: J. P. McGowan, Robert Watson. Story by Peter B. Kyne. CAST: Charles Starrett, Finis Barton, J. P. McGowan, Henry Mollison, LeStrange Millman, Arthur Kerr, Reginald Hincks, Ted Mapes, James McGrath.

A Mountie (Starrett) is sent to investigate a series of logging accidents and murder at a lumber camp.

1774. The Secret Seven (8/15/40) B&W—62 mins. (Crime). DIR: James Moore. PRO: Ralph Cohn. SP: Robert Tasker. Story by Robert Tasker, Dean Jennings. CAST: Bruce Bennett, Barton MacLane, Florence Rice, Joseph Crehan, Joseph Downing, Howard Hickman, Edward Van Sloan, Don Beddoe, Patrick J. Kelly, William Forrest, Danton Ferrero, George Anderson.

A reformed crook (Bennett) forms a secret society of seven forensic scientists to aid the police in their war on the underworld by using scientific methods to solve crime.

1775. The Secret Witness (12/12/31) B&W—68 mins. (Mystery). DIR: Thornton Freeland. SP: Samuel Spewack. Based on *Murder in the Gilded Cage* by Samuel Spewack. A Famous Attractions Corporation Production. CAST: William Collier, Jr., Una Merkel, Zasu Pitts, Purnell Pratt, Clyde Cook, Ralf Harolde, June Clyde, Rita La Roy, Hooper Atchley, Paul Hurst, Nat Pendleton, Greta Granstedt, Clarence Muse.

A young girl (Merkel) puts her life on the line as she tries to prove a young man (Collier, Jr.) innocent of murder of the man (Atchley) who drove his sister to suicide and almost becomes a victim of the murderer herself. *NOTES*: This film was previewed in October 1931 as *Terror by Night* by Famous Attractions Corporation before being released by Columbia.

1776. Secrets of the Lone Wolf (6/9/41) B&W—62 mins. (Mystery). *DIR*: Edward Dmytryk. *PRO*: Jack Fier. *SP*: Stuart Palmer. Based on characters created by Louis Joseph Vance. *CAST*: Warren William, Ruth Ford, Roger Clark, Victor Jory, Eric Blore, Thurston Hall, Fred Kelsey, Victor Kilian, Marlo Dwyer, Lester Scharff, Irving Mitchell, John Harmon, Joe McGuinn.

The Lone Wolf (William) is suspected of stealing the famous Napoleon jewels, while his butler, Jamison (Blore) pretends he is the Lone Wolf so he can lead the gang to his boss. [British title: *Secrets*].

1777. See No Evil (9/71) Eastman Color—89 mins. (Mystery-Thriller). *DIR*: Richard Fleischer. *PRO*: Martin Ransohoff, Leslie Linder. *SP*: Brian Clemens. A Filmways-Genesis Production. *CAST*: Mia Farrow, Dorothy Alison, Robin Bailey, Diane Grayson, Brian Rawlinson, Norman Eshley, Paul Nicholas, Christopher Matthews, Lila Kaye, Barrie Houghton, Michael Elphick, Donald Bisset.

A blind girl (Farrow) is trapped in a mansion with a psychotic killer (Nicholas) who has murdered her uncle (Bailey), aunt (Alison), and cousin (Grayson). [British title: *Blind Terror*].

1778. Seems Like Old Times (12/80) Metrocolor—102 mins. (Comedy). *DIR*: Jay Sandrich. *PRO*: Ray Stark. *SP*: Neil Simon. A Rastar Production. *CAST*: Goldie Hawn, Chevy Chase, Charles Grodin, Robert Guillaume, Harold Gould, George Griz-

zard, Yvonne Wilder, T. K. Carter, Marc Alaimo, Judd Omen, Fay Hauser, Ray Tracey, Sandy Lipton, Herb Armstrong.

A liberal lady lawyer (Hawn) hides her ex-husband (Chase) from the cops when he is mistaken for a bank robber, and tries to keep it a secret from her district attorney husband (Grodin).

1779. Seminole Uprising (5/55) Technicolor—74 mins. (Western). *DIR*: Earl Bellamy. *PRO*: Sam Katzman. *SP*: Robert E. Kent. Based on *Bugle's Wake* by Curt Brandon. *CAST*: George Montgomery, Karin Booth, William Fawcett, Kenneth MacDonald, Ed Coch, Steven Ritch, John Pickard, Ed Hinton, Jim Maloney, Rory Mallison, Howard Wright, Russ Conklin, Jonni Paris, Joanne Rio, Richard H. Cutting, Paul McGuire, Rube Schaffer.

An Army lieutenant (Montgomery) is sent to Texas to return a tribe of Seminole Indians to their Florida reservation.

1780. Senior Prom (12/58) B&W—82 mins. (Musical). *DIR*: David L. Rich. *PRO*: Harry Romm. *SP*: Hal Hackady. *CAST*: Jill Corey, Paul Hampton, Jimmie Komack, Barbara Bostock, Tom Laughlin, Frieda Inescort, Selene Walters, Francis De Sales, Marvin Miller, Louis Prima, Keely Smith, Sam Butera and the Witnesses, Ed Sullivan, Mitch Miller, Connie Boswell, Bob Crosby, Toni Arden, Freddy Martin and His Orchestra, Jose Melis, Les Elgart, Howard Miller.

A girl (Corey) falls for a college man (Hampton) when he cuts a popular record that tops the charts. *NOTES*: Tom Laughlin would later become famous for his portrayal of the character *Billy Jack*.

1781. Serafino (5/70) Technicolor—94 mins. (Comedy-Drama).

DIR/PRO: Pietro Germi, Lee Kresel. SP: Leo Benvenuti, Piero De Bernardi, Tullio Pinelli, Pietro Germi. Story by Alfredo Giannetti, Tullio Pinelli, Pietro Germi. An RPA-Rizzoli-Francoriz-Royal Films International Production. CAST: Adriano Celentano, Ottavia Piccolo, Saro Urzi, Francesca Romana Coluzzi, Benjamin Lev, Nazareno Natale, Giosue Ippolito, Ermelinda De Felice, Nerina Montagnani, Goffredo Canzano, Orlando D'Ubaldo, Oreste Palella.

A young man (Celentano), living in the mountains, comes into a sum of money and his uncle (Urzi) tries to have him committed to get his hands on it. When that fails, the uncle tries to marry him off to his daughter (Piccolo) but he is rescued by his friends and heads back to the mountains. NOTES: In Italian and French with English subtitles. Limited theatrical release. [Original French title: *Serafina ou l'Amour aux Champs*].

1782. Sergeant Mike (11/9/44) B&W—60 mins. (War-Drama). DIR: Henry Levin. PRO: Jack Fier. SP: Robert Lee Johnson. CAST: Larry Parks, Jeanne Bates, Loren Tindall, Jim Bannon, Robert Williams, Richard Powers, Larry Joe Olsen, Eddie Acuff, John Tyrrell, Charles Wagenheim, "Mike," the dog, "Pearl," the dog.

A machine gunner (Parks) is assigned to the Canine Corps where he trains dogs for the war, especially one dog, Mike, given him as a present by a boy (Olsen) whose father was killed in the war.

1783. Serpent of the Nile (5/53) Technicolor—81 mins. (Drama). DIR: William Castle. PRO: Sam Katzman. SP: Robert E. Kent. CAST: Rhonda Fleming, William Lundigan, Raymond Burr, Jean Byron, Michael Ansara, Michael Fox, Conrad Wolfe, John Craw-

ford, Jane Easton, Robert Griffin, Frederic Berest, Julie Newmar.

When Marc Antony (Burr) plots with Cleopatra (Fleming) to unite Rome and Egypt, she decides to kill him, but her plans are thwarted by a Roman soldier (Lundigan) who brings in the Roman Army which leads to her committing suicide. NOTES: The sets used in this film were the sets used for the Columbia film *Salome*.

1784. 711 Ocean Drive (7/14/50) B&W—102 mins. (Crime). DIR: Joseph M. Newman. PRO: Frank N. Seltzer. SP: Richard English, Francis Swann. An Essaness Production. CAST: Edmond O'Brien, Joanne Dru, Don Porter, Sammy White, Dorothy Patrick, Barry Kelley, Otto Kruger, Howard St. John, Robert Osterloh, Bert Freed, Carl Milletaire, Charles La Torre, Fred Aldrich, Charles Jordan, Sidney Dubin.

A telephone repairman (O'Brien) is lured into the bookmaking racket through his knowledge of electronics; he eventually murders and cheats his way to the top, only to be gunned down in a chase at Hoover Dam by syndicate killers. NOTES: This film was released at the time that U.S. newspapers were filled with bookmaking scandals.

1785. 7 Guns for the MacGregors (11/68) Technicolor/Scope—94 mins. (Western-Comedy). DIR: Frank Garfield (Franco Giraldi). PRO: Dario Sabatello. SP: Fernando Lion, Vincent Eagle, David Moreno, Duccio Tessari. An Italo-Spanish Co-Production. CAST: Robert Wood, Fernando Sancho, Agatha Flory, Leo Anchoriz, Perla Cristal, Manuel Zarzo, Nick Anderson, Paul Carter, Albert Waterman, Harry Cotton, Georges Rigaud, Julio Perez Tabernero.

A Scottish family, living on the Mexican border, find themselves at war with Mexican bandits when their horses are stolen. *NOTES:* A sequel to the 1967 film *Up the MacGregors.* [Original Italian title: *Sette Pistole per i MacGregor*]. [Original Spanish title: *Siete Pistolas para los MacGregors*].

1786. Seven Samurai (11/20/56) B&W—160 mins. (Historical-Drama-Action). *DIR:* Akira Kurosawa. *PRO:* Shojiro Motoki. *SP:* Shinobu Hashimoto, Hideo Oguni, Akira Kurosawa. A Toho Company Production. *CAST:* Takashi Shimura, Toshiro Mifune, Yoshio Inaba, Seiji Miyaguchi, Minoru Chiaki, Daisuke Kato, Isao Kimura, Kunihori Kodo, Kamatari Fujiwara, Yoshio Tsuchiya, Bokuzen Hidari, Keiko Tsushima, Yoshio Kosugi, Keiji Sakakida, Jiro Kumagai, Haruko Toyama.

In 1600 Japan, a group of seven Samurai are recruited to help a village pillaged by bandits. *NOTES:* In Japanese with English subtitles. Originally released by Columbia with the title *The Magnificent Seven,* the title was changed to the above to avoid confusion with the United Artists picture of the same name. Distribution later went to Kingsley International. The complete 208 min. Japanese version of this film has been recently restored. [Original Japanese title: *Shichinin No Samurai*].

1787. 1776 (11/72) Eastman Color/Panavision—141 mins. (Musical). *DIR:* Peter H. Hunt. *PRO:* Jack L. Warner. *SP:* Peter Stone. Based on the musical play by Peter Stone. *CAST:* William Daniels, David Ford, Howard Da Silva, Donald Madden, Emory Bass, Ken Howard, Ronald Holgate, Rex Robbins, Peter Forster, Frederic Downs, Howard Caine, John Myhers, Richard McMurray, John Cullum, Blythe Danner, Ray Middleton, Gordon DeVol, Virginia Vestoff.

Based on events surrounding the Declaration of Independence, John Adams (Daniels) tries to break down opposition to independence by allowing both free and slave states.

1788. 7th Cavalry (12/56) Technicolor—75 mins. (Western). *DIR:* Joseph H. Lewis. *PRO:* Harry Joe Brown. *SP:* Peter Packer. Based on *A Horse for Mrs. Custer* by Glendon F. Swarthout. *CAST:* Randolph Scott, Barbara Hale, Jay C. Flippen, Jeanette Nolan, Frank Faylen, Leo Gordon, Denver Pyle, Harry Carey, Jr., Michael Pate, Donald Curtis, Frank Wilcox, Pat Hogan, Russell Hicks, Peter Ortiz, William Leslie, Jack Parker, Edward F. Stidder, Al Wyatt.

A captain (Scott), absent from Custer's last stand, volunteers for the Little Big Horn burial detail.

1789. The 7th Voyage of Sinbad (12/58) Technicolor/Dynamation—87 mins. (Fantasy). *DIR:* Nathan Juran. *PRO:* Charles H. Schneer. *SP:* Kenneth Kolb. A Morningside Production. *CAST:* Kerwin Mathews, Kathryn Grant, Richard Eyer, Torin Thatcher, Alec Mango, Danny Green, Harold Kasket, Alfred Brown.

Sinbad (Mathews) encounters mythological beasts, a ruthless sorcerer (Thatcher), and a genie (Eyer) on the mystical island of Colossa while trying to rescue the princess (Grant). *NOTES:* Special effects by Ray Harryhausen and his first color film.

1790. A Severed Head (4/71) Eastman Color—98 mins. (Comedy-Drama). *DIR:* Dick Clement. *PRO:* Alan Ladd, Jr. *SP:* Frederic Raphael. Based on the book and play by Iris Murdoch and J. B. Priestley. A Winkast Production. *CAST:* Lee Remick, Richard Attenborough, Ian Holm, Claire Bloom, Jennie Linden, Clive Revill, Ann Firbank, Rosamunde Greenwood, Constance Lorne.

A black comedy about the sexual

escapades involving the upper crust of London society—the wife (Remick) of a wine-taster (Holm) has an affair with her psychologist (Attenborough), who is having an affair with his half-sister (Bloom).

Sex and the Teenager see **To Find a Man**

1791. The Shadow (12/22/37) B&W—59 mins. (Mystery). *DIR:* C. C. Coleman, Jr. *PRO:* Wallace MacDonald. *SP:* Arthur T. Horman. Story by Milton Raison. *CAST:* Charles Quigley, Rita Hayworth, Marc Lawrence, Arthur Loft, Dick Curtis, Dwight Frye, Vernon Dent, Marjorie Main, Donald Kirke, Bess Flowers, Bill Erving, Eddie Fetherstone, Sally St. Clair, Sue St. Clair, John Tyrrell, Beatrice Curtis, Ann Doran, Beatrice Blinn, Bud Jamison, Harry Strang, Francis Sayles, Edward Hearn, Edward J. LeSaint, Harry Bernard, Ernie Adams, Ted Mangen.

When a woman (Hayworth) inherits a debt-ridden circus from her father, the man (Kirke) to whom he owed the money, a horseman in the riding act, turns up dead and she and her press agent (Quigley) set out to find the killer. *NOTES:* The first film in which Rita Hayworth received star billing. Remade by Columbia in 1968 as *Berserk.* [British title: *The Circus Shadow*].

1792. Shadow of the Hawk (10/76) Eastman Color/Panavision—92 mins. (Fantasy). *DIR:* George McGowan. *PRO:* John Kemeny. *SP:* Norman Thaddeus Vane, Herbert J. Wright. Story by Peter Jensen, Lynette Cahill, Norman Thaddeus Vane. *CAST:* Jan-Michael Vincent, Marilyn Hassett, Chief Dan George, Pia Shandel, Marianne Jones, Jacques Hubert, Cindi Griffith, Anna Hagen, Murray Lowry.

The grandson (Vincent) of an Indian

medicine man (George) and a reporter (Hassett) battle supernatural Indian spirits.

1793. Shadow of the Past (5/50) B&W—83 mins. (Crime). *DIR:* Mario Zampi. *PRO:* Mario Zampi, Mae Murray. *SP:* Aldo di Benedetti, Ian Stuart Black. Story by Aldo di Benedetti. An Anglofilm Production. *CAST:* Joyce Howard, Terence Morgan, Michael Medwin, Andrew Osborn, Wylie Watson, Marie Ney, Ella Retford, Ronald Adam, Louise Gainsborough, Ian Fleming, Eve Ashley, Francis Roberts, John Warren.

A woman (Howard) poses as the ghost of her murdered sister in order to find out who killed her sister.

1794. The Shadow on the Window (3/57) B&W—73 mins. (Crime). *DIR:* William Asher. *PRO:* Jonie Taps. *SP:* Leo Townsend, David P. Harmon. Based on *The Missing Witness* by John and Ward Hawkins. *CAST:* Phil Carey, Betty Garrett, John Barrymore, Jr., Corey Allen, Gerald Sarracini, Jerry Mathers, Sam Gilman, Rusty Lane, Ainslie Pryor, Paul Picerni, William Leslie, Doreen Woodbury, Angela Stevens, Mort Mills, Carl Milletaire, Julian Upton, Nesdon Booth, Jack Lomas.

A young boy (Mathers) witnesses a murder and the kidnapping of his mother (Garrett) by three hoods (Barrymore, Jr., Allen, Sarracini) and is shocked into silence; his detective father (Carey) eventually tracks down the hoods and when the mother is freed, the boy returns to normal.

1795. Shadow Ranch (9/28/30) B&W—64 mins. (Western). *DIR:* Louis King. *PRO:* Sol Lesser. *SP:* Frank Howard Clark, Clarke Silvernail. Story by George M. Johnson and Clarke Silvernail. A Beverly Production. *CAST:* Buck Jones, Ernie Adams, Al Smith, Marguerite De La Motte,

Slim Whitaker, Kate Price, Fred Burns, Frank Rice, Ben Corbett, Ben Wilson, Hank Bell, Robert MacKenzie, Lafe McKee, Frank Ellis.

A cowboy (Jones) comes to the aid of a rancher (De La Motte) when an unscrupulous land grabber (Smith) tries to get her water rights.

1796. Shadowed (9/26/46) B&W—70 mins. (Crime). DIR: John Sturges. PRO: John Haggott. SP: Brenda Weisberg. Story by Julian Harman. CAST: Anita Louise, Lloyd Corrigan, Michael Duane, Robert Scott, Doris Houck, Helen Koford (Terry Moore), Wilton Graff, Eric Roberts, Paul E. Burns, Fred Graff, Jack Lee, Sarah Edwards, Jack Davis.

A millionaire (Corrigan) risks all to stop a gang of counterfeiters when stolen engraving plates fall into his hands.

1797. Shadows in the Night (7/27/44) B&W—67 mins. (Mystery). DIR: Eugene J. Forde. PRO: Rudolph C. Flothow. SP: Eric Taylor. Based on the CBS radio program *Crime Doctor* by Max Marcin. CAST: Warner Baxter, Nina Foch, George Zucco, Minor Watson, Ben Welden, Lester Matthews, Edward Norris, Charles Wilson, Charles Halton, Jeanne Bates, Arthur Hohl.

Dr. Ordway (Baxter), the Crime Doctor, helps an heiress (Foch) who is slowly being driven to madness and suicide by one of her relatives.

1798. Shadows of Sing Sing (2/14/34) B&W—63 mins. (Crime-Drama). DIR: Philip E. Rosen. PRO: Sid Rogell. SP: Albert DeMond. Story by Katherine Scola, Doris Maloy. CAST: Mary Brian, Bruce Cabot, Grant Mitchell, Harry Woods, Claire DuBrey, Bradley Page, Irving Bacon, Dewey Robinson, Fred Kelsey.

The son (Cabot) of a detective (Mitchell) is framed by a gangster (Page) when he falls in love with the gangster's sister (Brian).

1799. Shakedown (8/18/36) B&W—55 mins. (Crime-Drama). DIR: David Selman. PRO: Harry L. Decker. SP: Grace Neville. Story by Harry Shipman. CAST: Lew Ayres, Joan Perry, Thurston Hall, Victor Kilian, Henry Mollison, John Gallaudet, George McKay, Gene Morgan.

A young man (Ayres) prevents a plot to kidnap his sweetheart (Perry) when he goes to work for her father's (Hall) telegraph company as a messenger.

1800. Shampoo (2/75) Technicolor—109 mins. (Comedy). DIR: Hal Ashby. PRO: Warren Beatty. SP: Robert Towne, Warren Beatty. CAST: Warren Beatty, Julie Christie, Goldie Hawn, Lee Grant, Jack Warden, Tony Bill, Carrie Fisher, Jay Robinson, George Furth, Brad Dexter, William Castle, Doris Packer, Hal Buckley, Howard Hesseman, Michelle Phillips.

Set on the day Richard Nixon became President, a hairdresser (Beatty) sleeps with his women clients, tries to get a loan to start his own business and is turned down, loses the girl (Christie) he loves, and realizes how meaningless and empty his life has become. NOTES: The film debut of Carrie Fisher.

1801. Shamus (2/73) Eastman Color/Panavision—98 mins. (Crime-Comedy). DIR: Buzz Kulik. PRO: Robert M. Weitman. SP: Barry Beckerman. CAST: Burt Reynolds, Dyan Cannon, John Ryan, Joe Santos, Georgio Tozzi, Ron Weyland, Larry Block, Kevin Conway, John Glover, Frank Silvero, Beeson Carroll, Merwin Goldsmith, Kay Frye.

A private detective (Reynolds) finds a warehouse full of stolen munitions while searching for stolen diamonds.

1802. Shanghaied Love (9/6/31) B&W—75 mins. (Drama). *DIR:* George B. Seitz. *SP:* Roy Chanslor, Jack Cunningham. Based on *Then Hell Broke Loose* by Norman Springer. *CAST:* Richard Cromwell, Noah Beery, Sr., Sally Blane, Willard Robertson, Sidney Bracey, Richard Alexander, Edwin J. Brady, Erville Alderson, Lionel Belmore, Jack Cheatham, Fred "Snowflake" Toones.

A seaman (Robertson) seeks revenge on the cruel sea captain (Beery, Sr.) who stole his wife and daughter (Blane) and then caused the death of the wife.

1803. She Couldn't Take It (10/8/35) B&W—89 mins. (Crime-Comedy). *DIR:* Tay Garnett. *PRO:* B. P. Schulberg. *SP:* Oliver H. P. Garrett. Story by Gene Towne, Graham Baker. *CAST:* George Raft, Joan Bennett, Walter Connolly, Billie Burke, Lloyd Nolan, Wallace Ford, James Blakely, Alan Mowbray, William Tannen, Donald Meek, Frank Conroy, Tom Kennedy, Ivan Lebedeff, Franklin Pangborn, Thomas Jackson, Robert Middlemass, Stanley Andrews, Wyrley Birch, Irving Bacon, Olaf Hytten, George McKay, Edgar Dearing, Gene Morgan, George Lloyd, Emmett Vogan, Vic Potel, Lee Shumway, Bess Flowers, John Ince, Kernan Cripps, Frank LaRue, Oscar Rudolph.

While in prison, a bootlegger (Raft) is made executor of a fellow prisoner's (Connolly) will, who promptly drops dead of a heart attack. When the bootlegger is released from prison, he goes to the man's house to assume his duties and both the wife (Burke) and daughter (Bennett) vow to make his life miserable. *NOTES:* Oscar Rudolph, in the role of the newsboy, grew up to be a successful TV director in the 1950's and 1960's. [British title: *Woman Tamer*].

1804. She Has What It Takes (4/15/43) B&W—66 mins. (Musical). *DIR:* Charles Barton. *PRO:* Colbert Clark. *SP:* Paul Yawitz. Story by Paul Yawitz, Robert Lee Johnson. *CAST:* Jinx Falkenburg, Tom Neal, Constance Worth, Douglas Leavitt, Joe King, Matt Willis, Daniel Ocko, George McKay, George Lloyd, Joseph Crehan, John Dilson, Barbara Brown, Robert E. Homans, Harry Hayden, Jack Rice, Ernie Adams, Frank Hagney, Eddie Chandler, Ray Teal, William Haade, Netta Packer, Milton Kibbee, Eddie Kane, The Radio Rogues, The Vagabonds.

An unknown singer (Falkenburg) uses a columnist (Neal) to help her land a part in a Broadway play as she pretends to be the daughter of a famous deceased star.

1805. She Knew All the Answers (5/20/41) B&W—85 mins. (Comedy). *DIR:* Richard Wallace. *PRO:* Charles R. "Buddy" Rogers. *SP:* Harry Segall, Kenneth Earl, Curtis Kenyon. Based on *A Girl's Best Friend Is Wall Street* by Jane Allen. *CAST:* Joan Bennett, Franchot Tone, John Hubbard, Eve Arden, William Tracy, Pierre Watkin, Almira Sessions, Thurston Hall, Grady Sutton, Luis Alberni, Francis Compton, Dick Elliott, Selmer Jackson, Roscoe Ates, Chester Clute, Frank Sully, Billy Benedict, Fern Emmett, Don Beddoe, Byron Foulger.

A woman (Bennett) tries to show up her guardian (Tone) by obtaining a job on Wall Street when he refuses to let her marry a playboy (Hubbard).

1806. She Married an Artist (3/1/38) B&W—78 mins. (Drama). *DIR:* Marion Gering. *PRO:* Sidney Buchman. *SP:* Delmer Daves, Gladys Lehman. Based on *I Married an Artist* by Avery Strakosch. *CAST:* John Boles, Luli Deste, Frances Drake, Helen Westley, Albert (Van) Dekker, Alexander D'Arcy, Mavek Windheim, Franklin Pangborn, Jacqueline Wells (Julie Bishop).

An artist (Boles), in love with his model (Drake), decides to marry his art-school friend (Deste), but seeing the error of his ways and on the advice of his housekeeper (Westley), makes the choice to divorce his wife and marry his model.

1807. She Married Her Boss (9/27/35) B&W—85 mins. (Comedy). *DIR*: Gregory LaCava. *PRO*: Everett Riskin. *SP*: Sidney Buchman. Story by Thyra Samter Winslow. *CAST*: Claudette Colbert, Michael Bartlett, Melvyn Douglas, Raymond Walburn, Jean Dixon, Katharine Alexander, Edith Fellows, Clara Kimball Young, Charles Arnt, Selmer Jackson, John Hyams, Geneva Mitchell, Georgia Caine, Robert E. Homans, Sam Ash, Dave O'Brien, Ernie Adams, John Ince, Lloyd Whitlock.

A woman (Colbert) marries her boss (Douglas) and proceeds to straighten out her sister-in-law (Alexander) and step-daughter (Fellows).

1808. She Played with Fire (9/58) B&W—95 mins. (Suspense-Drama). *DIR*: Sidney Gilliat. *PRO*: Sidney Gilliat, Frank Launder. *SP*: Sidney Gilliat, Frank Launder, Val Valentine. Based on *Fortune Is a Woman* by Winston Graham. A Launder-Gilliat Production. *CAST*: Jack Hawkins, Arlene Dahl, Dennis Price, Violet Farebrother, Ian Hunter, Malcolm Keen, Geoffrey Keen, Patrick Holt, John Robinson, Michael Goodliffe, Martin Lane, Bernard Milks, Christopher Lee, Greta Gynt, John Phillips, Patricia Marmont.

An insurance investigator (Hawkins) discovers that the husband (Price) of his old girlfriend (Dahl) is selling valuable paintings and substituting forged paintings for those presumably destroyed in fires. [British title: *Fortune Is a Woman*].

1809. She Wouldn't Say Yes (11/29/45) B&W—87 mins. (Comedy). *DIR*: Alexander Hall. *PRO*: Virginia Van Upp. *SP*: Virginia Van Upp, John Jacoby, Sarett Tobias. Story by Laslo Gorog, William Thiele. *CAST*: Rosalind Russell, Lee Bowman, Adele Jergens, Charles Winninger, Harry Davenport, Sara Haden, Percy Kilbride, Lewis Russell, Mabel Paige, George Cleveland, Charles Arnt, Almira Sessions, Mantan Moreland, Willie Best, John Tyrrell, Arthur Q. Bryan, Cora Witherspoon, Doris Houck, Darren McGavin, Clarence Muse, Nick Stewart, Carl "Alfalfa" Switzer, Edward Gargan, Tom Dugan.

A psychiatrist (Russell) uses a cartoonist (Bowman) to prove her theory that one should keep one's emotions under control.

1810. Sheena (8/84) Metrocolor/Panavision—117 mins. (Adventure). *DIR*: John Guillermin. *PRO*: Paul Aratow. *SP*: Lorenzo Semple, Jr., David Newman. Story by David Newman and Leslie Stevens. A Columbia-Delphi II Production. *CAST*: Tanya Roberts, Ted Wass, Donovan Scott, Trevor Thomas, Clifton Jones, John Forgeham, Errol John, Sylvester Williams, Bob Sherman, Michael Shannon, Nancy Paul.

An American TV producer (Wass) falls in love with a jungle queen (Roberts) and joins her in her attempt to stop an unscrupulous native (Thomas) from usurping the throne of an African kingdom.

1811. She's a Soldier Too (6/29/44) B&W—67 mins. (Drama). *DIR*: William Castle. *PRO*: Wallace MacDonald. *SP*: Melvin Levy. Story by Hal Smith. *CAST*: Beulah Bondi, Nina Foch, Jess Barker, Lloyd Bridges, Percy Kilbride, Ida Moore, Erik Rolf,

Jeanne Bates, Shelley Winters, Marilyn Johnson.

A cab driver (Foch) is enlisted by a soldier (Bridges) to help him locate the son he left behind years ago.

1812. She's a Sweetheart (12/7/44) B&W—69 mins. (Musical). *DIR:* Del Lord. *PRO:* Ted Richmond. *SP:* Muriel Roy Bolton. *CAST:* Jane Frazee, Larry Parks, Jane Darwell, Nina Foch, Ross Hunter, Jimmy Lloyd, Loren Tindall, Carole Mathews, Eddie Bruce, Pat Lane, Danny Desmond, Ruth Warren, Dave Willock.

A landlady (Darwell) turns her boardinghouse into a haven for soldiers and initiates a romance between a soldier (Parks) and a singer (Frazee).

1813. Ship of Fools (9/65) B&W—148 mins. (Drama). *DIR/PRO:* Stanley Kramer. *SP:* Abby Mann. Based on the book by Katherine Anne Porter. *CAST:* Vivien Leigh, Simone Signoret, Jose Ferrer, Lee Marvin, Elizabeth Ashley, Oskar Werner, George Segal, Jose Greco, Michael Dunn, Charles Korvin, Heinz Ruehmann, Lilia Skala, Barbara Luna, Christine Schmidtmer, Alf Kjellin, Werner Klemperer, Gila Golan, Stanley Adams, Henry Calvin, Karen Verne, Oscar Beregi, Paul Daniel, Anthony Brand, Charles de Vries.

In 1932, a varied group of passengers set sail on a German passenger ship from Vera Cruz, Mexico, to Bremerhaven, Germany. *NOTES:* The last film of Vivien Leigh.

1814. Shockproof (1/25/49) B&W—79 mins. (Crime). *DIR:* Douglas Sirk. *PRO:* S. Sylvan Simon, Helen Deutsch. *SP:* Helen Deutsch, Samuel Fuller. *CAST:* Cornel Wilde, Patricia Knight, John Baragrey, Esther Minciotti, Howard St. John, Russell Collins, Charles Bates, Gilbert Barnett, Frank Jacquet, Ann Shoemaker,

King Donovan, Claire Carleton, Fred F. Sears, Jimmy Lloyd, Isabel Withers, Crane Whitley, Richard Benedict, Arthur Space.

A parole officer (Wilde) gives a woman (Knight), newly released from prison, the job of caring for his blind mother (Minciotti); eventually they fall in love and marry, but when she accidentally shoots her ex-lover (Baragrey), they both take it on the run.

1815. Shopworn (4/3/32) B&W—72 mins. (Drama). *DIR:* Nick Grinde. *PRO:* Harry Cohn. *SP:* Jo Swerling, Sarah Y. Mason, Robert Riskin. Story by Sarah Y. Mason. *CAST:* Barbara Stanwyck, Regis Toomey, Zasu Pitts, Lucien Littlefield, Clara Blandick, Robert Alden, Oscar Apfel, Maude Turner Gordon, Albert Conti, James Durkin, Wallis Clark, Edwin Maxwell, Joe Sawyer, Joan Standing.

A mother (Blandick) decides that the woman (Stanwyck) her son (Toomey) wants to marry is beneath her station, so she has her sent to a prison workhouse. When she is released she becomes a musical sensation and the mother now consents to the marriage.

1816. Shotgun Pass (11/1/31) B&W—58 mins. (Western). *DIR:* J. P. McGowan. *SP:* Robert Quigley. *CAST:* Tim McCoy, Monte Vandergrift, Virginia Lee Corbin, Ben Corbett, Frank Rice, Albert J. Smith, Dick Stewart, Archie Ricks, Joe Marba.

A rancher (McCoy) tries to secure a right-of-way for his herd of horses across another rancher's land.

1817. Shut My Big Mouth (2/19/42) B&W—71 mins. (Western-Comedy). *DIR:* Charles Barton. *PRO:* Robert Sparks. *SP:* Oliver Drake, Karen DeWolf, Francis Martin. Story by Oliver Drake. *CAST:* Joe E. Brown, Adele Mara, Lloyd Bridges, Victor Jory, Don Beddoe, Joan Woodbury, Fritz Feld, Noble Johnson, Forrest

Tucker, Russell Simpson, Chief Thunder Cloud, Pedro de Cordoba, Earle Hodgins, Joe McGuinn, Ralph Peters, Dick Curtis, Edmund Cobb, Edward Piel, Sr., Art Mix, Blackjack Ward, John Tyrrell, Georgia Backus, Fern Emmett, Hank Bell, Eddy Waller.

An Easterner (Brown) arrives out West, is made sheriff, and goes after a gang of outlaws.

1818. Siddhartha (7/73) Eastman Color/Panavision—95 mins. (Drama). *DIR/PRO/SP*: Conrad Rooks. Based on the book by Herman Hesse. A Lotus Production. *CAST*: Shashi Kapoor, Simi Garewal, Romesh Sharma, Pincho Kapoor, Zul Vellani, Amrik Singh, Shanti Hiranand, Kunal Kapoor.

In India, a young Indian (Kapoor) searches for the meaning of life.

1819. The Sideshow (12/22/28) B&W—70 mins. (Drama). *DIR*: Erle C. Kenton. *PRO*: Harry Cohn. *SP*: Howard J. Green. *CAST*: Marie Prevost, Ralph Graves, Little Billy, Alan Roscoe.

When the midget boss (Little Billy) of a traveling circus refuses to sell to a rival circus, accidents begin to happen.

1820. Siege of the Saxons (8/63) Technicolor—85 mins. (Adventure). *DIR*: Nathan Juran. *PRO*: Jud Kinberg. *SP*: Jud Kinberg, John Kohn. An Ameran Production. *CAST*: Ronald Lewis, Janette Scott, Ronald Howard, Mark Dignam, John Laurie, Jerome Willis, Richard Clarke, Charles Lloyd Pack, Francis DeWolf, John Gabriel, Peter Mason, Gordon Boyd.

When King Arthur (Dignam) is killed, his daughter (Scott), Merlin (Laurie), and an outlaw (Lewis) seek to drive the false king, Edmund of Cornwall (Howard), and the Saxons from England.

1821. Sierra Stranger (5/1/57) B&W—74 mins. (Western). *DIR*: Lee Sholem. *PRO*: Norman T. Herman. *SP*: Richard J. Dorso. An Acirema Production. *CAST*: Howard Duff, Gloria McGhee, Dick Foran, John Hoyt, Barton MacLane, George E. Stone, Ed Kemmer, Henry Kulky, Byron Foulger, Robert C. Foulk, Eve McVeagh.

A stranger (Duff) rescues a man (Kemmer) from a beating, but comes to realize that he is no good when he robs a stagecoach and turns on him.

1822. The Sign of the Ram (2/2/48) B&W—88 mins. (Drama). *DIR*: John Sturges. *PRO*: Irving Cummings. *SP*: Charles Bennett. Based on the book by Margaret Ferguson. *CAST*: Susan Peters, Alexander Knox, Phyllis Thaxter, Peggy Ann Garner, Ron Randell, Dame May Whitty, Allene Roberts, Ross Ford, Diana Douglas, Margaret Tracy, Paul Scardon, Gerald Hamer, Doris Lloyd.

A woman (Peters), confined to a wheelchair and born under the astrological sign of the Ram, alienates herself with her new husband (Knox) and step-children (Garner, Roberts, Ford). In the end she slowly descends into madness and wheels herself off a cliff. *NOTES*: This film marked Susan Peters' return to films after she lost the use of her legs in a hunting accident.

1823. The Silencers (3/66) Pathe Color—103 mins. (Action-Comedy). *DIR*: Phil Karlson. *PRO*: Irving Allen. *SP*: Oscar Saul. Based on *The Silencers* and *Death of a Citizen* by Donald Hamilton. A Meadway-Claude Production. *CAST*: Dean Martin, Stella Stevens, Daliah Lavi, Victor Buono, Robert Webber, Arthur O'Connell, James Gregory, Nancy Kovack, Roger C. Carmel, Cyd Charisse, Beverly Adams, Richard Devon, Ray Montgomery, Frank Hagney.

Matt Helm (Martin) sets out to stop

a madman (Buono) from destroying America's missile defense system.

1824. Silent Men (3/3/33) B&W— 68 mins. (Western). *DIR:* D. Ross Lederman. *SP:* Jack Cunningham, Stuart Anthony, Gerald Geraghty. Based on a story by Walt Coburn. *CAST:* Tim McCoy, Florence Britton, Wheeler Oakman, J. Carrol Naish, Walter Brennan, Mathew Betz, Lloyd Ingraham, Syd Saylor, Joe Girard, Steve Clark, William V. Mong.

A special agent (McCoy) of the Cattleman's Association sets out to prove his innocence when he is accused of being a cattle rustler and escaped convict.

1825. Silent Rage (4/82) Metrocolor—100 mins. (Action). *DIR:* Michael Miller. *PRO:* Anthony B. Unger. *SP:* Joseph Fraley. A Topkick Production. *CAST:* Chuck Norris, Ron Silver, Steven Keats, Toni Kalem, William Finley, Brian Libby, Stephen Furst, Stephanie Dunnam, Joyce Ingle, Jay DePland.

A sheriff (Norris) goes after a killer (Libby) made indestructible by a scientist (Keats) testing out a new serum.

1826. The Silent World (1/56) Technicolor—86 mins. (Documentary). *DIR:* Louis Malle, Jacques-Yves Cousteau. *PRO/SP:* Jacques-Yves Cousteau. *CAST:* Narrated by Jacques-Yves Cousteau.

A documentary of the Cousteau-National Geographic expeditions to the Red and Mediterranean seas, Persian Gulf and Indian Ocean in 1954–1955. [Original French title: *Le Monde du Silence*].

1827. Silver Bears (4/78) Technicolor—113 mins. (Comedy). *DIR:* Ivan Passer. *PRO:* Alex Wintsky, Arlene Sellers. *SP:* Peter Stone. Based on the book by Paul E. Erdman. *CAST:* Michael Caine, Cybill Shepherd, Louis Jourdan, Stephane Audran, David Warner, Tom Smothers, Martin Balsam, Jay Leno, Tony Mascia, Charles Gary, Joss Ackland, Jeremy Clyde, Moustache, Mike Falco.

A con man (Caine), out to purchase a bank in Switzerland for a mobster (Balsam) in order to launder money, gets involved in a scheme with a silver mine in Iran, the silver market, and a clerk (Smothers) and his wife (Shepherd) from a California bank.

1828. Silver Canyon (6/20/51) Sepiatone—70 mins. (Western). *DIR:* John English. *PRO:* Armand Schaefer. *SP:* Gerald Geraghty. Story by Alan James. A Gene Autry Production. *CAST:* Gene Autry, Gail Davis, Pat Buttram, Jim Davis, Bob Steele, Edgar Dearing, Dick Alexander, Terry Frost, Steve Clark, Stanley Andrews, Boyd Stockman, Kenne Duncan, Pat O'Malley, John Merton, Stanley Blystone, John R. McKee, Peter Mamakos, Duke York, Eugene Borden, Bobby Clark, Frankie Marvin, Sandy Sanders, William Haade, Jack O'Shea, Frank Matts, Jack Pepper, James Magill, Martin Wilkins.

Gene, a scout for the Union Army, goes after a renegade guerrilla leader (Davis) operating in Utah.

1829. Silver City Raiders (11/4/43) B&W—55 mins. (Western). *DIR:* William Berke. *PRO:* Leon Barsha. *SP:* Ed Earl Repp. *CAST:* Russell Hayden, Alma Carroll, Dub Taylor, Edmund Cobb, Jack Rockwell, Jack Ingram, Merrill McCormack, Art Mix, John Tyrrell, George Morrell, Horace B. Carpenter, Luther Wills, Paul Sutton, Tex Palmer, Bob Wills and His Texas Playboys.

A rancher (Hayden) goes after a land grabber (Ingram) using a phoney Spanish land grant to swindle the ranchers out of their land. [British title: *Legal Larceny*].

1830. **Silverado** (6/85) Technicolor/Super Techniscope—132 mins. (Western). *DIR/PRO:* Lawrence Kasdan. *SP:* Lawrence Kasdan, Mark Kasdan. *CAST:* Kevin Kline, Scott Glenn, Kevin Costner, Danny Glover, John Cleese, Todd Allen, Rosanna Arquette, Brian Dennehy, Linda Hunt, Jeff Goldblum, Sheb Wooley, Ray Baker, Kenny Call.

In the 1880's, the lives of four unlikely heroes (Glenn, Kline, Glover, Costner) converge when they team up to rid the town of Silverado of their crooked sheriff (Dennehy).

The Sin *see* **White Sister**

1831. **Sinbad and the Eye of Tiger** (6/77) Metrocolor—113 mins. (Fantasy). *DIR:* Sam Wanamaker. *PRO:* Charles H. Schneer, Ray Harryhausen. *SP:* Beverley Cross. Story by Ray Harryhausen and Beverley Cross. A Morningside Production. *CAST:* Patrick Wayne, Jane Seymour, Taryn Power, Margaret Whiting, Kurt Christian, Patrick Troughton, Nadim Sawaiha, Damien Thomas, Bruno Barnabe, Bernard Kay, David Sterne, Salami Coaker.

Sinbad (Wayne) battles dangerous creatures in his journey to remove the spell of an evil sorceress (Whiting) that keeps a prince (Thomas) from his rightful place on the throne. *NOTES:* Special effects by Ray Harryhausen.

1832. **Sing for Your Supper** (11/4/41) B&W—66 mins. (Musical). *DIR:* Charles Barton. *PRO:* Leon Barsha. *SP:* Harry Rebuas. *CAST:* Jinx Falkenburg, Charles R. "Buddy" Rogers, Bert Gordon, Eve Arden, Don Beddoe, Bernadene Hayes, Henry Kolker, Benny Baker, Dewey Robinson, Luise Squire, Larry Parks, Lloyd Bridges, Harry Barris, Walter Sande, Berni Gould, Don Porter, Sig Arno, Earle Hodgins.

A band leader (Rogers) has his dance hall saved by a wealthy socialite (Falkenburg).

1833. **Sing Me a Song of Texas** (2/8/45) B&W—66 mins. (Western-Musical). *DIR:* Vernon Keays. *PRO:* Colbert Clark. *SP:* J. Benton Cheney, Elizabeth Beecher. *CAST:* Tom Tyler, Rosemary Lane, Slim Summerville, Guinn "Big Boy" Williams, Carole Mathews, Noah Beery, Sr., Pinky Tomlin, Marie Austin, The Hoosier Hotshots, Foy Willing and the Riders of the Purple Sage, Hal McIntyre and His Orchestra.

A rancher (Beery, Sr.) pretends to be dead to decide which of his nieces (Lane, Mathews) is worthy of his wealth. [British title: *Fortune Hunter*].

1834. **Sing While You Dance** (7/25/46) B&W—88 mins. (Musical-Comedy). *DIR:* D. Ross Lederman. *PRO:* Leon Barsha. *SP:* Robert Stephen Brode. Story by Lorraine Edwards. *CAST:* Ellen Drew, Robert Stanton, Andrew Tombes, Edwin Cooper, Robert Stevens, Ethel Griffies, Amanda Lane, Eddy Waller, Paul E. Burns, Eddie Parks, Bert Roach, Mary Gordon, Walter Baldwin, Trevor Bardette, Jean Donahue.

A musical composer (Drew) persuades a widow (Griffies) to let her publish her deceased husband's music with minor changes.

1835. **Singin' in the Corn** (12/26/46) B&W—65 mins. (Musical). *DIR:* Del Lord. *PRO:* Ted Richmond. *SP:* Isabel Dawn, Monte Brice. Story by Richard Weil. *CAST:* Allen Jenkins, Judy Canova, Al Bridge, Guinn "Big Boy" Williams, George Chesebro, Ethan Laidlaw, Charles Halton, Robert Dudley, Nick Thompson, Francis Rel, Si Jenks, Pat O'Malley, Chester Conklin, Mary Gordon, Jay Silverheels, Rodd Redwing, Frank Lackteen, The Singing Indian Braves.

A carnival mind reader (Canova)

inherits her uncle's estate on the provision that a ghost town be given back to the Indians. [British title: *Give and Take*].

1836. Singing on the Trail (9/12/46) B&W—60 mins. (Western-Musical). *DIR:* Ray Nazarro. *PRO:* Colbert Clark. *SP:* J. Benton Cheney. *CAST:* Ken Curtis, Jeff Donnell, Guy Kibbee, Guinn "Big Boy" Williams, Ian Keith, Dusty Anderson, Matt Willis, Joe Haworth, Sam Flint, Eddy Waller, Jody Gilbert, Carolina Cotton, The Plainsmen, The Hoosier Hotshots, Four Chicks and Chuck.

A radio singer (Curtis) comes to the aid of the Hoosier Hotshots when they learn that the ranch they own is not legally theirs. [British title: *Lookin' for Someone*].

1837. Singing Spurs (9/23/48) B&W—62 mins. (Western-Musical). *DIR:* Ray Nazarro. *PRO:* Colbert Clark. *SP:* Barry Shipman. *CAST:* Kirby Grant, Patricia Knox, Lee Patrick, Jay Silverheels, Dick Elliott, Fred F. Sears, Marion Colby, Red Enger, Chester Clute, Riley Hill, Billy Wilkerson, The Shamrock Cowboys, The Hoosier Hotshots.

The Hoosier Hotshots help a neighbor (Grant) raise money to irrigate Indian lands.

1838. Sinner's Parade (9/14/28) B&W—58 mins. (Crime-Drama). *DIR:* John G. Adolfi. *PRO:* Harry Cohn. *SP:* Beatrice Van. Story by David Lewis. *CAST:* Victor Varconi, Dorothy Revier, John Patrick, Edna Marion, Marjorie Bonner, Clarissa Selwynne, Jack Mower.

A schoolteacher (Revier) moonlights as a dancer at a nightclub and helps the club owner (Varconi) when she realizes that the man she loves (Patrick) is the leader of the local crime ring.

1839. The Siren (3/11/28) B&W—58 mins. (Drama). *DIR:* Byron Haskin. *PRO:* Jack Cohn. *SP:* Elmer Harris. Story by Harold Shumate. *CAST:* Tom Moore, Dorothy Revier, Norman Trevor, Jed Prouty.

A society girl (Revier), charged with the murder of a gambler, is proven innocent by his partner (Moore).

1840. Siren of Bagdad (6/53) Technicolor—77 mins. (Comedy). *DIR:* Richard Quine. *PRO:* Sam Katzman. *SP:* Robert E. Kent, Larry Rhine. Story by Robert E. Kent. *CAST:* Paul Henreid, Hans Conreid, Patricia Medina, Charlie Lung, Laurette Luez, Anne Dore, George Keymas, Vivian Mason, Michael Fox, Karl Davis, Carl Milletaire.

A magician (Henreid) and his assistant (Conreid) set out to rescue the daughter (Medina) of a deposed sultan (Fox).

1841. Sirocco (6/12/51) B&W—98 mins. (Drama). *DIR:* Curtis Bernhardt. *PRO:* Robert Lord. *SP:* A. I. Bezzerides, Hans Jacoby. Based on *Coup De Grace* by Joseph Kessel. A Santana Pictures Production. *CAST:* Humphrey Bogart, Marta Toren, Lee J. Cobb, Everett Sloane, Gerald Mohr, Zero Mostel, Nick Dennis, Onslow Stevens, Ludwig Donath, David Bond, Vincent Renno, Martin Watkins, Peter Ortiz, Peter Brocco, Jay Novello, Leonard Penn, Harry Guardino, Edward Colemans, Al Eben.

In 1925 Syria, a gunrunner (Bogart) falls in love with the local police chief's girl (Toren), gets into trouble with the rebels when he quits supplying arms to them, and eventually has to rescue the police chief (Cobb) from the rebel leader (Stevens) at the cost of his own life.

1842. A Sister to Assist'er (3/38) B&W—72 mins. (Comedy). *DIR:* Widgey R. Newman, George Dewhurst. *PRO:* Widgey R. Newman. *SP:* George Dewhurst. Based on the play by John Le Breton. An Associated Industries Production. *CAST:* Muriel George, Pollie Emery, Charles Paton, Billy Percy, Harry Herbert, Dorothy Vernon, Dora Levis.

An old woman (George) skips out on her landlady (Emery), then pretends to be her own rich sister in order to get her trunk back. *NOTES:* Filmed twice as a silent film in 1922 and 1927, and once again in 1930 and 1948. Pollie Emery played the landlady in the 1922, 1927, 1930, and 1938 versions of this film. George Dewhurst was either director or co-writer on all versions.

1843. Sisters (6/29/30) B&W—66 mins. (Drama). *DIR:* James Flood. *PRO:* Harry Cohn. *SP:* Jo Swerling. Story by Ralph Graves. *CAST:* Sally O'Neil, Molly O'Day, Russell Gleason, Jason Robards, Sr., Morgan Wallace, John Lee, Carl Stockdale.

A country boy (Gleason) falls in love with a Manhattan model (O'Neil) and helps her sister (O'Day) when a crook (Wallace) tries to come between her and her husband (Robards, Sr.).

1844. Sisters Under the Skin (6/8/34) B&W—70 mins. (Drama). *DIR:* David Burton. *PRO:* Samuel J. Briskin. *SP:* Jo Swerling. Story by S. K. Lauren. *CAST:* Elissa Landi, Frank Morgan, Joseph Schildkraut, Doris Lloyd, Clara Blandick, Shirley Grey, Samuel S. Hinds, Henry Kolker, Arthur Stewart Hull, C. Montague Shaw, Howard Hickman, Robert Graves, Selmer Jackson.

A married man (Morgan) feels that he is losing his mistress (Landi) to a younger man (Schildkraut). [British title: *The Romantic Age*].

1845. Six-Gun Law (1/4/48) B&W—54 mins. (Western). *DIR:* Ray Nazarro. *PRO:* Colbert Clark. *SP:* Barry Shipman. *CAST:* Charles Starrett, Nancy Saunders, Smiley Burnette, Paul Campbell, Pierce Lyden, George Chesebro, Bob Wilke, John Cason, Bud Osborne, Ethan Laidlaw, Hugh Prosser, Budd Buster, Billy Dix, Curly Clements and His Rodeo Rangers.

A cowboy (Starrett), framed by an outlaw (Prosser) into thinking he killed the sheriff, becomes the new sheriff and goes undercover as the Durango Kid to prove his innocence and rid the town of the outlaws.

1846. Skatetown, U.S.A. (10/79) Metrocolor—98 mins. (Comedy). *DIR:* William A. Levey. *PRO:* William A. Levey, Lorin Dreyfuss. *SP:* Nick Castle. Story by Nick Castle, William A. Levey, Lorin Dreyfuss. A Rastar Production. *CAST:* Scott Baio, Flip Wilson, Ron Palillo, Ruth Buzzi, Dave Mason, Greg Bradford, Maureen McCormick, Patrick Swayze, Billy Barty, David Landsberg, Joe E. Ross, Lenny Bari, Kelly Lang, Sandra Gould, Murray Langston, Dorothy Stratten.

The good guy (Bradford) takes on the bad guy (Swayze) in a roller skating contest. *NOTES:* The film debut of Patrick Swayze; the first film to cash in on the roller-disco fad of the late 70's.

1847. Sky Commando (8/21/53) B&W—69 mins. (War-Drama). *DIR:* Fred F. Sears. *PRO:* Sam Katzman. *SP:* Samuel Newman. Story by William B. Sackheim, Arthur E. Orloff, Samuel Newman. *CAST:* Dan Duryea, Francis Gifford, Michael Conners, Michael Fox, Freeman Morse, William R. Klein, Dick Paxton, Selmer Jackson, Dick Lerner, Morris Ankrum, Paul McGuire.

A squadron leader (Duryea), disliked by his men, proves himself by flying a dangerous mission.

1848. Sky Raiders (5/31/31) B&W—59 mins. (Adventure-Aviation). *DIR:* Christy Cabanne. *SP:* Harvey Gates. *CAST:* Lloyd Hughes, Marceline Day, Wheeler Oakman, Walter Miller, Kit Guard, Ashley Buck, Jerome J. Jerome, William H. O'Brien, Jay Eaton, Dick Rush.

A pilot (Hughes) causes the death of his sweetheart's (Day) brother, but redeems himself when he rounds up a gang of sky pirates.

1849. Slaves of Babylon (10/53) Technicolor—82 mins. (Biblical). *DIR:* William Castle. *PRO:* Sam Katzman. *SP:* DeVallon Scott. *CAST:* Richard Conte, Linda Christian, Maurice Schwartz, Terence Kilburn, Michael Ansara, Leslie Bradley, Ruth Storey, John Crawford, Ric Roman, Robert Griffin, Beatrice Maude, Wheaton Chambers, Paul Purcell, Julie Newmar, Ernestine Barrier.

Daniel (Schwartz) battles wits with Nebuchadnezzar (Bradley) as he strives to free the Israelites from Babylonian captivity.

1850. The Sleeping Beauty (4/66) Technicolor/Scope—90 mins. (Ballet). *DIR:* Appolinari Dudko, Konstantin Sergeyev. *SP:* Appolinari Dudko, Konstantin Sergeyev, Josif Shapiro. A Lenfilm-Royal Films International Production. *CAST:* Alla Sizova, Yuri Soloviev, Natalia Dudinskaya, Irina Bazhenova, Vsevolod Ukhov, O. Zabotkina, Natalia Makasova, Valeri Panov, V. Raizanova, E. Minchenok, I. Korneyeva, S. Kuznetsov.

A filmed version of the Tchaikovsky ballet. *NOTES:* Limited theatrical release. [Original Russian title: *Spyashchaya Krasavitsa*].

1851. Slightly French (2/16/49) B&W—81 mins. (Musical-Comedy). *DIR:* Douglas Sirk. *PRO:* Irving Starr. *SP:* Karen DeWolf. Story by Herbert Fields. *CAST:* Dorothy Lamour, Don Ameche, Janis Carter, Willard Parker, Adele Jergens, Jeanne Manet, Frank

Ferguson, Myron Healey, Leonard Carey, Earle Hodgins, William Bishop, Patricia Barry, Jimmy Lloyd, Michael Towne, Fred F. Sears, Frank Mayo, Hal K. Dawson, Carol Hughes, Frank Wilcox, Al Hill, Pierre Watkin, Will Stanton.

A dancer (Lamour) is transformed into a French movie actress. *NOTES:* A remake of the 1934 Columbia film *Let's Fall in Love.*

1852. Slogan (3/70) Eastman Color—90 mins. (Drama). *DIR/SP:* Pierre Grimblat. An Orphee-Hamster-Royal Films International Production. *CAST:* Serge Gainsbourg, Jane Birkin, Andrea Parisy, Daniel Gelin, Juliette Berto, James Mitchell, Gilles Millinaire, Henri-Jacques Huet, Pierre Doris.

A middle-aged television producer (Gainsbourg), deciding that he has fulfilled this period of his life, turns to filmmaking and the companionship of young girls. *NOTES:* Limited theatrical release.

1853. The Slugger's Wife (3/85) Metrocolor—105 mins. (Comedy). *DIR:* Hal Ashby. *PRO:* Ray Stark. *SP:* Neil Simon. *CAST:* Michael O'Keefe, Rebecca De Mornay, Martin Ritt, Randy Quaid, Lisa Langlois, Cleavant Derricks, Loudon Wainwright III, Georgann Johnson, Danny Tucker, Lynn Redfield.

A home run hitter for the Atlanta Braves (O'Keefe) marries a rock singer (De Mornay), but because of the demanding pressure on their careers, they eventually break up.

1854. Smashing the Spy Ring (1/19/39) B&W—59 mins. (Spy-Drama). *DIR:* Christy Cabanne. *PRO:* Jack Fier. *SP:* Arthur T. Horman, Dorrell McGowan, Stuart E. McGowan. Story by Dorrell McGowan, Stuart E. McGowan. *CAST:* Ralph Bellamy, Fay Wray, Regis Toomey, Walter Kingsford, Ann Doran, Warren Hull, Forbes Murray, Lorna Gray, Paul Whitney, John Tyrrell, May Wallace.

A government agent (Bellamy) poses as a scientist to infiltrate a gang of spies and thwarts their plans to steal military equipment.

1855. Smith of Minnesota (10/15/42) B&W — 66 mins. (Sports-Drama). *DIR:* Lew Landers. *PRO:* Jack Fier. *SP:* Robert D. Andrews. *CAST:* Bruce Smith, Arline Judge, Warren Ashe, Don Beddoe, Kay Harris, Robert Stevens.

A famous football star (Smith) signs with Columbia Pictures for a biography of his career.

1856. Smoky Canyon (1/22/52) B&W — 55 mins. (Western). *DIR:* Fred F. Sears. *PRO:* Colbert Clark. *SP:* Barry Shipman. *CAST:* Charles Starrett, Dani Sue Nolan, Smiley Burnette, Jock Mahoney, Tristram Coffin, Forrest Taylor, Larry Hudson, LeRoy Johnson, Chris Alcaide, Charles Stevens, Sandy Sanders, Boyd Morgan.

The Durango Kid (Starrett) prevents a range feud between the cattle men and sheep men by exposing a crooked cattle syndicate.

1857. Smoky Mountain Melody (12/16/48) B&W — 61 mins. (Western-Musical). *DIR:* Ray Nazarro. *PRO:* Colbert Clark. *SP:* Barry Shipman. *CAST:* Roy Acuff, Sybil Merritt, Russell Arms, Guinn "Big Boy" Williams, Jason Robards, Sr., Fred F. Sears, Jock Mahoney, Jack Ellis, Tommy Ivo, Harry Cheshire, Sam Flint, Lonnie Wilson, Eddie Acuff, Carolina Cotton, John Elliott, Ralph Littlefield, Heinie Conklin, Olin Howlin, Peter Kirby, Jimmy Riddle, Joe Zinkan, Tommy Magness, The Smoky Mountain Boys.

Roy Acuff and the Smoky Mountain Boys inherit a ranch and have to

outwit the former owner's two sons in order to keep it.

1858. Smoky River Serenade (8/21/47) B&W — 67 mins. (Western-Musical). *DIR:* Derwin Abrahams. *PRO:* Colbert Clark. *SP:* Barry Shipman. *CAST:* Paul Campbell, Ruth Taylor, Virginia Hunter, Emmett Vogan, Paul E. Burns, Russell Hicks, Carolina Cotton, Cottonseed Clark, The Boyd Triplets, The Hoosier Hotshots.

The Hoosier Hotshots put on a benefit to help a ranch owner keep his ranch. [British title: *The Threat*].

1859. Smuggler's Gold (5/51) B&W — 64 mins. (Crime-Drama). *DIR:* William Berke. *PRO:* Milton Feldman. *SP:* Daniel B. Ullman. Story by Al Martin. *CAST:* Cameron Mitchell, Amanda Blake, Carl Benton Reid, Peter Thompson, William "Bill" Phillips, William Forrest, Robert Williams, Harlan Warde, Al Hill, Paul Campbell.

A deep sea diver (Mitchell) gets into trouble with smugglers when he is forced to dive for gold thrown overboard by a ship's captain (Reid).

1860. Snafu (11/22/45) B&W — 82 mins. (Comedy). *DIR/PRO:* Jack Moss. *SP:* Louis Solomon, Harold Buchman. *CAST:* Robert Benchley, Vera Vague (Barbara Jo Allen), Conrad Janis, Nanette Parks, Janis Wilson, Jimmy Lloyd, Enid Markey, Eva Puig, Ray Meyer, Marcia Mae Jones, Winfield Smith, John Souther, Byron Foulger, Kathleen Howard.

The parents (Benchley, Vague) of a 15-year-old soldier (Janis) have him honorably discharged from the Army and sent home where he has a hard time adjusting to civilian life. [British title: *Welcome Home*].

1861. The Snake People (3/71) Eastman Color — 90 mins. (Horror). *DIR:* Jack Hill, Juan Ibanez. *PRO:*

Luis Enrique Vergara. *SP:* Jack Hill. *CAST:* Boris Karloff, Julissa, Carlos East, Rafael Bertrand, Santanon, Quentin Bulnes, Tongolele.

The mysterious leader (Karloff) of a snake cult kidnaps and sacrifices his victims to the poison of a snake in possession of the reptile woman (Tongolele). The victims are then turned into zombies to terrorize the countryside. *NOTES:* This was the first of four films Karloff agreed to make for producer Luis Vergara. (For further information see *Notes* section under *Incredible Invasion*). Originally filmed in 1968. [Original Spanish titles: *Isla De Los Muertos*; *La Muerte Viviente*].

1862. Snake River Desperadoes (5/30/51) B&W—54 mins. (Western). *DIR:* Fred F. Sears. *PRO:* Colbert Clark. *SP:* Barry Shipman. *CAST:* Charles Starrett, Don Kay Reynolds, Smiley Burnette, Tommy Ivo, Monte Blue, Boyd Morgan, George Chesebro, John Pickard, Sam Flint, Duke York, Charles Horvath.

The Durango Kid (Starrett), with the help of a couple of youngsters (Reynolds, Ivo), prevents a range war between the whites and Indians and exposes a crooked trader (Blue).

1863. The Sniper (3/19/52) B&W—87 mins. (Crime). *DIR:* Edward Dmytryk. *PRO:* Stanley Kramer. *SP:* Harry Brown. Story by Edward and Edna Anhalt. *CAST:* Eduard Franz, Adolphe Menjou, Gerald Mohr, Marie Windsor, Frank Faylen, Richard Kiley, Mabel Paige, Marlo Dwyer, Geraldine Carr, Jay Novello, Ralph Peters, Max Palmer, Sidney Miller, Harry Cheshire, Kernan Cripps, Rory Mallison, Byron Foulger, Danny Mummert, Carl Benton Reid, Paul Marion, Grandon Rhodes, Harlan Warde, John Eldredge, Jessie Arnold, Nolan Leary, Harry Harvey, Frank Sully, Ralph Smiley, Victor Sen Yung, Gaylord Pendleton, George Chesebro, Al Hill.

A policeman (Menjou) in San Francisco tracks down a mentally disturbed young man (Franz) who is randomly killing women with whom he has come in contact.

1864. The Snorkel (7/58) B&W—92 mins. (Crime). *DIR:* Guy Green. *PRO:* Michael Carreras. *SP:* Peter Meyers, Jimmy Sangster. Story by Anthony Dawson. A Hammer-Clarion Production. *CAST:* Peter Van Eyck, Betta St. John, Mandy Miller, Gregoire Aslan, William Franklyn, Marie Burke, Irene Prador, Henry Vidon, David Ritch.

A man (Van Eyck) kills his wife (St. John) and tries to make it look like suicide, but is eventually found out by his stepdaughter (Miller).

1865. So Dark the Night (9/12/46) B&W—70 mins. (Crime). *DIR:* Joseph H. Lewis. *PRO:* Ted Richmond. *SP:* Martin Berkeley, Dwight V. Babcock. Story by Aubrey Wisberg. *CAST:* Steven Geray, Micheline Cheirel, Eugene Borden, Ann Codee, Egon Brecher, Helen Freeman, Theodore Gottlieb, Gregory Gay, Jean Del Val, Paul Marion, Emil Ramu, Louis Mercier, Billy Snyder, Frank Arnold.

A Parisian detective (Geray) sets out to solve the murder of his fiancee (Cheirel), her lover (Marion), and mother (Codee), unaware that he is the killer.

1866. So This Is Africa (4/22/33) B&W—68 mins. (Comedy-Adventure). *DIR:* Edward Cline. *SP:* Norman Krasna. *CAST:* Robert Woolsey, Bert Wheeler, Raquel Torres, Esther Muir, Berton Churchill, Henry Armetta, Spencer Charters, Clarence Moorehouse.

A pair of lion tamers (Wheeler, Woolsey) land in Africa as movie extras and resort to dressing in drag to avoid the native women. *NOTES:* Bert Wheeler and Robert Woolsey's only Columbia film.

1867. So This Is Love? (2/6/28) B&W—60 mins. (Comedy). *DIR:* Frank Capra. *PRO:* Harry Cohn. *SP:* Elmer Harris, Rex Taylor. Story by Norman Springer. *CAST:* Shirley Mason, William (Buster) Collier, Jr., Johnnie Walker, Ernie Adams, Carl Gerard, William H. Strauss, Jean Leverty.

A dress designer (Collier) becomes a prize fighter in order to win the love of his sweetheart (Mason).

1868. So You Won't Talk? (10/17/40) B&W—69 mins. (Crime-Comedy). *DIR:* Edward Sedgwick. *PRO:* Robert Sparks. *SP:* Richard Flournoy. *CAST:* Joe E. Brown, Frances Robinson, Vivienne Osborne, Bernard Nedell, Tom Dugan, Dick Wessel, Anthony Warde.

A bookstore clerk (Brown) is mistaken for a gangster (Brown) when he shaves off his beard. *NOTES:* Joe E. Brown played a dual role in this film.

1869. Social Register (8/19/34) B&W—72 mins. (Drama). *DIR:* Marshall Neilan. *SP:* Grace Perkins, Clara Beranger, James Ashmore Creelman. Based on the play by John Emerson, Anita Loos. *CAST:* Colleen Moore, Charles Winninger, Pauline Frederick, Alexander Kirkland, Robert Benchley, Ross Alexander, Margaret Livingston, Roberta Robinson, Olive Olsen, John Miltern, Edward Garvie, Georgette Harvey, Hans Hansen.

A chorus girl (Moore) falls in love with a society fellow (Kirkland) and must prove herself to his mother (Frederick) before they can marry.

1870. Soldiers and Women (5/18/30) B&W—69 mins. (Mystery). *DIR:* Edward Sloman. *PRO:* Harry Cohn. *SP:* Dorothy Howell. Based on

The Soul Kiss by Paul Hervey Fox, George Tilton. *CAST:* Aileen Pringle, Grant Withers, Helen Johnson, Walter McGrail, Emmett Corrigan, Blanche Frederici, Wade Boteler, Raymond Largay, William Colvin, Sam Nelson.

Two women (Pringle, Johnson), having an affair with a soldier (Withers) at an Army post, become implicated in murder when the husband of one of the women is found dead.

1871. Soldiers of the Storm (5/18/33) B&W—69 mins. (Crime). *DIR:* D. Ross Lederman. *SP:* Charles R. Condon, Horace McCoy. Story by Thomson Burtis. *CAST:* Regis Toomey, Anita Page, Barbara Weeks, Robert Ellis, Wheeler Oakman, Barbara Barondess, Dewey Robinson, George Cooper, Arthur Wanzer, Henry Wadsworth.

A border patrolman (Toomey) uses his plane to round up a gang of smugglers.

1872. A Soldier's Story (9/84) Metrocolor—102 mins. (Mystery-Drama). *DIR:* Norman Jewison. *PRO:* Norman Jewison, Ronald L. Schwary, Patrick Palmer. *SP:* Charles Fuller. Based on the play *A Soldier's Play* by Charles Fuller. *CAST:* Harold E. Rollins, Jr., Adolph Caesar, Art Evans, David Allen Grier, David Harris, Dennis Lipscomb, Larry Riley, Robert Townsend, Denzel Washington, William Allen Young, Patti LaBelle, Wings Hauser, Scott Paulin, Trey Wilson.

When a black Army sergeant (Caesar) is shot to death at an Army base, further racial tensions are increased when a black Army attorney (Rollins) is sent to investigate.

1873. The Solid Gold Cadillac (10/56) B&W—99 mins. (Comedy). *DIR:* Richard Quine. *PRO:* Fred Kohlmar. *SP:* Abe Burrows. Based on the play by George S. Kaufman, Howard Teichmann. *CAST:* Judy Holliday,

Paul Douglas, Fred Clark, John Williams, Hiram Sherman, Neva Patterson, Ralph Dumke, Ray Collins, Arthur O'Connell, Richard Deacon, Marilyn Hanold, Anne Loos, Harry Antrim, Bud Osborne, George Burns.

The ex-president (Douglas) of a corporation helps a stockholder (Holliday), with only 10 shares of stock, shake up the board of directors by campaigning for the rights of others like her.

Sombra de Pancho Villa, La see **La Sombra de Pancho Villa**

1874. Somebody Killed Her Husband (9/78) Movielab Color/Panavision—97 mins. (Comedy-Crime). *DIR:* Lamont Johnson. *PRO:* Martin Poll. *SP:* Reginald Rose. A Melvin Simon Production. *CAST:* Jeff Bridges, Farrah Fawcett-Majors, John Wood, Tammy Grimes, John Glover, Patricia Elliott, Mary McCarty, Laurence Guittard, Beeson Carroll, Eddie Lawrence, Vincent Robert Santa Lucia.

A Macy's clerk (Bridges) and his girlfriend (Fawcett-Majors) turn sleuths to locate the killer of her husband and two of her neighbors.

1875. Someone to Watch Over Me (10/87) DeLuxe Color—106 mins. (Romance-Thriller). *DIR:* Ridley Scott. *PRO:* Thierry de Ganay, Harold Schneider. *SP:* Howard Franklin. *CAST:* Tom Berenger, Mimi Rogers, Lorraine Bracco, Jerry Orbach, John Rubenstein, Andreas Katsulas, Tony DiBenedetto, James Moriarty, Mark Moses, Daniel Hugh Kelly, Harley Cross, Joanne Baron.

A married Manhattan detective (Berenger) becomes romantically involved with the socialite murder witness (Rogers) he's been assigned to protect.

1876. Something to Shout About (4/8/43) B&W—88 mins. (Musical).

DIR/PRO: Gregory Ratoff. *SP:* Lou Breslow, Edward Eliscu, George Owen. Story by Fred Schiller. *CAST:* Don Ameche, Janet Blair, Jack Oakie, William Gaxton, Veda Ann Borg, Cobina Wright, Jr., Hazel Scott, Jaye Martin, Lily Norwood (Cyd Charisse), James "Chuckles" Walker, The Bricklayers, Teddy Wilson and His Band.

A girl (Blair) becomes a Broadway star when she replaces the lead star (Wright, Jr.) on opening night.

1877. The Son of Davy Crockett (7/15/41) B&W—59 mins. (Western). *DIR/SP:* Lambert Hillyer. *PRO:* Leon Barsha. *CAST:* Bill Elliott, Iris Meredith, Dub Taylor, Kenneth MacDonald, Richard Fiske, Eddy Waller, Donald Curtis, Edmund Cobb, Steve Clark, Lloyd Bridges, Frank Ellis, Dick Botiller, Jack Ingram, Frank LaRue, Tom London, Charles Hamilton, Paul Scardon, Harrison Greene, Curley Dresden, Ray Jones, John Tyrrell, Nick Thompson, Merrill McCormack, Martin Garralaga, Lew Meehan, Francis Sayles.

Dave Crockett (Elliott), son of Alamo hero Davy Crockett, is sent by President Grant (Greene) to persuade the citizens of Yucca Strip to vote for admittance into the Union. [British title: *Blue Clay*].

1878. The Son of Dr. Jekyll (10/31/51) B&W—77 mins. (Horror). *DIR:* Seymour Friedman. *SP:* Mortimer Braus, Jack Pollexfen. *CAST:* Louis Hayward, Jody Lawrence, Alexander Knox, Lester Matthews, Gavin Muir, Paul Cavanagh, Rhys Williams, Doris Lloyd, Claire Carleton, Patrick O'Moore, Robin Camp, Holmes Herbert, Wheaton Chambers, Olaf Hytten, Joyce Jameson, Robin Hughes, Frank Hagney, Guy Kingsford, Leonard Mudie.

The son (Hayward) of Dr. Jekyll sets out to prove that his father was a serious scientist and not a monster.

1879. The Son of Rusty (8/7/47) B&W — 69 mins. (Drama). DIR: Lew Landers. PRO: Wallace MacDonald. SP: Malcolm Stuart Boylan. Based on characters created by Al Martin. CAST: Ted Donaldson, Tom Powers, Stephen Dunne, Ann Doran, Thurston Hall, Matt Willis, Rudy Robles, Teddy Infuhr, Mickey McGuire, Dwayne Hickman, David Ackles, Harlan Briggs, Griff Barnett, "Flame," the dog.

A boy (Donaldson) gets involved with a soldier (Dunne) when the boy's dog falls in love with the soldier's dog.

1880. Song of Idaho (3/30/48) B&W — 69 mins. (Comedy). DIR: Ray Nazarro. PRO: Colbert Clark. SP: Barry Shipman. CAST: Kirby Grant, June Vincent, Tommy Ivo, Dorothy Vaughn, Eddie Acuff, Emory Parnell, Maudie Prickett, The Starlighters, The Sunshine Boys, The Sunshine Girls, The Hoosier Hotshots.

A hillbilly crooner (Grant) tries to get his show back on the air by winning over the sponsor's son (Ivo).

1881. Song of India (2/28/49) B&W — 77 mins. (Adventure). DIR/PRO: Albert S. Rogell. SP: Art Arthur, Kenneth Perkins. Story by Jerome Odlum. CAST: Sabu, Gail Russell, Turhan Bey, Anthony Caruso, Aminta Dyne, Fritz Leiber, Trevor Bardette, Robert H. Barrat, David Bond, Rodd Redwing, Ted Hecht.

An Indian prince (Bey) and princess (Russell), on a hunting expedition in a sacred jungle where hunting is forbidden, are stopped by a jungle native (Sabu).

1882. The Song of Love (11/25/29) B&W — 76 mins. (Musical). DIR: Erle C. Kenton. PRO: Harry Cohn. SP: Howard J. Green, Henry McCar-

thy, Dorothy Howell. Story by Norman Houston. CAST: Belle Baker, Ralph Graves, David Durand, Eve Arden, Arthur Housman, Charles Wilson.

A mother (Baker) breaks up the family act when she decides that her son (Durand) is lacking education but, when the father (Graves) strays, the son is responsible for getting everyone back together. NOTES: Released as both a silent and sound film.

1883. Song of the Prairie (9/27/45) B&W — 62 mins. (Western). DIR: Ray Nazarro. PRO: Colbert Clark. SP: J. Benton Cheney. CAST: Ken Curtis, June Storey, Andy Clyde, Guinn "Big Boy" Williams, Jeff Donnell, Grady Sutton, Robert Williams, Dick Curtis, John Tyrrell, Deuce Spriggins, Thurston Hall, Carolina Cotton, The Town Criers, The Hoosier Hotshots.

The Hoosier Hotshots help a rancher (Curtis), who wants to be a bandleader, open a show place. [British title: *Sentiment and Song*].

1884. A Song to Remember (8/16/44) Technicolor — 113 mins. (Biography-Musical). DIR: Charles Vidor. PRO: Louis F. Edelman. SP: Sidney Buchman. Story by Ernst Marischka. CAST: Paul Muni, Merle Oberon, Cornel Wilde, Stephen Bekassy, Nina Foch, George Coulouris, Sig Arno, Howard Freeman, George Macready, Claire DuBrey, Frank Puglia, Fern Emmett, Sybil Merritt, Ivan Triesault, Fay Helm, Charles Wagenheim, Paul Zaremba, Gregory Gay, Ian Wolfe, Darren McGavin, Eugene Borden.

The story of composer-pianist Frederic Chopin (Wilde), his struggle with his music teacher (Muni), and his encounter with novelist George Sand (Oberon). NOTES: Stephen Bekassy played the role of Franz Liszt.

1885. Song Without End (8/60) Technicolor/Scope — 145 mins. (Biography-Musical). *DIR*: Charles Vidor, George Cukor. *PRO*: William Goetz. *SP*: Oscar Millard. *CAST*: Dirk Bogarde, Capucine, Genevieve Page, Patricia Morison, Ivan Desny, Marita Hunt, Lou Jacobi, Albert Rueprecht, Marcel Dalio, Lyndon Brook, Walter Rilla, Alex Davion, Katherine Squire.

The story of composer-pianist Franz Liszt (Bogarde), his loves (Capucine, Page), and his decision to compose his own music. *NOTES*: George Cukor took over direction after Charles Vidor died in 1959; the film debut of Capucine; Alex Davion played the role of Chopin and Patricia Morison played the role of George Sand.

1886. The Song You Gave Me (8/33) B&W — 86 mins. (Musical). *DIR*: Paul Stein. *PRO*: John Maxwell. *SP*: Clifford Grey. Based on the play *The Song Is Ended* by Walter Reisch. A British International Production. *CAST*: Bebe Daniels, Victor Varconi, Claude Hulbert, Lester Matthews, Frederick Lloyd, Eva Moore, Iris Ashley, Walter Widdop.

A secretary (Daniels) is won over by a singer (Varconi). *NOTES*: The first British film distributed by Columbia in the U.S. with the Columbia logo.

1887. Sons of New Mexico (1/14/50) B&W — 71 mins. (Western). *DIR*: John English. *PRO*: Armand Schaefer. *SP*: Paul Gangelin. A Gene Autry Production. *CAST*: Gene Autry, Gail Davis, Robert Armstrong, Dick Jones, Frankie Darro, Clayton Moore, Russell Arms, Irving Bacon, Pierce Lyden, Kenne Duncan, Mary Blake, Sandy Sanders, Roy Gordon, Frankie Marvin, Paul Raymond, Harry Mackin, Bobby Clark, Gaylord Pendleton, Billy Lechner.

Gene sets out to lead a juvenile delinquent (Jones) on the right path and keep him from getting mixed up with a gambler (Armstrong). *NOTES*:

The first appearance of Gail Davis in a Gene Autry film. [British title: *The Brat*].

1888. Sotto ... Sotto (Softly ... Softly) (11/85) Eastman Color — 105 mins. (Drama-Comedy). *DIR*: Lina Wertmuller. *PRO*: Mario Cecchi Gori, Vittorio Cecchi Gori. *SP*: Lina Wertmuller, Enrico Oldoini. Story by Lena Wertmuller. An Intercapital-Triumph Films Production. *CAST*: Enrico Montesano, Veronica Lario, Luisa De Santis, Massimo Wertmuller, Mario Scarpetta, Isa Danieli, Elena Fabrizi, Antonia Dell'Atte, Renato D'Amore, Alfredo Bianchini.

A man (Montesano) suspects his wife (Lario) of having an affair and goes about trying to learn the identity of her lover. *NOTES*: Limited theatrical release; in Italian with English subtitles.

1889. The Soul of a Monster (8/17/44) B&W — 61 mins. (Mystery-Horror). *DIR*: Will Jason. *PRO*: Ted Richmond. *SP*: Edward Dein. *CAST*: Rose Hobart, George Macready, Jim Bannon, Jeanne Bates, Erik Rolf, Ernest Hilliard.

A doctor (Macready) is forced to perform evil deeds for a spiritualist (Hobart) while under her spell.

Sound of the City: London 1964-1973 *see* **Rock City**

1890. Sound Off (5/52) Super CineColor — 83 mins. (Comedy). *DIR*: Richard Quine. *PRO*: Jonie Taps. *SP*: Richard Quine, Blake Edwards. *CAST*: Mickey Rooney, Anne James, Sammy White, John Archer, Gordon Jones, Wally Cassell, Arthur Space, Pat Williams, Marshall Reed, Helen Ford, Mary Lou Geer, Boyd "Red" Morgan.

A nightclub singer (Rooney) finds himself inducted in the Army and gets involved in a series of scrapes before he is sent to entertain the troops.

1891. South American George (12/41) B&W—93 mins. (Comedy). *DIR:* Marcel Varnel. *PRO:* Ben Henry. *SP:* Leslie Arliss, Norman Lee, Austin Melford. A Columbia-British Production. *CAST:* George Formby, Linden Travers, Enid Stamp-Taylor, Jacques Brown, Felix Aylmer, Ronald Shiner, Alf Goddard, Gus McNaughton, Mavis Villiers, Eric Clavering, Beatrice Varley, Herbert Lomas, Muriel George, Cameron Hall, Charles Paton, Rita Grant, Norman Pierce.

A man (Formby) assumes the identity of a famous South American tenor (Formby), falls in love with the tenor's press agent (Travers), and is pursued by gangsters. *NOTES:* George Formby played a dual role in this film.

1892. South of Arizona (7/28/38) B&W—55 mins. (Western). *DIR:* Sam Nelson. *PRO:* Harry L. Decker. *SP:* Bennett R. Cohen. *CAST:* Charles Starrett, Iris Meredith, Bob Nolan, Dick Curtis, Robert Fiske, Dick Botiller, Lafe McKee, Ed Coxen, Art Mix, Edmund Cobb, Hank Bell, John Tyrrell, Hal Taliaferro (Wally Wales), Steve Clark, George Morrell, Sons of the Pioneers (Bob Nolan, Pat Brady, Hugh Farr, Karl Farr, Lloyd Perryman).

A cowboy (Starrett) breaks a vow of silence and exposes two killers (Fiske, Curtis).

1893. South of Death Valley (8/18/49) B&W—54 mins. (Western). *DIR:* Ray Nazarro. *PRO:* Colbert Clark. *SP:* Earle Snell. Story by James Gruen. *CAST:* Charles Starrett, Gail Davis, Smiley Burnette, Clayton Moore, Lee Roberts, Fred F. Sears, Jason Robards, Sr., Richard Emory, Tommy Duncan and His Western All Stars.

The Durango Kid (Starrett) prevents a range war between miners and ranchers and exposes the outlaws behind it. [British title: *River of Poison*].

1894. South of the Chisholm Trail (1/30/47) B&W—58 mins. (Western). *DIR:* Derwin Abrahams. *PRO:* Colbert Clark. *SP:* Michael L. Simmons. *CAST:* Charles Starrett, Nancy Saunders, Smiley Burnette, Frank Sully, Jack Ingram, George Chesebro, Jock Mahoney, Frank LaRue, Eddie Parker, Jim Diehl, Fred F. Sears, Victor Holbrook, Thomas Kingston, Hank Newman and the Georgia Crackers.

A cowboy (Starrett) goes to work for a rancher and organizes a large cattle drive north to Abilene, and as the Durango Kid, he stops cattle rustlers from getting the herd and prevents a robbery of the Cattleman's Association.

1895. South of the Rio Grande (3/5/32) B&W—61 mins. (Western). *DIR:* Lambert Hillyer. *PRO:* Irving Briskin. *SP:* Milton Krims. Story by Harold Shumate. *CAST:* Buck Jones, Mona Maris, Philo McCullough, Doris Hill, Paul Fix, George J. Lewis, Charles Reque, James Durkin, Harry Semels, Charles Stevens.

A Mexican Army captain (Jones) sets out to find those responsible for the murder of his brother (Fix). *NOTES:* Paul Fix reprises his earlier role from the 1931 Columbia film *The Avenger*.

1896. The Southern Star (5/69) Technicolor/Scope—105 mins. (Adventure). *DIR:* Sidney Hayers. *PRO:* Roger Duchet. *SP:* David Pursall, Jack Seddon. Based on *L'Etoile du Sud, le Pays des Diamants* by Jules Verne. *CAST:* George Segal, Ursula Andress, Orson Welles, Ian Hendry, Johnny Sekka, Michael Constantin, Harry Andrews, Georges Geret, Charles Lamb, Guy Delorme.

In Africa, a geologist (Segal), his

fiancee (Andress), and crooks go on a mad chase after a fabulous diamond, the "Southern Star," when it is stolen. [Original French title: *L'Etoile Du Sud*].

1897. Spacehunter: Adventures in the Forbidden Zone (5/83) Metrocolor/Twin Panavision/3-D—90 mins. (Science Fiction). *DIR*: Lamont Johnson. *PRO*: Don Carmody, Andre Link, John Dunning. *SP*: Edith Rey, David Preston, Dan Goldberg, Len Baum. Story by Stewart Harding, Jean La-Fleur. *CAST*: Peter Strauss, Molly Ringwald, Ernie Hudson, Andrea Marcovicci, Michael Ironside, Beeson Carroll, Deborah Pratt, Aleisa Shirley, Cali Timmins, Paul Boretski, Patrick Rowe, Reggie Bennett.

A mercenary salvage ship captain (Strauss) and his companion (Ringwald) go in search of three girls lost on planet Terra Eleven.

1898. Special Delivery (9/55) B&W—86 mins. (Comedy). *DIR*: John Brahm. *PRO*: Stuart Schulberg, Gilbert de Goldschmidt. *SP*: Dwight Taylor, Phil Reisman, Jr. Based on an idea by Geza Radvanyi. A Trans-Rhein Production. *CAST*: Joseph Cotten, Eva Bartok, Joerg Becker, Rene Deltgen, Bruni Loebel, Niall MacGinnis, Lexford Richards, Don Hanmer, Robert Cunningham, Gert Frobe, Ursula Herking.

A U.S. diplomat (Cotten), stationed behind the Iron Curtain, gets the responsibility of caring for a baby left at the embassy and runs into trouble when the local communist government wants the baby back. [Original German title: *Vom Himmel Gefallen*].

1899. Special Inspector (11/1/39) B&W—65 mins. (Crime). *DIR*: Leon Barsha. *PRO*: Kenneth J. Bishop. *SP*: Edgar Edwards. A Central Film Production. *CAST*: Charles Quigley, Rita Hayworth, George McKay, Edgar Ed-

wards, Eddie Laughton, Bob Rideout, Grant MacDonald, Bill Irving, Virginia Coomb, Fred Bass, Vincent McKenna, Don Douglas.

The sister (Hayworth) of a murdered trucker teams with a Treasury man (Quigley) to stop a gang of fur smugglers who kill truckers and transport the furs across the border. *NOTES*: This film, considered a turkey by Columbia, never officially had a release date in the United States. It was completed late in 1937 and released in England in 1938 as a "Syndicate Production distributed by Warwick Films." It played one downtown Los Angeles theater in 1939, double billed with an earlier 1937 Rita Hayworth film, Crescent Pictures' *Old Louisiana* (retitled *Louisiana Gal*). Both films were offered as first-run attractions to exploit Rita Hayworth's popularity.

1900. Speed Demon (12/30/32) B&W—64 mins. (Drama). *DIR*: D. Ross Lederman. *SP*: Charles R. Condon. *CAST*: William Collier, Jr., Joan Marsh, Wheeler Oakman, Robert Ellis, George Ernest, Frank Sheridan, Wade Boteler.

Barred from racing, a race car driver (Collier, Jr.) turns to a life of crime. He befriends an orphan (Ernest), and when the boy is kidnapped, he straightens himself out and goes to his rescue.

1901. Speed Mad (7/15/25) B&W—50 mins. (Drama). *DIR*: Jay Marchant. *PRO*: Harry Cohn. *SP*: Dorothy Howell. *CAST*: William Fairbanks, Edith Roberts, Lloyd Whitlock, Florence Lee, Melbourne MacDowell, John Fox, Jr., Charles K. French.

A speed-crazy youth (Fairbanks) wins a big race, saves his sweetheart's (Roberts) home from foreclosure, and wins the respect of his father (MacDowell).

1902. Speed to Spare (6/14/37) B&W — 60 mins. (Drama). *DIR:* Lambert Hillyer. *PRO:* Ralph Cohn. *SP:* Bert Granet, Lambert Hillyer. *CAST:* Charles Quigley, Dorothy Wilson, Eddie Nugent, Patricia Farr, Gene Morgan, John Gallaudet, Gordon (Bill) Elliott, Jack Gardner.

Two brothers (Quigley, Nugent), separated at birth, are reunited on the race track as professional drivers.

1903. Speed Wings (2/12/34) B&W — 60 mins. (Action). *DIR:* Otto Brower. *PRO:* Irving Briskin. *SP:* Horace McCoy. *CAST:* Tim McCoy, Evalyn Knapp, William Bakewell, Ward Bond, Vincent Sherman, Hooper Atchley, Jack Long, Ben Hewlett.

A pilot (McCoy) takes to the air to foil a kidnapping.

1904. Spin a Dark Web (10/56) B&W — 76 mins. (Crime). *DIR:* Vernon Sewell. *PRO:* George Maynard, M. J. Frankovich. *SP:* Ian Stuart Black. Based on *Wide Boys Never Work* by Robert Westerby. A Film Locations Production. *CAST:* Faith Domergue, Lee Patterson, Rona Anderson, Martin Benson, Robert Arden, Joss Ambler, Peter Hammond, Peter Burton, Sam Kydd, Russell Westwood, Patricia Ryan, Bernard Fox.

A man (Patterson) is seduced into a life of crime by the sister (Domergue) of a powerful mobster (Benson). [British title: *Soho Incident*].

1905. The Spirit of Stanford (10/8/42) B&W — 74 mins. (Drama). *DIR:* Charles Barton. *PRO:* Sam White. *SP:* Howard J. Green, William Brent, Nick Lucats. Story by Nick Lucats, William Brent. *CAST:* Frankie Albert, Marguerite Chapman, Matt Willis, Shirley Patterson, Kay Harris, Robert Stevens, Lloyd Bridges, Forrest Tucker, Billy Lechner, Harold Landon, Volta Boyer, Ernie Nevers, Dale Van Sickel, John Gallaudet, Arthur Loft, James Westerfield, Stanley Brown, Eddie Laughton, John Tyrrell, Ray Walker, Doodles Weaver, Frank Ferguson, Ralph Brooks, Lester Dorr, Knox Manning, Jack Gardner.

A football player (Albert) leaves college to turn professional, but returns to win the big game when his roommate cannot play.

1906. Spoilers of the Range (4/27/39) B&W — 57 mins. (Western). *DIR:* C. C. Coleman, Jr. *PRO:* Harry L. Decker. *SP:* Paul Franklin. *CAST:* Charles Starrett, Iris Meredith, Bob Nolan, Dick Curtis, Kenneth MacDonald, Forbes Murray, Edward J. LeSaint, Ethan Laidlaw, Charles Brinley, Edmund Cobb, Hank Bell, Art Mix, Joe Weaver, Horace B. Carpenter, Edward Piel, Sr., Sons of the Pioneers.

When a crooked gambler (MacDonald) tries to stop the local ranchers from getting their cattle to market to pay off a loan, a cowboy (Starrett) comes to their rescue.

1907. Sport of Kings (6/26/47) B&W — 68 mins. (Drama). *DIR:* Robert Gordon. *PRO:* William Bloom. *SP:* Edward Huebsch. Based on *Major Denning's Trust Estate* by Gordon Grand. *CAST:* Paul Campbell, Gloria Henry, Harry Davenport, Mark Dennis, Harry Cheshire, Clinton Rosemond, Louis Mason, Oscar O'Shea, Ernest Anderson.

Two Northerners (Campbell, Dennis) win a Kentucky plantation as settlement of a bet and have a rough time from the locals and the plantation owner (Davenport) until they enter his horse in a race and he wins. [British title: *Heart Royal*].

1908. The Sporting Age (3/2/28) B&W — 56 mins. (Drama). *DIR:* Erle C. Kenton. *PRO:* Harry Cohn. *SP:* Peter Milne, Elmer Harris. Story by Armand Kaliz. *CAST:* Belle Bennett,

Holmes Herbert, Carroll Nye, Josephine Borio.

A husband (Herbert) pretends to be blind so he can spy on his wife (Bennett) who is having an affair with his secretary (Nye). He later invites his niece (Borio) to live with them so that she will fall for the secretary and he and his wife can get back together.

1909. Spring Break (3/83) Metrocolor—101 mins. (Comedy). *DIR/PRO:* Sean S. Cunningham. *SP:* David Smilow. *CAST:* David Knell, Perry Lang, Paul Land, Steve Bassett, Jayne Modean, Corinne Alphen, Donald Symington, Mimi Cozzens, Jessica James, Daniel Faraldo, Richard B. Shull.

Four college students head to Ft. Lauderdale for spring break and find romance, while one of the students (Knell) tries to stay one step ahead of his stepfather (Symington).

Spy in the Pantry *see* **Missing Ten Days**

1910. Squadron of Honor (6/28/38) B&W—62 mins. (Crime). *DIR:* C. C. Coleman, Jr. *PRO:* Ralph Cohn. *SP:* Michael L. Simmons. Story by Martin Mooney. *CAST:* Don Terry, Mary Russell, Thurston Hall, Arthur Loft, Robert Warwick, Marc Lawrence, Dick Curtis, George McKay, Eddie Fetherstone, Edward J. LeSaint, Ivan Miller, Harry Strang.

At an American Legion convention, Legionnaires come to the aid of the Legion commander (Hall) when he is accused of murder by a crooked armament manufacturer (Warwick).

1911. Square Shooter (1/21/35) B&W—57 mins. (Western). *DIR:* David Selman. *SP:* Harold Shumate. *CAST:* Tim McCoy, Jacqueline Wells (Julie Bishop), Erville Alderson, Charles Middleton, John Darrow, J.

Farrell MacDonald, Wheeler Oakman, Steve Clark, William V. Mong.

A cowboy (McCoy) returns home after five years in prison to find those who framed him.

1912. The Squealer (9/14/30) B&W—67 mins. (Crime-Drama). *DIR:* Harry Joe Brown. *PRO:* Harry Cohn. *SP:* Dorothy Howell, Casey Robinson, Jo Swerling. Story by Mark Linder. *CAST:* Jack Holt, Dorothy Revier, Davey Lee, Matt Moore, Zasu Pitts, Robert Ellis, Mathew Betz, Arthur Housman, Louis Natheaux, Eddie Kane, Eddie Sturges, Elmer Ballard.

A gangster (Holt), believing that his pal (Moore) turned him in to the cops, breaks out of jail to get revenge and learns that it was his wife (Revier) who squealed on him to protect him from a rival mob. He sacrifices his life when he realizes that his son (Lee) will be better off with his wife and his pal. *NOTES:* Portions of the script were used for the 1937 MGM film *The Last Gangster.*

1913. Stage Kisses (11/2/27) B&W—56 mins. (Drama). *DIR:* Albert Kelly. *PRO:* Harry Cohn. *SP:* Dorothy Howell. Story by L. A. Brown. *CAST:* Kenneth Harlan, Helene Chadwick, John Patrick, Phillips Smalley, Ethel Wales, Frances Raymond.

A chorus girl (Chadwick) causes her husband's (Harlan) parents to disinherit him but in the end she wins them over and all is forgiven.

1914. Stage to Tucson (12/50) Technicolor—82 mins. (Western). *DIR:* Ralph Murphy. *PRO:* Harry Joe Brown. *SP:* Bob Williams, Frank Burke, Robert Libott. Based on *Lost Stage Valley* by Frank Bonham. *CAST:* Rod Cameron, Kay Buckley, Wayne Morris, Sally Eilers, Roy Roberts, Carl Benton Reid, Harry Bellaver, Douglas Fowley, John Pickard, Olin

Howlin, Boyd Stockman, John Sheehan, Reed Howes, James Kirkwood.

During the Civil War, Union agents (Cameron, Morris) are sent to investigate the theft of government stagecoaches by a Southern sympathizer (Roberts). [British title: *Lost Stage Valley*].

1915. Stagecoach Days (6/20/38) B&W — 58 mins. (Western). *DIR:* Joseph Levering. *PRO:* Larry Darmour. *SP:* Nate Gatzert. *CAST:* Jack Luden, Eleanor Stewart, Harry Woods, Slim Whitaker, Jack Ingram, Hal Taliaferro (Wally Wales), Lafe McKee, Bob Kortman, Dick Botiller, Blackjack Ward.

A cowboy (Luden) helps a girl (Stewart) secure a mail contract by winning a stagecoach race.

1916. Stampede   (11/27/36) B&W — 58 mins. (Western). *DIR:* Ford Beebe. *SP:* Robert Watson. Story by Peter B. Kyne. *CAST:* Charles Starrett, Finis Barton, J. P. McGowan, LeStrange Millman, James McGrath, Arthur Kerr, Jack Atkinson, Michael Heppell, Ted Mapes, Reginald Hincks.

A rancher (Starrett) goes after those responsible for the murder of his brother.

1917. Stand by All Networks (10/29/42) B&W — 64 mins. (Drama). *DIR:* Lew Landers. *PRO:* Jack Fier. *SP:* Maurice Tombragel, Doris Malloy, Robert Lee Johnson. Story by Maurice Tombragel. *CAST:* John Beal, Florence Rice, Alan Baxter, Margaret Hayes, Lloyd Bridges.

A radio announcer (Beal) exposes a group of fifth columnists.

1918. Stand by Me (7/86) Technicolor/Panavision — 87 mins. (Comedy-Drama). *DIR:* Rob Reiner. *PRO:* Andrew Scheinmann, Bruce A. Evans, Raynold Gideon. *SP:* Raynold Gideon, Bruce A. Evans. Based on the novella *The Body* by Stephen King. An Act III

Production. *CAST:* Wil Wheaton, River Phoenix, Corey Feldman, Jerry O'Connell, Richard Dreyfuss, Kiefer Sutherland, Casey Siemaszko, Gary Riley, Bradley Gregg, John Cusack, Jason Oliver, Marshall Bell, Frances Lee McCain, Bruce Kirby.

When a writer (Dreyfuss) learns of a friend's death, he reminisces about the summer in 1959 when he (Wheaton) and his friends (Phoenix, Feldman, O'Connell) journeyed across the countryside to see a corpse, and through their adventures together, became even closer.

1919. Stand Up and Be Counted (5/72) Eastman Color — 99 mins. (Comedy-Drama). *DIR:* Jackie Cooper. *PRO:* M. J. Frankovich. *SP:* Bernard Slade. *CAST:* Jacqueline Bisset, Stella Stevens, Steve Lawrence, Gary Lockwood, Lee Purcell, Loretta Swit, Hector Elizondo, Anne Francine, Madlyn Rhue, Alex Wilson, Michael Ansara, Dr. Joyce Brothers, Jessica Rains, Meredith Baxter Birney, Gregg Mullavey, Nancy Walker, Jeff Donnell, Kathleen Freeman, Edith Atwater.

A magazine journalist (Bisset) is dispatched to Denver to cover the Women's Liberation movement in the area. *NOTES:* Jackie Cooper's debut as a director.

1920. Stardust (3/75) Eastman Color — 111 mins. (Drama). *DIR:* Michael Apted. *PRO:* David Puttnam, Sandford Lieberson. *SP:* Ray Connolly. A Nat Cohen-EMI-Goodtimes Enterprises Production. *CAST:* David Essex, Adam Faith, Larry Hagman, Keith Moon, Marty Wilde, Paul Nicholas, Dave Edmunds, Karl Howman, Peter Duncan, Edd Byrnes, Rosalind Ayres, James Hazeldine, Claire Russell, John Normington, Ines Des Longchamps.

A pop star (Essex) cannot cope with

fame and success and sinks slowly into the world of drugs. NOTES: A sequel to the 1973 EMI film *That'll Be the Day*.

1921. Starman (12/84) MGM Color/Panavision—115 mins. (Science Fiction-Romance). *DIR*: John Carpenter. *PRO*: Larry J. Franco. *SP*: Bruce A. Evans, Raynold Gideon. *CAST*: Jeff Bridges, Karen Allen, Charles Martin Smith, Richard Jaeckel, Robert Phalen, Tony Edwards, John Walter Davis, Dirk Blocker, Ted White, Lu Leonard, Russ Benning.

When an alien (Bridges) arrives on Earth and assumes the form of a woman's (Allen) dead husband, she finds herself becoming attracted to him as they travel cross country so he can rendezvous with his mother ship.

1922. Stars and Bars (3/88) Eastman Color—94 mins. (Comedy). *DIR*: Pat O'Conner. *PRO*: Sandy Lieberson. *SP*: William Boyd. Based on the book by William Boyd. *CAST*: Daniel Day Lewis, Harry Dean Stanton, Kent Broadhurst, Maury Chaykin, Matthew Cowles, Joan Cusack, Spalding Gray, Glenne Headly, Laurie Metcalf, Will Patton.

A British art expert (Lewis), newly arrived in America, is sent to a Southern plantation to purchase a long-lost painting of Renoir from an eccentric (Stanton) and winds up in a series of misadventures. NOTES: Limited theatrical release.

1923. Stars on Parade (5/25/44) B&W—63 mins. (Musical). *DIR*: Lew Landers. *PRO*: Wallace MacDonald. *SP*: Monte Brice. *CAST*: Larry Parks, Lynn Merrick, Ray Walker, Jeff Donnell, Robert Williams, Selmer Jackson, Edythe Elliott, Mary Currier, Danny O'Neil, Frank Hubert, Jean Hubert, The Chords, The Nat "King" Cole Trio, The Ben Carter Choir.

Two Hollywood hopefuls (Parks, Merrick) try to convince Los Angeles producers of the talent in their own town.

1924. Start Cheering (3/3/38) B&W—78 mins. (Musical-Comedy). *DIR*: Albert S. Rogell. *PRO*: Nat Perrin. *SP*: Eugene Solow, Philip Rapp, Richard E. Wormser. Story by Corey Ford. *CAST*: Jimmy Durante, Joan Perry, Walter Connolly, Charles Starrett, Edward Earle, Broderick Crawford, Ernest Truex, Minerva Urecal, Raymond Walburn, Virginia Dale, The Three Stooges (Moe Howard, Larry Fine, Curly Howard), Charley Chase, Louise Stanley, Gertrude Niesen, Hal LeRoy, Jimmy Wallington, Romo Vincent, Gene Morgan, Arthur Hoyt, Howard Hickman, Arthur Loft, Nick Lucats, Dr. Craig E. Earle (Professor Quiz), Louis Prima and His Band, Johnny Green and His Orchestra.

When a matinee idol (Starrett) decides to quit the screen and go back to campus for a rest, his sidekick (Durante) and manager (Connolly) try to convince him to come back to acting.

1925. State Penitentiary (6/8/50) B&W—66 mins. (Drama-Crime). *DIR*: Lew Landers. *PRO*: Sam Katzman. *SP*: Howard J. Green, Robert Libott, Frank Burt. Story by Henry E. Helseth. *CAST*: Warner Baxter, Onslow Stevens, Karin Booth, Robert Shayne, Richard Benedict, Brett King, John Bleifer, Leo T. Cleary, Rick Vallin, William Fawcett, Rusty Wescoatt, John Hart.

An airplane engineer (Baxter), falsely imprisoned for embezzlement, escapes from prison, and with his wife (Booth), goes after the real culprit (Shayne). NOTES: Photographed on location at the Nevada State Penitentiary. Warner Baxter's last film.

1926. State Trooper (3/27/33) B&W – 68 mins. (Crime-Drama). *DIR:* D. Ross Lederman. *SP:* Stuart Anthony. Story by Lambert Hillyer. *CAST:* Regis Toomey, Evalyn Knapp, Raymond Hatton, Mathew Betz, Edwin Maxwell, Walter McGrail, Lew Kelley, Don Chapman, Eddie Chandler.

A motorcycle cop (Toomey) goes to work for an oil tycoon (Maxwell) and stops a sabotage plot by his general manager (McGrail).

1927. Steaming (4/85) Eastman Color – 96 mins. (Drama). *DIR:* Joseph Losey. *PRO:* Paul Mills. *SP:* Patricia Losey. Based on the play by Nell Dunn. A World Film Services Production. *CAST:* Vanessa Redgrave, Sarah Miles, Diana Dors, Patti Love, Brenda Bruce, Felicity Dean, Sally Sagoe.

Women in a rundown steambath open up their private lives to each other. *NOTES:* Limited theatrical release.

1928. The Stepford Wives (2/75) TVC Color – 114 mins. (Science Fiction). *DIR:* Bryan Forbes. *PRO:* Edgar J. Scherick. *SP:* William Goldman. Based on the book by Ira Levin. A Palomar Pictures International Production. *CAST:* Katharine Ross, Paula Prentiss, Peter Masterson, Nanette Newman, Patrick O'Neal, Tina Louise, Carol Rosson, William Prince, Paula Trueman, Remak Ramsay, John Aprea, Carole Mallory, Judith Baldwin, Toni Reid, Barbara Rucker, George Coe, Michael Higgins, Joanna Cassidy, Simon Deckard, Josef Sommer, Martha Greenhouse.

Two suburban housewives (Ross, Prentiss) try to find out why the wives in Stepford, Connecticut, are perfect in every respect. *NOTES:* Followed by two television movies, *Revenge of the Stepford Wives,* 1980, and *The Stepford Children,* 1987.

1929. The Steppe (10/63) Eastman Color/Scope – 100 mins. (Drama). *DIR:* Alberto Lattuada. *PRO:* Moris Ergas. *SP:* Enzo Currelli, Tullio Pinelli, Alberto Lattuada. Based on the book by Anton Chekhov. A Zebra-Aera-Royal Films International Production. *CAST:* Daniele Spallone, Pavle Vujisic, Charles Vanel, Milan Bosiljcic, Marina Vlady, Pero Kvrgic, Hermina Pipinic, Marianna Leibl, Cristina Gajoni, Milan Djurdjevic, Ljuba Tadic, Michele Bally, Milorad Majic, Fernando Cicero, Natasia Petrovna.

A young man (Spallone) experiences many adventures as he journeys with his father and uncle from his Russian farm to the city, where he will go to school. [Original French title: *La Steppe*]. [Original Italian title: *La Steppa*].

1930. Steppin' Out (10/15/25) B&W – 57 mins. (Comedy). *DIR:* Frank R. Strayer. *PRO:* Harry Cohn. *SP:* George Verhouse. *CAST:* Dorothy Revier, Ford Sterling, Robert Agnew, Cissy Fitzgerald, Ethel Wales.

Complications develop when a secretary (Revier) poses as the wife of her boss (Angew).

1931. Stewardess School (8/86) DeLuxe Color/Panavision – 84 mins. (Comedy). *DIR/SP:* Ken Blancato. *PRO:* Phil Feldman. A Summa Entertainment Group-Columbia-Delphi V Production. *CAST:* Brett Cullen, Mary Cadorette, Donny Most, Sandahl Bergman, Wendie Jo Sperber, Judy Landers, Dennis Burkley, Julia Montgomery, Vicki Frederick, Corinne Bohrer, Rob Paulsen.

A group of misfits, after failing at their regular occupations, decide to enroll in flight attendant school.

1932. Stir Crazy (12/80) Metrocolor – 114 mins. (Comedy). *DIR:* Sidney Poitier. *PRO:* Hannah Weinstein.

328 The Columbia Checklist

SP: Bruce Jay Friedman. *CAST:* Gene Wilder, Richard Pryor, Georg Stanford Brown, JoBeth Williams, Craig T. Nelson, Barry Corbin, Charles Weldon, Nicolas Coster, Joel Brooks, Lee Purcell, Esther Sutherland, Erland Van Lidth de Jeude.

Two losers (Pryor, Wilder), on their way to California, get mistaken for robbers and land in prison where they plot their escape.

1933. Stolen Pleasures (1/5/27) B&W—58 mins. (Drama). *DIR:* Philip E. Rosen. *PRO:* Harry Cohn. *SP:* Leah Baird. *CAST:* Helene Chadwick, Gayne Whitman, Dorothy Revier, Ray Ripley, Harlan Tucker.

After two married couples separate, the husband (Ripley) of one winds up with the wife (Chadwick) of the other, gets stranded at a roadhouse during a storm, and there sees his wife (Revier) with another man (Tucker).

1934. The Stone Killer (8/73) Technicolor—95 mins. (Crime-Action). *DIR/PRO:* Michael Winner. *SP:* Gerald Wilson. Based on *A Complete State of Death* by John Gardner. A Dino De Laurentiis Presentation. *CAST:* Charles Bronson, Martin Balsam, David S. Sheiner, Norman Fell, Ralph Waite, Eddie Firestone, Walter Burke, David Moody, Stuart Margolin, John Ritter, Alfred Ryder, Paul Koslo, Charles Tyner, Frank Campanella, Robert Emhardt, Kelly Miles.

A former New York cop (Bronson) works with the Los Angeles police to find out why an underworld kingpin (Balsam) is recruiting Vietnam veterans.

1935. Stool Pigeon (10/25/28) B&W—56 mins. (Crime). *DIR:* Renaud Hoffman. *PRO:* Harry Cohn. *SP:* Stuart Anthony. Story by Edward Meagher. *CAST:* Olive Borden,

Charles Delaney, Lucy Beaumont, Louis Natheaux.

A young man (Delany) joins a criminal gang and creates trouble when he falls for the gang leader's girl (Borden).

1936. Stop! Look! and Laugh! (7/60) B&W—78 mins. (Comedy). *DIR:* Jules White, Edward Bernds, Charley Chase, Del Lord. *PRO:* Harry Romm. *SP:* Felix Adler, Edward Bernds, Clyde Bruckman, Monty Collins, Al Giebler, Thea Goodman, Searle Kramer, Zion Meyers, Elwood Ullman, Saul Ward, Jack White. *CAST:* Paul Winchell, Jerry Mahoney, The Marquis Chimps, The Three Stooges (Moe Howard, Larry Fine, Curly Howard).

Ventriloquist Paul Winchell and his dummy, Jerry Mahoney, along with the Marquis Chimps, link together ten "Three Stooges" shorts.

1937. Stop Me Before I Kill (6/61) B&W/Scope—109 mins. (Mystery-Drama). *DIR/PRO:* Val Guest. *SP:* Ronald Scott Thorn, Val Guest. Based on *The Full Treatment* by Robert Scott Thorn. A Hilary-Falcon-Hammer Production. *CAST:* Claude Dauphin, Diane Cilento, Ronald Lewis, Francoise Rosay, Katya Douglas, Bernard Braden, Barbara Chilcott, Ann Tirard, Edwin Styles, George Merritt.

A psychiatrist (Dauphin) tries to convince a mentally unstable man (Lewis) that he is trying to kill his wife (Cilento). [British title: *The Full Treatment*].

1938. The Stork Pays Off (11/12/41) B&W—68 mins. (Comedy). *DIR:* Lew Landers. *PRO:* Jack Fier. *SP:* Fanya Foss, Aleen Leslie. *CAST:* Victor Jory, Rochelle Hudson, Maxie Rosenbloom, Horace MacMahon, George McKay, Ralf Harolde, Danny Mummert, Arthur Loft, Bonnie Irma Dane.

A gangster (Jory) and his men are inadvertently put in charge of a day care center, which leads to their reformation and his becoming a city alderman.

1939. Storm Center (9/56) B&W—85 mins. (Drama). *DIR:* Daniel Taradash. *PRO:* Julian Blaustein. *SP:* Daniel Taradash, Elick Moll. A Phoenix Production. *CAST:* Bette Davis, Brian Keith, Kim Hunter, Paul Kelly, Kevin Coughlin, Joe Mantell, Sallie Brophy, Howard Wierum, Curtis Cooksey, Michael Raffetto, Edward Platt, Kathryn Grant, Howard Wendell, Burt Mustin, Edith Evanson, Joseph Kearns.

A librarian (Davis) creates a storm of controversy when she refuses to remove a book entitled "The Communist Dream" from her library shelves.

1940. Storm Over the Nile (6/56) Technicolor/Scope—107 mins. (Adventure). *DIR:* Zoltan Korda, Terence Young. *PRO:* Zoltan Korda. *SP:* R. C. Sheriff. Based on the screenplay by R. C. Sheriff, Lajos Biro, Arthur Wimperis, and based on *The Four Feathers* by A. E. W. Mason. A London Films Production. *CAST:* Laurence Harvey, Anthony Steel, James Robertson Justice, Geoffrey Keen, Ronald Lewis, Ian Carmichael, Michael Hordern, Jack Lambert, Mary Ure, Christopher Lee, Ferdy Mayne, John Wynne, Avis Scott, Roger Delgado.

A British officer (Steel) resigns his commission before his unit is shipped to the Sudan. He is given a single feather by each of his fellow officers (Harvey, Carmichael, Lewis) and his fiancée (Ure), a symbol of cowardice. He decides to prove his bravery by going to the Sudan, assuming native garb, and saving the lives of his fellow officers. *NOTES:* A remake of 1939 United Artists film *The Four Feathers.* Footage from the 1939 film was incorporated in this film version.

1941. Storm Over Tibet (7/52) B&W—87 mins. (Action). *DIR:* Andrew Marton. *PRO:* Ivan Tors, Laslo Benedek. *SP:* Ivan Tors, Sam Meyer. A Summit Production. *CAST:* Rex Reason, Diana Douglas, Myron Healey, Robert Karnes, Strother Martin, Harold Fong, Harald Dyrenforth, Jarmila Marton, William Schallert, John Dodsworth.

A pilot (Reason) steals a sacred mask from a Tibetan temple only to learn it is cursed and is believed to have caused the death of his fellow flier (Healey). *NOTES:* In 1936, Andrew Marton and his wife shot a documentary of the first Himalayan expedition entitled *Demon of the Himalayas.* This film was seen only in Germany by a limited audience and the war wiped out any trace of it. After the war, Mr. Marton located the negative, culled fifty minutes of footage from it, and released it with the above title. It was later re-released in August 1953, under the new title *Mask of the Himalayas.*

1942. The Story of Esther Costello (10/57) B&W—104 mins. (Drama). *DIR:* David Miller. *PRO:* Jack Clayton, David Miller. *SP:* Charles Kaufman. Based on the book by Nicholas Monsarrat. A Romulus-Valiant Production. *CAST:* Joan Crawford, Rosanno Brazzi, Heather Sears, Lee Patterson, Ron Randell, Fay Compton, John Loder, Denis O'Dea, Sidney James, Bessie Love, Robert Ayres, Maureen Delaney, Estelle Brody, June Clyde, Sally Smith, Megs Jenkins, Andrew Cruickshank, Diana Day, Victor Rietti, Sheila Manahan, Tony Quinn, Janina Faye.

A traumatic blind and deaf girl (Sears) is cared for by an American socialite (Crawford), but when her husband (Brazzi) rapes the girl, the girl is shocked back to reality and is able to see and communicate. The girl then leaves with the man (Patterson) who loves her and the wife gets revenge by killing herself and her husband in an auto accident.

1943. Straightaway (1/2/34) B&W — 60 mins. (Crime-Action). DIR: Otto Brower. PRO: Irving Briskin. SP: Lambert Hillyer. CAST: Tim McCoy, Sue Carol, William Bakewell, Ward Bond, Samuel S. Hinds, Francis McDonald, Arthur Rankin, Charles Sullivan.

A race driver (McCoy) is threatened to be charged with murder if his kid brother (Bakewell) wins the big race.

1944. Strait-Jacket (1/64) B&W — 89 mins. (Horror). DIR/PRO: William Castle. SP: Robert Bloch. CAST: Joan Crawford, Diane Baker, Leif Erickson, Howard St. John, John Anthony Hayes, Rochelle Hudson, George Kennedy, Edith Atwater, Mitchell Cox, Lee Yeary, Patricia Krest, Vickie Cos.

An axe-murderess (Crawford), released after twenty years in an asylum, returns home to her daughter (Baker) and the axe murders begin again. NOTES: William Castle's gimmick for this film was to have selected theaters give patrons cardboard axes.

1945. Strange Affair (10/5/44) B&W — 78 mins. (Mystery). DIR: Alfred E. Green. PRO: Burt Kelly. SP: Oscar Saul, Eva Greene, Jerome Odlum. Based on *Stalk the Hunter* by Oscar Saul. CAST: Allyn Joslyn, Evelyn Keyes, Marguerite Chapman, Edgar Buchanan, Nina Foch, Hugo Haas, Shemp Howard, Frank Jenks, Erwin Kalser, Tonio Selwart, John Wengraf, Erik Rolf, Carole Mathews, Edgar Dearing, Ray Teal.

A cartoonist (Joslyn), who enjoys being an amateur detective and proving the police wrong, sets out to prove that the death of a fund raiser (Kalser) was murder.

1946. The Strange Case of Dr. Meade (1/26/39) B&W — 64 mins. (Drama). DIR: Lewis D. Collins. PRO: Larry Darmour. SP: Gordon Rigby. Story by Gordon Rigby, Carleton Sand. CAST: Jack Holt, Beverly Roberts, Noah Beery, Jr., John Qualen, Paul Everton, Charles Middleton, Helen Jerome Eddy, Arthur Aylesworth, Barbara Pepper, Vic Potel, Harry Woods, George Cleveland, Claire DuBrey, Jay Walter Ward, Hollis Jewell.

A New York doctor (Holt), on vacation in the hills, saves many lives during a typhoid epidemic when the country doctor (Everton) wants to use herbs to fight it.

1947. Strange Fascination (12/52) B&W — 80 mins. (Drama). DIR/PRO/SP: Hugo Haas. CAST: Cleo Moore, Hugo Haas, Mona Barrie, Rick Vallin, Karen Sharpe, Marc Krah, Genevieve Aumont, Patrick Holmes, Maura Murphy, Brian O'Hara, Anthony Jochim, Gayne Whitman, Roy Engel, Robert Knapp.

A concert pianist (Haas) loses his money, his backer (Barrie), and his wife (Moore), and when he mangles his hands to collect the insurance on them, he loses that also and ends up playing piano one-handed in a dive.

1948. The Strange One (5/57) B&W — 100 mins. (Drama). DIR: Jack Garfein. PRO: Sam Spiegel. SP: Calder Willingham. Based on *End as a Man* by Calder Willingham. A Horizon Production. CAST: Ben Gazzara, Pat Hingle, Peter Mark Richman, Arthur Storch, Paul Richards, Larry Gates, Clifton James, Geoffrey Horne, James Olson, Julie Wilson, George Peppard.

A student leader (Gazzara) at a Southern military academy wields his power over the other students and faculty. [British title: *End as a Man*].

1949. The Stranger (12/87) De-Luxe Color—88 mins. (Crime-Drama). *DIR:* Adolfo Aristarain. *PRO:* Hugo Lamonica. *SP:* Dan Gurkis. A Tusi-tala-Nolin Co. Production. *CAST:* Bonnie Bedelia, Peter Riegert, Barry Primus, David Spielberg, Marcos Woinski, Julio de Grazia, Cecila Roth.

A psychiatrist (Riegert) probes the mind of an amnesiac witness (Bedelia) to a triple murder in order to learn what it was she actually saw.

1950. The Stranger and the Gunfighter (4/76) Technicolor/Pana-vision—107 mins. (Western). *DIR:* Anthony Dawson. *PRO:* Run Run Shaw, Gustave Berne. *SP:* Barth Jules Sussman. A Shaw Bros.-Compagnia Cinematografica Champion-Midega Film-Harbor Production. *CAST:* Lee Van Cleef, Lo Leih, Karen Yeh, Julian Ugarte, Goyo Peralto, Al Tung, Paty Shepard, Erika Blanc, Georges Rigaud, Richard Palacios, Alfred Boreman, Bart Barry, Paul Costello.

A gunfighter (Van Cleef) searches for hidden treasure by locating the map which has been tatooed on the backs of four women.

1951. The Stranger from Arizona (11/22/38) B&W—54 mins. (Western). *DIR:* Elmer Clifton. *PRO/SP:* Monroe Shaff. *CAST:* Buck Jones, Dorothy Fay, Hank Mann, Roy Barcroft, Hank Worden, Bob Terry, Horace Murphy, Budd Buster, Stanley Blystone, Ralph Peters, Dot Farley, Walter Anthony, Loren Riebe, Horace B. Carpenter.

A cowboy (Jones) helps a rancher (Fay) whose cattle are being rustled.

1952. The Stranger from Ponca City (7/3/47) B&W—56 mins. (Western). *DIR:* Derwin Abrahams. *PRO:* Colbert Clark. *SP:* Ed Earl Repp. *CAST:* Charles Starrett, Virginia Hunter, Smiley Burnette, Paul Campbell, Jock Mahoney, Jim Diehl, Ted Mapes, Forrest Taylor, Tom McDonough, John Carpenter, Bud Osborne, Charles Hamilton, Texas Jim Lewis and His Lone Star Cowboys.

The Durango Kid (Starrett) helps to clean up a town split in half by honest businessmen and criminal elements.

1953. The Stranger from Texas (12/18/39) B&W—54 mins. (Western). *DIR:* Sam Nelson. *PRO:* Harry L. Decker. *SP:* Paul Franklin. Based on *The Mysterious Avenger* by Ford Beebe. *CAST:* Charles Starrett, Lorna Gray, Bob Nolan, Dick Curtis, Edmund Cobb, Richard Fiske, Al Bridge, Jack Rockwell, Hal Taliaferro (Wally Wales), Edward J. LeSaint, Art Mix, George Chesebro, Buel Bryant.

A cowboy (Starrett) prevents a range war by bringing to justice the outlaws responsible for looting the local ranches. [British title: *The Stranger*].

1954. The Stranger Wore a Gun (8/53) Technicolor/3-D—83 mins. (Western). *DIR:* Andre De Toth. *PRO:* Harry Joe Brown, Randolph Scott. *SP:* Kenneth Gamet. Based on *Yankee Gold* by John Cunningham. A Scott-Brown Production. *CAST:* Randolph Scott, Claire Trevor, Joan Weldon, George Macready, Alfonso Bedoya, Lee Marvin, Ernest Borgnine, Pierre Watkin, Clem Bevans, Roscoe Ates, Franklyn Farnum, Frank Ellis, Francis McDonald, Terry Frost, Richard Benjamin, Harry Seymour, Joseph Vitale, Paul Maxey, Frank Scannell, Reed Howes, Edward Earle, Guy Wilkerson, Mary Newton, Mary Lou Holloway, Barry Brooks, Tap Canutt, Al Haskell, Frank Hagney, Phil Tulley, Al Hill, Harry Mendoza, Diana Dawson, Herbert Rawlinson, Britt Wood, James Millican, Jack Woody, Rudy Germaine, Rayford Barnes, Edith Evanson, Guy Teague.

After serving as a spy for Quantrill during the Civil War, a cowboy (Scott) heads for Arizona. He joins forces with an outlaw (Macready) to rob a gold shipment, but decides to go straight and pits the outlaw against a Mexican bandit (Bedoya), and finally, kills the outlaw in a gun duel.

1955. Strangers When We Meet (7/60) Eastman Color/Scope—117 mins. (Drama). *DIR/PRO:* Richard Quine. *SP:* Evan Hunter. Based on the book by Evan Hunter. A Bryna-Quine Production. *CAST:* Kirk Douglas, Kim Novak, Ernie Kovacs, Barbara Rush, Walter Matthau, Virginia Bruce, Kent Smith, Helen Gallagher, John Bryant, Roberta Shore, Nancy Kovack, Carol Douglas, Paul Picerni, Ernest Sarracino, Harry Jackson, Betsy Jones Moreland, Sue Anne Langdon, Dick Crockett, Ray Ferrell, Douglas Holmes, Audrey Swanson, Bart Patton, Robert Sampson.

An architect (Douglas), tiring of his marriage, has an affair with a married woman (Novak).

1956. The Stranglers of Bombay (7/60) B&W/Scope—80 mins. (Horror-Drama). *DIR:* Terence Fisher. *PRO:* Anthony Hinds. *SP:* David Zelag Goodman. A Hammer Production. *CAST:* Guy Rolfe, Allan Cuthbertson, Andrew Cruickshank, Marne Maitland, George Pastell, Jan Holden, Paul Stassino, Tutte Lemkow, David Spenser, Margaret Gordon, Roger Delgado, Michael Nightingale, Marie Devereux.

In 1820 India, two British officers (Rolfe, Cuthbertson) set out to break the Kali-worshipping cult of the Thugee.

1957. The Strawberry Roan (8/15/48) CineColor—79 mins. (Western). *DIR:* John English. *PRO:* Armand Schaefer. *SP:* Dwight Cummins, Dorothy Yost. Story by Julian Zimet. A Gene Autry Production. *CAST:* Gene Autry, Gloria Henry, Pat

Buttram, Jack Holt, Dick Jones, Jack Ingram, Eddy Waller, Ted Mapes, Sam Flint, John McGuire, Rufe Davis, Rodd Harper, Eddie Parker.

When the son (Jones) of a rancher (Holt) is injured by a wild horse, Gene saves the horse from the wrath of the rancher, and helps his son to ride again. *NOTES:* Gene Autry's first color western and his first picture with Pat Buttram. This film also marked Jack Holt's return to Columbia after an absence of 7 years, and was his first Columbia feature to be cast in a co-starring role. [British title: *Fools Awake*].

1958. Street of Illusion (9/3/28) B&W—65 mins. (Drama). *DIR:* Erle C. Kenton. *PRO:* Harry Cohn. *SP:* Dorothy Howell, Harvey Thew. Story by Channing Pollack. *CAST:* Virginia Valli, Ian Keith, Henry Meyers, Kenneth Thompson.

An egotistical actor (Keith) substitutes real bullets for prop bullets when he finds his leading lady (Valli) in the arms of another man (Thompson).

Street of Missing Women *see* **Cafe Hostess**

1959. Streets of Ghost Town (8/3/50) B&W—54 mins. (Western). *DIR:* Ray Nazarro. *PRO:* Colbert Clark. *SP:* Barry Shipman. *CAST:* Charles Starrett, Mary Ellen Kay, Smiley Burnette, Stanley Andrews, John Cason, Frank Fenton, George Chesebro, Jack Ingram, Don Kay Reynolds, Ozie Waters and His Colorado Rangers.

The Durango Kid (Starrett) and a sheriff (Andrews) help a boy (Reynolds) and his sister (Kay) locate a million dollars in stolen money in an old ghost town.

1960. Stripes (6/81) Metrocolor—106 mins. (Comedy). *DIR:* Ivan Reitman. *PRO:* Ivan Reitman, Dan Goldberg. *SP:* Len Blum, Dan Goldberg,

Harold Ramis. CAST: Bill Murray, Harold Ramis, Warren Oates, P. J. Soles, Sean Young, John Larroquette, John Volstad, John Diehl, Judge Reinhold, Robert Klein, Robert J. Wilke, Lance LeGault, Roberta Leighton, Conrad Dunn, Antone Pagan.

A New York cab driver (Murray) and his pal (Ramis) join the Army and end up in a misfit platoon, commanded by a tough drill sergeant (Oates).

1961. A Study in Terror (4/66) Eastman Color–95 mins. (Mystery). DIR: James Hill. PRO: Henry E. Lester. SP: Donald and Derek Ford. Based on characters created by Sir Arthur Conan Doyle. A Compton-Tekli-Planet-Sir Nigel Production. CAST: John Neville, Donald Houston, John Fraser, Anthony Quayle, Robert Morley, Barbara Windsor, Adrienne Corri, Frank Finlay, Judi Dench, Cecil Parker, Georgia Brown, Barry Jones, Kay Walsh, Edina Ronay, Terry Downes.

Sherlock Holmes (Neville) and Dr. Watson (Houston) embark on the search for London's Jack the Ripper. NOTES: The second Sherlock Holmes to be filmed in color. (The first was the 1959 United Artists-Hammer film *The Hound of the Baskervilles*. [Original German title: *Sherlock Holmes Grosster Fall*].

1962. Submarine (11/12/28) B&W–93 mins. (Adventure). DIR: Frank Capra. PRO: Harry Cohn. SP: Dorothy Howell, Winifred Dunn. Story by Norman Springer. An Irvin Willat Production. CAST: Jack Holt, Dorothy Revier, Ralph Graves, Clarence Burton, Arthur Rankin.

Two Navy buddies (Holt, Graves) who love the same girl (Revier) have a falling out until one of them becomes trapped in a submarine disaster. NOTES: Columbia's first picture with special sound effects and the second

Columbia picture to premiere at a major New York theater.

1963. Submarine Raider (6/22/42) B&W–65 mins. (War-Drama). DIR: Lew Landers. PRO: Wallace MacDonald. SP: Aubrey Wisberg. CAST: John Howard, Marguerite Chapman, Bruce Bennett, Warren Ashe, Nino Pipitone, Eileen O'Hearn, Philip Ahn, Larry Parks, Rudy Robles, Roger Clark, Forrest Tucker, Eddie Laughton, Stanley Brown, Jack Shay, Gary Breckner.

When a sub picks up a woman (Chapman) whose yacht has been sunk by the Japanese, she and the sub commander (Howard) try to warn the American forces at Pearl Harbor of the impending Japanese attack.

Submarine Zone *see* **Escape to Glory**

1964. Subway Express (3/29/31) B&W–68 mins. (Mystery). DIR: Fred Newmeyer. SP: Earle Snell. Based on the play by Eva Kay Flint and Martha Madison. CAST: Jack Holt, Aileen Pringle, Jason Robards, Sr., Fred Kelsey, Alan Roscoe, Sidney Bracey, Selmer Jackson, Lilliane Leighton, James Goss, Mason Williams, Harry Semels, Robert St. Angelo, John Kelly, Bob Kortman, Mary Gordon, Ethel Wales.

Inspector Killian (Holt) and his partner (Kelsey) investigate the murder of a passenger on the New York subway system.

Success *see* **The American Success Company**

1965. Such a Gorgeous Kid Like Me (3/73) Eastman Color–98 mins. (Drama). DIR: Francois Truffaut. PRO: Marcel Berbert. SP: Francois Truffaut, Jean-Loup Dabadie. Based on the book by Henry Farrell. A Les Films du Carrosse Production. CAST: Bernadette Lafont,

Claude Brasseur, Charles Denner, Guy Marchand, Andre Dussollier, Philippe Leotard, Anne Kreis, Daniele Girard.

A murderess (Lafont) relates her life story to a sociologist (Dussollier) and slowly draws him into her web. [British title: *A Gorgeous Bird Like Me*]. [Original French title: *Une Belle Fille Comme Moi*].

1966. The Sucker (10/66) Eastman Color/Scope—101 mins. (Comedy). *DIR*: Gerard Oury. *PRO*: Yves Laplanche, Enzo Provenzale. *SP*: Marcel Jullian, Georges Tabet, Andre Tabet, Gerard Oury. Story by Gerard Oury. A Les Films Corona-Explorer-Royal Films International Production. *CAST*: Bourvil, Louis de Funes, Walter Chiari, Venantino Venantini, Beba Loncar, Daniela Rocca, Lando Buzzanca, Jose-Luis de Vilallonga, Saro Urzi, Pierre Roussel, Michel Galabru, Jean Lefebvre.

A man (Bourvil) is given a car to drive while on vacation, unaware that it contains contraband. *NOTES*: Limited theatrical release. [Original French title: *Le Corniaud*]. [Original Italian title: *Colpo Grosso ma Non Troppo*].

1967. Suddenly Last Summer (12/59) B&W—114 mins. (Drama). *DIR*: Joseph L. Mankiewicz. *PRO*: Sam Spiegel. *SP*: Gore Vidal, Tennessee Williams. Based on *Garden District* and *Something Unspoken* by Tennessee Williams. A Horizon-Academy-Camp Production. *CAST*: Elizabeth Taylor, Montgomery Clift, Katharine Hepburn, Albert Dekker, Mercedes McCambridge, Gary Raymond, Mavis Villiers.

A brain surgeon (Clift) tries to determine what happened to a wealthy woman's (Hepburn) son and cousin (Taylor) while the two were abroad on vacation. *NOTES*: The last film of Albert Dekker.

1968. Suicide Mission (11/56) B&W—70 mins. (War-Drama). *DIR/PRO*: Michael Forlong. *SP*: Michael Forlong, David Howarth, Sidney Cole. Based on *The Shetland Bus* by David Howarth. A Warwick-North Sea Production. *CAST*: Leif Larson, Michael Aldridge, Atle Larsen, Per Christansen, T. W. Southam, Oscar Egede Nissen. Narrated by Anthony Oliver.

During World War II, a group of Norwegians, with the help of the Royal Navy, ferry arms and men across the North Sea in mid-winter to their homeland.

1969. Summer Wishes, Winter Dreams (10/73) Technicolor—87 mins. (Drama). *DIR*: Gilbert Cates. *PRO*: Jack Brodsky. *SP*: Stewart Stern. A Rastar Production. *CAST*: Joanne Woodward, Martin Balsam, Sylvia Sidney, Dori Brenner, Win Forman, Tresa Hughes, Peter Markin, Ron Richards, Charlotte Oberley.

A middle-aged couple (Balsam, Woodward) try to get their lives back together after the death of the wife's mother (Sidney).

1970. Summertree (4/71) Eastman Color—89 mins. (Drama). *DIR*: Anthony Newley, Don Record. *PRO*: Kirk Douglas. *SP*: Edward Hume, Stephen Yafa. Based on the play by Ron Cowen. A Bryna Production. *CAST*: Michael Douglas, Jack Warden, Brenda Vacarro, Barbara Bel Geddes, Kirk Callaway, Rob Reiner, William Smith, Bill Vint, Jeff Siggens, Gary Goodrow, Dennis Clark Fimple.

During the late 60's, a young man (Douglas) tries unsuccessfully to avoid the draft and is killed in Vietnam.

1971. Sundays and Cybele (3/63) B&W—110 mins. (Drama). *DIR*: Serge Bourguignon. *PRO*: Romain Pines. *SP*: Serge Bourguignon, Antoine Tudal, Bernard Eschasseriaux. Based on *Les Dimanches de Ville D'Avary* by

Bernard Eschasseriaux. A Terra-Fides-Orsay-Les Films Du Trocadero Production. CAST: Hardy Kruger, Patricia Gozzi, Nicole Courcel, Daniel Ivernal, Andre Oumansky, Michel de Re.

A shell-shocked veteran (Kruger) becomes friendly with a 12-year-old orphan girl (Gozzi) with tragic results. NOTES: In French with English subtitles. [Original French title: *Les Dimanches de Ville D'Avray*].

1972. The Sundown Rider (12/30/33) B&W—65 mins. (Western). DIR/SP: Lambert Hillyer. Story by John Thomas Neville. CAST: Buck Jones, Barbara Weeks, Pat O'Malley, Wheeler Oakman, Ward Bond, Niles Welch, Bradley Page, Frank LaRue, Ed Brady, Harry Todd.

A cowboy (Jones) gets mistaken for a rustler while trying to help a rancher (Weeks) save her ranch from outlaws.

1973. Sundown Valley (3/23/44) B&W—55 mins. (Western). DIR: Benjamin Kline. PRO: Jack Fier. SP: Luci Ward. CAST: Charles Starrett, Jeanne Bates, Dub Taylor, Jimmy Wakely, Clancy Cooper, Wheeler Oakman, Jack Ingram, Forrest Taylor, Eddie Laughton, Jessie Arnold, Grace Lenard, Joel Friedkin, The Tennessee Ramblers.

The manager (Starrett) of a gunsight plant and his sidekick (Taylor) go after a group of Nazis who try to stop their operation.

1974. Sunny Side of the Street (9/51) Super CineColor—71 mins. (Musical). DIR: Richard Quine. PRO: Jonie Taps. SP: Lee Loeb. Story by Harold Conrad. CAST: Frankie Laine, Billy Daniels, Terry Moore, Jerome Courtland, Toni Arden, Audrey Long, Dick Wesson, Lynn Bari, William Tracy, Willard Waterman, Jonathan Hale, Amanda Blake, Benny Payne, Paul Dubov, Peter Price.

A singer (Courtland) tries to break into TV with the help of a couple of singers (Laine, Daniels) and his girl (Moore).

1975. Superargo Vs. Diabolicus (6/66) Eastman Color/Scope—88 mins. (Action). DIR: Nick Nostro. PRO: Ottavio Poggi, J. J. Balcazar. SP: J. J. Balcazar. Story by Mino Giarda. A Liber Balcazar P.C.-S.E.C. Production. CAST: Ken Wood (Giovanni Cianfriglia), Gerard Tichy, Loredana Nusciak, Monica Randal, Francisco Castillo Escalona, Emilio Messina, Valentino Macchi, Geoffrey Copleston.

Superargo (Wood), the wrestler turned superhero, battles a mad scientist (Tichy) planning to take over the world using artificial gold. NOTES: Limited theatrical release. [Original Italian title: *Superargo Contro Diabolikus*]. [Original Spanish title: *Superargo Contra Diabolicus: Superargo el Hombre Enmascarado*].

1976. Superspeed (12/2/35) B&W—56 mins. (Action). DIR: Lambert Hillyer. PRO: Irving Briskin. SP: Harold Shumate. CAST: Norman Foster, Florence Rice, Mary Carlisle, Charley Grapewin, Arthur Hohl, Robert Middlemass, George McKay.

A man (Foster) invents a "superspeed" car formula, almost has it sabotaged by an auto plant manager (Hohl), but manages to use his formula to win a motorboat race.

1977. Surprise Package (11/60) B&W—100 mins. (Comedy). DIR/PRO: Stanley Donen. SP: Harry Kurnitz. Based on *A Gift from the Boys* by Art Buchwald. CAST: Yul Brynner, Bill Nagy, Mitzi Gaynor, Lionel Burton, Barry Foster, Eric Pohlmann, Noel Coward, George Coulouris, "Man Mountain" Dean, Warren Mitchell, Guy Deghy, Lyndon Brook.

An exiled mobster (Brynner) tries to

buy some crown jewels from a king (Coward), but when he wires home for his gang to send him the money he has stashed away, they mistakenly send him a girl (Gaynor), a gift from the boys.

1978. The Survivors (6/83) Metrocolor—102 mins. (Comedy). *DIR:* Michael Ritchie. *PRO:* William B. Sackheim. *SP:* Michael Leeson. A Rastar Production. *CAST:* Robin Williams, Walter Matthau, Jerry Reed, James Wainwright, Annie McEnroe, Kristen Vigard, Bernard Barrow, Anne Pitoniak, Meg Mundy, Marian Hailey, John Goodman, Joseph Carberry.

A gas-station owner (Matthau) and a business executive (Williams) lose their jobs and become the quarry of a hit man (Reed) after they witness a robbery.

1979. Swan Lake (11/57) Eastman Color—81 mins. (Ballet-Documentary). *DIR:* Serge Tulubyeva. *SP:* Serge Tulubyeva, A. Messerer. A Central Documentary Film Studio of Moscow Production. *CAST:* Nikolai Fadeyechev, Maya Plisetskaya, Vladimir Fadeyechev, V. Khomyakov, The Bolshoi Theatre Ballet.

A filmed documentary of the Tchaikovsky museum and the Bolshoi Ballet performing the Tchaikovsky "Swan Lake" ballet. *NOTES:* Limited theatrical release. [Original Russian title: *Lebedinole Ozero*].

1980. Swedish Wedding Night (11/65) B&W—95 mins. (Drama). *DIR:* Ake Falck. *PRO:* Tore Sjoberg, Lorens Marmstedt. *SP:* Lars Widding. Based on *Brollopsbesvar* by Stig Halvard Dagerman. A Minerva-Royal Films International Production. *CAST:* Jarl Kulle, Lena Hansson, Christina Schollin, Edvin Adolphson, Isa Quensel, Catrin Westerlund, Tor Isedal, Peter Thelin, Lars Ekborg, Margareta Krook, Yvonne Lombard, Georg Arlin,

Ove Tjernberg, Lars Passgard, Lars Lind, Sigge Fischer, Tommy Nilsson, Ulla Edin. Narrated by Ake Falck.

At a couple's (Kulle, Schollin) wedding feast, the guests bear their own private secrets and the wife's ex-lover (Passgard) hangs himself. *NOTES:* In Swedish with English subtitles. Limited theatrical release. [British title: *Wedding—Swedish Style*]. [Original Swedish title: *Brollopsbesvar*].

1981. Sweet Genevieve (10/29/47) B&W—68 mins. (Comedy). *DIR:* Arthur Dreifuss. *PRO:* Sam Katzman. *SP:* Arthur Dreifuss, Jameson Brewer. *CAST:* Jean Porter, Jimmy Lydon, Gloria Marlen, Ralph Hodges, Lucien Littlefield, Tom Batten, Kirk Alyn, Al Donahue and His Orchestra.

A girl basketball player (Porter) gets mixed up with racketeers when she thinks her father has been kidnapped.

1982. Sweet Inniscarra (3/34) B&W—72 mins. (Romance). *DIR/PRO/SP:* Emmett Moore. *CAST:* Sean Rogers, Mae Ryan.

In 1930 Ireland, a millionaire (Rogers) pretends to be a schoolmaster to win the girl (Ryan) he loves.

1983. Sweet Rosie O'Grady (10/7/26) B&W—69 mins. (Comedy). *DIR:* Frank R. Strayer. *PRO:* Harry Cohn. *SP:* Dorothy Howell, Harry O. Hoyt. Story by Maude Nugent. *CAST:* Shirley Mason, Cullen Landis, E. Alyn Warren, William Conklin.

A young girl (Mason), who has been raised by a cop (Conklin) and a pawnbroker (Warren), grows up to marry a wealthy man (Landis).

1984. Sweetheart of the Campus (6/30/41) B&W—67 mins. (Musical). *DIR:* Edward Dmytryk. *PRO:* Jack Fier. *SP:* Robert D. Andrews, Edmund L. Hartmann. Story by Robert D. Andrews. *CAST:* Ruby Keeler, Harriet Hilliard, Gordon Oliver, Don Beddoe, Charles Judels, Kathleen Howard, Byron Foulger, George Lessey, Frank Gaby, Leo Watson, Ozzie Nelson and His Band, The Four Spirits of Rhythm.

A band leader (Nelson) and his singer (Keeler) help a run-down college remain open by attracting enrollment when they open a nightclub on the campus. NOTES: Ruby Keeler's final starring role after a three year absence. [British title: *Broadway Ahead*].

1985. Sweetheart of the Fleet (8/17/42) B&W—65 mins. (Musical-Comedy). DIR: Charles Barton. PRO: Jack Fier. SP: Albert Duffy, Maurice Tombragel, Ned Dandy. Story by Albert Duffy. CAST: Joan Davis, Jinx Falkenburg, Joan Woodbury, Brenda and Cobina (Blanche Stewart, Elvia Allman), William Wright, Robert Stevens, Tim Ryan, George McKay, Walter Sande, Charles Trowbridge, Tom Seidel, Dick Elliott, Irving Bacon, Lloyd Bridges, Stanley Brown, Boyd Davis, John Tyrrell, Gary Breckner.

At a USO benefit, a publicist (Davis) for an ad agency runs into trouble when she hires two models (Falkenburg, Woodbury) to lip-sync songs sung by two ugly singers (Brenda and Cobina), hidden from view.

1986. Sweethearts on Parade (9/28/30) B&W—65 mins. (Musical-Drama). DIR: Marshall Neilan. PRO: Al Christie. SP: Colin Clements. Story by Al Cohn, James A. Starr. CAST: Alice White, Lloyd Hughes, Marie Prevost, Kenneth Thompson, Ray Cooke, Wilbur Mack, Ernest Wood, Max Asher.

A girl (White) rejects a proposal of marriage from a Marine (Hughes) for a millionaire (Thompson), and when she discovers he is already married, she returns to the Marine.

1987. The Swell-Head (8/5/27) B&W—59 mins. (Drama). DIR: Ralph Graves. PRO: Harry Cohn. SP: Robert Lord. CAST: Ralph Graves, Johnnie Walker, Eugenia Gilbert, Mildred Harris, Mary Carr, Tom Dugan.

A prizefighter (Graves) goes into the ring, wins a couple of bouts and thinks he can lick the world. He ignores all the rules of the ring and soon gets some sense knocked into him. [British title: *Counted Out*].

1988. Swell-Head (5/4/35) B&W—62 mins. (Comedy). DIR: Ben Stoloff. PRO: Bryan Foy. SP: William Jacobs. Story by Gerald Beaumont. CAST: Wallace Ford, Dickie Moore, Barbara Kent, J. Farrell MacDonald, Marion Byron, Sammy Cohen, Frank Moran, Mike Donlin.

An egotistical baseball player (Ford) finally comes down to earth when he gets hit on the head by a pitch.

1989. The Swimmer (5/68) Technicolor—94 mins. (Drama). DIR: Frank Perry. PRO: Frank Perry, Roger Lewis. SP: Eleanor Perry. Based on the story by John Cheever. A Horizon Picture Production. CAST: Burt Lancaster, Janet Landgard, Janice Rule, Tony Bickley, Marge Champion, Bill Fiore, John Garfield, Jr., Kim Hunter, Charles Drake, Bernie Hamilton, House Jameson, Jimmy Joyce, Michael Kearney, Richard McMurray, Jan Miner, Diana Muldaur, Joan Rivers, Cornelia Otis Skinner, Dolph Sweet, Louise Troy, Keri Oleson, Diana Van Der Vlis.

A man (Lancaster), finding himself miles from home and clad only in swimming trunks, decides to swim home via his neighbors' pools only to arrive home and find that it hasn't been lived in for years.

1990. Swing in the Saddle (8/31/44) B&W—58 mins. (Western-Musical). DIR: Lew Landers. PRO: Jack Fier. SP: Elizabeth Beecher, Morton Grant, Bradford Ropes. Story by Maurice Leo. *CAST:* Jane Frazee, Guinn "Big Boy" Williams, Slim Summerville, Sally Bliss, Mary Treen, Carole Mathews, Byron Foulger, Cousin Emmy, The Nat "King" Cole Trio, Red River Dave, The Hoosier Hotshots, Jimmy Wakely and His Oklahoma Cowboys.

Two girls (Frazee, Bliss) head west to learn the identity of a secret admirer and, mistaken for kitchen help, wind up working on a ranch. [British title: *Swing and Sway*].

1991. Swing Out the Blues (12/23/43) B&W—73 mins. (Musical-Comedy). *DIR:* Mal St. Clair. *PRO:* Sam White. *SP:* Dorcas Cochran. Story by Doris Malloy. *CAST:* Bob Haymes, Lynn Merrick, Janis Carter, Tim Ryan, Joyce Compton, Arthur Q. Bryan, Kathleen Howard, John Eldredge, Dick Elliott, Lotte Stein, Tor Johnson, The Vagabonds.

A press agent (Carter) tries to stop the marriage of her singing group's (Vagabonds) lead singer (Haymes) to a socialite (Merrick).

1992. Swing the Western Way (6/26/47) B&W—66 mins. (Western-Musical). *DIR:* Derwin Abrahams. *PRO:* Colbert Clark. *SP:* Barry Shipman. Story by Bert Horswell. *CAST:* Jack E. Leonard, Mary Dugan, Thurston Hall, Sam Flint, Regina Wallace, Ralph Littlefield, Johnny Bond, Lane Bradford, Tristram Coffin, Lyn Craft, George Lloyd, Eddie Acuff, Earl Brown, Rube Schaefer, George Dockstader, The Hoosier Hotshots, The Crew Chiefs, Jerry Wald and His Orchestra.

A man (Leonard) pretends to be a ranch owner so that he can marry a rich woman (Dugan). [British title: *The Schemer*].

1993. The Swingin' Maiden (1/64) Eastman Color—98 mins. (Comedy). *DIR:* Gerald Thomas. *PRO:* Peter Rogers. *SP:* Vivian A. Cox, Leslie Bricusse. Story by Harold Brooks, Kay Bannerman. A Gregory-Hake-Walker Production. *CAST:* Michael Craig, Anne Helm, Jeff Donnell, Alan Hale, Jr., Noel Purcell, Cecil Parker, Roland Culver, Joan Sims, Judith Furse, John Standing, Brian Oulton, Sam Kydd, Jim Dale, Peter Burton, Richard Thorp.

Two aircraft engine designers (Craig, Standing) compete for a contract from a tycoon (Hale, Jr.). [British title: *The Iron Maiden*].

1994. Sword of Sherwood Forest (1/61) Eastman Color/Scope—80 mins. (Adventure). *DIR:* Terence Fisher. *PRO:* Richard Greene, Sidney Cole. *SP:* Alan Hackney. A Hammer-Yeoman Production. *CAST:* Richard Greene, Peter Cushing, Richard Pasco, Niall MacGinnis, Jack Gwillim, Sarah Branch, Nigel Green, Oliver Reed, Dennis Lotis, Derren Nesbitt.

Robin Hood (Greene) and his band thwart the plans of the Sheriff of Nottingham (Cushing) and an earl (Pasco) to murder the Archbishop of Canterbury (Gwillim). *NOTES:* This film was based on the popular television series.

Sword of Vengeance III *see* **Lightning Swords of Death**

1995. The Swordsman (1/2/48) Technicolor—81 mins. (Drama). *DIR:* Joseph H. Lewis. *PRO:* Burt Kelly. *SP:* Wilfrid H. Pettitt. *CAST:* Larry Parks, Ellen Drew, George Macready, Edgar Buchanan, Marc Platt, Ray Collins, Michael Duane, Holmes Herbert, Billy Bevan, Nedrick Young, Robert Shayne, Lumsden Hare, Tom Stevenson, Harry Allen.

The son (Parks) and daughter (Drew) of two rival Scottish clans try to find romance amidst the fighting of their clans.

1996. Sylvester (3/85) Metrocolor—103 mins. (Drama). *DIR:* Tim

Hunter. *PRO:* Martin Jurow. *SP:* Carol Sobieski. A Rastar Production. *CAST:* Richard Farnsworth, Melissa Gilbert, Michael Schoeffling, Constance Towers, Pete Kowanko, Yankton Hatten, Shane Sherwin, Chris Pedersen, Angel Salazar, Arliss Howard, Richard Jamison, James Gammon.

In Kentucky, a girl (Gilbert) teams up with a crusty old codger (Farnsworth) to turn an unmanageable ex-rodeo horse into an Olympic champion.

1997. Synanon (5/65) B&W — 105 mins. (Drama). *DIR/PRO:* Richard Quine. *SP:* Ian Bernard, S. Lee Pogostin. Story by Barry Oringer, S. Lee Pogostin. *CAST:* Chuck Conners, Stella Stevens, Alex Cord, Richard Conte, Eartha Kitt, Edmond O'Brien, Barbara Luna, Alejandro Rey, Richard Evans, Gregory Morton, Chanin Hale, Casey Townsend, Larry Kert, Bernie Hamilton, Mark Sturges, Lawrence Montaigne, Patricia Huston.

Amidst the residents at Synanon House trying to kick the drug habit, an ex-con (Cord) has an affair with a prostitute (Stevens), leaves when they are harassed by a fellow inmate (Conners), and dies of an overdose in a sleazy hotel, leaving the prostitute to return and continue her therapy. *NOTES:* Edmond O'Brien played the role of Charles Dederich, who founded Synanon House in 1958, and some of the actual residents of Synanon House appear in the film. [British title: *Get Off My Back*].

1998. Tahiti Nights (2/5/45) B&W — 63 mins. (Musical). *DIR:* Will Jason. *PRO:* Sam White. *SP:* Lillie Hayward. *CAST:* Jinx Falkenburg, Dave O'Brien, Mary Treen, Florence Bates, Cy Kendall, Eddie Bruce, Pedro de Cordoba, Hilo Hattie, Carole Mathews, Isabel Withers, Peter Cusa-

nelli, Charles Opunui, Chris Willowbird, The Vagabonds.

A band leader (O'Brien) lands on a Tahitian island and learns that there are plans for him to wed the princess (Falkenburg) of a local tribe.

1999. Tainted Money (11/1/24) B&W — 50 mins. (Drama). *DIR:* Henry MacRae. *SP:* Stuart Payton. *CAST:* William Fairbanks, Eva Novak, Bruce Gordon, Edwards Davis.

A son (Fairbanks) and daughter (Novak) help to end a feud between two lumber magnates (Gordon, Davis).

2000. The Take (5/74) Metrocolor — 91 mins. (Action-Drama). *DIR:* Robert Hartford-Davis. *PRO:* Howard Brandy. *SP:* Del Reisman, Franklin Coen. Based on *Sir, You Bastard* by G. F. Newman. A World Film Services Production. *CAST:* Billy Dee Williams, Eddie Albert, Frankie Avalon, Sorrell Booke, Tracy Reed, Albert Salmi, Vic Morrow, James Luisi, A. Martinez.

A black cop (Williams) tries to break up the syndicate while being on the take.

2001. Take a Girl Like You (10/70) Technicolor — 101 mins. (Comedy). *DIR:* Jonathan Miller. *PRO:* Hal E. Chester. *SP:* George Melly. Based on the book by Kingsley Amis. An Albion Film Production. *CAST:* Hayley Mills, Oliver Reed, Noel Harrison, Sheila Hancock, John Bird, Aimi MacDonald, Ronald Lacey, Geraldine Sherman.

A playboy (Reed) becomes obsessed with a young teacher (Mills) and vows to get her in bed, but she will have nothing to do with him.

2002. Take Me Over (3/63) B&W — 60 mins. (Comedy). *DIR:* Robert Lynn. *PRO:* William McLeod. *SP:* Dail Ambler. *CAST:* John Paul, John Rutland, Diane Aubrey, Mark

Burns, Mildred Mayne, Totti Truman Taylor, Temperance Seven.

A hotel builder (Paul) sets out to buy a coffee house and antique store as part of his scheme to better his business.

2003. Talk About a Lady (3/28/46) B&W—71 mins. (Musical). DIR: George Sherman. PRO: Michael Kraike. SP: Richard Weil, Ted Thomas. Story by Robert D. Andrews, Barry Trivers. CAST: Jinx Falkenburg, Forrest Tucker, Joe Besser, Trudy Marshall, Richard Lane, Jimmy Little, Frank Sully, Jack Davis, Robert Regent, Mira McKinney, Robin Raymond, Stan Kenton and His Orchestra.

A country girl (Falkenburg) inherits a nightclub and a million dollars and comes into contact with a socialite (Marshall) who thinks it should be hers.

2004. Talk of the Town (7/21/42) B&W—118 mins. (Comedy). DIR/PRO: George Stevens. SP: Irwin Shaw, Sidney Buchman. Story by Sidney Harmon. Adapted by Dale Van Every. CAST: Cary Grant, Jean Arthur, Ronald Colman, Edgar Buchanan, Glenda Farrell, Charles Dingle, Emma Dunn, Rex Ingram, Leonid Kinskey, Tom Tyler, Don Beddoe, George Watts, Lloyd Bridges, Patrick McVey, Eddie Laughton, Billy Benedict, John Tyrrell, Bud Geary, Ralph Dunn, William Gould, Lee "Lasses" White, Joe McGuinn, Lelah Tyler, Georgia Backus, Gino Corrado, Frank Sully, Dan Seymour, Lee Prather, Clarence Muse, Al Bridge, Leslie Brooks.

A factory worker (Grant), falsely accused of arson and murder, takes refuge in a boarding house, falls in love with his landlady (Arthur), and meets a law professor (Colman) who agrees to help him prove his innocence.

2005. The Tall T (4/57) Technicolor—78 mins. (Western). DIR: Budd Boetticher. PRO: Harry Joe Brown. SP: Burt Kennedy. Based on *The Captives* by Elmore Leonard. CAST: Randolph Scott, Maureen O'Sullivan, Richard Boone, Arthur Hunnicutt, Skip Homeier, Henry Silva, John Hubbard, Chris Olsen, Robert Anderson, Robert Burton, Fred Sherman.

A rancher (Scott) and a pair of newlyweds (O'Sullivan, Hubbard) plot their escape from a trio of bandits (Boone, Homeier, Silva).

2006. The Taming of the Shrew (3/67) Technicolor/Panavision—122 mins. (Comedy). DIR: Franco Zeffirelli. PRO: Richard Burton, Elizabeth Taylor, Franco Zeffirelli. SP: Paul Dehn, Suso Cecchi D'Amico, Franco Zeffirelli. Adapted from the play by William Shakespeare. A Royal Films International-F.A.I. Production. CAST: Richard Burton, Elizabeth Taylor, Michael York, Alfred Lynch, Vernon Dobtcheff, Michael Hordern, Natasha Pyne, Alan Webb, Victor Spinetti, Roy Holder, Cyril Cusack, Anthony Garner, Ken Parry, Mark Dignam.

Based on the play by William Shakespeare, Petruchio (Burton) tries to tame the shrew Katharina (Taylor). [Original Italian title: *La Bisbetica Domata*].

2007. The Taming of the West (12/7/39) B&W—55 mins. (Western). DIR: Norman Deming. PRO: Leon Barsha. SP: Charles F. Royal, Robert Lee Johnson. Story by Robert Lee Johnson. CAST: Bill Elliott, Iris Meredith, Dick Curtis, Dub Taylor, James Craig, Stanley Brown, Ethan Allen, Kenneth MacDonald, Victor Wong, Don Beddoe, Lane Chandler, Charles King, Hank Bell, Irene Herndon, John Tyrrell, Art Mix, George Morrell, Bob Woodward, Richard Fiske.

Wild Bill Saunders (Elliott) rides into the town of Prairie Port and is persuaded by a cafe owner (Meredith) to become sheriff and clean up the town of cattle rustlers.

Tampico *see* **The Woman I Stole**

2008. Tank Force (8/58) Technicolor/Scope—103 mins. (War). *DIR:* Terence Young. *PRO:* Irving Allen, Albert R. Broccoli. *SP:* Richard Maibaum, Terence Young. Story by Merle Miller. A Warwick Films Production. *CAST:* Victor Mature, Leo Genn, Bonar Colleano, Luciana Paluzzi, George Coulouris, Robert Rietty, Martin Boddey, Alfred Burke, David Lodge, George Pravda, Percy Herbert, Kenneth Cope, Anne Aubrey, Anthony Newley, Maxwell Shaw.

An American sergeant (Mature) and five men escape from a desert prison camp during World War II, are captured by a pro-Nazi sheik (Shaw), and have to fight their way to freedom. [British title: *No Time to Die*].

2009. Tarawa Beachead (11/58) B&W—77 mins. (War). *DIR:* Paul Wendkos. *PRO:* Charles H. Schneer. *SP:* Richard Alan Simmons. A Morningside Production. *CAST:* Kerwin Mathews, Julie Adams, Ray Danton, Karen Sharpe, Onslow Stevens, Russell Thorsen, Eddie Ryder, John Baer, Michael Garth, Larry Thor, Buddy Lewis, Lee Farr, Bill Boyett, Don Reardon.

A Marine sergeant (Mathews) sees his commanding officer (Danton) murder a fellow officer in combat and must decide whether to remain silent or tell his superiors.

2010. Target Hong Kong (2/53) B&W—66 mins. (Action). *DIR:* Fred F. Sears. *PRO:* Wallace MacDonald. *SP:* Herbert Purdum. *CAST:* Richard Denning, Nancy Gates, Richard Loo, Soo Yong, Ben Astar, Michael Pate, Philip Ahn, Henry Kulky, Victor Sen Yung, Weaver Levy, Kam Tong, Robert W. Lee.

An American mercenary (Denning) and his pals (Kulky, Pate) are persuaded by Hong Kong Nationals to stop a Red leader (Astar) and his men from taking over Hong Kong.

2011. Tars and Spars (1/10/46) B&W—88 mins. (Musical). *DIR:* Alfred E. Green. *PRO:* Milton H. Bren. *SP:* John Jacoby, Sarett Tobias, Decia Dunning. Story by Barry Trivers. *CAST:* Janet Blair, Alfred Drake, Marc Platt, Jeff Donnell, Sid Caesar, Ray Walker, James Flavin.

A sailor (Drake) is labeled a hero even though he has never been to sea. *NOTES:* The film debut of Sid Caesar and Alfred Drake.

2012. Taxi Driver (2/76) Metrocolor/Panavision—113 mins. (Crime-Drama). *DIR:* Martin Scorsese. *PRO:* Michael and Julia Phillips. *SP:* Paul Schrader. A Bill-Phillips Production. *CAST:* Robert DeNiro, Cybill Shepherd, Peter Boyle, Jodie Foster, Albert Brooks, Leonard Harris, Harvey Keitel, Norman Matlock, Harry Northrup, Joe Spinnell, Martin Scorsese.

A moralistic Vietnam veteran (DeNiro), working as a cabbie in New York, decides to make a name for himself by assassinating a political figure, but when that fails, he decides to clean up the city when he kills a pimp (Keitel) and his assistant and liberates a 14-year-old prostitute (Foster).

2013. Teen-Age Crime Wave (11/55) B&W—77 mins. (Crime). *DIR:* Fred F. Sears. *PRO:* Sam Katzman. *SP:* Harry J. Essex, Ray Buffum. Story by Ray Buffam. A Clover Production. *CAST:* Tommy Cook, Mollie McCart, Sue England, Frank Griffin, James Bell, Kay Riehl, Guy Kingsford, Larry

Blake, James Ogg, Robert Bice, Helen Brown, Sidney Mason.

A teenager (Cook) kills a county sheriff when he frees his girl (McCart) and another prisoner (England) while en route to the state reformatory. They take it on the run and hold a family hostage in a farm house but are eventually caught.

2014. Tell It to the Judge (11/18/49) B&W—87 mins. (Comedy). *DIR:* Norman Foster. *PRO:* Buddy Adler. *SP:* Nat Perrin, Roland Kibbee. Story by Devery Freeman. *CAST:* Rosalind Russell, Robert Cummings, Gig Young, Marie McDonald, Harry Davenport, Fay Baker, Katherine Warren, Douglass Dumbrille, Clem Bevans, Louise Beavers, Grandon Rhodes, Thurston Hall, Jay Novello, William Newell, Harlan Warde, Lee Phelps, Lester Dorr, Billy Bevan, Steven Geray.

A woman judge (Russell) wants her ex-husband (Cummings) back, but every time they try to get together a blonde (McDonald) enters into their lives at the most inopportune time.

2015. Tempest (8/82) Metrocolor—140 mins. (Drama). *DIR/PRO:* Paul Mazursky. *SP:* Paul Mazursky, Leon Capetanos. Based on the play by William Shakespeare. *CAST:* John Cassavetes, Gena Rowlands, Susan Sarandon, Vittorio Gassman, Raul Julia, Molly Ringwald, Sam Robards, Paul Stewart, Jackie Gayle, Anthony Holland, Jerry Hardin, Paul Mazursky, Betty Mazursky, Peter Lombard.

A middle-aged tycoon (Cassavetes) moves to a Greek island with his daughter (Ringwald) and a singer (Sarandon) to re-examine his life. *NOTES:* The film debut of Molly Ringwald.

2016. Temptation (3/1/23) B&W—65 mins. (Drama). *DIR/SP:* Edward J. LeSaint. *PRO:* Harry Cohn.

Story by Lenore Coffee. A C.B.C. Release. *CAST:* Bryant Washburn, Eva Novak, June Eldridge, Phillips Smalley, Vernon Steele.

A stockbroker (Smalley) sets out to prove that a young couple (Washburn, Novak) can be corrupted by wealth.

2017. Temptation (6/29/30) B&W—72 mins. (Drama). *DIR:* E. Mason Hooper. *SP:* Leonard Praskins. *CAST:* Lois Wilson, Lawrence Gray, Billy Bevan, Eileen Percy, Gertrude Bennett, Bodil Rosing.

A young man (Gray) jumps parole, ends up in New York where he falls in love with a cafe waitress (Wilson), and she eventually persuades him to give himself up so they can start life anew. [British title: *So Like a Woman*].

2018. Ten Cents a Dance (3/8/31) B&W—75 mins. (Drama-Romance). *DIR:* Lionel Barrymore. *PRO:* Harry Cohn. *SP:* Jo Swerling, Dorothy Howell. Based on the song by Lorenz Hart, Richard Rodgers. *CAST:* Barbara Stanwyck, Ricardo Cortez, Monroe Owsley, Sally Blane, Blanche Frederici, Phyllis Crane, Vic Potel, Al Hill, Jack Byron, Pat Harmon, Bess Flowers, Martha Sleeper, Sidney Bracey, Hal Price, David Newell, Harry Todd, Peggy Doner.

A dance hall hostess (Stanwyck) unknowingly marries a crook (Owsley) and when she tries to borrow money from a friend (Cortez) to get him out of trouble, he leaves her and she ends up married to the friend.

2019. Ten Cents a Dance (6/7/45) B&W—60 mins. (Comedy). *DIR:* Will Jason. *PRO:* Michael Kraike. *SP:* Morton Grant. *CAST:* Jane Frazee, Jimmy Lloyd, Robert Scott, Joan Woodbury, John Calvert, George McKay, Edward Hyams, Dorothea Kent, Carole Mathews, Muriel Morris, Pattie Robbins, Marilyn Johnson, Jewel McGowan, Billy Nelson.

Two dance hall hostesses (Frazee, Woodbury) fall in love with a couple of GI's (Lloyd, Scott) when they try to lure them into a crooked card game. [British title: *Dancing Ladies*].

2020. 10 Rillington Place (5/71) Eastman Color—111 mins. (Crime). *DIR*: Richard Fleischer. *PRO*: Martin Ransohoff, Leslie Linder. *SP*: Clive Exton. Based on the book by Ludovic Kennedy. A Genesis-Filmways Production. *CAST*: Richard Attenborough, Judy Geeson, John Hurt, Pat Heywood, Isobel Black, Phyllis McMahon, Ray Barron, Douglas Blackwell, Andre Morell, Robert Hardy, Gabrielle Day, Jimmy Gardner, Edward Evans, Tenniel Evans.

The true story of mass murderer John Reginald Christie (Attenborough), who committed seven murders between 1944 and 1950, and whose perjured testimony led to the execution of an innocent man (Hurt) and the eventual abolishment of capital punishment in England.

2021. Ten Tall Men (1/26/51) Technicolor—97 mins. (Adventure-Comedy). *DIR*: Willis Goldbeck. *PRO*: Harold Hecht. *SP*: Roland Kibbee, Frank Davis. Story by Willis Goldbeck, James Warner Bellah. A Norma Production. *CAST*: Burt Lancaster, Jody Lawrence, Gilbert Roland, Kieron Moore, George Tobias, John Dehner, Nick Dennis, Mike Mazurki, Gerald Mohr, Ian MacDonald, Mari Blanchard, Donald Randolph, Robert Clary, Henry Rowland, Michael Pate, Stephen Bekassy, Raymond Greenleaf, Paul Marion, Philip Van Zandt, Nick Cravat, Mickey Simpson.

A sergeant (Lancaster) in the Foreign Legion sets out with nine men as they kidnap the daughter (Lawrence) of a sheik to stop a Riff invasion.

2022. Ten Wanted Men (2/55) Technicolor—80 mins. (Western). *DIR*: Bruce Humberstone. *PRO*: Harry Joe Brown. *SP*: Kenneth Gamet. Story by Irving Ravetch, Harriet Frank, Jr. A Ranown Production. *CAST*: Randolph Scott, Jocelyn Brando, Richard Boone, Alfonso Bedoya, Skip Homeier, Leo Gordon, Tom Powers, Dennis Weaver, Lee Van Cleef, Denver Pyle, Francis McDonald, Jack Perrin, Terry Frost, Franklyn Farnum, Minor Watson, Kathleen Crowley, Donna Martell, Clem Bevans, Lester Matthews, Louis Jean Heydt, Boyd "Red" Morgan, Pat Collins, Paul Maxey, Julian Rivero, Carlos Vera, Edna Holland, Reed Howes, George Boyce.

A rancher (Scott) tries to rule his land by lawful means but meets opposition in another rancher (Boone) who rules by the gun.

Terminal Station Indiscretion *see* **Indiscretion of an American Wife**

2023. The Terrace (11/64) B&W—90 mins. (Drama). *DIR*: Leopoldo Torre Nilsson. *PRO*: German Szulem. *SP*: Beatriz Guido. An Internacional-Royal Films International Production. *CAST*: Belita, Graciela Borges, Leonardo Favio, Marcela Lopez Rey, Hector Pellegrini, Dora Baret, Norberto Suarez, Enrique Leoporace, Luis Walmo, Mirtha Dubner, Oscar Caballero, Bernardo Kullock, Fernando Vegal, Maria Esther Duckse, Alfredo Tobares.

A group of youths rebel against parental authority and take over the roof of a Buenos Aires apartment building. When things get out of hand, they take a 10-year-old girl (Belita) hostage and throw her off the roof when their elders try to break up their party. *NOTES*: Limited theatrical release. [Original Argentinian title: *La Terraza*].

Terror by Night *see* **The Secret Witness**

2024. The Terror of the Tongs (5/61) Technicolor—79 mins. (Adventure). *DIR:* Anthony Bushell. *PRO:* Kenneth Hyman. *SP:* Jimmy Sangster. A Hammer-Merlin Production. *CAST:* Geoffrey Toone, Christopher Lee, Yvonne Monlaur, Brian Worth, Marne Maitland, Richard Leech, Burt Kwouk, Ewen Solon, Michael Hawkins, Marie Burke, Milton Reid, Roger Delgado, Eric Young.

In 1910 Hong Kong, a seaman (Toone) and a slave girl (Monlaur) go after the leader (Lee) of the Tong drug-slave traders when they murder his wife and daughter.

2025. The Terror of Tiny Town (12/1/38) B&W—62 mins. (Western). *DIR:* Sam Newfield. *PRO:* Jed Buell. *SP:* Fred Myton, Clarence Marks. Story by Fred Myton. *CAST:* Billy Curtis, Yvonne Moray, Little Billy, Johnny Bambury, Billy Platt, Charles Becker, Joseph Herbert, Nita Krebs, Fern McDill.

An outlaw (Little Billy) tries to stir trouble with a range war but is thwarted by a cowboy (Curtis). *NOTES:* The first western to feature an all-midget cast.

2026. Terror Trail (11/21/46) B&W—55 mins. (Western). *DIR:* Ray Nazarro. *PRO:* Colbert Clark. *SP:* Ed Earl Repp. *CAST:* Charles Starrett, Barbara Pepper, Smiley Burnette, Lane Chandler, Ted Mapes, Budd Buster, Tommy Coates, George Chesebro, Zon Murray, Elvin Eric Field, Robert Barron, Bill Clark, Ozie Waters and His Colorado Rangers.

The Durango Kid (Starrett) prevents a range war between cattlemen and sheepmen and helps to reform an outlaw (Field). [British title: *Hands of Menace*].

2027. Tess (12/80) Eastman Color/Panavision—170 mins. (Drama). *DIR:* Roman Polanski. *PRO:* Claude Berri. *SP:* Roman Polanski, Gerard Brach, John Brownjohn. Based on *Tess of the D'Urbervilles* by Thomas Hardy. A Renn-Burrill Production. *CAST:* John Collin, Tony Church, Nastassia Kinski, Peter Firth, John Bett, Tom Chadbon, Rosemary Martin, Leigh Lawson, Sylvia Coleridge, Richard Pearson, Carolyn Pickles, Suzanna Hamilton, Caroline Embling, David Markham.

A farm girl (Kinski) is sent to a wealthy estate where she is seduced by the owner (Lawson), becomes pregnant and loses the baby. She then weds a dairy farmer (Firth), but he leaves when he learns about her past, and she returns to her former lover, eventually kills him and goes on the run with her husband.

2028. The Texan Meets Calamity Jane (11/15/50) TruColor—71 mins. (Western). *DIR/PRO/SP:* Ande Lamb. *CAST:* James Ellison, Evelyn Ankers, Ruth Whitney, Lee "Lasses" White, Jack Ingram, Frank Pharr, Walter Strand, Hugh Hooker, Sally Weldman, Paul Barney, Rudy de Saxe, Ferrell Lester, Ronald Marriott, Bill Orisman, Lou W. Pierce, Elmer Herzberg, Ray Jones.

A Texas lawyer (Ellison) helps Calamity Jane (Ankers) to get her gambling hall back.

2029. Texans Never Cry (3/15/51) Sepiatone—70 mins. (Western). *DIR:* Frank McDonald. *PRO:* Armand Schaefer. *SP:* Norman S. Hall. A Gene Autry Production. *CAST:* Gene Autry, Gail Davis, Pat Buttram, Mary Castle, Russell Hayden, Don C. Harvey, I. Stanford Jolley, Richard Powers, Minerva Urecal, Frank Fenton, John R. McKee, Harry McKim, Sandy Sanders, Richard Flato, Michael Ragan, Roy Gordon, Duke York, Roy Cutler.

A Texas Ranger (Autry) puts an end to a counterfeit lottery ticket racket.

2030. Texas (10/16/41) Sepiatone — 93 mins. (Western). *DIR:* George Marshall. *PRO:* Samuel Bischoff. *SP:* Michael Blankfort, Lewis Meltzer, Horace McCoy. Story by Lewis Meltzer, Michael Blankfort. *CAST:* William Holden, Claire Trevor, Glenn Ford, George Bancroft, Edgar Buchanan, Don Beddoe, Addison Richards, Edmund Cobb, Raymond Hatton, Edmund MacDonald, Andrew Tombes, Joseph Crehan, Willard Robertson, Duke York, Patrick Moriarity, James Flavin, Carleton Young, Jack Ingram, Ethan Laidlaw, William Gould.

A ranch foreman (Ford) and his outlaw friend (Holden), both in love with the rancher's daughter (Trevor), join forces to drive a herd of cattle through Texas.

2031. Texas Cyclone (2/4/32) B&W — 58 mins. (Western). *DIR:* D. Ross Lederman. *PRO:* Irving Briskin. *SP:* Randall Faye. Story by William Colt MacDonald. *CAST:* Tim McCoy, Shirley Grey, Wheeler Oakman, John Wayne, Vernon Dent, Wallace MacDonald, Walter Brennan, Mary Gordon, James Farley, Harry Cording.

A cowboy (McCoy) rides into a strange town called Stampede and is mistaken for a rancher who disappeared five years before, and who is thought dead. A head wound restores his memory and proves him to be the missing rancher.

2032. Texas Dynamo (6/1/50) B&W — 54 mins. (Western). *DIR:* Ray Nazarro. *PRO:* Colbert Clark. *SP:* Barry Shipman. *CAST:* Charles Starrett, Lois Hall, Smiley Burnette, Jock Mahoney, Slim Duncan, John Dehner, Lane Bradford, Fred F. Sears,

Emil Sitka, Gregg Barton, George Chesebro, Ethan Laidlaw.

The Durango Kid (Starrett) puts an end to a crooked citizen's committee by posing as a hired killer. [British title: *Suspected*].

2033. Texas Panhandle (12/20/45) B&W — 55 mins. (Western). *DIR:* Ray Nazarro. *PRO:* Colbert Clark. *SP:* Ed Earl Repp. *CAST:* Charles Starrett, Nanette Parks, Tex Harding, Edward Howard, Dub Taylor, Ted Mapes, George Chesebro, Jack Kirk, Forrest Taylor, Budd Buster, Jody Gilbert, William Gould, Hugh Hooker, Spade Cooley, Carolina Cotton.

The Durango Kid (Starrett) helps a young girl (Parks) keep her ranch and exposes a gang of land swindlers. *NOTES:* It is in this movie that Starrett explains the existence of the Durango Kid.

2034. The Texas Ranger (5/10/31) B&W — 61 mins. (Western). *DIR:* D. Ross Lederman. *PRO:* Sol Lesser. *SP:* Forrest Sheldon. A Beverly Production. *CAST:* Buck Jones, Harry Todd, Carmelita Geraghty, Budd Fine, Harry Woods, Bert Woodruff, Ed Brady, Edward Piel, Sr., Nelson McDowell, Blackie Whiteford, Billy Bletcher, Lew Meehan.

A Texas Ranger (Jones) helps a woman vigilante (Geraghty) to regain her ranch.

2035. The Texas Rangers (6/1/51) Super CineColor — 74 mins. (Western). *DIR:* Phil Karlson. *PRO:* Edward Small. *SP:* Richard Schayer. Story by Frank Gruber. *CAST:* George Montgomery, Gale Storm, Jerome Courtland, Noah Beery, Jr., John Litel, William Bishop, Douglas Kennedy, John Dehner, Ian MacDonald, Jock Mahoney, John Doucette, Myron Healey, Trevor Bardette, Stanley Andrews, Joseph Fallon, Julian Rivero, Edward Earle.

A Texas Ranger (Montgomery) and his men go after Sam Bass (Bishop) and the notorious "Hole-in-the-Wall" gang.

2036. Texas Stagecoach (5/23/40) B&W—59 mins. (Western). DIR: Joseph H. Lewis. PRO: Leon Barsha. SP: Fred Myton. CAST: Charles Starrett, Iris Meredith, Bob Nolan, Kenneth MacDonald, Edward J. LeSaint, Dick Curtis, Harry Cording, Pat Brady, Don Beddoe, Fred Burns, Francis Walker, Eddie Laughton, George Chesebro, Lillian Lawrence, George Becinita, Blackie Whiteford, George Morrell, Sons of the Pioneers.

A cowboy (Starrett) comes to the aid of two rival stagecoach lines when a crooked banker (Curtis) forces foreclosure on them. [British title: *Two Roads*].

2037. Texas Stampede (2/9/39) B&W—57 mins. (Western). DIR: Sam Nelson. PRO: Harry L. Decker. SP: Charles F. Royal. Based on *The Dawn Trail* by Forrest Sheldon. CAST: Charles Starrett, Iris Meredith, Bob Nolan, Fred Kohler, Jr., Lee Prather, Ray Bennett, Blackjack Ward, Blackie Whiteford, Ernie Adams, Edmund Cobb, Hank Bell, Edward Hearn, Ed Coxen, Charles Brinley, Sons of the Pioneers.

A sheriff (Starrett) tries to keep the peace when cattlemen and sheepmen battle over water rights.

2038. The Texican (11/66) Technicolor/Scope—91 mins. (Western). DIR: Lesley Selander. PRO: John C. Champion, Bruce Balaban. SP: John C. Champion, Jose Antonio de la Loma. An M.C.R.-Balcazar Production. CAST: Audie Murphy, Diana Lorys, Broderick Crawford, Aldo Sambrell, John Peral, Anthony Casas, Luz Marquez, Gerard Tichy, Anthony Molino, Helga Genth.

An ex-lawman (Murphy) goes after a crooked saloon owner (Crawford) when he learns that he murdered his brother. [Original Spanish title: *El Tejano*].

2039. Thank God It's Friday (5/78) Metrocolor—100 mins. (Musical). DIR: Robert Klane. PRO: Robert Cohen. SP: Barry Armyan Bernstein. A Motown-Casablanca Production. CAST: Valerie Landsburg, Terri Nunn, Chick Vennera, Donna Summer, Ray Vitte, Mark Lonow, Andrea Howard, Jeff Goldblum, Debra Winger, Robin Menker, John Friedrich, Paul Jabara, Marya Small, Chuck Sacci, Hilary Beane, DeWayne Jesse.

On a Friday night, a varied group of people spend the night dancing at the local disco. NOTES: The film debut of Donna Summer.

2040. Thank You All Very Much (8/69) Technicolor—106 mins. (Drama). DIR: Waris Hussein. PRO: Max J. Rosenberg, Milton Subotsky. SP: Margaret Drabble. Based on *The Millstone* by Margaret Drabble. A Palomar-Amicus Production. CAST: Sandy Dennis, Ian McKellen, Eleanor Bron, John Standing, Michael Coles, Rachel Kempson, Deborah Stanford, Sarah Whalley, Maurice Denham.

A graduate student (Dennis) has an affair with a TV announcer (McKellen) and decides to have her baby against the advice of her friends. [British title: *A Touch of Love*].

2041. That Certain Thing (1/1/28) B&W—69 mins. (Drama). DIR: Frank Capra. PRO: Harry Cohn. SP: Elmer Harris. CAST: Ralph Graves, Viola Dana, Burr McIntosh, Aggie Herring, Carl Gerard, Sydney Crossley.

A millionaire's son (Graves) and his wife (Dana) open a box-lunch business that proves a lively competition to the father's (McIntosh) restaurant business. *NOTES:* Frank Capra's first Columbia film.

That Man Flintstone *see* **The Man Called Flintstone**

2042. That Man in Istanbul (2/66) Technicolor/Scope—117 mins. (Adventure). *DIR/PRO:* Antonio Isasi Isasmendi. *SP:* Nat Wachsberger, George Simonelli, Luis Comeron, Antonio Isasi Isasmendi, Jorge Illa. An E.D.I.C.-C.C.M.-Isasi Production. *CAST:* Horst Buchholz, Sylva Koscina, Mario Adorf, Perette Pradier, Klaus Kinski, Alvaro de Luna, Gustavo Re, Christiane Maybach, Gerard Tychy, Georges Rigaud, Umberto Raho.

An international playboy (Buchholz) is recruited by a secret service agent (Koscina) to help rescue a scientist (Raho) from an evil faction seeking world control. [Original Spanish title: *Estamboul '65*]. [Original French title: *L'Homme d'Istambul*]. [Original Italian title: *Colpo Grosso a Galata Bridge*].

2043. That Summer (4/79) Eastman Color—94 mins. (Drama). *DIR:* Harley Cokliss. *PRO:* Davina Belling, Clive Parsons. *SP:* Janey Preger. Story by Tony Attard. *CAST:* Ray Winstone, Tony London, Emily Moore, Julie Shipley, Jon Morrison, Andrew Byatt, Ewan Stewart, John Judd, John Junkin, Stephanie Cole.

A teenager (Winstone), just released from reform school, travels to the seaside with his friends (Shipley, Moore, London) for a summer of fun. *NOTES:* Limited theatrical release.

2044. That Texas Jamboree (5/16/46) B&W—59 mins. (Western-Musical). *DIR:* Ray Nazarro. *PRO:* Colbert Clark. *SP:* J. Benton Cheney. Story by Paul Gangelin. *CAST:* Ken Curtis, Jeff Donnell, Andy Clyde, Guinn "Big Boy" Williams, Kenneth MacDonald, George Chesebro, Curt

Barrett, Dick Elliott, Robert Stevens, Nolan Leary, Claire Carleton, Carolina Cotton, The Plainsmen, The Dinning Sisters, The Hoosier Hotshots, Deuce Spriggins and His Band.

A woman (Donnell) and her husband (Curtis) both run for mayor of a small Texas town. [British title: *Medicine Man*].

2045. That's Gratitude (10/27/34) B&W—67 mins. (Comedy). *DIR/SP:* Frank Craven. *PRO:* Bryan Foy. *CAST:* Frank Craven, Mary Carlisle, Arthur Byron, John Buckler, Sheila Mannors, Charles Sabin, Helen Ware, Blythe Daley, Franklin Pangborn, John Sheehan.

When the leader (Craven) of a musical comedy troupe meets a homely girl, who has a beautiful singing voice but an ugly face, he takes her to a plastic surgeon who turns her into a beauty and she then marries the tenor (Buckler) of the troupe.

2046. That's Life! (9/86) DeLuxe Color/Panavision—102 mins. (Comedy). *DIR:* Blake Edwards. *PRO:* Tony Adams. *SP:* Milton Wexler, Blake Edwards. A Paradise Cove-Ubilam Production. *CAST:* Jack Lemmon, Julie Andrews, Sally Kellerman, Robert Loggia, Chris Lemmon, Jennifer Edwards, Rob Knepper, Felicia Farr, Matt Lattanzi, Cynthia Sikes, Dana Sparks, Emma Walton, Jordan Christopher, Biff Elliott.

An architect (Lemmon) begins to question life as his family plans his sixtieth birthday.

2047. That's My Boy (11/19/32) B&W—71 mins. (Drama). *DIR:* Roy William Neill. *SP:* Norman Krasna. Based on the book by Francis Wallace. *CAST:* Richard Cromwell, Dorothy Jordan, Mae Marsh, Arthur Stone, Douglass Dumbrille, Lucien Littlefield, Leon Ames, Russell Saunders,

Sumner Getchell, Otis Harlan, Dutch Hendrian.

A football player (Cromwell) gets involved in a crooked stock scheme which could affect his career, but he redeems himself by paying back the investors and winning the big game.

2048. Theodora Goes Wild (11/5/36) B&W—94 mins. (Comedy). *DIR*: Richard Boleslawski. *PRO*: Everett Riskin. *SP*: Sidney Buchman. Story by Mary E. McCarthy. *CAST*: Irene Dunne, Melvyn Douglas, Thomas Mitchell, Thurston Hall, Rosalind Keith, Spring Byington, Elisabeth Risdon, Margaret McWade, Nana Bryant, Henry Kolker, Leona Maricle, Mary Forbes, Frank Sully, Billy Benedict, Harry Harvey, Eddie Fetherstone, Lee Phelps, Dennis O'Keefe, Sven-Hugo Borg, Laura Treadwell.

A New England woman (Dunne) writes a steamy best seller about the morals in a sleepy little town, goes to New York and meets the illustrator (Douglas) of her book, and proceeds on a series of adventures while in the big city.

2049. There's a Girl in My Soup (12/70) Eastman Color—96 mins. (Comedy). *DIR*: Roy Boulting. *PRO*: John Boulting, M. J. Frankovich. *SP*: Terence Frisby, Peter Kortner. Based on the play by Terence Frisby. An Ascot Production. *CAST*: Peter Sellers, Goldie Hawn, Tony Britton, Nicky Henson, Diana Dors, John Comer, Judy Campbell, Thorley Walters, Gabrielle Drake, Geraldine Sherman, Nicola Pagett, Christopher Cazenove.

In London, a lecherous TV gourmet (Sellers) pursues an Americn woman (Hawn), who has just broken up with her boyfriend (Henson), as his latest conquest.

2050. There's Always a Woman (4/29/38) B&W—82 mins. (Comedy-Crime). *DIR*: Alexander Hall. *PRO*: William Perlberg. *SP*: Gladys Lehman. Story by Wilson Collinson. *CAST*: Joan Blondell, Melvyn Douglas, Mary Astor, Frances Drake, Jerome Cowan, Robert Paige, Thurston Hall, Pierre Watkin, Walter Kingsford, Lester Matthews, Rita Hayworth, Wade Boteler, Arthur Loft, Bud Jamison, Robert Emmett Keane, John Gallaudet, Eddie Fetherstone, Gene Morgan, Tom Dugan, Bud Geary, Billy Benedict, Lee Phelps, George McKay, Edward F. Dunn.

The wife (Blondell) of an investigator (Douglas) with the district attorney's office gets involved in double murder when she decides to help her husband with a case. *NOTES*: Columbia planned this film to be the first of a series, and not wanting to have a third character committed to the series, Rita Hayworth's part was cut to only 30 seconds of screen time, but Joan Blondell withdrew from any subsequent films and only a sequel was produced, *There's That Woman Again*.

2051. There's Something About a Soldier (11/30/43) B&W—81 mins. (Drama). *DIR*: Alfred E. Green. *PRO*: Samuel Bischoff. *SP*: Horace McCoy, Barry Trivers. *CAST*: Tom Neal, Evelyn Keyes, Bruce Bennett, John Hubbard, Jeff Donnell, Frank Sully, Lewis Wilson, Robert Stanford, Jonathan Hale, Hugh Beaumont, Kane Richmond, Douglas Drake, Craig Woods.

A tough guy (Neal), who rebels at authority, enlists at Officer Candidate School and is turned into a decent soldier by his girl (Keyes) and a North African campaign veteran (Bennett).

2052. There's That Woman Again (1/6/39) B&W—70 mins. (Comedy-Mystery). *DIR*: Alexander

Hall. *PRO:* B. B. Kahane. *SP:* Philip G. Epstein, James Edward Grant, Ken Englund. Based on the screenplay by Gladys Lehman and the story by Wilson Collinson. *CAST:* Melvyn Douglas, Virginia Bruce, Margaret Lindsay, Stanley Ridges, Gordon Oliver, Tom Dugan, Don Beddoe, Jonathan Hale, Pierre Watkin, Paul Harvey, Marc Lawrence, Charles Wilson, Donald "Red" Barry, Vivian Oakland, Dick Curtis, William Newell, Pat Flaherty, John Dilson, Mantan Moreland, Lee Shumway.

An investigator (Douglas) and his wife (Bruce) get involved in a double murder as they go after stolen gems. *NOTES:* A sequel to the 1938 Columbia film *There's Always a Woman.* [British title: *What a Woman!*].

2053. These Are the Damned (6/65) B&W/Scope—77 mins. (Science Fiction). *DIR:* Joseph Losey. *PRO:* Anthony Hinds. *SP:* Evan Jones. Based on *The Children of Light* by H. L. Lawrence. A Hammer-Swallow Production. *CAST:* Macdonald Carey, Shirley Anne Field, Viveca Lindfors, Alexander Knox, Oliver Reed, Walter Gotell, James Villiers, Thomas Kempinski, Kenneth Cope, Brian Oulton, Barbara Everest, Alan McClellend, James Maxwell, Rachel Clay, David Palmer, John Thompson, Kit Williams.

In a British seaside resort, an American tourist (Carey) and the sister (Field) of a motorcycle thug (Reed) set out to free a group of children made radioactive by a scientist (Knox) perfecting a race of humans capable of surviving a nuclear blast. *NOTES:* Originally filmed in 1961 and released in England in 1963 at a running time of 96 mins. [British title: *The Damned*].

2054. They All Kissed the Bride (6/1/42) B&W—85 mins. (Comedy). *DIR:* Alexander Hall. *PRO:* Edward Kaufman. *SP:* P. J. Wolfson, Henry Altimus, Andrew Solt. Story by Gina Kaus, Andrew Solt. *CAST:* Joan Crawford, Melvyn Douglas, Roland Young, Billie Burke, Allen Jenkins, Andrew Tombes, Helen Parrish, Emory Parnell, Mary Treen, Nydia Westman, Ivan Simpson, Roger Clark, Gordon Jones, Edward Gargan, Larry Parks, Tom Dugan, John Dilson, George Pembroke, Wyndham Standing, Shirley Patterson, Douglas Wood, Boyd Irwin, Ann Doran, Ralph Sanford, Dale Van Sickel, Harry Strang, Ernie Adams, Lyle Latell, George McKay, Norman Willis.

A career woman (Crawford) inherits a trucking firm on her father's death, proceeds to run it with an iron hand, but when she meets a reporter (Douglas) at her sister's (Parrish) wedding she goes weak in the knees and realizes she has met her match. *NOTES:* This film was released six months after Pearl Harbor, and when Crawford tells Douglas "When I want a sneak, I'll get the best and hire a Jap" audiences roared, but by today's standards, this line is considered in questionable taste and is clipped from some existing TV prints. This film was originally slated to star Carole Lombard but was given to Miss Crawford when Lombard died in a plane crash in January 1942.

2055. They Came to Cordura (6/59) Eastman Color/Scope—123 mins. (Drama). *DIR:* Robert Rossen. *PRO:* William Goetz. *SP:* Ivan Moffat, Robert Rossen. Based on the book by Glendon F. Swarthout. *CAST:* Gary Cooper, Rita Hayworth, Van Heflin, Tab Hunter, Richard Conte, Michael Callan, Dick York, Robert Keith, Cesar Romero, Jim Bannon, Edward Platt, Maurice Jara, Sam Buffington, Arthur Hanson.

In 1916 Mexico, an "Awards officer" (Cooper) leads five Medal of Honor candidates (Heflin, Hunter, Conte, Callan, York) and a suspected traitor (Hayworth) across the desert to the town of Cordura and on the journey each shows their true character.

2056. They Dare Not Love (5/16/41) B&W—75 mins. (War-Drama). DIR: James Whale. PRO: Samuel Bischoff. SP: Charles Bennett, Ernest Vajda. Story by James Edward Grant. CAST: George Brent, Martha Scott, Paul Lukas, Egon Brecher, Roman Bohnen, Edgar Barrier, Kay Linaker, Frank Reicher, Lloyd Bridges.

An Austrian prince (Brent) is reunited with his love (Scott) when he goes to a German officer (Lukas) and offers himself in exchange for seven prisoners.

2057. They Live in Fear (10/6/44) B&W—65 mins. (Drama). DIR: Josef Berne. PRO: Jack Fier. SP: Michael L. Simmons, Damuel Ornitz. Story by Wilfrid H. Pettitt. CAST: Otto Kruger, Clifford Severn, Pat Parrish, Jimmy Carpenter, Erwin Kalser, Danny Jackson, Jimmy Zaner, Jimmy Clark, Danny Desmond, Billy Benedict, Kay Dowd, Eileen McClory, Douglas Wood, Frederick Giermann.

A refugee (Kruger) escapes from Nazi oppression, comes to America, and worries about the family he left behind.

2058. They Met in a Taxi (9/9/36) B&W—69 mins. (Comedy). DIR: Alfred E. Green. PRO/SP: Howard J. Green. Story by Octavius Roy Cohen. CAST: Chester Morris, Fay Wray, Lionel Stander, Raymond Walburn, Henry Mollison, Kenneth Harlan, Ann Merrill, Ward Bond, Frank Melton.

A cab driver (Morris) helps a woman (Wray) clear her name when she is accused of stealing a strand of pearls.

2059. They Rode West (12/54) Technicolor—84 mins. (Western).

DIR: Phil Karlson. PRO: Lewis J. Rachmil. SP: DeVallon Scott, Frank Nugent. Story by Leo Katcher. CAST: Robert Francis, Donna Reed, May Wynn, Phil Carey, Onslow Stevens, Roy Roberts, Jack Kelly, Stuart Randall, Eugene Iglesias, James Best, Peggy Converse, Frank DeKova, John War Eagle, Ralph Dumke, Julia Montoya, George Keymas, Maurice Jara.

A medical officer (Francis) loses the trust of his men when he treats the local Indian tribe during an outbreak of malaria. NOTES: The last film of Robert Francis.

2060. The Thief of Damascus (4/52) Technicolor—78 mins. (Adventure). DIR: Will Jason. PRO: Sam Katzman. SP: Robert E. Kent. CAST: Paul Henreid, John Sutton, Jeff Donnell, Lon Chaney, Jr., Elena Verdugo, Robert Clary, Edward Colmans, Nelson Leigh, Philip Van Zandt, Leonard Penn, Larry Stewart, Robert Conte.

A deposed Arabian general (Henreid) joins forces with Sinbad (Chaney, Jr.), Aladdin (Clary), and Ali Baba (Van Zandt) to save the city of Damascus from invaders. NOTES: This film used extensive footage from the 1948 RKO film *Joan of Arc.*

2061. Things Are Tough All Over (8/82) Eastman Color/Panavision—92 mins. (Comedy). DIR: Thomas K. Avildsen. PRO: Howard Brown. SP: Richard "Cheech" Marin, Thomas Chong. A C&C-Brown Production. CAST: Richard "Cheech" Marin, Thomas Chong, Toni Attell, Mike Bacarella, Billy Beck, Richard Calhoun, Rikki Marin, John Paragon, Lance Kinsey, Rip Taylor.

Two rock musicians (Cheech, Chong) have numerous misadventures while driving an Arab-owned, money-filled van to Las Vegas.

2062. Things Change (10/88) DeLuxe Color—105 mins. (Crime-Comedy). *DIR*: David Mamet. *PRO*: Michael Hausman. *SP*: David Mamet, Shel Silverstein. A Filmhaus Production. *CAST*: Don Ameche, Joe Mantegna, Robert Prosky, J. J. Johnston, Ricky Jay, Mike Nussbaum.

A Mafia underling (Mantegna) takes an old Chicago shoeshiner (Ameche), who resembles a Mafia don, out to Lake Tahoe for a final fling before he goes to jail, in place of the real don.

2063. The Things of Life (8/70) Eastman Color—90 mins. (Drama). *DIR*: Claude Sautet. *PRO*: Roland Girard, Jean Bolvary. *SP*: Paul Guimard, Jean-Loup Dabadie, Claude Sautet. Based on *Les Choses de la Vie* by Paul Guimard. A Lira-Fida-Sonocam Production. *CAST*: Romy Schneider, Michel Piccoli, Lea Massari, Jean Bouise, Herve Sand, Henri Nassiet, Gerard Lartigau.

An architect (Piccoli) has an affair with a younger woman (Schneider) and she demands that he give up his family and the things of his past life for her. [Original French title: *Les Choses de la Vie*].

2064. 13 Frightened Girls (7/63) Eastman Color—89 mins. (Spy-Adventure). *DIR/PRO*: William Castle. *SP*: Robert Dillon. Story by Otis L. Guernsey. *CAST*: Kathy Dunn, Murray Hamilton, Joyce Taylor, Hugh Marlowe, Khigh Dhiegh, Charlie Briggs, Norma Varden, Garth Benton, Lynne Sue Moon, Maria Cristina Servera, Janet Mary Prance, Penny Anne Mills, Alexandra L. Bastedo, Ariane Glaser, Ilona Schultze, Anna Baj, Aiko Sakamoto, Judy Pace, Luz Gloria Hervias, Marie-Louise Bielke, Ignacia Farias Luque, Emil Sitka, Jon Alvar, Walter Rode, Gina Trikonis.

A teenage girl (Dunn) stumbles into a murder, informs a CIA man (Hamilton) on whom she has a crush, and

with her friends, helps him to uncover an international spy ring.

2065. 13 Ghosts (7/60) B&W-Eastman Color—85 mins. (Horror). *DIR/PRO*: William Castle. *SP*: Robb White. *CAST*: Charles Herbert, Jo Morrow, Martin Milner, Rosemary DeCamp, Donald Woods, Margaret Hamilton, John Van Dreelan.

A family (Woods, DeCamp, Herbert, Morrow) moves into a haunted house where the 12 ghosts there are trying to recruit a thirteenth. *NOTES*: William Castle's gimmick for this film was using the "Illusion-O" ghost viewer, a pair of red and blue colored glasses, in which the audience was able to see the color ghost sequences by using the red lens, and remove the ghosts by using the blue lens.

2066. 13 West Street (5/62) B&W—80 mins. (Drama). *DIR*: Philip Peacock. *PRO*: William Bloom. *SP*: Bernard C. Schoenfeld, Robert Presnell, Jr. Based on *The Tiger Among Us* by Leigh Brackett. A Ladd Enterprises Production. *CAST*: Alan Ladd, Rod Steiger, Michael Callan, Dolores Dorn, Kenneth MacKenna, Margaret Hayes, Stanley Adams, Chris Robinson, Jeanne Cooper, Arnold Merritt, Mark Slade, Henry Beckman, Robert Cleaves, Bernie Hamilton, Ted Knight, Olan Soule.

An aerospace engineer (Ladd) takes the law into his own hands when he is attacked by a gang of youths and the leader (Callan) threatens his wife (Dorn).

2067. The Thirteenth Hour (3/6/47) B&W—65 mins. (Crime-Mystery). *DIR*: William Clemens. *PRO*: Rudolph C. Flothow. *SP*: Raymond L. Schrock, Edward Bock. Story by Leslie Edgley. Based on *The Whistler* radio program. *CAST*: Richard Dix, Karen Morley, Mark Dennis, John Kellogg, Bernadene Hayes, Jim Bannon, Regis

Toomey, Nancy Saunders, Lillian Wells, Michael Towne, Anthony Warde, Jack Carrington, Charles Jordan, Ernie Adams, Selmer Jackson, Pat O'Malley, Cliff Clark, Ed Park.

The owner of a trucking firm (Dix) sets out to prove his innocence when he is framed for murder. NOTES: The last film of Richard Dix.

2068. The 30 Foot Bride of Candy Rock (8/59) B&W/Scope — 75 mins. (Comedy). DIR: Sidney Miller. PRO: Lewis J. Rachmil. SP: Rowland Barber, Arthur A. Ross. Story by Lawrence L. Goldman from an idea by Jack Rabin, Irving Block. A D.R.B. Production. CAST: Lou Costello, Dorothy Provine, Gale Gordon, Jimmy Conlin, Charles Lane, Robert Burton, Will Wright, Lenny Kent, Ruth Perrott, Peter Leeds, Joey Faye, Doodles Weaver, Jack Rice, Veola Vonn.

A rubbish collector (Costello), who is also an inventor, accidentally causes his girl (Provine) to grow 30 feet in height. NOTES: This film was advertised as filmed in "Wonderama and Mattascope"; the last film of Lou Costello and his only film without Bud Abbott.

2069. 30 Is a Dangerous Age, Cynthia (3/68) Technicolor — 85 mins. (Comedy-Musical). DIR: Joseph McGrath. PRO: Walter Shenson. SP: Dudley Moore, John Wells, Joseph McGrath. CAST: Dudley Moore, Eddie Foy, Jr., Suzy Kendall, John Bird, Duncan MacRae, Patricia Routledge, Peter Bayliss, John Wells, Harry Towb, Frank Thornton, Derek Farr, Michael MacLaimmoir.

A young man (Moore) decides to get married and have his musical comedy produced before he reaches the age of 30.

2070. This Angry Age (5/58) Technicolor/Technirama — 111 mins. (Drama). DIR: Rene Clement. PRO:

Dino De Laurentiis. SP: Rene Clement, Irwin Shaw. Based on Sea Wall by Marguerite Duras. CAST: Anthony Perkins, Silvana Mangano, Richard Conte, Jo Van Fleet, Nehemiah Persoff, Yvonne Sanson, Alida Valli, Guido Celano, Chu Shao Chuan.

In Indochina, a mother (Van Fleet) and her two children (Perkins, Mangano) fight to keep their rice farm from a government agent (Conte), another landowner (Persoff), and the sea. [British title: The Sea Wall]. [Original Italian title: La Diga Sul Pacifico].

2071. This Man Is Mine (9/46) B&W — 103 mins. (Comedy). DIR/PRO: Marcel Varnel. SP: Doreen Montgomery, Norman Lee, Nicholas Phipps, Reginald Beckwith, Mabel Constanduros, Val Valentine, David Evans. Based on A Soldier for Christmas by Reginald Beckwith. A Columbia-British Production. CAST: Tom Walls, Glynis Johns, Jeanne de Casalis, Hugh McDermott, Nova Pilbeam, Barry Morse, Rosalyn Boulter, Ambrosine Phillpotts, Mary Merrall, Bernard Lee, Charles Victor.

In 1942, a Canadian soldier (McDermott) stays with an eccentric English family and is pursued by the daughter (Pilbeam) and the maid (Johns).

2072. This Sporting Age (10/1/32) B&W — 67 mins. (Drama). DIR: Andrew Bennison, A. F. Erickson. SP: Dudley Nichols. Story by J. K. McGuinness. CAST: Jack Holt, Evalyn Knapp, Hardie Albright, Walter Byron, Ruth Weston, J. Farrell MacDonald, Nora Lane, Shirley Palmer, Hal Price.

An Army captain (Holt), who is an avid polo player, engages the man (Byron) who wronged his daughter (Knapp) to a game of polo and kills him on the polo field.

2073. This Thing Called Love (2/2/41) B&W — 98 mins. (Comedy).

DIR: Alexander Hall. *PRO:* William Perlberg. *SP:* George Seaton, Ken Englund, P. J. Wolfson. Based on the play by Edwin Burke. *CAST:* Melvyn Douglas, Rosalind Russell, Allyn Joslyn, Gloria Holden, Lee J. Cobb, Gloria Dickson, Binnie Barnes, Paul McGrath, Leona Maricle, Don Beddoe, Rosina Galli, Sig Arno.

A pair of newlyweds (Douglas, Russell) have a problem with their marriage and decide on a three month platonic relationship. NOTES: This film was banned by the Catholic Legion of Decency for its uninhibited approach to sex. A remake of the 1929 Pathe film of the same name. [British title: *Married—But Single*].

2074. Thomasine and Bushrod (4/74) Eastman Color—93 mins. (Crime-Drama). *DIR:* Gordon Parks, Jr. *PRO:* Max Julien, Harvey Bernhard. *SP:* Max Julien. *CAST:* Max Julien, Vonetta McGee, George Murdock, Juanita Moore, Glynn Turman, Joel Fluellen, Jackson D. Kane, Bud Conlan, Kip Allen, Ben Zeller, Herb Robins, Harry Luck, Jason Bernard.

A black "Bonnie and Clyde" team (McGee, Julien) operate in 1911 Texas and New Mexico as they try to help the Mexicans, Indians, and poor whites.

2075. Those High Grey Walls (6/20/39) B&W—81 mins. (Prison-Drama). *DIR:* Charles Vidor. *PRO:* B. B. Kahane. *SP:* Lewis Meltzer. Story by William A. Ullman, Jr. *CAST:* Walter Connolly, Onslow Stevens, Paul Fix, Bernard Nedell, Iris Meredith, Oscar O'Shea, Nicholas Soussanin, Don Beddoe.

A doctor (Connolly) ends up in prison when he treats a convict he had delivered as a baby. He tries to work with the prison doctor (Stevens) who resents him, but is accepted in time and is later paroled when he is mis-takenly implicated in a prison break which he thwarts.

2076. A Thousand and One Nights (7/26/45) Technicolor—92 mins. (Comedy). *DIR:* Alfred E. Green. *PRO:* Samuel Bischoff. *SP:* Richard English, Jack Henley, Wilfrid H. Pettitt. Story by Wilfrid H. Pettitt. *CAST:* Cornel Wilde, Evelyn Keyes, Phil Silvers, Adele Jergens, Dusty Anderson, Dennis Hoey, Philip Van Zandt, Gus Schilling, Nestor Paiva, Rex Ingram, Richard Hale, Carole Mathews, Pat Parrish, Shelley Winters, Trevor Bardette, Dick Botiller, Cy Kendall, Frank Lackteen, John Abbott.

Aladdin (Wilde) is thwarted in his attempt to marry a princess (Jergens) by the genie (Keyes) of the lamp. NOTES: Rex Ingram reprised his giant genie role from the 1940 London Films-United Artists film *The Thief of Baghdad.*

2077. Three for the Show (4/55) Technicolor/Scope—93 mins. (Musical). *DIR:* H. C. Potter. *PRO:* Jonie Taps. *SP:* Edward Hope, Leonard Stern. Based on the play *Too Many Husbands* by W. Somerset Maugham. *CAST:* Betty Grable, Marge Champion, Gower Champion, Jack Lemmon, Myron McCormick, Paul Harvey, Robert Bice, Hal K. Dawson, Charlotte Lawrence, Willard Waterman, Gene Wesson, Aileen Caryle, Eugene Borden.

A showgirl (Grable) marries her late husband's partner (Gower Champion) but her first husband (Lemmon) shows up and she decides to set up house with both since she cannot decide which one she loves more. NOTES: A musical remake of the 1940 Columbia film *Too Many Husbands.* This film was banned by the Catholic Legion of Decency for its approach to the subject of polygamy.

2078. Three Girls About Town
(12/21/41) B&W — 71 mins. (Comedy).
DIR: Leigh Jason. PRO: Samuel Bis-
choff. SP: Richard Carroll. CAST:
Joan Blondell, Janet Blair, Binnie
Barnes, John Howard, Robert Bench-
ley, Eric Blore, Hugh O'Connell, Una
O'Conner, Paul Harvey, Frank Mc-
Glynn, Almira Sessions, Dorothy
Vaughn, Walter Soderling, Ben Tag-
gart, Chester Clute, Eddie Laughton,
Dick Elliott, Charles Lane, Bess
Flowers, Larry Parks, Bruce Bennett,
Lloyd Bridges, John Tyrrell, Lester
Dorr, Ray Walker, William Newell, Ar-
thur Loft, Jessie Arnold, Barbara
Brown, Sarah Edwards.

A reporter (Howard) helps two hotel
employees (Barnes, Blondell) and their
sister (Blair) out of a jam when they
find a dead body in the hotel during a
convention.

2079. Three Hours to Kill (10/
54) Technicolor — 77 mins. (Western).
DIR: Alfred L. Werker. PRO: Harry
Joe Brown. SP: Richard Alan Sim-
mons, Roy Huggins, Maxwell Shane.
Story by Alex Gottlieb. CAST: Dana
Andrews, Donna Reed, Dianne Fos-
ter, Stephen Elliott, Laurence Hugo,
Richard Webb, Carolyn Jones, Whit
Bissell, Francis McDonald, Richard
Coogan, James Westerfield, Charlotte
Fletcher, Felipe Turich, Arthur Fox,
Syd Saylor, Frank Hagney, Paul E.
Burns.

A man (Andrews) returns to the
town that tried to lynch him for a
murder he did not commit, determined to find the real killer.

2080. Three on a Couch (3/66)
Pathe Color — 109 mins. (Comedy).
DIR/PRO: Jerry Lewis. SP: Bob Ross,
Samuel A. Taylor. Story by Arne Sul-
tan, Marvin Worth. A Jerry Lewis Pro-
duction. CAST: Jerry Lewis, Janet
Leigh, Gila Golan, Fritz Feld, Buddy
Lester, Renzo Cesana, Kathleen Free-

man, Leslie Parrish, Mary Ann Mobley, James Best, Renie Riano, Scatman
Crothers.

Before an artist (Lewis) can take a
scholarship in Paris with his fiancee
(Leigh), he decides to cure three of her
female patients (Golan, Mobley, Parrish) with "men" trouble by donning
disguises and pretending to be their
boy friends. NOTES: Jerry Lewis' first
film for Columbia.

**2081. The Three Stooges Fol-
lies** (6/74) B&W — 106 mins. (Comedy-
Action).

A collection of Three Stooges
shorts, Buster Keaton shorts, and Vera
Vague (Barbara Jo Allen) shorts,
Chapter 1 of the 1949 serial Batman
and Robin, and a 1942 musical short,
America Sings, with Kate Smith.

**2082. The Three Stooges Go
Around the World in a Daze** (9/63)
B&W — 94 mins. (Comedy-Adven-
ture). DIR/PRO: Norman Maurer.
SP: Elwood Ullman. Story by Norman
Maurer. Based on Around the World in
80 Days by Jules Verne. A Normandy
Production. CAST: The Three
Stooges (Moe Howard, Larry Fine, Joe
DeRita), Jay Sheffield, Joan Freeman,
Walter Burke, Peter Forster, Maurice
Dallimore, Richard Devon, Anthony
Eustrel, Murray Alper, Don Lamond,
Jack Greening, Emil Sitka, Ramsay
Hill, Colin Campbell, Ron Whelan.

The Three Stooges embark on an
around the world trip with Phileas
Fogg III (Sheffield) as he wagers he can
make the same trip as his great-grand-
father.

**2083. The Three Stooges in Or-
bit** (7/62) B&W — 87 mins. (Comedy-
Science Fiction). DIR: Edward
Bernds. PRO: Norman Maurer. SP:
Elwood Ullman. Story by Norman
Maurer. A Normandy Production.
CAST: The Three Stooges (Moe How-
ard, Larry Fine, Joe DeRita), Carol

Christensen, Edson Stroll, Emil Sitka, George N. Neise, Rayford Barnes, Norman Leavitt, Nestor Paiva, Peter Dawson, Peter Brocco, Don Lamond, Thomas Glynn, Maurice Manson, Bill Dyer, Roy Engel.

The Three Stooges become involved with Martians trying to steal a rocket-tank-sub invention.

2084. The Three Stooges Meet Hercules (1/62) B&W—89 mins. (Comedy). *DIR*: Edward Bernds. *PRO*: Norman Maurer. *SP*: Elwood Ullman. Story by Norman Maurer. A Normandy Production. *CAST*: The Three Stooges (Moe Howard, Larry Fine, Joe DeRita), Vicki Trickett, Quinn Redeker, George N. Neise, Samson Burke, Mike McKeever, Marlan McKeever, Emil Sitka, Hal Smith, John Cliff, Lewis Charles, Barbara Hines, Terry Huntington, Diana Piper, Gregg Martell, Gene Roth, Rusty Wescoatt, Don Lamond, Edward Foster, Cecil Elliott.

The Three Stooges return to Ithaca, Greece, in 961 B.C. via a time machine where they meet Hercules (Burke), Ulysses (Cliff) and other figures of Greek literature.

2085. Three Stripes in the Sun (11/55) B&W—93 mins. (Drama). *DIR*: Richard Murphy. *PRO*: Fred Kohlmar. *SP*: Richard Murphy, Albert Duffy. Based on *The Gentle Wolfhound* by E. J. Kahn, Jr. *CAST*: Aldo Ray, Phil Carey, Dick York, Mitsuko Kimura, Chuck Conners, Camille Janclaire, Henry Okawa, Tatsuo Saito.

In 1949, an Army sergeant (Ray), stationed in Japan, undergoes a change of heart against the Japanese as he tries to help Japanese orphans. [British title: *The Gentle Sergeant*].

2086. 3:10 to Yuma (7/57) B&W—92 mins. (Western). *DIR*: Delmer Daves. *PRO*: David Heilwell. *SP*: Halsted Welles. Story by Elmore Leon-

ard. *CAST*: Glenn Ford, Felicia Farr, Van Heflin, Leora Dana, Henry Jones, Richard Jaeckel, Robert Emhardt, Ford Rainey, Sheridan Comerate, George Mitchell, Robert Ellenstein, Barry Curtis, Jerry Hartleben.

A rancher (Heflin), in desperate need of money, decides to deliver an outlaw (Ford) to the state prison at Yuma, but when his gang shows up, the rancher is abandoned by the townspeople and has to face the gang alone.

2087. Three Wise Girls (2/7/32) B&W—68 mins. (Drama). *DIR*: William Beaudine. *SP*: Agnes C. Johnson, Robert Riskin. Based on *Blonde Baby* by Wilson Collinson. *CAST*: Jean Harlow, Mae Clarke, Walter Byron, Marie Prevost, Andy Devine, Natalie Moorhead, Jameson Thomas, Lucy Beaumont, Katherine Claire Ward, Robert Dudley, Marcia Harris, Walter Miller, Armand Kaliz.

The story of three girls in New York. One (Clarke) commits suicide when her lover (Thomas) won't give up his wife for her, another (Prevost) marries a chauffeur (Devine), and the third (Harlow) becomes disillusioned and heads back home only to be followed by her lover (Byron) who promises to give up his wife for her. *NOTES*: Jean Harlow's final film for Columbia.

2088. The Three Worlds of Gulliver (12/60) Eastman Color/Dynamation—98 mins. (Fantasy-Adventure). *DIR*: Jack Sher. *PRO*: Charles H. Schneer. *SP*: Arthur A. Ross, Jack Sher. Based on *Gulliver's Travels* by Jonathan Swift. A Morningside Production. *CAST*: Kerwin Mathews, Jo Morrow, June Thorburn, Lee Patterson, Gregoire Aslan, Basil Sydney, Charles Lloyd Pack, Martin Benson, Mary Ellis, Peter Bull, Alec Mango, Sherri Alberoni, Marian Spencer.

Gulliver (Mathews), shipwrecked

during a storm at sea, encounters adventures on the islands of Lilliput and Brobdingnag. NOTES: Special effects by Ray Harryhausen.

2089. The Thrill Hunter (5/1/26) B&W—57 mins. (Comedy). DIR: Eugene De Lue. PRO: Harry Cohn. CAST: William Haines, Kathryn McGuire, Alma Bennett, E. J. Ratcliffe, Frankie Darro.

An author (Haines), mistaken for a foreign king and forced to marry a princess (Bennett), escapes and ends up with the daughter (McGuire) of his publisher (Ratcliffe).

2090. The Thrill Hunter (4/30/33) B&W—60 mins. (Western-Comedy). DIR: George B. Seitz. PRO: Irving Briskin. SP: Harry O. Hoyt. CAST: Buck Jones, Dorothy Revier, Edward J. LeSaint, Frank LaRue, Arthur Rankin, Robert Ellis, Al Smith, Harry Semels, Eddie Kane, Harry Todd, John Ince, Alf James, Willie Fung.

A cowboy (Jones) becomes a movie star, rounds up a gang of outlaws, and wins the leading lady (Revier).

2091. The Thrill of Brazil (9/11/46) B&W—91 mins. (Musical). DIR: S. Sylvan Simon. PRO: Sidney Biddell. SP: Allen Rivkin, Harry Clork, Devery Freeman. CAST: Evelyn Keyes, Keenan Wynn, Ann Miller, Allyn Joslyn, Tito Guizar, Felix Bressart, Sid Tomack, Eugene Borden, George J. Lewis, Robert Conte, Nino Bellini, Martin Garralaga, Alex Montoya, Frank Yaconelli, Enric Madriguera and His Orchestra, Veloz and Yolanda.

In Brazil, a Broadway producer (Wynn) tries to prevent his ex-wife (Keyes) from marrying a toothpaste magnate (Joslyn).

2092. Throw a Saddle on a Star (5/14/46) B&W—60 mins. (Western-Musical). DIR: Ray Nazarro. PRO:

Colbert Clark. SP: J. Benton Cheney. CAST: Ken Curtis, Jeff Donnell, Andy Clyde, Guinn "Big Boy" Williams, Emmett Lynn, Earl Duane, Frank Sully, Jack Parker, Robert Stevens, Eddie Bruce, Adelle Roberts, The Dinning Sisters, The Hoosier Hotshots, Foy Willing and the Riders of the Purple Sage.

The Hoosier Hotshots help a rodeo rider (Curtis) win the rodeo championship and the girl (Donnell).

2093. Thunder at the Border (11/67) Technicolor/Scope—94 mins. (Western). DIR: Alfred Vohrer. PRO: Horst Wendlandt. SP: Harald G. Petersson, David Dereszke, C. B. Taylor. Story by Karl Friedrich May. A Rialto-Jardan-Preben-Philipsen Production. CAST: Rod Cameron, Pierre Brice, Nadia Gray, Todd Armstrong, Marie Versini, Harald Peipnitz, Rik Battaglia.

Winnetou (Brice) and his friend Firehand (Cameron) help defend a Mexican village against bandits. [Original German title: *Winnetou und Sein Freund Old Firehand*].

2094. Thunder in the City (4/27/37) B&W—76 mins. (Comedy). DIR: Marion Gering. PRO: Alexander Esway, Akos Tolnay. SP: Akos Tolnay, Aben Kandel, Robert Sherwood, Walter Hackett. Story by Robert Sherwood, Aben Kandel. An Atlantic Production. CAST: Edward G. Robinson, Luli Deste, Nigel Bruce, Constance Collier, Ralph Richardson, Annie Esmond, Arthur Wontner, Elizabeth Inglis, Cyril Raymond, Nancy Burne, Billy Bray, James Carew, Everley Gregg, Elliott Nugent, Roland Drew.

An American promoter (Robinson) goes to London and helps an English couple (Bruce, Collier) promote a new mineral, "Magnelite," and ends up marrying their daughter (Deste).

2095. Thunder Over the Prairie (7/30/41) B&W—61 mins. (Western). DIR: Lambert Hillyer. PRO: William Berke. SP: Betty Burbridge. Based on *The Medico Rides* by James L. Rubel. CAST: Charles Starrett, Eileen O'Hearn, Cliff Edwards, Stanley Brown, David Sharpe, Donald Curtis, Jack Rockwell, Budd Buster, Danny Mummert, Ted Adams, Horace B. Carpenter, Joe McGuinn, Cal Shrum and His Rhythm Rangers.

Dr. Steven Monroe (Starrett) comes to the aid of an Indian medical student (Mummert) accused of murder.

2096. Thunderhoof (7/8/48) B&W—77 mins. (Western). DIR: Phil Karlson. PRO: Ted Richmond. SP: Hal Smith, Kenneth Gamet. CAST: Preston Foster, Mary Stuart, William Bishop, "Thunderhoof."

A rancher (Foster), his wife (Stuart), and his adopted son (Bishop) go in search of a black-and-white stallion. [British title: *Fury*].

2097. Thundering Frontier (12/5/40) B&W—57 mins. (Western). DIR: D. Ross Lederman. PRO: Jack Fier. SP: Paul Franklin. CAST: Charles Starrett, Iris Meredith, Bob Nolan, Carl Stockdale, Fred Burns, John Dilson, Blackie Whiteford, Pat Brady, Francis Walker, John Tyrrell, Ray Bennett, Alex Callam, Sons of the Pioneers.

A cowboy (Starrett) aids a young woman (Meredith) and her father (Stockdale) when a gang of outlaws begin sabotaging their business.

2098. The Thundering West (1/12/39) B&W—56 mins. (Western). DIR: Sam Nelson. PRO: Harry L. Decker. SP: Bennett R. Cohen. CAST: Charles Starrett, Iris Meredith, Dick Curtis, Robert Fiske, Bob Nolan, Hal Taliaferro (Wally Wales), Edward J. LeSaint, Blackie Whiteford, Clem Horton, Edmund Cobb, Hank Bell, Art Mix, Bud Osborne, Edward Piel, Sr., Slim Whitaker, Steve Clark, Fred Burns.

A former outlaw (Starrett) is made sheriff and is blackmailed by his former gang members to help them rob a gold shipment. NOTES: A remake of the 1934 Columbia film *The Man Trailer*.

2099. The Tiger Makes Out (10/67) Eastman Color—94 mins. (Comedy). DIR: Arthur Hiller. PRO: George Justin. SP: Murray Schisgal. Based on the play *The Tiger* by Murray Schisgal. CAST: Eli Wallach, Anne Jackson, Bob Dishy, John Harkins, Ruth White, Roland Wood, Rae Allen, Bibi Osterwald, Charles Nelson Reilly, David Doyle, Dustin Hoffman, John Ryan, Francis Sternhagen, David Burns, Edgar Stehli, Alice Beardsley, Kim August, Jack Fletcher.

A frustrated mailman (Wallach) decides to lash back at society by terrorizing his landlords (White, Wood) until they treat him right, and kidnapping a suburban housewife (Jackson) who agrees with his philosophy.

2100. Tight Spot (5/55) B&W—97 mins. (Crime-Drama). DIR: Phil Karlson. PRO: Lewis J. Rachmil. SP: William Bowers. Based on the play *Dead Pigeon* by Leonard Kantor. CAST: Edward G. Robinson, Ginger Rogers, Brian Keith, Lucy Marlow, Lorne Greene, Katherine Anderson, Allen Nourse, Peter Leeds, Doye O'Dell, Eve McVeagh, Helen Wallace, Frank Gerstle, Gloria Ann Simpson, Robert Shield, Norman Keats, Kathryn Grant, John Larch.

A U.S. attorney (Robinson) and police detective (Keith) use a woman (Rogers), wrongly put behind bars, as a key witness against a powerful crime kingpin (Greene).

2101. The Tigress (10/21/27) B&W—54 mins. (Drama). DIR:

George B. Seitz. *PRO:* Harry Cohn. *SP:* Harold Shumate. *CAST:* Jack Holt, Dorothy Revier, Frank Leigh, Philippe De Lacy, Howard Truesdell, Frank Nelson.

A gypsy (Revier) sets out to avenge the murder of her father (Truesdell), and prove that the owner of the estate (Holt) they had been camping on is innocent of the murder. *NOTES:* Jack Holt's first Columbia film.

2102. The Tijuana Story (10/57) B&W — 72 mins. (Crime). *DIR:* Leslie Kardos. *PRO:* Sam Katzman. *SP:* Lou Morheim. *CAST:* Rudolfo Acosta, James Darren, Robert McQueeney, Jean Willes, Joy Stoner, Paul Coates, Paul Newlan, George E. Stone, Robert Blake, Michael Fox, William Fawcett, Rick Vallin.

When a Tijuana newspaper reporter (Acosta) is assassinated by the mob, his son (Blake) takes up the crusade and sees that they are brought to justice. *NOTES:* Based on the real-life assassination of Tijuana newspaperman Manuel Acosta Mesa.

2103. Tillie the Toiler (8/13/41) B&W — 67 mins. (Comedy). *DIR:* Sidney Salkow. *PRO:* Robert Sparks. *SP:* Karen DeWolf, Francis Martin. Story by Karen DeWolf. Based on the newspaper comic strip created by Russ Westover. *CAST:* Kay Harris, William Tracy, George Watts, Daphne Pollard, Jack Arnold, Marjorie Reynolds, Bennie Bartlett, Stanley Brown, Ernest Truex, Franklin Pangborn, Sylvia Field, Edward Gargan, Harry Tyler.

Tillie (Harris) goes to work in her boyfriend's (Tracy) office as a stenographer, manages to almost ruin his business through her incompetence, but redeems herself and impresses the boss (Watts). *NOTES:* A remake of the 1927 MGM film with Marion Davies in the role of Tillie the Toiler. This film was planned as a series by Columbia

but poor box-office reception cancelled the idea. The film debut of Kay Harris.

2104. A Time for Killing (11/67) Pathe Color/Panavision — 88 mins. (Western). *DIR:* Phil Karlson. *PRO:* Harry Joe Brown. *SP:* Halsted Welles. Based on *The Southern Blade* by Nelson Wolford, Shirley Wolford. A Sage Production. *CAST:* Glenn Ford, Inger Stevens, Paul Peterson, Timothy Carey, George Hamilton, Richard X. Slattery, Emile Meyer, Marshall Reed, Kenneth Tobey, Max Baer, Todd Armstrong, Dick Miller, Harrison Ford, Kay E. Kuter, Duke Hobbie, Harry Dean Stanton, James Davidson, Charlie Briggs, Craig Curtis, Jay Ripley.

A Confederate major (Hamilton) and his men escape from a Union prison camp and are pursued by a Union captain (Ford) who seeks vengeance when they take his wife (Stevens) hostage. *NOTES:* The film's original director was Roger Corman who was replaced by Phil Karlson. [British title: *The Long Ride Home*].

2105. A Time of Destiny (2/88) DeLuxe Color — 118 mins. (Drama). *DIR:* Gregory Nava. *PRO:* Anna Thomas. *SP:* Anna Thomas, Gregory Nava. A Nelson-Alive Films Production. *CAST:* William Hurt, Timothy Hutton, Melissa Leo, Francisco Rabal, Stockard Channing, Megan Follows, Frederick Coffin.

A soldier (Hurt) vows revenge against his brother-in-law (Hutton) for marrying his sister (Leo) and accidentally killing his father (Rabal).

2106. Time Out for Rhythm (6/2/41) B&W — 74 mins. (Musical). *DIR:* Sidney Salkow. *PRO:* Irving Starr. *SP:* Edmund L. Hartmann, Bert Lawrence, Bert Granet. Based on the play *Show Business* by Alex Ruben. *CAST:* Ann Miller, Rudy Vallee, Rosemary

Lane, Allen Jenkins, Joan Merrill, Richard Lane, Stanley Andrews, The Three Stooges (Moe Howard, Larry Fine, Curly Howard), Six Hits and a Miss, Brenda and Cobina (Blanche Stewart, Elvia Allman), Eddie Durant and His Rhumba Orchestra, Glen Gray and His Casa Loma Band.

Two theatrical booking agents (Richard Lane, Vallee) each decide to go their separate ways and book their new discoveries (Rosemary Lane, Miller).

2107. The Tingler (10/59) B&W — 80 mins. (Horror). *DIR/PRO:* William Castle. *SP:* Robb White. *CAST:* Vincent Price, Judith Evelyn, Darryl Hickman, Patricia Cutts, Pamela Lincoln, Philip Coolidge.

A scientist (Price) discovers that fear will grow inside people, become an insectlike creature called "The Tingler" and attach itself to the spinal column, but if the person screams the creature dies. *NOTES:* William Castle's gimmick for this film was "Percepto," the attaching of vibrating motors to selected theater seats that would vibrate the seats during a crucial part of the film where the audience is supposed to scream.

To Elvis, with Love *see* **Touched by Love**

2108. To Find a Man (1/72) B&W — 90 mins. (Drama). *DIR:* Buzz Kulik. *PRO:* Irving Pincus. *SP:* Arnold Schulman. Based on the book by S. J. Wilson. A Pincus-Abrahams-Kulik Production. *CAST:* Pamela Sue Martin, Darren O'Conner, Lloyd Bridges, Phyllis Newman, Tom Ewell, Tom Bosley, Miles Chapin, Schell Rasten, Antonia Rey.

A boy (O'Conner) attempts to help a girl (Martin) get an abortion. [British title: *The Boy Next Door*].

2109. To Sir, with Love (6/67) Technicolor — 105 mins. (Drama).

DIR/PRO/SP: James Clavell. Based on the book by E. R. Braithwaite. *CAST:* Sidney Poitier, Judy Geeson, Christian Roberts, Suzy Kendall, Faith Brook, Geoffrey Bayldon, Rita Webb, Lulu, Fiona Duncan, Patricia Routledge, Christopher Chittell, Adrienne Posta, Edward Burnham.

A black engineer (Poitier), unable to find work, takes a job as a schoolteacher, is assigned to a London slum school where the students are rowdy and undisciplined, and eventually earns the respect of his students through his teaching methods.

2110. To the Ends of the Earth (2/27/48) B&W — 109 mins. (Crime). *DIR:* Robert Stevenson. *PRO:* Sidney Buchman. *SP:* Jay Richard Kennedy. *CAST:* Dick Powell, Signe Hasso, Maylia, Ludwig Donath, Vladimir Sokoloff, Edgar Barrier, John Hoyt, Marcel Journet, Luis Van Rooten, Fritz Leiber, Vernon Steele, Peter Virgo, Lou Krugman, Eddie Lee, Ivan Triesault, Leon Lenoir, George Volk, Robert Malcolm, Commissioner Harry J. Anslinger.

A Treasury agent (Powell) follows clues to Shanghai, Egypt, Cuba, and New Jersey as he tries to stop an international gang of opium smugglers.

2111. Together Again (10/30/44) B&W — 93 mins. (Comedy). *DIR:* Charles Vidor. *PRO:* Virginia Van Upp. *SP:* Virginia Van Upp, F. Hugh Herbert. Story by Stanley Russell, Herbert Biberman. *CAST:* Irene Dunne, Charles Boyer, Charles Coburn, Mona Freeman, Jerome Courtland, Elizabeth Patterson, Charles Dingle, Walter Baldwin, Fern Emmett, Janis Carter, Frank Puglia, Adele Jergens, Virginia Sale, Jessie Arnold, Isabel Withers, Virginia Brissac, Sam Flint, Carole Mathews, Shelley Winters, Adelle Roberts, Carl "Alfalfa" Switzer, Jimmy Lloyd, Ralph Dunn,

James Flavin, Charles Arnt, Milton Kibbee, Paul E. Burns, Hobart Cavanaugh, William Newell.

When the widow mayor (Dunne) of a small town and a New York sculptor (Boyer) get together, complications develop in the form of her father-in-law (Coburn), her teenage daughter (Freeman) and her daughter's boyfriend (Courtland). NOTES: The film debut of Jerome Courtland.

2112. Together We Live (3/1/35) B&W—70 mins. (Drama). DIR/SP: Willard Mack. CAST: Willard Mack, Ben Lyon, Esther Ralston, Sheila Mannors, Hobart Bosworth, Wera Engels, Charles Sabin, William Bakewell, Claude Gillingwater, William V. Mong, Richard Carle, Lou Tellegen, Carlyle Moore, Jr.

During the San Francisco strike of 1934, a Civil War veteran (Mack) tries to show his two older boys the error of their ways when they take an interest in Communism. NOTES: The last film of Willard Mack. He died after production was completed which delayed the film's release.

2113. Toilers of the Sea (2/36) B&W—83 mins. (Adventure). DIR: Selwyn Jepson, Ted Fox. PRO: L. C. Beaumont. SP: Selwyn Jepson. Based on *Toilers of the Sea* by Victor Hugo. A Beaumont Production. CAST: Cyril McLaglen, Mary Lawson, Ian Colin, Andrews Engelmann, Walter Sondes, Wilson Coleman, William Dewhurst.

A seaman (McLaglen) salvages the first steamship after the captain (Engelmann) abandons it for personal gains. NOTES: Cyril McLaglen was Victor McLaglen's brother.

2114. Tokyo Joe (10/11/49) B&W—88 mins. (Drama). DIR: Stuart Heisler. PRO: Robert Lord. SP: Cyril Hume, Walter Doniger, Bertram Millhauser. Story by Steve Fisher. A Santana Pictures Production. CAST:

Humphrey Bogart, Alexander Knox, Florence Marly, Sessue Hayakawa, Jerome Courtland, Gordon Jones, Teru Shimada, Hideo Mori, Charles Meredith, Rhys Williams, Lora Lee Michel, Harold Goodwin, James Cardwell, Kyoko Kama, Gene Gondo, Frank Kumagai, Otto Han.

An American serviceman (Bogart) returns to Tokyo after the war to locate his missing wife (Marly), gets involved with a Japanese Secret Service agent (Hayakawa), and sacrifices his life to save his daughter (Michel).

2115. Tol'able David (11/16/30) B&W—65 mins. (Drama). DIR: John Blystone. SP: Benjamin Glazer. Story by Joseph Hergesheimer. CAST: Richard Cromwell, Joan Peers, Noah Beery, Sr., John Carradine, Tom Keene, Henry B. Walthall, Edmund Breese, Barbara Bedford, Helen Ware, Richard Carlyle, Harlan E. Knight, James Bradbury, Jr.

The son (Cromwell) of a hillbilly family, the Kinemons, proves himself a man when he rescues the U.S. Mail from the Hatburn family. NOTES: A remake of the 1921 Associated First National (AFN) silent film. The film debut of Richard Cromwell in his first starring role.

2116. Tommy (3/75) Metrocolor— 111 mins. (Musical). DIR/SP: Ken Russell. PRO: Robert Stigwood, Ken Russell. Based on the musical drama by Robert Townshend. A Hemdale Production. CAST: Ann-Margret, Oliver Reed, Roger Daltry, Elton John, Eric Clapton, Keith Moon, Jack Nicholson, Robert Powell, Paul Nicholas, Tina Turner, Barry Winch, Victoria Russell, Ben Aris, Arthur Brown, Mary Holland, The Who.

The rock opera, told entirely in song, about a deaf and blind boy (Daltry) who enters a world of his own after his father dies.

2117. Tonight and Every Night (1/9/45) Technicolor—92 mins. (Musical). *DIR/PRO:* Victor Saville. *SP:* Lesser Samuels, Abem Finkel. Based on the play *Heart of a City* by Lesley Storm. *CAST:* Rita Hayworth, Lee Bowman, Janet Blair, Marc Platt, Leslie Brooks, Professor Lamberti, Dusty Anderson, Stephen Crane, Jim Bannon, Florence Bates, Ernest Cossart, Philip Merivale, Patrick O'Moore, Gavin Muir, Shelley Winters, Marilyn Johnson, Mildred Law, Jeanne Bates, Adele Jergens, Queenie Leonard, Richard Hayden, Robert Williams.

During World War II, despite Nazi bombings and personal hardships, a singer (Hayworth) makes the decision to give up the man (Bowman) she loves in order to continue entertaining the troops at the Music Box theater in London.

2118. Too Many Husbands (3/21/40) B&W—84 mins. (Comedy). *DIR/PRO:* Wesley Ruggles. *SP:* Claude Binyon. Based on the play *Too Many Husbands* by W. Somerset Maugham. *CAST:* Jean Arthur, Fred MacMurray, Melvyn Douglas, Harry Davenport, Dorothy Peterson, Melville Cooper, Edgar Buchanan, Tom Dugan, Gary Owen, Lee "Lasses" White, Mary Treen, William Brisbane, Sam McDaniels, Walter Soderling.

A widow (Arthur) marries a publisher (Douglas) when her husband (MacMurray) is reported drowned on a cruise. He later shows up and they both vie for her affections till a judge rules that she is still married to her first husband. *NOTES:* Remade by Columbia in 1955 as *Three for the Show*. [British title: *My Two Husbands*].

2119. Too Tough to Kill (12/20/35) B&W—58 mins. (Drama). *DIR:* D. Ross Lederman. *PRO:* Ben Pivar. *SP:* Lester Cole, Griffin Jay. Story by Robert D. Speers. *CAST:* Victor Jory,

Sally O'Neil, Thurston Hall, Johnny Arthur, Robert Gleckler, George McKay, Robert Middlemass, Dewey Robinson, Ward Bond.

An engineer (Jory) is sent to the Southwest to speed progress on a tunnel, and with the help of a girl reporter (O'Neil) and her cameraman (Arthur) gets rid of the criminals impeding construction.

2120. Tootsie (12/82) Technicolor/Panavision—116 mins. (Comedy). *DIR:* Sydney Pollack. *PRO:* Sydney Pollack, Dick Richards. *SP:* Larry Gelbart, Murray Schisgal. Story by Don McGuire and Larry Gelbart. *CAST:* Dustin Hoffman, Jessica Lange, Teri Garr, Dabney Coleman, Charles Durning, Bill Murray, Sydney Pollack, George Gaynes, Geena Davis, Doris Belack, Ellen Foley, Lynne Thigpen, Murray Schisgal, Estelle Getty.

Determined to get into show business, a man (Hoffman) disguises himself as a woman and becomes an overnight star on a TV soap. *NOTES:* Yes, co-author Don McGuire is the same Don McGuire who was a bit player at Columbia in the 40's and the star of the 1948 serial *Congo Bill*.

2121. Torero! (11/57) B&W—75 mins. (Documentary). *DIR:* Carlos Velo. *PRO:* Manuel Barbachano Ponce. *SP:* Carlos Velo, Hugo Mozo. *CAST:* Luis Procuna, Senora Procuna, Angel Procuna, Antonio Sevilla, Jose Farjat, Arturo Fregoso, Ponciana Diaz, Paco Malgetso, Manolete, Carlos Arruza, Luis Briones, Manuel Dos Santos, Luis Castro, Lorenz Garza.

A docudrama about bullfighting, based on the life of the great Mexican bullfighter Luis Procuna, as told through newsreel clips and Procuna himself.

2122. A Tornado in the Saddle (12/15/42) B&W—59 mins. (Western).

DIR: William Berke. PRO: Leon Barsha. SP: Charles F. Royal. CAST: Russell Hayden, Alma Carroll, Dub Taylor, Tristram Coffin, Donald Curtis, Blackie Whiteford, George Morrell, Jack Evans, Art Mix, Jack Kirk, Leon McAulfie, Tex Cooper, Jack Baxley, Hailey Higgins, John Merton, Ted Mapes, Carl Sepulveda, Rube Dalroy, Bob Wills and His Texas Playboys.

A sheriff (Hayden) goes after a crooked saloon owner (Coffin) when he hijacks a gold claim. [British title: Ambushed].

2123. Torture Garden (3/68) Technicolor—93 mins. (Horror). DIR: Freddie Francis. PRO: Max J. Rosenberg, Milton Subotsky. SP: Robert Bloch. An Amicus Production. CAST: Jack Palance, Burgess Meredith, Beverly Adams, Peter Cushing, John Standing, Maurice Denham, Michael Bryant, Robert Hutton, Bernard Kay, Niall MacGinnis, John Phillips, Michael Ripper, Catherine Finn, Roy Stevens, James Copeland, Barbara Ewing, Ursula Howells, Geoffrey Wallace, Hedger Wallace.

A series of four short stories linked together by a carnival barker (Meredith) who gives a group of people a glimpse into their future; Enoch—a playboy (Bryant) falls under the spell of a demon cat and is forced to kill people so that the cat can eat their heads; Terror Over Hollywood—a would-be movie star (Adams), in love with her robot leading man (Hutton), is turned into a robot and achieves everlasting fame; Mr. Steinway—a female reporter (Ewing) falls in love with a concert pianist (Standing) and is killed by his piano which contains the spirit of his dead mother; The Man Who Collected Poe—a collector (Palance) of Edgar Allen Poe memorabilia murders a fellow collector (Cushing) for his collection and learns that his greatest trea-

sure was Poe (Hedger Wallace) himself.

2124. Touched by Love (4/80) Metrocolor—95 mins. (Drama). DIR: Gus Trikonis. PRO: Michael Viner. SP: Hesper Anderson. Based on To Elvis, With Love by Lena Canada. A Rastar Production. CAST: Deborah Raffin, Diane Lane, Michael Learned, John Amos, Christina Raines, Mary Wickes, Clu Gulager, Twyla Volkins.

Based on a true story, a nurse (Raffin) encourages a cerebral palsy victim (Lane) to write to her idol, Elvis Presley, which she does. He responds, and they start a correspondence with each other until her death.

2125. The Tougher They Come (11/16/50) Sepiatone—69 mins. (Action-Drama). DIR: Ray Nazarro. PRO: Wallace MacDonald. SP: George Bricker. CAST: Wayne Morris, Preston Foster, Kay Buckley, William Bishop, Frank McHugh, Gloria Henry, Mary Castle, Joseph Crehan, Frank O'Conner, Al Bridge, Al Thompson.

Two loggers (Morris, Foster) inherit a logging camp and have to stop a corporation and their camp foreman (Bishop) from sabotaging their operation.

2126. Town on Trial! (8/57) B&W—96 mins. (Crime-Mystery). DIR: John Guillermin. PRO: Maxwell Setton. SP: Robert Westerby, Ken Hughes. A Marksman Films Ltd. Production. CAST: Charles Coburn, John Mills, Barbara Bates, Derek Farr, Alec McCowen, Elizabeth Seal, Geoffrey Keen, Margaretta Scott, Fay Compton, Meredith Edwards, Harry Locke, Maureen Connell, Magda Miller, Oscar Quitak, Newton Blick, Grace Arnold, Dandy Nichols, Raymond Huntley, Totti Truman Taylor.

A Scotland Yard detective (Mills) investigates a double murder in a small town; his list of suspects includes a blackmailer (Farr), a doctor (Coburn), the mayor (Keen), and a mental patient (McCowen).

2127. The Toy (12/82) DeLuxe Color—110 mins. (Comedy). *DIR:* Richard Donner. *PRO:* Phil Feldman. *SP:* Carol Sobieski. Based on the 1976 French film *Le Jouet* by Francis Veber. A Rastar Production. *CAST:* Richard Pryor, Jackie Gleason, Ned Beatty, Scott Schwartz, Teresa Ganzel, Wilfrid Hyde-White, Annazette Chase, Tony King, Don Hood, Virginia Capers, B. J. Hopper, Linda McCann, Ray Spruell.

A millionaire father (Gleason) buys his son (Schwartz) a human (Pryor) for a "toy," and the boy comes to learn that friendship must be earned, not bought.

2128. Traffic (12/72) Eastman Color—89 mins. (Comedy). *DIR:* Jacques Tati. *PRO:* Robert Dorfmann. *SP:* Jacques LaGrange, Jacques Tati. A Corona Production. *CAST:* Jacques Tati, Maria Kimberly, Marcel Fraval, Tony Kneppers, Honore Bostel, Francoise Maisongrosse.

Mr. Hulot (Tati) has several misadventures with automobiles and traffic problems when he drives his camper from Paris to Amsterdam to an auto show. *NOTES:* This was Jacques Tati's fifth film as director in a span of 25 years. His fourth, *Playtime*, was completed in 1967, but not released until 1973. [Original French title: *Trafic*].

2129. Traffic in Hearts (7/1/24) B&W—57 mins. (Drama). *DIR:* Scott R. Dunlap. *PRO:* Harry Cohn. *SP:* Jack Sturmwasser. Story by Jack Stone, Dorothy Yost. A C.B.C. Release. *CAST:* Robert Frazer, Mildred Harris, Don Marion, Charles Wellesley.

An architect (Frazer) is prevented from building model tenements for the poor by the politician father (Wellesley) of his sweetheart (Harris).

2130. Trail of the Rustlers (2/2/50) B&W—55 mins. (Western). *DIR:* Ray Nazarro. *PRO:* Colbert Clark. *SP:* Victor Arthur. *CAST:* Charles Starrett, Gail Davis, Smiley Burnette, Tommy Ivo, Myron Healey, Don C. Harvey, Gene Roth, Mira McKinney, Chuck Roberson, Eddie Cletro and His Roundup Boys.

The Durango Kid (Starrett) stops a mother (McKinney) and her two sons (Harvey, Healey) from stealing the ranch lands and gaining control of the valley when it is discovered that an underground river runs through the ranches. [British title: *Lost River*].

2131. Trail to Laredo (8/12/48) B&W—54 mins. (Western). *DIR:* Ray Nazarro. *PRO:* Colbert Clark. *SP:* Barry Shipman. *CAST:* Charles Starrett, Virginia Maxey, Smiley Burnette, Jim Bannon, Tommy Ivo, Ethan Laidlaw, Hugh Prosser, John Merton, George Chesebro, Mira McKinney, Bob Wilke, Ted Mapes, John Cason, The Cass County Boys.

The Durango Kid (Starrett) helps an old friend (Bannon) to clear himself of a robbery charge and stops a gold smuggling operation. [British title: *Sign of the Dagger*].

2132. Traitor's Gate (11/66) B&W—80 mins. (Crime-Drama). *DIR:* Freddie Francis. *PRO:* Ted Lloyd. *SP:* John Samson. Based on *The Traitor's Gate* by Edgar Wallace. A Summit-Rialto Production. *CAST:* Albert Lieven, Gary Raymond, Margot Trooger, Catherina Von Schell, Eddi Arent, Klaus Kinski, Anthony James, Tim Barrett, Heinz Bernard, Dave Birks, Edward Underdown, Alec Ross, Peter Porteous, Maurice Good.

A businessman (Lieven) sets out to rob the Tower of London of its crown jewels by replacing a guard with a look-alike convict (Raymond). [Original German title: *Das Verratertor*].

2133. Tramp, Tramp, Tramp (4/2/42) B&W – 68 mins. (Comedy). DIR: Charles Barton. PRO: Wallace MacDonald. SP: Harry Rebuas, Ned Dandy. Story by Shannon Day, Hal Braham, Marian Grant. CAST: Jackie Gleason, Jack Durant, Florence Rice, Bruce Bennett, Hallene Hill, Billy Curtis, Mabel Todd, Forrest Tucker, James Seay, John Tyrrell, John Harmon, Eddie Foster, Al Hill, Heinie Conklin, Kenneth MacDonald, Eddie Kane, William Gould, Herbert Rawlinson, Bud Jamison, James Millican, John Dilson, Harry Strang, George Turner, Lloyd Bridges, Eddie Laughton, Walter Sande, Bud Geary, The Harmonica Rascals, Borrah Minevitch.

Two barbers (Gleason, Durant) form a home guard unit when they start losing their customers to the draft.

2134. Trapped (3/5/37) B&W – 58 mins. (Western). DIR: Leon Barsha. PRO: Harry L. Decker. SP: John Rathmell. Story by Claude Rister. CAST: Charles Starrett, Peggy Stratford, Robert Middlemass, Ted Oliver, Lew Meehan, Edward Piel, Sr., Jack Rockwell, Alan Sears, Edward J. LeSaint, Francis Sayles, Art Mix.

A cowboy (Starrett) suspects a crippled rancher (Middlemass) of killing his brother.

2135. Trapped by Boston Blackie (5/13/48) B&W – 67 mins. (Crime-Mystery). DIR: Seymour Friedman. PRO: Rudolph C. Flothow. SP: Maurice Tombragel. Story by Charles R. Marion, Edward Bock. Based on the characters created by Jack Boyle. CAST: Chester Morris, June Vincent, George E. Stone, Richard Lane, Patricia White (Patricia Barry), Edward Norris, Frank Sully, Fay Baker, William

Forrest, Sarah Selby, Mary Currier, Pierre Watkin, Ben Welden, Abigail Adams, Ray Harper.

Blackie (Morris) and the Runt (Stone) are suspected of stealing a priceless collection of jewelry and set out after the real thieves.

2136. Trapped by G-Men (9/9/37) B&W – 63 mins. (Crime-Drama). DIR: Lewis D. Collins. PRO: Larry Darmour. SP: Tom Kilpatrick. Story by Bernard McConville. CAST: Jack Holt, Wynne Gibson, Jack LaRue, Edward Brophy, C. Henry Gordon, Arthur Hohl, Robert Emmett O'Conner, William Bakewell, William Pawley, Charles Lane, Eleanor Stewart, Frank Darien, Lucien Prival, Richard Tucker, Wallis Clark, George Cleveland.

An FBI agent (Holt) poses as a criminal to infiltrate a gang of crooks and bring them to justice. NOTES: Four years later, Jack Holt would play a similar role, as a Treasury agent, in the Columbia serial *Holt of the Secret Service*.

2137. Trapped by Television (6/16/36) B&W – 63 mins. (Drama). DIR: Del Lord. PRO: Ben Pivar. SP: Lee Loeb, Harold Buchman. Story by Sherman L. Lowe, Al Martin. CAST: Mary Astor, Lyle Talbot, Nat Pendleton, Joyce Compton, Thurston Hall, Henry Mollison, Wyrley Birch, Robert Strange, Marc Lawrence.

A television pioneer and inventor (Talbot) gets mixed up with the criminal element when they try to exploit his television inventions. [British title: *Caught by Television*].

Trapped by Wireless *see* **You May Be Next**

2138. Trapped in the Sky (2/16/39) B&W – 61 mins. (Action-Aviation). DIR: Lewis D. Collins. PRO: Larry Darmour. SP: Eric Taylor, Gordon

Rigby. Story by Eric Taylor. *CAST:* Jack Holt, Katherine DeMille, Sidney Blackmer, C. Henry Gordon, Ralph Morgan, Ivan Lebedeff, Paul Everton, Regis Toomey, Holmes Herbert, Guy D'Ennery.

A pilot (Holt) goes undercover to trap a gang of saboteurs and foreign agents when they try to destroy a secret, noiseless airplane.

2139. The Traveling Saleswoman (1/5/50) B&W—75 mins. (Western-Comedy). *DIR:* Charles F. Reisner. *PRO:* Tony Owen. *SP:* Howard Dimsdale. *CAST:* Joan Davis, Andy Devine, Joe Sawyer, Adele Jergens, Dean Riesner, John Cason, Chief Thunder Cloud, Harry Hayden, Charles Halton, Minerva Urecal, Eddy Waller, Teddy Infuhr, Robert Cherry, William Newell, Harry Woods, Ethan Laidlaw, Harry Tyler, Al Bridge, Emmett Lynn, Stanley Andrews, George Chesebro, Heinie Conklin, Chief Yowlachie, Bill Wilkerson, Nick Thompson, Jessie Arnold, Robert Wilke.

A saleswoman (Davis) and her fiance (Devine) head west and get involved with Indians and outlaws as she tries to promote her father's ailing soap business.

Traviata, La *see* **La Traviata**

2140. Treason (2/10/33) B&W— 63 mins. (Western). *DIR:* George B. Seitz. *SP:* Gordon Battle. *CAST:* Buck Jones, Shirley Grey, Edward J. LeSaint, Robert Ellis, Frank Lackteen, Charles Brinley, Art Mix, Frank Ellis, Ivar McFadden, Nick Cogley, T. C. Jacks, Charles Hill Mailes, Edwin Stanley.

A Union scout (Jones) infiltrates a gang of Confederate sympathizers whose leader is a woman (Grey).

2141. Treasure of Silver Lake (11/65) Eastman Color/Scope—82 mins. (Western). *DIR:* Harald Reinl.

PRO: Leif Feilberg. *SP:* Harald G. Petersson. Based on *Die Schatz im Silbersee* by Karl Friedrich May. An S.N.C.-Rialto-Jadran Production. *CAST:* Lex Barker, Herbert Lom, Gotz George, Pierre Brice, Karin Dor, Eddi Arent, Marianne Hoppe, Jan Sid, Ralf Wolter, Mirko Boman.

Old Shatterhand (Barker) and Winnetou (Brice) go after an outlaw (Lom) when he steals a treasure map. *NOTES:* This film was one of the first in the "Winnetou" series of westerns. His partner came to be known as "Old Shatterhand," "Old Surehand," or "Old Firehand" in various films of the series. [Original German title: *Der Schatz im Silbersee*]. [Original French title: *Le Tresor du Lac D'Argent*]. [Original Yugoslavian title: *Blago u Srebrnom Jezeru*].

2142. Trial Marriage (3/10/29) B&W—68 mins. (Drama). *DIR:* Erle C. Kenton. *PRO:* Harry Cohn. *SP:* Sonya Levien. Story by Elizabeth Alexander. *CAST:* Norman Kerry, Sally Eilers, Jason Robards, Sr., Thelma Todd.

A woman (Eilers), who had entered into a trial marriage, is divorced by her husband (Robards). After several years and several spouses, they meet and remarry for a second time. *NOTES:* Released as both a silent film and sound with music score and sound effects.

2143. Triple Threat (9/30/48) B&W—71 mins. (Drama). *DIR:* Jean Yarbrough. *PRO:* Sam Katzman. *SP:* Joseph Carole, Don Martin. *CAST:* Richard Crane, Gloria Henry, Mary Stuart, John Litel, Pat Phelan, Joseph Crehan, Regina Wallace, Syd Saylor, Dooley Wilson, Harry Wismer, Tom Harmon, Bob Kelly, Sammy Baugh, Johnny Clement, "Boley" Dancewicz, Paul Christman, Bill Dudley, Paul Governall, "Indian" Jack Jacobs, Sid

Luckman, Charles Trippi, Steve Van Buren, Bob Waterfield.

A college football player (Crane) turns professional and wins the big game for the team.

2144. Trouble in Morocco (3/9/37) B&W – 62 mins. (Adventure). *DIR:* Ernest B. Schoedsack. *PRO:* Larry Darmour. *SP:* Paul Franklin. Based on *Sowing Glory* by J. D. Newsom. *CAST:* Jack Holt, Mae Clarke, Harold Huber, C. Henry Gordon, Paul Hurst, Victor Varconi, Bradley Page, Oscar Apfel.

Two newspaper reporters (Holt, Clarke) go undercover in Cairo to stop an arms smuggling gang operating on the Moroccan border.

2145. The Trouble with Angels (4/66) Pathe Color – 111 mins. (Comedy). *DIR:* Ida Lupino. *PRO:* William Frye. *SP:* Blanche Hanalis. Based on *Life with Mother Superior* by Jane Trahey. *CAST:* Rosalind Russell, Binnie Barnes, Camilla Sparv, Mary Wickes, Marge Redmond, Hayley Mills, Gypsy Rose Lee, Kent Smith, Harry Harvey, Portia Nelson, June Harding, Marjorie Eaton, Barbara Hunter, Delores Sutton, Margalo Gillmore, Jill Hutton.

A Mother Superior (Russell) has to deal with two troublemakers (Mills, Harding), who get into all sorts of mischievous adventures at her convent school. *NOTES:* A sequel followed in 1968, *Where Angels Go, Trouble Follows.*

2146. The Trout (9/82) Fuji Color – 105 mins. (Drama). *DIR:* Joseph Losey. *PRO:* Yves Rousset-Rouard. *SP:* Joseph Losey, Monique Lange. Based on *La Truite* by Roger Vailland. A Triumph Films Production. *CAST:* Isabelle Huppert, Jean-Pierre Cassel, Jeanne Moreau, Daniel Olbrychski, Jacques Speisser, Isao Yamagata, Lisette Malidor, Jean-Paul Roussillon, Roland Bertin, Craig Ste-

vens, Alexis Smith, Ruggero Raimondi.

A woman (Huppert) goes to Japan to start a trout farm with her husband (Cassel) after a series of serious setbacks in her life. *NOTES:* Limited theatrical release; in French with English subtitles. [Original French title: *La Truite*].

2147. The True Glory (10/4/45) B&W – 85 mins. (Documentary). *DIR:* Sir Carol Reed, Garson Kanin. *PRO:* Governments of Great Britain and the United States.

A documentary testimonial to the Allied soldiers who fought in World War II from D-Day to V-E Day.

2148. The True Story of Lynn Stuart (3/58) B&W – 78 mins. (Crime). *DIR:* Lewis Seiler. *PRO:* Bryan Foy. *SP:* John H. Kneubuhl. Based on newspaper articles by Pat Michaels. *CAST:* Betsy Palmer, Jack Lord, Barry Atwater, Kim Spalding, Karl Lukas, Casey Walters, Harry Jackson, Claudia Bryar, John Anderson, Rita Duncan, Lee Farr, Louise Towers.

A Santa Ana housewife (Palmer) volunteers to work undercover to stop a gang of dope pushers after her nephew, under the influence of drugs, is killed in a car crash.

2149. The Trunk (10/61) B&W – 72 mins. (Crime). *DIR/SP:* Donovan Winter. *PRO:* Lawrence Huntington. Story by Edward Abraham, Valerie Abraham. A Donwin Production. *CAST:* Phil Carey, Julia Arnall, Dermot Walsh, Vera Day, Peter Swanwick, John Atkinson, Betty LeBeau, Tony Quinn, Robert Sansom, Pippa Stanley, Richard Nellor, Nicholas Tanner.

A blackmailer (Carey) is framed for murder when he tries to lead his ex-girl (Arnall) into believing she has killed her husband's (Walsh) ex-mistress (Day).

Feature Films

2150. Trust the Navy (12/35) B&W–71 mins. (Comedy). DIR: Henry W. George. PRO: Ian Sutherland. SP: Reginald Long, Arthur Rigby. Story by Arthur Rose. A St. George's Production. CAST: Lupino Lane, Nancy Burne, Wallace Lupino, Guy Middleton, Miki Hood, Ben Welden, Fred Leslie, Doris Rogers, Reginald Long, Arthur Rigby, Arthur Stanley, Charles Sewell.

A pair of sailors (Lupino Lane, Wallace Lupino), aboard the HMS *Improbable*, make life hectic for their Chief Petty Officer (Leslie) and also try to stop a gang of smugglers.

2151. The Truthful Sex (11/20/26) B&W–58 mins. (Drama). DIR: Richard Thomas. PRO: Harry Cohn. SP: Albert Shelby LeVine. CAST: Mae Busch, Huntley Gordon, Ian Keith, Leo White.

A couple (Busch, Gordon) grow tired of each other and drift apart, but later, are reunited and resume their life together.

2152. Tugboat Princess (12/16/36) B&W–69 mins. (Drama). DIR: David Selman. PRO: Kenneth J. Bishop. SP: Robert Watson. Story by Dalton Trumbo, Isadore Bernstein. CAST: Walter C. Kelly, Valerie Hobson, Edith Fellows, Clyde Cook, Lester Matthews, Reginald Hincks.

The captain (Kelly) of a tugboat borrows money from his rival (Cook) to secure an operation for his ward (Fellows), and races against time to pay it back before he loses his tugboat to the rival.

2153. 12 to the Moon (6/60) B&W–74 mins. (Science Fiction). DIR: David Bradley. PRO: Fred Gebhardt. SP: DeWitt Bodeen. Story by Fred Gebhardt. CAST: Ken Clark, Michi Kobi, Tom Conway, Anthony Dexter, John Wengraf, Anna-Lisa, Phillip Baird, Roger Til, Corey Devlin,

Tema Bey, Richard Weber, Robert Montgomery, Jr., Francis X. Bushman.

An international crew of 12 people head to the moon where they encounter trouble from a race of lunar people who seek peace.

2154. Twentieth Century (5/11/34) B&W–91 mins. (Comedy). DIR/PRO: Howard Hawks. SP: Charles MacArthur, Ben Hecht. Based on the play *Napoleon on Broadway* by Charles Bruce Millholland. CAST: John Barrymore, Carole Lombard, Roscoe Karns, Walter Connolly, Ralph Forbes, Dale Fuller, Etienne Girardot, Herman Bing, Lee D. Kohlmar, Billie Seward, Charles Lane, Mary Jo Mathews, Edward Gargan, Edgar Kennedy, Gigi Parrish, Fred Kelsey, Cliff Thompson, Nick Copeland, Howard Hickman, Harry Semels, Fred "Snowflake" Toones, George Offerman, Jr., Gaylord Pendleton, Eddy Chandler, James Burke.

On board the *Twentieth Century Limited* to New York, a Broadway director (Barrymore) tries to win back his once leading lady (Lombard) from her fiance (Forbes) and star her in his new show.

2155. 20 Million Miles to Earth (7/57) B&W–84 mins. (Science Fiction). DIR: Nathan Juran. PRO: Charles H. Schneer. SP: Bob Williams, Christopher Knopf. Story by Charlotte Knight, Ray Harryhausen. A Morningside Production. CAST: William Hopper, Joan Taylor, Frank Puglia, John Zaremba, Tito Vuolo, Thomas B. Henry, Jay Arvan, Arthur Space, Bart Bradley, George Peeling, George Khoury.

A rocket ship, returning from Venus, crash-lands in Italy and the only survivor (Hopper) tries to locate a missing alien creature that soon grows to huge proportions and begins to destroy everything it comes in contact with. NOTES: Special effects by Ray Harryhausen.

2156. 21 Days Together (5/27/40) B&W—75 mins. (Drama). DIR: Basil Dean. PRO: Alexander Korda. SP: Graham Greene, Basil Dean. Based on the play *The First and the Last* by John Galsworthy. A London Films-Denham Production. CAST: Vivien Leigh, Laurence Olivier, Leslie Banks, Francis L. Sullivan, Hay Petrie, Esme Percy, Robert Newton, Victor Rietti, Morris Harvey, Meinhart Maur, Lawrence Hanray, David Horne, Wallace Lupino, Muriel George, William Dewhurst, Frederick Lloyd, Elliot Mason, Arthur Young, Fred Groves, Aubrey Mallalieu, John Warwick.

When a mentally deranged man is taken to jail for a crime he did not commit, and will be held 21 days before he comes to trial, the real murderer (Olivier) and his girl (Leigh) decide to spend the three weeks together and then he will confess and free the man. [British title: *Twenty-One Days*].

2157. The 27th Day (7/57) B&W—75 mins. (Science Fiction). DIR: William Asher. PRO: Helen Ainsworth. SP: John Mantley. Based on the book by John Mantley. A Romson Production. CAST: Gene Barry, Valerie French, George Voskovec, Arnold Moss, Stefan Schnabel, Ralph Clanton, Frederick Ledebur, Paul Birch, Azemat Janti, Ed Hinton, Grandon Rhodes, David Bond, Theo Marcuse, Emil Sitka, Philip Van Zandt, Paul Frees, Marui Tsien.

An alien (Moss) from a dying planet gives each of five people (Barry, French, Voskovec, Janti, Tsien) a capsule that, when opened, will kill instantly, but will lose its power after 27 days.

Twinkle and Shine *see* **It Happened to Jane**

2158. Twist Around the Clock (12/61) B&W—86 mins. (Musical). DIR: Oscar Rudolph. PRO: Sam Katzman. SP: James B. Gordon. A Four Leaf Production. CAST: Chubby Checker, Dion, Vicki Spencer, The Marcels, Clay Cole, John Cronin, Mary Mitchell, Maura McGiveney, Tol Avery, Alvy Moore, Lenny Kent, Tom Middleton, Jefferson Parker, John Bryant, Barbara Morrison, Barry O'Hara.

A rock 'n' roll manager (Cronin) attempts to popularize a new dance craze, the "Twist." NOTES: A remake of the 1956 Columbia film *Rock Around the Clock*.

2159. Two Blondes and a Redhead (11/6/47) B&W—69 mins. (Musical). DIR: Arthur Dreifuss. PRO: Sam Katzman. SP: Victor McLeod, Jameson Brewer. Story by Harry Rebuas. CAST: Jean Porter, Jimmy Lloyd, June Preisser, Judy Clark, Rick Vallin, Douglas Wood, Charles Smith, Regina Wallace, John Meredith, Diane Fauntelle, Joanne Wayne, Tony Pastor and His Orchestra.

A society girl (Porter) plays hooky from an exclusive girls' school to star in a Broadway chorus. When the play closes, she goes back to school and brings two of the show-girls (Preisser, Clark) with her.

2160. Two-Fisted Gentleman (8/25/36) B&W—63 mins. (Comedy). DIR: Gordon Wiles. PRO: Ben Pivar. SP: Tom Van Dycke. CAST: James Dunn, June Clayworth, Thurston Hall, George McKay, Gene Morgan, Paul Guilfoyle, Harry Tyler, Muriel Evans, Charles Lane.

A female fight promoter (Clayworth) turns a nobody (Dunn) into a champion, but he forsakes the ring for a society girl (Evans). NOTES: The plot line was almost the same as the 1932 Columbia film *The Big Timer*.

2161. Two-Fisted Law (6/8/32) B&W—64 mins. (Western). *DIR:* D. Ross Lederman. *PRO:* Irving Briskin. *SP:* Kurt Kempler. Story by William Colt MacDonald. *CAST:* Tim McCoy, Alice Day, John Wayne, Wheeler Oakman, Tully Marshall, Wallace MacDonald, Walter Brennan, Richard Alexander.

A rancher (McCoy) is cheated out of his ranch by a crooked cattleman and land grabber (Oakman). After striking gold, he returns home and puts an end to the cattleman's activities. *NOTES:* John Wayne's last film for Columbia.

2162. Two-Fisted Rangers (1/4/40) B&W—60 mins. (Western). *DIR:* Joseph H. Lewis. *PRO:* Leon Barsha. *SP:* Fred Myton. *CAST:* Charles Starrett, Iris Meredith, Bob Nolan, Kenneth MacDonald, Hal Taliaferro (Wally Wales), Dick Curtis, Bill Cody, Jr., Ethan Laidlaw, James Craig, Bob Woodward, Francis Walker, Pat Brady, Sons of the Pioneers.

A cowboy (Starrett), with the help of a girl (Meredith), goes after the land baron (MacDonald) who killed his brother and the girl's father.

2163. Two-Fisted Sheriff (6/15/37) B&W—58 mins. (Western). *DIR:* Leon Barsha. *PRO:* Harry L. Decker. *SP:* Paul Perez. Story by William Colt MacDonald. *CAST:* Charles Starrett, Barbara Weeks, Bruce Lane, Edward Piel, Sr., Alan Sears, Al Bridge, Art Mix, Ernie Adams, Frank Ellis, Walter Downing, Claire McDowell, Robert Walker, George Chesebro, Dick Botiller, Richard Alexander, Maston Williams, Edmund Cobb, Fred Burns, Wally West, Ethan Laidlaw, George Morrell, Merrill McCormack, Tex Cooper, Dick Cramer, Steve Clark.

A sheriff (Starrett) loses his job when he allows his friend (Lane), framed for murder, to escape a lynch mob.

2164. Two-Fisted Stranger (5/30/46) B&W—50 mins. (Western). *DIR:* Ray Nazarro. *PRO:* Colbert Clark. *SP:* Robert Lee Johnson. Story by Peter Whitehead, Robert Lee Johnson. *CAST:* Charles Starrett, Doris Houck, Smiley Burnette, Lane Chandler, Charles Murray, Ted Mapes, I. Stanford Jolley, George Chesebro, Edmund Cobb, Jack Rockwell, Davidson Clark, Maudie Prickett, Zeke Clements, Herman Hack, Nolan Leary, Frank Ellis, Frank O'Conner.

The Durango Kid (Starrett) sets out to prove that diamonds found on ranch land were really placed there by a land swindler (Chandler) who is leader of a gang of outlaws. [British title: *High Stakes*].

2165. Two Gun Law (4/7/37) B&W—58 mins. (Western). *DIR:* Leon Barsha. *PRO:* Harry L. Decker. *SP:* John Rathmell. Story by Norman Sheldon. *CAST:* Charles Starrett, Peggy Stratford, Hank Bell, Edward J. LeSaint, Charles Middleton, Al Bridge, George Chesebro, Art Mix, Dick Curtis, Vic Potel, George Morrell, Tex Cooper.

Complications arise when an ex-outlaw (Starrett) tries to go straight and meets opposition from the townspeople.

2166. The Two-Headed Spy (3/59) B&W—93 mins. (Spy-Drama). *DIR:* Andre De Toth. *PRO:* Bill Kirby, Hal E. Chester. *SP:* James O'Donnell. Based on *Britain's Two Headed Spy* by J. Alvin Kugelmass. A Sabre Production. *CAST:* Jack Hawkins, Gia Scala, Erik Schumann, Alexander Knox, Felix Aylmer, Walter Hudd, Edward Underdown, Laurence Naismith, Geoffrey Bayldon, Kenneth Griffith, Robert Crewdsen, Michael Caine, Harriet Johns, Martin Benson, Victor Woolf, Richard Grey, Ronald Hines, Donald Pleasence, Martin Boddey,

Bernard Fox, Deering Wells, Peter Swanwick, Desmond Roberts, Ian Colin, Nada Beale.

Based on a true story, a British agent (Hawkins) infiltrates the German High Command and becomes a German general. When his contact (Aylmer) is found out and murdered, he comes under suspicion and has to flee home when he is found out by his German aide (Schumann).

2167. Two in a Taxi (9/18/41) B&W — 63 mins. (Drama-Comedy). *DIR*: Robert Florey. *PRO*: Irving Briskin. *SP*: Howard J. Green, Morton Thompson, Malvin Wald. *CAST*: Anita Louise, Russell Hayden, Noah Beery, Jr., Dick Purcell, Chick Chandler, Fay Helm, George Cleveland, Frank Yaconelli, Ben Taggart, Paul Porcasi, Henry Brandon, John Harmon, Ralph Peters, James Seay.

Everything goes wrong when a taxi driver (Hayden) tries to get enough money to buy a gas station and marry his sweetheart (Louise).

2168. Two Latins from Manhattan (9/25/41) B&W — 65 mins. (Musical-Comedy). *DIR*: Charles Barton. *PRO*: Wallace MacDonald. *SP*: Albert Duffy. *CAST*: Joan Davis, Jinx Falkenburg, Joan Woodbury, Fortunio Bonanova, Don Beddoe, Marquita Madero, Carmen Morales, Lloyd Bridges, Sig Arno, Boyd Davis, Antonio Moreno, John Dilson, Tim Ryan, Lester Dorr, Bruce Bennett, Ralph Dunn, Stanley Brown, Eddie Kane, Dick Elliott, Eddie Fetherstone, Ernie Adams.

When a Cuban sister act fails to show up at a New York nightclub, the public relations girl (Davis) at the club substitutes her two roommates (Falkenburg, Woodbury) for the act. Complications develop when the real sisters (Madero, Morales) show up.

2169. Two-Man Submarine (3/16/44) B&W — 62 mins. (War-Drama). *DIR*: Lew Landers. *PRO*: Jack Fier. *SP*: Griffin Jay, Leslie T. White. *CAST*: Tom Neal, Ann Savage, J. Carrol Naish, Robert Williams, Abner Biberman, George Lynn, J. Alex Havier, Lloyd Bridges.

During World War II, Nazis and Japanese join forces to steal a secret penicillin formula from American researchers on a Pacific island.

2170. Two of a Kind (7/51) B&W — 75 mins. (Suspense-Drama). *DIR*: Henry Levin. *PRO*: William Dozier. *SP*: Lawrence Kimble, James Gunn. Story by James Edward Grant. *CAST*: Edmond O'Brien, Lizabeth Scott, Terry Moore, Alexander Knox, Griff Barnett, Robert Anderson, Virginia Brissac, J. M. Kerrigan, Claire Carleton, Louis Jean Heydt.

A con-man (Knox) tries to pass off a carnival worker (O'Brien) to a middle-aged couple (Barnett, Brissac) as their long lost son.

2171. Two Rode Together (7/61) Eastman Color — 109 mins. (Western). *DIR*: John Ford. *PRO*: Stan Shpetner. *SP*: Frank Nugent. Based on *Comanche Captives* by Will Cook. *CAST*: James Stewart, Shirley Jones, Richard Widmark, Linda Cristal, Andy Devine, John McIntire, Paul Birch, Henry Brandon, Willis Bouchey, Harry Carey, Jr., Ken Curtis, Jeanette Nolan, John Qualen, Ford Rainey, Woody Strode, Olive Carey, Chet Douglas, Annelle Hayes, David Kent, Anna Lee, O. Z. Whitehead, Cliff Lyons, Mae Marsh, Frank Baker, Ted Knight, Ruth Clifford, Sam Harris, Jack Pennick, Chuck Roberson, Dan Borzage, Bill Henry, Chuck Hayward, Edward Brophy.

A sheriff (Stewart) and a cavalry officer (Widmark) set out for Comanche territory to ransom two white captives (Cristal, Kent). *NOTES*: James

tives (Cristal, Kent). *NOTES*: James Stewart's first appearance in a John Ford directed film.

2172. Two Senoritas from Chicago (8/12/43) B&W — 68 mins. (Musical-Comedy). *DIR*: Frank Woodruff. *PRO*: Wallace MacDonald. *SP*: Stanley Rubin, Maurice Tombragel. Story by Steven Vas. *CAST*: Joan Davis, Jinx Falkenburg, Ann Savage, Leslie Brooks, Ramsay Ames, Bob Haymes, Emory Parnell, Douglas Leavitt, Muni Saroff, Max Willenz, Stanley Brown, Frank Sully, Charles C. Wilson, Romaine Callender, George McKay, Harry Strang, Constance Worth, Eddie Laughton, Wilbur Mack, Anne Loos, Sam Ash.

A hotel refuse collector (Davis) gets into trouble when she produces a play without knowing who the authors were, and for passing off two actresses (Falkenburg, Savage), with phoney Portuguese accents, as sisters of the authors and stars of the play. *NOTES*: Similar in plot to the 1941 film *Two Latins from Manhattan*. [British title: *Two Senoritas*].

2173. Two Tickets to Paris (10/62) B&W — 90 mins. (Musical). *DIR*: Greg Garrison. *PRO*: Harry Romm. *SP*: Hal Hackady. *CAST*: Joey Dee, Gary Crosby, Kay Medford, Jeri Lynne Fraser, Lisa James, Charles Nelson Reilly, Richard Dickens, Nina Paige, Sal Lombardo, Jeri Archer, Michele Monet, Jay Burton, The Starlifters.

A shipboard romance between a singer (Dee) and a society girl (Fraser) sets the stage for a variety of musical numbers.

2174. Two Yanks in Trinidad (3/26/42) B&W — 84 mins. (War-Comedy). *DIR*: Gregory Ratoff. *PRO*: Samuel Bischoff. *SP*: Sy Bartlett, Richard Carroll, Harry Segall. Story by Sy Bartlett. *CAST*: Pat O'Brien, Brian Donlevy, Janet Blair, Roger Clark, John Emery, Donald MacBride, Frank Jenks, Frank Sully, Veda Ann Borg, Clyde Fillmore, Dick Curtis, Sig Arno, Dewey Robinson, Al Hill, Bud Geary, Ralph Peters, William Newell, Julius Tannen.

When two hoods have a falling out, one hood (O'Brien) enlists in the Army to escape the wrath of the other hood (Donlevy) who also enlists, along with his two bodyguards (Jenks, Sully). They follow him to Trinidad, where they become friends again when they capture a Nazi spy.

2175. Tyrant of the Sea (4/6/50) B&W — 70 mins. (War-Adventure). *DIR*: Lew Landers. *PRO*: Sam Katzman. *SP*: Robert Libott, Frank Burt. *CAST*: Rhys Williams, Ron Randell, Valentine Perkins, Doris Lloyd, Lester Matthews, Harry Cording, Terry Kilburn, Maurice Marsac, William Fawcett, Ross Elliott, Don C. Harvey, James Fairfax.

During the Napoleonic Wars, a sea captain (Williams) stops Napoleon's forces from invading England, but ultimately causes a mutiny with his stern dictatorial authority.

2176. U-Boat Prisoner (7/25/44) B&W — 65 mins. (War). *DIR*: Lew Landers. *PRO*: Wallace MacDonald. *SP*: Aubrey Wisberg. Based on *U-Boat Prisoner: The Life of a Texas Sailor* by Archie Gibbs. *CAST*: Bruce Bennett, Erik Rolf, John Abbott, John Wengraf, Robert Williams, Kenneth MacDonald, Erwin Kalser, Egon Brecher, Frederick Giermann, Arno Frey, Sven-Hugo Borg, Nelson Leigh, Fred Graff, Trevor Bardette, Paul Conrad, Eric Feldary.

An American seaman (Bennett) single-handedly captures a Nazi sub and its crew. [British title: *Dangerous Mists*].

2177. U-Boat 29 (10/11/39) B&W — 82 mins. (War-Spy Drama).

DIR: Michael Powell. PRO: Irving Asher. SP: Emeric Pressburger, Roland Pertwee. Based on The Spy in Black by J. Storer Clouston. A Harefield Production. CAST: Conrad Veidt, Valerie Hobson, Sebastian Shaw, Marius Goring, June Duprez, Athole Stewart, Agnes Lauchlan, Helen Haye, Cyril Raymond, Grant Sutherland, Robert Rendel, Torin Thatcher, Bernard Miles, Skelton Knaggs.

A WWI German submarine commander (Veidt) gets orders to go to the Orkney Islands off Scotland to await further orders. Once there he has to deal with triple agents and must abandon his mission. [British title: The Spy in Black].

2178. The Ugly Duckling (7/59) B&W — 84 mins. (Comedy). DIR: Lance Comfort. PRO: Tommy Lyndon-Hayes. SP: Sid Colin, Jack Davies. Based on characters created by Robert Louis Stevenson. A Hammer Production. CAST: Bernard Bresslaw, Reginald Beckwith, Jon Pertwee, Maudie Edwards, Jean Muir, Richard Wattis, Elwyn Brook-Jones, Michael Ripper, David Lodge.

A descendant (Bresslaw) of Dr. Jekyll mixes a potion that creates a suave, gentlemanly Mr. Hyde.

Ultima cita, La see **La Ultima cita**

2179. Under Age (5/21/41) B&W — 60 mins. (Crime). DIR: Edward Dmytryk. PRO: Ralph Cohn. SP: Robert D. Andrews. Story by Stanley Roberts. CAST: Nan Grey, Tom Neal, Mary Anderson, Alan Baxter, Leona Maricle, Don Beddoe, Yolande Mollot, Richard Terry, Wilma Francis, Patti McCarty, Billie Roy, Gwen Kenyon, Barbara Kent, Nancy Worth.

A group of young girls, forced to work for mobsters after their release from detention centers, lure wealthy men to bogus tourist traps.

2180. Under Suspicion (11/22/37) B&W — 61 mins. (Crime-Drama). DIR: Lewis D. Collins. PRO: Larry Darmour. SP: Joseph Hoffman, Jefferson Parker. Story by Philip Wylie. CAST: Jack Holt, Katherine DeMille, Luis Alberni, Purnell Pratt, Esther Muir, Rosalind Keith, Maurice Murphy, Morgan Wallace, Granville Bates, Craig Reynolds, Robert Emmett Keane, Margaret Irving, Clyde Dilson, George Anderson.

An automobile manufacturer (Holt) sets himself up for murder when he decides to leave his company and turn his stock over to his employees.

2181. Under the Yum Yum Tree (11/63) Eastman Color — 110 mins. (Comedy). DIR: David Swift. PRO: Frederick Brisson. SP: Lawrence Roman, David Swift. Based on the play by Lawrence Roman. A Sonnis-Swift Production. CAST: Jack Lemmon, Carol Lynley, Dean Jones, Edie Adams, Imogene Coca, Paul Lynde, Robert Lansing, James Milhollin, Pamela Curran, Asa Maynor, Jane Wald, Bill Bixby.

Two college students (Lynley, Jones) have a trial marriage in an apartment building run by a lecherous landlord (Lemmon).

2182. The Undercover Man (3/21/49) B&W — 85 mins. (Crime). DIR: Joseph H. Lewis. PRO: Robert Rossen. SP: Sydney Boehm, Malvin Wald, Jerry Rubin. Based on the article Undercover Man: He Trapped Capone by Frank J. Wilson. CAST: Glenn Ford, Nina Foch, James Whitmore, Barry Kelley, David Wolfe, Howard St. John, John Hamilton, Leo Penn, Anthony Caruso, Joan Lazer, Esther Minciotti, Angela Clarke, Robert Osterloh, Kay Medford, Patricia White (Patricia Barry), Peter Brocco, Joe Mantell.

Treasury agents try to prove an underworld crime boss, known as "Big Fellow," guilty of tax evasion. NOTES: A semi-documentary based on the methods used to convict Al Capone of tax evasion.

2183. Underground Agent (12/3/42) B&W — 70 mins. (Spy Drama). DIR: Michael Gordon. PRO: Sam White. SP: J. Robert Bren, Gladys Atwater. CAST: Bruce Bennett, Leslie Brooks, Frank Albertson, Julian Rivero, George McKay, Rhys Williams, Henry Victor, Addison Richards, Rosina Galli, Warren Ashe, Hans Conreid, Hans Schumm, Kenneth MacDonald, Lloyd Bridges, Ralph Sanford, John Tyrrell.

A government agent (Bennett) stops a group of Axis saboteurs from eavesdropping at a defense plant by inventing a word scrambler.

2184. Underground Guerrillas (3/10/44) B&W — 82 mins. (War-Drama). DIR: Sergei Nolbandov. PRO: Michael Balcon. SP: John Dighton, Monja Danischewsky, Sergei Nolbandov, Milosh Sokulich. Story by George Slocombe. An Ealing Studios Production. CAST: John Clements, Tom Walls, Mary Morris, Godfrey Tearle, Michael Wilding, Niall MacGinnis, Robert Harris, Rachael Thomas, Stephen Murray, Charles Victor, Ben Williams, Stanley Baker, Finlay Currie.

The Petrovitch family in Yugoslavia fights the invading Nazi troops. NOTES: Originally released in England in 1943, the original title of this film was *Chetnik,* named for the resistance freedom fighters of Yugoslavia, but the name was changed when 20th Century–Fox released *Chetniks* the same year. [British title: *Undercover*].

2185. The Underwater City (2/62) Eastman Color/Scope — 78 mins. Science Fiction). DIR: Frank McDon-

ald. PRO: Alex Gordon. SP: Owen Harris. Based on an idea by Alex Gordon, Ruth Alexander. A Neptune Production. CAST: William Lundigan, Julie Adams, Roy Roberts, Carl Benton Reid, Chet Douglas, Paul Dubov, George DeNormand, Edmund Cobb.

An engineer (Lundigan) builds an experimental domed city beneath the sea that eventually collapses. NOTES: Originally filmed in Eastman Color, the film was released to the theatres in Black and White; TV prints are in color.

2186. Underworld, U.S.A. (3/61) B&W — 98 mins. (Crime). DIR/PRO/SP: Samuel Fuller. Based on *Saturday Evening Post* articles by Joseph F. Dinneen. A Globe Enterprises Production. CAST: Cliff Robertson, Dolores Dorn, Beatrice Kay, Paul Dubov, Robert Emhardt, Larry Gates, Richard Rust, Neyle Morrow, Peter Brocco, Tom London, Bernie Hamilton, Don Douglas, Gerald Milton, Allan Gruener.

A son (Robertson) sets up an elaborate plan of revenge against the four mobsters who murdered his father.

2187. The Unknown (7/29/46) B&W — 70 mins. (Mystery). DIR: Henry Levin. PRO: Wallace MacDonald. SP: Malcolm Stuart Boylan, Julian Harmon. Based on the *I Love a Mystery* radio program and book by Carleton E. Morse. Adapted by Charles O'Neal, Dwight V. Babcock. CAST: Jim Bannon, Jeff Donnell, Barton Yarborough, Karen Morley, Robert Scott, Robert Wilcox, James Bell, Wilton Graff, Boyd Davis, Helen Freeman, J. Louis Johnson.

An amnesiac heiress (Morley) returns to her family mansion after twenty years for the reading of a will.

2188. The Unknown Ranger (12/1/36) B&W — 57 mins. (Western). DIR: Spencer G. Bennet. PRO: Larry

Darmour. SP: Nate Gatzert. CAST: Bob Allen, Martha Tibbetts, Hal Taliaferro (Wally Wales), Harry Woods, Edward Hearn, Robert "Buzz" Henry.
A cowboy (Allen) goes undercover at a ranch to stop a gang of rustlers.

2189. Unknown Valley (5/5/33) B&W—69 mins. (Western). DIR/SP: Lambert Hillyer. Story by Donald W. Lee. CAST: Buck Jones, Cecilia Parker, Carlotta Warwick, Bret Black, Ward Bond, Wade Boteler, Alf James, Frank McGlynn, Gaylord Pendleton, Arthur Wanzer, Charles Thurston.
An ex-Army scout (Jones), searching for his father, becomes lost in the desert and is rescued by a religious sect living in an isolated community in the desert.

2190. Unknown Woman (6/21/35) B&W—66 mins. (Crime-Drama). DIR: Albert Rogell. SP: Albert DeMond, Fred Niblo, Jr. Story by W. Scott Darling. CAST: Richard Cromwell, Marian Marsh, Douglass Dumbrille, Henry Armetta, Arthur Hohl, George McKay, Robert Middlemass, Nana Bryant, Arthur Vinton, Jerry Mandy, Ben Taggart, Nellie V. Nichols, Bob Wilbur, Eddie Chandler.
While on the trail of stolen bonds, an attorney (Cromwell) falls in love with a woman (Marsh) who turns out to be a federal agent.

2191. Unpublished Story (2/42) B&W—92 mins. (War-Drama). DIR: Harold French. PRO: Anthony Havelock-Allan. SP: Lesley Storm, Anatole de Grunwald, Patrick Kirwan, Sidney Gillat. Story by Anthony Havelock-Allan, Allan Mackinnon. A Twin Cities Production. CAST: Richard Greene, Valerie Hobson, Basil Radford, Roland Culver, Brefni O'Rorke, Miles Malleson, Andre Morell, Frederick Cooper, Renee Gadd, Henry Jorell, Muriel George, George Thorpe.
A war correspondent (Greene) uncovers information on a Nazi group operating as a peace organization and nearly gets killed while trying to break the story. NOTES: Screenwriter Sidney Gillat was uncredited.

2192. The Untamed Breed (10/21/48) Cinecolor—79 mins. (Western). DIR: Charles Lamont. PRO: Harry Joe Brown. SP: Tom Reed. Story by Eli Colter. A Sage Western Picture Production. CAST: Sonny Tufts, Barbara Britton, George "Gabby" Hayes, Edgar Buchanan, William Bishop, George E. Stone, Joe Sawyer, Gordon Jones, Reed Howes, James Kirkwood, Virginia Brissac, Harry Tyler.
A rancher (Tufts) comes up with the idea to breed his Brahma bull with Texas cattle in the hope of improving the strain.

2193. Unwelcome Stranger (4/6/35) B&W—65 mins. (Drama). DIR: Phil Rosen. PRO: Bryan Foy. SP: Crane Wilbur. Story by William Jacobs. CAST: Jack Holt, Mona Barrie, Jackie Searl, Ralph Morgan, Frankie Darro, Bradley Page, Sam McDaniel, Frank Orth.
A horse owner (Holt) trains an orphan (Searl) to become a jockey.

2194. The Unwritten Law (8/1/25) B&W—65 mins. (Crime-Drama). DIR: Edward J. LeSaint. PRO: Harry Cohn. SP: Thomas J. Hopkins. CAST: Elaine Hammerstein, Forrest Stanley, William V. Mong, Mary Alden.
A secretary (Hammerstein), tricked into marriage with her employer (Stanley), is arrested for his murder when he is found dead.

2195. The Unwritten Code (10/26/44) B&W—61 mins. (Drama). DIR: Herman Rotsten. PRO: Sam White. SP: Leslie T. White, Charles Kenyon. Story by Charles Kenyon, Robert Wilmot. CAST: Ann Savage, Tom Neal, Roland Varno, Howard Freeman,

Mary Currier, Bobby Larson, Teddy Infuhr, Otto Reichow, Fred Essler, Tom Holland, Philip Van Zandt, Al Bridge.

A Nazi (Varno) assumes the identity of a dead British soldier and plans to sneak into the U.S. to free Nazi prisoners.

2196. Up the MacGregors (11/67) Technicolor/Scope—93 mins. (Western-Comedy). DIR: Frank Garfield (Franco Giraldi). PRO: Dario Sabatello. SP: Fernando Lion, Paul Levy, Vincent Eagle, Jose Maria Rodriguez. A D.S.-Jolly-Talia Production. CAST: David Bailey, Agatha Flory, Leo Anchoriz, Georges Rigaud, Cole Kitosh, Nick Anderson, Paul Carter, Hugo Blanco, Harry Cotten, Kathleen Parker, Julie Fair, Roberto Camardiel, Julio Perez Tabernero.

Two families, one from Scotland and the other from Ireland, settle in Texas in the 1880's and join forces to fight a bandit gang. NOTES: A sequel followed in 1968, Seven Guns for the MacGregors. [Original Italian title: Sette Donne per i MacGregor]. [Original Spanish title: Siete Mujeres para los MacGregors].

2197. Uranium Boom (3/56) B&W—66 mins. (Drama). DIR: William Castle. PRO: Sam Katzman. SP: George F. Slavin, George W. George, Norman Retchin. Story by George F. Slavin, George W. George. CAST: Dennis Morgan, Patricia Medina, William Talman, Tina Carver, Philip Van Zandt, Bill Henry, Mel Curtis, Henry Rowland, Ralph Sanford, Frank Wilcox, Nick Tell, Michael Bryant.

Two prospectors (Morgan, Talman), searching for uranium, have a falling out over a woman (Medina).

2198. Used Cars (8/80) Metrocolor—113 mins. (Comedy). DIR: Robert Zemeckis. PRO: Bob Gale. SP: Robert Zemeckis, Bob Gale. CAST:

Kurt Russell, Jack Warden, Gerrit Graham, Frank McRae, Deborah Harmon, Joseph P. Flaherty, David L. Lander, Michael McKean, Michael Talbott, Harry Northup, Alfonso Arau, Al Lewis, Andrew Duncan, Dub Taylor, Claude Earl Jones, Dan Barrows, Marc McClure, Dick Miller.

A car salesman (Russell) tries to keep his car lot open by using extreme methods to sell cars.

2199. Utah Blaine (2/57) B&W—75 mins. (Western). DIR: Fred F. Sears. PRO: Sam Katzman. SP: Robert E. Kent, James B. Gordon. Based on the book by Louis L'Amour. A Clover Production. CAST: Rory Calhoun, Susan Cummings, Max Baer, Angela Stevens, Paul Langton, Ray Teal, Gene Roth, Terry Frost, Steve Darrell, Dennis Moore, Jack Ingram, George Keymas, Norman Frederic, Ken Christy.

A saddle tramp (Calhoun) saves the life of a ranch owner (Roth) left for dead by land grabbers and eventually inherits his ranch when the land grabbers succeed in killing him.

2200. The Valachi Papers (11/72) Eastman Color—125 mins. (Crime). DIR: Terence Young. PRO: Dino De Laurentiis. SP: Stephen Geller. Based on the book by Peter Maas. A DD-Euro-France Production. CAST: Charles Bronson, Mario Pilar, Fred Valleca, Jill Ireland, Joseph Wiseman, Gerald S. O'Loughlin, Walter Chiari, Arny Freeman, Lino Ventura, Amedeo Nazzari, Guido Leontini, Angelo Infanti, Fausto Tozzi.

A quasi-documentary covering almost 32 years as told by a "soldier" in the Mafia, Joe Valachi (Bronson). [Original Italian title: Joe Valachi: I Segreti di Cosa Nostra].

2201. Valentino (4/51) Technicolor—102 mins. (Biography). DIR: Lewis Allen. PRO: Edward Small. SP:

George Bruce. CAST: Eleanor Parker, Richard Carlson, Patricia Medina, Joseph Calleia, Dona Drake, Lloyd Gough, Anthony Dexter, Otto Kruger, Marietta Canty, Paul Bryar, Eric Wilton.

A fictionalized account of silent screen idol Rudolph Valentino (Dexter).

2202. Valley of Fire (11/20/51) Sepiatone—70 mins. (Western). DIR: John English. PRO: Armand Schaefer. SP: Gerald Geraghty. Story by Earle Snell. A Gene Autry Production. CAST: Gene Autry, Gail Davis, Pat Buttram, Russell Hayden, Terry Frost, Harry Lauter, William Fawcett, Bud Osborne, Barbara Stanley, Gregg Barton, Syd Saylor, Pat O'Malley, Victor Sen Yung, Christine Larson, Riley Hill, Duke York, Teddy Infuhr, Marjorie Liszt, Sandy Sanders, Fred Sherman, James Magill, Frankie Marvin, Wade Crosby, John Miller.

Autry is mayor of a frontier town without women. He sends for a wagon train of women willing to settle in the area, and has to come to their rescue when they are kidnapped.

2203. Valley of the Dragons (11/61) B&W/Scope—79 mins. (Science Fiction). DIR/SP: Edward Bernds. PRO: Byron Roberts. Based on *Career of a Comet* by Jules Verne, and a story by Donald Zimbalist. A ZRB Production. CAST: Cesare Danova, Sean McClory, Joan Staley, Danielle De Metz, Gregg Martell, Gilbert V. Perkins, I. Stanford Jolley, Mike Lane, Roger Til, Mark Dempsey, Jerry Sunshine, Dolly Gray.

Two 19th-century duellists (Danova, McClory) are swept onto a passing comet by a violent windstorm. On the comet they encounter a world populated by cave men and dinosaurs.

2204. Valley of the Headhunters (8/53) B&W—67 mins. (Jungle-Adven-

ture). DIR: William Berke. PRO: Sam Katzman. SP: Samuel Newman. Based on the *Jungle Jim* newspaper comic strip created by Alex Raymond. CAST: Johnny Weissmuller, Christine Larson, Nelson Leigh, Robert C. Foulk, Steven Ritch, Joseph Allen, Jr., George Eldredge, Neyle Morrow, Vince M. Townsend, Jr., Don Blackman, Paul Thompson.

Jungle Jim (Weissmuller) must secure valuable mineral rights from a group of natives.

Valor de Vivar, El *see* **El Valor de Vivar**

The Vampire Girls *see* **The Vampires**

2205. The Vampires (5/69) Eastman Color—91 mins. (Horror). DIR: Federico Curiel. PRO: Luis Enrique Vergara. SP: Federico Curiel, Adolfo Torres Protillo. A Vergara Production. CAST: John Carradine, Pedro Armendariz, Jr., Mil Mascaras, Maria Duval, Maura Monti, Martha Romero, Elsa Maria, Dagoberto Rodriguez, Jessica Munguia, Visney Larriaga, Manuel Garay, Sara Bentz.

A Mexican wrestler (Mascaras) saves the world from a group of female vampires and their leader (Carradine). NOTES: This movie played to Spanish-language theaters, but was later dubbed and released to television. [Original Spanish title: *Las Vampiras*].

2206. Vanity (12/35) B&W—76 mins. (Drama). DIR/SP: Adrian Brunel. PRO: A. George Smith. Based on the play by Ernest Denny. A GS Enterprises Production. CAST: Jane Cain, Percy Marmont, John Counsell, H. F. Maltby, Moira Lynd, Nita Harvey.

An egotistical actress (Cain) stages her own death to bask in the sorrow of her fans.

2207. Vanity Street (10/18/32) B&W—68 mins. (Drama). *DIR:* Nick Grinde. *SP:* Gertrude Purcell. Story by Frank Cavett, Edward Roberts. *CAST:* Charles Bickford, Helen Chandler, Mayo Methot, George Meeker, Arthur Hoyt, Raymond Hatton, Ruth Channing, Dolores Ray, Claudia Morgan, Ann Fay, Katherine Claire Ward, May Beaty, Dutch Hendrian, Eddie Boland.

A cop (Bickford) saves a young girl (Chandler) from jail, gets her a job, and has to save her again when she is accused of murder.

2208. Vengeance (3/9/30) B&W—66 mins. (Drama). *DIR:* Archie Mayo. *PRO:* Harry Cohn. *SP:* F. Hugh Herbert. Story by Ralph Graves. *CAST:* Jack Holt, Dorothy Revier, Philip Strange, George Pearce, Irma A. Harrison, Hayden Stevenson, Onest A. Conly.

When a man (Holt) is relieved of his job by an Englishman (Strange), he responds by relieving the Englishman of his wife (Revier).

2209. Vengeance of the West (8/16/42) B&W—60 mins. (Western). *DIR:* Lambert Hillyer. *PRO:* Leon Barsha. *SP:* Luci Ward. Based on the screenplay by George Morgan, Jack Townley. *CAST:* Bill Elliott, Adele Mara, Tex Ritter, Eddie Laughton, Frank Mitchell, Stanley Brown, Robert Fiske, Steve Clark, Dick Curtis, John Tyrrell, Edmund Cobb, Ted Mapes, Eva Puig, Jose Tortosa, Guy Wilkerson.

Rancher Joaquin Murietta (Elliott) seeks revenge for the murderous attacks on his family by a bandit gang. He joins forces with a Ranger (Ritter) to bring the bandits to justice. *NOTES:* A remake of the 1931 Columbia film *The Avenger*. [British title: *The Black Shadow*].

2210. Venus Makes Trouble (5/18/37) B&W—58 mins. (Drama). *DIR:* Gordon Wiles. *PRO:* Wallace MacDonald. *SP:* Michael L. Simmons. *CAST:* James Dunn, Patricia Ellis, Gene Morgan, Thurston Hall, Beatrice Curtis, Donald Kirk, Astrid Allwyn, Tom Chatterton, Spencer Charters, Howard Hickman, Charles Lane.

A promoter (Dunn), with a gift of gab, lands a job in New York and becomes the top promotions man in the city.

Verbena Tragica, La *see* **La Verbena Tragica**

2211. Verboten! (4/59) B&W—93 mins. (Drama). *DIR/PRO/SP:* Samuel Fuller. A Globe Enterprises-RKO Production. *CAST:* James Best, Susan Cummings, Tom Pittman, Paul Dubov, Harold Daye, Dick Kallman, Stuart Randell, Steven Geray, Anna Hope, Robert Boon, Neyle Morrow, Joseph Turkel, Charles Horvath, Sasha Harden, Paul Busch.

A weaving of two separate stories into one taking place in post-war Germany. An American soldier (Best) marries a German girl (Cummings) who saved him from the Gestapo, and the girl takes her younger brother (Daye), who is a member of a Neo-Nazi group, to the Nuremberg trials to make him aware of the atrocities of Hitler's Germany during the war. *NOTES:* Although this picture was an RKO film, the distribution of this film went to Columbia when RKO ceased production in 1958.

2212. Vibes (7/88) DeLuxe Color—99 mins. (Comedy). *DIR:* Ken Kwapis. *PRO:* Deborah Blum, Tony Ganz. *SP:* Lowell Ganz, Babaloo Mandel, Deborah Blum. An Imagine Entertainment Production. *CAST:* Jeff Goldblum, Cyndi Lauper, Peter Falk, Julian Sands, Googy Gress, Michael

Learned, Ramon Bieri, Elizabeth Pena, Ronald G. Joseph, Susan Bugg, Ahron Ipale, John Kapelos, Karen Akers.

An entrepreneur (Falk) hires a pair of mismatched psychics (Lauper, Goldblum) to locate his missing son, but in reality they are hunting for lost treasure.

2213. Vice Versa (3/88) DeLuxe Color—98 mins. (Comedy). *DIR:* Brian Gilbert. *PRO/SP:* Dick Clement, Ian La Frenais. *CAST:* Judge Reinhold, Fred Savage, Swoosie Kurtz, Corinne Bohrer, Jane Kaczmarek, David Proval, William Prince, Gloria Gifford, Harry Murphy, Richard Kind, Kevin O'Rourke.

A father (Reinhold) and son (Savage) end up exchanging places through the power of a mystical skull from the Far East.

2214. The Victors (12/63) B&W—175 mins. (War). *DIR/PRO/ SP:* Carl Foreman. Based on *The Human Kind* by Alexander Baron. A Highroad-Open Road Production. *CAST:* Vince Edwards, Albert Finney, George Hamilton, Melina Mercouri, Jeanne Moreau, George Peppard, Maurice Ronet, Rosanna Schiaffino, Romy Schneider, Elke Sommer, Eli Wallach, Michael Callan, Peter Fonda, Senta Berger, James Mitchum, Mervyn Johns, Tutte Lemkow, Peter Vaughn, Alf Kjellin.

Interwoven with newsreel footage, the film follows the exploits of a group of Allied soldiers from the invasion of Sicily through the occupation of Germany. *NOTES:* Recut and re-released at 156 minutes.

Vie Continue, La *see* **La Vie Continue**

Vie de Château, La *see* **La Vie de Château**

2215. The Vigilantes Ride (2/3/ 44) B&W—56 mins. (Western). *DIR:* William Berke. *PRO:* Leon Barsha. *SP:* Ed Earl Repp. *CAST:* Russell Hayden, Shirley Patterson, Dub Taylor, Jack Rockwell, Bob Kortman, Tristram Coffin, Dick Botiller, Jack Kirk, Stanley Brown, Blackie Whiteford, Bob Wills and His Texas Playboys.

A cowboy (Hayden) and his sidekick (Taylor) infiltrate a gang of outlaws in order to bring them to justice for the murder of his brother. [British title: *Hunted*].

2216. The Villain (7/79) Metrocolor—93 mins. (Comedy-Western). *DIR:* Hal Needham. *PRO:* Mort Engleberg. *SP:* Robert G. Kane. A Rastar Production. *CAST:* Kirk Douglas, Ann-Margret, Arnold Schwarzenegger, Paul Lynde, Ruth Buzzi, Foster Brooks, Jack Elam, Strother Martin, Robert Tessier, Mel Tillis, Laura Lizer Sommers, Ray Bickel, Jan Eddy, Mel Todd, James Anderson, Ed Little, Dick Dickenson, Richard Brewer, Charles Haigh, Ron Duffy.

An incompetent outlaw (Douglas) rides from one disaster to another while trying to abduct a fair damsel (Ann-Margret).

2217. The Violent Men (1/55) Technicolor/Scope—96 mins. (Western). *DIR:* Rudolph Mate. *PRO:* Lewis J. Rachmil. *SP:* Harry Kleiner. Based on *Smoky Valley* by Donald Hamilton. *CAST:* Glenn Ford, Barbara Stanwyck, Edward G. Robinson, Dianne Foster, Brian Keith, May Wynn, Warner Anderson, Basil Ruysdael, Lita Milan, Richard Jaeckel, Willis Bouchey, Jack Kelly, James Westerfield, Harry Shannon, Peter Hanson, Don C. Harvey, Carl Andre, James Anderson, Katharine Warren, Thomas B. Henry, William Phipps, Edmund Cobb, Frank Ferguson, Raymond Greenleaf, Ethan

Laidlaw, Kenneth Patterson, John Halloran, Robert Bice, Walter Beaver.

An aging land baron (Robinson), spurred on by his wife (Stanwyck) and brother (Keith), attempts to drive the ranchers and farmers out of a nearby valley. NOTES: Columbia's first CinemaScope release. [British title: *Rough Company*].

2218. Violets Are Blue (4/86) DeLuxe Color—88 mins. (Romance-Drama). *DIR*: Jack Fisk. *PRO*: Mary-kay Powell. *SP*: Naomi Foner. A Ra-star-Columbia-Delphi IV Production. *CAST*: Kevin Kline, Sissy Spacek, Bonnie Bedelia, John Kellogg, Jim Standiford, Augusta Dabney, Kate McGregor-Stewart, Adrian Sparks, Annalee Jefferies, Mike Starr.

Two former high school sweethearts (Kline, Spacek) try to pick up where they left off years before, only one is married and the other is a globe trotting photographer.

A Virgin for the Prince *see* **A Maiden for the Prince**

2219. Virgin Lips (7/25/28) B&W—59 mins. (Drama). *DIR*: Elmer Clifton. *PRO*: Harry Cohn. *SP*: Dorothy Howell, Harvey Thew. Story by Charles Beahan. *CAST*: Olive Borden, John Boles, Marshall Ruth, Alexander Gill, Richard Alexander, Arline Pretty.

A soldier of fortune (Boles) is hired to protect mining concerns in Central America from a bandit leader (Richard Alexander).

2220. The Virgin Soldiers (2/70) Technicolor—96 mins. (Comedy-Drama). *DIR*: John Dexter. *PRO*: Leslie Gilliat, Ned Sherrin. *SP*: John Hopkins. Based on the book by Leslie Thomas. An Open Road-Highroad Production. *CAST*: Lynn Redgrave, Nigel Davenport, Hywel Bennett, Nigel Patrick, Jack Shepherd, Rachel

Kempson, Geoffrey Hughes, Roy Holder, Don Hawkins.

British recruits in Malaya, naive about romance as well as war, try their hand at both. NOTES: A sequel was released by Warner Bros. in 1977, *Stand Up Virgin Soldiers*.

2221. Virtue (10/26/32) B&W—87 mins. (Drama). *DIR*: Edward Buzzell. *SP*: Robert Riskin. Story by Ethel Hill. *CAST*: Carole Lombard, Pat O'Brien, Ward Bond, Willard Robertson, Shirley Grey, Edward J. LeSaint, Jack LaRue, Mayo Methot.

A cab driver (O'Brien) helps to clear his wife (Lombard), a reformed street girl, of murder charges.

2222. Voice in the Night (3/24/34) B&W—60 mins. (Action-Drama). *DIR*: C. C. Coleman, Jr. *SP*: Harold Shumate. *CAST*: Tim McCoy, Billie Seward, Joseph Crehan, Ward Bond, Kane Richmond, Francis McDonald, Guy Usher, Frank Layton, Alphonse Ethier.

A telephone lineman (McCoy), installing lines across the desert, lands in the middle of a war between two companies.

2223. A Voice in the Night (2/4/41) B&W—95 mins. (Drama-War). *DIR*: Anthony Asquith. *PRO*: Mario Zampi. *SP*: Anatole de Grunwald, Basil Woon, Jeffrey Dell, Louis Golding, Gordon Wellesley, Bridget Boland, Roland Pertwee. Based on *Freedom Radio* by Wolfgang Wilhelm, George Campbell. A Two Cities Production. *CAST*: Clive Brook, Diana Wynyard, Raymond Huntley, Derek Farr, Joyce Howard, Howard Marion-Crawford, John Penrose, Morland Graham, Ronald Squire, Reginald Beckwith, Clifford Evans, Bernard Miles, Muriel George, Marita Hunt, Abraham Sofaer, George Hayes.

A Viennese doctor (Brook), held in high regard by the Nazis, eventually becomes disillusioned and sets up an underground radio station to broadcast condemnation of Germany. [British title: Freedom Radio].

2224. Voice of the Whistler (10/30/45) B&W—60 mins. (Drama-Mystery). DIR: William Castle. PRO: Rudolph C. Flothow. SP: William Castle, Wilfrid H. Pettitt. Story by Allan Rader. Based on The Whistler radio program. CAST: Richard Dix, Lynn Merrick, Rhys Williams, James Cardwell, Tom Kennedy, Donald Woods, Egon Brecher, Gigi Perreau.

Thinking he only has six months to live, a man (Dix) persuades a woman (Merrick) to marry him for his wealth when he dies. They go to live in a lighthouse and eventually he regains his health but not before his wife has plotted with her lover (Cardwell) to kill him. He kills the lover and is taken to jail leaving the wife to pass her days alone in the lighthouse.

2225. Voodoo Tiger (11/52) B&W—67 mins. (Jungle-Adventure). DIR: Spencer G. Bennet. PRO: Sam Katzman. SP: Samuel Newman. Based on the Jungle Jim newspaper comic strip created by Alex Raymond. CAST: Johnny Weissmuller, Jean Byron, James Seay, Jeanne Dean, Robert Bray, Rick Vallin, Paul Hoffman, John Cason, Frederic Berest, Alex Montoya, Richard Kipling, Charles Horvath, Michael Fox, William R. Klein.

Jungle Jim (Weissmuller) battles headhunters, gangsters, and Nazis to uncover an art treasure hidden in the jungle during World War II.

2226. The Wackiest Ship in the Army (1/61) Eastman Color/Scope—99 mins. (Comedy). DIR: Richard Murphy. PRO: Fred Kohlmar. SP: Richard Murphy, Herbert Margolis, William Raynor. Based on Big Fella Wash-Wash by Herbert Carlson.

CAST: Jack Lemmon, Rick Nelson, John Lund, Chips Rafferty, Tom Tully, Joby Baker, Warren Berlinger, Patricia Driscoll, Mike Kellin, Alvy Moore, Richard Anderson.

During World War II in the South Pacific, an inexperienced captain (Lemmon) and his crew sail a broken-down ship through Japanese-occupied waters to deliver an Australian coast watcher (Rafferty) to his destination.

2227. Wagon Team (9/30/52) Sepiatone—61 mins. (Western). DIR: George Archainbaud. PRO: Armand Schaefer. SP: Gerald Geraghty. A Gene Autry Production. CAST: Gene Autry, Gail Davis, Pat Buttram, Dick Jones, Gordon Jones, George J. Lewis, John Cason, Gregg Barton, Pierce Lyden, Syd Saylor, Henry Rowland, Harry Harvey, Carlo Tricoli, Sandy Sanders, Cass County Boys.

A stagecoach agent (Autry) goes under cover to recover an Army payroll taken by bandits.

2228. Walk a Crooked Mile (9/2/48) B&W—91 mins. (Spy-Drama). DIR: Gordon Douglas. PRO: Grant Whytock. SP: George Bruce. Story by Bertram Millhauser. An Edward Small Production. CAST: Louis Hayward, Dennis O'Keefe, Louise Allbritton, Carl Esmond, Onslow Stevens, Raymond Burr, Art Baker, Lowell Gilmore, Philip Van Zandt, Charles Evans, Frank Ferguson, Ray Teal, Arthur Space, John Hamilton, Reed Hadley (Narrator).

Told in documentary style, a Scotland Yard investigator (Hayward) and an FBI agent (O'Keefe) join forces to stop the Communists from stealing America's atomic secrets.

2229. Walk, Don't Run (7/66) Technicolor/Panavision—114 mins. (Comedy). DIR: Charles Walters. PRO: Sol C. Siegel. SP: Sol Saks. Story by Robert Russell and Frank Ross. A

Granley Company Production. *CAST:* Cary Grant, Samantha Eggar, Jim Hutton, John Standing, Miiko Taka, Ted Hartley, Ben Astar, George Takei, Teru Shimada, Lois Kiuchi.

A British industrialist (Grant) plays matchmaker to a young couple (Eggar, Hutton) during the 1964 Olympics in Tokyo. *NOTES:* Remake of the 1943 Columbia film *The More the Merrier.* This was Cary Grant's last feature film before retiring.

2230. Walk East on Beacon (4/29/52) B&W — 98 mins. (Spy-Drama). *DIR:* Alfred L. Werker. *PRO:* Louis deRochemont. *SP:* Leo Rosten, Virginia Shaler, Emmett Murphy, Leonard Heidemann. Based on the magazine article *The Crime of the Century* by J. Edgar Hoover. *CAST:* George Murphy, Finlay Currie, Virginia Gilmore, Karel Stepanek, Louisa Horton, Peter Capell, Bruno Wick, Karl Weber, Jack Manning, Vilma Kurer, Michael Garrett, Robert Carroll, Ernest Graves, Rosemary Pettit, George Roy Hill, Bradford Hatton.

Told in documentary style, an FBI agent (Murphy) and his men track down a Communist spy ring in the U.S. [British title: *The Crime of the Century*].

2231. A Walk in the Spring Rain (4/70) Technicolor/Panavision — 98 mins. (Romance). *DIR:* Guy Green. *PRO/SP:* Stirling Silliphant. Based on the book by Rachel Maddux. *CAST:* Ingrid Bergman, Anthony Quinn, Fritz Weaver, Katherine Crawford, Tom Fielding, Virginia Gregg, Mitchell Silberman.

A happily married woman (Bergman) finds herself falling in love with a mountain man (Quinn) while on vacation with her husband (Weaver).

2232. Walk on the Wild Side (2/62) B&W — 114 mins. (Drama). *DIR:* Edward Dmytryk. *PRO:* Charles K. Feldman. *SP:* John Fante, Edmund Morris. Based on the book by Nelson Algren. A Famous Artists Production. *CAST:* Laurence Harvey, Capucine, Jane Fonda, Anne Baxter, Joanna Moore, Barbara Stanwyck, Richard Rust, Karl Swenson, Donald "Red" Barry, Juanita Moore, John Anderson, Ken Lynch, Todd Armstrong.

A Texan (Harvey) learns that his former girlfriend (Fonda) has become a prostitute in a New Orleans brothel.

2233. The Walking Hills (3/1/49) B&W — 78 mins. (Western). *DIR:* John Sturges. *PRO:* Harry Joe Brown. *SP:* Alan LeMay, Virginia Roddick. *CAST:* Randolph Scott, Ella Raines, William Bishop, Edgar Buchanan, Arthur Kennedy, John Ireland, Jerome Courtland, Josh White, Russell Collins, Reed Howes, Charles Stevens, Houseley Stevenson.

A group of treasure hunters search for a wagon load of gold buried somewhere in Death Valley.

2234. Wall Street (12/1/29) B&W — 68 mins. (Drama). *DIR:* Roy William Neill. *PRO:* Harry Cohn. *SP:* Norman Houston. Story by Paul Ganglein, Jack Kirkland. *CAST:* Aileen Pringle, Ralph Ince, Sam De Grasse, Philip Strange, Ernest Hilliard, James Finlayson, Freddie Burke Frederick, George MacFarlane, Camille Rovelle, Grace Wallace.

A wealthy businessman (Ince) destroys all in his rise to power and the wife (Pringle) of one of the men he drove to suicide vows to destroy him.

2235. The Walls Came Tumbling Down (5/27/46) B&W — 82 mins. (Mystery). *DIR:* Lothar Mendes. *PRO:* Albert J. Cohen. *SP:* Wilfrid H. Pettitt. Based on the book by Jo Eisinger. *CAST:* Lee Bowman, Marguerite Chapman, Edgar Buchanan, Lee Patrick, Jonathan Hale, George Macready, J. Edward Bromberg, Mary

Field, Miles Mander, Moroni Olsen, Noel Cravat.

A Broadway columnist (Bowman) and a socialite (Chapman) search for the killer of a priest.

2236. Wandering Girls (1/20/27) B&W—58 mins. (Drama). *DIR:* Ralph Ince. *PRO:* Harry Cohn. *SP:* Harry O. Hoyt. Story by Dorothy Howell. *CAST:* Dorothy Revier, Eugenie Besserer, Frances Raymond, Robert Agnew, William Welsh, Armand Kaliz, Mildred Harris.

A young girl (Revier) runs away from home, falls in with crooks (Kaliz, Harris), and gets accused of robbery. Her name is cleared and she returns home having learned her lesson.

2237. War Correspondent (8/13/32) B&W—77 mins. (War). *DIR:* Paul Sloane. *SP:* Jo Swerling. Story by Keene Thompson. *CAST:* Jack Holt, Lila Lee, Ralph Graves, Victor Wong, Tetsu Komai.

A newspaperman (Graves) and mercenary pilot (Holt) compete for the affections of a woman (Lee) in war-torn Shanghai. [British title: *Soldiers of Fortune*].

2238. The War Lover (11/62) B&W—105 mins. (War). *DIR:* Philip Leacock. *PRO:* Arthur Hornblow, Jr. *SP:* Howard Koch. Based on the book by John Hersey. *CAST:* Steve McQueen, Robert Wagner, Shirley Anne Field, Gary Cockrell, Michael Crawford, Billy Edwards, Robert Easton, Al Waxman, Bob Kanter.

In 1943, an American bomber pilot (McQueen) tries to steal his co-pilot's (Wagner) girl (Field) and causes the death of one of his men (Cockrell) through his recklessness.

2239. Warlords of Atlantis (5/78) Technicolor—96 mins. (Science Fiction). *DIR:* Kevin Conner. *PRO:* John Dark. *SP:* Brian Hayles. An EMI Film

Production. *CAST:* Doug McClure, Peter Gilmore, Shane Rimmer, Lea Brodie, Michael Gothard, Hal Galili, John Ritzenberger, Derry Power, Donald Bisset, Ashley Knight, Robert Brown, Cyd Charisse, Daniel Massey.

Turn-of-the-century explorers (McClure, Bisset, Gilmore) find the lost city of Atlantis.

2240. The Warning (11/26/27) B&W—56 mins. (Adventure). *DIR/SP:* George B. Seitz. *PRO:* Harry Cohn. Story by Lillian Ducey and H. Milner Kitchin. *CAST:* Jack Holt, Dorothy Revier, Frank Lackteen, Pat Harmon, Eugene Strong, George Kuwa, Norman Trevor.

A secret agent (Holt) poses as an opium smuggler, saves the life of another secret agent (Revier), and in a blazing gun-battle defeats the drug czar's (Harmon) forces.

2241. The Warrior and the Slave Girl (11/59) Eastman Color/Scope—89 mins. (Adventure). *DIR:* Vitorrio Cottafavi. *PRO:* Virgilio De Blasi. *SP:* Ennio De Concini, Francesco De Feo, Gian Paolo Callegari, Francesco Thellung. An Alexandra Produziono Cinematografiche Production. *CAST:* Gianna Maria Canale, Georges Marchal, Ettore Manni, Rafael Calvo, Vera Cruz.

A wicked queen (Canale) and her armies are vanquished and the lawful ruler is put on the throne. [Original Italian title: *La Rivolta del Gladiatori*].

2242. The Warrior Empress (5/61) Eastman Color/Scope—101 mins. (Adventure). *DIR:* Pietro Francisci. *PRO:* Gianni Hecht Lucari. *SP:* Ennio De Concini, Pietro Francisci, Luciano Martini. An Orsay-Documento Production. *CAST:* Kerwin Mathews, Tina Louise, Ricardo Garrone, Antonio Batistella, Enrico Maria Salerno, Susi Golgi, Alberto Farenese.

Phaon (Mathews) and Sappho

(Louise) lead the people of a village in revolt against Rome over unfair taxes. [Original Italian title: *Saffo, Venere di Lesbo*]. [Original French title: *Sapho*].

Warrior's Rest see **Love on a Pillow**

2243. Washington Merry-Go-Round (9/29/32) B&W—78 mins. (Drama). *DIR:* James Cruze. *SP:* Jo Swerling. Story by Maxwell Anderson. *CAST:* Lee Tracy, Constance Cummings, Walter Connolly, Alan Dinehart, Clarence Muse, Arthur Vinton, Frank Sheridan, Arthur Hoyt, Clay Clement.

A congressman (Tracy) tries to stop a corrupt gang of politicians, gets booted out of office, and with the help of an elder statesman (Connolly) and his granddaughter (Cummings), regains his seat in congress and exposes the corrupt politicians. [British title: *Invisible Power*].

2244. Watch It Sailor! (1/62) B&W—81 mins. (Comedy). *DIR:* Wolf Rilla. *PRO:* Maurice Cowan. *SP:* Falkland Cary, Philip King. Based on their stage play. A Cormorant-Hammer Production. *CAST:* Dennis Price, Liz Fraser, Irene Handl, Graham Stark, Vera Day, Marjorie Rhodes, John Meillon, Cyril Smith, Frankie Howerd, Miriam Karlin.

A sailor's (Price) impending marriage is in danger when he has a bogus paternity suit filed against him.

2245. Watch Out, We're Mad (5/76) Eastman Color—91 mins. (Comedy-Crime). *DIR:* Marcello Fondato. *PRO:* Mario Cecchi Gori. *SP:* Marcello Fondato, Francesco Scarmaglia. Story by Marcello Fondato. A Capital-Filmayer Production. A Rizzoli Film. *CAST:* Terence Hill, Bud Spencer, Donald Pleasence, John Sharp, Paty Shepard, Manuel De Blas, Luis Barbero, Giancarlo Bastianoni, Roberto Alessandri, Ada Pometti.

Two stock car drivers (Spencer, Hill) take on the mob when the mobsters wreck their new dune buggy. *NOTES:* Limited theatrical release. [Original Italian title: *...Altrimenti Ci Arrabiamo*].

2246. Watermelon Man (5/70) Eastman Color—97 mins. (Comedy). *DIR:* Melvin Van Peebles. *PRO:* John B. Bennett. *SP:* Herman Raucher. A Johanna Production. *CAST:* Godfrey Cambridge, Estelle Parsons, Howard Caine, D'Urville Martin, Mantan Moreland, Kay Kimberly, Erin Moran, Emil Sitka, Lawrence Parke, Ray Ballard, Vivian Rhodes, Irving Selbst, Kay E. Kuter, Scott Garrett.

A bigoted white insurance salesman (Cambridge) wakes up one morning to discover he's suddenly black.

2247. Wattstax (2/73) Eastman Color—102 mins. (Documentary-Musical). *DIR:* Mel Stuart. *PRO:* Larry Shaw, Mel Stuart. A Stax Films-Wolper Pictures Production. *CAST:* Richard Pryor, The Dramatics, Staple Singers, Kim Weston, Isaac Hayes, Freddy Robinson.

A musical documentary centered around the L.A. community of Watts.

2248. The Way of the Strong (6/19/28) B&W—61 mins. (Crime-Drama). *DIR:* Frank Capra. *PRO:* Harry Cohn. *SP:* Peter Milne, William Conselman. *CAST:* Mitchell Lewis, Alice Day, Margaret Livingston, Theodore Von Eltz, William Norton Bailey.

An ugly racketeer (Lewis) falls in love with a blind girl (Day), but because of his ugliness, dupes her into thinking he is the handsome piano player (Von Eltz) in his cafe. Realizing the error of his ways, he sacrifices his life so that the blind girl and piano player can find happiness.

2249. The Way We Were (10/73) Eastman Color/Panavision—118 mins.

(Romance). *DIR:* Sydney Pollack. *PRO:* Ray Stark. *SP:* Arthur Laurents, Alvin Sargent, David Rayfiel. Based on the book by Arthur Laurents. A Rastar Production. *CAST:* Barbra Streisand, Robert Redford, Bradford Dillman, Lois Chiles, Patrick O'Neal, Viveca Lindfors, Murray Hamilton, Herb Edelman, Diana Ewing, Dan Seymour, George Gaynes, James Woods, Allyn Ann McLerie, Sally Kirkland, Marcia Mae Jones, Susan Blakely.

The lives and loves of a young couple (Streisand, Redford), she a political activist and he a novelist, from college days in the 30's to Hollywood in the 50's.

2250. We of the Never Never (2/83) Technicolor/Technovision—132 mins. (Drama). *DIR:* Igor Auzins. *PRO:* Greg Tepper, John B. Murray. *SP:* Peter Schreck. Based on the book by Jane Taylor Gunn. An Adams-Packer-Mainline-Triumph Films Production. *CAST:* Angela Punch McGregor, Arthur Dignam, Tony Barry, Tommy Lewis, Lewis Fitz-Gerald, Martin Vaughan, John Jarratt, Donald Blitner, Kim Chiu Kok, Cecil Parkee, Brian Granrott, Mawuyul Yanthalawuy, Danny Adcock, John Cameron, Sibina Willy, Jessie Roberts, Christine Conway, Ray Pattison, George Jadarku, Sally McKenzie, Sarah Craig, Fincina Hopgood.

A white woman (McGregor) becomes the first to travel Australia's aborigine wilderness, known as the "Never Never." *NOTES:* Limited theatrical release.

2251. We Were Strangers (4/21/49) B&W—106 mins. (Adventure-Drama). *DIR:* John Huston. *PRO:* Sam Spiegel. *SP:* John Huston, Peter Viertel. Based on *Rough Sketch* by Robert Sylvester. A Horizon Production. *CAST:* Jennifer Jones, John Gar-

field, Pedro Armendariz, Gilbert Roland, Ramon Navarro, Wally Cassell, David Bond, Morris Ankrum, Robert Malcolm, Roberta Haynes, Rodolfo Hoyos, Paul Marion, Rodd Redwing.

In 1933 Cuba, an American-born Cuban (Garfield) returns home to help his people in their revolutionary fight.

2252. A Weekend with Lulu (4/61) B&W—91 mins. (Comedy). *DIR:* John Paddy Carstairs. *PRO/SP:* Ted Lloyd. Story by Ted Lloyd, Val Valentine. A Hammer Production. *CAST:* Bob Monkhouse, Leslie Phillips, Alfred Marks, Shirley Eaton, Irene Handl, Sidney James, Kenneth Connor, Eugene Deckers, Graham Stark, Tutte Lemkow, Sidney Tafler.

A pair of young lovers (Phillips, Eaton) take off on a romantic weekend, but complications arise when the girl's mother (Handl) comes along and they mistakenly arrive in Paris.

2253. Welcome to the Club (9/71) Eastman Color—88 mins. (Comedy). *DIR:* Walter Shenson. *PRO:* Sam Lomburg, Walter Shenson. *SP:* Clement Biddle Wood. Based on the book by Clement Biddle Wood. *CAST:* Brian Foley, Jack Warden, Andy Jarrell, Kevin O'Conner, Francesca Tu, Al Mancini, David Toguri, Art Wallace, Louis Quinn, Marsha Hunt, Lee Meredith, Lon Satton, Christopher Malcolm, Joyce Wilford.

In 1945 Tokyo, a Quaker morale officer (Foley) tries to get his black friends better treatment and upsets military protocol.

2254. We'll Bury You (11/62) B&W—75 mins. (Documentary). *DIR/SP:* Jack W. Thomas. *PRO:* Jack W. Thomas, Jack Leewood. *CAST:* Narrated by William Woodson.

A study of Communism from Marx through Khrushchev as detailed in rare film clips from Russian newsreels and captured footage.

2255. We'll Meet Again (11/42) B&W — 84 mins. (Musical). *DIR:* Phil Brandon. *PRO:* Ben Henry, George Formby. *SP:* James Seymour, Howard Thomas. Story by Derek Sheils. A Columbia-British Production. *CAST:* Vera Lynn, Geraldo, Patricia Roc, Ronald Ward, Donald Gray, Betty Jardine, Frederick Leister, Brefni O'Rorke, Marian Spencer, Lesley Osmond, John Watt, John Sharman, Alvar Liddell.

A singer (Lynn) rises to a popular BBC star during World War II, loses her Scottish soldier (Gray) to her best friend (Roc), and decides to devote herself to entertaining military forces throughout Europe. *NOTES:* Loosely based on the real-life career of Vera Lynn.

2256. The Werewolf (7/56) B&W — 83 mins. (Horror). *DIR:* Fred F. Sears. *PRO:* Sam Katzman. *SP:* Robert E. Kent, James B. Gordon. A Clover Production. *CAST:* Steven Ritch, Don Megowan, Joyce Holden, Eleanore Tanin, Kim Charney, Harry Lauter, Larry Blake, Ken Christy, James Gavin, Don C. Harvey, Ford Stevens, Marjorie Stapp.

After taking an experimental serum, a man (Ritch) turns into a werewolf. *NOTES:* The werewolf makeup was used previously in the 1944 Columbia film *Return of the Vampire*.

2257. West of Abilene (10/21/40) B&W — 57 mins. (Western). *DIR:* Ralph Cedar. *PRO:* Leon Barsha. *SP:* Paul Franklin. *CAST:* Charles Starrett, Marjorie Cooley, Bob Nolan, Bruce Bennett, Forrest Taylor, Don Beddoe, William Pawley, Pat Brady, George Cleveland, Bud Osborne, Al Bridge, Frank Ellis, Sons of the Pioneers.

Two brothers (Starrett, Bennett)

stake a land claim and have to fight a gang of land grabbers trying to get it from them. [British title: *The Showdown*].

2258. West of Cheyenne (6/30/ 38) B&W — 59 mins. (Western). *DIR:* Sam Nelson. *PRO:* Harry L. Decker. *SP:* Ed Earl Repp. *CAST:* Charles Starrett, Iris Meredith, Bob Nolan, Dick Curtis, John Tyrrell, Edward J. LeSaint, Pat Brady, Jack Rockwell, Art Mix, Edmund Cobb, Ernie Adams, Tex Cooper, Sons of the Pioneers.

A rancher (Starrett) goes after a gang of cattle rustlers.

2259. West of Dodge City (3/ 27/47) B&W — 57 mins. (Western). *DIR:* Ray Nazarro. *PRO:* Colbert Clark. *SP:* Bert Horswell. *CAST:* Charles Starrett, Nancy Saunders, Smiley Burnette, Fred F. Sears, I. Stanford Jolley, Glenn Stuart, George Chesebro, Bob Wilke, Nolan Leary, Steve Clark, Marshall Reed, Zon Murray, Mustard and Gravy.

The Durango Kid (Starrett) stops a land swindler (Sears) and proves a boy (Stuart) innocent of robbery. [British title: *The Sea Wall*].

2260. West of Santa Fe (10/3/38) B&W — 60 mins. (Western). *DIR:* Sam Nelson. *PRO:* Harry L. Decker. *SP:* Bennett R. Cohen. *CAST:* Charles Starrett, Iris Meredith, Bob Nolan, Dick Curtis, Robert Fiske, Dick Botiller, Edward J. LeSaint, LeRoy Mason, Clem Horton, Edmund Cobb, Hank Bell, Edward Hearn, Bud Osborne, Buck Conners, Blackie Whiteford, Hal Taliaferro (Wally Wales), Sons of the Pioneers.

A sheriff (Starrett) comes to the aid of a rancher (Meredith) accused of murder by a gang of cattle rustlers.

2261. West of Sonora (3/25/48) B&W — 55 mins. (Western). *DIR:* Ray Nazarro. *PRO:* Colbert Clark. *SP:*

Barry Shipman. CAST: Charles Starrett, Anita Castle, Smiley Burnette, Steve Darrell, Hal Taliaferro (Wally Wales), George Chesebro, Bob Wilke, Emmett Lynn, Lynn Farr, Lloyd Ingraham, The Sunshine Boys.

The Durango Kid (Starrett) helps settle a family feud between two old men (Chesebro, Darrell), one of whom thinks the other an outlaw, by bringing the real outlaw (Taliaferro) to justice.

2262. West of Tombstone (1/15/42) B&W — 59 mins. (Western). DIR: Howard Bretherton. PRO: William Berke. SP: Maurice Geraghty. CAST: Charles Starrett, Marcella Martin, Cliff Edwards, Gordon DeMain, Russell Hayden, Jack Kirk, Budd Buster, Lloyd Bridges, Tom London, Eddie Laughton, Francis Walker, Ernie Adams, Clancy Cooper, Ray Jones, George Morrell.

When a sheriff (Starrett) goes after stagecoach robbers, he learns that Billy the Kid (DeMain) is alive and is now a respectable businessman.

2263. Westbound Mail (1/22/37) B&W — 57 mins. (Western). DIR: Folmer Blangsted. PRO: Harry L. Decker. SP: Francis Guihan. Story by James P. Hogan. CAST: Charles Starrett, Rosalind Keith, Edward Keane, Arthur Stone, Ben Welden, Al Bridge, George Chesebro, Art Mix.

A sheriff (Starrett) helps a postmistress (Keith) round up a gang of bandits who have been robbing her mail runs.

2264. Western Caravans (1/15/39) B&W — 58 mins. (Western). DIR: Sam Nelson. PRO: Harry L. Decker. SP: Bennett R. Cohen. CAST: Charles Starrett, Iris Meredith, Bob Nolan, Dick Curtis, Russell Simpson, Hal Taliaferro (Wally Wales), Sammy McKim, Ethan Laidlaw, Charles Brinley, Edmund Cobb, Hank Bell, Steve Clark, Herman Hack, Sons of the

Pioneers (Pat Brady, Bob Nolan, Tim Spencer, Hugh Farr, Karl Farr).

A sheriff (Starrett) stops a range war between the homesteaders and ranchers.

2265. The Western Code (9/16/32) B&W — 61 mins. (Western). DIR: John P. McCarthy. SP: Milton Krims. Story by William Colt MacDonald. CAST: Tim McCoy, Nora Lane, Mischa Auer, Wheeler Oakman, Gordon DeMain, Mathew Betz, Dwight Frye, Bud Osborne, Emilio Fernandez, Chuck Baldra, Cactus Mack.

A cowboy (McCoy) comes to the aid of a woman (Lane) who has lost her ranch to an outlaw.

2266. Western Courage (1/29/35) B&W — 61 mins. (Western). DIR: Spencer G. Bennet. PRO: Larry Darmour. SP: Nate Gatzert. Story by Charles F. Royal. CAST: Ken Maynard, Geneva Mitchell, Ward Bond, Wally West, Dick Curtis, Betty Blythe, Renee Whitney, E. H. Calvert, Bud McClure, Roy Bucko, Buck Bucko, Arkansas Johnny, Bart Carre, Charles K. French, Cornelius Keefe.

A spoiled brat (Mitchell) from the big city gets a dude ranch foreman (Maynard) in trouble with outlaws.

2267. Western Frontier (8/7/35) B&W — 59 mins. (Western). DIR: Al Herman. PRO: Larry Darmour. SP: Nate Gatzert. Story by Ken Maynard. CAST: Ken Maynard, Lucile Browne, Nora Lane, Robert "Buzz" Henry, Art Mix, Slim Whitaker, Frank Ellis, Dick Curtis, Frank Yaconelli, Otis Harlan, Nelson McDowell, Frank Hagney, Harold Goodwin, Gordon S. Griffith, Jim Marcus, Tom Harris, William Gould, Budd Buster, Herman Hack, Horace B. Carpenter, Oscar Gahan, Joe Weaver.

A sheriff (Maynard) goes after a gang of outlaws who are led by his missing sister (Browne).

2268. The Westerner (12/1/34) B&W—58 mins. (Western). *DIR:* David Selman. *PRO:* Irving Briskin. *SP:* Harold Shumate. Based on *Burnt Ranch* by Walt Coburn. *CAST:* Tim McCoy, Marion Shilling, Joe Sawyer, Edward J. LeSaint, Harry Todd, Slim Whitaker, Lafe McKee, Bud Osborne, Edmund Cobb, Hooper Atchley, John Dilson, Albert J. Smith, Merrill McCormack.

A cowboy (McCoy) buys a ranch and finds himself framed for murder by a gang of cattle rustlers.

2269. What a Woman! (12/28/43) B&W—94 mins. (Comedy). *DIR/PRO:* Irving Cummings. *PRO:* Sidney Buchman. *SP:* Therese Lewis, Barry Trivers. Story by Erik Charell. *CAST:* Brian Aherne, Rosalind Russell, Willard Parker, Ann Savage, Alan Dinehart, Norma Varden, Edward Fielding, Grady Sutton, Russell Hicks, Douglas Wood, Irving Bacon, Shelley Winters, Isabel Withers, Byron Foulger, Hobart Cavanaugh, Selmer Jackson, Pierre Watkin, Mary Forbes.

A literary agent (Russell) unknowingly selects the author (Parker) of the book she has just purchased to be the lead in the Hollywood production of the book. [British title: *The Beautiful Cheat*].

2270. What Price Innocence? (6/24/33) B&W—64 mins. (Drama). *DIR/SP:* Willard Mack. *CAST:* Willard Mack, Minna Gombell, Jean Parker, Betty Grable, Bryant Washburn, Ben Alexander, Beatrice Banyard, Louise Beavers.

A family physician (Mack) observes that the lives of children he has delivered into the world become a shambles upon their adolescence because their parents have failed to inform them of the facts of life. [British title: *Shall the Children Pay?*].

2271. What's Buzzin' Cousin? (7/30/43) B&W—75 mins. (Musical). *DIR:* Charles Barton. *PRO:* Jack Fier. *SP:* Harry Sauber, John P. Medbury. Story by Aben Kandel. *CAST:* Ann Miller, Eddie "Rochester" Anderson, John Hubbard, Jeff Donnell, Leslie Brooks, Carol Hughes, Theresa Harris, Freddy Martin, Roy Gordon, Dub Taylor, Bradley Page, Erville Alderson, Warren Ashe, Walter Soderling, Eddie Fetherstone, John Tyrrell, Freddy Martin and His Orchestra.

A girl (Miller) inherits a hotel in a ghost town and with the help of her three friends and a band of stranded musicians turns it into a hot spot.

2272. When a Girl's Beautiful (9/25/47) B&W—68 mins. (Musical). *DIR:* Frank McDonald. *PRO:* Wallace MacDonald. *SP:* Brenda Weisberg. Story by Henry K. Moritz. *CAST:* Adele Jergens, Marc Platt, Patricia White (Patricia Barry), Stephen Dunne, Steven Geray, Mona Barrie, Jack Leonard, Paul Harvey, Nancy Saunders, Doris Houck, Lela Bliss, Amelita Ward, Peggie Call, Vera Stokes, Thomas Louden.

An advertising man (Platt) creates the world's most beautiful girl by combining the best parts of a number of pictures, and then has to find a girl to fit the picture.

2273. When a Stranger Calls (10/79) Eastman Color—97 mins. (Horror). *DIR:* Fred Walton. *PRO:* Doug Chapin, Steve Feke. *SP:* Steve Feke, Fred Walton. *CAST:* Carol Kane, Rutanya Alda, Carmen Argenziano, Kirsten Larkin, Bill Boyett, Charles Durning, Ron O'Neal, Rachel Roberts, Tony Beckley, Colleen Dewhurst, Michael Champion, Joe Reale.

A psycho (Beckley) murders two children after terrorizing their babysitter (Kane) and then returns seven years later to extend his crime to the baby-sitter's family.

2274. When G-Men Step In (3/17/38) B&W—61 mins. (Crime). DIR: C. C. Coleman, Jr. PRO: Wallace MacDonald. SP: Arthur T. Horman. Story by Arthur T. Horman, Robert C. Bennett. CAST: Don Terry, Jacqueline Wells (Julie Bishop), Robert Paige, Gene Morgan, Paul Fix, Stanley Andrews, Edward Earle, Horace MacMahon, Huey White.

A government agent (Paige) sets out to break up a gang of racketeers of which his brother (Terry) is the head.

2275. When Husbands Flirt (1/1/26) B&W—57 mins. (Comedy). DIR: William A. Wellman. PRO: Harry Cohn. SP: Paul Gangelin. CAST: Dorothy Revier, Forrest Stanley, Tom Ricketts, Ethel Wales.

A wife (Revier) suspects her husband (Stanley) of playing around when she finds evidence that another woman has been in his car, not knowing that her husband lent his car to his partner (Ricketts).

2276. When Strangers Marry (5/25/33) B&W—65 mins. (Drama). DIR: Clarence Badger. SP: J. K. McGuinness. Story by Maximilian Foster. CAST: Jack Holt, Lillian Bond, Arthur Vinton, Barbara Barondess, Ward Bond, Paul Porcasi, Gustav von Seyffertitz, Rudolph Amendt, Charles Stevens.

A man (Holt) working on a railroad at the straits of Malay finds himself married to a spoiled rich woman (Bond), while his adversary (Vinton) tries to stop the railroad from being completed.

When the Devil Commands see **The Devil Commands**

2277. When the Devil Was Well (3/37) B&W—67 mins. (Comedy-Romance). DIR: Maclean Rogers. PRO:

A. George Smith. SP: W. Lane Crawford. A GS Enterprises Film Production. CAST: Jack Hobbs, Vera Lennox, Eva Gray, Gerald Rawlinson, Annie Esmond, Max Adrian, Aubrey Mallalieu, Bryan Powley.

A mother (Esmond) tries to get her son (Hobbs) to marry a socialite (Gray), but he manages to get her fixed up with his best friend (Rawlinson) and he marries his sweetheart (Lennox).

2278. When the Redskins Rode (5/30/51) Super Cinecolor—78 mins. (Western). DIR: Lew Landers. PRO: Sam Katzman. SP: Robert E. Kent. CAST: Jon Hall, Mary Castle, James Seay, Sherry Moreland, John Dehner, Pedro de Cordoba, Lewis Russell, William Bakewell, Milton Kibbee, Gregory Gay, Rusty Wescoatt, Rick Vallin, John Ridgely.

Set during the French and Indian War, the English try to enlist the aid of the Delaware Indians in defeating the Indians who have sided with the French, but a French spy (Castle) tries to thwart their plans.

2279. When the Wife's Away (10/25/26) B&W—57 mins. (Comedy). DIR: Frank R. Strayer. PRO: Harry Cohn. SP: Douglas Bronston. CAST: George K. Arthur, Dorothy Revier, Tom Ricketts, Ina Rorke, Ned Sparks, Harry Depp, Lincoln Plummer, Bobby Dunn.

A young couple (Arthur, Revier) set out to impress the husband's uncle (Ricketts) and gain their inheritance. Complications arise and they have to deal with crooks but eventually they get the money.

2280. When You Comin' Back Red Ryder? (2/79) Eastman Color/Panavision—118 mins. (Drama). DIR: Milton Katselas. PRO: Marjoe Gortner. SP: Mark Medoff. Based on the play by Mark Medoff. CAST: Candy Clark, Marjoe Gortner, Stephanie

Faracy, Dixie Harris, Anne Ramsey, Lee Grant, Hal Linden, Peter Firth, Pat Hingle, Bill McKinney, Riley Hill, Leon Russell, Audray Lindley, Sherry Unger, Mark Medoff, Ron Sobel.

An enraged Vietnam veteran (Gortner) terrorizes a group of people in a New Mexico roadside diner.

2281. When You're in Love (2/16/37) B&W–110 mins. (Musical). *DIR/SP*: Robert Riskin. *PRO*: Everett Riskin. Based on an idea by Ethel Hill, Cedric Worth. *CAST*: Grace Moore, Cary Grant, Aline MacMahon, Henry Stephenson, Thomas Mitchell, Catherine Doucet, Luis Alberni, Emma Dunn, Frank Puglia, Billy Gilbert, Arthur Hoyt, Gerald Oliver Smith, George Pearce, Edward Keane.

An international opera star (Moore) attempts to marry a U.S. citizen (Grant) in order to gain admittance to the country to attend a music festival. [British title: *For You Alone*].

2282. When You're Smiling (8/30/50) B&W–75 mins. (Musical). *DIR*: Joseph Santley. *PRO*: Jonie Taps. *SP*: Karen DeWolf, John R. Roberts. *CAST*: Jerome Courtland, Lola Albright, Jerome Cowan, Margo Wood, Collette Lyons, Robert Shayne, Ray Teal, Jimmy Lloyd, Donna Hamilton, Edward Earle, Frank Nelson, Neyle Morrow, Frankie Laine, Bob Crosby, Kay Starr, Billy Daniels, The Modernaires, The Mills Brothers.

A cowboy (Courtland) goes to Hollywood in the hopes of getting into show business, and with the help of a girl (Albright), eventually becomes a recording star.

2283. Where Angels Go ... Trouble Follows (3/68) Pathe Color–95 mins. (Drama). *DIR*: James Neilson. *PRO*: William Frye. *SP*: Blanche Hanalis. Based on characters created by Jane Trahey. *CAST*: Rosalind Russell, Stella Stevens, Binnie Barnes, Mary Wickes, Dolores Sutton, Milton Berle, Arthur Godfrey, Van Johnson, Robert Taylor, William Lundigan, Susan Saint James, Barbara Hunter, Alice Rawlings, Hilarie Thompson, Devon Douglas, Ellen Moss, Cherie Lamour, June Fairchild.

A young, rebellious nun (Stevens) tries to introduce new teaching methods while the Mother Superior (Russell) wants to keep the old ones. *NOTES*: A sequel to the 1966 Columbia film *The Trouble with Angels*.

2284. Where Are the Children? (12/86) Metrocolor/Panavision–92 mins. (Drama). *DIR*: Bruce Malmuth. *PRO*: Zev Braun. *SP*: Jack Sholder. Based on the book by Mary Higgins Clark. *CAST*: Jill Clayburgh, Max Gail, Harley Cross, Elisabeth Harnois, Bernard Hughes, Elizabeth Wilson, Frederic Forrest, James Purcell, Clifton James, Eriq LaSalle, Joseph Hindy, Zev Braun, Bruce Malmuth, Christopher Murney.

Foul play is suspected when it is learned that a woman's (Clayburgh) two children (Cross, Harnois) are missing because nine years before, her first two children from a previous marriage wound up missing and were found murdered.

2285. The Whirlpool (7/29/34) B&W–72 mins. (Drama). *DIR*: Roy William Neill. *PRO*: Robert North. *SP*: Dorothy Howell, Ethel Hill. Story by Howard Emmett Rogers. *CAST*: Jack Holt, Jean Arthur, Lila Lee, Rita La Roy, Donald Cook, John Miljan, Ward Bond, Allen Jenkins, Willard Robertson, Oscar Apfel.

A man (Holt) goes to prison on a murder charge and serves twenty years. When he is released he opens a nightclub, and there, meets the daughter (Arthur) whom he has never seen.

2286. The Whirlwind (4/14/33) B&W–62 mins. (Western). *DIR*: D.

Ross Lederman. *SP*: Stuart Anthony. Story by Walt Coburn. *CAST*: Tim McCoy, Alice Dahl, Pat O'Malley, J. Carrol Naish, Mathew Betz, Joe Girard, Lloyd Whitcomb, William McCall, Stella Adams, Theodore Lorch, Hank Bell, Mary Gordon, Joe Dominguez.

A cowboy (McCoy) is turned against his father (O'Malley) by a crooked lawyer (Naish) who is after their ranch.

2287. Whirlwind (4/1/51) Sepiatone—70 mins. (Western). *DIR*: John English. *PRO*: Armand Schaefer. *SP*: Norman S. Hall. A Gene Autry Production. *CAST*: Gene Autry, Gail Davis, Smiley Burnette, Thurston Hall, Harry Lauter, Dick Curtis, Harry Harvey, Tommy Ivo, Boyd Stockman, Kenne Duncan, Gregg Barton, Pat O'Malley, Al Wyatt, Gary Goodwin, Bud Osborne, Frankie Marvin, Stan Jones, Leon DeVoe.

A postal inspector (Autry) is out to get the goods on a Western crime syndicate.

2288. Whirlwind Raiders (5/13/48) B&W—54 mins. (Western). *DIR*: Vernon Keays. *PRO*: Colbert Clark. *SP*: Norman S. Hall. *CAST*: Charles Starrett, Nancy Saunders, Smiley Burnette, Fred F. Sears, Jack Ingram, Eddie Parker, Lynn Farr, Don Kay Reynolds, Arthur Loft, Philip Morris, Patrick Hurst, Maudie Prickett, Frank LaRue, Russell Meeker, Herman Hack, Doye O'Dell and the Radio Rangers.

The Durango Kid (Starrett) helps put an end to the notorious "Texas State Police" and their criminal activities. [British title: *State Police*].

2289. Whispering Enemies (3/24/39) B&W—62 mins. (Drama). *DIR*: Lewis D. Collins. *PRO*: Larry Darmour. *SP*: Gordon Rigby, Tom Kilpatrick. Story by John Rawlins and Harold Tarshis. *CAST*: Jack Holt,

Dolores Costello, Addison Richards, Joseph Crehan, Donald Briggs, Pert Kelton, Paul Everton.

Two rival owners of cosmetic companies (Holt, Costello) try to put each other out of business by spreading rumors about one another's products.

2290. The Whistle at Eaton Falls (8/2/51) B&W—96 mins. (Drama). *DIR*: Robert Siodmak. *PRO*: Louis deRochemont. *SP*: Lemist Esler, Virginia Shaler. Based on the research of J. Sterling Livingston. *CAST*: Lloyd Bridges, Dorothy Gish, Carleton Carpenter, Murray Hamilton, James Westerfield, Lenore Lonergan, Russell Hardie, Helen Shields, Doro Merande, Ernest Borgnine, Parker Fennelly, Diana Douglas, Anne Francis, Anne Seymour, Arthur O'Connell, Donald McKee.

After the president of a plastics plant has been killed in a plane crash, the new plant manager (Bridges) must lay off workers. Eventually labor and management get together and resolve their differences when new orders come in. [British title: *Richer Than the Earth*].

2291. The Whistler (3/30/44) B&W—59 mins. (Mystery-Crime). *DIR*: William Castle. *PRO*: Rudolph C. Flothow. *SP*: Eric Taylor. Story by J. Donald Wilson. Suggested by the radio program *The Whistler*. *CAST*: Richard Dix, Gloria Stuart, J. Carrol Naish, Joan Woodbury, Don Costello, Alan Dinehart, Cy Kendall, Otto Forrest, Byron Foulger, Trevor Bardette, Clancy Cooper, Robert Emmett Keane, Billy Benedict, George Lloyd.

A man (Dix) puts out a contract on his own life when he learns his wife has died. When he later learns that his wife may be alive, he tries to find the killer and stop him but he doesn't know who the killer will be.

2292. White Eagle (10/7/32) B&W—64 mins. (Western). *DIR:* Lambert Hillyer. *SP:* Fred Myton. *CAST:* Buck Jones, Barbara Weeks, Ward Bond, Robert Ellis, Jim Thorpe, Jason Robards, Sr., Frank Campeau, Bob Kortman, Robert Elliott, Clarence Geldert, Jimmy House, Frank Hagney, Russell Simpson.

White Eagle (Jones), an Indian Pony Express rider, tracks down an outlaw gang who have been stealing the organization's ponies and blaming it on the Indians. He later learns that he is a white man who was abducted and raised by the Indians. *NOTES:* Jones reprised his role of White Eagle for the 1941 serial of the same name.

2293. White Lies (1/7/35) B&W—63 mins. (Crime). *DIR:* Leo Bulgakov. *PRO:* Irving Briskin. *SP:* Harold Shumate. *CAST:* Walter Connolly, Fay Wray, Victor Jory, Leslie Fenton, Irene Hervey, Robert Allen, William Demarest, Robert Emmett O'Conner, Oscar Apfel, Mary Foy, Katherine Claire Ward, Jessie Arnold.

When a newspaper publisher (Connolly) uses yellow journalism to have a cop (Jory) demoted for arresting his daughter (Wray) for murder, the cop sets out to find the real killer.

2294. White Line Fever (8/75) Metrocolor—89 mins. (Action). *DIR:* Jonathan Kaplan. *PRO:* John Kemeny. *SP:* Ken Friedman, Jonathan Kaplan. An International Cinemedia Center Production. *CAST:* Jan-Michael Vincent, Kay Lenz, Slim Pickens, L. Q. Jones, Don Porter, Sam Laws, R. G. Armstrong, Dick Miller, John D. Garfield, Johnny Ray McGhee, Leigh French, Martin Kove.

A trucker (Vincent) battles corruption in the trucking industry on and off the road.

2295. White Mischief (1/88) Agfa Color—107 mins. (Mystery-Romance). *DIR:* Michael Radford. *PRO:* Simon Perry. *SP:* Michael Radford, Jonathan Gems. Based on the book by James Fox. A Goldcrest-Umbrella-Power Tower Investments-BBC Production. *CAST:* Sarah Miles, Joss Ackland, John Hurt, Greta Scacchi, Charles Dance, Susan Fleetwood, Jacqueline Pearce, Catherine Neilson, Murray Head, Ray McAnally, Geraldine Chaplin, Trevor Howard.

Murder and infidelity abound among the British colony living in Kenya's "Happy Valley" during the early days of World War II.

2296. White Nights (11/85) Metrocolor—136 mins. (Dance-Spy-Drama). *DIR:* Taylor Hackford. *PRO:* Taylor Hackford, William S. Gilmore. *SP:* James Goldman, Eric Hughes. Story by James Goldman. A New Visions-Columbia-Delphi V Production. *CAST:* Mikhail Baryshnikov, Gregory Hines, Jerzy Skolimowski, Helen Mirren, Geraldine Page, Isabella Rossellini, John Glover, Stefan Gryff, William Hootkins, Shane Rimmer, Maryam D'Abo.

A Russian ballet star (Baryshnikov), who defected to the U.S., finds himself back in Russia when his plane crashes. With the help of an American expatriate tap dancer (Hines) and his wife (Rossellini), he escapes to freedom.

2297. White Sister (3/73) Eastman Color—96 mins. (Drama). *DIR:* Alberto Lattuada. *PRO:* Carlo Ponti. *SP:* Iaia Fiastri, Alberto Lattuada, Tonino Guerra, Ruggero Maccari. *CAST:* Sophia Loren, Adriano Celentano, Fernando Rey, Luis Marin, Juan Luis Galiardo, Sergio Fasanelli, Giuseppe Maffoli.

A woman (Loren) becomes a nun when her lover is killed. She returns to Italy to assume a position as head nurse in a hospital where the administration is all Communist.

[Original Italian title: *Bianco, Rosso E...*].

2298. The White Squaw (11/1/56) B&W—75 mins. (Western). *DIR:* Ray Nazarro. *PRO:* Wallace Mac-Donald. *SP:* Les Savage, Jr. Based on *The Gun Witch of Wyoming* by Larabie Sutter (Les Savage, Jr.). A Screen Gems Incorporated Production. *CAST:* David Brian, May Wynn, William Bishop, Nancy Hale, Myron Healey, Frank DeKova, Roy Roberts, Grant Withers, Wally Vernon, Paul Birch, William Leslie, Robert Ross, George Keymas, Neyle Morrow, Guy Teague.

A half-breed white woman (Wynn) raised by the Indians helps stop a rancher (Brian) who is trying to drive the Indians from their land.

The White Stallion *see* **The Outlaw Stallion**

2299. White Water Summer (7/87) Technicolor—90 mins. (Drama). *DIR:* Jeff Bleckner. *PRO:* Mark Tarlov. *SP:* Manya Starr, Ernest Kinroy. A Columbia-Delphi V Production from Polar Entertainment. *CAST:* Kevin Bacon, Sean Austin, Jonathan Ward, K. C. Martel, Matt Adler, Caroline McWilliams, Charles Siebert, Joseph Piassarelli.

A leader (Bacon) takes it upon himself to instill self confidence in a city boy (Austin) during a three week camping trip. *NOTES:* Originally filmed in 1985, but never released to theaters. It went directly to cable TV.

2300. Who Cares? (6/15/24) B&W—59 mins. (Drama). *DIR:* David Kirkland. *PRO:* Harry Cohn. *SP:* Douglas Z. Doty. *CAST:* Dorothy Devore, William Haines, Lloyd Whitlock, Beverly Bayne.

A couple is reunited when the husband (Haines) rescues his wife (Devore) from a gigolo (Whitlock).

2301. Who Killed Gail Preston? (5/11/38) B&W—61 mins. (Mystery). *DIR:* Leon Barsha. *PRO:* Ralph Cohn. *SP:* Robert E. Kent, Henry Taylor. Based on the screen story *Murder in Swingtime* by Henry Taylor. *CAST:* Don Terry, Rita Hayworth, Robert Paige, Dwight Frye, Gene Morgan, Marc Lawrence, Arthur Loft, Wyn Cahoon, John Gallaudet, John Spacey, Eddie Fetherstone, John Millican, John Dilson, Vernon Dent, Lee Shumway, Dick Curtis.

A detective (Terry) searches for the killer of a nightclub singer (Hayworth).

2302. Who Was That Lady? (6/60) B&W—115 mins. (Comedy). *DIR:* George Sidney. *PRO/SP:* Norman Krasna. Based on the play *Who Was That Lady I Saw You With* by Norman Krasna. An Ansark-Sidney Production. *CAST:* Tony Curtis, Janet Leigh, Dean Martin, James Whitmore, John McIntire, Barbara Nichols, Larry Keating, Larry Storch, Simon Oakland, Joi Lansing, Kan Tong, Snub Pollard.

A professor (Curtis) and his friend (Martin), a television writer, pretend to be FBI agents to fool the professor's wife (Leigh) and get involved with real spies.

2303. The Whole Town's Talking (2/7/35) B&W—95 mins. (Comedy-Crime). *DIR:* John Ford. *PRO:* Lester Cowan. *SP:* Jo Swerling, Robert Riskin. Based on the book by William R. Burnett. *CAST:* Edward G. Robinson, Jean Arthur, Arthur Hohl, Wallace Ford, Arthur Byron, Donald Meek, Paul Harvey, Edward Brophy, Etienne Girardot, James Donlan, J. Farrell MacDonald, Robert Emmett O'Conner, Frank Sheridan, Francis Ford, Lucille Ball, Walter Long, Mary Gordon, Charles King, Tom London.

When a timid clerk (Robinson) gets mistaken for his double, "Killer" Mannion (Robinson), he is given a pass by the police to avoid another case of mistaken identity, but confusion develops when his double gets hold of the pass. *NOTES:* Edward G. Robinson played a dual role in this film. [British title: *Passport to Fame*].

2304. The Whole Truth (9/58) B&W—85 mins. (Mystery-Thriller). *DIR:* John Guillermin. *PRO:* Jack Clayton. *SP:* Jonathan Latimer. Based on the stage and television play by Philip Mackie. A Romulus-Valient Film Production. *CAST:* Stewart Granger, Donna Reed, George Sanders, Gianna Maria Canale, Michael Shillo, Richard Molinas, Peter Dyneley, John Van Eyssen, Philip Vickers, Jimmy Thompson.

A movie producer (Granger) tries to prove his innocence when he is accused of the murder of an actress (Canale) with whom he has been having an affair.

2305. Wholly Moses! (6/80) Metrocolor/Panavision—109 mins. (Comedy). *DIR:* Gary Weis. *PRO:* Freddie Fields. *SP:* Guy Thomas. *CAST:* Dudley Moore, Laraine Newman, James Coco, Paul Sand, Jack Gilford, Dom DeLuise, John Houseman, Madeline Kahn, David L. Lander, Richard Pryor, John Ritter, Richard B. Shull, Tanya Boyd, Tom Baker, Andrea Martin.

A shepherd (Moore) overhears God talking to Moses and thinks that he himself has been given the task of leading the people out of Egypt.

2306. Whom the Gods Destroy (7/13/34) B&W—74 mins. (Drama). *DIR:* Walter Lang. *PRO:* Felix Young. *SP:* Fred Niblo, Jr., Sidney Buchman. Story by Albert Payson Terhune. *CAST:* Walter Connolly, Robert Young, Doris Kenyon, Macon Jones, Scotty Beckettt, Rollo Lloyd, Hobart Bosworth, Akim Tamiroff, Charles

Middleton, Walter Brennan, Mary Carr, Jack Mulhall, Hugh Huntley.

An actor (Connolly) helps to save women and children from a sinking ship, and then dresses as a woman to save himself. When he returns home he learns that he is presumed dead and mourned as a hero.

2307. Who's Minding the Mint (10/67) Technicolor—98 mins. (Comedy). *DIR:* Howard Morris. *PRO:* Norman Maurer. *SP:* Ray S. Allen, Harry Bullock. *CAST:* Jim Hutton, Dorothy Provine, Milton Berle, Joey Bishop, Bob Denver, Walter Brennan, Victor Buono, Jack Gilford, Jamie Farr, David J. Stewart, Luther James, Robert Ball, Corinne Cole.

A money checker (Hutton) at the U.S. Mint loses $50,000 and hires a group of misfit thieves to help him print up a replacement.

2308. Who's Your Father? (3/35) B&W—63 mins. (Comedy). *DIR:* Henry W. George. *PRO:* Lupino Lane. *SP:* Lupino Lane, Arthur Rigby, Reginald Long. Based on the play *Turned Up* by Mark Melford. A St. George's Production. *CAST:* Lupino Lane, Peter Haddon, Nita Harvey, Jean Kent, Margaret Yarde, James Carew, Peter Gawthorne, James Finlayson, Eva Hudson.

When a man (Lane) prepares to get married, he learns that his mother (Yarde) has married an undertaker (Haddon), and his father (Gawthorne), thought lost at sea, has turned up with a new wife, a black woman (Harvey).

2309. Why Rock the Boat? (1/75) Eastman Color—112 mins. (Comedy). *DIR:* John Howe. *PRO/SP:* William Weintraub. Based on the book by William Weintraub. A National Film Board of Canada Production. *CAST:* Stuart Gillard, Tiiu Leek, Ken James, Bud Knapp, Henry Beckman, Sean Sullivan, Patricia Gage, Ruben

Morena, Cec Linder, Harry Ramer, Maurice Podbrey, Patricia Hamilton, Anna Reiser, Robert Rivard.

In the 1940's, a cub reporter (Gillard) ends up campaigning for the newspaper union when he can't bring in a story.

2310. Wicked As They Come (2/57) B&W — 94 mins. (Drama). *DIR:* Ken Hughes. *PRO:* Maxwell Setton, M. J. Frankovich. *SP:* Ken Hughes, Robert Westerby, Sigmund Miller. Based on *Portrait in Smoke* by William S. Ballinger. A Film Locations Production. *CAST:* Arlene Dahl, Phil Carey, Herbert Marshall, Michael Goodliffe, David Kossoff, Marvin Kane, Sidney James, Gilbert Winfield, Patrick Allen, Ralph Truman, Faith Brook, Jacques Brunius.

A woman (Dahl), from the slums of London, wins a beauty contest and vows to stop at nothing in her climb to the top. When she accidentally kills her husband (James) she is put in jail, but is exonerated and continues her evil ways.

2311. Wide Open Faces (4/18/38) B&W — 67 mins. (Comedy). *DIR:* Kurt Neumann. *PRO:* David L. Lowe. *SP:* Earle Snell, Clarence Marks, Joe Bigelow, Pat C. Flick. Story by Richard Flournoy. *CAST:* Joe E. Brown, Jane Wyman, Alison Skipworth, Lyda Roberti, Alan Baxter, Lucien Littlefield, Sidney Toler, Barbara Pepper, Berton Churchill, Joseph Downing, Stanley Fields, Horace Murphy.

A soda jerk (Brown) outwits a gang of crooks when they converge on an inn to search for stolen money.

2312. The Wife Takes a Flyer (4/28/42) B&W — 86 mins. (Comedy). *DIR:* Richard Wallace. *PRO:* B. P. Schulberg. *SP:* Gina Kaus, Jay Dratler, Harry Segall. Story by Gina Kaus. *CAST:* Joan Bennett, Franchot Tone, Allyn Joslyn, Cecil Cunningham,

Roger Clark, Lloyd Corrigan, Lyle Latell, Georgia Caine, Barbara Brown, Chester Clute, Lloyd Bridges, Hans Conreid, James Millican, Cy Kendall, Carl Ekberg.

A British pilot (Tone) is shot down over Nazi-occupied Holland during World War II and winds up pretending to be the crazy husband of a Dutch woman (Bennett) in whose home is also billeted a Nazi major (Joslyn). [British title: *A Yank in Dutch*].

2313. The Wife's Relations (2/13/28) B&W — 58 mins. (Comedy). *DIR:* Maurice Marshall. *PRO:* Harry Cohn. *SP:* Stephen Cooper. Story by Adolph Unger. *CAST:* Shirley Mason, Gaston Glass, Ben Turpin, Armand Kaliz.

A young man (Glass) gets into trouble when he takes a job as caretaker of a large estate and, when the owner is away, pretends to be the owner and invites his friends for a visit.

2314. The Wild One (2/54) B&W — 79 mins. (Drama). *DIR:* Laslo Benedek. *PRO:* Stanley Kramer. *SP:* John Paxton. Based on *The Cyclist's Raid* by Frank Rooney. *CAST:* Marlon Brando, Mary Murphy, Robert Keith, Lee Marvin, Jerry Paris, Jay C. Flippen, Peggy Maley, Ray Teal, Will Wright, Robert Osterloh, Robert Bice, Alvy Moore, Pat O'Malley, Timothy Carey, Angela Stevens.

A gang of motorcyclists terrorize a small town. *NOTES:* This film was based on a true incident. In 1947, 4,000 motorcyclists took over the small town of Hollister, California, for the 4th of July weekend and destroyed it.

2315. The Wild Westerners (6/62) Eastman Color — 70 mins. (Western). *DIR:* Oscar Rudolph. *PRO:* Sam Katzman. *SP:* Gerald Drayson Adams. A Four Leaf Production. *CAST:* James Philbrook, Nancy Kovack, Duane Eddy, Guy Mitchell, Hugh Sanders,

Elizabeth McRae, Marshall Reed, Nestor Paiva, Harry Lauter, Bob Steele, Terry Frost, Don C. Harvey, Pierce Lyden, Joe McGuinn, Lisa Burkert, Hans Wedemeyer, Elizabeth Harrower, Frances Osborne, Tim Sullivan, Charles Horvath, Marjorie Stapp. A U.S. Marshal (Philbrook) fights Indians and outlaws while trying to get a gold shipment from Montana to the Union troops in the East.

2316. Wildcat of Tucson (12/31/40) B&W — 59 mins. (Western). DIR: Lambert Hillyer. PRO: Leon Barsha. SP: Fred Myton. CAST: Bill Elliott, Evelyn Young, Dub Taylor, Kenneth MacDonald, Stanley Brown, Ben Taggart, George Lloyd, Edmund Cobb, George Chesebro, Sammy Stein, Forrest Taylor, Francis Walker, Murdock McQuarrie, Robert Winkler, Dorothy Andre, Bert Young, Johnny Daheim, Newt Kirby. Wild Bill Hickok (Elliott) helps his brother (Brown) clear himself of an attempted murder charge, reforms a crooked judge (Taggart), and rids the town of claim-jumpers. [British title: *Promise Fulfilled*].

Winnetou *see* **Apache Gold**

Winnetou and His Old Friend Firehand *see* **Thunder at the Border**

Winnetou II *see* **Last of the Renegades**

Winnetou III *see* **The Desperado Trail**

2317. Winning of the West (1/20/53) Sepiatone — 57 mins. (Western). DIR: George Archainbaud. PRO: Armand Schaefer. SP: Norman S. Hall. A Gene Autry Production. CAST: Gene Autry, Gail Davis, Smiley Burnette, Richard Crane, Robert Livingston, House Peters, Jr., Gregg Barton, William Fawcett, Ewing Mitchell, Rodd Redwing, George Chesebro, Eddie Parker, Terry Frost, Boyd Morgan, Bob Woodward, James Kirkwood, Frank Jacquet, Charles Delaney, Charles Soldani. A Ranger (Autry) sets out to stop a protection racket of which his kid brother (Crane) is a member.

2318. Winter a Go-Go (10/65) Pathe Color — 88 mins. (Musical). DIR: Richard Benedict. PRO: Reno Carell. SP: Bob Kanter, Reno Carell. Story by Reno Carell. CAST: James Stacy, William A. Wellman, Jr., Beverly Adams, Anthony Hayes, Jill Donohue, Tom Nardini, Duke Hobbie, Julie Parrish, Nancy Czar, Linda Rogers, Judy Parker, Bob Kanter, Walter Maslow, H. T. Tsiang, Buck Holland, The Nooney Rickett Four, Joni Lyman, The Reflections. Teenagers turn a ski resort into a hot spot where they can play their kind of music.

2319. Woman Against the World (5/11/38) B&W — 66 mins. (Drama). DIR: David Selman. PRO: Lew Golder. SP: Edgar Edwards. CAST: Ralph Forbes, Alice Moore, Edgar Edwards, Collette Lyons, Sylvia Welsh, Ethel Reese-Burns, George Hallett, James McGrath, Grant MacDonald, Fred Bass, Harry Hay, Enid Cole, Reginald Hincks. When her husband (Edwards) dies, a woman (Moore) has her infant baby taken from her by her aunt (Reese-Burns), whom she accidentally kills. She is convicted of murder, pardoned, and jailed again before she finds her baby, with the help of an attorney (Forbes).

2320. The Woman Eater (7/59) B&W — 71 mins. (Horror). DIR: Charles Saunders. PRO: Guido Coen. SP: Brandon Fleming. A Fortress Film Production. CAST: George Coulouris,

Vera Day, Joy Webster, Peter Wyan, Jimmy Vaughn, Sara Leighton, Joyce Gregg, Maxwell Foster, Edward Higgins, Robert MacKenzie.

A mad doctor (Coulouris) feeds women to his flesh-eating plant and uses the serum from the plant to revive the dead. [British title: *Womaneater*].

2321. The Woman from Tangier (2/12/48) B&W—66 mins. (Crime). *DIR*: Harold Daniels. *PRO*: Martin Mooney. *SP*: Irwin Franklyn. *CAST*: Adele Jergens, Stephen Dunne, Michael Duane, Denis Green, Ivan Triesault, Curt Bois, Ian MacDonald, Donna Demario, Anton Kosta, Maurice Marsac.

An insurance investigator (Dunne), with the help of a cafe entertainer (Jergens), sets out to recover stolen money and solve a double slaying.

2322. The Woman I Stole (6/30/33) B&W—68 mins. (Adventure). *DIR*: Irving Cummings. *SP*: Jo Swerling. Based on *Tampico* by Joseph Hergesheimer. *CAST*: Jack Holt, Fay Wray, Noah Beery, Sr., Donald Cook, Raquel Torres, Edwin Maxwell, Ferdinand Munier, Charles Browne, Lee Phelps.

In North Africa, an undercover agent (Holt) wins the heart of the wife (Wray) of his best friend (Cook), but in the end he gives her up and prevents desert bandits from taking over his friend's oil company.

2323. Woman in Distress (1/19/37) B&W—68 mins. (Crime). *DIR*: Lynn Shores. *PRO*: Ralph Cohn. *SP*: Albert DeMond. Story by Edwin Olmstead. *CAST*: May Robson, Irene Hervey, Dean Jagger, Douglas Dumbrille, George McKay, Gene Morgan, Paul Fix, Frank Sheridan, Charles Wilson, Arthur Loft, Wallis Clark.

Two newspaper reporters (Jagger, Hervey) come to the aid of an old lady (Robson) when thieves set out to steal a valuable Rembrandt painting from her, believed to have been destroyed years before.

2324. A Woman Is the Judge (10/3/39) B&W—62 mins. (Drama). *DIR*: Nick Grinde. *PRO*: Ralph Cohn. *SP*: Karl Brown. *CAST*: Frieda Inescort, Otto Kruger, Rochelle Hudson, Mayo Methot, Gordon Oliver, Arthur Loft, Walter Fenner, John Dilson, Bentley Hewlett, Beryl Mercer.

A lady judge (Inescort) acts as defense lawyer for her daughter (Hudson) when she is accused of murder.

2325. A Woman of Distinction (3/1/50) B&W—85 mins. (Comedy). *DIR*: Edward Buzzell. *PRO*: Buddy Adler. *SP*: Charles Hoffman, Frank Tashlin. Story by Hugo Butler, Ian McClellan Hunter. *CAST*: Ray Milland, Rosalind Russell, Edmund Gwenn, Janis Carter, Mary Jane Saunders, Francis Lederer, Jerome Courtland, Alex Gerry, Charles Evans, Charlotte Wynters, Clifton Young, Gale Gordon, Jean Willes, Lucille Ball, Myron Healey, Charles Trowbridge, Harry Strang, Walter Sande.

A visiting astronomy professor (Milland) causes a scandal when he romances the dean (Russell) of a woman's college.

2326. Woman of the River (9/54) Technicolor—92 mins. (Drama). *DIR*: Mario Soldati. *PRO*: Basilio Franchina. *SP*: Basilo Franchina, Giorgio Bassani, Pier Paolo Pasolini, Florestano Vancini, Antonio Altoviti, Mario Soldati, Ben Zavin. An EX-Les Films de Centaur Production. *CAST*: Sophia Loren, Gerard Oury, Lise Bourdin, Rik Battaglia, Enrico Oliveri.

When a woman (Loren) is scorned by her lover (Battaglia), a smuggler, she has him sent to prison from whence he escapes and seeks revenge against her. [Original Italian title: *La Donna del Fiume*].

2327. A Woman's Way (2/13/28) B&W–57 mins. (Drama). DIR: Edmund Mortimer. PRO: Harry Cohn. SP: Will M. Ritchie, Elmer Harris. Story by Izola Forrester. CAST: Margaret Livingston, Warner Baxter, Armand Kaliz, Mathilde Comont.
A Parisian Opera star (Livingston) falls in love with a wealthy American (Baxter) and, when she is threatened by a criminal (Kaliz) she once helped, she assists the police in his capture.

2328. Women First (12/15/24) B&W–51 mins. (Drama). DIR: B. Reeves Eason. PRO: Harry Cohn. SP: Wilfred Lucas. CAST: William Fairbanks, Eva Novak, Lydia Knott, Bob Rhodes.
An ex-jockey (Fairbanks), with the help of a stable owner (Novak), wins the big race and stops a bribery attempt.

2329. Women in Prison (3/2/38) B&W–59 mins. (Crime). DIR: Lambert Hillyer. SP: Saul Elkins. Story by Mortimer Braus. CAST: Wyn Cahoon, Scott Colton, Arthur Loft, Mayo Methot, Ann Doran, Sarah Padden, Margaret Armstrong, John Tyrrell, Bess Flowers, Dick Curtis, Eddie Fetherstone, John Dilson, Lee Prather.
A woman (Methot) is sent to prison for her part in a robbery and one of the gang members (Loft) goes to extremes to get to her since only she knows where the stolen money is hidden.

2330. Women of Glamour (3/9/37) B&W–68 mins. (Drama-Comedy). DIR: Gordon Wiles. SP: Lynn Starling, Mary C. McCall, Jr. Based on the play Ladies of the Evening by Milton Herbert Gropper. CAST: Virginia Bruce, Melvyn Douglas, Reginald Denny, Pert Kelton, Leona Maricle, Thurston Hall, Mary Forbes, John Spacey, Maurice Cass, Bess Flowers, Miki Morita.
A gold-digger (Bruce) competes with a socialite (Maricle) for the affections of a wealthy playboy (Douglas). NOTES: A remake of the 1930 Columbia film Ladies of Leisure.

2331. Women's Prison (2/55) B&W–80 mins. (Prison Drama). DIR: Lewis Seiler. PRO: Bryan Foy. SP: Crane Wilbur, Jack DeWitt. CAST: Ida Lupino, Jan Sterling, Cleo Moore, Audrey Totter, Howard Duff, Phyllis Thaxter, Warren Stevens, Barry Kelley, Gertrude Michael, Vivian Marshall, Ross Elliott, Mae Clarke, Adelle August, Eddie Foy III, Juanita Moore, Don C. Harvey, Edna Holland, Mira McKinney.
A psychopathic prison superintendent (Lupino) takes out her frustrations on the women inmates until a riot proves her undoing.

The World of Space see **Battle in Outer Space**

The World of Yor see **Yor, the Hunter from the Future**

2332. The World Was His Jury (1/58) B&W–82 mins. (Drama). DIR: Fred F. Sears. PRO: Sam Katzman. SP: Herbert Abbott Spiro. A Clover Production. CAST: Edmond O'Brien, Mona Freeman, Karin Booth, Robert McQueeney, Paul Birch, John Beradino, Richard H. Cutting, Harvey Stephens, Carlos Romero, Hortense Petra, Gary Goodwin, Kelly Junge, Jr.
An attorney (O'Brien) loses his friends when he defends a ship's captain (McQueeney) of negligence in a sea disaster.

2333. World Without Sun (12/64) Technicolor–93 mins. (Documentary). DIR/PRO/SP: Jacques-Yves Cousteau. CAST: Narrated by Jacques-Yves Cousteau.
An underwater exploration of the flora and fauna of the Red Sea and a descent to 1000 feet in a two man sub-

marine. [Original French title: *Le Monde sans Soleil*]. [Original Italian title: *Il Mondo senza Sole*].

2334. The Wreck (2/5/27) B&W — 56 mins. (Drama). *DIR*: William James Craft. *PRO*: Harry Cohn. *SP*: Arthur Statter, Mary Alice Scully. Story by Dorothy Howell. *CAST*: Shirley Mason, Malcolm McGregor, James Bradbury, Jr., Francis McDonald.

A girl (Mason) unknowingly marries a thief (McGregor) and is accused as his accomplice.

2335. The Wreck of the Hesperus (2/5/48) B&W — 70 mins. (Adventure). *DIR*: John Hoffman. *PRO*: Wallace MacDonald. *SP*: Aubrey Wisberg. Story by Edward Huebsch. Based on the poem by Henry Wadsworth Longfellow. *CAST*: Willard Parker, Edgar Buchanan, Patricia White (Patricia Barry), Holmes Herbert, Jeff Corey, Wilton Graff, Boyd Davis, Paul Campbell, Paul E. Burns, Eddy Waller.

In the 1830's, a sea captain (Parker) learns that his employer (Buchanan), a ship salvager, has been deliberately wrecking ships for salvage.

2336. The Wrecker (8/5/33) B&W — 72 mins. (Drama). *DIR*: Albert S. Rogell. *SP*: Jo Swerling. Story by Albert S. Rogell. *CAST*: Jack Holt, Genevieve Tobin, George E. Stone, Sidney Blackmer, Ward Bond, Irene White, Russell Waddle, Wally Albright, Edward J. LeSaint, Clarence Muse, P. H. Levy.

A building demolisher (Holt) loses his wife (Tobin) to another man (Blackmer), and when an earthquake traps the couple, he contemplates leaving them there.

2337. The Wrecking Crew (2/69) Technicolor — 105 mins. (Action-Drama). *DIR*: Phil Karlson. *PRO*: Irving Allen. *SP*: William P. McGivern.

Based on the book by Donald Hamilton. A Meadway-Claude 4 Production. *CAST*: Dean Martin, Elke Sommer, Sharon Tate, Nancy Kwan, Nigel Green, Tina Louise, John Larch, John Brascia, Weaver Levy, Bill Saito.

Matt Helm (Martin) is sent after a crime ring that's hijacked a train carrying one billion dollars in gold bullion.

2338. The Wrong Box (8/66) Eastman Color — 108 mins. (Comedy). *DIR/PRO*: Bryan Forbes. *SP*: Larry Gelbart, Burt Shevelove. Based on the book by Robert Louis Stevenson, Lloyd Osborne. A Salamander Production. *CAST*: John Mills, Ralph Richardson, Michael Caine, Peter Cook, Dudley Moore, Nanette Newman, Tony Hancock, Peter Sellers, Thorley Walters, John Le Mesurier, Norman Rossington, Tutte Lemkow, James Villiers, Graham Stark, Andre Morell, Leonard Rossiter, Hamilton Dyce, Gwendolyn Watts, Roy Murray.

Two elderly brothers (Mills, Richardson) try to do each other in for an inheritance, but end up causing confusion to all concerned.

2339. Wrong Is Right (4/82) Metrocolor/Panavision — 117 mins. (Satire-Drama). *DIR/PRO/SP*: Richard Brooks. Based on *The Better Angels* by Charles McCarry. A Rastar Production. *CAST*: Sean Connery, George Grizzard, Robert Conrad, Katharine Ross, John Saxon, G. D. Spradlin, Henry Silva, Leslie Nielsen, Robert Webber, Rosalind Cash, Hardy Kruger, Dean Stockwell, Ron Moody, Cherie Michan, Tony March, Jennifer Jason Leigh, Ivy Bethune, Tom McFadden.

A TV reporter (Connery) finds himself up against revolutionaries, the CIA, the FBI, and the President (Grizzard) when he tries to tie the U.S. to a terrorist group. [British title: *The Man with the Deadly Lens*].

2340. Wyoming Hurricane (4/20/44) B&W — 58 mins. (Western). DIR: William Berke. PRO: Leon Barsha. SP: Fred Myton. CAST: Russell Hayden, Alma Carroll, Dub Taylor, Paul Sutton, Tristram Coffin, Bob Kortman, Hal Price, Benny Petti, Bob Wills and His Texas Playboys.

A cowboy (Hayden) sets out to prove his innocence when he is framed for the murder of the sheriff by a crooked cafe owner (Coffin). [British title: *Proved Guilty*].

2341. Wyoming Renegades (3/27/55) Technicolor — 73 mins. (Western). DIR: Fred F. Sears. PRO: Wallace MacDonald. SP: David Lang. CAST: Phil Carey, Martha Hyer, Gene Evans, William Bishop, Douglas Kennedy, Roy Roberts, Don Beddoe, Aaron Spelling, Harry Harvey, John Cason, Don C. Harvey, Boyd Stockman, George Keymas, Mel Welles, Henry Rowland, Guy Teague, Don Carlos.

A former outlaw (Carey) tries to go straight but gets drawn back into an outlaw gang. His girl (Hyer) and the town women finally stage an ambush that finishes the gang.

2342. X, Y & Zee (1/72) Eastman Color — 110 mins. (Drama). DIR: Brian G. Hutton. PRO: Jay Kanter, Alan Ladd, Jr. SP: Edna O'Brien. A Zee Films Production. CAST: Elizabeth Taylor, Michael Caine, Susannah York, Margaret Leighton, John Standing, Mary Larkin, Michael Cashman, Gino Melvazzi.

A successful architect (Caine) constantly battles with his wife (Taylor) and seeks an affair with a woman (York) whose personality is opposite that of his wife's. [British title: *Zee & Co.*].

2343. A Yank in Indo-China (4/3/52) B&W — 67 mins. (War-Action). DIR: Wallace A. Grissell. PRO: Sam Katzman. SP: Samuel Newman. An Esskay Production. CAST: John Archer, Douglas Dick, Jean Willes, Maura Murphy, Harold Fong, Don C. Harvey, Rory Mallison, Leonard Penn, Pierre Watkin, Hayward Soo Hoo, Kam Tong, Peter Chang.

Two pilots (Archer, Dick) operating a freight service in Indochina make war on the Communist guerrillas. [British title: *Hidden Secret*].

2344. A Yank in Korea (2/14/51) B&W — 73 mins. (War-Action). DIR: Lew Landers. PRO: Sam Katzman. SP: William B. Sackheim. Story by Leo Lieberman. CAST: Lon McCallister, William "Bill" Phillips, Brett King, Larry Stewart, William Tannen, Tommy Farrell, Norman Wayne, Rusty Wescoatt, William Haade, Sunny Vickers, Richard Paxton, Ralph Hodges.

A soldier (McCallister) nearly gets his whole platoon killed due to his carelessness but redeems himself by blowing up a munitions dump. [British title: *Letter from Korea*].

2345. Yesterday's Enemy (11/59) B&W/Scope — 95 mins. (War). DIR: Val Guest. PRO: Michael Carreras. SP: Peter R. Newman. Based on the television play by Peter R. Newman. A Hammer Production. CAST: Stanley Baker, Guy Rolfe, Leo McKern, Gordon Jackson, David Oxley, Richard Pasco, Russell Waters, Philip Ahn, Bryan Forbes, Percy Herbert, David Lodge, Barry Lowe.

In 1942 Burma, a British unit takes over a village after finding a coded Japanese map.

2346. Yesterday's Wife (3/15/23) B&W — 56 mins. (Comedy-Drama). DIR/SP: Edward J. LeSaint. PRO: Harry Cohn. Story by Evelyn Campbell. A C.B.C. Release. CAST: Irene Rich, Josephine Crowell, Lottie Williams, Lewis Dayton, Eileen Percy, Philo McCullough, William Scott.

When a couple (Rich, Dayton) get a divorce and end up at the same resort, a boating accident helps to bring them back together.

2347. Yol (The Trek of Life) (10/ 82) Fuji Color—111 mins. (Drama). *DIR:* Serif Goren. *PRO:* Edi Hubschmid, K. L. Puldi. *SP:* Yilmaz Guney. A Guney-Cactus-Artificial Eye-Triumph Films Production. *CAST:* Tarik Akan, Halil Ergun, Nocmettin Cobanoglu, Serif Sezer, Meral Orhousoy, Semra Ucar, Hikmet Celik, Sevda Aktolga, Tuncay Akca.

Five Turkish prisoners are given their freedom for one week to visit their loved ones, only to discover that tragedy awaits each man. *NOTES:* Limited theatrical release; in Turkish with English subtitles.

2348. Yor, the Hunter from the Future (8/83) Eastman Color—88 mins. (Science Fiction-Adventure). *DIR:* Anthony Dawson. *PRO:* Michele Marsala. *SP:* Anthony Dawson, Robert Bailey. Based on *Yor* by Juan Zanotto and Ray Collins. A Diamant Film Production. *CAST:* Reb Brown, Corinne Clery, John Steiner, Carole Andre, Alan Collins, Ayshe Gul, Marina Rocchi, Sergio Nicolai.

After nuclear destruction has wiped out modern civilization, a caveman (Brown) is caught in a time warp that mixes elements of the prehistoric era with elements of the future. [Original Italian title: *Il Mondo di Yor*].

2349. You Belong to Me (10/28/ 41) B&W—94 mins. (Romantic Comedy). *DIR/PRO:* Wesley Ruggles. *SP:* Claude Binyon. Story by Dalton Trumbo. *CAST:* Barbara Stanwyck, Henry Fonda, Edgar Buchanan, Roger Clark, Ruth Donnelly, Melville Cooper, Ralph Peters, Maude Eburne, Gordon Jones, Fritz Feld, Paul Harvey, Stanley Brown, Lloyd Bridges,

Byron Foulger, Arthur Loft, Larry Parks, Grady Sutton.

A millionaire playboy (Fonda) ends up marrying a lady doctor (Stanwyck) and, jealous of her male patients, buys a bankrupt hospital and puts her in charge so he can keep an eye on her. *NOTES:* Remade by Columbia in 1950 as *Emergency Wedding* [British title: *Good Morning, Doctor*].

2350. You Can't Do Without Love (7/44) B&W—89 mins. (Musical Comedy). *DIR:* Walter Forde. *PRO:* Ben Henry, Culley Forde. *SP:* Howard Irving Young, Peter Fraser, Margaret Kennedy, Emery Bonnett. A Columbia-British Production. *CAST:* Vera Lynn, Donald Stewart, Mary Clare, Frederick Leister, Richard Murdoch, Phyllis Stanley, Cyril Smith, Mavis Villiers.

A would-be singer (Lynn) tries to impress a producer (Stewart) at a benefit concert, and winds up stopping a gang of crooks and winning over the producer. [British title: *One Exciting Night*].

2351. You Can't Run Away from It (11/56) Technicolor/Scope— 95 mins. (Musical). *DIR/PRO:* Dick Powell. *SP:* Claude Binyon, Robert Riskin. Based on the screenplay *It Happened One Night* by Robert Riskin and *Night Bus* by Samuel Hopkins Adams. *CAST:* June Allyson, Jack Lemmon, Charles Bickford, Paul Gilbert, Jim Backus, Stubby Kaye, Henny Youngman, Allyn Joslyn, Bryon Foulger, Howard McNear, Jack Albertson, Frank Sully, Dub Taylor, Larry Blake.

An heiress (Allyson) runs away from a marriage arranged by her father (Bickford) and falls in love with a reporter (Lemmon). *NOTES:* A musical remake of the 1934 Columbia film *It Happened One Night.*

2352. You Can't Take It with You (8/23/38) B&W—127 mins.

(Comedy). *DIR/PRO:* Frank Capra. *SP:* Robert Riskin. Based on the play by George S. Kaufman and Moss Hart. *CAST:* James Stewart, Jean Arthur, Lionel Barrymore, Edward Arnold, Mischa Auer, Ann Miller, Spring Byington, Samuel S. Hinds, Dub Taylor, Donald Meek, H. B. Warner, Halliwell Hobbes, Mary Forbes, Eddie "Rochester" Anderson, Josef Swickard, Ann Doran, Charles Lane, Ward Bond, Harry Davenport, Pierre Watkin, Russell Hicks, Irving Bacon, Dick Curtis, Byron Foulger.

The daughter (Arthur) of a highly eccentric New York family falls for a rich man's son (Stewart) and the family winds up reforming the son's parents (Arnold, Forbes), showing them that money does not always bring happiness. *NOTES:* James Stewart's first Columbia film.

2353. You Can't Win Them All (7/70) Technicolor/Panavision—99 mins. (Adventure). *DIR:* Peter Collinson. *PRO:* Gene Corman. *SP:* Leo Gordon. *CAST:* Tony Curtis, Charles Bronson, Michele Mercier, Gregoire Aslan, Tony Bonner, Leo Gordon, John Achleson, John Alderton, Horst Jansen, Patrick Magee.

Two soldiers of fortune (Curtis, Bronson) agree to escort three girls and a shipment of gold across Turkey, but through a series of misadventures wind up losing both the girls and the gold.

2354. You Light Up My Life (8/77) Technicolor—90 mins. (Musical-Drama). *DIR/PRO/SP:* Joseph Brooks. *CAST:* Didi Conn, Joe Silver, Michael Zaslow, Stephan Nathan, Melanie Mayron, Jerry Keller, Lisa Reeves, John Gowans, Joseph Brooks, Simmy Bow, Bernice Nicholson, Ed Morgan, Marty Zagon.

The daughter (Conn) of an entertainer (Silver) tries to get her life in order and establish herself as a singer.

2355. You May Be Next! (2/25/36) B&W—67 mins. (Crime). *DIR:* Albert S. Rogell. *PRO:* Sid Rogell. *SP:* Fred Niblo, Jr., Ferdinand Reyher. Story by Henry Wales and Ferdinand Reyher. *CAST:* Ann Sothern, Lloyd Nolan, Douglass Dumbrille, John Arledge, Berton Churchill, Nana Bryant, Robert Middlemass, George McKay, Gene Morgan, Clyde Dilson.

A gang of crooks blackmail a radio engineer (Nolan) into using a high frequency transmitter to jam the frequency of his radio station. [British title: *Panic on the Air*].

2356. You Must Be Joking! (10/65) B&W—99 mins. (Comedy). *DIR:* Michael Winner. *PRO:* Charles H. Schneer. *SP:* Alan Hackney. Based on a story by Alan Hackney and Michael Winner. *CAST:* Michael Callan, Lionel Jeffries, Denholm Elliott, Bernard Cribbins, Wilfrid Hyde-White, Terry-Thomas, Gabriella Licuci, Patricia Viterbo, Lee Montague, Tracy Reed, James Robertson Justice, Leslie Phillips, Irene Handl, Richard Wattis, Gwendolyn Watts, Peter Bull, Miles Malleson, Clive Dunn, James Villiers, Graham Stark, Norman Vaughn.

A psychologist (Jeffries) rounds up five British soldiers and puts them through special tests to find the perfect soldier.

2357. You Were Never Lovelier (10/5/42) B&W—97 mins. (Musical). *DIR:* William A. Seiter. *PRO:* Louis F. Edelman. *SP:* Michael Fessier, Ernest S. Pagano, Delmer Daves. Based on the screenplay and story *The Gay Senorita* by Carlos Olivari and Sixto Pondal Rios. *CAST:* Fred Astaire, Rita Hayworth, Adolphe Menjou, Leslie Brooks, Adele Mara, Isobel Elsom, Gus Schilling, Barbara Brown, Douglas Leavitt, Catherine Craig, Kathleen Howard, Mary Field, Larry Parks, Stanley Brown, Kirk Alyn, Lina

Romay, Ralph Peters, Xavier Cugat and His Orchestra.

An American dancer (Astaire), stranded in Buenos Aires, is hired by the owner (Menjou) of a hotel to woo and wed his daughter (Hayworth).

2358. You'll Never Get Rich (9/12/41) B&W—88 mins. (Musical). DIR: Sidney Lanfield. PRO: Samuel Bischoff. SP: Michael Fessier, Ernest S. Pagano. CAST: Fred Astaire, Rita Hayworth, John Hubbard, Robert Benchley, Osa Massen, Frieda Inescort, Guinn "Big Boy" Williams, Donald MacBride, Cliff Nazarro, Marjorie Gateson, Frank Ferguson, Emmett Vogan, Martha Tilton.

A Broadway choreographer (Astaire) gets drafted into the Army while he is putting on a show, and by utilizing a great deal of ingenuity, he manages to successfully complete his show.

2359. Young Americans (10/67) Technicolor—103 mins. (Documentary). DIR/SP: Alex Grasshoff. PRO: Robert Cohn. CAST: The Young Americans, Milton C. Anderson.

A feature on "The Young Americans" singing group. NOTES: Nominated for and winner of the 1968 Oscar for Best Documentary Feature. The Oscar was withdrawn and the feature declared ineligible May 7, 1969, when it was learned that the feature was first released in 1967. This was the first and only time in Academy history that an Oscar had to be withdrawn.

2360. The Young Don't Cry (8/57) B&W—89 mins. (Drama). DIR: Alfred L. Werker. PRO: Philip A. Waxman. SP: Richard Jessup. Based on *The Cunning and the Haunted* by Richard Jessup. CAST: Sal Mineo, James Whitmore, J. Carrol Naish, Gene Lyons, Paul Carr, Thomas Carlin, Leigh Whipper, James Reese, Ruth Attaway, Leland Mayforth, Dick

Wigginton, Stanley Martin, Josephine Smith, Joseph Killorin, Phillips Hamilton, Victor Johnson.

An escaped convict (Whitmore) persuades an unwitting teenager (Mineo) to aid him in his getaway.

2361. The Young Land (5/59) Technicolor—89 mins. (Western). DIR: Ted Tetzlaff. PRO: Patrick Ford. SP: Norman S. Hall. Based on *Frontier Frenzy* by John Reese. A C. V. Whitney Production. CAST: Patrick Wayne, Yvonne Craig, Dennis Hopper, Dan O'Herlihy, Ken Curtis, Pedro Gonzalez-Gonzalez, Roberto de la Madrid, Cliff Ketchum, Edward Sweeny, Miguel Camacho, Cliff Lyons.

In 1848 California, a gunman (Hopper) is put on trial for killing a Mexican and the trial is watched closely by the populace as a test of the Anglo system of justice. NOTES: This film was originally intended to be released by Buena Vista in 1957, but was finally released by Columbia. This was C. V. Whitney's third and final film to deal with the American West, the other two being *The Searchers* (Warner Bros., 1956) and *The Missouri Traveller* (Buena Vista, 1958).

2362. The Young One (6/60) B&W—94 mins. (Drama). DIR: Luis Bunuel. PRO: George P. Werker. SP: Luis Bunuel, H. B. Addis (Hugo Butler). Based on *Travelin' Man* by Peter Matthiessen. A Producciones Olmeca-Valiant-Vitalite Production. CAST: Zachary Scott, Kay Meersman, Bernie Hamilton, Claudio Brook, Crahan Denton.

A black musician (Hamilton), falsely accused of having raped a white woman, seeks refuge on a small island, used by hunters, and is befriended by a young girl (Meersman) and a racist gameskeeper (Scott). [British title: *Island of Shame*]. [Original Spanish title: *La Joven*].

2363. Young Winston (10/72) Eastman Color/Panavision—145 mins. (Biography-Adventure). *DIR:* Richard Attenborough. *PRO/SP:* Carl Foreman. Based on *My Early Life: A Roving Commission* by Winston Churchill. A High Road/Hugh French Production. *CAST:* Simon Ward, Peter Cellier, Ronald Hines, John Mills, Anne Bancroft, Russell Lewis, Robert Shaw, Laurence Naismith, Basil Dignam, Jack Hawkins, Pat Heywood, William Dexter, Robert Hardy, Colin Blakely, Ian Holm, Richard Leech, Patrick Magee, Jane Seymour, Thorley Walters, Patrick Holt, Edward Woodward, James Cossins, Norman Rossington, Anthony Hopkins.

The adventurous life of Winston Churchill (Ward) from the time he was a junior officer in India, his journalistic experiences during the Boer War, and finally his election to Parliament.

2364. Younger Generation (3/4/29) B&W—75 mins. (Drama). *DIR:* Frank Capra. *PRO:* Jack Cohn. *SP:* Sonya Levien, Howard J. Green. Based on the play *It Is to Laugh* by Fannie Hurst. A Frank Capra Production. *CAST:* Jean Hersholt, Lina Basquette, Ricardo Cortez, Rex Lease, Rosa Rosanova, Syd Crossley, Martha Franklin, Julanne Johnston, Jack Raymond, Otto Fries, Julia Swayne Gordon.

A young man (Cortez), ashamed of his Jewish background, tries to remove himself from his origins and his ghetto heritage. *NOTES:* Columbia's first part-talking picture.

2365. Youth in Revolt (5/16/39) B&W—91 mins. (Drama). *DIR:* Jean Benoit-Levy. *SP:* Jean Benoit-Levy, Marie Epstein. Story by Julien Luchaire. A Transcontinental Films Production. *CAST:* Jean-Louis Barrault, Fabien Loris, Charles Daurat, Odette Joyeux, Dolly Mollinger, Jacqueline

Porel, Blanchette Brunoy, Bernard Blier, Jacqueline Pacud, Claude Sainval, Dina Vierny, Tony Jacqot, Maurice Bacquet, Fernand Ledoux.

A group of young men and women, disillusioned and fed up with civilization, flee to a cabin in the Maritime Alps to set up their own ideal community. *NOTES:* In French with English subtitles.

2366. Youth on Trial (1/11/45) B&W—59 mins. (Drama). *DIR:* Oscar (Budd) Boetticher. *PRO:* Ted Richmond. *SP:* Michel Jacoby. *CAST:* Cora Sue Collins, David Reed, Eric Sinclair, Georgia Bayes, Robert Williams, Mary Currier, John Calvert, Boyd Bennett, William Forrest, Boyd Davis, Joseph Crehan, Edwin Stanley, Florence Auer.

A woman judge (Currier) realizes she's neglected her home life when her own daughter (Collins) is caught in a raid and brought before her in court.

2367. Youthful Folly (11/34) B&W—72 mins. (Romance). *DIR:* Miles Mander. *PRO:* Norman Loudon. *SP:* Heinrich Frankel. Based on a play by Gordon Davis. A Sound City Production. *CAST:* Irene Vanbrugh, Jane Carr, Mary Lawson, Grey Blake, Arthur Chesney, Eric Maturin, Fanny Wright.

A working class musician (Maturin) falls in love with a rich society girl (Carr) over the objections of his sister (Lawson).

2368. Zarak (12/56) Technicolor/Scope—99 mins. (Adventure). *DIR:* Terence Young. *PRO:* Irving Allen, Albert R. Broccoli. *SP:* Richard Maibaum. Based on *The Story of Zarak Khan* by A. J. Bevan. A Warwick Production. *CAST:* Victor Mature, Michael Wilding, Anita Ekberg, Finlay Currie, Bonar Colleano, Bernard Miles, Frederick Valk, Peter Illing,

Andre Morell, Patrick McGoohan, Eunice Gayson, Eddie Byrne.

A bandit chief (Mature) whose outlaw gang roams India's northwest frontier is captured by the British. While a prisoner, he gains respect for the British officer (Wilding) who captured him. He escapes and when the British garrison is attacked he saves the officer at the cost of his own life.

2369. Zelly and Me (4/88) Technicolor—87 mins. (Drama). DIR/SP: Tina Rathborne. PRO: Sue Jett, Tony Mark. A Cypress Production. CAST: Alexandra Johnes, Isabella Rossellini, Glynis Johns, Kaiulani Lee, David Lynch, Joe Morton, Courtney Vickery, Lindsay Dickon, Jason McCall, Aaron Boone.

The trials and tribulations of an orphaned eight-year-old (Johnes) and the friendship she shares with her nanny (Rossellini). NOTES: Limited theatrical release.

2370. Zombies of Mora-Tau (3/57) B&W—70 mins. (Horror). DIR: Edward L. Cahn. PRO: Sam Katzman. SP: Raymond T. Marcus. Story by George H. Plympton. A Clover Production. CAST: Gregg Palmer, Allison Hayes, Autumn Russell, Joel Ashley, Morris Ankrum, Marjorie Eaton, Gene Roth, Leonard Geer, Lewis Webb, Ray "Crash" Corrigan, Mel Curtis, Frank Hagney, Karl Davis, William Baskin.

A diver (Palmer) plans to salvage a diamond treasure off the coast of Africa that is guarded by zombies. [British title: *The Dead That Walk*].

2371. Zotz! (7/62) B&W—87 mins. (Comedy). DIR/PRO: William Castle. SP: Ray Russell. Based on the book by Walter Karig. CAST: Tom Poston, Julia Meade, Jim Backus, Fred Clark, Cecil Kellaway, Zeme North, Margaret Dumont, Louis Nye, Mike Mazurki, Albert Glasser, James Millhollin, Carl Don.

A professor (Poston) finds an ancient coin that gives him unusual powers and he tries to convince everyone that he is a new secret weapon when he points his index finger and says "Zotz." NOTES: Although there was no audience participation for this film, William Castle's gimmick was to have selected theaters give its patrons plastic "Zotz" coins.

Serials
(1937–1956)

Following is a complete list of serials produced and distributed by Columbia Pictures. Columbia was the last studio to enter the serial field, and it was also the last studio to leave, climaxing almost twenty years of serial production, which consisted of fifty-five 15-chapter serials, one 12-chapter serial, and one 13-chapter serial. Dates given are approximate release dates.

2372. Adventures of Captain Africa (6/9/55) B&W—15 chapters. *DIR*: Spencer G. Bennet. *PRO*: Sam Katzman. *SP*: George H. Plympton. *CAST*: John Hart, Rick Vallin, Ben Welden, June Howard, Bud Osborne, Paul Marion, Lee Roberts, Terry Frost, Ed Coch, Michael Fox. *CHAPTER TITLES*: (1) Mystery Man of the Jungle, (2) Captain Africa to the Rescue, (3) Midnight Attack, (4) Into the Crocodile Pit, (5) Jungle War Drums, (6) Slave Traders, (7) Saved by Captain Africa, (8) The Bridge in the Sky, (9) Blasted by Captain Africa, (10) The Vanishing Princess, (11) The Tunnel of Terror, (12) Fangs of the Beast, (13) Renegades at Bay, (14) Captain Africa and the Wolf Dog, (15) Captain Africa's Final Move.

Captain Africa (Hart) faces many dangers as he helps a deposed caliph to regain his throne.

2373. Adventures of Sir Galahad (12/22/48) B&W—15 chapters. *DIR*: Spencer G. Bennet. *PRO*: Sam Katzman. *SP*: George H. Plympton, Lewis Clay, David Mathews. *CAST*: George Reeves, Charles King, William Fawcett, Pat Barton, Hugh Prosser, Lois Hall, Nelson Leigh, Jim Diehl, Don C. Harvey, Marjorie Stapp, John Merton, Pierce Lyden, Rick Vallin, Leonard Penn, Ray "Crash" Corrigan. *CHAPTER TITLES*: (1) Stolen Sword, (2) Galahad's Daring, (3) Prisoners of Ulric, (4) Attack on Camelot, (5) Galahad to the Rescue, (6) Passage of Peril, (7) Unknown Betrayer, (8) Perilous Adventure, (9) Treacherous Magic, (10) The Sorcerer's Spell, (11) Valley of No Return, (13) The Wizard's Vengeance, (14) Quest for the Queen, (15) Galahad's Triumph.

Galahad (Reeves) cannot take his place at the Round Table until he recovers the missing sword, Excalibur. He must combat a villainous magician (Fawcett), Saxon bandits, and an outlaw known as the "Black Knight" (?????) before he can succeed.

2374. Atom Man Vs. Superman (6/19/50) B&W—15 chapters. *DIR*: Spencer G. Bennet. *PRO*: Sam Katzman. *SP*: George H. Plympton, David Mathews, Joseph F. Poland. Based on the *Superman* adventure appearing in *Superman* and *Action* comics magazine. Adapted from the *Superman* radio program. *CAST*: Kirk Alyn, Noel Neill, Lyle Talbot, Tommy Bond, Pierre Watkin, Jack Ingram, Don C. Harvey, Rusty Wescoatt, Terry Frost, Wally West, Paul Stader, George Robotham. *CHAPTER TITLES*: (1) Superman Flies Again, (2) Atom Man Appears, (3) Ablaze in the Sky, (4) Superman Meets Atom Man, (5) Atom Man Tricks Superman, (6) Atom Man's Challenge, (7) At the Mercy of Atom Man, (8) Into the Empty Room, (9) Superman Crashes Through, (10) Atom Man's Heat Ray, (11) Luthor's Strategy, (12) Atom Man Strikes, (13) Atom Man's Flying Saucer, (14) Rocket of Vengeance, (15) Superman Saves the Universe.

Luthor (Talbot), secretly the Atom Man, plans to destroy Metropolis with his various inventions, but is thwarted at every turn by Superman (Alyn).

2375. Batman (7/16/43) B&W — 15 chapters. *DIR*: Lambert Hillyer. *PRO*: Rudolph C. Flothow. *SP*: Victor McLeod, Leslie Swabacker, Harry Fraser. Based on the *Batman* adventure appearing in *Detective* comics and *Batman* magazine, created by Bob Kane. *CAST*: Lewis Wilson, Douglas Croft, Shirley Patterson, J. Carrol Naish, William C. P. Austin, Charles Middleton, Robert Fiske, Michael Vallon, Gus Glassmire, Kenne Duncan, Sam Flint, George Chesebro, Stanley Price, Frank Shannon, I. Stanford Jolley, Anthony Warde, Terry Frost, Tom London, Dick Curtis, Bud Osborne, Pat O'Malley, George J. Lewis, Jack Ingram, Earle Hodgins, Charles Wilson, John Maxwell. *CHAPTER TITLES*: (1) The Electrical Brain, (2) The Bat's Cave, (3) Mark of the Zombies, (4) Slaves of the Rising Sun, (5) The Living Corpse, (6) Poison Peril, (7) The Phoney Doctor, (8) Lured by Radium, (9) The Sign of the Sphinx, (10) Flying Spies, (11) A Nipponese Trap, (12) Embers of Evil, (13) Eight Steps Down, (14) The Executioner Strikes, (15) Doom of the Rising Sun.

Batman (Wilson) and Robin (Croft) go after an enemy undercover spy ring aiding the Axis powers whose leader, Dr. Daka (Naish), maintains his power by turning men into zombies. *NOTES*: In 1965, Columbia released all 15 chapters of this serial to theaters in a single screening and entitled it "An Evening with Batman and Robin."

2376. Batman and Robin (5/26/49) B&W — 15 chapters. *DIR*: Spencer G. Bennet. *PRO*: Sam Katzman. *SP*: George H. Plympton, Joseph F. Poland, Royal K. Cole. Based on the *Batman* comic appearing in *Detective* comics and *Batman* magazine, created by Bob Kane. *CAST*: Robert Lowery, John Duncan, Jane Adams, Lyle Talbot, Ralph Graves, Don C. Harvey, William Fawcett, Leonard Penn, Rick Vallin, Michael Whalen, Greg McClure, House Peters, Jr., Jim Diehl, Eric Wilton, Marshall Bradford. *CHAPTER TITLES*: (1) Batman Takes Over, (2) Tunnel of Terror, (3) Robin's Wild Ride, (4) Batman Trapped, (5) Robin Rescues Batman, (6) Target-Robin, (7) The Fatal Blast, (8) Robin Meets the Wizard, (9) The Wizard Strikes Back, (10) Batman's Last Chance, (11) Robin's Ruse, (12) Robin Rides the Wind, (13) The Wizard's Challenge, (14) Batman Vs. Wizard, (15) Batman Victorious.

Batman (Lowery) and Robin (Duncan) search for a remote-control machine stolen by a mysterious figure known as "The Wizard" (?????).

2377. Black Arrow (10/20/44) B&W—15 chapters. *DIR:* Lew Landers. *PRO:* Rudolph C. Flothow. *SP:* Sherman L. Lowe, Jack Stanley, Leighton Brill, Royal K. Cole. *CAST:* Robert Scott, Adele Jergens, Kenneth MacDonald, Robert Williams, Charles Middleton, George J. Lewis, I. Stanford Jolley, Martin Garralaga, Nick Thompson, George Navarro, Harry Harvey, John Laurenz, Dan White, Edwin Parker, Stanley Price, Ted Mapes. *CHAPTER TITLES:* (1) A City of Gold, (2) Signal of Fear, (3) The Seal of Doom, (4) Terror of the Badlands, (5) The Secret of the Vault, (6) Appointment with Death, (7) The Chamber of Horror, (8) The Vanishing Dagger, (9) Escape from Death, (10) The Gold Cache, (11) The Curse of the Killer, (12) Test by Torture, (13) The Sign of Evil, (14) An Indian's Revenge, (15) The Black Arrow Triumphs.

Black Arrow (Scott), son of a Navajo chief, sets out to prevent white men from stealing the tribe's gold.

2378. Blackhawk (7/24/52) B&W—15 chapters. *DIR:* Spencer G. Bennet, Fred F. Sears. *PRO:* Sam Katzman. *SP:* George H. Plympton, Sherman L. Lowe, Royal K. Cole. Based on the *Blackhawk* comic magazine drawn by Reed Crandall. *CAST:* Kirk Alyn, Carol Forman, John Crawford, Michael Fox, Rick Vallin, Don C. Harvey, Larry Stewart, Weaver Levy, Zon Murray, Nick Stuart, Marshall Reed, Pierce Lyden, William Fawcett, Rory Mallison, Frank Ellis. *CHAPTER TITLES:* (1) Distress Call from Space, (2) Blackhawk Traps a Traitor, (3) In the Enemy's Hideout, (4) The Iron Monster, (5) Human Targets, (6) Blackhawk's Leap for Life, (7) Mystery Fuel, (8) Blasted from the Sky, (9) Blackhawk Tempts Fate, (10) Chase for Element X, (11) Forced Down, (12) Drums of Doom, (13) Blackhawk's Dar-

ing Plan, (14) Blackhawk's Wild Ride, (15) The Leader Unmasked.

Blackhawk (Alyn) sets out to stop a gang of saboteurs led by the notorious sabotage chief Laska (Forman), and her boss, the mysterious "Leader" (?????).

2379. Blazing the Overland Trail (8/4/56) B&W—15 chapters. *DIR:* Spencer G. Bennet. *PRO:* Sam Katzman. *SP:* George H. Plympton. *CAST:* Dennis Moore, Lee Roberts, Norma Brooks, Gregg Barton, Lee Morgan, Don C. Harvey, Pierce Lyden, Ed Coch, Reed Howes, Kermit Maynard, Pete Kellett, Al Ferguson. *CHAPTER TITLES:* (1) Gun Emperor of the North, (2) Riding the Danger Trail, (3) The Black Raiders, (4) Into the Flames, (5) Trapped in a Runaway Wagon, (6) Rifles for Redskins, (7) Midnight Attack, (8) Blast at Gunstock Pass, (9) War at the Wagon Camp, (10) Buffalo Stampede, (11) Into the Fiery Blast, (12) Cave-In, (13) Bugle Call, (14) Blazing Peril, (15) Raiders Unmasked.

Army scout Jim Bridger (Moore) sets out to stop an unscrupulous rancher (Harvey) from gaining control of the Overland Trail. *NOTES:* Columbia's last serial release.

2380. Brenda Starr, Reporter (1/26/45) B&W—13 chapters. *DIR:* Wallace W. Fox. *PRO:* Sam Katzman. *SP:* George H. Plympton, Ande Lamb. Based upon the comic feature *Brenda Starr, Reporter,* created by Dale Messick. *CAST:* Joan Woodbury, Kane Richmond, Syd Saylor, Joe Devlin, George Meeker, Wheeler Oakman, Clay Forrester, Marion Burns, Lottie Harrison, Ernie Adams, Jack Ingram, Anthony Warde, John Merton, Billy Benedict. *CHAPTER TITLES:* (1) Hot News, (2) The Blazing Trap, (3) Taken for a Ride, (4) A Ghost Walks, (5) The Big Boss Speaks, (6) Man Hunt, (7) Hideout of Terror, (8) Killer at Large,

(9) Dark Magic, (10) A Double-Cross Backfires, (11) On the Spot, (12) Murder at Night, (13) The Mystery of the Payroll.

Brenda Starr (Woodbury) is hunted by gangsters as she tries to solve a coded message leading to a missing payroll.

2381. Brick Bradford (1/5/48) B&W—15 chapters. *DIR:* Spencer G. Bennet. *PRO:* Sam Katzman. *SP:* George H. Plympton, Arthur Hoerl, Lewis Clay. Based on the newspaper feature *Brick Bradford* owned and copyrighted by King Features Syndicate. *CAST:* Kane Richmond, Rick Vallin, Linda Johnson, Pierre Watkin, Charles Quigley, Jack Ingram, Fred Graham, John Merton, Leonard Penn, Wheeler Oakman, Carol Forman, Charles King, John Hart, Helene Stanley, Nelson Leigh, Robert Barron, George DeNormand. *CHAPTER TITLES:* (1) Atomic Defense, (2) Flight to the Moon, (3) Prisoners of the Moon, (4) Into the Volcano, (5) Bradford at Bay, (6) Back to Earth, (7) Into Another Century, (8) Buried Treasure, (9) Trapped in the Time Top, (10) The Unseen Hand, (11) Poison Gas, (12) Door of Disaster, (13) Sinister Rendezvous, (14) River of Revenge, (15) For the Peace of the World.

Brick Bradford (Richmond) travels to the moon through the "Crystal Door," and backwards into time via the "Time Top," as he helps a professor (Merton) protect and perfect his invention, the Interceptor Ray.

2382. Bruce Gentry (2/10/49) B&W—15 chapters. *DIR:* Spencer G. Bennet, Thomas Carr. *PRO:* Sam Katzman. *SP:* George H. Plympton, Joseph F. Poland, Lewis Clay. Based on the newspaper feature *Bruce Gentry*, distributed by the New York Post Syndicate, Inc. *CAST:* Tom Neal, Judy Clark, Ralph Hodges, Forrest Taylor, Hugh Prosser, Tristram Coffin, Jack Ingram, Terry Frost, Eddie Parker, Charles King, Stephen Carr, Dale Van Sickel. *CHAPTER TITLES:* (1) The Mysterious Disc, (2) The Mine of Menace, (3) Fiery Furnace, (4) Grade Crossing, (5) Danger Trail, (6) A Flight for Life, (7) The Flying Disc, (8) Fate Takes the Wheel, (9) Hazardous Heights, (10) Over the Falls, (11) Gentry at Bay, (12) Parachute of Evil, (13) Menace of the Mesa, (14) Bruce's Strategy, (15) The Final Disc.

Bruce Gentry (Neal) pursues an enemy agent known as "The Recorder" (?????), who uses mysterious flying discs as weapons of destruction.

2383. Captain Midnight (2/15/42) B&W—15 chapters. *DIR:* James W. Horne. *PRO:* Larry Darmour. *SP:* Basil Dickey, George H. Plympton, Jack Stanley, Wyndham Gittens. Based on the radio serial *Captain Midnight*. *CAST:* Dave O'Brien, Dorothy Short, James Craven, Sam Edwards, Guy Wilkerson, Bryant Washburn, Luana Walters, Joe Girard, Ray Teal, George Pembroke, Charles Hamilton, Al Ferguson. *CHAPTER TITLES:* (1) Mysterious Pilot, (2) The Stolen Range Finder, (3) The Captured Plane, (4) Mistaken Identity, (5) Ambushed Ambulance, (6) Weird Waters, (7) Menacing Fates, (8) Shells of Evil, (9) The Drop to Doom, (10) The Hidden Bomb, (11) Sky Terror, (12) Burning Bomber, (13) Death in the Cockpit, (14) Scourge of Revenge, (15) The Fatal Hour.

Captain Midnight (O'Brien) battles the dreaded Ivan Shark (Craven) as he attempts to steal a range finder to aid him in his plans to bomb the United States.

2384. Captain Video (12/17/51) B&W-CineColor—15 chapters. *DIR:* Spencer G. Bennet, Wallace A. Grissell. *PRO:* Sam Katzman. *SP:* Royal K. Cole, Sherman L. Lowe, Joseph F. Poland, George H. Plympton. Based on characters from the television series *Captain Video and His Video Rangers*. *CAST:* Judd Holdren, Larry Stewart, George Eldredge, Gene Roth, William Fawcett, Don C. Harvey, Jack Ingram, I. Stanford Jolley, Skelton Knaggs, Jimmy Stark, Rusty Wescoatt, Zon Murray, George Robotham, Oliver Cross, Bill Bailey. *CHAPTER TITLES:* (1) Journey Into Space, (2) Menace of Atoma, (3) Captain Video's Peril, (4) Entombed in Ice, (5) Flames of Atoma, (6) Astray in the Stratosphere, (7) Blasted by the Atomic Eye, (8) Invisible Menace, (9) Video Springs a Trap, (10) Menace of the Mystery Metal, (11) Weapon of Destruction, (12) Robot Rocket, (13) Mystery of Station X, (14) Vengeance of Vultura, (15) Video Vs. Vultura.

Captain Video (Holdren) and his Ranger (Stewart) set out to prevent the planet Atoma from conquering Earth.

2385. Chick Carter, Detective (7/11/46) B&W — 15 chapters. *DIR:* Derwin Abrahams. *PRO:* Sam Katzman. *SP:* George H. Plympton, Harry Fraser. Adapted from the Smith and Street character *Chick Carter* appearing in *Shadow* magazine and *Shadow* comics and based on the radio program. *CAST:* Lyle Talbot, Douglas Fowley, Julie Gibson, Pamela Blake, Eddie Acuff, Robert Elliott, George Meeker, Leonard Penn, Charles King, Jack Ingram, Joel Friedkin, Eddie Parker. *CHAPTER TITLES:* (1) Chick Carter Takes Over, (2) Jump to Eternity, (3) Grinding Wheels, (4) Chick Carter Trapped, (5) Out of Control, (6) Chick Carter's Quest, (7) Chick Carter's Frame-Up, (8) Chick Carter Gives Chase, (9) Shadows in the Night, (10) Run to Earth, (11) Hurled Into Space, (12) Chick Carter Faces Death, (13) Rendezvous with Death, (14) Chick Carter Sets a Trap, (15) Chick Carter Wins Out.

Chick Carter (Talbot) battles ruthless gangsters as he sets out to find a missing gem, known as the "Blue Diamond."

2386. Cody of the Pony Express (3/4/50) B&W — 15 chapters. *DIR:* Spencer G. Bennet. *PRO:* Sam Katzman. *SP:* David Mathews, Lewis Clay, Charles R. Condon. Story by George H. Plympton, Joseph F. Poland. *CAST:* Jock Mahoney, Dickie Moore, Peggy Stewart, William Fawcett, Tom London, Helena Dare, George J. Lewis, Pierce Lyden, Jack Ingram, Rick Vallin, Frank Ellis, Ross Elliott, Ben Corbett, Rusty Wescoatt. *CHAPTER TITLES:* (1) Cody Carries the Mail, (2) Captured by Indians, (3) Cody Saves a Life, (4) Cody Follows a Trail, (5) Cody to the Rescue, (6) The Fatal Arrow, (7) Cody Gets His Man, (8) Renegade Raiders, (9) Frontier Law, (10) Cody Tempts Fate, (11) Trouble at Silver Gap, (12) Cody Comes Through, (13) Marshal of Nugget City, (14) Unseen Danger, (15) Cody's Last Ride.

Young Pony Express rider Bill Cody (Moore) joins forces with an Army investigator (Mahoney) and his aide (London) to stop an unscrupulous lawyer (Lewis) from seizing control of the frontier territory.

2387. Congo Bill (10/12/48) B&W — 15 chapters. *DIR:* Spencer G. Bennet, Thomas Carr. *PRO:* Sam Katzman. *SP:* Arthur Hoerl, George H. Plympton, Lewis Clay. Based on the comic strip *Congo Bill* appearing in *Action* comics magazine and created by Whitney Ellsworth. *CAST:* Don McGuire, Cleo Moore, Jack Ingram, I. Stanford Jolley, Leonard Penn, Nelson Leigh, Charles King, Armida, Hugh Prosser, Neyle Morrow,

Fred Graham, Rusty Wescoatt, Anthony Warde, Stephen Carr. CHAPTER TITLES: (1) The Untamed Beast, (2) Jungle Gold, (3) A Hot Reception, (4) Congo Bill Springs a Trap, (5) White Shadows in the Jungle, (6) The White Queen, (7) Black Panther, (8) Sinister Schemes, (9) The Witch Doctor Strikes, (10) Trail of Treachery, (11) A Desperate Chance, (12) The Lair of the Beast, (13) Menace of the Jungle, (14) Treasure Trap, (15) The Missing Letter.

Congo Bill (McGuire) sets out in search of a missing heiress (Moore) in the jungles of Africa.

2388. Deadwood Dick (7/19/40) B&W—15 chapters. DIR: James W. Horne. PRO: Larry Darmour. SP: Wyndham Gittens, Morgan B. Cox, George Morgan, John Cutting. CAST: Don Douglas, Lorna Gray, Harry Harvey, Marin Sais, Lane Chandler, Jack Ingram, Charles King, Ed Cassidy, Robert Fiske, Lee Shumway, Edmund Cobb, Tom London, Kenne Duncan, Yakima Canutt, Roy Barcroft. CHAPTER TITLES: (1) A Wild West Empire, (2) Who Is the Skull? (3) Pirates of the Plains, (4) The Skull Baits a Trap, (5) Win, Lose or Draw, (6) Buried Alive, (7) The Chariot of Doom, (8) The Secret of Number 10, (9) The Fatal Warning, (10) Framed for Murder, (11) The Bucket of Death, (12) A Race Against Time, (13) The Arsenal of Revolt, (14) Holding the Fort, (15) The Deadwood Express.

Dick Stanley (Douglas), editor of the *Deadwood Pioneer Express* newspaper, assumes the identity of Deadwood Dick, the Robin Hood of the Plains, as he tries to stop a mysterious figure known as "The Skull" (?????) from gaining control of the Dakota territory.

2389. The Desert Hawk (7/7/44) B&W—15 chapters. DIR: B. Reeves

Eason. PRO: Rudolph C. Flothow. SP: Sherman L. Lowe, Leslie Swabacker, Jack Stanley, Leighton Brill. CAST: Gilbert Roland, Mona Maris, Ben Welden, Kenneth MacDonald, Frank Lackteen, I. Stanford Jolley, Charles Middleton, Egon Brecher, George Remarent, Kermit Maynard. CHAPTER TITLES: (1) The Twin Brothers, (2) The Evil Eye, (3) The Mark of the Scimitar, (4) A Caliph's Treachery, (5) The Secret of the Palace, (6) The Feast of the Beggars, (7) Double Jeopardy, (8) The Slave Traders, (9) The Underground River, (10) The Fateful Wheel, (11) The Mystery of the Mosque, (12) The Hand of Vengeance, (13) Swords of Fate, (14) The Wizard's Story, (15) The Triumph of Kasim.

The caliph of Ahad (Roland), overthrown by his evil brother (Roland), assumes the guise of "The Desert Hawk" as he fights his way back to his rightful place on the throne. NOTES: Gilbert Roland plays a dual role in this serial.

2390. Flying G-Men (1/24/39) B&W—15 chapters. DIR: Ray Taylor, James W. Horne. PRO: Jack Fier. SP: Robert E. Kent, Basil Dickey, Sherman L. Lowe. CAST: Robert Paige, Robert Fiske, James Craig, Lorna Gray, Sammy McKim, Don Beddoe, Forbes Murray, Dick Curtis, Ann Doran, Nestor Paiva, George Chesebro, Bud Geary, Tom Steele, George Turner, Hugh Prosser. CHAPTER TITLES: (1) Challenge in the Sky, (2) Flight of the Condemned, (3) The Vulture's Nest, (4) The Falcon Strikes, (5) Flight from Death, (6) Phantom of the Sky, (7) Trapped by Radio, (8) The Midnight Watch, (9) Wings of Terror, (10) Flaming Wreckage, (11) While a Nation Sleeps, (12) Sealed Orders, (13) Flame Island, (14) Jaws of Death, (15) The Falcon's Reward.

A government agent (?????) assumes

the guise of the "Black Falcon" as he fights a spy ring bent on destroying the nation's air defenses.

2391. The Great Adventures of Captain Kidd (9/17/53) B&W — 15 chapters. *DIR:* Derwin Abbe, Charles S. Gould. *PRO:* Sam Katzman. *SP:* Arthur Hoerl, George H. Plympton. *CAST:* Richard Crane, David Bruce, John Crawford, George Wallace, Lee Roberts, Paul Newlan, Nick Stuart, Terry Frost, John Hart, Marshall Reed, Eduardo Cansino, Jr., Willetta Smith, Lou Merrill, Ray "Crash" Corrigan, Charles King, Bud Osborne, Gene Roth. *CHAPTER TITLES:* (1) Pirate Vs. Man-of-War, (2) The Fatal Shot, (3) Attacked by Captain Kidd, (4) Captured by Captain Kidd, (5) Mutiny on the Adventure's Galley, (6) Murder on the Main Deck, (7) Prisoners of War, (8) Mutiny Unmasked, (9) Pirate Against Pirate, (10) Shot from the Parapet, (11) The Flaming Fortress, (12) Before the Firing Squad, (13) In the Hands of the Mohawks, (14) Pirate Gold, (15) Captain Kidd's Last Chance.

Two British Naval officers (Crane, Bruce) join the crew of the infamous Captain Kidd (Crawford) to help prove that the acts of piracy leveled against him are false.

2392. The Great Adventures of Wild Bill Hickok (6/30/38) B&W — 15 chapters. *DIR:* Mack V. Wright, Sam Nelson. *PRO:* Jack Fier. *SP:* George Rosener, Charles A. Powell, G. A. Durlam, Dallas M. Fitzgerald, Tom Gibson. Story by John Peere Miles. *CAST:* Bill Elliott, Carole Wayne, Monte Blue, Frankie Darro, Dickie Jones, Sammy McKim, Kermit Maynard, Roscoe Ates, Monty Collins, Reed Hadley, Chief Thunder Cloud, George Chesebro, Ray Mala, Al Bridge, Slim Whitaker, Edmund Cobb, Robert Fiske, Hal Taliaferro (Wally Wales), Blackie Whiteford, Jack Perrin, Walter Wills, J. P. McGowan, Eddy Waller, Walter Miller, Lee Phelps, Art Mix, Earle Hodgins, Earl Dwire, Ed Brady, Ray Jones, Frank Lackteen. *CHAPTER TITLES:* (1) The Law of the Gun, (2) Stampede, (3) Blazing Terror, (4) Mystery Canyon, (5) Flaming Brands, (6) The Apache Killer, (7) Prowling Wolves, (8) The Pit, (9) Ambush, (10) Savage Vengeance, (11) Burning Waters, (12) Desperation, (13) Phantom Bullets, (14) The Lure, (15) Trail's End.

Wild Bill Hickok (Elliott) organizes the "Flaming Arrows" to assist him in stopping a renegade band of outlaws.

2393. The Green Archer (11/2/40) B&W — 15 chapters. *DIR:* James W. Horne. *PRO:* Larry Darmour. *SP:* Morgan B. Cox, John Cutting, Jesse A. Duffy, James W. Horne. Based on the book *The Green Archer* by Edgar Wallace. *CAST:* Victor Jory, Iris Meredith, James Craven, Robert Fiske, Dorothy Fay, Forrest Taylor, Jack Ingram, Joseph Girard, Fred Kelsey, Kit Guard. *CHAPTER TITLES:* (1) Prison Bars Beckon, (2) The Face at the Window, (3) The Devil's Dictograph, (4) Vanishing Jewels, (5) The Fatal Spark, (6) The Necklace of Treachery, (7) The Secret Passage, (8) Garr Castle Is Robbed, (9) The Mirror of Treachery, (10) The Dagger That Failed, (11) The Flaming Arrow, (12) The Devil Dogs, (13) The Deceiving Microphone, (14) End of Hope, (15) The Green Archer Exposed.

A mysterious figure, known as "The Green Archer" (?????), thwarts the attempts of a gang of jewel thieves as they plan murder to protect their identities.

2394. Gunfighters of the Northwest (3/18/53) B&W — 15 chapters. *DIR:* Spencer G. Bennet. *PRO:* Sam Katzman. *SP:* Arthur Hoerl, George H. Plympton, Royal K. Cole. *CAST:*

Jock Mahoney, Clayton Moore, Phyllis
Coates, Don C. Harvey, Rodd Red-
wing, Marshall Reed, Lyle Talbot,
Tommy Farrell, Terry Frost, Lee Rob-
erts, Joseph Allen, Jr., Gregg Bar-
ton, Chief Yowlachie, Pierce Lyden.
CHAPTER TITLES: (1) A Trap for the
Mounties, (2) Indian War Drums, (3)
Between Two Fires, (4) Midnight
Raiders, (5) Running the Gauntlet, (6)
Mounties at Bay, (7) Plunge of Peril, (8)
Killer at Large, (9) The Fighting
Mounties, (10) The Sergeant Gets His
Man, (11) The Fugitive Escapes, (12)
Stolen Gold, (13) Perils of the
Mounted Police, (14) Surprise Attack,
(15) Trail's End.
   The Canadian Mounties set out to
stop a band of outlaws, known as the
"White Horse Rebels," and renegade
Indians from gaining control of the
Canadian territory. NOTES: Colum-
bia's only serial to be filmed entirely
outdoors without the use of a single in-
terior set.

   2395. Holt of the Secret Service
(12/28/41) B&W—15 chapters. DIR:
James W. Horne. PRO: Larry Dar-
mour. SP: Basil Dickey, George H.
Plympton, Wyndham Gittens. CAST:
Jack Holt, Evelyn Brent, C. Montague
Shaw, Tristram Coffin, John Ward,
Ted Adams, Joe McGuinn, Edward
Hearn, Ray Parsons, Jack Cheatham,
Jack Perrin. CHAPTER TITLES: (1)
Chaotic Creek, (2) Ramparts of Re-
venge, (3) Illicit Wealth, (4) Menaced
by Fate, (5) Exits to Terror, (6) Deadly
Doom, (7) Out of the Past, (8) Escape
to Peril, (9) Sealed in Silence, (10)
Named to Die, (11) Ominous Warning,
(12) The Stolen Signal, (13) Prison of
Jeopardy, (14) Afire Afloat, (15) Yielded
Hostage.
   Jack Holt, Secret Service agent, as-
sumes the identity of Nick Farrel, a
dangerous criminal, as he and his partner Kay (Brent) track down a gang of

counterfeiters who are flooding the
country with bogus money.

   2396. Hop Harrigan (3/24/46)
B&W—15 chapters. DIR: Derwin Ab-
rahams. PRO: Sam Katzman. SP:
George H. Plympton, Ande Lamb.
Adapted from the Hop Harrigan
adventure strip by John Blummer, ap-
pearing in All American comics and
the Hop Harrigan radio program.
CAST: William Bakewell, Jennifer
Holt, Robert "Buzz" Henry, Emmett
Vogan, Sumner Getchell, Claire
James, John Merton, Wheeler Oak-
man, Ernie Adams, Peter Mitchell,
Terry Frost, Anthony Warde, Jackie
Moran, Bobby Stone, Jim Diehl, Jack
Buchanan. CHAPTER TITLES: (1) A
Mad Mission, (2) The Secret Ray, (3)
The Mystery Plane, (4) Plunging Peril,
(5) Betrayed by a Madman, (6) A Flam-
ing Trap, (7) One Chance for Life, (8)
White Fumes of Hate, (9) Dr. Tobor's
Revenge, (10) Juggernaut of Fate, (11)
Flying to Oblivion, (12) Lost in the
Skies, (13) No Escape, (14) The Chute
That Failed, (15) The Fate of the
World.
   Hop Harrigan (Bakewell) sets out to
stop a mysterious figure known as the
"Chief Pilot" (?????) from stealing the
invention of an eccentric scientist.

   2397. The Iron Claw (8/11/41)
B&W—15 chapters. DIR: James W.
Horne. PRO: Larry Darmour. SP:
Basil Dickey, George H. Plympton,
Jesse A. Duffy, Charles R. Condon,
Jack Stanley. Story by Arthur Stringer.
CAST: Charles Quigley, Joyce Bryant,
Forrest Taylor, Walter Sande, Norman
Willis, Alex Callam, James Metcalfe,
Allen Doone, Edythe Elliott, John
Beck, Charles King, James Morton,
Hal Price, Jack Perrin. CHAPTER TI-
TLES: (1) The Shaft of Doom, (2) The
Murderous Mirror, (3) The Drop to
Destiny, (4) The Fatal Fuse, (5) The
Fiery Fall, (6) The Ship Log Talks, (7)

The Mystic Map, (8) The Perilous Pit, (9) The Cul-De-Sac, (10) The Curse of the Cave, (11) The Doctor's Bargain, (12) Vapors of Evil, (13) The Secret Door, (14) The Evil Eye, (15) The Claw's Collapse.

A mysterious figure known as the "Iron Claw" (?????) sets out to murder the members of the Benson family in order to gain control of a huge fortune in hidden gold. In addition, two outlaw gangs are also after the gold along with the Benson brothers (Taylor, Willis, Metcalfe, Callam).

2398. Jack Armstrong (2/6/47) B&W—15 chapters. *DIR:* Wallace W. Fox. *PRO:* Sam Katzman. *SP:* Arthur Hoerl, Lewis Clay, Leslie Swabacker, Royal K. Cole. Adapted from the radio feature *Jack Armstrong, the All-American Boy.* *CAST:* John Hart, Rosemary La Planche, Joe Brown, Jr., Claire James, Pierre Watkin, Wheeler Oakman, Jack Ingram, Eddie Parker, Hugh Prosser, John Merton, Frank Marlo, Charles Middleton, Russ Vincent, Gene Roth. *CHAPTER TITLES:* (1) Mystery of the Cosmic Ray, (2) The Far World, (3) Island of Deception, (4) Into the Chasm, (5) The Space Ship, (6) Tunnels of Treachery, (7) Cavern of Chance, (8) The Secret Room, (9) Human Targets, (10) Battle of the Warriors, (11) Cosmic Annihilator, (12) The Grotto of Greed, (13) Wheels of Fate, (14) Journey Into Fate, (15) Retribution.

Jack Armstrong (Hart), together with Uncle Jim (Watkin) and Billy (Brown), thwarts the attempts of a mad scientist to take over the world.

2399. Jungle Menace (8/7/37) B&W—15 chapters. *DIR:* George Melford, Harry Fraser. *PRO:* Jack Fier. *SP:* George Rosener, Sherman L. Lowe, Harry O. Hoyt, George Melford, George M. Merrick. Story by Arthur Hoerl, Dallas M. Fitzgerald, Gordon S.

Griffith. *CAST:* Frank Buck, Reginald Denny, Sasha Siemel, Esther Ralston, William Bakewell, Charlotte Henry, Clarence Muse, Willie Fung, LeRoy Mason, Mathew Betz, Duncan Renaldo, Fred Kohler, Jr., Robert Warwick, Snub Pollard, George Rosener, John St. Polis, Richard Tucker. *CHAPTER TITLES:* (1) River Pirates, (2) Deadly Enemies, (3) Flames of Hate, (4) One-Way Ride, (5) Man of Mystery, (6) Shanghaied, (7) Tiger Eyes, (8) The Frame-Up, (9) The Cave of Mystery, (10) Flirting with Death, (11) Ship of Doom, (12) Mystery Island, (13) The Typhoon, (14) Murder at Sea, (15) Give 'Em Rope.

Frank Hardy (Buck), jungle explorer and wild animal trapper, joins forces to solve the murder of a rubber plantation owner (St. Polis), and bring the murdering rubber pirates to justice. *NOTES:* Columbia's first serial release.

2400. Jungle Raiders (9/14/45) B&W—15 chapters. *DIR:* Lesley Selander. *PRO:* Sam Katzman. *SP:* Ande Lamb, George H. Plympton. *CAST:* Kane Richmond, Eddie Quillan, Veda Ann Borg, Carol Hughes, Janet Shaw, John Elliott, Jack Ingram, Charles King, Ernie Adams, I. Stanford Jolley, Kermit Maynard, Budd Buster, George Turner, Nick Thompson, Jim Aubrey. *CHAPTER TITLES:* (1) Mystery of the Lost Tribe, (2) Primitive Sacrifice, (3) Prisoners of Fate, (4) Valley of Destruction, (5) Perilous Mission, (6) Into the Valley of Fire, (7) Devil's Brew, (8) The Dagger Pit, (9) Jungle Jeopardy, (10) Prisoners of Peril, (11) Vengeance of Zara, (12) The Key to Arzec, (13) Witch Doctor's Treachery, (14) The Judgement of Rana, (15) The Jewels of Arzec.

Bob Moore (Richmond) and Ann Reed (Shaw) join forces to locate their missing parents and search for a hidden treasure in the jungles of Africa.

2401. King of the Congo (1/3/52) B&W—15 chapters. *DIR:* Spencer G. Bennet, Wallace A. Grissell. *PRO:* Sam Katzman. *SP:* George H. Plympton, Royal K. Cole, Arthur Hoerl. Based on the adventures of the dynamic hero of *Thunda* comics magazine. *CAST:* Buster Crabbe, Gloria Dea, Leonard Penn, Jack Ingram, Rusty Wescoatt, Nick Stuart, Rick Vallin, Neyle Morrow, Bart Davidson, Alex Montoya, Bernie Gozier, William Fawcett, Lee Roberts, Frank Ellis. *CHAPTER TITLES:* (1) Mission of Menace, (2) Red Shadows in the Jungle, (3) Into the Valley of Mist, (4) Thunda Meets His Match, (5) Thunda Turns the Tables, (6) Thunda's Desperate Chance, (7) Thunda Trapped, (8) Mission of Evil, (9) Menace of the Magnetic Rocks, (10) Lair of the Leopard, (11) An Ally from the Sky, (12) Riding Wild, (13) Red Raiders, (14) Savage Vengeance, (15) Judgement of the Jungle.

Captain Roger Drum (Crabbe) of the United States Air Force crashes in the jungles of Africa while in pursuit of a subversive group. He is rescued by the native Rock People and renamed "Thunda" because of his strength. He enlists the aid of the Rock People in helping him capture the subversive group.

2402. The Lost Planet (5/7/53) B&W—15 chapters. *DIR:* Spencer G. Bennet. *PRO:* Sam Katzman. *SP:* Arthur Hoerl. *CAST:* Judd Holdren, Vivian Mason, Ted Thorpe, Forrest Taylor, Michael Fox, Gene Roth, Karl Davis, Leonard Penn, John Cason, Nick Stuart, Joseph Mell, Jack George, Frederic Berest, I. Stanford Jolley, Pierre Watkin. *CHAPTER TITLES:* (1) The Mystery of the Guided Missile, (2) Trapped by the Axial Propeller, (3)

Blasted by the Thermic Disintegrator, (4) The Mind Control Machine, (5) The Atomic Plane, (6) Disaster in the Stratosphere, (7) Snared by the Prysmic Catapult, (8) Astray in Space, (9) The Hypnotic Ray Machine, (10) To Free the Planet People, (11) Dr. Grood Defies Gravity, (12) Trapped in a Cosmic Jet, (13) The Invisible Enemy, (14) In the Grip of the De-Thermo Ray, (15) Sentenced to Space.

Two reporters (Holdren, Mason) try to stop the evil Dr. Grood (Fox), an electronics genius from the planet Ergo, from conquering the universe.

2403. Mandrake, the Magician (5/2/39) B&W—12 chapters. *DIR:* Sam Nelson, Norman Deming. *PRO:* Jack Fier. *SP:* Joseph F. Poland, Basil Dickey, Ned Dandy. Based on the King Features newspaper character created by Lee Falk and Phil Davis. *CAST:* Warren Hull, Doris Weston, Al Kikume, Rex Downing, Edward Earle, Forbes Murray, Kenneth MacDonald, Don Beddoe, Dick Curtis, John Tyrrell, Ernie Adams, George Chesebro, George Turner. *CHAPTER TITLES:* (1) Shadow on the Wall, (2) Trap of the Wasp, (3) City of Terror, (4) The Secret Passage, (5) The Devil's Playmate, (6) The Fatal Crash, (7) Gamble for Life, (8) Across the Deadline, (9) Terror Rides the Rails, (10) The Unseen Monster, (11) At the Stroke of Eight, (12) The Reward of Treachery.

Mandrake (Hull), world famous magician, and his servant Lothar (Kikume), set out to stop an underworld gang leader known as "The Wasp" (?????) as he plans to steal a radium energy machine.

2404. The Monster and the Ape (4/20/45) B&W—15 chapters. *DIR:* Howard Bretherton. *PRO:* Rudolph C. Flothow. *SP:* Sherman L. Lowe, Royal K. Cole. *CAST:* Robert Lowery, George Macready, Ralph Morgan,

Carole Mathews, Willie Best, Jack Ingram, Anthony Warde, Ted Mapes, Eddie Parker, Stanley Price, Kit Guard. *CHAPTER TITLES:* (1) The Mechanical Terror, (2) The Edge of Doom, (3) Flames of Fate, (4) The Fatal Search, (5) Rocks of Doom, (6) A Friend in Disguise, (7) A Scream in the Night, (8) Death in the Dark, (9) The Secret Tunnel, (10) Forty Thousand Volts, (11) The Mad Professor, (12) Shadows of Destiny, (13) The Gorilla at Large, (14) His Last Flight, (15) Justice Triumphs.

Professor Ernst (Macready), an enemy agent, uses a trained ape named Thor to kill his colleagues and gain control of the Metalogen Man, a robot, and the supply of Metalogen. He is pursued by Ken Logan (Lowery), a representative of the firm that manufactures the robot.

2405. Mysterious Island (8/23/51) B&W — 15 chapters. *DIR:* Spencer G. Bennet. *PRO:* Sam Katzman. *SP:* George H. Plympton, Lewis Clay, Royal K. Cole. Based on *L'Ile Mysterieuse* by Jules Verne. *CAST:* Richard Crane, Marshall Reed, Karen Randle, Ralph Hodges, Gene Roth, Hugh Prosser, Terry Frost, Rusty Wescoatt, Bernie Hamilton, Leonard Penn. *CHAPTER TITLES:* (1) Lost in Space, (2) Sinister Savages, (3) Savage Justice, (4) Wild Man at Large, (5) Trail of the Mystery Man, (6) The Pirates Attack, (7) Menace of the Mercurians, (8) Between Two Fires, (9) Shrine of the Silver Bird, (10) Fighting Fury, (11) Desperate Chances, (12) Mystery of the Mine, (13) Jungle Deadfall, (14) Men from Tomorrow, (15) The Last of Mysterious Island.

Captain Nemo (Penn) aids Captain Harding (Crane) and his fellow travelers in their fight against the island's natives, pirates, and visitors from the planet Mercury.

2406. The Mysterious Pilot (12/7/37) B&W — 15 chapters. *DIR:* Spencer G. Bennet. *PRO:* Jack Fier. *SP:* George M. Merrick, George Rosener. Based on *The Silver Hawk* by William B. Mowery. *CAST:* Captain Frank Hawks, Dorothy Sebastian, Rex Lease, Guy Bates Post, Kenneth Harlan, Yakima Canutt, Frank Lackteen, Robert Terry, George Rosener, Clara Kimball Young, Harry Harvey, Tom London, Ted Adams, Earl Douglas, Robert Walker, Roger Williams, Esther Ralston, Jack Perrin. *CHAPTER TITLES:* (1) The Howl of the Wolf, (2) The Web Tangles, (3) Enemies of the Air, (4) In the Hands of the Law, (5) The Crack-Up, (6) The Dark Hour, (7) Wings of Destiny, (8) Battle in the Sky, (9) The Great Flight, (10) Whirlpool of Death, (11) The Haunted Mill, (12) The Lost Trail, (13) The Net Tightens, (14) Vengeance Rides the Airways, (15) Retribution.

Jim Dorn (Hawks), a cartographer for the Royal Canadian Air Force, helps a young girl (Sebastian) escape to safety after she overhears a murder plot. *NOTES:* At the end of each chapter Frank Hawks would conduct a demonstration on some aerial topic to an attentive young boy.

2407. Overland with Kit Carson (8/1/39) B&W — 15 chapters. *DIR:* Sam Nelson, Norman Deming. *PRO:* Jack Fier. *SP:* Joseph F. Poland, Morgan B. Cox, Ned Dandy. *CAST:* Bill Elliott, Iris Meredith, Richard Fiske, LeRoy Mason, Trevor Bardette, James Craig, Olin Francis, Kenneth MacDonald, Francis Sayles, Dick Botiller, Dick Curtis, Hal Taliaferro (Wally Wales), Ernie Adams, Flo Campbell. *CHAPTER TITLES:* (1) Doomed Men, (2) Condemned to Die, (3) The Fight for Life, (4) The Ride of Terror, (5) The Path of Doom, (6) Rendezvous with Death, (7) The Killer

Stallion, (8) The Devil's Nest, (9) Blazing Peril, (10) The Black Raiders, (11) Foiled, (12) The Warning, (13) Terror in the Night, (14) Crumbling Walls, (15) Unmasked.

Kit Carson (Elliott) sets out to stop a mysterious outlaw known as "Pegleg" (?????) and his band of outlaws, the Black Raiders.

2408. Perils of the Royal Mounted (5/24/42) B&W — 15 chapters. DIR: James W. Horne. PRO: Larry Darmour. SP: Basil Dickey, Scott Littleton, Louis Heifetz, Jesse A. Duffy. CAST: Robert Stevens (Robert Kellard), Nell O'Day, Herbert Rawlinson, Kenneth MacDonald, John Elliott, Nick Thompson, Art Miles, Richard Fiske, Rick Vallin, Forrest Taylor, Kermit Maynard, George Chesebro, Jack Ingram, Iron Eyes Cody. CHAPTER TITLES: (1) The Totem Talks, (2) The Night Raiders, (3) The Water God's Revenge, (4) Beware, the Vigilantes, (5) The Masked Mountie, (6) Underwater Gold, (7) Bridge to the Sky, (8) Lost in the Mine, (9) Into the Trap, (10) Betrayed by Law, (11) Blazing Beacons, (12) The Mountie's Last Chance, (13) Painted White Man, (14) Burned at the Stake, (15) The Mountie Gets His Man.

Renegade outlaws join forces with the Indians as they try to wipe out the Royal Canadian Mounted Police.

2409. Perils of the Wilderness (1/6/56) B&W — 15 chapters. DIR: Spencer G. Bennet. PRO: Sam Katzman. SP: George H. Plympton. CAST: Dennis Moore, Richard Emory, Eve Anderson, Kenneth MacDonald, Rick Vallin, John Elliott, Don C. Harvey, Terry Frost, Al Ferguson, Bud Osborne, Rex Lease, Pierce Lyden, John Mitchum, Lee Roberts, Stanley Price, Ed Coch, Kermit Maynard. CHAPTER TITLES: (1) The Voice from the Sky, (2) The Mystery Plane, (3) The

Mine of Menace, (4) Ambush for a Mountie, (5) Laramie's Desperate Chance, (6) Trapped in the Flaming Forest, (7) Out of the Trap, (8) Laramie Rides Out, (9) Menace of the Medicine Man, (10) Midnight Marauders, (11) The Falls of Fate, (12) Rescue from the Rapids, (13) Little Bear Pays a Debt, (14) The Mystery Plane Flies Again, (15) Laramie Gets His Man.

A ruthless overlord of crime, Bart Randall (MacDonald), in the wilds of the Canadian Northwest, is pursued by Marshal Laramie (Moore) of Montana and Sergeant Gray (Emory) of the Canadian Mounties. NOTES: John Mitchum is Robert Mitchum's brother.

2410. The Phantom (12/24/43) B&W — 15 chapters. DIR: B. Reeves Eason. PRO: Rudolph C. Flothow. SP: Morgan B. Cox, Victor McLeod, Sherman L. Lowe, Leslie Swabacker. Based on the King Features newspaper cartoon strip created by Lee Falk and Ray Moore. CAST: Tom Tyler, Jeanne Bates, Kenneth MacDonald, Frank Shannon, Guy Kingsford, Joe Devlin, Ernie Adams, John S. Bagni, George Chesebro, "Ace," the dog. CHAPTER TITLES: (1) The Sign of the Skull, (2) The Man Who Never Dies, (3) A Traitor's Code, (4) The Seat of Judgement, (5) The Ghost Who Walks, (6) Jungle Whispers, (7) The Mystery Well, (8) In the Quest of the Keys, (9) The Fire Princess, (10) The Chamber of Death, (11) The Emerald Key, (12) The Fangs of the Beast, (13) The Road to Zoloz, (14) The Lost City, (15) Peace in the Jungle.

The Phantom (Tyler) sets out to help a professor (Shannon) and his daughter (Bates) locate the Lost City of Zoloz and its hidden treasure, and to prevent an international crook, Dr. Bremmer (MacDonald), from building a secret air base at Zoloz.

2411. Pirates of the High Seas (10/4/50) B&W — 15 chapters. *DIR:* Spencer G. Bennet, Thomas Carr. *PRO:* Sam Katzman. *SP:* David Mathews, Joseph F. Poland, George H. Plympton, Charles R. Condon. *CAST:* Buster Crabbe, Lois Hall, Tommy Farrell, Gene Roth, Tristram Coffin, Neyle Morrow, Stanley Price, Hugh Prosser, Symona Boniface, Terry Frost, Lee Roberts, William Fawcett, Rusty Wescoatt, Pierce Lyden, Charles Quigley, I. Stanford Jolley, Marshall Reed, John Hart. *CHAPTER TITLES:* (1) Mystery Mission, (2) Attacked by Pirates, (3) Dangerous Depths, (4) Blasted to Atoms, (5) The Missing Mate, (6) Secret of the Ivory Case, (7) Captured by Savages, (8) The Vanishing Music Box, (9) Booby Trap, (10) Savage Snare, (11) Sinister Cavern, (12) Blasted from the Depths, (13) Cave In, (14) Secret of the Music Box, (15) Diamonds from the Sea.

Captain Jeff Drake (Crabbe) sails his ship to the Pacific island of Taluha in search of lost diamonds and a phantom pirate ship.

2412. Riding with Buffalo Bill (11/11/54) B&W — 15 chapters. *DIR:* Spencer G. Bennet. *PRO:* Sam Katzman. *SP:* George H. Plympton. *CAST:* Marshall Reed, Rick Vallin, Joanne Rio, Shirley Whitney, Jack Ingram, William Fawcett, Gregg Barton, Ed Coch, Steve Ritch, Pierce Lyden, Michael Fox, Lee Roberts, John Truex. *CHAPTER TITLES:* (1) The Ridin' Terror from St. Joe, (2) Law of the Six Gun, (3) Raiders from Ghost Town, (4) Cody to the Rescue, (5) Midnight Marauders, (6) Under the Avalanche, (7) Night Attack, (8) Trapped in the Powder Shack, (9) Into an Outlaw Trap, (10) Blast of Oblivion, (11) The Depths of the Earth, (12) The Ridin' Terror, (13) Trapped in the Apache Mine, (14) Railroad Wreckers, (15) Law Comes to the West.

Famous hunter and Indian Scout Bill Cody (Reed) sets out to prevent a gang of outlaws from destroying the new railroad in the territory.

2413. Roar of the Iron Horse (5/15/51) B&W — 15 chapters. *DIR:* Spencer G. Bennet, Thomas Carr. *PRO:* Sam Katzman. *SP:* Royal K. Cole, George H. Plympton, Sherman L. Lowe. *CAST:* Jock Mahoney, Virginia Herrick, William Fawcett, Hal Landon, Jack Ingram, Mickey Simpson, George Eldredge, Myron Healey, Rusty Wescoatt, Frank Ellis, Pierce Lyden, Dick Curtis, Hugh Prosser, Rick Vallin, Bud Osborne. *CHAPTER TITLES:* (1) Indian Attack, (2) Captured by Redskins, (3) Trapped by Outlaws, (4) In the Baron's Stronghold, (5) A Ride for Life, (6) White Indians, (7) Fumes of Fate, (8) Midnight Marauders, (9) Raid of the Pay Train, (10) Trapped on a Trestle, (11) Redskin's Revenge, (13) Plunge of Peril, (14) When Killers Meet, (15) The End of the Trail.

Sent to investigate mysterious accidents on a railroad, Jim Grant (Mahoney), government investigator, finds they are being caused by a renegade outlaw known as "The Baron" (?????) who is searching for a meteor filled with diamonds.

2414. The Sea Hound (9/11/47) B&W — 15 chapters. *DIR:* Walter B. Eason, Mack V. Wright. *PRO:* Sam Katzman. *SP:* Lewis Clay, George H. Plympton, Arthur Hoerl. Based on *The Sea Hound* comic magazine and radio program. *CAST:* Buster Crabbe, James Lloyd, Pamela Blake, Ralph Hodges, Spencer Chan, Robert Barron, Hugh Prosser, Rick Vallin, Jack Ingram, Milton Kibbee, Al Baffert, Stanley Blystone, Robert Duncan, Pierce Lyden, Emmett Lynn, Rusty

Wescoatt, William Fawcett. *CHAP-
TER TITLES*: (1) Captain Silver Sails
Again, (2) Spanish Gold, (3) The Mys-
tery of the Map, (4) Menaced by
Ryaks, (5) Captain Silver's Strategy, (6)
The Sea Hound at Bay, (7) Rand's
Treachery, (8) In the Admiral's Lair, (9)
On the Water Wheel, (10) On the
Treasure Trail, (11) The Sea Hound
Attacked, (12) Dangerous Waters, (13)
The Panther's Prey, (14) The Fatal
Double-Cross, (15) Captain Silver's
Last Stand.

Captain Silver (Crabbe) sails his
schooner "The Sea Hound" to Typhoon Cove and learns of a secret treasure. He battles pirates, natives, and a
sea robber known as the "Admiral"
(?????) before he finds the treasure.

2415. The Secret Code (9/4/42)
B&W—15 chapters. *DIR:* Spencer G.
Bennet. *PRO:* Larry Darmour. *SP:*
Basil Dickey, Leighton Brill, Robert
Beche. *CAST:* Paul Kelly, Anne
Nagel, Clancy Cooper, Trevor Bar-
dette, Robert O. Davis, Gregory Gay,
Louis (Ludwig) Donath, Eddie Parker,
Beal Wong, Jacqueline Dalya, Alex
Callam, Eddie Woods, Selmer Jackson.
CHAPTER TITLES: (1) Enemy Pass-
port, (2) The Shadow of the Swastika,
(3) Nerve Gas, (4) The Sea Spy Strikes,
(5) Wireless Warning, (6) Flaming Oil,
(7) Submarine Signal, (8) The Missing
Key, (9) The Radio Bomb, (10) Blind
Bombardment, (11) Ears of the Enemy,
(12) Scourge of the Orient, (13) Pawn
of the Spy Ring, (14) Dead Men of the
Deep, (15) The Secret Code Smashed.

Police Lieutenant Dan Barton
(Kelly) assumes the guise of the "Black
Commando" as he goes undercover to
smash a Nazi spy ring trying to obtain
a synthetic rubber formula by secret
code. *NOTES:* At the end of each
chapter, Selmer Jackson as "Major
Henry Burton" would give lessons in
breaking various secret codes.

**2416. The Secret of Treasure Is-
land** (3/2/38) B&W—15 chapters.
DIR: Elmer Clifton. *PRO:* Jack Fier.
SP: George Rosener, Elmer Clifton,
George M. Merrick. Story by L. Ron
Hubbard. *CAST:* Don Terry, Gwen
Gaze, Grant Withers, Hobart Bos-
worth, Yakima Canutt, William Far-
num, Walter Miller, George Rosener,
Dave O'Brien, Warner Richmond,
William Boyle, Sandra Karina, Joe
Caits, Colin Campbell, Patrick J. Kelly,
Jack Perrin. *CHAPTER TITLES:* (1)
The Isle of Fear, (2) The Ghost Talks,
(3) The Phantom Duel, (4) Buried
Alive, (5) The Girl Who Vanished, (6)
Trapped by the Flood, (7) The Cannon
Roars, (8) The Circle of Death, (9) The
Pirate's Revenge, (10) The Crash, (11)
Dynamite, (12) The Bridge of Doom,
(13) The Mad Flight, (14) The Jaws of
Destruction, (15) Justice.

Larry Kent (Terry), reporter, journeys to Treasure Island in search of
lost treasure and fights a mysterious
figure known as "Dr. X" (?????).

2417. The Shadow (1/1/40)
B&W—15 chapters. *DIR:* James W.
Horne. *PRO:* Larry Darmour. *SP:* Jo-
seph F. Poland, Ned Dandy, Joseph
O'Donnell. Based upon stories pub-
lished in *The Shadow* magazine. Adap-
ted from the *Shadow* radio program.
CAST: Victor Jory, Veda Ann Borg,
Roger Moore, Robert Fiske, John Paul
Jones, Jack Ingram, Charles Hamilton,
Edward Piel, Sr., Frank LaRue, Jack
Perrin. *CHAPTER TITLES:* (1) The
Doomed City, (2) The Shadow At-
tacks, (3) The Shadow's Peril, (4) In the
Tiger's Lair, (5) Danger Above, (6) The
Shadow's Trap, (7) Where Horror
Waits, (8) The Shadow Rides the Rails,
(9) The Devil in White, (10) The
Underground Trap, (11) Chinatown at
Dark, (12) Murder by Remote Control,
(13) Wheels of Death, (14) The Sealed
Room, (15) The Shadow's Net Closes.

Lamont Cranston (Jory), scientist and criminologist, assumes the guise of "The Shadow" as he tracks down a mastermind of the underworld known as the "Black Tiger" (?????).

2418. Son of Geronimo (11/5/52) B&W—15 chapters. *DIR:* Spencer G. Bennet. *PRO:* Sam Katzman. *SP:* George H. Plympton, Royal K. Cole, Arthur Hoerl. *CAST:* Clayton Moore, Rodd Redwing, Tommy Farrell, Eileen Rowe, Marshall Reed, Bud Osborne, John Crawford, Zon Murray, Rick Vallin, Lyle Talbot, Wally West, Chief Yowlachie, Frank Matts, Sandy Sanders, Bob Cason. *CHAPTER TITLES:* (1) War of Vengeance, (2) Running the Gauntlet, (3) Stampede, (4) Apache Allies, (5) Indian Ambush, (6) Trapped by Fire, (7) A Sinister Scheme, (8) Prisoners of Portico, (9) On the Warpath, (10) The Fight at Crystal Springs, (11) A Midnight Marauder, (12) Trapped in a Flaming Tepee, (13) Jim Scott Tempts Fate, (14) A Trap for Geronimo, (15) Peace Treaty.

Jim Scott (Moore), Indian Scout, with the help of Porico (Redwing), who claims to be the son of Geronimo, seeks to bring peace between the white men and Indians.

2419. Son of the Guardsman (10/24/46) B&W—15 chapters. *DIR:* Derwin Abrahams. *PRO:* Sam Katzman. *SP:* George H. Plympton, Harry Fraser, Royal K. Cole, Lewis Clay. *CAST:* Robert Shaw, Daun Kennedy, Robert "Buzz" Henry, Jim Diehl, Hugh Prosser, Leonard Penn, Wheeler Oakman, Charles King, John Merton, Ray Bennett, I. Stanford Jolley, Belle Mitchell, Frank Ellis, Al Ferguson. *CHAPTER TITLES:* (1) Outlaws of Sherwood Forest, (2) Perils of the Forest, (3) Blazing Barrier, (4) The Siege of Bullard Hall, (5) A Dagger in the Dark, (6) A Fight for Freedom, (7) Trial by

Torture, (8) Mark Crowell's Treachery, (9) Crushed to Earth, (10) A Throne at Stake, (11) Double Danger, (12) The Secret of the Treasure, (13) Into the Depths, (14) The Lost Heritage, (15) Free Men Triumph.

A young nobleman (Shaw) turns outlaw to save the throne of England.

2420. The Spider Returns (5/5/41) B&W—15 chapters. *DIR:* James W. Horne. *PRO:* Larry Darmour. *SP:* Jesse A. Duffy, George H. Plympton. Story by Morgan B. Cox, Lawrence Edmund Taylor, John Cutting, Harry Fraser. Based on *The Spider* magazine stories. *CAST:* Warren Hull, Mary Ainslee, Dave O'Brien, Kenne Duncan, Joe Girard, Alden Chase, Corbet Harris, Bryant Washburn, Charles Miller, Harry Harvey, Jack Perrin. *CHAPTER TITLES:* (1) The Stolen Plans, (2) The Fatal Time-Bomb, (3) The Secret Meeting, (4) The Smoke Dream, (5) The Gargoyle's Trail, (6) The X-Ray Eye, (7) The Radio Boomerang, (8) The Mysterious Message, (9) The Cup of Doom, (10) The X-Ray Belt, (11) Lips Sealed by Murder, (12) A Money Bomb, (13) Almost a Confession, (14) Suspicious Telegrams, (15) The Payoff.

Richard Wentworth (Hull), celebrated criminologist, assumes the guise of the "Spider" as he tracks down "The Gargoyle" (?????), a mysterious foreign agent, bent on destroying the nation's defense projects.

2421. The Spider's Web (10/10/38) B&W—15 chapters. *DIR:* James W. Horne, Ray Taylor. *PRO:* Jack Fier. *SP:* Robert E. Kent, Basil Dickey, George H. Plympton, Martie Ramson. Based on *The Spider* magazine stories. *CAST:* Warren Hull, Iris Meredith, Richard Fiske, Kenne Duncan, Forbes Murray, Don Douglas, Charles C. Wilson, Marc Lawrence, Lane Chandler, Nestor Paiva, Ernie Adams, Al Ferguson, Tom London, Edmund Cobb. CHAPTER TITLES: (1) Night of Terror, (2) Death Below, (3) High Voltage, (4) Surrender or Die, (5) Shoot to Kill, (6) Sealed Lips, (7) Shadows of the Night, (8) While the City Sleeps, (9) Doomed, (10) Flaming Danger, (11) The Road to Peril, (12) The Spider Falls, (13) The Man Hunt, (14) The Double Cross, (15) The Octopus Unmasked.

Richard Wentworth (Hull), celebrated criminologist, assumes the guise of the "Spider" as he tracks down "The Octopus" (?????), a mysterious figure bent on destroying the nation's transportation system.

2422. Superman (7/15/48) B&W – 15 chapters. DIR: Spencer G. Bennet, Thomas Carr. PRO: Sam Katzman. SP: Arthur Hoerl, Lewis Clay, Royal K. Cole. Based on the *Superman* adventure feature appearing in *Superman* and *Action* comics. Adapted from the *Superman* radio program. CAST: Kirk Alyn, Noel Neill, Tommy Bond, Pierre Watkin, Carol Forman, George Meeker, Jack Ingram, Terry Frost, Charles King, Charles Quigley, Herbert Rawlinson, Forrest Taylor, Stephen Carr, Rusty Wescoatt. CHAPTER TITLES: (1) Superman Comes to Earth, (2) Depths of the Earth, (3) The Reducer Ray, (4) Man of Steel, (5) A Job for Superman, (6) Superman in Danger, (7) Into the Electric Furnace, (8) Superman to the Rescue, (9) Irresistible Force, (10) Between Two Fires, (11) Superman's Dilemma, (12) Blast in the Depths, (13) Hurled to Destruction, (14) Superman at Bay, (15) The Payoff.

Superman (Alyn) battles the "Spider Lady" (Forman), an underworld queen who seeks the powerful Reducer Ray.

2423. Terry and the Pirates (4/3/40) B&W – 15 chapters. DIR: James W. Horne. PRO: Larry Darmour. SP:

Mark Layton, George Morgan, Joseph Levering. Based upon the cartoon strip characters created by Milton Caniff. CAST: William Tracy, Granville Owens, Joyce Bryant, Allen Jung, Victor De Camp, Sheila Darcy, Dick Curtis, John Paul Jones, Forrest Taylor, Jack Ingram. CHAPTER TITLES: (1) Into the Great Unknown, (2) The Fang Strikes, (3) The Mountain of Death, (4) The Dragon Queen Threatens, (5) At the Mercy of a Mob, (6) The Scroll of Wealth, (7) Angry Waters, (8) The Tomb of Peril, (9) Jungle Hurricane, (10) Too Many Enemies, (11) Walls of Doom, (12) No Escape, (13) The Fatal Mistake, (14) Pyre of Death, (15) The Secret of the Temple.

Terry Lee (Tracy), Pat Ryan (Owens), Big Stoop (De Camp), and Connie (Jung) join forces with the Dragon Lady (Darcy) as they search for Terry's father, seek to recover a stolen treasure, and battle the dreaded warlord "Fang" (Curtis) and his Tiger Men.

2424. Tex Granger (4/1/48) B&W – 15 chapters. DIR: Derwin Abrahams. PRO: Sam Katzman. SP: Arthur Hoerl, Lewis Clay, Harry Fraser, Royal K. Cole. Based on the *Tex Granger* adventure featured in *Calling All Boys* and *Tex Granger* comics magazine. CAST: Robert Kellard, Peggy Stewart, Robert "Buzz" Henry, Smith Ballew, Jack Ingram, I. Stanford Jolley, Terry Frost, Jim Diehl, Britt Wood, Bill Brauer, Eddie Parker, Rusty Wescoatt, "Duke," the wonder dog. CHAPTER TITLES: (1) Tex Finds Trouble, (2) Rider of Mystery Mesa, (3) Dead or Alive, (4) Dangerous Trails, (5) Renegade Pass, (6) A Crooked Deal, (7) The Rider Unmasked, (8) Mystery of the Silver Ghost, (9) The Rider Trapped, (10) Midnight Ambush, (11) Renegade Roundup, (12) Carson's Last Draw, (13)

Blaze Takes Over, (14) Riding Wild, (15) The Rider Meets Blaze.

Tex Granger (Kellard) assumes the guise of the "Midnight Rider of the Plains" as he goes after land grabbers and gold rustlers.

2425. The Valley of Vanishing Men (12/17/42) B&W – 15 chapters. *DIR:* Spencer G. Bennet. *PRO:* Larry Darmour. *SP:* Harry Fraser, Lewis Clay, George Gray. *CAST:* Bill Elliott, Carmen Morales, Slim Summerville, Jack Ingram, Kenneth MacDonald, George Chesebro, John Shay, Tom London, Arno Frey, Julian Rivero, Roy Barcroft, I. Stanford Jolley, Ted Mapes, Lane Chandler, Lane Bradford, Ernie Adams, Robert Fiske, Blackie Whiteford, Chief Thunder Cloud. *CHAPTER TITLES:* (1) Trouble in Canyon City, (2) The Mystery of Ghost Town, (3) Danger Walks by Night, (4) Hillside Horror, (5) Guns in the Night, (6) The Bottomless Well, (7) The Man in the Gold Mask, (8) When the Devil Drives, (9) The Traitor's Shroud, (10) Death Strikes at Seven, (11) Satan in the Saddle, (12) The Mine of Missing Men, (13) Danger on Dome Rock, (14) The Door That Has No Key, (15) Empire's End.

Riding into New Mexico, Bill Tolliver (Elliott) and his sidekick Missouri (Summerville) learn that Bill's father is working as a slave in a gold mine run by an outlaw gang. He sets out to free his father and smash the slave mine and outlaw gang.

2426. The Vigilante (5/22/47) B&W – 15 chapters. *DIR:* Wallace W. Fox. *PRO:* Sam Katzman. *SP:* George H. Plympton, Lewis Clay, Arthur Hoerl. Based on *The Vigilante* adventure feature appearing in *Action* comics magazine. *CAST:* Ralph Byrd, Ramsay Ames, Lyle Talbot, George Offerman, Jr., Robert Barron, Frank Marlo, Hugh Prosser, Jack Ingram, Eddie Parker, George Chesebro, Bill Brauer, Frank Ellis, Edmund Cobb, Terry Frost. *CHAPTER TITLES:* (1) The Vigilante Rides Again, (2) Mystery of the White Horses, (3) Double Peril, (4) Desperate Flight, (5) In the Gorilla's Cage, (6) Battling the Unknown, (7) Midnight Rendezvous, (8) Blasted to Eternity, (9) The Fatal Flood, (10) Danger Ahead, (11) X-1 Closes In, (12) Death Rides the Rails, (13) The Trap That Failed, (14) Closing In, (15) The Secret of the Skyroom.

The Vigilante (Byrd), government undercover agent, goes after a mysterious gang leader known only as "X-1" (?????), who will stop at nothing to obtain a strand of pearls known as the "100 Tears of Blood."

2427. White Eagle (1/31/41) B&W – 15 chapters. *DIR:* James W. Horne. *PRO:* Larry Darmour. *SP:* Arch Heath, Morgan B. Cox, John Cutting, Lawrence W. Taylor. Story by Fred Myton. Adapted from the 1932 feature *White Eagle*. *CAST:* Buck Jones, Dorothy Fay, Raymond Hatton, James Craven, Jack Ingram, Chief Yowlachie, Charles King, John Merton, Roy Barcroft, Edward Hearn, George Chesebro, Kenne Duncan, Edmund Cobb, Edward Piel, Sr., Steve Clark, Yakima Canutt, Hank Bell, Bud Osborne. *CHAPTER TITLES:* (1) Flaming Teepees, (2) The Jail Delivery, (3) The Dive Into Quicksands, (4) The Warning Death Knife, (5) Treachery at the Stockade, (6) The Gun-Cane Murder, (7) The Revealing Blotter, (8) Bird-Calls of Deliverance, (9) The Fake Telegram, (10) Mystic Dots and Dashes, (11) The Ear at the Window, (12) The Massacre Invitation, (13) The Framed-Up Showdown, (14) The Fake Army General, (15) Treachery Downed.

White Eagle (Jones), an Indian Pony Express rider, tracks down an outlaw gang who are making it look as if the Indians are to blame for murder and robbery.

2428. Who's Guilty? (12/13/45) B&W—15 chapters. *DIR:* Howard Bretherton, Wallace A. Grissell. *PRO:* Sam Katzman. *SP:* Ande Lamb, George H. Plympton. *CAST:* Robert Kent, Amelita Ward, Tim Ryan, Jayne Hazard, Minerva Urecal, Belle Mitchell, Charles Middleton, Davidson Clark, Sam Flint, Bruce Donovan, Jack Ingram, Milton Kibbee, Nacho Galindo, Roberto Tafur, Wheeler Oakman, Charles King, Anthony Warde. *CHAPTER TITLES:* (1) Avenging Visitor, (2) The Unknown Strikes, (3) Held for Murder, (4) A Killer at Bay, (5) Human Bait, (6) The Plunge of Doom, (7) A Date with Fate, (8) Invisible Hands, (9) Fate's Vengeance, (10) The Unknown Killer, (11) Riding to Oblivion, (12) The Tank of Terror, (13) White Terror, (14) A Cry in the Night, (15) The Guilty One.

A mysterious figure known as the "Voice" (?????) plans to kill the members of the Calvert family and get their fortune. Through the investigation of a private detective (Kent), the "Voice" is finally tracked down and unmasked.

Cartoons
(1928–1965)

Following is a complete list of theatrical cartoons produced and or distributed by Columbia Pictures, from the beginning of the sound era, including those of Walt Disney (1928–1932), United Productions of America (1948–1959), and William Hanna and Joseph Barbera (1959–1965).

Producer and Director are given, where known; the earlier Columbia produced cartoons carried no director credit. Dates given are approximate release dates.

2429. The Air Hostess (10/22/37) Technicolor – 7 mins. PRO: Charles Mintz. A Color Rhapsodies cartoon.

2430. Alaskan Knights (5/23/30) B&W – 7 mins. DIR: Ben Harrison, Manny Gould. PRO: Charles Mintz. A Krazy Kat cartoon.

2431. Amoozin But Confoozin' (4/3/44) Technicolor – 7 mins. DIR: Sid Marcus. PRO: Charles Mintz. A Li'l Abner cartoon.

2432. Animal Cracker Circus (9/23/38) Technicolor – 7 mins. DIR: Ben Harrison. PRO: Charles Mintz. A Color Rhapsodies cartoon.

2433. Antique Antics (6/14/33) B&W – 7 mins. DIR: Ben Harrison, Manny Gould. PRO: Charles Mintz. A Krazy Kat cartoon.

2434. The Apache Kid (10/9/30) B&W – 7 mins. DIR: Ben Harrison,

Manny Gould. PRO: Charles Mintz. A Krazy Kat cartoon.

2435. Artic Antics (6/14/33) B&W – 7 mins. DIR: Ub Iwerks. PRO: Walt Disney. A Silly Symphonies cartoon.

2436. As the Fly Flies (11/17/44) B&W – 7 mins. DIR: Howard Swift. A Phantasies cartoon.

2437. The Auto Clinic (3/4/38) B&W – 7 mins. DIR: Ben Harrison, Manny Gould. PRO: Charles Mintz. A Krazy Kat cartoon.

2438. Auto Show (12/8/33) B&W – 7 mins. DIR: Dick Huemer. PRO: Charles Mintz. A Scrappy cartoon.

2439. The Autograph Hunter (1/5/34) B&W – 7 mins. DIR: Ben Harrison, Manny Gould. PRO: Charles Mintz. A Krazy Kat cartoon.

2440. Autumn (2/15/30) B&W – 7 mins. DIR: Ub Iwerks. PRO: Walt Disney. A Silly Symphonies cartoon.

2441. Aw, Nurse (3/9/34) B&W— 7 mins. *DIR:* Sid Marcus, Art Davis. *PRO:* Charles Mintz. A Scrappy cartoon.

2442. Babes at Sea (11/30/34) Technicolor—7 mins. *PRO:* Charles Mintz. A Color Rhapsodies cartoon.

2443. Baby Boogie (5/19/55) Technicolor—7 mins. *DIR:* Paul Julian. *PRO:* Stephen Bosustow. A UPA cartoon Special.

2444. The Bad Genius (12/1/32) B&W—7 mins. *DIR:* Dick Huemer. *PRO:* Charles Mintz. A Scrappy cartoon.

2445. Ballet-Oops (2/11/54) Technicolor—7 mins. *DIR:* Robert Cannon. *PRO:* Stephen Bosustow. A UPA cartoon Special.

2446. The Band Master (9/8/30) B&W—7 mins. *DIR:* Ben Harrison, Manny Gould. *PRO:* Charles Mintz. A Krazy Kat cartoon.

2447. Bare Faced Flatfoot (4/26/51) Technicolor—7 mins. *DIR:* Pete Burness. *PRO:* Stephen Bosustow. A Mr. Magoo UPA cartoon.

2448. The Barn Dance (11/15/28) B&W—7 mins. *DIR/PRO:* Walt Disney. A Mickey Mouse cartoon.

2449. Barnyard Babies (6/14/40) B&W—7 mins. *DIR:* Sid Marcus. A Fables cartoon.

2450. The Barnyard Battle (7/2/29) B&W—7 mins. *DIR/PRO:* Walt Disney. A Mickey Mouse cartoon.

2451. The Barnyard Broadcast (9/30/31) B&W—7 mins. *DIR:* Burt Gillett. *PRO:* Walt Disney. A Mickey Mouse cartoon.

2452. The Barnyard Concert (4/5/30) B&W—7 mins. *DIR/PRO:* Walt Disney. A Mickey Mouse cartoon.

2453. Barnyard Olympics (4/13/32) B&W—7 mins. *DIR:* Wilfred Jackson. *PRO:* Walt Disney. A Mickey Mouse cartoon.

2454. Bars and Stripes (10/15/31) B&W—7 mins. *DIR:* Ben Harrison, Manny Gould. *PRO:* Charles Mintz. A Krazy Kat cartoon.

2455. A Battle for a Bottle (5/29/42) B&W—7 mins. *DIR:* Frank Tashlin. A Phantasies cartoon.

2456. Battle of the Barn (5/31/32) B&W—7 mins. *DIR:* Dick Huemer. *PRO:* Charles Mintz. A Scrappy cartoon.

2457. Be Patient, Patient (10/27/44) Technicolor—7 mins. *DIR:* Bob Wickersham. A Fox and the Crow cartoon.

2458. The Beach Party (10/28/31) B&W—7 mins. *DIR:* Burt Gillett. *PRO:* Walt Disney. A Mickey Mouse cartoon.

2459. Bear Hug (3/5/64) Technicolor—7 mins. *DIR/PRO:* William Hanna, Joseph Barbera. A Loopy de Loop cartoon.

2460. Bear Knuckles (10/15/64) Technicolor—7 mins. *DIR/PRO:* William Hanna, Joseph Barbera. A Loopy de Loop cartoon.

2461. Bear Up! (11/7/63) Technicolor—7 mins. *DIR/PRO:* William Hanna, Joseph Barbera. A Loopy de Loop cartoon.

2462. Bearly Able (6/28/62) Technicolor—7 mins. *DIR/PRO:* William Hanna, Joseph Barbera. A Loopy de Loop cartoon.

2463. Beef For and After (3/1/62) Technicolor—7 mins. *DIR/PRO:* William Hanna, Joseph Barbera. A Loopy de Loop cartoon.

2464. The Beer Parade (3/4/33) B&W—7 mins. *DIR:* Dick Huemer. *PRO:* Charles Mintz. A Scrappy cartoon.

2465. The Big Birdcast (5/13/38) Technicolor—7 mins. *PRO:* Charles Mintz. A Color Rhapsodies cartoon.

2466. Big House Blues (3/6/47) Technicolor—7 mins. *DIR:* Howard Swift. A Color Rhapsodies cartoon featuring Flippy.

2467. Big Mouse Take (6/17/65) Technicolor—7 mins. *DIR/PRO:* William Hanna, Joseph Barbera. A Loopy de Loop cartoon.

2468. The Bill Poster (11/24/33) B&W—7 mins. *DIR:* Ben Harrison, Manny Gould. *PRO:* Charles Mintz. A Krazy Kat cartoon.

2469. The Bird Man (2/1/35) B&W—7 mins. *DIR:* Ben Harrison, Manny Gould. *PRO:* Charles Mintz. A Krazy Kat cartoon.

2470. The Bird Store (1/5/32) B&W—7 mins. *DIR:* Wilfred Jackson. *PRO:* Walt Disney. A Silly Symphonies cartoon.

2471. Bird Stuffer (2/1/36) B&W—7 mins. *DIR:* Ben Harrison, Manny Gould. *PRO:* Charles Mintz. A Krazy Kat cartoon.

2472. Birds in Love (10/28/36) Technicolor—7 mins. *PRO:* Charles Mintz. A Color Rhapsodies cartoon.

2473. Birds of a Feather (1/23/31) B&W—7 mins. *DIR:* Burt Gillett. *PRO:* Walt Disney. A Silly Symphonies cartoon.

2474. Birth of Jazz (4/13/32) B&W—7 mins. *DIR:* Ben Harrison, Manny Gould. *PRO:* Charles Mintz. A Krazy Kat cartoon.

2475. The Birthday Party (1/2/31) B&W—7 mins. *DIR:* Burt Gillett.

PRO: Walt Disney. A Mickey Mouse cartoon.

Black and Blue Market *see* **The Cocky Bantam**

2476. Black Sheep (9/17/32) B&W—7 mins. *DIR:* Dick Huemer. *PRO:* Charles Mintz. A Scrappy cartoon.

2477. Blackboard Revue (3/15/40) Technicolor—7 mins. *DIR:* Ub Iwerks. A Color Rhapsodies cartoon.

2478. Blue Rhythm (8/7/31) B&W—7 mins. *DIR:* Burt Gillett. *PRO:* Walt Disney. A Mickey Mouse cartoon.

2479. Bluebird's Baby (1/21/38) Technicolor—7 mins. *PRO:* Charles Mintz. A Color Rhapsodies cartoon.

2480. Bon Bon Parade (10/10/35) Technicolor—7 mins. *PRO:* Charles Mintz. A Color Rhapsodies cartoon.

2481. Booby Socks (7/12/45) B&W—7 mins. *DIR:* Howard Swift, Bob Wickersham. A Phantasies cartoon.

2482. Boston Beany (12/4/47) Technicolor—7 mins. *DIR:* Sid Marcus. A Color Rhapsodies cartoon.

2483. Bowery Daze (3/30/34) B&W—7 mins. *DIR:* Ben Harrison, Manny Gould. *PRO:* Charles Mintz. A Krazy Kat cartoon.

2484. A Boy, a Gun and Birds (1/12/40) Technicolor—7 mins. *DIR:* Ben Harrison. A Color Rhapsodies cartoon.

2485. A Boy and His Dog (12/23/36) Technicolor—7 mins. *PRO:* Charles Mintz. A Color Rhapsodies cartoon.

2486. Bringing Up Mother (1/14/54) Technicolor—7 mins. *DIR:* William Hurtz. *PRO:* Stephen Bosustow. A UPA cartoon Special.

2487. The Broadway Malady (4/18/33) B&W—7 mins. *DIR:* Ben Harrison, Manny Gould. *PRO:* Charles Mintz. A Krazy Kat cartoon.

2488. The Bulldog and the Baby (7/3/42) B&W—7 mins. *DIR:* Alec Geiss. A Fables cartoon.

2489. Bungle Uncle (1/18/62) Technicolor—7 mins. *DIR/PRO:* William Hanna, Joseph Barbera. A Loopy de Loop cartoon.

2490. Bungled Bungalow (12/28/50) Technicolor—7 mins. *DIR:* Pete Burness. *PRO:* Stephen Bosustow. A Mr. Magoo UPA cartoon.

2491. Bunnies Abundant (12/13/62) Technicolor—7 mins. *DIR/PRO:* William Hanna, Joseph Barbera. A Loopy de Loop cartoon.

2492. Bunnies and Bonnets (3/29/33) B&W—7 mins. *DIR:* Ben Harrison, Manny Gould. *PRO:* Charles Mintz. A Krazy Kat cartoon.

2493. The Busy Beavers (6/22/31) B&W—7 mins. *DIR:* Wilfred Jackson. *PRO:* Walt Disney. A Silly Symphonies cartoon.

2494. Busy Bus (4/20/34) B&W—7 mins. *DIR:* Ben Harrison, Manny Gould. *PRO:* Charles Mintz. A Krazy Kat cartoon.

2495. Bwana Magoo (1/9/59) Technicolor—7 mins. *DIR:* Tom McDonald. *PRO:* Stephen Bosustow. A Mr. Magoo UPA cartoon.

2496. The Cactus Kid (5/10/30) B&W—7 mins. *DIR/PRO:* Walt Disney. A Mickey Mouse cartoon.

2497. Cagey Bird (7/18/46) Technicolor—7 mins. *DIR:* Howard Swift. A Color Rhapsodies cartoon featuring Flippy.

2498. Calling Dr. Magoo (5/24/56) Technicolor/Scope—7 mins. *DIR:* Pete Burness. *PRO:* Stephen Bosustow. A Mr. Magoo UPA cartoon.

2499. Camping Out (8/10/32) B&W—7 mins. *DIR:* Dick Huemer. *PRO:* Charles Mintz. A Scrappy cartoon.

2500. Canine Capers (9/16/37) B&W—7 mins. *DIR:* Sid Marcus, Art Davis. *PRO:* Charles Mintz. A Scrappy cartoon.

2501. Canned Music (9/12/29) B&W—7 mins. *DIR:* Ben Harrison, Manny Gould. *PRO:* Charles Mintz. A Krazy Kat cartoon.

2502. Cannibal Capers (3/15/30) B&W—7 mins. *DIR:* Burt Gillett. *PRO:* Walt Disney. A Silly Symphonies cartoon.

2503. Captains Outrageous (12/25/52) Technicolor—7 mins. *DIR:* Pete Burness. *PRO:* Stephen Bosustow. A Mr. Magoo UPA cartoon.

2504. Carnival Courage (9/6/45) Technicolor—7 mins. *DIR:* Howard Swift. A Color Rhapsodies cartoon featuring Willoughby Wren.

2505. Case of the Screaming Bishop (8/4/44) B&W—7 mins. A Phantasies cartoon.

2506. The Castaway (3/27/31) B&W—7 mins. *DIR:* Wilfred Jackson. *PRO:* Walt Disney. A Mickey Mouse cartoon.

2507. A Cat, a Mouse, and a Bell (5/10/35) Technicolor—7 mins. *PRO:* Charles Mintz. A Color Rhapsodies cartoon.

2508. Catch Meow (9/14/61) Technicolor—7 mins. *DIR/PRO:* William Hanna, Joseph Barbera. A Loopy de Loop cartoon.

2509. Catnipped (2/14/46) Technicolor—7 mins. *DIR:* Howard Swift.

A Color Rhapsodies cartoon featuring Flippy.

2510. The Cat's Meow (1/2/30) B&W−7 mins. *DIR*: Ben Harrison, Manny Gould. *PRO*: Charles Mintz. A Krazy Kat cartoon.

The Cat's Nightmare *see* **The Cat's Out**

2511. The Cat's Out (7/20/31) B&W−7 mins. *DIR*: Wilfred Jackson. *PRO*: Walt Disney. A Silly Symphonies cartoon.

2512. Cat-Tastrophy (6/30/49) Technicolor−7 mins. *DIR*: Sid Marcus. A Color Rhapsodies cartoon.

2513. The Chain Gang (8/18/30) B&W−7 mins. *DIR*: Burt Gillett. *PRO*: Walt Disney. A Mickey Mouse cartoon.

2514. The Charm Bracelet (9/1/39) B&W−7 mins. *DIR*: Sid Marcus, Art Davis. *PRO*: Charles Mintz. A Scrappy Phantasies cartoon.

2515. Chicken Fraca-See (10/11/62) Technicolor−7 mins. *DIR/PRO*: William Hanna, Joseph Barbera. A Loopy de Loop cartoon.

2516. Chicken Hearted Wolf (3/14/63) Technicolor−7 mins. *DIR/PRO*: William Hanna, Joseph Barbera. A Loopy de Loop cartoon.

2517. Child Sock-Cology (8/10/61) Technicolor−7 mins. *DIR/PRO*: William Hanna, Joseph Barbera. A Loopy de Loop cartoon.

2518. The China Plate (5/16/31) B&W−7 mins. *DIR*: Wilfred Jackson. *PRO*: Walt Disney. A Silly Symphonies cartoon.

2519. Chinatown Mystery (1/4/32) B&W−7 mins. *DIR*: Dick Huemer. *PRO*: Charles Mintz. A Scrappy cartoon.

2520. Cholly Polly (12/18/42) B&W−7 mins. *DIR*: Alec Geiss. A Phantasies cartoon.

2521. Christopher Crumpet (6/25/53) Technicolor−7 mins. *DIR*: Robert Cannon. *PRO*: Stephen Bosustow. A Jolly Frolics UPA cartoon.

2522. Christopher Crumpet's Playmate (9/8/55) Technicolor−7 mins. *DIR*: Robert Cannon. *PRO*: Stephen Bosustow. A UPA cartoon Special.

2523. Cinder Alley (3/9/34) B&W−7 mins. *DIR*: Ben Harrison, Manny Gould. *PRO*: Charles Mintz. A Krazy Kat cartoon.

2524. Cinderella (8/14/30) B&W−7 mins. *DIR*: Ben Harrison, Manny Gould. *PRO*: Charles Mintz. A Krazy Kat cartoon.

2525. Cinderella Goes to a Party (5/3/42) Technicolor−7 mins. *DIR*: Frank Tashlin. A Color Rhapsodies cartoon.

2526. The City Slicker (7/8/38) B&W−7 mins. *DIR*: Sid Marcus, Art Davis. *PRO*: Charles Mintz. A Scrappy cartoon.

2527. The Clock Goes Round and Round (11/6/37) B&W−7 mins. *DIR*: Sid Marcus, Art Davis. *PRO*: Charles Mintz. A Scrappy cartoon.

2528. The Clock Store (9/16/31) B&W−7 mins. *DIR*: Wilfred Jackson. *PRO*: Walt Disney. A Silly Symphonies cartoon.

2529. Cockatoos for Two (2/13/47) Technicolor−7 mins. *DIR*: Bob Wickersham. A Color Rhapsodies cartoon.

2530. The Cocky Bantam (11/12/43) B&W−7 mins. *DIR*: Paul Sommer. A Phantasies cartoon.

2531. Common Scents (5/10/62) Technicolor—7 mins. DIR/PRO: William Hanna, Joseph Barbera. A Loopy de Loop cartoon.

2532. The Concert Kid (11/2/34) B&W—7 mins. DIR: Sid Marcus, Art Davis. PRO: Charles Mintz. A Scrappy cartoon.

2533. Concerto in B-Flat Minor (3/20/42) Technicolor—7 mins. DIR: Frank Tashlin. A Color Rhapsodies cartoon.

2534. Coo-Coo Bird Dog (2/3/49) Technicolor—7 mins. DIR: Sid Marcus. A Phantasies cartoon.

2535. Count Down Clown (1/5/61) Technicolor—7 mins. DIR/PRO: William Hanna, Joseph Barbera. A Loopy de Loop cartoon.

2536. Creepy Time Pal (5/19/60) Technicolor—7 mins. DIR/PRO: William Hanna, Joseph Barbera. A Loopy de Loop cartoon.

2537. Crook Who Cried Wolf (12/12/63) Technicolor—7 mins. DIR/PRO: William Hanna, Joseph Barbera. A Loopy de Loop cartoon.

2538. Crop Chasers (9/22/39) Technicolor—7 mins. DIR: Ub Iwerks. PRO: Charles Mintz. A Color Rhapsodies cartoon.

2539. Crow's Fete (4/14/65) Technicolor—7 mins. DIR/PRO: William Hanna, Joseph Barbera. A Loopy de Loop cartoon.

2540. The Crystal Gazebo (11/7/32) B&W—7 mins. DIR: Ben Harrison, Manny Gould. PRO: Charles Mintz. A Krazy Kat cartoon.

2541. The Crystal Gazer (9/26/41) B&W—7 mins. A Phantasies cartoon.

2542. The Cuckoo I.Q. (7/3/41) Technicolor—7 mins. DIR: Sid Marcus. A Color Rhapsodies cartoon.

2543. The Curio Shop (12/15/33) B&W—7 mins. DIR: Ben Harrison, Manny Gould. PRO: Charles Mintz. A Krazy Kat cartoon.

2544. The Cute Recruit (5/2/41) B&W—7 mins. A Phantasies cartoon.

2545. The Delivery Boy (6/6/31) B&W—7 mins. DIR: Burt Gillett. PRO: Walt Disney. A Mickey Mouse cartoon.

2546. Desert Sunk (3/27/30) B&W—7 mins. DIR: Ben Harrison, Manny Gould. PRO: Charles Mintz. A Krazy Kat cartoon.

2547. Destination Magoo (12/16/54) Technicolor—7 mins. DIR: Pete Burness. PRO: Stephen Bosustow. A Mr. Magoo UPA cartoon.

2548. Disarmament Conference (4/27/31) B&W—7 mins. DIR: Ben Harrison, Manny Gould. PRO: Charles Mintz. A Krazy Kat cartoon.

2549. Disillusioned Bluebird (5/26/44) Technicolor—7 mins. DIR: Howard Swift. A Color Rhapsodies cartoon.

2550. Dizzy Ducks (11/28/36) B&W—7 mins. DIR: Sid Marcus, Art Davis. PRO: Charles Mintz. A Scrappy cartoon.

2551. Dizzy Newsreel (8/27/43) B&W—7 mins. DIR: Alec Geiss. A Phantasies cartoon.

2552. Doctor Bluebird (2/5/36) Technicolor—7 mins. PRO: Charles Mintz. A Color Rhapsodies cartoon.

2553. The Do-Good Wolf (7/14/60) Technicolor—7 mins. DIR/PRO: William Hanna, Joseph Barbera. A Loopy de Loop cartoon.

2554. The Dog, Cat and Canary (1/5/45) Technicolor—7 mins. DIR: Howard Swift. A Color Rhapsodies cartoon featuring Flippy.

2555. Dog Meets Dog (3/6/42) B&W−7 mins. *DIR:* Frank Tashlin. A Phantasies cartoon.

2556. The Dog Snatcher (10/15/31) B&W−7 mins. *DIR:* Dick Huemer. *PRO:* Charles Mintz. A Scrappy cartoon.

2557. Dog Snatcher (5/29/52) Technicolor−7 mins. *DIR:* Pete Burness. *PRO:* Stephen Bosustow. A Mr. Magoo UPA cartoon.

2558. The Dream Kids (2/5/44) Technicolor−7 mins. *DIR:* Bob Wickersham. A Fox and the Crow cartoon.

2559. Dreams on Ice (10/20/39) Technicolor−7 mins. *DIR:* Sid Marcus. *PRO:* Charles Mintz. A Color Rhapsodies cartoon.

2560. Drum-Sticked (10/3/63) Technicolor−7 mins. *DIR/PRO:* William Hanna, Joseph Barbera. A Loopy de Loop cartoon.

2561. The Duck Hunt (1/28/32) B&W−7 mins. *DIR:* Burt Gillett. *PRO:* Walt Disney. A Mickey Mouse cartoon.

2562. The Dumb Conscious Mind (10/23/42) B&W−7 mins. *DIR:* Paul Sommer, John Hubley. A Phantasies cartoon.

2563. Dumb Like a Fox (7/18/41) B&W−7 mins. A Fables cartoon.

2564. Duty and the Beast (5/28/43) B&W−7 mins. *DIR:* Alec Geiss. A Phantasies cartoon.

2565. The Early Bird (9/16/38) B&W−7 mins. *DIR:* Sid Marcus, Art Davis. *PRO:* Charles Mintz. A Scrappy cartoon.

2566. The Egg Hunt (5/31/40) Technicolor−7 mins. *DIR:* Ub Iwerks. A Color Rhapsodies cartoon.

2567. The Egg Yegg (12/8/44) Technicolor−7 mins. *DIR:* Bob Wickersham. A Fox and the Crow cartoon.

2568. Egyptian Melodies (8/19/31) B&W−7 mins. *DIR:* Wilfred Jackson. *PRO:* Walt Disney. A Silly Symphonies cartoon.

2569. El Terrible Toreador (9/7/29) B&W−7 mins. *DIR/PRO:* Walt Disney. A Mickey Mouse cartoon.

2570. Elephantastic (2/6/64) Technicolor−7 mins. *DIR/PRO:* William Hanna, Joseph Barbera. A Loopy de Loop cartoon.

2571. The Emperor's New Clothes (4/30/53) Technicolor−7 mins. *DIR:* Ted Parmelee. *PRO:* Stephen Bosustow. A Jolly Frolics UPA cartoon.

2572. The Explosive Mr. Magoo (5/8/58) Technicolor−7 mins. *DIR:* Pete Burness. *PRO:* Stephen Bosustow. A Mr. Magoo UPA cartoon.

2573. A Fallible Fable (5/16/63) Technicolor−7 mins. *DIR/PRO:* William Hanna, Joseph Barbera. A Loopy de Loop cartoon.

2574. The False Alarm (4/22/33) B&W−7 mins. *DIR:* Dick Huemer. *PRO:* Charles Mintz. A Scrappy cartoon.

2575. The Family Circus (1/25/51) Technicolor−7 mins. *DIR:* Art Babbitt. *PRO:* Stephen Bosustow. A Jolly Frolics UPA cartoon.

2576. Fare-Play (7/2/32) B&W−7 mins. *DIR:* Dick Huemer. *PRO:* Charles Mintz. A Scrappy cartoon.

2577. Farm Relief (12/30/29) B&W−7 mins. *DIR:* Ben Harrison, Manny Gould. *PRO:* Charles Mintz. A Krazy Kat cartoon.

2578. Farmer Tom Thumb (9/27/40) B&W−7 mins. A Fables cartoon.

2579. Fee Fie Foes (6/9/61) Technicolor—7 mins. DIR/PRO: William Hanna, Joseph Barbera. A Loopy de Loop cartoon.

Fiddlin' Around see **Just Mickey**

2580. Fiesta Time (4/4/45) Technicolor—7 mins. DIR: Bob Wickersham. A Color Rhapsodies cartoon featuring Tito.

2581. The Fire Fighters (6/20/30) B&W—7 mins. DIR: Burt Gillett. PRO: Walt Disney. A Mickey Mouse cartoon.

2582. The Fire Plug (10/16/37) B&W—7 mins. DIR: Sid Marcus, Art Davis. PRO: Charles Mintz. A Scrappy cartoon.

2583. Fish Follies (5/10/40) Technicolor—7 mins. A Color Rhapsodies cartoon.

2584. Fishin' Around (9/1/31) B&W—7 mins. DIR: Burt Gillett. PRO: Walt Disney. A Mickey Mouse cartoon.

2585. Flop House (11/9/32) B&W—7 mins. DIR: Dick Huemer. PRO: Charles Mintz. A Scrappy cartoon.

2586. Flora (3/18/48) Technicolor—7 mins. DIR: Alex Lovy. A Color Rhapsodies cartoon.

2587. The Fly in the Ointment (7/23/43) B&W—7 mins. DIR: Paul Sommer. A Phantasies cartoon.

2588. The Foolish Bunny (3/26/38) Technicolor—7 mins. DIR: Art Davis. PRO: Charles Mintz. A Color Rhapsodies cartoon.

2589. Football Bugs (4/29/36) Technicolor—7 mins. PRO: Charles Mintz. A Color Rhapsodies cartoon.

2590. Four Wheels and No Brake (1/27/55) Technicolor—7 mins. DIR: Ted Parmelee. PRO: Stephen Bosustow. A UPA cartoon Special featuring Pete Hothead.

2591. Fowl Brawl (1/19/47) Technicolor—7 mins. DIR: Howard Swift. A Phantasies cartoon.

2592. The Fox and the Grapes (12/5/41) Technicolor—7 mins. DIR: Frank Tashlin. A Color Rhapsodies cartoon featuring the Fox and the Crow.

2593. The Fox Hunt (11/10/31) B&W—7 mins. DIR: Wilfred Jackson. PRO: Walt Disney. A Silly Symphonies cartoon.

2594. Foxey Flatfoots (4/11/46) Technicolor—7 mins. DIR: Bob Wickersham. A Fox and the Crow cartoon.

2595. The Foxy Pup (5/21/37) Technicolor—7 mins. DIR: Ub Iwerks. PRO: Charles Mintz. A Color Rhapsodies cartoon.

2596. The Frog Pond (8/12/38) Technicolor—7 mins. DIR: Ub Iwerks. PRO: Charles Mintz. A Color Rhapsodies cartoon.

2597. Frolicking Fish (5/23/30) B&W—7 mins. DIR: Burt Gillett. PRO: Walt Disney. A Silly Symphonies cartoon.

2598. Fuddy Duddy Buddy (10/18/51) Technicolor—7 mins. DIR: John Hubley. PRO: Stephen Bosustow. A Mr. Magoo UPA cartoon.

2599. Fudget's Budget (6/17/54) Technicolor—7 mins. DIR: Robert Cannon. PRO: Stephen Bosustow. A UPA cartoon Special.

2600. Gallopin' Gaucho (8/7/28) B&W—7 mins. DIR/PRO: Walt Disney. A Mickey Mouse cartoon.

2601. Garden Gaieties (8/1/35) B&W—7 mins. DIR: Ben Harrison,

Manny Gould. *PRO:* Charles Mintz. A Krazy Kat cartoon.

2602. Georgie and the Dragon (9/27/51) Technicolor—7 mins. *DIR:* Robert Cannon. *PRO:* Stephen Bosustow. A Jolly Frolics UPA cartoon.

2603. Gerald McBoing Boing (1/25/51) Technicolor—7 mins. *DIR:* Robert Cannon. *PRO:* Stephen Bosustow. A Jolly Frolics UPA cartoon featuring Gerald McBoing Boing.

2604. Gerald McBoing Boing on the Planet Moo (2/9/56) Technicolor—7 mins. *DIR:* Robert Cannon. *PRO:* Stephen Bosustow. A Gerald McBoing Boing UPA cartoon.

2605. Gerald McBoing Boing's Symphony (7/15/53) Technicolor—7 mins. *DIR:* Robert Cannon. *PRO:* Stephen Bosustow. A Gerald McBoing Boing UPA cartoon.

2606. Giddy Yapping (4/7/44) B&W—7 mins. *DIR:* Howard Swift. A Phantasies cartoon.

2607. Giddyap (7/27/50) Technicolor—7 mins. *DIR:* Art Babbitt. *PRO:* Stephen Bosustow. A Jolly Frolics UPA cartoon.

2608. Gifts from the Air (1/1/37) Technicolor—7 mins. *PRO:* Charles Mintz. A Color Rhapsodies cartoon.

2609. Glee Worms (6/24/36) Technicolor—7 mins. *PRO:* Charles Mintz. A Color Rhapsodies cartoon.

2610. The Gloom Chasers (1/18/35) B&W—7 mins. *DIR:* Sid Marcus, Art Davis. *PRO:* Charles Mintz. A Scrappy cartoon.

2611. Gold Getters (3/1/35) B&W—7 mins. *DIR:* Sid Marcus, Art Davis. *PRO:* Charles Mintz. A Scrappy cartoon.

2612. Golf Chumps (4/6/39) B&W—7 mins. *DIR:* Ben Harrison,

Manny Gould. *PRO:* Charles Mintz. A Krazy Kat cartoon.

2613. Goofy Gondolas (12/21/34) B&W—7 mins. *DIR:* Ben Harrison, Manny Gould. *PRO:* Charles Mintz. A Krazy Kat cartoon.

2614. Goofy News Views (4/27/45) B&W—7 mins. *DIR:* Sid Marcus. A Phantasies cartoon.

2615. The Gorilla Hunt (2/24/39) Technicolor—7 mins. *DIR:* Ub Iwerks. *PRO:* Charles Mintz. A Color Rhapsodies cartoon.

2616. The Gorilla Mystery (9/22/30) B&W—7 mins. *DIR:* Burt Gillett. *PRO:* Walt Disney. A Mickey Mouse cartoon.

2617. Graduation Exercises (4/12/35) B&W—7 mins. *DIR:* Sid Marcus, Art Davis. *PRO:* Charles Mintz. A Scrappy cartoon.

2618. Grape Nutty (4/14/49) Technicolor—7 mins. *DIR:* Alex Lovy. A Color Rhapsodies cartoon featuring the Fox and the Crow.

2619. The Great Bird Mystery (10/20/32) B&W—7 mins. *DIR:* Dick Huemer. *PRO:* Charles Mintz. A Scrappy cartoon.

2620. The Great Cheeze Mystery (10/27/41) B&W—7 mins. *DIR:* Art Davis. A Fables cartoon.

2621. The Great Experiment (7/27/34) B&W—7 mins. *DIR:* Sid Marcus, Art Davis. *PRO:* Charles Mintz. A Scrappy cartoon.

2622. The Greyhound and the Rabbit (4/19/40) Technicolor—7 mins. A Color Rhapsodies cartoon.

2623. Grizzly Golfer (12/20/51) Technicolor—7 mins. *DIR:* Pete Burness. *PRO:* Stephen Bosustow. A Mr. Magoo UPA cartoon.

2624. The Grocery Boy (2/8/32) B&W—7 mins. *DIR:* Wilfred Jackson. *PRO:* Walt Disney. A Mickey Mouse cartoon.

2625. The Gullible Canary (9/18/42) B&W—7 mins. *DIR:* Alec Geiss. A Phantasies cartoon.

2626. Gumshoe Magoo (11/6/58) Technicolor—7 mins. *DIR:* Gil Turner. *PRO:* Stephen Bosustow. A Mr. Magoo UPA cartoon.

2627. Gym Jams (9/9/38) B&W—7 mins. *DIR:* Ben Harrison, Manny Gould. *PRO:* Charles Mintz. A Krazy Kat cartoon.

2628. Habit Rabbit (12/31/63) Technicolor—7 mins. *DIR/PRO:* William Hanna, Joseph Barbera. A Loopy de Loop cartoon.

2629. Habit Troubles (11/19/64) Technicolor—7 mins. *DIR/PRO:* William Hanna, Joseph Barbera. A Loopy de Loop cartoon.

2630. Happy Birthday (10/7/38) B&W—7 mins. *DIR:* Sid Marcus, Art Davis. *PRO:* Charles Mintz. A Scrappy cartoon.

2631. Happy Butterfly (12/20/34) B&W—7 mins. *DIR:* Sid Marcus, Art Davis. *PRO:* Charles Mintz. A Scrappy cartoon.

2632. A Happy Family (9/27/35) B&W—7 mins. *DIR:* Ben Harrison, Manny Gould. *PRO:* Charles Mintz. A Krazy Kat cartoon.

2633. Happy Go Loopy (3/2/61) Technicolor—7 mins. *DIR/PRO:* William Hanna, Joseph Barbera. A Loopy de Loop cartoon.

2634. Happy Holidays (10/25/40) B&W—7 mins. A Phantasies cartoon.

2635. Happy Tots (3/31/39) Technicolor—7 mins. *DIR:* Ben Har-

rison. *PRO:* Charles Mintz. A Color Rhapsodies cartoon.

2636. The Happy Tots' Expedition (2/9/40) Technicolor—7 mins. *DIR:* Ben Harrison. A Color Rhapsodies cartoon.

2637. Hash House Blues (11/2/31) B&W—7 mins. *DIR:* Ben Harrison, Manny Gould. *PRO:* Charles Mintz. A Krazy Kat cartoon.

2638. The Haunted House (12/2/29) B&W—7 mins. *DIR/PRO:* Walt Disney. A Mickey Mouse cartoon.

2639. He Can't Make It Stick (6/11/43) Technicolor—7 mins. *DIR:* Paul Sommer, John Hubley. A Color Rhapsodies cartoon.

2640. Hell's Bells (11/11/29) B&W—7 mins. *DIR:* Ub Iwerks. *PRO:* Walt Disney. A Silly Symphonies cartoon.

2641. A Helping Paw (1/7/41) Technicolor—7 mins. *DIR:* Sid Marcus. A Color Rhapsodies cartoon.

2642. Here, Kiddie, Kiddie (9/1/60) Technicolor—7 mins. *DIR/PRO:* William Hanna, Joseph Barbera. A Loopy de Loop cartoon.

2643. The Herring Murder Mystery (12/30/43) Technicolor—7 mins. *DIR:* Don Roman. A Color Rhapsodies cartoon.

2644. Hic-Cups the Champ (5/28/32) B&W—7 mins. *DIR:* Ben Harrison, Manny Gould. *PRO:* Charles Mintz. A Krazy Kat cartoon.

2645. Highway Snobbery (8/9/36) B&W—7 mins. *DIR:* Ben Harrison, Manny Gould. *PRO:* Charles Mintz. A Krazy Kat cartoon.

2646. Holiday Land (11/9/34) Technicolor—7 mins. *DIR:* Sid Marcus, Art Davis. *PRO:* Charles Mintz. A

Color Rhapsodies cartoon featuring Scrappy.

2647. Hollywood Babies (11/10/33) B&W — 7 mins. *DIR:* Dick Huemer. *PRO:* Charles Mintz. A Scrappy cartoon.

2648. A Hollywood Detour (1/23/42) Technicolor — 7 mins. *DIR:* Frank Tashlin. A Color Rhapsodies cartoon.

2649. Hollywood Goes Krazy (2/13/32) B&W — 7 mins. *DIR:* Ben Harrison, Manny Gould. *PRO:* Charles Mintz. A Krazy Kat cartoon.

2650. Hollywood Graduation (8/26/38) Technicolor — 7 mins. *DIR:* Art Davis. *PRO:* Charles Mintz. A Color Rhapsodies cartoon.

2651. Hollywood Picnic (12/18/37) Technicolor — 7 mins. *PRO:* Charles Mintz. A Color Rhapsodies cartoon.

2652. Hollywood Sweepstakes (6/28/39) Technicolor — 7 mins. *DIR:* Ben Harrison. *PRO:* Charles Mintz. A Color Rhapsodies cartoon.

2653. Honolulu Wiles (8/17/30) B&W — 7 mins. *DIR:* Ben Harrison, Manny Gould. *PRO:* Charles Mintz. A Krazy Kat cartoon.

2654. The Horse on the Merry-Go-Round (2/17/38) Technicolor — 7 mins. *DIR:* Ub Iwerks. *PRO:* Charles Mintz. A Color Rhapsodies cartoon.

2655. Horse Shoo (1/7/65) Technicolor — 7 mins. *DIR/PRO:* William Hanna, Joseph Barbera. A Loopy de Loop cartoon.

2656. Hot Dogs on Ice (10/21/38) B&W — 7 mins. *DIR:* Ben Harrison, Manny Gould. *PRO:* Charles Mintz. A Krazy Kat cartoon.

2657. Hot Foot Lights (8/2/45) Technicolor — 7 mins. *DIR:* Howard Swift. A Color Rhapsodies cartoon.

2658. Hotcha Melody (3/15/35) B&W — 7 mins. *DIR:* Ben Harrison, Manny Gould. *PRO:* Charles Mintz. A Krazy Kat cartoon.

2659. Hotsy Footsy (10/23/52) Technicolor — 7 mins. *DIR:* William Hurtz. *PRO:* Stephen Bosustow. A Mr. Magoo UPA cartoon.

2660. House Cleaning (6/1/33) B&W — 7 mins. *DIR:* Ben Harrison, Manny Gould. *PRO:* Charles Mintz. A Krazy Kat cartoon.

2661. The House That Jack Built (4/14/39) Technicolor — 7 mins. *DIR:* Sid Marcus. *PRO:* Charles Mintz. A Color Rhapsodies cartoon.

2662. How Now Boing Boing (9/9/54) Technicolor — 7 mins. *DIR:* Robert Cannon. *PRO:* Stephen Bosustow. A Gerald McBoing Boing UPA cartoon.

2663. A Hunting We Won't Go (8/23/43) Technicolor — 7 mins. *DIR:* Bob Wickersham. A Color Rhapsodies cartoon featuring the Fox and the Crow.

2664. I Want to Be an Actress (7/18/37) B&W — 7 mins. *DIR:* Sid Marcus, Art Davis. *PRO:* Charles Mintz. A Scrappy cartoon.

2665. Imagination (10/29/43) Technicolor — 7 mins. *DIR:* Bob Wickersham. A Color Rhapsodies cartoon.

In a Clock Store *see* **The Clock Store**

2666. In My Gondola (9/3/36) Technicolor — 7 mins. *PRO:* Charles Mintz. A Color Rhapsodies cartoon.

2667. Indian Serenade (7/16/37) Technicolor — 7 mins. *PRO:* Charles Mintz. A Color Rhapsodies cartoon.

2668. It Happened to Crusoe (3/14/41) B&W — 7 mins. A Fables cartoon.

2669. The Jaywalker (5/31/56) Technicolor—7 mins. *DIR:* Robert Cannon. *PRO:* Stephen Bosustow. A UPA cartoon Special.

2670. The Jazz Fool (10/15/29) B&W—7 mins. *DIR/PRO:* Walt Disney. A Mickey Mouse cartoon.

2671. Jazz Rhythm (6/19/30) B&W—7 mins. *DIR:* Ben Harrison, Manny Gould. *PRO:* Charles Mintz. A Krazy Kat cartoon.

2672. Jitterbug Knights (8/11/39) Technicolor—7 mins. *DIR:* Sid Marcus. *PRO:* Charles Mintz. A Color Rhapsodies cartoon.

2673. Jungle Rhythm (11/15/29) B&W—7 mins. *DIR/PRO:* Walt Disney. A Mickey Mouse cartoon.

2674. Just a Wolf at Heart (2/14/63) Technicolor—7 mins. *DIR/PRO:* William Hanna, Joseph Barbera. A Loopy de Loop cartoon.

2675. Just Mickey (3/6/30) B&W—7 mins. *DIR/PRO:* Walt Disney. A Mickey Mouse cartoon.

2676. Kangaroo Courting (7/22/54) Technicolor—7 mins. *DIR:* Pete Burness. *PRO:* Stephen Bosustow. A UPA cartoon Special.

2677. The Kangaroo Kid (12/23/38) Technicolor—7 mins. *DIR:* Ben Harrison. *PRO:* Charles Mintz. A Color Rhapsodies cartoon.

2678. Kannibal Kapers (12/27/35) B&W—7 mins. *DIR:* Ben Harrison, Manny Gould. *PRO:* Charles Mintz. A Krazy Kat cartoon.

2679. The Karnival Kid (7/31/29) B&W—7 mins. *DIR/PRO:* Walt Disney. A Mickey Mouse cartoon.

2680. Katnips of 1940 (10/12/34) B&W—7 mins. *DIR:* Ben Harrison, Manny Gould. *PRO:* Charles Mintz. A Krazy Kat cartoon.

2681. Kickapoo Juice (12/1/44) Technicolor—7 mins. *DIR:* Howard Swift. *PRO:* Charles Mintz. A Li'l Abner cartoon.

2682. Kindly Scram (3/5/43) B&W—7 mins. *DIR:* Alec Geiss. A Phantasies cartoon.

2683. King Midas, Junior (12/18/42) Technicolor—7 mins. *DIR:* Paul Sommer, John Hubley. A Color Rhapsodies cartoon.

2684. The King's Jester (5/20/35) B&W—7 mins. *DIR:* Ben Harrison, Manny Gould. *PRO:* Charles Mintz. A Krazy Kat cartoon.

2685. Kitty Caddy (11/6/47) Technicolor—7 mins. *DIR:* Sid Marcus. A Phantasies cartoon.

2686. Kitty Gets the Bird (6/13/41) B&W—7 mins. A Fables cartoon.

2687. Kongo-Roo (4/18/46) B&W—7 mins. *DIR:* Howard Swift. A Phantasies cartoon.

2688. Kooky Loopy (11/16/61) Technicolor—7 mins. *DIR/PRO:* William Hanna, Joseph Barbera. A Loopy de Loop cartoon.

2689. Krazy Magic (5/20/38) B&W—7 mins. *DIR:* Ben Harrison, Manny Gould. *PRO:* Charles Mintz. A Krazy Kat cartoon.

2690. Krazy Spooks (10/13/33) B&W—7 mins. *DIR:* Ben Harrison, Manny Gould. *PRO:* Charles Mintz. A Krazy Kat cartoon.

2691. Krazy's Bear Tales (1/27/39) B&W—7 mins. *DIR:* Ben Harrison, Manny Gould. *PRO:* Charles Mintz. A Krazy Kat cartoon.

2692. Krazy's Newsreel (10/24/36) B&W—7 mins. *DIR:* Ben Harrison, Manny Gould. *PRO:* Charles Mintz. A Krazy Kat cartoon.

2693. Krazy's Race of Time (5/6/37) B&W–7 mins. *DIR*: Ben Harrison, Manny Gould. *PRO*: Charles Mintz. A Krazy Kat cartoon.

2694. Krazy's Shoe Shop (5/12/39) B&W–7 mins. *DIR*: Ben Harrison, Manny Gould. *PRO*: Charles Mintz. A Krazy Kat cartoon.

2695. Krazy's Travel Squawks (6/4/38) B&W–7 mins. *DIR*: Ben Harrison, Manny Gould. *PRO*: Charles Mintz. A Krazy Kat cartoon.

2696. Krazy's Waterloo (11/16/34) B&W–7 mins. *DIR*: Ben Harrison, Manny Gould. *PRO*: Charles Mintz. A Krazy Kat cartoon.

2697. Ku-Kunuts (3/30/45) Technicolor–7 mins. *DIR*: Bob Wickersham. A Fox and the Crow cartoon.

2698. Lambs Will Gamble (11/1/30) B&W–7 mins. *DIR*: Ben Harrison, Manny Gould. *PRO*: Charles Mintz. A Krazy Kat cartoon.

2699. The Land of Fun (4/18/41) Technicolor–7 mins. *DIR*: Sid Marcus. A Color Rhapsodies cartoon.

2700. Leave Us Chase It (5/5/47) Technicolor–7 mins. *DIR*: Howard Swift. A Phantasies cartoon.

2701. Let's Go (4/10/37) Technicolor–7 mins. *PRO*: Charles Mintz. A Color Rhapsodies cartoon.

2702. Let's Ring Doorbells (11/7/35) B&W–7 mins. *DIR*: Sid Marcus, Art Davis. *PRO*: Charles Mintz. A Scrappy cartoon.

2703. Life with Loopy (4/7/60) Technicolor–7 mins. *DIR/PRO*: William Hanna, Joseph Barbera. A Loopy de Loop cartoon.

2704. Lighthouse Keeping (8/15/32) B&W–7 mins. *DIR*: Ben Harrison, Manny Gould. *PRO*: Charles Mintz. A Krazy Kat cartoon.

2705. Li'l Anjil (3/19/36) B&W–7 mins. *DIR*: Ben Harrison, Manny Gould. *PRO*: Charles Mintz. A Krazy Kat cartoon.

2706. Lionel Lion (4/3/44) B&W–7 mins. *DIR*: Paul Sommer. A Phantasies cartoon.

2707. Little Bo Bopped (12/3/59) Technicolor–7 mins. *DIR/PRO*: William Hanna, Joseph Barbera. A Loopy de Loop cartoon.

2708. Little Boy with a Big Horn (3/26/53) Technicolor–7 mins. *DIR*: Robert Cannon. *PRO*: Stephen Bosustow. A Jolly Frolics UPA cartoon.

2709. Little Buckaroo (4/11/38) B&W–7 mins. *DIR*: Ben Harrison, Manny Gould. *PRO*: Charles Mintz. A Krazy Kat cartoon.

2710. Little Lost Sheep (10/6/39) B&W–7 mins. *PRO*: Charles Mintz. A Fables cartoon featuring Krazy Kat.

2711. The Little Match Girl (11/5/37) Technicolor–7 mins. *PRO*: Charles Mintz. A Color Rhapsodies cartoon.

2712. Little Moth's Big Flame (11/3/38) Technicolor–7 mins. *DIR*: Sid Marcus. *PRO*: Charles Mintz. A Color Rhapsodies cartoon.

2713. The Little Pest (8/15/31) B&W–7 mins. *DIR*: Dick Huemer. *PRO*: Charles Mintz. A Scrappy cartoon.

2714. Little Rover (6/28/35) Technicolor–7 mins. *PRO*: Charles Mintz. A Color Rhapsodies cartoon.

2715. The Little Theatre (2/7/41) B&W–7 mins. *DIR*: Sid Marcus, Art Davis. *PRO*: Charles Mintz. A Phantasies cartoon featuring Scrappy.

2716. The Little Trail (12/3/30) B&W−7 mins. *DIR:* Ben Harrison, Manny Gould. *PRO:* Charles Mintz. A Krazy Kat cartoon.

2717. Lo, the Poor Buffal (11/4/48) Technicolor−7 mins. *DIR:* Alex Lovy. A Color Rhapsodies cartoon.

2718. Loco Lobo (1/9/47) Technicolor−7 mins. *DIR:* Howard Swift. A Color Rhapsodies cartoon featuring Tito.

2719. The Lone Mountie (12/10/38) B&W−7 mins. *DIR:* Ben Harrison, Manny Gould. *PRO:* Charles Mintz. A Krazy Kat cartoon.

2720. Looney Balloonists (9/24/36) B&W−7 mins. *DIR:* Sid Marcus, Art Davis. *PRO:* Charles Mintz. A Scrappy cartoon.

2721. Loopy's Hare-Do (12/14/61) Technicolor−7 mins. *DIR/PRO:* William Hanna, Joseph Barbera. A Loopy de Loop cartoon.

2722. Love Comes to Magoo (10/2/58) Technicolor−7 mins. *DIR:* Tom McDonald. *PRO:* Stephen Bosustow. A Mr. Magoo UPA cartoon.

2723. Love Krazy (1/30/32) B&W−7 mins. *DIR:* Ben Harrison, Manny Gould. *PRO:* Charles Mintz. A Krazy Kat cartoon.

2724. Lucky Pigs (5/26/39) Technicolor−7 mins. *DIR:* Ben Harrison. *PRO:* Charles Mintz. A Color Rhapsodies cartoon.

2725. The Lyin' Hunter (2/12/37) B&W−7 mins. *DIR:* Ben Harrison, Manny Gould. *PRO:* Charles Mintz. A Krazy Kat cartoon.

2726. The Mad Dog (2/27/32) B&W−7 mins. *DIR:* Burt Gillett. *PRO:* Walt Disney. A Mickey Mouse cartoon.

2727. The Mad Hatter (11/3/40) Technicolor−7 mins. *DIR:* Sid Marcus. A Color Rhapsodies cartoon.

2728. Madcap Magoo (6/23/55) Technicolor−7 mins. *DIR:* Pete Burness. *PRO:* Stephen Bosustow. A Mr. Magoo UPA cartoon.

2729. Madeline (11/27/52) Technicolor−7 mins. *DIR:* Robert Cannon. *PRO:* Stephen Bosustow. A Jolly Frolics UPA cartoon.

2730. The Magic Fluke (3/27/49) Technicolor−7 mins. *DIR:* John Hubley. *PRO:* Stephen Bosustow. A Fox and the Crow UPA cartoon.

2731. Magic Strength (2/4/44) B&W−7 mins. *DIR:* Bob Wickersham. A Phantasies cartoon featuring Willoughby Wren.

2732. Magoo Beats the Heat (6/21/56) Technicolor/Scope−7 mins. *DIR:* Pete Burness. *PRO:* Stephen Bosustow. A Mr. Magoo UPA cartoon.

2733. Magoo Breaks Par (6/27/57) Technicolor/Scope−7 mins. *DIR:* Pete Burness. *PRO:* Stephen Bosustow. A Mr. Magoo UPA cartoon.

2734. Magoo Goes Overboard (2/21/57) Technicolor/Scope−7 mins. *DIR:* Pete Burness. *PRO:* Stephen Bosustow. A Mr. Magoo UPA cartoon.

2735. Magoo Goes Skiing (3/11/54) Technicolor−7 mins. *DIR:* Pete Burness. *PRO:* Stephen Bosustow. A Mr. Magoo UPA cartoon.

2736. Magoo Goes West (4/19/56) Technicolor/Scope−7 mins. *DIR:* Pete Burness. *PRO:* Stephen Bosustow. A Mr. Magoo UPA cartoon.

2737. Magoo Makes News (12/12/55) Technicolor−7 mins. *DIR:* Pete Burness. *PRO:* Stephen Bosustow. A Mr. Magoo UPA cartoon.

2738. Magoo Saves the Bank (9/26/57) Technicolor/Scope—7 mins. *DIR:* Pete Burness. *PRO:* Stephen Bosustow. A Mr. Magoo UPA cartoon.

2739. Magoo Slept Here (11/19/53) Technicolor—7 mins. *DIR:* Pete Burness. *PRO:* Stephen Bosustow. A Mr. Magoo UPA cartoon.

2740. Magoo's Caine Mutiny (3/8/56) Technicolor—7 mins. *DIR:* Pete Burness. *PRO:* Stephen Bosustow. A Mr. Magoo UPA cartoon.

2741. Magoo's Check Up (2/24/55) Technicolor—7 mins. *DIR:* Pete Burness. *PRO:* Stephen Bosustow. A Mr. Magoo UPA cartoon.

2742. Magoo's Cruise (9/11/58) Technicolor—7 mins. *DIR:* Rudy Larriva. *PRO:* Stephen Bosustow. A Mr. Magoo UPA cartoon.

2743. Magoo's Express (5/19/55) Technicolor—7 mins. *DIR:* Pete Burness. *PRO:* Stephen Bosustow. A Mr. Magoo UPA cartoon.

2744. Magoo's Glorious Fourth (7/25/57) Technicolor/Scope—7 mins. *DIR:* Pete Burness. *PRO:* Stephen Bosustow. A Mr. Magoo UPA cartoon.

2745. Magoo's Homecoming (3/5/59) Technicolor—7 mins. *DIR:* Gil Turner. *PRO:* Stephen Bosustow. A Mr. Magoo UPA cartoon.

2746. Magoo's Lodge Brother (5/7/59) Technicolor—7 mins. *DIR:* Rudy Larriva. *PRO:* Stephen Bosustow. A Mr. Magoo UPA cartoon.

2747. Magoo's Masquerade (8/15/57) Technicolor/Scope—7 mins. *DIR:* Rudy Larriva. *PRO:* Stephen Bosustow. A Mr. Magoo UPA cartoon.

2748. Magoo's Masterpiece (7/30/53) Technicolor—7 mins. *DIR:* Pete Burness. *PRO:* Stephen Bosustow. A Mr. Magoo UPA cartoon.

2749. Magoo's Moose Hunt (11/28/57) Technicolor—7 mins. *DIR:* Robert Cannon. *PRO:* Stephen Bosustow. A Mr. Magoo UPA cartoon.

2750. Magoo's Private War (12/19/57) Technicolor—7 mins. *DIR:* Rudy Larriva. *PRO:* Stephen Bosustow. A Mr. Magoo UPA cartoon.

2751. Magoo's Problem Child (10/18/56) Technicolor/Scope—7 mins. *DIR:* Pete Burness. *PRO:* Stephen Bosustow. A Mr. Magoo UPA cartoon.

2752. Magoo's Puddle Jumper (7/26/56) Technicolor/Scope—7 mins. *DIR:* Pete Burness. *PRO:* Stephen Bosustow. A Mr. Magoo UPA cartoon.

2753. Magoo's Three-Point Landing (6/5/58) Technicolor—7 mins. *DIR:* Pete Burness. *PRO:* Stephen Bosustow. A Mr. Magoo UPA cartoon.

2754. Magoo's Young Manhood (3/13/58) Technicolor—7 mins. *DIR:* Pete Burness. *PRO:* Stephen Bosustow. A Mr. Magoo UPA cartoon.

2755. Major Google (5/24/36) Technicolor—7 mins. *PRO:* Charles Mintz. A Barney Google cartoon.

2756. The Make-Believe Revue (3/22/35) Technicolor—7 mins. *PRO:* Charles Mintz. A Color Rhapsodies cartoon.

2757. Malice in Slumberland (11/20/42) B&W—7 mins. *DIR:* Alec Geiss. A Phantasies cartoon.

2758. Man of Tin (2/23/40) B&W—7 mins. *DIR:* Sid Marcus, Art Davis. *PRO:* Charles Mintz. A Phantasies cartoon featuring Scrappy.

2759. The Man on the Flying Trapeze (4/8/54) Technicolor—7 mins. *DIR:* Ted Parmelee. *PRO:*

Stephen Bosustow. A UPA cartoon Special.

2760. The Masque Raid (6/25/37) B&W—7 mins. *DIR:* Ben Harrison, Manny Gould. *PRO:* Charles Mintz. A Krazy Kat cartoon.

2761. The Masquerade Party (5/11/34) B&W—7 mins. *DIR:* Ben Harrison, Manny Gould. *PRO:* Charles Mintz. A Krazy Kat cartoon.

2762. Mass Mouse Meeting (6/25/43) B&W—7 mins. *DIR:* Alec Geiss. A Phantasies cartoon.

2763. Matador Magoo (3/30/57) Technicolor/Scope—7 mins. *DIR:* Pete Burness. *PRO:* Stephen Bosustow. A Mr. Magoo UPA cartoon.

2764. The Match Kid (5/9/33) B&W—7 mins. *DIR:* Dick Huemer. *PRO:* Charles Mintz. A Scrappy cartoon.

2765. The Medicine Show (2/7/32) B&W—7 mins. *DIR:* Ben Harrison, Manny Gould. *PRO:* Charles Mintz. A Krazy Kat cartoon.

2766. Meet Mother Magoo (12/27/56) Technicolor/Scope—7 mins. *DIR:* Pete Burness. *PRO:* Stephen Bosustow. A Mr. Magoo UPA cartoon.

2767. Merry Cafe (12/26/36) B&W—7 mins. *DIR:* Ben Harrison, Manny Gould. *PRO:* Charles Mintz. A Krazy Kat cartoon.

2768. The Merry Dwarfs (12/1/29) B&W—7 mins. *DIR:* DIR/PRO: Walt Disney. A Silly Symphonies cartoon.

2769. Merry Mannequins (3/19/37) Technicolor—7 mins. *DIR:* Ub Iwerks. *PRO:* Charles Mintz. A Color Rhapsodies cartoon.

2770. Merry Minstrel Magoo (4/9/59) Technicolor—7 mins. *DIR:*

Rudy Larriva. *PRO:* Stephen Bosustow. A Mr. Magoo UPA cartoon.

2771. Merry Mouse Cafe (8/15/41) B&W—7 mins. A Phantasies cartoon.

2772. Merry Mutineers (10/2/36) Technicolor—7 mins. *PRO:* Charles Mintz. A Color Rhapsodies cartoon.

2773. Mickey Cuts Up (11/25/31) B&W—7 mins. *DIR:* Burt Gillett. *PRO:* Walt Disney. A Mickey Mouse cartoon.

2774. Mickey in Arabia (7/20/32) B&W—7 mins. *DIR:* Wilfred Jackson. *PRO:* Walt Disney. A Mickey Mouse cartoon.

2775. Mickey Steps Out (7/10/31) B&W—7 mins. *DIR:* Burt Gillett. *PRO:* Walt Disney. A Mickey Mouse cartoon.

2776. Mickey's Choo-Choo (10/1/29) B&W—7 mins. *DIR/PRO:* Walt Disney. A Mickey Mouse cartoon.

2777. Mickey's Follies (8/28/29) B&W—7 mins. *DIR/PRO:* Walt Disney. A Mickey Mouse cartoon.

2778. Mickey's Orphans (12/5/31) B&W—7 mins. *DIR:* Burt Gillett. *PRO:* Walt Disney. A Mickey Mouse cartoon.

2779. Mickey's Revue (5/12/32) B&W—7 mins. *DIR:* Wilfred Jackson. *PRO:* Walt Disney. A Mickey Mouse cartoon.

2780. Midnight Frolics (11/24/38) Technicolor—7 mins. *DIR:* Ub Iwerks. *PRO:* Charles Mintz. A Color Rhapsodies cartoon.

Midnight in a Toy Shop *see* **Midnite in a Toy Shop**

2781. Midnite in a Toy Shop (7/28/30) B&W—7 mins. *DIR:* Wilfred

Jackson. *PRO:* Walt Disney. A Silly Symphonies cartoon.

2782. Millionaire Hobo (11/24/39) B&W—7 mins. *DIR:* Sid Marcus, Art Davis. *PRO:* Charles Mintz. A Phantasies cartoon featuring Scrappy.

2783. Minding the Baby (11/16/31) B&W—7 mins. *DIR:* Dick Huemer. *PRO:* Charles Mintz. A Scrappy cartoon.

2784. The Miner's Daughter (5/25/50) Technicolor—7 mins. *DIR:* Robert Cannon. *PRO:* Stephen Bosustow. A Jolly Frolics UPA cartoon.

2785. The Minstrel Show (11/21/32) B&W—7 mins. *DIR:* Ben Harrison, Manny Gould. *PRO:* Charles Mintz. A Krazy Kat cartoon.

2786. Mr. Elephant Goes to Town (10/4/40) Technicolor—7 mins. *DIR:* Art Davis. A Color Rhapsodies cartoon.

2787. Mr. Fore by Fore (7/7/44) B&W—7 mins. *DIR:* Howard Swift. A Phantasies cartoon.

2788. Mr. Moocher (9/8/44) Technicolor—7 mins. *DIR:* Bob Wickersham. A Fox and the Crow cartoon.

2789. Monkey Love (9/12/35) Technicolor—7 mins. *PRO:* Charles Mintz. A Color Rhapsodies cartoon.

2790. Monkey Melodies (9/2/30) B&W—7 mins. *DIR:* Burt Gillett. *PRO:* Walt Disney. A Silly Symphonies cartoon.

2791. The Moose Hunt (4/30/31) B&W—7 mins. *DIR:* Burt Gillett. *PRO:* Walt Disney. A Mickey Mouse cartoon.

2792. Mother Goose in Swingtime (12/18/39) Technicolor—7 mins. *DIR:* Manny Gould. *PRO:* Charles Mintz. A Color Rhapsodies cartoon.

2793. Mother Goose Melodies (4/11/31) B&W—7 mins. *DIR:* Burt Gillett. *PRO:* Walt Disney. A Silly Symphonies cartoon.

2794. Mother Hen's Holiday (5/7/37) Technicolor—7 mins. *PRO:* Charles Mintz. A Color Rhapsodies cartoon.

2795. Mother Hubba-Hubba Hubbard (5/29/47) Technicolor—7 mins. *DIR:* Bob Wickersham. A Color Rhapsodies cartoon.

2796. Mountain Ears (11/3/39) Technicolor—7 mins. *DIR:* Manny Gould. *PRO:* Charles Mintz. A Color Rhapsodies cartoon.

2797. The Mouse Exterminator (1/26/40) B&W—7 mins. A Phantasies cartoon featuring Krazy Kat.

2798. Mouse Meets Lion (10/25/40) B&W—7 mins. A Fables cartoon.

2799. Movie Struck (9/8/33) B&W—7 mins. *DIR:* Dick Huemer. *PRO:* Charles Mintz. A Scrappy cartoon.

2800. Musical Farmer (6/8/32) B&W—7 mins. *DIR:* Wilfred Jackson. *PRO:* Walt Disney. A Mickey Mouse cartoon.

2801. Mutt 'N Bones (8/25/44) B&W—7 mins. *DIR:* Paul Sommer. A Phantasies cartoon.

2802. Mysto Fox (8/29/46) Technicolor—7 mins. *DIR:* Bob Wickersham. A Fox and the Crow cartoon.

2803. Neighbors (8/15/35) Technicolor—7 mins. *PRO:* Charles Mintz. A Color Rhapsodies cartoon.

2804. Nell's Yells (6/30/39) Technicolor—7 mins. *DIR:* Ub Iwerks. *PRO:* Charles Mintz. A Color Rhapsodies cartoon.

2805. **The New Homestead** (1/ 7/38) B&W—7 mins. *DIR*: Sid Marcus, Art Davis. *PRO*: Charles Mintz. A Scrappy cartoon.

2806. **News Oddities** (7/19/40) B&W—7 mins. A Phantasies cartoon.

2807. **No Biz Like Shoe Biz** (9/ 8/60) Technicolor—7 mins. *DIR/ PRO*: William Hanna, Joseph Barbera. A Loopy de Loop cartoon.

2808. **Not in Nottingham** (9/5/ 63) Technicolor—7 mins. *DIR/PRO*: William Hanna, Joseph Barbera. A Loopy de Loop cartoon.

2809. **The Novelty Shop** (8/15/ 36) Technicolor—7 mins. *PRO*: Charles Mintz. A Color Rhapsodies cartoon.

2810. **Nursery Crimes** (10/8/43) B&W—7 mins. *DIR*: Alec Geiss. A Phantasies cartoon.

2811. **Old Blackout Joe** (8/27/42) B&W—7 mins. *DIR*: Paul Sommer. A Phantasies cartoon.

2812. **An Old Flame** (4/24/30) B&W—7 mins. *DIR*: Ben Harrison, Manny Gould. *PRO*: Charles Mintz. A Krazy Kat cartoon.

2813. **The Oompahs** (1/24/52) Technicolor—7 mins. *DIR*: Pete Burness. *PRO*: Stephen Bosustow. A Jolly Frolics UPA cartoon.

2814. **The Opry House** (3/20/29) B&W—7 mins. *DIR/PRO*: Walt Disney. A Mickey Mouse cartoon.

2815. **Out of the Ether** (9/5/33) B&W—7 mins. *DIR*: Ben Harrison, Manny Gould. *PRO*: Charles Mintz. A Krazy Kat cartoon.

2816. **The Paper Hanger** (6/21/ 32) B&W—7 mins. *PRO*: Charles Mintz. A Krazy Kat cartoon.

2817. **Park Your Baby** (12/22/39) B&W—7 mins. *DIR*: Sid Marcus, Art Davis. *PRO*: Charles Mintz. A Fables cartoon featuring Scrappy.

2818. **Patch Mah Britches** (12/ 19/35) Technicolor—7 mins. *PRO*: Charles Mintz. A Barney Google cartoon.

2819. **Paunch 'N' Judy** (12/13/40) B&W—7 mins. *DIR*: Ben Harrison. A Fables cartoon.

2820. **The Peace Conference** (4/26/35) B&W—7 mins. *DIR*: Ben Harrison, Manny Gould. *PRO*: Charles Mintz. A Krazy Kat cartoon.

2821. **Peaceful Neighbors** (1/26/ 39) Technicolor—7 mins. *DIR*: Sid Marcus. *PRO*: Charles Mintz. A Color Rhapsodies cartoon.

2822. **A Peekoolyr Sitcheeayshun** (8/11/44) Technicolor—7 mins. *DIR*: Sid Marcus. *PRO*: Charles Mintz. A Li'l Abner cartoon.

2823. **A Peep in the Deep** (8/23/ 40) B&W—7 mins. *DIR*: Sid Marcus, Art Davis. *PRO*: Charles Mintz. A Fables cartoon featuring Scrappy.

2824. **The Pet Shop** (4/28/32) B&W—7 mins. *DIR*: Dick Huemer. *PRO*: Charles Mintz. A Scrappy cartoon.

2825. **Pete Hothead** (9/25/52) Technicolor—7 mins. *DIR*: Ted Parmelee. *PRO*: Stephen Bosustow. A Jolly Frolics UPA cartoon featuring Pete Hothead.

2826. **Phoney Baloney** (9/13/45) Technicolor—7 mins. *DIR*: Bob Wickersham. A Fox and the Crow cartoon.

2827. **Piano Mover** (1/4/32) B&W—7 mins. *DIR*: Ben Harrison, Manny Gould. *PRO*: Charles Mintz. A Krazy Kat cartoon.

2828. **Pickled Puss** (9/2/48) Technicolor—7 mins. *DIR*: Howard Swift. A Color Rhapsodies cartoon.

2829. **The Picnic** (10/9/30) B&W—7 mins. *DIR:* Burt Gillett. *PRO:* Walt Disney. A Mickey Mouse cartoon.

2830. **Picnic Panic** (6/20/46) Technicolor—7 mins. *DIR:* Bob Wickersham. A Color Rhapsodies cartoon.

2831. **Picnics Are Fun and Dino's Serenade** (1/16/59) Technicolor—7 mins. *DIR:* Lew Keller. *PRO:* Stephen Bosustow. A Ham and Hattie UPA cartoon.

2832. **Pink and Blue Blues** (8/28/52) Technicolor—7 mins. *DIR:* Pete Burness. *PRO:* Stephen Bosustow. A Mr. Magoo UPA cartoon.

2833. **Pioneer Days** (11/20/30) B&W—7 mins. *DIR:* Burt Gillett. *PRO:* Walt Disney. A Mickey Mouse cartoon.

2834. **Plane Crazy** (5/15/28) B&W—7 mins. *DIR/PRO:* Walt Disney. A Mickey Mouse cartoon.

2835. **Playful Pan** (12/16/30) B&W—7 mins. *DIR:* Burt Gillett. *PRO:* Walt Disney. A Silly Symphonies cartoon.

2836. **The Playful Pest** (12/3/43) B&W—7 mins. *DIR:* Paul Sommer. A Phantasies cartoon.

2837. **Playing Politics** (7/8/36) B&W—7 mins. *DIR:* Sid Marcus, Art Davis. *PRO:* Charles Mintz. A Scrappy cartoon.

2838. **Playing the Pied Piper** (8/8/41) B&W—7 mins. *DIR:* Lou Lilly. A Fables cartoon.

2839. **Plenty Below Zero** (5/14/43) Technicolor—7 mins. *DIR:* Bob Wickersham. A Color Rhapsodies cartoon featuring the Fox and the Crow.

2840. **The Plow Boy** (6/28/29) B&W—7 mins. *DIR/PRO:* Walt Disney. A Mickey Mouse cartoon.

2841. **Polar Playmates** (4/25/46) Technicolor—7 mins. *DIR:* Howard Swift. A Color Rhapsodies cartoon.

2842. **Polly Wants a Doctor** (1/6/44) B&W—7 mins. *DIR:* Howard Swift. A Phantasies cartoon.

2843. **Pooch Parade** (7/19/40) B&W—7 mins. *DIR:* Sid Marcus, Art Davis. *PRO:* Charles Mintz. A Fables cartoon featuring Scrappy.

2844. **Poor Elmer** (7/22/38) Technicolor—7 mins. *DIR:* Sid Marcus. *PRO:* Charles Mintz. A Color Rhapsodies cartoon.

2845. **Poor Little Butterfly** (7/4/38) Technicolor—7 mins. *DIR:* Ben Harrison. *PRO:* Charles Mintz. A Color Rhapsodies cartoon.

2846. **Popcorn Story** (11/30/50) Technicolor—7 mins. *DIR:* Art Babbitt. *PRO:* Stephen Bosustow. A Jolly Frolics UPA cartoon.

2847. **Pork Chop Phooey** (3/18/65) Technicolor—7 mins. *DIR/PRO:* William Hanna, Joseph Barbera. A Loopy de Loop cartoon.

2848. **Porkuliar Piggy** (10/13/44) Technicolor—7 mins. *DIR:* Bob Wickersham. *PRO:* Charles Mintz. A Li'l Abner cartoon.

2849. **Port Whines** (10/10/29) B&W—7 mins. *DIR:* Ben Harrison, Manny Gould. *PRO:* Charles Mintz. A Krazy Kat cartoon.

2850. **Practice Makes Perfect** (4/5/40) B&W—7 mins. *DIR:* Sid Marcus, Art Davis. *PRO:* Charles Mintz. A Fables cartoon featuring Scrappy.

2851. **Professor Small and Mister Tall** (3/26/43) Technicolor—7 mins. *DIR:* Paul Sommer, John Hubley. A Color Rhapsodies cartoon.

2852. **Prosperity Blues** (10/8/32) B&W—7 mins. *DIR:* Ben Harrison,

Manny Gould. *PRO:* Charles Mintz. A Krazy Kat cartoon.

2853. Punch de Leon (1/12/50) Technicolor—7 mins. *DIR:* John Hubley. *PRO:* Stephen Bosustow. A Jolly Frolics UPA cartoon featuring the Fox and the Crow.

2854. The Puppet Murder Case (6/21/35) B&W—7 mins. *DIR:* Sid Marcus, Art Davis. *PRO:* Charles Mintz. A Scrappy cartoon.

2855. Puttin' Out the Kitten (3/26/37) B&W—7 mins. *DIR:* Sid Marcus, Art Davis. *PRO:* Charles Mintz. A Scrappy cartoon.

2856. Raggedy Rug (1/2/64) Technicolor—7 mins. *DIR/PRO:* William Hanna, Joseph Barbera. A Loopy de Loop cartoon.

2857. The Ragtime Bear (9/8/49) Technicolor—7 mins. *DIR:* John Hubley. *PRO:* Stephen Bosustow. A Jolly Frolics UPA cartoon featuring Mr. Magoo.

2858. Railroad Rhythm (11/20/37) B&W—7 mins. *DIR:* Ben Harrison, Manny Gould. *PRO:* Charles Mintz. A Krazy Kat cartoon.

2859. Railroad Wretch (3/31/32) B&W—7 mins. *DIR:* Dick Huemer. *PRO:* Charles Mintz. A Scrappy cartoon.

2860. Rancid Ransom (11/15/62) Technicolor—7 mins. *DIR/PRO:* William Hanna, Joseph Barbera. A Loopy de Loop cartoon.

2861. Ratskin (8/15/29) B&W—7 mins. *DIR:* Ben Harrison, Manny Gould. *PRO:* Charles Mintz. A Krazy Kat cartoon.

2862. Red Riding Hood Rides Again (12/5/41) Technicolor—7 mins. *DIR:* Sid Marcus. A Color Rhapsodies cartoon.

2863. The Restless Sax (12/1/31) B&W—7 mins. *DIR:* Ben Harrison, Manny Gould. *PRO:* Charles Mintz. A Krazy Kat cartoon.

2864. Rippling Romance (6/21/45) Technicolor—7 mins. *DIR:* Bob Wickersham. A Color Rhapsodies cartoon.

2865. Rise of Duton Lang (12/1/55) Technicolor—7 mins. *DIR:* Osmond Evans. *PRO:* Stephen Bosustow. A UPA cartoon Special.

2866. Ritzy Hotel (5/9/32) B&W—7 mins. *DIR:* Ben Harrison, Manny Gould. *PRO:* Charles Mintz. A Krazy Kat cartoon.

2867. River Ribber (10/4/45) Technicolor—7 mins. *DIR:* Paul Sommer. A Color Rhapsodies cartoon featuring Professor Small and Mr. Tall.

2868. Robin Hoodlum (12/23/48) Technicolor—7 mins. *DIR:* John Hubley. A Fox and the Crow UPA cartoon.

2869. Rock Hound Magoo (10/24/57) Technicolor—7 mins. *DIR:* Pete Burness. *PRO:* Stephen Bosustow. A Mr. Magoo UPA cartoon.

2870. The Rocky Road to Ruin (9/16/43) Technicolor—7 mins. *DIR:* Paul Sommer. A Color Rhapsodies cartoon.

2871. Rodeo Dough (2/13/31) B&W—7 mins. *DIR:* Ben Harrison, Manny Gould. *PRO:* Charles Mintz. A Krazy Kat cartoon.

2872. Room and Bored (9/30/43) Technicolor—7 mins. *DIR:* Bob Wickersham. A Fox and the Crow cartoon.

2873. Rooty Toot Toot (3/27/52) Technicolor—7 mins. *DIR:* John Hubley. *PRO:* Stephen Bosustow. A Jolly Frolics UPA cartoon.

2874. **Russian Dressing** (5/1/33) B&W—7 mins. *DIR*: Ben Harrison, Manny Gould. *PRO*: Charles Mintz. A Krazy Kat cartoon.

2875. **Sad Little Guinea Pigs** (2/22/38) B&W—7 mins. *DIR*: Ben Harrison, Manny Gould. *PRO*: Charles Mintz. A Krazy Kat cartoon.

2876. **Sadie Hawkins Day** (5/4/44) Technicolor—7 mins. *DIR*: Bob Wickersham. *PRO*: Charles Mintz. A Li'l Abner cartoon.

2877. **Safety Spin** (5/21/53) Technicolor—7 mins. *DIR*: Pete Burness. *PRO*: Stephen Bosustow. A Mr. Magoo UPA cartoon.

2878. **Sailing and Village Sand** (2/27/58) Technicolor—7 mins. *DIR*: Lew Keller. *PRO*: Stephen Bosustow. A Ham and Hattie UPA cartoon.

2879. **Sandman Tales** (10/6/33) B&W—7 mins. *DIR*: Dick Huemer. *PRO*: Charles Mintz. A Scrappy cartoon.

2880. **Sassy Cats** (1/25/33) B&W—7 mins. *DIR*: Dick Huemer. *PRO*: Charles Mintz. A Scrappy cartoon.

2881. **Scary Crows** (8/20/37) Technicolor—7 mins. *PRO*: Charles Mintz. A Color Rhapsodies cartoon.

2882. **Schoolboy Dreams** (9/24/40) B&W—7 mins. *DIR*: Sid Marcus, Art Davis. *PRO*: Charles Mintz. A Phantasies cartoon featuring Scrappy.

2883. **The Schooner the Better** (7/4/46) B&W—7 mins. *DIR*: Howard Swift. A Phantasies cartoon.

2884. **Scoutmaster Magoo** (4/10/58) Technicolor—7 mins. *DIR*: Robert Cannon. *PRO*: Stephen Bosustow. A Mr. Magoo UPA cartoon.

2885. **Scrappy's Added Attraction** (1/13/39) B&W—7 mins. *DIR*: Sid Marcus, Art Davis. *PRO*: Charles Mintz. A Scrappy cartoon.

2886. **Scrappy's Art Gallery** (1/12/34) B&W—7 mins. *DIR*: Sid Marcus, Art Davis. *PRO*: Charles Mintz. A Scrappy cartoon.

2887. **Scrappy's Band Concert** (4/29/37) B&W—7 mins. *DIR*: Sid Marcus, Art Davis. *PRO*: Charles Mintz. A Scrappy cartoon.

2888. **Scrappy's Big Moment** (7/28/35) B&W—7 mins. *DIR*: Sid Marcus, Art Davis. *PRO*: Charles Mintz. A Scrappy cartoon.

2889. **Scrappy's Boy Scouts** (1/2/36) B&W—7 mins. *DIR*: Sid Marcus, Art Davis. *PRO*: Charles Mintz. A Scrappy cartoon.

2890. **Scrappy's Camera Troubles** (6/5/36) B&W—7 mins. *DIR*: Sid Marcus, Art Davis. *PRO*: Charles Mintz. A Scrappy cartoon.

2891. **Scrappy's Dog Show** (5/18/34) B&W—7 mins. *DIR*: Sid Marcus, Art Davis. *PRO*: Charles Mintz. A Scrappy cartoon.

2892. **Scrappy's Expedition** (8/27/34) B&W—7 mins. *DIR*: Sid Marcus, Art Davis. *PRO*: Charles Mintz. A Scrappy cartoon.

2893. **Scrappy's Ghost Story** (5/24/35) B&W—7 mins. *DIR*: Sid Marcus, Art Davis. *PRO*: Charles Mintz. A Scrappy cartoon.

2894. **Scrappy's Music Lesson** (6/4/37) B&W—7 mins. *DIR*: Sid Marcus, Art Davis. *PRO*: Charles Mintz. A Scrappy cartoon.

2895. **Scrappy's News Flashes** (12/8/37) B&W—7 mins. *DIR*: Sid Marcus, Art Davis. *PRO*: Charles Mintz. A Scrappy cartoon.

2896. **Scrappy's Party** (11/13/33) B&W—7 mins. *DIR*: Dick Huemer.

PRO: Charles Mintz. A Scrappy cartoon.

2897. Scrappy's Playmates (3/27/38) B&W — 7 mins. DIR: Sid Marcus, Art Davis. PRO: Charles Mintz. A Scrappy cartoon.

2898. Scrappy's Pony (2/27/36) B&W — 7 mins. DIR: Sid Marcus, Art Davis. PRO: Charles Mintz. A Scrappy cartoon.

2899. Scrappy's Relay Race (7/7/34) B&W — 7 mins. DIR: Sid Marcus, Art Davis. PRO: Charles Mintz. A Scrappy cartoon.

2900. Scrappy's Rodeo (6/2/39) B&W — 7 mins. DIR: Sid Marcus, Art Davis. PRO: Charles Mintz. A Scrappy cartoon.

2901. Scrappy's Side Show (3/3/39) B&W — 7 mins. DIR: Sid Marcus, Art Davis. PRO: Charles Mintz. A Scrappy cartoon.

2902. Scrappy's Television (1/29/34) B&W — 7 mins. DIR: Sid Marcus, Art Davis. PRO: Charles Mintz. A Scrappy cartoon.

2903. Scrappy's Theme Song (6/15/34) B&W — 7 mins. DIR: Sid Marcus, Art Davis. PRO: Charles Mintz. A Scrappy cartoon.

2904. Scrappy's Toy Shop (4/13/34) B&W — 7 mins. DIR: Sid Marcus, Art Davis. PRO: Charles Mintz. A Scrappy cartoon.

2905. Scrappy's Trailer (8/29/35) B&W — 7 mins. DIR: Sid Marcus, Art Davis. PRO: Charles Mintz. A Scrappy cartoon.

2906. Scrappy's Trip to Mars (2/4/38) B&W — 7 mins. DIR: Sid Marcus, Art Davis. PRO: Charles Mintz. A Scrappy cartoon.

2907. Seeing Stars (9/12/32) B&W — 7 mins. DIR: Ben Harrison, Manny Gould. PRO: Charles Mintz. A Krazy Kat cartoon.

2908. Sheep Stealers Anonymous (6/13/63) Technicolor — 7 mins. DIR/PRO: William Hanna, Joseph Barbera. A Loopy de Loop cartoon.

2909. The Shindig (7/11/30) B&W — 7 mins. DIR: Burt Gillett. PRO: Walt Disney. A Mickey Mouse cartoon.

2910. The Shoemaker and the Elves (1/20/35) Technicolor — 7 mins. PRO: Charles Mintz. A Color Rhapsodies cartoon.

2911. Short Snorts on Sports (6/3/48) Technicolor — 7 mins. DIR: Alex Lovy. A Phantasies cartoon.

2912. Show Time (11/30/32) B&W — 7 mins. DIR: Ben Harrison, Manny Gould. PRO: Charles Mintz. A Krazy Kat cartoon.

2913. Showing Off (11/11/31) B&W — 7 mins. DIR: Dick Huemer. PRO: Charles Mintz. A Scrappy cartoon.

2914. Showtime (4/14/38) Technicolor — 7 mins. DIR: Ub Iwerks. PRO: Charles Mintz. A Color Rhapsodies cartoon.

2915. Silent Tweetment (9/19/46) Technicolor — 7 mins. DIR: Bob Wickersham. A Color Rhapsodies cartoon featuring Flippy.

2916. Simple Siren (9/20/45) B&W — 7 mins. DIR: Paul Sommer. A Phantasies cartoon.

2917. The Skeleton Dance (5/10/29) B&W — 7 mins. DIR/PRO: Walt Disney. A Silly Symphonies cartoon.

2918. Skeleton Frolic (1/29/37) Technicolor — 7 mins. DIR: Ub Iwerks. PRO: Charles Mintz. A Color Rhapsodies cartoon.

2919. **Slay It with Flowers** (1/8/43) Technicolor—7 mins. *DIR:* Bob Wickersham. A Color Rhapsodies cartoon featuring the Fox and the Crow.

2920. **Slippery Slippers** (9/7/62) Technicolor—7 mins. *DIR/PRO:* William Hanna, Joseph Barbera. A Loopy de Loop cartoon.

2921. **Sloppy Jalopy** (2/21/52) Technicolor—7 mins. *DIR:* Pete Burness. *PRO:* Stephen Bosustow. A Mr. Magoo UPA cartoon.

2922. **Slow Beau** (2/27/30) B&W—7 mins. *DIR:* Ben Harrison, Manny Gould. *PRO:* Charles Mintz. A Krazy Kat cartoon.

2923. **Snap Happy Traps** (6/6/46) B&W—7 mins. *DIR:* Bob Wickersham. A Phantasies cartoon.

2924. **Snoopy Loopy** (6/16/60) Technicolor—7 mins. *DIR/PRO:* William Hanna, Joseph Barbera. A Loopy de Loop cartoon.

2925. **Soda Poppa** (5/29/31) B&W—7 mins. *DIR:* Ben Harrison, Manny Gould. *PRO:* Charles Mintz. A Krazy Kat cartoon.

2926. **Soldier Old Man** (4/2/32) B&W—7 mins. *DIR:* Ben Harrison, Manny Gould. *PRO:* Charles Mintz. A Krazy Kat cartoon.

2927. **Sole Mates** (11/7/29) B&W—7 mins. *DIR:* Ben Harrison, Manny Gould. *PRO:* Charles Mintz. A Krazy Kat cartoon.

2928. **Song of Victory** (9/4/42) Technicolor—7 mins. *DIR:* Bob Wickersham. A Color Rhapsodies cartoon.

2929. **Southern Exposure** (2/5/34) B&W—7 mins. *DIR:* Ben Harrison, Manny Gould. *PRO:* Charles Mintz. A Krazy Kat cartoon.

2930. **Spare the Child** (1/27/55) Technicolor—7 mins. *DIR:* Abe Liss.

PRO: Stephen Bosustow. A UPA cartoon Special.

2931. **Spark Plug** (4/12/36) Technicolor—7 mins. *PRO:* Charles Mintz. A Barney Google cartoon.

2932. **Spellbound Hound** (3/16/50) Technicolor—7 mins. *DIR:* John Hubley. *PRO:* Stephen Bosustow. A Mr. Magoo UPA cartoon.

2933. **The Spider and the Fly** (10/13/31) B&W—7 mins. *DIR:* Wilfred Jackson. *PRO:* Walt Disney. A Silly Symphonies cartoon.

2934. **Spook Easy** (1/30/30) B&W—7 mins. *DIR:* Ben Harrison, Manny Gould. *PRO:* Charles Mintz. A Krazy Kat cartoon.

2935. **Spring and Saganaki** (10/16/58) Technicolor—7 mins. *DIR:* Lew Keller. *PRO:* Stephen Bosustow. A Ham and Hattie UPA cartoon.

2936. **Spring Festival** (8/6/37) Technicolor—7 mins. *PRO:* Charles Mintz. A Color Rhapsodies cartoon.

2937. **Springtime** (10/4/29) B&W—7 mins. *DIR:* Ub Iwerks. *PRO:* Walt Disney. A Silly Symphonies cartoon.

2938. **Stage Door Magoo** (10/6/55) Technicolor—7 mins. *DIR:* Pete Burness. *PRO:* Stephen Bosustow. A Mr. Magoo UPA cartoon.

2939. **Stage Krazy** (11/13/33) B&W—7 mins. *DIR:* Ben Harrison, Manny Gould. *PRO:* Charles Mintz. A Krazy Kat cartoon.

2940. **Steamboat Willie** (7/29/28) B&W—7 mins. *DIR/PRO:* Walt Disney. A Mickey Mouse cartoon.

2941. **Stepping Stones** (5/17/32) B&W—7 mins. *DIR:* Dick Huemer. *PRO:* Charles Mintz. A Scrappy cartoon.

2942. The Stork Market (7/11/31) B&W—7 mins. *DIR:* Ben Harrison, Manny Gould. *PRO:* Charles Mintz. A Krazy Kat cartoon.

2943. The Stork Takes a Holiday (6/11/37) Technicolor—7 mins. *PRO:* Charles Mintz. A Color Rhapsodies cartoon.

2944. The Streamlined Donkey (1/17/41) B&W—7 mins. *DIR:* Sid Marcus. A Fables cartoon.

2945. Summer (1/4/30) B&W—7 mins. *DIR:* Ub Iwerks. *PRO:* Walt Disney. A Silly Symphonies cartoon.

2946. Sunday Clothes (9/15/31) B&W—7 mins. *DIR:* Dick Huemer. *PRO:* Charles Mintz. A Scrappy cartoon.

2947. Svengarlic (8/3/31) B&W—7 mins. *DIR:* Ben Harrison, Manny Gould. *PRO:* Charles Mintz. A Krazy Kat cartoon.

2948. Swash Buckled (4/5/62) Technicolor—7 mins. *DIR/PRO:* William Hanna, Joseph Barbera. A Loopy de Loop cartoon.

2949. Swing Monkey Swing (9/10/37) Technicolor—7 mins. *PRO:* Charles Mintz. A Color Rhapsodies cartoon.

2950. Swiss Movements (4/4/31) B&W—7 mins. *DIR:* Ben Harrison, Manny Gould. *PRO:* Charles Mintz. A Krazy Kat cartoon.

2951. Swiss Tease (9/11/47) Technicolor—7 mins. *DIR:* Sid Marcus. A Color Rhapsodies cartoon.

2952. Taken for a Ride (1/31) B&W—7 mins. *DIR:* Ben Harrison, Manny Gould. *PRO:* Charles Mintz. A Krazy Kat cartoon.

2953. Tale of a Wolf (3/3/60) Technicolor—7 mins. *DIR/PRO:* William Hanna, Joseph Barbera. A Loopy de Loop cartoon.

2954. The Tangled Angler (12/26/41) B&W—7 mins. *DIR:* Frank Tashlin. A Fables cartoon.

2955. Tangled Television (8/30/40) Technicolor—7 mins. *DIR:* Sid Marcus. A Color Rhapsodies cartoon.

2956. Tangled Travels (6/9/44) B&W—7 mins. *DIR:* Alec Geiss. A Phantasies cartoon.

2957. Technoracket (5/20/33) B&W—7 mins. *DIR:* Dick Huemer. *PRO:* Charles Mintz. A Scrappy cartoon.

2958. The Tell-Tale Heart (1/54) Technicolor/3-D—7 mins. *DIR:* Ted Parmelee. *PRO:* Stephen Bosustow. A UPA cartoon Special based on the Edgar Allen Poe story. Narrated by James Mason. *NOTES:* Sources quote this cartoon as being released in both flat and 3-D versions. It was released on the same bill with *Drums of Tahiti.*

Terrible Toreador, El *see* **El Terrible Toreador**

2959. Terror Faces Magoo (7/9/59) Technicolor—7 mins. *DIR:* Chris Ishii. *PRO:* Stephen Bosustow. A Mr. Magoo UPA cartoon.

2960. Tetched in the Head (10/24/35) Technicolor—7 mins. *PRO:* Charles Mintz. A Barney Google cartoon.

2961. There's Music in Your Hair (3/28/41) B&W—7 mins. A Phantasies cartoon.

2962. There's Something About a Soldier (2/26/43) Technicolor—7 mins. *DIR:* Alec Geiss. A Color Rhapsodies cartoon.

2963. This Changing World—Broken Treaties (1941) B&W—7

mins. *DIR*: Paul Fennell. A Cartoon Films Ltd. Special.

2964. This Changing World – How War Came (1941) B&W – 7 mins. *DIR*: Paul Fennell. A Cartoon Films Ltd. Special.

2965. This Changing World – The Carpenters (1941) B&W – 7 mins. *DIR*: Paul Fennell. A Cartoon Films Ltd. Special.

2966. This Is My Ducky Day (5/4/61) Technicolor – 7 mins. *DIR/PRO*: William Hanna, Joseph Barbera. A Loopy de Loop cartoon.

2967. The Timid Pup (8/1/40) Technicolor – 7 mins. *DIR*: Ben Harrison. A Color Rhapsodies cartoon.

2968. Tito's Guitar (10/30/42) Technicolor – 7 mins. *DIR*: Bob Wickersham. A Color Rhapsodies cartoon featuring Tito.

2969. Toll Bridge Troubles (11/27/42) Technicolor – 7 mins. *DIR*: Bob Wickersham. A Color Rhapsodies cartoon featuring the Fox and the Crow.

2970. Tom Thumb (2/16/34) B&W – 7 mins. *DIR*: Ben Harrison, Manny Gould. *PRO*: Charles Mintz. A Krazy Kat cartoon.

2971. Tom Thumb's Brother (6/12/41) Technicolor – 7 mins. *DIR*: Sid Marcus. A Color Rhapsodies cartoon.

2972. Tooth or Consequences (6/5/47) Technicolor – 7 mins. *DIR*: Howard Swift. A Phantasies cartoon.

2973. Topsy Turkey (2/5/48) Technicolor – 7 mins. *DIR*: Sid Marcus. A Phantasies cartoon.

2974. Traffic Troubles (3/7/31) B&W – 7 mins. *DIR*: Burt Gillett. *PRO*: Walt Disney. A Mickey Mouse cartoon.

2975. Trailblazer Magoo (9/13/56) Technicolor/Scope – 7 mins. *DIR*: Pete Burness. *PRO*: Stephen Bosustow. A Mr. Magoo UPA cartoon.

2976. The Trapeze Artist (9/1/34) B&W – 7 mins. *DIR*: Ben Harrison, Manny Gould. *PRO*: Charles Mintz. A Krazy Kat cartoon.

2977. Treasure Hunt (2/25/32) B&W – 7 mins. *DIR*: Dick Huemer. *PRO*: Charles Mintz. A Scrappy cartoon.

2978. Treasure Jest (8/30/45) Technicolor – 7 mins. *DIR*: Howard Swift. A Fox and the Crow cartoon.

2979. Tree for Two (6/21/43) Technicolor – 7 mins. *DIR*: Bob Wickersham. A Color Rhapsodies cartoon featuring the Fox and the Crow.

2980. Trees and Jamaica Daddy (1/30/58) Technicolor – 7 mins. *DIR*: Lew Keller. *PRO*: Stephen Bosustow. A Ham and Hattie UPA cartoon.

2981. Trouble Bruin (9/17/64) Technicolor – 7 mins. *DIR/PRO*: William Hanna, Joseph Barbera. A Loopy de Loop cartoon.

2982. Trouble Indemnity (9/14/50) Technicolor – 7 mins. *DIR*: Pete Burness. *PRO*: Stephen Bosustow. A Mr. Magoo UPA cartoon.

2983. Two Faced Wolf (4/6/61) Technicolor – 7 mins. *DIR/PRO*: William Hanna, Joseph Barbera. A Loopy de Loop cartoon.

2984. Two Lazy Crows (11/26/36) Technicolor – 7 mins. *PRO*: Charles Mintz. A Color Rhapsodies cartoon.

2985. The Ugly Duckling (12/12/31) B&W – 7 mins. *DIR*: Wilfred Jackson. *PRO*: Walt Disney. A Silly Symphonies cartoon.

2986. **Uncultured Vulture** (2/6/47) Technicolor—7 mins. *DIR:* Bob Wickersham. A Phantasies cartoon.

2987. **Under the Shedding Chestnut Tree** (2/22/42) B&W—7 mins. *DIR:* Bob Wickersham. A Fables cartoon.

2988. **A Unicorn in the Garden** (9/24/53) Technicolor—7 mins. *DIR:* William Hurtz. *PRO:* Stephen Bosustow. A UPA cartoon Special based on the James Thurber story.

2989. **Unsure Runts** (5/16/46) Technicolor—7 mins. *DIR:* Howard Swift. A Fox and the Crow cartoon.

2990. **Untrained Seal** (7/26/36) Technicolor—7 mins. *PRO:* Charles Mintz. A Color Rhapsodies cartoon.

2991. **Up 'N Atom** (7/10/47) Technicolor—7 mins. *DIR:* Sid Marcus. A Color Rhapsodies cartoon.

2992. **The Vitamin G-Man** (1/22/43) B&W—7 mins. *DIR:* Paul Sommer, John Hubley. A Phantasies cartoon.

2993. **Wacky Quacky** (3/20/47) Technicolor—7 mins. *DIR:* Alex Lovy. A Phantasies cartoon.

2994. **Wacky Wigwams** (2/22/42) Technicolor—7 mins. *DIR:* Alec Geiss. A Color Rhapsodies cartoon.

2995. **The Wallflower** (7/3/41) B&W—7 mins. A Phantasies cartoon.

2996. **Watcha Watchin'** (4/18/63) Technicolor—7 mins. *DIR/PRO:* William Hanna, Joseph Barbera. A Loopy de Loop cartoon.

2997. **Way Down Yonder in the Corn** (11/25/43) Technicolor—7 mins. *DIR:* Bob Wickersham. A Fox and the Crow cartoon.

2998. **Way of All Pests** (2/28/41) Technicolor—7 mins. *DIR:* Art Davis. A Color Rhapsodies cartoon.

2999. **Wedding Bells** (1/10/33) B&W—7 mins. *DIR:* Ben Harrison, Manny Gould. *PRO:* Charles Mintz. A Krazy Kat cartoon.

3000. **The Weenie Roast** (9/14/31) B&W—7 mins. *DIR:* Ben Harrison, Manny Gould. *PRO:* Charles Mintz. A Krazy Kat cartoon.

3001. **Whacks Museum** (9/29/33) B&W—7 mins. *DIR:* Ben Harrison, Manny Gould. *PRO:* Charles Mintz. A Krazy Kat cartoon.

3002. **What a Knight** (3/14/32) B&W—7 mins. *DIR:* Ben Harrison, Manny Gould. *PRO:* Charles Mintz. A Krazy Kat cartoon.

3003. **When Magoo Flew** (1/6/55) Technicolor—7 mins. *DIR:* Pete Burness. *PRO:* Stephen Bosustow. A Mr. Magoo UPA cartoon.

3004. **When the Cat's Away** (5/3/29) B&W—7 mins. *DIR/PRO:* Walt Disney. A Mickey Mouse cartoon.

3005. **Who's Zoo in Hollywood** (10/17/41) Technicolor—7 mins. *DIR:* Art Davis. A Color Rhapsodies cartoon.

3006. **Wild and Woozy West** (4/30/42) B&W—7 mins. *DIR:* Allen Rose. A Phantasies cartoon.

3007. **Wild Waves** (12/21/29) B&W—7 mins. *DIR:* Burt Gillett. *PRO:* Walt Disney. A Mickey Mouse cartoon.

3008. **Willie the Kid** (6/26/52) Technicolor—7 mins. *DIR:* Robert Cannon. *PRO:* Stephen Bosustow. A Jolly Frolics UPA cartoon.

3009. **Willoughby's Magic Hat** (4/30/43) B&W—7 mins. *DIR:* Bob Wickersham. A Phantasies cartoon featuring Willoughby Wren.

3010. **Window Shopping** (6/3/38) Technicolor—7 mins. *DIR:* Sid

Marcus. *PRO:* Charles Mintz. A Color Rhapsodies cartoon.

3011. Winter (10/22/30) B&W – 7 mins. *DIR:* Burt Gillett. *PRO:* Walt Disney. A Silly Symphonies cartoon.

3012. Wise Owl (12/6/40) Technicolor – 7 mins. *DIR:* Ub Iwerks. A Color Rhapsodies cartoon.

3013. The Wolf at the Door (12/29/32) B&W – 7 mins. *DIR:* Dick Huemer. *PRO:* Charles Mintz. A Scrappy cartoon.

3014. Wolf Chases Pig (4/20/42) B&W – 7 mins. *DIR:* Frank Tashlin. A Fables cartoon.

3015. Wolf Hounded (11/5/59) Technicolor – 7 mins. *DIR/PRO:* William Hanna, Joseph Barbera. A Loopy de Loop cartoon.

3016. Wolf in Sheep Dog's Clothing (7/11/63) Technicolor – 7 mins. *DIR/PRO:* William Hanna, Joseph Barbera. A Loopy de Loop cartoon.

3017. Wonder Gloves (11/29/51) Technicolor – 7 mins. *DIR:* Robert Cannon. *PRO:* Stephen Bosustow. A Jolly Frolics UPA cartoon.

3018. Wooden Shoes (2/25/33) B&W – 7 mins. *DIR:* Ben Harrison, Manny Gould. *PRO:* Charles Mintz. A Krazy Kat cartoon.

3019. Woodman Spare That Tree (7/2/42) Technicolor – 7 mins. *DIR:* Bob Wickersham. A Color Rhapsodies cartoon.

3020. The World's Affair (6/5/33) B&W – 7 mins. *DIR:* Dick Huemer. *PRO:* Charles Mintz. A Scrappy cartoon.

3021. A Worm's Eye View (4/28/39) B&W – 7 mins. *DIR:* Sid Marcus, Art Davis. *PRO:* Charles Mintz. A Scrappy cartoon.

3022. Ye Olde Swap Shop (6/28/40) Technicolor – 7 mins. *DIR:* Ub Iwerks. A Color Rhapsodies cartoon.

3023. Yelp Wanted (7/16/31) B&W – 7 mins. *DIR:* Dick Huemer. *PRO:* Charles Mintz. A Scrappy cartoon.

3024. Zoo Is Company (7/6/61) Technicolor – 7 mins. *DIR/PRO:* William Hanna, Joseph Barbera. A Loopy de Loop cartoon.

Miscellaneous Short Subjects (1922–1965)

Following is a complete list of miscellaneous live action short subject series produced and or distributed by Columbia Pictures. They are listed here to give the reader a reference as to the other short subjects released by Columbia in addition to its cartoon and comedy shorts.

No available information exists on the individual titles of the series shorts, with the exception of *Fools Who Made History*. All shorts were either 1 or 2 reels in length and were released in black and white except where noted. Descriptions are given where known.

The reader will note that Columbia did not produce a weekly newsreel for theaters.

3025. **America Speaks** (1942).

3026. **Animal Cavalcade** (1952–53).

3027. **Around the World in Color** (1937).

3028. **Assorted Favorites** (1952, 1961, 1963).

3029. **Broadway Follies** (1937).

3030. **Can You Top This?** (1948).

3031. **Candid Microphone** (1949–54, 1961, 1963).

3032. **Cavalcade of Broadway** (1949–51).

3033. **Cinemascope Featurettes** (1956–57).

3034. **Cinescopes** (1939–41).

3035. **Color Favorites** (Re-issues) (1947–52).

3036. **Color Favorites** (1961, 1963, 1965).

3037. **Color Featurettes** (1959, 1961–62).

3038. **Color Sensations** (1929).

3039. **Color Specials** (1963).

3040. **Columbia "Quiz" Reels** (1940–42).

3041. **Columbia Tours** (1936, 1938–42).

3042. **Columbia-Victor Gems** (1929).

3043. **Community Sings** (1937–49) (Musical-Singalong). A series of audience participation musical shorts.

3044. **Court of Human Relations** (1936).

3045. **A Day with the FBI** (1951).

3046. Edward Buzzell's Bedtime Stories (1930-31) (Drama-Comedy). A series of "Radio Bedtime Stories" shot silent with voices dubbed by Edward Buzzell.

3047. Famous Bands (1942) (Musical). A series of musical shorts featuring name bands of the day.

3048. Featurettes (1936).

3049. Film Novelties (1947, 1949-50).

3050. Film-Vodvil (1943-46).

3051. Fools Who Made History—"The Story of Charles Goodyear" (9/39) (Biography). DIR/SP: Jan Leman. PRO: Hugh McCollum. CAST: Robert Sterling, Richard Fiske, Hal Taliaferro (Wally Wales).
This story deals with Charles Goodyear's (Taliaferro) attempt to develop a process to vulcanize rubber, his first association with the Baker Chemical Co., his success at vulcanizing, and his court battles to patent his process.

3052. Fools Who Made History—"The Story of Elias Howe" (10/39) (Biography). DIR/SP: Jan Leman. PRO: Hugh McCollum. CAST: Richard Fiske, Lucille Brown. Narrated by Lindsay Macharrie.
This story deals with Elias Howe's (Fiske) development of the sewing machine and his fight to prove that machine-made garments were equal to those that were hand-made. NOTES: The series was discontinued with this release.

3053. Football Thrills (1931).

3054. Great Moments in Football (1928).

3055. Happy Hour Specials (1937, 1939).

3056. The Heart of Show Business Technicolor (1957). Various screen stars present a history of Variety Clubs International.

3057. Historical Reels (1941).

3058. Holiday Series (1965).

3059. International Forum (1941).

3060. Kate Smith Special— "America Sings" (1942). A musical short featuring songs by Kate Smith.

3061. Lambs Gambols (1932). A series of comedies made by the Lambs Club and released by Columbia.

3062. Laughing with Medbury (1933-35) (Comedy-Travelogues). A series of travelogues with comic commentaries by John P. Medbury.

3063. Life's Last Laughs (1934-35).

3064. March of the Years (1933). A series of historical shorts.

3065. Mickey McGuire (1933) (Comedy). A series of comedy shorts starring Joe Yule, Jr. (Mickey Rooney).

3066. Minute Mysteries (1933).

3067. Monkeyshines (1931) (Comedy). A series featuring an all-simian cast, with over-dubbed dialogue.

3068. The Movies and You (1950).

3069. Music Hall Vanities (1939).

3070. Music to Remember (1951).

3071. Musical Travelarks (1958, 1960).

3072. Musicals (1933).

3073. New Sport Thrills (1937).

3074. New York Parade (1941).

3075. O.W.I. Shorts (1943). A series of shorts on the Office of War Information.

3076. One Reel Special (1948).

3077. Panoramics (1941–43, 1945).

3078. Radiograms (1928).

3079. **Rambling Reporter** (1930).

3080. **Screen Snapshots** B&W/ Color (1922–1958) (Candid Biography). DIR/PRO: Ralph Staub. These shorts began as a production of C.B.C. Film Sales in 1920 in New York and were continued by Harry Cohn when he formed Columbia Pictures. The Screen Snapshots were a kind of "Candid Camera" catching Hollywood at play, at work, or at leisure. They lasted 38 years and were the longest running of the Columbia shorts.

3081. **Special Color Featurettes** (1963).

3082. **Special Musical Featurettes** (1947–48).

3083. **Specials** (1936, 1962–63).

3084. **Specialties** (1930).

3085. **Spice of Life** (1934–35).

3086. **Sport Thrills** (1938).

3087. **Sports Reels** (1939, 1942–46).

3088. **Stars of Tomorrow** (1935–36, 1951).

3089. **Strange as It Seems** (1937) (Oddity-Travelogue). A series of shorts depicting oddities from around the world. The series was picked up by Columbia when Universal Studios decided to drop this series in favor of a new type of series short.

3090. **Sunrise Comedies** (1932) (Comedy). A series of comedies made by the Lambs Club and released by Columbia.

3091. **Thrills of Music** (1946–50).

3092. **Thrills of Music** (Re-issues) (1952).

3093. **Topnotchers** (1953–54).

3094. **Variety Favorites** (Re-issues) (1950–52).

3095. **Vera Vague's Laff Tours** (1948–49) (Comedy-Travelogue). This was a short-lived series that combined comedy with a travelogue and was narrated by Vera Vague (Barbara Jo Allen).

3096. **Victory Shorts** (1943).

3097. **Voice of Experience** (1935–36).

3098. **Walter Futter's Curiosities** (1930–32).

3099. **Walter Futter's Travelaughs** (1931–32).

3100. **Washington Parade** (1938–41).

3101. **The World of Sports** (1932–36, 1940–41, 1947–63, 1965) (Sports). A series of sports shorts, narrated by Bill Stern, covering all facets of sports.

Independent Short Subjects
(1959–1971)

Following is a list of independently produced short subjects distributed by Columbia Pictures. During the years 1959 to 1971 independent producers would often release their product through a major studio until they were able to go through an independent releasing company.

The independent short subjects listed here, animated and live action, were nominated for Academy Awards. Release of additional short subjects is unknown, since yearly motion picture reference periodicals did not list independently produced shorts.

There is no available information on the individual titles of the shorts, with the exception of *The Critic*, which the author has seen. The shorts, listed by category, were in color and were either 1 or 2 reels in length.

Animated Short Subjects

3102. The Critic (1963). *PRO:* Ernest Pintoff. A Pintoff-Crossbow Production. *CAST:* Voice of Mel Brooks. A cynic makes comments while watching a film in a movie theater.

3103. Evolution (1971). *PRO:* Michael Mills. A National Film Board of Canada Production.

3104. The House That Jack Built (1968). *PRO:* Wolf Koenig, Jim McKay. A National Film Board of Canada Production.

3105. Walking (1969). *PRO:* Ryan Larkin. A National Film Board of Canada Production.

3106. What on Earth! (1967). *PRO:* Robert Verral, Wolf Koenig. A National Film Board of Canada Production.

Live Action Short Subjects

3107. Duo (1968). *PRO:* National Film Board of Canada.

3108. The Golden Fish (1959). *PRO:* Jacques-Yves Cousteau. A Les Requins Associes Production.

3109. People Soup (1969). *PRO:* Marc Merson. A Pangloss Production.

3110. A Place to Stand (1967). *PRO:* Christopher Chapman. A T.D.F.

455

Production for the Ontario Department of Economics and Development. NOTES: Nominated in two categories, Live Action Short Subject, and Documentary Short Subject.

3111. Rooftops of New York (1961). PRO: Robert Gaffney. A Robert Gaffney-McCarty-Rush Production.

Appendix A
The Columbia Movie Series

Blondie

Blondie (1938)
Blondie Meets the Boss (1939)
Blondie Takes a Vacation (1939)
Blondie Brings Up Baby (1939)
Blondie on a Budget (1940)
Blondie Has Servant Trouble (1940)
Blondie Plays Cupid (1940)
Blondie Goes Latin (1941)
Blondie in Society (1941)
Blondie Goes to College (1942)
Blondie's Blessed Event (1942)
Blondie for Victory (1942)
It's a Great Life (1943)
Footlight Glamour (1943)
Leave It to Blondie (1945)
Blondie Knows Best (1946)
Life with Blondie (1946)
Blondie's Lucky Day (1946)
Blondie's Big Moment (1947)
Blondie's Holiday (1947)
Blondie in the Dough (1947)
Blondie's Anniversary (1947)
Blondie's Reward (1948)
Blondie's Secret (1948)
Blondie's Big Deal (1949)
Blondie Hits the Jackpot (1949)
Blondie's Hero (1950)
Beware of Blondie (1950)

Boston Blackie

Meet Boston Blackie (1941)
Confessions of Boston Blackie (1941)
Alias Boston Blackie (1942)
Boston Blackie Goes Hollywood (1942)
After Midnight with Boston Blackie (1943)
The Chance of a Lifetime (1943)
One Mysterious Night (1944)
Boston Blackie Booked on Suspicion (1945)
Boston Blackie's Rendezvous (1945)
A Close Call for Boston Blackie (1946)
The Phantom Thief (1946)
Boston Blackie and the Law (1946)
Trapped by Boston Blackie (1948)
Boston Blackie's Chinese Venture (1949)

Bulldog Drummond

Bulldog Drummond at Bay (1947)
Bulldog Drummond Strikes Back (1947)

Crime Doctor

Crime Doctor (1943)
Crime Doctor's Strangest Case (1943)
Shadows in the Night (1944)
The Crime Doctor's Courage (1945)
The Crime Doctor's Warning (1945)
Crime Doctor's Man Hunt (1946)
Just Before Dawn (1946)
The Millerson Case (1947)
The Crime Doctor's Gamble (1947)
Crime Doctor's Diary (1949)

David Harding

David Harding, Counterspy (1950)
Counterspy Meets Scotland Yard (1950)

Ellery Queen

Ellery Queen, Master Detective (1940)
Ellery Queen and the Perfect Crime (1941)
Ellery Queen and the Murder Ring (1941)
Ellery Queen's Penthouse Mystery (1941)
A Close Call for Ellery Queen (1942)
A Desperate Chance for Ellery Queen (1942)
Enemy Agents Meet Ellery Queen (1942)

Five Little Peppers

Five Little Peppers and How They Grew (1939)
Five Little Peppers at Home (1940)
Five Little Peppers in Trouble (1940)
Out West with the Peppers (1940)

Gasoline Alley

Gasoline Alley (1951)
Corky of Gasoline Alley (1951)

Gidget

Gidget (1959)
Gidget Goes Hawaiian (1961)
Gidget Goes to Rome (1963)

I Love a Mystery

I Love a Mystery (1945)
The Devil's Mask (1946)
The Unknown (1946)

Inspector Killian

The Donovan Affair (1929)
Subway Express (1931)

Inspector Trent

Before Midnight (1934)
One Is Guilty (1934)
Crime of Helen Stanley (1934)
Girl in Danger (1934)

Jungle Jim

Jungle Jim (1948)
The Lost Tribe (1949)
Pygmy Island (1950)
Captive Girl (1950)
Mark of the Gorilla (1950)
Fury of the Congo (1951)
Jungle Manhunt (1951)
Jungle Jim in the Forbidden Land (1952)
Voodoo Tiger (1952)
Killer Ape (1953)
Savage Mutiny (1953)
Valley of the Headhunters (1953)
Jungle Man-Eaters (1954)
Cannibal Attack (1954)
Jungle Moon Men (1955)
Devil Goddess (1955)

The Lone Wolf

The Lone Wolf Returns (1926)
Alias the Lone Wolf (1927)
The Lone Wolf's Daughter (1928)
Last of the Lone Wolf (1930)
The Lone Wolf Returns (1936)
The Lone Wolf in Paris (1938)
The Lone Wolf Spy Hunt (1939)
The Lone Wolf Strikes (1940)
The Lone Wolf Meets a Lady (1940)
The Lone Wolf Takes a Chance (1941)
The Lone Wolf Keeps a Date (1941)
Secrets of the Lone Wolf (1941)

Counter-Espionage (1942)
One Dangerous Night (1943)
Passport to Suez (1943)
The Notorious Lone Wolf (1946)
The Lone Wolf in Mexico (1947)
The Lone Wolf in London (1947)
The Lone Wolf and His Lady (1949)

Matt Helm

The Silencers (1966)
Murderer's Row (1966)
The Ambushers (1967)
The Wrecking Crew (1969)

Nero Wolfe

Meet Nero Wolfe (1936)
The League of Frightened Men (1937)

Rusty

Adventures of Rusty (1945)
The Return of Rusty (1946)
For the Love of Rusty (1947)
The Son of Rusty (1947)
My Dog Rusty (1948)
Rusty Leads the Way (1948)

Rusty Saves a Life (1949)
Rusty's Birthday (1949)

Thatcher Colt

Night Club Lady (1932)
The Circus Queen Murder (1933)

The Three Stooges

Have Rocket, Will Travel (1959)
The 3 Stooges Meet Hercules (1962)
The 3 Stooges in Orbit (1962)
The 3 Stooges Go Around the World
   in a Daze (1963)
The Outlaws Is Coming (1965)

The Whistler

The Whistler (1944)
The Mark of the Whistler (1944)
The Power of the Whistler (1945)
The Voice of the Whistler (1945)
Mysterious Intruder (1946)
The Secret of the Whistler (1946)
The 13th Hour (1947)
Return of the Whistler (1948)

Appendix B
The Columbia
Westerns and Stars

Bob Allen

The Unknown Ranger (1936)
Rio Grande Ranger (1936)
Ranger Courage (1937)
Law of the Ranger (1937)
Reckless Ranger (1937)
The Rangers Step In (1937)

Gene Autry

The Last Round-Up (1947)
The Strawberry Roan (1948)
Loaded Pistols (1949)
The Big Sombrero (1949)
Riders of the Whistling Pines (1949)
Rim of the Canyon (1949)
The Cowboy and the Indians (1949)
Riders in the Sky (1949)
Sons of New Mexico (1950)
Mule Train (1950)
Cow Town (1950)
Beyond the Purple Hills (1950)
Indian Territory (1950)
The Blazing Sun (1950)
Gene Autry and the Mounties (1951)
Texans Never Cry (1951)
Whirlwind (1951)
Silver Canyon (1951)
Hills of Utah (1951)
Valley of Fire (1951)
The Old West (1952)
Night Stage to Galveston (1952)

Apache Country (1952)
Barbed Wire (1952)
Wagon Team (1952)
Blue Canadian Rockies (1952)
Winning of the West (1953)
On Top of Old Smoky (1953)
Goldtown Ghost Raiders (1953)
Pack Train (1953)
Saginaw Trail (1953)
Last of the Pony Riders (1953)

Ken Curtis

Rhythm Round-Up (1945)
Song of the Prairie (1945)
Throw a Saddle on a Star (1946)
That Texas Jamboree (1946)
Cowboy Blues (1946)
Singing on the Trail (1946)
Lone Star Moonlight (1946)
Over the Santa Fe Trail (1947)

Bill Elliott

In Early Arizona (1938)
Frontiers of '49 (1939)
Lone Star Pioneers (1939)
The Law Comes to Texas (1939)
Overland with Kit Carson (1939)
The Return of Daniel Boone (1941)
The Son of Davy Crockett (1941)
North of the Rockies (1942)

Vengeance of the West (1942)
The Valley of Vanishing Men (1942)

Bill Elliott
as Wild Bill Hickok

The Great Adventures of Wild Bill
  Hickok (1938)
Prairie Schooners (1940)
Beyond the Sacramento (1940)
Wildcat of Tucson (1940)
Across the Sierras (1941)
North from the Lone Star (1941)
Hands Across the Rockies (1941)
King of Dodge City (1941)
Roaring Frontiers (1941)
Lone Star Vigilantes (1942)
Bullets for Bandits (1942)
The Devil's Trail (1942)
Prairie Gunsmoke (1942)

Bill Elliott
as Wild Bill Saunders

Taming of the West (1939)
Pioneers of the Frontier (1940)
The Man from Tumbleweeds (1940)
The Return of Wild Bill (1940)

Russell Hayden (as Star)

The Lone Prairie (1942)
A Tornado in the Saddle (1942)
Riders of the Northwest Mounted
  (1943)
Saddles and Sagebrush (1943)
Silver City Raiders (1943)
The Vigilantes Ride (1944)
Wyoming Hurricane (1944)
The Last Horseman (1944)

Russell Hayden (as Co-Star)

The Royal Mounted Patrol (1941)
Riders of the Badlands (1941)

West of Tombstone (1942)
Lawless Plainsman (1942)
Down Rio Grande Way (1942)
Riders of the Northland (1942)
Bad Men of the Hills (1942)
Overland to Deadwood (1942)

Jack Holt (as Star)

End of the Trail (1936)
North of Nome (1936)
Roaring Timber (1937)

Jack Holt (as Co-Star)

The Strawberry Roan (1948)
Loaded Pistols (1949)

Buck Jones

The Lone Rider (1930)
Shadow Ranch (1930)
Men Without Law (1930)
The Dawn Trail (1930)
Desert Vengeance (1931)
The Avenger (1931)
The Texas Ranger (1931)
The Fighting Sheriff (1931)
Branded (1931)
Border Law (1931)
The Deadline (1931)
The Range Feud (1931)
Ridin' for Justice (1932)
One Man Law (1932)
South of the Rio Grande (1932)
Hello Trouble (1932)
McKenna of the Mounted (1932)
White Eagle (1932)
Forbidden Trail (1932)
Treason (1933)
The California Trail (1933)
The Thrill Hunter (1933)
Unknown Valley (1933)
The Fighting Code (1933)
The Sundown Rider (1933)
The Fighting Ranger (1934)

The Man Trailer (1934)
Hollywood Round-Up (1937)
Headin' East (1937)
The Overland Express (1938)
Law of the Texan (1938)
The Stranger from Arizona (1938)
California Frontier (1938)
White Eagle (1941)

Jack Luden

Rolling Caravans (1938)
Stagecoach Days (1938)
Pioneer Trail (1938)
Phantom Gold (1938)

Tim McCoy

The One Way Trail (1931)
Shotgun Pass (1931)
The Fighting Marshall (1931)
The Fighting Fool (1932)
Texas Cyclone (1932)
The Riding Tornado (1932)
Two-Fisted Law (1932)
Daring Danger (1932)
Cornered (1932)
The Western Code (1932)
Fighting for Justice (1932)
End of the Trail (1932)
Man of Action (1933)
Silent Men (1933)
The Whirlwind (1933)
Rusty Rides Alone (1933)
Beyond the Law (1934)
The Prescott Kid (1934)
The Westerner (1934)
Square Shooter (1935)
Law Beyond the Range (1935)
The Revenge Rider (1935)
Fighting Shadows (1935)
Justice of the Range (1935)
Riding Wild (1935)

Ken Maynard

Western Courage (1935)
Western Frontier (1935)

Lawless Riders (1935)
Heir to Trouble (1935)
The Cattle Thief (1936)
Avenging Waters (1936)
Heroes of the Range (1936)
The Fugitive Sheriff (1936)

George Montgomery

The Texas Rangers (1951)
Indian Uprising (1952)
Cripple Creek (1952)
The Pathfinder (1953)
Jack McCall, Desperado (1953)
Fort Ti (1953)
Battle of Rogue River (1954)
Masterson of Kansas (1955)
Seminole Uprising (1955)

Audie Murphy

The Guns of Fort Petticoat (1957)
The Quick Gun (1964)
Arizona Raiders (1965)
The Texican (1966)
40 Guns to Apache Pass (1967)

Tex Ritter (as Co-Star)

King of Dodge City (1941)
Roaring Frontiers (1941)
The Lone Star Vigilantes (1942)
Bullets for Bandits (1942)
North of the Rockies (1942)
The Devil's Trail (1942)
Prairie Gunsmoke (1942)
Vengeance of the West (1942)
Cowboy Canteen (1944)
Apache Ambush (1955)

Randolph Scott

The Desperadoes (1943)
The Gunfighters (1947)
Coroner Creek (1948)

The Walking Hills (1949)
The Doolins of Oklahoma (1949)
The Nevadan (1950)
Santa Fe (1951)
Man in the Saddle (1951)
Hangman's Knot (1952)
The Stranger Wore a Gun (1953)
Ten Wanted Men (1955)
A Lawless Street (1955)
7th Cavalry (1956)
The Tall T (1957)
Decision at Sundown (1957)
Buchanan Rides Alone (1958)
Ride Lonesome (1959)
Comanche Station (1960)

Charles Starrett

Gallant Defender (1935)
The Mysterious Avenger (1936)
Secret Patrol (1936)
Code of the Range (1936)
The Cowboy Star (1936)
Stampede (1936)
Dodge City Trail (1936)
Westbound Mail (1937)
Trapped (1937)
Two Gun Law (1937)
Two-Fisted Sheriff (1937)
One Man Justice (1937)
The Old Wyoming Trail (1937)
Outlaws of the Prairie (1937)
Cattle Raiders (1938)
Call of the Rockies (1938)
Law of the Plains (1938)
West of Cheyenne (1938)
South of Arizona (1938)
The Colorado Trail (1938)
West of Santa Fe (1938)
Rio Grande (1938)
The Thundering West (1939)
Western Caravans (1939)
Texas Stampede (1939)
North of the Yukon (1939)
Spoilers of the Range (1939)
The Man from Sundown (1939)
Riders of Black River (1939)
Outpost of the Mounties (1939)

The Stranger from Texas (1939)
Two-Fisted Rangers (1940)
Bullets for Rustlers (1940)
Blazing Six Shooters (1940)
Texas Stagecoach (1940)
West of Abilene (1940)
Thundering Frontier (1940)
The Pinto Kid (1941)
Outlaws of the Panhandle (1941)
The Royal Mounted Patrol (1941)
Riders of the Badlands (1941)
West of Tombstone (1942)
Lawless Plainsman (1942)
Down Rio Grande Way (1942)
Riders of the Northland (1942)
Bad Men of the Hills (1942)
Overland to Deadwood (1942)
Riding Through Nevada (1942)
Pardon My Gun (1942)
The Fighting Buckaroo (1943)
Law of the Northwest (1943)
Frontier Fury (1943)
Robin Hood of the Range (1943)
Hail to the Rangers (1943)
Cowboy in the Clouds (1943)
Cowboy Canteen (1944)
Sundown Valley (1944)
Riding West (1944)
Cowboy from Lonesome River (1944)
Cyclone Prairie Rangers (1944)
Saddle Leather Law (1944)
Sagebrush Heroes (1945)
Rough Ridin' Justice (1945)

Charles Starrett
as Dr. Steven Monroe

The Medico of Painted Springs (1941)
Thunder Over the Prairie (1941)
Prairie Stranger (1941)

Charles Starrett
as The Durango Kid

The Durango Kid (1940)
Return of the Durango Kid (1945)

Both Barrels Blazing (1945)
Rustlers of the Badlands (1945)
Blazing the Western Trail (1945)
Outlaws of the Rockies (1945)
Lawless Empire (1945)
Texas Panhandle (1945)
Frontier Gunlaw (1946)
Roaring Rangers (1946)
Gunning for Vengeance (1946)
Galloping Thunder (1946)
Two-Fisted Stranger (1946)
The Desert Horseman (1946)
Heading West (1946)
Landrush (1946)
Terror Trail (1946)
The Fighting Frontiersman (1946)
South of the Chisholm Trail (1947)
The Lone Hand Texan (1947)
West of Dodge City (1947)
Law of the Canyon (1947)
Prairie Raiders (1947)
The Stranger from Ponca City (1947)
Riders of the Lone Star (1947)
Buckaroo from Powder River (1947)
Last Days of Boot Hill (1947)
Six-Gun Law (1948)
Phantom Valley (1948)
West of Sonora (1948)
Whirlwind Raiders (1948)
Blazing Across the Pecos (1948)
Trail to Laredo (1948)
El Dorado Pass (1948)
Quick on the Trigger (1948)
Challenge of the Range (1949)
Laramie (1949)
The Blazing Trail (1949)
South of Death Valley (1949)
Bandits of El Dorado (1949)
Desert Vigilante (1949)
Horsemen of the Sierras (1949)
Renegades of the Sage (1949)

Frontier Outpost (1949)
Trail of the Rustlers (1950)
Outcast of Black Mesa (1950)
Texas Dynamo (1950)
Streets of Ghost Town (1950)
Across the Badlands (1950)
Raiders of Tomahawk Creek (1950)
Lightning Guns (1950)
Prairie Roundup (1951)
Ridin' the Outlaw Trail (1951)
Fort Savage Raiders (1951)
Snake River Desperadoes (1951)
Bonanza Town (1951)
Cyclone Fury (1951)
The Kid from Amarillo (1951)
Pecos River (1951)
Smoky Canyon (1952)
The Hawk of Wild River (1952)
Laramie Mountains (1952)
The Rough, Tough West (1952)
Junction City (1952)
The Kid from Broken Gun (1952)

Jimmy Wakely (as Co-Star)

Cowboy Canteen (1944)
Sundown Valley (1944)
Swing in the Saddle (1944)
Cowboy from Lonesome River (1944)
Cyclone Prairie Rangers (1944)
Saddle Leather Law (1944)
Rough Ridin' Justice (1945)

John Wayne (as Co-Star)

The Range Feud (1931)
Texas Cyclone (1932)
Two-Fisted Law (1932)

Appendix C
The Columbia Comedy
Shorts and Stars*

Max Baer and Maxie Rosenbloom

Two Roaming Champs (1950)
Wine, Women and Bong (1951)
The Champ Steps Out (1951)
Rootin' Tootin' Tenderfoot (1952)

Joe Besser

Waiting in the Lurch (1949)
Dizzy Yardbird (1950)
Fraidy Cat (1951)
Aim, Fire, Scoot (1952)
Caught on the Bounce (1952)
Spies and Guys (1953)
The Fire Chaser (1954)
G.I. Dood It (1955)
Hook a Crook (1955)
Army Daze (1956)

Herman Bing

Oh, What a Knight! (1937)

Brendel, El see El Brendel

Wally Brown and Tim Ryan

French Fried Frolic (1949)

Billie Burke

Silly Billie (1948)
Billie Gets Her Man (1948)

Walter Catlett

Elmer Steps Out (1934)
Get Along Little Hubby (1934)
Fibbing Fibbers (1936)
Static in the Attic (1939)
You're Next (1940)

Charley Chase

The Grand Hooter (1937)
From Bad to Worse (1937)
The Wrong Miss Wright (1937)
Calling All Doctors (1937)
The Big Squirt (1937)
Man Bites Lovebug (1937)
Time Out for Trouble (1938)
The Mind Needer (1938)
Many Sappy Returns (1938)

The history of the Columbia comedy shorts and their stars is to be found in The Columbia Comedy Shorts *by Ted Okuda and Edward Watz (McFarland, 1986).*

465

The Nightshirt Bandit (1938)
Pie a la Maid (1938)
The Sap Takes a Wrap (1939)
The Chump Takes a Bump (1939)
Rattling Romeo (1939)
Skinny the Moocher (1939)
Teacher's Pest (1939)
The Awful Goof (1939)
The Heckler (1940)
South of the Boudoir (1940)
His Bridal Fright (1940)

Andy Clyde

It's the Cats (1934)
In the Dog House (1934)
I'm a Father (1935)
Old Sawbones (1935)
Tramp Tramp Tramp (1935)
Alimony Aches (1935)
It Always Happens (1935)
Hot Paprika (1935)
Caught in the Act (1936)
Share the Wealth (1936)
The Peppery Salt (1936)
Mister Smarty (1936)
Am I Having Fun! (1936)
Love Comes to Mooneyville (1936)
Knee Action (1937)
Stuck in the Sticks (1937)
My Little Feller (1937)
Lodge Night (1937)
Gracie at the Bat (1937)
He Done His Duty (1937)
The Old Raid Mule (1938)
Jump, Chump, Jump (1938)
Ankles Away (1938)
Soul of a Heel (1938)
Not Guilty Enough (1938)
Home on the Rage (1938)
Swing, You Sinners! (1939)
Boom Goes the Groom (1939)
Now It Can Be Sold (1939)
Trouble Finds Andy Clyde (1939)
All-American Blondes (1939)
Andy Clyde Gets Spring Chicken (1939)
Mr. Clyde Goes to Broadway (1940)

Money Squawks (1940)
Boobs in the Woods (1940)
Fireman, Save My Choo Choo (1940)
A Bundle of Bliss (1940)
The Watchman Takes a Wife (1941)
The Ring and the Belle (1941)
Yankee Doodle Andy (1941)
Host to a Ghost (1941)
Lovable Trouble (1941)
Sappy Birthday (1942)
How Spry I Am (1942)
All Work and No Pay (1942)
Sappy Pappy (1942)
Wolf in Thief's Clothing (1943)
A Maid, Made Mad (1943)
Farmer for a Day (1943)
He Was Only Feudin' (1943)
His Tale Is Told (1944)
You Were Never Uglier (1944)
Gold Is Where You Lose It (1944)
Heather and Yon (1944)
Two Local Yokels (1945)
A Miner Affair (1945)
Spook to Me (1945)
The Blonde Stayed On (1946)
You Can't Fool a Fool (1946)
Andy Plays Hookey (1946)
Two Jills and a Jack (1947)
Wife to Spare (1947)
Eight-Ball Andy (1948)
Go Chase Yourself (1948)
Sunk in the Sink (1949)
Marinated Mariner (1950)
A Blunderful Time (1950)
Blonde Atom Bomb (1951)
Pleasure Treasure (1951)
A Blissful Blunder (1952)
Hooked and Rooked (1952)
Love's A-Poppin' (1953)
Oh Say Can You Sue (1953)
Tooting Tooters (1954)
Two April Fools (1954)
Scratch Scratch Scratch (1955)
One Spooky Night (1955)
Andy Goes Wild (1956)
Pardon My Nightshirt (1956)

Monte Collins

Unrelated Relations (1936)

Monte Collins
and Tom Kennedy

Gum Shoes (1935)
Stage Frights (1935)
Gobs of Trouble (1935)
Oh, My Nerves! (1935)
Just Speeding (1936)
Midnight Blunders (1936)
Free Rent (1936)
New News (1937)
Bury the Hatchet (1937)
Calling All Curtains (1937)
Fiddling Around (1938)

Joe DeRita

Slappily Married (1946)
The Good Bad Egg (1947)
Wedlock Deadlock (1947)
Jitter Bughouse (1948)

Johnny Downs

Groom and Bored (1942)
Kiss and Make Up (1942)

El Brendel

Ay Tank Ay Go (1936)
Super Snooper (1937)
Yumpin' Yimminy! (1941)
Ready, Willing But Unable (1941)
Love at First Fright (1941)
The Blitz Kiss (1941)
Sweet Spirits of the Nighter (1941)
Olaf Laughs Last (1942)
Phoney Cronies (1942)
Ham and Yeggs (1942)
His Wedding Scare (1943)
I Spied for You (1943)

Boobs in the Night (1943)
A Rookie's Cookie (1943)
Defective Detectives (1944)
Mopey Dope (1944)
Pick a Peck of Plumbers (1944)
Snooper Service (1945)
Pistol Packin' Nitwits (1945)

Leon Errol

Hold Your Temper (1933)
Perfectly Mismated (1934)
One Too Many (1934)
Honeymoon Bridge (1935)

Eddie Foy, Jr.

Dance, Dance, Dance (1945)
Foy Meets Girl (1950)
Wedding Yells (1951)

Billy Gilbert

Shot in the Escape (1943)
Crazy Like a Fox (1944)
Wedded Bliss (1944)

George Givot
and Cliff Nazarro

Two Saplings (1943)

The Glove Slingers

Glove Slingers (1939)
Pleased to Mitt You (1940)
Fresh as a Freshman (1941)
Glove Affair (1941)
Mitt Me Tonight (1941)
Kink of the Campus (1941)
Glove Birds (1942)
A Study in Socks (1942)
College Belles (1942)
The Great Glover (1942)

Socks Appeal (1943)
His Girl's Worst Friend (1943)

Hugh Herbert

Pitchin' in the Kitchen (1943)
Who's Hugh? (1943)
Oh, Baby! (1944)
His Hotel Sweet (1944)
A Knight and a Blonde (1944)
Woo, Woo! (1945)
Wife Decoy (1945)
The Mayor's Husband (1945)
When the Wife's Away (1946)
Get Along Little Zombie (1946)
Honeymoon Blues (1946)
Hot Heir (1947)
Nervous Shakedown (1947)
Should Husbands Marry? (1947)
Tall, Dark and Gruesome (1948)
A Pinch in Time (1948)
Trapped by a Blonde (1949)
Super-Wolf (1949)
One Shivery Night (1950)
A Slip and a Miss (1950)
Woo-Woo Blues (1951)
Trouble In-Laws (1951)
The Gink at the Sink (1952)

Sterling Holloway

Mr. Wright Goes Wrong (1946)
Moron Than Off (1946)
Scooper Dooper (1947)
Hectic Honeymoon (1947)
Man or Mouse (1948)
Flat Feat (1948)

Shemp Howard

Pick a Peck of Plumbers (1944)
Open Season for Saps (1944)
Off Again, On Again (1945)
Where the Pest Begins (1945)
A Hit with a Miss (1945)
Mr. Noisy (1946)

Jiggers, My Wife (1946)
Society Mugs (1946)
Bride and Gloom (1947)

Roscoe Karns

Black Eyes and Blues (1941)
Half Shot at Sunrise (1941)

Buster Keaton

Pest from the West (1939)
Mooching Through Georgia (1939)
Nothing But Pleasure (1940)
Pardon My Berth Marks (1940)
The Taming of the Snood (1940)
The Spook Speaks (1940)
His Ex Marks the Spot (1940)
So You Won't Squawk (1941)
Good Nuisance (1941)
She's Oil Mine (1941)

Tom Kennedy
and Johnny Arthur

Half-Way to Hollywood (1938)

Muriel Landers

Tricky Chicks (1957)

Richard Lane
and Gus Schilling

High Blood Pleasure (1945)
Ain't Love Cuckoo? (1946)
Hot Water (1946)
Pardon My Terror (1946)
Training for Trouble (1947)
Wedding Belle (1947)
Two Nuts in a Rut (1948)
Pardon My Lamb Chop (1948)
He's in Again (1949)

Flung by a Fling (1949)
Hold That Monkey (1950)

Harry Langdon

Counsel on De Fence (1934)
Shivers (1934)
His Bridal Sweet (1935)
The Leather Necker (1935)
His Marriage Mixup (1935)
I Don't Remember (1935)
A Doggone Mixup (1938)
Sue My Lawyer (1938)
Cold Turkey (1940)
What Makes Lizzy Dizzy? (1942)
Tireman, Spare My Tires (1942)
Carry Harry (1942)
Piano Mooner (1942)
A Blitz on the Fritz (1943)
Blonde and Groom (1943)
Here Comes Mr. Zerk (1943)
To Heir Is Human (1944)
Defective Detectives (1944)
Mopey Dope (1944)
Snooper Service (1945)
Pistol Packin' Nitwits (1945)

Una Merkel

Quack Service (1943)
To Heir Is Human (1944)

Harry Mimmo

Down the Hatch (1953/3-D)

The Mischief Makers

Kids Will Be Kids (1954)

Polly Moran

Oh, Duchess! (1936)
Sailor Maid (1937)

Alan Mowbray

French Fried Patootie (1941)

Charlie Murray

His Old Flame (1935)

"Musical Novelties"

Roamin' Thru the Roses (1933)
Um-Pa (1933)
School for Romance (1934)
Love Detectives (1934)
When Do We Eat? (1934)
Woman Haters (1934)
Susie's Affairs (1934)
Tripping Through the Tropics (1934)
Hollywood Here We Come (1934)

Franklin Pangborn

The Captain Hits the Ceiling (1935)

The Radio Rogues

Do Your Stuff (1935)
Star Gazing (1935)
Yoo Yoo Hollywood (1935)

George Sidney
and Charlie Murray

Ten Baby Fingers (1934)
Radio Dough (1934)
Stable Mates (1934)
Fishing for Trouble (1934)
Plumbing for Gold (1934)
Back to the Soil (1934)

Joe Smith
and Charlie Dale

A Nag in the Bag (1938)
Mutiny on the Body (1939)

Slim Summerville

Garden of Eatin' (1943)
Bachelor Daze (1944)

The Three Stooges
(Moe, Larry, Curly)

Woman Haters (1934)
Punch Drunks (1934)
Men in Black (1934)
Three Little Pigskins (1934)
Horses' Collars (1935)
Restless Knights (1935)
Pop Goes the Easel (1935)
Uncivil Warriors (1935)
Pardon My Scotch (1935)
Hoi Polloi (1935)
Three Little Beers (1935)
Ants in the Pantry (1936)
Movie Maniacs (1936)
Half-Shot Shooters (1936)
Disorder in the Court (1936)
A Pain in the Pullman (1936)
False Alarms (1936)
Whoops, I'm an Indian (1936)
Slippery Silks (1936)
Grips, Grunts and Groans (1937)
Dizzy Doctors (1937)
Three Dumb Clucks (1937)
Back to the Woods (1937)
Goofs and Saddles (1937)
Cash and Carry (1937)
Playing the Ponies (1937)
The Sitter Downers (1937)
Termites of 1938 (1938)
Wee Wee Monsieur (1938)
Tassels in the Air (1938)
Flat Foot Stooges (1938)
Healthy, Wealthy and Dumb (1938)
Violent Is the Word for Curly (1938)
Three Missing Links (1938)
Mutts to You (1938)
Three Little Sew and Sews (1939)
We Want Our Mummy (1939)
A-Ducking They Did Go (1939)
Yes, We Have No Bonanza (1939)
Saved by the Belle (1939)

Calling All Curs (1939)
Oily to Bed, Oily to Rise (1939)
Three Sappy People (1939)
You Nazty Spy! (1940)
Rockin' Thru the Rockies (1940)
A-Plumbing We Will Go (1940)
Nutty But Nice (1940)
How High Is Up? (1940)
From Nurse to Worse (1940)
No Census, No Feeling (1940)
Cookoo Cavaliers (1940)
Boobs in Arms (1940)
So Long, Mr. Chumps (1941)
Dutiful But Dumb (1941)
All the World's a Stooge (1941)
I'll Never Heil Again (1941)
An Ache in Every Stake (1941)
In the Sweet Pie and Pie (1941)
Some More of Samoa (1941)
Loco Boy Makes Good (1942)
Cactus Makes Perfect (1942)
What's the Matador? (1942)
Matri-Phony (1942)
Three Smart Saps (1942)
Even as I.O.U. (1942)
Sock-a-Bye Baby (1942)
They Stooge to Conga (1943)
Dizzy Detectives (1943)
Spook Louder (1943)
Back from the Front (1943)
Three Little Twerps (1943)
Higher Than a Kite (1943)
I Can Hardly Wait (1943)
Dizzy Pilots (1943)
Phony Express (1943)
A Gem of a Jam (1943)
Crash Goes the Hash (1944)
Busy Buddies (1944)
The Yoke's on Me (1944)
Idle Roomers (1944)
Gents Without Cents (1944)
No Dough Boys (1944)
Three Pests in a Mess (1945)
Booby Dupes (1945)
Idiots Deluxe (1945)
If a Body Meets a Body (1945)
Micro-Phonies (1945)
Beer Barrel Polecats (1946)
A Bird in the Head (1946)

Uncivil Warbirds (1946)
Three Troubledoers (1946)
Monkey Businessmen (1946)
Three Loan Wolves (1946)
G.I. Wanna Home (1946)
Rhythm and Weep (1946)
Three Little Pirates (1946)
Half-Wits Holiday (1946)

The Three Stooges
(Moe, Larry, Shemp)

Fright Night (1947)
Out West (1947)
Hold That Lion (1947)
Brideless Groom (1947)
Sing a Song of Six Pants (1947)
All Gummed Up (1947)
Shivering Sherlocks (1948)
Pardon My Clutch (1948)
Squareheads of the Round Table (1948)
Fiddlers Three (1948)
Hot Scots (1948)
Heavenly Daze (1948)
I'm a Monkey's Uncle (1948)
Mummy's Dummies (1948)
Crime on Their Hands (1948)
The Ghost Talks (1949)
Who Done It? (1949)
Hokus Pokus (1949)
Fuelin' Around (1949)
Malice in the Palice (1949)
Vagabond Loafers (1949)
Dunked in the Deep (1949)
Punchy Cowpunchers (1950)
Hugs and Mugs (1950)
Dopey Dicks (1950)
Love at First Bite (1950)
Self-Made Maids (1950)
Three Hams on Rye (1950)
Studio Stoops (1950)
Slaphappy Sleuths (1950)
A Snitch in Time (1950)
Three Arabian Nuts (1951)
Baby Sitter Jitters (1951)
Don't Throw That Knife (1951)
Scrambled Brains (1951)

Merry Mavericks (1951)
The Tooth Will Out (1951)
Hula-La-La (1951)
Pest Man Wins (1951)
A Missed Fortune (1952)
Listen, Judge (1952)
Corny Casanovas (1952)
He Cooked His Goose (1952)
Gents in a Jam (1952)
Three Dark Horses (1952)
Cuckoo on a Choo Choo (1952)
Up in Daisy's Penthouse (1953)
Booty and the Beast (1953)
Loose Loot (1953)
Tricky Dicks (1953)
Spooks (1953/3-D)
Pardon My Backfire (1953/3-D)
Rip, Sew and Stitch (1953)
Bubble Trouble (1953)
Goof on the Roof (1953)
Income Tax Sappy (1954)
Musty Musketeers (1954)
Pals and Gals (1954)
Knutzy Knights (1954)
Shot in the Frontier (1954)
Scotched in Scotland (1954)
Fling in the Ring (1955)
Of Cash and Hash (1955)
Gypped in the Penthouse (1955)
Bedlam in Paradise (1955)
Stone Age Romeos (1955)
Wham Bam Slam (1955)
Hot Ice (1955)
Blunder Boys (1955)
Husbands Beware (1956)
Creeps (1956)
Flagpole Jitters (1956)
For Crimin' Out Loud (1956)
Rumpus in the Harem (1956)
Hot Stuff (1956)
Scheming Schemers (1956)
Commotion on the Ocean (1956)

The Three Stooges
(Moe, Larry, Joe Besser)

Hoofs and Goofs (1957)
Muscle Up a Little Closer (1957)

A Merry Mix-Up (1957)
Space Ship Sappy (1957)
Guns A-Poppin (1957)
Horsing Around (1957)
Rusty Romeos (1957)
Outer Space Jitters (1957)
Quiz Whizz (1958)
Fifi Blows Her Top (1958)
Pies and Guys (1958)
Sweet and Hot (1958)
Flying Saucer Daffy (1958)
Oil's Well That Ends Well (1958)
Triple Crossed (1959)
Sappy Bull Fighters (1959)

Let Down Your Aerial (1949)
House About It (1950)
He Flew the Shrew (1951)
Fun on the Run (1951)
A Fool and His Money (1952)
Heebie Gee-Gees (1952)
Strop, Look and Listen (1952)
He Popped His Pistol (1953)
A-Haunting They Did Go (1953)
Doggie in the Bedroom (1954)
His Pest Friend (1955)
Nobody's Home (1955)
He Took a Powder (1955)
Come on Seven (1956)

Vera Vague
(Barbara Jo Allen)

You Dear Boy (1943)
Doctor, Feel My Pulse (1944)
Strife of the Party (1944)
She Snoops to Conquer (1944)
The Jury Goes Round 'N' Round (1945)
Calling All Fibbers (1945)
Hiss and Yell (1946)
Headin' for a Weddin' (1946)
Reno-Vated (1946)
Cupid Goes Nuts (1947)
A Miss in a Mess (1949)
Clanked in the Clink (1949)
Wha' Happened? (1949)
Nursie Behave (1950)
She Took a Powder (1951)
Happy Go Wacky (1952)

Wally Vernon
and Eddie Quillan

Crabbin' in the Cabin (1948)
Parlor, Bedroom and Wrath (1948)

Harry Von Zell

So's Your Antenna (1946)
Meet Mr. Mischief (1947)
Rolling Down to Reno (1947)
Radio Romeo (1947)
The Sheepish Wolf (1948)
Radio Riot (1949)
Microspook (1949)
His Baiting Beauty (1950)

Danny Webb

A Star Is Shorn (1939)

Bert Wheeler

Innocently Guilty (1950)
The Awful Sleuth (1951)

Guinn "Big Boy" Williams

The Champ's a Chump (1936)

Appendix D
The Columbia Awards

(Winners in bold letters)

Best Picture

1932/33 Lady for a Day
1934 It Happened One Night
1934 One Night of Love
1936 Mr. Deeds Goes to Town
1937 The Awful Truth
1937 Lost Horizon
1938 You Can't Take It with You
1939 Mr. Smith Goes to Washington
1941 Here Comes Mr. Jordan
1942 The Invaders
1942 The Talk of the Town
1943 The More the Merrier
1949 All the King's Men
1950 Born Yesterday
1953 From Here to Eternity
1954 The Caine Mutiny
1954 On the Waterfront
1955 Picnic
1957 The Bridge on the River Kwai
1959 Anatomy of a Murder
1961 The Guns of Navarone
1962 Lawrence of Arabia
1964 Dr. Strangelove
1965 Ship of Fools
1966 A Man for All Seasons
1967 Guess Who's Coming to Dinner
1968 Funny Girl
1968 Oliver!
1970 Five Easy Pieces
1971 The Last Picture Show
1971 Nicholas and Alexandra

1976 Taxi Driver
1978 Midnight Express
1979 Kramer Vs. Kramer
1980 Tess
1982 Gandhi
1982 Tootsie
1983 The Big Chill
1983 The Dresser
1984 A Passage to India
1984 A Soldier's Story
1987 Hope and Glory
1987 The Last Emperor

Best Foreign Language Film

1962 Sundays and Cybele
1970 Investigation of a Citizen Above Suspicion

Best Actor

1934 Clark Gable – It Happened One Night
1936 Gary Cooper – Mr. Deeds Goes to Town
1939 James Stewart – Mr. Smith Goes to Washington
1941 Cary Grant – Penny Serenade
1941 Robert Montgomery – Here Comes Mr. Jordan
1945 Cornel Wilde – A Song to Remember
1946 Larry Parks – The Jolson Story

1949 Broderick Crawford—All the King's Men
1951 Fredric March—Death of a Salesman
1953 Montgomery Clift—From Here to Eternity
1953 Burt Lancaster—From Here to Eternity
1954 Humphrey Bogart—The Caine Mutiny
1954 Marlon Brando—On the Waterfront
1957 Alec Guinness—The Bridge on the River Kwai
1959 Paul Muni—The Last Angry Man
1959 James Stewart—Anatomy of a Murder
1962 Peter O'Toole—Lawrence of Arabia
1964 Peter Sellers—Dr. Strangelove
1965 Lee Marvin—Cat Ballou
1965 Oskar Werner—Ship of Fools
1966 Paul Scofield—A Man for All Seasons
1967 Spencer Tracy—Guess Who's Coming to Dinner
1968 Ron Moody—Oliver!
1970 Melvyn Douglas—I Never Sang for My Father
1970 Jack Nicholson—Five Easy Pieces
1973 Jack Nicholson—The Last Detail
1976 Robert DeNiro—Taxi Driver
1978 Gary Busey—The Buddy Holly Story
1979 Dustin Hoffman—Kramer vs. Kramer
1979 Al Pacino— . . . And Justice for All
1979 Jack Lemmon—The China Syndrome
1981 Paul Newman—Absence of Malice
1982 Ben Kingsley—Gandhi
1982 Dustin Hoffman—Tootsie
1983 Michael Caine—Educating Rita

1983 Tom Courtenay—The Dresser
1983 Albert Finney—The Dresser
1984 Jeff Bridges—Starman
1985 James Garner—Murphy's Romance

Best Actress

1932/33 May Robson—Lady for a Day
1934 Claudette Colbert—It Happened One Night
1934 Grace Moore—One Night of Love
1936 Irene Dunne—Theodora Goes Wild
1937 Irene Dunne—The Awful Truth
1942 Rosalind Russell—My Sister Eileen
1943 Jean Arthur—The More the Merrier
1950 Judy Holliday—Born Yesterday
1952 Julie Harris—The Member of the Wedding
1953 Deborah Kerr—From Here to Eternity
1959 Katharine Hepburn—Suddenly, Last Summer
1959 Elizabeth Taylor—Suddenly, Last Summer
1963 Leslie Caron—The L-Shaped Room
1965 Samantha Eggar—The Collector
1965 Simone Signoret—Ship of Fools
1966 Lynn Redgrave—Georgy Girl
1967 Katharine Hepburn—Guess Who's Coming to Dinner
1968 Barbra Streisand—Funny Girl
1971 Janet Suzman—Nicholas and Alexandra
1973 Barbra Streisand—The Way We Were

1973	Joanne Woodward – Summer Wishes, Winter Dreams
1975	Ann-Margret – Tommy
1979	Jane Fonda – The China Syndrome
1979	Marsha Mason – Chapter Two
1980	Gena Rowlands – Gloria
1981	Marsha Mason – Only When I Laugh
1983	Julie Walters – Educating Rita
1984	Judy Davis – A Passage to India
1985	Anne Bancroft – Agnes of God

Best Supporting Actor

1937	Ralph Bellamy – The Awful Truth
1937	H. B. Warner – Lost Horizon
1939	Harry Carey – Mr. Smith Goes to Washington
1939	Claude Rains – Mr. Smith Goes to Washington
1941	James Gleason – Here Comes Mr. Jordan
1943	**Charles Coburn – The More the Merrier**
1943	J. Carrol Naish – Sahara
1946	William Demarest – The Jolson Story
1949	John Ireland – All the King's Men
1951	Kevin McCarthy – Death of a Salesman
1953	**Frank Sinatra – From Here to Eternity**
1954	Lee J. Cobb – On the Waterfront
1954	Karl Malden – On the Waterfront
1954	Rod Steiger – On the Waterfront
1954	Tom Tully – The Caine Mutiny
1955	Arthur O'Connell – Picnic
1957	Sessue Hayakawa – The Bridge on the River Kwai
1959	Arthur O'Connell – Anatomy of a Murder

1959	George C. Scott – Anatomy of a Murder
1962	Omar Sharif – Lawrence of Arabia
1963	John Huston – The Cardinal
1965	Michael Dunn – Ship of Fools
1966	James Mason – Georgy Girl
1966	Robert Shaw – A Man for All Seasons
1967	Cecil Kellaway – Guess Who's Coming to Dinner
1968	Jack Wild – Oliver!
1969	Elliott Gould – Bob & Carol & Ted & Alice
1969	Jack Nicholson – Easy Rider
1970	Gene Hackman – I Never Sang for My Father
1971	Jeff Bridges – The Last Picture Show
1971	**Ben Johnson – The Last Picture Show**
1973	Randy Quaid – The Last Detail
1975	Jack Warden – Shampoo
1978	John Hurt – Midnight Express
1979	Justin Henry – Kramer Vs. Kramer
1981	James Coco – Only When I Laugh
1984	Adolph Caesar – A Soldier's Story
1984	Noriyuki "Pat" Morita – The Karate Kid
1985	Robert Loggia – Jagged Edge

Best Supporting Actress

1938	Spring Byington – You Can't Take It with You
1949	**Mercedes McCambridge – All the King's Men**
1951	Mildred Dunnock – Death of a Salesman
1953	**Donna Reed – From Here to Eternity**
1954	**Eva Marie Saint – On the Waterfront**
1966	Wendy Hiller – A Man for All Seasons

1967   Beah Richards—Guess Who's Coming to Dinner
1968   Kay Medford—Funny Girl
1969   Dyan Cannon—Bob & Carol & Ted & Alice
1969   **Goldie Hawn—Cactus Flower**
1970   Karen Black—Five Easy Pieces
1971   Ellen Burstyn—The Last Picture Show
1971   **Cloris Leachman—The Last Picture Show**
1971   Margaret Leighton—The Go-Between
1972   **Eileen Heckart—Butterflies Are Free**
1972   Susan Tyrrell—Fat City
1973   Sylvia Sidney—Summer Wishes, Winter Dreams
1975   **Lee Grant—Shampoo**
1976   Jodie Foster—Taxi Driver
1977   Melinda Dillon—Close Encounters of the Third Kind
1978   **Maggie Smith—California Suite**
1979   **Meryl Streep—Kramer Vs. Kramer**
1979   Jane Alexander—Kramer Vs. Kramer
1981   Melinda Dillon—Absence of Malice
1981   Joan Hackett—Only When I Laugh
1982   **Jessica Lange—Tootsie**
1982   Teri Garr—Tootsie
1983   Glenn Close—The Big Chill
1984   **Peggy Ashcroft—A Passage to India**
1985   Meg Tilly—Agnes of God

Best Director

1932/33 Frank Capra—Lady for a Day
1934   **Frank Capra—It Happened One Night**
1934   Victor Schertzinger—One Night of Love

1936   **Frank Capra—Mr. Deeds Goes to Town**
1937   **Leo McCarey—The Awful Truth**
1938   **Frank Capra—You Can't Take It with You**
1939   Frank Capra—Mr. Smith Goes to Washington
1941   Alexander Hall—Here Comes Mr. Jordan
1943   George Stevens—The More the Merrier
1949   Robert Rossen—All the King's Men
1950   George Cukor—Born Yesterday
1953   **Fred Zinnemann—From Here to Eternity**
1954   **Elia Kazan—On the Waterfront**
1955   Joshua Logan—Picnic
1957   **David Lean—The Bridge on the River Kwai**
1961   J. Lee Thompson—The Guns of Navarone
1962   **David Lean—Lawrence of Arabia**
1963   Otto Preminger—The Cardinal
1964   Stanley Kubrick—Dr. Strangelove
1965   William Wyler—The Collector
1966   Richard Brooks—The Professionals
1966   **Fred Zinnemann—A Man for All Seasons**
1967   Richard Brooks—In Cold Blood
1967   Stanley Kramer—Guess Who's Coming to Dinner
1968   **Carol Reed—Oliver!**
1971   Peter Bogdanovich—The Last Picture Show
1977   Steven Spielberg—Close Encounters of the Third Kind
1978   Alan Parker—Midnight Express
1979   **Robert Benton—Kramer Vs. Kramer**

1980   Roman Polanski—Tess
1982   Richard   Attenborough—Gandhi
1982   Wolfgang Petersen—Das Boot (The Boat)
1982   Sydney Pollack—Tootsie
1983   Peter Yates—The Dresser
1984   David Lean—A Passage to India
1987   Bernardo Bertolucci—The Last Emperor
1987   John Boorman—Hope and Glory

Writing—Adaptation

1930/31   Seton I. Miller, Fred Niblo, Jr.—The Criminal Code
1932/33   Robert Riskin—Lady for a Day
1934   Robert Riskin—It Happened One Night

Writing—Screenplay

1936   Robert Riskin—Mr. Deeds Goes to Town
1937   Vina Delmar—The Awful Truth
1938   Robert Riskin—You Can't Take It with You
1939   Sidney Buchman—Mr. Smith Goes to Washington
1941   Seton I. Miller, Sidney Buchman—Here Comes Mr. Jordan
1942   Rodney Ackland, Emeric Pressburger—The Invaders
1942   Sidney Buchman, Irwin Shaw—The Talk of the Town
1943   Richard Flournoy, Lewis R. Foster, Frank Ross, Robert Russell—The More the Merrier
1949   Robert Rossen—All the King's Men
1950   Albert Mannheimer—Born Yesterday

1953   Daniel Taradash—From Here to Eternity
1954   Stanley Roberts—The Caine Mutiny

Writing—Original Story

1939   Lewis R. Foster—Mr. Smith Goes to Washington
1941   Harry Segall—Here Comes Mr. Jordan
1942   Emeric Pressburger—The Invaders
1942   Sidney Harmon—The Talk of the Town
1943   Frank Ross, Robert Russell—The More the Merrier
1944   Alfred Neumann, Joseph Than—None Shall Escape
1945   Ernst Marischka—A Song to Remember

Writing—Original Screenplay

1940   Ben Hecht—Angels Over Broadway
1975   Robert Towne, Warren Beatty—Shampoo

Writing—Story and Screenplay

1949   Sidney Buchman—Jolson Sings Again
1954   Budd Schulberg—On the Waterfront

Writing—Motion Picture Story

1952   Edna Anhalt, Edward Anhalt—The Sniper
1956   Leo Katcher—The Eddy Duchin Story

Writing—Story and Screenplay—based on factual or unpublished material

1969 Paul Mazursky, Larry Tucker—Bob & Carol & Ted & Alice
1969 Dennis Hopper, Peter Fonda, Terry Southern—Easy Rider
1970 Bob Rafelson, Adrien Joyce—Five Easy Pieces
1971 Elio Petri, Ugo Pirro—Investigation of a Citizen Above Suspicion
1972 Carl Foreman—Young Winston

Writing—Screenplay—based on material from another medium

1957 Pierre Boulle—The Bridge on the River Kwai
1959 Wendell Mayes—Anatomy of a Murder
1961 Carl Foreman—The Guns of Navarone
1962 Robert Bolt—Lawrence of Arabia
1963 Serge Bourguignon, Antoine Tudal—Sundays and Cybele
1964 Stanley Kubrick, Terry Southern, Peter George—Dr. Strangelove
1965 Walter Newman, Frank R. Pierson—Cat Ballou
1965 Stanley Mann, John Kohn—The Collector
1965 Abby Mann—Ship of Fools
1966 Robert Bolt—A Man for All Seasons
1966 Richard Brooks—The Professionals
1967 Richard Brooks—In Cold Blood
1968 Vernon Harris—Oliver!

1970 Robert Anderson—I Never Sang for My Father
1971 Larry McMurtry, Peter Bogdanovich—The Last Picture Show
1973 Robert Towne—The Last Detail
1975 Ted Allan—Lies My Father Told Me
1978 Oliver Stone—Midnight Express
1978 Neil Simon—California Suite
1979 Robert Benton—Kramer Vs. Kramer
1982 Wolfgang Petersen—Das Boot (The Boat)
1983 Ronald Harwood—The Dresser
1983 Willy Russell—Educating Rita
1984 David Lean—A Passage to India
1984 Charles Fuller—A Soldier's Story
1986 Raynold Gideon, Bruce A. Evans—Stand by Me
1987 Mark Peploe, Bernardo Bertolucci, Enzo Ungari—The Last Emperor

Writing—Story and Screenplay—written directly for the screen

1958 Paddy Chayefsky—The Goddess
1967 William Rose—Guess Who's Coming to Dinner
1967 Robert Kaufman, Norman Lear—Divorce American Style
1976 Walter Bernstein—The Front
1979 Valerie Curtin, Barry Levinson—...And Justice for All
1979 Mike Gray, T. S. Cook, James Bridges—The China Syndrome
1981 Kurt Luedtke—Absence of Malice
1982 John Briley—Gandhi

1982 Don McGuire, Larry Gelbart, Murray Schisgal—Tootsie
1983 Lawrence Kasdan, Barbara Benedek—The Big Chill
1987 John Boorman—Hope and Glory

Cinematography—B&W

1938 Joseph Walker—You Can't Take It with You
1939 Joseph Walker—Only Angels Have Wings
1941 Joseph Walker—Here Comes Mr. Jordan
1941 Ted Tetzlaff—The Talk of the Town
1943 Rudolph Mate—Sahara
1951 Frank Planer—Death of a Salesman
1953 Hal Mohr—The Four Poster
1953 Burnett Guffey—From Here to Eternity
1954 Boris Kaufman—On the Waterfront
1955 Charles Lang—Queen Bee
1956 Burnett Guffey—The Harder They Fall
1959 Sam Levitt—Anatomy of a Murder
1965 Burnett Guffey—King Rat
1965 Ernest Laszlo—Ship of Fools
1966 Ken Higgins—Georgy Girl
1967 Conrad Hall—In Cold Blood
1971 Robert Surtees—The Last Picture Show

Cinematography—Color

1944 Rudolph Mate, Allen M. Davey—Cover Girl
1945 Anthony Gaudio, Allen M. Davey—A Song to Remember
1946 Joseph Walker—The Jolson Story
1948 William Snyder—The Loves of Carmen
1949 William Snyder—Jolson Sings Again

1956 Harry Stradling—The Eddy Duchin Story
1957 Jack Hildyard—The Bridge on the River Kwai
1959 Leon Shamroy—Porgy and Bess
1960 Joe MacDonald—Pepe
1963 Fred A. Young—Lawrence of Arabia
1963 Leon Shamroy—The Cardinal
1966 Ted Moore—A Man for All Seasons
1966 Conrad Hall—The Professionals
1968 Harry Stradling, Jr.—Funny Girl
1968 Oswald Morris—Oliver!
1969 Charles B. Lang—Bob & Carol & Ted & Alice
1969 Daniel Fapp—Marooned
1971 Freddie Young—Nicholas and Alexandra
1972 Charles B. Lang—Butterflies Are Free
1972 Harry Stradling, Jr.—1776
1973 Harry Stradling, Jr.—The Way We Were
1975 James Wong Howe—Funny Lady
1977 Vilmos Zsigmond—Close Encounters of the Third Kind
1979 Nestor Almendros—Kramer Vs. Kramer
1980 Nestor Almendros—The Blue Lagoon
1980 Geoffrey Unsworth, Ghislain Cloquet—Tess
1982 Jost Vacano—Das Boot (The Boat)
1982 Billy Williams, Ronnie Taylor—Gandhi
1982 Owen Roizman—Tootsie
1984 Ernest Day—A Passage to India
1985 William A. Fraker—Murphy's Romance
1987 Philippe Rousselot—Hope and Glory
1987 Vittorio Storaro—The Last Emperor

Art Direction/Set Decoration — B&W

1937 Stephen Goosson—Lost Horizon

1938 Stephen Goosson, Lionel Banks—Holiday

1939 Lionel Banks—Mr. Smith Goes to Washington

1940 Lionel Banks, Robert Peterson—Arizona

1941 Lionel Banks, George Montgomery—Ladies in Retirement

1942 Lionel Banks, Rudolph Sternad, Fay Babcock—The Talk of the Town

1944 Lionel Banks, Walter Holscher, Joseph Kish—Address Unknown

1954 Richard Day—On the Waterfront

1956 Ross Bellah, William Kiernan, Louis Diage—The Solid Gold Cadillac

1956 Takasai Matsuyama—Seven Samurai (The Magnificent Seven)

1959 Carl Anderson, William Kiernan—The Last Angry Man

1959 Oliver Messell, William Kellner, Scot Slimon—Suddenly, Last Summer

1965 Robert Emmett Smith, Frank Tuttle—King Rat

1965 Robert Clatworthy, Joseph Kish—Ship of Fools

Art Direction/Set Decoration — Color

1944 Lionel Banks, Cary Odell, Fay Babcock—Cover Girl

1945 Stephen Goosson, Rudolph Sternad, Frank Tuttle—A Thousand and One Nights

1956 William Flannery, Jo Mielziner, Robert Priestley—Picnic

1957 Walter Holscher, William Kiernan, Louis Daige—Pal Joey

1958 Cary Odell, Louis Daige—Bell, Book, and Candle

1960 Ted Haworth, William Kiernan—Pepe

1962 John Box, John Stoll, Dario Simoni—Lawrence of Arabia

1963 Lyle Wheeler, Gene Callahan—The Cardinal

1967 Robert Clatworthy, Frank Tuttle—Guess Who's Coming to Dinner

1967 Renzo Mongiardino, John Decuir, Elven Webb, Giuseppe Mariani, Dario Simoni, Luigi Gervasi—The Taming of the Shrew

1968 John Box, Terence Marsh, Vernon Dixon, Ken Muggleston—Oliver!

1971 John Box, Ernest Archer, Jack Maxsted, Gil Parrondo, Vernon Dixon—Nicholas and Alexandra

1972 Don Ashton, Geoffrey Drake, John Graysmark, William Hutchinson, Peter James—Young Winston

1973 Stephen Grimes, William Kiernan—The Way We Were

1975 Richard Sylbert, W. Stewart Campbell—Shampoo

1977 Joe Alves, Dan Lomino—Close Encounters of the Third Kind

1978 Albert Brenner, Marvin March—California Suite

1979 Arthur Jeph Parker, George Jenkins—The China Syndrome

1980 Pierre Guffroy, Jack Stevens—Tess

1982 Stuart Craig, Bob Laing, Michael Seirton—Gandhi

1982 Dale Hennesy, Marvin March—Annie

1984 John Box, Hugh Scaife—A Passage to India

1987 Anthony Pratt, Joan Woollard—Hope and Glory
1987 Ferdinando Scarfiotti, Bruno Caesari—The Last Emperor

Sound

1934—Paul Neal—One Night of Love
1935 John Livadary—Love Me Forever
1936 John Livadary—Mr. Deeds Goes to Town
1937 John Livadary—Lost Horizon
1938 John Livadary—You Can't Take It with You
1939 John Livadary—Mr. Smith Goes to Washington
1940 Jack Whitney, General Service—The Howards of Virginia
1940 John Livadary—Too Many Husbands
1941 John Livadary—The Men in Her Life
1942 John Livadary—You Were Never Lovelier
1943 John Livadary—Sahara
1944 John Livadary—Cover Girl
1945 John Livadary—A Song to Remember
1946 **John Livadary—The Jolson Story**
1953 **John Livadary—From Here to Eternity**
1954 John Livadary—The Caine Mutiny
1956 John Livadary—The Eddy Duchin Story
1957 John Livadary—Pal Joey
1959 Samuel Goldwyn—Sound Department—Gordon E. Sawyer, Todd-AO Sound Department—Fred Hynes—Porgy and Bess
1960 Charles Rice—Pepe
1961 Shepperton Studio Sound Department—John Cox—The Guns of Navarone

1962 Shepperton Studio Sound Department—John Cox—Lawrence of Arabia
1963 Charles Rice—Bye Bye Birdie
1968 Columbia Studio Sound Department—Funny Girl
1968 **Shepperton Studio Sound Department—Oliver!**
1969 Les Fresholtz, Arthur Piantadosi—Marooned
1972 Arthur Piantadosi, Charles Knight—Butterflies Are Free
1975 Arthur Piantadosi, Les Fresholtz, Richard Tyler, Al Overton, Jr.—Bite the Bullet
1975 Richard Portman, Don MacDougall, Curly Thirlwell, Jack Solomon—Funny Lady
1977 Robert Knudson, Robert J. Glass, Don MacDougall, Gene S. Cantamessa—Close Encounters of the Third Kind
1977 Walter Goss, Dick Alexander, Tom Beckert, Robin Gregory—The Deep
1978 Tex Rudloff, Joel Fein, Curly Thirlwell, Willie Barry Thomas—The Buddy Holly Story
1982 Milan Bor, Trevor Pyke, Mike Le-Mare—Das Boot (The Boat)
1982 **Gerry Humphreys, Robin O'Donoghue, Jonathan Bates, Simon Kaye—Gandhi**
1982 Arthur Piantadosi, Les Fresholtz, Dick Alexander, Les Lazarowitz—Tootsie
1984 Graham Hairstone, Nicholas Le Messurier, Michael A. Carter, John Mitchell—A Passage to India
1985 Donald Mitchell, Rick Kline, Kevin O'Donnell, David Ronne—Silverado
1985 Donald Mitchell, Michael Minkler, Gerry Humphreys, Chris Newman—A Chorus Line
1987 **Bill Rowe, Ivan Sharrock—The Last Emperor**

Film Editing

1934 Gene Milford — One Night of Love
1936 Otto Meyer — Theodora Goes Wild
1937 Al Clark — The Awful Truth
1937 Gene Milford, Gene Havlick — Lost Horizon
1938 Gene Havlick — You Can't Take It with You
1939 Gene Havlick, Al Clark — Mr. Smith Goes to Washington
1942 Otto Meyer — The Talk of the Town
1945 Charles Nelson — A Song to Remember
1946 William Lyon — The Jolson Story
1949 Robert Parrish, Al Clark — All the King's Men
1953 William Lyon — From Here to Eternity
1954 William Lyon, Henry Batista — The Caine Mutiny
1954 Gene Milford — On the Waterfront
1955 William Lyon, Charles Nelson — Picnic
1957 Viola Lawrence, Jerome Thoms — Pal Joey
1957 Peter Taylor — The Bridge on the River Kwai
1958 William Lyon, Al Clark — Cowboy
1959 Lewis R. Loeffler — Anatomy of a Murder
1960 Viola Lawrence, Al Clark — Pepe
1961 Alan Osbiston — The Guns of Navarone
1962 Anne Coates — Lawrence of Arabia
1963 Lewis R. Loeffler — The Cardinal
1965 Charles Nelson — Cat Ballou
1967 Robert C. Jones — Guess Who's Coming to Dinner
1968 Robert Swink, Maury Winetrobe, William Sands — Funny Girl
1968 Ralph Kemplen — Oliver!
1977 Michael Kahn — Close Encounters of the Third Kind
1978 Gerry Hambling — Midnight Express
1979 Jerry Greenberg — Kramer Vs. Kramer
1980 David Blewitt — The Competition
1982 Hannes Nikel — Das Boot (The Boat)
1982 John Bloom — Gandhi
1982 Frederic Steinkamp, William Steinkamp — Tootsie
1983 Frank Morris, Edward Abroms — Blue Thunder
1984 David Lean — A Passage to India
1985 John Bloom — A Chorus Line
1987 Gabriella Cristiani — The Last Emperor

Costume Design — B&W

1950 Jean Louis — Born Yesterday
1952 Jean Louis — Affair in Trinidad
1953 Jean Louis — From Here to Eternity
1954 Christian Dior — Indiscretion of an American Wife
1954 Jean Louis — It Should Happen to You
1955 Jean Louis — Queen Bee
1956 Kohei Ezaki — Seven Samurai (The Magnificent Seven)
1956 Jean Louis — The Solid Gold Cadillac
1965 Jean Louis, Bill Thomas — Ship of Fools

Costume Design — Color

1957 Jean Louis — Pal Joey
1958 Jean Louis — Bell, Book and Candle

1959 Irene Sharaff—Porgy and Bess
1960 Edith Head—Pepe
1963 Donald Brooks—The Cardinal
1966 **Elizabeth Haffenden, Joan Bridge—A Man for All Seasons**
1967 **Irene   Sharaff,   Danilo Donati— The Taming of the Shrew**
1968 **Phyllis Dalton—Oliver!**
1970 **Nino Novarese—Cromwell**
1971 **Yvonne Blake, Antonio Castillo—Nicholas and Alexandra**
1972 Anthony Mendleson—Young Winston
1973 Dorothy Jeakins, Moss Mabry—The Way We Were
1975 Ray Aghayan, Bob Mackie— Funny Lady
1980 **Anthony Powell—Tess**
1982 **John Mollo, Bhanu Athaiya— Gandhi**
1984 Judy Moorcroft—A Passage to India
1987 **James Acheson—The Last Emperor**

Music Scoring—Original—Drama or Musical

1934 **Louis Silvers, Victor Schertzinger, Gus Kahn—One Night of Love**
1937 Morris Stoloff, Dimitri Tiomkin—Lost Horizon
1938 Morris   Stoloff,   Gregory Stone—Girl's School
1939 Dimitri Tiomkin—Mr. Smith Goes to Washington
1939 Victor Young—Golden Boy
1940 Victor Young—Arizona
1940 Louis Gruenberg—The Fight for Life
1940 Richard Hageman—The Howards of Virginia
1941 Morris Stoloff, Ernst Toch— Ladies in Retirement

1941 Morris Stoloff—You'll Never Get Rich
1942 Morris Stoloff, Frederick Hollander—The Talk of the Town
1942 Leigh Harline—You Were Never Lovelier
1943 Morris Stoloff, Louis Gruenberg—The Commandos Strike at Dawn
1943 Morris Stoloff—Something to Shout About
1944 Morris Stoloff, Ernst Toch— Address Unknown
1944 **Morris   Stoloff,   Carmen Dragon—Cover Girl**
1945 Morris Stoloff, Miklos Rozsa— A Song to Remember
1945 Morris Stoloff, Marlin Skiles— Tonight and Every Night
1946 **Morris Stoloff—The Jolson Story**
1949 Morris   Stoloff,   George Duning—Jolson Sings Again
1950 George   Duning—No   Sad Songs for Me
1951 Alex North—Death of a Salesman
1953 Morris Stoloff, George Duning—From Here to Eternity
1953 Morris   Stoloff,   Frederick Hollander—The 5,000 Fingers of Dr. T
1954 Max Steiner—The Caine Mutiny
1954 Leonard Bernstein—On the Waterfront
1955 George Duning—Picnic
1956 Morris Stoloff, George Duning—The Eddy Duchin Story
1957 **Malcolm Arnold—The Bridge on the River Kwai**
1959 **Andre Previn, Ken Darby— Porgy and Bess**
1960 Johnny Green—Pepe
1960 **Morris Stoloff, Harry Sukman—Song Without End**
1961 Dimitri Tiomkin—The Guns of Navarone
1962 **Maurice Jarre—Lawrence of Arabia**

1963   John Green—Bye Bye Birdie
1963   Maurice Jarre—Sundays and
       Cybele
1965   DeVol—Cat Ballou
1966   John Barry—Born Free
1967   Quincy Jones—In Cold Blood
1968   Walter Schraf—Funny Girl
1968   John Green—Oliver!
1970   Frank Cordell—Cromwell
1971   Richard Rodney Bennett—
       Nicholas and Alexandra
1972   John Williams—Images
**1973   Marvin Hamlisch—The Way
       We Were**
1975   Gerald Fried—Birds Do It,
       Bees Do It
1975   Alex North—Bite the Bullet
1976   Bernard Herrmann—Obses-
       sion
1976   Bernard   Herrmann—Taxi
       Driver
1977   John Williams—Close Encoun-
       ters of the Third Kind
**1978   Giorgio Moroder—Midnight
       Express**
1980   Philippe Sarde—Tess
1982   Ravi Shankar, George Fen-
       ton—Gandhi
**1984   Maurice Jarre—A Passage to
       India**
1985   George Delerue—Agnes of
       God
1985   Bruce Broughton—Silverado
**1987   Ryuichi Sakamoto, Cong Su,
       David   Byrne—The   Last
       Emperor**

Music Scoring—Adaptation

1967   DeVol—Guess Who's Coming
       to Dinner
1975   Peter Matz—Funny Lady
1975   Peter Townshend—Tommy
**1978   Joe Renzetti—The Buddy
       Holly Story**
1982   Ralph Burns—Annie
1982   Tom Waits—One from the
       Heart

Best Song

1936   "Pennies from Heaven" from
       Pennies from Heaven—Music
       by Arthur Johnson, Lyrics by
       Johnny Burke
1938   "A Mist Over the Moon" from
       The Lady Objects—Music by
       Ben Oakland, Lyrics by Oscar
       Hammerstein II
1940   "It's a Blue World" from *Music
       in My Heart*—Music and Lyrics
       by Chet Forrest and Bob
       Wright
1941   "Since I Kissed My Baby Good-
       bye" from *You'll Never Get
       Rich*—Music and Lyrics by
       Cole Porter
1942   "Dearly Beloved" from *You
       Were Never Lovelier*—Music by
       Jerome Kern, Lyrics by Johnny
       Mercer
1943   "You'd Be So Nice to Come
       Home To" from *Something to
       Shout   About*—Music   and
       Lyrics by Cole Porter
1944   "Long Ago and Far Away" from
       Cover Girl—Music by Jerome
       Kern, Lyrics by Ira Gershwin
1945   "Anywhere" from *Tonight and
       Every Night*—Music by Jule
       Styne, Lyrics by Sammy Cahn
1953   "Blue Pacific Blues" (Sadie's
       song) from *Miss Sadie Thomp-
       son*—Music by Lester Lee,
       Lyrics by Ned Washington
1959   "Strange Are the Ways of Love"
       from *The Young Land*—Music
       by Dimitri Tiomkin, Lyrics by
       Ned Washington
1960   "Faraway Part of Town" from
       Pepe—Music by Andre Previn,
       Lyrics by Dory Langdon
1962   "Walk on the Wild Side" from
       Walk on the Wild Side—Music
       by Elmer Bernstein, Lyrics by
       Mack David
1965   "The Ballad of Cat Ballou"
       from *Cat Ballou*—Music by

Jerry Livingston, Lyrics by Mack David

1966 **"Born Free"** from *Born Free*—Music by **John Barry,** Lyrics by **Don Black**

1966 "Georgy Girl" from *Georgy Girl*—Music by Tom Springfield, Lyrics by Jim Dale

1967 "The Look of Love" from *Casino Royale*—Music by Burt Bacharach, Lyrics by Hal David

1968 "Funny Girl" from *Funny Girl*—Music by Jule Styne, Lyrics by Bob Merrill

1971 "Bless the Beasts and Children" from *Bless the Beasts and Children*—Music and Lyrics by Barry DeVorzon and Perry Botkin, Jr.

1973 **"The Way We Were"** from *The Way We Were*—Music by **Marvin Hamlisch,** Lyrics by **Alan and Marilyn Bergman**

1975 "How Lucky Can You Get" from *Funny Lady*—Music and Lyrics by Fred Ebb and John Kander

1977 **"You Light Up My Life"** from *You Light Up My Life*—Music and Lyrics by **Joseph Brooks**

1978 **"Last Dance"** from *Thank God It's Friday*—Music and Lyrics by **Paul Jabara**

1979 "Through the Eyes of Love" from *Ice Castles*—Music by Marvin Hamlisch, Lyrics by Carole Bayer Sager

1980 "People Alone" from *The Competition*—Music by Lalo Schifrin, Lyrics by Wilbur Jennings

1982 "It Might Be You" from *Tootsie*—Music by Dave Grusin, Lyrics by Alan and Marilyn Bergman

1984 **"Take a Look at Me Now"** from *Against All Odds*—Music and Lyrics by **Phil Collins**

1984 "Ghostbusters" from *Ghost-*

busters—Music and Lyrics by Ray Parker, Jr.

1985 "Separate Lives" from *White Knights*—Music and Lyrics by Stephen Bishop

1985 **"Say You, Say Me"** from *White Knights*—Music and Lyrics by **Lionel Ritchie**

1985 "Surprise, Surprise" from *A Chorus Line*—Music by Marvin Hamlisch, Lyrics by Edward Kleban

1986 "Glory of Love" from *The Karate Kid, Part II*—Music by Peter Cetera and David Foster, Lyrics by Peter Cetera and Diane Nini

1986 "Life in a Looking Glass" from *That's Life!*—Music by Henry Mancini, Lyrics by Leslie Bricusse

Best Make-Up

1982 Tom Smith—Gandhi
1987 Bob Laden—Happy New Year

Special Effects

1939 Roy Davidson, Edward C. Hahn—Only Angels Have Wings

1944 David Allen, Ray Corey, Robert Wright, Russell Malmgren, Harry Kusnick—Secret Command

1945 L. W. Butler, Ray Bomba—A Thousand and One Nights

1961 **Bill Warrington, Vivian C. Greenham**—The Guns of Navarone

Special Visual Effects

1969 Robbie Robertson—Marooned

Best Visual Effects

1977   Roy Arbogast, Douglas Trumbull, Matthew Yuricich, Gregory Jein, Richard Yuricich—Close Encounters of the Third Kind
1984   Richard Edlund, John Bruno, Mark Vargo, Chuck Gasper—Ghostbusters

Special Achievement—Sound Effects Editing

1977   Frank Warner—Close Encounters of the Third Kind

Best Sound Effects Editing

1982   Mike Le-Mare—Das Boot (The Boat)

Short Films—Comedies

1934   Jules White—Men in Black
1935   Jules White—Oh, My Nerves

Short Films—One Reelers (Screen Snapshots Series)

1943   Ralph Staub—Hollywood in Uniform
1944   Ralph Staub—50th Anniversary of Motion Pictures
1945   Ralph Staub—Screen Snapshots 25th Anniversary

Short Films—Two Reelers

1945   Jules White—The Jury Goes Round 'N' Round (Comedy)
1946   Jules White—Hiss and Yell (Comedy)
1947   Ben Blake—A Voice Is Born (Musical Featurette)

Short Films—Cartoons

1931/32   Walt Disney—Mickey's Orphans
1934   Charles Mintz—Holiday Land
1937   Charles Mintz—The Little Match Girl
1941   Columbia—How War Came (This Changing World series)
1943   Columbia—Imagination
1944   Columbia—The Dog, Cat and Canary
1945   Columbia—Rippling Romance
1948   Stephen Bosustow—Robin Hoodlum
1949   Stephen Bosustow—Magic Fluke
1950   Stephen Bosustow—Gerald McBoing Boing
1950   Stephen Bosustow—Trouble Indemnity
1951   Stephen Bosustow—Rooty Toot Toot
1952   Stephen Bosustow—Madeline
1952   Stephen Bosustow—Pink and Blue Blues
1953   Stephen Bosustow—Christopher Crumpet
1953   Stephen Bosustow—The Tell Tale Heart
1954   Stephen Bosustow—When Magoo Flew
1956   Stephen Bosustow—Gerald McBoing Boing on Planet Moo
1956   Stephen Bosustow—The Jaywalker
1956   Stephen Bosustow—Magoo's Puddle Jumper
1957   Stephen Bosustow—Trees and Jamaica Daddy
1963   Ernest Pintoff—The Critic
1967   Robert Verrall, Wolf Koenig—What on Earth!
1968   Wolf Koenig, Jim MacKay—The House That Jack Built
1969   Ryan Larkin—Walking
1971   Michael Mills—Evolution

Short Films—Live Action

1959   Jacques-Yves Cousteau—The Golden Fish
1961   Robert Gaffney—Rooftops of New York
1967   Christopher Chapman—A Place to Stand
1968   National Film Board of Canada—Duo
1969   Marc Merson—People Soup
1972   Richard Barclay—Norman Rockwell's World . . . An American Dream

Documentary— Short Subjects

1967   Christopher Chapman—A Place to Stand

Documentary—Features

1945   Governments of Great Britain and the USA—The True Glory
1956   Jacques-Yves Cousteau—The Silent World
1957   Manuel Barbachano Ponce—Torero!
1964   Jack Le Vien—The Finest Hours
1964   Jacques-Yves Cousteau—World Without Sun
1968   Robert Cohn—Young Americans
1969   Olympic Organizing Committee—The Olympics in Mexico

Assistant Director

1937   C. C. Coleman, Jr.—Lost Horizon

Honorary Award

1968   Onna White—for her outstanding choreography achievement for *Oliver!*

Scientific or Technical Award—Class II

1950   John Livadary, Floyd Campbell, Lloyd Russell, Columbia Studio Sound Department—for the development of a multitrack magnetic re-recording system

Scientific or Technical Award—Class III

1934   Columbia Pictures Corp.—for their application of the vertical cut disc method (hill and dale recording) to actual studio production, with their recording of the sound on the picture *One Night of Love*
1937   John Livadary—Director of Sound for Columbia Pictures Corp. for the application of the bi-planar light valve to motion picture sound recording
1944   John Livadary, Bernard B. Brown—for the design and engineering of a separate soloist and recording session
1944   Paul Zeff, S. J. Twining, George Seid—of the Columbia Studio Laboratory for the formula and application to production of a simplified variable area sound negative developer
1954   John Livadary, Lloyd Russell, Columbia Studio Sound Department—for an improved limiting amplifier as applied to sound level comparison devices
1960   Arthur Holcomb, Petro Vlahos, Columbia Studio Camera Department—for a camera flicker indicating device

Bibliography

Adams, Les, and Buck Rainey. *Shoot-Em-Ups*. New Rochelle, N.Y.: Arlington House, 1978.

Alicoate, Jack, ed. *Film Daily Yearbook of Motion Pictures*. New York: The Film Daily, 1922–1970.

Baer, Richard D. *The Filmbuff's Checklist of Motion Pictures (1912–1979)*. Hollywood, Ca.: Hollywood Film Archive, 1979.

Barbour, Alan G. *The Serials of Columbia*. New York: Screen Facts Press, 1967.

Bergan, Ronald, and Robyn Karney. *The Holt Foreign Film Guide*. New York: Henry Holt and Company, 1988.

Bojarski, Richard. *The Films of Bela Lugosi*. Secaucus, N.J.: The Citadel Press, 1980.

———. and Kenneth Beals. *The Films of Boris Karloff*. Secaucus, N.J.: The Citadel Press, 1976.

Carmen, Bob, and Dan Scapperotti. *The Adventures of the Durango Kid*. 1983.

Cline, William C. *In the Nick of Time*. Jefferson, N.C.: McFarland & Co., 1984.

Connelly, Robert B. *The Motion Picture Guide: Silent Film 1910–1936*. Evanston, Il.: Cinebooks, Inc., 1986.

Cross, Robin. *2000 Movies: The 1940's*. New York: Arlington House, 1985.

———. *2000 Movies: The 1950's*. New York: Arlington House, 1988.

Deschner, Donald. *The Films of Cary Grant*. Secaucus, N.J.: The Citadel Press, 1973.

Dimmitt, Richard B. *A Title Guide to the Talkies (1927–1963)*. New York: The Scarecrow Press, Inc., 1965.

Dooley, Roger. *From Scarface to Scarlett: American Films in the 1930's*. New York: Harcourt Brace Jovanovich, 1981.

Edera, Bruno, and John Halas, ed. *Full Length Animated Feature Films*. New York: Hastings House, Publishers, 1977.

Eyles, Allen. *John Wayne*. New York: A.S. Barnes & Co., 1979.

———, Robert Adkinson and Nicholas Fry. *The House of Horror: The Complete Story of Hammer Films*. London: Lorrimer Publishing Ltd., 1971.

Finler, Joel W. *The Hollywood Story*. New York: Crown Publishers, 1988.

Gifford, Denis. *The British Film Catalogue 1895–1985, A Reference Guide*. New York: Facts on File Publications, 1986.

Hirschhorn, Clive. *The Hollywood Musical*. New York: Crown Publishers, 1981.

Larkin, Rochelle. *Hail Columbia*. New Rochelle, N.Y.: Arlington House, 1975.

Lenburg, Jeff. *The Encyclopedia of Animated Cartoon Series*. Westport, Ct.: Arlington House, 1981.

Maltin, Leonard. *Of Mice and Magic: A History of American Animated Cartoons*. New York: McGraw-Hill, 1980.

———. *Selected Short Subjects*. New York: Da Capo Press, 1972.

———. *TV Movies and Video Guide*. New American Library, 1967–1989.

McCarthy, Clifford. *Bogey: The Films of Humphrey Bogart*. Secaucus, N.J.: The Citadel Press, 1965.

Miller, Don. *B Movies*. New York: Ballantine Books, 1973.

Nash, Jay Robert, and Stanley Ralph Ross. *The Motion Picture Guide: 9 Vols*. Evanston, Il.: Cinebooks, Inc., 1986.

490   Bibliography

The New York Times Directory of the Film. New York: Arno Press/Random House, 1971.
The New York Times Film Reviews 1913-1968: 6 Vols. New York: Arno Press/New York Times, 1970.
Okuda, Ted, and Edward Watz. *The Columbia Comedy Shorts.* Jefferson, N.C.: McFarland & Co., 1986.
Parish, James Robert. *Hollywood Character Actors.* Westport, Ct.: Arlington House, 1978.
Peary, Danny. *Cult Movies.* New York: Dell Publishing Co., Inc., 1981.
Pitts, Michael R. *Famous Movie Detectives.* Metuchen, N.J.: Scarecrow Press, 1979.
————. *Hollywood and American History.* Jefferson, N.C.: McFarland & Co., 1984.
Quigley, Martin, Jr., ed. *International Motion Picture Almanac.* New York: Quigley Publishing Co., 1959-1967.
Quirk, Lawrence J. *The Complete Films of William Holden.* Secaucus, N.J.: The Citadel Press, 1986.
Rainey, Buck. *Saddle Aces of the Cinema.* New York: A. S. Barnes & Co., 1980.
Ringgold, Gene. *The Films of Rita Hayworth.* Secaucus, N.J.: The Citadel Press, 1980.
Rothel, David. *The Gene Autry Book.* Madison, N.C.: Empire Publishing Co., Inc., 1988.
Scherle, Victor, and William Turner Levy. *The Films of Frank Capra.* Secaucus, N.J.: The Citadel Press, 1977.
Snyder, Robert L. *Pare Lorenz and the Documentary Film.* Norman, Oklahoma: University of Oklahoma Press, 1968.
Thomas, Bob. *King Cohn: The Life and Times of Harry Cohn.* New York: G. P. Putnam's Sons, 1967.
Turner, George E., and Michael H. Price. *Forgotten Horrors: Early Talkie Chillers from Poverty Row.* Canbury, N.J.: A. S. Barnes and Co., 1979.
Weiss, Ken, and Ed Goodgold. *To Be Continued.* New York: Crown, 1972.
Weldon, Michael. *The Psychotronic Encyclopedia of Film.* New York: Ballentine Books, 1983.
Willis, John. *Screen World.* New York: Crown Publishers, 1966-1989.
Zinman, David. *Saturday Afternoon at the Bijou.* New Rochelle, N.Y.: Arlington House, 1973.

Name Index

The number after each name refers to the film entry number, not the page number.

The spelling of some names varied from film to film (i.e., Douglas/Douglass Dumbrille); these have been noted wherever possible.

Alternate names (i.e., Jacqueline Wells [Julie Bishop]) are also given wherever possible.

Abbe, Derwin 2391
Abbot, Anthony 351, 1400
Abbott, Diahnne 981
Abbott, John 107, 178,
  425, 440, 453, 863,
  1318, 1438, 1461, 1580,
  2076, 2176
Abbott, Ruth 1466
Abbott, Vic 1206
Abdul-Jabbar, Kareem 723
Abel, Robert 1123
Abel, Walter 643, 1029,
  1312
Abraham, Edward 2149
Abraham, Valerie 2149
Abrahams, Derwin 246,
  699, 1582, 1664, 1687,
  1720, 1732, 1858, 1894,
  1952, 1992, 2385, 2396,
  2419, 2424
Abrams, Leon 1317
Abril, Victoria 1334
"Ace," the dog 19, 2410
Achard, Marcel 1069
Achleson, John 2353
Acker, Sharon 820
Ackerman, Jack 1207
Ackerman, Leslie 827,
  1100
Ackerman, Robert 970
Ackland, Joss 1827, 2295
Ackland, Rodney 951,
  1212
Ackles, David 1364, 1663,
  1733, 1735, 1736, 1879

Ackroyd, David 1343
Acosta, Rudolfo 1122,
  2102
Acuff, Eddie 203, 208,
  210, 214, 215, 216, 219,
  221, 222, 290, 314, 529,
  983, 1064, 1117, 1118,
  1137, 1314, 1438, 1461,
  1782, 1857, 1880, 1992,
  2385
Acuff, Roy 888, 1857
Acuff, Roy, and His
  Smoky Mountain Boys
  and Girls 408
Adair, Phyllis 804
Adaire, Josephine 1337,
  1477
Adam, Ronald 182, 1485,
  1569, 1793
Adames, Juan 762
Adams, Abigail 1264, 2135
Adams, Arthur 792
Adams, Beverly 51, 171,
  812, 1030, 1356, 1823,
  2123, 2318
Adams, Casey 965
Adams, Coolidge 144
Adams, Dorothy 129, 494,
  619, 802, 1425
Adams, Edie 2181
Adams, Ernie 38, 184,
  293, 517, 578, 592, 626,
  810, 840, 849, 891, 915,
  964, 1064, 1107, 1156,
  1187, 1232, 1234, 1248,

1289, 1290, 1452, 1468,
  1491, 1563, 1586, 1679,
  1704, 1738, 1791, 1795,
  1804, 1807, 1867, 2037,
  2054, 2067, 2163, 2168,
  2258, 2262, 2380, 2396,
  2400, 2403, 2407, 2410,
  2421, 2425
Adams, Gerald Drayson
  151, 468, 539, 807, 2315
Adams, Jane 2376
Adams, Julie 2009, 2185
Adams, Lillian 575
Adams, Nan 680
Adams, Nick 950, 1562
Adams, Samuel Hopkins
  964, 2351
Adams, Stanley 857, 1658,
  1813, 2066
Adams, Stella 2286
Adams, Ted 272, 810,
  1095, 1362, 1620, 1725,
  1739, 2095, 2395, 2406
Adams, Tony 637, 1244,
  1299, 2046
Adamson, Ewart 482
Adamson, Hans Christian
  853
Adamson, Joy 238, 1152
Adcock, Danny 2250
Addams, Charles 1450
Addington, Sarah 62
Addis, H. B. 2362; see
  also Hugo Butler
Addy, Wesley 727

491

Basil, Toni 648
Basinger, Kim 1244, 1373
Baskin, Elya 1338
Baskin, William 775, 2370
Basquette, Lina 635, 856, 2364
Bass, Alfie 920
Bass, Emory 1787
Bass, Fred 1899, 2319
Bassani, Giorgio 2326
Basserman, Albert 778
Bassett, Steve 1909
Bassett, William 1008
Bast, William 812
Bastedo, Alexandra L. 2064
Bastian, Stephan 616
Bastianoni, Giancarlo 2245
Baston, J. Thornton 285
Bateman, Charles 267
Bateman, Zillah 933
Bates, Alan 466, 736, 763, 1435, 1731
Bates, Barbara 43, 75, 2126
Bates, Charles 1814
Bates, Florence 1525, 1998, 2117
Bates, Granville 963, 1127, 2180
Bates, Jeanne 184, 331, 1538, 1626, 1665, 1782, 1797, 1811, 1889, 1973, 2117, 2410
Bates, Kathryn 814
Bates, Michael 525, 812, 1421
Bates, Rhonda 603
Bateson, Timothy 1345, 1698
Batistella, Antonio 2242
Battaglia, Rik 487, 2093, 2326
Batten, Tom 1981
Battiferri, Nino 1379
Battle, Gordon 2140
Battley, David 1035
Bauer, Belinda 55
Bauer, Fred 273
Bauer, John W. 1758
Bauer, Margaret 1178
Bauer, Steven 122
Baugh, Sammy 2143

Baum, Len 1897
Bauman, Joanne 1608
Baumer, Marie 599
Baur, Ellen 1244
Bausch, Pina 64
Baviera, Jose 559
Baxley, Jack 1095, 2122
Baxley, Paul 45
Baxter, Alan 579, 593, 1124, 1170, 1344, 1371, 1917, 2179, 2311
Baxter, Anne 671, 2232
Baxter, Charles 1189
Baxter, Eugene 1632, 1763
Baxter, George 1055, 1583
Baxter, Teresa 970
Baxter, Warner 12, 93, 262, 412, 419, 420, 421, 422, 423, 424, 425, 500, 733, 1000, 1307, 1596, 1797, 1925, 2327
Bay, Tom 631
Baye, Nathalie 1098
Bayes, Georgia 2366
Bayldon, Geoffrey 84, 320, 449, 1027, 1134, 1486, 2109, 2166
Bayler, Terence 1206
Bayley, Hilda 1346
Baylis, Peter 638, 1154, 2069
Bayne, Beverly 2300
Bazhenova, Irina 1850
Beach, Jim 273
Beahan, Charles 1472, 2219
Beal, John 87, 562, 912, 1013, 1129, 1370, 1917
Beal, Royal 473
Beale, Nada 2166
Beals, Jennifer 256
Bean, Orson 58
Beane, Hilary 2039
Beard, Stymie 273, 468
Beardsley, Alice 2099
Bearse, Amanda 695
Bearsley, Barney 484
Beatty, Ned 55, 162, 2127
Beatty, Robert 1574
Beatty, Warren 518, 685, 957, 1142, 1298, 1800
Beaty, May 2207
Beaudine, William 1287,

2087
Beaumon, Leon 703, 1102, 1564
Beaumont, Gerald 1590, 1988
Beaumont, Hugh 660, 795, 857, 1326, 1626, 2051
Beaumont, L. C. 2113
Beaumont, Lucy 1935, 2087
Beaumont, Robert 1152
Beaune, Michel 100
Beaver, Walter 2217
Beavers, Louise 755, 766, 2014, 2270
Beche, Robert 2415
Bechi, Gino 1045
Becinita, George 2036
Beck, Billy 2061
Beck, Glenn 514
Beck, James 688
Beck, John 1018, 2397
Becker, Ben 1191
Becker, Charles 2025
Becker, Jean 100
Becker, Joerg 1898
Beckerman, Barry 1801
Beckett, Scotty 194, 248, 389, 728, 778, 987, 1136, 2306
Beckley, Tony 2273
Beckley, William 368
Beckman, Henry 2066, 2309
Beckwith, Reginald 441, 650, 1001, 2071, 2178, 2223
Becue, Nathalie 1043
Beddoe, Don 48, 130, 154, 157, 158, 160, 199, 210, 211, 224, 234, 363, 389, 421, 515, 565, 579, 592, 728, 753, 758, 769, 776, 834, 891, 958, 999, 1033, 1165, 1169, 1170, 1171, 1200, 1234, 1236, 1240, 1281, 1292, 1305, 1316, 1372, 1434, 1438, 1501, 1556, 1579, 1715, 1738, 1762, 1763, 1774, 1805, 1817, 1832, 1855, 1984, 2004, 2007, 2030, 2036, 2052, 2073, 2075,

Besch, Bibi 827
Besnehard, Dominique 1
Besser, Joe 542, 871, 2003
Besserer, Eugenie 1589,
 1726, 2236
Besson, Luc 159, 1115
Best, Geoffrey 238
Best, James 291, 1344,
 1398, 1619, 1681, 2059,
 2080, 2211
Best, Willie 211, 1809,
 2404
Bethune, Ivy 2339
Bett, John 2027
Betti, Laura 1042, 1645
Bettinson, Ralph 1268,
 1414, 1713
Bettis, Valerie 21, 1125
Betton, George 1150
Betz, Mathew 628, 1290,
 1824, 1912, 1926, 2265,
 2286, 2399
Bevan, A. J. 2368
Bevan, Billy 398, 677,
 686, 1321, 1461, 1546,
 1665, 1713, 1770, 1995,
 2014, 2017
Bevans, Clem 816, 1153,
 1236, 1307, 1650, 1697,
 1954, 2014, 2022
Bevans, Philippa 1437
Bey, Tema 2153
Bey, Turhan 1598, 1881
Beymer, Richard 649, 946
Bezzerides, A. I. 1841
Bianchini, Alfredo 1888
Biava, Claudio 1207
Biberman, Abner 879,
 2169
Biberman, Herbert 1280,
 1474, 2111
Bice, Robert 37, 306, 401,
 433, 775, 800, 952, 993,
 1407, 1457, 1525, 1646,
 2013, 2077, 2217, 2314
Bick, Jerry 1297
Bickel, Ray 2216
Bickford, Charles 1083,
 1093, 1287, 1510, 1590,
 1715, 2207, 2351
Bickley, Tony 1989
Biddell, Sidney 468, 579,
 2091
Bielke, Marie-Louise 2064

Bieri, Ramon 266, 1623,
 2212
Bigelow, Joe 2311
Bilar, Celia 1718
Bilk, Acker, and His Para-
 mount Jazz Band 1698
Bill, Buffalo, Jr. (Jay Wil-
 sey) 91, 867, 1636, 1637,
 1643
Bill, Tony 321, 1800
Biller, Hal 519
Billings, George 456, 719
Billingsley, Barbara 36
Billingsley, Peter 932
Billington, Kevin 949
Bing, Herman 14, 374,
 1028, 1358, 1472, 2154
Bingham, John 691
Binns, Edward 595, 1198
Binyon, Claude 77, 565,
 1547, 2118, 2349, 2351
Binyon, Conrad 248, 778,
 1306
Birch, Paul 802, 803,
 2157, 2171, 2298, 2332
Birch, Wyrley 27, 34, 92,
 187, 783, 793, 1168,
 1183, 1321, 1358, 1516,
 1803, 2137
Bird, John 2001, 2069
Bird, Norman 319, 449,
 1254
Birell, Tala 34, 305, 418,
 1126, 1130, 1168, 1462,
 1580
Birkin, Jane 1852
Birks, Dave 2132
Birman, Len 1133
Birney, Meredith Baxter
 1919
Biro, Lajos 1940
Bischoff, Samuel 76, 314,
 392, 453, 579, 1322,
 1409, 1427, 2030, 2051,
 2056, 2076, 2078, 2174,
 2358
Bishop, Edward 128
Bishop, Jennifer 1213
Bishop, Joey 1547, 2307
Bishop, Kenneth J. 386,
 472, 1253, 1353, 1773,
 1899, 2152
Bishop, William 17, 68,
 180, 391, 433, 498, 832,

 1021, 1179, 1555, 1577,
 1851, 2035, 2096, 2125,
 2192, 2233, 2298, 2341
Bispo, Louis 658
Bissell, Whit 68, 291, 318,
 387, 421, 599, 966, 1021,
 2079
Bisset, Donald 1777, 2239
Bisset, Jacqueline 320,
 477, 1919
Bittins, Michael 462
Bixby, Bill 1680, 2181
Bizet, Georges 312
Black, Bret 2189
Black, Buck 1551
Black, Ian Stuart 1793,
 1904
Black, Isobel 2020
Black, Karen 352, 535,
 648, 1100
Black, Maurice 268
Black, Stephen 839, 913
Blackman, Don 1456,
 2204
Blackman, Honor 976,
 1134
Blackman, Joan 775
Blackman, Wanda 1443
Blackmer, Sidney 365,
 562, 791, 1352, 1447,
 1738, 1758, 2138, 2336
Blackmore, Barry 457
Blackmore, Richard D.
 1179
Blackwell, Carlyle, Jr. 299
Blackwell, Douglas 2020
Blain, Gerard 907
Blair, Betsy 310, 795
Blair, David 1642
Blair, Henry 1745
Blair, Janet 177, 204, 709,
 720, 916, 1368, 1461,
 1876, 2011, 2078, 2117,
 2174
Blair, Joyce 120, 977, 1022
Blair, Nicky 833
Blair, Patricia 353
Blaisdell, Anne 507
Blake, Amanda 401, 1859,
 1974
Blake, Anne 1355, 1766
Blake, Arthur 829
Blake, Beverly 416
Blake, Bobby 1095; see

also Robert Blake
Blake, Gladys 1054, 1128, 1712
Blake, Grey 2367
Blake, Larry 415, 437, 544, 577, 948, 979, 1263, 1727, 2013, 2256, 2351
Blake, Lucius 1571
Blake, Madge 151
Blake, Marie 194
Blake, Mary 366, 1887
Blake, Oliver 328
Blake, Pamela 1377, 2385, 2414
Blake, Richard 497
Blake, Robert 938, 1727, 2102; see also Bobby Blake
Blakely, Colin 854, 1175, 1228, 1384, 2363
Blakely, Gene 117, 586
Blakely, James 1309, 1803
Blakely, Susan 1178, 2249
Blanc, Erika 1950
Blanc, Mel (voice of) 872, 1226
Blanc, Michel 530
Blancato, Ken 1931
Blanchard, Mari 85, 259, 435, 523, 2021
Blanche, Francis 94
Blanche, Roland 458
Blanchon, J. H. 250
Blanco, Hugo 2196
Bland, Joyce 377
Bland, Trevor 143
Blandick, Clara 175, 705, 1325, 1530, 1815, 1844
Blane, Sally 31, 452, 1404, 1802, 2018
Blaney, Charles E. 1337, 1477
Blangsted, Folmer 323, 1452, 2263
Blankfort, Michael 12, 194, 461, 660, 991, 1370, 2030
Blanshard, Joby 851
Blanton, John 1002
Blasetti, Alessandro 917
Blass, Herman 1381
Blatt, Daniel H. 55
Blatty, William Peter 1233

Blauner, Steve 535
Blaustein, Julian 138, 405, 1939
Blazek, Vratislav 1067
Bleckner, Jeff 2299
Blees, Robert 89, 1767
Blees, William 855, 999, 1385
Bleifer, John 185, 731, 991, 1646, 1925
Bletcher, Billy 529, 956, 2034
Bleuze, Jean-Claude 930
Blevins, Michael 347
Blick, Newton 2126
Blier, Bernard 63, 907, 2365
Blinn, Beatrice 290, 388, 769, 890, 1512, 1791
Blinn, William E. 255
Bliss, Imogene 332, 1024
Bliss, Lela 2272
Bliss, Sally 448, 1279, 1732, 1990
Blitner, Donald 2250
Bloch, Robert 1944, 2123
Block, Irving 2068
Block, Kimberly 97
Block, Larry 827, 1801
Block, Martin 1222
Blocker, Dirk 1921
Blodgett, Michael 688
Blondell, Gloria 1006
Blondell, Joan 48, 392, 776, 1680, 2050, 2078
Bloom, Bill 1233
Bloom, Claire 1790
Bloom, Gaetan 530
Bloom, William 350, 659, 1308, 1907, 2066
Bloomfield, Derek 546
Blore, Eric 398, 1162, 1163, 1165, 1166, 1170, 1171, 1359, 1438, 1462, 1536, 1776, 2078
Blossom, Roberts 349
Blot, Jacques 1043
Blount, Sheraton 470
Blue, Edgar Washington 285
Blue, Monte 663, 816, 1093, 1862, 2392
Blue, Vida 181
Bluestone, Abby 1406

Blum, Deborah 2212
Blum, Edwin 105, 234, 529
Blum, Harry N. 1443
Blum, Jack 820
Blum, Len 846, 1960
Blum, Sammy 430
Blummer, John 2396
Bluthal, John 525
Blye, Maggie 825
Blystone, John 2115
Blystone, Stanley 293, 557, 719, 842, 862, 973, 1005, 1113, 1153, 1238, 1755, 1828, 1951, 2414
Blythe, Betty 131, 2266
Blythe, Erik 952
Boardman, Eleanor 663
Boardman, Virginia True 113, 706
Boccaccio, Giovanni 104
Bock, Edward 422, 1013, 1242, 1666, 2067, 2135
Bodart, Ada 464
Boddey, Martin 1022, 2008, 2166
Boddy, Michael 32
Bodeen, DeWitt 2153
Bodine, Luba 907
Boehm, Sydney 165, 2182
Boetticher, Oscar, Jr. (Budd) 270, 372, 476, 578, 807, 1317, 1471, 1681, 2005, 2366
Bogarde, Dirk 447, 647, 1885
Bogart, Humphrey 291, 468, 828, 937, 1032, 1188, 1746, 1841, 2114
Bogart, John Paul 312
Bogdanovich, Peter 1092, 1398
Bogeaus, Benedict 1201, 1339
Bogen, Sophie 1573
Bogetti, Vera 585
Bogle, Warren 170
Bogue, M. A. 314
Bohdalova, Jirina 1067
Bohnen, Roman 397, 1010, 1325, 2056
Bohrer, Corinne 1931, 2213
Bohringer, Richard 1549

Bohrman, Stan 342
Bois, Curt 686, 840, 1061, 2321
Bois, Jean 1043
Boisson, Christine 566
Boitard, Cyr 1
Bolam, James 1486
Boland, Bridget 1597, 2223
Boland, Eddie 1139, 1313, 2207
Boland, Gene 1543
Bolden, Harry 1285
Bolder, Robert 815
Bolding, Bonnie 1423
Boles, John 339, 412, 1806, 2219
Boleslawski, Richard 1087, 2048
Bolger, Ray 334, 1003
Bolin, Shannon 932
Bolkan, Florinda 8, 953, 1207
Bologna, Carmine 1645
Bologna, Joseph 332
Bolognini, Mauro 104, 310, 1616
The Bolshoi Theatre Ballet 1979
Bolster, Anita 1366
Bolt, Ben 169
Bolt, Charles 1422
Bolt, Robert 1114, 1228
Bolton, Guy 1063
Bolton, Joe 1494
Bolton, Muriel Roy 1279, 1366, 1812
Bolvary, Jean 2063
Bolzoni, Adriano 906
Boman, Mirko 2141
Bon, Richard 66
Bonacelli, Palo 1303
Bonanova, Fortunio 385, 880, 1719, 1731, 2168
Bond, Anson 343
Bond, David 46, 350, 770, 1268, 1727, 1841, 1881, 2157, 2251
Bond, Derek 743
Bond, Edward 1297, 1397
Bond, Johnny 698, 1007, 1695, 1708, 1992
Bond, Lillian 490, 849, 1567, 2276

Bond, Raymond 1140
Bond, Rudy 126, 269, 824, 1300, 1315, 1344, 1410, 1456
Bond, Sheila 1263
Bond, Timothy 820
Bond, Tommy 16, 354, 651, 652, 653, 1491, 2374, 2422
Bond, Ward 31, 91, 262, 324, 426, 502, 621, 623, 629, 630, 749, 793, 856, 875, 964, 1005, 1120, 1173, 1243, 1250, 1290, 1340, 1441, 1544, 1572, 1586, 1590, 1649, 1903, 1943, 1972, 2058, 2119, 2189, 2221, 2222, 2266, 2276, 2285, 2292, 2336, 2352
Bondarev, Yuri 786
Bondi, Beulah 1324, 1325, 1546, 1811
Bonds, Gary "U.S." 1698
Bonerz, Peter 1426
Bonfigli, Marina 1645
Bonham, Frank 1914
Bonham, Guy 527
Boniface, Symona 939, 1230, 1462, 1713, 2411
Bonifas, Paul 572
Bonisolli, Franco 1045
Bonn, Walter 1600
Bonnaire, Sandrine 1
Bonnell, Vivian 675
Bonner, Charles 12
Bonner, Marjorie 1539, 1838
Bonner, Patricia 598
Bonner, Priscilla 1539
Bonner, Tony 416, 2353
Bonnett, Emery 2350
Bono, Cher 780
Bono, Sonny 780
Booke, Sorrell 595, 2000
Boon, Robert 21, 1076, 2211
Boone, Aaron 2369
Boone, Richard 118, 727, 2005, 2022
Boorman, Charley 530
Boorman, John 530, 893
Boorman, Katrine 530
Boorman, Telshe 530

Booth, Anthony 380, 381, 382, 383, 393, 1036
Booth, Carol 1192
Booth, Connie 61
Booth, James 854, 942, 977
Booth, Karin 333, 433, 992, 996, 1085, 1125, 1779, 1925, 2332
Booth, Mary 753
Booth, Ned 761
Booth, Nesdon 1794
Boothe, Jon 1611
Bordeaux, Joe 875
Borden, Bill 1037
Borden, Eugene 350, 693, 759, 823, 1064, 1085, 1275, 1559, 1567, 1661, 1745, 1828, 1865, 1884, 2077, 2091
Borden, Lynn 227
Borden, Olive 580, 1935, 2219
Bordoff, Trudy 835
Boreman, Alfred 1950
Boretski, Paul 1897
Boretz, Allen 962
Borg, Ariane 1039
Borg, Sven-Hugo 641, 686, 1126, 1755, 2048, 2176
Borg, Veda Ann 758, 1102, 1137, 1312, 1352, 1721, 1876 2174, 2400, 2417
Borgaze, Frank 1416
Borgaze, Raymond 1280
Borges, Graciela 2023
Borges, Yamil 347
Borgnine, Ernest 110, 340, 696, 792, 990, 1100, 1239, 1327, 1639, 1954, 2290
Bori, Diane 67
Borio, Josephine 1908
Borkon, Jules 1260
Borman, Bibs 1525
Borras, Eduardo 1718
Bory, Jean-Marc 1195
Borzage, Dan 1082, 2171
Borzage, Frank 1249
Bosetti, Giulio 1651
Bosiljcic, Milan 1929
Bosley, Tom 511, 2108

2259, 2261, 2288
Clark, Dane 1390
Clark, Davidson 410, 528,
810, 1693, 2164, 2428
Clark, Dick 126
Clark, Don 918
Clark, Edward 655, 1750
Clark, Ernest 321, 499,
587, 1414, 1435
Clark, Frank Howard 624,
628, 1157, 1795
Clark, Fred 442, 1873,
2371
Clark, Harvey 474, 1249
Clark, Jameson 1012, 1174
Clark, Jimmy 751, 2057
Clark, John 1071
Clark, Judy 123, 2159,
2382
Clark, Judy, and Her
Rhythm Cowgirls 1158
Clark, Judy, and the Solid
Senders 871
Clark, Ken 1227, 2153
Clark, Mary Higgins 2284
Clark, P. G. 240
Clark, Roger 491, 891,
1064, 1099, 1245, 1281,
1462, 1776, 1963, 2054,
2174, 2312, 2349
The Clark Sisters (voice
of) 1473
Clark, Steve 158, 191,
323, 409, 505, 528, 541,
814, 866, 1006, 1023,
1095, 1160, 1241, 1276,
1407, 1429, 1467, 1496,
1497, 1498, 1503, 1563,
1581, 1582, 1586, 1660,
1664, 1695, 1732, 1739,
1758, 1824, 1828, 1877,
1892, 1911, 2098, 2163,
2209, 2259, 2264, 2427
Clark, Susan 1426
Clark, Wallis 88, 330, 374,
429, 634, 681, 921, 925,
964, 1058, 1383, 1403,
1546, 1572, 1815, 2136,
2323
Clarke, Angela 830, 950,
1021, 1325, 2182
Clarke, David 1230
Clarke, Davidson 1105
Clarke, Donald Hender-

son 1308
Clarke, Geoffrey 897
Clarke, John 489
Clarke, Lydia 101
Clarke, Macrea 457
Clarke, Mae 82, 634, 774,
1495, 1526, 1682, 2087,
2144, 2331
Clarke, Richard 1820
Clarke, Robert 1054
Clarke, T. E. B. 743
Clarke-Smith, D. A. 614
Clarkson, Patricia 1711
Clary, Charles 573, 1578
Clary, Robert 2021, 2060
Claudio, Jean 250
Clausen, Carl 1020
Clavell, Aurora 1221
Clavell, James 1027, 2109
Clavering, Eric 951, 1346,
1891
Clavier, Francois 1043
Clay, Cassius 1658; see
also Muhammad Ali
Clay, Charles 1345
Clay, Lewis 2373, 2381,
2382, 2386, 2387, 2398,
2405, 2414, 2419, 2422,
2424, 2425, 2426
Clay, Rachel 2053
Clayburgh, Jill 970, 2284
Claydon, George 145
Clayman, Larry 971
Clayton, Eddie 369, 796
Clayton, Jack 1606, 1942,
2304
Clayworth, June 2160
Cleall, Peter 382
Cleary, Leo T. 1925
Cleaves, Robert 2066
Cleese, John 61, 949,
1333, 1830
Clemens, Brian 771, 1610,
1777
Clemens, William 2067
Clement, Aurore 954
Clement, Clay 1534, 2243
Clement, Dick 1486,
1790, 2213
Clement, Johnny 2143
Clement, Rene 2070
Clemente, Steve 629
Clements, Colin 298,
860, 1986

Clements, Curly, and His
Rodeo Rangers 1845
Clements, John 2184
Clements, Stanley 236,
750, 1306, 1325, 1336,
1625
Clements, Zeke 2164
Clery, Corinne 906, 2348
Cletro, Eddie, and His
Roundup Boys 2130
Cleveland, Carol 61, 1333
Cleveland, George 189,
433, 888, 1010, 1031,
1033, 1314, 1430, 1809,
1946, 2136, 2167, 2257
Clever, Edith 1528
Cliff, John 980, 1109,
1119, 2084
Clifford, Jack 158, 323,
371, 719, 1467, 1474,
1627, 1671, 1712
Clifford, Ruth 580, 2171
Clift, Montgomery 696,
946, 1967
Clifton, Dorinda 751
Clifton, Elmer 293, 1108,
1492, 1620, 1951, 2219,
2416
Clifton, Peter 1710
Clifton, Vala 583
Clifton, Wallace 113
Cline, Edward 1526, 1866
Clitheroe, Jimmy 1346,
1675
Clive, E. E. 86
Clive, Henry 1441
Clive, Robert 839
Clork, Harry 2091
Close, Del 169
Close, Glenn 161, 974
Clough, John Scott 604
Clouse, Robert 57, 723
Clouston, J. Storer 2177
Clowes, St. John L. 784
Clute, Chester 215, 221,
488, 515, 582, 734, 1064,
1266, 1281, 1336, 1419,
1805, 1837, 2078, 2312
Clutesi, George 1412
Clyde, Andy 1883, 2044,
2092
Clyde, Jeremy 1827
Clyde, June 1286, 1775,
1942

Dagerman, Stig Halvard 1980
Da Gray, Slim 32, 479
Daheim, Johnny 2316
Dahl, Alice 2286
Dahl, Arlene 1071, 1808, 2310
Dailey, Dan 1547
Dailey, Irene 648
Daily, Elizabeth 1422
Daily, Mary 814
Daine, Lois 319
Dainton, Leonard 1229
Daix, Didier 902
Dakan, Jimmy 1434
Dalbert, Suzanne 689, 1055, 1257
D'Albrook, Sidney 1272
Dale, Alan 522
Dale, Esther 93, 204, 205, 388, 1066, 1352
Dale, Jim 1154, 1384, 1993
Dale, Virginia 1424, 1924
Daley, Blythe 2045
Dalgarno, Dolores 1483
Dalio, Marcel 493, 660, 823, 1885
Dallimore, Maurice 368, 2082
Dalmas, Herbert 13, 1089, 1432
Dalroy, Rube 2122
Dalrymple, Ian 361, 1520
Dalton, Audrey 1323
Dalton, Jeff 923
Dalton, Ken 826
Dalton, Timothy 434
Daltry, Roger 2116
Daly, Jack 913, 1527, 1560
Daly, James 911
Daly, Pat 551
Dalya, Jacqueline 2415
D'Ambricourt, Adrienne 1287
d'Ambrose, Jacques 1304
D'Amico, Cecchi 1752
D'Amico, Suso Cecchi 1616, 1753, 2006
Damon, Mark 70, 948, 1135, 1651
D'Amore, Renato 1888
Dana, Leora 2086
Dana, Vic 523
Dana, Viola 2041

Danare, Malcolm 349
Dance, Charles 2295
Dance, Patsy 899
Dance, Reginald 532
Dancewicz, "Boley" 2143
D'Andrea, Tom 1018
Dandridge, Dorothy 830, 1575
Dandridge, Ruby 468, 610
Dandy, Ned 891, 1099, 1985, 2133, 2403, 2407, 2417
Dane, Alexandra 393
Dane, Bonnie Irma 1938
Dane, Lawrence 121, 820
Dane, Lois 851
D'Angelo, Beverly 170
Dangler, Anita 1100
Daniel, Paul 1813
Daniel, Susan 312
Danieli, Isa 1888
Daniell, Henry 93, 107, 883, 1087, 1437, 1770
Daniels, Bebe 365, 1886
Daniels, Billy 437, 1632, 1974, 2282
Daniels, Harold 2321
Daniels, Mark 1095
Daniels, Mickey 964
Daniels, Phil 256
Daniels, Roderick E. 337
Daniels, William 225, 1787
Danischewsky, John 1728
Danischewsky, Monja 2184
Dann, Larry 132
Dann, Roger 422
Dannay, Frederic *see* El-lery Queen
Danner, Blythe 1198, 1787
Danning, Joseph 1431
Danny and the Juniors 1123, 1131
Dano, Royal 247
Danon, Raymond 1062
Danova, Cesare 746, 2203
Danson, Linda 373
Danson, Ted 637
Dante, Anthony 1197
Dante, Michael 78, 600, 979

Dantine, Helmut 616
Danton, Mark 169
Danton, Ray 2009
Danza, Tony 885
Da Pron, Louis 42
D'Arbanville, Patti 694
Darby, Susan Jane 658
Darcel, Denise 655
D'Arcy, Alexander 93, 199, 662, 776, 1806
D'Arcy, Gene 1296, 1756
Darcy, Georgine 523
D'Arcy, Roy 152
Darcy, Sheila 2423
Darden, Severn 352, 467, 1204, 1213, 1328
Dare, Danny 1220
Dare, Helena 2386
Darget, Chantal 106, 1267
Darien, Frank 77, 135, 1029, 1290, 2136
Darin, Bobby 1547
Dark, John 2239
Darling, W. Scott 773, 2190
Darmond, Grace 510
Darmour, Larry 91, 324, 358, 427, 490, 561, 562, 563, 564, 571, 659, 702, 703, 704, 706, 788, 791, 847, 867, 873, 939, 1102, 1107, 1112, 1159, 1224, 1430, 1495, 1500, 1534, 1554, 1564, 1636, 1637, 1643, 1649, 1701, 1706, 1714, 1915, 1946, 2136, 2138, 2144, 2180, 2188, 2266, 2267, 2289, 2383, 2388, 2393, 2395, 2397, 2408, 2415, 2417, 2420, 2423, 2425, 2427
Darnell, Linda 355
Darrell, Steve 190, 192, 304, 329, 404, 463, 557, 701, 993, 1109, 1542, 1684, 1687, 2199, 2261
Darren, James 45, 126, 269, 506, 731, 744, 745, 746, 802, 806, 1122, 1484, 1727, 2102; (voice of) 872
Darrieux, Danielle 7, 1180

Darro, Frankie 262, 612,
632, 1006, 1416, 1624,
1649, 1887, 2089, 2193,
2392
Darrow, John 552, 1911
Darwell, Jane 35, 195,
339, 412, 936, 1011,
1082, 1312, 1340, 1460,
1472, 1812
Da Silva, Howard 1205,
1787
Dauphin, Claude 1937
Daurat, Charles 2365
Davalos, Dick 45, 898
Davalos, Ellen 950
Davenport, Gail 1712
Davenport, Harry 936,
1011, 1523, 1809, 1907,
2014, 2118, 2352
Davenport, Nigel 1134,
1152, 1228, 1310, 2220
Daves, Delmer 405, 990,
1806, 2086, 2357
Davi, Jana 803
David, Eleanor 554
David, Thayer 1116
Davidson, Bart 2401
Davidson, Bert 253
Davidson, James 2104
Davidson, Lawford 1533
Davidson, Martin 932,
1178
Davidson, Max 459, 1004,
1570
Davidson, Tito 559
Davidson, William B. 873,
963, 1293, 1438
Davies, Brian 128
Davies, David 1479
Davies, Desmond 546
Davies, Howard 367
Davies, Jack 524, 874,
920, 2178
Davies, Janet 949
Davies, Marion 2103
Davies, Richard 1361
Davies, Rupert 931, 1012
Davies, Stephen 1640
Davies, Windsor 381
Davila, Raul 868
Davion, Alex 1885
Davis, Ann B. 1547
Davis, Art 939, 1554,
1564, 2441, 2500, 2514,

2526, 2527, 2532, 2550,
2565, 2582, 2588, 2610,
2611, 2617, 2620, 2621,
2630, 2631, 2646, 2650,
2664, 2702, 2715, 2720,
2758, 2782, 2786, 2805,
2817, 2823, 2837, 2843,
2850, 2854, 2855, 2882,
2885, 2886, 2887, 2888,
2889, 2890, 2891, 2892,
2893, 2894, 2895, 2897,
2898, 2899, 2900, 2901,
2902, 2903, 2904, 2905,
2906, 2998, 3005, 3021
Davis, Bette 1293, 1939
Davis, Blair 790
Davis, Boyd 208, 565,
581, 755, 834, 999, 1281,
1642, 1669, 1985, 2168,
2187, 2335, 2366
Davis, Brad 1303, 1617
Davis, David 892
Davis, Donald 355, 855,
1462, 1663
Davis, Edwards 1578,
1999
Davis, Eleanore 1632
Davis, Fitzroy 845
Davis, Frank 2021
Davis, Gail 224, 404, 772,
944, 1451, 1457, 1509,
1828, 1887, 1893, 2029,
2130, 2202, 2227, 2287,
2317
Davis, Geena 2120
Davis, George 422
Davis, Gordon 2367
Davis, Ilah 827
Davis, J. Edwards 1215
Davis, Jack 216, 1401,
1771, 1796, 2003
Davis, Jim 1828
Davis, Jimmy 445
Davis, Jimmy, and His
Rainbow Ramblers 1693
Davis, Jimmy, and His
Singing Buckaroos 698
Davis, Joan 123, 829,
1007, 1985, 2139, 2168,
2172
Davis, Joel 1136
Davis, John Walter 1921
Davis, Judy 1532
Davis, Karl 1567, 1751,

1840, 2370, 2402
Davis, Lisa 714
Davis, Michael 45
Davis, Nancy 413, 853
Davis, Norbert 814
Davis, Ossie 308, 396,
898, 1765
Davis, Owen 520, 1415
Davis, Phil 2403
Davis, Richard 1218, 1304
Davis, Richard Harding
533
Davis, Robert O. 999,
1688, 2415
Davis, Roger 1683
Davis, Rufe 1957
Davis, Sammi 893
Davis, Sammy, Jr. 1547,
1575
Davis, Stringer 928
Davis, Tom 1470
Davis, Tyrrell 1591, 1631
Davis, Wray 857
Davo, Jose Marco 583
Daw, Marjorie 113
Dawkins, Paul 1154
Dawn, Isabel 1835
Dawn, Katherine 1004
Dawn, Norman 1004
Dawson, Anthony 647,
1864, 1950, 2348
Dawson, Billy 16
Dawson, Diana 1954
Dawson, Doris 265
Dawson, Hal K. 216, 593,
1113, 1851, 2077
Dawson, Ingard 955
Dawson, Peter 593, 2083
Dawson, Richard 1027
Day, Alice 1284, 2161,
2248
Day, Ambrose 1458
Day, Diana 1942
Day, Doris 965
Day, Gabrielle 2020
Day, Lillian 1488
Day, Marceline 533, 624,
1659, 1848
Day, Max 713
Day, Price 1056
Day, Shannon 2133
Day, Susan 166
Day, Vera 2149, 2244,
2320

Marshall, Tully 113, 1224, 1404, 1477, 2161
Marshall, Vivian 745, 2331
Marshall, Zena 144
Marshe, Vera 167
Marson, Ania 1397
Marston, Joel 1402, 1609
Martel, K. C. 2299
Martell, Donna 770, 877, 1097, 2022
Martell, Gregg 21, 1271, 2084, 2203
Marter, Ian 513
Marth, Frank 1543
Martin, A. Z. 1213
Martin, Al 19, 209, 314, 678, 1364, 1625, 1663, 1733, 1735, 1736, 1859, 1879, 2137
Martin, Allen, Jr. 861
Martin, Andrea 2305
Martin, Barney 898
Martin, Bill 1758
Martin, Charles G. 1742
Martin, Chris-Pin 296, 720, 1550
Martin, D'Urville 794, 2246
Martin, Dean 51, 903, 1356, 1547, 1823, 2302, 2337
Martin, Dewey 1032
Martin, Don 1186, 2143
Martin, Ernest 347
Martin, Francis 1817, 2103
Martin, Fred S. 1457, 1690
Martin, Freddy, and His Orchestra 1780, 2271
Martin, Jaye 1876
Martin, Jean 1399
Martin, Lewis 190, 401, 413
Martin, Lucy 1395
Martin, Marcella 2262
Martin, Marcelle 1245
Martin, Marion 542, 563
Martin, Millicent 1435
Martin, Pamela Sue 282, 2108
Martin, Paul A. 1134
Martin, Quinn 203

Martin, Rosemary 2027
Martin, Ross 588
Martin, Stanley 2360
Martin, Steve 1723
Martin, Strother 267, 671, 825, 1412, 1941, 2216
Martin, Tony 1359
Martindale, Edward 53, 1631
Martindale, Wink 1131
Martindel, Edward 330, 482
Martinez, A. 2000
Martinez, Paco 438
Martinez, Tony, and His Band 1709
Martinez-Casado, Juan Jose 438
Martini, Luciano 2242
Martins, Orlando 1022, 1741
Marton, Andrew 171, 1941
Marton, Jarmila 1941
Marton, Paul 401
Marvin, Frankie 112, 157, 190, 404, 944, 1095, 1451, 1509, 1697, 1828, 1887, 2202, 2287
Marvin, Lee 165, 291, 322, 553, 799, 816, 1601, 1681, 1813, 1954, 2314
Marvin, Michelle 1648
Marx, Arthur 208
Marx, Sam 85, 754, 1403
Mascaras, Mil 2205
Mascia, Tony 1827
Mascorieto, Jeddu 868
Maskell, Virginia 949, 1479
Maslow, Walter 2318
Mason, A. E. W. 1940
Mason, Basil 933, 1511
Mason, Dave 1846
Mason, Elliot 2156
Mason, Gladys 1070
Mason, Haddon 464
Mason, James (American actor) 40, 237, 323, 1755
Mason, James (English actor) 32, 470, 540, 732, 736, 1177, 1594, 1606, 1642, 2958
Mason, LeRoy 11, 2260,

2399, 2407
Mason, Louis 880, 1388, 1755, 1907
Mason, Marsha 332, 336, 1480
Mason, Peter 1820
Mason, Reginald 258
Mason, Sarah Y. 769, 1815
Mason, Shirley 665, 1676, 1730, 1750, 1867, 1983, 2313, 2334
Mason, Sidney 73, 1538, 2013
Mason, Sully 314
Mason, Tom 1116
Mason, Vivian 1007, 1840, 2402
Mason, William 150
Massari, Lea 1214, 1399, 2063
Massen, Osa 184, 440, 734, 2358
Massey, Anna 279, 743, 1176
Massey, Daniel 691, 2239
Massey, Raymond 951, 1208
Massie, Robert K. 1397
Masterson, Peter 1928
Mastovoy, Leo 1464
Mastroianni, Marcello 1042
Mastrosimone, William 122
Masur, Richard 818
Matania, Clelia 650
Mate, Rudolph 461, 962, 1420, 1538, 1576, 1662, 2217
Matelli, Dante 1098
Mather, Aubrey 678, 1136, 1770
Mather, Berkely 732, 1175
Mather, George Edward 186
Mathers, Jerry 1794
Mathers, Jimmy 1394
Matheson, Murray 105
Matheson, Richard 507
Mathews, Allen 463, 1362
Mathews, Carl 1111
Mathews, Carole 191, 750, 915, 1317, 1498,

Thorpe, Richard 98, 1022
Thorpe, Ted 655, 1759, 2402
Thorsen, Russell 775, 2009
Thrasher, J. Leslie 677
The Three Stooges 305, 778, 836, 1368, 1494, 1712, 1924, 1936, 2081, 2082, 2083, 2084, 2106
Thring, Frank 32
Thulin, Ingrid 28
"Thunderhoof," the horse 2096
Thurber, James 2988
Thurman, Bill 1092
Thurn-Taxis, Alexis 245, 734, 751, 1595, 1721
Thursby, Dave 274
Thurston, Carol 385, 1019, 1095
Thurston, Charles 2189
Tibbetts, Martha 430, 1636, 2188
Tichy, Gerard 640, 1975, 2038
Tierney, Gene 20
Til, Roger 2153, 2203
Tilbury, Zeffie 963
Tillis, Mel 2216
Tillotson, Johnny 1001
Tilly, Jennifer 1422
Tilly, Meg 33, 161
Tilsley, Frank 447
Tilton, Edwin Booth 1302, 1624
Tilton, George 1870
Tilton, Martha 2358
Timmerman, Chad 225
Timmins, Cali 1897
Tindall, Loren 751, 1278, 1314, 1490, 1504, 1580, 1721, 1782, 1812
Tinling, James 663, 677
Tinsley, Theodore 1253, 1516, 1353
Tirard, Ann 1937
Tissier, Jean 23, 1517
Tiven, Sally 1470
Tjader, Cal, Band 676
Tjernberg, Ove 1980
Toal, Maureen 808, 1486
Tobares, Alfredo 2023
Tobey, Kenneth 96, 666,

688, 960, 2104
Tobias, George 1216, 1359, 1368, 2021
Tobias, Sarett 1809, 2011
Tobin, Dan 1075
Tobin, Genevieve 887, 1415, 2336
Tobin, Mark 1233
Tobisch, Lotte 1096
Todd, Ann 1288, 1766
Todd, Beverly 266
Todd, Bob 382
Todd, Harry 113, 469, 624, 625, 628, 964, 1101, 1313, 1468, 1972, 2018, 2034, 2090, 2268
Todd, James 1161
Todd, Lola 1652
Todd, Mabel 2133
Todd, Mel 2216
Todd, Richard 854, 1192
Todd, Ruth 390
Todd, Thelma 27, 35, 98, 168, 475, 2142
Todman, Bill 1680
Toeplitz, Ludovico 142
Toguri, David 2253
Toland, Virginia 728
Toler, Sidney 330, 1409, 2311
Tolnay, Akos 2094
Tolo, Marilu 1030
Tomack, David 838
Tomack, Sid 196, 219, 244, 421, 678, 693, 708, 916, 1032, 1222, 1390, 1747, 2091
Tombes, Andrew 129, 204, 358, 1365, 1669, 1834, 2030, 2054
Tombragel, Maurice 244, 1163, 1593, 1666, 1917, 1985, 2135, 2172
Tomelty, Joseph 848, 851, 1599
Tomita, Tamlyn 1009
Tomlin, Pinky 1833
Tomlinson, David 713
Tomlinson, Martin 1641
Tompkins, Angel 600
Tone, Franchot 20, 862, 916, 1028, 1298, 1805, 2312
Toner, Tom 760

Toney, Jim 1056
Tong, Kam 2010, 2302, 2343
Tongolele 1861
Toni, Viviana 590
Tooker, William H. 173
Toomey, Regis 77, 491, 500, 873, 879, 1171, 1370, 1377, 1386, 1815, 1854, 1871, 1926, 2067, 2138
Toone, Geoffrey 1212, 1459, 2024
Toones, Fred "Snowflake" 852, 1057, 1324, 1546, 1802, 2154
Tophe, Chris 1262
Topol 132
Toren, Marta 85, 1841
Torena, Juan 1047
Toretzka, Ludmila 1288
Torey, Hal 413
Toriel, Caprice 1348
Torino, Cosimo 1752
Tork, Peter 841
Torme, Mel 1128
Torn, Rip 414
The Tornados 1001
Torokvei, Peter 80
Torrence, David 632, 1183
Torrente, Ugo 1752
Torres, Miguel Contreras 989, 1041, 1044
Torres, Raquel 1866, 2322
Torrey, Len 1690
Tors, Ivan 171, 689, 761, 1941
Tortosa, Jose 252, 1108, 2209
Totman, Wellyn 580
Totter, Audrey 85, 437, 1235, 1269, 1319, 2331
Tourangeau, Jacques 33
Tourneur, Jacques 441, 1410
Tovar, Loretta 1481
Tovar, Lupita 237, 420
Towb, Harry 1599, 2069
Towers, Constance 261, 604, 1996
Towers, Harry Alan 367; *see also* Peter Welbeck
Towers, Louise 2148
The Town Criers 407, 1883